THE
THESAURUS OF
SLANG

Revised and Expanded Edition

ESTHER LEWIN AND ALBERT E. LEWIN

☑® Facts On File, Inc.

To Talia and Ian
and in memory of
dear Natalie

3 1969 01229 3725

The Thesaurus of Slang: Revised and Expanded Edition

Copyright © 1997 First paperback edition.
Copyright © 1994 by Esther Lewin and Albert E. Lewin

Facts On File, Inc.
11 Penn Plaza
New York NY 10001

Library of Congress Cataloging-in-Publication Data
Lewin, Esther.
    The thesaurus of slang: over 165,000 uncensored contemporary
  slang terms, common idioms, and colloquialisms, updated for the
  1990's and arranged for quick and easy reference / Esther Lewin and
  Albert E. Lewin. — Rev. and expanded ed.
        p. cm.
    Includes bibliographical references.
    ISBN 0-8160-3661-6
    1. English language—Slang—Dictionaries. 2. English language—
Synonyms and antonyms.   I. Lewin, Albert E.   II. Title.
PE3721.L45   1997
427'.09—dc20   93–42890

Facts On File books are available at special discounts when purchased in bulk
quantities for businesses, associations, institutions, or sales promotions. Please call
our Special Sales Department in New York at 212/967-8800 or 800/322-8755.

You can find Facts On File on the World Wide Web at **http://www.factsonfile.com**

Cover design by Cathy Rincon

Printed in the United States of America

VB VC 10 9 8 7 6 5 4 3 2

This book is printed on acid-free paper.

PREFACE TO THE SECOND EDITION

With the publication of the original edition, one of the questions often asked was, why a thesaurus and not a dictionary of slang? It was a dictionary that inspired the creation of *The Thesaurus of Slang*. Some years ago I was given a fine slang dictionary as a birthday gift. Being a writer of fiction in its various forms I am always looking for informal language especially to use when writing dialogue. To my great disappointment, I found the dictionary of slang, as complete as it was, to be the most useless book on my reference shelf. It listed slang words and defined them, which, of course, is what a dictionary is meant to do. Therefore, to find a slang word, it was necessary to know the word to look up. And that's the joker. If you knew the slang word to look for, usually you knew its definition. The dictionary was fine for idle browsing but for anyone seriously in search of a slang word right now, it was a loser.

It occurred to me that what I really needed was a thesaurus devoted to slang, one which listed a standard English word and offered a selection of slang synonyms for that word. In a sense, I wanted a book that translated English into slang, At that time, there was no such book in the market place. After several years of haunting bookstores and expecting a thesaurus of slang to appear, Esther and I decided to do the job ourselves. We estimated it might take a year or two to put such a book together. Six years later, in 1987, we closed the file on the first edition of our *Thesaurus of Slang*. Simultaneously, we opened a new file for the collection of additional slang, colloquialisms, jargon, etc., for a future revised edition. After six more years and some 15,000 additions, changes and deletions, the time has come to close the file on the revised edition. As of this writing, there is very little slang in general use in America that is not listed somewhere in this book.

The six years have revealed some interesting insights. There is a popular misconception regarding slang: slang changes rapidly. Not so. We have found that slang is generational. The slang that we learn as we grow up, we tend to use for the rest of our lives adding new words and dropping a few as we go. The greatest change is in the youth groups: Young people invent, change and misconstrue language as they pass through the brief period from adolescence to adulthood. African Americans introduce many of the new words and phrases that come into general use. As a group they are lovers of language, playing with words, creating the innovative phrase, rhyming catch phrases such as "In it to win it." "When you're hot you're hot. When you're not you're not." Advertising not only creates new words and phrases, it popularizes its creations through widespread campaigns. If any one area can be pinpointed as the source of change in language, ad copywriters could well be the leaders. Probably the most important change introduced by advertising is the way words are spelled or misspelled for attention-getting effect. Night is often spelled nite. You is seen as U. Kleen for clean. Flo for flow. The result is confusion as to the acceptable way to spell. Purists may deplore this development but this simplification in spelling is finding its way into the language. George Bernard Shaw, the great playwright and critic, tried, unsuccessfully, to introduce a phonetic method of spelling. He must be chuckling in his grave.

Ad copy has contributed more than spelling. Ad slogans often find their way into common usage. "Where's the beef?" grew from a hamburger commercial into a political phrase that certainly helped elect a president of the United States.

New language comes from new industry. Computers, space programs and genetic engineering have all contributed slang to the language and we expect a spate of new expressions to come from multimedia, interactive television and the possible revolution in health care. Some of it is already in the language and in this revised edition.

With 15,000 new words, phrases and deletions, 10 percent of the volume is new. That bears out our finding that slang is generational. If we were to revise this work every six years, we might expect that the entire book will be changed in sixty years. In reality it doesn't happen that way. Many words, we wouldn't risk a guess how many, but a considerable number found in the original edition will still be in use in the mid-twenty-first century. Americans, today, are still using slang that predates Shakespeare. *Bird* meaning *woman* is still used today. *Bird* dates back to 1300 and it has various forms in daily use: *chick, chicken, biddy. Moll* is another word for *woman* from the early 1500s.

Shakespeare and old words aside, the six years of collected slang reveal much about our society. This is not to be construed as a scientific survey. While one might expect that the 10 percent change from the first edition would be evenly distributed throughout the entries, changes do not take place overall. Some categories grew far beyond the average.

The most change appears to be in the drug culture. There are more new terms for *marijuana* than in any other category: 98 new words amounting to a 46 percent increase. *Amphetamine* has a higher percentage, 55 percent with 39 new words. *Cocaine* language jumps by 44 percent with 42 new words. The entire drug category has grown to the largest general group in the book. The category *drugged* gained 46 percent new words. *Drunk* gained less than 7 percent, but since it is our largest single category with over 800 slang terms selected from more than 2,000, the 7 percent gain amounts to 52 new entries.

All this use of drugs and alcohol has a natural result, *vomit*, with a 48 percent gain in new words and phrases, accounting for 44 various ways to throw up, not to mention a 35 percent gain in words for *death*. If society is not shooting itself enough with drugs there are 19 percent more words for guns. It is not surprising that there are 85 new terms amounting to 30 percent for the word *stupid*. What is surprising is that *outstanding* shows a 32 percent increase, 31 new words, although many of them are derogatory. Some of those words are also found in *disliked person*, which adds 43 nasty new words, a 34 percent change. *Bad* finishes with 34 more words, a 22 percent jump.

Police gains 26 new slang synonyms, a 17 percent increase. *Prisoner* held by law enforcement increased by 43 percent with 36 new slang terms. No wonder our prisons are overpopulated. The *jail cell* occupied 50 percent more of the language with 10 new words.

Reflecting our preoccupation with the '80s the word *merger* added 9 new words for a 56 percent rise.

As always, sex is a popular topic. *Sexual intercourse* found 35 percent more ways of describing the act of love and its variations with 69 new expressions. No pun intended. *Promiscuous* added 32 percent new words with 20 more entries, all derogatory references to women. *Prostitute* picks up 20 percent additional labels. *Woman* increases her share of new language with 44 new words and phrases amounting to 18 percent, many of which are obscene. *Vagina* receives 30 more descriptions for 29 percent, while *penis* rises higher by 32 percent with 63 new obscene references.

All these statistics suggest what has and has not been occupying our minds in the last six years. However, before the reader draws a set of cynical conclusions from all this, consider those categories with little or no change. *Crime, commit a;* defeat; hit; ineffective; aggressive; and attack all show less than 2 percent change. *Admire, alert, apprehensive, risk, thief,* and *robbery* show zero change.

A few of the most significant areas that have not seen change and therefore are not on the minds of the general public are *advocate, question* (the verb), and *prohibit*.

Racial words and phrases are almost entirely derogatory. We take no sides in reporting what people call one another. What appears in this volume is the way America talks today. There are 36 new words for *African Americans*, a 22 percent increase, all derogatory. Likewise there are 17 new words for *whites*, a 24 percent change. Asians have 24 percent more and Mexicans are known by 30 percent more terms. All are derogatory.

Lest you think there is no fun in this volume, to the contrary. *The Thesaurus of Slang* is chock full of America's most picturesque speech, wit and the humor that springs from being who we are.

Some of the delightful new expressions in this book are:

Joygerm fever—happy.
Glass widow—husband is an alcoholic.
Cherry tree—a tall virgin.
Club Fed—federal prison, low security.
Napkin notion—idea written during a power lunch.
Flunkenstein—a failing student.
Bottle fatigue—a hangover.
Broken rib—an ex-wife.

And left over from the first edition, one of our favorites:

Walking on rocky socks—drunk.

The Thesaurus of Slang is full of them. See for yourself. Enjoy.

—Albert E. Lewin

PREFACE TO THE FIRST EDITION

The Thesaurus of Slang is made up of 12,000 standard English words listed alphabetically; each is followed by one or more of the 150,000 slang words or phrases contained in this volume. That simple arrangement is what makes this book a useful tool for writers, speakers, students of language and anyone else who might need a quick and easy source of slang.

It has been said that a thesaurus is a book in which you look up the wrong word in order to find the right one. That definition fits this book perfectly. As a thesaurus, it offers a convenient translation from standard English to its slang equivalent. It is by no means a slang dictionary, nor is it meant to be. Using this thesaurus, all or part of a formal English sentence can be rewritten in slang, something almost impossible to do using a slang dictionary. This is not to say that slang dictionaries should be considered superfluous. It is the basic premise that is different; a dictionary is meant to define words, but if the user doesn't know the slang word for which a definition is sought, a slang dictionary is reduced to little more than a volume for browsing. If anything, *The Thesaurus of Slang* should make slang dictionaries more useful. Except in a few instances where the use of an obscure slang term is demonstrated, this thesaurus, since it is not a dictionary, does not define slang words beyond giving them a formal English synonym. For a more precise definition of the words found in this book, a slang dictionary should be used.

In a sense, this volume is similar to a foreign-language dictionary in that it "translates" formal English into the language of slang. To some readers slang can seem like a foreign language and, like a foreign language, there are times when it doesn't translate exactly. The same word or phrase can differ subtly in meaning in different contexts. In an extreme instance a word can be its own antonym; for example, *baddest* can mean "best" or "worst."

While attempting to determine the right formal synonym of a slang term, we often asked which formal English word was the one most likely to occur to a reader searching for a slang synonym. For example, it is not likely a reader would think to find *pot likker* under the entry *residue. Soup stock* was more credible. Therefore, for some entries, precision has been sacrificed for ease of use. Where a widely used slang term is not easily translated into standard English, the slang itself is listed as the subject heading. Such a case is *blind date.*

The slang in this collection is based on actual usage culled from a wide variety of sources, such as newspapers, magazines, fiction and nonfiction books, television, radio, trade papers, industry, casual conversation. For the most part, the slang terms in this thesaurus are in current general usage; however, the reader will also find many of the most recent words appearing particularly in the language of young people, technical workers and politicians. In these pages, most readers will discover unfamiliar words and phrases, as well as old words with surprising new definitions.

All of language was once "nonstandard," until the invention of the printing press created the need for standardization and inspired the first dictionary. Slang also originates out of need. New words are continually coming into the language, to stay only as long as they are useful. No attempt was made in this book to rule out "vogue" words. Deciding which of these words are merely passing through the language and which are taking up more-or-less permanent residence was not part of our editorial criteria. Slang is created by all social classes in every kind of circumstance as a more convenient, more private, or more entertaining means of communication. Groups create their own language within a language. The various kinds of slang are a means of identification. Peers recognize each other through its use. Slang is a way of belonging, of "speaking the same language."

The word *slang* itself is said to have once meant "to be abusive." And much slang is abusive, chauvinistic, irreverent, profane, and sexually explicit. This book includes all types of slang, uncensored. For better or worse, this is the slang commonly used in America today.

Experts in linguistics disagree among themselves over matters of definition, and they are certain to disagree with some of the definitions in this work. It is a risk anyone who prepares such a text must take. In those instances where it can be pointed out that we are in error, corrections will be made most gratefully, but for the moment, what the reader finds within these pages is as close to the correct usage of slang, colloquialisms, and American idiom as we could presently determine.

—Esther and Albert E. Lewin

HOW TO USE THIS BOOK

For speakers, writers of fact or fiction, playwrights, screen and television writers, journalists, advertising copy writers, publicists, politicians, members of the clergy—anyone who deals with the expression of ideas through words, *The Thesaurus of Slang* is simple to use. Standard English words are listed in alphabetical order. Under each of these words is a collection of slang synonyms. Suppose you are preparing a speech or an essay and you want to make the following statement less formal, "Freedom of speech is basic to democracy." The operational word is *basic*. Look up the word *basic*.

BASIC adj.   plain vanilla, bottom line, nitty-gritty, where it's at, name, name of the game, nub, key, meat and potatoes, coal and ice. See also VITAL.

Depending on the level of informality desired, you find a wide range of choices, so the sentence can be written, "Freedom of speech is the meat and potatoes of democracy," or "Freedom of speech is the nub of democracy."

In addition to the listing of slang synonyms under a particular word, the thesaurus also offers a broader selection of words to assist you in finding exactly the sense you seek.

ENACT v.   1. jam, jam through, railroad, railroad through, steamroller through. 2. be on, go on, do a turn, do one's stuff, do a number. See EXECUTE. See also PERFORM.

Enact illustrates three of these features. The word *enact* is synonymous with "legislate." Synonyms for that sense of the word are listed under the numeral 1. "Enact" also means to "act." Number 2 provides a selection of "act" words. Following the slang terms there appears "See EXECUTE." and "Sec also PERFORM." "See" references offer a broader selection of slang synonyms. If you don't find the word you are seeking in the first group, the "See" category can provide more choices. "See also" references provide a broader selection still, directing you to collateral meanings of the word. As a convenience, there are no listings simply referring the reader to another category without some slang synonyms listed, allowing the reader a choice of synonyms without having to look further.

Still another refinement is offered to aid your search for exactly the right word. A semicolon separates specialized references from the general. Such words as might refer only to males as opposed to females or might differentiate activities from objects. Wherever possible, the most current, widely used words are listed first.

It is agreed among lexicographers that finding exactly the right synonym for a word is an inexact pursuit. In standard English, no two words carry precisely the same meaning and it is no different with slang, where exact definitions are often as varied as the locales in which the words are used. In many cases, parts of speech are mixed; nouns are listed with adjectives; verbs become nouns and nouns verbs; positives are used as negatives. That's the way you will find it here. Except for the sake of clarity, no attempt has been made to define slang beyond the category heading. The thesaurus should not be considered a dictionary. Where definition is necessary, reference to a good slang dictionary is recommended.

ACKNOWLEDGMENTS

No work of this size is complete without the help of others.

Eliza Lewin lent her sharp editorial skills and was always ready to double check references and prepare lists for our bibliography.

As with the earlier edition, Professor Herbert Turman was our technical adviser—generous with his time, reading manuscript whenever we sought his help and generally cheering us on.

Joseph Simon, tasteful publisher of the Ward Ritchie Press, shared his wide experience and technical expertise.

We arc forever indebted to Anthony Borras, who, back in the early days of personal computing, before IBM had a PC on the market, programmed a database system, DBM5, to manage the many sorts and searches required to assemble this book.

Helen G. Mochedlover, manager of the Literature and Fiction Department of the Los Angeles Public Library, provided us with a great many sources of information and material.

We must mention Susan Schwartz, our editor, for her encouragement, guidance and attention to detail in a manuscript filled with opportunities for error.

Finally, to our many friends and readers who sent us lists of words that have added to the comprehensive quality of this thesaurus, we thank you.

LIST OF ABBREVIATIONS

Acad.	academy	Mus.	musical
adj.	adjective	n.	noun
adv.	adverb	N.	Navy
A.F.	Air Force	News.	newspaper
Af. Am.	African American	N.Y.	New York
Anon.	anonymous	N.Y.C.	New York City
Art.	article	Obs.	obsolete
Ass't.	assistant	Obsc.	obscene
Bsbl.	baseball	Photo.	photographic
Bus.	business	Pl.	plural
CB.	Citizen's Band Radio	Pol.	political
C.I.A.	Central Intelligence Agency	Porno.	pornographic
Conj.	conjunction	Pref.	prefix
Derog.	derogatory	Prep.	preposition
Elec.	electrical	pron.	pronoun
Esk.	Eskimo	Rel.	religious
Fem.	female	Rest.	restaurant
Fin.	financial	Rom.	romantic
Fr.	French	R.R.	railroad
Ftbl.	football	Sch.	school
Ger.	German	Sgt.	Sergeant
Govt.	government	So.	southern
Hum.	humorous	Sp.	Spanish
Ind.	Indian American	suff.	suffix
interj.	interjection	Stu.	student use
I.R.S.	Internal Revenue Service	The.	theatrical use
Jap.	Japanese	TV.	television
L.A.	Los Angeles	U.	underworld
Lt.	lieutenant	Usu.	usually
M.	male	v.	verb
Medic.	medical	V.D.	venereal disease
Mex.	Mexican	WWI	World War I
Mil.	military	WWII	World War II
Ms.	manuscript	Yid.	Yiddish

A

A n. Able, Alfa.

ABANDON v. bail out, bow out, chicken out, check out, punk out, drop out, opt out, count out, cop out, sell out, storm out, pull out, push out, flake out, snake out, bug out, nix out, ooze out, peel out, ship out, burn out, ding, walk out on, run out on, blow off, leg, leg it out, break out (Af. Am.), ease out, fade, fade out, do a fade, fade away, hat up, drift away, dust, fly the coop, ease on, put it to the wind, slide, take French leave (without permission), scratch gravel, duck, heel, haul one's freight, quit the scene, sniff a powder, take a powder, screw, walk, fuck off, bug off, kick off, knock off, slam off, come off, cry off, swear off, skidoo, go over the side, slough, book, time to book, time to bail, bottle up and go, up stakes, pull up stakes, cheese it, take a walk, dump, cut loose, ditch, shake, leave flat, leave high and dry, leave holding the bag, bag it, leave in the lurch; pass, pass on, pass up, take the oath, pack in, give in, cave in, granny dumping, grandpa dumping (forcing government to care for elderly); give up, give up the ghost, give up the ship, throw in the sponge, throw in the towel, pull the pin, pull the plug, pull in one's horns, cry uncle, hang up one's spurs, pack it in, rat, chuck, chuck it, fold, quit cold, quit cold turkey, kick, drop, ankle, hang it up, bog down, binch (job), kiss goodbye, throw over, toss over, throw overboard, wash one's hands of, change one's tune, change one's song, drop like a hot potato, stand down, back down, pigeonhole, sideline, sidetrack. See also DESERT, RENOUNCE, RESIGN.

ABANDONED adj. godforsaken, passed up, pigeonholed, sidelined, sidetracked, on the rocks, out in left field, left in the lurch.

ABBREVIATE v. cut, cut down, cut to the bone, nutshell, put in a nutshell, boil down, trim, get to the meat. See also SHORTEN.

ABBREVIATED adj. for short. See also SHORT.

ABDICATE v. walk out on, wash one's hands of, chuck, ding, drop like a hot potato, bail out, opt out, cop out, sell out, leave high and dry, bag it, leave holding the bag, leave in the lurch, give it up. See RESIGN. See also QUIT.

ABDOMEN n. tummy, gut, pot, belly, potbelly, banjobelly (So.), spare tire, corporation, alderman, breadbasket, bay window. See STOMACH.

ABDOMINAL ORGANS n. guts, innards, inners, insides, department of the interior, inner man, inner workings, inner works, spaghetti.

ABDUCT v. grab, shanghai, snatch, put the snatch on one, sneeze, dognap (dog abduction).

ABERRANT adj. flaky, weirdo, psycho, mental, section 8, off-base, off-color, out-of-line. See also ABNORMAL.

ABHOR v. have no use for, have an allergy to, be allergic to, be down on, be grossed out on. See DISLIKE.

ABHORRENT adj. gross, shucky, yucky, icky, total shuck, awful, beastly. See DESPICABLE.

ABIDE v. 1. live with, bear with, suck it up, hear of, put up with, hang in, hang in there, hang tough, sit tight, be big, stand for. See ENDURE. 2. bunk, bunk out, crash, hang out, nest, cocoon, perch, roost, squat. See INHABIT.

ABILITY n. the stuff, the right stuff, what it takes, cutting the mustard, savvy, the goods, on the ball. See SKILL.

ABJURE v. swear off, knock off, lay off, turn it off, blow off, pass by, pass on, pass up, stay away from, cool it, can it, chuck it, stow it, cut it out, break it off, break it up, drop, drop it, get on the wagon, kick, pigeonhole, shake, sideline.

ABLE adj. all-around, paid one's dues, there, right there, up to it, up to speed, up to snuff, up to the mark, have savvy, take care of business, just what the doctor ordered, mad (jazz), wicked, know one's onions, know the ropes, know all the ins and outs, know the score, know all the answers, know one's fruit, know one's (practically anything), fool (e.g., dancing fool, flying fool). See CAPABLE. See also SKILLFUL.

ABNEGATION n. no way, nix, not (used at end of a positive sentence), forget it, November Foxtrot Whiskey (no fucking way), fuck that noise, bump that, yank on that, who me?, not by a long shot, fat chance, nothing doing, stonewall.

ABNORMAL adj. abb, screwy, bogus, for weird, weirdo, flaky, off-base, off-color, out-of-line, spaz, grody, grody to the max, gross, fantasmo, funny. See ECCENTRIC, CRAZY.

ABODE n. pad, crash pad, crib, condo, co-op, coop, joint, den, domi, dommy, flop; cradle, hat (Af. Am.); digs, diggings, hole. See HOUSE.

ABOLISH v. scrub, nix, call off, call all bets off, kill, blow off, kibosh, put the kibosh on, zap. See CANCEL, DESTROY.

ABOMINABLE adj. gross, grody, grody to the max, gagger, mutant, sleazeball, cocksucking, awful, hellish, pail, bucket, it rots, poxy, scurvy, scuzzo, scuzzy, shitsky, beastly, grim, hairy, lousy, rotten, stinking. See BAD.

ABORT v. scrub, call it quits, terminate, knock it off, break off, break it off, cut off, blow off, lay off. See CANCEL. See also STOP.

ABORTION n. pro choice, pro choicer (pro); right to life, right to lifer, pro life, pro lifer (anti); Mom and Pop meets (birth control meetings). See also FAILURE.

ABORTION CLINIC n. abortuary.

ABORTION, PERFORM v. pull a rabbit, terminate, D. and C., scrape.

ABOUND v. have a full plate, be up to here with, be up to one's ass in, be up to one's ears in, be knee deep in, be alive with, crawl with, be filthy with, no end of, no end to, be thick with, be thick as flies, more than you can shake a stick at.

ABOUT adv. pretty near, on the bubble (borderline), practically, craptically, in the neighborhood of, in the ball-park of. See also NEAR.

ABOVEBOARD adj. up front, right on, call a spade a spade, make no bones about it, straight from the shoulder. See HONEST.

ABRASIVE adj. rub the wrong way, spiky. See IRRITAT-ING.

ABRIDGE v. chop, cut, nutshell, put in a nutshell, snip, blue-pencil. See SHORTEN.

ABROGATE v. do in, finish off, forget it, knock out, nix, not (used at end of a sentence), renig, torpedo, scrub, blow off. See REPEAL; CANCEL.

ABRUPT adj. snippy, snappy, short.

ABSCOND v. absquatulate, take a powder, take a run-out powder, split, slide (Af. Am.), take off, hightail, fade, fade out, fade away, git, get, fly the coop, exfiltrate, breeze, clear out, skin out, duck out, duck and run, cut out, cut and run, pull out, dog it, make feet, take a walk, vamoose, skedaddle, make oneself scarce, get the hell out, make a break for it, take French leave, go AWOL, go south with, skip, skip out, jump, beat it, blow, scram, lam, take it on the lam.

ABSENCE n. no show, hooky, AWOL, A.W.O.L., cut, over the hill, French leave.

ABSENT adj. no-show, hooky, cutting, blitz, bag (Sch.) AWOL, French, French leave, over-the-hill, out, out-of-pocket, out-of-touch, ghost (counted as present), nobody home.

ABSENT v. cut, cut class, bag, ditch, dust, skip class, no show, dope off, blow off, fuck off, goof off, lay out of, punt, play hooky, skip, AWOL, go AWOL, go A.W.O.L., go over the hill, make oneself scarce, not show up, stay away in droves, take French leave, on French leave, turn up missing, flush, buck.

ABSENTMINDED adj. out-to-lunch, popcorn-headed, airheaded, helium-headed, absentminded professor, Suzie (Fem.), mooning, moony, pipe-dreaming, woolgathering, goofing off, looking out the window, the lights are on but nobody's home, spacey, space cadet. See also FORGETFUL.

ABSOLUTELY adv. absofuckinglutely, right on, posolutely, absitively, fucking-A, flat-ass, cert, def, but def, downright, flat out, straight out, no catch, no fine print, no fine print at the bottom, why sure, for sure, fer shure, fer sher, fer shirr, sure thing, surest thing you know, sure as shootin', sure enough, sure as death and taxes, sure as fate, sure as hell, sure as the devil, sure as I live and breathe, sure as can be, sure as God made little green apples, dead sure, dead cert, for dang sure, for a fact, and no mistake, no buts about it, no ifs ands or buts, come hell or high water, flat, flat out, you know, you know it, you better believe it, you can say that again, you're not kidding, you're darn tootin', you betcha, you betcher life, you bet, you said it, straight out, no strings attached, no holds barred, no catch, no kicker, with knobs on, with tits on, the real McCoy, I'll tell the world, I'll tell the cockeyed world, in spades, check, with bells on, on the button, on the money, on the nose, that's the ticket, on the lemon, on the noggin, it, is the Pope Catholic?, does a bear shit in the woods?, is a bear Catholic?, does the Pope shit in the woods?, honest to God, indeedy, real, for real, really truly, right-o, right on, right as rain, right you are, rather, stone (stone-deaf).

ABSOLVE v. let off, let one off this time, let one off the hook, let one off easy, let up on, let go, let it go, whitewash, launder, sanitize, bleach, clear, wipe the slate clean, wipe it off, write off, go easy on, blink at, wink at, lifeboat, hand out clemo, spring.

ABSOLVED adj. beat the rap, walked, off-the-hook, let go, let off, clemo.

ABSORB v. 1. co-opt, take over. 2. get, get into, follow, fershtay, latch onto, soak up, take in. See UNDERSTAND. 3. eat (eat the cost).

ABSORBED adj. up to here in, eat sleep and breathe (something), really into, gone, head over heels in. See EN-GROSSED.

ABSTAIN v. 1. take the pledge, take the cure, go on the wagon, go on the water wagon. 2. pass, pass up, sit on the fence, sit on one's ass, sit on one's butt, sit on one's duff, sit on one's hands, sit out, fence-sit, go by, give the go-by, give one or something the go-by, quit.

ABSTINENT adj. dry, A.A., teetotaler, on the dry, on the wagon, on the water wagon, took the pledge.

ABSTRACTED adj. daydreaming, pipe-dreaming, mooning, moony, woolgathering, staring into the middle distance. See PREOCCUPIED.

ABSTRUSE adj. clear as mud, clear as dishwater, it beats me, you've got me, it's Greek to me, I give up, I pass. See OBSCURE.

ABSURD adj. camp, campy, jokey, joshing, yokky, gagged up, for grins, flaky, freaky, freaked out, goofy, kooky, wacky, screwy, loony, off the wall, batty, cockamamie, cool, crazy, daffy, nutty, sappy, dippy, dizzy, goofus. See also FOOLISH.

ABSURDITY n. jive, jazz, bull, shit, bullshit, BS, bull-pucky, horseshit, total cahcah, crap, applesauce, sour grapes, vanilla, phedinkus, hot air, piss and wind, balloon juice, flapdoodle, flumadiddle. See NONSENSE.

ABUNDANT adj. no end, up to one's ass in, up the ying-yang in, lousy with, filthy with, stink with, crawling with, drug on the market, rolling in, mucho, heavy, fat, plate is full. See PLENTY.

ABUSE n. bad mouthing, shitting on, pissing on, kicking around, pushing around, lousing around, screwing, screwing around, fucking over, buckwheats, honey, hosing, humping, knifing, quinine, skinning alive, signifying, signifyn', shucking and jiving, S'ing 'n' J'ing.

ABUSE v. 1. mess up, manhandle, roughhouse, rough up, bung, bung up, cut up, shake up, total, wax, hose, hump. 2. trash, bash, bad-mouth, peg, punk, jack, cap, back cap, back bite, rip up the back, bitter-mouth, cut down to size, do a number on, dog on (verbal), crack on (Hum., Af. Am.), pick on, dump on, rag, rag on, rip on, tool on, knock, put down, run down, tear down, burn down, burn one down, smear, ride, hurl a brickbat, dozens, play the dozens, play dirty dozens, sound dozens, sound, signify, shuck and jive, give one the finger, give five fingers to one, give a black eye, zing, give one a zinger, give one the cold shoulder, cut to the quick, blow off, cut, chop, get bent, do one wrong, rank out, gross out, cuss out, dish out, dish it out, slam, dig at, pooh-pooh, slap at, swipe, hassle, rag, break one's balls, push around, louse around, kick one around, mess around with, screw around, screw, yentz, buckwheat, hit with buckwheats, knock up, shag, haircut (by a woman), take over the hurdles, shit on, piss on, fuck over.

ABUSED adj. dogged, caught shit, picked-on, shafted, walking wounded, had to scrape one off the sidewalk. See also BATTERED.

ACADEME n. cacademia.

ACADEMICIAN n. prof, teach, brain, egghead, hardboiled egghead (tough-minded), scrambled egghead (fuzzy-minded), Dr. Nytol (boring), gnurd, gome, grind, pencil geek, tool, power tool, throat, wonk, auger, book-worm, cereb, cutthroat, grub, ink squirter, spider, squid. See also TEACHER.

ACADEMY n. alma mater, old Siwash, brainery, halls of ivy, aggie, cow college, fem sem. See SCHOOL.

ACCEDE v. 1. okay, OK, go along with, play ball with, be game for, give the go-ahead, give the green light. 2. cave in, give in, cry uncle, fold, throw in the towel, roll over and play dead. See AGREE.

ACCELERATE v. put the pedal to the metal, punch it, gun, rev, rev up, open 'er up, drop the hammer down, hammer on, nail it, peel rubber, dust, roll, tool, fire up, step on the gas, lay scratch, lay rubber, lay a batch, batch out, make tracks. See SPEED.

ACCELERATOR PEDAL n. hammer.

ACCENTUATE v. spot, spotlight, limelight, highlight, resonate, underline, hit, headline.

ACCEPT v. 1. okay, OK, buy, lap up, eat up, set store by, sign, sign off on, thumbs up, check out, check up, put one's John Hancock on, get behind, go for, have eyes for, got to hand it to one, give the nod, give the go ahead, give the green light, give the stamp of approval, rubber-stamp, stroke, pat on the back, hats off to. See also APPROVE. 2. live with, bear with, suck it up, go along with, put up with, stomach something, stand for, sit still for, take, don't make waves, don't rock the boat, fit in, play the game, swim with the tide, toe the mark, when in Rome do as the Romans do. See also ENDURE. 3. take one up on. 4. take as gospel truth, take stock in, swallow, swallow hook line and sinker, take one's lumps, lump it.

ACCEPTABLE adj. cool, coolville, coolsville, cas, cazh, A-OK, A-okay, fucking-A, OK, ok, okay, okey-dokey, okee-doke, up to speed, level, reat, all reet, all root, all righty, right on, I can live with that, Jake, that'll work, not half bad, swell, dory, okey-dory, hunky-dory, ducky, just ducky, George, jake, peachy, peachy-keen, sharp, hitting on all six, all to the mustard, on the beam, on the ball, on the right track, up to code, up to snuff, big, large, drooly, kimble (tries to be), lulu, one of the boys, pop, selling, sizzler, tuff, trendy, happenin', in the swim, faddy, masscult, it's the berries, crazy, copacetic, kopasetic, cooking with gas, close, in the groove, groovy, groove, far out, on the beam, on the right track, on the ball, on target, right on the money, frantic, fab, home cooking, hotsic-totsie, in there, icc, ready, sharp, right guy, okay people, kosher, regular.

ACCEPTANCE n. go-ahead, green light, okay. See APPROVAL.

ACCEPTED adj. 1. okayed, go down. 2. in, in the loop, made it, in like Flynn, that's it, pass, pass current, won one's spurs, arrived. 3. touted, highly touted, okay people, kosher, legit, according to the book, boy scout, good Joe, aces, straight, straight arrow, in line, playing their game, playing it safe, in the groove, according to Hoyle.

ACCESS n.   connection, contact, in, open arms, open door.

ACCESSIBLE adj.   the door's always open, come-at-able, gettable, get-in-able.

ACCESSORY n.   stall, insider, plant.

ACCIDENT n.   pile-up, crack-up, fender-bender, bumper-thumper, bam and scram (hit and run), total, fender tag, rear ender, stack-up, smash, smash-up, rack-up, wrack-up, event (nuclear), fluke, mess 'em up, slip-up, bang 'em up, crack 'em up; ride-out, squat (fraudulent).

ACCIDENT-PRONE adj.   klutzy, Calamity Jane.

ACCLAIM n.   strokes, stroking, pat on the back, pat on the head, PR, puff, puffing up, pumping up, rave, abreaction route.

ACCLAIM v.   hear it for, kudo, rave, root, beat one's skin, beat one's drum, blow one's horn, stroke, boost, push, puff up, brag about, give a bouquet, give a posy, hand it to, have to hand it to.

ACCLAIMED adj.   hot, highly touted, touted, a somebody, belled. See also CELEBRITY.

ACCLAMATION n.   hand, big hand, mitt-pound, bring down the house, have 'em on their feet.

ACCLIMATED adj.   settled in, sea legs, get one's sea legs. See also ACCUSTOMED.

ACCOMMODATE v.   go with the flow, go by the book, don't make waves, don't rock the boat, play the game, shape up, shape up or ship out, bend over backwards, meet halfway. See CONFORM.

ACCOMMODATING adj.   user-friendly, handy, all-around, on deck, on tap, be a sport, be a regular fellow. See also INDULGENT.

ACCOMMODATION n.   deal, fifty-fifty, one's own sweet time, whenever. See also COMPROMISE.

ACCOMMODATIONS n.   crash pad, pad, digs, diggings, crib, roof over one's head. See HOUSE.

ACCOMPANIMENT n.   backup, backing, back.

ACCOMPANY v.   1. drag, take out, furp, squire, date. 2. dog, dog one's heels, string along, tag after, tag along, draft, spook, schlep along, stick to.

ACCOMPLICE n.   stall, insider, plant.

ACCOMPLISH v.   make it, pull off, do the trick, put it over, take care of, score, hit, break out with, bust out with (surprisingly or suddenly), get there, unzip, arrive, bring home the bacon, nail it, do a bang-up job, do one proud, do

justice, get someplace, get to first base, make hay, make hay while the sun shines, sew up. See ACHIEVE.

ACCOMPLISHED adj.   1. buttoned-up, that's history, cashed, a wrap, wrapped-up, cleaned-up, wound-up, mopped-up, pow, dealt with, have under one's belt, knocked off, pulled it off, polished off, put away, did the trick, turned the trick, put across, put over, came through with, fixed, home, set, shot, wired, all over but the shouting, done for, done to a T, done to a finish, done to a frazzle, all set, almost home (nearly), home free. See also FINISHED. 2. brainy, savvy, wised up, hep, hip, hip to the jive, cool, sharp, sharp as a tack, tack, with it, book-smart, all woke up, know one's business. See SKILLED, SKILLFUL.

ACCORD n.   pact, okay, deal, dicker, drop-dead conditions (firm or final); Big 10-4. 2. good vibrations, good vibes, on the same wave length. See AGREEMENT.

ACCORDION n.   squeeze box, box of teeth, groan box, wind box, lap organ.

ACCOST v.   run into, face off, brace, cross, flag, flag down, whistle for, whistle down. See also CONFRONT.

ACCOUNT n.   1. the picture, the whole picture, rundown, lowdown, ABC's, blow by blow, play by play, score, tab, take, make, megillah, whole megillah. See also STORY. 2. tab, cuff, bad news, check, checkeroo, damages, grunt, IOU, score. See also STATEMENT.

ACCOUNT v.   count heads, count noses, cut ice, cut some ice, dope out, figure in, keep tabs, keep score, run down, take account of, tote, tote up. See also COUNT.

ACCOUNTABLE adj.   count on one, on the hook, carry the load, kosher, right guy, Rock of Gibraltar, straight, surefire. See also RESPONSIBLE.

ACCOUNTANT n.   pencil pusher, sharp pencil pusher, pencil shover, pen pusher, pen driver, bean counter, CPA, number cruncher.

ACCOUNTING n.   1. the books, count. 2. score, tab.

ACCULTURATE v.   go native, hit the beach, fit in.

ACCUMULATE v.   round up, scare up, rack up, clean up, pile up, make a pile, make a bundle. See also GET, INCREASE, SAVE.

ACCUMULATION n.   1. buildup, up, upping. 2. chunk, gob, pile, hunk. See also SUM.

ACCURATE adj.   on the nose, on the button, on the numbers, on the money, right on the money, right on, keerect, reet, reat, solid. See CORRECT.

ACCURSED adj.   snake-bit, jinxed, damned, all-fired, hellfire, hoodooed, voodooed.

ACCUSATION n.   beef, beefing, bitch, gripe, holler, roar, bum rap (false).

ACCUSE v. finger, point the finger at, put the finger on, hang something on, pin on one, pin it on one, name, front, front off, blow the whistle on one, whistle-blow, frame, frame up, spell, spell for, put up a job, lay at one's door, let one have it. See also DENOUNCE.

ACCUSED n. goat, butt, patsy, fall guy.

ACCUSER n. whistle-blower, fink. See also INFORMER.

ACCUSTOM v. get one's sea legs, roll with the punches, swim with the tide, come up to scratch, fit in. See CONFORM.

ACCUSTOMED adj. grooved, in the groove, sea legs, get one's sea legs, settled in. See CONFORM.

ACHIEVE v. go to town, go over big, perk, percolate, tear off, tick, make it, make it big, make one's mark, make a name for oneself, make hay, make the grade, make well, make out, make a noise in the world, earn one's wings, have one's wings, pull off, pull it off, beat out, knock off, polish off, romp off with, do the trick, turn the trick, do up brown, do a turn, do to a turn, do to a T, do a number, do oneself proud, do the job, be on, go on, as advertised, get it across, put across, put over, put it over, put away, put the lid on, put it together, one down, one down and two to go, sail through, take care of, T.C.B. (take care of business), deal with, come through with, come out on top of the heap, strut, strut one's stuff, do one's stuff, come on, come on like gangbusters, score, hit, break out with, bust out with (surprisingly or suddenly), bring down the house, be home free, get away with, get fat, get rich, get well, get over, get ahead, get there, get to first base, clean up, wind up, button up, wrap up, mop up, tape, unzip, ring the bell, hack it, arrive, bring home the bacon, bring home the groceries, feather one's nest, line one's nest, hit the bull's-eye, fly, nail it, drive it home, win one's spurs, squeak by (barely), go places, go great guns, luck, step into the shoes of.

ACHIEVED adj. under one's belt, knocked off, polished off, dealt with, put away, that's history, pulled off, put across, put over, cleaned up, wound up, wrapped up, mopped up. See also ACCOMPLISHED, FINISHED.

ACHIEVEMENT n. track record.

ACHING adj. hurting. See PAINFUL.

ACKNOWLEDGE v. 1. I'll be back to you, I'll get back to you; not give one a flop, not give one a rumble or tumble, pass up (fail to). See also ANSWER. 2. own up, come out of the closet, cop a plea, fess, fess up, out with it, open up, crack, come clean, get it off one's chest. See CONFESS.

ACNE n. crater face, pizza puss, pizza face (severe).

ACQUAINT v. intro, knock down, give a knockdown, do the honors, bring out, come out with, fix up, spring with. See also INTRODUCE.

ACQUIESCE v. 1. okay, pass, pass on, shake on, cut a deal, buy, set, yes one, ditto, play ball with, that works for me, give one five (slap hands), jibe. 2. come across, come around, give out, put out (sexual); give in, cave in, cry uncle, say uncle, roll over and play dead, fold. See AGREE.

ACQUIESCENT adj. yes-man, ass kisser, on a string, henpecked, tied to one's apron strings, on a leash, weak sister, Milquetoast, Caspar Milquetoast, tail between one's legs, schnook, dance, dance to one's tune, eat crow, eat humble pie, eat shit, putty in one's hands, wimpy, wet rag, wet sock, when in Rome do as the Romans do. See also SUBMISSIVE.

ACQUIRE v. promote, corral, access, hustle, wangle, grab, get hold of, get one's hands on, latch on to, pick up, lock up, rack up, scare up, bag, snag, catch, cop. See GET.

ACQUIRED IMMUNE DEFICIENCY SYNDROME n. AIDS, PWA (person with AIDS), gatoraids (Florida), switchblaids (gang).

ACQUISITIVE adj. grabby, poligot, greedy guts.

ACQUISITIVENESS n. the grabs, the gimmies.

ACQUIT v. clear, let go, let off, let one off the hook, let one off easy, wipe it off, blink at, wink at, whitewash. See ABSOLVE.

ACQUITTED adj. beat the rap, walked, let off, let off the hook.

ACRIMONIOUS adj. bitchy, cussed, mean, ornery, salty. See SARCASTIC.

ACT n. 1. routine, shtick, gag, bit, blackout, piece, after piece, spot, stand-up comedy, dumb act (without words), hoke act. See also PERFORMANCE. 2. shuck and jive, stall, put on, stunt, bit, false front, fake, phony, crocodile tears, soft soap, sweet talk, chaser, mitzvah (good). 3. papers (legal).

ACT v. 1. go for it, go for broke, go in for, go that route, go to town, move on (to something else), move, make one's move, make with (the eyes, feet, etc.), do a number, do one's thing, double, do double duty (two roles), TCB (take care of business), take a flier (impulsively), pull off, fish or cut bait, shit or get off the pot, get in there, get with it, chill hard, kickin' it, kick it live (Af. Am., do it well), large and in charge (Af. Am.), boogie, time to boogie (time to get started), take up, whip up, whip out, tear off, knock off, perk, percolate, cook, it cooks, that dog'll hunt, tick, bag, click, break out with, bust out with (surprisingly or suddenly), stooge, operate, run with the ball, come on, come on like, do one's stuff, whittle. 2. be on, go on, do a turn, do one's bit, knock off, strut, strut one's stuff, do one's stuff, say one's piece, play one's role, play one's gig, go into one's song and dance, chew the scenery, mug, ham, ham it up, tread the boards, stooge, emote, do black; go over big, put it over, bring down the house, come on like gangbusters (well), beat out, blow, bomb, lay a bomb, lay an egg, go into the toilet. See also PRETEND, IMITATE.

ACTING n. ham acting, hammy acting, hamming, hamming up, improv (improvisation), stooging, thesping. See also ACT.

ACTION n. game, ball game, bag, scene, play (Af. Am.), trip, where the action is, where the rubber hits the road, comin' down, comin' off, goin' down, going, happenin', movin', movin' out, rollin', do, whoop-de-do, whoop-la, hoop-a-doop, hoop-de-doop, hoopla, hoopty-do, racket, plan, stunt, bit, followthrough, big idea, deal, hopper, pipeline, proposition, works, in full swing.

ACTIVATE v. put into play, demothball, take out of mothballs, trigger, call up. See also ACTUATE, ENERGIZE.

ACTIVE adj. hyper, ball of fire, fireball, whiz, eager beaver, busy as a beaver, busy as a bee, busier than a one-armed paperhanger, perky, chipper, burn, clocked-up, in full swing, jumping, on the go, on a merry go round, on the hop, on the jump, work one's tail off, run one's ass ragged, running around like a chicken with its head cut off, whirling dervish. See also SPIRITED, INDUSTRIOUS.

ACTIVIST n. trendinista (mostly Stu.).

ACTIVITY n. bag, game, ball game, scene, trip, where the action is, what's comin' down, what's comin' off, what's goin' down, what's going, what's happening, racket, stunt, bit, works, zoo. See ACTION.

ACTOR n. ham, hambone, ham fatter, trouper, legiter, lead, talent, matinee idol, bit player, moppet (child), star, thesp, straight man, feeder, stooge, foil, mugger, baddie, finger wringer, greaseball, barnstormer, dog (bad), hulligan (foreigner), stand-in, extra, lot hopper (film extra), atmosphere, scene chewer, scene sweller, spear carrier, supe, super, walk-on, heat (box office power). See also ACTRESS.

ACTOR'S AGENT n. flesh peddler, ten percenter.

ACTRESS n. fem lead, star, love interest, T and A, tits and ass, wampus. See also ACTOR.

ACTUAL adj. for real, honest-to-God, kosher, sure enough. no buts about it, no ifs ands or buts.

ACTUALITY n. what it is, like it is, telling it like it is, the emess, the real world, the real deal (Af. Am.), live, in the flesh, brass tacks, down to earth, no shit, the straight shit, the straight stuff, for real, too good to be true. See also REALITY; TRUTH.

ACTUATE v. turn on, egg on, fire up, key up, work up, work up into a lather, put up to. See also ACTIVATE, ENERGIZE.

ADAMANT adj. hard-nosed, hang tough, tough nut, set in concrete, carved in stone, pat, stand-pat, burly, take no prisoners, murder (he's murder). See STUBBORN.

ADAM'S APPLE n. gargle, google (not common).

ADAPT v. play the game, shape up, shape up or ship out, get one's act together, get it all together, get all the pieces in place, come around, come over, if you can't beat 'em join 'em, roll with the punches. See CONFORM.

ADAPTABLE adj. all-around, AC/DC, ac/dc, cosplug, switch hitter, go every which way, can do it all, hang loose, roll with the punches, putty in one's hands.

ADD v. 1. pad, pyramid, tag, tag on, slap on, tack on, hitch on, pour it on, cue in, figure in, piggyback, bump, bump up, beef up, soup up, hop up, heat up, hike, hike up, step up, jazz up, jack up, jump up, put up, run up, charge up, punch up, heat up, hot up, juice up, up, build, build up, spike, flesh out, add bells and whistles, snowball, sweeten, sweeten the pot, ante, up the ante, parlay, speed up, boost, press a bet, join together, join up with, hook up with, hook on, plug into, add fuel to the fire. 2. tot, tot up, tote, tote up, reckon up. See also INCREASE.

ADDICT n. junkie, junker, greasy junkie, AD, A-head, user, doper, space cadet, mainliner, zone, zoner, freak, piper (crack smoker), head, hop, hophead, hopper, drughead, coke head, basehead (freebases), acid head, acid freak, dust head, stoner, gomer, weedhead, pothead, pillhead, meth-head, fiend, dope fiend, hooked, hype, hypo, banger, bangster, jabber, jaboff, needle man, needle knight, smack slammer, smokey, tripper, dirty, dopenik, straight (after injection), viper, wasted, dynamiter, artillery man, jug, jug man, on the jug (injects into jugular vein), sick (needs injection), cokey, cokomo, kokomo, snifter, tooter, ice creamer, student, Skag Jones, snowbird, snow snorter, station worker, Saturday night habit (occasional), bean popper, joy popper (new or occasional user), joy boy, campfire boy, Cap'n Toke, tea toker, from Mount Shasta (not common), goof, goofball, aspirin hound, speedo, speed freak, horse; globetrotter, boomer, drifter, floater, boot and shoe (always moving), author, scribe (both able to write prescriptions). See also DRUG USER.

ADDICTED v. hooked, hooked on, on the needle, hyped, sprung (on rock cocaine), dusted (high on PCP), spaced-out, wiped-out, strung-out.

ADDICTION n. habit, hook, monkey, monkey on one's back, Jones, jones, sweet tooth, thing, to be into, hang up, one's bag, shot, kick; boss habit, ape sitting on one's neck, crapping on one's brain (heavy); chickenshit habit, ice-cream habit (minimal).

ADDITION n. options, all the options, bells, bells and whistles, upping, boost, hike.

ADDITIONAL adj. on the side, option, all the options, bells and whistles, perks, padding, spare tire, plus God knows what, and (implied: coffee and), and such, and such and such, and so on, all that sort of thing, and all that, and like that, stuff like that, and what-not, and what-have-you, widow, lagniappe. See also EXTRA.

ADDITIONALLY adv. one mo' time, una mas, come again, chew one's cabbage twice.

ADDLE v. get to, discomboberate, discumbobulate, ball up, rattle, rattle one's cage, throw, throw one, put one on a crosstown bus. See CONFUSE.

ADDLED adj. unglued, defrosted, slap-happy, punchy, shook, shook-up, up, balled-up, fouled-up, fucked-up, mixed-up, farmisht, fertummeled, farshimmelt, woozy, thrown, rattled, out to lunch, gone. See CONFUSED.

ADDRESS n. pitch, spiel, chalk talk, pep talk, soapbox oration. See SPEECH.

ADDRESS v. 1. pitch, spiel, spout, stump, get on a soapbox. See SPEAK. 2. dig, hammer away, plug, peg away, go at, go for, have a go at, have at, pitch into. See APPLY ONESELF. See also ATTEMPT. 3. flag, flag down, whistle for, whistle down, flop, give one a flop, give one a toss, give one the glad eye, give one the glad hand, highball, shoulder, tumble. See also GREET.

ADDRESS BOOK n. little black book, trick book (used by prostitutes).

ADEPT adj. sharp, sharp as a tack, tack, smart as a whip, brainy, brain, got it up here (head), no dumbbell, no dummy, nobody's fool, not born yesterday, quick on the trigger, quick on the uptake, crazy like a fox, clean, heads up, on the ball, on the beam, up to speed, phenom, pro, there, whiz, whiz kid, whiz bang, wizard, boss player, has enough ducks in a row, hot, hotshot, know one's onions, know one's stuff, have know-how, slick, smooth, crack, crackerjack, cute, no slouch, savvy. See also SKILLED.

ADHERE v. stick like a barnacle, stick like a leech, stick like glue, stick like a wet shirt, stick like a limpet, freeze to, cling like a burr, cling like ivy, hold on like a bulldog, stay put.

ADHERENT n. flunky, buff, echo, fan, freak, frenzies, nut, hanger-on, ho-dad, ho-daddy, plaster, shadow, stooge, tail.

ADHESIVE n. stickum, gunk, gummy, spit.

AD HOC adj. ad hockery. See also TEMPORARY.

ADJUST v. 1. fix up, doctor, fine-tune, tweek, fiddle with. See also CHANGE; MODIFY. 2. get one's act together, get one's shit together, get it together. 3. fit in, play the game, roll with the punches, swim with the tide, grin and bear it, when in Rome do as the Romans do. See CONFORM.

ADJUSTABLE RATE MORTGAGE n. ARM.

ADJUSTER n. go-between, fixer.

ADMINISTER v. ride herd on, boss, run, run the show, head, head up, hold the reins, sit on top of, be in the driver's seat, be in the saddle, crack the whip, pull the strings, pull the wires. See MANAGE.

ADMINISTRATION n. brass, top brass, front office, people in the front office, upstairs, people upstairs, big brother, one's watch, D.C., the digger, the mighty dome, the Union, Uncle Sam, U.S., U.S.A., Washington, the Feds (also Federal Reserve Bank). See also MANAGEMENT.

ADMINISTRATION BUILDING n. ad building, tower of power, HQ, GHQ, CP.

ADMINISTRATOR n. exec, CEO, boss, Prez, prex, prexy (Usu. college), POTUS (President of the U.S.), Great White Father (U.S.), big brother, head, head man, head honcho, brass, man upstairs, front office, suit. See also EXECUTIVE.

ADMIRABLE adj. killer, a 10, A, A-1, A-number one, A-plus, A-OK, okay, fresh, sweet, dyno, aggro, ace, aces, ace high, ace of spades, cas, cazh, def, daddy, super, super-duper, smashing, brutal, gnarly, mega-gnarly, righteous, unreal, Jake, not half bad, cool, zero cool, cold, wicked, out of this world, out of sight, gilt-edged, drooly, flash, lampin', like wow, best ever, crack, cracking, crackerjack, peacherino, peach, peachy, ginger-peachy, peachy-keen, keen, salt of the earth, top, tops, topnotch, topnotcher, top-flight, top-drawer, top-of-the-line, tip-top, first-class, first-chop, first-rate, star, boss, stunning, corking, a corker, solid, solid sender, great, greatest, a doozie, a daisy, dilly, bo, boo, tickety-boo, deadly, deadly-boo, bong, sly, copacetic, kopasetic, the bee's knees, the cat's meow, the cat's whiskers, the cat's pajamas, the butterfly's book, the caterpillar's kimono, George, the real George, down, good show, golden, hard, hummer, humdinger, knockout, mad, mess, mezz, nasty, nifty, the nuts, the nerts, ripping, rip-snorter, sanitary, heavenly, bang-up, like dynamite, fab, in fat city, in orbit, murder, neat, neato, hunky-dory, all wool and a yard wide, jam-up, slap-up, dandy, fine and dandy, just dandy, jim-dandy, but good, strictly, a sweetheart, catch, find, plenty, zanzy, beautiful, cuspy, check-plus, stellar, dream, living doll, lollapaloosa, whiz, killer-diller, mean, ducky, hot, spiffy, spiffing, ripping, nobby, delicious, scrumptious, not too shabby, something else, groovy, tough, heavy, bad, evil, marvy, winner, choice, reet, gasser, Jake, ginchy, slammin', fabu, it's to die for, dynamite, major, far-out, funky, state-of-the-art, too much, swell, savage, shirt, shirty, tawny, a whale of a, world-beater, pip, pippin, lulu, darb, a honey, a beaut, this is some kinda ———, it's the berries, bully, sharp, the best.

ADMIRE v. be crazy for, be crazy over, be crazy about, be nuts about, be daffy about, be wild about, be whacky about, be mad about, be mad for, go for, fall for, moon for, have the hots, be hot for, have eyes for, carry the torch for, torching, have it for one, sprung on, be gone on, be far gone on, be sweet on, be stuck on, groove on, be hipped on, get high on, freak out on, have a crush on, have a mash on, have a case on, goof on, take to, be smitten by, rings one's bell, be keen about, have a thing about. See also LOVE, APPROVE.

ADMIRED adj. pop, drooly, okay people, big, large, large charge, big man on campus, BMOC, kimble (tries to be).

ADMIRER n. rooter, groupie, buff, fan, skeezer (hip-hop), wannabee, autograph hound, booster, bug, freak, junkie, nut, frenzie, crank, culture vulture, fiend, flip, hound, alligator, gator, gate, cat, hepcat, stargazer, blue farouq. See also DEVOTEE, LOVER, SUPPORTER.

ADMISSION, HOSPITAL n. hit.

ADMISSION TICKET n. admish, board, stub, two-fer (half price), pasteboard, chit, deadwood (unsold); pass, freebee, paper, Annie Oakley, Chinee, Chinee ducat (Derog.), comp (free); dukie, dookie (meal ticket); duck (social event); bid, invite (invitation).

ADMIT v. spill, spill it, spill one's guts, spill the beans, cop a plea, get it off one's chest, get it out of one's system, bring it out into the daylight, let it all hang out, open up, fess up, own up, out with it, spit it out, blab, blabber, come clean, give away, give away the show, let the cat out of the bag. See also CONFESS, ALLOW, CONCEDE.

ADMONISH v. speak to, talk to, tell a thing or two, rag, rag on, gig, give what for, give a going over, give a piece of one's mind, give one his comeuppance, call to task, call down, jack up, hoist, growl, rap, dance the carpet, call on the carpet, slap one's wrist, rap on the knuckles, glue, ding, draw the line. See also SCOLD, REBUKE.

ADOLESCENT n. weenie bopper, bobby soxer, juve, punk, yoot, jailbait (Fem.), teen, teeny, teenybop, teenybopper, petiteen, subdeb, sweet sixteen, twixt teen. See TEENAGER.

ADOPT v. go in for, go native, take up, go down the line, opt, tap.

ADORABLE adj. cute, dishy, hot stuff, hot item, sure-fire, sexy, lulu, suave, superfly, dream bait, highly salable, good enough to eat up, good enough to eat with a spoon, a catch (usually husband or wife), after one's own heart, wouldn't kick (him/her) outta bed.

ADORATION n. amore, mash, pash, weakness, yen, shine, beaver fever (Obsc.), calf love, puppy love, hankering.

ADORE v. be crazy for, be crazy over, be crazy about, be nuts about, be daffy about, be wild about, be wacky about, be mad about, be mad for, dig, go for, fall for, sprung on, flip over, be gone on, be far gone on, be sweet on, be stuck on, groove on, goof on, be serious, be smitten with, got it bad, have one's nose open, be that way. See LOVE.

ADORN v. doll up, fix up, gussy up, spruce up.

ADORNMENT n. dingbat, doodad, thing, fandangle, jazz, floss, seagoing (large, absurd). See DECORATION.

ADROIT adj. quick on the trigger, quick on the uptake, savvy, have know-how, sharp, slick, crack, crackerjack, cute, cutie, foxy, hot tamale, neat, nifty, been there, sharp as a tack, smart as a whip, good hands, clean, heads-up, on the ball, on the beam, up to speed, whiz, wizard. See also SKILLED.

ADULATE v. suck ass (Obsc.), suck up to, kiss up to, kiss ass, brown-nose (Obsc.), bootlick, massage, curry below the knee. See FLATTER.

ADULATION n. strokes, bouquet, posy, eyewash, oil, soap, soft soap, blarney, bunkum, butter salve, sweet talk, shot in the arm, shot in the ass. See FLATTERY.

ADULTERATE v. doctor, doctor up, phony up, plant, spike, water, water down, baptize, irrigate, cook, cut, needle, lace, shave.

ADULTERATOR n. needleman (liquor).

ADULTEROUS adj. extracurricular, fast, fast-and-loose, speedy, messy, two-timing, sneakin' deacon, moonlighting, cheating, cheat on, double-crossing, two-faced.

ADULTERY n. affair, fling, relationship, musical beds, carrying on, hanky-panky, playing around, nooner, matinee, two-timing, doggin', getting some on the side, a little something on the side, dog one around, tip, tip out, working late at the office, yard on, extracurricular activity, extracurricular sex, extracurricular relations, Roman spring (late in life), thing, your place or mine?

ADULTHOOD n. prime, prime of life, dry behind the ears, ripe age, age of consent, drinking age.

ADVANCE n. 1. breakthrough, a break, go-ahead. 2. boost, buildup, Mexican raise (promotion without raise in pay). See also PROMOTION. 3. front money, in front, front-end loading, hike, angel dust, bite, floater, grubstake, jawbone, juice (usurious), score, scratch, take, touch, stake to. See also LOAN. 4. tip, tip-off, feeler, pass, proposition. See also OFFER. 5. up, upping, upgrade. See also IMPROVE.

ADVANCE v. 1. get the green light, get the go-ahead, get over, get well, get ahead, get there, get with it, go places, go great guns, make the grade, make a hit, romp off with, skyrocket, take off, fly, move out, strike a vein, strike a rich vein, hit, come through with, cream, cream up, step into the shoes of, catch on, score, arrive, nail it, hack it, do oneself proud, come on, come along, come out on top of the heap, win one's spurs. See also ACHIEVE; SUCCEED; IMPROVE. 2. up, up one's pay, upgrade, boost, boost one's pay, get fat, get rich, strike it rich, strike gold, make a killing, make out, pan out, turn out, go crazy large (Af. Am.), break the bank, hit the jackpot, hit pay dirt, kick upstairs. 3. plug, hype, push, splash, spot, throw the spotlight on, puff, boost, ballyhoo, put on the map, make a pitch for, beat the drum for, thump the tub for, get ink for. See SUPPORT. 4. stake, loan shark. See LOAN.

ADVANCED adj. avant-garde, leading-edge, cutting-edge, state-of-the-art, break, breakthrough, far-out, radical (not political), out-of-sight.

ADVANCING adj. upbeat, on the rise, on the lift, up-scaling, looking good, looking up, making it, on the upswing, on a roll, rolling.

ADVANTAGE n. edge, break, bulge, drag, pull, suction, string, ropes, weight, wire, wire-pulling, clout, winner, a lock, over, drop, have the drop on, jump, have a jump on, have a leg up on, bargaining chip, big chip, ace in the hole, card up one's sleeve, play the card, born with a silver spoon in one's mouth, head start, jump start, flying start, running start, nose out, in, in on the ground floor, inside track, what's in it for one, in pocket, the percentage, the upper hand, whip hand, a foot in the door, sitting pretty, sitting in the driver's seat, sitting in the catbird seat, steal a march, al joe, alzo, fix, gaff, gimmick, nuts, spot, spark, zinger, all sewed up, loose change (temporary), a lot to do with, a lot to say about.

ADVANTAGE, TAKE v. steamroll, bulldoze, bleed, give one the short end of the stick, get one by the balls, get one by the short hairs, make hay, make hay while the sun shines, kick around, pack it in, trade on, cash in on, pour it on, push, push one's luck, burn up, hump, knock up, put one over, pull a fast one, push around, screw, screw around, cop a heel, cop a sneak, double bank, piece off; rim, reem (Obsc.), shave, skin, play for a sucker, mooch (commodity scam), take for a ride, take for a sleighride, take the bull by the horns, strike while the iron is hot, not be caught flatfooted.

ADVENTURE n. happening, hap, happenso, cranking, a trip, a real trip, scene, a gas.

ADVENTURE v. go out on a limb, go for broke, go off the deep end, step off the deep end, go to sea in a sieve, leave oneself wide open, play with fire, be a fire eater.

ADVERSARY n. bad guy, opposish, oppo, opposite number, bandit, buddy (sarcasm), buddy-buddy, buddy fucker (Obsc.), crip.

ADVERSE adj. agin, down on, nasty, sick, allergic, have no use for, ornery, stuffy, debit side, on the debit side, down side, the bad news.

ADVERSE REACTION adj. backlash.

ADVERSITY n. bummer, downer, ran into a buzz saw (unexpected), shit happens, bad scene, can of worms, trouble in River City, hobble, crunch, be clobbered, shit, deep shit, shit out of luck, shit outta luck, S.O.L., nightmare, crisis mode, lame, up shit creek, up shit creek without a paddle, tough shit, TS, shit hit the fan, one's ass is grass, down on one's luck, rotten luck, rough, tough, tough luck, rotten break, tough break, bad break, total shuck, drag, grabber, hurting, the worst, kiss of death, can't even get arrested, cold, hard time, hard knocks, hard row to hoe, up against it, on the skids, pull in one's belt, gone to pot, gone to the dogs, it shouldn't happen to a dog, unload, rain, rainin', rainy day, run for cover, bugaboo, double whammy, jinx, jonah, evil eye, stink eye, poison, that's the way the ball bounces, that's the way the cookie crumbles, a bitch, payin' dues, raw deal, tit caught in the wringer, tit in the wringer, tail in a gate, holy mess, unholy mess, messed up, stew, devil to pay, hell to pay, pain in the ass, pain in the neck, bad news, clutch, jam, your court (your problem), pretty pass, pickle, pretty pickle, fine kettle of fish, how-do-you-do, fine how-do-you-do, ticklish spot, tricky spot, sticky wicket, scrape, double trouble, tar baby, headache, heat's on, hot water, hot grease, jackpot, messed up, screw-up, tsuris, tumul, need it like a hole in the head, rum go, deadman's hand, it's your funeral, they're peeing on us and telling us it's raining, next week East Lynne.

ADVERTISE v. plug, pitch, make a pitch for, drum, beat the drum for, hard-sell, soft-sell, tub-thump, thump the tub for, ballyhoo, bill, billboard, boost, promote, puff, put on the map, hype, push, splash, spot, build up, press agent, throw the spotlight on, get on a soapbox for.

ADVERTISEMENT n. ad, plug, envelope stuffer, flyer, throwaway, literature, squib, want ad, commercial, advert, advid (video), Bambi (uses a cute animal), art (graphic), bleed (extends to edge of page), double-truck (two-page ad), hymns (hidden messages), sizzle (image), teaser, videocart (grocery shopping cart), kickapoo (product).

ADVERTISER n. fairy godfather, sponsor.

ADVERTISING n. Madison Avenue, Mad Avenue, blurb, hype, PR, promo, puff, plug, pluggery, ballyhoo, buildup, pitch, dynamiting, hard sell, blasting, bulldogging, blitz, roadblock (saturation campaign), hoopla, pizzazz, squib, screamer, spread, puffery. See also PUBLICITY.

ADVERTISING AGENCY n. ad agency, pluggery, shop.

ADVERTISING FRAUD n. scam, hype, limb, tap, tap game, con, con game, on the bite.

ADVERTISING MAN n. huckster, adman, ad writer, ballyhooer, ballyhoo man, booster, pitchman, plugger, spieler. See also PUBLICIST.

ADVICE n. tip, tip-off, steer, bum steer (bad), kibitz, flea in the ear, two cents' worth, word to the wise, telltale.

ADVISE v. steer, tout, update, level with, clue one in on, lay it on one, lay it on the line, put it on the line, lay it out for, lay a rap, let in on, let in on the know, put next to, put one on to, put one on to something hot, put one in the picture, put hip, put hep, put a bug in one's ear, put a bug up one's ass, put a flea in one's ear, put in one's two cents, put one wise, wise one up, put through the grind, put through the mill, tip, tip off, give one a tip, give one a pointer, give a pointer to, give one the word, post, keep one posted, pull one's coat, show one the ropes, kibitz, fold an ear, break in, break it to one, lace one's boots.

ADVISOR n. spin doctor, handler (Pol.), policy wonk, tout, tipster, clubhouse lawyer, jailhouse lawyer, guard-house lawyer, kibitzer, armchair general, Monday morning quarterback, second guesser, Dutch uncle, rabbi, buttinski, backseat driver, God committee, God squad (both Medic.).

ADVISORS, GROUP OF n. think tank, skunk works (usually secret), kitchen cabinet, groupthink, brain trust.

ADVOCATE v. root for, stump for, thump the tub for, bless, boost, give a boost to, give a leg up, give a lift, go for, go to bat for, hold a brief for, plump for, ride shotgun for, stick up for, run interference for, put a flea in one's ear about, put a bug in one's ear about, push, juice up, build up, plug, tout, spread it around, be in one's corner, back, back up, buck up, brace up, hold with, go with, get on the bandwagon, stick by, say so. See also RECOMMEND, SUPPORT.

AFFABLE adj. clubby, clubbable, breezy, Joe Nice Guy, Mr. Nice Guy, a real butt-kicker, one of the boys, one of the guys.

AFFAIR n. 1. goings-on, hanky-panky, fling, carrying on, unholy bedlock, a thing together, a relationship, getting some on the side, playing around, nooner, matinee, two-tim-ing, doggin', extracurricular activity, extracurricular sex, ex-tracurricular relations, tip out. 2. hap, happening, happenso, cranking, come off. See also PARTY.

AFFECT v. play-act, put up a front, do a bit, fake, lay it on thick, make out like. See IMITATE, PRETEND.

AFFECTATION n. front, false front, put-on, putting on the dog, putting on the ritz, show, showing out, showing off, Flash Gordon, going Hollywood, neon ribbons. See PRETENSION.

AFFECTED adj. ham, hammy, schmaltzy, tear-jerk-ing, false, fraud, phony, bogus, play actor, gone Hollywood, camp around, campy, artsy, artsy-crafty, artsy-fartsy, chichi, putting on the dog, putting on the ritz, ritzy, gold card, stuck up, airish, crooker, pinky crooker, highfalutin, play the————, put the hat on. See also PRETENTIOUS.

AFFECTING adj. mind-blowing, out of this world, on the move, feel in one's guts, turned on by, turned on to. See MOVING.

AFFECTION n. soft spot, crush, case, hooked, amore, mash, pash, mad pash, weakness, yen, mad for, crazy for, wild for, shine, beaver fever (Obsc.), calf love, puppy love, hankering, partial to, spoiling for, itch for.

AFFECTIONATE adj. lovey-dovey, huggy-huggy, mushy, nutty about, nutty over, all over one, partial to, soft on, big, big for, crazy for, crazy about, crazy over, heart in the right place.

AFFIANCED n. old lady, old man, main squeeze, dolly, daddy-o, intended, steady, going steady, pinned, bird, donah, donar, future, asked-for.

AFFILIATE n. 1. affil (TV), branch, branch house, off-shoot. 2. clubber, joiner. See ASSOCIATE.

AFFILIATE v. team up, team up with, tie up, tie up with, line up with, throw in together, throw in with, go partners with, hook up with, come aboard, plug into. See ASSOCIATE.

AFFILIATED adj. hooked up with, in cahoots with, joined up with, lined up with, partners with, thrown in with, tied in with, plugged into,

AFFILIATION n. tie-up, tie-in, have an in with, hookup, gang, mob, ring, syndicate, clan, bunch, crew, crowd, plunderbund, outfit, Old Boy network, cahoots. See ASSOCIATION.

AFFINITY n. thing, bag, groove, in the groove, groovy, turned on to, cotton to, flash, weakness for, cup of tea, druthers, hit it off, on the same wavelength, good vibes, good vibrations, simpatico. See INCLINATION.

AFFIRM v. swear up and down, swear on a stack of bibles, swear till one is blue in the face, cross one's heart and hope to die, cross one's heart and hope to spit, say-so, okay, put one's John Hancock on, rubber-stamp. See also AGREE.

AFFIRMATION n. go-ahead, green light, okay, right on, stamp of approval. See CONFIRMATION. See also AP-PROVAL.

AFFIRMED interj. alrighty, all reet, right on, absofuckinglutely (Obsc.), solid, O.K., thumbs up, Rodger Dodger, that'll work, crazy. See AGREED.

AFFIX v. tack on, tag, tag on, hitch on, slap on. See also FASTEN.

AFFLICTION n. bug, crud, creeping crud, the runs, what's going around, the pip, dose, double dose.

AFFLUENCE n. Easy Street, lap of luxury, the life of Riley, velvet, high on the hog, on top of the heap, bed of roses, clover.

AFFLUENT adj. uptown, upscale, in the chips, livin' high, have money to burn, shittin' in the tall grass, stinking rich, well-heeled, well-fixed, rollin', have the wherewithal, flush, fat cat, livin' large, clockin', big boys, upper-class, the main line, the haves. See WEALTHY.

AFFRONT n. put-down, brickbat, left-handed compli-ment, backhanded compliment, dump, dump on, dirty deed, dozens, dirty dozens. See INSULT.

AFFRONT v. diss, cap, pop junk, put down, dump on, give one the finger, give one a zinger, give one the cold shoulder, hit one where he lives. See INSULT.

AFRAID adj. 'fraidy cat, scaredy cat, run scared, scared stiff, scared witless, scared spitless, scared shitless, shit green, have cold feet, brick, shit a brick, shit in one's pants, piss in one's pants, spooked, frozen, goose-bumpy, asshole suckin' wind, pecker-assed, clutched up, D and D (deaf and dumb, afraid to testify). See FRIGHTENED.

AFRICAN AMERICAN n. Afro-American, black, brother, sister, bro, blood, youngblood, blood brother, soul, soul brother, soul sister, member; groid (So. Stu.), molonjohn, spade, ace of spades, moke, smoke, smoky, scrub, nigger, colored, colored negative, negative, coon, darky, darkie, buck, buck nigger, boy, beige, ape, blue, blue gum, blue skin, boogie, faded boogie, boogerboo, clink, bones, Mr. Bones, boot, satchel, satchel mouth, dark cloud, dark meat (sexual), shadow, shad, shad mouth, shine, spook, skillet, squasho, scobe, spill, splib, watermelon, zulu, ditty bop, ditty bob, domino, eightball, eight-rock, chocolate, chocolate bar, chocolate drop, ground ape, charcoal, charcoal nigger, chimney chops, Hershey bar, dew baby (dark-skinned), alligator bait (Fla., La.), article (slave, Obs.), cuh, cuz, bongo lips, boat lip, jig, moon cricket, mud flop, porch monkey, prune, rug, rughead, scrub, titre, toad, yanta, negative, Gange, Kange, Geechee, boojie, moolie, clown, cluck, cuffee, Mose, original, suede, shvartzeh, goonie (Virgin Islands), Mau Mau, jungle bunny, chungo bunny, moss, burrhead, hardhead, jarhead, kinkyhead, nap, nappy, nappyhead, woolly head, velcro head, butterhead, headlight, hod, scuttle, shot, Ethiopian, Guinea, snowball, raisin, ink, inky-dink, jazzbo, jig, jigaboo, zig, zigaboo, smear hoofer, Jim Crow, jit, peola, pink toes, pinky, red bone (light-skinned), dinge, conk buster (intellectual), bedbug (Pullman porter), bright (light), kelt, keltch (passing as white), tush (mulatto), black and tan, bleached ebony, sepe, sepia, banana, high yella, high yellow, bird's-eye maple (Fem. mulatto); spear carrier, handkerchief head, Uncle Tom, Mr. Tom (middle class), Dr. Thomas, Aunt Tom, Aunt Jane, Aunt Jemima, uncle, aunt, auntie, uppity black, pancake (subservient), HN (house nigger), Sam, Sambo, Stepin Fetchit, load of coal (group) (all Derog.).

AFRICAN AMERICAN, FEMALE n. sister, soul sister, band, bantam, barbecue, covess dinge, dange broad, black and tan, banana, bird's-eye maple, high yella, high yeller, high yellow, lemon (Derog.); poon tang, poontang (sexual Derog.); Aunt, auntie, Aunt Jane, Aunt Jemima, Aunt Tom, Sapphire.

AFTER-EFFECT n. spin-off, fallout, chain reaction, flak (bad), waves, can of worms, it's your funeral.

AFTERMATH n. chain reaction, waves, flak (bad), upshot, blow-off, payoff. See RESULT.

AFTERNOON n. this aft.

AGAIN adv. one mo' time, come again, una mas, chew one's cabbage twice. See REPEAT.

AGAINST adj. agin, down on, anti, con, copper a tip (act against advice). See OPPOSED.

AGAINST, BE v. knock, pan, bag on (Hum.), base on, put down, thumb down, turn thumbs down on, slam, blackball, be agin, hold no brief for, hit, take a dim view of. See OPPOSE.

AGE n. mileage, wear and tear.

AGE v. put mileage on, push, take hair off the dog, pull pages off the calendar.

AGED adj. senior citizen, golden ager, ager, gray, gray-haired, blue-haired, gray power, WOOP (well-off older people), on the shady side, over-the-hill, been around, bent, the dwindles, geed-up, gone, hairy, passé, ——— years young, oldie, older than dirt, worse for wear, wrinklie, rusty, creaky, hinges creaking, motheaten, got a few miles on one, shot, back number, antique, oldish, relic, from way back, P., peep (parent), pop, pops, pappy guy, dad, grandpa, grampa, gramps, grandma, gramma, gramms, grans, granny, old lady, old girl, old bag, haybag, hag, old dame, old hen, old battle-ax, warhorse, old frump, biddy, O.M., old gent, old chap, old cuss, coot, old bat, old dog, old goat, dodo, old dodo, fogey, old fogey, regular old fogey, old folks, old-timer, old softy, old smoothie, foozle, fossil, old fossil; old fart, old poop, old crock (Derog.); codger, duffer, old as Methuselah, old as the hills, oldster, alter cocker, A.K., duddy, fuddy-duddy, no chicken, no spring chicken, buzzard, desert rat, mossback, second childhood, the dwindles, on one's last legs, one foot in the grave, have one foot in the grave and the other on a banana peel, raisin, pruneface, baldie, baldy, chrome-dome, gink, gummer, long in the tooth, upper plates, on one's last legs, gerk (fool).

AGENDA n. hit list, lineup.

AGENT n. flesh peddler, ten percenter. See also OPERATIVE.

AGGRANDIZE v. boost, ballyhoo, hike, hike up, hype, lay it on with a trowel. See EXAGGERATE.

AGGRAVATE v. get to, bug, needle, hack, wig, utz (Yid.), drive up the wall, dog, nag, get in one's face, be on the back of, be at, pick on, chew on, give a bad time to. See ANNOY.

AGGRAVATION n. aggro, headache, tsuris, agita, pet peeve, a pain, pain in the ass, hang up, botheration. See ANNOYANCE.

AGGREGATE n. the works, whole enchilada, whole ball of wax, whole schmear, whole megillah, whole shooting match. See WHOLE.

AGGRESSION n. blitz, blitzkrieg, push, dirty deed. See ATTACK.

AGGRESSIVE adj. pushy, aggro, ambish, ballsy, bogard, cheeky, cocky, flip, fresh, crusty, gally, nervy, chutzpadik, biggety, sassy, smart-alecky, smart-ass, wise-ass, brassy, bold as brass, hungry, come on, come on like gangbusters, come on strong, enforcer, get up and go, be a go getter, go after, play for keeps, play hard ball, hard sell, heller, take charge, take over, take the bull by the horns, shoot from the hip. See also AMBITIOUS, ENTERPRISING, BELLIGERENT.

AGGRESSIVELY adv. in your face, woofing, taking it to 'em.

AGGRESSIVENESS n. guts, push, punch, steam, moxie, spunk, gumption, balls, drive, the stuff, the goods, what it takes, taking it to 'em, in there punching, get up and go, get out and go.

AGGRESSOR n. bushwhacker, mugger.

AGILE adj. nimble, quick on the draw, quick on the trigger, twinkletoes. See also FAST.

AGITATE v. psych, adjy, spook, get to, make one flip, flip one out, craze, bug, bug up, burn one up, egg on, push one's buttons, turn one on. See DISTURB. See also EXCITE.

AGITATED adj. antsy, uptight, defrosted, shittin' bricks, shook, shook up, creeped out, wired up, hopped up, hyper, freak out, spazz, spazz out, don't trip, hissy, clutched, clutched up, be a wreck, be a basket case. See DISTURBED.

AGITATION n. creeps, fidgets, jitters, heebie-jeebies, jimjams, jumps, shakes, quivers, trembles, dithers, agita, all-overs, flap, fuss, lather, flusteration, flustration, pucker, swivet, tizzy, stage fright, buck fever, needles, stew, to-do, zingers, fuzzbuzz (commotion), fuzzbuzzy, haroosh, scene, big scene, foofaraw, wingding, rhubarb, rowdy-dow, rumpus, ruckus, ruction, shindy, shivaree, stir, row, rumble.

AGITATOR n. adjy, spark plug, pusher, fireman, hatchet man, needle man, steam-up ghee, kochleffl (Yid.), stormy petrel, wave maker.

AGO adv. back, from way back, back when, time was, ages ago, from the year one, since God knows when, since Hector was a pup. See also PAST.

AGONIZE v. carry on, bleed, hurt, eat one's heart out, sing the blues, take it big. See LAMENT.

AGREE v. 1. okay, pass, pass on, shake on, shake hands on, sign on, take one up on, clinch, clinch the deal, make a deal, firm a deal, cut a deal, buy, buy into, set, yes one, ditto, take kindly to, get on the bandwagon, go along with, go along with the crowd, play ball with, hold with, we're all on the same page, be in tune with, be on the same wavelength with, get some brains wrapped around an idea, be game for, give the go-ahead, give the green light, give one a blank check, give one carte blanche, give one's blessing, give one's stamp of approval, give off good vibes, bury the hatchet, check, be

game for, give one five (slap hands), jibe, jive with, crazy, solid, that'll work, that works for me, way to go, there you go, you sold me, you got it, you ain't just whistling Dixie, you said a mouthful, it's a deal, me too, sure thing, I'll drink to that, I hear you, I hear you talkin, like you say, groovy, all the way. See also APPROVE, ENDORSE. 2. come across, come around, give out, put out (sexual); give in, cave in, cry uncle, say uncle, say the word, roll over and play dead, fold, gleek it, throw in the sponge, throw in the towel, toss in the sponge, toss in the towel, toss it in, give away the store, give up, quit, knuckle under, knuckle to, lie down and roll over for, string along. See also SUBMIT.

AGREEABLE adj. easy, breezy, Mr. Nice Guy, Joe Nice Guy, be a prince, a real butt-kicker, be a good joe, be a pussycat, upper, nervous, wild, reet, all reet, all root, all-righty, all-rightie, cool, coolsville, Jake, crazy, copacetic, kopasetic, okay, A-OK, fucking-A, okey-dokey, okey-doke, I can live with that, that'll work, ding-ho, ding-how, swell, dory, okey-dory, hunky-dory, right, righteous, snazzy, ducky, just ducky, George, jake, sharp, so-so, fine, fine as wine, dandy, fine-and-dandy, just dandy, jim-dandy, peach, peachy, peacherino, peachy-keen, keen, swell, fat, neat, nifty, spiffy, spiffing, ripping, nobby, delicious, flyin', creamy, orgasmic, cushy, fetching, home cooking, buzz, buscar (unexpected), but good, up to code, up to snuff, it's the berries, big deal, chop-chop, gas, a gas, gasser, far-out, in orbit, groove, in the groove, groovy, hip, on the beam, on the right track, on the ball, on target, on the button, on the nose, right on, right on the money, hitting on all six, all to the mustard, just what the doctor ordered, that's the ticket, frantic, fab, in there, in line, ice, ready, hotsie-totsie. See also ACQUIESCENT, CONTENT, WILLING.

AGREED interj. uh-huh, um-huh, I can live with that, yeah, yeah man, yep, yup, yowzah, yessiree, yes indeedy, indeedy, yea bo, si si, shoot, fer sure, sure, sure thing, surest thing you know, shore, check, right, right on, alrighty, right-o, reet, all reet, all rightee, okay, okie-doakie, okie bebe doakie, sweet, awesome, you betcha, you bet, you bet your life, you bet your ass, you bet your sweet ass, you bet your boots, that'll work, A, fuckin'-A, absofuckinglutely, for it, give the nod, thumbs up, Rodger Dodger, crazy, fine, like you say, good deal, keerect, solid, Charlie, Uncle Charlie, jake with me, you're damn tootin', you're darn tootin', you're the doctor, natch.

AGREEMENT n. good vibrations, good vibes, on the same wavelength, okay, deal, done deal, handshake, pact, ticket, piece of paper, drop-dead conditions (firm or final), Big 10-4, Four Roger for sure, Ten Roger Four, Ten Roger D, Four Roger, Roger Dodger, me too, go-ahead, green light, get the nod.

AGRICULTURAL COLLEGE n. aggie, cow college.

AGRICULTURAL STUDENT n. aggie.

AGRICULTURE n. agrimation (automated).

AID n. leg, leg up, shot in the arm, hand, handout, boost, juice, on the reservation, security blanket, backup, backing.

AID v. go with, go for, go to bat for, go the route for, stick up for, open doors for, lend a hand, bail out, straighten one out. See HELP. See also SUPPORT.

AIDE n. girl Friday, man Friday, stooge, shop, crew, troops. See ASSISTANT.

AIL v. gross out, feel awful, feel under the weather, look green around the gills, not feel like anything, come down with, take one's death.

AILING adj. down, run down, down with, got a bug, under the weather, below par, feeling awful, be off one's feed, feel like death warmed over, rocky, seedy, sick as a dog. See ILL.

AILMENT n. bug, crud, creeping crud, the runs (diarrhea), that's what's going around, the flu, the pip, dose, double scrudfantods, fascinoma (Medic.), willies (mythical).

AIM n. where one's heading, ambish. See also OBJECTIVE.

AIM v. target, zero in, move in, sight, sight on, get one in the crosshairs.

AIMLESSLY adv. hit or miss, by bits and pieces, by fits and starts, any which way. See ERRATICALLY.

AIR BATTLE n. dogfight, fur ball (air-to-air melee), raid, air raid, scramble, arrows (bullet holes in a plane).

AIRCRAFT n. plane, jet, ramjet, scramjet, crate, boxcar, can, big iron (multiengine), cab, kite, cloud buster, hedgehopper. See AIRPLANE.

AIRCRAFT CARRIER n. flattop, covered wagon, bird farm, mother, jeep carrier, blackshoe (crew).

AIR-CUSHION VEHICLE n. hovercraft, ACV.

AIRFIELD n. strip, air strip, landing strip, runway, home plate (A.F.).

AIR FORCE ACADEMY CADET n. Doolie, Mister Doolie, gadget, gomer, gomar.

AIR FORCE PERSONNEL flyboy, goofer, goopher, gimper, kiwi, sky winder, penguin.

AIR FREIGHT n. birdieback.

AIRPLANE n. plane, jet, ramjet, scramjet, stretch DC-9, crate, boxcar, fat Albert (jumbo jet), ship, airship, can, big iron (multiengine), big iron fever (desire to fly big aircraft), equipment, bug smasher, Indian, cab, cloudbuster, crop duster, clay pigeon, coffee grinder, coffin, flying coffin (unsafe), beast, bogie (enemy, target), bus (WWI, WWII), tail-ass Charlie, bird, bird in the air (unidentified), bird dog (WWII), gooney bird (DC-3), chicken, chicks (friendly), bandit (enemy), backfires (bomber), drone, flivver, flying jenny, grasshopper, heap, hedgehopper, Jenny, Jerry (German), Mig (Russian), pea shooter (WWII), seagull, soup job, wind wagon, Willie Fudd, flying banana, flying boxcar, killer, mosquito, spotter plane, spy plane, zoo (press), animal; dumbo (rescue sea plane), kneecap (NEACP plane), blue room, skycar (small commuter).

AIRPLANE CONTROLS n. joystick, joy knob; fly by wire (autopilot).

AIRPLANE CRASH n. pancake, belly landing, ditch, down, in the drink, splash, augers in, bites hard, buys the farm, plant in the yard, thud, washout, wipeout, prang, Chinese three-point landing (one wing low), dumbo (rescue sea plane).

AIRPLANE DEPARTURE n. takeoff, wheels up, scramble (A.F.).

AIRPLANE FLIGHT n. jump, hop, red-eye (overnight flight), hedgehop (low), flip, roach coach (to tropics), angels——(altitude in thousands of feet, e.g., angels 2 = 2,000 feet), contrail (high-altitude vapor trail).

AIRPLANE FLIGHT RESERVATION n. bump (cancellation of prebooked passenger reservation).

AIRPLANE GROUND CREW PERSON n. grease monkey, blisterfoot, dust eater, ground gripper, paddlefoot.

AIRPLANE LANDING n. three-point, three-pointer, touchdown, touch and go (practice), put her down, catch a wire (aircraft carrier), slam dunk, grease it in, dangle the dunlops (lower the wheels), dead stick, power off; splash, splash down, go in, pancake, ditch (crash). See also AIRPLANE, CRASH.

AIRPLANE PARTS n. eve (rib of wing), flaps (ailerons), howgozit (fuel gauge), greenhouse (cockpit cover), stick, joystick, zip fuel (high-energy), hush kit (muffler).

AIRPLANE PASSENGER n. PAX, dogs, hawk, deadhead (free), carry-on (luggage).

AIRPLANE, TO TAKE OFF IN AN v. scramble (A.F.).

AIRPORT n. strip, airstrip, landing strip, runway, home plate (A.F.), birdcage (traffic-controlled airspace).

AIRPORT HOTEL n. airtel.

AIR RAID n. alert, flap (also alert or alarm), BDA (bomb damage assessment), mission.

AIRS n. front, false front, put on. See also PRETENSION.

AIR TRAVEL n. flight, hop, red-eye (midnight). See also TRAVEL.

AIR VICTORY n. down one, splash one, splash the zeros (WWII).

AKRON, OHIO Rubber City.

ALABAMA Cotton State, Lizard State, the Heart of Dixie, Yellow Hammer State.

ALABAMAN n. Bama.

ALARM n. Mayday, SOS, flap, flash, high sign, sign, wigwag, wink, nod, tip, tip off, tooter, scramble, a bug in one's ear; bug, dinger (burglar).

ALARM v. scare to death, scare stiff, scare silly, throw a scare into, spook, chill, chill off, give one a turn, make one jump a mile, make one jump out of his skin, toot the tooter (set off mechanical). See FRIGHTEN.

ALARM CLOCK n. alarm, clock radio, chimer, tattler.

ALARMED adj. scared stiff, scared shitless, spooked, uptight, hung-up, frozen, pushed the panic button, goose-bumpy, jumped a mile, jumped out of one's skin, given a turn, struck all of a heap. See FRIGHTENED.

ALARMING adj. hairy, hair-raising, furry, scary, white-knuckle, spooky, hot, loaded, dynamite, chancy, dicey, unhealthy, heavy, rugged, on the spot, put on the spot.

ALASKA Last Frontier, Great Land, North Star State, Sourdough State, Up Over, Seward's Folly.

ALASKAN Sourdough, Cheechako (newly arrived).

ALBUQUERQUE, NEW MEXICO Big A, the Kirk.

ALCATRAZ PRISON n. the Rock.

ALCOHOL n. hooch, hootch, hall, booze, sauce, alky, idiot oil, idiot juice, juice, scrap iron, moonshine, medicine, doctor, antifreeze, oil, rotgut, red-eye, rerun, canned heat, smoke, firewater, giggle-soup (So.). See LIQUOR.

ALCOHOLIC n. drunk, heavy drinker, brown bagger, boozer, dip, dipso, stew, stewbum, rummy, rumbum, wino, lush, barfly, shikker. See DRINKER.

ALCOHOLISM, CURE n. A.A., dry out, kick the habit, go on the wagon, go on the water wagon, take the cure, quit cold turkey.

ALERT adj. 1. sharp, wired, with it, bright-eyed and bushy-tailed, jazzed, switched on, on the job, on one's toes, on the qui vive, on the lookout, on the ball, quick on the draw, quick on the trigger, fast on the draw, good hands, fly, no flies on, on the beam, Johnny-on-the-spot, keep one's eye on the ball, fly, salty, heads-up, hopped-up, psyched-up, wise, wised-up, cagey, leery, hip. See also AWARE, INTELLIGENT, KNOWLEDGEABLE. 2. all ears, have one's ear to the ground, have eyes in the back of one's head, have a weather eye open, have one's eyes peeled, mind one's p's and q's, scramble.

ALERT n. Mayday, SOS, flap, high sign, tipoff, tooter, scramble. See ALARM.

ALERT v. flag, wave a red flag, cloud up, give one the high sign, toot the tooter (set off mechanical), pull one's coat, tip, tip off. See also ADVISE.

ALEUTIAN ISLANDS Chain.

ALIAS n. AKA (also known as), handle, nickname, summer name.

ALIBI n. cop-out, cover, cover-up, stall, fish story, song and dance, airtight alibi. See EXCUSE.

ALIBIER n. Alibi Ike.

ALIEN n. furriner, FOB (fresh off the boat), greenhorn, ginzo, guinzo, gringo, goum, greaseball, jaboney, jiboney, wetback, geepo, strange weed (all Derog.).

ALIENATED adj. turned-off, on one's shitlist, on the shit parade, in bad with, on the outs, at outs, at sixes and sevens, at loggerheads. See also ALONE.

ALIKE adj. ditto, double, xerox, fax, carbon copy, clone, dead ringer, look-alike, spittin' image, S.O.S. (same old shit), same difference. See SAME.

ALIMONY n. palimony (unmarried).

ALIVE adj. alive and kicking, ticking, warm, here, in the lifestream.

ALL n. jackpot, the works, lock stock and barrel, whole enchilada, whole ball of wax, whole nine yards, whole works, whole schmear, whole show, whole shooting match, wall-to-wall, across-the-board. See WHOLE.

ALLAY v. cool, cool out, make nice, play up to, pour oil on troubled waters, schmear, square, take the sting out, take the bite out. See PACIFY.

ALLENTOWN, PENNSYLVANIA Mack City.

ALLEVIATE v. soft-pedal, take the bite out, take the edge off, pour oil on troubled waters, take the sting out. See also PACIFY.

ALLIANCE n. hookup, tie-up, gang, mob, ring, syndicate, clan, family, bunch, crowd, Old Boy network, zoo, outfit. See ASSOCIATION.

ALLIGATOR n. gator.

ALLOCATE v. dish out, divvy, divvy up, cut, crack, slice, slice the melon, split up. See DIVIDE.

ALLOCATION n. piece, a piece of the action, end, divvy, bite, cut, slice, rake off, fifty-fifty, the lion's share. See SHARE.

ALLOT v. cut, cut the pie, cut the melon, crack, slice, shell out, split up, divvy, divvy up. See DIVIDE.

ALLOTMENT n. cut, bite, slice, chunk, split, end, piece, a piece of the action, a cut of the pie, a cut of the melon, rake-off. See SHARE.

ALLOW v. pass on, okay, yes one, ditto, take kindly to, be big, free up, suck it up, go along with, live with, hold with, sit still for, be game for, hear of, give the go-ahead, give the green light, give one a blank check, give one carte blanche, give one's blessing, give one's stamp of approval, give one five (slap hands), check, come around. See also CONCEDE, GRANT.

ALLOWANCE n. cut, cut in, cut up, cut a melon (profits), share, drag, P.C., piece, rake-off, taste. See SHARE.

ALL RIGHT adj. no slouch, all reet, okey-dokey, okey-doke, O.K. A-OK, ding-how, easy, I can live with that, not half bad, swell, hunky-dory, shoot, ducky, fucking-A, George. See ACCEPTABLE.

ALLURE n. bedroom eyes, come-hither look, come-on, the jazz.

ALLURE v. hook, pull, vamp, suck in, turn one on, come on, give one the come-on, sweep off one's feet. See ATTRACT.

ALLURING adj. stacked, built, curvy, be whistle bait, schwing!, be a looker, be a pussycat, be a sex kitten, be a mink, be a stone, be a stone fox, be a head rush, be a stunner, zimmer, drop-dead beautiful, knockout (all Fem.); lady-killer, tall dark and handsome (both M.). See BEAUTIFUL.

ALLY n. friendly, ours, us. See also FRIEND.

ALLY v. play ball with, plug into, line up with, tie in with, throw in with, go partners with, play footsie with, join up with, hook up with, interface with. See ASSOCIATE.

ALMOST adv. by the skin of one's teeth, on the bubble, pretty near, practically, craptically, virtual. See NEARLY.

ALMS n. handout, hand, helping hand, do one's part. See DONATION.

ALONE adj. stag, solo, be a loner, be a lone wolf, dolo, doe, shag, onliest, Herman the hermit, Crusoe, Robinson Crusoe, traveling light, in solitary; batch, batching it (living alone); all by one's lonesome, me and my shadow, me myself and I, to chew something over alone, on one's own hook, on one's own say so, ace (Rest.).

ALOOF adj. cool, cool cat, cold, cold fish, loner, lone wolf, dog it, dog up, stuck up, uppity, laid-back, offish, standoffish, on ice, put on airs, thick-skinned, hard-boiled, I should worry, hardhearted, Herman the hermit. See also ARROGANT.

ALPHABET n. ABC's.

ALTER v. doctor, play with, phony up, cook, take it in a little, mid-course correction, revamp, tweek, give it a tweek (small), fine-tune, dink, dial back, pencil-whip (documentation), recalibrate. See CHANGE.

ALTERATION n. mid-course correction, about-face, flip-flop, switch, switch-over. See MODIFICATION.

ALTERCATION n. fracas, brawl, brush, flap, hassle, punch out, rhubarb, rumble, run-in, go, set-to, bone of contention, fuss, wrangle, beef, blowup, spat, tiff, words. See ARGUMENT.

ALTERED adj. doctored, cooked, spiked.

ALTERNATE n. backup, sub.

ALTERNATE v. yo-yo, blow hot and cold, shilly-shally, hem and haw.

ALTERNATING CURRENT n. AC.

ALTERNATIVE n. 1. backup, redundancy, sub. 2. other side of the coin, other fish to fry, other fish in the sea, other pebbles on the beach, druthers, go down the line, take it or leave it. See also CHOICE.

ALTIMETER n. air log.

ALTITUDE n. angels——(aircraft altitude in thousands of feet, e.g., angels 2 = 2,000 feet).

ALTRUIST n. do-gooder, bleeding heart, good scout, Robin Hood. See also PHILANTHROPIST.

ALTRUISTIC adj. big, bighearted, all heart, bleeding heart, heart in the right place, do-gooder.

ALUMNUS n. alum, old grad.

ALWAYS adv. for keeps, for ever so long, for a coon's age, for a dog's age, for a month of Sundays, till hell freezes over, till you're blue in the face, till the cows come home, till shrimps learn to whistle, since God was young, since Hector was a pup.

AMALGAM n. combo, mishmash, mishmosh, soup (liquid), lorelei, everything but the kitchen sink, Duke's Mixture (strange).

AMALGAMATE v. pool, team up with, tie up, tie in with, tie up with, join together, come together, hook up with, interface with, network with. See ASSOCIATE.

AMALGAMATION n. megacorp, multinational, pool, bunch, crew, crowd, gang, mob, plunderbund, outfit, ring. See ASSOCIATION.

AMANUENSIS n. sec, girl Friday, man Friday.

AMARILLO, TEXAS Big A, Cactus City.

AMASS v. round up, scare up, clean up, pile up, corral, make a pile, make a killing. See also INCREASE.

AMATEUR n. ham (radio), bush, bush-league, am, ammie, jackleg, Sunday —— (Sunday driver, etc.).

AMATEURISH adj. half-assed, artsy-fartsy, half-baked, half-cocked, Mickey Mouse, Sunday —— (Sunday driver, etc.). See INCOMPETENT.

AMATEUR RADIO n. rig.

AMATEUR RADIO OPERATOR n. ham, ham operator.

AMAZE v. put one away, blow one away, blow one's mind, bowl down, bowl over, flabbergast. See ASTONISH.

AMAZED adj. blown away, mind-blown, bug-eyed, floored, could have been knocked over with a feather. See ASTONISHED.

AMAZEMENT n. one for the book, something else, stunner, stopper.

AMAZING adj. mind-blowing, stunning, something else, something to shout about, something to write home about, one for the book, stunner, grabber, megadual, helluva note.

AMBASSADOR n. cookie pusher.

AMBIGUOUS adj. clear as mud, clear as dishwater, clear as ditch water.

AMBITION n. fire in the belly, push, right stuff, in there punching, moxie, get-up-and-go, get-out-and-go.

AMBITIOUS adj. hungry, ambish, ballsy, bogard, pushy, pushy hotshot, come on, come on like gangbusters, come on strong, get-up-and-go, go-getter, hard-sell, play for keeps, take-charge, takeover, on the make, out for a rep, ball of fire, fireball, eager beaver, spark plug, self-starting, self-starter, full of get up and go, looking to glom the stepping dough (U.), raise one's sights, set one's sights high, take the bull by the horns, heller. See also AGGRESSIVE.

AMBLE v. hoof it, ank, ankle, toddle, sashay, gander, percolate, gumshoe, ooze, mope, mooch, boogie. See WALK.

AMBULANCE n. meat wagon, Band-Aid wagon, butcher wagon, crash wagon, fruit wagon, blood box, bone box.

AMBUSH v. jump, box in, get one in a box, lay for, lay for one, bushwhack, dry-gulch, jap, pull a jap (Derog.). See also ATTACK.

AMELIORATE v. step up, upgrade. See IMPROVE.

AMEND v. square, square up, square a beef, square things, make up for, pay one's dues. See CORRECT. See also IMPROVE, EDIT.

AMERICAN n. Joe, G.I. Joe, Uncle Sam, Yank, Yankee, yanqui, Americano; gringo (Derog.).

AMERICAN FLAG n. Old Glory, Red White and Blue, Star-Spangled Banner, Stars and Stripes, Stars and Bars (Confederate).

AMERICAN INDIAN n. redskin; apple, Uncle Tomahawk (friendly to the white establishment) (all Derog.).

AMERICAN INDIAN MOVEMENT red power, AIM.

AMERICAN LEAGUE n. junior circuit (Bsbl.).

AMERICAN LEGION n. the heroes' union (Derog.).

AMIABLE adj. 1. buddy-buddy, clubby, mellow, tight, palsy-walsy, cozy, downright neighborly. See FRIENDLY. 2. Joe Nice Guy, Mr. Nice Guy, prince, pussycat, sweet, a sweetie, a sweetheart, so sweet she can give you cavities, so sweet he can give you diabetes (too nice), breezy, cool, coolsville, crazy, copacetic, swell, right, righteous, home cooking.

AMICABLE adj. clubby, mellow (close), cozy, right nice, white, regular, square shooter. See FRIENDLY.

AMISS adj. glitched-up, haywire, gone haywire. See WRONG, CROOKED.

AMITY n. good vibes, good vibrations, hit it off, in sync, on the same wavelength, simpatico, together. See also HARMONIOUS, SYMPATHETIC.

AMMUNITION n. ammo, iron rations, confetti.

AMMUNITION DEPOT n. ammo dump.

AMNESIA n. blackout, out of it, out to lunch, draw a blank. See also FORGETFULNESS.

AMOROUS adj. horny, pash, sexy, hot, hot for, hot pants, heavy, hot and heavy, hot baby, hot number, hot patootie, sweet for, sweet on, turned on, rammy, have a crush on, lovey-dovey, boy-crazy, girl-crazy. See also FOREPLAY, SEXUALLY AROUSED.

AMOROUS ADVANCE, MAKE AN v. hit on, crack on, pick up, come on to, move, put the move on, move in on, make one's move, make a play for, make a pass at, go for it. See FLIRT.

AMOROUS PLAY n. making out, coo, pass, make a pass, suck face, doing face time, face rape, suck heads, box tonsils, play tonsil hockey, go for sushi, grovel, maw, canoodle, consent, kneesies, footsies, cop a feel, feel one up, dry hump, dry dock, petting, necking, party, petting party, get physical, parking, monkey business, pitch woo, fling woo, spoon, smooch, perch, lallygag, lollygag, spark, billing and cooing, night baseball. See also SEXUAL RELATIONS.

AMORPHOUS adj. baggy, blobby.

AMOUNT n. 1. price tag, score, tab, list, net, come to, bad news, damage, set one back, to the tune of, tidy sum, what the traffic will bear. See COST. 2. hunk, chunk, gob, heap, mess, pack, hit, load, passel, pile, slat. See also WHOLE.

AMOUNT, LARGE n. ton, mucho, mucho mucho, heap, load, buttload, loads, shitload, shit bag, lots, grip, bags, heavy, heavy duty, bocoo, boocoo, bookoos, bocooz, pack, peck, pot, passle, flock, raft, slew, whole slew, scads, score, zillion, jillion, bazillion, skillion, umpteen, umptieth, umpty-umpth, kind (that kind of money), mint, wad, whopper, whopping, bundle, man-sized, king-sized, mess, gang, sockful, shithouse full, fistful, aplenty, good 'n' plenty, gob, jallop (serving of food), lollop, oodles, oodles and oodles, stinking with, crawling with, alive with, thick with, thick as flies, thick as hail, thick as fleas on a hound dog, drug on the market, galore, money to burn, rolling in, up to one's ass in, coming out of one's ears, knee deep in, all over the place, more than you can shake a stick at, would choke a horse, no end of, no end to.

AMOUNT, SMALL n. titch, smidge, smidgen, skoshe, skoshe more, spot, taste, un poco, weenchy, teensy-weensy, teeny-weeny, diddly, diddly-shit, shit, chickenshit, chickenfeed, peanuts, small change, penny ante, two cents' worth, tad, shoestring, gnat's heel, bite, cut, nip, slice, a hoot, drop in the bucket, drop in the ocean, small beer, hill of beans, row of buttons, row of pins, dribs and drabs, damn, darn, tinker's damn, smithereen, stump. See also NOTHING.

AMPERE n. amp.

AMPHETAMINE n. A, speed, amp, black widow, Catholic aspirin, amphets, boosters, trucker, peps, black beauties, blackbird, black mollies, browns, bumblebees, chicken powder, coast-to coasts, L.A. turnabouts, West Coast turnabouts, cranks, doll, fives, footballs, green dragon, greenie, jelly baby, jug, lightning, minibennies, nuggets, road dope, root, rosas, roses, sparkle-plenty, sweet, uppie, whites, white cross, whitey, zoom, bam, liquid bam, bombita, cartwheel, real fast, chalk, chaulkers, cotton (saturated with Benzedrine), copilot, diet pills, double blue, driver, eye opener, forwards, French blue, hearts, jellybeans, jollybeans, leapers, leepers, lid popper, light-footed, peaches, pepper, pep pill, ripper, splash, thrusters, truck drivers, up, uppers, wake up, obie.

AMPHETAMINE USE v. amp, overamp.

AMPHETAMINE USER n. A-head, speed freak.

AMPHIBIOUS VEHICLE n. duck (WWII).

AMPLE adj. heavy, galore, no end, up to one's ass in, plate is full. See PLENTY. See also AMOUNT, LARGE.

AMPLIFICATION n. boost, buildup, upping, padding. See also EXAGGERATION.

AMPLIFIED adj. beefed-up, built-up, souped-up, hiked-up, jacked-up, boosted, padded, upped, pyramided. See also EXAGGERATED.

AMPLIFIER n. hamburger helper (linear radio).

AMPLIFIER, LINEAR n. afterburner.

AMPLIFY v. 1. boost, up, beef up, build up, hike, hike up, jack up, jump up, put up, pyramid. See EXPAND. 2. flesh out, spell out. 3. puff, ballyhoo, lay it on thick, blow, blow smoke, make a federal case out of something. See EXAGGERATE.

AMUSE v. crack one up, break one up, fracture one, grab, tumul, panic, put away, wow, slay, kill, knock dead, knock them in the aisles, lay 'em in the aisles, have 'em in the aisles.

AMUSEMENT n. laughs, lots of laughs, ball, action, fun and games, grins, get some grins, just for grins, big time, high time, high old time, picnic, cold chillin', shits and giggles, field day, whoopee, hoopla, just for laughs, just for the heck of it, just for the hell of it, just for the devil of it. See also ENTERTAINMENT.

AMUSE ONESELF v. have a ball, have a few grins, have lots of laughs, laugh it up, party, get one's kicks, get one's jollies.

AMUSING adj. crackup, ball, for grins, fun, gas, more fun than a barrel of monkeys, cutup, he had 'em in the aisles, knock 'em in the aisles, lay 'em in the aisles, hooper-dooper, hooper-doo, boffo, break one up, tear one apart, a scream, camp, campy, jokey, joshing, yok, yokky, zetser, a hoot, laffer, riot, gagged-up, priceless, a million laughs, a million laffs, screaming, screamingly funny, too funny for words, too killing for words, gut-busting, side-splitting.

AMYL NITRITE n. amy, amies, amys, aimless amy, posies, popper, blue, blue angel, blue bird, blue devil, blue heaven, pear, snapper, pearls, poppsies, Dr. Bananas, whiffenpopper.

ANALINGUS v. browning, bite the brown, reem, rim job (all Obsc.). See also CUNNILINGUS; FELLATIO.

ANAL INTERCOURSE v. ace-fuck, butt, bufu, back-scuttle, brown, brown-hole, cornhole, goin' up the mustard road, Greek, Hershey bar way, bugger, shirtlift, tube, lay tube, sit on it, up the old dirt road, up the chocolate highway (all Obsc.). See also SEXUAL INTERCOURSE.

ANALYSIS n. the couch, on the couch.

ANALYST n. shrink, shrinker, head shrinker, couch doctor, guy with the net, guy in the white coat, bug doctor (prison), guru, squirrel.

ANALYST, FINANCIAL n. numbers cruncher, bean counter, quant, quan.

ANALYZE v. figure, figure out, sort out, rap, confab, hash, rehash, hash over, chew over, kick around, knock around, get down to cases, get down to brass tacks, spell out, let the daylight in, let the sunlight in, talk game. See also DELIBERATE.

ANCHOR n. hook, mud hook.

ANCHOR v. drop the hook.

ANCHORAGE, ALASKA Los Anchorage, the Iceberg.

ANCIENT adj. been around, bent, got a few miles on, a lot of mileage, relic, antique, creak, creaker, back number, from way back, oldie, old dodo, fossil, old fossil, old goat, older than dirt, worse for wear, rusty, moth-eaten. See also AGED; OLD.

AND conj. 'n', nuh.

AND THEN? So? Nu? What then? Vah den?

ANECDOTE n. gag, yarn, long and the short of it, tall story, fish story, cock-and-bull story, cock and bull, tall tale, fairy tale, line of cheese, megillah, wheeze, chestnut, old chestnut, old touches, touches.

ANESTHESIOLOGIST n. goo man, gasser, gas passer.

ANESTHETIC n. dope, gas, shot, spinal.

ANESTHETIZE v. knock out, KO, kayo, dope, drug, gork, put to sleep, put under, freeze.

ANEW adv. one mo' time, una mas, come again. See REPEAT.

ANGER n. mad, sore, huff, dander, Irish, pet, tiff, miff, stew, storm, slow burn, conniption, conniption fit, cat fit, duck fit, blow-up, flare-up, boiling point, rise, get a rise out of, more heat than light.

ANGER v. brown off, burn up, rile, miff, make mad, make sore, that grinds my gears, piss one off, tick off, T off, frost, utz (Yid.), needle, give one the needle, push one's key, blow up, blow one's top, blow one's stack, blow a fuse, blow a gasket, cop an attitude (Af. Am.), flip, flip out, flip one's lid, fly off the handle, chap, get sore, see red, push one's buttons, get one's back up, get one's balls in an uproar, get hot under the collar, get under one's skin, get in one's hair, get a rise out of one, get one's goat, get into a dither, get into a stew, get one's dander up, get one's Irish up, get one's mad up, get one hot under the collar, make one's blood boil, work up, work oneself into a lather, work oneself into a sweat, have a hemorrhage, have a shit hemorrhage, whip up, fire up, key up, kick up a row, kick up a dust, kick up a shindy, put one's Irish up, put one's dander up, raise one's dander, raise cain, raise hell, raise the devil, raise the roof, hack, hit the ceiling, egg on, turn on, turn one on, go on make my day, make waves, make a scene, ask for it, stick in one's craw, sound, sound off, burn one off, bitch one off, do a slow burn, reach boiling point, boil over, go into a tailspin.

ANGLE n. dogleg, slant, take, twist.

ANGLO-SAXON n. WASP, anglo, whitey, ofay, white bread; goy, goyim, shicksa, shagetz (Yid.) (all Derog.).

ANGRY adj. pissed off, go ballistic, browned off, pissy, p'd off, p.o.'d, cheesed off, lose it, bullshit, burned one's head, aerated, chewed, aggro, bent, bent out of shape, flexed out of shape, pushed outta shape, torqued (A.F.), blown out, blow, blow one's cool, blow a fuse, blow a gasket, blow one's stack, blow one's top, blow one's topper, blow one's cork, blow one's noggin, blow one's cap, blow one's wig, blow the roof, blow it out, bouncing, bugged, bummed out, mad, good and mad, mad as a hornet, mad as a wet hen, mad as hops, hacked, sore, steamed, steamed up, let off steam, at the boiling point, boiling over, fried, brassed off, ticked off, tee'd off, t'd off, t.o.'d, see red, shit blue, shit green, shit hemorrhage, shit on one or something, go ape, go apeshit, have a shit fit, go into a tailspin, go up in the air, huffy, miffed, peeved, have a hemorrhage, have a shit hemorrhage, shit bricks, have it in for one, have a conniption, have a conniption fit, have a cat fit, have a kitten, have kittens, cast a kitten, have pups, have tight cheeks, have tight jaws, have wind in his jaws (Af. Am.), throw a fit, duck fit, fit to be tied, hit the ceiling, hopped up, hopping mad, sizzling, burned, slow burn, burnt up, burned up, smoke, smoking, hot, get hot, get hot under the collar, get hot in the biscuit, get one's back up, get one's dander up, get one's gauge up, get one's bowels in an uproar, get up on one's ear, got a wild hair up one's ass, flipped, flip one's wig, flipped one's lid, flip one's razzberry, fly off the handle, so mad one could spit nails, on a short fuse, on the war path, on the outs, in a stew, in a sweat, in a swivet, in a tizzy, in a lather, in a dither, in a pucker, race one's motor, raise cain, raise hell, raise the devil, raise the roof, ranting and raving, raving mad, red-assed, riled-up, ripped-up, roaring mad, run a temperature, salty, jumpin' salty, loaded for bear, look daggers at, geed up, get one's monkey up, plugged, porky, evil, fighting, flare, scream bloody murder, yell bloody murder.

ANGUISHED adj. hurting, cut up, tore up, ripped, worried sick, worried stiff. See DISTRESSED. See also DISTURBED.

ANIMAL n. critter, dog (inferior), mutt, stray (orphaned, deserted), varmint, bad actor (vicious), bum, cob roller, road pizza (dead on the road).

ANIMAL DOCTOR n. horse doctor, vet.

ANIMAL EXCREMENT n. turd, terd, do, do-do, dog-do, dog-dew, doggy-do, bird turd, cow-plop, cow-flop, droppings; golden apples, road apples (horse), hooky, horse hocky.

ANIMATED adj. peppy, zingy, snappy, zippy, zappy, full of piss and vinegar. See SPIRITED.

ANKLETS n. bobby socks, bobby sox.

ANNAPOLIS, MARYLAND Crabtown, Crab (resident).

ANNEX v. tack on, tag, tag on, hitch on, slap on, take on, take over, hook on, hook up, hitch up. See also FASTEN, APPROPRIATE.

ANNEXATION n. takeover, grab.

ANNIHILATE v. wipe out, take out, rub out, do in, finish off. See KILL.

ANNIHILATED adj. totaled, wiped out, kaput, dusted, hashed-up, cooked, sunk, zapped. See KILLED.

ANNOUNCE v. put it out, put it on the street, trumpet, call, blast, drum, spread it around, pass the word, sound off, run off at the mouth. See also DECLARE, PROCLAIM.

ANNOUNCEMENT n. poop, poop sheet, flyer.

ANNOUNCER n. deejay, disc jockey, veejay, rip and reader, spieler, talker.

ANNOY v. bug, needle, put the needle in, ride, miff, push, push one's button, push all the buttons, push the right button, that grinds my gears, cop an attitude (Af. Am.), hit one where he lives, chew on, dog on, be at, be in one's face, get in one's face, sweat, be on the back of, gross out, eat, shiv, chiv, chivey, chivvy, henpeck, chap, nag; noodge, nudzh, utz (Yid.); sound, sound off, brown off, tick off, T off, brass off, cheese off, piss one off, bitch one off, push one's key, turn one off, talk one's ear off, ask for it, go on make my day, make waves, heat up, hot up, fire up, burn up, burn one off, peeve, cool, give one the finger, flip one the finger, give one hemorrhoids, give a bad time to, give one a hard time, give one the business, give one the needle, give one a turn, turn one on, egg on, work on, hit on, what's with, bend one's ear, bore stiff, burn out, put one to sleep, fuck with one's head, get, get to, get in one's face, get in one's hair, get a rise out of one, get one's goat, put one's dander up, get one's dander up, get one's Irish up, get one's mad up, get one hot under the collar, get under one's skin, make it tough for, make it tough for all, discombobulate, throw into a swivet, throw into a tizzy, flummox, fuzzbuzz, drive one bananas, drive up the wall, drive one up a tree, rile, rattle one's cage, hack, hassle, hound, dog, bulldog, penny dog, worry, wig, ride, dump on, dog one's case, jump on one's case, get on one's case, get on one's back, put the heat on, start in on, drive up the wall, hock a charnik, hock one's charnik, put the squeeze on one, put the screws on, put one through the wringer, play cat and mouse, pick at, pick on, pressure, rub, rub the wrong way, rub salt in the wound, bone, all right already, gnaw, yap at, on one's tail, tail, bring one up short, pull one up short, rag, rag on, rip on, curdle, gripe, gripe one's ass, gripe one's back, gripe one's balls, gripe one's butt, gripe one's left nut, gripe one's middle kidney, nitpick, picky-picky, break one's balls, stick in one's craw, add insult to injury, what's eating one?

ANNOYANCE n. drag, downer, beef, bellyache, bitch, headache, buzz crusher, vid, gripe, grouse, holler, howl, kick, rip, tsuris, pet peeve, a pain, pain in the ass, pain in the neck, a nag, nudge, nudzh, noodge, worriment, worriation, hang-up, rough go, handful, drip, flat tire, blister, pill, botheration, bad news.

ANNOYED adj. bugged, hacked, blown out, rousted, steamed, defrosted, frosted over, get off my case, get outta town, give me a break, cut me some slack, don't sweat me (Af. Am.), uptight, tightened-up, unglued, choked, zonkers, clutched, clutched-up, hacked, hacked off, brassed off, cheesed off, sketched, discombobulated, pissin', pissed off, peed off, tee'd off, brassed off, browned off, aggro, drove, way drove, bummed out, strung out, burned-up, hung, hung-up, dogged, miffed, peeved, riled, rubbed the wrong way, spooked, all hot and bothered, at the end of one's rope, buffaloed, hard put to it, put to it, picked on, torn down, up the wall, driven up the wall, on edge, bleeding, what's eating one?, fit to be tied.

ANNOYING adj. uncool, hefty, blivit, bugs one, weenie, from hell, that gives one a pain, one gives one a pain, pain in the neck, pain in the ass, bitch, son of a bitch, son of a gun, a bit much, too much, flea, pesky, pestiferous. See also WORRY.

ANNUL v. scrub, nix, call off, kill, get off the hook. See CANCEL.

ANNULMENT n. breakup, dedomiciling, go phftt, split, split up, couldn't make it, marriage on the rocks. See also DIVORCE.

ANOINT v. lube, slick, slick on.

ANON adv. by 'n' by, by and by, come Sunday, down the line, coming down the pike, in a short, short-short.

ANONYMITY n. what's-its-name, whatsis, whatzit, whatchamacallit, what d'ye call it, what's-his-face, what's-his-name, I'll never forget what's-his-name, so-and-so, such-and-such, you know who, a whoozit.

ANONYMOUS adj. incog, bearding, a certain person, Joe Doaks, Jane Doe, John Doe, Cheap John, Joe Blow, pig in a poke, X, X factor, Mr. X, unk, George Spelvin, so-and-so, such-and-such, whatchamacallit, what's-his-name, I'll never forget what's-his-name, what's-his-face, whatsis, whatzit, you know who.

ANSWER n. 1. owning up. 2. comeback, feedback, snappy comeback, backcap, backtalk, crackback, topper, cooler, lip, guff, parting shot, thank-you note. 3. all the right moves, Band-Aid (temporary, too little), quick fix, on target, pay dirt, the ticket. See also SOLUTION.

ANSWER v. 1. talk back, answer back, backtalk, shoot back, snappy comeback, come back at, get back at, come right back at, back at you, get back to one, I'll be back to you, I'll get back to you, be in touch with one, feedback, own up, 'fess up, field the question, sass, squelch, top, settle. 2. crack, deal with, dope, dope out, lick, unzip, work through. See also SOLVE.

ANTAGONIST n. opposite number, opposish, oppo, meat, me and you, bad guy, bandit, buddy (sarcasm), buddy-buddy, buddy fucker, crip, whose side are you on?, angries.

ANTAGONISTIC adj. anti, agin, be agin, con, ran into a buzz saw (unexpected), balky, bitchy; turbobitch, stanky (woman), cussed, mean, ornery, scrappy, snorky, limber, flip, catty, waspish, be down on, have no use for, have a chip on one's shoulder, have a bone to pick, have it in for, hard on for (Obsc.), on the muscle, on the outs, at outs, out for a rep, at loggerheads, allergic to, turned off by. See also BELLIGERENT, CONTRARY.

ANTENNA n. rabbit ears (indoor), whip, bullwhip, bird snapper, feelers, sky wire, spike, big mama, ballet dancer, chopped top, hustler, scatterstick, tuning forks, twangers, twin huskies.

ANTI-AIRCRAFT ARTILLERY n. AAA, flak, SAM (USSR), silkworm (China).

ANTI-AIRCRAFT GUN n. AAA, AA, ack-ack, able-able, pom-pom, 88 (Ger.), archie, chatterbox, flak hack.

ANTI-BALLISTIC MISSILE n. ABM, MX.

ANTIBIOTICS n. bug juice.

ANTICIPATE v. jump the gun, count one's chickens before they're hatched, cross the bridge before one comes to it, take the words out of one's mouth, lick one's chops, figure, in the cards, it's looking to, see it coming, be afraid, wait for the other shoe to drop. See also PREDICT.

ANTICIPATED adj. as advertised, no big surprise, be just like one, be one all over, not put it past, looking for, in the cards, in the wind, waitin' on, the noose is hanging. See also FORETOLD.

ANTI-COMMUNIST n. red-baiter, right-winger; hard hat, real 'merkin, boss class, Archie Bunker, redneck (all Derog.).

ANTIDOTE n. fix, quick fix.

ANTI-ENVIRONMENTAL adj. basic brown.

ANTI-ESTABLISHMENT adj. underground, hippie, yippie.

ANTI-INTELLECTUALISM n. meatballism, know-nothing.

ANTINUCLEAR adj. antinuke, antinuker, antibomb.

ANTITANK ROCKET n. bazooka (rocket and launcher).

ANTI-WHITE PREJUDICE n. Crow Jim, Crow Jimism.

ANTI-WOMEN'S LIBERATION Aunt Jane, Aunt Jemima, Aunt Tabby, Aunt Thomasina, Aunt Tom (all Derog.).

ANTIPATHY n. allergy, no use for.

ANTITHESIS n. flip side, other side of the coin. See OPPOSITE. See also CONTRARY.

ANUS n. servant's entrance, asshole, ass, A-hole, crack, rear, rear end, backside, ying-yang, keister, kazoo, back hole, back way, rip, rosebud, back garden, bucket, snatch, gig, gigi, geegee, hole, bumhole, bunghole, brown hole, little brown eyeball, round eye, third eye, rocky road, dirt road, tube, O-ring, round pussy, the safe, the suitcase, the tomb, exhaust pipe, chocolate highway, Hershey bar route, poop shoot, hoop, food dropper, moon, where the sun doesn't shine. See also BUTTOCKS.

ANXIETY n. worriment, worriation, botheration, downer, drag, jitters, shakes, sweat, cold sweat, shivers, cold shivers, cold creeps, creeps, willies, agita, goose bumps, all-overs, needles, pins and needles, pucker, fidgets, ants, ants in one's pants, nail-biter, heebie-jeebies, jimjams, jumps, quivers, trembles, dithers, butterflies, flap, fuss, lather, stew, zingers, stage fright, buck fever, cliff-hanging. See also NERVOUSNESS.

ANXIOUS adj. uptight, creeped out, jittery, jumpy, the jumps, jitters, shaky, bugged, choked, defrosted, hissy, zonkers, pissin', shittin', shittin' bricks, shit green, scared shit-less, strung out, twigged out, unglued, hyper, spooked, twitty, fidgety, wreck, nervous wreck, bundle of nerves, nervy, all-overish, wired, wired up, yantsy, antsy, antsy-pantsy, ants in one's pants, about to piss in one's pants, clutched, clutched-up, shook-up, all shook up, shaking in one's boots, shivery, quivery, hacked, buggin', dragged (following drugs), have a short fuse, butterflies, butterflies in one's stomach, coffee head, the jams, the jims, the jimmies, jim-jams, heebie-jeebies, the screaming meemies, the meemies, fall apart, torn down, shot to pieces, basket case, hung up with, tightened up, up the wall, in crisis mode, in a lather, in a stew, in a sweat, sweaty, sweat it, sweating bullets, in a swivet, in a tizzy, in a state, in a dither, in one's hair, on edge, on the ragged edge, have one's teeth on edge, on pins and needles, on tenterhooks, on the gog, jumpy as a cat on a hot tin roof, have kittens, cast a kitten, having the leaps, worried sick, worried stiff, biting one's nails, beside oneself, put to it, hard put to it, at the end of one's rope, rarin' to go. See also AFRAID, APPREHENSIVE, NERVOUS.

ANY adj. any which way, whatever, any old ———.

ANYHOW adv. anyhoo.

ANYTHING pron. all, whatever.

APART adj. solo, loner, lone wolf. See ALONE.

APARTMENT n. condo, co-op, coop, crash pad, crib, blue denim crib (nice), dommy, turf, digs, diggings; cradle, hat (Af. Am.), pad, padhouse, cave, den, flop, joint, box, flat, dump drum, heave, camp, kip, scatter, walk-up, walk-back (rear), go-down (basement), cold-water flat, cubby, cubby-hole (small), place to hang your hat, place to lay your head and a few friends, roof over one's head, granny flat (for elderly parents in same house). See also HOUSE.

APATHETIC adj. laid-back, blah, have the blahs, could care less, couldn't care less, flat, have spring fever, June around, dopey, drippy, draggy, nebbish, wimpy, moony, don't give a shit, don't give a damm, don't give a hoot, what's the diff?, what the hell, so what?, I should worry?, it's all the same to me. See also INDIFFERENT, LANGUID.

APE v. do, do like, go like, make like, mirror, ditto. See IMITATE.

APEX n. the max, ape, far out, the most, tops, the greatest, up there, really up there.

APHRODISIAC n. love drug, popper, Spanish fly, turn-on, wampole.

APIECE adv. a pop.

APOLOGIZE v. cop a plea, cop out, crawl, square oneself, square a beef, square things, make up for, get down on one's marrowbones. See also EXCUSE.

APPALL v. gross out, throw, get to, faze. See DISCONCERT. See also INSULT.

APPALLING adj. bummer, gross, grody, grody to the max, downer, bad scene, mean, heavy, the end. See BAD. See also DREADFUL.

APPARATUS n. gismo, widget, outfit, idiot box, black box, conjerod, job, jobby, jobbie, contraption, dealie bob, sucker, bugger, mother, motherfucker, mothafucka (Obsc.), mofo, mother grabber, grabber, gimmick, gaff, stuff, setup, whatchamacallit, whatsis, whatzis, what's-its-name, what's-it, whatchee, whatchy, whoziz, whoose-it, whosis, whoosis, whoosamajiggle, jigamaree, gimcrack, thigamajig, thinga-majig, thingamajigger, thingumajugfer, thingum, thing-ummy, thingadad, thingumabob, thingumadad, thingumadoo, thingamadoodle, whangdoodle, thing-amadodger, thingamadudgeon, thingamananny, thing-amaree, turnout, doo, doo-da-dad, doodad, do funny, dofunny, jigger, dojigger, doojigger, dojiggy, domajig, domajigger, hickey, dohickey, doohickey, do hinkey, do-whacky, dowillie, doowillie, dowhistle, doowhistle, doomaf-logy, dingbat, dingus, goofus, gasser, gigamaree, gilguy, gilhickey, gilhooley, fandangle, flumadiddle, frobnitz, frob-nitzem, kit and kaboodle, hootenany, hootmallalie, wing-ding, coil, can opener (vault), Armstrong (requires strength).

APPAREL n. threads, glad rags, rig, getup, drapery, duds, feathers. See CLOTHING.

APPARENT adj. barefaced, plain as the nose on one's face, clear as the nose on one's face, under one's nose, clear-cut, crystal-clear, big as life, open-and-shut, open-and-shut case, goes without saying, out in the open, makes no bones about it, talks turkey, that's a fact Jack, you ain't just whistling Dixie, if it were a snake it would bite you, cheesecloth (person), commando (sex), jazzy, is the Pope Catholic?, does a bear shit in the woods? See also CERTAIN.

APPARITION n. spook, haunt, hant, haint, things that go bump in the night.

APPEAL v. hit on, strike. See also BEG, PLEAD.

APPEALING adj. dishy, dreamy, a honey, cher, cool whip, pussycat, head rush, delicious, fetcher, but good, okay. See BEAUTIFUL.

APPEAR v. make the scene, make it, pop up, bob up, turn up, roll up, clock in, check in, time in, come to light, drop in, blow in, breeze in, roll in, pop in, punch in, punch the clock, ring in, show up, speak of the devil, show a leg, turn out. See also ACT.

APPEARANCE n. image, front, get one's game together (best), screen (deceptive), blind. See also COUNTENANCE.

APPEARANCES n. front, show, window dressing, put on, fake, phony. See PRETENSION.

APPEASE v. make matters up, patch things up, meet halfway, pour oil on troubled waters. See PACIFY.

APPELLATION n. handle, John Doe, John Hancock, John Henry, monicker, tag, what's-'is-name, what's-his-face, brand, flag (assumed), front name, label, tag, tab.

APPETITE n. big eyes, itch, sweet tooth, yen, chucks, chuckers, zazzle. See DESIRE.

APPETIZERS n. finger food, dip, spread, munchies.

APPETIZING adj. delish, grinds, scrumptious, sweetened, sugar-coated, yummy, nummy, divine, heavenly, got the juices flowing. See also DELICIOUS.

APPLAUD v. beat one's skin, give a hand, give a big hand, hear it for, kudo, rave, root. See also ACCLAIM.

APPLAUSE n. hand, big hand, mitt-pound, bring down the house, O (ovation), standing O, have 'em on their feet. See also ACCLAIM.

APPLE PIE n. Eve with the lid on (Rest.).

APPLIANCES n. white goods.

APPLICABLE adj. on the button, on the nose, right on, on target, kosher, legit, that's the idea, that's the ticket, just what the doctor ordered. See also SUITABLE.

APPLY v. put in for. See also ASK.

APPLY ONESELF v. take one's best shot, give it one's best shot, give it all one's got, give it the ol' college try, in it to win it (Af. Am.), bear down on it, buckle down, knuckle down, hump, bust one's hump, hump it, hump oneself, put one's back into it, hustle, scratch, sweat, hit the ball, pour it on, grind, dig, hammer away, plug, peg away, pull out all the stops. See also ATTEMPT, STRIVE.

APPOINTMENT n. 1. date, heavy date, blind date, blind drag, rendezvous, gig, double date, meet, your place or mine; miss a meet, stand one up, stand one on a corner, flake, no show (fail to keep an); zero hour, triff, treff (secret). 2. plum (political), prune (appointee with experience).

APPOINTMENT, KEEP AN v. keep a meet, make a meet, take a meet, shape, show.

APPRAISE v. check, check out, dig it, eye, look over, windshield appraisal (superficial, from a car), peg, read, size, size up, dope out, take account of, figure, figure in, figure out, cut in, cut some ice, guesstimate, have one's number, take one's measure.

APPRECIATE v. 1. flip, flip for, flip over, get high on, freak out on, groove on. See ENJOY. See also GAIN. 2. savvy, with it, catch the drift, see daylight, dig, read, can you relate (Af. Am.). See UNDERSTAND. See also KNOW.

APPREHEND v. 1. collar, take in, bag, grab, nail, pop, run in. See ARREST. 2. get, catch, blow wise, collar the jive, tumble, get the picture, read. See UNDERSTAND.

APPREHENSIVE adj. worried sick, worried stiff, feel in one's bones, feel in one's guts, get the vibes, have a funny feeling, have a hunch, biting one's nails, jitters, jittery, jumpy, shaky, shivery, cold shivers, quivery, trembles, dithers, in a dither, sweat, in a sweat, cold sweat, in a cold sweat, have cold feet, frozen, 'fraidy cat, scaredy cat, run scared, scared buck fever, stage fright, heebie-jeebies, jumps, allovers, butterflies, uptight, hung-up, on the ragged edge, have butterflies in one's stomach, stiff, push the panic button, the willies, spooked, goose-bumpy, rabbity, mousy, pucker-assed, pecker-assed, asshole-puckerin', asshole-suckin' wind, gutless, shake in one's boots, ague, creeps, heebies, leaping heebies, jams, jims, jimjams, jimmies, clutch-up, D and D (deaf and dumb, afraid to testify), punk out. See also ANXIOUS, FEARFUL.

APPRENTICE n. newie, new kid on the block, rookie, rook, greenhorn, tenderfoot, boot, freshie, turkey, flunky, heel, heeler (reporter), peg boy, pratt boy, new blood, student. See also NOVICE.

APPRENTICESHIP n. paying one's dues, learning the ropes.

APPRISE v. tip, tip off, wise up, put next to, put one in the picture. See ADVISE. See also INSTRUCT.

APPRISED adj. plugged-in, in the picture, in the know, wise to, all woke up, know the score, on the beam, double digs, kept posted. See AWARE. See also KNOWLEDGEABLE.

APPROACH n. wrinkle, new wrinkle, crack, fling, go, lick, stab, shot, whack. See also CONCEPT, PLAN, IDEA, OFFER.

APPROACH v. 1. belly up to, buzz, move in on, come at, contact. 2. make up to, feel, feel one out, give one a flop, give one a play, give one a promote, give one a rumble, give one a tumble, give one a toss, thumb, tumble. See also GREET, PLAN.

APPROACHABLE adj. come-at-able, gettable, get-in-able, the door's always open. See also OBTAINABLE.

APPROBATION n. go-ahead, get the nod, okay, OK, crazy, bells. See APPROVAL.

APPROPRIATE adj. just what the doctor ordered, on the button, on the money, on the nose, that's the idea, that's the ticket. See also SUITABLE.

APPROPRIATE v. take over, annex, grab, grab hold of, glom on to, snatch, confiscate, liberate, moonlight requisition, borrow, take a five-finger discount (shoplift), clap hands on, get one's fingers on, get one's hands on, rough off, swipe, kipe, highjack, hijack, high-grade. See also CONFISCATE, STEAL, PLAGIARIZE.

APPROPRIATION n. takeover, grab.

APPROVAL n. 1. strokes, stroking, abreaction route, commercial, cow sociology, Dr. Spocking the help, opening up, pat on the back, pat on the head, one's stock has gone up, eyes for, PR, puff, puffing up, pumping up, tasty, dual, megadual, bold rave, rave, radical, way sweet, mondo choice, bells, atta boy, atta girl, that's the boy, that's the girl, that's my boy, that's my girl, George, by George, hubba-hubba, keen, wow. See also AGREE, ENDORSE. 2. okay, OK, get the nod, green light, get the green light, crazy, the go-ahead, get the go-ahead, good going, that'll work. See also ACCEPT.

APPROVE v. 1. buy, buy into, back, bless, dig, groove, okay, OK, lap up, sign, sign off on, thumbs up, check out, check up, check up on, ditto, get behind, go for, go along with, have eyes for, plump for, push, stump for, hold a brief for, thump the tub for, hear it for, whoop it up for, boost, booster, give a boost to, give the nod, give the go-ahead, give the green light, give the stamp of approval, rubber-stamp, put one's John Hancock on, carry on over, make a to-do over, take on over, go on about, stroke, hats off to, push, puff up, rave, root for, cracked up to be, brag about, give a bouquet, give a posy, hand it to, have to hand it to. 2. live with, go along with, string along with, suck it up, put up with, cope, handle, lump it, lump it and like it, stomach something, grin and bear it, face it, take one up on, be big on, roll with the punches.

APPROVED adj. kosher, okay, okay people, OK'd, touted, highly touted.

APPROXIMATELY adv. around, guesstimate, ballpark figure, in the ballpark of, upwards of. See NEARLY.

APRICOTS n. cots, elephant ears (not common).

APT adj. quick on the uptake, nobody's fool, no dumbbell, not born yesterday, quick on the trigger, savvy, smart, sharp as a tack, smart as a whip. See also SKILLED, APPLICABLE, SUITABLE.

APTITUDE n.   smarts, savvy, stuff, what it takes, plenty on the ball. See SKILL.

ARAB n.   A-rab, raghead, camel jockey, gyppo (WWII), rab, sand nigger (all Derog.).

ARBITER n.   go-between, fixer, holdout, maven, middleman. See ARBITRATOR.

ARBITRAGEUR n.   arb.

ARBITRARY adj.   bossy, downright, flat-ass, flat-out, straight-out, no ifs ands or buts, no joke, no joker in the deck.

ARBITRATE v.   come to school, make a deal, hammer out a deal, hack out a deal, work out a deal, meet halfway, play ball with, strike a happy medium, trade off. See also NEGOTIATE.

ARBITRATOR n.   go-between, fixer, maven, middleman (labor).

ARCH SUPPORTERS n.   happies, arch supports.

ARDOR n.   hot pants, weakness, turn-on, jazz, oomph, pep talk. See LOVE. See also DESIRE.

ARDUOUS adj.   uphill, heavy, murder, pisser, tough, ballbuster, no picnic. See DIFFICULT.

AREA n.   neck of the woods, the zone, turf, nabe, hood, pit (racing, gambling).

ARENA n.   gridiron, bowl (Ftbl.), diamond (Bsbl.), boards (basketball), ice, rink (hockey), ring, pit.

ARGOT n.   doublespeak, bafflegab, lingo, jive, street talk. See JARGON.

ARGUABLE adj.   iffy.

ARGUE v.   hassle, cross, buck, nix, zap, take on, lock horns, set to, sock, sock it to one, stick it to one, top, talk back, talk game, in one's face, be agin, go agin, sass, pick a bone, pick an argument, put up an argument, put up a fight, put up a struggle, argufy, row, break with, rhubarb, pettifog, bump heads, cross swords, face off, face down, go one on one, one to one, mano a mano, go at, come at, lay at, have at, have at it, have at each other, fly in the face of, pitch into, light into, lay into, wade into, lace into, sail into, lean on, take on, jump, jump on, jump on one's case, jump down one's throat, lay out, straighten out, let have it, let have it with both barrels, give one both barrels, blast, mix it up with, tangle with, knock the chip off one's shoulder, push around, make a stink, gripe, griping, gritch, pop off, sound off, squawk, put up a squawk, bellyache, blast, crab, cut a beef, grouse, growl, kick, speak one's piece, haul into court, drag into court, beat a dead horse, flog a dead horse (moot). See also CONTEST.

ARGUMENT n.   row, tiff, spat, words, rumpus, ruckus, ruction, brawl, brush, brush-off, shindy, scene, set-to, run-in, scrap, hassle, talking heads, rhubarb, bone, bone of contention, bone to pick, face-off, fuss, flap, go, stew, wrangle, static, beef, romp, dustup, hoedown, knockdown, knockdown and drag-out, jihad, sockdolager, flack session, clincher, crusher, finisher, blow, blowup, branigan, brannigan, catamaran, donnybrook, Donnybrook, rowdy-dow, rowdy-dowdy, battle royal, jackpot, gin.

ARGUMENTATIVE adj.   scrappy, salty, spiky, chip on one's shoulder, fire eater, forecastle lawyer. See BELLIGERENT.

ARID adj.   bone-dry, dry as a bone, dry as dust.

ARISE v.   roll out, rise and shine, hit the deck, pile out, show a leg, turn out, drop your cocks and grab your socks (Obsc.), keep banker's hours (late).

ARISTOCRAT n.   upper cruster, ritzy, blueblood, silk stocking, lace curtain, swell.

ARIZONA   Apache State, Aztec State, Baby State, Grand Canyon State, Sand Hill State, Sunset State, Valentine State.

ARKANSAS   Bear State, Bowie State, hog country, Hot Water State, Land of Opportunity, Toothpick State, Wonder State.

ARKANSAS CITY, ARKANSAS   Ark City.

ARM n.   1. bender, flapper, flipper, fin, wing, hook arm. See also WEAPON. 2. offshoot, affil (TV), branch, branch house.

ARM v.   equalize, heel, pack, pack a rod, tote, rod up, heel up, load up, lug iron.

ARMAMENT n.   hardware, heat (gun).

ARMED adj.   equalized, wired, carrying, carrying the difference, carrying iron, totin', toting a gun, packing a gun, packed, strapped, gat up, heeled, heeled-up, well-heeled, loaded, armed to the teeth, lugging, lugging iron, lugging a rod, rodded up, packing a rod, packing a heater, packing heat.

ARM INJURY n.   glass arm, winged.

ARMORED TRUCK n.   money bus, fort.

ARMORY n.   dump.

ARMY DISCHARGE n.   the paper, ruptured duck, section 8 (mental), blue ticket (dishonorable), bobtail, bob tail (dishonorable, WWI), early out (medical).

ARMY OFFICER n.   ossifer, brass, brass hat, gold braid, barbed wire, chicken colonel, light colonel (Lt. Colonel), skipper, skip, old man, buck general (brigadier); shavetail, looey, john, missing link, butter bar, brown bar (2d Lt.), 90-day wonder (2d Lt., WWI), rail (1st Lt.), butcher

(M.D.) buggy bitchers (field artillery, cavalry, 1930), mustang (risen from the ranks), goat, O.D. (officer of the day), X.O. (executive officer), dust-dust (newly promoted).

ARMY OFFICER, NONCOMMISSIONED n.
NCO, one-striper, PFC (private first class), two-striper (corporal), sarge, kick, topkick, first man, first shirt, first soldier (1st sergeant).

ARMY PLATOON n. toon, able, baker, charlie.

ARMY TRUCK n. blitzbuggy.

ARMY UNIFORM n. O.D., olive drab, G.I., pinks (officer), full dress, fatigues, khakis, peacoat, A uniform, B uniform, cammies (camouflage clothing), chicken guts (gold braid).

ARMY UNIT n. divarty (division artillery), hundred and worst (101st Airborne), big red one (1st Infantry Division), blood and fire (63d Infantry Division), Green Berets (special forces), snake eaters (Green Berets).

AROUSE v. turn on, heat up, wake up, work up, send, fire up. See EXCITE.

AROUSED adj. turned-on, hot, hot to trot, hopped-up, steamed-up, worked-up, rammy. See EXCITED.

ARRAIGN v. point the finger, point the finger at, lay at one's door, pin on, pin it on one, hang something on one. See also ACCUSE.

ARRANGE v. 1. get all the pieces in place, put in shape, put in good shape, whip into shape, put to rights, put in apple-pie order, clear the decks, fix up, police, police up, spruce up. 2. hammer out a deal, hack out a deal, work out, work out a deal, iron out, make a connection, promote, quarterback, get one's act together, get one's head together, get one's shit together, pull things together, shape up, straighten up and fly right, pull a wire, put the fix in, frame, tailor. See also PLAN, SCHEME.

ARRANGED adj. packed, stacked, cooked-up, in the bag, fixed, framed, set-up, wired, cut and dried. See also ORGANIZED, PREARRANGED.

ARRANGEMENT n. 1. game plan, layout, package, package deal, setup, frameup, pecking order, T.O. (table of organization), down the line. 2. chart, score, lead sheet (music). See also AGREEMENT.

ARRAY n. threads, drapes, duds, feathers, getup, California chic (expensive casual), glad rags, rig. See CLOTHING.

ARRAY v. doll up, dog out, dud, dude up, dode (bad fit), fit out, rag out, rag up, rig out, rig up, suit up, deck, deck out, turn out, tog, drape.

ARREST n. collar, bust, heat, mitt, the mitt, nab, grab, pickup, pinch, pull, pull-in, run-in, sweep, bag, bite, drop, gaff, glom, glom on to, hook, nail, nick, nip, fall, booby pinch, brodie, crimp, flop, jackpot, jam, knockoff, rumble, slough, slough up, snare, snatch, trip, tumble, pickle, accommodation collar (to fill a quota or meet social or political pressure), humbug (unjustified), IBAR (immediate booking and release).

ARREST v. 1. collar, bust, pick up, pinch, pull, pull in, run in, bag, brace, book, hook, get, grab, nab, nail, net, nick, nip, kick, tab, tag, vag, snag, sneeze, slough, slough up, round up, roust, drop, gaff, glom, gloon to, sidetrack, put the arm on, put the claw on, put the cuffs on, put the bite on, put the sleeve on, put the snare on, snatch, put the snatch on, land, come down on, take in, haul in, toss in jail, throw in the clink, slap in the piss can, knock off, knock over, belt out, get one's fingers on, get one's hands on, throw the book at one, accommodation collar (to fill a quota or meet social or political pressure), humbug (unjustified), pluck chickens, red light, looks like rain (imminent), chill (submit to arrest). 2. knock off, scrub, drop, can it, shut down, freeze. See STOP.

ARRESTED adj. booked, collared, nabbed, nailed, corralled, cornered, hooked, dog meat, dropped, flopped, popped, guzzled, hit the pits, ill, in the pokey with smokey, go down, jammed, jammed-up, on the peg, sneezed, dead to rights, got one dead to rights, I'm dead, one move and you're dead, come out with your hands up, take a brodie, walk into a collar. See also STOPPED.

ARREST, ESCAPE v. miss a collar, duck a pinch.

ARREST IN THE ACT n. catch red-handed, catch dead to rights, dead bang, dead bang rap, right fall, right rap. See CAUGHT IN THE ACT.

ARREST ON SUSPICION v. pickup, forty-eight, forty-eighter, highway mopery, mopery, mopery collar, mopery in the first degree, mopery pinch, mopery rap.

ARREST, UNJUST n. bum beef, bum rap, frame, frame-up, hummer, phony collar, phony drop, phony fall, phony grab, phony knock, phony pinch, phony snatch, plant, stiff, wrong drop, wrong fall, wrong pinch.

ARRIVE v. clip off, make it, make the scene, hit, hit town, blow in, sky in, breeze in, come breezing in, barge in, bust in, roll in, check in, sign in, time in, clock in, punch in, punch the clock, drop in, pop in, ring in, spring in, mooch in, drag in, look what the cat dragged in, fall in, fall up, fall by, fall out, fall down, roll up, show, show up, bob up, pop up, wind up at, bum-rush, buzz (to announce an arrival). See also APPEAR, ENTER.

ARROGANCE n. brass, cheek, chutzpah, crust, gall, nerve.

ARROGANT adj. cool, cocky, biggety, bossy, dicty, sidity, sidity, sniffy, snippy, snooty, snotty, puffed-up, uppish, uppity, upstage, stuck-up, stuck on oneself, chesty, too big for one's britches, ego trip, ego-tripping, king shit, high-and-mighty, high-hat, high-hatted, high-hatty, high-toned, high-flown, high-headed, high-nosed, highfalutin, on one's high horse, put on airs, pull rank, have one's glasses on (Af. Am.), top-lofty, hoity-toity, cold shoulder, crack the whip, throw one's weight around, dog it, cheeky, know-it-all, snotnose, smarty, smarty pants, smart-aleck, smart-alecky, smart guy, smart ass, wise ass, wise guy.

ARSENAL n. dump.

ARSON n. torching, touch off, Greek lightning.

ARSONIST n. firebug, match, spark, torch, touch-off man, fiero, feero, fire buff, sparkie.

ART n. the farts (fine arts), Prop Art (propaganda), outsider art, raw art.

ARTERY n. red pipe, sewer.

ARTFUL adj. foxy, crazy like a fox, slick, smooth, playing politics, politician. See also SLY.

ARTICLE n. 1. piece, think piece, column, scoop, spread, beat, blurb, write-up, story. 2. thingamajig, dojigger, jigger, dohickey, gismo, jobbie, thingamabob. See APPARATUS.

ARTICULATE v. verbalize, mouth, sound off. See also SPEAK.

ARTIFICIAL adj. fake, faked, falsie, plastic, hyped-up, bogus, phony, queer. See also COUNTERFEIT.

ARTIFICIAL GRASS n. Astroturf, carpet, rug.

ARTIFICIAL LEG n. peg, peg leg.

ARTILLERY n. AA's, Arty, Divarty (division artillery), big bertha, Big Bertha (WWI), how, grandmother (howitzer, WWI), 88, long Tom, big guns, heavy stuff, tree bursts, rainmakers, bazooka, stovepipe.

ARTILLERYMAN n. guns (gunnery sergeant), gun bunny, gunny.

ARTILLERY TERMS ack-ack, ash can, ashcan, coal box, crump (WWI); the cosmolines (WWII), incoming mail (enemy fire), fireworks, flak, G can.

ARTIST n. bomber (graffiti).

ARTISTIC adj. arty, arty-crafty, arty-farty, artsy-craftsy, artsy-fartsy, art fag, long-haired.

ARTLESS adj. up-front, call a spade a spade, make no bones about it, open, straight shit, call it like it is, talk turkey. See FRANK.

ASCENDANCY n. 1. on top. See AUTHORITY. 2. upper hand, whip hand, drop on one, edge on one, jump on one, leg up on one. See ADVANTAGE.

ASCERTAIN v. check, check out, check up on, doublecheck, look-see, make sure, eye, eyeball, read, see, dig it, peg, size, size up, pick up, pick up on, get hold of, get into one's head, get it down, get down pat, get down cold,

get the hang of, learn the ropes, go through the school of hard knocks.

ASCERTAINED adj. nailed-down, dead sure, for sure, fer sher, fer shirr, for a fact, cold, all locked up. See PROVEN.

ASIAN n. Chinaman, Chink, Chinx, gook, Jap, nip, dink, gooney, gooney bird, Buddha-head, raghead, skibby, skibo, slant, slant-eyes, slope, slope eyes, ricer, rice puppy, eggrolls, yellow peril; banana, Twinkie (favors whites, yellow on the outside white inside), mango, zip (all Derog.). See also CHINESE, JAPANESE, PHILIPPINE.

ASIDE n. throwaway.

AS IF adv. like (It's like I might die).

AS IS adj. as advertised, pat, stand pat, what you see is what you get, WYSIWYG.

ASK v. 1. grill, roast, sweat, sweat it out of one, sweat out, So?, buzz, give one the third, give one the third degree, put one through the wringer, put the heat on one, put the screws on, go over, pick one's brains, cat-haul, hit, strike, pop the question, whistle for (but won't get). See also QUESTION. 2. hit, touch, bite, bum, hustle, promote, mooch, knock. See BEG.

ASKEW adj. topsy-turvy, catawampus, zigzag, cock-eyed, yaw-ways. See CROOKED.

ASLANT adj. slaunchways, slaunchwise.

ASLEEP adj. crashed, snoozing, out, out cold, out like a light, out of it, flaked out, sacked out, getting some sack time, getting some shut-eye, bat caving, making zzz's, making a few z's, catchin' some zees, taking forty winks, on the kip, on the nod, dead, dead to the world, in dreamland, in the land of Nod, collaring a nod, in the arms of Morpheus, in the lap of Morpheus, sawing wood, sawing logs, pounding one's ear.

ASPARAGUS n. sparrowgrass.

ASPECT n. slant, twist, gimmick, angle, take, switch.

ASPERSE v. slam, knock, put down, burn, burn down, burn one down, dig at, slap at, rag, rag on, cap, slice up, rank, give a black eye. See SLANDER.

ASPERSION n. rap, slam, smear, dump, hit, knock, put-down, black eye, backhanded compliment, dirty dig, raspberry, bazoo. See DEFAMATION.

ASPIC n. nervous pudding.

ASPIRANT n. tyro, hopeful, white hope.

ASPIRATION n. fire in the belly, push, right stuff.

ASPIRING adj. hungry, ambish, eager beaver, go-getter, on the make, out for a rep. See AMBITIOUS. See also HOPEFUL.

ASS n.   Rocky Mountain canary.

ASSAIL v.   bash, bust, blister, blast on, lambaste, trash, work over, have at, come at. See ATTACK.

ASSAILANT n.   mugger, hit man, trigger man, goon, bushwhacker, oppo, opposite number, meat. See also ENEMY.

ASSASSIN n.   hit man, trigger man, piece man, torpedo, enforcer, gorilla, gun, gunman, gunsel, bumpman, button man, hatchet man, bang man, apache, shootist, clipper, plugger, soldier, troop, butcher, knock-off ghee, red-hot, dropper (hired), wad agent.

ASSASSINATE v.   liquidate, neutralize, waste, do in, burn, off, take out, erase, kiss off top, top off, compromise (espionage use), take care of. See KILL.

ASSASSINATION n.   hit, offing, wasting, liquidation, neutralization, taking out, a ride, croaking. See KILLING.

ASSAULT v.   1. bash, blast, haul off on one, slam, trash, wilding (gang), zap, jump, go for, slap around, work over, come down on, meat-ax, bushwhack, let one have it, light into. 2. shoot down, jump on one's case, jump down one's throat, take one over the hurdles, blitz. See ATTACK.

ASSAULT AND ROB v.   mug, arm, car-jack, bushwhack, put the arm on, put the muscle on, put the mug on, put the slug on.

ASSAULTER n.   mugger, hit man, car-jacker, bushwhacker.

ASSAY v.   check, check out, eyeball, read, see, peg, size, size up. See APPRAISE. See also ANALYZE; ATTEMPT.

ASSEMBLE v.   round up, scare up, meet up, bunch up, gang up, corral, hang around, hang out, make the scene, poke, punch, capture. See also MEET.

ASSEMBLY n.   confab, clambake, coffee klatsch, meet, get-together, huddle, sit-in, turnout. See MEETING. See also CROWD.

ASSENT v.   1. okay, pass on, shake on, cut a deal, done deal, buy, ditto, that works for me, give one five (slap hands). 2. give in, cave in, say uncle, knuckle under. See AGREE.

ASSERT v.   shoot one's wad, shoot one's bolt, shoot off one's mouth, mouth off, pop off, butt in, horn in. See also PROCLAIM.

ASSERTION n.   say-so, one's stamp of approval, mouthful (you said a mouthful), two cents' worth. See AFFIRMATION.

ASSESS v.   check, check out, dig it, figger, figure, nick, peg, size, size up, take one's measure. See also APPRAISE.

ASSESSMENT n.   1. Irish dividend (Derog.). 2. value judgment.

ASSETS n.   bankroll, nut, nest egg, rainy day, sock, stash, stache, mattressful, kitty, stake, backing, budget, ace in the hole, ace up one's sleeve (hidden), a little something put away, a little something put aside, stuff, goods.

ASSIDUOUS adj.   grind, plugger, nose to the grindstone, springbutt, eager beaver, work one's tail off, whiz. See INDUSTRIOUS.

ASSIGN v.   1. name, slot, tab, tag, reference, hang something on, pin on, credit. See also NAME. 2. dish out, fork out, hand out, shell out. See also DIVIDE. 3. buck off, task.

ASSIGNATION n.   affair, date, heavy date, love nest, matinee, noonie, one-night stand, quickie, rendezvous, triff, treff (secret), your place or mine. See RENDEZVOUS.

ASSIGNMENT n.   beat, bum out. See also TASK.

ASSIMILATE v.   go native, hit the beach.

ASSIST n.   shot in the arm, shot in the ass, boost, leg, leg up, hand, handout, lift, backup. See also SUPPORT.

ASSIST v.   boost, give a boost to, give a leg up, give a lift, lend a hand, plug, hype, push, hold a brief for, go with, go for, go to bat for, go to the mat for, go down the line for, go the route for, make a pitch for, beat the drum for, plump for, run interference for, grease the wheels for, thump the tub for, root for, stump for, front for, stand up for, stick up for, ride shotgun for, take care of one for, backup, bail out. See also SUPPORT.

ASSISTANT n.   girl Friday, gal Friday, man Friday, sec, help, temp, backup, flunky, furp, apparatchick, squeak, straw boss, home guard, peon, savage, serf, slave, slavey; shop, crew, troops (Pl.).

ASSOCIATE n.   1. affil (TV), branch, branch house, offshoot. 2. buddy, chum, pal, sidekick, playmate, matie, pard, pardner, kissing cousin, one of the boys; shop, crew, troops (Pl.). See FRIEND. 3. clubber, joiner. 4. dweeb (junior or senior).

ASSOCIATE v.   team up, team up with, pool, tie up, tie in, tie-in, tie-up, tie in with, tie up with, throw in together, throw in with, line up with, swing in with, go partners with, go in partners with, be in cahoots with, go in cahoots with, bunch up, gang up, gang up with, pal up with, buddy up with, hang around, hang out with, run with, run around with, truck with, play footsie with, go along with, string along with, take up with, kick it, get into, get in on, get in with, get together, come together, join together, join up with, hook up, hook on, hook up with, stand up with, stand in with, get on the in with, interface, interface with, network with, meld with, play ball, play ball with, suit up with (team), sign up, sign on, tag on, tack on, slap on, hitch on, come aboard, deal one in, include me in, plug into, glue oneself to, fraternize.

ASSOCIATED adj. hooked up with, in cahoots with, joined up with, lined up with, partners with, thrown in with, tied in with, plugged into.

ASSOCIATION n. Old Boy network, syndicate, outfit, tie-up, tie-in, tie-in tie-up, hookup, gang, mob, bunch, crew, ring, circle, clan, tribe, troupe, troops, those one runs with, strange bedfellows (unlikely), combination, combo, pool, megacorp, multinational, plunderbund, the company, family, famiglia, rat pack, yoot (teenage), bunch, crowd, zoo.

ASSORTMENT n. mixed bag, combo, everything but the kitchen sink, mishmash, mishmosh, garbage, kludge (parts). See also MIXTURE.

ASSUAGE v. cool, cool out, make nice, pour oil on troubled waters, take the edge off, take the sting out of. See PACIFY.

ASSUME v. 1. take over, glom on to, snatch, liberate, confisticate, moonlight requisition, take a five-finger discount (shoplift), annex, swipe, grab, grab hold of, borrow, clap hands on, get one's fingers on, get one's hands on, highjack, hijack, kipe, high-grade. 2. be afraid, have a hunch, have a sneaking suspicion. See also BELIEVE. 3. take on, take over.

ASSUMPTION n. 1. shot, shot in the dark, hunch, stab, sneaking suspicion. See also BASIS. 2. takeover, grab.

ASSURANCE n. sure thing, lock, lock and win, have a lock on, license to print money, sewed up, cold lay, shoo-in, rain or shine. See CERTAINTY.

ASSURE v. 1. buck up, brace up. See SUPPORT. See also AFFIRM, AVER. 2. ice, put on ice, lock, lock on, lock and win, have a lock on, lock up, cinch, clinch, nail down, set. 3. sell, sell one on, bag, bet on. See also PERSUADE.

ASSURED adj. 1. cocksure, iceman, ice in one's veins, gutsy, got the faith baby, gung-ho, high, high on something, gamble on, keeping the faith, rosy, upbeat, bullish, all puffed up, pumped up, glad-hander (overly), looking at the world with rose-colored glasses, looking at something through rose-colored glasses. See also IMPERTURBABLE. 2. sure as shit, surefire, nailed-down, lock-and-win situation, on ice, bet one's bottom dollar on, in the bag, racked, boat race (horse racing). See CERTAIN.

ASTERISK n. bug.

ASTEROID n. doomsday rock, killer asteroid, shocked quartz.

ASTONISH v. floor, rock, gork, blow away, blow one's mind, boggle the mind, bowl down, bowl over, flabbergast, knock one over, knock one over with a feather, set one on one's ass, strike all of a heap, throw on one's beam ends, spring something on one, throw one a curve, put one away. See also SURPRISE.

ASTONISHED adj. floored, stuck, stumped, thrown, blown away, boggled, bowled down, bowled over, bug-eyed, whomper-jawed, discombobulated, flabbergasted, could've knocked one over with a feather, set on one's ass, struck all of a heap, thrown off one's beam ends, caught off base, caught with one's pants down, flatfooted, shit-blue, shit-green, bit one in the ass. See also SURPRISED.

ASTONISHMENT n. toxic, stunner, one for the book, something else, something to shout about, something to write home about.

ASTOUND v. blow away, bowl over, flabbergast, knock one over with a feather, set on one's ass, strike all of a heap, throw on one's beam ends. See ASTONISH.

ASTOUNDED adj. bug-eyed, set on one's ass, boggled, bowled down, bowled over, flabbergasted, whomper-jawed, struck all of a heap, blown away, put away.

ASTOUNDING adj. mind-blowing, far-out, stunning, megadual. See AMAZING.

ASTRONAUT n. moonman, spaceman.

ASTRONAUT LAUNCH n. eyeballs in eyeballs out (physical effect).

ASTUTE adj. brainy, foxy, sharp as a tack, have smarts, brill, on the ball, quick on the uptake, not born yesterday. See INTELLIGENT; SHREWD.

ASYLUM n. 1. booby hatch, funny farm, nuthouse, rubber room, soft wall. See INSANE ASYLUM. 2. hideaway, hideout, hole in, hole up, place to hole up, safehouse, blowout center, ivory tower, den.

AT prep. by.

ATHLETE n. jock, superjock, shoulders, strap, V man, iron man, muscle man, muscle head, meathead, jockey, animal, ape, gorilla, Neanderthal (Derog.); redshirt (elegibility extended), speed merchant, white hope (white contender), sport.

ATHLETIC SUPPORTER n. jock.

ATLANTA, GEORGIA Big A, Big Peach, Big South, Hot Lanta, Hotlanta, Hot Town.

ATLANTIC CITY, NEW JERSEY the Boardwalk.

ATLANTIC OCEAN n. big drink, the pond, big pond, herring pond, Big Ditch.

ATMOSPHERE n. scene, space, place, mood, color, local color, color man (TV sports).

ATOM BOMB n. A-bomb, nucular bomb, the bomb, doomsday machine, nuke, backpack nuke.

ATOMIC WAR n. A-war, H-war, nucular war, the unthinkable, MAD (mutually assured destruction).

ATONE v. make up for, pay one's dues, square, square a beef, square things, take one's medicine. See also APOLOGIZE, CORRECT, PAY.

ATROCIOUS adj. gross, grody, grody to the max, awful, beastly, godawful, goshawful, hellish, hairy, lousy, rotten. See BAD. See also DREADFUL.

ATTACH v. hitch up, hitch on, hook on, hook up, slap on, tag on. See also FASTEN.

ATTACHED adj. anchored, nailed, built in.

ATTACHMENT n. crush, case, amore, mad pash, weakness, yen, shine, hankering, beaver fever (Obsc.), calf love, puppy love. See LOVE.

ATTACK n. blitz, blitzkrieg, mugging, push, dirty deed, surgical mission (quick) attempting a creep.

ATTACK v. 1. mug, bang (gang), bat, bash, bust, biff, blister, boff, bop, bean, beat, beat the shit out of, beat one to a frazzle, blast, blast on, brain, break one's face, bam, wham, whop, soak, slog, storm, wallop, haul off on one, land a haymaker, lambaste, K.O., slam, swat, push, paste, sock, smack, split, trash, whack, wing, zap, zapper, zetz, larrup, yerk, plunk, jump, jump on, slug, heel, punch out, wipe out, work out, work over, lay out, read one out, throw a punch, tangle ass with, gang up, get, shellack, guzzle, go at, go for, go for it, go in for, go out for, go after, go to town on, heat, have at, have a go at, lay at, take a swing at, take a crack at, crack down on, poke, take a poke at, take a swipe at, whack, take a whack at, rush, come at, come down on, come down hard on one, put the bee on one, belt, belt out, blind, blindside, bushwhack, dry-gulch, banjax, boot, boot around, bloop, bonk, conk, clout, clip, hit a clip, clump, clunk, clonk, clock, crown, chop down, chill, cold-cock, cold-pack, cook, Chinese, cop, double-bank, drop, deck, dump, dust off, flip, flatten, give 'em hell, give one a fat lip, give one both barrels, let one have it with both barrels, let one have it, give one the blanket, give one the works, give a deal to, sock it to one, stick it to one, hand it to one, kick ass, kick the shit out of one, kick the daylights out of one, kick the living daylights out of one, kick the bejesus out of, kick one ass-over-teakettle, kick one on one's ear, kick one into next week, kick one's cruller in, kick one's lemon in, kick one's sconce in, put out one's lamp, put one in the hospital, tip over, knock over, knock off, knock cold, knock dead, knock the bejesus out of one, knock one on one's ass, knock one ass-over-teakettle, knock one on one's ear, knock on one's keister, knock one into next week, knock one's block off, knock one for a loop, knock for a row of (anything), knock the beholden out of one, knock the daylights out of one, knock the shit out of one, whale the daylights out of one, floor one, land all over one, measure, meatball, lump, lump up, put the boots to, roast, scorch, skin alive, lace, lace into, lay into, pitch into, light into, sail into, wade into, rip, rip into, rip up, rip up one side and down the other, slap down, fire on, hang one on, lean on, lean against, take on, lay on sap, lay a finger on, lay a glove on, land on, put the slug on, put the slough on, slough, slough around, woof, push around, ring one's bell, pull a joint, pull a Jap (surprise, Derog.), pepper, plant one. See also SCOLD. 2. shoot down, shoot down an idea, shoot down a thing, jump on one's case, jump down one's throat, you gonna jump on my chest?, shade, throw shade, do a razor job on, stretch, take one over the hurdles, timber up, blitz, fly in the teeth of.

ATTACKER n. mugger, bushwhacker, dry gulcher.

ATTAIN v. 1. snag, cop, get one's hands on, glom on to, latch on to, promote. See GET. See also EFFECT. 2. make it, pull off, come through with, score, get fat, get there, unzip, arrive. See ACHIEVE.

ATTAINABLE adj. no sweat, no problem, duck soup, cherry pie, cake, cakewalk, sleepwalk, walk, piece of cake, can o' corn. See EASY. See also OBTAINABLE.

ATTEMPT n. all one's got, crack, fling, go, jelly go, header, lick, one's all, one's damnedest, one's darnedest, one's level best, shot, stab, try, whack, dry run, tryon, tryout, have a fling at, shakedown, shakedown cruise, workout. See also ENDEAVOR.

ATTEMPT v. make a run at, tackle, take on, look to, make a try, cut and try, try on for size, do it or bust a gut, bust one's ass, break one's ass, break one's neck, break one's back, break one's heart, try one's damnedest, try one's darnedest, bring in the heavy artillery, in it to win it (Af. Am.), give it the old college try, try on for size, give it a try, give it a go, give a it a fling, give it one's best shot, take one's best shot, give it a whirl, give a go, give a fling, give it one's all, give it all one's got, bend over backward, lay oneself out, push, knock oneself out, take the bull by the horns, take a shot at, take a fling at, take a crack, take a crack at, take a whack at, cut, take a cut at, take a stab at, make a stab at, have a go at, have a fling at, have a shot at, on the make, pitch into, in there pitching, do one's level best, go in for, go out for, go all out, go for it, go for broke, go the limit, shoot the works. See also APPLY ONESELF.

ATTEND v. 1. catch, make the scene, bob up, pop up, turn up, show, show up, punch in, punch the clock, clock in, time in, drop in, ring in, check in, speak of the devil. See also APPEAR. 2. listen up, pick up, catch, get a load of this, get a load of that, are you ready for this?, give ears, have one's ears on, knock on your lobes. 3. doctor.

ATTENDANCE n. box office, draw, house.

ATTENDANT n. bird dog, alarm clock, baby sitter.

ATTENTION interj. looky, heads up, tenhut.

ATTENTION n. big rush, brace, drop a line on one, listen up, pop to, spotlight, tender loving care, TLC.

ATTENTION GETTER n. grabber, hook, billboard, promo.

ATTENTION, PAY v. see to, TCB (take care of business), be on the ball, get one's head out of one's ass, keep a weather eye open, keep one's ears to the ground, keep one's eye on the ball, keep one's eye peeled, listen up, clue in, keg, not miss a trick, not overlook a bet, pay mind to, shine me on (to me), watch out. See also HEED.

ATTENTIVE adj. on one's toes, on the lookout, on the qui vive, hang on every word, listen up, on the ball, on the job, Johnny on the spot, with a weather eye open, with one's eyes peeled, all ears, glued, hooked, not miss a trick, not overlook a bet, see after, see to. See also WARY.

ATTIC n. sky parlor.

ATTIRE n. threads, glad rags, bib and tucker, California chic (expensive casual), drapes, duds, feathers. See CLOTHING.

ATTIRE v. rag out, rag up, dud, tog, doll up, dog out, turn out, deck, deck out, fit out, outfit, dode (bad fit), drape, dude up, suit up.

ATTIRED adj. dolled-up, decked out, rigged out, dressed fit to kill. See DRESSED.

ATTITUDE n. tude, cop a tude (bad), head-set, mind-set, mind trip, routine, where one's head is, where one is at, where it's at, like it is, the size of it, say so, slant, take, angle, twist, sound, pov (point of view), P.O.V. See also OPINION.

ATTITUDINIZE v. do a bit, lay it on thick, play-act, put up a front, fake, make out like. See POSTURE. See also PRETEND.

ATTORNEY n. man's mouth, mouthpiece, shyster, ack-ack, ambulance chaser, legal eagle, legal beagle, beagle, beak, fixer, lip, patch, the L.A., tongue, pleader, pettifogger, Philadelphia lawyer, squeal, pelican (appellate), bomber (divorce), front, mugger, spieler, spouter, tangle jaw, warble, springer, dump truck (public defender), ghost (writes briefs), D.A., cuter, cutter (prosecutor).

ATTORNEY GENERAL n. the A.G.

ATTORNEY, PUBLIC DEFENDER n. state lawyer, state mouthpiece.

ATTORNEY'S FEE n. fall dough, knock-off, nut.

ATTRACT v. turn on, turn one on, pull, grab, draw, bait, mousetrap, shill, steer, tout, freak out, knock dead, send, come on, give one the come-on, give one a come-hither look, make a hit with, sweep off one's feet, vamp, hook, bat one's eyes at, bat the eyes at, suck in, rope in, score, wow, humbug, go over big, lead up the garden path. See also LURE.

ATTRACTION, SEXUAL adj. chemistry, it.

ATTRACTIVE adj. tasty, ten, 10, oochie, mobile, drop-dead gorgeous, wukka, stud muffin, dyno, Clydesdale (male), industrial, hunk, beauhunk, beefcake, beef-a-roni, Greek God, demigod, drool over, living doll, schwing!, hooky, around-the-way girl, portable, looker, good looker, hottie, freak, flygirl, flyboy, ankle, stone, head rush, knock one's eyes out, stunning, beaut; freak mama, freak mommy (sexually attractive), tall dark and handsome. See BEAUTIFUL.

ATTRIBUTE v. hang something on, pin on, credit, reference. See ASSIGN.

AUCTION v. jam, under the hammer.

AUDACIOUS adj. gutty, nervy, brassy, ballsy, smart-ass, wise-ass, chutzpahdik, cheeky, rind. See DARING.

AUDACIOUSNESS n. balls, guts, guttiness, gutsiness, chutzpah, cheek, brass, nerve, moxie, stuff, crust, gall, spunk.

AUDIENCE n. fan, moviegoer, playgoer, showgoer, theatergoer, first-nighter, showcase, standee, turnout, sports fan, buff, clacker, clapper, deadhead, paper (free pass), paper house, one who catches a show, kibitzer, heckler, aficionado, fence-hanger, bleacher bum, knothole gang. See also SPECTATOR.

AUDIT v. sit in.

AUDITION n. demo, tryout, read, try on, cattle call.

AUDITORIUM n. hall, barn, house.

AUGER n. corkscrew.

AUGMENT v. beef up, pad, boost, bump (poker), tag on, piggyback, add bells and whistles, sweeten. See INCREASE.

AUGMENTATION n. buildup, beefing up, fleshing out, boost, hike, up, upping. See also ADDITION.

AUGUR v. read, crystal ball it, call it, call the shots, have a hunch, figure out, psych it out. See PREDICT.

AUGUST adj. highfalutin, high-minded, high-nosed, high-toned, stiff-necked. See also POMPOUS.

AUSPICIOUSLY adv. at the eleventh hour, in the nick of time. See also TIMELY, CONVENIENT.

AUSTERE adj. clean, vanilla, bare-bones, what you see is what you get. See PLAIN.

AUSTRALIA Down Under, Oz, Aussie land, Outback.

AUSTRALIA AND NEW ZEALAND Anzas.

AUSTRALIAN n. Aussie, Auzzie, Anzac, Ossie; Bill-Jim, Billjim (soldier, WWI), Digger, dinkum (soldier); down under, Sooner.

AUTHENTIC adj. for real, genuine article, legit, absolute, the emess, straight from the horse's mouth, twenty-four-carat. See TRUE.

AUTHOR n. scribbler, scribe, scripter, telewriter (TV), ghost, ghostwriter, columnist, ink slinger, word slinger, wordsmith. See WRITER.

AUTHOR v. script, pen, put down, bang out, bat out, make hen tracks, See WRITE.

AUTHORITATIVE adj. 1. legit, on the legit, the emess, the righteous, out of the horse's mouth, straight from the horse's mouth. See FACTUAL. 2. got the horses to do it, Norwegian steam, powerhouse. See POWERFUL.

AUTHORITIES n. establishment, the feds, the law, brass, top brass, in-group, ins, people in the front office, people upstairs, higher-ups, the top, the bosses, power elite, powers that be, them, they, city hall, the man. See also ADMINISTRATOR, MANAGEMENT.

AUTHORITY n. 1. boss, bosslady, bossman, A-number 1, chief, C.O., CEO, exec, executive suite, front office, suit, the old man, czar, governor, the commish, hot stuff, head, head honcho, head man, hammer-man, lead-off man, general, queen bee, the brass, brass hat, top brass, gold braid, rug rank (high), Mr. Big, big player, big chew, big shot, big shit, big weenie, big cheese, the whole cheese, big wig, bigwigged, top, on top, top dog, topper, top-hand, top-kick, upstairs, high up, higher ups, high priest, king, kingfish, kingpin, king of the hill, bull of the woods, big league, shark, brain, brains, guru, pro, pundit, egg head, ivory dome, ol' professor, old pro, old hand, old war-horse, trained seal, maven, whiz, wizard, buff, bone man, heart man, big nose man, freak, nut; the fuzz, the man, pig, the long arm of the law, oink (police, Derog.); biggest frog in the pond, buddy seat. See also EXECUTIVE; COMMANDER; SUPERVISOR; POLICE. 2. juice, zap, pow, kicker, pizzazz, the force, moxie, powerhouse, poop, punch, clout, steam, might and main, beef, strong arm, the stuff, the goods, what it takes, upper hand, whip hand, drop on one, edge on one, jump on one, leg up on one, the say, the say-so, a lot to say about, a lot to do with, the word, bible, righteous, geets, guts, string, ropes, weight.

AUTHORIZATION n. go-ahead, green light, okay, OK. See CONSENT.

AUTHORIZE v. okay, OK, say the word, give the go-ahead, give the green light, give the word, put one's John Hancock on, rubber-stamp, bless. See APPROVE.

AUTHORIZED adj. okayed, OK'd, kosher, legit.

AUTO n. wheels, mobe, bug, van, boom car (loud radio or tape), jeep, bus, clunker, jalopy, crate, heap, buggy, hot rod. See AUTOMOBILE.

AUTOCRAT n. a Hitler, Simon Legree, slave driver, czar.

AUTOCRATIC adj. bossy, driver, pusher, whip cracker, ass-kicker. See IMPERIOUS.

AUTOGRAPH SEEKER n. autograph hound.

AUTOMATED adj. autofacturing.

AUTOMATIC adj. knee-jerk reaction.

AUTOMATIC PILOT n. George, Iron Mike.

AUTOMATIC TELLER MACHINE n. money-puker, ATM.

AUTOMOBILE n. wheels, mobe, boom car (loud radio or tape), hoopty, ride, trans, smart car (computerized), four-wheeler, fastback, hatchback, go-cart, hard top; ragtop, droptop, straw hat, no top (convertible); bent eight (V-8), bumblebee (small foreign), rice burner (Japanese), cherry, chrome dome, super skate, compact, roller skate (subcompact), pony car, pony (medium-sized), short, limo, stretch limo, stretch car (extra length), van, cock wagon, sin-bin (van), wagon, jeep, peep (jeep), hauler (fast), rail job (dragster), Detroit iron (American), Model T (Ford), tin lizzie, quad (four headlights), long John Silver (one headlight), tank, fox trap, bus, mean machine, 'chine, clean 'chine, sheen (Af. Am.), cream puff, preacher's car (no options), wheel chair, meat grinder, oil burner, blown gasser, buff (great-looking), banger, junker, clunker, iron, piece, lemon, crutch, jalopy, ark, canoe, bomb, bagel (poorly maintained), cement mixer, tuna wagon, rattletrap, death trap, coffin, cage, hoopy, hooptie (still runs), chugalong, wreck, wreck of the Hesperus; ark, beater (old), bucket, bucket of bolts, guzzler, gas guzzler, grizzler, crate, egg crate, heap, heap of junk, junk heap, cheap heap, scrap heap, motheaten (corroded), boat, boiler, hot boiler (stolen), can, bone shaker, breezer, golfer, gondola, nerdmobile (family car), load, rig, rubber, sled, dead sled (nonworking or abandoned), slicker, buggy, gas buggy, gasoline buggy, blitz buggy, zoom buggy, buzz buggy, love buggy, dune buggy, struggle buggy, chopped, chopped car, low rider, raked, stocker, art cart, funny car, scout car, jeepers-creepers, Easter egg (decorated), conobox (small, inexpensive), pimpmobile, pimp ride, pussy-wagon (large, gaudy), midget, midgie, bantam car, muscle car, soup job, hot rod, bomb, buzz wagon, chariot, job, flivver, fliv, gig, goat, go it all, grinder, hayburner, one-lunger, kemp, Jimmie, jitney, Leaping Lena (Obs.), puddle jumper, tub; bear bait, bear food, bear meat (unequipped with citizens band radio), orphan (no longer manufactured), turtle (armored). See also VEHICLE.

AUTOMOBILE ACCIDENT n. total, smashup, smackup, stack-up, pileup, bumper-thumper, fender-bender, fender tag, nerf (nudge another car), crack-up, rack-up, wrack-up; ride-out, squat (fraudulent), dimple (dent), rubberneck (look at accident). See ACCIDENT.

AUTOMOBILE BRAKES n. binders, clinchers, anchor, cliches, grabbers, kill switch (automatic), grab a handful of air.

AUTOMOBILE, ELECTRIC n. juicemobile.

AUTOMOBILE ENGINE n. big banger, four-banger (four cylinder), six-banger, six-holer (six cylinder), forked-eight (V-8), shillelagh (Chevrolet), lump, mill.

AUTOMOBILE HOOD n. doghouse.

AUTOMOBILE HORN n. beeper, honker, tooter.

AUTOMOBILE INSURANCE FRAUD bull and cows (two cars in fake accident), bucket (car in fraud), swoop and squat (fraudulent accident), consent job, owner's job (theft), ghost (unpaid passenger).

AUTOMOBILE, NAMES n. beamer, Bimmer (BMW), Benzo (Mercedes Benz), Rati (Mazerati), Roller (Rolls Royce), Vet (Corvette), Jag (Jaguar), Merc (Mercury), 5.0 (Mustang G.T.), Olds (Oldsmobile), T-bird (Thunderbird) Bug, Beatle, VW, V-dub (Volkswagen), Chevy (Chevrolet), deuce and a quarter (Buick Electra 225), goat (Pontiac GTO), Cad, Caddy, Caddie, golfer, cat, kitty, cattle train, hog (all Cadillac), rodda (Af. Am., Cadillac), ducker (Dodge), Model T (Ford), deuce (1932 Ford), A-bone (model A Ford), T-bone (Model T Ford).

AUTOMOBILE PARTS n. moonroof (transparent roof section), buggy whip (radio antenna), stick, dash (dashboard), big hole (gear), mag (magneto), banger barrel, (cylinder); jug, pot (carburetor); wrinkle-rod (crankshaft), busted lung (spark plug) blower, huffers and puffers (supercharger), roll bar, spaghetti (excess trim), squint (tinted windshield glass), turtle shell (trunk or trunk lid), wires (wheels), nerf bars (special bumpers).

AUTOMOBILE SHOW n. Motorama.

AUTOMOBILE, STOLEN n. a short, hot car, bent one, rinky, trap, slick, G-ride, gondola (not common); consent job, owner's job (theft insurance fraud); move a job, push hot boilers, push hot ones (dispose of), on the schlep, car jacking (stealing), chop shop (cars dismantled for parts).

AUTOMOBILE TERMS Georgia credit card, Okie credit card, Tijuana credit card (hose for siphoning gasoline), DWI (driving while intoxicated), ride shotgun (front seat), light it up (start), run hard and put away, wet-tail, tailgate, slipstreaming, drafting (too close to car in front) smoked choked and croaked (abused); raked, California tilt (front end lower); jumper cable, booster cable, boom car (loud radio or tape), pits (service area), guts (interior), stack, down in the kitchen (low gear), bottom end; shunpiking (using the back roads), fishtail, black box puke, blow lunch (blow an engine), blown engine (serious breakdown), muscle (power), pull (remove a part), blue book (value), boneyard (junkyard), Botts' dots (pavement markers), dimple, ocean fenders (dent), car clout (break-in), flea (buyer out for bargain), roach (buyer with no credit), happy man (finance company), idiot lights (flashing dashboard lights), mud doggin' (off road), make (brand name), Italian mausoleum (trunk, Derog.).

AUTOMOBILE TIRE n. rubber, baldy (worn), retread, skins, hides, shoe, boots, sneakers, snowballs (whitewall), sticker (new), donuts, flat, flat hoop, sore foot (punctured), pumpkin (flat), barefoot (worn-out), carcass (old), slicks (racing).

AUTOMOBILE TRANSMISSION n. tranny, stick (manual), box slush, slush box, mashed-potato drive (automatic).

AUTOMOBILE WAREHOUSE n. doghouse, drop off, dump, hole, hot boiler farm, hot car farm, plant, stash.

AUTO RACEWAYS n. Indy, brickyard (Indianapolis), hairpin turn, groove, line (best route around track), marbles (slippery spot).

AUTO RACING TERMS back off (decelerate), consy (consolation race), dice (close race), endo (end over end crash), fishtail, squirrel (both skid side to side), green flag, grid start, heel and toe (driving technique), hooligan race, nerf (bump during race), pace lap, pick off (pass a car), pole sitter (pole position starter), red flag, reverse start, shunt (collide), slingshot (passing strategy), spinout.

AVAILABLE adj. on tap, come-at-able, gettable, get-in-able, up for grabs, on deck, ready willing and able. See OBTAINABLE.

AVANT-GARDE adj. leading-edge, state-of-the-art, far out, beat, way out, hep, hip, fly, po-mo (postmodern), new wave. See VANGUARD.

AVARICIOUS adj. grabby, piggy, tight, big-eyed, skinflint, screw, pinchy, poligot. See STINGY. See also GREEDY.

AVENGE v. get even with, come back at, get back at, get hunk, stick it in and break it off, square accounts, give one a dose of one's own medicine. See REVENGE.

AVERAGE adj. so-so, vanilla, white bread, fair, fair to middling, middle-of-the-road, middlebrow, run-of-the-alley, run-of-the-mill, everyday, plastic, boilerplate, garden, garden variety, no great shakes, dime a dozen, nowhere, strictly union, humdrum, rumdum, cotton-pickin', mainstream, starch, boojy, ham and egger, hoddy-doddy, journeyman, in and outer (sports), man on the street, Billy Sixpack, Joe Lunchbucket, Sammy Smith concept, Susie Smith concept, John Smith, Mr. Smith, Mrs. Smith, Mrs. Brown, Mr. Brown, ordinary Joe, Joe Doakes, plebe.

AVERSION n. allergy, no eyes for, no use for.

AVIATOR n. flyboy, hot shot, jockey, throttle jockey, truck driver, bird legs, birdman, barnstormer, eagle. See PILOT.

AVIATRIX n. birdwoman.

AVID adj. creaming to, dying to, gotta have. See IMPATIENT.

AVOCATION n. bag, one's bag, into, kick, schtick, shot, thing, be into, do one's thing.

AVOID v. 1. duck, duck out of, deke, hide, lay low, run for cover, bob, weave; janck, jink (enemy planes); juke, stutter-step, fake one out, shake, shake off, shake and bake, fish, flicker, ditch, give the slip, skip out on, get around, sashay around, tiptoe around, dodge, give one the run-around, hang one out to dry, palm off, steer clear of, run for cover, circumlocute, beat the rap, beat around the bush. See also RETREAT. 2. cut, cut dead, cold-shoulder, give the cold shoulder to, chill, shine one on, freeze, blow off, have no truck with. 3. bag, skip, give a miss to, not touch with a ten-foot pole, give the go-by, give a wide berth, pass the buck, buck-pass, buck it over, pass up, stay shy of. See also SNUB.

AVOW v. swear up and down, swear on a stack of bibles, swear till one is blue in the face, cross one's heart and hope to die. See also AFFIRM.

AWAIT v. hang in, hang around, hang out, sweat, sweat it, sweat it out, cool one's heels, it's looking to, wait for the other shoe to drop. See WAIT.

AWAKEN v. roll out, rise and shine, hit the deck, pile out, show a leg, turn out, drop your cocks and grab your socks (Obsc.), keep banker's hours (late).

AWARD n. the gold, gold star, the cookies, feather in one's cap, Oscar. See also DONATION.

AWARD v. hand out, dish out, fork out, shell out, gift, gift with, put something in the pot, sweeten the kitty. See GIVE.

AWARDS n. Oscar (film), Tony (theater), Emmy (TV), Grammy (phono record), Obie (Off-Broadway), Clio (TV commercial), Effie (advertising), Arkie (computer games), E (for efficiency, WWII).

AWARE adj. plugged-in, tuned-in, chilly, in the picture, be up on, grounded, with it, cool, savvy, sharp, been there, wise to, wised-up, on to, fly, hep, hip, hip to the jive, hipped, on the beam, tuned in, into, really into, go-go, all woke up, know-how, groovy, latched on, in the know, know one's stuff, know the ropes, know all the ins and outs, know the score, know all the answers, know what's what, know one's onions, know it all, know one's business, knows one's P's and Q's, knows one's p's and q's, on the beam, double digs, hear tell of, hear say, kept posted, ear to the ground, wake up and smell the coffee. See also KNOWLEDGEABLE.

AWAY adj. out, out-of-pocket, out-of-touch. See also ABSENT.

AWE v. blow away, blow one away, knock one's socks off, make one's teeth fall out, showboat, showtime, grandstand, hotdog. See IMPRESS.

AWESOME adj. killer, zero cool, far-out, megadual, frantic, mean, mind-blowing, gone, real gone, hairy, nervous, something else, clean outta sight. See IMPRESSIVE. See also AMAZING.

AWFUL adj. sucks, sucks a big one, sux, sucky, dank, beat, rotted, rottissimo (very bad), Rott, it rots, poxy, bunk, pail, bucket, scurvy, scuzzo, scuzzy, shitsky, skewy, grody, grody to the max, gross, grungy, raunchy, stinking, synthetic, burly, tough, tough nuggies. See BAD.

AWKWARD adj. klutzy, bogus, all thumbs, wally, butterfingers, two left hands, two left feet, a newt, clodhopper. See CLUMSY.

AWRY adj. cockeyed, catawampus, slaunchways, slaunchwise, zigzag, hell west and crooked. See CROOKED.

AXIOM n. daffodil.

B

B n. Benny, Bravo.

BABBLE v. go on, run on, run off at the mouth, have diarrhea of the mouth, yakkety-yak, yakking, gas, talk through one's hat, spill the beans, bibble-babble, bull, bullshit, BS, throw the bull. See also SPEAK.

BABY n. crawler, toddler, kid, babe, bottle baby, babykins, bambino, cheese factory, tot, tad, in diapers, nipper, papoose, drape ape, rug rat, preemie, baster baby (by artificial insemination), button, Michelin baby (fat), bundle, bundle from heaven, little darling, little angel, little doll, little cherub, little deduction, little dividend, little write-off, write-off, tax benefit, expense, youngster, angelface, dumpling, buttercup, chick, honeychild, lollipop, rosebud, snooky, snookums, sugar, sugarplum; Boomer, Baby Boomer (post-WWII); wet behind the ears, Irish twins (both born within a year, Derog.).

BABYISH adj. kid stuff.

BACHELOR n. batch, old bach, bachelor girl, old maid, single, single-o, single man, stag, unattached, available, eligible.

BACHELOR v. bach it, batch it.

BACK n. lats (muscles).

BACK v. 1. angel, bankroll, bank, greenback, grubstake, stake. See FINANCE. 2. boost, give a boost, give a leg up, give a lift, go to bat for, stick by, stick up for. See SUPPORT.

BACKACHE n. backacky, back gone out, crick.

BACKER n. the money, angel, greenback, sponsor, rabbi, Chinaman, fairy godmother, grubstaker, staker, meal ticket. See BENEFACTOR.

BACK TALK n. comeback, snappy comeback, feedback, you get it, guff, lip. See ANSWER.

BACKUP adj. spillback, safety copy.

BACKWARDS adj. ass backwards, bass ackwards, ass over elbows, arsy-varsy, off the cob, topsy-turvy, catawampus, catawhompus. See also REVERSE.

BACKWOODS n. boonies, boondocks, tullies, B.F.E., butt-fucking Egypt, B.F.A., butt-fucking Africa, sticks. See COUNTRY.

BACON n. grunts, sow belly.

BACON AND EGGS ON TOAST n. Adam and Eve on a raft, bride and groom on a raft, cackleberries and grunts (Rest.).

BACON, LETTUCE AND TOMATO n. BLT, BLT on wheels (to take out, Rest.).

BACTERIA n. bug.

BAD adj. sucks, sux, sucky, beat, rotted, rottissimo (very bad), Rotterdam, it rots, poxy, bunk, pail, bucket, grody, grody to the max, gross, gagger, bad scene, scurvy, scuzzo, scuzzy, shitsky, skewy, greasy, beastly, dead-ass, rat's-ass, bad-assed, barfy, bald, grunge, grungy, raunchy, scuzzy, sleazy, sleazeball, sludgeball, cocksucking (Obsc.), burly, foul ball, shitty, crappy, crap, dreck, crud, cruddy, crusty, burnt, cheesy, Velveeta, Cap'n Chedda, cheap, cheapie, diddly, diddly-shit, diddly-poo, doodly, doodly-poo, shitbox, shitbag, shitburger, chickenshit, ain't worth shit, ain't worth the powder to blow it to hell, ain't worth a hoot, ain't worth a plugged nickel, bad news, bummer, downer, dank, downside, grabber, the pits, the dogs, bottom out, blah, crummy, rough, sad, stinking, synthetic, tough, tough nuggies, eighteen-carat, fierce, something fierce, godawful, goshawful, wacked, whacked, lame, bonk, fiddlefucking, worst-case scenario, garbage, icky, yucky, lousy, rotten, murder, murderous, nuts, poison, tripe, bum, dirty, dirty-minded, doin' dirt, low-down, mangy, measly, damn, damned, darn, darned, cotton-pickin', stiffo, tin, wood, not so hot, no bargain, no account, no count, no good, N.G., tripe, turkey, dud, hellish, hell of a note, hipper-dipper, dinger, ech, flukum, flookum, on the fritz, white elephant, punk, humpty-dumpty, jeasley, crab, ice, pretzels, bogus, junk, junky, the least, lousy, beans, hill of beans, a lemon, peanuts, bad apple, two-bit, short end of the stick, bottom of the barrel, number ten (Korean War), one thou, one thousand (Vietnam War).

BAD BREATH n. dragon breath, dragon (person with bad breath).

BADGE n. shield, button, buzzer, cookie cutter, flash, potsy, tin, white tin, yellow tin, lost-and-found badges (Gulf War, Marine term for Army name tags). See also IDENTIFICATION.

BADGER v. bug, ride, be at, be on the back of, eat, chiv, noodge, give one the business, work on, fuzzbuzz, hassle. See ANNOY.

BAD PERSON n. bad guy, bastard, prick, sleazeball, slimeball, slime bucket, bub; mother, motherfucker M.F., mofo, fuckface, cocksucker (Obsc.); shower scum, jive turkey, son of a bitch, SOB, maggot, shithead, megabitch. See SCOUNDREL.

33

BAD-TEMPERED adj. bitchy, cussed, mean, ornery, stanky (Fem.), ugly. See IRRITABLE.

BAFFLE v. stick, stump, throw, floor, get, rattle, buffalo. See PUZZLE.

BAFFLED adj. thrown, in a fog, spaced out, beat, bamboozled, buffaloed. See PUZZLED.

BAG n. jiffy bag, keister, valpack, carry-on, tote bag, gear, swag bag, diddie bag (Army), doggie bag (Rest.). See also LUGGAGE.

BAGGAGE n. bags, carry-on, tote, tote bag, things, fortnighter, gear, two-suiter, garment bag, duffel, duffel bag, valpack, keister, meter, peter, slough, jiffy bag, swag bag, turkey.

BAGGAGE HANDLER n. baggage smasher, baggage masher, redcap, skycap. See also PORTER.

BAGGAGE THIEF n. keisterman, keister mark (victim).

BAIL BOND TERMS spring, springer (bondsman); buy new shoes, hop bail, lam, jump bail (run away); charge account (access to bail money), half in stir (free on bail).

BAILIWICK n. turf, territory, stamping grounds, stomping grounds, old stomping grounds, neck of the woods. See NEIGHBORHOOD.

BAIL VIOLATOR n. hot foot, jumper.

BAIT n. come-on, drag, shill, puffer, B-girl. See LURE.

BAKER n. doughboy, dough head, dough puncher. See also COOK.

BALANCE n. hang, even-steven.

BALANCE v. come out, come out even.

BALCONY, THEATER n. peanut gallery, bloody-nose gallery, paradise; nigger heaven, Ethiopian paradise (both Derog.).

BALD adj. baldy, bald as a coot, bald as an egg, bald as an eagle, chrome-dome, cueball, curly, egghead, skinhead.

BALK v. cramp, cramp one's style, crimp, throw one a curve, throw a monkey wrench into the works, spike one's guns, upset one's apple cart, See HINDER.

BALL n. apple, pellet, pill, sphere.

BALL (DANCE) n. prom, hop, jump, mingle, shindig, boogie, hoedown, hoedig, hoodang, hog-wrestle, brawl. See also PARTY.

BALLET STUDENT n. rat.

BALLOON n. bladder, sky hook.

BALLOON VENDOR n. bag guy.

BALLROOM n. frolic pad, track.

BALTIMORE AND OHIO R.R. n. Beefsteak and Onions, old B. and O.

BALTIMORE, MARYLAND Bal City, Balto, B.W., Dollar Bills and Brick Houses.

BALTIMORE RESIDENTS n. Baltimorons.

BAN n. no-no, a don't, off-limits, outta bounds, a thou-shalt-not.

BAN v. blackball, ice out, pass by, pass up, shut out, close down, close up.

BANAL adj. dumb, noplace, nowhere, square, stupid, corn, cornball, corn-fed, corny, hokum, hokey, tripe, blah, draddy, dull as dishwater, flat, flat as a pancake, ho-hum, nothing, pablum, Barbie and Ken, zero. See also TRITE.

BANALITY n. buzzword, boilerplate, dullsville, high camp, hokum, corn, familiar tune, chestnut, old chestnut, saw, old saw, old song, old story, potboiler.

BAND n. 1. combo, group, big band, jazz band, jump band, swing band, blue blowers, jazz blowers, sidemen, backup, ork. 2. those one runs with, bunch, crowd, mob, gang, gang bangers, ring, clan, outfit, tribe, troupe, troops, rat pack, yoot (teenage). See GROUP.

BANDANA n. snotrag, wipe, blower, duster, tear duster, sneezer, sniffer.

BAND LEADER n. professor, monkey.

BANISH v. kick out, chuck out, chucker out, boot out, throw out on one's ear, bounce, give one the heave-ho, give one the old heave-ho, give one the bum's rush, give the mitten, give the hook, fire, kiss off, can. See also EJECT, OSTRACIZE.

BANISHED adj. blackballed, cold-shouldered, left out in the cold, left on the outside looking in, out of the loop, not in the picture, shut-out, sidelined. See EXCLUDED.

BANJO n. banjer.

BANJOIST n. banjo man, banjo picker, banjo strummer, banjo thrummer, banjo twanger, picker.

BANJO-UKULELE n. banjo uke, banjuke.

BANK n. damper, jay, jug, big-top, ATM (automatic teller machine).

BANK ACCOUNT n. nest egg, rainy day, sock, mattressful.

BANKBOOK n. damper pad.

BANKER n. loan shark, Shylock, shy, juice dealer, megadink (young). See also FINANCIER.

BANKROLL n. roll, wad, bundle, shoestring, the bank, glory roll, Michigan roll, Philadelphia bankroll. See also MONEY.

BANKRUPT adj. belly-up, toes-up, toes, broke, busted, chapter 11, on the rocks, to the wall, cleaned-out, go to the cleaners, go to the poorhouse. See also DESTITUTE.

BANKRUPT v. go belly up, go toes up, go toes, go bust, go chapter 11, go broke, go under, go up, go the wall, fold, fold up, close one's doors.

BANKRUPTCY n. chapter 11, chapter 7, chapter 13, belly-up, go belly up, toes-up, toes, go under, in the toilet, in the tub, take a bath, close the doors.

BANNED adj. blackballed, no-no, shut out, left out in the cold, not in the picture, out of bounds, left on the outside looking in. See also PROHIBITED, EXCLUDED.

BANNER n. streamer, screamer.

BANQUET n. big feed, blow, blowout.

BANTAM n. banty.

BANTER v. rap, jive, jolly, josh, kid, kid around, goof on, needle, play the dozens, put on, rag, razz, rib, roast. See also JOKE; TEASE.

BANTERER n. rapper, jiver, jollier, josher, kidder, kibitzer, needler, ragger, razzer, ribber, roaster.

BAR n. snake ranch, office, meat rack, meat market (singles bar), beaver palace (Obsc.), candy store, fern bar, fernie, fleshpot, free and easy; gay bar; fruit stand, bird circuit (homosexual, Derog.); titty shake (topless), draft board, guzzlery, guzzery, guzzle shop, dramshop, grogshop, grog mill, gin mill, fill mill, hideaway, room, rum room, night spot, nitery, dive, joint, after-hours joint, juke joint, juice joint, hop joint, beer joint, taproom, grocery, waterhole, the nineteenth hole, gutbucket, bucket shop, suds shop, slop, slop shop (beer), barrelhouse, barrel house, gashouse, alehouse, beerhouse, mug house, washer, cheap John, creep dive, deadfall, honky-tonk, speakeasy, blind pig, blind tiger, scatter, gargle factory, chain locker (dockside), shine box (Af. Am.).

BAR v. blackball, ice out, shut out, pass by, pass up. See EXCLUDE.

BARB n. needle.

BARBECUE n. cookout, smoke-out, cue, BBQ, B.B.Q., rib joint, slab house.

BARBED WIRE n. gooseberry, gooseberry bush (entanglement).

BARBER n. hair stylist, axman, butcher, chin polisher, scraper, hair bender.

BARBER v. get one's ears raised, get one's head scratched, get one's rug beat, mow the lawn.

BARBITURATE n. barb, blue devils, blue heaven, candy, down, goofball, peanuts, Phennies, Christmas tree, Christmas roll, rainbow roll, blockbuster, blunt, fender-bender, goofer, marshmallow reds, Mexican red, red and blue, sleeper, sex, stum, stumbler, tuie, tus, twos, pink lady, purple heart, yellow jacket, abbot, geronimos, blockbuster, nimby, nebbie, nemmy.

BARE adj. 1. bare-assed, B.A., buck naked, naked as a jaybird, naked as the day one was born, without a stitch, nudie, in one's birthday suit, in the altogether, in the raw, skinny. See NUDE. 2. clean, vanilla, what you see is what you get. See PLAIN.

BARE v. 1. let it all hang out, bring it out into the daylight, bring it out into the open, show, show up, whip out, do a fruit salad (expose genitals), flash (also used in cards). See EXPOSE. 2. spill, spill one's guts, blab, sing, crack, get it off one's chest, come clean, open up, blow the whistle on. See CONFESS.

BARELY adv. squeak by, by a hair, by the skin of one's teeth, pretty near, close shave, practically.

BARGAIN n. steal, a real steal, deal, buy, more bang for the buck, dicker, a run for one's money, loss leader. See also AGREEMENT, CHEAP.

BARGAIN v. dicker, deal, hack out a deal, hammer out a deal, make a deal, work out a deal, hondle, Jew down (Derog.), knock down the price. See NEGOTIATE.

BARITONE n. bary.

BARRACKS n. hooch (Quonset), jeep town.

BARRED adj. blackballed, cold-shouldered, left out in the cold, left on the outside looking in, out of the loop, not in the picture, shut out, baldhead, sidelined. See also PROHIBITED.

BARRED WINDOWS n. burglar bars.

BARRIER n. Chinese wall.

BARTENDER n. barkeep, apron, B-girl, bar girl, beer jerker, beer slinger, fizzical culturist, interior decorator, pour man.

BARTER v. horse-trade, swap, swap horses. See NEGOTIATE.

BASE adj. sucks, sux, sucky, beat, rotted, rottissimo (very bad), Rotterdam, it rots, poxy, pail, bucket, grody, grody to the max, gross, beastly, dead-ass, rat's-ass, bad-assed, raunchy, scuzzy, sleazy, sleazeball, slimeball.

BASE n. HQ, GHQ, CP. See also HEADQUARTERS.

BASEBALL, BALL n. apple, horsehide, cowhide, pill, sphere, spheroid, cantaloupe, casaba, egg, radish, hand grenade, globule (Obs.), emery ball (rough-sided, illegal), shine ball (smoothed, illegal), voodoo ball, die (fail to roll or bounce).

BASEBALL, BASE n. bag, sack, cushion; hassock, keystone, keystone sack (second base), hot corner (third base), plate, platter (home).

BASEBALL, BASE ON BALLS n. walk, free transportation, free ticket, free trip, give up a walk, handout, four wide ones.

BASEBALL BAT n. lumber, wood, stick, pole, club, war club, Black Betsy, fungo, fungo stick, swat stick, banana stick.

BASEBALL, BAT v. up (at bat), take one's cut, switch-hit, choke, choke up (grip bat high on handle), hit the dirt (drop to avoid a bad pitch), ahead of the count, looking (not swinging), K (strikeout), buck ten (low batting average).

BASEBALL ERROR n. bobble, boot, lose the handle, muff, miscue.

BASEBALL HIT n. 1. poke, pole, belt, clout, touch, fly, pop fly, pop out, pop up, pull (he pulled it to left), fungo, punch, chop, Baltimore chop (high bounce), roller, comebacker, sacrifice, sacrifice fly, bloop single, dying swan, smash, swat (Babe Ruth was the Sultan of Swat), paste, blast, bleeder, scratch hit, fluke, flair, bouncer, Leaping Lena, pinch hit, hopper, hammer, shell (Lefty was shelled for ten hits), safety, slam, lace one (hard hit), sip one, scorcher, smoke one, scald one, atom ball (hit right atom), pull the trigger, lather, banjo hit, can o' corn (high fly), cloudbuster, tater (fly ball), sinker, Texas Leaguer (short fly), cat, frozen rope, clothesline (low hard), hang out the wash, hang out the hump, a rope, drive, line drive, drive in (he drove in a run), blue dart, grounder, daisy cutter, grass cutter, lawnmower, slow roller, skimmer, tag one, crank one out, cream, leg hit, fence buster, go for the fences, get good wood on it, in one's wheelhouse (preferred hitting zone), slug fest, slugging average, pepper, scatter (they scattered six hits against Ryan). 2. bunt, drag bunt, squeeze, squeeze bunt, suicide squeeze, dump one, lay down a, sacrifice bunt. 3. single, beat out (race to first base before the throw), bleeder, seeing-eye single. 4. double, two-bagger, two-ply poke. 5. triple, go for three, three-bagger, three-ply poke. 6. home run, homer, four-bagger, grand slam (with bases full), grand slammer, lose one, lose one over the fence, money smash, out of the park, take one downtown, over the fence, round-tripper, Babe Ruth, circuit blow, circuit clout, circuit wallop, clean the bases, clean off the bases, dial 8, dial long-distance, dinger, tape measure, revved, revved up, salami, over the fence, take one deep.

BASEBALL PITCH n. deal, fire, hurl, twirl, stuff, stuff on the ball, stuff on it, Sunday pitch, bringing it to 'em, hummer, hump it in, good cheese, the express, aspirin, beebees, fast ball, fastballing, fireballing, blow, blow one by, burn one over, smoke, smoke ball, throw smoke, gas, throw gas, steam, canned heat, heater, fog, fog it in, split-fingered fast ball, breaking ball, curve, nickel curve, Uncle Charlie (curve), chuck 'n' duck (hanging curve), yellow hammer, yakker (curve), crossfire (sidearm), slider, slurve (sliding curve), fader (swerve), jug-handle curve, roundhouse (slow curve), hook, fadeaway, junk, throw junk, floater, flutterball, butterfly ball, palm ball, hesitation pitch, slip pitch (off-speed), change-up, let-up, let-up pitch, let-up ball, pull the string, Clyde's ball (slow ball), sinker, sinker ball, drop, submarine (underhand), screwball, turn the ball over (screwball), knuckleball, knuckler, spitball, spitter, Cuban forkball (spitball, Derog.), forkball, emery ball, grease ball, dipsy-do, dipsy-doodle, knockdown, brush-back, chin music, dust, dust-off (high inside), duster, knuckle duster, ear duster, beanball, head hunter, inshoot, jam (in on the hands), floater, fat (perfect to hit), hanger (failed to curve), gofer ball, gopher ball, groove one (heart of the strike zone), over the plate, nibble (pitch around the edges), automatic take (three balls, no strikes), cripple (thrown with three balls, no strikes), away (wide), four wide ones, cheese express, airing it out (pitching well), pinching (umpire's conservative call).

BASEBALL PITCHER n. hurler, knuckler, flinger, southpaw, portsider, lefty, chucker, starter, stopper (able to beat any team), fireman (relief), reliever (sub), middle reliever, long man, short man, ace (best), arm (ability, a great arm), side wheeler, fastballer, fireballer, smoke (he throws smoke), junkman (throws slowballs), submariner (underhand), hose (throwing arm), rubber arm (durable), glass arm, barber, cockeye, crooked arm, croakie, fork hander, forkballer, hook arm, hand grenader, cousin (easy to hit); go the route, go the distance, go all the way, in a hole (at a disadvantage); derrick, yank, send him to the showers, chase (replace pitcher); Iron Mike (pitching machine).

BASEBALL PLAY n. on, aboard (on base); jammed, juiced, drunk (bases loaded), die (runner left on base), around the horn (ball thrown third to second to first base), triple play (three outs in one play), double play, double steal, steal, take a lead (move toward next base), go with the pitch, squeeze, safety squeeze, suicide squeeze, safe, beat out, out, cut down (out, he was cut down stealing), pick off, run down (caught off base), gun down, nail (out, nailed at second), hit the dirt (slide), fadeaway slide, fallaway slide, fielder's choice, force, force out, shade (adjust field position, Dusty shaded a little to the left), sacrifice, sacrifice fly, shag (chase a ball), caught on the fly, corral, trap, take, gobble, wait for, one hand, under it, a chance, shoestring catch, circus catch (catch a ball); peg, flip (throw); assist, take (fail to swing at a pitch), bail out (drop away from a wild pitch), bat around (full team bats in an inning), break (unexpected favorable action).

BASEBALL PLAYER n. big leaguer, bush leaguer, bush, busher, sandlotter, baseballer, boys of summer, first sacker, second sacker, third sacker, battery (pitcher/catcher), first string, second string, leadoff, leadoff man (first to bat), slugger, cannon, woodman, fence buster, heavy sticker, clouter, power hitter, long-ball hitter, pinch hitter, pinch runner, pull hitter, punch hitter, spray hitter, switch hitter, guess hitter, cleanup (fourth batter); Desi, DH (designated hitter); a good eye; cream puff, banjo hitter (weak); ball hawk, fly catcher, center (centerfielder), back-up infielder, leatherman, glove man (fielder), utility man, platoon player, gardener, butterfingers, bark (coach).

BASEBALL SCORE n. safe, save (relief pitcher game credit), away (one out = one away), die (left on base), behind (balls or strikes to one's disadvantage), blank, pitcher's duel, shutout (held scoreless), laugher (easy win), bring in (a hit brings in a run), give up a run, go-ahead run; full count, long count (three balls, two strikes); ribby (RBI, run batted in).

BASEBALL STADIUM n. ball park, park, diamond (infield); pasture, Hogan's brickyard, the rock pile (bad infield); daisies, garden (outfield).

BASEBALL STRIKEOUT n. fan, K, caught looking, punched out, retire, whiff (also strike).

BASEBALL TERMS national pastime, horsehide, nine, play hardball, rounders, piggy, piggy move-up; the majors, the show (major leagues), cactus league, grapefruit league, minors (minor leagues), farm, farm team, farm out (transfer a player to a farm team), sandlot (amateur), cup of coffee (short stay on a team), home stand (play on home grounds), pitching duel, slugfest, hitfest, doubleheader, twin bill (two games), twi-night double header, nightcap (2d game of double header); raincheck, rainout (postponement); pennant (league championship, they took the pennant), flag (pennant), magic number (formula of victories needed to win pennant), cellar (last place in team standings), lifetime (career record), come off (record of recent past, he comes off a big slump), cousin (easily beaten opponent), chapter (inning), bottom (last half of an inning, the bottom of the sixth); hill, mound, (pitching box); rag, pup (glove); retire the side, pull (remove, he pulled the pitcher), bullpen, slab (pitcher's rubber bar), lineup (batting order), on deck, in the slot (awaiting a turn at bat), bat in a bucket, come through, fungo circle, pepper; scout (talent scout), greenfly (fan), Baseball Annie (dates players).

BASEBALL UMPIRE n. ump, the boys in blue, homer, arbiter, blind Tom, the call (decision), the count (balls and strikes), clubhouse lawyer (player).

BASELESS adj. hot air, just talk, bullshit, BS, piss and wind, whataya talking?, my eye, you're talking like a man with a paper ass, you're talking through your hat. See GROUNDLESS.

BASHFUL adj. wallflower, mousy, ratty.

BASIC adj. bottom line, plain vanilla, nitty-gritty, where it's at, name, name of the game, nub, key, meat and potatoes, coal and ice. See also VITAL.

BASICS n. ABC's, three R's, nitty-gritty, nuts and bolts, brass tacks, get down, get down to brass tacks, groceries, guts, meat and potatoes, beginners, coal and ice, primo, cut, gutty.

BASIS n. bottom line, nitty-gritty, nuts and bolts, rock bottom, meat and potatoes. See FOUNDATION.

BASKETBALL n. B-ball, roundball, the pill, rock (Af. Am.), smashmouth basketball (very aggressive), ball.

BASKETBALL PLAY n. hawk some ball, one on one, low post, high post, assist, give and go, blindside (he blindsided him and stole the ball), fast break, flip pass, hook pass, jump pass, outlet, blind pass (without looking), dish it off (pass), pull the trigger (shoot), turnover (lose possession of the ball), bogart, bogarde (keep possession), put the ball on the floor (dribble), sag (they sagged to cut off Alajuan), softball pass (underhand), steal (Magic reached in and stole the ball), pick one's drawers (steal the ball), put him in the popcorn machine (outmaneuver and score), camp (establish position).

BASKETBALL PLAYER n. cager, baller, basketballer, basket hanger, hoop man; big man, aircraft carrier (center), nose bleeder, post man, the tall trees, front line, front liner (forwards and center); swing man (plays more than one position), greyhound, playmaker.

BASKETBALL SHOT n. hoop, lay-up, jumper, jump shot, J (jump shot), set shot, flip, finger roll, fallaway, hook, trey, three-pointer, downtown, scoop, stuff, swish, swisher, take it to the hole, pull the trigger, can one, get one to go down, bomb (long), long-distance dedication, rainmaker (high arc), chippie (easy open shot), bust (good shot), run and gun, garbage (score loose ball), alley oop, dunk, slam dunk, bash on, tomahawk (dunk), shoot a pair, shoot the eyes out, charity shot, brick (miss off the rim), air ball (complete miss).

BASKETBALL TERMS cage (the game), five, quint (the team), casaba (ball); the iron, the rack, hoop, hole, (basket); the paint, the key (free-throw line); shoot some hoops (play), sellout (bad play) sweet (smooth player), lineup (players in game), hoop man, the big man, low post, high post, ref, the dirt part (defense), hijack (blocked play), jump ball, bring it in (from out of bounds), outlet pass, pass off, ball handler, hot hand (playing well); flip, bury it, drain it (score); box out, screen, tickytack foul, T (technical foul), foul out, bonus situation, charity stripe (free-throw line), go to the line, shoot a pair, kill the clock (timeout), run out the clock (stall), sit on a lead, sit on the ball, let the air out of the ball (slow down the play), junks (shoes).

BASQUE n. basco.

BASS FIDDLE n. bass, bull fiddle, gut bucket, doghouse, old boomer, vein (double bass).

BASTE v. slather, slop on.

BATH n. tub, shower, Jacuzzi, hot tub, spa, splash, light splash.

BATHE v. shower, dunk, tub, splash, swab down.

BATHING SUIT n. bikini, monokini (topless), string, thong, tank suit, kneebusters, clamdiggers, baggies, jammies.

BATHROOM n. can, john, restroom, ladies, ladies' room, women's room, girls' room, little girls' room, ruth, powder room, library, sandbox, biffy, throne room, back, backhouse, cacatorium, chapel, crapper, crappery, craphouse, honey house, necessarium, privy, shithouse, shitter, where the dicks hang out, tea room (for homosexual acts). See TOILET.

BATHTUB n. tub, Jacuzzi, hot tub, spa, plunger.

BATON n. stick, nightstick, bat, billy club (policeman's).

BATON ROUGE, LOUISIANA B.R. Town.

BATTER v. mug, bat, bash, bust, beat the shit out of, blast, lambaste, paste, trash, punch out, work out, work over, kick ass, take one over the hurdles. See HIT.

BATTERED adj. 1. bashed, bashed-up, beat-up, bunged-up, worked over, roughed-up. See also ABUSED. 2. geed-up, g'd-up (coin).

BATTERY n. juice box, can (WWII).

BATTLE n. rumble, rhubarb, knockdown and dragout, battle royal, brawl, branigan, brannigan, hey rube. See FIGHT.

BATTLE v. brawl, hassle, scrap, roughhouse, bang heads, mix it up, pitch a bitch, raise sand.

BATTLESHIP n. battlewagon, man-o'-war.

BAUBLE n. gewgaw, junk jewelry.

BAWDY adj. dirty, raunchy, blue, rough, lowdown and dirty, purple, off-color, salty. See OBSCENE.

BAYONET n. can opener, toothpick, pig sticker, frog sticker, cheese toaster, toasting fork, Rosalie.

BEADS n. junk jewelry, brass (cheap or fake), stones, rocks, sparklers, ice, glass, Christmas, hardware, pennyweight, chocker, choker.

BEAM n. glim, dimmer.

BEAM v. crack a smile, grin from ear to ear, grin like a Cheshire cat, grin like a Chessy cat.

BEANS n. musical fruit, bullets, rib stickers, Arizona strawberries, Arkansas strawberries, Boston strawberries, Mexican strawberries, prairie strawberries.

BEANS AND FRANKFURTERS n. Army chicken, beans and tubesteak, beans and franks.

BEAR v. live with, bear with, suck it up, put up with, roll with the punches, hang on, ride out, stay the course, stand for, be big, grin and bear it. See ENDURE.

BEARD n. beaver, brush, muff, peach fuzz, pez, spinach, face spinach, face lace, bush, shrubbery, alfalfa, chin whiskers, Castro; gallaway (false), galways (stage Irishman). See WHISKERS.

BEARDED adj. brush-faced, muffed, wearin' a muff, alfalfa'd, beavered, brushy, brush peddler, chin-whiskered, Castro; galwayed, gallawayed (false); Santa Clausish.

BEARER n. boy, shlepper, Typhoid Mary (disease). See also BAGGAGE HANDLER.

BEARING n. 1. that away, every which way, forty ways to Sunday, forty ways from Sunday. 2. brace, brush (Army). 3. how it is, how the land lies, fix, the lay of the land (all Pl.).

BEAST n. 1. critter, dog (inferior), stray (orphaned, deserted), varmint. 2. bad actor (vicious), bum, cob roller.

BEAT v. 1. bash, trash, drub, flax, wax, lather, cane, dot (precise blow), dog, wipe, hide, rock one's world, punk, jack, tan one's hide, brain, kayo, clobber, cream, paste, waste, beat the shit out of one, put one in the hospital, break one's face. See HIT. 2. bury, smoke, blank, skunk, schneider, murder, kill, cook, trim, skin, shellack, squelch, squash, bulldoze, torpedo, put away. See DEFEAT.

BEATEN adj. aced, dogged on, blanked, burned, busted, beatsville, creamed, clobbered, hosed, licked, ripped, fixed, shut down, roof fell in (sudden), you can't buck city hall, you can't beat the system. See DEFEATED.

BEATEN-UP adj. 1. bashed, bashed-up, beat-up, mopped up, bunged-up, roughed-up, worked over. 2. geed-up, g'd-up (coin).

BEATING n. paddling, licking, larruping, walloping, whaling, buttwoopin' (Af. Am.), lathering, leathering, hiding, tanning, shellacking, roof fell in (sudden), waxing, lumps, get one's lumps, barrel punishment, dressing-down, strap oil, hazel oil, hickory oil, birch oil, dose of strap oil, dose of hazel oil, dose of birch oil, dose of hickory oil. See also DEFEAT.

BEAT (RHYTHMIC) n. pitapat, tick, ticktock.

BEAU n. old man, main squeeze, flame, boy friend, honey man, lovebird, big moment. See BOY FRIEND.

BEAUTIFUL adj. sweet, sweeta, ten, 10, dyno, oochie, wukka, babelicious, boss, righteous, such a Mona, beddy, betty, bet, nugget, nuggy, nectar, gooey nectar, necky, freak mama, schwing!, talent, traffic stopper, hardbody, stacked, constructed, built, well-built, built for comfort, built like a brick shithouse, brick house, hottie, freak, flygirl, flyboy, zimmer, hammer, burger, double burger, triple burger with cheese, curvy, a honey, a lulu, cool, glam, cher, diddly, drooly, dishy, dazzler, dream, dreamy, dreamboat, dream puss, dream bait, drop-dead gorgeous, vicious, whistle bait, angel, angel face, angel puss, living doll, ankle, phat chick, piece, piece of furniture, nice little piece of furniture, piece of ass, flavor (Af. Am.), geranium, daisy, glamour girl, looker, good looker, hammer, bunny, pussycat, sex kitten, mink, stone, stone fox, foxy, head rush, crazy, sharp, slick, slick chick, cute, smooth, scrumptious, ducky, nobby, snappy, snappy number, snazzy, solid sender, stunner, stunning, cunning, tip, nifty, number, gimme, peach, peacherino, peachy-keen, delicious, pinup, pinup girl, playmate, oomph girl, sweater girl, spiffy, spiffing, ripping, pip, pippin, pipperoo, poundcake, right, reet, reat, neat, fetcher, biscuit, beaut, raving, raving beauty, go-getter, hot shit, keen, look like a million, look fit to kill, looking fit to kill, killer, killer-diller, lady-killer, killing, knockout, knock dead, knock one dead, knock one's eyes out, eye-filling, eyeful, easy on the eyes, treat for sore eyes, not hard to look at, long on looks, a picture, pretty as a picture, centerfold, swell, dandy, fine and dandy, just dandy, jim-dandy, fat, hunky-dory, but good, good enough to eat up, good enough to eat with a spoon, okay, OK, A-OK, oh yeah, freak mama, freak mommy (sexually attractive), crush'n' (clothes).

BEAUTIFY v.   doll up, fix up, gussy up, pretty up, spruce up.

BEAUTY SALON n.   body-and-fender shop.

BEAUTY TREATMENT n.   blow job, blow dry, the works, color, hair done, nails done, perm.

BECOME v.   morph, turn, snowball, mushroom, shoot up.

BED n.   hay, pad, sack, fart sack, rack, rack monster, shoe, flop, joint, kip, snooze bin, work bench (Obsc.), rock, barnacle, camp, dreamer, safety, doss, flea bag.

BEDBUG n.   chinch, crum, crumb, pillow pigeon, wild life.

BEDDING n.   crash pad, roll, California blanket.

BEDEVIL v.   hoodoo, voodoo, put the whammy on one or something, put the horns on one or something, 2. ride, bug, be on the back of, noodge, give one the needle, hit on, chew on, get, get to, be in one's face, fuzzbuzz, rile, hassle, hound, dog, bulldog, worry, push, push one's key, push one's button. See ANNOY.

BEDEVILED adj.   spooked, bugged, bummed out, hacked, catch shit, hung-up, uptight, picked on. See ANNOYED.

BED, GO TO v.   crash, flake out, get some shut-eye, hit the hay, hit the sack, sack out, turn in. See RETIRE.

BEDLAM n.   all hell broke loose, to-do, snarl-up, mishmosh, mishmash, rumpus, ruckus, ruction, shivaree, hoopla, holy mess, unholy mess, bloody mess, mess and a half, rat's nest, every which way, every which way but up, forty ways from Sunday, galley west, hectic, hassle, pretty kettle of fish, pretty piece of business, nice piece of work, free-for-all. See also TURMOIL.

BEDPAN n.   turnpike cruiser, New York tureen, banjo.

BED ROLL n.   balloon, biddle, bindle.

BEDROOM SLIPPERS n.   mules, scuffs.

BED SHEETS n.   lily whites, dreamer.

BEEF n.   shoe sole, tiger meat, bossy (roast beef, stew), cow, bull, leather, moo (steak), young horse.

BEER n.   brew, suds, a chill, chilly, cool one, cold one, frosty, bud (Budweiser or any beer), sauce, tube, foam, drafty, gusto, honey, greenie (Heineken), skat, slosh, slops (inferior), oil, Alaskan martini, barley pop, belly wash, draw one, blow one, boilermaker (with whiskey chaser), brown bottle, cold coffee, Coney Island head, Coney Island (mostly foam), fluids and electrolytes (Medic. Stu.), head (foam), hops, horse collar, beevo, liquid bread, reeb, brewha, brewski, brewsky, swill, Kool-Aid; Colorado Kool-Aid, road brew, road sauce, near beer (nonalcoholic); needle beer, needled beer (alcohol added), pig sweat, pony, sixer (six-pack), twack (twelve pack).

BEER, DRINK v.   have a few, raise a few, pound a few brews, brewhaha, brewha, pop tops, chugalugging, crack a tube, do some stewing, bust some suds, slam some beers, suck out a few heads, slosh, brews brothers, budhead, yeaster (drinkers), brew-out (party); micro, pub-crawling, brew pub (small brewery in a restaurant).

BEFALL v.   come down, go down, action, jell, gel, cook, cook up a storm, cook with gas, shake, smoke. See OCCUR.

BEFITTING adj.   on the button, on the nose, right on, just what the doctor ordered, according to Hoyle, kosher. See SUITABLE.

BEFOULED adj.   cooked (radiation), dirty, exposed, mucked up.

BEFRIEND v.   buddy up, get in with, get on the in with, get chummy with, take up with, case out, come on to, cotton to, hit it off, tuck under one's wing. See also CULTIVATE.

BEFRIENDED adj.   made it with one, on the in with, hit it off.

BEFUDDLED adj.   shook, shook up, dopey, punchy, punch-drunk, slap-happy, in a botheration. See CONFUSED.

BEG v.   bum, panhandle, hustle, sponge, schnor, score, cadge, chisel, tap, touch, make, make a touch, mooch, promote, bite, put the bite on, put the bee on one, put the touch on, put the arm on, put the sleeve on, pass the hat, brace, batter, burn, buzz, ding, nick, nickel up, dime up, hit, hit on, hit up, hit the bricks, hit the stem, hit the turf, freeload, pivot, pling, grub, knock, needle, hold out for, whistle for (but won't get), drop the lug on one, flag down, slam a gate.

BEGGAR n.   bum, bummer, stumblebum, slum bum, rubber bum, moocher, panhandler, promoter, ragbag, bag lady, bag woman, schnorrer, sponger, scab, freeloader, lumberman (with crutches), crip (crippled, Derog.), peggy (one-legged), plinger, professor, rustler, muzzler, bindle man, bindlestiff, stiff, mission stiff, bit borrower, blinkie (fakes blindness), chiseler, chronicker, cipher, wingding, dingbat, ding-dong, ding-donger, dinger, dino, geezo, greaseball, heister, guttersnipe, gutter pup, in the gutter, bo. See also VAGRANT.

BEGGARLY adj. broke, busted, flat, flat broke, to the curb, stony, piss-poor, hard-up, bag lady, truly needy, strapped, pinched, down-and-out, down-at-the-heel, on one's uppers, poor as a church mouse, looking for a handout. See DESTITUTE.

BEGIN v. kick it, bow, open, open up, come out, coming out, roll 'em, let it roll, phase in, start the ball rolling, get rolling, get things rolling, get going, get into, get in there, get in on the ground floor, start from scratch, get one's feet wet, get the show on the road, get under way, get with it, get on the job, get cracking, let's get cracking, get squared away, buckle down, knuckle down, tackle, from the top, take it from the top, take it from the edge, count down, take off, kick off, blast off, sail off, send off, push off, jump off, jump to it, go to it, hop to it, have at it, light into, head into, tear into, sail into, wade into, fall to, cut one's teeth, rev, rev up, fire up, goose, hit for, hit the ground running (in full operation), break in, clock in, ring in, pitch in, dive in, blast away, batch out (accelerate), begin the beguine, break the seal, right out of the gate, break the ice, let fly, play ball, shoot, hang up one's shingle.

BEGINNER n. starter, boot, student, freshie, newie, new boy, new boy on the block, new kid on the block, break in, gremlin, gremmie, fish, tyro, tenderfoot, foot in the door, green, greenie, greenhorn, rookie, rook, turkey, punk, jice, new jice, heel, heeler (reporter), peg boy, pratt boy, buckwheater, cheechako, chukoko, Johnny-come-lately, new blood, blow-in. See also NOVICE.

BEGINNING n. preem, bow, curtain-raiser, opener, openers, for openers, opener-upper, open up, devirginize (first time), break one's cherry, top, from scratch, square one, day 1, day one, phase zero, first crack out of the box, countdown, for starters, flying start, running start, jump start, right off the bat, from out front, from the top, from the gate, from the word go, the get-go, git-go, from the gitty-up (Af. Am.), jump-off, kickoff, takeoff, send-off, start-off, blast-off, first off, first round, coming out, coming-out party, virgin territory.

BEGRUDGE v. turn green, eat one's heart out, to die over, I should have such luck.

BEGUILE v. 1. gyp, flam, flimflam, screw, have, take, stick, burn, chisel, con, scam, shave, rook, snow, blow smoke up one's ass, play for a sucker, diddle, string along, suck in, rope in. See TRICK. 2. vamp, sweep off one's feet, knock

dead, knock out, slay, tickle to death, tickle pink, send, wow, turn on. See also ATTRACT.

BEHAVE v. shape up, shape up or ship out, toe the mark, mind your p's and q's, watch one's step, keep one's nose clean.

BEHAVIOR n. bag, style.

BEHIND adv. trailing, backyard, have to play catch up, off the pace, bringing up the rear, eat one's dust.

BEHOLD v. lay eyes on, catch, glim, glom, spot, spy, eye, eyeball, give with the eyes, flash, lamp, pipe, gun. See SEE.

BEHOLDEN adj. into, on the tab, in hock, owe one (I owe you one), on the cuff, on the arm, into the shylock, on a string.

BEING n. life, lifing, rat race, world, journey, the big game, hand (one is dealt).

BELCH v. burp, repeat.

BELGIAN n. Belgie, Blemish, Belgeek, flamingo (all Derog.).

BELIEF n. op, say-so, slant, POV (point of view), P.O.V., take, gospel truth, stock, store, judgment call, two cents' worth.

BELIEVABLE adj. straight, straight shit, no shit, no bullshit, up-front, aboveboard, honest-to-God, one's stock has gone up. See also TRUSTWORTHY.

BELIEVE v. feel, hold, stomach (can't stomach something), swallow, swallow it hook line and sinker, take as gospel truth, take stock in, set store by, swear by, okay, OK, buy, bank on, bet on, bet one's bottom dollar on, lay money on, lap up, be afraid, have a hunch, have a sneaking suspicion, got to hand it to one, pat on the back, go along with, string along with.

BELIEVER n. freak (strong), bug, nut. See DEVOTEE.

BELITTLE v. run down, put down, downplay, play down, take down, take down a peg, take down a peg or two, take the starch out of, take the shine out of, tear down, shoot down, cut down to size, cut-rate, cut to the quick, burn, burn down, burn one down, cap, slice up, rip, pan, slam, smear, rag, rag on, bag on (Hum.), base on, rank, snappin (Af. Am.), shade, throw shade, squash, squelch, hit, blister, roast, scorch, rap, take a rap at, take a swipe at, take the shine out of, fluff off, brush off, dump on, shit on, do a number on, shred, mud-sling, needle, give one the needle, knock, knock down, poor-mouth, bad-mouth, bitter mouth, peg, back cap, back bite, rip up the back, give a black eye, give one one's comeuppance, thumb one's nose at, pooh-pooh, rubbish, sour grapes, mark lousy, put the crimpers in, put the hooks in, put the needles in, put the zingers in, put away, put a tuck in one's tail, poke full of holes, shoot full of holes, prick one's balloon, puncture one's balloon, take the wind out of one's sails, blow sky high, knock the bottom out of, knock the chocks out from under, knock the props out from under, knock one off his perch, make one sing small. See also EMBARRASS.

BELITTLED adj. eat crow, eat dirt, eat humble pie, sing small, come out moldy, crawl, faced, lost face, took down, put down, comedown, dumped on, drummed out, draw in one's horns, egg on one's face, knocked from one's high horse, knocked off one's perch, have a tuck in one's tail, got one's comeuppance. See also DISCREDITED.

BELITTLING n. sour grapes, crow, humble pie.

BELL n. ding-dong, dinger, tinkler; hit the dinger, toot the tooter (ring a bell).

BELL BOTTOMS n. bells.

BELLBOY n. bellhop, hop, boy, button, baggage smasher, pack rat. See also BAGGAGE HANDLER.

BELLIGERENT adj. in your face, ornery, scrappy, snorky, bitchy, turbobitch, cussed, flip, tetchy, salty, spiky, limber, mean, bad-ass, cantankerous, fire-eater, out for a rep, have a bone to pick, have a chip on one's shoulder, have it in for, at loggerheads, at outs, on the outs, on the muscle, hard on for, forecastle lawyer. See also AGGRESSIVE.

BELLOW n. holler, beller, blast, yawp, yell.

BELLOW v. holler, holler out, blow at, beller, beller out, yell, yell out, blast, yawp.

BELLY n. tummy, gut, pot, potbelly, melon belly, swagbelly, beerbelly, tank, spare tire, corporation, breadbasket, bay window, front porch; innie, outie (belly button). See STOMACH.

BELONG v. in, in with, run with, swing, swing with, one of the boys.

BELOVED n. number one, numero uno, B.F., G.F., old lady, old man, one and only, O and O, honey, hon, dearie, baby, doll, doll face, puddin', sweetie, sweetie pie, sweets, sweet pea, sugar, sugar bowl, sugar daddy, daddy, candyleg, money honey, honey man, biscuit, gold mine, generous keeper, steady, big moment, heartbeat, heart throb, love, love of my life, flame, oyster, jane, toots, tootsie, turtle dove, roller, mule, skinner, hat, mat, date, mate, significant other, patootie, hot patootie, sweet patootie, lambie pie, rave. See also BOY FRIEND, GIRL FRIEND.

BELT n. squeeze, stretcher.

BEMOAN v. sing the blues, beat one's breast, cry me a river, cry over spilled milk, go for a crying towel. See LAMENT.

BEMUSED adj. mooning, moony, daydreaming, pipedreaming, woolgathering, staring into the middle distance.

BENEFACTION n. writeoff, handout, gifting, lump, poke-out.

BENEFACTOR n. the money, angel, sponsor, backer, greenback, sugar daddy, rabbi, Chinaman, fairy godmother, lady bountiful, meal ticket, Santa Claus, staker, grubstaker, pigeon, live one, believer, mark, fan, front. See also PHILANTHROPIST.

BENEFICENT adj. big, bighearted, be big, loose, softie, soft touch, a marshmallow, Santa Claus, good Joe, have a heart, heart in the right place, prince of a person.

BENEFICIAL adj. good for what ails you, what the doctor ordered.

BENEFIT n. benie, gravy, mitzvah, perk, extras, cakes and ale, gravy train, cream, cream at the top, egg in one's beer, stuff, golden coffin (benefits to heirs). See also PROFIT.

BENEFIT v. pay, pay off, make it, do for one, do the trick, fill the bill, make a killing. See PROFIT. See also HELP.

BENEVOLENT adj. big, bighearted, bleeding heart, all heart, heart in the right place, do-gooder, Santa Claus. See also BENEFICENT.

BENT n. thing, thing for, bag, head-set, mind-set, groove, tilt, druthers, weakness for, have a bump for. See INCLINATION.

BENZEDRINE n. bennie, benny, benz, benzie, bean, B, speed, upper, brother Ben, copilot Ben, hi-ball, pep pill, peachies, white, blancas, crosses.

BENZEDRINE USE v. benny jag.

BERATE v. kick ass and take names, fire on, rip on, chew, chew ass, chew out, eat out, cuss out, jump all over, rake over the coals, call down, tell off, give what for, give one hell, scorch, blister. See SCOLD.

BERKELEY, CALIFORNIA Berzerkely.

BESET adj. bugged, dogged, rousted, catch shit, picked on, driven up the wall. See ANNOYED.

BESIEGE v. come at from all sides, bug, buttonhole, work on, work over, put the bee on. See also PERSUADE.

BESPECTACLED adj. four-eyed, four-eyes, wearing cheaters.

BEST adj. 1. killer, A, A-1, A-number 1, A-one, number one, numero uno, the fat, the cream, primo, ten, 10, ace, ace-hi, ace-high, aces, bump'n', world-class, greatest, out-of-sight, out-of-this-world, far-out, gonest, hundred-proof, mostest, evil, wicked, bad, baaaadest, brutal, bitchin', twitchin', boss, cool, coolsville, coolville, crack, crackerjack, murder, daddy, cherry, deffest, dope, dual, fierce, fresh, fully on, fully, mint, nitro, on the strength, raw, sick, stupid fresh, master (Af. Am.), righteous, first-chop, super, gilt-edged, gilt-edge, all-time, all-time haymaker, key, stone,

stone groove, terrible, terrific, stokin', tubular, vicious, wailing, whaling, dope on a rope, hype, stink, be all that, tops, top gun, top dog, top drawer, topflight, top-notch, tip-top, top of the class, top of the list, the most, the almost, endsville, the end, savage, solid gold, winner, champ, king o' the hill, white hope, white knight. See also EXCELLENT. 2. all one's got, all out, balls out, in it to win it (Af. Am.), ain't half steppin' (Af. Am.), one's all, one's damnedest, one's darnedest, one's level best, best shot, Sunday best.

BEST v. drub, trash, flax, wax, dog on, punk, jack, lather, larrup, leather, lambaste, whop, whomp, whip, wipe, hide, tan, tan one's hide, brain, bop, K.O., kayo, drop, deck, dish, total, powder, clobber, cream, zap, paste, waste, hurt, kick ass, whip ass, bust up, clean on, take the wind out of one's sails, take one, take it all, take out, take care of, take down, put down, smack down, shoot down, shoot down in flames, dress one down, shut down, shut out, psych out, rank out, fake out, lay one out, lay one low, wipe out, wipe up the floor with, wipe up the place with, wipe off the map, beat one out, beat up, beat the bejesus out of, beat the tar out of, beat the beholden out of, beat the shit outta, beat the living tar out of, beat the living daylights out of, make mince meat out of, knock cold, knock off, knock the beholden out of, knock the daylights out of, knock the living daylights out of, knock the shit out of, knock into the next county, knock for a row of (anything), knock one on one's ass, knock one ass over teakettle, knock one on one's ear, knock one into next week, knock one for a loop, deal a knockout blow to, make hamburger out of one, wallop, blast, sock it to one, let have it, floor one, down one, land a haymaker, put one away, put on ice, put it in their eye, put one in the hospital, give a going over, bury, blank, ace, skunk, murder, kill, trim, swamp, skin, bulldoze, roll over, torpedo, meatball. See DEFEAT. See also TRIUMPH.

BESTIALITY n. animal training.

BEST MAN, BE A v. stand up for one.

BESTOW v. gift, gift with, kick in, put out, come through, get it up, get it on. See GIVE.

BET n. action, ante, parlay, play, down-on, odds-on, long shot, shot. See WAGER.

BET v. make book, book the action, take a flier, play, plunge, put up, put up or shut up, shoot, back, cover, get down on (on a horse). See WAGER.

BETHLEHEM, PENNSYLVANIA Steel City, Steel Town.

BETRAY v. knife, stab one in the back, rat, rat on, fink, fink on, sing, sing on, snitch, belch, squeal, stool, spill, finger, double-cross, fuck, blow the whistle, drop a dime on one. See INFORM.

BETRAYED adj. buried, beat out of, double-cross, fucked, fucked over, fucked without a kiss, giveaway, got it up the ass, Judas kiss, letting down, sellout.

BETRAYER n. rat, rat fink, fink, narc, snitch, snitcher, squealer, stoolie, stool pigeon, snout, yellow dog (gang), blabbermouth, preacher, singer. See INFORMER. See also TRAITOR.

BETROTHED n. intended, asked-for, steady, going steady, pinned, bird, donah, donar, future.

BETTER adj. souped-up, sharpened, over the hump, on the mend, out of the woods, on the comeback trail.

BETTER v. boost, upgrade, look up, pick up, perk up, dress up, snap up. See IMPROVE.

BETWEEN prep. in the seam, between a rock and a hard place, between sixes and sevens, between the devil and the deep blue sea, betwixt and between, Catch-22, damned if you do and damned if you don't, the rub.

BEVERAGE n. bug juice, chaser, pop, cooler, drink, ham, giggle-soup (So.). See also DRINK, LIQUOR.

BEVERLY HILLS, CALIFORNIA n. Poshopolis.

BEWAIL v. sing the blues, take on, eat one's heart out. See LAMENT.

BEWARE v. keep a weather eye open, keep one's eye peeled, keep one's distance, keep on one's toes, keep one's ears to the ground, watch one's step, watch out, mind one's p's and q's, bend over backwards, handle with kid gloves, walk on eggs.

BEWHISKERED adj. alfalfa'd, beavered, brushy, brush-faced, brush peddler, chin-whiskered, Castro; galwayed, gallawayed (false); Santa Clausish, muffed, wearin' a muff.

BEWILDER v. rattle, throw, take one's mind, fuck with one's head, mess with one's head, snow, floor. See PUZZLE.

BEWILDERED adj. unglued, unzipped, unscrewed, punchy, shook-up, floored, flipped-out, farmisht, thrown, dopey, out to lunch. See PUZZLED.

BEWILDERMENT n. mix-up, foul-up, fuck-up, snafu, who's minding the store? See CONFUSED.

BEWITCH v. hoodoo, voodoo, put the whammy on one or something, put the horns on one or something. 2. sweep off one's feet, vamp, knock dead, knock out, slay, tickle to death, tickle pink, send, wow, turn on. See ENRAPTURED. See also ENRAPTURE, ATTRACT.

BEWITCHED adj. hooked, bugged, gone on, fallen for, mad about, gaga about, hung-up, head over heels, sprung on, turned-on, have one's nose open, have a bee in one's bonnet, have a bug in one's ear, have a bug up one's ass, have an ax to grind, have a thing about. See also CHARMED.

BEWITCHING adj.   traffic-stopping, a lulu of a, mink, fox, drop-dead beautiful. See BEAUTIFUL.

BIAS n.   head-set, mind-set, mind-trip, tude, cop a tude (bad), spin, spin control, tilt, flash. See INCLINATION.

BIASED adj.   agin, tilted, weighted, down on, one-sided, cold-deck, feel a draft, flash, Jane Crow (against women), homer (umpire favoring home team), redneck, red-baiter, Jew-baiter, black-baiter, a regular Archie Bunker.

BIBLE n.   the Word, the Good Book, the good news, sword, dagger (pocket-sized).

BICARBONATE OF SODA n.   bicarb.

BICEPS n.   guns, ceps.

BICKER v.   scrape, pick at, trade zingers, dig, hassle each other. See ARGUE.

BICKERING n.   hassle, scene, tempest in a teapot. See ARGUMENT.

BICYCLE n.   bike, cycle, two-wheeler, wheel, wheels.

BICYCLE v.   pedal, bike, cycle.

BICYCLING n.   biking, cycling, pedaling, wheeling.

BICYCLIST n.   biker, cyclist, scorcher, crackerjack.

BID n.   feeler, proposition, pass, hit, offer.

BID v.   l. give the nod, shill; puffer, boost (false auctioneering). 2. make a play for, make a pass at, hit on, make a pitch, come up with, pop the question, proposition, speak one's piece.

BIDE v.   hang in, hang around, cool it, hold the phone, sit tight, sweat it. See WAIT.

BIG adj.   humongous, humongoid, humungous, humongo, mungo, bahugen, gross, honking, butt-kicking, bonzai, king size, monster, monstro, moby, mother, motherfucker (Obsc.), mofo, big mother, big mama, big daddy, biggy, big-ass, big-time, big-wiz, heavyweight, heavy duty, beefy, hefty, high-powered, major-league, big-league, overgrown, overblown, tall, super, super-duper, super-colossal, seagoing, jumbo, man-sized, lunker, hoss, buster, bull, blimp, barn door, a whale of a, whaling, whacking, walloping, lolloping, whopping, whopper, hulking, spanking, slapping, strapping, thumper, thumping, thundering, bumping, banging, tidy.

BIGAMIST n.   Brigham Young, captain's paradise.

BIGOT n.   redneck, no-neck, good old boy, good old boys' network, male chauvinist pig, MCP, pig, sexist porker, McCarthyite, Archie Bunker, jingoist, flag waver, patrioteer, superpatriot.

BIGOTRY n.   Jim Crow, Jim Crowism, Jane Crowism, feel a draft (recognition of), glass ceiling (invisible barrier to promotion).

BIKINI n.   floss (thong bikini).

BILK v.   rip off, rook, screw, shaft, frig, jive, shuck, shuck and jive, fleece, burn, bleed, bleed white, con, pluck, take, take one to the cleaners, milk, sting. See CHEAT.

BILL n.   bad news, check, checkeroo, damages, grunt, IOU, score, tab. See ACCOUNT.

BILL v.   put the squeeze on, put the arm on, put the bite on, chase, bone, see you in the alley.

BILLBOARD n.   three-sheet, twenty-four-sheet.

BILL OF SALE n.   papers.

BIND n.   box, in a box, crunch, squeeze, tight squeeze, tight spot, hot water, lose-lose situation, no-win situation, pickle, between a rock and a hard place. See PREDICAMENT.

BIND v.   hog-tie, put a half-nelson on, put a lock on, lock up.

BIOGRAPHY n.   bio, biog, close-up, profile, résumé.

BIOLOGY n.   bio, bugs.

BIPHETAMINE n.   black beauties.

BIRD n.   birdie, birdy, feathered friend, boid, banty, biddy, chick, chickabiddy, chickadee.

BIRMINGHAM, ALABAMA   Magic City.

BIRTH n.   blessed event, producing, visit from the stork, drop one.

BIRTH CONTROL n.   Vatican roulette (rhythm method), on the pill, Norplanted, MOM and POP meets (birth control meetings), Memos on Marriage, Policy on Population, family planning.

BIRTH CONTROL DEVICE n.   the pill, Norplanted BC, IUD, bag, scum bag, cundrum, Trojan, skin, fish skin, rubber, Ramses, safety. See CONTRACEPTIVE.

BISCUIT n.   bullet, cathead, clanker, dingbat, hard tack, sinker, tooth buster, dry cush.

BISEXUAL n.   switch hitter, ac/dc, AC/DC, ambidextrous, ambisextrous, bi, bicycle, combo, half and half, double-gaited, he/she, swings both ways, hits both ways, have it both ways, ki-ki.

BIT n.   1. smithereen, bite, gob, blob, chunk, hunk, lump, stump; cut, slice, rake off, nibble (computer), piece of the pie, slice of the melon, slice of the pie. See also SHARE. 2. chewed fine, itsy-bitsy pieces (Pl.).

BITE n.   1. gob, chaw, chomp. 2. guts, kick, zap, zip.

BITE v. sink one's teeth into, take a chunk out of, chaw on, fling a fang into, nab at.

BIZARRE adj. funky, grody, grody to the max, kooky, off-the-wall, offbeat, camp, wild, far-out, way-out. See STRANGE. See also ECCENTRIC.

BLABBER v. go on, run on, run off at the mouth, yakkety-yak, yakking, blah-blah, blad, gas, have diarrhea of the mouth, beat one's gums, talk through one's hat, spill the beans, bibble-babble, bull, bullshit, throw the bull, shoot the breeze. See also SPEAK.

BLACK adj. black 360 degrees, Man Tan black.

BLACK n. Afro-American, brother, sister, bro, blood, youngblood, blood brother, soul, soul brother, soul sister, member, groid (So. Stu.), molonjohn; spade, ace of spades, moke, smoke, smoky, scrub, nigger, colored, colored negative, negative, coon, darky, darkie, buck, buck nigger, boy, beige, ape, blue, blue gum, blue skin, boogie, faded boogie, boogerboo, clink, Bones, Mr. Bones, boot, satchel, satchel mouth, dark cloud, dark meat (sexual), shadow, shad, shad mouth, shine, spook, skillet, squasho, scobe, spill, splib, watermelon, Zulu, ditty-bop, ditty-bob, domino, eightball, eight-rock, chocolate, chocolate bar, chocolate drop, ground ape, charcoal, charcoal nigger, chimney chops, Hershey bar, dew baby (dark-skinned), alligator bait (Fla., La.), article (slave, Obs.), cuh, cuz, bongo lips, boat lip, jig, moon cricket, mud flop, porch monkey, prune, rug, rughead, scrub, titre, toad, yanta, negative, Gange, Kange, Geechee, boojie, moolie, clown, cluck, cuffee, Mose, original, suede, shvartzeh, goonie (Virgin Islands), Mau Mau, jungle bunny, chungo bunny, moss, burrhead, hardhead, jarhead, kinkyhead, nap, nappy, nappyhead, woolly head, velcro head, butterhead, headlight, hod, scuttle, shot, Ethiopian, Guinea, snowball, raisin, ink, inky-dink, jazz-bo, jig, jigaboo, zig, zigaboo, smear, hoofer, Jim Crow, jit, peola, pink toes, pinky, red bone (light-skinned), dinge, conk buster (intellectual), bedbug (Pullman porter), bright (light), kelt, keltch (passing as white), beige, tush (mulatto); black and tan, bleached ebony, sepe, sepia, banana, high yella, high yellow, bird's eye maple (Fem. mulatto); spear carrier, handerkerchief head, Uncle Tom, Mister Tom (middle-class), Dr. Thomas, Aunt Tom, Aunt Jane, Aunt Jemima, uncle, aunt, auntie, uppity black, pancake (subservient), HN (house nigger), Sam, Sambo, Stepin Fetchit, load of coal (group) (all Derog.).

BLACKBALL n. ding, thumbs down. See also BANISH, OSTRACIZE.

BLACKBALL v. ding, zing, thumbs down on one. See also BANISH, OSTRACIZE.

BLACKEN v. bad-mouth, do a number on, peg, rip, rip up and down, knock, give a black eye, rag, rag on, pop junk, pan, smear. See SLANDER.

BLACK EYE n. shiner, mouse, goog, shanty.

BLACK, FEMALE n. sister, soul sister; band, bantam, barbecue, covess dinge, dange broad, black and tan, banana, bird's eye maple, high yella, high yellow, lemon, peola, pink toes, poon tang, poontang (sexual), Aunt, Auntie, Aunt Jane, Aunt Jemima, Aunt Tom, Sapphire (all Derog.).

BLACKGUARD n. sleazoid, sleaze ball, bad ass, bad news, bastard, prick, dick, shit, low-life, bounder, rounder, rotter, scalawag. See SCOUNDREL.

BLACKJACK TABLE POSITIONS first base, second base, third base, nine o'clock, ten o'clock, eleven o'clock, twelve o'clock, noon, high noon, one o'clock (etc).

BLACKJACK TERMS George (generous player), hit (card request), hole card, snapper (make blackjack).

BLACKLIST n. hit list, shit list. See also BANISH, OSTRACIZE.

BLACKLIST v. hit list, pipe one off, siwash.

BLACKMAIL v. shake down, shake, put the shake on one, badger, play the badger game.

BLACKMAILER n. bloodsucker, leech, shakedown artist, shark.

BLACK MARKET adj. under-the-counter, under-the-table.

BLACK OUT v. 1. pass out, zone out, draw a blank, go out like a light. 2. cover up, cut off, hold back, squelch, squash.

BLACKS AND WHITES n. black and tan, salt and pepper.

BLACKSMITH n. smithy, smitty, darby cove, iron burner.

BLACKSMITH SHOP n. pig joint.

BLACK STUDIES n. Chitlins 101.

BLADDER n. water tank, bag.

BLADE n. shank.

BLAME v. finger, point the finger, blow the whistle on, cap on, can, carry the can, tie the can on one, blast, blast on, lay on, lay a bad trip on one, lay the body at one's doorstep, put the whammy on one, lower the boom, pass the buck, knock, paste, roast, rap, rap on the knuckles, slap on the wrist, rap one's knuckles, slap one's wrist, let one have it, climb all over, jump all over one, jump down one's throat, put the slug on one, throw the book at one, sock it to one, stick it to one, give one hell, catch it, catch hell, bitch, read one out, chew out, go after, take down, call down, come down on, come down hard on, rip, peg, bad-mouth, poor-mouth, trash, zing, zap, knock, rap, give one both barrels, rake over the coals, frame, frame-up, jacket. See also ACCUSE, DENOUNCE.

BLAMED PERSON n. fall guy, butt, goat, pigeon, who shot John.

BLAND adj. vanilla, diddly-bop, jerky, nerdy, wuss, wimpy, tame, blah, dull as dishwater, flat, flat as a pancake, ho-hum, nothing, pablum, white bread, zero. See also MILD.

BLANDISHMENT n. eyewash, soap, soft soap, a line, sweet talk, baloney, blarney. See FLATTERY.

BLASÉ adj. cool, laid-back, mellow, fed up, done it all, been around twice, what's the big deal?, BFD (big fucking deal). See INDIFFERENT.

BLASPHEME v. cuss, damn, darn, drat, flame, put the horns on, put the whammy on one, put the double whammy on one, hoodoo one, voodoo one, talk dirty.

BLAST n. energetic disassembly.

BLATANT adj. loud, flashy, screaming, glitzy, pizzazz, snazzy, zappy, showy. See also FLAGRANT, GAUDY, CONSPICUOUS, NOISY.

BLAZE n. rapid oxidation.

BLEACHER SEATS n. blues (circus), Ruthville (Bsbl.).

BLEMISH n. zit, goob, goober, goophead, pip, blem, second, beauty spot, bloom, doohickey, dohinky, hickey, sight, dump, blot on the landscape, bug.

BLEMISHED adj. rank, a few bugs, a glitch, gremlins, a lemon, seconds. See IMPERFECT.

BLEND n. combo, mishmash, mishmosh, mixed bag, soup (liquid), stew, goulash, lorelei, everything but the kitchen sink.

BLEND v. feather in, interface, camouflage, marry; dissolve, cross-dissolve (film).

BLIGHT n. eyesore, sight, dump, blot on the landscape.

BLIGHT v. trash, foul up, fuck up, mess up, glitch up. See also DAMAGE.

BLIND DATE n. stranger date, grab bag.

BLINK v. bat the eyes.

BLISS n. gone, far out, cool, Nadaville.

BLISSFUL adj. crazy, grokked, mad, cool, zero cool, gone, real gone, sent, stoned, dreamy, floating, flying, high, wicked, wigged, wild, weird, weirded out, out, far-out, spaced-out, wigged-out, blissed-out, flipped-out, turned-on, walking on air, on cloud seven, on cloud nine, in seventh heaven, in Nadaville, twilight zone. See also HAPPY.

BLITHE adj. up, upbeat, high, jazzed, perky, chipper, sunny. See CHEERFUL.

BLIZZARD n. whiteout.

BLOCK n. hang-up, jam-up, catch, joker, monkey wrench, gridlock (traffic). See HINDRANCE.

BLOCK v. hang up, hold up, shut out, shut off, close out, close off, stall, stymie, stonewall. See HINDER.

BLOCKAGE n. lock, jam-up, backup, gridlock.

BLOCKHEAD n. twit, airbrain, goof, dogburger, ninny, nincompoop, dimbo (girl), oofus. See also STUPID.

BLONDE n. dizzy blonde, bottled blonde, bleached blonde, platinum blonde, decided blonde (bleached), peroxide blonde, ash blonde, whitey, towhead, goldilocks (all Derog.).

BLOOD n. claret, goo, gravy, red gravy, people juice.

BLOODHOUNDS n. catsup hounds, ketchup dogs, ketchup hounds, beat the pups (evade).

BLOOD VESSEL n. main line.

BLOOMINGDALE'S n. Bloomie's; Bloomies (customers).

BLOUSE n. body shirt, tank top, top.

BLOW n. belt, bash, sock, slug, zap, zetz, clip, Sunday punch, blindside (unexpected). See HIT.

BLUDGEON n. club, billy, billy club, stick, nightstick, blackjack, sap, conk crusher. See CLUB.

BLUEPRINT n. blue. See also PLAN.

BLUFF v. psych out, bull, bullshit, BS, bunco, bunko, cheek it, con, fake, fake it, fake one out, four-flush, goof on, jive, shuck, shucking and jiving, muscle, stiff, throw the bull. See also DECEIVE.

BLUNDER n. flub, flub-up, fluff, muff, gaff, boner, blooper, bloomer, howler, goof, dumb trick, dumb move, dumb thing to do, fool mistake. See MISTAKE.

BLUNDER v. flub, fluff, muff, blow, blow one's lines, foul up, fuck up, mess up, blow it, blow it big time, juke, drop the ball, drop one's buckets. See ERR.

BLUNDERER n. goof, goofball, goofer, goof off, goof up, foul ball, foul-up, fuck-off, fuck-up, a newt, muff, muffer, butterfingers, fumble fist, foozler, stumblebum, stumblebunny, klutz, dub, duffer, hick, lummox, lump, rube, slob, Swede.

BLUNT adj. snippy, snappy, short.

BLUNT, BE v. lay it on the line, put all one's cards on the table, talk turkey, talk like a Dutch Uncle, call a spade a spade. See also FRANK.

BLUNTLY adv. cold turkey.

BLUR v. fuzz, fuzzy up.

BLUSTER n. bull, bullshit, BS, bull-pucky, bunk, bunco, bunkum, talk, big talk, fancy talk, fine talk, tall talk, tall story, fish story, gas, hot air, piss and wind, balls, guts, macho. See also DECEIT.

BLUSTER v. jive, shuck, shuck and jive, hot-dog, grandstand, showboat. See BOAST. See also RANT.

BLUSTERER n. bullshitter, bullshooter, bullshit artist, gasbag, blowhard, windbag, big bag of wind. See BRAGGART.

BLUSTERING n. talk, big talk, tall talk, baloney, bull, bullskating (Af. Am.), bullshit, BS, shittin'. See BRAGGING.

B.M.W. n. BMW, beemer, bimer.

BOARD A TRAIN v. hop on board, hop a choo-choo, hop a freight, catch a rattler, flip (free, hobo use).

BOARDINGHOUSE n. bed and breakfast, bread and board, crumb joint, crumb house, cathouse, flophouse, rooming house, doss house, doss, cheap John, chinch pad, fleabag, flea trap, fort (Stu.).

BOARD OF DIRECTORS n. execs, exec suite, front office, toppers, brass, upstairs, scenery, dummy (holds proxy).

BOARDS n. load of sticks.

BOAST n. drag, bull, bullshit, BS, shittin', bunk, bunco, bunko, bunkum, baloney, talk, big talk, fancy talk, fine talk, tall talk, tall story, fish story, gas, hot air, piss and wind, highfalutin, high-siding.

BOAST v. drag, woof, jive, shuck, shuck and jive, hot dog, grandstand, showboat, fake, fake it, fake one out, psych out, stiff, four-flush, bull, bullshit, BS, throw the bull, sling the bull, sling, sling the crap, shovel the shit, shoot the shit, lay it on thick, sound off, noise off, show off, cheek it, con, muscle, toot one's own horn, blow one's own horn, blow one's own trumpet, blow, blow off, blow hard, smoke, crow, signify, pitch, advertise, three-sheet, big-mouth, talk, talk big, spread oneself, brag oneself up, pat oneself on the back, crack one's jaw, gam, yam, lick one's chops, rub one's nose in, splash, sport, bog-wog.

BOASTER n. grandstander, hot dogger, showoff, hotshot, key swinger, blowhard, bullshit artist (Obsc.), hot-air artist. See BRAGGART.

BOASTFUL adj. hot stuff, hotshot; hot shit, bullshit, bullshitting (Obsc.); big-talking, biggety, ho-dad, ho-daddy, key swinging, loudmouth, know-it-all, smart-alecky, phony, hub cap, crack one's jaw, crapper, cocky, cock, cock of the walk, chesty, gutbucket, stuffy, stuffed shirt, stuck up, puffed up, gassy, windbag, windy, load of wind, full of hot air, blowhard, blow smoke, gall, ham, hifalutin, highfalutin, high-hatty, hincty, his nibs, snooty, on an ego trip, swell-headed, swell-head, big-head, big I am, stuck on oneself, a regular I love me, think one is it, think one's shit doesn't stink, too big for one's shoes, too big for one's britches.

BOAT n. tub, bateau, bucket, hooker, cat (catamaran), dink (dinghy), cigarette (racing powerboat). See also SHIP.

BOATSWAIN n. bos'n, pipes.

BODY n. 1. bod, build, built, shape, shaft, chassis, classy chassis, beefcake, meatwave, Diesel, built like a brick shithouse, frame, coke frame (Fem.), anatomy, bag of bones, booty. 2. dead meat, cold meat, stiff, loved one, remains, cage, carcass, corpus, croppy (R.R.).

BODY-BUILDING TERMS Nautilust (machine exerciser), cacti (shaves body), sponge (too much salt), float (displays muscles).

BODYGUARD n. sidewinder, jaboney, jiboney, trigger man. See also GUARD.

BODY ODOR n. B.O., gapo, GAPO.

BOGUS adj. phony, bogue, queer, fake, ersatz, plastic, not what it's cracked up to be. See COUNTERFEIT.

BOISE, IDAHO Spud Town.

BOISTEROUS adj. rambunctious, roughhouse, rowdy-dowdy, cowboy, hoopla, loudmouth, rootin'-tootin', raise hell, raise cain, raise the roof, ziggy, off-base, out-of-line, out-of-order.

BOLD adj. gutsy, gritty, nervy, chutzpahdik, spunky, I'm shakin' (response to threat, sarcasm), brassy, cheeky, fire-eater, come on strong, smart-ass, in your face. See FEARLESS. See also DARING.

BOLOGNA n. boloney, horse cock.

BOLSTER v. brace up, buck up, pick up. See SUPPORT.

BOLT v. take off, jump off, drop out, bail out, cut out, opt out, cop out, hightail, hotfoot, skedaddle, make tracks, make a break for it, step on it, run like a scared rabbit, run out on, walk out on, kiss good-bye, cut loose, quit cold, ditch, ding, leave flat, leave high and dry, leave holding the bag, leave in the lurch, dump, give up the ghost, give up the ship. See also GO, FLEE.

BOMB n. the bomb, A-bomb, H-bomb, nucular bomb, slow flyer (cruise missile), doomsday machine, buzz bomb, smart bomb, nuke, backpack nuke, physics package, egg, block buster, daisy cutter, firecracker; football, Italian football, guinea football (gangster, Derog.); Molotov cocktail (homemade), pill, pineapple, ticker, Lazy Dog, hamburger.

BOMB v. lay an egg, lay a bomb, blitz, prang, torch (firebomb).

BOMBARDIER n. bubble chaser (WWII).

BOMBARDMENT n. blitz.

BOMBAST n. balderdash, gobbledygook, hifalutin, highfalutin, hot air. See also BLUSTER.

BOMBASTIC adj. big-talking, biggety, bullshitting, loudmouth, stuffed shirt, gassy, windbag, windy, piss and wind, full of hot air. See BOASTFUL.

BOMBING n. blitz.

BOMBING MISSION n. milk run (easy), prang (successful).

BOMB MAKER n. can maker.

BONA FIDE adj. for real, kosher, legit, on the legit, all wool and a yard wide, card-carrying. See TRUE.

BOND n. 1. gunk, stickum, spit. 2. network, tie-in, hook up. See also ASSOCIATION.

BONDS n. 1. Fannie Mae, Ginnie Mae, Sallie Mae, Freddie Mac, Farmer Mac, muni, municipals, baby bond (less than $1,000), James Bond (matures in 2007); Bo Derek, ten (treasury bond maturing in the year 2010); junk bond (high-risk), double-barreled bond (two sources of repayment), Yankee bond (foreign), T-Bill, Zebras (zero coupon-based rate adjustment securities), zeroes, Tiger/Tigr, CATS, stiffs, strips, SLOB (secured lease obligation bond), puds (public utility districts), wash tub (Washington Suburban Sanitary District), gorilla (trader). See also STOCKS. 2. cuffs, darbies, derbies.

BONUS n. fringe benefit, goodies, gravy, perk, perks, golden parachute, tin parachute (nonmanagement employee), golden handcuffs (deferred), button, hat, ice, PM, spiff (salesman). See also EXTRA, GRATUITY.

BOO n. Bronx cheer, raspberry, razz, razzberry, zerbert, the bird.

BOOK n. best-seller, book with legs, page-turner, potboiler, spyboiler, bible (authoritative).

BOOK v. line up, sew up, pencil in, set up.

BOOKING AGENT n. flesh peddler, ten percenter.

BOOKKEEPER n. bean counter, CPA, number cruncher, sharp pencil pusher, pencil shover, pen pusher, pen driver.

BOOKKEEPING n. books, count.

BOOKMAKER n. book, bookie, customer's man, runner, scalper, banker, C (commission); horseroom, poolroom, wire room (place of business).

BOOKWORM n. grind, greasy grind.

BOON n. mitzvah (Yid.), windfall.

BOORISH adj. bad-assed, bad-ass, dank, off-base, out-of-line, out-of-order, bitchy, turd poodle, cantankerous, cussed, grouchy, grumpy, mean, ornery, tetchy, ugly, loud, loudmouthed, rough. See also COARSE.

BOOST n. buildup, backup, lift, shot in the arm, shot in the ass, leg, leg up, hand, handout, goose. See also SUPPORT.

BOOST v. goose, goose up, pick up, put one on cloud nine, put one on top of the world, give a lift, gazumph (price after sale). See also SUPPORT.

BOOTLEG v. moonlight, moonshine, under the counter, rum run.

BOOTLEGGER n. moonshiner, rumrunner, gangster, legger, dynamiter.

BOOTLEG LIQUOR n. moonshine, shine, mountain dew, white lightning, white mule, corn, corn likker, panther piss, bathtub gin, Dago red (wine), home brew, hootch, just off the boat. See also LIQUOR.

BOOTS n. waders, waffle stompers, monkey boots (ankle boots), waters.

BOOTY n. goods, hot goods, hot items, graft, take, make, pickings, swag, boodle, squeeze.

BORDELLO n. house, cathouse, call house, poontang palace, snake ranch, chicken ranch, call joint, beaver base, hook shop, body shop. See BROTHEL.

BORDERLINE adj. on the bubble.

BORE n. yawn, major yawn, downer, bummer, wimp, creep, drag, drip, frog, grind, grub, grunge, grunch, Jeff (Af. Am.), meatball, sklonk, flat tire, headache, a pain, pain in the ass, pain in the neck, wet blanket, blister, deadwood, deadhead, nudge, nag, pill, crashing bore, snooze act, lump, drone, spare tire, stuffed shirt, mince.

BORE v. turn one off, bend one's ear, bore stiff, burn out, drag, put one to sleep, talk one's ear off.

BORED adj. bored stiff, fed up, full up, up to here, had it up to here, ho-hum, so what else is new?, done it all, been around twice, just going through the motions. See also UNINTERESTED, LANGUID.

BOREDOM n. ho-hums, the blahs, blah-blahs.

BORING adj. bor-ring, MEGO (mine eyes glaze over), blah, cozy, flat, flat tire, flat as a pancake, cheesy, ho-hum, nothing, nothing doing, zero, big zero, drag, draggy, draddy, a yawn, big yawn, yawner, snooze, gasser, icky, the least, downer, bummer, dead, really deadsville, Dullsville, noplaceville, Nadaville, go over like a lead balloon, lay an egg, bomb, diddly-bop, nowhere, bore one stiff, tired, wonky, gummy, pablum, beige, drip, grass, grass out, wiped-out, grunch, grunge, grungey, neb, nebbish, Irving, Melvin, party pooper, dull as dishwater, stick-in-the-mud, wet blanket.

BORROW v. touch, tap, hit, hit up, hit one for, hit on, bum, burn, appropriate, jawbone, knock, mooch, smooch, sponge, scrounge, cadge, cuff, crab, float one, brace, blitzkrieg, soak, lift, lug, put the lug on one, bite, put the bite on one, put the bee on one, put the arm on one, put the sleeve on one, put the claw on one, dog it, four-flush, go on the hook for, feel a dollar, feel some bread, steal one's stuff, get on the cuff, get on tick.

BORROWER n. moocher, smoocher, sponge, sponger, scrounger, desperado, four-flusher (does not repay), leech.

BOSOM n. boobs, boobies, bubs, bubbies, tits, titties, hooters, tatas, bodacious tatas (large), knockers, bazooms, babaloos, cans, jugs, headlights, mosquito bites (small). See BREASTS.

BOSS n. exec, chief, suit, bosshead, boss lady, boss man, honcho, head honcho, head, head man, big shit, big weenie, big cheese, big man, big gun, wheel, top dog, hellmaster, whip hand. See EXECUTIVE.

BOSSY adj. pulling rank.

BOSTON, MASSACHUSETTS Beantown, Highbrow, Highbrowville, Hub.

BOSTON RESIDENT n. Beantowner, Bean Eater, Beaner, Baked Bean, Bowwow.

BOTCH n. flub, muff, boner, boo-boo, blooper, boot, bobble, fumble, dumb trick, fool mistake, fuck-up, put one's foot in it. See MISTAKE.

BOTCH v. goof, goof up, hash up, screw up, bollix up, mess up, queer, boot, bobble, no way to run a railroad, juke. See ERR.

BOTHER n. headache, pain in the ass, pain in the neck, drag, bellyache, bitch, tsimmes, a nag, nudge, vid, worriment. See ANNOYANCE.

BOTHER v. be in one's face, bug, ride, eat, nudge, make waves, sweat, hassle, dog, bulldog, give one a hard time, give one hemorrhoids, get in one's hair, push one's key, push one's button, rub the wrong way. See ANNOY.

BOTHERED adj. bugged, hacked, blown out, uptight, hacked-off, brassed-off, cheesed-off, aggro, pissed-off, peed-off, tee'd-off, browned-off, drove, way drove, get a rash, bummed out, burned-up, hung-up, in a stew, in one's hair, dogged, miffed, peeved, riled, rubbed the wrong way, spooked, screaming meemies, all hot and bothered, at the end of one's rope, buffaloed, hard put to it, put to it, picked on, on pins and needles, on tenterhooks, worried sick, worried stiff, driven up the wall, rousted, sweat it, steamed. See also DISTURBED.

BOTHERSOME adj. be in one's face, pain, pain in the ass, pain in the neck, bitchy, son of a bitch, son of a gun, ———— from hell, messy, pesky, pestiferous, flea, tar baby. See TROUBLESOME. See also ANNOYING.

BOTTLE n. bot, soldier; corpse, M.T., em, dummy, dead soldier, dead man, dead marine, dead one (empty).

BOTTOM n. the pits, cellar, bottom line, bottom dollar, rock bottom, scraping the bottom of the barrel, low man on the totem pole, ain't no more, that's all there is.

BOUFFANT adj. boofed (hair).

BOUND adj. hog-tied.

BOUNDLESS adj. no end of, no end to, wide-open, more than you can shake a stick at, no strings, no strings attached, you name it you got it, no holds barred, no catch, no kicker, no joker, no joker in the deck, no ifs ands or buts. See also PLENTY.

BOUNTEOUS adj. 1. big, bighearted, be big, loose, Santa Claus, good Joe, have a heart, heart in the right place. 2. dime-a-dozen, aplenty, galore, no end in sight, stink with, crawling with, up to one's ass in. See PLENTY.

BOUNTIFUL adj. 1. loose, softie, soft touch, be big, Santa Claus, good Joe, have a heart, heart in the right place. 2. dime-a-dozen, aplenty, galore, no end, no end in sight, stink with, crawling with, up to one's ass in. See PLENTY.

BOURGEOIS adj. boojy.

BOUT n. set-to, bat, bender, binge, bust, go, tear, toot, wingding. See also BOXING, FIGHT, EVENT, REVEL.

BOVINE n. Bossie, Bossy, moo cow, moo-moo, Elsie, Nellie.

BOWEL MOVEMENT n. shit, crap, dump, caca, cahcah, kak, B.M., number two, poop, duker, call, nature's call, turds, dingleberries, big one, boom-boom, business, poo-poo, aah-aah, honey, drek, jobby, being regular, the shits, the runs, trots, shits, GI's, GI shits, turistas, Montezuma's revenge, liquid cork (Medic.), bird turd, doggy-do, buffalo chips, cow chips, cow flops, cow plops, cow pats, golden apples, horse apples, road apples, alley apples, hocky, horse hocky. See DIARRHEA.

BOWEL MOVEMENT, HAVE A v. shit, crap, dump, poop, go to the can, go to the john, shake a few clinkers out, do one's business. See DEFECATE.

BOWLEGGED adj. rainbow.

BOWLING, SPLITS half Worcester (3, 9 or 2, 8 pins left standing), horsemen (1, 2, 4, & 7 or 1, 3, 6, & 10); lily, sour apple (5, 7, & 10); spread eagle (2, 3, 4, 6, 7, & 10), washout (1, 2, & 10), baby split (2 & 7 or 3 & 10 standing), bedpost, goalpost, fencepost (all 7 & 10 left), big four (4, 6, 7, 10), Christmas tree (3, 7, 10 or 2, 7, 10), Cincinnati (8, 10), dodo (1 & 7 or 10), double pinochle (4, 6, 7, & 10), rob the cradle (pick up only one).

BOWLING TERMS big ball (powerful), blow (miss), carry (knockdown pins), cheesecake (a lane grooved for strikes), cherry (miss a spare), the count (pins downed by first ball), creeper (slow ball), flat apple, flat ball, kegler, kegling, maples (pins), pie alley (grand for strikes), spare, strike.

BOX n. clamshell (fast food).

BOXER n. palooka, pug, mug, lug, slugger, scrapper, punching bag, cauliflower ear, plug. See PRIZEFIGHTER.

BOXING n. the fights, battle, prelim, scrap, slugfest, mill, throw leather. See also FIGHT.

BOXING, KNOCKOUT KO, kayo, TKO, flatten, stopper, stiffener, chill, down for the count, take the count, kiss the canvas, kiss the resin, lower the boom, throw in the towel.

BOXING MATCH n. go, bout.

BOXING PUNCHES n. KO, stopper (knockout), lower the boom, stiffener, bolo, jab, smear, right cross, rabbit punch, roundhouse punch, sizzler, tee off, uppercut.

BOXING TERMS put on the gloves, go a coupla rounds, swap leather, one-two punch, punchy, duke (win), garden (arena), inning, heat (round), handle (manage); leather, mitt, pillow (glove); thumb (get finger in opponent's eye) dance, rock on one's heels, cauliflower ear, listener, tin ear, potato trap (mouth), glass jaw, chops (jaw), slam-bang (hard fight), waltz (easy fight), do-se-do (dull), TKO (technical knockout), back-pedal, on the ropes, hit the canvas, take the count, saved by the bell; fix (bribed to lose), throw a fight, take a dive, splash, tank act, tank fight, tank job, go in the tank, dump (loss, all fixed).

BOX OFFICE n. wicket, window, B.O.

BOY n. guy, dude, cat, shemp, feller, man, boyo, boychik, lad, tad, tadpole, kid, kiddo, sonny, sonnyboy, juvie, JD (juvenile delinquent), punk, punk kid, bub, bubba, bud, buddy, squirt, chap, buck, buster, chip, chip off the old block, cub, sprout, small fry, young fry, bird, duck, stud, Fred, joker, character, clown, jasper, runt, half-pint, little shaver, yupster, booger, bugger, chicken, wet behind the ears, cokey, gunsel, monkey, pecker, pisser, Peck's bad boy. See also CHILD, YOUNG MAN, YOUTH.

BOYCOTT v. blackball, ice out, pass by, pass up, shut out. See also OSTRACIZE.

BOY FRIEND n. main dude, main man, main squeeze, squeeze, my guy, my man, old man, b-friend, total babe, baby, stud, John, ace, ace lane, beau, best fella, best fellow, big moment, Fred, Fred Smith (perfect imaginary), snag, hooky, flame, heart throb, passion ration, sofa lizard, papa, sweet papa, sweet back (Af. Am.), daddy, sugar daddy, sugar bowl, body and soul, Casanova, Lothario, Don Juan, companion, constant companion, jelly roll, kissing cousin, back-door man, honey man, money honey, generous keeper, gold mine, big game, biscuit roller, masher, mule skinner, oyster, lovebird, turtle dove, sponsored (has girl friend).

BRACE v. buck up, perk up, pick up, chirk up.

BRACES n. tin grin, tinsel teeth.

BRACER n. pickup, pick-me-up, shot in the arm, tonic, eye-opener, hair of the dog, hair of the dog that bit one.

BRAG v. drag, woof, jive, shuck, shuck and jive, hot dog, grandstand, showboat, blow one's own horn, pat oneself on the back. See BOAST.

BRAGGADOCIO n. drag, talk, big talk, fancy talk, tall talk, bullshit, BS, shittin', hot air. See BLUSTER.

BRAGGART n. grandstander, hot dogger, showoff, hotshot, blowhard, blower, big timer, big mouth, bullshitter, bullshooter, bullshit artist, hot-air artist, crock of shit, pile of shit, earbanger, gasbag, windbag, big bag of wind, windjammer, windy, lover boy, know-it-all, blatherskite, big I am, big I love me, big head, swellhead, swelled head, be on an ego trip, think one is it, think one's shit doesn't stink, hot-shot Charlie, get too big for one's britches, biggety, ho-dad, ho-daddy, key swinging, loudmouth, hubcap, crack one's jaw, crapper, cocky, cock, cock of the walk, chesty, gutbucket, stuffy, stuffed shirt.

BRAGGING n. jive, jazz, snow job, hard sell, blow job, build, buildup, line, spiel, talk, talk big, tall tale, tall story, fish story, fancy talk, fine talk, baloney, phony boloney, phonus bolonus, crap, bull, bullskating (Af. Am.), bullshit, BS, bull-pucky, crock of shit, pile of shit, piece of shit, shit for the birds, shittin', cock-and-bull story, bunk, bunkum, gas, smoke, hot air, piss and wind, highfalutin, high-siding, riff, garbage, hocky, horse hocky, hogwash, malarkey, marmalade.

BRAIN n. head, bean, noodle, noggin, pate, sconce, thinker, box, think box, think pot, think tank, knowledge box, dream box, upper story, upstairs, wig, gray matter, little gray cells, wetwave, wetwear. See also HEAD.

BRAIN-DAMAGED adj. exceptional, gork, pinhead, spaz, retardo, not all there, soft in the head, weak in the upper story, vegetable. See RETARDED. See also FEEBLE-MINDED.

BRAINY adj. brain, genius, egghead, hardboiled egghead (tough-minded), scrambled egghead (fuzzy-minded), brill, whiz kid, Einstein, sharp as a tack, tack, have smarts, smart as a whip, technotrash (social idiot), no dumbbell. See INTELLIGENT.

BRAKE v. anchor it, lay down rubber, leave a stripe, nail the brakes, give on the wind (suddenly), in short pants, skuffling. See also STOP.

BRAKEMAN n. brakie.

BRAKES n. anchor, binders, cinchers, clinchers, clichés, grabbers, kill switch (automatic), grab a handful of air.

BRAMBLE n. sticker.

BRANDISH v. flash, sport, show off, come on strong, throw one's weight around. See FLAUNT.

BRAND NAME n. make (usually automobile), label. See also AUTOMOBILE, NAMES.

BRASH adj. brassy, cheeky, flip, get previous, fly. See also BRAZEN, FEARLESS.

BRA PADDING n. falsies, cheaters, deceivers, gay deceivers, props.

BRASS n. Dutch gold.

BRASSIERE n. bra, harness, lung hammock, uplift, boulder-holder, falsies, flopper-stopper.

BRASS KNUCKLES n. brass knucks, knucks.

BRAT n. JD (juvenile delinquent), punk, punk kid, holy terror, wild one, snotnose, snotnose kid. See also CHILD, BOY, GIRL.

BRAVADO n. balls, guts, macho, talk, big talk, fancy talk, fine talk, tall talk.

BRAVE adj. game, gritty, gutsy, gutty, spunky, nervy, I'm shakin' (response to threat, sarcasm), fire-eater, hairy, stand tall, walk tall, bigger 'n life. See FEARLESS. See also DARING.

BRAVE v. defi, face off, face down, fly in the face of, jam up, put one's life on the line, meet eyeball to eyeball, stand up to, take one on, knock the chip off one's shoulder, step over the line. See CHALLENGE.

BRAVERY n. balls, guts, heart, corazón, nerve, stomach, what it takes, grit, true grit, spunk, backbone, moxie, starch, clock, Dutch courage (intoxicated).

BRAWL n. scrap, rumble, free-for-all, rhubarb, knockdown and drag-out, battle royal, duke out, pluggin', scruff up, Donnybrook, donnybrook, hell broke loose. See FIGHT.

BRAWL v. buck, kick up a row, roughhouse, put up a fight, bang heads, raise cain, rumble. See FIGHT.

BRAWN n. beef, clout, muscle, punch, sock, kick, moxie, steam, steamroller, strong arm.

BRAWNY adj. husky, hefty, beefy, hunk, hulk, pumped-up, hoss (muscular), muscle man, he-man, industrial, beauhunk, beefcake, beef-a-roni, Greek god, crushman, powerhouse. See MUSCULAR. See also STRONG.

BRAZEN adj. cocky, gritty, grit, gutsy, gutty, nervy, spunky, hot-shot, come on strong, bold as brass, brassy, smart, smart-alecky, smart-ass, wise-ass, chutzpahdik, crusty, chit, spetters, salty, cheeky, flip, fly, hell of a, hell of a note, helluva nerve. See also FEARLESS.

BRAZIL NUT n. nigger toe (Derog.).

BREACH v. crash, crash the gates, break in, bust in, kick in, barge in, butt in, chisel in, horn in, muscle in, penetrate, mess over, put in one's oar, shove in one's oar, put one's two cents in. See also PENETRATE.

BREAD n. slab, staff of life, double-o, duffer, dummy, gum wadding, punk, shingle (toasted slice).

BREAD AND BUTTER n. punk and plaster, dough well done with cow to cover (also toast).

BREAD AND WATER n. piss and punk, angel cake and wine, cake and wine, dry.

BREAK n. 1. total bust. 2. coffee break, breakoff, time, time out, time off, downtime, letup, take five, take ten, come up for air, breather, take a breather, breathing spell, cutoff, happy hour, attitude adjustment hour (cocktail hour), layoff.

BREAK v. 1. bust, bust up, bust in, rack up, goof up, bung, bung up, break up, break to smothereens, total, torpedo, trash, fix, fritz, put on the fritz, jim up. See also DAMAGE. 2. break out. See also ESCAPE. 3. break in, break out, kick in, bust in, crack, crack open, jimmy. 4. gentle (animal). 5. break-break, break in, barge in. See also INTERRUPT.

BREAK AND ENTER v. penetrate, crash, toss. See also BURGLARIZE, PENETRATE.

BREAK DOWN v. come apart at the seams, crack up, conk out, strung out, schizzed out, psyched out, gronk out, basket case.

BREAKFAST n. brekkie, morning chow, brunch (late morning), eat one's Wheaties, put on the feedbag.

BREASTS n. boobs, boobies, kajoobies, bubs, bubbies, tits, titties, tatas, bodacious tatas (large), knockers, bazooms, torpedoes, babaloos, boobulars, cans, jugs, eyes, brown eyes, big brown eyes, hands, globes, headlights, knobs, nobs, nugs, lungs, maracas, mamas, upper frontal superstructure, racks, tonsils, bags, fun bags, teacups, plates, buckets, bazoongies, bazongas, breastworks, chestnuts, grapes, cantaloupes, melons, twins, pair, peach of a pair, apples, papayas, lemons, oranges, grapefruits, honeydew melons, watermelons, fried eggs, garbonzas, gazongas, gazungas, kettledrums, love bubbles, milkers, milk bottles, dairy farm, pumps, hooters, orbs, balloons, sweaterful, bra busters, bumpers, front bumpers, beauts, blubbers, endowed, chichi, droopers, pillows (Obs.), top-heavy, diddies, nacks, nards, dugs, flapjacks, flops tetitas, growths, bee bites, bee stings, mosquito bites (small), raisins, pimples, warts (Derog.).

BREECHES n. jeans, slacks, shorts, Levi's, hip huggers, whites, bells, bell bottoms, britches, ducks. See PANTS.

BREED n. likes, likes of, lot, number.

BREEZY adj. hawk stretch.

BREWERY n. micro, brew-pub (small brewery in a restaurant).

BRIBE n. fringe benefit, goodies, juice, graft, gravy, perk, perks, payoff, bad notes, payola, plugola, drugola, gayola, kickback, big one, fix, hush money, envelope, ice, nut, contribution, take, on the take, cream, under the table, mordida, contract, cush, baksheesh, salve, sugar, sweetener, sweetening, shake, soap, hat, smear, schmeer, grease, palm oil, touch, boodle, street money, walking-around money, chop, fall dough, freight; laying pipes, Abscam (Pol.); influence peddling, protection, protection money.

BRIBE v. pay off, fix, fix the alzo, put in the fix, take care of, smear, shmeer, grease, grease one's palm, oil, oil one's palm, slip one a buck, reach, get to, get at, get it on the line, put in the bag, come across, take an envelope, take a chicken, fit the mitt, buzz, do business, crack business, make a deal, buy, buy off, piece one off, kick in, put in the zingers, sweeten the pot, sweetener, sweeten one up, see, see the cops, grass eater (police officer who will take), meat eater (police officer who demands), gaff, barry (hiring boss), black market, swing for bread. See also PAY.

BRIBE MONEY n. the payoff, the envelope, payola, drugola, gayola, bad notes, cough syrup, grease, schmeer, smear, ice, protection, protection money, kickback, the fix, contribution, a chicken, mordida, boodle, pound, chop, freight, take, slush, slush fund, sugar. See also PROTECTION MONEY.

BRIBER n. fixer, apple polisher, greasy.

BRIBERY n. juice, payola, drugola, gayola, contribution, on contract (police), on the pad, on the take, under the table.

BRICKS n. confetti, Irish confetti (Derog.), load of rocks, alley apple.

BRIDEGROOM n. man, my man, old man, main man, main on the hitch, ace lane, breadwinner, buffalo. See also BOY FRIEND.

BRIDGE, DENTAL n. mouth jewelry.

BRIEF adj. short and sweet, in a nutshell, boiled-down, make a long story short, the long and the short of it, snippy.

BRIEF v. update one, let in on, put next to, put one in the picture, put one wise, tip off, fill one in, show one the ropes. See ADVISE.

BRIEFCASE n. elephant bag (large).

BRIEFING n. backgrounder, rundown, update.

BRIER n. sticker.

BRIG n. cooler, can, clink, clinker, tank, hard room, lockup, lock up, slam, slammer, Club Fed, jug, crate, pokey, hoosegow, iron house. See also JAIL, PRISON.

BRIGHT adj. 1. glitzy, flashy, showy, razzle-dazzle. 2. sharp, brain, egghead, whiz kid, Einstein, have smarts, smart as a whip. See INTELLIGENT.

BRIGHTEN v. punch up, shine, buff up.

BRILLIANT adj. 1. brill, razzle-dazzle, glitzy, flashy, showy. 2. brainy, genius, egghead, hard-boiled egghead (tough-minded), scrambled egghead (brilliant but fuzzy-minded), sharp, sharp as a tack, tack, whiz kid, Einstein, technotrash (social idiot), smart as a whip. See INTELLIGENT.

BRING v. lug, pack, piggyback, ride, shlep, tote, truck, back, birdie-back, buck, gun, heel, hump, jag, shoulder.

BRING YOUR OWN BEER v. B.Y.O.B. (also bring your own bottle).

BRING YOUR OWN LIQUOR v. B.Y.O.L.

BRING YOUR OWN WHISKEY v. B.Y.O.W.

BRITAIN n. Blighty, John Bull, Merry Old, Albion, Limeyland, tight little island.

BRITISH n. beefeater, Brit, Britisher, Cockney, Limey; Tommy, Tommy Atkins (soldier).

BRITISH FLAG n. Union Jack.

BROADCAST v. colorcast, get out, go on the air, go on the air waves, telecast, televise. See also INFORM, SPEAK.

BROADCASTER n. deejay, disc jockey, veejay, rip and reader, spieler, talker, airer.

BROADCASTING n. air time.

BROADCAST NETWORK n. web, net, skein, feed (source), pubcaster (public).

BROAD-MINDED adj. open.

BROAD-SCALE adj. shotgun.

BROADSIDE n. literature, flier, handbill, handout.

BROADWAY n. Great White Way, Mazda Alley, dream street, the big time.

BROCHURE n. flier, handout.

BROKE adj. flat, flat broke, dead broke, strapped, cleaned out, tapped out, on one's ass, on one's uppers, to the curb, down to one's last penny. See DESTITUTE.

BROKEN adj. busted, dusted, down, downtime, out, out of commission, on the blink, on the fritz, in the shop, on the shelf, wracked dead, kaput. See DAMAGED.

BROKERAGE, ILLEGAL n. clearinghouse, stiff joint, bucket shop.

BRONCHOSCOPE v. bronck.

BROOD v. eat one's heart out, bleed, stew over, sweat over, chew the cud. See LAMENT. See also THINK.

BROOKLYN, NEW YORK City of the Dead, Crookland (dangerous areas, Af. Am.).

BROTH n. dishwater, bowl, splash, water.

BROTHEL n. house, cathouse, can house, call house, massage parlor, rap club, rap parlor, rap studio, poontang palace, snake ranch, chicken ranch, meat market, camp, zoo, bagnio, beauty parlor, joint, call joint, hook shop, maison de joie, house of joy, joy house, nautch joint, notchery, notch house, parlor house, sporting house, bawdyhouse, fancy house, gay house, barrelhouse, bedhouse, peg house (male), house of ill repute, house of ill fame, house of delight, beaver base, rib joint, jazz joint, sugar hill, blacksmith's shop (Af. Am.), body shop, stew, dive, den of vice, den of iniquity, sink of iniquity, gooseberry den, doss, doss house, juke, juke house; jag, jag house (homosexual); intimaterie, man trap, pad, place, red-light, red-lighterie, service station, shooting gallery, sin spot, sin bin, slut hut, crib; case, birdcage (not common); cheap john, chippie joint, fleshpot, honky-tonk, camp, casa, chamber of commerce, shop, nunnery.

BROTHEL PROPRIETOR n. head pimp, sporting girl's manager, stable boss.

BROTHEL PROPRIETRESS n. madame, housemother, landlady, mama-san, mother, Aunt, Auntie.

BROTHELS, CHAIN OF n. line, stable.

BROTHER n. breed, bro, broh, brah, bub, bubba, bud, buddy.

BROWBEAT v. bulldoze, lean on, put the heat on, put one through the wringer, put the chill on, woof, bad-eye. See INTIMIDATE.

BROWNING AUTOMATIC RIFLE B.A.R.

BROWSE v. hit the high spots, get the cream, give the once-over, once over lightly.

BRUISE v. bung, bung up, cut up, do a number on one, hit one where one lives, lay a bad trip on one, zing. See WOUND. See also HIT.

BRUSH v. brush down (clothes), brush up.

BRUSQUE adj. snippy, snappy, short.

BRUTAL adj. bad-ass, kill-crazy.

BRUTALITY n. bear hug, choke hold (police), third degree.

BRUTALLY adv. something fierce, something terrible.

BUCKET n. billy can, growler, gutbucket.

BUFFALO, NEW YORK the Buffer, Polack Town.

BUFFOONERY n. camp, high camp, low camp, pratfall comedy, slapstick, monkeyshines, shenanigans. See also FOOLISHNESS, ACTING.

BUG n. seam squirrel, cootie, cutie, cootie garage (hair puffs in which cootie lives), grayback.

BUGLE n. misery pipe.

BUGLER n. hell cat (plays reveille).

BUILD v. throw up, throw together, knock together, fudge together, whom up, cobble up, fab, prefab.

BUILDING n. high-rise, skyscraper, tower, towers, pile o' bricks, rockpile, see-through, going dark (vacant), the blindfold lady (court).

BULGARIAN n. Bugger, Burglar, Vulgarian (all Derog.).

BULGE v. pop out, bug out, blob, googly.

BULKY adj. beefy, hefty.

BULL n. duke.

BULLDOZER n. dozer.

BULLET n. slug, lead, dose, rocket, love letter, pickle, pill, stumer, cap, cop killer, devastator, teeth, Black Talon, Dragon's Breath, Blammo Ammo, Safety Slug, Bolo, Desert Eagle (Israeli), corset (bulletproof vest), arrows (holes in a plane).

BULLETIN n. what's going down, what's happenin', a flash, break, scoop, skinny, handout, the dope, hot wire. See NEWS. See also REPORT.

BULLETPROOF VEST n. corset.

BULLY v. lean on, push around, bulldoze, buffalo, enforce, showboat, turn on the heat, walk heavy, woof, jackboot. See INTIMIDATE.

BUM n. bummer, bag lady, guttersnipe, gutter pup, in the gutter, bo. See BEGGAR.

BUMBLER n. klutz, dub, bagger, a newt, all thumbs, butterfingers, two left hands, two left feet, stumblebum, bogus, clodhopper, goofball, not cut out for. See CLUMSY.

BUMP v. bang into, crash, nerf, bumper-thumper, fender-bender, fender tag, rowdy-dowdy, rough-and-tumble, bump heads. See also HIT.

BUMS' LODGINGS n. jungle, skid row, bughouse square, the scratch park, flophouse, flea bag.

BUNCH n. chunk, hunk.

BUNDLE n. a roll, biddle, bindle, load.

BUNGLE n. boo-boo, blooper, boot, bobble, muff, goof-up, fuck-up, louse-up, screw-up, bonehead play, dumb trick. See MISTAKE.

BUNGLE v. flub, muff, boot, bobble, couldn't get a handle on it, lost the handle, drop the ball, blow it, blow it big time, go at it ass backwards. See ERR.

BUNGLER n. foul-up, fuck-up, bagger, dub, goof, goofball, stumblebum. See BLUNDER.

BUNGLING adj. awful, amateur night, amateur night in Dixie. See also CLUMSY.

BUNK n. hay, sack, rack, kip, doss, fleabag (N.). See also BED.

BUNKHOUSE n. bullpen, dump, dice house. See also HOUSE.

BUNK MATE n. bunkie, chum, roomie, roomy, old lady, old miss, wife, old man, O.M.

BUOYANCY n. bounce, vim and vigor, zip, feelgood.

BUOYANT adj. high wide and handsome, laid-back. See CHEERFUL.

BURDEN n. excess baggage, schlepper, ball and chain, albatross, albatross around one's neck. See HINDRANCE. See also RESPONSIBILITY.

BURDEN v. snow, snow under, dump on, give it to one, dish it out, dish out, stick it to one. See also HINDER.

BURDENSOME adj. bitch, ballbreaker, ballbuster, tough, tough proposition, headache. See TROUBLESOME.

BUREAU n. setup, cave, foundry, salt mines, front office, shop, store.

BUREAUCRACY n. red tape, red tapism, red tapery, foolocracy, gynocracy, mediocracy, moneyocracy. See also ADMINISTRATION, MANAGEMENT, ESTABLISHMENT.

BUREAUCRAT n. paper shuffler, paper pusher, buck passer, space cadet (young), apparatchik, empty suit, cee gee (cradle-to-grave bureaucrat), acabu (academic bureaucrat), milicrat (Mil.), polibu (pol.), probu (professional).

BURGLAR n. prowler, crook, second-story man, second-story worker, porch-climber, crasher, flat worker, fly, midnight, midnighter, moonlighter, owl, spider (of house and apartment); cracksman, safecracker. See THIEF.

BURGLAR ALARM n. dinger, bug; slap on a jumper, kill a bug (divert a); bug, put a bug on (install).

BURGLARIZE v. burgle, rip off, lift, liberate, moonlight requisition, promote, take a five-finger discount (shoplift), appropriate, hustle, touch, rough off, snatch, snitch, swipe, house (money), pinch, boost. See ROB. See also CRIME, COMMIT A.

BURGLAR'S TOOLS n. jimmy, jumper, nippers, bar, bar spreader, spreader, blade, briars, chopper, double, hardware, james, outsiders, pig, screw, shamus, stem, stick, wire gun.

BURGLARY n. break-in, caper, heist, owl job, prowl, on the prowl, crashing in joints, pushing joints, safeblowing, safecracking, second-story work, shack, sting, garage hopping (teenage).

BURGLARY, SAFE OR VAULT n. box work, busting petes, cracking cribs, heavy, heavy time, knocking off peters, peter racket, pete job, pete work, safeblowing, safecracking, taking boxes, the rip.

BURIAL n. cold meat party, deep-six, planting.

BURIAL GROUND n. boneyard, bone factory, bone orchard, marble orchard, marble town, cold storage, headstone city.

BURIAL PLACE n. cold storage, deep-six, dustbin, planted, pushing up daisies, a daisy, six, six feet under.

BURLESQUE n. burlesk, burlap, burlicue, burly, burlyque, burlesk, camp, cooch show, coochie show, girl show, girlie show, hootchy-kootchy show, leg show, peep show, skin show, skin house, topless, T and A, takeoff.

BURLY adj. husky, hefty, beefy, hunk, hulk, gorilla, hoss (muscular), beefcake, beef-a-roni, crushman, industrial, bruiser, muscle man. See MUSCULAR.

BURNISH v. shine, buff up.

BURRO n. mountain canary, Rocky Mountain canary.

BURY v. adios it, cover up, deep-six, plant, put six feet under.

BUS n. minibus, microbus, avenue tank (double deck), clunker, coffin (unsafe), hack, jitney, jitney bus, kidney buster, rig, rubberneck wagon (sightseeing), two-story lorry; iron pimp, brain train, kiddie car (school). See also AUTOMOBILE.

BUS DRIVER n. bus jockey, hack skinner, skip.

BUSHFIGHTER n. bushwacker.

BUSINESS n. 1. game, racket, bag, dodge, line, what one is into, rat race, biz, show biz, gesheft. See OCCUPATION. 2. megacorp, multinational, plunderbund, outfit; set up, set up shop (start); shop, small-time, Ma and Pa, Mom and Pop, front door, turnkey operation, shoestring operation, fly-by-night operation, bucket shop, coffee-and-cake joint, coffee-and-cake layout, coffee-and-cake place, coffee-and-cake spot (petty), white elephant (unsuccessful), gold mine (successful). See also CORPORATION. 3. beeswax, carrying on, goings-on, hanky-panky, hap, happening, ongoing.

BUSINESS ADMINISTRATION n. bizad.

BUSINESS, GO INTO v. set up shop, open up, get into, take a fling at, take a flier, hang up one's shingle.

BUSINESSMAN n. suit, pinstriper, vest, rainmaker, big-time operator, BTO, big wheel, wheeler-dealer, tycoon; cockroach, nickel-and-dime operator, small potatoes (small); tradester, baron, robber baron, big butter-and-egg man, the money.

BUSINESS OPPORTUNITY n. contact, in.

BUSINESS, TRANSACT v. buy out, close, deal, done deal, wheel and deal, hard sell, make a buck, make a buy, make a killing, put one over, bring home the bacon, raid, take over, cash in one's chips, chase, fold.

BUS STOP n. flag spot, flag stop, dog pound (Greyhound station).

BUST n. boobs, boobies, tits, hooters, tatas, bodacious tatas (large), knockers, jugs, globes, headlights, knobs, maracas, mosquito bites (small), See BREASTS.

BUSTLE n. 1. fuzzbuzz, do, fuss, rumpus. See ACTION, TURMOIL. 2. bishop (1775–1875), birdcage (1870).

BUSY adj. in warp one, up to speed, at the speed of heat, run one's ass ragged, clocked up, busy as a beaver, busy as a bee, busier than a one-armed paperhanger, on a merry-go-round, on the hop, on the jump, like Grand Central Station, whirling dervish, tied up, have other fish to fry, head over heels in, up to one's ass in, up to here in, overloaded, snowed, swamped, full plate, enough on one's plate.

BUSYBODY n. buttinsky, kibitzer, nosy Parker, snoop, snooper, yenta, backseat driver, Paul Pry, little pitcher with big ears, bugger. See also NEWSMONGER.

BUTCHER v. 1. beef up (cow). 2. goof up, hash up, louse up, screw up, bollix up, make a mess of. See ERR.

BUTT n. turkey, pigeon, clay pigeon, goat, patsy, mark, believer, easy mark, vic, chump, tool, set-up, softie, fall guy. See VICTIM.

BUTT v. buck.

BUTTE, MONTANA Big Butte, Brass.

BUTTER n. butta, high-priced spread, grease, axle grease, goober grease (peanut), lube, lubricant, marfak, plaster, cow, cow salve, salve.

BUTTOCKS n. buns, fanny, ass, arse, ass end, assterior, A-hole, behind, bottom, backside, bucket, bum, butt, bubblebutt (large and rounded), can, cheeks, moon, tail, tailbone, tail end, keester, keister, kazoo, wazoo, derriere, prat, rump, rumpus, seat, cakes, rumbleseat, sitter, fern, heinie, heinder, hind end, rear, rear end, tush, tushy, tuchis, tokus, dokus, duff, frances, labonza, gazonga, gazoo, winkie, culo, backporch, back yard, balcony, beam, biscuit, canetta, duster, getaway, pads, spread, rusty-dusty, satchel, vestibule, nether cheeks, stern, booty, boody, doo-doo, caboose, hams, pressed ham, goldmine, moneymaker, parking place, poop, Sunday face, handlebars of love; moon, gaucho, hang a B.A. (bare ass), red eye (expose the buttocks, usually an insult). See ANUS.

BUTTRESS v. beef up, build up, step up, hop up, soup up, jazz up, jack up, heat up, hot up, spike (drink). See SUPPORT.

BUXOM adj. busty, curvy, zaftig, built, stacked, well-stacked, built like a brick shithouse, built for comfort. See also FAT.

BUY v. blow oneself to, cop, score, land, make a buy, buy off, buy out, buy into, take up.

BUYER n. live one, float, walk in, front, head, believer, mark, chump, easy make, pigeon, sucker, ultra (insists on best), end user.

BYGONE adj. olden days, water under the bridge, water over the dam, down memory lane, when Hector was a pup, when one was knee high to a grasshopper. See PAST.

BYPASS n. circumbendibus.

BYPASS v. finesse it, go 'round the barn, go by way of.

BYPASS SURGERY n. rich man's tonsillectomy, senior citizen tonsillectomy.

BYSTANDER n. gaper, kibitzer, nark, sidewalk superintendent, watcher.

C

C n. Charlie.

CABBAGE n. violets, geraniums.

CABARET n. night spot, nitery, disco, after-hours joint, dive, speakeasy, hideaway. See NIGHTCLUB.

CABIN CRUISER n. stinkpot.

CABOOSE n. clown wagon, glory wagon, little red caboose, bed house, doghouse, bouncer, brain box, crib, crumb, diner, go-cart, hack, hearse, hut, kitchen, palace, parlor, perambulator, shack, shanty, van, way car, saloon. See also TRAIN.

CACHE n. kitty, nest egg, stake, stash, stache, plant, drop, drop joint, drop-off, hideout, shade. See also ASSETS.

CACHE v. stash, stache, stash away, plant, park, ditch, duck, bury, squirrel, squirrel away, put in the hole, stick in the hole.

CACOPHONY n. clinker, sour note.

CAD n. shit, shitheel, heel, sleazeball, slimebucket, worm, maggot, bounder, rounder, rotter, dog, rake.

CADAVER n. stiff, cold meat, dead meat, fly bait, body, loved one, remains, cage, carcass, croppy.

CADAVEROUS adj. skin-and-bones, skeleton, bag of bones, stack of bones, peaked, peaky. See THIN.

CADENCE n. beat, count.

CADET n. kaydet, beast; doolie, Mr. Doolie, gadget, gomer, gomar (A.F. Acad.); foundling, find (dismissed), gray legs (West Point), middy (N.).

CADGER n. bum, moocher, panhandler, promoter, bag lady, schnorrer, sponger, scab, freeloader. See BEGGAR.

CADILLAC n. Cad, Caddie, Caddy, golfer, cat, kitty, cattle train, hog.

CAFE n. eatery, pit stop, after joint, rib joint, slab house, burger joint, grease joint, coffee bar, coffeepot, soup house, bistro, noshery. See RESTAURANT.

CAFETERIA n. caf, one-arm joint. See also RESTAURANT.

CAISSON WORKER n. sandhog.

CAJOLE v. stroke, snow, massage, soap, soft-soap, simonize, con, jolly, oil, dooze, spread it on, lay it on, lay it on thick, lay it on with a trowel, lay a rap, get around, get next to, play up to, shine up to, make up to, act up to, butter, butter up, soften up, schmeikle (Yid.), sweeten up, sweet-talk, loud talk, dialogue one, honey, schmeer, rub the right way, work on, work over, brown-nose, suck around, suck up to; suck off, suck ass, kiss ass, kiss one's ass, lick ass (all Obsc.); blow smoke up one's ass, kiss butt, bootlick, boost, pat on the back, build, build up, toss a bouquet, give a posy, give the man a big cigar, gold star, have to hand it to one, puff up, trade last, TL, blarney, buzz, charm, buck, contract, cream, bag play, hand one a line, shoot a line, shoot the crap, shoot the bull, sling the bull, sling it, sell, shit, bullshit, BS, pull one's leg, overdo it, string along, kid along, stooge, yes, be a yes-man, fall all over, fish, play footsie, footsie-wootsie, footie-footie, footsie-footsie, handshake, heel, play Mr. Nice Guy, politic, run after, polish the apple, apple polish, kowtow, caboodle, buddy up, carpet-bag, curry below the knee.

CAJOLERY n. eyewash, grease, oil, snow job, soap, soft soap, sweet talk, blarney, bunkum, butter, banana oil, shit, salve. See FLATTERY.

CAJUN n. coon ass, cree-owls, swamp-rat.

CAKE PREPARATION n. mix, cake mix.

CALAMITY n. shit, deep shit, total shuck, the worst, blue ruin, one's ass is grass, curtains, Waterloo, trouble in River City, holy mess, unholy mess. See DISASTER.

CALCULATE v. dope out, figure in, figure out, figure up, reckon up, take account of, tote, tote up, tot, tot up, keep tab, keep tabs, size up, take one's measure, work out.

CALCULATOR n. brain, number cruncher,

CALCULUS n. calc.

CALENDAR n. lineup, pipeline.

CALENDAR, SET v. line up, get on line, pencil in, set, set up.

CALIFORNIA Cali (Af. Am.), Shakyside, the Golden State, slow track, the Coast.

CALISTHENICS n. aerobics, jazzercise, monkey drill.

CALL n. holler, blow, yawp.

CALL v. 1. blast, give one a blast, give one a blow, beep, bleep, contact, get back to, figure, swing by, fall by, fall down, hit, play, pay a call, drop in, drop by, crash (uninvited). See also TELEPHONE. 2. holler, holler out, blow at, yawp, yoo-hoo.

CALLIGRAPHY n. chicken tracks, hen tracks, mark, scrawl, scribble.

CALLING n. racket, line, bag, do, dodge, go, grift, play, hang, nine-to-five shit, rat race, slot, swindle, gig, day gig. See OCCUPATION.

CALLIOPE n. goopus, horse piano,

CALLOUS adj. cold, cool, cool cat, laid back, chill, iceman, arctic, cold fish, cold-blooded, ice water in one's veins, hard as nails, hard-boiled, thick-skinned, rhinoceros hide, dead-ass, mean machine, no heart, butter wouldn't melt in his mouth, got lead balls for eyes, tough.

CALLOUSLY adv. in cold blood.

CALLOW adj. kid, low-tech, sophomore, jellybean, green ass, don't know shit from Shinola, not dry behind the ears. See UNSOPHISTICATED.

CALM adj. cool, cool as a cucumber, keep one's cool, keep one's shirt on, unflappable, not turn a hair, ah-ah head, laid-back, all quiet on the western front, all quiet on the Potomac. See also ASSURED, IMPERTURBABLE, DISPASSIONATE.

CALM v. cool, cool out, cool it, cool off, take a chill pill, stroke, pour oil on troubled waters, take the edge off, take the bite out, take the sting out of, take it easy, take it down a thousand, lay back, soft-pedal, simmer down. See PACIFY.

CALM DOWN v. cool it, cool off, take a pill, take a chill pill, take it easy, take it down a thousand.

CALORIES n. lite (fewer calories), fat pill (high calories).

CAMBODIAN n. Cambo.

CAMEL n. hump, ship of the desert.

CAMERA n. box, pop bottle (inferior), wobblyscope (hand-held movie).

CAMERAMAN n. lenser, photog, shutterbug, coffee grinder (silent films).

CAMOUFLAGE n. cover-up, beard, camel flags (WWI).

CAMOUFLAGE v. cover up, beard, wear cheaters, slap on some glims, flash the gogs, throw on a makeup, phony up one's get-up.

CAMPAIGN v. run, politick, press the flesh, stump, take the stump, stump the country, hit the campaign trail, whistle-stop, take to the hustings, shake hands and kiss babies, ring doorbells, mend one's fences, mud-sling, muckrake.

CAMPAIGNER n. baby kisser, stumper, stump speaker, stump orator, whistle-stopper. See also POLITICIAN.

CAMPAIGN FUNDS n. war chest, slush fund, rainmaker (fund raiser).

CAMPER adj. sourdough tourist, tenderfoot (first time).

CAN n. pop top, gutbucket, gunboat, growler (large for beer).

CANADIAN n. Canuck, Kanuck, Jack Canuck, stew-eater Frite, Jean Baptiste, Pepsi (Fr. Canadian); hoser (north) (all Derog.).

CANAL n. choke point, bottleneck.

CANAPÉS n. finger food, dip, spread, munchies.

CANCEL v. scrub, not (used at end of a sentence), nix, kill, cut, trim, zap, X-out, do in, do one in, dial back, off, trash, total, torpedo, ax, sink, bog, crab, queer, squash, smash, smash up, finish off, forget it, knock off, knock out, knock the bottom out of, knock the chocks out from under, knock the props out from under, call off, call all bets off, scratch, break, break the lease, blow off, blow sky high, dust, tear down, come down on, shoot, shoot down, shoot down in flames, put down, torpedo, spike one's gun, kibosh, put the kibosh on, kayo, KO, blue pencil, rub out, take out, launder, wash out, wipe out, weasel out, worm one's way out of, welsh, crawfish, renig, nig, go back on one's word, put something out of action, cook, cook one's goose, upset one's apple cart.

CANCER n. C, big C.

CANDID adj. up front, right up front, frontal, open, call it like it is, straight shit, the real deal (Af. Am.), talk turkey. See FRANK.

CANDIDACY n. running, throwing one's hat in the ring, on the ticket.

CANDIDATE n. hopeful, political hopeful, presidential timber, dark horse, favorite son, handshaker, stalking horse, write-in, lame duck. See also POLITICIAN.

CANDY n. sweets, sweets to the sweet, pogey bait, poggie bait, commo (prison), hokey-pokey, hokum, jawbreaker.

CANDY FLECKS adj. ants, dots, jimmies, shots, sparkles, sprinkles.

CANDY STORE n. gedunk, sweet shoppe.

CANE n. stick, gimp stick, skinned mush.

CANINE n. mutt, pooch, doggy, pup, puppy, man's best friend, flea hotel, tail wagger. See DOG.

CANNON n. AA's, Arty, Divarty (division artillery), how, 88, long Tom, big guns, heavy stuff, rainmakers, big bertha, Big Bertha, grandmother (WWI). See ARTILLERY.

CANNY adj. foxy, crazy like a fox, cagey, fancy footwork, full of fancy footwork, slick, slippery, sly boots, smooth, smarts, street smarts, streetwise. See SHREWD.

CANONICALS n. clericals, backward collars.

CAN OPENER n. church key (beer).

CANTANKEROUS adj. bitchy, bad-assed, ornery, stuffy, snappish, waspish. See IRRITABLE.

CANTEEN n. slop chute (N.).

CANTON, OHIO Fame Town.

CAP n. beanie, dink, sky piece; cunt cap, tit cap (Army, Obsc.).

CAP v. put the lid on, top it off, wrap, wrap up, button up, button down, do to a T, do to a frazzle, clinch, can.

CAPABLE adj. A, 1-10 (degree: he's a 7), pro, vet, the right stuff, stuff, know one's stuff, dynamite, fireball, one-man band, has what it takes, the formula, the goods, green thumb, fool (e.g., dancing fool), mad, (jazz), there, on the ball, something on the ball, know one's way around, know the ropes, know the score, know-how, know one's onions, crisp, up, up to it, up to snuff, up to speed, up to the mark, up one's alley, a pistol, old hand, old-timer, old war-horse, won one's spurs, been around the block a few times. See also QUALIFIED.

CAPACITY n. 1. standing room only, SRO, jam-packed, sardined, up to the rafters, chock full. See FULL. 2. what it takes, the goods, up to it. See SKILL.

CAPER n. rib, gag, put-on, high jinks, hi jinks, hot foot, hot one, monkeyshines, shenanigans. See also REVEL.

CAPER v. let loose, cut loose, go on a tear, horse around, kick up one's heels, whoop it up, raise hell, blow off the lid. See REVEL.

CAPITAL n. 1. kitty, nest egg, stake. See ASSETS. 2. cap, small cap. 3. the Hill, D.C. (Washington).

CAPITALIST n. the money, money bags, the boss, the boss class, the one who signs the checks, angel (The.), backer, robber baron, Daddy Warbucks.

CAPITALIZE v. angel, back, bankroll, bank, juice, grubstake, stake, pick up the check, pick up the tab. See FINANCE.

CAPITALIZED adj. uppercased.

CAPITULATE v. cave in, fold, give away the store, knuckle under; come across, put out, give out (sexual). See SURRENDER.

CAPRICE n. fool notion, flea in one's ear, rib, gag, put-on, caper.

CAPRICIOUS adj. flaky, kinky, fantasmo, gaga, punchy, yo-yo, any way the wind blows, blow hot and cold, up and down, picky, picky-picky, etched in sand, helter-skelter, higgledy-piggledy, every which way. See WHIMSICAL.

CAPRICIOUSLY adv. any which way, fast and loose, hit or miss, all over the shop, by fits and starts. See ERRATICALLY.

CAPSULE n. cap.

CAPTAIN n. C.O., boss, skip, skipper (Army, N.), old man, cap, chief, four-striper, owner (N.), head honcho, head man, top, top dog, topkick, topper, higher-up, A-1, A-number 1. See also COMMANDER, EXECUTIVE.

CAPTIVATE v. rope in, hook, vamp, bat one's eyes at, give one the come-on, make a hit with, sweep off one's feet, turn one on. See ATTRACT. See also PERSUADE.

CAPTIVATED adj. turned-on, head over heels in, hooked, have one's nose open, fallen for, gaga about, gone on, sprung on, mad about, crazy about. See also BEWITCHED.

CAPTIVATING adj. dishy, pussycat, stone fox, head rush, whistle bait, solid sender, stunner, number, living doll, oh yeah. See BEAUTIFUL.

CAPTURE n. collar, bust, nab, grab, pickup, pinch, pull, pull in, run in, sweep, bag, drop, gaff, glom, gloon to, hook, nail, nick, nip, fall, booby pinch, brodie, crimp, flop, jackpot, jam, knockoff, pinch, rumble, slough, slough up, snare, snatch, trip, tumble, pickle, accommodation collar (to fill a quota or because of social or political pressure), humbug (unjustified).

CAPTURE v. collar, bust, round up, pinch, pick up, pull in, run in, land, snatch, grab, nab. nail, put the cuffs on. See ARREST.

CAPTURED adj. collared, nabbed, nailed, cornered, hauled in, picked up, dog meat, I'm dead, come out with your hands up. See ARRESTED.

CAR n. wheels, ride, mobe, muscle car, bug, beetle, stretch car (extra length), boom car (loud radio or tape), van, peep (jeep), bus, jalopy, bucket, gas guzzler, crate, heap, boat. See AUTOMOBILE. See also VEHICLE.

CARBOHYDRATE n. carbo.

CARBONATED adj. bubbly, fizzy, fizzly, sparkling.

CARBONATED WATER n. soda, club soda, clear soda, white soda; back soda, soda back (chaser); seltzer, sizz water, fizz water, fizzy stuff, for two cents plain, ammonia, maiden's delight (cherry), mixer. See also SODA.

CARBON COPY n. tissue, cc, flimsy.

CARBON MOLECULE, SPHERICAL n. bucky ball, bucky, buckminster fullerene, fullerene.

CARBURETOR n. duals, pot, carbos.

CARCASS n. body, loved one, remains, stiff, cold meat, dead meat, croppy. See BODY.

CARCINOMA n. growth, the big C.

CARDIAC MASSAGE n. CPR, pump a patient (Medic.).

CARDSHARP n. mechanic, card shark, capper (Obs.).

CARE n. 1. tender loving care, TLC. 2. worriation, worriment.

CAREER n. racket, game, bag, number, thing, dodge. See OCCUPATION.

CARE FOR v. 1. sit, baby-sit, keep an eye on, keep tabs on, ride herd on, watch out for, watch over, watch the store, mind the store. See HEED. 2. crazy about, nuts about, mad for, go for, hot for, gone on, stuck on, groove on, got it bad, nose open. See LOVE.

CAREFREE adj. laid-back, cool, cas, cazh, feel-good, high wide and handsome.

CAREFUL, BE v. cover one's ass, play it cool, bend over backwards, handle with kid gloves, hedge one's bets, play safe, walk on eggs, back and fill, pussyfoot. See CAUTIOUS.

CARELESS adj. slapdash, sloppy, any old way, any which way, by halves, fast and loose, helter-skelter, harum-scarum, devil-may-care, go out on a limb, fail to cover one's ass, leave oneself wide open, stick one's neck out, play with fire, fire-eating, go for broke, go off the deep end, step off the deep end, jump off the deep end, get in over one's head, goofing off, pay no mind, looking out the window, out to lunch, asleep at the switch, asleep on the job, not on the job, daydreaming, woolgathering, go overboard, go to sea in a sieve, buy a pig in a poke.

CARELESSLY adv. any old way, any which way, do by halves, knock off, knock out, bat out, shove out, slap out, slap up, slapdash, throw off, toss off, toss out, mess around, fast and loose, half-assed, helter-skelter, higgledy-piggledy. See also ERRATICALLY.

CARESS v. stroke, feel up, feel out, cop a feel, fool around, paw, playing footsie, bear hug, clinch, clutch, grab, grab ass, squeeze.

CARETAKER n. sitter, baby-sitter, house-sitter, super, swamper, crumb boss (hobo and logger).

CARGO n. stow (dockworker use).

CARGO HATCH n. bellyhold (airplane).

CARGO PLANE n. goon, pregnant guppy.

CARGO SHIP n. crock, tub, rust bucket, tramp.

CARICATURE n. takeoff, put-on, send-up.

CARNAGE n. offing, wasting, taking out, liquidation, blitz, search and destroy, S and D, a ride, croaking.

CARNIVAL n. carny, carnie (also worker), gilly show, grind show, ragbag.

CAROM v. sideswipe, kiss off.

CAROUSAL n. tear, bender, binge, toot, bat, drunk, jag, on the town, blowout, wingding, bust. See also PARTY; REVEL.

CAROUSE v. go on a toot, go on a bat, go on a spree, whoop it up, hell around, raise Cain, paint the town red. See REVEL.

CAROUSEL n. whirligig, merry-go-round.

CAROUSER n. playboy, good-time Charlie, man about town, rake.

CARP v. lint-pick, nitpick, bitch, noodge. See also QUIBBLE.

CARPENTER n. wood butcher, carps (stage), chips (ship).

CARPET n. wall-to-wall.

CAR, RECONNAISSANCE n. recon car, beep, jeep, peep, half track.

CARRIAGE n. brace, brush (Army).

CARRIER n. boy, shlepper, Typhoid Mary. See also BAGGAGE HANDLER.

CARRY v. lug, pack, back, backpack, piggyback, birdie back, heft, hoist, ride, shlep, shlep along, tote, truck, buck, gun, heel, hump (bags of coffee), jag, shoulder.

CARTEL n. megacorp, multinational, plunderbund, bunch, crew, crowd, gang, mob, outfit, ring. See also CORPORATION.

CARVE v. whack, hack, chiv, shiv.

CASH n. cold cash, hard cash, spot cash, buck, bread, long bread, dough, oday (pig Latin), dinero, ends (Af. Am.), the ready, the necessary, loot, lucre, filthy lucre, skins, gelt, green, green money, greenery, folding money, billys, cabbage, roll, bankroll, the bank, wad, paper, soft money, happy money, mad money, bundle, change, feed, chickenfeed, hard money, hard stuff, coin, iron (silver coin), iron men, piece of change, jack, mazumah, mezonny, mint, peanuts, poke, dead president, rocks, shorts, small bread, small potatoes, simoleons, spending snaps, spinach, wampum, adobe dollar, alfalfa, bait, biscuit, bite, spon, spondoolicks, spondoolix, tusherony, tucheroon. See also MONEY.

CASH v. break a bill, make change.

CASH A CHECK v. float one, smash.

CASH DRAWER n. damper.

CASHIER n. broad on the damper, ghee on the damper, on the damper, on the gun, box man, stick man, man behind the gun, man behind the stick.

CASHIER v. bounce, give the ax, give the gate, give the air, give one his walking papers, pink-slip, sack, drum out. See DISCHARGE.

CASHIERED adj. unfrocked (any profession), drummed out, turned off, fired, selected out, canned, laid-off, sacked. See DISCHARGED.

CASH ON DELIVERY n. C.O.D.

CASH REGISTER n. register, cash box, chip, damper, dinger, stick.

CASINO n. house, joint, shop, store, big store, toilet, trap, bust-out joint, creep joint, creep dive, frolic pad, track.

CASKET n. box, cold-meat box, crate, pinto, pine overcoat, wood overcoat, wooden overcoat, Chicago overcoat, wooden coat, wooden kimono, pine drape, pine pajamas, bird's-eye maple pajamas, tree suit.

CASPER, WYOMING Ghost Town.

CASSETTE n. cassingle (single).

CAST v. heave, lob, peg, pitch, chuck, chunk, fire, sling, toss.

CASTIGATE v. kick ass and take names, fire on, rip on, chew out, eat out one's ass, bawl out, jump down one's throat, come down on, read the riot act. See PUNISH.

CAST OFF v. cut loose. See DISCARD.

CASTRATE v. cut off one's balls, deball, fix, alter, arrange, doctor, domesticate, trim, work on.

CASUAL adj. cas, cazh, caj, laid-back, cool, mellow, breezy, easygoing, down-home, homey, haimish, folksy, pokesy, sporty, let one's hair down, throwaway, loose, loose as a goose.

CASUAL WEAR n. jeans, denims, dress down, sporty, sports clothes, sweats, come as you are.

CAT n. kitty, kitty cat, puss, pussy, pussy cat, meow-meow, Chessycat, coon cat.

CATACLYSM n. deep shit, total shuck, curtains, Waterloo, holy mess, unholy mess, double trouble. See DISASTER.

CATALOGUE n. charts, drop-dead list (fired, expelled, excluded), enemies list, hit list (punished or ostracized), shit list, S-list. See DIRECTORY.

CATALOGUE v. 1. tab, button down, peg, chart, spell out, pigeonhole, put away, put down as, put down for. See also ITEMIZE. 2. lane, track (Stu.).

CATALOGUED adj. by the numbers, chapter and verse.

CATALYST n. fireman, hatchetman, needle man, adjy, spark plug, pusher, steam-up ghee, stormy petrel, wavemaker.

CATAMITE n. chicken, punk, boy, pratt boy, bindle boy, brat, gazooney, bronc, bronco, brat, bo, cherry-picker, gonsel, lamb, kid lamb, nephew, peddle snatch, punk, punk kid, road kid, roundeye, twidget, Willie. See also HOMOSEXUAL.

CATASTROPHE n. total shuck, bad news, the worst, blue ruin, curtains, Waterloo, dead man's hand, tit in the wringer. See DISASTER.

CATCALL n. raspberry, razzberry, razz, Bronx cheer, zerbert, the bird.

CATCH n. Catch-22, joker, nigger in the woodpile (Derog.). See HINDRANCE.

CATCH v. 1. corral, collar, bust, bag, get one's fingers on, grab, nail, snag, sneeze, looks like rain (imminent). See ARREST. 2. savvy, get, take in, tumble to, wise up to, catch on, catch the drift, get the drift, get the hang of, see daylight. See UNDERSTAND. 3. be on to, be hep to, have one's number, have the goods on, catch with one's pants down, catch flat-footed, catch one dead to rights, get one dead to rights.

CATCH COLD v. take one's death.

CATCH UNAWARE v. blindside, sandbag, snooker.

CATEGORICAL adj. all-out, flat-ass, flat-out, straight-out, no strings attached, no holds barred, no kicker. See UNCONDITIONAL. See also CERTAIN.

CATEGORIZE v. tab, peg, typecast, button down, pigeonhole, put down as, put down for, rank out, size up.

CATERING TRUCK n. roach coach, garbage truck.

CATERPILLAR TRACTOR n. Cat.

CATHARTIC n. cc pills.

CATHOLIC adj. RC; Romish, papish, papist, papistic, popish (all Derog.).

CATHOLIC n. fish eater, Jesus lover, cat lick, mackerel snapper, Mick, pape, right foot, right-handed, bead puller, bead counter (all Derog.); Roman; Jack Catholic (lapsed).

CATHOLICISM n. papism, papistry, popeism, popery (all Derog.).

CATSKILL RESORTS n. Borscht Belt, Jewish Alps.

CATSUP n. red lead, red paint, kid stuff, growley.

CATTLE n. dogie, longhorn, moo cow, shorthorn, whiteface, dinge (substandard, unbranded), stray. See also COW, BULL.

CATTLE BRAND n.   iron, brand, running iron.

CAUCASIAN n.   paleface, ofay, Anglo, honky, ball face; monkey, peckerwood silk, gray (Af. Am.); greyhounding (Af. Am. dating a white), WASP, white bread, whitey, blue-eyed, blue-eyed devil, round eyes (all Derog.). See also WHITES.

CAUGHT adj.   nabbed, nailed, booked, collared, corralled, cornered, dog meat, dead to rights, got one dead to rights, I'm dead, one move and you're dead, hooked, hook line and sinker, dropped, flopped, guzzled, hit the pits, ill, in the pokey with smokey, in a fix, in a hole, jammed up, on the peg, sneezed, take a brodie, walk into a collar, come out with your hands up, stiffed in, swamped. See also ARRESTED.

CAUGHT IN THE ACT v.   caught red-handed, caught with one's hand in the cookie jar, caught with the smoking gun, caught flat-footed, caught with jeans at half mast, caught with one's pants down, caught dead to rights, caught dead bang to rights, caught dead bang, banged to rights, snared flat-footed, snared dead bang, dead pigeon, turkey, had, buried, in the barrel, washed up.

CAUSE v.   start the ball rolling, get things rolling, break the ice, break in, kick off, intro, father, egg on, ring in, bow, kick it, open, open up.

CAUSTIC adj.   bitchy, cussed, mean, sticking the zingers in, wise-guy, smart-ass. See SARCASTIC.

CAUTION n.   tip, tip-off, flea in one's ear, bug in one's ear. See also ALARM.

CAUTION v.   put one wise, wise one up, tip, tip off, give the high sign, flag, wave a red flag, cloud up, pull one's coat. See also ADVISE.

CAUTIOUS adj.   cagey, pussyfoot, leery, been hit before, play it cool, play safe, watch one's step, watch out, pay mind to, keep on one's toes, walk on eggs, walk wide, think twice, hedge one's bets, play it close to the vest, take it easy, take it slow, bend over backwards, cover one's ass, not miss a trick, not overlook a bet, not go out on a limb, not stick one's neck out, on the lookout, shine me on, listen up, all ears, keep one's ear to the ground, keep one's eye peeled, keep one's eye on the ball, be on the ball, with a weather eye open, with one's eyes peeled, handle with kid gloves, mind one's p's and q's.

CAVE EXPLORER n.   potholer.

CAVIL v.   nitpick, lint-pick, split hairs, make a big thing about, make a mountain out of a molehill, catch at straws. See also QUIBBLE.

CAVORT v.   carry on, go places and do things, fool around, horse around, monkey around, cut loose, cut up. See REVEL.

CB OPERATOR n.   apple, CB Stud, channel chump, Dixie cup (So.), fox jaws (Fem.), signal stopper.

CB RADIO n.   ears.

CEASE v.   wind up, pack in, drop, drop it, cut it out, nip, break off, back off, knock off, leave off, call it a day, quit cold turkey, close out, shut down. See STOP.

CEASED adj.   fini, kaput, finished-up, washed-up, wound-up, wrapped-up, dusted, that's history, written off, all over but the shouting, signed sealed and delivered, when the fat lady sings. See also STOPPED.

CEASELESSLY adv.   round the clock, day and night, on a treadmill. See CONTINUOUSLY.

CEDE v.   fold, give in, hand over, fork over, come across with, drop, throw in the sponge, throw in the towel, toss in the sponge, toss in the towel. See also GIVE UP, SURRENDER.

CELEBRATE v.   open a bottle, break out the bubbly, paint the town red, raise hell, tie one on, party, party down, go on a bender, go on a binge, go on a spree, go on the town. See also REVEL.

CELEBRATED adj.   w.k. (well-known), number 1, number one, numero uno, large, up there, right up there, big, high-powered, double-barreled, touted, highly touted, cut a dash, in the limelight, make a splash, flash in the pan (brief), not to be sneezed at. See also CELEBRITY.

CELEBRATION n.   blowout, bash, blast, brawl, hullabaloo, hoopla, jamboree, paint the town red, whoopee, whooper-dooper, wingding. See PARTY. See also REVEL.

CELEBRITY n.   celeb, star, superstar, monster, name, champ, a somebody, VIP, face, face card, lion, page-one-er, prima donna, great, brass hat, hot shot, hot dog, the late great ———, Mr. Showbiz, Mr. ———, Miss ———, Mr. Big, big name, bigwig, big gun, big noise, big shot, big shit, big timer, big time, big-time operator, B.T.O., wheel, big wheel, big number, big man, big man on campus, B.M.O.C., big stuff, biggie, big boy, big-league, major-league, big deal, big chew, big player, big one, big ghee, big spud, big cheese, big piece of cheese, real cheese, the cheese, whole cheese, A-list, hooper-dooper, knocker, large charge, magoo, talent, shout, visiting fireman, heavy, heavy stuff, heavyweight, gun, high-muck, high-muck-a-muck, high-muckety-muck, high-mucky-muck, high-monkey-monk, high pillow.

CELLULITE n.   cottage cheese, oatmeal.

CEMENT n.   mud, stickum, gunk.

CEMETERY n.   boneyard, bone factory, bone orchard, marble orchard, marble town, marble city, cold storage, headstone city, boot hill, dead center, necropolis, rest camp.

CENSOR v.   bleep, black out, blue-pencil, scissor out, cork, put the lid on, decontaminate, launder, sanitize, sterilize, squelch. See REPRESS. See also SUPPRESS.

CENSORSHIP n.   blackout, hush-up, iron curtain. See SUPPRESSION.

CENSURE v. blow the whistle on, blast, blast on, lay on, lay a bad trip on one, put the whammy on one, have someone's ass, lower the boom, drop the boom, paste, roast, rap, tell off, tell one where to get off, speak to, talk to, take down, call down, come down on, come down hard on, turn thumbs down, thumb down, blackball, call to task, call on the carpet, dance the carpet, put one on the carpet, have one on the carpet, have one on the mat. See SCOLD. See also CRITICIZE.

CENSUS n. head count, nose count.

CENT n. Indian head, red cent, brown, brown Abe, copper, brownie, peanuts, red, silver, meter money, throw money, wampum, washers.

CENTS, FIVE n. nickel, blip, jit, jitney, buffalo, fish scale, flat.

CENTS, TEN n. dime, thin dime, thin, thin one, thin man, deemar, deemer, demon, dimmer, deece, liberty, sow.

CENTS, TWENTY-FIVE n. two bits, quarter, cuter, kyuter, queter, big George, gas meter, light piece (silver), meter, ruff, shin plaster (paper), squirt.

CENTS, FIFTY n. four bits, half a buck, silver wing.

CENTS, SEVENTY-FIVE n. six bits.

CENTER n. mainstream, middle of the road, straddle the fence. See also MIDDLE.

CENTRAL AMERICAN n. banana (Derog.).

CENTRAL EUROPEAN n. Bohunk, Hunky (Derog.).

CENTRAL INTELLIGENCE AGENCY n. CIA, the company, the Company, the Agency, Langley, Mother K, farm (training camp), spook (agent), spook factory, toy factory, the pit (basement at Langley) the firm (British Secret Service).

CENTRAL INTELLIGENCE AGENCY TERMS mole, block program (more secret than top secret), bigot list (allowed to know block program), witting (knows secret), humint (humanly gathered intelligence), plumbing (agent's field support structure), fumigate (search for listening devices), honey trap, lady (both women sent to compromise the opposition), legend (fictional cover story), gray man (inconspicuous, the perfect agent), knuckle dragger (paramilitary working with CIA), CI-nick (counter-intelligence, pronounced see-nick), dry cleaning (avoiding pursuit, or testing to see if being followed), make (identifying one's surveillant), flaps and seals (course of instruction in surreptitious letter opening), the loot (info gained through intelligence operation), noise (useless information to confuse relevant information), vacuum cleaner (informant who supplies overabundant details), cousin (British Intelligence; also, Israeli Intelligence reference to an Arab), lion tamer (one who deals with a former agent who threatens trouble);

harmonica bug (telephone listening device may also be explosive), music box (radio transmitter), musician (wireless operator); naked (alone without help), biographic leverage (blackmail), black-bag job (bribery or burglary); family jewels (illegal activities), jockstrap medal (secretly awarded), L-pill (suicide pill), demote maximally, measles (murder looks like natural causes), terminate (purge by killing), granny (non-Agency employee whose premises are used for observation), Aunt Minnie (tourist photo that includes a strategic location), letter drop (secret message depository).

CEREAL n. grits, mush, cush, birdseed.

CERTAIN adj. sure, sure thing, cocksure, sure as shit, for certain, on ice, cold, have down cold, pat, have down pat, nailed down, all locked up, have a lock on, lock-and-win situation, license to print money, got the faith baby, keepin' the faith, count on it, no buts about it, no ifs ands or buts, open-and-shut, set, right on, odds-on, gamble on, bet on, bet one's bottom dollar on, put your money on, bet the house on, bet the rent on, passed the litmus test, checked and double-checked, racked, taped, cinch, lead-pipe cinch, cinched, clinched, come hell or high water, in the bag, that's death, and no mistake, know damn well, know darn well, boat race (horse racing), the fix is in, is the Pope Catholic?, does a bear shit in the woods?, is a bear Catholic?, does the Pope shit in the woods?, do they grow corn in Iowa?

CERTAINLY adv. absofuckinglutely, absitively, posolutely, cert, sure as God made little green apples, fer sher, for a fact Jack, you better believe it, right on, in a heartbeat. See ABSOLUTELY.

CERTAINTY n. lock, lockup, lock and win, have a lock on, sure thing, dead sure thing, sure bet, sure card, for sure, fer sher, fer shirr, sure fire, as sure as shooting, cinch, sewed up, all sewed up, open-and-shut, open-and-shut case, pushover, stock, store, put stock in, put store by, score, set up, soft touch, wrap-up, nuts, pipe, cinch, lead-pipe cinch, candy, cold lay, bet your ass, bet your boots, bet your bottom dollar, bet your life, bet your sweet life, shoo-in, gospel truth, ironclad contract, rain or shine.

CERTIFICATE n. shingle, paper.

CERTIFICATE OF DEPOSIT n. CD.

CERTIFICATE OF OWNERSHIP n. pink, pink slip (car).

CERTIFIED PUBLIC ACCOUNTANT n. CPA, bean counter, number cruncher, sharp pencil pusher, pencil shover, pen pusher, pen driver.

CERTIFY v. okay, OK, rubber-stamp, put one's John Hancock on. See CONFIRM.

CESAREAN SECTION n. C section, emergency exit.

CESSATION n. freeze, downtime, time out, come up for air, breather, break, break-off, cutoff, layoff, letup, screaming halt, shuddering halt, grinding halt.

CHAIN n. clinker.

CHAIN GANG GUARD n. chain gang Charley, long chain Charley, long line skinner, johnny creep, the johnny.

CHAIN GANG LEG CHAIN n. bull chain, rattler, G-string (leash).

CHAIR n. seat, sling, squatter.

CHAIRMAN n. the chair.

CHAIRPERSON n. the chair.

CHALLENGE n. defi, defy, have one's work cut out for one, when push comes to shove, when you separate the men from the boys.

CHALLENGE v. defi, face off, face down, in your face, face to face, fuck with, fuck around with, jam up, brace, cross, fly in the face of, fly in the teeth of, put one's life on the line, eyeball to eyeball, meet eyeball to eyeball, hang in, hang in there, hang tough, stick it out, stick to one's guns, stand up to, stand up and be counted, go one on one, mano a mano, take out, take on, take one on, take one up on, call one's bluff, knock the chip off one's shoulder, make something out of, step over the line, make my day, go on make my day, bite the bullet, keep a stiff upper lip, keep one's chin up, drop a lug, zap.

CHALLENGING adj. furry, hairy. See also EXCITING.

CHAMPAGNE n. bubbly, the bubbly, giggle juice, giggle water, grape, the grape, angel foam, Minnehaha, laughing water, sparkle water, whoopee water.

CHAMPION adj. world-class, tops, greatest, killer, cool, 'motor, out-of-sight, out-of-this-world, first-chop, tip-top, top-notch, topflight, top-drawer, super, gilt-edged, gilt-edge. See BEST.

CHAMPION n. champ, number one, numero uno, the greatest, top dog, king o' the hill, king shit, white hope, white knight. See also BEST.

CHAMPION v. back, go to bat for, ride shotgun for, thump for, beat the drum for. See SUPPORT.

CHANCE adj. dicey, iffy, risky, chancy, fluky. See RISKY.

CHANCE n. 1. shot at, long shot, break, breaks, fair shake, fighting chance, avs (law of averages). See WAGER. See also OPPORTUNITY. 2. in the cards, that's the way the cookie crumbles, lucky break, streak of luck, luck out. See LUCK.

CHANCE v. stick one's neck out, put it on the line, plunge, take the plunge, put one's money where one's mouth is. See WAGER. See also RISK.

CHANGE n. about-face, flip-flop, turnaround, mid-course correction, switch, switch over, new ball game, new deal, new shuffle, big bang (dramatic), quantum leap (major). See also MODIFICATION.

CHANGE v. switch, switch over, doctor, phony up, shift gears, cook, take it in a little, mid-course correction, monkey around with, bottom out, transmogrify, do up, revamp, kite stiffs (checks), tweak, give it a tweek (small), fine tune, yo-yo, butcher, dink, dial back, recalibrate. See also SHIFT. 2. see the light, come to Jesus, hit the sawdust trail. 3. turn over a new leaf, turn the corner, turn the tables, turn around, turn one around, do up, about face, flip-flop, sing a different tune. 4. shoot a twenty, break a ten, make change. See also CASH.

CHANGEABLE adj. yo-yo, seesaw, wishy-washy, etched in sand.

CHANGED adj. born again, newborn Christian, got religion, saw the light.

CHANT n. belly music, shout.

CHANT v. shout.

CHAOS n. mix-up, holy mess, rat's nest, free-for-all, can of worms, who's minding the store? See CONFUSION.

CHAOTIC adj. helter-skelter, harum-scarum, skimble-skamble, every which way, arsy-varsy, topsy-turvy. See CONFUSED. See also ERRATICALLY.

CHAPEL n. dirge factory, god box, amen corner.

CHAPERON n. bird dog, alarm clock, baby-sitter.

CHAPLAIN n. Holy Joe, sky pilot, sky scout, preacher man, sin hound, buck, fire insurance agent, gospel pusher, turn-around collar. See CLERGYMAN.

CHAPTER n. branch, branch house, offshoot, affil. See ASSOCIATE.

CHARACTER n. card, creepo, oddball-type, weirdo. See ECCENTRIC.

CHARACTERISTIC n. 1. slant, twist, gimmick, shtick, bit, bag, one's bag, thing, one's thing, nature of the beast, the way of it, the name of that tune, that's one all over, just like one. 2. thumbprint. See also NATURE.

CHARACTERIZE v. typecast, tab, peg, pigeonhole, button down, put down as, put down for, put away, rank out, size up, take one's measure.

CHARGE n. 1. price tag, bad news, damage, bite, what the traffic will bear. click charge (metered), tick, nick, to the tune of, squeeze. See COST. See also FEE. 2. blitz, blitzkrieg, mugging, push, dirty deed, surgical mission (quick), attempting a creep. 3. the gripes, beef, beefing, bitch, gripe, a hoo-ha, stink, big stink, dido, kick, blast. See ACCUSATION. See also CRIMINAL CHARGE.

CHARGE v. 1. put it on one's card, cuff, cuffo, put on the cuff, put on the tab, put on tick, nick, paste, go in hock for. 2. finger, point the finger at, hang something on, whistle-blow, blow the whistle on one, turn on the heat, burn one's ass, drag into court, haul into court, have the law on, law, have up, put one away, pull up, take out after. See also ACCUSE. 3. mug, storm, haul off on one, jump on, blindside, bushwhack, land all over one, lace into. See ATTACK.

CHARISMA n. pizazz, flash, it, got it, star quality, glamour, the jazz, something, chrismo, chismo, razzle-dazzle, animal magnetism.

CHARITABLE adj. big, be big, big-hearted, all heart, heart in the right place, bleeding heart, do-gooder, good scout, Robin Hood, Santa Claus.

CHARITY n. handout, a hand, helping hand, do one's part, chickadee checkoff (donation), write-off, gift, gifting, lump, poke-out.

CHARLATAN n. fake, faker, fraud, four-flusher, phony. See QUACK.

CHARLESTON, SOUTH CAROLINA Charlie.

CHARLOTTE, NORTH CAROLINA Queen City.

CHARM n. 1. whammy, chemistry, star quality, something, it, pizazz, the jazz. 2. evil eye, stink eye, go, hoodoo, jinx, whack, whammy, hocus-pocus, mumbo-jumbo, abracadabra.

CHARM v. send, grab, kill, slay, turn on, wow, do cute, knock dead, knock out, sweep off one's feet, make a hit with, vamp, bat the eyes at, blow one out of the water, tickle to death, tickle pink. See also PERSUADE, ATTRACT.

CHARMED adj. sold on, hooked, wowed, turned on, tickled pink, tickled to death, head over heels in, pleased as punch. See also BEWITCHED.

CHARMER n. vamp, man trap, velvet trap, beaver trap, fetcher, killer, lady-killer, lulu, operator, player, swinger, joy boy, sheik.

CHARMING adj. righteous, dreamy, dishy, drop-dead gorgeous, flavor (Af. Am.), scrumptious, delicious, good enough to eat with a spoon. See also BEAUTIFUL.

CHASE v. take out after, go after, shag, run down, track down, bird dog (scout), play catch up. See FOLLOW. 2. troll, pussy patrol, give one the eye, give one the cyclops, go for the cheese,

CHASTENED, ACT v. eat crow, eat dirt, eat humble pie, get one's comeuppance. See HUMILIATED.

CHASTISE v. fire on, rip on, chew out, ream out, lay into, lean on, climb all over, rake up one side and down the other, slap down, ding, settle one's hash. See PUNISH.

CHAT n. rap, rap session, rapping rash; mack, lip music (Af. Am.), yak, yakkety-yak, blah-blah, chinfest, chin music, chitchat, gas, guff, hot air, talkee-talkee, visit. See also SPEAK.

CHAT v. rap, gab, gas, jaw, chin, confab, mack (Af. Am.), yak, yakkety-yak, yakking, go on, run on, bull, bullshit, BS, throw the bull, throw the bullshit, shoot the bull, shoot the shit, shoot the bullshit, shoot the breeze, bat the breeze, bat the chat, bat one's gums, beat one's gums, chew, chew the fat, chew the rag, parley-voo, twiddle, visit with. See also SPEAK.

CHATTANOOGA, TENNESSEE Choo Choo Town.

CHATTER n. gab, gas, yak, yakkety-yak, talkee-talkee, guff, hot air, blah-blah, bibble-babble. See also SPEECH.

CHATTER v. gas, gab, jaw, yak, yakkety-yak, go on, go on and on, run on, run off at the mouth, have diarrhea of the mouth, shoot off one's mouth, shoot off one's face, shoot the breeze, bat the breeze, bat the chat, beat one's gums, talk through one's hat, bull, bullshit, BS, throw the bull, bibble-babble, twiddle. See also SPEAK.

CHATTERBOX n. gabber, gasbag, windbag, windjammer, hot-air artist.

CHAUFFEUR n. wheelman. See also DRIVER.

CHAUTAUQUA n. Brown Top.

CHAUVINIST n. male chauvinist pig, MCP, pig, sexist porker, Archie Bunker, hard hat, hundred percenter, redneck, flag-waver, jingoist, patrioteer, superpatriot.

CHEAP adj. 1. dirt-cheap, cheapie, el cheapo, cheap as dirt, dog-cheap, steal, real steal, buy, real buy, tourist, low-cost, low budget, cost nothing, cost next to nothing, more bang for the buck, easy on the pocketbook, bought for a song, pick up for a song, cut-rate, low-tariff, dime a dozen, price is right. 2. cheesy, chickenshit, crap, crappy, crud, cruddy, crusty, mangy (fur), borax, shit, dime-a-dozen, dreck, drecky, piece of shit, pile of shit, shitbox, shitbag, shitburger, rinky-inky, dog, scroungy, piss-assed, small, small time, two-bit, raunchy, quick-and-dirty, kinky, ratty-tatty, rat's ass, sleazy, gummy, gook, low-rent, diddly, diddly-poo, diddly-shit, doodly, doodly-shit, doodly-poo, ain't worth diddly-shit, ain't worth doodly-shit, ain't worth shit, ain't worth the powder to blow it to hell, ain't worth a hoot, ain't worth a plugged nickel, cheapie, el cheapo, Mickey Mouse, cotton-pickin', garbage, schlock, schlocky, plastic, slimpsey, junk, junky, no-good, N.G., dunnage (dockworker use), no bargain, no-account, no-count, not so hot, the least, lousy, jelly bean, beans, hill of beans, ain't worth a hill of beans, piss-poor, lemon, peanuts, dud, blah, ham, from hunger, fluky, flookum, white elephant, G, jeasley, jitney, bogus, minus, punk, stiffo, wood, tripe, turkey, abortion, bum, clinker, crackerbox (house), tin, tinhorn. 3. tight, penny-pinching, close, close-fisted, chintzy, stingy, cheap John. See STINGY. 4. glitzy, snazzy, flashy, ticky-tacky, flukum, frog, fishball, gook. See GAUDY.

CHEAPLY adj. nickel and dime it, run on the rims.

CHEAT n. hustle, con game, short con, big con, big store, sting, bogus, bunk, bunco, bunko, flam, flimflam, flimflammery, all hat and no cattle (Texas), jip, gip, gyp, scam, racket, dodge, stunt, shady deal, sharp deal, wrong number, not kosher, crooked deal, crooked stick, cheatin' heart, Honest John, doberman (Af. Am.), play dirty, lowdown and dirty, dirty work, grandstand, razzmatazz, razzle-dazzle, fast shuffle, royal fucking, royal screwing, sellout, bait and switch, the pilgrim drop, handkerchief switch, bum steer, curve ball, jazz, jive, shuck, total shuck, balls, hooey, hocky, hokey-pokey, hokum, hogwash, malarkey, marmalade, spinach, banana oil, baloney, bulldog, garbage, cover, cover-up, snow job, whitewash, whitewash job, doesn't wash, down and dirty, dirty dealing, dirty work, dirty pool, dirty trick, taradiddle, diddling, fix, Barney, frame, frame-up, plant, flake (plant false evidence), hookup, put-on, spoof, stab in the back, two-timing, Judas kiss, cross, double-cross, double-X, XX, double banker, doubletalk, double-speak, double shuffle, fast shuffle, shell game, skin game, Murphy game, the old army game, bill of goods, trick, fool, fast one, run around, cutie, claptrap, line of cheese, borax, song, song and dance, string, smoke, tripe, vanilla, bitch, skunk, cake cutter (circus), hanky-panky, hocus-pocus, hugger-muggery, graft, grift, autograph, kiting checks, bucket shop, boiler room, Carrie Watsons, the engineer's daughter, double trays, dipsy-doodle, shenanigans, monkeyshines, monkey business, funny business; limb, shit kicker, tap, tap game (advertising).

CHEAT v. rip off, rook, fuck, screw, bone, shaft, frig, fork, hype, fudge, deke, hose, hump, pratt, rim, ream, shine one on, jerk one off, jerk one around, dick, dick one around, job, fuck one over, run a game on one, blow smoke up one's ass, jive, shuck, shuck and jive, frontin', team xerox (on a test), run a game on, scrog, gaffle, snake one in, rope in, do a number on one, disinform, mooch (commodity scam), sell wolf cookies, throw the bull, bullskating (Af. Am.), bullshit, bunco, bunko, cheek it, fake, fake one out, four-flush, cross, cross up, cross one up, two-time, trim, caboodle, fast talk, fleece, gas, gum, flam, flimflam, stick, burn, beat, bleed, bleed white, bilk, clip, con, chisel, gouge, gyp, scam, stiff, sting, sandbag, bait and switch, low ball, throw one a curve, wrong steer, bum steer, give one a bum steer, hurdy, give one the runaround, see one coming, Murphy, pigeon drop, ike, pluck, rope in, take, take one to the cleaners, take one for a ride, take for a sucker, take a dive, splash, throw a fight, throw a game, play games with, play the nine of hearts, play for a sucker, sucker, suck in, sucker into, cream, milk, pull something on one, pull one's leg, pull a quickie, pull a fast one, pull a fast shuffle, double-shuffle, double-cross, XX, double-clock, double-deal, second deal, give one a raw deal, bottom-deal, deal from the bottom of the deck, pack the

deal, stack the cards, stack the deck, shave the deck, shave, sting, strip bare, skin, slice, skunk, crib, crimp, set up, doctor, cook up, deacon, duff, hoke up, frame, load, salt, salt a mine, fudge, plant, flake (plant false evidence), phony up, queer, promote, string, string along, snow, snow job, cold haul, cold deck, cold cock, buffalo, bamboozle, gazoozle, hocus-pocus, slip one over on, put something over, put something across, put on, put on the check, make a patsy of, make a monkey of, hold up, soak, sell one a bill of goods, sell gold bricks, goldbrick, do in, do out of, chouse, chouse out of, fake out, bust out, kiss out, psych out, outfox, fox, kid, fleece, pull the wool over one's eyes, have, humbug, hornswoggle, ice, grift, on the grift, rinkydink, score, shag, single-o, ride a pony, diddle, vamp, hook, throw the hooks into, gaff, lead one up the garden path, they're peeing on us and telling us it's raining, go South.

CHEATED adj. stung, been had, taken, been taken, taken for a bundle, taken for a ride, taken for a sleighride, took, been took, took a hosing, hosed, get hosed, aced out, jobbed, fucked, fucked over, jerked around, boned, screwed, screwed blewed and tattooed, gypped, stiffed, stuck, stuck with, get played (Af. Am.), skinned, shafted, get the shaft, dicked, gaffled, foxed, conned, disinformed, mousetrapped, strung along, set up, got it up the ass, weenie, wiener, got the short end of the stick, got the dirty end of the stick, got a raw deal, got a haircut, got trimmed, jived, shucked and jived, sandbagged, suckered, sucked in, sold, believer, sold a bill of goods, saw one coming, easy mark, bearded, fell for, took the bait, flammed, flimflammed, roped in, double-crossed, diddled, clipped, burned, fleeced, shaved, gouged, chiseled, juiced, gassed, bilked, buffaloed, hippoed, snookered, snowed, snowed under, hornswoggled, laid relaid and parlayed.

CHEATER n. 1. hustler, shark, sharp, sharpie, mechanic, faker, fake, phoney, fraud, con man, con artist, chiseler, flimflammer, flimflam man, doberman (Af. Am.), jive ass, gyp, jip, gyp artist, gypper, gypster, crook, crooked stick, bunco, bunco steerer, bunco artist, burn artist, clip artist, short-change artist, play actor, double-dealer, double-crosser, gouge, whip, stiff, smoothie, smooth apple, smooth article, smooth operator, operator, suede-shoe operator, slick operator, grifter, grafter, blackleg, bilker, diddler, two-timer, two-faced, moonlighter, fast talker, four-flusher, feather merchant, bent, shady, jackleg, horse trader, burglar, Jesse James, Honest John, sneakin' deacon, broadsman, boogerboo, shiver, S.L.O.B. (silver-lipped operator of bullshit), worm, hoser, wrong, wrong number, crust, city slicker, wolf in sheep's clothing, cheese eater, skunker, dingo, not kosher. 2. he had a pony, he used an airplane, equestrian (test cheating)

CHECK n. damper, grunt, holdup, map, rubber check (bad).

CHECK v. 1. knock off, break off, lay off, leave off, shut off, close off, choke, choke off, cut off, cut the shit, cut the crap, cut it out, kick over, call it quits, freeze, box in, get one in a box, bring to a screaming halt, come to a screaming halt, come to a grinding halt, come to a shuddering halt, hold the horses, cool it, can it, turn it off, come off it, let up, break it up, cramp one's style, cut off one's water, turn off one's water, shut out, shut down, close out, peter out, tune out, want out, stonewall, stall, fix one's wagon, take the air out of the ball, saddle with, weigh down, hang like a millstone round one's neck. See also STOP. 2. check out, check it out, double O, O.O., case, frisk, look-see, read, candle, scout it out, squack. See also ASCERTAIN. 3. play for time, conk out, die. See also DELAY.

CHECK, BAD n. rubber check, scrip, stiff (also forged), bad paper; bouncer, check bouncer, kiter (writer), pusher.

CHECKBOOK n. damper pad.

CHECKERED adj. checkeroo.

CHEEKS n. choppers.

CHEER v. 1. buck up, pick up, brace up, chirk up, perk up, give a lift, put one on top of the world, put one on cloud nine, snap out of it, let the sunshine in. See also ENLIVEN. 2. hear it for, sound off for, root for, plug. See ENCOURAGE. 3. bring down the house, have 'em on their feet.

CHEERFUL adj. chipper, chirpy, corky, perky, high, sunny, sunny-side up, up, upbeat, upper, jazzed, joygerm fever, little merry Sunshine, little Mary Sunshine, grooving, peppy, zippy, zingy, zappy, snappy, rosy, looking at the world with rose-colored glasses, looking at (something) through rose-colored glasses, go-go, bouncy, jumping, rocking, swinging, swingle, juiced up full, glad-hander (overly), high, high on something. See also HAPPY.

CHEERLESS adj. draggy, mopey, blue, ass in a sling, down in the mouth, in the dumps. See UNHAPPY.

CHEF n. cookie, hasher, hash slinger, belly robber, belly burger, biscuit roller, builder, stew builder, grub chocker, grease pot, pot slinger, sizzler, jeppo, ninety-nine, boiler (logger). See also BAKER.

CHEMICAL MIXTURE n. soup.

CHEMICAL RESIDUE n. soup.

CHEMICAL SPRAY n. yellow rain (war).

CHEMISE n. shimmy.

CHERRY PIE n. George Washington pie.

CHERRY SODA n. maiden's delight.

CHESS PLAYER n. woodpusher (lacks skill).

CHEST n. brisket.

CHEVROLET n. Chev, Chevie.

CHEW v. chaw, chomp, munch, gum, fling a fang into, trape (chew gum loudly).

CHEYENNE, WYOMING Rodeo Town.

CHIC adj. sharp, dap, clean, last word, latest thing, spinach, natty. See STYLISH.

CHICAGO, ILLINOIS Chi, Second City, Windy City, Wind City, Big Wind, Big Windy, Chi Town, Big C, Cattle Town, Toddlin' Town, the Village, the Loop.

CHICAGO RESIDENT n. Chicagoan, Chicagorilla, hog, South Sider, North Sider, West Sider, gangster.

CHICANERY n. hanky-panky, monkey business, song and dance, run-around, dirty pool, whitewash job. See TRICK.

CHICKEN n. biddy, banty, buzzard, chick, chicky, chickadee, chickabiddy, gull, gump, seagull, albatross (WWII), bird, pigeon, yard-bird (fried, prison).

CHICKEN PARTS n. part that goes over the fence last, pope's nose, pup's nose (So.), parson's nose (tail); white meat, dark meat.

CHICKEN SOUP n. Jewish penicillin, doodle soup (with noodles, So.).

CHIDE v. call on the carpet, take down, take down a peg, rap one's knuckles, slap on the wrist, speak to, talk to. See REBUKE.

CHIEF n. key player, head honcho, head man, top brass, big shit, big weenie, big gun, big wheel. See EXECUTIVE.

CHILD n. kid, little kid, seed, half-pint, crumb crusher, shaver, little shaver, squirt, little squirt, little guy, little bugger, little dickens, little darling, little angel, little doll, yupster, juvenile delinquent, JD, punk, punk kid, snotnose kid, kiddo, pup, puppy, cub, sonny, sonny boy, bud, buddy, bub, bubba, drape ape (Stu.), house ape, rug ape, rug rat, young chit, sprout, bambino, nipper, small fry, young fry, tad, tadpole, chip off the ole block, ankle biter, kinch, kinchen, latchkey child, boomerang (adult who returns to live with parents). See also BOY; GIRL.

CHILDBIRTH n. blessed event, producing, visit from the stork, drop one.

CHILDISH adj. kid stuff, Mickey Mouse.

CHILD MOLESTER n. short, short eyes, chicken hawk, cho-mo, Chester the Molester, diddler, pamper pirate, pamper sniffer.

CHILD PRODIGY n. boy wonder, natural, whiz kid, quiz kid, brain.

CHILDREN n. seed, crumb crushers, crumb snatchers, mice, small fry, young fry, offspring, get (animal), skotey (spoiled kid of the eighties), rug rats, boomerang kid (returns home to live).

CHILD TENDER n. sitter, baby sitter, nanny.

CHILI CON CARNE n. bowl of red.

CHILLS n. the shakes, the shivers.

CHILLY adj. 1. snappy, creeps, cold creeps, coolth, two-dog night, icebox (place). 2. cool, frost one, frosty, cold tit, arctic, tight-assed, butter wouldn't melt in his mouth. See COLD.

CHIMERA n. fool's paradise, pipe dream.

CHIMPANZEE n. chimp.

CHIN n. button, on the button, point, China chin, glass chin, glass jaw (easily knocked out).

CHINA n. bamboo curtain, Red China.

CHINESE n. Chinaman, Chink, chink, Chinky, Chinx, Chinee, chino, chow, chow-chow, chopsticks, fortune cookie (Fem.), ding, almond eyes, flange head (WWII), Buddha head, pigtail, John, monk, pong, rice belly, riceman, slant, slanthead, slant eyes, slope, coosie, yellow peril, yellow fish (all Derog.).

CHINESE DINNER n. Chinks, Chinx, eat at Chinx (Derog.).

CHINESE IDEOLOGICAL DIVISION n. Bamboo Curtain.

CHINESE RESTAURANT n. Chinks, Chinx (Derog.), chop suey joint.

CHIP v. whack, hack.

CHIPPED BEEF ON TOAST n. shit on a shingle.

CHIPS n. barber pole (stacked by color), buy in, checks; blacks ($100), greens, quarters ($25); reds, nickel ($5); stack (20), bingle (single).

CHIROPRACTOR n. bonecracker.

CHITTERLINGS n. chit'lins, soul food.

CHLORAL HYDRATE n. knockout drops, Mickey, Mickey Finn, Lipton tea, little Michael.

CHOCOLATE n. choc.

CHOCOLATE LOVER n. chocoholic.

CHOCOLATE PUDDING n. ant paste.

CHOICE adj. A-one, ten, aces, bitchin', twitchin', stone, terrible, top drawer, bump'n, solid gold, daddy, winner. See EXCELLENT.

CHOICE n. bag, cup of tea, druthers, go down the line, flash groove, turned on to, weakness for, say-so, take it or leave it, other side of the coin, other fish to fry, other fish in the sea, other pebbles on the beach.

CHOKE v. yoke.

CHOLERIC adj. bent out of shape, go ballistic, lose it, hot under the collar, blow one's cool, ranting and raving, red-assed, hacked, steamed, ticked off. See ANGRY.

CHOOSE v. opt, name, slot, tab, tag, tap, finger, creaming (selecting the best), go down the line, fish or cut bait. See SELECT.

CHOOSY adj. picky, picky-picky, choicy, pernickety, persnickety, fussy. See also PARTICULAR.

CHOP v. whack, hack.

CHOPPED MEAT n. burger, beefburger, cheeseburger, Big Mac, big boy, hamburg, superburger, Wimpy, Salisbury steak, ground round, chewed fine, clean up the kitchen (order for hamburger, hash or stew).

CHORAL MUSIC, n. sing, sing-in, folk sing, hootenanny.

CHORE n. grind, workout, bone breaker, ball-breaker, ball racker, ball-buster, conk buster, fun and games, funsey, funsies, scud, scut, scutwork, shitwork, KP (Army), chickwork (household). See also WORK.

CHOREOGRAPHER n. terper.

CHORUS GIRL n. hoofer, gypsy, in the line, pony, chorine. See DANCER.

CHOSEN adj. get the nod, tabbed, pegged, called.

CHRONIC FATIGUE SYNDROME n. CFS, Iceland disease, Royal Free disease, yuppie flu.

CHRYSANTHEMUM n. mum.

CHUBBY adj. fatty, hefty, chunky, husky, big, full-figured, ample, pleasingly plump, zaftig, roly-poly, tubby, butterball, chubbo, Bertha, candidate for pigginess. See FAT.

CHUCKHOLE n. chughole, pothole, bump.

CHURCH n. dirge factory, god box, amen corner.

CHURLISH adj. snippy, bitchy, stanky (woman), bad-assed, bad-ass, cantankerous, cussed, grouchy, grumpy, mean, ornery, tetchy, ugly. See IRRITABLE.

CIA n. Company, the Agency, Langley. See CENTRAL INTELLIGENCE AGENCY.

CIGAR n. seegar, stogie, Havana, rope, el ropo, boxfire, broom, gage, gagger, heater, hemp, the hemp, jitney, punk, stinker, torch, weed, Guinea, twofer (cheap).

CIGAR BUTT n. curbstone cigar, old soldier, snipe.

CIGARETTE n. butt, burn, cig, ciggie, ret, heater, smoke, tube, kings, Q.B. (quick butt), ready-made, tailor-made, slim, straight, nail, coffin nail, skag (Mil.), fag, faggot, maggot, bonfire, boxfire, brain tablet, stick, cancer stick, chalk, commo (prison), deck, deck of butts (package), duck, fire, lung duster, quirley (cowboy), square, roll yer own, weed, snipe, gage, gasper, hump (Camel), pill, slow burners, fast burners (stale), root, cigaroot, drag, spark, ready roll; dope stick, pimp stick, punk, reefer, joint, rope joint, box (carton).

CIGARETTE BUTT n. roach, snipe, corpse, clipper, clincher, dincher, grounder, hopper, lip burner, bonfire, maggot, old soldier.

CIGARETTE LIGHTER n. light (also act of lighting cigarette), zippo, cricket.

CIGARETTE PAPER n. blanket, joint staff, the makings (includes tobacco), tube.

CINCH adj. snap, no sweat, no problem, no biggie, pushover, picnic, biscuit, cinchy, slam dunk, soft, doable, cake, cakewalk, sleepwalk, walk, walkover, easy as pie. See EASY.

CINCINNATI, OHIO Cincy, Queen City, Death Valley (U.).

CINEMA n. 1. the movies, silver screen, big screen, pictures, show, picture show, flicks, bijou, nabes. 2. movie theater, drive-in, ozoner (drive-in), skin house, adult movies, porn house, porn palace, local fleabag, bughouse (cheap), grindhouse, quadriplex, sixplex. See MOTION PICTURE THEATER.

CINNAMON ROLL n. snail, Danish.

CIPHER n. 1. squat, diddly-squat, zip, zippo, zip city, goose egg, zot, zilch. 2. empty suit, wimp, zero, dunnage (dockworker use), nebbish, pipsqueak, squirt, shrimp, punk, nobody. See NOTHING.

CIRCLE n. bunch, click, crew, crowd, crush, gang, insiders, mob, outfit, Old Boy network, ring. See also ASSOCIATION.

CIRCLE THE EARTH v. orbit.

CIRCUITOUS adj. go round the barn, went by way of, long way, long way home.

CIRCULAR n. handout, handbill, broadside, flyer, insert, literature, throwaway, zap art (for a cause).

CIRCUMCISION n. putzilectomy, cut.

CIRCUMSCRIBE v. nail it down, call a spade a spade.

CIRCUMSPECT adj. cagey, play safe, watch one's step, handle with kid gloves. See CAUTIOUS.

CIRCUMSTANCE n. action, hap, happenin', happenso, situash, scene, like it is, where it's at. See CONDITION. See also EVENT.

CIRCUMVENT v. get around, queer, crimp, cramp, stymie, stump. See PREVENT.

CIRCUS n. big top, gilly (small), three-ring.

CIRCUS TERMS big top, big rag, Clown Alley, come-in (waiting crowd), cut cake (short change); Clem, hey Rube (call for help, fight, riot, small town resident), dead cat (lion, tiger, etc., that does not perform), front door (administration), backyard (performers), geek (freak act), with it (circus help), cooch (dancer), gaffer (manager), grifter (sideshow concessionaire), barker, grind show, strike it (pull up stakes).

CITATION n. quote, saying, ticket (traffic).

CITE v. get down to cases, get down to brass tacks, spell out, reference.

CITIZEN n. cit, John Q., John Q. Public, Yank, Yankee.

CITY n. urb, burg, apple, Big Town, Big Time, boomer, boom town, dump, slab, two-stemmer, tough town, wide-open joint, right tank, wrong tank.

CITY DISTRICTS n. barrio, Bowery, Chinatown, hell's half acre, hell's kitchen, tartown, shantytown, Japantown, Koreatown, Little Italy, black belt, niggertown (Derog.), wrong side of the tracks, other side of the tracks, red-light district, skid road, skid row, inner city, tenderloin, high-rent district, gold coast, mainline, mainstreet, downtown.

CITY DWELLER n. city slicker, cliff dweller, cave dweller, subway rider, strap hanger, street people, Broadway baby, townee, towner.

CIVIL AERONAUTICS ADMINISTRATION n. CAA.

CIVIL AIR PATROL n. CAP.

CIVIL SERVANT n. paper shuffler, buck passer, apparatchik, cee gee.

CIVILIAN n. feather merchant (WWII), civ, civvie.

CIVILIAN CONSERVATION CORPS n. C.C.C., peavie.

CIVILIAN DRESS n. cits, civvies, mufti, plain clothes, street clothes.

CLAIM v. hit, hit up, hold out for, knock, pop the question, whistle for (but won't get), dibs on something.

CLAIRVOYANCE n. sixth sense, ESP.

CLAIRVOYANT n. mitt reader.

CLAMOR n. hubba-hubba, buzz-buzz, hoo-ha, clinker, rowdydow, ruckus, hullabaloo.

CLAMOR v. howl, put up a howl, put up a squawk, holler, raise Cain, raise sand. See COMPLAIN.

CLAMOROUS adj. jumping, yakky, ear-popping. See also NOISY.

CLAN n. folks, home folks, kinfolks, insiders, bunch, click, crew, crowd, crush, gang, mob, outfit, ring. See also ASSOCIATION.

CLANDESTINE adj. under wraps, undercover, hush-hush, tref, treff, triff, creep (mission), skunk works (secret manufacturing plant or laboratory, originally Lockheed). See SECRET.

CLANDESTINELY adv. on the Q.T., on the quiet, on the sly, undercover, under wraps, hush-hush, strictly hush-hush, in a hole-and-corner way, in holes and corners.

CLAP v. give a hand, give a big hand, hear it for, beat one's skins.

CLAPTRAP n. bafflegab, gobbledygook, poppycock, bosh, bunk, tommyrot, baloney, narrishkeit. See NONSENSE.

CLAQUE n. groupie, buff, fan, frenzie, rooter. See DEVOTEE. See also SUPPORTER.

CLARIFY v. spell out, draw one a picture, paint a picture, make perfectly clear, give a for-instance. See EXPLAIN.

CLARINET n. licorice stick, black stick, stick, gob stick, wop stick (Derog.), agony pipe.

CLASH n. mix-up, jam, run-in, have a go at each other, brawl, pluggin', scruff-up, Donnybrook, jump. See FIGHT.

CLASH v. bang heads, buck, brawl, row, mix it up, raise sand. See FIGHT.

CLASP v. grab, grab ass, squeeze, clinch, clutch, bear hug, glom onto. See also GRAB.

CLASS adj. classy, touch of class, chic; tourist (cheap).

CLASS n. pecking order, place, slot, likes, likes of, lot, number, lot number, down the line, the right stuff, the right people.

CLASS DISTINCTION n. pecking order, place, slot.

CLASSICAL adj. long-hair, long-haired.

CLASSICAL MUSIC n. long-hair, long-haired, long underwear.

CLASSIFIED adj. hush-hush, under one's hat, under wraps, family jewels (Govt., CIA), wildcat (plan). See SECRET.

CLASSIFY v. button down, peg, pigeonhole, put one in a box, put away, put down as, put down for, rank out, size up, take one's measure, typecast, tab.

CLAUSE n. catch, joker, kicker, string, a string to it, a string attached to it, fine print, small print, fine print at the bottom, small fine print at the bottom.

CLAUSTROPHOBIA n. stir crazy, stir daffy, stir simple, stir bugs, cabin fever.

CLEAN adj. apple-pie, apple-pie order, neat as a button, neat as a pin, Bonnie Brillo (neat person), slick, squeaky-clean, vanilla.

CLEAN v. straighten up, police, police up, police the area, spruce up, crumb up, pick up, side up the table (clear), get one's shit together, once over, once over lightly, dobie, doby (by hand), button chop, soogie, sujee, soogie-moogie, sujee mujee, swab, swab down, (N. and maritime), do the dishes, G, G party, clamp down (N.), garbage collecting, G.C., bus (Rest.); launder, wash, smurfing (money, title), white money (laundered). See also TIDY.

CLEAR adj. open-and-shut, clear-cut, crystal-clear, spelled out plain as the nose on one's face, barefaced. See APPARENT.

CLEAR v. let off, let one off the hook, let go, defog. See ABSOLVE.

CLEARED adj. beat the rap, walked, let off, let go, clemo, off the hook.

CLEARHEADED adj. sharp, all there, glued (antonym: unglued), together, got one's act together, got one's head together, got one's shit together, with it. See REASONABLE.

CLEAVE v. 1. whack, hack. 2. freeze to, stay put, stick like a barnacle. See ADHERE.

CLEMENCY n. spring, clemo, lifesaver.

CLERGYMAN n. padre, the rev, reverend, Holy Joe, sky pilot, sky scout, sky merchant, Bible beater, Bible basher, Bible puncher, Bible thumper, bish, abbey, black coat, buck, deac, devil dodger, devil driver, preacher man, fire proofer, fire escape, fire insurance agent, gospel ghee, gospel pusher, salvation rancher, harp polisher, long-haired boy, right buck, sin hound, turn-around collar, glory roader.

CLERICAL WORKER n. white collar, pink collar, bright collar (intelligent, well-educated, young), desk jockey, pencil pusher, pencil shover, pen driver, pen pusher, paper pusher, paper shuffler, company monkey (Army). See also SECRETARY.

CLEVELAND, OHIO Dirty City, Iron Town, Yap Town.

CLEVER adj. savvy, slick, fly, crack, crackerjack, brain, brainy, egghead, got the smarts, have a head on one's shoulders, have one's head screwed on right, have savvy, have the smarts, nobody's fool, no dummy, no dumbbell, not born yesterday, not so dumb, on the ball, sharp, sharp as a tack, tack, smart as a whip, got it up here, quick on the trigger, quick on the uptake, cute, hot tamale, neat, nifty, quick, foxy, crazy like a fox, phenom, pro, there, whiz-bang, whiz kid, wizard, with it, boss player, enough ducks in a row, hot, hotshot, know-how, know one's onions, know one's stuff. See also SKILLED, INTELLIGENT, SHREWD.

CLICHÉ n. buzzword, boiler plate, corn, familiar tune, high camp, chestnut, old chestnut, saw, old saw, old song, old story, played-out, potboiler.

CLIENT n. believer, pigeon, sucker, live one, mark, chump, easy make, float, front, head, walk-in.

CLIMAX n. blowoff, payoff, capper, topper, ape, bitter end, far-out, critical mass (dramatic).

CLIMAX (SEXUAL) v. come, cum, blow, spew, spooch, splooge, go off, get off, get off one's rocks, shoot, shoot one's load, haul one's ashes, cream one's jeans, get over the mountain, have one's ticket punched, ring one's bell, ring one's chimes (Fem.). See SEXUAL CLIMAX.

CLIMB v. ape up.

CLING v. hang on to, hang in, freeze to, cling like a burr, cling like ivy, hold on like a bulldog, stay put, stick like glue, stick like a barnacle, stick like a leech, stick like a limpet, stick like a wet shirt.

CLINIC n. bone factory, butcher shop, pogey (prison), alley (corridor).

CLIQUE n. insiders, bunch, click, circle, crew, crowd, crush, gang, mob, outfit, Old Boy network, ring. See also DEVOTEE.

CLIQUISH adj. high-hat, uppity. See also SNOBBISH.

CLITORIS n. clit, clitty, button, little man in the boat, spare tongue (Obsc.).

CLOCK n. tick-tock, chronicker, tattler, ticker, turnip, timepiece, Big Ben.

CLONE n. pod.

CLOSE adj. 1. tight, skinflint, pinch-fist, chintzy, skimpy, stingy, Scotch. See STINGY. 2. cozy with, tight with, just like this (fingers intertwined), making it with, thick, thick as thieves, chummy, buddy-buddy, pally, palsy, palsy-walsy, in bed with, roommates, sleepin' together, kissin' cousins, trade spit, swap spit. 3. warm, in spitting distance, in the ball park, give or take a little, slicing it thin. See NEAR. 4. clam, clam up, hush-hush, on the q.t., zip one's lips, mum's the word, button up, button up one's lip, between one and the lamppost, tight chops. 5. close shave, slicing it thin, near miss, right apartment house wrong apartment, close but no cigar (miss). See also NEARLY.

CLOSE n. wrap, wind-up, signoff, swan song, el foldo, that's all folks. See END.

CLOSE v. 1. wrap up, wrap a joint up, fold, fold a joint, fold up, close down, shut down, wind down, ring down, drop the curtain, shutter, slough a joint, put a lid on, cap, tape, call off, call all bets off, cut loose. 2. clinch, clinch the deal,

done deal, button down, button up, sew up. See CONSUMMATE. 3. go the route, put to bed, call it a day, clear, down to the short strokes, pack it in. See FINISH.

CLOSED adj. dark (The., sports), gone fishing.

CLOSELY adv. by the skin of one's teeth, stuck to one like glue, fit like wallpaper, any closer he'd be on the other side, the jeans look like they were painted on.

CLOSEMOUTHED adj. clam-up, clammed-up, dried-up, dummied-up, hush-hush, on the q.t., zip one's lips, button up, button up one's lip, between one and the lamppost, tight chops, tight-lipped, garbo.

CLOT v. glop up, clabber, lopper.

CLOTHE v. drape, dud, tog, fit out, deck, deck out, dog out, rag out, rag up, rig out, rig up, turn out, doll up, dude up, dode (bad fit), suit up.

CLOTHED adj. togged, decked out, rigged out, gussied-up, all dolled up, in fine feather, in one's best bib and tucker, in one's Sunday best, dressed fit to kill, dressed to the nines. See DRESSED.

CLOTHES n. threads, togs, duds, gear, glad rags, Barbie and Ken (conventional), California chic (expensive casual), vines, schmotte, drapes, drag, hand-me-downs, Sunday go-to-meetin' clothes. See CLOTHING.

CLOTHES HORSE n. Captain Hipness, Beau Brummell, fashion plate.

CLOTHING n. threads, set of threads, togs, toggery, duds, outfit, rags, glad rags, gutter wear, getup, get-out, turnout, feathers, fine feather, full feather, Barbie and Ken (conventional), vine, weeds, silks, flute, dry goods, schmotte (Yid), sack, tents, granny dress, duster, frame, front, fronts, flash, frock, sock frock, rig, gray flannel, pantsuit, jumpsuit, sweats, skinsuits, triathard, preps, grubbies, grubbers, micro, mini, miniskirt, midi, maxi, maxicoat, maxidress, wraparound, pallazzios, honking brown (flashy), California black tie (any colorful variation of formal wear), California chic (expensive casual), basic black, fofarraw, foofooraw, Christmas (ostentatious), ready-made, tailor-made, civvies, cits, mufti, fatigues, Port Arthur tuxedo, khakis, dress blues, whites, drape, drapery, drapes, set of drapes, draped-down (wearing gold), drape shape, drape shape with a reet pleat, zoot suit, zoot suit with a reet pleat, cool suit with a loop droop, Nehru jacket, Nehru suit, clobber, harness (leather, especially motorcycle), bomber jacket, drag, boondock (outdoor), racket jacket, Sunday clothes, Sunday suit, Sunday best, Sunday go-to-meeting, bib and tucker, best bib and tucker, secondhand, handout, hand-me-downs, reach-me-downs, bull's wool (stolen), felon sneakers, harem pants, hot pants, pedal pushers, hip huggers, see-through blouse, tie-dyes, knee-hi's, legwarmers, bobbysox, Mary Janes, Buster Browns, white ducks, Dr. Dentons.

CLOTHING INDUSTRY n. rag trade, rag business, schmotte business, garmento (buyer, jobber).

CLOTHING STORE n. toggery.

CLOTTED adj. clabbered, loppered, glopped-up.

CLOUD n. ol' buttermilk sky, ground clouds.

CLOWN n. 1. Bozo, Joey, paleface, whiteface. 2. cutup, gagman, gagster, jokesmith, madcap, wisecracker, life of the party. See also JOKER.

CLOYING adj. sticky, gooey, sappy, sloppy, schmaltzy, mushy, gushy, gushing, teary, beery, namby-pamby. See SENTIMENTAL.

CLUB n. 1. billy, billy club, blackjack, sap, sapstick, stick, nightstick, rosewood, business, cosh, conk buster, conk crusher, convincer, duffy silencer, mace, persuader, rosh, works, shill. 2. hangout, stamping ground, bottle club, henhouse (WWII officer). See also NIGHTCLUB. 3. crew, gang, ring, mob, bunch, outfit. See ASSOCIATION. 4. wood, iron (golf).

CLUBHOUSE n. hangout, stamping ground, the nineteenth hole.

CLUE n. lead, hot lead, tip-off, telltale, dead giveaway, print, bum steer (false).

CLUMP n. blob, chunk, hunk.

CLUMSY adj. klutz, klutzy, doyburger, dingleberry, bagger, one-bagger, a newt, clunker, clunky, bogus, dub, jerk, jerky, flub-dub, amateur, amateur night in Dixie, all thumbs, butterfingers, half-assed, ham-fisted, ham-handed, two left hands, two left feet, lead-footed, stumblebum, clodhopper, galoot, goaty (Army), goofball, garbage, garbage time, not cut out for, walrus, bo.

CLUSTER n. blob, chunk, hunk.

CLUSTER v. bunch up, crowd around, gang around.

CLUTCH v. grab, collar, hook, glom, glaum, glom onto, put the snare on, snatch, snag. See GRAB. See also HOLD.

COACH n. old man, skipper.

COACH v. ready, toot, lick into shape, hone, break, break in, put through the grind, put through the mill, pull one's coat, lay it out for. See also ADVISE.

COAGULATE v. glop up, clabber, lopper.

COAL n. black diamonds, diamonds, estate, real estate.

COALESCE v. join up with, hook up with, tie in with, join together, come together.

COALITION n. hookup, tie up, affil. See ASSOCIATION.

COARSE adj. cheap, raw, raunchy, blue, dirty, lowdown and dirty, filthy, off-color, rough, foulmouthed, loudmouthed. See OBSCENE.

COAST v. smooth along, skate.

COAST GUARD n. hooligan navy, freshwater navy, coasties, SPARS (Women's Auxiliary).

COAST GUARDSMAN n. bungalow sailor.

COAT n. threads, flogger, peacoat, greatcoat, broad (jive, 1935).

COAX v. arm-twist, work on, jawbone, come on, con, hook, rope in. See PERSUADE.

COAXIAL CABLE n. co-ax, main line.

COBALT THERAPY n. deep fry.

COCA-COLA n. Coke, dope, fuzz-fuzz, drag one through Georgia (chocolate), frown (lemon), maiden's delight (cherry), freak (not common).

COCAINE n. C, Cee, sea, coke, cokey, candy, nose candy, crack, rocks (hard), eight-track (2.5 grams), sugar, snow, cloud walk, snowball, speedball (plus morphine or heroin), snowbird, white, white cross, white mosquitoes, white Christmas, old lady white, white girl, white stuff, Doctor White, sleighride, toot, toots, Charlie, Cecil, Connie, Corinne, Bernice, Pearl, girl, girlfriend, her, lady, uptown, angel, angie, Bernies, Burnese, Burese, crank, blow, blower, blow in the snow, little Joe in the snow, snowcaine, snow stuff, cane, candycane, blast, bullet, coca, croak (plus speed), evil, jolt, bazooka, icicles, star stuff, supercharge, rails, rock candy, snort, sneeze, jimbo soda, moon rock, gin, jam, flake, joy flakes, joy powder, gold dust, happy dust, heaven dust, pimp dust, pogo-pogo, pony, tootonium, tootuncommon, Peruvian, reindeer dust, cookie, leaf, trey, wings, bloke, big bloke, live (sniffed), whiff, balloon (bag), Cadillac (ounce), row, line (dose).

COCAINE ADDICT n. cokehead, base head, Charlie, on the pipe (freebasing), piper (crack smoker), snifter, snow snifter, snowbird, snow snorter, jammer, tooter.

COCAINE AND HEROIN n. C and H, cold and hot, speedball (also cocaine and morphine), dynamite, parachute, whizbang.

COCAINE CARRIER n. mule, body packing.

COCAINE SELLING v. slangin' 'caine, bartender (seller).

COCAINE USE v. sleigh ride, boola, line, do lines, go down the line, sniff, snort, blow, toot, beaming up, blasted, jam; wired for sound, pack a nose sweep, sweep with both barrels, ski trip, jam; jam house, rock house, stash house, snow shed, cokeland (source); hit, row (single dose), geek out (seek crumbs of cocaine).

COCAINE USER n. cokie, cokehead, crackhead, base head, piper (crack smoker), jammer, snowbird, snow snorter, snow snifter, snifter, sniffer, snooter, toothead, tooter, horner (tender nose), on the pipe (freebasing), pinned (high), high beams on (high), coke bugs (hallucination).

COCKPIT n. cab, greenhouse, hut, pulpit, office.

COCKSURE adj. hotdogger, hotshot, smart-ass, wise-ass, wise-guy, smart-guy, smart-aleck, smarty, smarty-pants, know-it-all. See SURE. See also CERTAIN, ARROGANT.

COCKTAIL INGREDIENTS n. garbage (olive, cherry, etc.), mixer, setups.

COCKTAIL LOUNGE n. juice joint, ginmill, spot, office, gargle factory, meat market (singles bar), taproom, fill-mill. See BAR.

COCKY adj. hotdogger, hotshot, snotnose, smart-ass, wise-ass, wise-guy, smart-guy, smart-aleck, smarty, smarty-pants, know-it-all. See SURE. See also CERTAIN, ARROGANT.

CODDLED adj. spoiled, spoiled rotten, played up to, made much over, stroked.

CODEINE n. schoolboy.

CODFISH n. Cape Cod turkey, sleeve buttons, Hollywood stew (creamed).

COERCE v. lean on, twist one's arm, hold one's feet to the fire, strong-arm, pull rank, put the squeeze on, high-pressure, make one an offer one can't refuse. See FORCE.

COERCION n. arm, strong arm, strong-arm tactics, bulldozing, steamroller, beef, clout, punch, kick, sock, pressure, high pressure, squeeze, chill, heat, gaff, gueril, mugg, nuts, shake, moxie, poop, steam. See also FORCE.

COFFEE n. java, decaf, cup a, mocha, moke, jamoke, jo, brew (Mil.), dope, mud, unleaded (decaf), cawfee, perk, perc, Joe, draw one (Rest. order); draw one in the dark, barefoot (black); with socks on (cream), blonde and sweet (cream and sugar); slop and slugs (coffee and doughnuts), coffee and (doughnut, Danish, cake), forty-four, forty-weight, hot stuff, cowboy coffee, road tar (truck stop), alkali, battery acid, fluid, embalming fluid, paint remover, varnish remover, belly wash, mouthwash, blackout, black strap, ink, bootleg, flit, smoke, black soup, black water, Brazil water; dishwater, blanko water (WWII), bilge water, stump water, driddle water (weak); Norwegian, creek bank, sawmill, shanty, sheepherder's 100-mile coffee (strong), laced (with liquor), travelin', to go (outgoing order), with a splash (dark).

COFFEE CAKE n. bear claw, Danish, snail, coffee and.

COFFIN n. box, cold meat box, bone box, crate, Chicago overcoat, pine overcoat, wood overcoat, wooden overcoat, wooden coat, wooden kimono, wooden suit, pine drape, pine pajamas, bird's-eye maple pajamas, tree suit, pinto.

COGITATE v. flash on, kick around, brainstorm, head trip, noodle it around, stew over, crunch, figger, chew the cud. See THINK.

COGNITIVE adj. hip, hip to the jive, hep, hep to, tuned-in, plugged-in, fly, with it, chilly, on the beam, grounded. See AWARE.

COGNIZANT adj. got, hipped, hip to, hep to, on to, wise to, in the know, in the picture, tuned in, plugged-in, fly, up on, been there, savvy, on the beam, wake up and smell the coffee. See AWARE. See also KNOWLEDGEABLE.

COGNOMEN n. handle, handle to one's name, brand, front name, label, moniker, monicker, tab, tag, flag (assumed), John Doe, John Hancock, John Henry.

COHABITERS n. apartmates, convivants, mingles, roomies, live-ins, LTR.

COHORT n. stall. See ACCOMPLICE.

COIFFURE n. 1. women's: do, hairdo, blow-dry, 2. men's: trim, cut, razor cut, fuzz cut, cueball (just had a haircut). See HAIR STYLE.

COIN n. change, small change, silver, chickenfeed, meter money. See also CASH.

COIN v. dream up, make up, think up, trump up, spark, spitball, brainstorm, head trip, take it off the top of one's head. See CREATE.

COINCIDE v. sync, sync up, lip sync.

COINCIDENCE n. coinkidink.

COIN PURSE n. jitney bag.

COITUS n. fuck, screw, lay, hump, boff, bang, jazz, shag, action, balling, roll in the hay, jump in the sack, lay pipe, dirty deed, bed and breakfast, fooling around (all Obsc.). See SEXUAL INTERCOURSE.

COLD adj. snappy, arctic, bitter, have duck bumps, have goose bumps, have party hats (goose bumps), lay chilly, creeps, cold creeps, coolth, colder 'n a witch's tit, colder than a frozen fish's asshole, colder than a well digger's ass, freeze one's ass off, cold enough to freeze the balls off a brass monkey, freeze one's tits off, freeze one's balls off, one-dog night, two-dog night, three-dog night, icebox (place). 2. frosty, arctic, tight-assed, cold tit, butter wouldn't melt in his mouth, ice water in one's veins, cool, frost one, fish-eyed.

COLD n. sniffles, snuffles, common cold.

COLD CUTS n. delicatessen, deli, sandwich fixings, horse cock.

COLDHEARTED adj. cold, cold fish, iceman, mean machine, got lead balls for eyes. See CALLOUS.

COLLABORATE v. team up, team up with, tie in, tie in with, tie up with, throw in together, throw in with, go partners with, go in partners with, be in cahoots with, go in cahoots with, truck with, get together, come together, join together, join up with, hook up, hook on, hook up with, get in bed with, interface, interface with, be hand in glove with, do business with, glue oneself to.

COLLABORATOR n. team player, running dog, fellow traveler, quisling (Pol.). See also WRITER.

COLLAPSE n. crackup, breakdown, conk out, basket case, meltdown.

COLLAPSE v. break down, break up, melt down, belly up, crack up, fold, fold up, cave in, conk out, give out, drop, fall apart, come apart at the seams, go to pieces.

COLLAPSIBLE adj. breakaway (The.).

COLLAR n. choker, dog collar (priest), horse collar (protective).

COLLECT v. round up, get hold of, scare up, corral, dig up, pass the hat, put down (wine), moonlight requisition. See also ASSEMBLE.

COLLECTED adj. cool, cool as a cucumber, keep one's cool, keep one's shirt on, not turn a hair, unflappable. See CALM.

COLLECTIVE n. family, co-op.

COLLECTOR n. nut, buff, freak, bag man (gangster), skip tracer (loan). See also DEVOTEE.

COLLEGE n. alma mater, brainery, old Siwash, halls of ivy, aggie, cow college, East Jesus State (small), fem sem, kindergarten. See UNIVERSITY.

COLLEGE COURSE, EASY n. breeze, snap, piece of cake, crip course, crib course, Sandbox 101, skate, slide.

COLLEGE GRADES n. A: ace, smoke, blitz, kick butt. B: B-out. C: hook. D: donut, dog. F: bomb, blow, punch-out, wave.

COLLEGIATE adj. rah-rah.

COLLIDE v. crash, crunch, nerf, jolt, crack up, pile up, rack up, smash up, smash into, bang into, plow into, sideswipe, fender-bend, fender-tag.

COLLISION n. smash-up, smash, crash, crunch, shunt, sideswipe, pileup, rack-up, wrack-up, crack-up, stack-up head-on, bumper-thumper, rear ender, fenderbender, fender tag, a tuckis full of fenders.

COLLOQUIALISM n. jive, jive talk, street talk, lingo, weasel words, flash (thieves).

COLLOQUY n. confab, groupthink, rap, rap session, buzz session, clambake, flap (urgent), gam, huddle, powwow, think-in, chinfest, talkfest, talkee-talkee. See also TALK.

COLLUDE v. finagle, frame, buy off, cook up, put in a fix, be in cahoots with, work hand in glove with. See SCHEME.

COLLUSION n. con, con game, short con, big con, sting, bunco, bunko, flam, flimflam, gyp, gip, jip, scam, racket, RICO (racketeering), dodge, all hat and no cattle (Texas), royal fucking, royal screwing, bait and switch, fast shuffle, double shuffle, double banker, double-cross, shell game, skin game, the old army game, bill of goods, bitch, skunk, whitewash, diddling, graft, grift. See also SCHEME.

COLOGNE n. smell well.

COLOR v. cook, cook up, doctor, fudge, hoke up.

COLORADO Centennial State.

COLORFUL adj. flaky, jazzy, glamorous.

COLOSSAL adj. humongous, humongoid, humungous, humongo, mungo, monstro, honking, super, superduper, supercolossal, bonzai, jumbo, blimp, butt-kicking, barn door, a whale of a. See BIG.

COLUMBUS, OHIO Capital City, Louse Town.

COMATOSE adj. out, out cold, out to lunch, loxed-out, veged-out, dead, dead-to-the-world, gone, gone under, gorked. See UNCONSCIOUS.

COMB v. beat the bushes, leave no stone unturned, geek out (seek crumbs of cocaine), look high and low, search high heaven, turn upside down. See SEARCH.

COMBAT n. battle royal, brush, brush-off, flap, mix-up, shootout, jackpot, run-in. See FIGHT.

COMBAT v. buck, put up a fight, cross swords with, shoot it out with, go up against. See FIGHT.

COMBATANT n. 1. champ, mug, pug, lug, palooka, heavy, slugger, tiger, punching bag, cauliflower ear, dancer (coward), plug ugly. See PRIZEFIGHTER. 2. GI, GI Joe; grunt, hump, leg (infantry, Vietnam); dogface, yardbird, sad sack, buck private, buck-ass private, doughfoot, doughboy, paddlefoot, foot soldier, footslogger, snuff, jazzbo (Af. Am.), trooper, Yank, government-inspected meat (homosexual use), bullet bait, cannon fodder, bunion breeder, galoot, gravel agitator, gravel crusher (WWI), red legs artilleryman (WWI), bluebelly (Union soldier, Derog.), Fed (Union); Johnny Reb, reb (Confederate); Fritz, Jerry (German); Tommy, Tommy Atkins (English).

COMBATIVE adj. bitchy, cantankerous, cussed, ornery, scrappy, hawkish, fire-eater, trigger-happy. See BELLIGERENT.

COMBINATION n. combo (incl. safe and musical group), mishmash, mishmosh, stew, soup (liquid), lorelei, dog's breakfast (unpalatable), duke's mixture, everything but the kitchen sink. See MIXTURE.

COMBINE n. bunch, crew, crowd, gang, mob, syndicate, outfit, ring, hook-up, tie-up, tie-in tie-up, Old Boy network, plunderbund. See ASSOCIATION.

COMBINE v. 1. team up with, tie up with, throw in together, bunch up, get together, hook on. See ASSOCIATE. 2. stand in with, interface, interface with, network with, tag on, tack on, slap on, hitch on, plug into, glue oneself to. 3. cross-dissolve (film), cue in (scripts, mss., songs), dub, hook in, marry (film), mix (recording).

COMBUSTIBLE n. juice, go juice, motion lotion, motion potion, soup, synfuel (synthetic).

COME v. hit, hit town, blow in, sky in, breeze in, roll in, roll up, check in, sign in, time in, clock in, punch in, punch the clock, drop in, pop in, ring in, spring in, drag in, look what the cat dragged in, fall in, fall up, fall by, fall out, fall down, make it, make the scene, show, show up, bob up, pop up, wind up at, buzz (to announce an arrival). See ARRIVE.

COMEDIAN n. stand-up comic, stooge, banana, top banana, clown, Bozo, cutup, million laughs, wisecracker. See JOKER.

COMEDIC adj. horseplay, howl, hot one, needle, nifty, rib, rib-tickling, a million laughs, a million laffs, screaming, screamingly funny, too funny for words, too killing for words, gut-busting, side-splitting.

COMEDOWN n. flop, dive, cropper, pratfall, comeuppance, get one's comeuppance. See FAILURE.

COMEDY n. slapstick, camp, campy, high camp, low camp, baggy-pants comedy, pratfall comedy, in-one-door-and-out-another comedy, send-up, blackouts, sitcom, dromedy (dramatic comedy), afterpieces, boffo, schtick, stationhouse bits, takeoff, play-on, burlesk, burlap, burly, burlecue, burlycue, ball, action, fun and games, grins, for grins, laughs, lots of laughs, just for laughs, just for the heck of it, just for the hell of it, just for the devil of it, big time, high time, high old time, picnic, field day, whoopee, hoopla, merry-go-round. See also JOKE, AMUSEMENT.

COMELY adj. dishy, ten, 10, boss, righteous, wukka, head rush, oochie, dreamboat, whistle bait, piece, looker, stunner, living doll, gimme. See BEAUTIFUL.

COMESTIBLES n. eats, feed, grub, scoff, go juice, pecks, vittles, goodies. See FOOD.

COMFORT v. buck up, pick up, brace up, chirk up, perk up, give a lift, snap out of it, let the sunshine in. See SUPPORT.

COMFORTABLE adj. fat, fat dumb and happy, comfy, cushy, snug as a bug in a rug, can't complain, have no kick coming. See also WEALTHY.

COMIC adj. jokey, joshing, yokky, boffo, camp, campy, gagged-up, for grins, flaky, freaky, freaked-out, goofy, kooky, wacky, screwy, loony, off-the-wall, batty, cockama-

mie, cockamainie, cockeyed, cool, crazy, daffy, nutty, sappy, dippy, dizzy, goofus, gump, horse's ass, horse's collar, horse's neck, horse's tail, Mickey Mouse, nerky, jerky, do the crazy act, do the crazy bit, do the crazy shtick, tomfool, fool around, make a monkey of oneself, fool, foolheaded. See also AMUSING.

COMIC n. stand-up comic, stooge, banana, top banana, clown, Bozo, life of the party, card, a million laughs. See JOKER.

COMIC SECTION n. comics, the comics, comix, funnies, funny paper, funny papers.

COMIC STRIP n. comics, the comics, comix, funnies (also comic-strip page or section), funny paper, funny papers.

COMMAND v. head, head up, mastermind, run, run the show, deal, deal with, kick ass, kick butt, call the play, call the signals, call the shots, call the tune, take over, take her, sit on top of, sitting pretty, be in the driver's seat, be in the saddle, hold the reins, wear the pants, pull the strings, pull the wires, have the say, have the say-so, throw one's weight around, walk heavy, lay down the law, push the buttons, crack the whip, pussywhip (Fem.), conn, take the conn (Navy vessel). See also MANAGE.

COMMANDEER v. liberate, moonlight requisition, take over, grab, snatch.

COMMANDER n. CO, skipper, boss, A-number one, head, head honcho, head man, old man, point man, lead-off man, the man, boss man, boss lady, mother, main squeeze, don, mastermind, hellmaster, Mister Big, Mister Right, the brass, top brass, top, top dog, topkick, top hand, top banana, kingfish, kingpin, king, czar, exec, queen bee, guru, rishi, high priest, higher-up, cook, his nibs, digger, spark plug, avatar.

COMMANDER ATLANTIC FLEET n. CINCLANT.

COMMANDER PACIFIC FLEET n. CINCPAC.

COMMANDING adj. bossy, in charge, high-and-mighty, throw one's weight around, out of the horse's mouth, straight from the horse's mouth, on one's high horse.

COMMANDING OFFICER n. CO, CINC, CINCLANT, CINCPAC, skipper, boss, A-number one, head, head honcho, head man, old man, point man, lead-off man, the man, hellmaster, boss man, boss lady, first skirt (WACS, WAVES), mother, main squeeze, the brass, brass hat, top brass, top, top dog, top kick.

COMMAND POST n. CP.

COMMENCE v. start the ball rolling, phase in, get going, get one's feet wet, get the show on the road, get cracking, tear into, jump into, hit the ground running (in full operation). See BEGIN.

COMMENCEMENT n. opener, preem, bow, tee off, first crack out of the box, curtain-raiser, countdown, from the top, git-go, kickoff. See BEGINNING.

COMMEND v. boost, give a boost to, stroke, pat on the back, build, build up, toss a bouquet, give a bouquet, give a posy, give the man a big cigar, hand it to, have to hand it to, gold star, puff up, trade last, TL, hear it for, hats off to. See also APPROVE, ENDORSE.

COMMENDATION n. stroke, strokes, stroking, points, Brownie points, bouquet, posy, shot in the arm, plum, abreaction route, commercial, cow sociology, Dr. Spocking the help, opening up, pat on the back, pat on the head, trade last, TL, PR, puff, puffing up, pumping up, rave. See also APPROVAL.

COMMENT n. crack, backtalk, comeback, wisecrack, one's two cents' worth, input, mouthful (you said a mouthful).

COMMENTATOR n. talking head.

COMMERCIAL adj. slick, potboiler, pulp, hack.

COMMERCIAL n. plug, spot, mersh, teleblurb, pitch.

COMMINGLE v. come together, throw in together, throw in with, swing in with, mix in with, network, pool. See ASSOCIATE.

COMMISSION n. vigorish, spiff, commish, ante, bite, chunk, end, juice, piece, piece of the action, rake-off, share, skig, slice, cut, cut-in, cutup, cut a melon (profits), drag, P.M., taste. See also SHARE.

COMMISSIONED OFFICER n. top brass, the brass, five-star general, four-star general (etc.), chicken colonel, shavetail, looey, lieut, 90-day wonder.

COMMISSIONER n. commish.

COMMIT v. 1. go in for, go out for, go for broke. See ACT. 2. put away, take one away, put on ice, hold, lag.

COMMITTED adj. locked-in, set, set in concrete, bound, bound and determined, go for broke, go for it, mean business. See DETERMINED.

COMMON adj. everyday, vanilla, plastic, garden, garden variety, mainstream, low, cheap, no great shakes, loudmouthed, so-so, dime-a-dozen, run-of-the-mill, run-of-the-alley, rum-dum, starch, masscult, cottonpickin', ham and egger, hoddy-doddy, plebe, Billy Sixpack, Joe Lunchbucket, ordinary Joe, Joe Doakes, Jane Doe, John Doe, John Q. Public, John Smith, Mr. Smith, Mrs. Smith, Mrs. Brown, Mr. Brown, any Tom Dick or Harry. See also AVERAGE.

COMMON MAN n. ordinary Joe, Joe Doakes, John Q. Public, John Smith, Mr. Brown, Mr. Smith, Tom Dick and Harry, Brown Jones and Robinson, Billy Sixpack, Joe Lunchbox, the great unwashed, plebe, vox pop, boojy. See also AVERAGE.

COMMONPLACE adj. everyday, garden, garden variety, corn, chestnut, dime-a-dozen, vanilla, rumdum, starch, mainstream, middle-of-the-road, run-of-the-alley, run-of-the-mill, boilerplate, familiar tune. See also TRITE.

COMMON SENSE adj. cool, commonsensical.

COMMOTION n. commo, flap, stir, big stink, rumpus, all hell broke loose, big scene. See TURMOIL. See also CONFUSION, BEDLAM.

COMMUNE n. family.

COMMUNICATE v. 1. contact, interact, interface, network, connect, mesh, outreach, reach out, reach out and touch someone, relate, touch, touch base, raise, keep in touch, be on the same wavelength, have good vibes, have good vibrations, have truck with, get across, get the message, grok (sympathetically), back channel (secretly). 2. drop a line, drop a note, give one a ring, give one a jingle, give one a call, give one the horn, get one on the horn. See also CORRESPOND. 3. Sound off, jaw, confab, put in the loop, put in the know, give a meeting, hold a meet, buzz, open one's face, modjitate, modulate, soapbox. See SPEAK.

COMMUNICATION n. info, scoop, poop, the hot poop, the inside story, the hot story, pipeline, skinny, hot skinny, lowdown, dope, dope sheet, goods, flaming (Obsc., computer conversations). See INFORMATION. See also TALK.

COMMUNICATIONS SATELLITE n. COMSAT.

COMMUNIQUÉ n. handout, break, beat, scoop, the latest, what's happenin', what's going down, chip, poop, hot poop, dope.

COMMUNIST n. commie, comrade, red, fellow traveler, lefto, leftist, left-winger, lefty, linky-dink, pink, pinko, radical, bolshie, bolshevik, comsymp, card-carrying. See also RADICAL.

COMMUNIST SYMPATHIZER n. comsymp, fellow traveler, parlor pink, pink, pinko, lefto, left-winger, red fellow.

COMMUNITY n. 1. hood, neighborhood, neck of the woods, stomping ground, territory, turf, ghetto, inner city, jungle, shanty town, skid row, slum, zoo. See also DISTRICTS. 2. family.

COMMUNITY SING n. sing, sing-in, folk-sing, hootenanny.

COMMUTATION n. lifeboat, lifesaver, clemo, commute, spring.

COMMUTED (SENTENCE) adj. beat the chair, beat the rope, got a commute, got a lifeboat, got an anchor, got bugged, got clemo, made the bughouse.

COMMUTER n. straphanger.

COMPACT adj. boiled-down, in a nutshell, short and sweet, make a long story short.

COMPACT n. handshake, deal, dicker, ticket, paper, piece of paper. See AGREEMENT.

COMPANION n. amigo, pal, brother, sister, cuz, cousin, bud, buddy, roomie, pard, mellow (close), shadow, ghost (rarely seen), playmate, home biscuit, goombah, side-kick, crew (group), tribe (group). See FRIEND.

COMPANIONABLE adj. clubby, cozy, cozy with, tight, tight with, buddy-buddy, mellow, pally, palsy, palsy-walsy, chuchula-muchula. See INTIMATE. See also SOCIABLE.

COMPANY n. megacorp, multinational, outfit, syndicate, plunderbund, socks and stocks (nonbanking company such as Sears offering financial services), bunch, crew, crowd, gang, jungle, zoo, mob, ring, clan. See CORPORATION.

COMPANY SPY n. fink, company man.

COMPARE v. hang (how does that hang?), hold a candle to, stack up against, match up.

COMPARTMENTALIZE v. pigeonhole, slot, niche, place, split, piece, break up, divvy, divvy up.

COMPASSIONATE adj. softhearted, all heart, bleeding-heart (Derog.), old softie, soft-shell, be big, live with, go easy with, go easy on.

COMPATIBLE adj. in sync with, hit it off, get along with, on the same wavelength, good vibes, good vibrations, cotton to, in the groove, groovy, simpatico, mix, togetherness.

COMPATRIOT n. landsman, compadre, holmes (from home boy), campesino.

COMPEL v. put the arm on, squeeze, put the chill on, turn on the heat, crack down, throw one's weight around. See FORCE.

COMPELLED adj. hung-up, bugged, have a bug up one's ass, have a thing about, have a tiger by the tail. See OBSESSED.

COMPELLING adj. come on strong, push, punch, steamroller, husky, hefty, beefy, gutty, gutsy, take over, take charge. See also URGENT.

COMPENSATE v. comp, shell out, come down with, plank out, pony up, tickle the palm, pay up, take care of. See PAY.

COMPENSATION n. 1. take, take-home, pay, payoff, groceries, bread, sugar, salt, scale, shake, soap, touch, bacon, bacon and eggs, bring home the bacon, eagle shit; boost, hike, jump (raise); peanuts, coffee and cakes, chicken feed (small); fogy, fogey (Mil.), double dipping (compensation from two government agencies), golden parachute, golden handcuffs (deferred). 2. walking-around money, cash on the nail, cash on the barrelhead, money on the side, boodle, hat, hush money, ice, laying pipes (Pol.), street money, chop, fall dough, freight, bad notes, grease, palm oil, knock-off, rake-off, nut, schmear, big one, a fix, influence peddling, under the table, on the take, cream, mordida, contribution, contract, cush, graft, juice, salve, baksheesh, sweetener, sweetening, piece, split, kickback, payoff, plug-ola, payola, drugola, gayola. See also BRIBE. 3. strokes, brownie button (Hum.), feather in one's cap, gold star, plum, what's in it for one?

COMPETE v. jockey for position, scramble for, go for, go for broke, go for the gold, go for the throat, go for the jugular, go after, in the hunt. See also CONTEST.

COMPETENCE n. hacking it, the right stuff, what it takes, cutting it, cutting the mustard, know-how, makings, making the grade, moxie, savvy, the goods. See SKILL.

COMPETENT adj. crisp, dynamite, fireball, on the ball, one-man band, a pistol, know one's onions, know one's stuff, know one's business, know one's goulash, know one's beans, know backwards and forwards, know the ropes, know all the ins and outs, know the score, know all the answers, know one's oats, know one's bananas, know one's goods, know one's fruit, know one's groceries, know one's oil, know one's (practically anything), have savvy, take care of business, just what the doctor ordered, all-around, paid one's dues, mad (jazz), there, up to it, up to snuff, up to speed, up to the mark, wicked, fool (e.g., dancing fool, flying fool), more bang for one's buck, chakra-gonged. See also ABLE, CAPABLE.

COMPETING adj. in the hunt, in the rat race, on the merry-go-round.

COMPETITION n. competish, rat race, horse race (close), dog eat dog, a regular jungle out there, do or die, one on one, go, go for it, go for the gold, run, a dick-measuring contest (needless).

COMPETITIVE adj. dog-eat-dog, killer, killer instinct, streetwise.

COMPETITOR n. oppo, opposish, opposite number, meat, me and you, angries, dark horse (unknown).

COMPLAIN v. beef, where's the beef?, cut a beef, bitch, pitch a bitch, bleed, make a stink, gripe, gripe one's cookies, pop off, sound off, growl, gritch, squawk, put up a squawk, take on, kvetch, bellyache, blast, buck, crab, grouse, growl, kick, yammer, sing, sing the blues, cry the blues, get out the crying towel, rain, run one's mouth, speak one's piece, squeal, carry on, blow the whistle, blow at, holler, howl, raise a howl, put up a howl, piss up a storm, push out one's lips, eat one's heart out, raise Cain, raise sand.

COMPLAINER n. bitcher, beefer, bellyacher, griper, kicker, kvetch, squawker, whiner, crab, crank, crybaby, grouse, grouch, unhappy camper, hog caller, pill, 'plainer, rapper, sorehead, squealer, whistle-blower, blues singer, heat merchant, forecastle lawyer, sourpuss, lemon puss.

COMPLAINT n. beef, where's the beef?, gripe, kick, rap, guff, stink, rumble, CC (chief complaint). See GRIEVANCE.

COMPLETE adj. the works, whole nine yards, whole enchilada, whole megillah, lock stock and barrel, hook line and sinker. See WHOLE. 2. finished-off, fini, that's it, all over but the shouting, home free, you've seen my whole spring line, see daylight (near completion). See FINISHED.

COMPLETE v. wrap up, sew up, wind it up, call it a day, put to bed, put away, button down, go the route, tape, get it under one's belt. See FINISH.

COMPLETED adj. set, wired, a wrap, wound-up, mopped-up, pow, under one's belt, home free. See FINISHED.

COMPLETELY adv. all (all dolled up), big-time, from A to Z, from A to izzard, top to bottom, plenty, royal, whole hog, to a fare-you-well, to a fare-thee-well, galley west, shoot the works, six ways to Sunday, slam-bang, stone (stone deaf), tote, up the ass, cold turkey, dead, dead right, dead to rights, smack, smack out, flat-ass, flat out, from soup to nuts, from hell to breakfast, all the way, all hollow.

COMPLETION n. wrap-up, wind-up, curtains, that's all folks, that's all there is there ain't no more, Say goodnight Gracie, hips, swan song. See END.

COMPLEX adj. 1. hi-tech, can of worms, zoo, gasser, rat's nest, snake pit, wheels within wheels, Rube Goldberg, mega factor. See also DIFFICULT. 2. hang-up, a thing about something.

COMPLEXION n. looks, mug, phiz, cut of one's jib, front.

COMPLEXIONED adj. complected.

COMPLIANT adj. pussy-whipped, putty in one's hands, ac/dc, AC/DC, cosplug, wimpy, wet rag, wet sock, when in Rome do as the Romans do. See SUBMISSION. See also OBEDIENT.

COMPLICATE v. make waves, open up a can of worms, foul up, screw up, snafu, add fuel to the fire, make the cheese more binding. See CONFUSE.

COMPLICATED adj. hi-tech, can of worms, gasser, rat's nest, snake pit, wheels within wheels, mind blower, mega factor, Rube Goldberg.

COMPLIMENT v. toss a bouquet, give a bouquet, give a posy, pat on the back, trade last, TL, warm fuzzy, blow sunshine up one's ass. See PRAISE.

COMPLIMENTARY adj. on-the-house, comp, Annie Oakley, free lunch (seems free but isn't). See FREE.

COMPLY v. 1. go along with, go along with the crowd, yes one, ditto, play the game, play ball, See AGREE. 2. come across, come around, give out, put out (sexual); give in, cave in, cry uncle, say uncle, roll over and play dead, fold, gleek it, throw in the sponge, throw in the towel, toss in the sponge, toss in the towel, toss it in, don't make waves, don't rock the boat, go with the flow, go social, give away the store, give up, quit, knuckle under, knuckle to, shape up, shape up or ship out, clean up one's act, come up to scratch, straighten up and fly right, do it according to Hoyle, go by the book, by the numbers, go through channels, fit in, follow the beaten path, stay in line, not get out of line, toe the line, toe the mark, lie down and roll over for, when in Rome do as the Romans do, crazy, solid, way to go, there you go, you sold me, you got it, it's a deal, I hear you, I hear you talkin', groovy, all the way.

COMPLY, FAIL TO v. drop out, opt out, cop out, get out of line, rock the boat, make waves, leave the beaten path, kick over the traces, look the other way, let it go, let one off easy, let one off this time, wink at, pay no mind, pay no never mind, play past, pooh-pooh. See also REFUSE.

COMPONENT n. part and parcel, makings, makin's, fixings, fixin's, board, plug-in, peripheral.

COMPOSE v. comp, clef, tune, author, coin a phrase, cook up, dream up, whip up, whomp up, fudge together, bang out, bat out, scratch out, knock out, knock off, knock out a few pages, knock off hen tracks on a rolltop piano (typing), make hen tracks, put down, note down, pen, put pen to paper, script, scriven, scribble, drive a pen, drive a pencil, push a pen, push a pencil, stain a paper, spoil a paper, shed ink, spill ink, Grub Street (hack), ghost, ghostwrite.

COMPOSED adj. together, have one's act together, glued (antonym: unglued), cool, cool as a cucumber, keep one's cool, keep one's shirt on, keep a stiff upper lip, not turn a hair, unflappable, commonsensical, ah-ah head, ice maiden (Fem.), roll with the punches. See also ASSURED, CALM.

COMPOSER n. tunester, tunesmith, songsmith.

COMPOSITE n. combo, duke's mixture (strange), stew, paste-up.

COMPOSITION n. comp, piece, tune, chart, arrangement, number, score, setup, getup, lead sheet (music).

COMPOSURE n. cool, keep one's cool, polish.

COMPOUND n. combo, mishmash, mishmosh, soup (liquid), lorelei, duke's mixture, stew, goulash.

COMPREHEND v. get, gotya, get the picture, catch, click, tumble, savvy, capeesh, fershtay, dig, can you relate?

(Af. Am.), read, dawned on one, light dawned. See UNDERSTAND.

COMPREHENSION n. aha reaction, double-take, slow take, take, take it big.

COMPREHENSIVE adj. across-the-board, the works, lock stock and barrel, whole shebang, wall-to-wall, the picture, the big picture. See WHOLE.

COMPRESSED adj. telescoped, stuffed, crash.

COMPROMISE n. trade-off, deal, fifty-fifty, half and half, third way, happy medium, sellout, copout, win-win situation.

COMPROMISE v. trade off, make a deal, meet halfway, go fifty-fifty, if you can't fight 'em join 'em, strike a happy medium, come to school, play ball with, sell out, whore, cop out, give in. See also RECONCILE.

COMPULSION n. hang-up, monkey, have on the brain, tiger, tiger by the tail. See OBSESSION.

COMPUTE v. dope out, figure, figure in, figure out, input (enter), output (product), log on (begin), take account of, tot, tote, tote up, tot up, count heads, count noses, cut ice, keep tabs, run down, run down some numbers, number-crunch, size up, take one's measure.

COMPUTER n. brain, PC, number cruncher, micro, mini, mainframe, big iron, CPU, laptop; clone, a compatible (using same architecture and operating codes as a leading brand), crufty (poorly made).

COMPUTER BULLETIN BOARD n. BBS (bulletin board services), on line, net-nerd (uses as a substitute for real relationship), compubabe (Fem.), hot tub (channel to talk sex), forum (topic), lurker (noncontributing listener), thread (single subject), topic drift (forum is off designated subject), chat (private conversation), emoticon (punctuation-based symbols).

COMPUTER CONTROL n. joystick, mouse.

COMPUTER: FAIL v. down, go down, crash, gronk out, barf, cold fault (immediate), lock, lock-up, deadlock, hang, fry, glitch, up (repaired and operational), kludge (patch or fix computer program).

COMPUTER OPERATOR n. gweep, hacker, user, wirehead, chiphead (enthusiastic), techie. See COMPUTER USER.

COMPUTER PROGRAMS n. DDT (debugging program), humongous (large, unmanageable), artware (design); time bomb, Trojan horse (programmed to cause destruction at a prescribed time); worm (destructive endless cycle); crufty, kludgy (badly written program); machoflops, teraflops (performs multitrillion calculations per second).

COMPUTER TERMS K (kilobyte), down, go down, crashed, gronked (inoperative); cuspy (excellent), bug,

debug (error correction), crunching numbers (numerically intensive processing), demon (a background operating program), tweek, dink (modify), mung (change), bagbiter (failure), deadlock, locked up (jammed), GIGO (garbage in, garbage out), gubbish (useless information), GUI (graphical user interface), footprint (tabletop area occupied), docs (instructions), expansion slot, board, breadboard (fits into an expansion slot), macro (one or two keystrokes that reproduce a series of keystrokes at high speed), gulp (multiple bytes), Moby (large), hash (unwanted, meaningless data), trapdoor (bypasses security), windows (divided or superimposed monitor screens), icon (pictographic utility label), floppy, flippy (disks), iron (hardware), AI (artificial intelligence), pull-down menu, download (retrieve a file from another computer or source), backup (safety copy), E-mail (electronic mail), snailmail (postal service), multitasking, multiuser (network unit), Big Floyd (FBI crime network), transparent (unobtrusive program operation), LAN (local area network), cybercrud (tech-talk), flame war (dispute), residence (file location); jewel box, eco-pack (holds disks); Trojan horse, shoulder surfing, dumpster diving (spying techniques); worm (sabotage by eating away files), WYSIWYG (what you see is what you get), WISIWYS (what I see is what you see, networking computers); bar (temporary name), wallpaper (lengthy fanfold printout), on-line, Silicon Valley.

COMPUTER USE n. hackerdom.

COMPUTER USER n. end user, hacker, gweep, digithead, propeller head (engineer), gearhead (programmer), techno-nerd, wirehead, cyberpunk, chiphead (enthusiastic), nerdling (unskilled), hedgehog (limited to one system), zipperhead (closed mind), digerati (intellectuals), cyberphobe (fears computers), lurker (illegal), handle (computer name).

COMRADE n. amigo, bud, buddy, bosom buddy, buddyroo, asshole buddy, home biscuit, brah, chum, matie, pal, sidekick tribe (group), crew (group), ghost (rarely seen). See FRIEND.

CON adj. agin, be agin, no way, fuck that noise, over my dead body.

CONCEAL v. 1. bury, cover up, duck, stash, bag, flatten out, hide out, hole up, plant, put in the hole, stick in the hole. 2. finesse it, launder, white money (laundered), palm, paper over, fig-leaf it, hold out on, skim (income), keep buttoned up, keep it under one's hat, keep under wraps, con, jerk around, fuck over, put something across, put something over on one, pull the wool over one's eyes. 3. wear cheaters, cover up, slap on some glims, flash the gogs, throw on a makeup, phony up one's get-up, beard. 4. put on an act, put up a front, put on a front, put on a false front, stonewall, whitewash, pull up a bluff, put up a bluff, play possum, four-flush, blow smoke, make like, let on, let on like. See also DISGUISE, HIDE.

CONCEALED adj. under wraps, incog, on the Q.T., hush-hush, hushed-up, covered-up, holed-up, planted, stashed, doggo, put in the hole.

CONCEALMENT n. cover-up, beard, fig leaf; drop, dubock, front, laundromat (places used to hide illegal transactions), skunk works (secret manufacturing plant or laboratory).

CONCEDE v. go along with, play ball with, yes one, ditto, bury the hatchet. See AGREE. 2. give in, cave in, say uncle, fold, throw in the sponge, toss in the towel, go with the flow, quit, knuckle under. See SURRENDER.

CONCEITED adj. hot shit, hot stuff, hot shot, bullshit, lip gloss, bullshitting, bullskating (Af. Am.), big-talking, biggety, ho-dad, ho-daddy, key swinging, loudmouth, know-it-all, snotnose, smart-ass, smart-alecky, phony, hubcap, crack one's jaw, crapper, cocky, cock, cock of the walk, chesty, gutbucket, stuffy, stuffed shirt, stuck-up, puffed-up, gassy, windbag, windy, load of wind, full of hot air, blowhard, blow smoke, gall, ham, hog, highfalutin, high-muck-a-muck, high-hat, hincty, his nibs, snooty, on an ego trip, ego-tripping, swell-headed, big-head, high-nosed, big I am, stuck on oneself, a regular I love me, think one is it, think one's shit doesn't stink, too big for one's shoes, too big for one's britches.

CONCEIVE v. 1. cook up, dream up, make up, think up, trump up, brainstorm, head trip, spark, spitball, take it off the top of one's head. See CREATE. 2. get knocked up (pregnant).

CONCENTRATE v. 1. sweat, head trip, hammer, hammer away at, crack one's brains, pour it on. See THINK. 2. cut, cut down, cut to the bone, nutshell, put in a nutshell, boil down, trim, sharpen, get to the meat, get to home in, move in, zero in.

CONCENTRATED adj. telescoped, crashed, stuffed, boiled-down.

CONCEPT n. slant, twist, approach, big idea, brain child, wrinkle, brain wave, take, flash on it, wienie, fool notion, the name of that tune. See IDEA.

CONCERN n. 1. tender loving care, TLC. 2. megacorp, multinational, plunderbund, jungle, zoo, bunch, crew, crowd, gang, mob, outfit, ring. See CORPORATION.

CONCERNED adj. worried sick, in a stew, up tight, biting one's nails, on pins and needles, butterflies in one's stomach, coffee head, all-overish. See ANXIOUS.

CONCERT n. rockfest, gig, rave (techno concert with Ecstasy and other drugs), show.

CONCESSION n. 1. store, stand, hole in the wall. 2. rollback, buyback, giveback, takeaway (labor union bargaining), give, give in, cop out, deal, fifty-fifty, half and half, happy medium, sell out, trade-off, win-win situation.

CONCIERGE n. super, swamper, watchdog.

CONCILIATE v. cool, fix up, bury the hatchet, kiss and make up, make up, make it up, make matters up, patch things up, get together on, come together, meet halfway. See PACIFY.

CONCILIATOR n. rent-a-judge.

CONCISE adj. in a nutshell, short and sweet, make a long story short, boiled down, cut to the bone.

CONCLAVE n. clambake, confab, meet, flap (urgent), huddle, powwow, eyeball-to-eyeball encounter, buzz session, rap, rap session, gam, get-together. See MEETING.

CONCLUDE v. 1. wrap it up, wind up, close out, drop the curtain, put the lid on, call it a day, knock off, put to bed. See FINISH. 2. add up to, boil down to, figure, figger, have a hunch, be afraid, what one is saying is, the way one sees it. See also BELIEVE.

CONCLUDED adj. wrapped-up, fini, that's history, buttoned-up, home, in the bag, all over but the shouting, signed sealed and delivered. See FINISHED.

CONCLUSION n. wrap, payoff, down to the short strokes, end of the line, that's all folks, when the fat lady sings. See END.

CONCLUSIVE adj. all-out, flat-ass, flat-out, straight-out, no ifs ands or buts, what you see is what you get, litmus test.

CONCOCT v. fab, prefab, throw together, slap together, fudge together, hatch, ad lib. See CREATE.

CONCUR v. 1. okay, pass on, shake on, cut a deal, set, hold with, that works for me, give one five (slap hands), jibe. See AGREE. 2. you sold me, you got it, you ain't just whistlin' Dixie, you said a mouthful, it's a deal, I'll drink to that, I hear you, I hear you talkin', groovy, all the way. See also SURRENDER.

CONCURRENCE n. nod, big 10-4, Four Roger, for sure, stamp of approval, on the same wavelength, go-ahead, green light, get the nod. See AGREEMENT.

CONCURRENTLY adv. dead heat, in sync, on the beat, with the beat.

CONDEMN v. put down, come down on, thumbs down on, call down, rap on the knuckles, slap on the wrist, name, hang something on, blow the whistle on one, whistle-blow, finger, point the finger, point the finger at, put the finger on, lay at one's door, pin it on one, frame, frame up, let one have it, put away, send up, send up the river, throw the book at, break one's license, clean up the calendar. See also ACCUSE.

CONDENSE v. cut, cut down, cut to the bone, nutshell, put in a nutshell, boil down, trim, get to the meat, chop, snip, blue-pencil. See SHORTEN.

CONDENSED adj. telescoped, crashed, stuffed, boiled-down.

CONDESCEND v. high-hat, toss a few crumbs, act like one of the boys.

CONDESCENDING adj. snooty, uppish, uppity, king shit, have one's glasses on (Af. Am.), smart-ass. See ARROGANT.

CONDITION n. 1. action, hap, happenin', situash, spot, riff, ball game, scene, way it shapes up, how things shape up, way things are, way of the world, like it is, what it is, where it's at, where one is at, size of it, lay of the land, how the land lies, how things stand, how things stack up, how it goes, how it is, how things are, how-de-do, how-do-you-do, the go-along. 2. catch, joker, kicker, string, a string attached to it, fine print, small print, fine print at the bottom, small fine print at the bottom. 3. ——— city (fat city), cherry (perfect), mint, showroom perfect.

CONDITION v. 1. warm up, loosen up, shape up, toughen up, build up, work up, work over, whip into shape, sharpen. 2. program, brainwash, mind-fuck, head-fuck, fuck with one's head, fuck over one's mind, break down. See also TRAIN.

CONDITIONALLY adv. with a grain of salt, with a catch to it, with a joker to it, with a kicker to it, with a string to it, with a string attached.

CONDITIONED adj. programmed, brainwashed, head-fucked.

CONDITIONING n. warmup, sharpening up, shaping up, an edge, readying, daily dozen. See PREPARATION.

CONDOM n. rubber, rubber boots, pro, night cap, shower cap, raincoat, hat, party hat, jimmy hat, jimmie, life jacket, bone cover, protection, cadet, safety, bag, scumbag, jolly bag, joy-bag, jo-bag, baggie, Trojan, horse, rough rider, Ramses, armor, skin, fish skin, eel, Manhattan eel, Coney Island whitefish, Hudson River whitefish, Magnum, Manhattan eel, Port Said garter, propho, safe, glove, stud glove, French letter, French tickler, Frenchy, purse.

CONDOMINIUM n. condo, condomarinium (beside a marina), lollipop (N.Y.).

CONDONE v. okay, OK, buy, lap up, give the green light, go along with, put the Good Housekeeping Seal of approval on, let it come. See also ACCEPT; ENDURE.

CONDUCT n. channels, red tape, bag, by the numbers, by the book.

CONDUCT v. run, run things, shepherd, ride herd on, call the tune, trailblaze. See MANAGE.

CONFECTION n. cush, sweets, g'dong, gedunk, hickey.

CONFEDERATE SOLDIER n. butternut, reb, Johnny Reb, Gray, the Gray.

CONFEDERATE SYMPATHIZER n. butternut.

CONFER v. 1. confab, give a meeting, take a meeting, have a meet, hold a meet, brainstorm, blitz, toss some ideas around, kick some ideas around, groupthink, put in the loop, put in the know, get heads together, huddle, go into a huddle, run something by one, pick one's brains, rap, mack (Af. Am.), jaw, gab, chin, chew, chew over, chew the fat, chew the rag, rag around, bump one's gums, bat the chat, breeze, bat the breeze, shoot the breeze, shoot the shit, shoot the bull, bull, bullshit, BS, throw the bull, talk turkey, gobble, flap, mouth off. See also DISCUSS. 2. lay on, gift with, put something in the pot, sweeten the kitty. See GIVE.

CONFERENCE n. confab, meet, breakout meeting (brainstorm session), groupthink, think-in, huddle, pow-wow, eyeball-to-eyeball encounter, chalk talk (prof. and students, informal, or sports). See MEETING.

CONFESS v. fess, fess up, rat, rat on, fink, fink on, unload, unload on, croon, sing, sing on, weasel on, sing like a canary, chirp, talk, snitch, dry snitch, squeal, squawk, stool, spill, spill the beans, spill one's guts, finger, leak, buzz (in secret), bury, deal, hose, split, belch, blow, blow the whistle, blow the gaff, drop a dime on one, clue one in, noise off, sound off, pop off, do one dirt, drum, come clean, come through, come out, come out of the closet, dump on, post, keep one posted, put the finger on, put one in the picture, put hep, put hip, put next to, put on to, put a bug in one's ear, put a bug up one's ass, put one wise to, put it on the line, put it on the street, let it all hang out, bring it out into the daylight, bring it out into the open, cop out, spit it out, crack, crack on, let next to, let down, let one's hair down, let down one's side, let the cat out of the bag, take a load off one's mind, take a load off one's chest, spring, spring one's duke, spring with a crack, tip, tip off, tip one's hand, tip one's duke, peach, holler, open up, own up, cough up, dig up, get it off one's chest, get it out of one's system, out with it, switch, update, wise one up, give with, give away, give the show away, give one the word, give it to one up the ass, sock it to one, lay it on one, lay it on the line, sell out, sell down the river, pull a fast one, run one's mouth, have a big mouth, have a big bazoo, blab, bladder, cop a plea, break a story.

CONFESSION n. song, story, owning up, squawk, squeal.

CONFESSOR n. canary, crooner, singer.

CONFIDE v. crack to, buzz, lay the gaff, lay it on, unload on, spring with the score, bend an ear, spill to, let one in on. See also CONFESS.

CONFIDENCE n. stock, store, sure bet, guts.

CONFIDENCE GAME n. con, con game, sting, bunco, flimflam, Abscam, bait and switch, shell game, the old army game. See CHEAT.

CONFIDENCE MAN n. hustler, shark, mechanic, con man, con artist, burn artist, jive ass, slick operator, feather merchant, horse trader. See CHEAT.

CONFIDENT adj. 1. cocksure, sure as shit, gamble on, racked, got the faith baby, keeping the faith, bet on, bet one's bottom dollar on. See CERTAIN. 2. gutsy, rosy, bullish, upbeat, iceman, ice in one's veins, gung-ho, high, high on something, all puffed up, pumped-up, glad-hander (overly), looking at the world through rose-colored glasses, looking at (something) through rose-colored glasses.

CONFIDENTIAL adj. off-the-record, eyes-only, for your eyes only, hush-hush, top secret, classified, under one's hat, inside, skunk works (secret manufacturing plant or laboratory). See SECRET.

CONFIDENTIALLY adv. between you and me, between you me and the lamppost, between you and me and the bedpost, between us girls, don't even tell your mother, don't breathe it to a soul, don't spread this around, don't let this get around, the ground floor, let one in on it, on the cuff, off the cuff, off the record, on the q.t., take a tip. See also SECRET.

CONFIDING adj. blue-eyed, a mark, easy mark, easy, wide-eyed, yold, yo-yo, sucker, patsy, green.

CONFINE v. 1. ice, put on ice, put away, send up. See JAIL. 2. cool, cool off, cool down, hold down, keep the lid on, bottle up, cork, cork up, hog-tie, put a half nelson on. See RESTRAIN.

CONFINED adj. hog-tied, iced, on ice, chilled, bottled-up, corked-up. See also JAILED.

CONFIRM v. bless, buy, okay, OK, lap up, sign, sign off on, thumbs up, check out, check up on, double-check, size up, make sure, make doubly sure, put one's John Hancock on, give the nod, give the go-ahead, give the green light, give the stamp of approval, give the high sign, rubber-stamp, crack on one (or something), debunk (prove false). See also ASCERTAIN, VERIFY, AFFIRM.

CONFIRMATION n. go-ahead, fuckin'-A, green light, mouthful (you said a mouthful), okay, OK, right on, bet yer life, you bet, you betcha, you can say that again, you said it, say so, one's stamp of approval, Good Housekeeping stamp of approval, rubber stamp.

CONFISCATE v. contifisticate, annex, grab, glom on to, liberate, moonlight requisition, take over, swipe, kipe, hijack, high-grade, police up. See APPROPRIATE.

CONFLAGRATION n. rapid oxidation, up in smoke.

CONFLICT n. hassle, brush, dance, flap, rhubarb, run-in, row, ruckus jihad, fuss. See FIGHT.

CONFLICT v. tangle, tangle ass with, brawl, scrap, romp, slug, bump heads with, cross swords with, lock horns with, square off with. See FIGHT.

CONFORM v. go with the flow, go by the book, go through channels, don't make waves, don't rock the boat, play the game, shape up, shape up or ship out, get all the pieces in place, get one's act together, clean up one's act, by the numbers, come around, come over, come to school, come up to scratch, straighten up and fly right, if you can't beat 'em join 'em, lean over backwards, make room, meet halfway, move over, find the middle ground, follow the beaten path, swim with the tide, do it according to Hoyle, bend over backwards, fit in, roll with the punches, toe the mark, toe the line, stay in line, when in Rome do as the Romans do, grin and bear it, take it, make a deal, go fifty-fifty.

CONFORMIST n. straight, straight arrow, straight edge, a narb, narbo, square, L7, sheep, yes man, organization man, company man, plastic, plastic person, Barbie Doll, Barbie and Ken, Babbitt, Mr. Grundy, Mrs. Grundy. See CONVENTIONAL.

CONFOUND v. discombobulate, ball up, fuck up, screw up, bug, throw, take one's mind, fuck with one's head, fuddle, put one on a crosstown bus. See CONFUSE.

CONFOUNDED adj. unglued, balled-up, screwed-up, farmisht, thrown, rattled, in a fog, dizzy, kerflummoxed, stuck, stumped, drowning, hugger-mugger. See CONFUSED.

CONFRONT v. face down, jam up, in your face, go up against, meet eyeball-to-eyeball, go one-on-one, mano a mano, pop, tell off, call one's bluff, make my day, go on make my day. See BRAVE.

CONFRONT WITH A WEAPON v. draw on, draw down on, get the drop on, pin, front up, hit one with, smack with, spring with.

CONFUSE v. get, get to, discomboberate, discombobulate, ball up, foul up, fuck up, cross, louse up, mess up, muck up, screw up, snafu, blow up, bollix up, beat, lick, bug, rattle, rattle one's cage, throw, throw into a tizzy, throw into a swivet, throw a monkey wrench into the works, bamboozle, buffalo, lose momentum, psych out, gross out, take one's mind, fuck with one's head, mess with one's head, mess with one's mind, make a mess of, fuddle, play hob with, put one on a crosstown bus, make waves, open up a can of worms, add fuel to the fire, ball up, heat up, hot up, profundicate, synomaniac (one who complicates), muddy the waters, stir the waters, make hash out of, snow, stump, floor, put off, flummox, upset one's applecart.

CONFUSED adj. unglued, unzipped, unscrewed, come unglued, come unzipped, come apart, come apart at the seams, defrosted, gonzo, discombobulated, discombooberated, spaced-out, glassy-eyed, slap-happy, punch-drunk, punchy, mind is blown, shook, shook-up, all balled up, balled-up, fouled-up, fucked-up, snafu, comfu, tarfu, tuifu, fubb (fucked up beyond belief), loused up, messy, messed-up, mucked-up, mussy, mussed-up, sloppy, screwy, screwed-up, bugged-up, bollixed-up, hung, hung up, mixed-up, blaaed-up, gummixed-up, caught short, messed-up attic, helter-skelter, galley west, floored, flipped-out, farmisht, fertummeled, woozy, thrown, dopey, lost one's cool, fussed, fried (Stu.), rattled, rattlebrained, nuts, higgledy-piggledy, skimble-skamble, half-baked, half-assed, ass-backwards, bassackwards, backasswords, arsy-varsy, topsy-turvy, upside-down, foggy, wandering around in a fog, in a fog, kerflummoxed, flummoxed, don't know from nothing, don't know one's ass from a hole in the ground, don't know one's ass from first base, don't know shit from Shinola, don't know crossways from crosswise, don't know which way is up, licked, stuck, stumped, mocus, double-Dutch, boggily-woogily, drowning, hugger-mugger, bamboozled, thrown off one's beam ends, goat fuck (Mil.), Chinese fire drill. See also DISTURBED.

CONFUSION n. goulash, mix-up, foul-up, fuck-up, screw-up, snarl-up, mishmosh, mishmash, holy mess, unholy mess, bloody mess, mess and a half, all hell broke loose, horseshit and gunsmoke, topsy-turvy, arsy-varsy, ruckus, ruction, shindy, can of worms, who's minding the store?, flap, hoopla, rat's nest, discombobulation, discombooberation, flusteration, flustration, foofaraw, stew, free-for-all, etaoin shrdlu, every which way, every which way but up, forty ways to Sunday, forty ways from Sunday, all over hell, all over the shop, galley west, hectic, harum-scarum, pretty kettle of fish, pretty piece of business, nice piece of work.

CONFUTE v. tap, knock the props out from under, shoot full of holes, blow sky high. See REFUTE.

CONGEAL v. clabber, lopper, glop up.

CONGENIAL adj. clubby, mellow, right neighborly, regular fellow, mixer. See FRIENDLY.

CONGESTED adj. jam-packed, packed like sardines, sardined, mobbed, up to the rafters, fanny-bumper, gridlocked. See CROWDED.

CONGLOMERATION n. mixed bag, combo, everything but the kitchen sink, kludge (parts), duke's mixture (strange), mishmash, mishmosh.

CONGRATULATE v. stroke, boost, pat on the back, toss a bouquet, give a bouquet, give a posy, give the man a big cigar, gold-star, have to hand it to one, hear it for. See also PRAISE.

CONGREGATE v. corral, round up, meet up, bunch up, gang up, gang around, make the scene.

CONGREGATION n. get-together, sit-in, confab, meet, gam, turnout. See MEETING.

CONGRESS n. 1. the Hill, the mighty dome; the House, dark side of the moon (House of Representatives),

Hill rat (staff). 2. clambake, confab, meet, huddle, powwow, get-together. See MEETING.

CONJECTURE n. guesstimate, hunch, SWAG (slightly wild-assed guess), shot, shot in the dark, stab, stab in the dark, sneaking suspicion.

CONJECTURE v. take a stab, take a shot, take a shot in the dark, figure, guesstimate. See SPECULATE.

CONJUNCTIVITIS n. pinkeye.

CONNECT v. 1. tie in, tie up with, come aboard, get into, plug into, interface, join up with, meld with, network with. See ASSOCIATE. See also COMMUNICATE. 2. hook up, hook on, tag, tag on, tack on, slap on, hitch on. See also FASTEN. 3. hook in, cross-dissolve (film), cue in (scripts, ms., songs), dub, marry (film), mix (recording).

CONNECTICUT Constitution State, Nutmeg State, Wooden Nutmeg State.

CONNECTION n. tie-in, network, hookup. See also COMMUNICATION.

CONNECTIONS n. contacts, in, inside track, wires, ropes, strings, clout. See INFLUENCE.

CONNIVANCE n. scam, racket, flimflam, graft, whitewash job, diddle. See CHEAT.

CONNIVE v. operate, be in cahoots with, work hand in glove with, frame, frame up, cook up, finagle, yank one, angle, promote, wangle, wire, diddle. See SCHEME.

CONNIVER n. operator, hustler, burn artist, finagler, wire-puller, carpetbagger, on the make, velcroid (sticks to important people). See also CONSPIRATOR.

CONNOISSEUR n. maven, buff, fan, freak, into, nut. See also AUTHORITY.

CONQUER v. trash, total, drub, whip, kill (Mil., enemy aircraft down), clobber, cream, ace, zap, whip ass, shut down, wipe off the map. See DEFEAT.

CONQUEST n. big win, grand slam, score, splash, kill (Mil., enemy aircraft down), killing, takeover, clean sweep. See TRIUMPH.

CONSCIENTIOUS adj. tough, hanging tough, hanging in, heart and soul into, watch out, watch one's step, keep on one's toes, play safe, walk on eggs, mind one's p's and q's, bend over backwards, keep one's ear to the ground.

CONSCIENTIOUS OBJECTOR n. conchie, C.O., peacenik.

CONSCRIPT n. draftee, rookie, tenderfoot, chicken; barber bait, big Joe, big John, bimbo, bozo (WWII); boot (N.), draft bait (subject to conscription). See also RECRUIT.

CONSCRIPT v. sign on, sign up, call up.

CONSCRIPTION n. greetings, letter from Uncle Sam.

CONSENT n. go-ahead, green light, mouthful (you said a mouthful), okay, OK, right on, bet yer life, you bet, you can say that again, you said it, say-so, stamp of approval, blank check, carte blanche, blessing.

CONSENT v. 1. okay, bless, shake on, sign off on, make a deal, yes one, give the nod. 2. give in, cave in, cry uncle, say uncle, roll over and play dead, fold, gleek it, lump it, throw in the sponge, throw in the towel, toss in the sponge, toss in the towel, toss it in, give away the store, give up, quit, knuckle under, knuckle to, lie down and roll over for, crazy, solid, way to go, there you go, that works for me, like you say, you sold me, you got it, you just ain't whistling Dixie, you said a mouthful, done deal, it's a deal, me too, sure thing, I'll drink to that, I hear you, I hear you talkin, groovy, all the way. See AGREE.

CONSEQUENCE n. fallout, reaction, chain reaction, flak (bad), follow-up, follow-through, spin-off, waves, can of worms, bottom line, it's your funeral.

CONSERVATIONIST n. duck squeezer, eagle freak, ecofreak, econut, guppy, greeny, tree hugger, banana (build absolutely nothing anywhere near anything).

CONSERVATIVE adj. right, right-wing, right-winger, right-of-center, New Right, radical right, extreme right, hard right, rightist, right angle, right of Attila the Hun, neo-con, red-neck, red-baiter, good ol' boy, squish (uncommitted), real Amerikan, Archie Bunker, hard-hat, hard-shell, diehard, Bircher, Birchite, John Bircher, caveman, citizen (anyone more conservative than you are), Ivy League, straight arrow, white bread, white bread and mayonnaise, standpatter, old guard, old line, duddy, fuddy-dud, fuddy-duddy, plays close to the vest, storm trooper, witch hunter, Black Shirt, Brown Shirt, Ku Kluxer, lunatic fringe, McCarthyite, Posse Comitatus.

CONSERVE v. cut down on, cut back, sock away, stash, scrimp, skimp, squirrel, squirrel away. See SAVE.

CONSIDER v. kick around, feel, noodle, noodle it around, sweat, sweat over, cool something over, rack one's brains. See THINK.

CONSIDERABLE adj. fab, fat, something, something else, super, super-duper, monstro, mongo, unreal, to the max, a doozie, dynamite, like all-get-out, mad, man-sized, a pip, solid gold, tidy, tits, tuff. See also IMPORTANT.

CONSIDERATE adj. mellow, cool, a sport, regular fellow, a gent, a mensch. See also ACCOMMODATING.

CONSIDERATION n. a little slack, a little something to sweeten the pot. See also FEE, GRATUITY, PAY.

CONSOLIDATE v. 1. tie in, tie up with, pool, throw in together, plug into, bunch up, hook up with, team up with.

See ASSOCIATE. 2. hook up, hook on, tag, tag on, tack on, slap on, hitch on. 3. cross-dissolve (film), cue in (scripts, ms., songs), dub, hook in, marry (film), mix (recording).

CONSOLIDATED adj. telescoped, crashed, stuffed.

CONSORT v. run with, run around with, pal, pal with, pal up with, pal around with, take up with, tie up with, clique with, gang up with, hang around with, hang out with, chum with, chum together.

CONSORTIUM n. megacorp, multinational, plunderbund, bunch, crew, crowd, gang, mob, outfit, Old Boy network, ring. See CORPORATION.

CONSPICUOUS adj. flashy, splashy, make a big splash, glitzy, jazzy, showy, loud, screaming, splurgy, candy, candy kid, classy, flossy, toney, high-toned, belled, duded up, all spiffed up, put on the dog, hanging out, live in a glass house, spot one like a lead dime, stick out like a sore thumb. See also APPARENT.

CONSPIRACY n. fix, frame, frame-up, hookup, put-up job, game, little game, Barney. See SCHEME.

CONSPIRATOR n. finagler, operator, wire-puller, wangler, mastermind, brain.

CONSPIRE v. get in bed with, cook up, operate, promote, wangle, wire, hatch, work something out, be in cahoots, put out a contract. See SCHEME.

CONSTABLE n. cop, copper, Keystone Kop, bull, bubble-gum man, shamus, dick, hick dick, flic; cossack, pig, oink, flatfoot, fink, headbeater, roach, clown (all Derog.); big brother, boy scouts, county Joe, county mounty, county mountie, sparrow cop, law, John Law, Johnny Law, arm, long arm, long arm of the law, local boy, local yard, local yokel, local bear, bear, smokey, smokey the bear, little bear (local), road ranger, button, collar, badge, fuzz, fuzzy. See also POLICE OFFICER.

CONSTANT adj. cool, together, unflappable, solid as a rock, Rock of Gib, Rock of Gibraltar.

CONSTANTLY adv. round the clock, day and night.

CONSTITUENT n. 1. fixin's, makings, makin's, part and parcel, board, plug-in. See also BASIC. 2. goat (political).

CONSTRAIN v. cool, cool off, cool down, not go off the deep end, keep the lid on, bottle up, cork up, hog-tie, put a half nelson on, hold down. See RESTRAIN.

CONSTRAINT n. hang-up, jones, monkey, a no-no, a must; cuffs. See HINDRANCE.

CONSTRUCT v. whip up, trump up, cook up, cobble up, dream up, hoke up, whomp up, throw up, throw together, knock together, fudge together, fab, prefab, put out.

CONSTRUE v. be afraid, figure it to be, one's best guess.

CONSULT v. get heads together, brainstorm, confab, groupthink, put in the loop, put in the know, huddle, go into a huddle, flap, take a meeting, have a meet, toss some ideas around, kick some ideas around, run something by one, pick one's brains. See also CONFER.

CONSULTANT n. Beltway bandit, seagull model.

CONSULTATION n. confab, groupthink, breakout meeting (brainstorm session), rap, rap session, buzz session, skull session, clambake, eyeball-to-eyeball encounter, flap, gam, huddle, powwow, think-in, second opinion. See also MEETING.

CONSUME v. scarf, chow down, scoff, throw back, mow (mow a burger), nibble, snack, wolf, bolt, narf, trough out, grind, grease one's chops, grease down, stuff one's face. See EAT.

CONSUMED adj. down the tube, petered-out, shot.

CONSUMER n. end user, ultra (insists on best), See also BUYER.

CONSUMMATE v. wrap, wrap up, tape, button down, button up, clean up, mop up, sew up, wind up, fold up, can, jell, clinch, close, sign, come through, knock off, polish off, top it off, all the way, put away, put the lid on, put to bed, get it together, go the route, take care of, call it a day, drop the curtain, ring down the curtain, deal coming down, do to a 'T', do to a frazzle, do to a finish.

CONSUMMATION n. payoff, wind-up, wrap, wrap-up, cleanup, mop-up, to a T, to a finish, to a frazzle. See END.

CONTACT n. in, connection, cutout, head-to head, network, channel, rabbi. See INFLUENCE.

CONTACT v. interface, interact, network, connect, grok, reach out, relate, touch base. See COMMUNICATE.

CONTAIN v. cork, cork up, cool, cool off, cool down, hold down, bottle up, hog-tie, not go off the deep end, keep the lid on, put a half nelson on. See RESTRAIN.

CONTAINER n. bucket, hooker, tub, growler. See also BAG.

CONTAMINATED adj. cooked (radiation), dirty, exposed, mucked up, cruddy.

CONTEMPLATE v. 1. percolate, size up, take in, cool something over, chew over, kick around, bat it around. See THINK. 2. see it coming, be afraid, in the cards, it's looking to, wait for the other shoe to drop. See ANTICIPATE.

CONTEMPORARY adj. state-of-the-art, leading-edge, now, contempo, fire-new, hot off the press, just out. See NEW.

CONTEMPTIBLE adj. dirty, heel, shitheel, cocksucking (Obsc.), low-down no-good, hairball, gweebo, rat,

rat fink, fink, son of a bitch, SOB, fishball, chickenshit, the lowest, Melvin. See DESPICABLE.

CONTEMPTUOUS adj. cool, cold shoulder, biggety, dicty, sidity, siditity, sniffy, snippy, snooty, snotty, uppish, uppity, upstage, king shit, high-and-mighty, high-hat, high-hatted, high-hatty, high-headed, high-nosed, on one's high horse, have one's glasses on (Af. Am.), crack the whip, throw one's weight around, come down on, dog it, cheeky, hard, hard-nosed, sticking the zingers in (remark). See also ARROGANT.

CONTEND v. 1. jockey for position, scramble for, in it to win it (Af. Am.), go for, go for it, go for broke, go for the throat, go for the jugular, go after, make a play for, push, push for, knock oneself out, break one's neck, bust one's ass, shoot for, shoot at, shoot the works, give it one's all, give it all one's got. 2. handle, handle it, get a handle on something, hack, hack it, live with, make it, make a go of it. See ARGUE. 3. cross, take on, sock, sock it to one, break with, fly in the face of, in one's face, be agin, buck, nix, have a bone to pick, pettifog, put up an argument, set to, zap, zapper, pitch into, light into, lay into, wade into, lace into, sail into, come at, go at, lay at, have at, lean on, crack down on, gang up on, jump on, jump on one's case, jump down one's throat, come down on, come down hard on one, land on, land all over one, lay a finger on, lay out, let have it, let have it with both barrels, give one both barrels, blast, rip, rip into, rip up, rip up one side and down the other, put up a fight, mix it up with, tangle with, bump heads with, cross swords with, lock horns with, stick it to one, push around. See also FIGHT.

CONTENDER n. dark horse (unknown), white hope. See also COMPETING.

CONTENT adj. fat dumb and happy, can't complain, have no kick coming, I'm straight, happy camper, pleased as Punch, tickled, tickled pink, tickled to death. See HAPPY.

CONTENTION n. hassle, static, beef, run-in, scrap, scene, set-to, bone to pick, bone of contention, flak, flak session, rhubarb, shindy, dead horse, wrangle. See ARGUE, FIGHT.

CONTENTION, IN adj. in the hunt.

CONTENTIOUS adj. salty, spiky, scrappy, bitchy, cantankerous, cussed, ornery, crabby, touchy, tetchy, chip on one's shoulder, fire-eater, forecastle lawyer. See BELLIGERENT.

CONTENTS n. guts, innards, nub.

CONTEST n. hassle, static, beef, row, rumble, run-in, scrap, brawl, set-to, duke out, go, bone to pick, bone of contention, battle royal, squelcher, wrangle, when push comes to shove. See ARGUMENT. See also FIGHT.

CONTEST v. 1. in it to win it (Af. Am.), jockey for position, scramble for, go for, go for it, go for broke, go for the throat, go for the jugular, go after, go a couple of rounds, make a play for, push, push for, knock one's brains out, knock oneself out, break one's neck, bust one's ass, shoot for, shoot at, shoot the works, give it one's all, give it all one's got, jump on, jump on one's case, jump down one's throat, come down on, come down hard on one, land on, let have it with both barrels, give one both barrels, blast, tangle, tangle with, tangle ass with, mix it up with, bump heads with, cross swords with, lock horns with, shoot it out with, stick it to one, push around, raise sand. See also ARGUE. 2. square off, square up, row, scrap, kick up a row, hassle, cross, take on, take a poke, sock, sock it to one, break with, fly in the face of, be agin, buck, nix, have a bone to pick, pettifog, put up an argument, set to, zap, zapper, pitch a bitch, pitch into, light into, lay into, wade into, lace into, sail into, come at, go at, lay at, have at, have at it, lean on, crack down on, gang up on, lay a finger on, lay out, let have it, duke, duke it out, put up one's dukes, romp, rip, rip into, rip up, rip up one side and down the other, slug, put the slug on one, put on the gloves, put up a fight, go up against, hook up with, knuckle with. See also FIGHT. 3. have the law on, law, haul into court, drag into court.

CONTESTANT n. dark horse (unknown), white hope, hopeful. See also PRIZEFIGHTER.

CONTINGENCY n. if money, if it's cool.

CONTINUE v. get on with it, let it ride, keep on trucking. See also PERSIST.

CONTINUOUS adj. looped, no end of, no end to, on a treadmill, day and night.

CONTINUOUSLY adv. round the clock, day and night, right and left, for ever so long, for a coon's age, for a dog's age, for a month of Sundays, till hell freezes over, till you're blue in the face, till the cows come home, till shrimps learn to whistle.

CONTRABAND n. stuff, goods, swag.

CONTRACEPTIVE n. rubber, pro, pro pack, prophylactic, prophy, nightcap, raincoat, safety, bag, scumbag, Trojan, armor, skin, fish skin, French letter, Frenchy, purse, the pill, minipill, Norplant, IUD, B.C., shield; pussy butterfly, copper T (intrauterine device, Obsc.); rubber cookie, ring, catcher's mitt, plastic clam, jelly loop, shower cap (diaphragm).

CONTRACT n. pact, deal, dicker, handshake, papers, yellow-dog (employee agreement not to join a union), drop-dead conditions (firm or final). See AGREEMENT.

CONTRACT v. 1. pact, ink, sign, sign up, buy, set, re-up, hammer out a deal, hack out a deal, work out a deal, make a deal, firm a deal, clinch the deal, it's a deal, shake on, shake hands on, go along with, come around, you sold me, you got it, drop-dead conditions (firm or final). See also SHORTEN. 2. catch, come down with, take one's death.

CONTRADICT v. be agin, buck, cross, fly in the face of, have a bone to pick, take on, thumbs down, turn thumbs down on.

CONTRADICTION n. November Foxtrot Whiskey (no fucking way), not! (added to end of sentence), N.O., nix, no way, no way José, no sale, bump that, forget you, fat chance, stonewall, negatory, like fun, like hell.

CONTRADICTORY adj. ornery, stuffy, agin, anti, con, no go.

CONTRAPTION n. gismo, gadget, jobby, motherfucker (Obsc.), whatchamacallit, thingamajig, dohickey. See APPARATUS.

CONTRARY adj. ornery, stuffy, anti, con, no go, ass-backwards, bass-ackwards, topsy-turvy, arsy-varsy, on the other hand, be agin, be down on, have a bone to pick, have it in for, on the outs, at outs, at loggerheads, fly in the face of, copper a tip (act against advice), other side of the coin, flip side.

CONTRAST v. hang (how does that hang?), hold a candle to, stack up against, match up.

CONTRIBUTE v. 1. ante up, pony up, get it up, chip in, kick in, come through. See GIVE. 2. have a finger in, have a finger in the pie, get in the act, sit in on, put in one's two cents.

CONTRIBUTION n. handout, a hand, helping hand, write-off, gift, gifting, do one's part, chickadee checkoff, lump, poke-out, maxed-out (political limit).

CONTRIBUTOR n. angel, Santa Claus, sugar daddy, fairy godmother, lady bountiful, giver, heavy hitter, maxed-out (Pol.).

CONTRIVANCE n. 1. gimmick, angle, dodge, slant, trick, twist, switch. 2. widget, contraption, dealie bob, sucker, mother, whatsis, gimcrack. See APPARATUS.

CONTRIVE v. 1. finagle, angle, mastermind, jockey, play games. See SCHEME. 2. cook up, dream up, trump up, whip up, frame up, come up with, throw together. See PLAN.

CONTRIVER n. hustler, finagler.

CONTROL n. juice, string, ropes, weight, clout, the high ground, the driver's seat, a lot to do with, a lot to say about, inside track, wire pulling. See also AUTHORITY.

CONTROL v. head, head up, mastermind, run, run things, run the show, push the buttons, handle, henpeck, quarterback, call the signals, call the play, call the shots, call the tune, deal with, truck with, be in the driver's seat, be in the saddle, ride herd on, crack the whip, wear the pants, rule the roost, keep under one's thumb, lead by the nose, kick one around, throw one's weight around, throw a lot of weight, twist around one's little finger, wind around one's little finger, have the upper hand, have the whip hand, have it covered, have the say, have the say-so, have a lot to do with, have a lot to say about, do it your way, hold the aces, hold the reins, pull the ropes, pull the strings, pull the wires, wire-pull, reel one back in, bring to heel, box in, get one in a box, sit on top of, in front of, take the high ground, pussywhip (Fem.). See also MANAGE.

CONTROLLED adj. cool, cool and collected, cool cat, laid-back, dealing with, got a handle on it, hip, ice man, in charge, in the driver's seat. See CALM.

CONTROVERSY n. beef, row, scrap, scene, fuss, words, bone of contention, brush, flak, flak session, wrangle. See ARGUMENT.

CONTUSE v. bung, bung up, rough up, belt around, bang up. See WOUND. See also HIT.

CONVENE v. corral, round up, meet up, scare up, get together. See also MEET.

CONVENIENCE n. one's own sweet time, whenever.

CONVENIENT adj. user-friendly, handy, all-around, on deck, on tap.

CONVENTION n. confab, powwow, show, quadrennial circus, meet, clambake, get-together. See MEETING.

CONVENTIONAL adj. straight, straight arrow, straightedge, uptight, a narb, narbo, square, squaresville, L7, cubular, four-square, spiffy, white bread, plastic, Barbie and Ken, granola head, lame, stuffy, drippy, rube, Clyde, Babbitt, Elk (person), buster, boy scout, jock, in line, in the groove, in a rut, by the numbers, according to Hoyle, playing their game, playing it safe, chicken.

CONVERSANT adj. hip, hep, cool, into, plugged-in, all woke up, go-go, kept posted, on-the-beam. See KNOWL-EDGEABLE.

CONVERSATION n. rap, yack-yack; lines, mack (Af. Am.), gab, small talk, pillow talk (confidential), jive, chin music, eyeball-to-eyeball encounter, visit. See TALK.

CONVERSE v. chew the fat, rag around, gab, rap, yack, modjitate, shoot the shit, schmoose, fold one's ear, bat the chat. See SPEAK.

CONVERSION n. about-face, flip-flop, switch, switch-over.

CONVERT v. 1. switch, switch over. See CHANGE. 2. see the light, come to Jesus, hit the sawdust trail, be born again.

CONVERTED adj. born-again, got religion, newborn Christian, saw the light.

CONVERTIBLE n. rag top, chopped top, no top.

CONVEY v. lug, pack, back, piggyback, birdie-back, ride, shlep, shlep along, tote, truck, buck, heel, hump, jag, shoulder, duke, weed, pass it on over.

CONVICT n. con, jailbird, vic, ex-con, lifer, two time loser, yardbird, chain gang, rock crusher, PW, stir bird, rat, brig rat, goodie, hog, lag, robuck (bully), trusty, politician (privileged), merchant schoolmate (fellow convict), eel, slippery eel, center man, real man, right guy, gee, geezo, gorilla, tough, punk, hipster, spear chicken, apple knocker, lane, square John; cherry (new, no experience), fish, fresh one, jice, new jice, hoosier (new); hideout (escapist); short, short eyes (child molester); beast (sex offender).

CONVICT v. put away, send up, throw the book at, break one's license, frame, frame up. See SENTENCE.

CONVICTION n. 1. judgment call, op, say-so, slant, two cents' worth, vox pop. 2. rap, fall.

CONVINCE v. brainwash, sell one on, hook, hook in, put across, turn one's head around, schmeikle, hold one's feet to the fire, twist one's arm, make a believer out of one. See PERSUADE.

CONVINCED adj. sold, satisfied, bought it.

CONVIVIAL adj. glad-hander, clubby, elbow-bender.

CONVOCATION n. get-together, turnout, meet, clambake, confab, powwow. See MEETING.

CONVULSIVE adj. spaz, herky-jerky, have a fit, throw a fit.

COOK n. cookie, hasher, hash slinger, belly burglar, gut burglar, belly robber, biscuit roller, chocker, grease pot, grub chocker, jeppo, ninety-nine, boiler (logger), pot slinger, sizzler, builder, stew builder. See also BAKER.

COOK v. burn, cremate, nuke (microwave), doctor, ruin, spoil.

COOKIES n. dry cush.

COOLING adj. warming-down.

COOPER n. bungs, Jimmy Bungs (ship).

COOPERATE v. partner, go partners, get together, throw in together, be in cahoots with, do business with, work hand in glove with, team up with, throw in with, go along with, get in bed with, live with, play ball, play the game. See also COLLABORATE.

COOPERATIVE n. coop, co-op. See ASSOCIATION.

COOPERATIVE PERSON n. team player.

COORDINATE v. get it together, get one's act together, get one's ducks in a row, have all the pieces in place, pull together, pull things together, team up, shape up, quarterback. See ARRANGE.

COORDINATES n. fix, spot.

CO-OWNER n. pard, pardner, buddy, buddy-buddy.

CO-OWNERSHIP n. go partners, get-together, throw in together, in cahoots with, team up with, throw in with, join up with, line up with, in the same bed with.

COPE v. hack, hack it, handle, handle it, get a handle on something, make it, make a go of it, live with.

COPILOT n. meter reader, kid, stooge.

COPIOUS adj. heavy, aplenty, a mess, galore, no end, up to one's ass in, coming out of one's ears, alive with, crawling with, thick with. See PLENTY.

COPULATE v. fuck, screw, lay, hump, nail, ball, bang, boff, dork, pork, shtup, jazz, shag, pump, bump, boost, get together, get busy, get down, boogaloo, do it, do the wild thing, hoe hoppin' (promiscuous, Af. Am.), jab, knock boots with, plug, rock (someone's) world, slam, square (someone's) circle, thump, jump in the sack, make it, make out, go all the way, do the dirty deed, beating someone with an ugly stick, go to bed with, lay pipe, spread for (Fem.), get it on, hide the salami, parallel park (all Obsc.). See SEXUAL INTERCOURSE.

COPULATION n. fuck, screw, lay, nookie, balling, go the limit, score, laying pipe, matinee, bed and breakfast, nooner, quickie, parallel parking, night baseball, a little heavy breathing, roll in the hay, he'n' and she'n', fun and games, (all Obsc.). See SEXUAL INTERCOURSE.

COPY n. 1. ditto, dupe, fax, xerox, clone, carbon, carbon copy, mimeo, stat, repro, knockoff, flimsy. 2. look-alike, work-alike, ringer, dead ringer, copycat, spitting image, spit and image, chip off the old block, double, peas in a pod, twin, ——— compatible (P.C. compatible). 3. knock-off, fake, phony, plastic, bogus, bite, pirate.

COPY v. 1. dupe, fax, xerox, carbon, clone, mimeo, ditto, knock off, stat. 2. act like, do, do like, go like, make like, chomp, mirror, take off as, do a take-off, play the ——— (affect a role). 3. steal one's stuff, pirate, bite, fake, phony, knock off, take a leaf out of one's book, fax hacker (sends unrequested messages or advertisements).

COQUETTE n. operator, vamp, C.S.P. (casual sex partner), player, swinger, man trap, velvet trap, cruiser, gold digger, wolverine.

CORDIAL adj. buddy-buddy, clubby, mellow (close), cozy, palsy-walsy, red-carpet treatment. See FRIENDLY.

CORE n. bottom line, heart, meat and potatoes, nitty-gritty, nub. See BASIC.

CORNED BEEF n. Irish turkey (with cabbage), horse, red horse, salt horse, young horse.

CORNED BEEF HASH n. corn bill, corn willie, corned willie.

CORNER v. tree, have one up a tree, chase up a tree, chase up a stump, have one on the ropes, cut off, mousetrap.

CORNET n. quail.

CORNETIST n. brass officer, lip splitter.

CORPORATION n. the Company, syndicate, megacorp, multinational, plunderbund, clan, jungle, zoo, hookup, tie-in, tie-up, bunch, crew, crowd, gang, mob, outfit, ring, shell. See also ASSOCIATION; BUSINESS.

CORPORATION OFFICERS n. CEO, execs, exec suite, board, biggies, big shot, brass, front office, toppers, upstairs. See also EXECUTIVE.

CORPSE n. dead meat, cold meat, fly bait, body, loved one, remains, stiff, cage, carcus, goner, landowner, worm chow, worm food, croppy.

CORPULENT adj. hefty, fat city, fat slob, beef trust, baby elephant, bikini whale (girl), blimp, Mr. Five by Five. See FAT.

CORPUS CHRISTI, TEXAS Taco Town.

CORRAL v. poke, punch, sweep.

CORRECT adj. on the nose, on the button, on the numbers, on the money, right on the money, on the ball, on the beam, on target, on track, on the right track, dead on, right on, righteous, right you are, right as rain, right-o, keerect, that dog'll hunt, bull's-eye, good eye, hit the nail on the head, an A, fuckin' A, S.O.P., amen, you better believe it, that's for sure, kosher, okay, OK, right stuff, reet, solid, stone, cut it fine, draw it fine, dot the i's and cross the t's, cook with gas, cook on the front burner, chop-chop, you said a mouthful, you're darn tootin', according to Hoyle. See also CONVENTIONAL.

CORRECT v. 1. debug, doctor, flyspeck, launder, scrub, clean up, pick up, shape up, fix up, go over, fiddle with. 2. straighten up and fly right, straighten out, go straight, follow the straight and narrow, clean up one's act, get one's act together, get with it, get on the ball, shape up, upgrade, make first rate, recalibrate, dial back, turn around, turn things around, turn over a new leaf, mat down, take a brace. See also IMPROVE. 3. make up for, pay one's dues, square, square up, square the beef. See also RECOMPENSE.

CORRELATE v. tune in on, be on the same wavelength, have good vibes, have good vibrations.

CORRESPOND v. 1. sync up, sync, lip sync. 2. drop a note, drop a line, scribble a line, scribble a note, drop a kite, tab a kite, fly a kite (airmail, also a letter smuggled in or out of prison), knock out a tab, pen, put pen to paper.

CORRESPONDENT n. stringer, telewriter (TV), newshen, pen pal. See WRITER.

CORROBORATE v. check out, check up, check on, check up on, double-check, okay, OK, rubber-stamp, give the nod. See CONFIRM.

CORRUPT adj. wide-open, on the take, on the pad, money talks bullshit walks, open, meat-eater, racket up, tainted, something rotten in Denmark, gone to bad, gone to the dogs, gone to hell, fast-and-loose. See also DISHONEST.

CORRUPT v. brainwash, hook, get one hooked, lead one down the primrose path.

CORRUPTION n. juice, payoff, payoff money, bad notes, payola, drugola, gayola, under the table, oil, on the take, padding, shake, skimming, squeeze, boodle, hat. See also BRIBE; PROTECTION MONEY.

COSMETICS n. makeup, paint, war paint, drugstore complexion, glob, globby, glop, gloppy, goo, gook, goonk, goop, goopy, goup, gunk.

COST n. price tag, bad news, damage, score, tab, bite, nut, nick, dues, tick, ticket, squeeze, a throw, set one back, come to, what's it come to?, to the tune of, tidy sum, hummer, bigger bang for the buck, arm and a leg, what the traffic will bear, highway robbery, highway mopery, back, top dollar, bottom dollar, bottom line, below the line, line, nickel and dime (minor), outlay, paid the piper.

COST v. come to, move back, set one back, stood, to the tune of.

COSTLY adj. pricey, cher, dear, steep, stiff, executive, heavy sugar, what the traffic will bear. an arm and a leg, highway robbery, important. See EXPENSIVE.

COST OF LIVING ADJUSTMENT n. COLA.

COSTUME n. getup, outfit.

COTERIE n. groupies, bunch, click, crew, crowd, crush, gang, mob, outfit, ring, insiders, followers, fans, skeezer (hip-hop), buddies, rat pack.

COTTON GIN n. flying jinny, jenny.

COUCH n. davenport, sofa bed, day bed.

COUGH n. hack, bark, croup.

COUGH SYRUP n. terps, turps.

COUNCIL n. brain trust, kitchen cabinet, groupthink, gang, mob, ring, clan, outfit, confab, huddle, powwow, meet. See also GROUP, MEETING.

COUNSEL n. 1. steer, bum steer, kibitz, flea in the ear, two cents' worth, one's two cents' worth, tip, tip-off, word to the wise. 2. mouthpiece, beak, beagle, legal eagle, lip, patch, bomber (divorce). See ATTORNEY.

COUNSEL v. steer, tout, tip, tip off, give one a tip, give a pointer to, put in the loop, put in the know, put one in the picture, put on to, put on to something hot, put hip, put hep, put a bug in one's ear, put a flea in one's ear, fold an ear, put in one's two cents, put one wise, wise one up, keep posted, show one the ropes, lace one's boots, confab, get heads together, huddle. See also ADVISE.

COUNSELOR n. 1. mouthpiece, man's mouth, beak, beagle, legal beagle, legal eagle, squeal, bomber (divorce), ambulance chaser, shyster, front, lip, mugger, spieler, spouter, tangle-jaw, tongue, warble, fixer, springer, ghost (writes briefs), cuter, cutter (prosecutor), the D.A., pleader, pettifogger, Philadelphia lawyer. 2. tout, tipster, clubhouse lawyer, jailhouse lawyer, guardhouse lawyer, kibitzer, armchair general, Monday morning quarterback, Dutch uncle, buttinsky, backseat driver; God committee, God squad (both Medic.).

COUNT v. tot, tot up, tote, tote up, run down, tick off, count heads, count noses, count the house, cut ice, cut some ice, keep tab, keep tabs, dope out, figure in, figure out, take account of, reckon up.

COUNTENANCE n. looks, mug, phiz, phizog, kisser, puss, map, mush, moosh, pan, deadpan, poker face, dial, biscuit, clock, conk, Chevy Chase, gills, index, mask, potato, squash, sourpuss, picklepuss, sugarpuss, cut of one's jib, front.

COUNTENANCE v. 1. live with, go along with, put up with, suck it up, bear with, cope, handle, hear of, swallow, stomach something, grin and bear it, stand for, sit still for. See also ENDURE. 2. sign off on, okay, thumbs up, put one's John Hancock on, get behind, go for, have eyes for, give the nod, give the green light, give the stamp of approval. See ACCEPT.

COUNTER v. be agin, go agin, buck, cross, fly in the face of, have a bone to pick, take on, thumbs down, turn thumbs down on, sass, backtalk, top, put the blocks to. See OPPOSE. See also HINDER.

COUNTERCULTURE n. underground, flower children, hippy, yippy, yippie, street people, weathermen.

COUNTERFEIT adj. phony, queer, fake, faked, bogue, bogus, junque, pseud, pseudo, put on, autobogophobia (fear of bogosity), bogosity, bogotified, hokey, ersatz, plastic, pirate goods, pirate labels, bum, bent, falsie, wrong, wrong number, two-faced, fishy, frame, framed, plant, planted (evidence), crock, crock of shit, sincere, not kosher, not what it's cracked up to be, no such animal, soft shell, it won't fly, stiffing it, gil, Hollywood. See also FALSE.

COUNTERFEIT n. actor, bogus, bogue, bunco, bunko, bum, junque, phony, pseud, pseudo, put-on. See also FORGERY.

COUNTERFEIT v. fake, phony, phony up, dupe, knock off, xerox, carbon, clone, mimeo, stat, ditto, bite, pencil-whip (documentation), do, do like, act like, go like, make like, make out like.

COUNTERFEITER n. penman, raiser, designer, maker, scratcher, scratch man, one of a scratch mob, butterfly man, scrip, script writer, short-story writer, connection, queer hustler, cobbler, paper hanger; bill poster, cobbler (forges passports), shoe (also passports); penciler, tracer (crude).

COUNTERFEIT MONEY n.   paper, wallpaper, funny paper, funny money, phony money, queer, bogus, sourdough, boodle, backs, fronts, hot dough, shuffle, stiff, green goods, long green, gypsy bankroll; plug, slug, cluck, stumer (coin); scrip, stiff (check).

COUNTERFEIT MONEY, DISSEMINATE v. pass, pass the queer, shove, shove the queer, paper, lay paper, smack with.

COUNTERMAN n.   jerk, soda jerk.

COUNTERPART n.   carbon copy, ringer, dead ringer, ditto, spit and image, spitting image, look-alikes, peas in a pod, two of a kind. See COPY.

COUNTLESS adj.   zillion, jillion, bazillion, mucho, mega———(Pref., e.g. megabucks), eleventeen, umpteen, umptieth, umpty-umpth, load, loads, loaded, shit load, shit bag, raft, rafts, slew, whole slew, wad, gobs, scads, mess, mint, mucho, pack, peck, heap, pile, piles, bags of, oodles, lots of, bokoo, boku, lousy with, stack, stacks, passel, tidy sum, more than one can shake a stick at, no end of, no end to, thick as fleas on a hound dog, thick as flies, thick as hail.

COUNT ON v.   bank on, bet on, bet one's bottom dollar on, take as gospel truth, score, tab.

COUNTRY n.   boondocks, boonies, sticks, stix, B.F.E., butt-fucking Egypt, B.F.A., butt-fucking Africa, woods, outback, up country.

COUNTRYMAN n.   landsman, paesano, paisano.

COUPLE n.   item, duo, deuce it, couple, gruesome twosome, team, pair off, twosome, spic and span (Puerto Rican, and Af. Am., Derog.).

COURAGE n.   balls, brass balls, guts, gutsiness, guttiness, heart, nerve, stomach, what it takes, grit, true grit, spunk, backbone, moxie, starch, clock, corazón, chutzpah, huevos, intestinal fortitude, bottled courage, Dutch courage (intoxicated). See also DARING.

COURAGEOUS adj.   game, gritty, gutsy, gutty, spunky, nervy, stand tall, tough it out, I'm shakin' (response to threat, sarcasm), bigger 'n life, fire eater, hairy, cool hand. See FEARLESS.

COURIER n.   bagman, runner, mule, gofer, gopher, speedy, smurf (carries illegal money to launder it).

COURSE n.   1. groove, rut, boards, aisle, byway, stroll. 2. forty ways to Sunday, forty ways from Sunday, that-a-way, every which way. 3. channels, red tape, by the numbers, by the book. See also PROCEDURE.

COURSE (COLLEGE) n.   gut course, pipe course, snap course, cake, a mick, slider (easy); hardcore, killer,

grinder (hard); dead whore (easy college test), rip, pud, undergrad, grad, postgrad, doc, postdoc.

COURT n.   kangaroo court (mock or harsh small-town), train station (traffic).

COURT v.   coo, date, go together, go steady, go with, keep company, chase, run after, make time with, rush, head rush, sashay, sashay out with, walk out with, spark, squire, play up to, set one's cap for, snow.

COURTHOUSE n.   blindfolded lady with the scales.

COUSIN n.   cuz.

COVENANT n.   deal, dicker, handshake, pact, papers. See AGREEMENT.

COVER n.   fig leaf; drop, dubok, front (all places used to hide illegal transactions).

COVERED adj.   under wraps, doggo, q.t., incog.

COVERED WITH adj.   lousy with, mangy with, dripping with.

COVERT adj.   under wraps, undercover, hush-hush, creep (mission), tref, triff, doggo, incog, q.t., skunk works (secret manufacturing plant or laboratory), go black. See SECRET.

COVERTLY adv.   undercover, under wraps, hush-hush, strictly hush-hush, on the q.t., on the quiet, on the sly, in a hole-and-corner way, in holes and corners, wildcat.

COVER UP v.   1. beard, wear cheaters, slap on some glims, flash the gogs, throw on a makeup, phony up one's get-up. 2. cover for, stonewall, take the rap for, whitewash, put on an act, front, front for, put up a front, put on a front, put on a false front, blow smoke, play the goat. 3. finesse it, launder, whitewash, palm, paper over, squash, squelch, skunk works (secret manufacturing plant or laboratory), keep it under one's hat, keep under wraps, keep the lid on, put the lid on, sweep under the rug, pull the wool over one's eyes.

COVET v.   yen, yen for, have the hots for, hard-on for, jones for, itch for, spoil for, have one's mouth fixed for, lech, lech for. See DESIRE.

COVETOUS adj.   green-eyed, jelly.

COW n.   Bossie, Bossy, moo cow, moo-moo, Nellie, Elsie.

COW v.   bulldoze, buffalo, chicken out, enforce, lean on, push around, showboat, turn on the heat, woof, nut on one, walk heavy. See INTIMIDATE.

COWARD n.   chicken, chicken heart, chicken liver, lily liver, white liver, yellow, yellow-belly, candy ass, pecker ass, 'fraid cat, 'fraidy cat, scaredy cat, jellyfish, jelly-belly, weak sister, sissy, baby, big baby, dancer, deuce, piker, mouse, milksop, Milquetoast, Caspar Milquetoast, gutless, gutless wonder, nebbish, nerd, turkey. See also WEAKLING.

COWARDLY adj. yellow, wimp factor, 'fraidy cat, run scared, scared shitless, shit green, the willies, rabbity, chicken, lily-livered, milk candy ass, paper tiger. See AFRAID.

COXSWAIN n. cox.

COZY adj. comfy, cushy, snug as a bug in a rug, in clover, in velvet, on a bed of roses.

CRACKERS n. dog biscuits.

CRAFTY adj. foxy, crazy like a fox, smart, smarts, street smarts, street wise, cagey, fancy footwork, full of fancy footwork, slick, slippery, sly-boots, smooth. See also SHREWD.

CRAM v. 1. jam, jam-pack, pack 'em in, pack like sardines, sardine, ram in, chock, chockablock, stuff, fill to the brim, top off. 2. hit the books, megabook, heavy booking, shed, speed, pull an all-nighter, burn the midnight oil. See STUDY.

CRAMP n. charley horse.

CRANIUM n. biscuit, headbone, ivory. See HEAD.

CRANKY adj. bitchy, mean, ornery, tetchy, outa sorts, out of sorts, a bear, cantankerous, cussed, grouchy, grumpy, snappish, ugly, got up on the wrong side of the bed. See IRRITABLE.

CRAPS TERMS craps, floating crap game, dominoes; African dominoes, African golf (Derog.); hillbilly craps (private or street game), perfects, bones, ivories, flats (dice); snake eyes (two ones); little Joe, little Joe from Kokomo, little Dick (four); Phoebe, fever, fever in the South (five); Jimmy Hicks, sixty days (six), natural, 7 come 11 (seven or eleven); eighter from Decatur; 8 the hard way (eight); quinine, strychnine, ninety days, niner, niner from Carolina, Nina from Carolina (nine); Big Dick (ten), boxcars (pair of sixes), no dice, fade, you're faded, covered, come out, crap out, come, buy the back line, ice (protection money), boxcar numbers (large sum of money).

CRASH n. 1. total, crunch, crackup, pileup, rack-up, stack-up, smashup, smash into, sideswipe, fender-bender, fender tag, bumper thumper, rear ender. 2. washout, pancake, ditch, splashdown, prang (aircraft), kill (Mil., enemy aircraft down). See also AIRPLANE CRASH.

CRASH v. 1. crack up, pile up, smash up, rack up, crunch, sideswipe, fender-bend, fender-tag, rear-end, bang into, nerf. 2. bite the dust, pancake, washout, bites hard, buys the farm, plant in the yard, prang, ditch, splash down, go in, auger in (WWII, aircraft). See also AIRPLANE CRASH.

C RATIONS n. Charlie.

CRAVAT n. choker, chocker, noose, stretcher.

CRAVE v. itch for, yen for, hanker for, spoil for, give one's eyeteeth for, die for, eat one's heart out. See DESIRE.

CRAVEN adj. empty suit, wuss, wimp, wimpy, nebbish, weak-kneed. See WEAKLING.

CRAVING n. the munchies (food), yen, yen-yen, have one's tongue hanging out for, have one's mouth fixed for, carry a torch for, it is to die for, lech, itch, hurting. See DESIRE.

CRAZE n. kick, in, in-thing, the latest thing, the last word, newest wrinkle, wrinkle. See RAGE.

CRAZINESS n. cloud-cuckoo-land, battiness, daffiness, goofiness, nuttiness, sappiness, screwiness, whackiness.

CRAZY adj. dippy, dingy, ding-a-ling, kooky, head case, flaky, wacky, whacko, whacko city, wakilana, loco, loc, blue loco, bent, unglued, unzipped, unscrewed, screwy, screwball, screwed-up, screw-loose, have a screw loose, have a lugnut loose, loose in the bean, loose in the upper story, schizy, schizzed-out, schizoid, got a wild hair up one's ass, psycho, psyched-out, freaked-out, zonked-out, flippo, flipped, flipped-out, flipped one's lid, flipped one's wig, flipped one's stack, nobody home, light's on but nobody's home, one sandwich short of a picnic, belt does not go through all the loops, doesn't have both oars in the water, out to lunch, out of one's tree, out of one's gourd, out of one's head, out of one's skull, out of one's mind, baked, totally baked, fried, in the ozone, over the edge, crackers, bananas, banana pie, bonzo, bonkers, bonkus in the konkus, ape, apeshit, gone ape, gone apeshit, nertz, nerts, nutter, nutted up, nuts, nutsy, nutsy Fagan, just plain nuts, nutbag, nut cake, nutty, fruity, fruitcakey, nutty as a fruitcake, cockeyed, cockamamie, cracked, cracked-up crackpot, freak, freaky, off one's nut, off one's rocker, off one's head, off one's trolley, off the track, off one's hinges, off in the upper story, off the wall, up the wall, minus some buttons, missing a few buttons, not have all one's buttons, missing a few marbles, not have all one's marbles, lost one's marbles, half-deck, not playing with a full deck, tetched, touched, touched in the head, bats, batty, bats in the belfry, mad as a hatter, mad as a March Hare, mad as a weaver, mad as a coot, crazy as a coot, crazy as a loon, loony, Looney Tune, crazier than a bedbug, cutting out paper dolls, leak in the think tank, snakes in one's head, hairpin, haywire, funny, birdie (teenage), dotty, potty, cuckoo, in cloud-cuckoo-land, gone, not all there, not right in the head, meshuga, meshugana, around the bend, round the bend, squirrelly, yo-yo, sappy, goofy, scatterbrain, lame brain, dick-brained, a case, snap case, headcase, snapped, sickie, section 8, non compos, non compos mentis, balmy, barmy, loopy, beany, buggy, bugs, bughouse, slaphappy, gaga, daffy, daffydill, pixilated.

CRAZY, GO v. cow out, crack up, flip out, go ape, go apeshit, come unglued, come unzipped, flake out, schiz out, psych out, freak out, spazz, spazz out, snap, nut up. See INSANE, GO.

CREAM n. come, cum, cow juice, moo juice.

CREAM AND SUGAR n. blond 'n' sweet.

CREAM CHEESE n. shmeer (on a bagel).

CREASE v. dog-ear.

CREATE v. 1. cook up, dream up, whip up, whomp up, trump up, come up with, hatch, craft, fab, bat out, knock out, knock off, knock together, fudge together, throw together, throw up, blow, blow one's soul, dash off, pull off, get off, come through with, noodle, doodle around. See also DEVISE. 2. think up, make up, dream up, head trip, breakout meeting (brainstorm session), brainstorm, spark, break out with, bust out with (surprisingly or suddenly), spitball, take it off the top of one's head. 3. bat out, coin a phrase, author, pen, drive a pencil, knock off hen tracks on a rolltop piano (type), script, scriven, mount (theatrical). See WRITE.

CREATIVE adj. cool, far-out, fly, hep, hip, way-out, leading-edge.

CREATURE n. critter, varmint.

CREDENCE n. gospel, truth, stock, store.

CREDENTIALS, FORGED n. creed, button, flash, paper, tin.

CREDIBLE adj. up front, straight, straight shit, no shit, no bullshit, aboveboard, honest-to-God, one's stock has gone up. See BELIEVABLE.

CREDIT n. 1. plastic, on the tab, on the cuff, on the arm, on the muscle, on pump, on tick, tick, gold ball (good credit), a roach (a person with bad rating), extension (maximum), red ink, in the red, the nut, the cuff. See DEBT. 2. points, Brownie points, strokes, pat on the back. See COMMENDATION. 3. gospel truth, stock, store.

CREDIT v. buy, set store by, take as gospel truth, got to hand it to one, take stock in, pat on the back. See BELIEVE.

CREDITABLE adj. not too shabby, gnarly, nasty, organic, doin' a hundred, batting a thousand, a prince of a fellow, pillar of the church, Jesus bread, Christian, true Christian, salt of the earth. See PRAISEWORTHY.

CREDIT CARD n. plastic, plastic money, smartcard (containing computerized information).

CREDIT, EXTEND v. lug, finance.

CREDIT RATING n. gold ball (very good), a roach (a person with bad rating), D and B (Dun and Bradstreet).

CREDULOUS, BE v. fall for, swallow whole, swallow hook line and sinker, take the bait, be taken in, easy mark. See GULLIBLE.

CREEP v. pussyfoot, gumshoe, creepy, crawly.

CRESTFALLEN adj. down, taken down, blue, singing the blues, ass in a sling, down in the dumps. See DEPRESSED.

CREW n. bunch, crowd, gang, mob, hands, all hands, team.

CRIME n. racket, heavy racket, RICO (racketeering), caper, job, wrongdoing, hit, hit-and-run, case, caser, hustle, make, move, promote, beef, bloomer, fast one, quickie, sneak, lay, gaff, touch, grift, score, beat, piece of work, riffle, trick, keister, mooch, nick, crime in the suites (white collar), divorce (domestic shooting).

CRIME, COMMIT A v. cross the line, set up (plans for), spill the lay, lay out, lay the gaff, spring the gaff; give one a steer, give one a send in, tout (supply with leads); blind steer, bum steer, steer wrong, wrong steer, phony steer, steer, press (supply with faulty leads); spit on the sidewalk (minor), cut in for a gapper's bit, cut in on a touch, declare in, ring in, case, caser, case out, spot (inspect site for), throw bricks (felony), clock, peg a joint, smoke a joint, feeler, put the pike on, duke in, tip, tip off, wire (tip leading up to), beat, caper, clout, job, racket, RICO (racketeering), riffle, candy, make, a sweet make, nice thing, red one, tumul, tumuling (regularly engaged in), making a clean buck, turning a smart buck (nonviolent), bend the law, bang to rights; run the roads down, break out, charge out, mooch out on the grift, get out on the hustle, go out on a piece of work, go out on a touch, plunge out on a score, cut out on the stem, step out on a caper, stepping out, go on a trick, hit the heavy time, hit the hard way, hit and run, hit the turf (leave for scene of), in action, on the hustle, on the make, on the move, on the promote, on the turf, on the sail, out for a buck, racketeering, hip up on the score, pull off a job, pull a heist, pull a one-two play, pull a fast one, pull a quickie, pull a sneak, cop a sneak, play a matinee, stick, hump to death, smash and grab, cop and blow (swiftly); blow, bollix, boot, boot around, crab, crab a play, crimp, crumb a deal, jim, jim a deal, shape up, louse up, mess up, burn up, knock up, piss up, piss in a snowbank, play a bloomer, pull a bloomer, queer, rank, rank a joint, rank a mark, rank and lam, rank a play, screw up (bungle); rehash, reload, go back for seconds (against same victim); screw up (exhaust an area); a nice score, a good touch (profitable venture); blank, stiff, bloomer, fritzer, lemon, skunk, stiffo, a t.b., turkey (profitless venture); deadwood, four-cornered (caught).

CRIME, ORGANIZED n. Mafia, Mafiosi, Cosa Nostra, famiglia, family, organization, our organization, our outfit, outfit, the People, syndicate, the mob, the arm, the gang, bangers, gang bangers, crime cartel, the commission.

CRIME, PETTY n. fink caper, lousy caper, rat caper, spitting on the sidewalk, stabbing a horse and stealing his blanket.

CRIMINAL adj. crooked, heavy, off-base, out-of-line, racket, shady, caught red-handed, caught with one's hand in the cookie jar, dirty, hung-up, hung up with, smoking gun, wildcat.

CRIMINAL n. perp, crook, chiseler, hood, banger, gang banger, geester, car-jacker, con, ex-con, heavy, heel, hustler, hot, mug, mugger, dropper, IBM (Italian Business Man, Derog.), bad actor, bad egg, bad guy, critter, the boys, the boys uptown, deuce (small time), hair bag, dropper, eel, slippery eel, fagin, shylock, F.F.V., finger, finger man, finger mob (gang), fish, jailbird, yardbird, schoolmate (fellow convict), goodie, hog, hoosier (new), lag, vic, muzzler, arm man, blotto, cat burglar, gorilla, guerilla, hep broad, hep ghee, hipster, moll, gun moll, racketeer, in man, inside man, pick man, box man, second-story man, wrong, wrongo, wrong number, gangster, mobster, hoodlum, hooligan, wheel man (driver), mooner, plug-ugly, strong-arm man, muscle man, goon, gunsel, trigger man, piece man, button man, torpedo, hatchet man, marker; mob marker, prowler, spotter, steerer, ten percenter, tipster (spotter of victims), two-time loser, repeater. See also THIEF.

CRIMINAL CHARGE n. pinch, beef, right fall, right beef, stiff beef, stiff rap, right rap, tough rap (supported by ample evidence); jacked up, mopery in the first degree, mopery collar, mopery rap, walkout rap, wrap-up rap (supported by little evidence); bum beef, bum finger, bum rap, frameup, hummer, phony rap, plant, wrong beef, wrong rap (unjust); chill, chill a beef, chill a rap, fix, jerk off a rapper, spike, square a rapper, get the rapper to pull off, square, square a beef, square a pinch, squash a holler, squash a rap, yank a sticker, play the deuce of clubs (quash or withdraw charges); bank, make (guilty); walk (not guilty), street beef (new charges) fall, take a fall, ride the beef (accept all blame).

CRIMINAL, IDENTIFY v. finger, put the finger on, make, make one's kisser, make one's mug, make one's prints (at scene of crime), card, peg, aim, flop, toss, blow, give one a blow, call the turn, shag, tumble. See IDENTIFY.

CRIMINAL RECORD n. 1. pedigree, record, jacket, cherry (no record). 2. rap sheet, yellow sheet, fuzzbiz.

CRIMINAL'S TOOLS n. books, hardware, pig, stuff.

CRIMINAL VICTIM n. touch, square John, stiff, believer, sucker, turkey, yuld, grift, light time (nonviolent action), score, trick, blank, payoff ghee, sailor, scissorbill, springfield, come on, degenerate, hoosier, jay, keister mark, mooch; good giver-up, soft giver-up, lush, sweet mark, soft touch, sweetheart (docile victim); lush who won't go, sucker who kicks over, mark who kicks up, sleeper, tough giver-up (victim who resists).

CRIPPLED adj. crip, gimp, gimpy, game, g'd up, geed up, stiff, hamstrung, hog-tied, sidelined, out of commission.

CRISIS n. crisis mode, crunch, clutch, in a clutch, pinch, in a pinch, squeeze, in a squeeze, crash, bummer, bad scene, downer, drag, rub, trouble in River City, boxed in, in a box, in a corner, in a crack, in a fix, in a hole, jam, in a jam, spot, on the spot, put on the spot, tight spot, in a spot, in a tight spot, in a mess, in a pickle, in a scrape, in a stew, ass out, in deep water, in over one's head, up the creek, up the creek without a paddle, up shit creek, up shit creek without a paddle, up a tree, behind the eight ball, zero hour, flap, flashpoint, push the panic button, hit the panic button, when the shit hits the fan, fire in the belly, heat's on, hurry-up call, can of worms, matter of life and death, when push comes to shove, when the chips are down, when the going gets tough, when things get tough, tough going, hard going, hard time, tar baby, hot potato, bitch, hooker, grabber, joker, Catch-22, double trouble, hit a snag, cropper, come a cropper, have one's ass in a sling, one small difficulty, sticky wicket, large order, squeeze, crash, glitch; meltdown, China syndrome (nuclear).

CRISIS MANAGER n. trouble shooter, fireman, fixer.

CRITIC n. aisle-sitter, Monday morning quarterback, nitpicker, zapper, culture vulture, crix (Pl.).

CRITICAL adj. touch-and-go, touchy, hanging by a thread, on slippery ground, on thin ice, chips are down, fire in the belly, heat's on, hurry-up call, matter of life and death, behind the eight ball, up the creek, up the creek without a paddle, up shit creek without a paddle.

CRITICISM n. 1. call-down, putdown, rap, rap on the knuckles, slap on the wrist, cut, cutting, flak, catch flak, hit, knock. 2. write-up, notice, rave, pan, scorcher, sideswipe, slam, slap, sleighride, static, swipe, the bird, zapper, Bronx cheer, lemon, bullcrit (hasn't read or seen work).

CRITICIZE v. trash, bash, ping (Mil.), zing, zap, rap, pop, knock, dog, dog one out (Persian Gulf War), rag, rag on, crack on (Hum., Af. Am.), snappin' (Af. Am.), nitpick, pan, slam, slice up, slug, slog, hit, scorch, blister, burn, cap, roast, clobber, blast, blast on, lambaste, trim, fluff, take down, take down a peg, peg, shade, throw shade, come at one sideways, call down, dress down, put down, run down, burn down, burn one down, come down on, come down hard on, bag on (Hum.), base on, rank, land on, do a number on, sit on, lean on, jump on, jump all over, cut, cut down to size, cut in half, cut to bits, rip, skin alive, bad-mouth, poor-mouth, sock it to one, swipe at, snipe at, lay out, read one out, go after, let one have it, stick it to one, sail into, tear into, light into, throw the book at one, take a potshot at, take a swipe at, tee off on one, rake, rake up one side and down the other, rake over the coals, haul over the coals, jack up, needle, give one the needle, give one the heat, give a black eye, give it to, give a going over, give what for, give one the raspberry, boo, Bronx cheer, zerbert, attend to, bitch, bitch-bitch-bitch, sound off, pop off, dim view, take a dim view.

CRITIQUE n. takedown, putdown, pan, rap, flak, slam, slap, write-up, notice, zapper. See CRITICISM.

CROAT n. itch, itchy, tug (Derog.).

CRONY n. buddy, bosom buddy, good buddy, asshole buddy, pardner, mellow (close), old man, mate, pal, sidekick. See FRIEND.

CROOKED adj. zigzag, screwy, kinky, agee, agee-jawed, wamper-jawed, catawampus, slaunchways, slaunchwise, cockeyed, hell west and crooked, jack-deuce, skewed, skewgee, askewgee, topsy-turvy, yaw-ways.

CROOKED HORSE RACE n. boat race, fixed, the fix is in, jockey ring, doctor (one who drugs); hop up, slow pill, fast pill (drug); battery, buzzer, joint (all used to shock horse).

CROSS v. be agin, go agin, buck, sass, backtalk, queer, crimp, cramp, put a crimp in, stymie, crab, foul up, fuck up, louse up, snafu, bollix, stonewall, blow smoke, flummox, stump, gum, gum up the works, throw a monkey wrench into the works, spike one's guns, take on, take the wind out of one's sails, knock the bottom out of, knock the chocks from under one, knock the props from under one, have a bone to pick, put the blocks to, put one's nose out of joint, upset one's apple cart.

CROSS-EXAMINATION n. third, third degree.

CROSS-EXAMINE v. sweat, grill, put the screws to, third-degree, put through the third degree. See QUESTION.

CROSS-EYED adj. cockeyed, cockeye.

CROTCH n. snatch.

CROUPIER n. dealer, bank, book, box man, cutter, house, man behind the gun, man behind the stick, stick, stickman.

CROWBAR n. bar, James, jimmy, shamus, stick.

CROWD n. jam, jam up, jam-pack, mob, push, turnout, blowout, sellout, crush, fanny-bumper, everybody and his brother, everybody and his uncle, loaded to the rafters, wall-to-wall people, riffraff, cattle, ragtag, ragtag and bobtail, the great unwashed. See also GROUP, MEETING.

CROWD v. jam, jam-pack, pack 'em in, pack like sardines, sardine, stuff, ram in, chock, chockablock, top off.

CROWDED adj. mobbed, mob scene, packed, jammed, jam-packed, filled to the rafters, full up, up to the hilt, full as a tick, full house, right to the roof, SRO, standing room only, sold out; clean, gone clean (The.); topped off, lousy with, crumbed up with, crummy with, stiff with, swagged up with, up to here, fit to bust, packed like sardines, sardined, fanny bumper, wall-to-wall people.

CRUCIAL adj. showdown, faceoff, hanging by a thread, on slippery ground, on thin ice, touch and go, touchy, acid test. See CRITICAL.

CRUDE adj. grody, grody to the max, knuckle dragger, loud, loud-mouthed, raunchy, raw, tacky, cheap, bunk, skank. See also COARSE.

CRUDENESS n. raunch.

CRUEL adj. bad-ass, bad-assed, wild-assed, bitchy, cussed, dirty, mean, mean machine, ornery, rough, tough, nuts, poison, bum, lousy, murder, murderous, kill-crazy, hard, arctic, butter wouldn't melt in his mouth, got lead balls for eyes, doin' dirt, eighteen-carat, hellish.

CRUELLY adv. deadpan, in cold blood, with a poker face, with a straight face, something fierce, something terrible.

CRUISE v. gunkhole (sailing ad lib).

CRUSH v. squash, squish, scrunch, shmush, kablooey, romp, total. 2. put away, dump, dump on, shit on, hit, hurt. See HUMILIATE. 3. squelch, ice, kill, put the lid on, blow away, blow one out, snow under. See REPRESS.

CRUSHED adj. 1. crawling, draw in one's horns, come out moldy, eat crow, eat dirt, eat humble pie, sing small. See HUMILIATED. 2. busted, in smithereens, totaled, kablooey, scrunched, squished, squashed, bunged up, cut up. 3. down, a downer, down in the dumps, let-down, taken down, taken down a peg, blue, in a blue funk, singing the blues. See DEPRESSED. 4. blown away, blown out, blown out of the water, aced, zapped. See DEFEATED.

CRUTCH n. gimp stick.

CRUX n. nub, heart, key, meat and potatoes, bottom line, nitty-gritty.

CRY n. fuss, holler, blow, hoot and holler, yawp, ruckus.

CRY v. 1. blubber, bawl, break down, boo-hoo, let go, let it out, let it all out, shed bitter tears, weep bitter tears, turn on the water works, cry one's eyes out, cry me a river, sing the blues, crack up, die, laugh on the other side of one's face, put on the weeps. 2. holler, holler out, blow at, yawp.

CRYING n. waterworks, weeps.

CRYSTALLIZE v. gel, jell, set, set up.

CUBAN n. hatchet thrower, Spic (Derog.).

CUCKOLD v. creep, put the horns on, stretch the rubber, two-time.

CUCUMBER n. cuke, cowcumber (So.).

CUDGEL n. billy, nightstick, sap, mace, shill. See CLUB.

CUE n. 1. high sign, lead, hot lead, nod, tip-off. 2. feed, feed line.

CUE CARD n. idiot board, idiot cards, TelePrompTer.

CUL-DE-SAC n. dead end.

CULMINATE v. top it off, go the route, go over the mountain, blow one's wad, shoot one's wad. See also CONSUMMATE.

CULMINATION n. blowoff, capper, critical mass, payoff, all the way.

CULPABLE adj. caught in the act, caught red-handed, caught with one's hand in the cookie jar, dirty, hung up, hung up with, smoking gun, off-base, out-of-line.

CULPRIT n. con, jailbird, goodie, hog, hoosier (new), lag, vic, yardbird, beast (sex offender), ex-con. See also CRIMINAL.

CULTIST n. Moonie, frenzie, crazy. See also DEVOTEE.

CULTIVATE v. shine up to, make up to, play up to, suck up to, brown-nose, kiss ass, ass-kiss, get in with, get on the in with, get next to, get on the good side of, get on the right side of, run after. See also BEFRIEND.

CULTURED adj. long-haired, highbrow, hoity-toity. See also REFINED.

CUMBERSOME adj. clunky, clunk, clunker, galumphing. See CLUMSY.

CUNNILINGUS n. head, face, face man, face job, hat job, French, French job, French way, box lunch, fruit cup, fur burger, muff dive, seafood, sugar bowl pie, tongue wash, cunt lapping, tuna taco, fish dinner, yodeling in the gully, yodeling in the canyon, eating at the Y, blow, blow job, pearl diving, suck, talk to the canoe driver, clit licker (all Obsc.).

CUNNILINGUS v. eat it, eat out, eat pussy, eat at the Y, face job, French, French kiss, give face, give head, give skull (Af. Am.), go down on, go around the world, have hair pie, fur pie, muff-dive, cunt-lap, perform, sit on one's face, sixty-nine, clean up the kitchen (all Obsc.).

CUNNING adj. smooth, smarts, street smarts, streetwise, foxy, crazy like a fox, cagey, fancy footwork, full of fancy footwork, slick, slippery, sly boots. See also SHREWD.

CUNNING n. gamesmanship, one-upmanship, know-how, savvy, the big stick, hustle, hanky-panky, hokey-pokey, con, con game, short con, big con, big store, sting, bunk, bunco, bunko, flam, flimflam, flimflammery, jip, gyp, gyp joint, scam, stunt, fast shuffle, switch, bait and switch, taradiddle, diddling, cheat, frame, frame-up, double shuffle, fast shuffle, fast one, runaround, song and dance, monkey business, funny business, skullduggery.

CUR n. mutt, Heinz, Heinz 57, Heinz 57 Varieties, pooch, dorg, flea hotel. See DOG.

CURATE n. padre, the rev, Holy Joe, sky pilot, sin hound. See CLERGYMAN.

CURATIVE n. pick-me-up, shot in the arm, just what the doctor ordered.

CURB v. 1. ice, put on ice, put away, scrub, send up, box in, get one in a box, bring to a screaming halt. See REPRESS. See also STOP, PREVENT. 2. cool, cool off, cool down, hold down, bog, bog down, keep the lid on, bottle up, cork, cork up, hog-tie, put a half nelson on. See RESTRAIN.

CURDLE v. cheese up, glop up, clabber, lopper.

CURE n. fix, quick fix.

CURE v. kick, kick the habit, shake, sweat it out, take the cure, bogue, dry out, clear up, quit cold, quit cold turkey, become Mr. Fish.

CURIOUS adj. nosy, snoopy, lookie-lou, gawker, gawker's block (freeway slowdown at the scene of an accident), in one's crack. See INQUISITIVE.

CURRENCY n. cold cash, bread, dough, almighty dollar, dinero, moolah, mazuma, the wherewithal, skins, eagle shit, gelt, green stuff, long green, folding, folding money, happy cabbage, alfalfa, wad, chicken feed, dead president. See MONEY.

CURRENT adj. trendy, faddy, fly, chilly, bust fresh, hip, mod, now, state-of-the-art, the leading edge, happenin', what's happening, with it, on the front burner, up to speed, swinging, in the mainstream, in the swim. See NEW.

CURRENT n. AC, DC, juice.

CURRICULUM VITAE n. brag sheet, vita.

CURRY FAVOR v. suck up to, kiss ass, kiss butt, brown-nose, yes, apple-polish, buddy up, fall all over, play footsie, stroke, massage. See FLATTER.

CURSE n. whammy, double whammy, jinx, cuss, cuss word, dirty word, dirty name, four-letter word, no-no, swearword, kibosh, hoodoo, kiss of death.

CURSE v. cuss, damn, darn, drat, flame, jinx, put the horns on, put the whammy on one, put the double whammy on one, give one a kine ahora (Yid.), give one the evil eye, hoodoo, hoodoo one, voodoo, voodoo one, talk dirty.

CURSED adj. all-fired, hellfire, hoodooed, voodooed, snake-bit.

CURSING n. French, pardon my French, cussing, dirty language, dirty talk, cuss, cuss word, dirty word, four-letter word, swear word, no-no, dirty name, bleep.

CURSORY adj. half-assed, half-baked, by bits and pieces, by fits and starts, in dribs and drabs, hit or miss, sloppy. See CARELESS.

CURT adj. snippy, snappy, short.

CURTAIL v. 1. cut, cut down, cut to the bone, nutshell, put in a nutshell, boil down, trim, chop, get to the meat. See SHORTEN. 2. cut back, roll back, dig in, tighten one's belt, downsize, leblang (theater ticket price).

CURTAIN n. rag, oleo (both The.).

CURTAIN CALL n. take a bow, bend.

CURVACEOUS adj. curvy, curves, stacked, built, built for comfort, built like a brick shithouse. See also BEAUTIFUL.

CURVE n. hairpin.

CURVED adj. skewed, curvaceous, curvy.

CUSTARD n. g'dong, gedunk, glop, goop, pud.

CUSTARD PIE n. magoo (for throwing).

CUSTODIAN n. super, swamper, baby-sitter, house-sitter, sitter.

CUSTOM n. thing, into, hang-up, one's bag, shot, kick, swim, grind, daily grind, groove, one's p's and q's, Jones.

CUSTOMARY adj. regular, same old shit, SOS, according to the book, according to Hoyle, by the numbers, playing it safe, in the groove, in a rut, chicken, chickenshit.

CUSTOMER n. pigeon, sucker, live one, a laydown (pays full price), mark, chump, easy make, float, front, head, walk-in, grape (waiting to be squeezed).

CUSTOM-MADE adj. customized, tailor-made, special order, to order.

CUT v. whack, hack, chiv, shiv.

CUTE adj. oochie (person).

CYBERNETIC MACHINE n. brain, number cruncher, micro.

CYLINDER n. barrel, can.

CYMBALS n. highhat, potlids.

CZECH n. Chesky, Bohunk (Derog.), check, duke, Butchski, Czezski.

D

D n. Delta, Dog.

DABBLE v. mess around, fart around, fiddle with, monkey, monkey around, horse around, kid around, muck around, fool around, fool with, fuck around, play around, screw around, jerk off, dilly-dally, lollygag, go at it half-assed, go at it half-baked, go at it artsy-fartsy, potchky (Yid.), play games with.

DAFT adj. flaky, wacky, whacko, wakilana, screwy, in the ozone, baked, totally baked, fried, out of one's gourd, crackers, bonzo, bonkers, nutty, off the wall. See CRAZY.

DAIS n. soapbox, stump, bally stand (circus).

DALLAS Big D.

DALLIANCE n. hanky-panky, fling, carrying-on, relationship, making-out, nooner, fooling around, horsing around, kidding around, messing around, playing around, screwing around, mucking around, farting around, jerking off, billing and cooing, petting, necking, spooning, smooching, lollygagging, a little on the side, working late at the office, Roman spring (late in life). See also AFFAIR, ADULTERY.

DALLY v. 1. dilly-dally, monkey, monkey around, horse around, mess around, kid around, muck around, fart around, fool around, fuck around, play around, screw around, lollygag, jerk off, fool with, M.L.A. (major lip action), box tonsils, play tonsil hockey, a little smacky, play games with. 2. have a fling, carry on, play around, get some on the side. See also FLIRT.

DAMAGE v. ding, wing, tweak, glitch up, take a hit, bend the goods, total, louse up, mess up, muck up, crumb, crumb up, ball up, bollix, bollix up, bugger, bugger up, foul up, fuck up, rack up, goof up, gum up, hash up, screw up, jimmy up, slip up, rough up, shake up, snarl up, snafu, blansh, play hob with, play hell with, play merry hell with, play the devil with, cook, foozle, queer, sink, destabilize, do, do a number on one, hit on, do in, get, hit one where he lives, lay a bad trip on one, zing, lean on, wax.

DAMAGED adj. busted, dusted, kaput, dinged, totaled, gone, gone haywire, glitched, down, on down time, on the blink, on the bum, on the fritz, out of action, out of kilter, out of whack, no-go, run-down, had it, bent, queered, bobbled, bitched, bitched-up, buggered, buggered-up, racked-up, screwed-up, fouled-up, fucked-up, loused-up, gummed-up, balled-up, bollixed-up, messed-up, hashed-up, mucked-up, snafued, commfued, cooked, sunk, shot, flubbed, in smithereens.

DAMN v. jinx, put the horns on, put the whammy on one, put the double whammy on one, hoodoo, hoodoo one, voodoo, voodoo one.

DAMNED adj. all-fired, hellfire, hoodooed, voodooed, snake-bit. See CURSED.

DAMP adj. sticky, steamy, sweat box, steam bath.

DAMSEL n. chick, doll, babe, talent, frill, frail, skirt, miniskirt, queen, classy chassis, jill, li'l mama, granola (wears no makeup), tomato. See GIRL.

DANCE n. 1. prom, hop, sock hop (shoeless), disco, jump, mingle, shindig, boogie, hoedown, hoe-dig, hoodang, hog wrestle, brawl. 2. electric slide, break, rap, slamming, slam dance, soft shoe, clog, crawl, hip-hop, jitter, jitterbug, swing, rug cutter, shout, break, go-go, alley cat, pogo, rock, rock 'n' roll, shag, boogaloo, twist, frug, funky chicken, shuffle, hustle, square, artsport, the big apple, black bottom, boogie-woogie, topless, hooch, hootchy-cooch, shake, shimmy, bumps, grinds, bumps and grinds, toddle, circus (naked), ballin' the jack, breakdown, bunny hug, cakewalk, camel walk, Charleston, Lindy, Lindy hop.

DANCE v. get down, hip-hop, mosh, slam dance, body dance, break dance, touch dance, hoof it, groovin' and duckin', thrashin', hustle, conga, twist, frug, shuffle, boogie, boogie down, boogaloo, juke it, jive, rock, rock and roll, rock out, shake, shake one's skirt, spin, swing, jitter, jitterbug, truck, cut a rug, lay iron (tap), strut, strut one's stuff, shimmy, stomp, wrestle, bunny hop, trip the light fantastic, cheek to cheek, belly to belly, strip, grind, bump and grind.

DANCE HALL n. frolic pad, track.

DANCER n. hoofer, B-boy (break dancer), break, soft shoe, apache, jitterbug, rug cutter, alligator, stripper, strip tease, strip-tease artist, sizzler, bumper, grinder, coffee grinder, peeler, cement mixer, fanner, song-and-dance man, terper; the line, gypsy, pony, chorine (chorus).

DANDY n. dude, flash, dapper Dan, Beau Brummell, sport, swell, dap, toff, snappy dresser, clotheshorse, macaroni. See DUDE.

DANGER n. double trouble, thin ice, hot potato, dynamite, risky business.

DANGEROUS adj. hot, hairy, loaded, dynamite, unhealthy, file, widow maker, jungle, zoo, heavy, rugged, spot, on the spot, put on the spot, dicey, iffy, chancy, fat chance, hasn't got a Chinaman's chance, in the tube, not a prayer, a snowball in hell, play with fire, too hot to handle, hot potato, can get burned, go for broke, play Russian roulette, on thin ice, on slippery ground, on a wing and a prayer, out on a limb, Baker flying (N.), bell the cat, tweak the devil's nose, touchy, touch and go, hanging by a thread, go to sea in a sieve.

DANGER WARNING interj. watch it, heads up, freeze, jiggers, cheese it, mope, nix, six to five, smarten up, wise up, zex, snap out of your hop. See ALARM.

DANGER, WARN OF v. 1. flag, wave a red flag, give one the high sign, cloud up, toot the tooter (mechanical), highball, 2. tip, tip off, crack, hep up, hip up, smarten up, wise up. See also ADVISE, ALARM.

DANK adj. sticky, steamy, close, steam bath, sweat box.

DAPPER adj. classy, dap, snazzy, spiffy, clean, sharp, natty, nifty, nobby, swank, swanky, posh, ritzy, swell, dressed to kill, dressed to the teeth, dressed to the nines, turned out. See STYLISH.

DARE n. defi, defy.

DARE v. make my day, go on make my day, take one on, call one's bluff, knock the chip off one's shoulder, step over the line, face off, come with it (Af. Am.). See CHALLENGE.

DAREDEVIL n. fire-eater, cujo, harum-scarum.

DARING adj. gutsy, gutty, gritty, grit, spunky, nervy, cujo, pizzazz, I'm shakin' (response to threat, sarcasm), cocky, crusty, smart, smart-alecky, smart-ass, wise-ass, hot shot, cheeky, chutzpahdik, spetters, salty, brassy, bold as brass, come on strong, hell of a, hell of a note, helluva nerve, off the deep end, go off the deep end, step off the deep end, go for broke, go out on a limb, go to sea in a sieve, leave oneself wide open, play with fire, fire-eater. See also FEARLESS.

DARING n. nerve, guts, moxie, stuff, pizzazz, brass, chutzpah, grit, spunk, speed. See also COURAGE.

DARK GLASSES n. shades, sunshades, wraparounds, glims, mask, peepers, specs, bebop glasses.

DARVON n. enns (also Darvocet), vons.

DASH v. make a run for it, make it snappy, get on it, rush act, rush period. See also GO.

DASHBOARD n. dash.

DASHED adj. crumbed, down, a downer, down in the dumps, let down, taken down, taken down a peg, blue, in a blue funk, singing the blues. See DEPRESSED.

DASH OFF v. 1. knock off, throw off, toss off, toss out, knock out, bat out, slap out, shove out, slap up. See WRITE. 2. do by halves, slapdash, mess around, any which way, any old way, fast and loose, helter skelter, sloppy.

DATA n. info, poop, poop sheet, scoop, score, dope, goods, whole story, brass tacks, chapter and verse, the know, picture. See FACTS. See also INFORMATION.

DATE n. bird, blind date, blind drag, drag, shag, cradle snatcher, dream bait, egg (Dutch treat), import (out of town), Faust, John, lounge lizard, sofa lizard, earth pig (unattractive). See also APPOINTMENT.

DATE v. see, deuce it, go together, go around together, go around with, keep company, go steady, make time with, play around, step out, fix up, furp, rob the cradle, snatch the cradle.

DATED adj. tired, out, out of it, played-out (Af. Am.), not with it, crunchy granola (still living in the sixties), old hat, joanie, passe, bent, back number, hairy, moth-eaten, moldy, moldy fig, has-been, yesterday, a narb, narbo, square, squaresville, corn, corny, cornball, corn-fed, off the cob, clown, dinosaur, duddy, fuddy-duddy, foozle, fossil, frog, funky, horse-and-buggy, icky, razzmatazz, jazzy, of the old school, ticky, ricky-tick, rinky-dink, rinky-tinky, gasser, chintzy, mince. See also OLD.

DAUGHTER n. sprout, little beaver.

DAUNTED v. buffaloed.

DAVENPORT, IOWA Quad Cities.

DAWDLE v. get noplace fast, poke, poke around, poke along, mosey, toddle, schlep along, bum, bum around, hang out, hang around, goof around, stick around, mooch around, scrounge around, jack around, bat around, fool around, fuck around, fuck off, goof off, screw off, rat, rat fuck, R.F., fuck the dog, sit on one's ass, sit on one's butt, sit on one's duff, jelly, tool, tail, bail out, cat, warm a chair, press the bricks, lie down on the job.

DAWDLER n. slowpoke, foot dragger, stick-in-the-mud, sleepyhead, goof-off, fake-off, fuck-off, goldbrick, schlepper, slower than the seven-year itch, molasses in January. See also LOAFER.

DAWN n. sunup, bright, early bright, crack of dawn, day peep.

DAY n. bright, early bright.

DAYBREAK n. crack of dawn, day peep, bright, early bright, sunup.

DAYDREAM n. trip, head trip, mind trip, castle in the air, fool's paradise, pipe dream, stare into the middle distance, pie in the sky, in a zone.

DAYDREAM v. trip out, build castles in the air, moon, pipe-dream, woolgather, stare into the middle distance.

DAY-ORIENTED adj. day-people.

DAYTON, OHIO Gem City.

DAZE n. gauze, glaze, Nadaville, MEGO (my eyes glaze over).

DAZED adj. gorked, glazed, gone, dopey, out of it, out to lunch, nebular, spaced, spaced-out, spacey, trippy, tweeked out, woozy, foggy, in a fog, wandering around in a fog, slaphappy, punchy, punch-drunk; nodding, on the nod (narcotic). See also CONFUSED.

DAZZLE v. glitz, razzle-dazzle.

DAZZLING adj. glitzy, razzle-dazzle, flashy, showy.

DEACON n. deac.

DEAD adj. kaput, cold, stiff, bought the farm, had it, offed, dead meat, dog meat, belly-up, toes-up, toes, quartermaster material (Mil.), passed on, passed away, checked out, conked out, kicked the bucket, cashed in, cashed in one's chips, bit the dust, pushing up daisies, croaked, went, went to the last roundup, went west, went to the happy hunting grounds, gone, goner, gone west, gone to the happy hunting grounds, gone glimmering, gone to kingdom come, gone to that great (whatever) in the sky, dead and gone, done for, dead and done for, dead as a dodo, dead as a doornail, dead as a herring, dead as mutton, dead duck, stone dead, stone cold, on a slab, down the drain, finished, six feet under, in Davy Jones' locker, out of range, took one's last curtain call, at rest, crapped-out, flatlined, popped off, feet-first, pifted, boxed.

DEADLINE n. drop-dead date, time frame, time lock, the clock's running, under the gun.

DEADLOCK n. standoff, Mexican standoff, Catch-22, box, corner, dead end, gridlock, hole, damned if you do and damned if you don't, pickle.

DEAD ON ARRIVAL adj. D.O.A.

DEAD, THE n. the majority, the great majority.

DEAF-MUTE adj. deaf-and-dumb, D and D, dee and dee, dummy (Derog.).

DEAL v. 1. dicker, hack out a deal, hammer out a deal, make a deal, work out a deal, hondle, handle, horse-trade, swap, swap horses, Jew down (Derog.), knock down the price. See NEGOTIATE. 2. come across with, dish out, drop, fork over, network with, connect with, have truck with,

DEAL CARDS v. run 'em, deal out, deliver, hit, pitch.

DEALER, CARD n. clerk; mechanic, subway expert (cheaters).

DEALER, GAMBLING n. box man, stick man, fence, stop.

DEALS n. wires, wire pulling, ropes, strings, irons, irons in the fire, balls in the air.

DEAL WITH v. hack, hack it, handle, handle it, get a handle on something, make a go of it, make it, live with. See MANAGE.

DEAN n. tack, dick.

DEAR adj. pricey, steep, stiff, cher, high, fancy, out-of-sight, an arm and a leg, pretty penny, heavy sugar, important, See EXPENSIVE.

DEAR n. dearie, honey, baby, toots, tootsie, sugar, sweetie, sweet face, doll face, puddin', lovey, love of my life. See BELOVED.

DEARTH n. slim pickings.

DEATH n. curtains, curtains for one, celestial discharge, dirt nap, grim reaper, kiss-off, the end, fini, finish, lead poison (by shooting), holy ghost (gunshot wounds), floater, bobber (drowned), jumper, flyer, fried, crispy critters (burned), jam, strawberry jam, red blanket (massive injuries), lights out, lumps, crossing the bar, big jump, final thrill, last debt, last roundup, last out, ol' man Mose, -30-, taps, tap city, one's number is up, when the lights go out, buy the farm, a daisy, parole, cold storage, sweet by-and-by, the hard way; back-gate parlor, back door, back gate, back parole, pine-box release, pine-box parole (prison).

DEATH CHAMBER n. dance hall.

DEATH WALK n. last mile, last waltz, trip up back.

DEBACLE n. blue ruin, shit hit the fan. See DISASTER.

DEBASE v. take down, take down a peg, put down, burn down, burn one down, cap, shoot one down, put one away, dump on, shit on, slice up, fluff off. See BELITTLE.

DEBASED adj. put down, took down, dumped on, faced, eat humble pie, in the doghouse, in bad, in Dutch, lost face, gone to the dogs, gone to hell, gone to bad. See BELITTLED.

DEBATABLE adj. touch-and-go, chancy, iffy, betwixt and between, between sixes and sevens, between a rock and a hard place, the jury's out. See DOUBTFUL.

DEBATE n. hassle, wrangle, words, rap, rap session, powwow, bull yard, blah-blah, flack session, spat, tiff, bone, bone of contention, bone to pick. See also ARGUMENT.

DEBATE v. hassle, lock horns, set to, talk back, talk game, pick a bone, put up an argument, rhubarb, pettifog, kick around, knock around, hammer, hammer away at, chew over, confab, hash, rehash, hash over, bump heads, cross swords, have at it. See also ARGUE, DISCUSS.

DEBAUCHED adj. gone to the bad, gone to the dogs, gone to hell, down in the gutter. See WANTON.

DEBAUCHER n. high liver, playboy, swinger, rake, chaser, womanizer, cunt chaser (Obsc.). See LECHER.

DEBAUCHERY n. bender, tear, binge, toot, bat, blowout, wingding, bust, drunk, jag, high living, fast living, live in the fast lane, life in the fast lane, drive in the fast lane, drive in the fast lane with no brakes, la dolce vita, burn one's candle at both ends, hell-bent, go to hell, go to hell in a handbasket, merry-go-round, paint the town red, on the town. See also REVEL.

DEBRIS n. junk, shit, crap.

DEBT n. red ink, tab, cuff, bad news, damage, score, bite, price tag, chit, IOU, I owe you, in debt, in the red, in the ketchup, in a hole, in hock, in the barrel, living over one's head, nut, on the nut, off the nut, bottom line, below the line, set one back, come to, to the tune of, hummer, albatross, albatross around one's neck, baggage, dead horse, due bill, dues, stiffed one, highway mopery, nigger-rich (borrowing to buy luxuries, Derog.).

DEBTOR n. moocher, smoocher, leech, scrounger, sponge, sponger, rabbit, desperado; deadbeat, four-flusher (does not repay).

DEBUT n. opener, bow, coming out, coming-out party. See BEGINNING.

DEBUT v. come out, bow, open. See BEGIN.

DEBUTANTE n. deb, subdeb.

DECADENT adj. gone to the bad, gone to the dogs, gone to hell. See WANTON.

DECAY v. go to pot, go soft, go downhill, use it or lose it. See DETERIORATE.

DECEASE n. the end, curtains, grim reaper, crossing the bar, taps, buy the farm. See DEATH.

DECEASE v. go, buy the farm, croak, cool off, meet Mr. Jordan, pull the plug, flatline (medical), call off all bets, check out, turn it in, head for the last roundup, deep-six, head for a hearse, one-way ticket, dance on air (hang). See DIE.

DECEASED adj. dead meat, bought the farm, quartermaster material (Mil.), passed on, checked out, kicked the bucket, bit the dust, pushing up daisies, dirt napping, at rest, crapped out, flatlined, gone, gone to a better place, gone to meet one's maker, gave up the ghost, closed one's eyes for the last time. See DEAD.

DECEIT n. smoke and mirrors, dirty dealing, dirty work, dirty pool, dirty trick, sellout, two-timing, crocodile tears, soft soap, sweet talk, spoof, whitewash job. See CHEAT.

DECEITFUL adj. jive-ass, bent, shady, sharp, wrong, wrong number, double-crossing, snake in the grass, worm, two-faced, two-timing, dirty, low-down and dirty, dirty work, crooked, crooked stick, cheatin' heart, fishy, gyp, not kosher, honest John, feather legs, slick, slippery, speak with forked tongue.

DECEIVE v. run a game on one, shine one on, blow smoke up one's ass, screw, shaft, hose, dick, dick one around, jerk one around, fuck one over, lowball, goof on, jive, shuck, shuck and jive, disinform, sting, throw one a curve, give one a bum steer, pull one's chain, doctor, cook, cook up, deacon, duff, hoke, hoke up, load, salt, salt a mine, phony up. See CHEAT.

DECEIVED adj. been had, been taken, fucked, foxed, get played (Af. Am.), conned, disinformed, mousetrapped, set up, sandbagged, suckered, double-crossed, diddled, dicked, gaffled, snowed. See CHEATED.

DECEIVER n. con man, con artist, sharpie, smoothie, fake, faker, fraud, phony, play actor, fast talker, boogerboo, shiever, S.L.O.B. (silver-lipped operator of bullshit), bullskating (Af. Am.), worm, cheese-eater, skunker, hoser, whip, shark. See CHEATER.

DECENT adj. on the up and up, straight, straight arrow, straight shooter, white, regular, spiffy, a livin' doll. See VIRTUOUS.

DECEPTION n. 1. hustle, con, con game, sting, flam, scam, fast shuffle, blow smoke up one's ass, lip gloss, jive, shuck, total shuck, cover-up, snow job, whitewash, whitewash job, doesn't wash, down and dirty. See CHEAT. 2. crock, fib, story, terminological inexactitude, balls, hogwash, malarkey, baloney. See LIE.

DECEPTIVE adj. bum, off, way off, fishy, jivey, jive-ass, shuckin' and jivin', two-faced, gil, Hollywood, slick, sincere, snide, phony, plastic, huggery-muggery, reach-me-down, fake, fakey, out in left field. See also SHIFTY.

DECIBELS n. dB, dog biscuits.

DECIDE v. call the shots, cinch, clinch, nail down, take a decision, go down the line, fish or cut bait, shit or get off the pot, opt, tap. See DETERMINE.

DECIDED adj. nailed, on ice, all locked up, cinched, clinched, in the bag, set, taped, for sure, posolutely, absitively. See DETERMINED.

DECIDEDLY adv. absofuckinglutely, def, but def, cert, sure, real, really, jolly, bloody, stone (stone deaf), terribly, terrifically, almighty, powerful, right, woofing, for a fact, for a fact Jack, that's a fact Jack, you said it, no buts about it, no ifs ands or buts, no strings attached, no holds barred, no catch, no kicker, and no mistake, come hell or high water, flat-ass, flat out, straight out, in spades, sure as God made little green apples, is the Pope Catholic? See also ABSOLUTELY.

DECISION n. the nod, the call, showdown.

DECISIVE adj. all-out, flat-out, straight-out, litmus test, no ifs ands or buts.

DECKHAND n. roustabout.

DECK OF SHIP n. mat (usually aircraft carrier), topside.

DECLAIM v. get on a soapbox, spiel, spout, chew the scenery, blow hot air, pile it on, talk big. See ORATE.

DECLARATION n. spiel, pitch, story, hot air, piss and wind, say-so, two cents' worth, bomb. See also PROCLAIM, PROMULGATE, REPORT, ASSERT.

DECLARE v. put it out, blast, sound off, run off at the mouth, get on a soapbox, soapbox, spiel, spout. See PROCLAIM. See also SPEAK.

DECLINE n. flop, dive, cropper, pratfall, skids, on the skids. See also SLUMP, FAILURE.

DECLINE v. 1. go to pot, go downhill, go to the dogs, hit the skids, come apart at the seams, be on one's last legs, have one foot in the grave and the other on a banana peel. See DETERIORATE. 2. turn down, turn thumbs down on, pass on, spike, splash, back up (refuse to do something), not buy, not hear of, not think of. See also REJECT.

DECLINING adj. played-out, done, done up, in a bad way, on one's last legs, on the skids, running out of gas.

DÉCOLLETÉ adj. down to there, plunging neckline, let it all hang out.

DECOMPRESSION SICKNESS n. bends.

DECORATE v. doll up, fix up, gussy up, spruce up, jazz up, put on the bells and whistles.

DECORATION n. 1. gingerbread, bells and whistles, fuss, gewgaws, gimcracks, garbage (food), dingbat, do-dad, doodad, thing, fandangle, jazz, seagoing (large, absurd). 2. fruit salad, scrambled eggs, ruptured duck, purple hurt (purple heart), brag rags, chest hardware, chicken guts (Mil.).

DECOY n. 1. deek, nark, plant, come-on man, sitting duck, shill, puffer, stoolie, stool pigeon, booster, pusher, bunco steerer, blow off, 2. rubber duckie (N.). See also LURE.

DECOY v. come on, bait, con, mousetrap, shill, steer, tout, suck in, rope in, humbug, egg one on, lead up the garden path, chum (fishing). See LURE.

DECREE n. rap, the riot act, say, the word.

DECREE v. lay down the law, put one's foot down, read the riot act. See COMMAND.

DECRY v. pan, slam, hit, rap, snappin (Af. Am.), ping (Mil.), peg, bag on (Hum.), base on, take a swipe at, knock, poor-mouth, bad-mouth, do a number on. See CRITICIZE. See also CENSURE; BELITTLE.

DEDICATED adj. true blue, old faithful. See LOYAL.

DEDUCE v. figure, figger, add up to, boil down to, what one is saying is, have a hunch, be afraid, the way one sees it. See CONCLUDE. See also BELIEVE.

DEDUCT v. knock off, cut back, roll back.

DEDUCTION n. deduck (income tax item), cut. See also INFERENCE.

DEED n. 1. papers. 2. stunt, mitzvah (good). 3. happenin', plan, stunt, game, ball game, bit, do, follow through, big idea. See also ACTION.

DEEM v. be afraid, feel, set store by. See BELIEVE.

DEEMPHASIZE v. downplay, play down, gloss over, soft-pedal, throw away, cover up, make light of. See UNDERPLAY.

DEEMPHASIZED adj. downplayed, played-down, glossed-over, low-keyed, low-profile, soft-pedaled, kept under one's hat. See also UNIMPORTANT.

DEER AREA n. antler alley.

DEFACE v. tag, write (graffiti); trash, mess up, hash up, screw up, foul up, fuck up, louse up, gum up, muck up tagger, writer (person). See also DAMAGE.

DEFAMATION n. dirt, dirty linen, dirty wash, dirty laundry, dirty dig, cheap shot, dynamite, mud, slime, smear, sizzler, scorcher, dirty shame, low-down dirty shame, crying shame, burning shame, put-down, rap, slam, brickbat, dump, hit, knock, dozens, dirty dozens, woofing, slap in the face, black eye, backhanded compliment, left-handed compliment, skeleton in the closet, skeleton in the cupboard, low rent.

DEFAME v. pan, slam, smear, blister, roast, scorch, burn, knock, rag, rag on, bad-mouth, hit on, crack on (Hum., Af. Am.), bag on (Hum.), base on, cap, slice up, slag, rank, snappin (Af. Am.), shade, throw shade, pop junk, do a number on, put the zingers in. See SLANDER.

DEFAMER n. knocker, mudslinger, cat, backbiter.

DEFAULT v. stiff, welch, welsh, skate, skip, skip out on, run out on, see in the alley, meet under the arch, give one the arm, bet on the muscle, put on the cuff, put the sleeve on, shirk out of, button up one's pocket, draw the purse string.

DEFAULTER n. deadbeat, stiff, welcher, welsher, behind, desperado, rabbit, skipper, skedaddler, no-show.

DEFEAT n. beating, whipping, licking, paddling, trimming, shellacking, drubbing, embarrassment, trashing, hiding, lathering, lambasting, smearing, pasting, clobbering, larruping, leathering, tanning, walloping, whopping, whomping, whitewashing, waxing, whaling, shutout, washout, Waterloo, disaster, flunk, foozle, lumps, gets one's lumps, cuttin' (jazz), upset, shuck, total shuck, total loss, bloody murder, blue murder, poke in the eye, pratfall, shoot one's wad, fizzle, body blow, dressing-down, come-down, come down in the world, down for the count, down on one's luck, down and out, fall, take a fall. See also TRIUMPH.

DEFEAT v. 1. bash, trash, ace, smoke, drub, dish, dog on, flax, wax, lather, larrup, leather, lambaste, roof fell in (sudden), workover, whop, whomp, whack, whip, whipsaw, tan, tan one's hide, take it all, take it out of one's hide, take it out of one's skin, brain, bloop, bonk, conk, KO, kayo, bust, shred, drop, deck, total, powder, pepper, clobber, cream, zap, zetz, paste, waste, wing, bump, hurt, kick ass, whip ass, clean on, take one, take out, take care of, take the wind out of one's sails, take down, put down, smack down, shoot down, shoot down in flames, tear down, dress one down, shut down, shut out, rank out, punch one out, lay one low, lay one out, wipe out, wipe up the floor with, wipe up the place with, wipe off the map, beat up, beat the bejesus out of one, beat the tar out of, beat the beholden out of one, beat the shit outta, beat the living tar out of, beat the living daylights out of, make mincemeat out of, knock, knock cold, knock off, knock around, knock one out, knock the beholden out of one, knock the daylights out of, knock the living daylights out of, knock the shit out of, knock the bottom out of, knock the chocks out from under, knock the props out from under, knock into the next county, knock for a row of (anything), knock on the head, knock one on one's ass, knock one ass over teakettle, knock one on one's ear, knock one into next week, knock one's block off, knock one's socks off, knock one for a loop, deal a knockout blow to, make hamburger out of one, whale, whale the daylights out of, whale the (anything) out of, wallop, let have it, dust one's jacket, banjax, blast, put on ice, put the slug on one, put one away, floor one, down one, floor, put it in their eye, put one in the hospital. 2. blow one's doors off, bury, blank, plunk, skunk, schneider, mug, murder, murdalize, kill, cook, cook one's goose, eat one's lunch, go upside one's head, trim, trounce, cap, top, fix, fix one's wagon, swamp, scuttle, sconce, skin, shave, massage, oil, smear, shellac, shellack, whitewash, squelch, squash, steamroller, bulldoze, roll over, torpedo, tube, meatball, make one say uncle, do in, lick, lick to a frazzle, beat all hollow, beat the game, beat the system, beat by a nose, nose out, edge out, sneak past, upset, sink the opposition, destabilize, put the skids to, snow, snow under, plow under, put the kibosh on, finish, finish off, shut off, tee off on, rack up, blow away, blow off, blow one out, blow one out of the water, blow sky-high, pin one's ears back, have it all over, bring home the bacon, take the cake, poke full of holes, shoot full of holes, run rings around, run circles around, clean on, clean one's clock, throw for a loop, throw a monkey wrench into the works, upset one's apple cart, give one the business, put away, settle, settle one's hash, spike one's guns.

DEFEATED adj. creamed, dogged on, aced out, blanked, clocked, burned, busted, beatsville, bit the dust, clobbered, cooked, hosed, scooped, topped, trimmed, trounced, lathered, lambasted, licked, lick one's wounds, whipped, whitewashed, murdered, ripped, fixed, zapped, skinned, skinned alive, snowed, snowed under, settled, down, down and out, done in, done for, stymied, shut down, shut off, flameout, get one's lumps, cry uncle, say uncle, all up with, mind-blown, blown away, blown out, blown out of the water, been through the mill, thrown for a loss, tail between one's legs, have one's ass in a sling, on the chin, take it, take it on the chin, you can't buck something, you can't buck city hall, you can't beat the system.

DEFECATE v. crap, shit, go caca, go, caca, poop, poo-poo, go poo-poo, go ah-ah, go to the the can, go to the bathroom, go to the john, go to the Chic Sale, go to the two-holer, have a BM, make number two, make caca, make ah-ah, capoop, squat, take a squat, take a shit, take a crap, play in the sandbox, haul ashes, shake the ashes out, shake a few clinkers out, drop a turd, dunk, dump, take a dump, dump a load, drop a load, answer a call, have a hurry-up call, answer nature's call, do one's business, grunt.

DEFECATION n. BM (bowel movement), stool, shit, crap, caca, dump, number two, turd, terd, business, call, jobby, nature's call. See BOWEL MOVEMENT.

DEFECT n. glitch, bug, kink, catch, gremlin, hiccup factor, irregular, second, blem, not up to scratch, not come up to scratch, not make it, not pass muster, not cut the mustard. See also BLEMISH.

DEFECT v. pull out, sell out, run out, take a walk, go over the fence, go over the hill. See also GO.

DEFECTIVE adj. glitched, a few bugs, gremlins, schlock, blems, seconds, on the bum. See IMPERFECT.

DEFEND v. back, ride shotgun for, go to bat for, go to the mat for, thump for, beat the drum for, stand up for, stick up for, cover, cover up, cover one's ass, stonewall. See also SUPPORT.

DEFENSE n. copout, jive, song, song and dance, story, whitewash, cleanup, fish, fish story, fish tale, have to see a man about a dog, off-time, cover one's ass, Twinkie defense (mental impairment due to eating sweets). See EXCUSE.

DEFENSE DEPARTMENT TERMS MAD (Mutually Assured Destruction), megadeaths (millions killed), bonus kill, collateral damage, body count, theater war, MIRVed, MARVed, strategic hamlet (target city), surgically clean strike, ERD, Enhanced Radiation Device (neutron bomb), SDI, Star Wars.

DEFENSELESS adj. naked, ass out, sitting duck, out on a limb, wide open, one's hands are tied, on the line, in the line of fire, on the spot, pigeon, clay pigeon, stick one's neck out, ready to be taken, sucker for a left, up the creek without a paddle, caught with one's pants down, caught with the smoking gun, caught in the open, with one's face hanging in the breeze.

DEFER v. 1. shelve, put on the back burner, put on hold, hold off, hang fire, cool it, give one a rain check. See DELAY. 2. kiss ass, give into, kowtow to.

DEFERRED adj. scrubbed, pigeonholed, on hold, on the shelf, on the back burner, in a wait state.

DEFIANCE n. big talk, tall talk, backtalk, defi, defy, balls, gas, guts, hot air, macho, sass, lip.

DEFICIENCY n. glitch, bug, hack it, not make it, black mark.

DEFICIENT adj. not up to scratch, not hack it, not make it, not cut out for, outta gas, second-fiddle, second-string, third-string. See also IMPERFECT.

DEFICIT n. red ink, in the red, in the ketchup, in the hole, in hock, due bill, dues, dead horse. See DEBT.

DEFILE v. trash, crud up, crumb up, scuzz up, skank, muck up, sleaze up, mess up, piss on, give one a black eye, make one lose face. See also SLANDER.

DEFILED adj. mucked-up, cooked (radiation), trashed, dirty, exposed.

DEFINE v. label, tag, nail it down, call a spade a spade, lay it out, map out.

DEFINITE adj. absofuckinglutely, on ice, cold, lock and win situation, no ifs ands or buts, license to print money, set, checked and double-checked, in the bag. See CERTAIN.

DEFINITELY adv. absitively, posolutely, cert, come hell or high water, no buts about it, with tits on, in spades. See ABSOLUTELY.

DEFINITIVE adj. flat-out, straight-out, nailed-down, what you see is what you get, downright. See ULTIMATE. See also ABSOLUTE.

DEFLATE v. debunk, knock down, take down, shoot down, cut down to size, slice up, let down easy, break one's heart, kick one in the heart, kick in the ass, kick in the stomach, puncture one's balloon, let the air out of one's tires, let the wind out of one's sails. See HUMILIATE.

DEFLATION n. comeuppance, knock, knockdown, takedown, put-down, touché, pan, debunk, kick one in the heart, kick in the ass, kick in the stomach.

DEFLECT v. bounce, bounce off, slip, cover up, give one the hip.

DEFLOWER v. pop one's cherry, cop a cherry, pick her cherry, break one's cherry, break in, pluck. See also SEDUCE.

DEFRAUD v. run a game on one, rook, screw, shaft, hose, rip off, shuck and jive, double-clock, fleece, burn, clip, take one to the cleaners, sucker into, mooch (commodity scam). See CHEAT.

DEFRAY v. pay up, foot the bill, cough up, pony up, ante up, come up with the necessary, plunk down, shell out, fork over. See PAY.

DEFRAYAL n. payoff, cash on the line, cash on the nail, cash on the barrelhead, kickback, the wherewithal, the necessary, the needful. See also PAYMENT.

DEFT adj. crackerjack, crack, good hands, have know-how, cute.

DEFUNCT adj. dead and done for, dusted, done for, down the drain, gone, gone glimmering, had it, kaput. See DEAD.

DEFY v. defi, fly in the face of, meet eyeball to eyeball, make my day, go on make my day, hang tough, take one on, stick, stick fast, won't take no for an answer, kick over the traces. See CHALLENGE.

DEGENERATE n. bad guy, bub, motherfucker (Obsc.), M.F., mofo, mother-humper, mother-jumper, mother-jammer, mammy-jammer, mother-lover, mother-rucker, bad-ass, sleazeball, barf bag, slimebucket, mutant, maggot, creep, turd, shit, shithead, shitheel, bad news, freak, geek, mutant. See VILLAIN.

DEGENERATE v. go to pieces, go downhill, go to the dogs, come apart at the seams, die on the vine. See DETERIORATE.

DEGRADE v. bump, bust, bench, mud-sling, pan, bag on (Hum.), base on, slam, burn, burn down, burn one down, cap, slice up, rank, take down, take down a peg or two, shoot down, tear down, run down, put down, cut down to size. See HUMILIATE.

DEGRADED adj. gone to bad, gone to the dogs, gone to hell, crawling, in bad, lost face, drummed out, put down. See DISGRACED.

DEGRADING adj. infra dig.

DEGREE n. sheepskin, shingle, PHT (putting hubby through).

DEHYDRATED adj. cotton-mouth, mouth full of cotton, spitting dust.

DEITY n. Dad, Head Knock, Lordy, Man Upstairs.

DEJECTED adj. bummed-out, dragged, down-in-the-mouth, hurtin', in the pits, shot down, all torn up, mopey. See DEPRESSED.

DEJECTION n. blahs, blues, blue devils, blue funk, funk, bad scene, bummer, dolefuls, letdown, downer, down trip, dumps, mumps, mopes, mulligrubs, the mokers.

DELAWARE Blue Hen State, Diamond State, First State.

DELAY n. hangup, holdup, slowup, tie-up, bind, downtime, jam, logjam, showstopper, holding, holding pattern. back burner, limbo.

DELAY v. 1. fool around, fuck around, futz around, fart around, play around, screw around, stooge around, hang around, hang about, lollygag, play for time, conk out, die, stall, pull a stall, hang, hang back, hang fire, dally, dilly-dally, shilly-shally, sit on one's hands, sit on one's ass, sit on one's butt, sit on one's duff, give one the runaround (repeatedly), goldbrick, goof off, fuck off, hold on, sit tight, stonewall, drag out, drag one's feet, drag one's heels, drag one's ass, have lead in one's pants, string out, stretch out, let go to pot, let slide, vamp, piddle-diddle (So.), take the air out of the ball. See also DAWDLE. 2. shelve, put on the shelf put on the back burner, put on hold, put on ice, put off, hold off, hold up, hold on, hang, hang up, hang fire, pigeonhole, cool, cool it, cool one's heels, blow things off.

DELAYED adj. scrubbed, stabbed, sidelined, sidetracked, passed up, pigeonholed, buttonholed, shelved, on the shelf, on hold, on the back burner. 2. hung-up, held-up, in a bind, jammed, jammed-up, strapped for time, burn the midnight oil, snooze you lose.

DELECTABLE adj. scrumptious, yummy, nummy, delish, grinds, divine, heavenly.

DELEGATE n. front, rep.

DELETE v. cut, sterilize, sanitize, decontaminate, bleep, bleep out, blue-pencil, knock out, X-out, trim, gut, clean up, launder, snip, pass up, drop, rub, squash, squelch. See also EDIT.

DELIBERATE v. noodle it around, hammer away at, cool something over, stew over, sweat over, chew over, chew the cud, rack one's brains, put on one's thinking cap, kick around, knock around, bat it around, run it up the flagpole, pour it on. See also ANALYZE; DISCUSS; THINK.

DELICATESSEN n. deli, delly, dellie, goulash, cold cuts.

DELICIOUS adj. delish, grinds, yummy, yummy in the tummy, nummy, divine, heavenly, scrumptious.

DELIGHT v. turn on, freak out, knock out, knock dead, send, slay, grooving, score, wow, hit the spot, be just the ticket, just what the doctor ordered, go over big, tickle pink, tickle to death. See also AMUSE.

DELIGHTED adj. tickled pink, tickled to death, set up, blow one's mind, handsprings, backflips, flipping, lookin' good, pleased as Punch, sold on, wowed, a rush. See THRILLED.

DELIGHT IN v. groove on, grok, dig, get off on, get high on, get naked (not necessarily sexual), get a boot out of, live a little, live it up. See ENJOY.

DELINQUENT n. 1. JD, juvie, punk, stoner, cuddle bunny (young female). 2. welcher, welsher, behind, deadbeat, deadhead, stiff, desperado, rabbit, skipper, skedaddler, no show.

DELIRIOUS adj. off one's head, out of one's head, out of one's skull, got a wild hair up one's ass, flipped, flipped-out, dingy. See also HALLUCINATORY.

DELIRIUM TREMENS n. DT's, the shakes, the horrors, wormies, the heebie-jeebies, jimjams, beezie-weezies, screaming meemies, blue johnnies, blue devils, pink elephants, pink spiders, snakes, snakes in the boots, the clanks, the creeps.

DELIVER v. drop, fork over, pass it on over, hand-carry, hand-walk, put on, put out, dish out, come across with, duke, weed, gimme.

DELIVERANCE n. getaway, out, walk (escape punishment), powder, break, breakout, beat, figary, mooch, mope, spring, tear-away, getaway route.

DELIVERY n. drop.

DELIVERY BOY n. gopher, gofer, speedy, driver.

DELUDE v. disinform, jerk one around, dick one around, low-ball, goof on, jive, shuck, shuck and jive, shine one on, sell wolf cookies, job, do a number, caboodle, snow, hype, they're peeing on us and telling us it's raining. See TRICK.

DELUDED adj. jerked around, fucked over, sucked in, suckered, foxed, conned, get played (Af. Am.), disinformed, mousetrapped, strung along. See TRICKED.

DELUGE v. swamp, flood with, snow, snow under.

DELUSION n. pipe dream, Disneyland, trip, head trip, fool's paradise.

DELUXE adj. plush, posh, ritzy, swank, swanky, first-cabin. See LUXURIOUS.

DELVE v. really get into, leave no stone unturned, turn inside out. See SEARCH.

DEMAND v. hit, hit up, hit on, hold out for, knock, pop the question, whistle for (but won't get), dibs on something, fish or cut bait, shit or get off the pot, hurting for.

DEMANDING adj. ball breaker, back breaker, tough, separates the men from the boys. See DIFFICULT.

DEMEAN v. cut down to size, knock down, pan, poor-mouth, bad-mouth, snappin (Af. Am.), peg, bag on (Hum.), cut-rate, dump on, shit on. See HUMILIATE.

DEMEANED adj. eat crow, eat dirt, eat humble pie, crawl, put down, dumped on, shit on, come out moldy, faced, knocked from one's high horse, knocked off one's perch, have a tuck in one's tail, got one's comeuppance. See BELITTLED.

DEMEANING adj. infra dig.

DEMENTED adj. schizy, schizzed out, schizoid, psycho, flipped out, totally baked, in the ozone, bent, fruity, fruitcakey, nutty as a fruitcake, have a lug nut loose, whacko, ding-a-ling, unglued, out of one's tree, out of one's gourd, bananas, banana pie. See CRAZY.

DEMERIT n. demo, gig, ram, rip, rap, skin, Brownie (R.R.), black mark.

DEMEROL n. mcp, meps, cubes, morals.

DEMILITARIZE v. dcmob.

DEMILITARIZED ZONE n. DMZ.

DEMISE n. the end, lights out, big jump, final thrill, last roundup, last out, -30-, taps, one's number is up, buy the farm. See DEATH.

DEMOBILIZE v. demobe.

DEMOCRATIC PARTY n. Demos, donkeys, party of the people.

DEMOCRATS n. Demos, donkeys.

DEMOCRATS, SOUTHERN n. solid South, boll weevils, Dixiecrats, Dix.

DEMOLISH v. trash, total, torpedo, sink, put in the toilet, wipe off the map, take out, take apart, tear down, break the lease, blue ruin. See DESTROY.

DEMOLISHED adj. totaled, down the tube, down the toilet, done for, wiped off the map, kaput, hashed-up, shot, dusted. See DESTROYED.

DEMON n. fiend, hellion, little devil. See DEVIL.

DEMONSTRATE v. 1. show and tell, roll out, trot out. See DISPLAY. 2. walk one through, crack on one or something, give a for-instance, debunk (prove false). See EXPLAIN. 3. sit in, lie in, buck it over, march on, stage a walkout. See STRIKE.

DEMONSTRATION n. lie-in, sit-in, love-in, teach-in, walkout, march, rally. See also STRIKE.

DEMONSTRATOR n. angries, peaceniks, protestniks, Vietniks.

DEMORALIZE v. psych out, unglue, unzip, get to, blow up, blow out, take apart, take the steam out, send up, send up the balloon. See also DISTURB.

DEMORALIZED adj. unzipped, caved-in, come apart, come apart at the seams, psyched out, go to pieces, lost momentum. See DISCOURAGED.

DEMOTE v. bump, bust, break, rif, bench, layer, set back, hold back.

DEMOTED adj. busted, broken, benched, in the bag (police), set down, set back, held back.

DEMOTION n. rif, bust.

DEMUR v. wait and see, hem and haw, pussyfoot, pussyfoot around.

DEN n. rec room, rumpus room, playroom, family room.

DENIAL n. not (used at end of a positive sentence), nix, ixnay, no way, no way José, November Foxtrot Whiskey (no fucking way), no can do, no sale, no soap, no go, no dice, negatory, turndown, thumbs-down, lumps, slap in the face, kick in the teeth, kick in the ass, fubis, 86, like hell, shove it, shove it up your ass, stick it up your ass, stick it, stow it, fuck that noise!, frig it, forget it, bag that, bump that, forget you, who me?, you should live so long, include me out, ask me another, N.O., nope, no siree, unh-unh, uh-uh, ugh ugh, nah, naw, go take a running jump for yourself, go jump in the lake, over my dead body, not on your life, not by a long chalk, not by a long shot, not by a long sight, not by a darn sight, not by a damn sight, not by a darn, not by a damn, not a bit of it, not much, not a chance, not a Chinaman's chance, fat chance, nothing doing, like hell I will, I'll see you in hell first, stonewall, cold shoulder, cut, go-by, hard time (sexual).

DENIED adj. nixed, punched out, turned-down, no go, blackballed; 86, eighty-six (denied service, too drunk).

DENIGRATE v. run down, put down, tear down, blister, roast, mud-sling, knock, knock down, slam, rag, rag on, crack on (Hum., Af. Am.), burn, burn down, burn one down, snappin (Af. Am.), bad-mouth, peg, cap, slice up, slag, rank, shade, throw shade, rip up the back, give a black eye, put away, knock one off his perch, make one sing small. See SLANDER.

DENOMINATION n. moniker, handle, tag, slot, brand, flag (assumed), label, tab.

DENOTE v. flash, button down, put down for, tab, tag, make, peg, finger, put the finger on, put one's finger on, hang a sign on.

DENOUNCE v. rat, rat on, fink, fink on, sing on, stool on, name, drop a dime on one, finger, put the finger on, pin it on one, blow the whistle, lay at one's door. See INFORM.

DENTAL BRACES n. railroad tracks, tinsel teeth.

DENTAL OFFICE n. tooth booth.

DENTAL STUDENT n. dent.

DENTIST n. fanger, butcher, molar masher.

DENVER, COLORADO Mile High, Mile High City.

DENY v. stonewall, not (used at end of a sentence), nix, be agin, blackball, break with, buck, fly in the face of, turn down, thumbs down, turn thumbs down, take the fifth (plead the fifth amendment), plead a five.

DEODORANT n. smokescreen.

DEOXYRIBONUCLEIC ACID n. DNA.

DEPART v. split, beat it, scram, jet, cut out, cut and run, cut ass, haul ass, bag ass, barrel ass, drag ass, shag ass, color me gone, motor, motorvate, le-go, sko (let's go) air out, bread wide, slide (Af. Am.), bolt (quickly), blow, blow this joint, break camp, hoof it, be-bop, I'm out, I'm outtie, I'm Audi 5000, roll out, make feet, make a break, hit the road, hit the trail, hit the bricks, bop off, blast off, fuck off, kick off, shove off, move on, move out, ease on out, ooze out, flake out, peel out, skin out, get, git, get-git, take off, take a powder, take it on the lam. See GO.

DEPARTED adj. finished, boxed, bought the farm, passed away, kicked the bucket, cashed in one's chips, pushing up daisies, stone cold, on a slab, kaput, six feet under, popped off. See DEAD.

DEPARTMENT n. slot, wing.

DEPARTMENT OF ENERGY n. DOE.

DEPARTMENT OF TRANSPORTATION n. DOT.

DEPARTURE n. 1. getaway, takeoff, walkout, powder, vanishing act, bow out. 2. in thing, last word, latest thing, latest wrinkle, new wrinkle, newey, newie, newfangled contraption, what's happening, what's in. See NEW.

DEPENDABLE adj. carry the load, rock, Rock of Gibraltar, one who delivers, one who comes through, always there in a pinch, count on one. See TRUSTWORTHY.

DEPENDENCY n. habit, hook, monkey, monkey on one's back, jones, Jones, security blanket. See also ADDICTION.

DEPENDENT adj. on one's back, on one's coattails, carrying one, in one's power, in one's pocket, in one's clutches, under one's thumb, under one's spell, at one's mercy, at one's beck and call, at one's feet, a slave to, beholden to, hooked on, led by the nose, tied to one's apron strings, dance to one's tune.

DEPEND ON v. bank on, bet on, bet one's bottom dollar on, gamble on, lay money on, ride on one's coattails, carry the load, carry the mail.

DEPLETE v. bleed, bleed white, suck dry. See also SQUANDER.

DEPLORABLE adj. awful, dirty, godawful, goshawful, bald, grim, lousy, rotten, stinking, shitty, tough shit, TS, burnt, bad scene, bummer, downer, grabber. See also BAD.

DEPLORE v. carry on, take on, eat one's heart out, sing the blues, cry over spilled milk, cry me a river, hurting. See LAMENT.

DEPOSE v. bounce, boot out, kick out, drum out, freeze out, throw out on one's ear, run out of town, ride out on a rail, give the ole heave-ho, send packing. See EJECT.

DEPOSED v. unfrocked (any profession), drummed out, turned off, booted out, run out of town, sent packing.

DEPOSIT n. drop.

DEPOSIT v. drop, park, plant, plank, plank down, plunk, plunk down, plop, stash, stache, ditch, duck, squirrel, squirrel away, sock away.

DEPRAVED adj. kinky, dirty, feelthy, gone to the bad, gone to the dogs, gone to hell, dirty-minded. See WANTON.

DEPRECATE v. rip, put down, take down, run down, cut down to size, burn, burn down, burn one down, cap, slice up, rank, pooh-pooh, poor-mouth, mud-sling, give a black eye, take a dim view of, hold no brief for, not go for, not get all choked over, throw cold water on, throw a wet blanket on. See SLANDER.

DEPRESS v. bug, buzz crusher, drag, drug, turn one off, bum out, put down, run down, play down, beat, beat down, bring one down, damper, put a damper on, put the zingers in, put the hooks in, put the needle in, chill, chill off, faze, throw cold water on, throw a wet blanket on, act like a wet blanket.

DEPRESSANT n. downer, sleeper.

DEPRESSED adj. low, dragged, ripped, crumbed, destroyed, dragging ass, sorry-assed, ass in a sling, have one's ass in a sling, dick in the dirt, blue, blue funk, in a blue funk, funky, grim, got the blue devils, in the toilet, in the dumper, in the dumps, down, a downer, on a downer, let-down, taken down, taken down a peg or two, down in the dumps, in the doleful dumps, down-and-out, down in the mouth, downbeat (movie, song, etc.), low-down, crummy, cleek, sob story, sob stuff, tearjerker, weeper, tear-drop special, make like an crocodile, have the blues, singing the blues, crying the blues, hang crepe, on a bummer, bummed out, flaked out, put away, carry the torch, hurtin', bleeding, in pain, in the pits, down on all fours, shook, shot down, should have stood in bed, carry a heavy load, off one's feed, rhino, have the mulligrubs, have the dolefuls, have the blahs, clanked, clanked-up, cracked-up, tore-up, all torn up, droopy, mopey, mooney, gloomy Gus, wet blanket, raining on one's parade, sad-sacky, killjoy, prunefaced, sourpuss, spring fever.

DEPRESSED AREA n. ghetto, inner city, rig city, rigville, shanty town, ghost town, tar town, dinky town, skid row, barf city, tent city, rust belt.

DEPRESSION n. 1. hard times, bad times, bad scene, bust, slump, crash, rainy days, rainin', bear market, bottom out, slide, dead-cat bounce (false sign of recovery), the big trouble (the 1930s). 2. blahs, blah-blahs, blues, blue devils, blue funk, funk, bummer, downer, dolefuls, dismals, dumps, mumps, mopes, mokers, mulligrubs, down trip, letdown, go downhill, go to the dogs, go to pot, go to pieces, go soft, cave in, hit the skids, come apart at the seams, die on the vine.

DEPRIVE v. stiff, hold back, skim, cold turkey (suddenly and completely).

DEPRIVED adj. needy, underdeveloped (nation or district), have-nots, the poor, bag lady, truly needy. See also DESTITUTE.

DEPTH BOMB OR CHARGE n. ashcan, can, tin can.

DEPUTY n. backup, sub, dogcatcher, white cap.

DERANGED adj. unglued, unzipped, unscrewed, loco, loc, wacko, ape, apeshit, gone ape, gone apeshit, nuts, nutsy Fagan, bull-goose loony, loose in the upper story, flipped, flipped-out, baked, totally baked, fried, not have all one's marbles, leak in the think tank. See CRAZY.

DERELICT n. bum, bummer, stumblebum, skid-row bum, skid-row stiff, stiff, drifter, grifter, slimeball, bag lady, scumbag, floater. See also BEGGAR.

DERIDE v. put down, pan, cap, put on, dump on, do a number on, bag on (Hum.), base on, shoot on, slice up, jolly, kid, rag, roast, slam, slag, rank, shade, throw shade, thumb one's nose at one, give five fingers to one, burn, rip on, pooh-pooh, hurl a brickbat. See RIDICULE.

DERISION n. dig, dirty dig, slap, slam, swipe, jab, dump, put-down, Bronx cheer, the bird, raspberry, razzberry, zerbert, backhanded compliment, left-handed compliment, brickbat, crack, rank-out, comeback, parting shot, bazoo.

DERISIVE adj. fresh, sassy, flip, smart, smart-alecky, smart-ass, wise-ass, biggety, cocky, cheeky, crusty, gally, nervy, out-of-line. See SARCASTIC.

DERISIVE SOUND n. boo, bird, Bronx cheer, zerbert, raspberry, razzberry.

DERIVATION n. spin-off, waves.

DERMAL PATCH n. the patch, derms.

DERMATOLOGIST n. zit doctor, skin man.

DERRICK n. Christmas tree.

DESCENDANT n. chip off the old block.

DESCENDING ORDER n. pecking order, down the line.

DESCRIBE v. run through, track, picture, run down.

DESCRIPTION n. ABC's, blow-by-blow, rundown, make, picture, fingerprint. See also ACCOUNT.

DESECRATE v. trash, crud up, crumb up, scuzz up, skank, muck up, sleaze up, mess up, piss on, give one a black eye, make one lose face.

DESERT v. go AWOL, go A.W.O.L., go over the hill, go west, go over the side, hit the hump, split, ding, fuck off, take off, take the air, drop out, cut out, opt out, cop out, bail out, pull out, check out, flake out, snake out, crawl out, bug out, light, light out, give up the ship, give up the ghost, hightail, hotfoot, skedaddle, make tracks, run out on, walk out on, walk, take a walk, take French leave, kiss good-bye, cut loose, quit cold, ditch, shake, kick, wash one's hands of, leave flat, leave high and dry, leave holding the bag, leave in the lurch, dump, chuck, fade, do a fade, fade out, fade away, rat, duck, heel, collar a broom, cop a broom, quit the scene, take a powder, sniff a powder. See GO, ABSCOND, ABANDON.

DESERTER n. hooky player, AWOL, no-show.

DESERTS n. what is coming to one, what one has coming, what one was asking for, get hers, get his, comeuppance.

DESERVE v. rate, be in line for, what is coming to one, what one has coming, get one's comeuppance.

DESEXUALIZE v. cut off one's balls, deball, fix, alter.

DESIGN n. 1. layout, doodle, comp, paste-up, dummy. 2. picture, big picture, game, game plan, play, gimmick, angle, action, pitch proposition, setup, scenario, scene, story, recipe, trick, bit, child, brainchild, booby trap, lay of the land, what's cookin', how one figures it. See PLAN. See also SCHEME.

DESIGN v. cook up, dream up, sketch out, lay out, work something out. See PLAN.

DESIGNATE v. finger, name, slot, tab, tag, make, aim, peg, lay one's finger on, put one's finger on, put the finger on, button down, pin down, put down for.

DESIGNER n. garmento (clothing).

DESIRABLE adj. untouchable, drop-dead beautiful, ten, 10, piece, piece of furniture, piece of ass, mink, stone, stone fox, head rush, gimme, centerfold, good enough to eat with a spoon, living doll, oh yeah. See BEAUTIFUL.

DESIRE n. bag, itch, hard-on for, wide-on for (female), jones for, hots, hot pants, in heat, lech, nasties, the urge, amore, mash, pash, shine, hankering, eyes for, mad for, carry a torch for, have one's tongue hanging out for, have one's mouth fixed for, hurting for, die for, it's to die for, beaver fever, sweet tooth, cup of tea, druthers, go down the line, flash groove, turn on, weakness, fire in the belly, the munchies (food), yen, yen-yen, big eyes, calf love, puppy love, zazzle. See also INCLINATION, LOVE.

DESIRE v. go for, yen for, have the hots for, have hot pants for, hard-on for, jones for, cream for, lech for, itch, itch for, hanker for, fall for, have eyes for, big eyes for, spoil for, give one's kingdom in hell for, give one's eyeteeth for, have one's mouth fixed for, goof on, mad on, mad for, wild for, crazy for, die over, sweet tooth, sweet on, have a crush on, have a mash on, have a case on, have it bad, be smitten, take to, take a liking to, take a shine to, cotton to, partial to, zazzle.

DESIRED adj. wanted.

DESIROUS adj. horny, turned on, rammy, pash, sexy, heavy, hot, hot and heavy, hot baby, hot number, hot pants, hot patootie. See AMOROUS. See also SEXUALLY AROUSED, IMPATIENT.

DES MOINES, IOWA Dez Minnies.

DESK n. work station.

DESOLATE adj. 1. godforsaken, destroyed. 2. in pain, blue funk, crumbed, ass in a sling, dick in the dirt, down, crying the blues, hurting, in the pits. See DEPRESSED.

DESPAIR v. bum out, destroy, flatten, take down, take one down, let the air out, eat one's heart out, hit rock bottom, lay the blues on.

DESPAIRING adj. 1. sunk, at the end of one's rope, runnin' out of time, can't win for losin', no-win situation, not a prayer, up shit creek, up shit creek without a paddle, in the soup, shot down, no more cards to play. See HOPELESS. 2. bummed-out, have one's ass in a sling, down in the dumps, teardrop special, crumbed, crying the blues, hang crepe, in pain, in the pits, have the mulligrubs, clanked, clanked up, raining on one's parade. See DEPRESSED.

DESPERATE adj. in the soup, in the toilet, in deep shit, up shit creek, up shit creek without a paddle, up the creek, up the creek without a paddle, ass out, bust, hard-up, up against it, no way, no-win situation, no more cards to play, sunk, gone, goner, gone goose, dead duck, tryin' to stay alive, runnin' out of time, at the end of one's rope, scrapin' the bottom of the barrel, got one's back to the wall, fighting to keep one's head up, trying to keep one's head above water, can't win for losin', not a ghost of a chance, not a Chinaman's chance, not a prayer, not a snowball's chance in hell, not till hell freezes over.

DESPERATELY adv. like crazy, like mad.

DESPICABLE adj. sleazy, sleazeball, sludgeball, slime bucket, mutant, maggot, hairball, the lowest, low-life, low-down, low-down no-good, down, dirty, low-down and dirty, dirtbag, dirtball; fuckhead, buddy fucker, motherfucker, MF, mofo (all Obsc.); mother lover, mother rucker, mother grabber, mother jiver, mother dangler, lolla-lucka, dweeb, scurve, scurvy, scuzzo, scuzzbag, gross, pail, bucket, it rots, poxy, scuzzy, shitsky, shitburger, grody, grody to the max, icky, yicky, yucky, shucky, total shuck, beastly, dank, bunk, awful, godawful, goshawful, grim, hairy, rotten, gooky, gucky, grungy, bad-ass, bitchy, turbobitch, son of a b., son of a bitch, SOB, son of a gun, so-and-so, son of a so-and-so, bastard, momzer, snake, snake in the grass, triple clutcher, scumsucker, scumsucking, crummy, cruddy, lousy, shitty, shit-ass, shitheel, heel, shit-stick, chicken, chickenshit, cocksucking, shower scum, meanie, stinking, stinker, stinkeroo, stinky, schtoonk, fink, fink caper, rat caper, rat, rat fink; fuck pig, pig fucker (Obsc.); snide, slimy, pissant, pisshead, beats all, body robber.

DESPISE v. chill, allergic to, have no use for, down on, put down, run down, do a number on, trash, rubbish, wipe out, look down one's nose at, thumb one's nose at, turn up one's nose at, wouldn't touch something with a ten-foot pole.

DESPONDENT adj. crumbed, in the pits, sorry-assed, blue, blue funk, down-in-the-mouth, ass in a sling, low, bummed-out, shot down, all torn up. See DEPRESSED.

DESPOT n. a Hitler, Simon Legree, slave driver, czar.

DESPOTIC adj. bossy, driver, pusher, whip cracker, ass-kicker. See IMPERIOUS.

DESSERTS n. cush, sweets, g'dong, gedunk, hickey.

DESTINED adj. in the cards, que sera sera, the way the ball bounces, the way the cookie crumbles, the way the beads read, the handwriting on the wall.

DESTINY n. break, breaks, karma, the beads, the way the cookie crumbles, the way the ball bounces, handwriting on the wall, in the lap of the gods, Lady Luck, Lady Fortune, Dame Fortune, by and by, from now on in, from here in, from here out, just around the corner.

DESTITUTE adj. flat, flat broke, dead broke, stone broke, stony, busted, belly up, to the wall, totaled, total wipe, wipeout, wiped-out, truly needy, bag lady, disadvantaged, deprived, underdeveloped, (nation or district), blasted, hard-up, strapped, beat, oofless, wasted, clean, cleaned out, tapped, tapped out, melted out, locked out, played out, on one's ass, on the rocks, on the edge, on the ragged edge, on one's uppers, on the hog, on the turf, hurting, pinched, feeling the pinch, to the curb, down-and-out, down to the one's last cent, down to one's last penny, down-at-the-heel, run down at the heels, looking for a handout, have-nots, not have one dime to rub against another, at the end of one's rope, in dire straits, in Queer Street, seen better days, feeling the pinch, poor, dirt poor, poor as a church mouse, coffee-and-cake time, cold in hand (Af. Am.), rhino, for the yoke, on the rims, run on the rims.

DESTROY v. trash, total, nuke, cream, torpedo, kill, axe, sink, zap, bog, crab, squash, smash, smash up, bitch up, botch up, foul up, fuck up, crumb, crumb up, goof up, pile up, rack up, crack up, louse up, mess up, muck up, screw up, snarl up, bugger, bugger up, ball up, bollix up, hash up, put in the toilet, wipe out, wipe off the map, take out, take apart, tear down, break, break the lease, floor, destabilize, bolo (enemy target), nix, X out, wash out, KO, knock out, knock the bottom out of, knock the chocks out from under, knock the props out from under, stamp out, rub out, lose (files), queer, zing, blue ruin, blow sky high, poke full of holes, throw a monkey wrench into the works, put out of action, put out of commission, Dutch, flub up, flub the dub, gum, gum up, gum up the works, screw up the works, queer the works, deep-six (evidence), jim, pickle, rim rock, put the skids under one, spike one's gun, really fix it. 2. settle one's hash, do, do one in, do in, finish, finish off, fix, fix one's wagon, cook one's goose, blow one's doors off, clip one's wings, put in the toilet. See RUIN.

DESTROYED adj. totaled, down the tube, down the toilet, down the drain, down the spout, down the rathole, out the window, dusted, finished, dead and done for, done for, done in, taken out, wiped out, stamped out, wiped off the map, fragged, gone to rack and ruin, gone to the dogs, gone to pot, gone, had it, kaput, queered, screwed, fouled-up, fucked-up, mucked-up, racked-up, loused-up, buggered, buggered-up, gummed-up, snarled-up, balled-up, bollixed-up, hashed-up, messed-up, cooked, on the fritz, on the blink, sunk, shot, kiss (something) good-bye, to hell and gone, in smithereens, boloed (enemy target). See also RUINED.

DESTROYER n. baby sitter, can, tin can, garbage can, flivver, rust bucket (all N.).

DESULTORILY adv. any old way, any which way, do by halves, half-assed, slapdash, knock off, knock out, bat out, shove out, slap out, slap up, throw off, toss off, toss out, fast and loose, mess around, helter-skelter, by bits and pieces, by fits and starts, in dribs and drabs, hit or miss. See also ERRATICALLY.

DETACHED adj. cool, play it cool, cas, cazh, laid-back, far-out, out of it, out to lunch, spaced-out, spacey. See also ALOOF; INDIFFERENT.

DETAIL n. ABC's, ABC of it, blow-by-blow, rundown, spelled out, like it is, make, picture, the numbers, the goods, bottom line, meat and potatoes, chapter and verse, gospel, megillah, scud, scut, nitty-gritty, nuts and bolts, short stroke, what's what, where it's at, the size of it, the straight of it, cue, clue, dope, brass tacks. 2. kitchen police, KP, shit detail (Mil.).

DETAIL v. spell out, lay out, take it line by line, fly-speck, cross the t's and dot the i's, paint a picture, sweat the details, quote chapter and verse, get down to brass tacks, get down to cases, fine-tune.

DETAILS n. short strokes, down to the short strokes, nitty-gritty, touches, finishing touches.

DETAIN v. ice, put on ice, put away, hospitalized (CIA illegal detention), send up. See JAIL.

DETAINED adj. hung-up, held-up, buttonholed. See DELAYED.

DETECT v. uncover, spot, smoke out, smell out, nose out, dig up, hit upon, stumble on, tumble to, wise up to. See DISCOVER.

DETECTIVE n. dick, shamus, flatfoot, tec, private eye, P, eye, narc, man, G-man, T-man, revenuer, federal, fed, FBI; Pinkerton, Pink, Pinkie, the Eye, the eye (Pinkerton detective or Pinkerton National Detective Agency); peeper, snoop, shoe, gumshoe, gumboot, gumheel, rubber heel, brain, deek, elbow, fink, plumber, sleeper (male), bird dog, op, nab, eagle eye, hick dick, house dick, shadow, shagger, slewfoot, stag, star, tail, tin star, door knocker, pounder, bear tracker (plainclothes), hawkshaw, sleuth, sleuth-hound, beagle, skip tracer, spotter; fly ball, fly bob, fly bull, fly cop, fly dick, fly mug (aircraft); cinderball (R.R.). See also POLICE OFFICER, OPERATIVE.

DETECTIVE STORY n. whodunit, who-done-it, shocker, chiller, chiller-diller, thriller, cliff-hanger, mystery, spyboiler, grabber.

DETECTOR n. bird dog.

DETER v. cool, chill, turn off, put off, throw cold water on, throw a wet blanket on, act like a wet blanket, damper, put a damper on. See PREVENT.

DETERIORATE v. 1. fade, slide, skid, hit the skids, break, go to pot, go soft, go downhill, go to pieces, go to the dogs, go to hell in a handbasket, crack, crack up, fold, conk out, peter out, poop out, peg out, fizzle out, cave in, lose it, use it or lose it, over the hill, come apart at the seams, die on the vine, be on one's last legs, have one foot in the grave, have one foot in the grave and the other on a banana peel. 2. melt down.

DETERMINATION n. drive, guts, guttiness, intestinal fortitude, the right stuff, starch, backbone, heart, moxie, spunk.

DETERMINE v. 1. figure, figger, have a hunch, be afraid, add up to, boil down to, what one is saying is, size, size up, the way one sees it. 2. opt, tap, cinch, clinch, nail down, pin down, go down the line, be in the driver's seat, call the shots, give the litmus test, lay one's finger on, put one's finger on, fish or cut bait, take a decision.

DETERMINED adj. 1. nailed, nailed-down, set, on ice, in the bag, open-and-shut, all locked up, have a lock on, lock-and-win situation, take no prisoners, no buts about it, no ifs ands or buts, bet on, bet one's bottom dollar on, checked and double-checked, cinched, clinched, taped, for damn sure, surefire, sure, surest thing you know, for sure, fer shure, fer sher, that's for sure, posolutely, absitively, for a fact. 2. hang in, hang in there, hang tough, go for it, go for broke, go the whole hog, hustle, gritty, gutty, gutsy, game, set, dead set on, sot, bound, bound and determined, scratch, sweat, dig, hammer away, plug, peg away, chill out, do or die, have blood in one's eye, be out for blood, playing for blood, playing hard ball, playing for real, stick at nothing, mean business, strictly business, mean serious jelly, no shit, no bird turdin', not playing around, no fooling, getting it straight, set one's cap for, bent on, hell bent on, hell bent for breakfast, hell bent for leather, pour it on, grind, bear down on it, buckle down, knuckle down, hump it, put one's back into it, high water, come hell or high water, money talks bullshit walks, make no bones about it, unflappable, hard as nails, hard nut to crack, hard-boiled, hold the fort, hold the line, pat, brick wall, stay-put, stand-pat, stand by one's guns, stand one's ground, hold one's ground, dig in one's heels, put one's foot down, solid as a rock, stick it out, stick to one's guns, stick at nothing, stop at nothing, spunky, make no bones about it, knock down and drag out, hard-nosed, take the bit in one's mouth, take the bull by the horns, take the tiger by the tail. See also STUBBORN. 3. in the cards, que sera sera, the way the ball bounces, the way the cookie crumbles, that's the way the beads read.

DETEST v. grossed out on, have no use for, have an allergy to, have no use for, down on. See DISLIKE.

DETESTABLE adj. gross, grody, grody to the max, slimy, sleazy, sleazeball, sludgeball, slime bucket, shower scum, mutant, maggot, beastly, awful, godawful, lousy, rotten, triple-clutcher, low-down. See DESPICABLE.

DETONATABLE adj. ready to blow, hair-trigger, touchy, live (ammunition), live ammo.

DETONATE v. push the button, go off, go blooey, go flooey, kablooey, kaflooey, let go, va-voom.

DETONATED adj. set off, blown, energetically disassembled, launched.

DETONATION n. energetic disassembly.

DETOUR n. circumbendibus.

DETOUR v. finesse it, go round the barn, went by way of. See also DIGRESS.

DETOXIFICATION CENTER n. detox.

DETOXIFY v. get straight, detox, become Mr. Fink, bogue, normie, quit cold turkey, dry out, kick the habit, sweat it out, take the cure, clear up, have the shakes, have the wet-dog shakes.

DETRACT v. do a number on, pan, slam, blister, mudsling, run down, put down, tear down, shoot down, cut-rate, backbite, rip up the back, give a black eye, mark lousy. See SLANDER.

DETRACTION n. black eye, brickbat, putdown, rap, slam, dump, hit, knock, backhanded compliment, left-handed compliment. See DEFAMATION.

DETROIT, MICHIGAN Motown, Motor City.

DETUMESCE v. go flat, go limp.

DEVALUATE v. knock the bottom out of, nose-dive, take down, knock off, cut-rate.

DEVASTATE v. 1. trash, total, smash, hash up, put in the toilet, wipe off the map, take apart, break the lease, stamp out. See DESTROY. 2. make hash of, do one in, fix one's wagon, put something out of action, jim, put the skids under one. See RUIN.

DEVASTATED adj. totaled, shucked, trashed, dusted, down the tube, down the rathole, stamped out, had it, kaput, shot, fragged, to hell and gone. See DESTROYED.

DEVELOPER n. 1. builder, promoter, wheeler-dealer, operator. 2. hypo, soup.

DEVELOPING SOLUTION n. soup.

DEVELOPMENT n. buildup, boost, hike, up, upping, critical mass (dramatic). See ADVANCE.

DEVIANT n. pervo, prevert. See also HOMOSEXUAL.

DEVIATE v. circumlocute, bend the rules, get around, drift.

DEVICE n. 1. gimmick, angle, dodge, slant, trick, twist, switch. See also STRATEGY. 2. gismo, gadget, widget, idiot box, black box, dealie, dealie bob, mother, grabber, gimmick, whatzis, thingumabob. See also APPARATUS.

DEVIL n. fiend, hellion, little devil, debbil, dybbuk, the Deuce, the Dickens, diablo, Lucifer, Old Dad, Old Harry, Old Nick, Old Ned, Old Horny, Old Scratch, Old Gooseberry, Old Bendy, Old Blazes, Old Clootie, Old Poker, Old Gentleman.

DEVIOUS adj. fishy, shady, not kosher, playing games, playing politics, put on, the big put on, faking one out, fancy footwork, go round the barn, went by way of, long way. See also SLY, SHREWD.

DEVISE v. 1. brainstorm, head trip, spark, spitball, take it off the top of one's head, mastermind, hatch, make up, think up, come up with, cook up, dream up, trump up, craft, whip up, whomp up, frame up, line up, ready up, throw together, fudge together, get one's act together, get off, work something out, noodle, noodle around. See also PLAN. 2. ad lib, off the top of one's head, fake it, play it by ear. See IMPROVISE.

DEVOTED adj. gone, gone on, stuck on, hipped on, wild about, mad about, crazy about, nuts about, have a thing about, true blue, old faithful, behind one. See LOYAL. See also AFFECTIONATE.

DEVOTEE n. wannabee, groupie, skeezer (hip-hop), junkie, buff, bug, fan, freak, bug, crazies, nut, trendoid, punker (punk rock); B-boy, B-girl (rap music), head banger, metal head (heavy metal), frenzie, crank, culture vulture, fiend, flip, hound, rooter, booster, alligator, gate, gator, cat, hepcat, prophet, stargazer, blue farouq, flunky, stooge, eager beaver, great one for, demon, sucker for, filbert, fool, boo-bird (boos at games). See also SUPPORTER.

DEVOTEES n. fandom, groupies, frenzies.

DEVOUR v. scarf down, chow down, pig out, wolf, wolf down, garbage down, bolt down, throw back, narf, trough out, grease down, inhale, hoover, grind, kill, gulp, eat like it's going out of style. See EAT.

DEVOUT adj. Holy Joe, Jasper, knee bender, born-again, got religion, Jesus lover, Jesus freak, Mary, goody, goody-goody, goody two-shoes, scoutmaster.

DEXAMYL n. Christmas trees, purple heart.

DEXEDRINE n. dex, dexy, dexie, dexo, football, heart, orange, peach, pep pill, purple heart.

DEXEDRINE, USE v. dex, dexed.

DEXTEROUS adj. sharp, cute, good hands, have know-how, savvy, slick, crack, crackerjack. See SKILLFUL.

DEXTROAMPHETAMINE n. dex, dexie, dexy, football, heart, oranges.

DIAGRAM n. picture, big picture, game, game plan. See PLAN.

DIALECT n. lingo. See also LANGUAGE.

DIALOGUE n. rap, rap session, chinfest, small talk, confab, flap (urgent), powwow, talkee-talkee; lines, sides, book (The.).

DIAMOND n. ice, cracked ice, rock, rock candy, headlight, spark, sparkler, a girl's best friend, pennyweight, Simple Simon.

DIAPER n. didy, didic.

DIAPER COVER n. soaker.

DIAPHRAGM n. rubber cookie, ring, catcher's mitt, plastic clam, shower cap.

DIARRHEA n. runs, trots, turistas, shits, G's, G shits, Basra belly, Delhi belly, gypsy tummy, Hong Kong dog, Johnny Trots, Aztec two-step, quickstep, craps, Joe Trots, movies, squirts, Hershey squirts, Tijuana racetrack, Mexicali revenge, Montezuma's revenge, ride the porcelain bus, ride the porcelain Honda, ride the porcelain train, collywobbles, liquid cork (medicine). See also BOWEL MOVEMENT.

DIARY n. comic book, funny book, swindle sheet.

DICE n. craps, cubes, dominoes, galloping dominoes, African dominoes, African golf, Memphis dominoes, calipers, true dice, perfects, ivories, bones, devil's bones, devil's teeth, horses, Mississippi marbles.

DICE, CROOKED n. flats, bottoms, busters, bustouts, bevels, coolers, edgework, fading dice, wrong dice, right dice, missouts, platinum loaders, repeaters, peeties, shapes, tappers, tops, t's, downhills, uphills, dispatchers, sure pops, percentage dice, squeezes, tats, brick, flat, door pops, loads, cap dice, capped dice, gaffs, marbles, passers, rollers.

DICE GAMBLER n. roller, high roller, pad roller, cutter, gaffer, dice hustler, cowboy (reckless), dipsy (hustler).

DICE GAME TERMS snake eyes, boxcars, Big Dick (10), natural, fever, Phoebe (5), little Joe, eighter from Decatur; dominoes; African dominoes, African golf (Derog.); perfects, bones, ivories, flats (dice); come out, come, crap out, buy the back line. See CRAPS TERMS

DICKER v. hammer out a deal, hack out a deal, work out a deal, cut a deal, Jew down (Derog.), hondle. See NEGOTIATE.

DICTATE v. call the play, call the signals, call the tune, lay down the law, put one's foot down, read the riot act, walk heavy, bulldoze, take the reins. See COMMAND.

DICTATOR n. a Hitler, Simon Legree, slave driver, czar.

DICTATORIAL adj. bossy, crack the whip, throw one's weight around. See IMPERIOUS.

DICTATORSHIP n. garrison state.

DIDACTIC adj. preachy.

DIE v. go, kick off, kick the bucket, kick in, buy it, buy the farm, buy one's lunch, pass away, croak, cool, cool off, bump, bump off, beam up, meet one's maker, meet Mr. Jordan, give up the ghost, turn up one's toes, turn it in, get one's ticket punched, breathe one's last, OD, pull the plug, flatline (Medic.), box, go west, go north, go down the tube, go tits up, go to kingdom come, sprout wings, go home feet first, go home in a box, go to the wall, go flooey, go blooey, go belly up, bite the dust, kiss the dust, kiss off, knock off, pop off, slam off, drop off, pipe off, shove off, step off, step off the curb, step off the deep end, go off the deep end, cash in, cash in one's chips, pass in one's chips, pass in one's checks, hand in one's chips, call off all bets, check out, check in, quit the scene, eat it, have it, head for the last roundup, take the last count, take the long count, make the last muster, over the creek, gone across the creek, slip one's cable, push up daisies, grounded for good, strike bedrock, deep six, take a dirt nap, go to Davy Jones' locker (drown), hop the twig, cook, fry, shove over, quit it, up and die, peg out, pass out, strike out, chalk out, flake out, flack, flack out, head for a hearse, back gate, back-door parole, get a back-gate commute, one-way ticket, one-way ride, kayoed for keeps, trumped; dance, dance on air, dance on nothing, dance off (hang).

DIEHARD n. bitter ender, standpatter.

DIESEL ENGINE n. smudge pot.

DIET n. chow, snack, bite, eats, go juice, plastic cow (nondairy cream), peckings (Af. Am.), hots (hot meal, Mil.), grubbery, goodies, grub. See FOOD.

DIET v. skinny, skinny down, count calories, fall off (lose weight), watch one's weight, slim down.

DIET SPA n. fat farm.

DIFFER v. bump heads, lock horns, go at it, go after each other, hit a clinker, hit a sour note, sound a sour note. See also DISAGREE.

DIFFERENCE n. 1. dif, diff, different strokes, different strokes for different folks. 2. spat, tiff, words, bone to pick, beef, blowup, dustup, hassle, rhubarb, row, run-in, scrap, brawl, brannigan, blow-off, brush, brush-off, catamaran. See ARGUMENT.

DIFFERENT adj. dif, diff, far cry, funky, offbeat, poles apart, weird, quirky, whale of a difference, like night and day, march to the beat of a different drummer.

DIFFERENTIATE v. know what's what, know one's ass from a hole in the ground, know one's ass from one's elbow, know a rock from a hard place, know shit from Shinola, split hairs, redline (financial), Jim Crow.

DIFFICULT adj. hellish, wicked, uphill, uphill battle, burly, mean, heavy, hairy, murder, pisser, rough, stanky (woman), bitch, son of a bitch, son of a gun, stiff, tough, tough one, tough nut to crack, toughie, tough proposition, tough lineup to buck, rough go, dope, separates the men from the boys, hard job, hard pull, hard row to hoe, hard row of stumps, hard way, hi-tech, handful, ballbreaker, ballbuster, ass buster, conk buster, backbreaker, headache, large order, tall order, honey, no picnic, no piece of cake, sticky, sticky wicket, can of worms, bear, makes the cheese more binding, heavy sledding, roundabout way.

DIFFICULTY n. shit, deep shit, serious jelly, serious shit, crisis mode, bad news, bad scene, clutch, hang-up, drag, bind, double bind, tall order, large order, rough go, heavy sledding, rain, ticklish spot, tricky spot, tight spot, tight squeeze, lose-lose situation, no-win situation, one's ass is grass, ass out, gasser, pisser, rat's nest, snake pit, trouble in River City, box, crunch, downside, catch, Catch-22, bitch, handful, in your court (your problem), headache, bummer, downer, worriment, botheration, grabber, hooker, nightmare, double trouble, behind the eight ball, boxed in, in a box, in deep doo-doo, in a fix, in a hole, snafu, jam, in a jam, in a clutch, in a mess, in a pickle, scrape, in a scrape, in a spot, in a tight spot, in a hot spot, on the hot seat, in hot water, in deep water, in heavy water, stew, in a stew, in over one's head, up a tree, up the creek, up the creek without a paddle, up shit creek, up shit creek without a paddle, pain in the ass, pain in the neck, between a rock and a hard place, tail in a gate, tit in a wringer, mix, mess, holy mess, unholy mess, kettle of fish, fine kettle of fish, a fine mess you've got us into, how-do-you-do, fine how-do-you-do, hobble, pickle, pretty pickle, pretty pass, squeeze, sticky wicket, bummer, hard knocks, rotten luck, tough luck, raw deal, bad break, rotten break, tough break, up against it, on the skids, down on one's luck, hard row to hoe, hard row of stumps, hard time, hard pull, tar baby, heat's on, a mountain out of a molehill, heavy load to haul, the devil to pay, hell to pay, bug, glitch, hitch, hiccup factor, puzzler, can of peas, can of worms, Pandora's box, green hornet (Mil.), hot potato, stinker, tsuris, tumul, what's-with, sixty-four-dollar question, twister, teaser, sticker, floorer, stumper, bugaboo, crimp, crimp one's style, hump, stinger, hot grease, jackpot, mess up, screw up, need it like a hole in the head, rub, push comes to shove, when things get tough, toughie, tough proposition, tough to buck, tough nut to crack, tough going, hard going, it's your funeral, joker, scuffle, put on the spot, hit a snag, a holdup, cropper, come a-cropper, one small difficulty.

DIFFIDENT adj. mousy, rabbity.

DIG v. really get into, leave no stone unturned, look all over hell, search high heaven, geek out (seek crumbs of cocaine), shake, shake down, turn inside-out, turn upside-down. See SEARCH.

DIGEST v. cut, cut down, cut to the bone, nutshell, put in a nutshell, boil down, trim, get to the meat.

DIGESTIVE TRACT n. plumbing, guts, innards, inners, insides, gizzard, stuffings, spaghetti.

DIGGER n. groundhog, sandhog.

DIGIT n. claw, fang (musician), feeler (middle finger), fish hooks, forks, hooks, lunch hooks, meat hooks, pinkie, poppers, stealers.

DIGNIFIED adj. highfalutin, high-minded, high-nosed, high-toned, stiff-necked. See also MAJESTIC, POMPOUS.

DIGRESS v. circumlocute, get sidetracked, all over the map, go round the barn, go by way of, long way, long way home.

DILAPIDATED adj. beat-up, crummy, raunchy, tacky, ratty, ramshackle, rinky-dink, rinky-tinky, slummy, frowzy, fruit, dog-eared, used-up, in a bad way.

DILEMMA n. box, in a box, bind, double bind, up shit creek without a paddle, Catch-22, one small difficulty, grabber, hooker, pickle. See PREDICAMENT.

DILETTANTISH adj. half-assed, half-baked, half-cocked, fluffie, artsy-fartsy.

DILIGENT adj. grind, plugger, whiz, nose to the grindstone, springbutt, eager beaver, work one's tail off. See INDUSTRIOUS.

DILUTE v. doctor, doctor up, phony up, plant, spike, water, water down, baptize, irrigate, cook, cut, needle, lace, shave.

DIMETHYLTRYPTAMINE n. DMT.

DIMINISH v. 1. soft-pedal, take the bite out, take the edge off, take the sting out, throw a wet blanket on, throw cold water on, whitewash, water down. See QUIET. 2. dump on, slice up, run down, put down, tear down, cut down to size, burn, burn down, burn one down, rank, poor-mouth, bad-mouth, put away. See BELITTLE.

DIMINISHED adj. eat crow, eat dirt, eat humble pie, sing small, put down, egg on one's face, knocked from one's high horse, got one's comeuppance. See BELITTLED.

DIMINUTIVE adj. mini, teeny, teensy, bitty, bitsy, itsy-bitsy, wee, peewee, button, yea big, mite, pint-sized. See SMALL.

DIN n. hubba-hubba, hullaballoo, buzz-buzz, boom-boom, hoo-ha, rowdydow, hell broke loose, all hell broke loose.

DINE v. eat out, do lunch. See also EAT.

DINING ROOM n. caf, crumb hall. See also RESTAURANT.

DINNER n. eats, chow, chow fight, major munch, hots (hot meal, Mil.), din-din, feed bag, ribs, potluck, bean time, early bird special. See also FOOD.

DINNER PAIL n. nosebag, feedbag.

DIP v. dunk.

DIPHTHERIA n. dip.

DIPLOMA n. sheepskin, shingle, dip.

DIPLOMAT n. cookie pusher.

DIPPER n. bug (industrial or baker).

DIPROPYLTRYPTAMINE n. DPT.

DIPSOMANIAC n. dip, dipso, power drinker, drunk, boozer, boozehound, stewbum, rummy, wino, lush, barfly, souse, shikker, soak, tippler, long hitter, juice head. See DRINKER.

DIRECT adj. 1. open, straight, straight out, straight from the shoulder, from the horse's mouth, calling a spade a spade, talk turkey. See FRANK. 2. nonstop, beeline, as the crow flies, down the alley, down the pipe, in the groove, on the beam.

DIRECT v. 1. head up, boss, shepherd, run things, call the shots, quarterback, be in the driver's seat, conn (vessel, N.), take the reins, have the say. See MANAGE. 2. target, zero in, move in, sight, sight on.

DIRECT ADDRESS man, son, sonny, Doc, Mac, Bo, brother, sister, doll, jellybean, pussycat, pal, bub, bud, buddy, buddy boy, bucko, good buddy, pard, pardner, Jack, Jackson, Joe, Joe Blow, Jim, kid, kiddo, keed, lady (sarcastic), mate, matie, mister (Derog.), Melvin, Charley, Chester, hey, hey you, motherfucker (Derog.), mother grabber, mofo, mother, mother jiver, mother rucker, ma, mama, pop, pops, dad, daddio, sir, ma'am, baby, stinky, tubby, fatso, people, shortie, stupid, four-eyes, so-and-so (affectionate or Derog.), blood, cuh, cuz (Af. Am.), sweetheart, sweetie,

sweetie-pie, buttercup, toots, tootsie, dear, dearie, darling, old bean, old man, old friend, old chap, old boy, old fellow, old fruit, old fart, old goat, old sock, old thing, old top, son of a bitch, son of a gun, son of a sea cook.

DIRECT CURRENT n. DC.

DIRECTION n. 1. thataway, every which way, forty ways to Sunday, forty ways from Sunday, forty ways for Sunday. 2. steer, bum steer, tip. See also COUNSEL.

DIRECTION FINDER n. HFDF, huff-duff (high-frequency direction finder).

DIRECTIONS n. dope sheet, DWIM (do what I mean), DTRT (do the right thing), poop sheet.

DIRECTLY adv. slap, smack, plump, slam-bang, smack-dab, right outta the box.

DIRECTOR n. top brass, head honcho, skipper, old man, Big Daddy, big player, big chew, exec, man upstairs, kingpin, top dog, key player. See EXECUTIVE.

DIRECTORATE n. front office, people in the front office, man upstairs, people upstairs, executive suite, kiva, brass, top brass, Big Brother. See MANAGEMENT.

DIRECTORY n. laundry list (agenda), enemies list, blacklist (punished or ostracized), crap list, hit list, shitlist, S list, drop-dead list (fired, expelled, excluded), sucker list, short list, book (pimp's list), black book, little black book, scorecard, lineup, blue-book, white book, plum book (Govt. positions), charts, pap (Annapolis); white pages, yellow pages (telephone).

DIRIGIBLE n. blimp, gasbag.

DIRT n. 1. real estate, state. 2. gook, drek, crud, gunk, mung, grunge, grunch, prut, scuz, smut, sleaze, scrunge.

DIRTY adj. 1. crud, cruddy, crumb, crumby, crummy, crusty, grungy, scrungy, nappy, mung, icky, yecchy, yucky, chili bowl (person), pigpen, barn, stable, stall, scuzzy, skank, raunchy, messy, mess, mess-up, muss, muss-up, sleazy, sleaze-up, mucky, muck-up, crud-up, crum-up. 2. below the belt, not cricket, raw deal.

DIRTY ROOM n. pigpen, stable, stall, live-in wastebasket.

DISABLE v. total, wing, ding, tweak, bend the goods, hamstring, queer, shoot down, knock out, take out, hog-tie, bugger, kibosh, put the kibosh on, put out of commission, fuck up, screw up, screw up the works, queer the works, gum up the works, throw a monkey wrench into the works, throw a monkey wrench in the machinery, spike one's guns, put a spoke in one's wheels, clip the wings of, take the wind out of one's sails, knock the props out from under, cut the ground out from under, not leave a leg to stand on. See also SABOTAGE.

DISABLED adj. crip, gimp, gimpy, game, g'd up, geed up, stiff, hamstrung, hog-tied, taken out, sidelined, out of commission.

DISADVANTAGE, BE AT A v. be had by the balls, be had by the short hairs, be had by the tail, dead man's hand, hipped, underdog, knock.

DISADVANTAGED adj. down-and-out, hard-up (also sexual), have-nots, needy, truly needy, the poor, bag lady, locked-out. See DESTITUTE.

DISADVANTAGEOUS adj. downside, debit side, on the debit side, downtick, the bad news. See also UNPROFIT-ABLE.

DISAGREE v. cross, take on, sock, sock it to one, break with, fly in the face of, be agin, buck, nix, have a bone to pick, pettifog, put up an argument, set to, zap, zapper, pitch into, light into, lay into, wade into, lace into, sail into, come at, go at, lay at, have at, have at it, lean on, crack down on, gang up on, jump, jump on, jump on one's case, jump down one's throat, come down on, come down hard on one, land on, land all over, lay out, let have it, let have it with both barrels, give one both barrels, blast, rip, rip into, rip up, rip up one side and down the other, put up a fight, mix it up with, tangle with, bump heads with, cross swords with, lock horns with, stick it to one, hit a sour note, sound a sour note, hit a clinker, sound a clinker.

DISAGREEABLE adj. 1. bitchy, out of sorts, cantankerous, grouchy, uptight, Mr. Coffee Nerves, beefing, bellyaching. See IRRITABLE. 2. awful, drag, draggy, gummy, pain, pain in the ass, pain in the neck, sleazeball, sludgeball, turbobitch, sour, sourpuss, witch. See OBNOXIOUS.

DISAGREEMENT n. split, spat, tiff, beef, scrap, hassle, rhubarb, fuss, wrangle, brawl, brush, brush-off, row, rumpus, ruckus, ruction, words, flak, far cry, poles apart, whale of a difference, ain't with that (Af. Am.), blow-off, blowup, bone, pick a bone, bone to pick, bone of contention, no way, shindy, set-to, run-in, brannigan, catamaran. See also ARGUMENT.

DISALLOW v. kill, ding, zing, not (used at end of a sentence), nix, put down, pass on. See DISAPPROVE.

DISAPPEAR v. do a vanishing act, fade, fade out of sight, fade away, get small (from a crime), melt into the scenery, pull a Judge Crater.

DISAPPOINT v. let down, break a date, no show, stand one up, chill, flake. See also FRUSTRATE.

DISAPPOINTED adj. down, let down, a downer, bummed, crumbed, taken down, down in the dumps, in a blue funk. See also UNHAPPY.

DISAPPOINTMENT n. bummer, downer, drag, whacked, lame, bonk, bunk, letdown, anticipointment (after anticipation), fizzle, fizzle out, not hack it, not make it, also-ran, bringdown, half-assed, half-baked, a lemon, bitter pill, bitter pill to swallow, setback, the old one-two, that's it?, that's all there is there isn't any more?, this is what we came for?, this is what it's all about?, you want it should sing too?, what you see is what you get.

DISAPPROVAL, WORDS OF nix, ding, zing, square, nuts, balls, your mama (Af. Am.), calldown, rap on the knuckles, slap on the wrist, is that so, izzat so, shee-it, blow it out, not on your life, no siree, no way, no you don't, no eyes for.

DISAPPROVE v. pan, slam, knock, hit, rap, kill, ping (Mil.), ding, zing, nix, pass on, Pasadena, turn thumbs down, thumb down, blackball, call down, put down, take a dim view of, hold no brief for, not go for, not get all choked up over. See also REJECT, FROWN.

DISAPPROVED OF adj. damned, blasted, over, panned, killed, kissed-off, blooming, dadblamed, dadblasted, darn, drat, in the doghouse, out in the cold, left out.

DISARM v. skin.

DISARMAMENT n. take 'em down.

DISARRANGED adj. beat-up, messed-up, mussed-up, messy, mussy, sloppy, slobbed-out, grungy, grubby, scuzzed, scuzzed-up.

DISARRAY n. holy mess, unholy mess, all over hell, all over the shop, harum-scarum, bloody mess, topsy-turvy, arsy-varsy. See also CHAOS; MISFORTUNE.

DISASSOCIATE v. blow one off, cut loose, drop out, have no truck with, steer clear, back off, back away from. See DISENGAGE. See also SEPARATE.

DISASTER n. bummer, downer, grabber, shit, deep shit, shit hit the fan, total shuck, trouble in River City, bad scene, bad news, the worst, nightmare, one's ass is grass, blue ruin, bitch, rough, tough, hot water, curtains, Waterloo, screw-up, mess-up, holy mess, unholy mess, rainin', double trouble, hard time, headache, hot grease, jackpot, tsuris, need it like a hole in the head, can of worms, crunch. See also MISFORTUNE.

DISAVOW v. dial back, backwater, crawfish, crawfish out, drop out, nig, renig, wash one's hands of, welsh, go back on one's word, weasel out, worm one's way out of, worm out of.

DISAVOWAL, WORDS OF no way, no way José, not! (used at end of a sentence), no go, no dice, N.O. nope, ugh-ugh, fat chance, nothing doing. See DENIAL.

DISBARRED adj. unfrocked, drummed out.

DISBELIEF, WORDS OF come on, get real (Af. Am.), ain't buyin' it (Af. Am.), sheesh, balls, blow it out, bullfinch, bullshit, bullchitna (Esk.), horseshit, horse hockey, hockey pucks, get outta town, so's your old man, vanilla.

DISBELIEVING adj. cagey, leery, ain't buyin' it (Af. Am.), been hit before.

DISBURSE v. pay off, foot the bill, cough up, pony up, ante up, come through, come across, come up with, shell out, put out, fork out. See PAY.

DISCARD v. chuck, chuck out, eighty-six, lose, ditch it, junk, adios, dog, off-load, toss, dump, scrap, give the old heave-ho, throw over, throw overboard, deep-six, throw on the junk heap, toss onto the scrap heap, retire, round file, file it in the circular file, kiss, kiss off, kiss (something) good-bye, cut loose, chop out.

DISCERN v. 1. spot, dig, read, focus, take in, get a load of, rubberneck, give one the beady eye, give with the eyes, put the squint on. See SEE. 2. get, read, get the picture, see the light, blow wise, get wise to, can you relate (Af. Am.), dig, I know where you're comin' from, figure out, have one's number. See UNDERSTAND.

DISCERNMENT n. aha reaction, savvy, hep to, wise to, see the light, flash on it, get one's drift, on the same wavelength, I got it, it hit me, it just come to me.

DISCHARGE n. ax, boot, door, gate, pink slip, the bullet, walking papers, walking ticket, early retirement, payroll adjustment, released resources, reshaping, bounce, bum's rush, kicking-out, old heave-ho. See DISMISSAL.

DISCHARGE v. can, fire, bump, bounce, boot, boot out, kick, kick out, kick upstairs, lay off, downsize, rif (reduction in force), golden handshake (rich bonus guarantee), cut loose (dockworker use), bust, nix, X out, ax, give the ax, give the air, give one his walking papers, hand one his walking papers, sack, give the sack to, give one the old heave-ho, give the bum's rush, give the hook, give the pink slip, pink slip, give the gate, show the gate, show the door, wash out, drum out, freeze out, lock out, let out, let one go, throw out on one's ear, run out of town, ride out on a rail, get rid of, kiss off, kiss one good-bye, flush, dust, shake, scrub, send packing, send to the showers.

DISCHARGED adj. 1. fired, canned, kicked out, let out, selected out, let go, locked out, laid-off, cut loose (dockworker use), sacked, booted, bounced, dumped, axed, pink-slipped, got the ax, got one's walking papers, got the gate, got the sack, got the mat, got the burlap, got a pink slip, got it in the neck, shown the door, given the boot, given the heave-ho, got the bullet, kissed off, buck off, packed it in, unfrocked (by profession), drummed out, turned-off, written-off, heads rolled. 2. launched, set off, blown, energetically disassembled. 3. beat the rap, walked, let off, let go, section eight.

DISCHARGE NOTICE n. pink slip, the bullet, walking papers, walking ticket.

DISCIPLE n. booster, buff, bug, fan, freak, groupie, wannabee, junkie, nut, punker (punk rock), crank, culture vulture, fiend, hound, rooter, flunky, stooge. See DEVOTEE.

DISCIPLINARIAN n. chickenshit, chickenshit guy, sundowner.

DISCIPLINE n. chickenshit, lumps, catch hell, salt mines, back to the salt mines, pay through the nose, for it, going over, hell to pay, get yours, comeuppance, get what is coming to one, ass-kicking. See also PUNISHMENT.

DISCIPLINE v. chew, chew ass, chew out, eat out, ream out, straighten out, kick ass and take names, jump on one's shit, climb one's frame, jawbone, come down on. See PUNISH.

DISC JOCKEY n. deejay, D.J.

DISCLOSE v. fess, fess up, croon, snitch, belch, squeal, stool, spill, leak, buzz (in secret), drop a dime on one, come out of the closet, put it on the street, put one in the picture, go the hang-out road. See CONFESS.

DISCLOSURE n. tip, tip-off, ABC's, blow-by-blow, run-down, make, picture, handout, leak, showdown, squeal, snitch. See also REVELATION.

DISCONCERT v. bug, get to, discomboberate, discombobulate, discombooberate, ball up, foul up, fuck up, psych out, upset one's apple cart. See CONFUSE.

DISCONCERTED adj. unglued, defrosted, come unzipped, come apart, all shook up, creeped-out, spaced-out, hung-up, messed-up attic, hissy, in the twilight zone, in a botheration, psyched out. See CONFUSED.

DISCONNECT v. break it off, break it up, drop, drop it, sideline.

DISCONSOLATE adj. low, hurtin', destroyed, put away, in pain, in the pits, sorry-assed, cracked-up, cut-up, tore-up, ripped. See DEPRESSED.

DISCONTENTED adj. bitching, bitchy, crabby, kvetching, griping, picky, picky-picky, unhappy camper, that's it?, that's all there is there isn't any more?, this is what we came for?, this is what it's all about?, you want it should sing too?, what you see is what you get, down in the mouth, in the dumps, blue, the natives are restless. See UNHAPPY.

DISCONTINUE v. scrub, kill, pack in, drop, blow off, knock it off, break off, want out, dust, call all bets off, call it quits. See STOP.

DISCONTINUOUSLY adv. by bits and pieces, by fits and starts, hit or miss, in dribs and drabs, willy-nilly, herky-jerky. See ERRATICALLY.

DISCORD n. 1. diff, split, spat, hassle, static, beef, row, ruckus, ruction, rumpus, run-in, scrap, scene, set-to, fuss, dustup, hoedown, knockdown, bone, pick a bone, bone of contention, no way, far cry, bad vibes, poles apart, sockdolager, flak, clincher, crusher, finisher, rhubarb, shindy, squelcher, dead horse, wrangle, whale of a difference, like night and day, march to the beat of a different drummer. See also ARGUMENT. 2. clinker, sour note.

DISCORDANT adj. sour, sour note, clinker, hit a clinker, hit a sour note, sound a clinker, sound a sour note.

DISCOTHEQUE n. disco.

DISCOUNT n. deduck (income tax item), cut, cutback, rollback, knock off, gray market (selling imports at below list prices).

DISCOURAGE v. cool, chill, turn off, put off, kid out of, talk out of, bum out, bum one out, take the air out of one's balloon, throw cold water on, throw a wet blanket on, put a damper on, put the zingers in. See PREVENT.

DISCOURAGED adj. down, beat, downbeat, beat-down, down-in-the-mouth, down-in-the-dumps, crumbed, in a funk, in a blue funk, caved in, unzipped, unglued, come apart, come apart at the seams, fall apart at the seams, psyched-out, shot, shot to pieces, gone to pieces, lost momentum.

DISCOURSE n. rap, rap session, buzz session, hash session, rapping rash, talkfest, gabfest, bull fest, bull session, clambake, huddle, spiel. See SPEAK.

DISCOURSE v. chew, chew over, chew the fat, chew the rag, rag around, modulate, modjitate, kick the gong around, punch the gun, blow change, give a meeting, hold a meet, confab, talk turkey. See SPEAK.

DISCOURTEOUS adj. flip, fresh, sassy, smart-alecky, cheeky, crusty, base, roll over one, cut, cold shoulder, chit. See INSOLENT.

DISCOURTESY n. cheap shot, put-down, zinger, backhanded compliment, left-handed compliment, brickbat, dump, low rent.

DISCOVER v. pick up on, dig up, hit upon, be hep to, be on to, stumble on, trip over, tumble to, wise up to, right under one's nose, uncover, strike (oil, gold), spot, spark, smoke out, smell out, nose out, suss out, see the light, bring to light, catch flatfooted, catch red-handed, catch with one's pants down, catch with one's hand in the cookie jar, have dead to rights, have one's number.

DISCOVERY n. a find, luck out, luck into, fall into.

DISCREDIT v. mud-sling, shoot down, run down, put down, tear down, cut rate, burn, burn down, burn one down, cap, pooh-pooh, mark lousy, poke full of holes, knock one off one's perch. See BELITTLE.

DISCREDITED adj. lost face, in bad, in Dutch, in the doghouse, drummed-out, paper tiger, crawl, sing small, bad-ass. See also BELITTLED.

DISCREET adj. hush-hush, clam, clam up, on the Q.T., zip one's lips, button up, button up one's lip, between one and the lamppost, tight chops, handle with kid gloves, mind one's p's and q's, on the lookout.

DISCREPANCY n. far cry, poles apart, whale of a difference, split.

DISCRETIONARY adj. the call, the judge and jury, call it as one sees it.

DISCRIMINATE v. know what's what, know one's ass from one's elbow, know one's ass from first base, know one's ass from a hole in the ground, know shit from Shinola, know a rock from a hard place, make out, split hairs. 2. redline (financial), Jim Crow.

DISCRIMINATING adj. picky, picky-picky, choicy, choosy, pernickety, persnickety. See PARTICULAR.

DISCRIMINATION n. glass ceiling (invisible barrier to promotion).

DISCUSS v. rap, mack (Af. Am.), chew over, hash, re-hash, hash over, let the daylight in, let the sunlight in, talk game, figure, figure out, sort out, blitz, brainstorm, breakout meeting (brainstorm session), put in the loop, put in the know, confab, get heads together, groupthink, huddle, go into a huddle, flap, take a meeting, have a meet, toss some ideas around, kick some ideas around, kick around, knock around, rag around, run something by one, pick one's brains, flog a dead horse, whip a dead horse, blow, blow hot air, bounce off one. See also DELIBERATE; CONFER.

DISCUSSION n. powwow, meet, confab, huddle, think-in, groupthink, gam, rap, rap session, buzz session, clambake, eyeball-to-eyeball encounter, flap, bull yard, chalk talk (Stu. and professor use, informal sports). See also MEETING.

DISDAIN v. chill, put down, run down, look down one's nose at, turn up one's nose at, thumb one's nose at, wouldn't touch (anything) with a ten-foot pole, allergic to, down on.

DISDAINFUL adj. cool, dicty, on one's high horse, put on airs, have one's glasses on (Af. Am.), toplofty, snooty, king shit, high-hat, uppity. See ARROGANT.

DISEASE n. bug, crud, creeping crud, growth, the runs, the flu, the pip, what's going around, dose, double scrudfantods, fascinoma (Medic.). See ILLNESS.

DISEASE, MYTHICAL n. the bug, crud, creeping crud, scrud, double scrudfantods, willies, the pip, gaposis (gap in clothing), medical student's disease.

DISENGAGE v. pull the plug, back out, back out of, back off, back away from, opt out, drop out, cut out, cut loose, fink out, poop out, crawfish out, veg out, weasel out, worm out of, crawl out of, wangle out of, backpedal, backwater, draw in one's claws, draw in one's horns, kiss off, blow one off, have no truck with, steer clear, turn tail, turn tail and run, stand down, quit cold, eyes to cool it, leave flat, throw over, crash, pull in one's horns. See also SEPARATE.

DISENTANGLE v. bail one out, get out from under, let go, let off, let off the hook. See FREE.

DISFAVOR v. blackball, turn thumbs down on, put one on one's shitlist, scratch one off one's list, hold no brief for, not get all chocked up over. See DISAPPROVE.

DISFAVORED adj. left-out, baldheaded, off one's list, on one's list, one one's shitlist, on one's enemies list, on the shelf, in Dutch, in wrong, in bad, in the doghouse, in the shithouse, got one's ass in sidweays, out in the cold.

DISGORGE v. barf, puke, zuke, spew, throw up, up-chuck, Ralph, talk to Ralph on the big white phone, York, boag, bison, yak, to the curb, chunk, chew the cheese, toss one's tacos, flash one's cookies, pray to the porcelain god, drive the porcelain bus, laugh at the carpet. See VOMIT.

DISGRACE n. comedown, put-down, dump, in the doghouse, black eye, skeleton in the closet, skeleton in the cupboard. See also SCANDAL.

DISGRACE v. lose face, give a black eye. See HUMILI-ATE. See also DESECRATE.

DISGRACED adj. in bad, in Dutch, in the doghouse, bad-ass, gone to bad, gone to the dogs, gone to hell, took down, put down, come down, come out moldy, dumped on, faced, drummed out, crawl, draw in one's horns, eat dirt, eat crow, eat humble pie, lost face, egg on one's face, knocked from one's high horse, knocked off one's perch, put a tuck in one's tail, stumped, stymied, sing small.

DISGRUNTLED adj. beefing, bitching, not a happy camper, unhappy camper, kicking, bellyaching, crabbing, crabby, kvetching, cranky, gripping, grouchy, grousing. See UNHAPPY.

DISGUISE n. cover-up, beard, front, fig leaf, camel flags (WW1).

DISGUISE v. beard, whitewash, wear cheaters, cover up, slap on some glims, flash the gogs, throw on a makeup, phony one's getup, front, put up a front, put on a front, put on a false front, put on an act, put up a bluff, pull up a bluff, make like.

DISGUISED adj. incog, bearding.

DISGUSTED adj. scuzzed out, grossed out, turned-off, grody, grody to the max, frosted, blown out, aggro, have a bellyful, have a skinful, barfed out, browned off, brassed off, pissed off, cheesed off, T'd off, ech, eeoooh, fed up, full up, gives one a pain, gives one a pain in the neck, gives one a pain in the ass.

DISGUSTING adj. gross, grossed out, rotted, rottissimo (very bad), Rotterdam, it rots, poxy, gagger, pail, bucket, pukey, pukoid, grody, grody to the max, it stinks, it sucks, sux, sucky, scurvy, scuzzo, scuzzy, shitsky, shitburger, skewy, scuzzed out, stinking, skank, icky, yecchy, yucky, under the curb, up under the curb, lousy, rotten, mothering, motherfucking (Obsc.), mother-grabbing, mother-nudging, turn-off, faust, beastly, furry, awful, godawful, goshawful, grim, uncool, draggy, creepy, stinky, sleazy, sleazeball, sludgeball, shower scum, nerdy, twerpy, wimpy, spastic, funky (Af. Am.), Velveeta , Cap'n Chedda, drippy, simpy, lousy, specimen, bad case of the uglies, dumb cluck, dummy, gummy, cotton-picking, in one's hat, for the birds, gives one a pain, gives one a pain in the neck, gives one a pain in the ass, from hell, pesky, pestiferous, bitchy.

DISH n. manhole cover.

DISHEVELED adj. mangled, thrashed, beat-up, messed-up, mussed-up, messy, mussy, sleazy, sloppy, slobbed-out, grungy, grubby, scuzzy, scuzzed, scuzzed-up, hagged-out.

DISHONEST adj. crooked, crooked stick, bent, shady, fishy, fish, dog, gyp, racket, sneaky, slick, sharp, shifty, shifty-eyed, wrong, wrong number, wrong gee, not kosher, cheatin', cheatin' heart, dirty, lowdown and dirty, dirty work, on the make, on the take, on the pad, play hard, fink out, no-good, N.G., no-account, no-count, no bargain, honest John, shitheel, shit hook, doberman (Af. Am.), worm, tinhorn, convict, copperhearted, crum, crumb, slimy, trust one as far as one can swing a cat, trust one as far as one can throw an elephant.

DISHONOR v. give one a black eye, make one lose face. See also DESECRATE; PROFANE.

DISHONORABLE DISCHARGE n. kick, D.D.

DISHONORED adj. lost face, drummed out, in the doghouse, eat crow, eat dirt, eat humble pie. See DIS-GRACED.

DISHWASHER n. pearl diver, pot walloper, suds buster, deep sea chef (hobo).

DISILLUSION v. debunk, turn off, talk out of, kid out of, put off, let down easy, puncture one's balloon, kick in the ass, kick in the stomach, kick in the heart, break one's heart, throw cold water on, throw a wet blanket on.

DISINFORMATION n. bull, bullshit, BS, bullpucky, bullshitting, con, scam, spiel, a line, baloney, horseshit, the big lie (Pol.), borax, they're pissing on us and telling us it's raining.

DISJOINTED adj. fuzzy, spacey, spaced-out, out of it, out to lunch, play it cool, cool, far-out.

DISLIKE v. turned off by, grossed out on, have no use for, allergic to, have an allergy to, down on, turn thumbs down on, take a dim view of, hold no brief for, not go for, not get all choked over, put one on one's list, put one on one's shitlist, on the shit parade, scratch one off one's list, for the birds, gives one a pain, gives one a pain in the neck, gives one a pain in the ass, have a hate on for.

DISLIKED PERSON n. asshole, assface, asswipe, barney, geek, geekoid, scrounge, nightie (nightmare), smack (overachieving geek), sleaze, sleazeball, sludgeball, hairball, meatball, wanker, mother, muthuh; motherfucker, muthuhfuckuh, mother-humper, M.F., mofo, mother-jumper, mother-jammer, mammy-jammer, mother-lover, mother-rucker (Obsc.), mutant, barf bag, bub, corn dog, elrod, scoob, goob, goober, goobatron, yernt, nob, social zero, nothingburger, ho-dad, ho-daddy, rat, fink, rat fink, prick, cocksucker, peckerwood (Af. Am.), scumbag, shower scum, zod, droid, droob, drube, nerd, shit breath, quimp, remo, turdface, dexter, full hank, lop, narc, spud, squid, schmo, jerk, jerk-off, twerp, twink, woofie, cull, banana, creep, drip, dumb cluck, dummy, cheesehead, cheeseface, Captain Cheddar (Af. Am.), gross, scrub, dag, loser, winner, mince, mole, moron, nothing, simp, spastic, stinker, stinkpot, turkey, weenie, wimp, wimpy, yo-yo, zombie, corpse, droop, herkle, prune, specimen, cotton-picker, dipstick, bad case of the uglies, won't give one the time of day, louse, gerk (old).

DISLOCATED adj. in the wrong box, right church wrong pew, in the right church but the wrong pew, in the wrong pew, like a fish out of water, out of one's element, nowhere.

DISLOYAL adj. two-timing, cheater, double-crossing, two-faced, doggin', snaky, snake in the grass, worm. See UNFAITHFUL.

DISMAL adj. sorry-assed, low, ass in a sling, dick in the dirt, crying the blues, bummed-out, flaked-out, hurting, in the pits, barf city, down in the dumps, out, down in the mouth. See DEPRESSED.

DISMANTLE v. part out.

DISMAY n. blues, blahs, blue devils, blue funk, deep funk, funk, bummer, dolefuls, letdown, downer, down trip, dumps, mumps, mopes, miseries, mulligrubs, the mokers, mess and a half, bloody mess, holy mess, unholy mess, hassle, trouble in River City, who's minding the store?, pretty kettle of fish, pretty piece of business, nice piece of work. See also FEAR.

DISMAY v. faze, flummox, get to, throw, throw into a tizzy, ball up, bollix up, foul up, fuck up, louse up, mess up, muck up, screw up, snafu, play hob with. See FRIGHTEN. See also CONFUSE.

DISMAYED adj. scared stiff, push the panic button, pee in one's pants, spooked, goose-bumpy, pucker-assed, given a jar, crumbed, dragged, buggin', blue, got the blue devils, hang crepe, bummed-out, defrosted, shook, shot down, all torn up. See FRIGHTENED.

DISMISS v. 1. can, fire, bump, boot, lay off, cut loose (dockworker use), give the ax, give one his walking papers, sack, pink-slip, get the bullet, wash out, downsize, rif (reduction in force). See DISCHARGE. 2. throw out on one's ear, run out of town, ride out on a rail, get rid of, kiss one good-bye, kiss off, buck off, dust, flush, shake, scrub, send packing, send to the showers. See also EJECT; BANISH.

DISMISSAL n. ax, pink slip, sack, boot, the gate, door, bounce, grand bounce, layoff, payroll, adjustment, released resources, reshaping, cut loose (dockworker use), rif (reduction in force), early retirement, furlough (temporary), walking papers, walking ticket, the bullet, housecleaning, bum's rush, kicking out, old heave-ho, in the barrel, fluff, brush-off, kiss-off, cold shoulder.

DISMISSED adj. fired, canned, unfrocked (any profession), let out, drummed out, turned off, sacked, booted, bounced, cut loose (dockworker use), axed, selected out, See DISCHARGED, OUSTER.

DISORDER n. 1. mess, holy mess, rat's nest, topsy-turvy, arsy-varsy, every which way, discombobulation, discombooberation. See CONFUSION. 2. flap, fuss, to-do, stir, kick up, snarl-up, fuzzbuzzjihad, scene. See TURMOIL.

DISORDERLY adj. on a tear, raising a rumpus, raising a ruckus, kicking up a row, kicking up a shindy, off-base, out-of-line, out-of-order.

DISORGANIZATION n. foul-up, fuck-up, mix-up, screw-up, bloody mess, holy mess, unholy mess, rat's nest, topsy-turvy. See CONFUSION.

DISORGANIZED adj. screwed-up, spazzed-out, mussed-up, unglued, unscrewed, unzipped, zoo, Chinese fire drill. See CONFUSED.

DISPARAGE v. pan, slam, smear, ping (Mil.), rip on, rag, rag on, crack on (Hum., Af. Am.), bag on (Hum.), base on, roast, scorch, rap, slice up, rank, dump on, run down, put down, tear down, burn, burn down, burn one down, cap, slag, shade, throw shade, sour grapes, put the hooks in. See BELITTLE.

DISPARAGED adj. drummed-out, crawl, eat crow, eat dirt, eat humble pie, lost face, draw in one's horns, sing small. See BELITTLED.

DISPARATE adj. far cry, poles apart, whale of a difference, like night and day.

DISPARITY n. dif, diff, different strokes, different strokes for different folks.

DISPASSIONATE adj. iceberg, cold fish, cool cat, cool, cool as a cucumber, keep one's cool, arctic, unflappable, laid-back, cas, cazh, keep one's shirt on, not turn a hair, roll with the punches, could care less, flat, tough, fair to middling, butter wouldn't melt in his mouth, got lead balls for eyes, poker-faced, don't give a shit, don't give a damm, don't give a hoot, what's the diff?, what the hell, so what?, it's all the same to me, that's your lookout, that's your pigeon, I should worry?

DISPASSIONATELY adv. in cold blood, deadpan, with a poker face, with a straight face.

DISPATCH n. handout, poop sheet, beat, scoop, See NEWS.

DISPATCH v. railroad, railroad through, walk through, hand-carry, run with, run with the ball. See also SPEED.

DISPEL v. break up, break it up, bust up, split up, scramble.

DISPENSE v. dish out, fork out, shell out, hand out, come across with, give with, give away the store. See GIVE.

DISPERSE v. break up, break it up, bust up, split up, scramble, take off in all directions.

DISPERSED adj. all over the lot, all over the place, from hell to breakfast, every which way.

DISPIRITED adj. dragged, low, crumbed, dick in the dirt, blue, blue funk, downbeat, shot-down, funky, bummed-out, rhino. See DEPRESSED.

DISPLACE v. step into the shoes of, take over. See also REPLACE.

DISPLAY n. 1. expo, exbo, exhib, exhibish, flash (gaudy merchandise or prize), front, fireworks, an act, a scene, for show, frameup. 2. shine, dash, splash, splurge, grandstand, grandstand play, showboat, showtime, showoff.

DISPLAY v. showcase, flash, sport, grandstand, streak, let it all hang out, do a fruit salad (expose genitals), roll out, trot out, break out, whip out, carry on, show off, show and tell, hot-dog, fan it, wave it around, run up the colors, strut one's stuff, do one's stuff, go through one's paces, parade one's wares, make a scene, put on an act, do a number, hit one with, come up with, smack with, spring with, play to the gallery, take it big, come on strong, come the heavy, do the heavy, throw one's weight around, chuck one's weight about, style (Af. Am.).

DISPLEASE v. zing, wing, nick, turn off, cool, cut to the quick, sound, dozens, sounding dozens, play dirty dozens, signify, signify'n', shucking and jiving, S'ing 'n' J'ing, miff, cap, capping, gross out, curdle, get bent, blow off, lay a bad trip on one, hit one where one lives, hurt one where one lives. See also ANNOY, INSULT.

DISPOSE v. 1. put to rights, put in apple-pie order, tailor, promote. See ARRANGE. 2. shepherd, call the tune, ride herd on, lay down the law, put one's foot down, read the riot act. See MANAGE.

DISPOSED adj. game, game for, at the drop of a hat. See also READY.

DISPOSE OF v. 1. knock off, polish off, cut, cut off, chop, take care of, put away, deal with, do the trick, turn the trick. See FINISH. 2. chuck, chuck out, lose, eighty-six, junk, adios (something), throw over, throw overboard, deep-six, round-file, file it in the circular file, kiss off. See DISCARD. See also DISCHARGE.

DISPOSITION n. mind-set, bag, groove, flash, tude, cop a tude (bad), thing, type, cup of tea, druthers, turned on to, where one is at. See INCLINATION.

DISPOSSESS v. boot out, toss out on one's ear, throw out on the street, adios one, bounce, send packing, See EVICT. See also DISCHARGE.

DISPROVE v. blow sky high, knock the bottom out of, knock the chocks out from under, knock the props out from under, poke full of holes, shoot full of holes.

DISPUTANT n. oppo, opposish, opposite number, ran into a buzz saw (unexpected), meat, me and you, angries, bad guy, buddy (sarcasm), guardhouse lawyer, Philadelphia lawyer.

DISPUTE n. beef, tiff, words, row, fuss, a bone, bone of contention, rhubarb, wrangle. See ARGUMENT.

DISPUTE v. take on, lock horns, pick a bone, put up an argument, be agin, bump heads, have at, jump on one's case, haul into court, drag into court. See ARGUE.

DISQUALIFY v. eighty-six, not make the cut.

DISREGARD v. 1. ig., tune out, look the other way, let it go, let one off easy, let one off this time, wink at, live with, pay no mind, pay no never mind, play past, pooh-pooh. 2. cut, brush off, cool, chaunce, not give one the time of day, give the go-by, leave out in the cold, look right through. See IGNORE. 3. be asleep at the switch, let go to pot, let slide.

DISREPAIR, IN adj. busted, down, downtime, dusted, out of commission, on the fritz, wracked, dead, kaput. See DAMAGED.

DISREPUTABLE adj. dog, in the doghouse, in bad, in Dutch, bad-ass, no good. See also BAD.

DISREPUTE adj. sleaze factor.

DISRESPECTFUL adj. diss, fresh, sassy, smart-alecky, smart-ass, cheeky, base, pop junk, nervy, out-of-line, bold as brass. See INSOLENT.

DISROBE v. strip, strip to the buff, do a strip, do a strip tease, take it off, peel, get all naked, slip out of, shuck, husk.

DISRUPT v. discombobulate, ball up, rattle one's cage, psych out, muddy the waters, put off, upset one's apple cart. See CONFUSE.

DISRUPTED adj. unglued, come unglued, come unzipped, come apart, come apart at the seams, fall apart at the seams, discombobulated, discombooberated, hung-up, mixed-up, blaaed-up, gummixed-up, gummoxed-up, helter-skelter, galley west, farmisht, fertummeled, farshimmelt, thrown, fussed, rattled, higgledy-piggledy, skimble-skamble, harum-scarum, shot, shot to pieces, gone, haywire, go blooey, go kerflooie, kerflumixed, flommexed, flummoxed, flabbergasted, stuck, hugger-mugger, messy, bowled down, bowled over, struck all of a heap, thrown off one's beam ends. See also CONFUSED.

DISRUPTIVE adj. off-base, out-of-line, out-of-order, trouble-making. See also ROWDY.

DISSATISFIED adj. crabby, beefing, bitching, kvetching, griping, grousing, picky, picky-picky, unhappy camper, that's it?, that's all there is there isn't any more?, this is what we came for?, this is what it's all about?, you want it should sing too?, what you see is what you get. See UNHAPPY.

DISSEMBLE v. stonewall, cover up, whitewash, pass, goof on, shuck and jive, signify, blow smoke, gammon, talk trash, double-talk, double-speak, fake, fake it, wear cheaters, slap on some glims, flash the gogs, throw on a makeup, phony up one's getup, trip, beard, put a different face on, put up a front, put on a front, put on a false front, put up a smokescreen, put on an act, make like, let on, let on like, play possum, pussyfoot, put on the check, put up a bluff, pull up a bluff, four-flush.

DISSEMBLER n. smoothie, smoothy, phony, two-way ghee, wolf in sheep's clothing. See CHEATER.

DISSEMBLING n. crocodile tears, soft soap, sweet talk, an act. See also FAKERY.

DISSENSION n. bad vibes, static, sour note, beef, scene, fuss, flak, clinker. See DISCORD.

DISSENT n. 1. no way, N.O., nope, no siree, November Foxtrot Whiskey (no fucking way), bump that, yank on that, fuck that noise!, not on your life, not a chance, nothing doing, forget it. See DENIAL. 2. bad vibes, clinker, sour note, split, spat, bone, pick a bone, bone of contention, hassle, flak. 3. far cry, poles apart, whale of a difference.

DISSENT v. break with, fly in the face of, be agin, buck, ain't with that (Af. Am.), pettifog, put up an argument, jump on one's case, put up a fight. See DISAGREE.

DISSENTER n. maverick, marcher, swinger, dropout, angry, beatnik, hippie, yippie, freak, flower child, nature boy, street people, night people, offbeat, Bohemian, weirdo, weirdie, fish out of water, oddball, square peg in a round hole.

DISSENTING adj. anti, agin, con, no go. See NONCONFORMING.

DISSIDENCE n. bad vibes, clinker, sour note. See also DISCORD.

DISSIMILAR adj. far cry, funky, weird, offbeat, march to the beat of a different drummer, poles apart, whale of a difference, like night and day.

DISSIPATE v. piss away, go through, kiss good-bye, blow, dump, pump up (gambling). See SQUANDER, FRITTER AWAY.

DISSIPATED adj. 1. gone to bad, gone to the dogs, gone to seed, gone to hell, gone to hell in a bread basket, hellbent. 2. blown, blown out, burned out, played out, pissed away, diddled away, down the drain, down the toilet, down the rathole, down the spout, down the tube, kiss something good-bye, out the window.

DISSIPATER n. high liver, nighthawk, night owl, playboy, swinger, operator, player, speed. See LECHER.

DISSIPATION n. 1. life in the fast lane, live in the fast lane drive in the fast lane, drive in the fast lane with no brakes, high living, burn one's candle at both ends, hellbent, go to hell, go to hell in a handbasket. 2. bender, bat, binge, bust, circus, tear, toot, wingding. See REVEL. See also PARTY.

DISSOLUTE adj. high liver, nighthawk, night owl, playboy, swinger, operator, player, alley cat, meat-eater, on the pad, on the take, open, racket up, driving in the fast lane, driving in the fast lane with no brakes, living in the fast lane, life in the fast lane, high living, burn one's candle at both ends, gone to bad, gone to the dogs, gone to hell, go to hell, go to hell in a handbasket, hellbent, fast and loose, fast, swift, speedy. See also WANTON.

DISSONANT adj. clinker, sour, sour note.

DISSUADE v. faze, turn off, put off, kid out of, talk out of, chicken out, blink, throw cold water on, throw a wet blanket on, lean on, put the arm on. See also PREVENT.

DISTANCE n. a good ways, stone's throw, bit, spitting distance, Sunday run, tidy step, whoop, two whoops and a holler, a hoot and holler, a hop skip and a jump, a shlep, sleeper jump, piece, far piece, fer piece, fur piece, down the road a piece, country mile; click, klick (both kilometer).

DISTANT adj. 1. standoffish, cold, cool, cool cat, dog it, dog up, laid-back, offish, on ice, put on airs, stuck-up, uppity. See ALOOF. 2. ways, piece, far piece, sticks, boonies, tullies, B.F.E., butt-fucking Egypt, B.F.A, butt-fucking Africa, clear to hell and gone, middle of nowhere. See REMOTE.

DISTANT EARLY WARNING LINE n. DEW line.

DISTASTEFUL adj. grody, grody to the max, gagger, gross, pukey, pukoid, yucky, icky, yicky. See UNSAVORY.

DISTILL v. 1. boil down, cut, cut down, cut to the bone, nutshell, put in a nutshell, trim, get to the meat.

DISTILL ALCOHOL v. cook, rerun, turn over, moonlight, moonshine.

DISTINCTION n. diff, different strokes, different strokes for different folks.

DISTINCTIVE adj. 1. poles apart, far cry, offbeat, march to the beat of a different drummer. See also UNIQUE. 2. weird, whale of a difference, like night and day, like wow, super, gnarly, megagnarly, unreal, zero cool, cold, wicked, flash, this is some kinda ———. See EXCELLENT.

DISTINGUISH v. 1. make out, figure out, know what's what, know one's ass from one's elbow, know a rock from a hard place, know crossways from crosswise. See DISCRIMINATE. 2. flash, flash on, glom, glim, gun, beam, spot, spy, dig, read, lamp, pipe, catch, focus, eye, eagle eye, eyeball, take in, get a load of, get an eyeful of, get a hinge, put the squint on, pick up on. See SEE.

DISTINGUISHED adj. w.k. (well-known), name, champ, number 1, number one, numero uno, VIP, in the limelight, large, brass hat, big name, heavy, heavy stuff, heavyweight. See CELEBRITY.

DISTORT v. snow, give one a snow job, whitewash, doctor, cook, con, scam, put one on, bull, bullshit, fudge, throw one a curve, trump up, hoke up, phony up, fake, pencil-whip (documentation), gammon, make out like. See also LIE.

DISTORTED adj. cockeyed, double-talk, chewing gum, bum, off, way off, off base, off the beam, screwy, sour, all wet, bum steer, ass-backwards, back-asswards, bass-ackwards, lame.

DISTORTION n. jazz, jive, line, crap, crock of shit, bullshit, BS, phony boloney, smoke, the big lie (Pol.), tall story, latrine rumor. See LIE.

DISTRACT v. catch flies (The.), stall.

DISTRACTED adj. popcorn-headed, air-headed, empty-headed, absentminded professor, pipe-dreaming, daydreaming, in a world of one's own, out to lunch, wool-gathering, mooning, mooney, goofing off, looking out the window, here in body only, a million miles away, building castles in the air, have on the brain, have on one's mind, pay no mind, hung-up, asleep at the switch, asleep on the job, not on the job. See also PREOCCUPIED.

DISTRAUGHT adj. unglued, unzipped, unscrewed, defrosted, shook up, creeped out, hissy, fertummeled, thrown, fussed, rattled, in a panic, like a chicken with its head cut off. See CONFUSED.

DISTRESS n. 1. bummer, downer, drag, bad scene, grabber, double trouble, can of worms, agita, clutch, jam, shit, deep shit, rain, rainin', rainy day, scrape, hot water, hot grease, jackpot, screw-up, crunch, one's ass is grass, tumul, pickle, pretty pickle, pretty pass, trouble in River City, fine kettle of fish, fine how-do-you-do, ticklish spot, tricky spot, sticky wicket, tail in a gate, tit caught in the wringer, mess, holy mess, unholy mess, devil to pay, hell to pay, tar baby, hobble. 2. hard time, hard knocks, hard row to hoe, tough break, tough luck, rotten luck, rum go, can't even get arrested. 3. heartache, headache, blues, worriment, tsuris, stew, all-overs, cliff-hanging, pins and needles, need it like a hole in the head, pain in the ass, pain in the neck, bad news, downside, next week East Lynne. See also ADVERSITY; WORRY.

DISTRESS v. bug, hack, wig, burn up, brown off, tick off, be in one's face, bone, dog, eat, what's eating one?, ride, nag, needle, hound, nudzh, noodge, miff, chap, peeve, get, get to, get one's goat, get in one's hair, get under one's skin, hit on, flummox, fuck with one's head, rattle one's cage, push, push one's button, drive up the wall, be on the back of, be at, penny-dog, rile, nit-pick, pick on, picky-picky, break one's balls, do a number on one, hit one where he lives, on one's case, stick in one's craw, give one a hard time, give one a turn, give a bad time to, make it tough for, discombobulate, discomboberate, throw into a swivet, throw into a tizzy, lay a bad trip on one, zing. See also DISTURB.

DISTRESSED adj. uptight, tightened-up, in crisis mode, jittery, jumpy, the jumps, jitters, creeped-out, hissy, shaky, bugged, choked, zonkers, pissin', shittin', shittin' bricks, scared shitless, shit-green, strung-out, bummed-out, unglued, hyper, spooked, twitty, fidgety, wreck, nervous wreck, bundle of nerves, nervy, all-overish, hurting, wired, wired-up, yantsy, antsy, antsy-pantsy, ants in one's pants, about to piss in one's pants, don't trip, choke, choke in, choke up, clutched, clutched-up, shook-up, shook, all shook up, shaking in one's boots, shivery, quivery, hacked, hit where one lives, buggin', dragged (following drugs), butterflies, butterflies in one's stomach, the jams, the jims, the jimmies, jimjams, heebie-jeebies, the screaming meemies, fall apart, torn down, all torn-up, tore-up, ripped, cut-up, shot to pieces, shot down, basket case, miffed, peeved, riled, rubbed the wrong way, burned up, hung-up, tightened-up, up the wall, up against it, lose one's cool, in a lather, in a stew, in a sweat, sweaty, sweat it, sweating bullets, in a swivet, in a tizzy, in a state, in a dither, in a flap, on edge, on the ragged edge, have one's teeth on edge, on pins and needles, on tenterhooks, on the gog, jumpy as a cat on a hot tin roof, have kittens, cast a kitten, having the leaps, have a fit, discombobulated, worried sick, worried stiff, biting one's nails, a real nail-biter, turn gray, beside oneself, put to it, hard put to it, have a heart attack, at the end of one's rope, on the skids, gone to pot, gone to the dogs, down on one's luck.

DISTRIBUTE v. divvy up, cut up, cut the pie, cut the melon, crack, slice up, dish out, fork out, shell out. See DIVIDE.

DISTRIBUTOR n. distrib, middleman, jobber.

DISTRICT n. territory, turf, hood, neck of the woods, stomping ground, ghetto, inner city, jungle, shanty town, skid row, slum, zoo. See NEIGHBORHOOD.

DISTRICT ATTORNEY n. D.A., cutter.

DISTRICTS n. Shubert Alley, Tin Pan Alley, Broadway, the Great White Way (The.), West End, the City, Wall Street, the Street, do or die Bed Stuy (Bedford Stuyvesant), Back Bay, Mainline, gold coast, high-rent district, slurb, burbs, Rialto, old town, Storyville, Las Vegas Strip, Sunset Strip, the Strip, Bowery, Hell's Kitchen, the Loop, the yards, back o' the yards, Tenderloin, Sugar Hill, heavy lump (Sugar Hill), SoHo, NoHo, Bowash (Boston-to-Washington corridor), Automation Alley (between Ann Arbor and Detroit), Hashbury (Haight-Ashbury), Clown Alley (circus), Lunch Bucket City (working class), territory, turf, hood, neck of the woods, rust belt, black belt, black bottom, ghetto, down the line, garment district, red-light district, Track One (brothel), Track Two (homosexual), skid row, inner city, slum, the jungle (crowded city), shantytown, zoo, shoe-store alley, used-car alley, gasoline alley, drunk alley. See also NEIGHBORHOOD.

DISTRUSTFUL adj. cagey, leery, uptight, been hit before. See also CAUTIOUS.

DISTURB v. 1. get to, flip, flip out, adjy, psych, psych out, spook, rattle, floor, fuddle, craze, curdle, bug, bug up, burn up, ball up, fire up, steam up, stir up, key up, kick up a row, work up, work up into a lather, bring one up short, pull one up short, rile, give one a bad time, give one a hard time, give one a turn, turn off, turn on, pick on, egg on, sound off, make waves, make a scene, make a fuss, fuss, fuzzbuzz, make it a tough go, make it tough for all, put the zingers in, needle, give one the needle, put the needles in, ride, throw, throw into a snit, throw into a stew, throw one a curve, throw into a tizzy, throw into a swivet, throw wood on the fire, add fuel to the flames, raise Cain, raise hell, raise the devil, raise the roof, raise a rumpus, raise a ruckus, raise a ruction, rabble-rouse, rattle, floor, throw, get to, discomboberate, discombobulate, discombooberate, drive one bananas, drive one up a tree, drive one up a wall, bitch one off, piss one off, cop an attitude (Af. Am.), that grinds my gears, ask for it, go on make my day, stick in one's craw, get a rise out of one, get one's goat, get under one's skin, get in one's hair, brown off. See also EXCITE. 2. queer, foul up, fuck up, louse up, gum up the works, flummox, throw a monkey wrench into the works, upset one's apple cart, knock the chocks from under one, knock the props from under one, put a crimp in.

DISTURBANCE n. flap, fuss, commo, dustup, to-do, big scene, stink, big stink, haroosh, jihad, fuzzbuzz (commotion), foofaraw, rumpus, ruckus, stir, row, rumble. See AGITATION. See also RIOT.

DISTURBED adj. antsy, yantsy, uptight, tightened-up, choked, defrosted, zonkers, discombobulated, pissing, shitting, shitting bricks, shook, shook-up, all shook up, creeped out, wired, wired-up, hopped-up, hyper, clutched, clutched-up, all hot and bothered, all-overish, in a scrape, in a stew, in a sweat, in a swivet, in a tizzy, flustrated, in a flusteration, in a foofaraw, in a lather, in a pucker, in a botheration, fussed, fidgety, jittery, jumpy, jumpy as a cat on a hot tin roof, on pins and needles, on tenterhooks, on the gog, on edge, on the ragged edge, have one's teeth on edge, have kittens, cast a kitten, biting one's nails, having the leaps, heebie-jeebies, the screaming meemies, the meemies, the jams, the jims, jim-jams, the jumps, jitters, nervy, wreck, nervous wreck, bundle of nerves, beside oneself, worried stiff, shot to pieces, fall apart, basket case, spooked, twitty, sweaty, bum trip, thrown. See also BOTHERED, CONFUSED, EXCITED, TROUBLED, UNEASY.

DISUSED adj. godforsaken, shelved, on the shelf, in mothballs, mothballed, down.

DITCH DIGGER n. sewer hog.

DITHER n. flap, flusteration, flustration, foofaraw, don't trip, lather, pucker, stew, swivet, tizzy. See EXCITEMENT, NERVOUSNESS, ANXIETY.

DIVE n. header, belly bump, belly buster, belly flop, belly whacker, belly whopper, chewalloper.

DIVE v. rip one (perfect), brodie, gutter, header, take a header, belly-bump, belly-bust, belly-flop, belly-whack, belly-whop, chewallop, dump altitude (aircraft).

DIVERGENT adj. poles apart, far cry, whale of a difference.

DIVERSE adj. mixed bag, funky, like night and day, dif, diff.

DIVERSION n. 1. laughs, lots of laughs, grins, fun and games, ball, big time, high time, high old time, hoopla, whoopee, picnic, merry-go-round, field day. See AMUSEMENT. See also ENTERTAINMENT. 2. red herring, action, stutter step, fake-out.

DIVERSITY n. mixed bag, diff, different strokes, different strokes for different folks.

DIVERT v. 1. sidetrack, circumlocute, bend the rules, get around, send on a wild-goose chase, catch flies (The.), stall. 2. break one up, fracture one, wow, get one's kicks, get one's jollies, panic, kill 'em, knock 'em dead, put 'em away, slay, lay 'em in the aisles, have 'em in the aisles. See AMUSE.

DIVEST v. unload, dump, adios, 86, eighty-six, ditch, bleed, bleed white, milk, sell off.

DIVESTED adj. unloaded, minus, cut, dumped, eighty-sixed, bled, bled white, milked.

DIVIDE v. dish out, fork out, shell out, hand out, hand over, divvy, divvy up, go halfies, go halvers, go fifty-fifty, go even-steven, crack, slice, slice up, cut the pie, cut the melon, slice the melon, slice the pie, split, split up, cut, cut up, cut one in, duke one in, cut up the touches, cut up the pipes, cut up the jackpot, piece up, whack up, bump into, size into (chips).

DIVIDEND n. melon, pie, plum, divvy, lagniappe, taste. See also INTEREST; SHARE.

DIVINE adj. divoon.

DIVINE n. the rev, sky pilot, preacher man, harp polisher, glory roader. See CLERGYMAN.

DIVINE v. take a stab, take a stab in the dark, take a shot, take a shot in the dark, talk off the top of one's head, go out on a limb. See also PREDICT.

DIVINITY n. Dad, Head Knock, Lordy, Man Upstairs.

DIVISION n. 1. affil (TV), branch, branch house, offshoot. See ASSOCIATE. 2. piece, bite, divvy, cut, crack, slice, chunk, end, piece of the action, piece of the pie, slice of the melon, cut of the melon, rake-off, fifty-fifty, halver, bigger half, big end. See INTEREST; SHARE.

DIVORCE n. breakup, dedomiciling, pffft, phfft, go phftt, Mexicancellation, Reno-vation, split, split-up, splitsville, on the rocks, marriage on the rocks, come to a parting of the ways, couldn't make it, on the out and out, washed-up, holy deadlock, matchruptcy.

DIVORCE v. split, split up, dedomicile, break up, call it quits, phftt, go phftt, untie the knot, Reno-vate, go to Reno, Mexicancel. See also SEPARATE.

DIVORCEE n. ex (-wife or -husband), dumpee, grass widow, broken rib.

DIVULGE v. fess up, spill the beans, blow the whistle, put it on the street, go public with, let it all hang out, bring it out into the daylight, bring it out into the open, let one's hair down, spring, tip off, open up, own up, cough up, give the show away. See CONFESS.

DIZZY adj. gaga, rocky, woozy, dopey, punchy, punch-drunk, slap-happy, the room going around, head-spinning, light-headed.

DO v. go for it, move, do one's thing, TCB (take care of business), pull off, break out with, bust out with (surprisingly or suddenly), kickin' it, get with it, boogie, time to boogie (time to get started), shit or get off the pot, perk, cook, operate, that dog'll hunt, come on like. See ACT.

DOCILE adj. cool, mellow, laid-back. See also SUBMISSIVE.

DOCKHAND n. dock walloper, roustabout.

DOCTOR n. M.D., doc, bones, sawbones, bone bender, bone breaker, bone setter, pill pusher, pill roller, pill bag, pill peddler, pill slinger, big eye man, big nose man, big heart man, medic, medico, med, mediciner, croaker, stick croaker, butcher, quack, bolus (U.), barefoot doctor (rural); Dr. Feelgood, Feelgood, ice-tong doctor, right rocker, script writer (prescribe drugs illegally); cut-em-up, fix-em-up, pills, pill punk, iodine, salts (prison), baby catcher (obstetrician), rear admiral (proctologist), small-arm inspector, femme D (woman).

DOCTOR OF DIVINITY n. DD.

DOCTOR OF PHILOSOPHY n. Ph.D., Ph.T. (putting hubby through college).

DOCUMENT n. MS., Ms, ms., script, pages, language.

DOCUMENT v. leave a paper trail, crack on one or something, debunk (prove false), pan out. See VERIFY.

DOCUMENTARY FILM n. doc, docudrama, rockumentary (music).

DODGE v. duck, juke, shake, shake off, put the move on one, ditch, give the slip, skip out on, circumlocute, buck it over, get around; jank, jink (enemy planes). See AVOID.

DODGE CAR n. ducker.

DOER n. eager beaver, operator, big-time operator, BTO, workaholic, hustler, ball of fire, live wire. See MAN OF ACTION.

DOG n. mutt, pooch, poochy, pup, doggie, doggy, puppy dog, purp, dorg, fido, bowwow, goop, gyp (female), man's best friend, four-legged friend, hard dog (trained to attack), Heinz, Heinz 57, Heinz 57 Varieties, flea hotel, tail-wagger, bone polisher, bone eater, biscuit eater, pot licker, pot hound, soup hound, hound dog.

DOG EXCREMENT n. do, dog-do, doggy-do, dog-dew, dog turd, dog hockey, sidewalk obstacle course.

DOGGED adj. bullhead, bullheaded, bulletheaded, hardheaded, pigheaded, muleheaded, mule, mulish, stubborn as a mule, hard-nosed, stiff-necked, horse, sticky, Turk, tough nut, hang tough, murder (he's murder), has one's Dutch up, the game ain't over till the last man is out, ain't over till the fat lady sings. See also TENACIOUS, STUBBORN.

DOGGEDLY, ACT v. hang in, hang tough, stick it, go for broke, go for it, go all out. See OBSTINATE, BE.

DOGMATIC adj. bossy, flaky, iceman, got the faith baby, cocksure, sure as shit, come hell or high water, redneck, a regular Archie Bunker. See also STUBBORN, PREJUDICED.

DOGMATIST, RIGHT WING n. Archie Bunker, male chauvinist pig, MCP, pig, sexist porker, redneck, good old boy, good old boys' network, McCarthyite, jingoist, flag-waver, patrioteer, superpatriot.

DOG-RACING TERMS hamburger (inferior dog), the dogs.

DOLDRUMS n. blahs, blah-blahs, blues, blue devils, blue funk, funk, crumbed, bummer, downer, down trip, letdown, dolefuls, dismals, dumps, mumps, mopes, mokers, mulligrubs, miseries (Af. Am.).

DOLE n. handout.

DOLLAR n. bill, buck, clam, fish, fishskin, one, single, skin, smacker, ace, banana, berry, bob, boffo, bone, case, case buck, case dough, case note, check, cholly, clacker, coconut, cucumber, frog, frogskin, hog, hogs, Jewish flag (Derog.), last dollar, lizard, man, peso, pilaster, plunk, potato, rag, rock, rutabaga, scrip, simoleon, Simon, slab, slug, smack, scoot, year; cartwheel, iron man, ball, bullet, copek, D, hardtack, plug, shekel, shiner, sinker, wheel (silver).

DOLLAR, SILVER n. cartwheel, iron man, ball, bullet, copek, D, hardtack, plug, shekel, shiner, sinker, wheel, Suzzi.

DOLLARS, TWO n. two-spot, deuce, deucer, deuce spot, two-case note, two cents.

DOLLARS, FIVE n. fin, five, fiver, five-spot, Abe's Cabe, five-case note; finski, finif, pound, half-eagle (gold coin).

DOLLARS, TEN n. saw, sawbuck, ten, tenner, ten-spot, dews, dime note, dix, bean, eagle (gold coin).

DOLLARS, TWENTY n. double sawbuck, twenty, twenty cents, double eagle (gold coin).

DOLLARS, TWENTY-FIVE n. squirt.

DOLLARS, FIFTY n. fifty, half a C, half a century, half a yard.

DOLLARS, ONE HUNDRED n. C, century, century note, C note, hollow note, one bill, yard, dollar, hun.

DOLLARS, FIVE HUNDRED n. half grand, five yards, D, five centuries, five C's, half G. nickel, small nickel.

DOLLARS, ONE THOUSAND n. big one, one dollar, dime, G, C note, grand, horse, thou, yard, kilobucks.

DOLLARS, FIVE THOUSAND n. big nickel.

DOLLARS, ONE MILLION n. mil, megabucks.

DOLOPHINE n. dolly.

DOLT n. ditzo, hamburger, dork, dorf, lop, fuckbrain, lamebrain, dickhead, Fred, Barney, Wilma, beau, mutant, yo-yo, out-to-lunch, lunchie, lunchbox, lunchsack, feeb, dodo, dumdum, twillie, airhead, helium head, conehead, meathead, hamburger, jel, doesn't know from A to B, a few bricks shy of a load, one doughnut shy of a dozen, elevator doesn't run to the top floor, a low-watt bulb, a few sandwiches short of picnic, lorg, gump, zombie, stupe, boob, sap, simp, butthead, deadass, gink, cluck. See STUPID.

DOMAIN n. 1. territory, turf, stomping grounds, old stomping grounds, stamping grounds, home grounds, back home, neck of the woods, bailiwick. See also DISTRICTS. 2. slot, wing. See OCCUPATION.

DOMESTIC n. girl, help, woman, cleaning woman, cleaning lady, biddy, furp, tweeny, pillow punk, cabin girl (chambermaid), live-in, slavey, peon, serf, man, boy, houseboy, number one boy, pratt boy.

DOMESTICATE v. gentle, bust.

DOMESTIC CRISIS n. soap, soap opera.

DOMICILE n. domi, dommy, pad, crash pad, crib, condo, co-op, coop, joint, roof over one's head, dump, hooch (Vietnam), castle, home plate, rack, roost. See HOUSE. See also APARTMENT.

DOMINATE v. run the show, call the shots, call the tune, kick ass, kick butt, rule the roost, wear the pants, lay down the law, lead by the nose, have the whip hand, reel one back in, bring to heel, box in, get one in a box, sit on top of, serve, run, in front of, take the high ground. See MANAGE.

DOMINATED adj. henpecked, on a string, tied to one's apron strings, pussy-whipped, under one's thumb. See SUBJUGATED.

DOMINEER v. run things, run the show, push the buttons, serve, bulldoze, henpeck, pussy-whip (Fem.), shoot on, call the shots, call the tune, be in the driver's seat, be in the saddle, ride herd on, crack the whip, wear the pants, wear the trousers, rule the roost, keep under one's thumb, lead by the nose, kick one around, throw one's weight around, throw a lot of weight, have the whip hand, do it one's way, hold the aces, reel one back in, twist around one's little finger, wind around one's little finger, bring to heel, box in, get one in a box, sit on top of.

DOMINEERING adj. bossy, crack the whip, high-and-mighty, on one's high horse, throw one's weight around, wear the pants, in the driver's seat. See also ARROGANT.

DOMINION n. territory, turf, stomping grounds, old stomping grounds, stamping grounds, one's neck of the woods. See also DISTRICTS.

DON v. suit up, dud, dude, dude up, doll up, dog out, fit out, rag out, rag up, rig out, rig up, turn out, tog, drape.

DONATE v. 1. ante up, pony up, lay on, get it up, put something in the pot, sweeten the pot, sweeten the kitty, feed the kitty, pass the hat, do one's part. See GIVE. 2. have a finger in, have a finger in the pie, get in the act, sit in on, put in one's two cents.

DONATION n. handout, a hand, helping hand, write-off, chickadee checkoff (charity), gift, gifting, do one's part, lump, poke-out, maxed-out (political limit).

DONE adj. set, buttoned-up, wired, fixed, a wrap, cashed, pow, all over but the shouting, done to a T, done with. See FINISHED.

DONKEY n. Rocky Mountain canary.

DONOR n. angel, Santa Claus, sugar daddy, fairy godmother, lady bountiful, giver, heavy hitter, maxed-out (political limit), backer.

DO NOTHING v. sit on one's hands, let it come, let it go, stand by.

DOOM n. karma, the beads, the way the cookie crumbles, the way the ball bounces, handwriting on the wall, in the lap of the gods.

DOOMED adj. done, done-for, dead duck, dead meat, sunk, toast, in the cards, que sera sera, the way the ball bounces, the way the cookie crumbles, the way the beads read, the handwriting on the wall, kiss of death.

DOOMSAYER n. Calamity Jane, Alice under the ax.

DOOR n. slammer.

DOPAMINE n. L. Dopo, El Dopo.

DORIDEN n. doors, dories (sedative).

DORMANT adj. on the shelf, on the bench, on the beach, on ice, out of the rat race, out of action, out of the swim, closed-down, down.

DORMITORY n. dorm, fratority, sorenity, birdcage, bull pen, bullypen, frau shack, henranch, hencoop, quail roost, zoo.

DOSE n. hit, shot, fix, nip, slug, bang, dram.

DOSE v. dope, dope up, dose up, doctor, fix, hit.

DOSSIER n. sheet, rap sheet, dope, file. See DIRECTORY. See also RECORD.

DOUBLE n. 1. stand-in, ringer, dead ringer, look-alike, clone, twin, spitting image, angel (radar). See also COPY. 2. doubleheader (successful two ways), double in brass, wear two hats (two kinds of work), rule of twice, twofers.

DOUBLE BASS n. bull fiddle, doghouse, vcin.

DOUBTFUL adj. chancy, iffy, dicey, up for grabs, doubting Thomas, touchy, touch-and-go, on slippery ground, on ice, on thin ice, long-shot, fat chance, hanging by a thread, cagey, leery, been hit before, don't hold your breath, you should live so long, blow hot and cold, sit on the fence, waffling, shilly-shally, stuck, betwixt and between, at sixes and sevens, between a rock and a hard place, dipypdro, the jury's out, tics and twitches.

DOUBTLESS adj. posolutely, sure as hell, sure as I live and breathe, fer shirr, that's for sure, no ifs ands or buts, is the Pope Catholic? See CERTAIN.

DOUCHE BAG n. bag.

DOUGHNUT n. sinker, cruller, slug, submarine, knothole, mudball.

DOUSE v. dunk.

DOVETAIL v. lip-sync, sync, sync up.

DOVETAILED adj. 1. in sync. 2. co-ed.

DOWDY adj. frumpy, frowzy, run-down, down-at-the-heels, off-the-cob, mince, moldy.

DOWNCAST adj. singing the blues, dragged, ass in a sling, sorry-assed, down in the dumps, low, bummed out, in pain, in the pits, shot down. See DEPRESSED.

DOWNFALL n. the skids, on the skids, hit the skids, rack and ruin, on the rocks. See FAILURE.

DOWNGRADE v. bump, bust, break, rif, bench, set back, hold back.

DOWNGRADED adj. benched, busted, broken, in the bag (police), set down, set back, held back.

DOWNRIGHT adj. up front, open, straight, straight shit, talk like a Dutch Uncle, call a spade a spade, put all one's cards on the table, make no bones about it, talk turkey. See SINCERE.

DOWNTRODDEN adj. in one's power, in one's pocket, in one's clutches, under one's thumb, at one's mercy, at one's beck and call, at one's feet, a slave to, led by the nose, dance to one's tune.

DOWNTRODDEN n. have-nots, the underdog, bag lady, underdeveloped (nation or district), the needy, truly needy. See DESTITUTE.

DOZE v. snooze, grab a few Z's, bag some Z's, cop some Z's, blow Z's, flake out, rack duty, rack time, catnap, doss, dozz, doz, calk off, drop off, dope off, cork off, knock off, dig oneself a nod, collar a nod, catch a wink. See SLEEP.

DRAB adj. blah, grungy, run-down, dull as dishwater, dog, gummy, zero, big zero, flat. See BORING.

DRAFT n. greetings, letter from Uncle Sam.

DRAFT v. sign on, sign up, call up.

DRAFT BOARD n. trap.

DRAFTEE n. boot, rookie, tenderfoot, cannon fodder, sad sack. See also RECRUIT.

DRAG v. lug, schlep, truck.

DRAGONFLY n. mosquito hawk, snake doctor (So.).

DRAG-RACE TRACK n. drag strip, shutdown strip (past finish line), dragway.

DRAG-RACING CAR n. dragster, hot rod, a rail job (built on a bare frame), funny car, slingshot, fueler, gasser, altered.

DRAG RACING, MAINTENANCE burnout pit, bleach box, baldies, slicks (treadless tires), stuffer (supercharger), shoe (tire), wheelie bar.

DRAG RACING, START hole, hole job, hole shot (get a winning start); burnout (soften tires), drop the hammer (pop the clutch), wheelie, wheel stand.

DRAG RACING TERMS drag, dragging, banzai (all out), Top Fuel (race for fastest cars), bench racing (race analysis), Christmas tree (starting lights), heads-up (no handicap), altered (vehicle class), unload (lose a part such as a wheel), dump (win), ET (elapsed time).

DRAIN v. bleed, bleed white, suck dry, get every last drop.

DRAINED adj. dead, dead tired, beat, used-up, draggin' ass, hung, pooped, wiped-out, burned-out, hacked, hit the wall (marathon). See WEARY.

DRAMATIST n. scripter, play doctor, play fixer, telewriter (TV), teleplaywright, scribbler, scribe, scrivener, scratcher, word slinger, wordsmith, ghost, ghostwriter, knight of the pen, knight of the plume, knight of the quill. See also WRITER.

DRAMATIZE v. ham it up, play up, lay it on thick, make a production of, splash, play on the heartstrings, throw in the hook, the grabber, the rooting interest, play it don't say it.

DRAW n. standoff, Mexican standoff, push, even-steven, dead heat, dead end.

DRAWING n. 1. the numbers, the numbers game. 2. graphics, comp, layout, storyboard, doodle.

DRAWN adj. peaked, peaky, bag of bones, skin-and-bones, stack of bones. See also THIN.

DREAD n. cold feet, buck fever, goose bumps, creeps, cold creeps, cold shivers, jitters, worriment, stage fright. See FEAR.

DREADFUL adj. beastly, icky, yicky, yucky, mean, hellish, hairy, furry, wicked, heavy, gross, grody, grody to the max, godawful, goshawful, grim, lousy, rotten, hair-raising, white-knuckle, spooky, spooked, frozen, goose-bumpy, asshole-puckerin', asshole suckin' wind, pecker-assed, creepy.

DREAM n. pie in the sky, castles in Spain, castles in the air.

DREAM v. head-trip, dream up, make up, think up, trump up, spark, spitball, brainstorm, take it off the top of one's head.

DREAMER n. star gazer, scoutmaster.

DREDGER n. groundhog, sandhog.

DREGS adj. bottom-of-the-barrel, scrape the bottom of the barrel, gook, gunk.

DRESS n. 1. threads, set of threads, togs, toggery, duds, outfit, rags, glad rags, fresh dip, weeds, schmotte, schmatteh, frame, front, flash, frock, sock frock, bag, micro, mini, miniskirt, midi, maxi, maxicoat, maxidress, granny dress, Mother Hubbard, drape, drapery, drapes, set of drapes. 2. getup, get out, feathers, fine feather, full feather, Barbie and Ken (conventional), vine, flute, dry goods, rig, pantsuit, jumpsuit, California black tie (any colorful variation of formal wear), California chic (expensive casual), fofarraw, civvies, cits, mufti, fatigues, Port Arthur tuxedo, khakis, dress blues, whites, fishtail, drape shape, drape shape with a reet pleet, zoot suit, zoot soot, zoot suit with a reet pleat, cool suit with a loop droop, Nehru jacket, Nehru suit, clobber, harness (leather, especially motorcycle), drag, boondock (outdoor), racket jacket, Sunday best, Sunday go-to-meetings, bib and tucker, secondhand. See also CLOTHING.

DRESS v. turn out, fit out, rig out, rig up, rag out, rag up, tog, suit up, doll up, deck, deck out, dog out, dud, dude, dude up, dode (bad fit), drape, primp, prink, prank.

DRESSED adj. togged, togged-up, slicked-up, rigged-up, rigged-out, ragged-up, ragged-out, duded-up, duded-out, dap (Af. Am.), decked-out, deck-up, trick out, trick-up, tog out, tog-up, rag out, rag-up, fig out, fig-up, turned-out, tricked-out, dolled-up, fancied-up, gussied-up, slicked-up, spiffed-up, spruced-up, in fine feather, in high feather, in one's best bib and tucker, corporate (business), looking sharp, mellow back; laid-out, tied-back, clean back (Af. Am.), dressed fit to kill, Sunday go-to-church, put on the dog. See also WELL-DRESSED, STYLISH.

DRIFT v. kick around, float, go thataway, go every which way, go forty ways to Sunday, go forty ways from Sunday, go forty ways for Sunday, anywhere the wind blows. See also WANDER.

DRIFTER n. bum, on the bum, king of the road, bo, stiff, bindlestiff, floater, rolling stone, ragbag. See VAGRANT. See also BEGGAR.

DRILL n. 1. constitutional, daily dozen, workout, gym, warmup, jazzercise. 2. dry run, run-through, call, shakedown, shakedown cruise, tryout, workout, dress. See also TEST.

DRILL v. work out, tune up, lick into shape, get in shape, walk through, hone, break, break in. See PRACTICE.

DRILL INSTRUCTOR n. D.I., DI.

DRINK n. swig, slug, shot, bang, snort, snorter, snifter, ham, spot, nip, drop, wee drop, jigger, pint, pull, toast, fresh one, short one, short dog (cheap wine in a brown paper bag), double, finger, finger or two, cooler, juice, plasma, serum, shot in the arm, hooter, shooter, giggle-soup (So.), slam, taste, wash, quickie, quick one, one for the road, one too many, eye-opener, nightcap. See also LIQUOR.

DRINK v. guzzle, guz, down, swig, belt, put away, sponge, lick, liquor, liquor up, booze up, dab, lap, lap up, sop, sop it up, tank up, soak up, bottom, bottoms up, beer up, gin up, mug up (coffee), chug-a-lug, on the sauce, hit the sauce, hit the bottle, hit the booze, hit the red-eye, bend one's elbow, tip one's elbow, exercise the elbow, crook one's elbow, crook one's little finger, take a pull, go on a drunk, go on a bat, go on a binge, go on a toot, go on a bender, paint the town red, have one too many, drown one's troubles, crawl, pub-crawl, joint-hop, pound, knock back, juice back, juice down, crack a six-pack (beer), brewhaha (beer), brewha, dork off, do some stewing, slosh, throg, wash down, swill, bellywash, tipple, belt the grape, wet one's whistle, dip the beak, splice the main brace, get a bun on, get a buzz on, blast, scoff, slurp, pull, fight a bottle, growler rushing, hang a few on, hang on a few, inhale, irrigate, kill, knock off, fall off the wagon; blow-dried, closed, dammed, signed (drunk and refused additional drinks).

DRINKER n. lush, lushie, lusher, lushhound, souse, dip, dipso, barfly, stew, stewbum, stewie, wino, loady, loadie, big drunk, town drunk, brown bagger, boozer, boozehound, booze fighter, hoochhound, ginhound, tippler, alky, jick head, juice head, juicer, dip, dipso, power drinker, groghound, grog blossom, bum, rum, rummy, rumhound, pretzel bender, shikker, guzzler, swiller, soaker, tank, pot, rumpot, lovepot, tosspot, crock, swigger, soak, sponge, long hitter, elbow bender, elbow crooker, barrelhouse bum, bottle baby, bottle man, stiff, bust, busthead, copper nose, swillbelly, swillpot, swillbowl.

DRINK, SOFT n. pop, Coke, dope, bug juice, setup (for alcoholic mix), chaser, mixer, seltzer, penny plain, two cents plain, cooler.

DRIVE n. 1. get-up-and-go, push, guts, moxie, punch, clout, steam, the stuff, the right stuff, the goods, what it takes, spunk, gumption, fire in the belly. See also ATTACK. 2. spin, whirl, run, joyride, Sunday drive, airing, lift, pickup, burnout (high-speed), commute, hitch.

DRIVE v. 1. cruise, roll, roll by, tool, tootle around, tiptoe, bomb around, heel-and-toe (racing), burn rubber, burn up the road, burn the breeze, drag, floor it, step on it, lean on it, bear down on it, fire up, lay rubber down, fly, pour it on, pour on the coal, step on the gas, push, scat, tailgate, whoosh, hustle, make the sparks fly, go all out, go full steam ahead, break one's neck, bear down, poke, hump, get cutting. 2. bulldoze, pressure, high-pressure, steamroll, lean on, goose, goose up, nerf, nag, jawbone, egg on, sell, sell one, railroad through. See FORCE.

DRIVE-IN THEATER n. ozoner, drive-in, passion pit.

DRIVEL n. hogwash, gobbledygook, poppycock, tripe, rot, tommyrot. See NONSENSE.

DRIVER n. wheelman, cowboy, leadfoot, Harvey Wallbanger (reckless), charger, double clutcher, dump chump (truck), bottlecap (tank truck), dynamiter, fireman, fluffy foot, gypsy, coachy, skinner, mule skinner, hogger, hoghead, shithead, shoe, skate jockey, road jockey, road

runner roadhog, Willy Weaver (drunk). See also TRUCK DRIVER.

DRIVING, AUTOMOBILE n. cruising, at the wheel, buggy riding, chining, tooling.

DROLL adj. camp, campy, jokey, joshing, yok, yokky, gagged-up, for grins, zetser, laffer, riot, crack up, crack 'em up, break one up. See AMUSING.

DRONE n. mother (plane).

DROP v. 1. nose-dive, dive, flop, do a Brodie. 2. knock off, off, adios that, bag that, 86 that, eighty-six that, dog, kibosh, put the kibosh on, scrub, blow off, dust, wash out, wipe out, waste one, scratch. See also DISCARD.

DROPPED adj. scrubbed, adiosed, dogged, washed-out, washed-up, all washed up, scratched, eighty-sixed, offed, wasted.

DROWSE v. grab a few Z's, cop some Z's, zizz, catnap, doze, doz, calk off, drop off, dope off, cork off, cop a nod, did oneself a nod, collar a nod, catch a wink. See SLEEP.

DROWSY adj. dopey, out of it, sleepyhead, snoozy, stretchy, on the nod, eye trouble, in sleepsville.

DRUDGE n. workaholic, workhorse, nose to the grindstone, grind, greasy grind.

DRUDGE v. plug, dig, grind, peg away, slave, sweat, back to the salt mines, heel (Stu.), schlep. See PLOD.

DRUDGERY n. grind, daily grind, blunting, rat race, elbow grease, shitwork, donkeywork, gruntwork (Army), scud, scut, workout, ball breaker, ball racker, ball buster, bone breaker, back breaker, ass breaker, conk buster, bitch, bitch kitty, son of a bitch, fun and games.

DRUG n. A-bomb, Anywhere (possession), controlled substance, party favor, ammunition, blank (nonnarcotic), doll, downer, downs, Finn, hard stuff, knockout drops, bonaroo, fruit salad (mixture), little Michael, little Mike, Mickey Finn, starch, upper, ups, shroom (psychedelic), turkey (diluted), magic bullet (Medic.); dummy, the business, jaloney, flea powder, dust, dynamite, hype, mojo, sugar (bad or fake dope), designer drug, G.Q. (good quality).

DRUG ADDICTION n. habit, hook, Jones, jones, sweet tooth, monkey on one's back, boss habit, ape sitting on one's neck, crapping on one's brain (heavy); chickenshit habit, ice-cream habit (minimal). See ADDICTION.

DRUG BUY n. bag, dime bag, nickel bag, dime's worth, cap; matchbox, stick (cigarette); quarter bag, can, lid, O.Z., weight (ounce); key, kee, ki (kilogram); brick (compressed kilo).

DRUG CURE TERMS take the cure, kick the habit, kick, cold turkey, get the monkey off, get the monkey off one's back, off the habit, clear up, kill the Chinaman, normie, straight, crank handle, winder, hitchhiker (voluntary patient in a hospital), rifle range, shooting gallery (ward of hospital), croaker (doctor).

DRUGGED adj. stoned, high, on the nod, nodding, spaced, spaced-out, trip, tripping, flyin', stoned out of one's mind, stoned out of one's head, stoned out of one's gourd, ethereal, snowed, snowed-in, snowed-up, snowed under, caught in a snowstorm, sleigh riding, coked, coked-up, coasting, floating, twisted, jacked, blasted, blown away, blown-out, wigged-out, mellowed-out, strung-out, wiped-out, zonked-out, zootied, charged-up, gaged-up, geezed-up, junked-up, teaed-up, torn-up, hopped-up, heeled, high as a kite, loaded, smashed, happy, flying, joy-riding, ripped, out, out of it, on the needle, on the weed, on the hype, on the hype stick, on the light artillery, on a cloud, pinned (constricted pupils), contact high, geed-up, g'd-up, goofed, gow, gowed-up, in orbit, baked, crispy, amped, bent, beaming, blitzed, blitzed-out, bombed, bombed-out, blasted, blind, buzzed, boxed-up, fried, gone, gone under, jazzed, jazzed-up, laid-out, loaded, maxed-out, monolithic, potted, revved-up, racked, racked-up, riffed, schizzed, shermed (angel dust), hopped, killed, nodded out, org (drug rush), transcended, tweaked, tweeked, tweek out, gassed, tore-up, zoned, up high, x-out, zooty, skulled, tall.

DRUG MARKETPLACE n. rock house, cokeland, ice-cream truck, pizza parlor (Mafia), Alphabet City (N.Y.C.), Sherm Alley (L.A.).

DRUG OVERDOSE v. OJ, overjolt, overvamp, overamp, overcharge, OD, oh dee, burn out, freak out, jazz out, rock out, zone out, zonk out, jammed up, crystallized (methedrine).

DRUG PACKET n. lid, bag, deck, bindle, bird's-eye.

DRUG PARAPHERNALIA n. works, toys, spike, head kit, kit, fit, outfit, rig, the business, apps, joint (total equipment), necessities, flake spoon, cooker, gun, hook, ken ten (lamp for opium), artillery, banger, hype stick, light artillery, harpoon, needle, pin, pin gun, winky (freebase), quill (matchbook cover), bong (pipe), mary gin (seed remover), roach clip, crutch, Woodstock emergency pipe (aluminum foil); stash bag, stash box, stash jar (marijuana).

DRUG SELLER n. dealer, pusher, drug pusher, connection, peddler, dope peddler, source, roller, high roller, bartender, street pharmacist, one who's holding, pin, twirler, hyp, hype, mother, mule, junker, shover, viper, the man, heavy man, tea man, reefer man, candy man, swing man, bagman, big man, scag man, bingles, bingler, broker, house connections, juggler, OZ man, powder monkey, missionary, operator, trafficker, internal (smuggler), travel agent (LSD), beat artist, fixer, gazoonie (strong-arm).

DRUG TERMS cut, doctor, phony up (adulterate); cut deck (adulterated); charge, load, load plane (carries narcotics), skinful; shot, hit, piece, can, deck, phony bingle, carrying (possession); scag trade, golden triangle (opium poppy-growing area of Siam), factory, underground factory, basement lab, flake (plant drugs or illegal weapons).

DRUG TRAFFIC n. scag trade, clocking (selling crack); load plane (carries narcotics), whammer (woman smuggler, carries drugs in vagina).

DRUG USE adj. on the needle, on the nod, high, use, up, habit, belly habit (oral), mouth habit (smoke), nose habit, needle habit, needle park, chipping (occasional use), dusted (high on PCP), fried, reentry, blown, floating, wrecked, roasted, twisted, wired, sprung (on rock cocaine), strung-out, goon out, way out, wigged-out, mellowed-out, wiped-out, zonked-out, freaked-out, weird out, stoned out of one's gourd, whack attack, scratch a monkey, feed a monkey, slammin', blazed (marijuana), zerked-out, smacked-back (heroin), wired for sound (cocaine), car, in the car, out of the car, charged-up, gaged-up, geezed-up, junked-up, teaed-up, torn-up, hopped-up, heeled, high as a kite, loaded, smashed, fires, weedhead, the business, blown away, blown-out, skagged-out, happy, thrill, kick, charge, coasting, having a buzz, flying, joy-riding, sleigh-riding, blow weed, zoom, trip, trip out, freak out, flip out, X out, ripped, out of it, turn on, get there, get small, ping wing, pin shot, pothead, on the weed, on the hype, on the hype stick, on the light artillery, on a cloud, shooting the pin, pinned (constricted pupils), shooting gallery, snowed, caught in a snowstorm, snowstorm (party), tracks, dirty arm, service stripe, trapdoor, trapdoor scab (injecting under a scab to hide needle marks), cokie, coked, coked-up, pinned, doper, contact high, coast, drive, geed-up, g'd-up, geezer, goofed, gow, gowed-up, hold, hot shot, hype, in orbit, whistling (no money for a fix), chemical dependency.

DRUG USE v. shoot, shoot up, drop, pop, use, waste, space out, zone out, tweek out, nod, fix, take a fix, take a drag, hit, take a hit, toke, smoke a toke, smoke a bowl, blow major jaw (smoke buds), get high, get off, get up, go up, make, goon out, tall, floating, flying, gone, sniff, snort, blow, blast, bust a cat, boot, cook, mainline, bust the mainline, freebase, baseballing, the big drive, bang, bomb, bomb out, O.D., OJ (overjolt), hot shot (fatal), jab off, joy pop, skin pop, jolt, jolt of junk, kick the mooch around, kick the gong around, shoot the pin, reenter, chase the dragon, do up, do a blow, do a toot, do drugs, dabbling, dossing, dozzing, speedball, lit up, blind, beaming, beaming up, torn up, hit the pipe, hit the needle, hit the sewer, sewer, channel, home, ditch, pit, geez, geeze, bogart (get more than one's share), short, sick (need), whistling (no money for a fix), straighten one (administer), string out, sweet tooth, Tom, Tom Mix, trip, blow coke, blow snow, drop a bop (pill), chipping (occasional use), cork the air, blow one's mind, give one knockout drops, slip one a mickey, dope, dope up, dose, dose up.

DRUG USER n. A.D., AD, A-head, junkie, junker, greasy junkie, user, toxic waste dump, doper, piper (crack smoker), space cadet, mainliner, freak, head, loady, loadie, hop, hophead, drughead, coke head, basehead (freebase), acid head, acid freak, dust head, weedhead, pothead, pillhead, pinhead, meth head, fiend, dope fiend, shroom dog (mushroom user), hooked, hype, hypo, banger, bangster, jabber, jaboff, needle man, needle knight, use the needle, smack slammer, tripper, dirty, dopenik, straight (after injection), viper, wasted, dynamiter, Cap'n Toke, sick (needs injection), cokey, pinned (high), snifter, tooter (cocaine), ice creamer, student, Skag Jones, snowbird, snow snorter, station worker; Saturday night habit, chipper, chippy (occasional); weekend warrior, joy popper (new or occasional user), campfire boy, tea toker, from Mount Shasta (not common), goof, goofball, aspirin hound, bean popper, speed freak, globetrotter (always moving); author, scribe (both able to write prescriptions); boomer, drifter, floater, hopper, boot and shoe (always moving), Mighty Joe Young, artilleryman. See ADDICT.

DRUG-USE SITE n. headshop, gallery, ballroom, balloon room, parachute, spot.

DRUG WITHDRAWAL n. kicking the habit, drying out, sweating it out, taking the cure, hurting, shakes, wet-dog shakes, bogue, cold turkey, becoming Mr. Fink.

DRUGS n. D&N (drugs and narcotics), junk, shit, bang, narky, goofball, reds, uppers, downers, stuff, hard stuff, cement, goods, Jones, party favors, merchandise, fruit salad (mixture), the needle, shot, shot in the arm, fix, bag, lid, bop, charge, shot, card (portion), biddle, bindle, bingle, bing, birdsize, jolt, bundle, nickel bag, Z (ounce), deck, dime bag (ten dollars' worth), cap, West Coast cap, Tijuana cap, Mexican cap, Frisco cap, cold stuff (deadly), dust, dynamite (pure), fix up, bongs, check, fours, mojo, needle candy, score, sugar, candy, cubes, dust, starch, flea powder, ammunition, lucky seven (mixture), psychedelic jelly bean, nixon (poor quality), stallion stick, stums, sweet surrender, corporation cocktail (coal gas bubbled through milk), Allah Supreme, God's medicine, hokus, hook, hop, half load, happenings, ice cream (crystals), brown bomber, casa boom, 'cotics, death boy, death wish.

DRUGS: AMPHETAMINE n. A, bam, liquid bam, amp, black widow, Catholic aspirin, amphets, boosters, trucker, peps, black beauties, blackbird, black mollies, browns, bumblebees, chicken powder, coast-to-coasts, L.A. turnabouts, West Coast turnabouts, cranks, doll, fives, footballs, green dragon, greenie, jelly baby, jug, lightning, mimibennies, nuggets, road dope, root, rosas, roses, sparkle plenty, sweet, uppie, whites, white cross, whitey, zoom, bombita, cartwheel, chalk, cotton (saturated with Benzedrine), copilot, diet pills, double blue, driver, eye-opener, forwards, French blue, hearts, jellybeans, jolly beans, leapers, leepers, lid popper, lightfooted, peaches, pepper, pep pill, ripper, splash, speed, thrusters, truck drivers, up, uppers, wake up, obie.

DRUGS: AMYL NITRITE n. amy, amies, amys, aimless amy, posies, popper, blue, blue angel, blue bird, blue devil, blue heaven, pear, snapper, pearls, poppsies, Dr. Bananas, whiffenpopper.

DRUGS: BARBITURATE n. barb, blue devils, blue heaven, candy, down, goofball, peanuts, Phennies, Christmas tree, Christmas roll, rainbow roll, blunt, fender-bender, goofer, marshmallow reds, Mexican red, red and blue, sleeper, sex, stum, stumbler, tuie, tus, twos, pink lady, purple heart, yellow jacket, abbot, geronimos, blockbuster, nimby, nebbie, nemmy.

DRUGS: BENZEDRINE n. B, bennie, benny, benz, benzie, cheesy, bean, speed, upper, brother Ben, copilot Ben, hi-ball, pep pill, peachies, white, blancas, crosses.

DRUGS: BIPHETAMINE n. black beauties.

DRUGS: CHLORAL HYDRATE n. knockout drops, Mickey, Mickey Finn, Lipton tea, little Michael.

DRUGS: COCAINE n. C, Cee, sea, coke, cola, cokey, candy, nose candy, crack, rocks (hard), eight-track (2.5 grams), sugar, snow, snowball, cloud walk, speedball (plus morphine or heroin), snowbird, white, white cross, white mosquitoes, white Christmas, old lady white, white girl, white stuff, Doctor White, sleighride, toot, toots, Charlie, Cecil, Connie, Corinne, Bernice, Pearl, girl, girlfriend, her, lady, angel, angie, Bernies, Burnese, Burese, crank, blow, blower, blow in the snow, little Joe in the snow, snowcaine, snow stuff, cane, candy cane, blast, bullet, coca, croak (plus speed), evil, jolt, bazooka, icicles, star stuff, supercharge, rails, rock candy, snort, sneeze, jimbo soda, moonrock, uptown, gin, jam, flake, joy flakes, joy powder, gold dust, happy dust, heaven dust, pimp dust, pogo-pogo, pony, tootonium, tootuncommon, Peruvian, reindeer dust, cookie, leaf, trey, wings, bloke, big bloke, live (sniffed), whiff, balloon (bag), Cadillac (ounce), row, line (dose).

DRUGS: COCAINE AND HEROIN n. C and H, cold and hot, speedball (also cocaine and morphine), dynamite, whizbang.

DRUGS: DEMEROL n. mep, meps, cubes, morals.

DRUGS: DEXAMYL n. Christmas trees, purple heart.

DRUGS: DEXEDRINE n. dex, dexy, dexie, dexo, football, heart, oranges, peach, pep pill, purple heart.

DRUGS: DEXTROAMPHETAMINE n. dex, dexie, dexy, football, heart, greenies, oranges.

DRUGS: DIMETHYLTRYPTAMINE n. DMT.

DRUGS: DIPROPYLTRYPTAMINE n. DPT.

DRUGS: FENTANYL n. fen, China white.

DRUGS: HASHISH n. hash, heesh, sheesh, keep, candy, blond, blond hash, blond Lebanese, black Russian, carob chips, chocolate, fir, kif, Pakistan hash, sealing wax, shishi, soles, hashover (hangover), hash head (user).

DRUGS: HASHISH (ALCOHOL EXTRACT) n. oil, black oil, hash oil, Indian oil, honey oil, cherry leb, son of one, the one.

DRUGS: HEROIN n. C, H, aitch, the big H, the beast, horse, snow, sugar, smeck, smack, bag, cadillac, piece, weight (ounce), fix, shit, goma, A-bomb, Aunt Hazel, dog food, Big Daddy, his, ca-ca, hot shot (strong, maybe lethal), courage pills, dope, tootsie roll, carne (Mexican), downtown, peanut butter, foolish powder, gumball, globe trotter, gold dust, ferry dust, goods, Gulf P-funk, MPTP (synthetic), Henry, hero, shag, scat, rock candy, nose candy, nose powder, the tragic magic, liquid sky (with sex), Lady H, yen shee, stuff, hard stuff, white, white lady, white stuff, China white, triangle stuff (Burma, Laos, Thailand), junk, hook, hot shot (overdose), pack, blanks, bones, boy, brother, brown, brown sugar, brown rine, Persian brown, Mexican brown, Mexican mud, tar, black tar, Chinese, Chinese red, Chinese white, Chinese rocks, red chicken, chiva, cobics, crap, doojee, Dojee, doorjee, estuffa, first degree, heroina, powder, joy powder, flea powder, polvo, scag, scar, scramble, tecaba, thing, bombita, dynamite, cold .45, Colt .45, schmee, antifreeze, caballo, deck, salt, him, hero of the underworld, Harry, Big Harry, witch hazel, angel, noise, lemonade, poison, eye-opener (first of day), goldfinger (synthetic), cheeo (seed to be chewed).

DRUGS: HEROIN AND COCAINE n. speedball, dynamite.

DRUGS: HEROIN AND MARIJUANA n. atom bomb.

DRUGS: ISOBUTYL NITRITE n. popper.

DRUGS: JIMSON WEED n. devil's trumpet.

DRUGS: LUMINAL n. purple heart.

DRUGS: LYSERGIC ACID DIETHYLAMIDE n. LSD, acid, acido, the chief, big chief, cresto, tru, pellet, tab, paper, vitamin A, animal crackers, luggage, cid, sid, delysid, outer, Raggedy Ann, T, tee, the hawk, candy, cube, trip, ticket, LSD-25, 25, cap, flight, big D, coffee, instant Zen, Zen, peace, sugar, sugar lump, sunshine, California sunshine, Hawaiian sunshine, sunshine pill, orange, orange mushroom, orange wedges, wedges, orange sunshine, yellow sunshine, yellow, mellow yellow, pink, pink swirl, purple flats, purple haze, purple micro dots, blue acid, blue cheer, blue splash, royal blue, blue flag, blue heaven, blue mist, strawberry fields, gelatin, white lightning, clear light, haze, contact lens, Owsley's, Owsley acid, paper acid, flake acid, domes, dots, micro dots, brown dots, cherry top, chocolate chips, flats, Lucy in the Sky with Diamonds, pearly gate, barrels, blotters, frogs, lids, windowpanes, tab.

DRUGS: MANDRAKE n. devil's testicle, Satan's apple.

DRUGS: MARIJUANA n. pot, grass, joint, reefer, endo, boom, skunk, chocolate tide, indigo, tropicana, chronic, reefer weed, weed, lone weed, bud, Budd, Ty bud, endica bud, trom (Stu.), viper's weed, ragweed, killer weed, blunt (hollowed out cigar filled with marijuana), organic stuff, hash, shit, hooch, hemp, T, tea, jay, roach, Mary, Mary Jane, Mary Anne, Mary Wanna, Mary Warner, Mary and Johnnie, discipline, greefo, griefo, grefa, grafa, ganga, gangi, hay, Indian hay, alfalfa, mezz, the mighty mezz, cheese, Thai stick, Mexican red, Mexican brown, Cam, Cambodian red, Panamanian red, Panama red, gold, Panama gold, Acapulco gold, Colombian gold, Colombian red, Colombian, Santa Marta gold, African black, Jersey green, golden leaf, Maui-wowee, A-bomb, love blow, bambalacha, Margarita, Marjorie, bammy, michoocan, black gungeon, black gunny, black mo, black moat, brick, broccoli, tosca, charas, yedo, jeeba, Durbin poison (South Africa), dirt grass, Hawaiian, iceberg, icepack, kickstick, mess, laughing grass, lobo, locoweed, diambesta, M, light green, bone, smokables, oregano, boot, bule, collyweed, corn, cranny, early girl, stink weed, tripweed, wacky weed, wisdom weed, ses weed, food, hooter, ily, maroochie, ned, chub, red hair, wacky backy, wacky tabbacky, primo (best), skonk (bad-smelling), straw, stuff, beetle, birdwood, bomber, belt, drag, hit, bush, charge, beat, dynamite, fu, gage, stick, stick of gage, herb, dew, goofball, spliff, spleef, splim, jadja, Indian hemp, smoke, joy smoke, giggle smoke, giggle weed, juane, kef, keef, kif, moocah, mota, musta, mutah, mutha, muggles, mohasky, pod, Texas tea, splay, red dirt marijuana, salt and pepper, sinsemilla, sensemilla, sinsemella, stuff, snap, snop, boo, gungeon, gunion, black gunion, jabooby, Lipton's (fake), weed tea, yesca, yeska, Alice B. Toklas brownies, Jimmy dog, James Earl dog, hootch dog, Jim Jones (marijuana laced with cocaine dipped in PCP), frios, lovlies (dipped in PCP), bush, mootah, mu, panatella, dope, rope, seed, baby, blue sage, dagga, 13, 13-M, thirteen, pukalolo, bo-bo, bar, gold leaf, manicure, sweet Lucy, baby, Banji, bhang, catnip, Coli, sativa, ace cheeba, cheeo (seed to be chewed).

DRUGS: MESCALINE n. big chief, mesc, bean, botton, mescal, moon, pumpkin seed.

DRUGS: METHADONE n. meth, biscuits, dolls, dollies.

DRUGS: METHAMPHETAMINE n. tweak, go-fast medicine, ice (extra-potent smokable form), crystals, Cris, Cristine, crank, elephant, tranquilizer, dynamite, speed.

DRUGS: METHAQUALONE n. pillow, soap, soaper.

DRUGS: METHEDRINE n. crystals, love drug.

DRUGS: METHYLENEDIOXYAMPHETAMINE n. MDMA, MDA, Ecstasy, E., Epsom salts, adam, X.

DRUGS: METHYL FENTANYL n. China white.

DRUGS: MORNING GLORY SEED n. flying saucer, heavenly blue, blue star, glory seeds, pearly gate, pearly whites, summer skies.

DRUGS: MORPHINE n. M, morph, morf, cube juice, dime's worth, dreamer, medicine, God's own medicine, God's drug, soldier's drug, happy dust, Ixey, joy powder, Miss Emma, Em, Aunt Emma, emsel, coby, dope, junk, gunk, first line, glad stuff, stuff, happy stuff, happy powder, lent, reffi, hocus, unkie, sweet Jesus, red cross, sugar, snow, blue happiness, white stuff, white dust, white nurse, mojo, whiz-bang (mixed with cocaine).

DRUGS: NEMBUTAL n. purple heart, yellow jacket, blockbuster, pill, nebbie, nemish, nemmie, nimby, abbot.

DRUGS: NEMBUTAL AND MORPHINE n. purple heart.

DRUGS: OPIUM n. O, big O, pop, poppy, pox, grease, pill, Chinese tobacco, gow, ghow, gom, goma, hop, hops, mud, tar, gee, stem, yen, yen shee, pen yan, pen yen, bird's-eye, high hat, fire plug, black stuff, black pills, black silk, black smoke, brick, brick gum, dopium, gong, gonger, poppy train, dream beads, dream wax, dream gum, dreams, God's own medicine, midnight oil, yam-yam, smoke.

DRUGS: PAREGORIC n. blue velvet, black jack.

DRUGS: PEYOTE n. mescal, button, biscuits, dog biscuits, legume, plants, magic pumpkin.

DRUGS: PHENCYCLIDINE n. PCP, angel dust, Sherms (cigarette), P-stuff, busy bee, crystal, elephant, elephant tranquilizer, embalming fluid, black whack, cozmos, Detroit pink, herms, hog, horse trank, jet fuel, kaps, kools, puffy, zombie buzz, scuffle, skaffle, skuffle, killer weed, peace pill, rocket fuel, lovely, tic, mist, angel mist, magic mist, dust, rock dust, T dust, magic dust, monkey dust, fairy dust, devil dust, dummy dust, stardust, white dust, animal, pig killer, cadillac, C.J., K.J., goon, sheets, hog, mint, monkey, snorts, aurora borealis, dummy, ozone, soma, cyclone, horse, new magic; super joint, super grass (marijuana sprinkled with PCP), squeeze, Mr. Whipple, bomb (mixed with embalming fluid).

DRUGS: QUAALUDE n. lude, quad, quas, quacks, sopor, pillows, wallbanger, vitamin Q, lemon, Canadian quail.

DRUGS: SECONAL n. red devil, R.D., red bird, red, Sec, sex, Seccy, Seggy, Secos, pink lady.

DRUGS: TALWIN n. blue jeans and T-shirts (mixed with pyribenzamine).

DRUGS: TUINAL n. Christmas trees, double trouble, rainbows, tootsies, reds, blues, red and blue, T, tooie, tuie.

DRUGS: VALIUM n. ums, V, dies, dis, dyes, vals, volume, downer, mello yello, true blue, housewife's delight.

DRUGS: XANAX n. double X.

DRUGS, BUY v. make a buy, score, score some, keep the meet, cop, hit, re-up, sail, ten cents, trey, turn.

DRUGS, SELL v. peddle, push, clocking (selling crack), twirl, scag trade.

DRUM v. beat out some licks.

DRUMMER n. hide beater, skin beater.

DRUMMING v. press roll.

DRUMS n. skins, hides, snares, bamboula, bongos, booms, sock, suitcase, traps, tubs.

DRUMSTICKS n. boom sticks, brushes (wire), sticks.

DRUNK adj. tight, tipsy, bombed, bombed out, bombed out of one's skull, skulled, booty, blown, blitzed, bobo, crocked, cockeyed, wearing beer goggles, Coke bottle-eyed (all women look beautiful), soused, stewed, stiff, stinko, stinking, Mickey Finished, plastered, DWI (driving while intoxicated), potatoed, flat-lined, hammered, tattered, pie-eyed, wasted, trashed, squashed, totaled, totaled out, fractured, looped, loopy, high, high as a kite, higher than a kite, blind, blotto, giffed, gone, gone under, under the influence, DUI (driving under the influence), boozed-up, juiced, juiced-up, stoned, howled, tanked, tanked-up, roaring, roaring drunk, D.O.A., dead drunk, rolling drunk, stinking drunk, funky drunk, sloppy drunk, blind drunk, skunk-drunk, drunk as a skunk, drunk as a skunk in a trunk, drunk as a lord, potted, fried, faded, smashed, crashed, swacked, polluted, plootered, plotzed, turned on, tied one on, zonked, zonked out, zapped, zigzag, zooed, zoobang, zorked, zulued, loaded, carrying a load, carrying a heavy load, three bricks short of a load, feeling no pain, embalmed, on a tear, on a toot, on a bat, on a bender, on a binge, on a jag, on instruments, on the sauce, on the juice, on the shikker, schikker, shikkered, schnoggered, schnokkered, snokkered, snokkered up, stonkered, snootful, lubricated, mellow, ossified, paralyzed, petrified, pickled, pissed, pissed as a newt, pissed up to the eyebrows, pissed to the ears, pissy-eyed, pissy drunk, potsed, prestoned, padded, pasted, pied, pipped-up, racked-up, riffed, vulcanized, wall-eyed, well-oiled, wet, whooshed, woofled, woofy, woozy, ripped, put to bed with a shovel, faced, shit-faced, S.F., tuned, illuminated, lit, lit-up, lit up like a Christmas tree, lit a bit, lit to the gunnels, merry, hipped, out, out cold, out like a light, out on the roof, boiled, parboiled, balmy, behind the cork, bent, bleary eyed, boozed, boozy, bottled, bunned, buzzed, buzzy, blixed, stewed to the gills, boiled to the gills, fried to the gills, soused to the gills, lit to the gills, burned to the ground, slammed, canned, canned-up, comfortable, piffed, piffled, pifflicated, petrificated, pigeon-eyed, pixilated, plonked, potty, preserved, primed, pruned, rocky, rosy, rumdum, rummy, saturated, screaming, screeching, scronched, set-up, sent, shellacked, shot, shredded, soupy, sloppy, sloshed, slugged, smoked, snozzled, soaked, spiffed, spifflicated, spaced out, passed out, passed out cold, wicked-faced, giddy, fuddled, muddled, muzzy, dizzy, addled, seeing double, overtaken, corked, corned, cut, cut one's wolf loose, crocko, afflicted, jug-bitten, organized, elevated, heading into the wind, three sheets to the wind, three sheets in the wind and the other one flapping, six sheets to the wind, tiddly, full of Dutch courage, with a bun on, cooked, crashed and burned, daquifried, decayed, ding-swizzled, teed, twisted, torqued, bagged, bongoed, boxed, featured, frozen, glazed, have a brass eye, have a kick in the guts, have a skinful, have a rubber drink, have a skate on, have a slant on, have a flag out, have a bun on, have a can on, have a glow on, have an edge on; half-cocked, half-crocked, half-shot, half-slewed, half-sprung, half-stewed, half-seas-over, half under, half-shaved, half-snapped (half-drunk); hooted, hang one on, happy, heeled, dipsy, off the wagon, fallen off the wagon, horseback, in the bag, leaping, nimtopsical, over the bay, owled, plowed, snoozamorooed, sozzled, zozzled, bulletproofed, buzzed, hammered, laid-out, stretched, tired, walking on rocky socks, blasted, blewed, blued, blindo, boggled, guyed out, flannel-mouth, activated, adrip, afloat, aglow, alcoholized, alight, alkied, alkied up, antifreezed, ate the dog, back teeth afloat, baptized, bashed, basted, beerified, beery, bent out of shape, bent and broken, crashed, torn, tore-up, tore down, wiped out, aced, tubed, tweased, tweeked, tweaked, toasted, discomboobulated, discomfuddled, flying one wing low, foozlified, fossilized, gaffed, galvanized, giggled, greased, grogged, groggy, guttered, had one or two, holding up the wall, honked, honkers, hosed, impaired, inpixocated, in orbit, inked, inky-poo, intoxed, irrigated, jazzed up, jiggered, jugged up, juicy, Kentucky fried, southern fried, Mexican fried, muy tostado, knee-walking drunk, knockered, laced, likkerous, liquefied, listing to starboard, little 'round the corner, loud and proud, lushed, lushed up, lushington, spliced, main brace well spliced, mashed, mizzled, noddy-headed, oiled-up, pretty far gone, ripe, ripped and wrecked, ripped to the tits, schizzed out, seeing pink elephants, sewed, shot down, sizzled, slathered, slewed, smashed out of one's mind, snooted, squiffed, squiffy, starched, steamed, stiffed, stiffo, suffering no pain, swacko, tanked out, tight as a goat, tight as a drum, top-heavy, toxicated, trammeled, varnished, whiffled, whoozy, gassed, gassed-up, glassy, glass-eyed, glassy-eyed, had a bun on, had a skinful and a half, had one too many, marinated, maxed out, in the gutter, in one's cups, jagged, jazzed, jazzed-up, jolly, jugged, killed, limp, lathered, liquored, liquored-up, decks awash, ding-swizzled, feel good, fired-up, floating, frazzled, fuzzled, fuzzy, gay, geared-up, ginned, ginned-up, stitched, stone blind, stunned, tangle-footed, teed-up, under the table, under the weather.

DRUNKARD n. drinker, heavy drinker, drunk, big drunk, dip, dipso, boozer, booze artist, booze fighter, boozehound, stew, stewbum, stewie, souse, soak, squiff, toast, Otis, sponge, sop, shikker, bum, rummy, rumbum, rum hound, lush hound, lush, lusher, lushie, barfly, wino, wine jockey, brown bagger, juicehead, power drinker, swillbelly, swillpot, swillbowl, bottle nose, grog blossom, long hitter, hooch hound, ginhound, elbow bender, town drunk, pot, rumpot, tippler, stiff, big stiff, crock, alky, barrel house bum, bottle baby, bottle man, bottle sucker, bust, busthead, tank, copper nose, jick head, juicer, bingo-boy (gang). See also DRINKER.

DRUNKEN COURAGE n. Dutch courage.

DRY adj. 1. blah, draggy, dull as dishwater, ho-hum, bor-ring. See also TRITE. 2. ashy, flaky (skin).

DRYDOCK n. jaheemy, geehemy, jaheembie, geeheebee.

DRY-MOUTHED adj. cotton-mouth, mouth full of cotton.

DUAL adj. twin, doubleheader (successful two ways), double in brass (two kinds of work), rule of twice, wear two hats, twofers, double-dip (two incomes), switch hit (bisexual).

DUBIOUS adj. chancy, iffy, touch-and-go, hanging by a thread, don't hold your breath, you should live so long. See DOUBTFUL.

DUDE n. hot shot, flash, city slicker, candy kid, hep cat, sport, macaroni, swell, toff, snappy dresser, Dapper Dan, Beau Brummell, clotheshorse.

DUDGEON n. rise, get a rise out of, sore, huff, dander, Irish, pet, tiff, miff, stew, storm, ruckus, wingding, slow burn, conniption, conniption fit, cat fit, duck fit, blow-up, flare-up. See PIQUE.

DUE n. rate, be in line for, comeuppance, what is coming to one, what one has coming, what one was asking for, get hers, get his.

DUE BILL n. bad news, I.O.U.

DULL adj. blah, draggy, beige, cozy, ho-hum, bor-ring, big yawn, yawner, go over like a lead balloon, lay an egg, bombed, phoned in, dead, dealy, deadsville, dullsville, dragsville, white bread. See BORING.

DULLARD n. hamburger, dork, dorf, droid, nerd, full hank, lop, droob, drube, feeb, loser, winner, dexter, narc, spud, squid, grunge, grunch, birdbrain, rattleweed, nobody home, biff (girl), deadass, dumbo, deadass, turkey, spaz, schlemiel, schmuck, dip, dipstick, dill, dickhead, Gumbyhead, popcorn head, punter (easily defrauded), lorg, gump, hamburger, mutant, deadneck, flat tire, Gumby, doesn't know enough to come in out of the rain, Barbie and Ken. See STUPID.

DULUTH, MINNESOTA the Little Twin, Twin Forts.

DUMB adj. dodo, dummy, dumbo, dumdum, dumbbell, dumb bunny, dumb cluck, dumb Dora, dumb head, dumb ox, dumb fuck, dumb shit, mung shit, twillie, biff (girl), Barbie and Ken, four-letter man (D.U.M.B.), one doughnut shy of a dozen, elevator doesn't run to the top floor, a low-watt bulb, a few sandwiches short of picnic. See STUPID.

DUMBFOUND v. blow away, blow one's mind, bowl down, bowl over, flabbergast, knock one over with a feather, set one on one's ass, strike all of a heap, throw, throw into a tizzy, throw on one's beam ends. See ASTONISH.

DUMBFOUNDED adj. blown away, stuck, stumped, bamboozled, buffaloed, beat, floored, licked, bowled down, bowled over, flabbergasted, struck all of a heap, thrown, thrown off one's beam ends. See also ASTONISHED.

DUN v. lean on, put the squeeze on, put the arm on, put the bite on, chase, bone, hock one's charnik, noodge, see in the alley.

DUN AND BRADSTREET n. D & B.

DUNCE n. ditzo, dork, megadork, dorf, dickhead, Fred, Barney, Wilma, dimbo (girl), beau, lorg, gump, lunchbox, lunch sack, vacant lot, Z-head, nerd, lop, doyburger, assface, asswipe, deadass, feeb, lamebrain, jerk, twit, spaz, dodo, ninny, hairball, Airedale, algae head, pointyhead, stoop, yold, putz (Yid.), yutz, deadneck, butthead, goof ball, gink, jel, half-baked, a few bricks shy of a load, one doughnut shy of a dozen, his elevator doesn't go all the way to the top, isn't playing with a full deck, a low-watt bulb, a few sandwiches short of picnic, nuthin' upstairs. See STUPID.

DUNG n. buffalo chips, cow chips, cow flops, cow pats, cow puckey, road apples, golden apples, moose beans, moose nuggets, moose pecans, turd, shit, horseshit, horse hockey, dog dirt, dog-doo, droppings.

DUNGAREES n. jeans, blue jeans, docs, jeans and docs, Levi's, leaves, coveralls, Chinos.

DUPE n. believer, mark, easy mark, pigeon, patsy, sucker, vic, chump, mooch (commodity scam), tool, sitting duck, pigeon, clay pigeon, grape (waiting to be squeezed), fish, greeny. See VICTIM.

DUPE v. rook, screw, shaft, rip off, jerk one around, dick, dick one around, fuck one over, goof on, shuck and jive, rope in, do a number on one. See TRICK.

DUPED adj. stung, been had, taken, taken for a bundle, took, been took, get played (Af. Am.), boned, aced out, jobbed, fucked, fucked over, stiffed, suckered, diddled, burned. See TRICKED.

DUPLICATE n. 1. ditto, dupe, xerox, clone, carbon, carbon copy, mimeo, stat, repro, knockoff, flimsy. 2. lookalike, work-alike, ringer, dead ringer, copy cat, spitting image, spit and image, chip off the old block, double, peas in a pod, twin, ——compatible (P.C. compatible). 3. knockoff, fake, phony, bogus, pirate.

DUPLICATE v. 1. dupe, xerox, carbon, clone, mimeo, ditto, repro, knock off, stat, reinvent the wheel. 2. act like, do, do like, go like, make like, chomp, mirror, take off as, do a takeoff, play the ——(affect a role). 3. pirate, bite, fake, phony, knock off, steal one's stuff, take a leaf out of one's book, fax hacker (sends unrequested messages of advertising).

DUPLICITY n. dirty dealing, dirty work, dirty pool, dirty trick, Judas kiss, stab in the back, skulduggery, gamesmanship, one-upsmanship. See CHEAT.

DURABILITY n. backbone, grit, guts, gutsiness, heart, intestinal fortitude, moxie, starch, stick-to-itiveness, staying power, eat nails, hard as nails.

DUSK n. dimday.

DUST n. dustball, house moss, kittens, pussies, slut's wool, dust kitty, dust bunny, beggar's velvet, ghost turds.

DUTCHMAN n. butter box, Frank (Obs.).

DUTY n. taking care of business, TCB, hooked, on a string, owe one one, dues, minding the store. See also RESPONSIBLE, RESPONSIBILITY.

DWARF n. little people, little person, trial size, shrimp, runt, shorty, shortish, short pint, half-pint, half-portion, dusty butt, peanut, peewee, bantam, sawed-off, squirt, knee-high, knee high to a grasshopper.

DWELL v. bunk, bunk out, hang out, crash, nest, cocoon, perch, roost, squat, hang up one's hat, hang up one's shingle, hole up, locate, park. See INHABIT.

DWELLING n. pad, crib, cubbyhole, den, domi, flop, diggings, hole in the wall, dump, castle. See HOUSE. See also APARTMENT.

DYE n. rinse, touch up (hair).

DYING adj. done for, on one's last legs, checking out, at the end of one's rope, MFC (measure for coffin), heading for the last roundup, going down (Af. Am.), one foot in the grave, one foot in the grave the other on a banana peel.

DYNAMIC adj. ballsy, bogard, come on strong, play for keeps, go-getter, play hard ball. See ENTERPRISING.

DYNAMITE n. dinah, dine, grease, noise, stick.

E

E n. Easy, Echo.

EACH pron. a pop, per.

EAGER adj. hot to trot, rarin' to go, gung-ho, full on, self-starting, itchy, dying to, needles, ants, antsy, antsy-pantsy, ants in one's pants, not about to let any grass grow under one's feet, ready for Freddie. See IMPATIENT.

EAGERLY adv. at the drop of a hat.

EARDRUM n. drum, pop a drum (rupture).

EARLY adv. previous, a bit previous, bright and early, early bird, early on.

EARMARK v. name, slot, tab, tag. See DEDICATE.

EARN v. make, make a buck, pull, pull down, drag down, cop, clear, hustle, rate, sock, turn, bring home the bacon, bring home the groceries, get along, keep the wolf from the door, pay one's dues, be in line for, pick up, clean up, scare up, wangle, snag, score, cash in on, make a good thing of, make a killing, make it big, make hay, make money hand over fist, feather one's nest, line one's nest, grab, kipe, kype, latch on to something, double-dipping (compensation from two government agencies).

EARNEST adj. meaningful, no fooling, for real, serious jelly, no shit, mean business, playing hard ball, money talks bullshit walks. See SERIOUS.

EARNINGS n. payoff, net, bottom line, in the black, gate, melon, take-home, groceries, salt, piece of the pie. See INCOME. See also COMPENSATION.

EARPHONES n. cans.

EARRING n. dangler.

EARS n. flappers, flaps, flippers, lugs, mikes, sails, tin ear (deaf), cauliflower, pretty ear (deformed or cauliflower).

EARSPLITTING adj. leather-lunged.

EARTH n. apple, big blue marble, real estate, spaceship Earth, dust, old sod, terra firma.

EARTHQUAKE n. shaker.

EARTHY adj. 1. down, down-to-earth, down-home, funky, folksy, home folks, homey, haimish, meat-and-pota-toes man. See NATURAL. 2. cheap, raw, raunchy, blue, dirty, lowdown and dirty, filthy, off-color, rough, rough stuff, foul-mouth, foul-mouthed, loud-mouthed, in the gutter, salty. See OBSCENE.

EASE v. grease the wheels, run interference for, open doors, walk through, hand-carry.

EASE UP v. lighten up, don't sweat it, cool it, go with the flow, hang loose, let it all hang out, let it all happen, mellow out. See RELAX.

EASILY adv. no sweat, no biggie, hands down, like nothing, nothing to it, slick as a whistle, swimmingly, piece of cake, at the drop of a hat.

EAST n. dirty side, back East.

EAST COAST n. dirty side, East.

EASTERN EUROPEAN n. Bohunk, Hunk, Hunkie, Litvak (all Derog.).

EASY adj. snap, set-up, wired, slam-dunk, no biggie, no sweat, no problem, a no-brainer, nothing to it, like nothin', pushover, picnic, cinchy, doable, biscuit, cheeseball, soft, soft touch, sweet, velvet, pie, cherry pie, easy as pie, easy as falling off a log, easy make, easy digging, duck soup, sitting duck, like shooting fish in a barrel, turkey shoot, cake, cakewalk, sleepwalk, walk, a piece of cake, cream puff, cushy, knack, downhill, fluff, breeze, breeze in, stroll, walk-over, walk in the park, win in a walk, win hands down, waltz, picnic, gut course, dead whore (college test), snap course (college), pud (test or course); child's play, lead-pipe cinch, racket, white meat, whipsaw, whipsaw through, mick, Mickey Mouse, simple as ABC, clear sailing, can o' corn, laid-back, toss it off, throwaway, geranium, jelly, free ride, peach. See also OBTAINABLE.

EAT v. scarf, scarf back, throw back, scarf down, chow down, scoff, slurp, narf, snarf, squff, mow (mow a burger), grind, chomp, wedge, dig in, munch, munch out, nibble, snack, snack on, peck, peck at, pick at, Mac out, jug up, blimp out, pig out, trough out, pork out, make a pig of oneself, make a hog of oneself, dig into, chuck, board, gorm, gorp, graze, grease, grease one's chops, grease down, wolf, wolf down, garbage down, inhale, hoover, kill, gobble, gulp, bolt, dispatch, dispose, nosh, fress, fling a fang, chew, gum, grit, swabble, yam, brown-bag it, stuff one's face, feed one's face, fall to, get away with, pitch in, tuck in, tuck away, put away, put it away, pack it away, tie on, tie on the nosebag, tie on the feedbag, put on the feedbag, do lunch, break bread with, eat high on the hog, eat high on the joint, eat like a horse, eat one's head off, eat out of house and home, eat like it's going out of style, eat like there's no tomorrow, eat like a bird, eat Chinx (Chinese dinner, Derog.), go after it, come and get it, grits time, buzz around the barrel, lick the plate, polish off, knock off, collar a hot, surround oneself outside of, put oneself outside of, take it on, make with a knife and fork, foot under the table, mug up.

EATABLES n. chow, snack, eats, finger food, feedbag, grub pile, scoffings, chewings, movable feast, hots (hot meal, Mil.), home cooking. See FOOD.

EATER n. chow hound, nasher, nosher, star boarder, fresser, porker, oinker.

EATING PLACE n. eatery, pit stop, after joint, grease joint, beanery, bistro, noshery, cook shack, chow hall, chow line, mess, one-armed joint, pigpen, coffeepot, caf. See RESTAURANT.

EAVESDROP v. be all ears, tap, wiretap, bug, dippin', cars into, Erie, on the Erie, slurp, listen in, tune in on.

EAVESDROPPER n. bugger, kibitzer, nosy Parker, snoop, snooper, yenta, Paul Pry, little pitcher with big ears.

EBULLIENT adj. bouncy, chirpy, chipper, feeling one's oats, full of beans, full of piss and vinegar, zippy. See SPIRITED.

ECCENTRIC adj. funky, freak, freaky, freaked-out, geeky, kook, kooky, coo-coo, bent, beat, beatnik, beat generation, offbeat, off the beaten track, bent, weird, weirdo, weirdie, dudical, radical dude, wombat, quirky, funky, strange one, oddball, foul ball, goofball, special, avant-garde, cool, fringy, kinky, geeky, speed, hippy, flake, flaky, far out, way out, wild, crazy, funny, funny-looking, off the wall, out in left field, trippy, not wrapped real tight, fly ball, case, goony, gooney bird, birdy, chirp, queer fish, queer duck, strange duck, rare bird, jayhawk, gasser, loner, dolo, meshuga, meshuganah, potty, cockeyed, three-dollar bill, crackpot, gonzo, queer potato, queer in the head, herky, screwy, screwball, aired out, jell-brain, jelled, twerp, twirp, character, shaky, glick, creepy, wacky, whacko, whacky, wakilana, whacked out, yo-yo, nut, nutcake, nutroll, nutty, nutty as a fruitcake, fruity, fruitcake, full mooner, spacey, spaced out, California sprouts-eating, psychobabbler, Asiatic (WWII, N.).

ECCENTRICALLY adv. all over the shop, by fits and starts, every which way, here there and everywhere, hit or miss, right and left. See ERRATICALLY.

ECCLESIASTIC n. the Rev, Holy Joe, sky pilot, Bible thumper, Bible basher, Bible puncher, bish, devil driver, fire escape, fire insurance agent, gospel pusher, salvation rancher, harp polisher, long-haired boy, buck, right buck. See CLERGYMAN.

ECHO v. rubber-stamp, ditto, mirror, make like, do like, go like. See also COPY.

ECONOMICAL adj. 1. dirt cheap, cheap as dirt, dog cheap, cheapie, el cheapo, steal, real steal, buy, real buy, low-budget, low-cost, cost nothing, cost next to nothing, more bang for the buck, bought for a song, cut-rate, low-tar-

iff, dime-a-dozen, price is right. 2. tight, close, scrimpy, skimpy, stingy, on the rims, run on the rims, Scotch, nickel nurser. See THRIFTY.

ECONOMICS n. ec, eco, econ.

ECONOMIZE v. scrimp, skimp, penny-pinch, cut corners, cut to the bone, tighten one's belt, stretch a dollar, rub the print off a dollar bill. See SAVE.

ECSTASY n. Nadaville, twilight zone. See also ELATION.

ECSTATIC adj. cool, zero cool, gone, real gone, orgasmic, out, far out, spaced-out, wig, wigged-out, flipped-out, blissed-out, joygerm fever, sent, crazy, grokked, mad, wild, wicked, weird, weirded-out, dreamy, turned-on, stoned, high, high as a kite, sunny, sunny side up, shook-up, hopped-up, tea'd-up, up, upbeat, flyin', flyin' high, floating, floating on air, walking on air, on a joy ride, on a cloud, on cloud seven, on cloud nine, in seventh heaven, tickled to death, tickled pink, pleased as Punch, sold on, hummy, out of it, blowing one's top, blowing one's roof, popping one's nuts, in Nadaville, in the twilight zone.

EDIBLES n. eats, chow, bite, snack, feed, feedbag, grub, takeout, fast food, pogey, scoff, slop, garbage. See FOOD.

EDIFICE n. pile o' bricks, rock pile, skyscraper, towers.

EDIT v. massage, blue-pencil, clean up, cut, tighten, go over, dial back, recalibrate, fly-speck, debug, bleep, bleep out, launder, sanitize, sterilize, decontaminate, scrub, boil (bottom to top), bake (top to bottom).

EDITOR n. ed, blue penciler, cutter (film), play doctor, play fixer.

EDITORIAL n. thinkpiece, op ed piece, shirttail (column).

EDUCATE v. brainwash, let in on the know, put hip, put hep, put through the grind, show one the ropes, drum into. See INSTRUCT.

EDUCATED adj. double-dig, highbrow, brain, brains, brainy, savvy, book-smart, know all the answers, know what's what, know one's onions. See KNOWLEDGEABLE.

EDUCATION n. ed.

EERIE adj. spooky, spookish, scary.

EFFACE v. wipe out, wipe off the map, off, X out, zap, kayo, KO, launder, scrub, nix. See CANCEL.

EFFECT n. fallout, reaction, chain reaction, flak (bad), follow-up, follow-through, can of worms, spin-off, it's your funeral, waves. See RESULT.

EFFECT v. make waves, unzip, turn the trick, do the trick, do the job, do up brown, do to a turn, do to a T, do one's stuff, do one's thing, do a number, come through with, get to, buy, sell, get it across, put across, put it over, put away, make it, make it big, break out with, bust out with (surprisingly or suddenly), pull off, pull it off, knock off, polish off, tear off, tick, take care of, take care of business, T.C.B., deal with, hammer out, hack out, work out, hit, score, clean up, wind up, button up, wrap up, mop up, put the lid on, go to town, perk, percolate.

EFFECTIVE adj.   lead in one's pencil, powerhouse, large and in charge (Af. Am.), live, wicked, on the ball, play hardball. See also CAPABLE; POWERFUL.

EFFEMINATE adj.   gay, faggy, swish, swishy, flyer, flamer, fruity, pansy, pansified, pantywaist, fairy, loose in his loafers, Heblew, fagela, lost his cholla, ma, mother, old woman, womanish, nancy, nance, capon, cream puff, camp, sissy, sissified, cookie pusher, Ethel, bait, frame, goody-goody, lacy, lily, limp wrist, Nellie, pimp, pretty boy, puss, weak sister, milksop, music major, twinkie, lah-de-dah, mama's boy, mammy boy, Percy boy, Percy pants, fraidy cat, scaredy cat, chicken, chick (all Derog.).

EFFICIENT adj.   on the ball, dynamite, smoking, fireball, play hardball, one-man band, up, a pistol, crisp, more bang for one's buck, chakra-gonged. See COMPETENT.

EFFORT n.   all-out, push, try, go, fling, shot, crack, whack, stab, balls out, ain't half steppin' (Af. Am.), full-court press, Sunday punch (best), go the extra mile, go to the wall, in there pitching, mouse milking (maximum effort for minimum return). See ENDEAVOR.

EFFORTLESS adj.   snap, no-brainer, slam-dunk, no sweat, no problem, no biggie, picnic, cinchy, biscuit, easy as pie, duck soup, cake, cakewalk, sleepwalk, walk, walkover, piece of cake, child's play. See EASY.

EFFUSIVE adj.   all jaw, big-mouthed, gabby, gasser, gassy, windy, windbag, load of wind. See TALKATIVE.

EGG n.   hen fruit, hen apple, cackle, cackleberry; blindfold a pair, yellow eye, red eyes, over, over easy, sunny side up (fried); dropped (poached); wreck 'em, wreck a pair, wreck two (scrambled); cowboy with spurs (Western omelette with French fries).

EGGS AND HAM n.   cluck and grunt.

EGO n.   macho trip, power trip.

EGOTIST n.   big I am, big I love me, big timer, swellhead, be on an ego trip, go on an ego trip, think one's shit doesn't stink, snotnose, smart ass, jit, grandstander, hot dogger, blowhard, know-it-all. See BRAGGART.

EGOTISTIC adj.   stuck on oneself, on a ego trip, hubcap, look out for number one, look out for numero uno, take care of number one, take care of numero uno, out for yours truly, shirt up, single-o. See CONCEITED.

EGYPTIAN n.   Gyppo (WWII, Derog.).

EIGHT n.   eighter, eighter from Decatur.

EIGHTEEN-NINETIES n.   Gay Nineties, Naughty Nineties, Mauve Decade, Golden Age, Gilded Age.

EJACULATE v.   come, come off, cum, blow, spew, spooch, splooge, shoot, shoot off, shoot one's wad, cream, cream one's jeans, jis, go off, get off, get one's rocks off, get one's nuts off, get off the nut, get over the mountain, haul one's ashes, bust one's nuts, empty the trash, spend, drop one's load, pop one's cookies (all Obsc.).

EJACULATE n.   cum, come, spew, spoo, spooch, splooge, cream.

EJACULATION n.   cum, wad, shot, load, spew, spoo, spooch, splooge, number three, get a nut, blow (all Obsc.). See SEXUAL CLIMAX, ATTAIN.

EJECT v.   boot out, kick out, muscle out, chuck out, put out, bounce, can, dump, ditch, adios it, fire, flush, give one the old heave-ho, give 'em the old heave-ho, give one the bum's rush, give the mitten, give the gate, give the air, give 'em the hook, give 'em the 1-2-3, French walk, Spanish walk, get an early shower, send to the showers, send packing, show the door, throw out on one's ear, run out of town, ride out on a rail, kiss good-bye, kiss off, pack off.

EJECTION n.   rush, bum's rush, bounce, boot, heave-ho, kiss-off, the gate.

EJECTION SEAT n.   panic rack.

EJECTOR n.   bouncer, dude heaver, chucker, chucker-out, boot giver.

ELABORATE adj.   plush, posh, hi-tech, wheels within wheels, mega factor, with bells and whistles, with all the extras, with all the options, Rube Goldberg. See also ORNATE.

ELATED adj.   hopped-up, fired-up, flying, high, flying high, turned-on, lookin' good, set up. See also HAPPY.

ELATION n.   up, upper, cloud-nine land, high, buzz, charge, kick, kicks, flash, jollies. See EXCITEMENT.

ELAVIL n.   els (antidepressant).

ELBOW n.   crazy bone, funny bone, hinge, bow.

ELBOW v.   push around, rough-and-tumble.

ELDER n.   gray, gray-haired, blue-haired, golden ager, senior citizen, senior, pop, pops, dad, gramps, grampa, grandpa, grandma, gramma, gramms, granny, wrinklie, oldster, old fogy, old fart, old-timer, —— years young, A.K., alte kocker, gerk (fool). See OLD MAN, OLD WOMAN.

ELDERLY adj.   gray, gray-haired, blue-haired, gray power, been around, bent, lot of mileage, has seen better days, no spring chicken, tired, wrinklie, one foot in the grave, long in the tooth, over-the-hill, on one's last legs, g'd-up. See AGED.

ELECT v.   go down the line, opt, tap. See SELECT.

ELECTED adj. in the bag, a shoo-in, nailed down, on ice, open-and-shut, set, named, home free.

ELECTIONEER v. run, politick, press the flesh, hit the campaign trail, stump, shake hands and kiss babies, mud-sling. See CAMPAIGN.

ELECTIONEERING n. running, pressing the flesh, politicking, stumping, whistle-stopping.

ELECTION, LOSE v. go toes up (reelection loss).

ELECTRIC CHAIR n. the chair, hot seat, hot spot, hot shot, squat, hot squat, hot chair, juice chair, old sparky, old smokey, hummingbird, electric cure, hair curler, permanent wave, barbecue, barbecue stool, sizzle seat, manufactured lightning, baker (not common).

ELECTRIC CORD CONNECTOR n. juice box, plug, wall plug.

ELECTRIC CURRENT n. AC, DC, juice (electricity).

ELECTRIC GUITAR ATTACHMENT fuzzbox.

ELECTRICIAN n. gaffer (movie), grunt, hike, juice (stage), juicer.

ELECTROCUTE v. fry, burn, go, go to the chair, get a charge, get the hot seat, ride old smoky, ride the lightning, sizzle, squat, squat hot, topped, electric cure.

ELECTRONIC MAIL n. PROFS (professional office system), E-mail.

ELECTRONIC MONITOR n. CRT, tube, screen, readout.

ELECTRONIC SURVEILLANCE n. bug, bugging, tap, body mike, wire, run a wire (install tap or microphone) fumigate, sweep (search for surveillance), ELINT (information gathered by spy satellites).

ELECTROSHOCK THERAPY, DO v. zap a patient.

ELEGANT adj. spiffy, classy, snazzy, posh, plush, plushy, ritzy, swank, swanky, snarky, swellegant, splendiferous, splendacious, fancy-shmancy, dressed to kill, dressed to the teeth, dressed to the nines, done to the nines, nobby. See also STYLISH.

ELEMENT n. making, makin's, fixin's, part and parcel, board, plug-in.

ELEMENTARY adj. 1. ABC's, three r's, basics, meat and potatoes, primo. See also BASIC. 2. setup, like nothin', easy make, easy digging, duck soup, child's play, simple as ABC, can o' corn. See EASY.

ELEPHANT n. bull, punk (young).

ELEVATE v. boost, bring up, build up, fetch up, jump up, put up, run up, goose, goose up, hike, hike up, jack up, shoot up, pyramid.

ELEVATED adj. high-rise, big-time, heavy.

ELEVATED TRAIN n. el, elevated, L.

ELEVEN n. dinge.

ELICIT v. worm out of one, worm something out of one, wring out, arm-twist, shake, shake a joint, shake down, squeeze, badger, play the badger game, bite, pull one's leg, lean on, put the arm on, put on the muscle, put the bee on, put the gorilla on, put the handle on, rattle. See also PERSUADE.

ELIMINATE v. 1. junk, chuck, chuck out, adios, eighty-six, deep six, dog, heave-ho, throw away, throw overboard, throw on the junk heap. See ERADICATE. 2. ice out, elbow out, blackball, pass by, pass up, blow off, shut out, shake out. 3. do away with, executive fallout (business), ax, liquidate, wipe out, sanitize, sterilize, scrub, scratch, dust, waste. See KILL.

ELIMINATED adj. axed, washed-out, washed-up, all washed up, scratched, scrubbed, dogged, adiosed, eighty-sixed, offed, wasted, liquidated, blackballed, iced-out, shut-out. See also KILLED.

ELITE adj. 1. world-class, greatest, killer, cool, out-of-sight, out of this world, first-chop, tops, tip-top, topflight, top-drawer, topnotch, super, key, gilt-edged, Cliveden set, smart money, Boston Brahmins, reform crowd, DAR, coupon clippers. See BEST. 2. beautiful people, jet set, smart set, country club set, horsy set, Eurotrash, glitterati, cognoscenti, crowd, our crowd, in crowd, the establishment, blue blood, crème de la crème, FFV's, the 400, Four Hundred, main-line, old money, upper ten thousand, Brahmin, those in the know, carriage trade, swell, swanky, upper-cut, upper-crust, high-life, high-rise boys, high-society, lace curtain, lace-curtain swell, silk-stocking.

ELITIST n. Brahmin, egghead, highbrow, high-hat, stiff-neck, bluenose.

ELONGATE v. fill, pad, spin out, stretch out, put some rubber in it, drag out, drag one's feet. See also EXPAND.

ELONGATED adj. king-size, stretch (auto, airplane). See also PROLONGED.

ELOQUENT adj. stem winder (excellent).

EL PASO, TEXAS Border Town.

ELUDE v. 1. give the slip, get around, duck, ditch, dodge, give one the runaround, juke, steer clear of. See AVOID. 2. give a miss to, not touch with a ten-foot pole, give the go-by, give a wide berth, blow off, pass the buck, buck-pass, pass up, stay shy of. 3. cop out, cop a plea, jive, shuck, stonewall, goof on, blow smoke, hem and haw, run around, give one the run-around, stall off, get around, beat around, beat around the bush.

ELUSIVE adj. cagey, greasy, slippery, jivey, jukey, stonewalling.

EMACIATED adj. peaked, peaky, skinny, skin and bones, bag of bones, stack of bones, rattleboned. See THIN.

EMANATION n. vibe, vibes.

EMASCULATE v. cut off one's balls, deball, fix, alter.

EMBARRASS v. bug, burn down, burn one down, discombobulate, discomboberate, hang up, throw, throw into a swivet, throw into a tizzy, put on a spot, put in a spot, put in a hole, catch one short, catch with one's pants down, catch with egg on one's face, fuzz-buzz, give one a bad time, give one a hard time, low-grade, cramp one's style, make one sing small. See also BELITTLE.

EMBARRASSED adj. burned, egg on one's face, red-faced, caught short, molded, come out moldy, crawling, eat crow, eat dirt, eat humble pie, sing small. See HUMILIATED.

EMBARRASSMENT n. boo-boo, goof, drop a brick, hot potato, could have sunk into the floor, wished the floor would open up, egg on one's face, shoot oneself in the foot, takedown, put-down.

EMBELLISH v. doll up, fix up, gussy up, spruce up, add bells and whistles.

EMBELLISHMENT n. gingerbread, jazz, garbage (food), frill, frills, fuss, gewgaw, gimcracks, froufrou, spinach (excessive), bells and whistles, dingbat, doodad, thing, fandangle, seagoing (large, absurd), egg in one's beer, icing on the cake.

EMBEZZLE v. skim, put a hand in the till, put a hand in the cookie jar, work in a bank and take home samples. See also STEAL.

EMBEZZLER n. white-collar thief.

EMBLEM n. logo, brand.

EMBRACE n. bear hug, squeeze, clinch, lock.

EMBRACE v. 1. grab, grab ass, clinch, clutch, bear-hug, squeeze, glom onto. 2. go in for, take up, get into. See also APPROVE; ENDORSE.

EMBROIDER v. 1. doll up, fix up, gussie up, spruce up. 2. lay it on, spread it on thick, puff, blow, yeast, make a mountain out of a molehill, make a federal case out of something. See EXAGGERATE.

EMERALDS n. green ice.

EMERGENCY n. crisis mode, clutch, crunch, in a pinch, in a squeeze, when the shit hits the fan; meltdown, China syndrome (nuclear). See CRISIS.

EMERGENCY ROOM n. E.R., the pits.

EMERGENCY SWITCH n. panic button, chicken button, chicken switch, egads button, egads switch.

EMERITUS adj. on the shelf, out of circulation, over-the-hill, passed it, a once-was, has-been, hung up one's spurs, old-timer.

EMIGRATION n. brain drain, brawn drain.

EMINENT adj. celeb, star, superstar, name, champ, VIP, w.k. (well known), lion, page-oner, prima donna, gun, big gun, not to be sneezed at. See CELEBRITY. See also IMPORTANT.

EMISSARY n. hired gun, rep, front.

EMOTION n. gut reaction, vibes, where one is at, where one lives, drive.

EMOTIONAL adj. soap, soapy, syrupy, drippy, emote, emoting (simulate), dust 'em off, hoke, hokum, hokey, hissy, icky, mushy, razzmatazz, schmalzy, slush, softy, soppy, sloppy, soupy, sappy, sticky, gooey, gummy, gushing, teary, tearjerker, cry crocodile tears, corny, cornball, off the cob, hearts and flowers, beery, namby-pamby, all torn up, all tore up, all shook up, shook, shook-up, defrosted, choked, choked-up, feel stuff, fall apart, frantic, funky, touchy-funky, touchy, touchy-feely, get one's gage up, give out, gut reaction, gutty, hyper, wreck, nervous wreck, bundle of nerves, hopped-up, full up, shot down.

EMOTIONAL RELEASE n. safety valve, abreaction, blow off steam.

EMOTIONLESS adj. cool, cool cat, laid-back, flat, nowhere, chill, cold, cold turkey, cold fish, cold-blooded, in cold blood, iceman, deadpan, with a straight face, poker-face, stony-eyed, lead balls for eyes, thick-skinned, rhinoceros hide.

EMPATHETIC adj. good vibes, on the same beam, on the same wavelength. See COMPATIBLE.

EMPATHIZE v. tune in, feel for, I hear ya, can get behind it, be on the same wavelength, pick up on, be there for one.

EMPATHY n. soul, hit it off, on the same wavelength, good vibes, good vibrations, cotton to, in the groove, grooving, simpatico.

EMPHASIZE v. resonate, spot, spotlight, limelight, highlight, underline, hit, headline.

EMPHASIZED adj. hard-hitting, underlined, highlighted, headlined.

EMPHATIC adj. sure, sure enough, for a fact Jack, no ifs ands or buts, and no mistake, do they grow corn in Iowa? See CERTAIN.

EMPHATICALLY adv. absofuckinglutely, posolutety, absitively, mighty, terrifically, indeedy, really truly, woofing, sure, why sure, you know it. See ABSOLUTELY.

EMPLOY v. sign on, sign up, take on, ink, bring on board, come on board, truck with.

EMPLOYED adj. on board, come on board, inked, signed, in place. See also BUSY.

EMPLOYEE n. help, breadwinner, working stiff, company man, desk jockey, white collar, pink collar, bright collar (intelligent, well-educated, young), blue collar, peon, ham-and-egger. See WORKER.

EMPLOYEE REINFORCEMENT n. stroke sessions, opening up, abreaction route, cow sociology, Dr. Spocking the help.

EMPLOYEE STOCK OWNERSHIP PLAN n. ESOP.

EMPLOYER n. chief, C.O., meal ticket, head honcho, boss lady, boss man, hammer man, big shit, bull of the woods, old man, juice, slave driver. See EXECUTIVE.

EMPLOYMENT n. bag, beeswax, biz, game, gesheft, job, line, racket, setup, thing, what one is into, number, rat race, coffee-and-cake job. See OCCUPATION.

EMPLOYMENT AGENCY n. flesh peddler (employee or owner), body shop, people plucker (headhunter), headhunter, slave market.

EMPLOYMENT, SEEK v. pound the pavements, chase, knock on doors, out lookin', lookin' around, circle want ads.

EMPORIUM n. shlock joint, stand, chain store, outlet, outlet store, co-op, discount house, flea market, thrift shop, cut-rate store, super, superette, supermarket, five-and-ten, five-and-dime, Kress's, Kresge's, Woolworth's, 7–Eleven, the grab, boutique, bodega.

EMPOWER v. give the go-ahead, give the green light, give the nod, give the word, okay, OK, say the word. See also APPROVE.

EMPOWERED adj. okayed, OK'd, kosher, legit.

EMPTY adj. dead, dead soldier, dead marine (empty whiskey bottle), deadhead (empty return trip on bus, taxi, plane, etc.).

EMULATE v. play the ——— (affect a role), mirror, ditto, do, do like, go like, make like, steal one's stuff, take a leaf out of one's book, follow in one's footsteps.

EMULSIFY v. clabber, lopper.

EMULSION n. gook, gunk, goo, gooey, goop, goopy, glob, globby, gop, glop, gloppy.

ENACT v. 1. jam, jam through, railroad, railroad through, steamroller through. 2. be on, go on, do a turn, do one's stuff, do a number. See EXECUTE. See also PERFORM.

ENAMOR v. grab, kill, slay, turn on, bat the eyes at, sweep off one's feet, vamp, make a hit with. See ATTRACT.

ENAMORED adj. gone, gone on, hipped on, stuck on, smitten, has a thing about, has one's nose open, hooked, that way. See LOVE, IN.

ENCHANT v. send, wow, slay, kill, grab, turn on, sweep off one's feet, make a hit with, vamp. See ENRAPTURE. See also BEWITCH.

ENCHANTED adj. turned-on, head over heels in, hooked, gone goose. See also BEWITCHED.

ENCHANTER n. vamp, operator, player, swinger, joy boy, sheik, mantrap, velvet trap. See also LURE.

ENCHANTMENT n. abracadabra, hocus-pocus, mumbo-jumbo, open sesame, hoodoo, voodoo, evil eye, stink eye, jinx, whammy, double whammy.

ENCOMPASSING adj. wall-to-wall, across-the-board, all the options, whole ball of wax, whole nine yards, big-time, in a big way.

ENCOUNTER n. scrap, hassle, rumpus, run-in, set-to, flap, gin. See ARGUMENT.

ENCOUNTER v. bump into, run into, meet face to face, meet up with, rub eyeballs, run smack into. See MEET. See also FIGHT.

ENCOURAGE v. 1. go for it, get down, push, juice, psych up, back up, prop up, boost, give a leg up, egg on. 2. sound off for, root for, plump for, all the way, get behind, stick by. See SUPPORT.

ENCOURAGED adj. up, set-up, psyched-up, juiced-up, fired-up.

ENCROACH v. worm in, worm one's way in, squeeze in, elbow in, horn in, chisel in, muscle in, work in, barge in, butt in, put in one's oar, shove in one's oar, put one's two cents in, crash, crash the gates.

ENCUMBER v. saddle with, weigh down, hang up, hold up, hog-tie, drag one's foot, stall. See HINDER.

ENCUMBRANCE n. hangup, baggage, excess baggage, psychological baggage, foot dragging, catch, glitch, joker, one small difficulty. See HINDRANCE.

END n. wrap, wrap-up, wind-up, mop-up, cleanup, sign-off, blow-off, kiss-off, payoff, capper, tag, tag end, butt, butt end, tail end, fag end, bitter end, el foldo, thirty, -30-, hips, swan song, curtain, curtains, down to the short strokes, short stop, end of the line, history, rest is history, and that was all she wrote, all there is, there ain't no more, that's all, that's all folks, when the balloon goes up, when the fat lady sings. 2. mark, where one's heading.

END v. wrap, wrap up, tape, sew up, check it, hang it up, pack it in, close out, shut down, nuke, pull the plug, pull the pin, ring off, cut off, cut the crap, scrub, break off, call it a day, put to bed, send one south, close the books on, want out. See FINISH.

ENDANGER v. lay on the line, put on the spot, stick one's neck in the noose, stick one's neck out, play into one's hands, chance it.

ENDANGERED adj. on the line, on the spot, out on a limb, got one's neck out, caught with one's pants down, have one's ass out.

ENDEARMENT TERMS n. sweetie, sweets, sweet-kins, sweetie pie, sweetheart, sweet nothings, hon, honey, honey bunch, honey child, honey pie, sugar, sugar pie, love, luv, doll, baby doll, baby, babe, babyface, chick, chickabiddy, duck, duckling, dove, turtle dove, lamb, lamb-kins, lambie, lambie pie, snookums, bubie, buttercup, cutey, cupcake, one and only, stinker, little stinker, toots, tootsie-wootsie.

ENDEAVOR n. 1. crack, stab, try, whack, shot, best shot, fling, go, header, lick, all-out, all one's got, one's all, one's damnedest, one's darnedest, one's level best, full on, ain't half steppin' (Af. Am.), ol' college try, crash program, crash project, full steam, full blast, push, try, whirl, balls out, full-court press; dry run, try on, have a fling at. See also ATTEMPT. 2. baby, bag, bag one's into, thing, thing one's into, biggie (major), deal, pet project, proposition. See also ACTION.

ENDEAVOR v. make a run at, take on, in it to win it (Af. Am.), cut and try, buck, push, hassle, sweat, sweat it, scratch, grind, dig, plug, peg away, hammer away, ain't half steppin' (Af. Am.), hustle, hump, hump it, hump oneself, go for broke, pour it on, work one's head off, mouse milking (maximum time for minimum effort). See ATTEMPT.

ENDED adj. a wrap, wrapped up, pfft, wound-up, but-toned-up, that's history, done with, cashed, pow, in the bag, nailed-down, all over but the shouting, when the fat lady sings. See FINISHED.

ENDLESS adj. more than you can shake a stick at, no end of, no end to, on a treadmill.

ENDLESSLY adv. round the clock, day and night, for a month of Sundays, till hell freezes over, till you're blue in the face. See INTERMINABLY. See also ALWAYS.

ENDORSE v. back, bless, boost, give a boost to, give the nod, give the go-ahead, give the green light, stand behind, get behind, get on the bandwagon, push, okay, OK, go with, go along with, go along with the crowd, root for, stump for, thump the tub for, go for, plump for, hold a brief for, hold with, put a flea in one's ear, put a bug in one's ear, be big on, buy, sign, sign off on, put one's John Hancock on, thumbs up, take, take kindly to, ditto, rubber-stamp. See also APPROVE.

ENDORSEMENT n. 1. strokes, pat on the back, good going, abreaction route, commercial, cow sociology, hubba-hubba. 2. okay, OK, get the nod, green light, get the green light, crazy, go-ahead, get the go-ahead. See APPROVAL.

ENDOW v. lay on, gift with, come through with, put a buck one's way. See GIVE.

ENDOWMENT n. gifting, stake. See also DONATION.

ENDURANCE n. backbone, grit, guts, gutsiness, heart, corazón, moxie, starch, cool, hanging in there, hang tough, legs, intestinal fortitude, staying power, stick-to-itiveness, sitzfleisch. See also TENACITY.

ENDURE v. handle, lump, lump it, lump it and like it, live with, bear with, put up with, suck it up, roll with the punches, bite the bullet, hang in, hang in there, hang tough, hang on, stick, stick it out, stick with it, win out, ride out, go the limit, sit tight, sit and take it, sit out, sit still for, cool one's heels, sweat, sweat it, sweat it out, sweat out, wait out, staying power, stay the course, hold one's own, hear of, hack it, take it, take it on the chin, face it, face the music, take one's medicine, go along with, string along with, stand for, stand the gaff, stand up, stand up to it, shape up, show one's mettle, show one's stuff, show some starch, be big, be big about, eat shit, pay dues, grin and bear it, not let it get one down, cut it, bleed, hurt, hurting, carry the torch for one (love), eat one's heart out (envy).

ENDURING adj. set, set in concrete, in for the long haul, hang in, keep one's cool, keep one's shirt on, not hold one's breath.

ENDURINGLY adv. for ages, for a month of Sundays, forever and a day, till hell freezes over. See PERMANENT.

ENEMY n. oppo, opposish, opposite number, meat, bandit, bad guys, buddy (sarcasm), buddy-buddy, buddy fucker, crip, whose side are you on?, me and you, angries.

ENEMY LIST n. hit list, shit list.

ENERGETIC adj. zippy, zappy, snappy, peppy, got the horses to do it, ball of fire, fair hell, go-go, movers and shakers, wave makers, come on strong. See SPIRITED.

ENERGETICALLY adv. all out, full on, full tilt, full bore, in full swing, full steam ahead, like gangbusters, slam-bang, by storm.

ENERGIZE v. zap, jazz up, pep up, zip up, pump up, work up, juice up, turn on the juice, demothball, take out of mothballs, trigger, goose, prime. See STIMULATE. See also EXCITE.

ENERGIZED adj. juiced-up, pepped-up, powered-up, zipped-up, zapped-up, get a lift. See EXCITED.

ENERGY n. juice, go juice, zing, pow, sock, pizzazz, vim, pep, pepper, pepper-upper, piss and vinegar, full head of steam. See POWER.

ENERGY RESEARCH AND DEVELOPMENT ADMINISTRATION n. ERDA.

ENFEEBLE v. clip one's wings, shake up, soften up, wing.

ENFEEBLED adj. out of condition, out of shape, out of steam, out of gas, on the ropes, run down, run to seed, gone to seed, not what one used to be, rusty, soft, good and flabby. See also INCAPACITATED.

ENFOLD v. grab, grab ass, clinch, clutch, bear-hug, squeeze.

ENFORCE v. lean on, lean against, arm-twist, strong-arm, put the arm on, sweat one, take care of, high-pressure, pull rank, make one an offer one can't refuse. See FORCE.

ENGAGE v. 1. hook, grab, catch, turn on. 2. sign on, sign up, take on, ink, bring on board, come on board, truck with. 3. pitch into, tackle, go in for, go out for, go for broke, have a go at, have a shot at, have a fling at, take a fling at, take the bull by the horns, give a whirl, give a try, try on for size.

ENGAGED adj. 1. intended, asked-for, steady, going steady, pinned, bird, donah, donar, future. 2. tied-up, have other fish to fry, head over heels in, into. 3. on board, inked, signed, in place. See BUSY.

ENGAGEMENT n. date, heavy date, double date, blind date, blind drag, get-together, going out, seeing one, rendezvous, gig, meet; miss a meet, stand one up, stand one on a corner (fail to keep an), zero hour; trif, triff, tref, treff (secret). See also BETROTHED.

ENGAGEMENT, ENTERTAINMENT gig, turn, split week, one-night stand, date, play date.

ENGINE n. horses, power plant, power train, under the hood, barrel (cylinder), maud, pot, putt-putt, rubber band, fan (A.F.), one-lunger (one-cylinder).

ENGINE DRIVER n. hogger, hoghead.

ENGINEER n. techie, technie, technonerd, propeller head, FIDO (aerospace), tech-mech, technokraut (German), slide-ruley type, black gang (ship worker).

ENGINEER v. rig, angle, wangle, work, come up with, upstage, doctor, cook, plant, con, scam, put one on, put one over, jockey, operate, play games, pull strings, pull wires, wire-pull, yank one, finagle, fenagle, faniggle. See also MANAGE, PLAN, SCHEME.

ENGINE FAILURE n. flameout (jet), die.

ENGLAND n. Blighty, John Bull, Merrie Old, Albion, Limeyland, Tight Little Island.

ENGLISH n. the King's English, talkin' white (Af. Am.).

ENGLISH CHANNEL TUNNEL n. Chunnel.

ENGLISH MUFFIN n. burn the British (toasted).

ENGLISH PERSON n. beefeater, Brit, Britisher, Cockney, Limey, lime juicer; Tommy, Tommy Atkins (soldier).

ENGRAVING n. scratch.

ENGROSSED adj. gone, hung up, bugged, hooked, into, really into, heavily into, up to here in, head over heels in, all wound up in, wrapped up in, eat sleep and breathe something, turned on, tied up, fiend, have a bee in one's bonnet, have a bug in one's ear, have a bug up one's ass, have an ax to grind, have a thing about, have a tiger by the tail.

ENHANCE v. pad, pyramid, soup up, build up, upgrade, flesh out, add bells and whistles. See EXPAND.

ENIGMA n. twister, teaser, cliff-hanger, a grabber, sixty-four-dollar question, sticker, mind-boggler, stumper, hard nut to crack, tough nut to crack.

ENJOY v. groove on, have a ball, ball, funk, grok, suck it up, dig, dig one or something, dig the most, rat fuck, R.F., get some grins, get it on, adore, be big on, get off on, get high on, get naked (not necessarily sexual), flip, flip for, flip over, freak out on, get a charge out of, get a kick out of, get a lift out of, get a boot out of, get a bang out of, get one's rocks off, get one's cookies, drop the bomb, just for kicks, just for laughs, knock oneself out, have oneself a time, hit the high spots, eat up, eat it up, savvy, with it, kvell (Yid.), live a little, live it up, take it easy, make a day of it, make a night of it, on the town, out on the town, paint the town, paint the town red, down the primrose path, see the sights, step out.

ENJOYABLE adj. fun (fun party), groovy, just for kicks, just for grins, lots of laughs, just for laughs, just for the heck of it, just for the hell of it, just for the devil of it, fine and mellow, clear sailing.

ENLARGE v. pad, slap on, beef up, jazz up, jack up, blow up, build up, add bells and whistles, snowball. See EXPAND.

ENLARGED adj. boosted, hiked, hiked-up, jacked-up, jumped-up, built-up, blown-up, pyramided, beefed-up, padded, spun out, strung out, dragged out, run out. See also EXAGGERATED.

ENLIGHTEN v. give one the word, let in on the know, put hip, put one in the picture, put on to, update, pull one's coat. See ADVISE.

ENLIGHTENED adj. plugged-in, tuned-in, in the picture, savvy, sharp, wised up, hip to the jive, all woke up, wake up and smell the coffee, know what's what. See AWARE.

ENLIST v. join up, sign on, sign up, sign up for, call up, hitch, poggie, take on.

ENLISTED MAN n. G.I., G.I. Joe, Joe, Joe Blow, Blow Joe, doughfoot, (WWII), E.M., draftee, doughboy (WWI, Mexican War), dogface, enrollee, enlistee. See SOLDIER.

ENLIVEN v. jazz up, perk up, pep up, put pep into, zip up, put zip into, snap up, fire up, work up, buck up, pick up, brace up, chirk up, spice, spice up, juice up, juice, turn on the juice, zap, spark, jim-jam, give a lift, snap out of it, let the sunshine in. See also EXCITE.

ENMESH v. box in, get one in a box, lay for, lay a trap for.

ENMESHED adj. hooked into, conned into, sucked into, all wound up.

ENNUI n. ho-hums, the blahs, blah-blahs.

ENORMOUS adj. gross, humongous, humungous, humongo, mungo, monstro, honking, butt-kicking, bonzai, king-size, mother, motherfucker (Obsc.), big mother, big mama, big daddy, supercolossal, blimp, barn door, whopping. See BIG.

ENOUGH adj. bellyful, had it, had it up to here, that's it, that'll do, all right already, enough already, enough of that shit, fed up, have a skinful, have a snootful, sick and tired of, barfed-out, punched-out, last straw.

ENRAGE v. brown off, lose it, rile, piss one off, cop an attitude (Af. Am.), bitch one off, T off, needle, get under one's skin, utz (Yid.), get in one's hair, get one's mad up, that grinds my gears, whip up, hack, ask for it. See ANGER.

ENRAGED adj. p'd off, p.o.'d, bent, bent out of shape, aerated, blow a gasket, mad as a wet hen, steamed, t.o.'d, see red, bullshit, go ape shit, have a shit hemorrhage. See ANGRY.

ENRAPTURE v. turn on, freak out, knock out, knock dead, send, slay, grooving, score, wow, vamp, sweep off one's feet, make a hit with, hit the spot, be just the ticket, be just what the doctor ordered, go over big, tickle pink, tickle to death. See also ATTRACT.

ENRAPTURED adj. gone, real gone, zero cool, fallen for, gaga about, mad about, sprung on, turned on, gone on, head over heels, hooked, have one's nose open, freaked-out, far-out, spaced-out, wig, wigged-out, flipped-out, blissed-out, sent, crazy, grocked, mad, wild, wicked, weird, weirded-out, dreamy, high, high as a kite, sunny, sunny side up, shook-up, hopped-up, tea'd-up, up, upbeat, joy-germ fever, flyin', flyin' high, floating, floating on air, walking on air, on a joyride, on a cloud, on cloud seven, on cloud nine, all over oneself, come all over oneself, in seventh heaven, tickled to death, tickled pink, pleased as Punch, sold on, hummy, out of it, blowing one's top, blowing one's roof, popping one's nuts, in Nadaville, in the twilight zone.

ENRICH v. pad, pyramid, hitch on, pour it on, figure in, beef up, soup up, hop up, hike, hike up, step up, jazz up, jack up, jump up, run up, up, build, build up, builder-upper, upgrade, spike, flesh out, add bells and whistles, sweeten, sweeten the pot, parlay, press a bet.

ENROLL v. sign on, sign up, sign up for, join up, call up, take on.

ENROLLED PERSON n. enrollee, enlistee.

ENSIGN n. insect, ninety-day wonder, one-striper.

ENSLAVE v. get one's hook into, keep under one's thumb. See SUBJUGATE.

ENSNARE v. rope in, suck in, bag, hook, give a come-hither look, come on, bat the eyes at.

ENSUING adv. next off, coming up.

ENSURE v. ice, put on ice, cinch, clinch, lock on, lock up, nail down, set, okay, OK, put one's John Hancock on.

ENTANGLE v. bag, duke in, hook, rope in, embrangle, swindle in, swindle up, set up, foozle, give a come-hither look, lead on, come on, bat the eyes at. See INVOLVE.

ENTANGLED adj. all wound up in, dragged into, hooked into, sucked into, wrapped up in.

ENTER v. penetrate, access, bum-rush, barge in, blow in, bust in, pop in, mooch in, ace in, breeze in, come breezing in, come barging in, come, come busting in, break in, crack, crack a safe. See also ARRIVE.

ENTERPRISE n. happenin', plan, stunt, game, ball game, bit, do, baby, bag, bag one's into, thing, thing one's into, big idea, biggie (major), deal, pet project, proposition, flier, plunge. See also ACTION, CORPORATION.

ENTERPRISING adj. ambish, ballsy, bogard, come on, come on like gangbusters, come on strong, enforcer, gumption, spunk, balls, drive, guts, go-go, spanking, snappy, zappy, zippy, full of piss and vinegar, full of hot air, full of beans, full of hops, full of prunes, peppy, full of pep, full of get-up-and-go, get-up-and-go, get-out-and-go, go-getter, get up a head of steam, have lead in one's pencil, push, pushy, fair hell, heller, moxie, in there punching, taking it to 'em, take charge, take over, take the bull by the horns, hard-sell, hardball, play hardball, play for keeps, ball of fire, hot-shot, hungry, moving out, spark plug, self-starting, self-starter.

ENTERTAIN v. crack one up, grab, tumul, slay, knock dead, knock them in the aisles. See AMUSE.

ENTERTAINER n. 1. standup comic, baggy-pants comic, straight man, stooge, top banana, second banana, clown, a million laughs, gagman. See COMIC. 2. trouper, legiter, ham, matinee idol, bit player, moppet (child), foil, baddie, stand-in, extra, scene chewer, walk on. See ACTOR. 3. hoofer, B-boy (break dancer), jitterbug, stripper, song-

and-dance man, terper, the line, gypsy, chorine (chorus). See DANCER. 4. long hair, long underwear, cat, blowing cat, gate, lip splitter, solid sender, side man, ear man, faker (illiterate); rocker, monster (popular). See MUSICIAN.

ENTERTAINING adj. crack-up, ball, fun, gas, a scream, yok, a riot, priceless, screamingly funny, too funny for words, gut-busting. See AMUSING.

ENTERTAINMENT n. 1. ball, laughs, lots of laughs, grins, big time, fun and games, high time, high old time, big time, bash, bat, blowout, wingding, brawl, clambake, shindig. See PARTY. 2. hot stuff, long hair, long-haired, tearjerker, show biz.

ENTERTAINMENT FAILURE n. turkey, bomb, bomb out, flop, stinker, stinkeroo, stiff, go down like the Titanic.

ENTERTAINMENT INDUSTRY n. show biz, Broadway, Hollywood, the movies, the Industry.

ENTERTAIN (SOCIAL) v. throw a party, give a party, put on a party, toss a party, have a get-together, have a do, blow one to, on one, I'm buyin', I'll get it (pay the check), pick up the check, pick up the tab, pop, pop for, spring for, stand for.

ENTHRALL v. grab 'em, hook 'em. See ATTRACT.

ENTHUSE v. pump up, carry on over, make a to-do over, take on over, go on about, whoop it up for, turn on.

ENTHUSIASM n. pep talk, jazz, oomph, turn-on.

ENTHUSIAST n. nut, fan, freak, crazies, frenzie, fiend, rooter, gate, great one for, gearhead (computer enthusiast). See DEVOTEE.

ENTHUSIASTIC adj. hot, hot for, hot shit, hot to trot, large for, nuts for, nuts over, nutty about, nutty over, bugged, booster, enthuse, dig, flip, flipped, flip one's lid, freaked-out, turned on, sprung on, cracked on, big on, bugs on, gone on, full on, hipped on, up, jacked-up, shook-up, fired-up, steamed-up, hepped-up, hopped-up, upbeat, stoked, all hopped-up about, worked-up about, steamed-up about, stoned, eager beaver, springbutt, in a big way, wig out, overboard, go overboard about, crazy about, wild about, mad about, ape over, ape about, looking good, looking great, glad-hander (overly), gung-ho, high, high on something, keeping the faith, rosy, looking at the world through rose-colored glasses, looking at something through rose-colored glasses, cooking, cooking with gas, full of piss and vinegar, full of ginger, rarin' to go, eat this shit, fall apart, hung up on, keen, knock oneself out, carry on over, starry-eyed over, gaga over.

ENTICE v. grab, draw, bait, mousetrap, shill, tout, turn on, give one the come-on, bat the eyes at, make with bedroom eyes. See ATTRACT. See also PERSUADE.

ENTICEMENT n. come-on, come-hither, sweetening, sweetener, bait, mousetrap. See LURE.

ENTICER n. come-on man, deek, nark, plant, sitting duck, shill, puffer. See also SEDUCER.

ENTIRETY n. the works, whole enchilada, whole ball of wax, whole nine yards, whole bit, whole schmear, whole megillah, everything including the kitchen sink. See WHOLE.

ENTITLED TO, BE v. rate, be in line for, what one has coming, finders keepers losers weepers.

ENTOMB v. put six feet under, plant, adios it, cover up, deep-six.

ENTOMBMENT n. cold-meat party, planting.

ENTOMOLOGIST n. bugologist, bug hunter, bug chaser, man with the net, butterfly chaser.

ENTOMOLOGY n. bugology.

ENTRAILS n. chitlins, guts, insides, innards.

ENTRANCE n. slammer.

ENTRANCE HALL n. squat pad.

ENTRAP v. duke in, rope in, swindle in, suck in, box in, bag, hook, get one in a box, lay for, set up, swindle up. See LURE.

ENTRAPPED adj. cornered, hooked, hooked into, dragged into, sucked into, suckered into, left holding the bag.

ENTREE n. connection, contact, in, pull, yank, suction, open arms, open door. See INFLUENCE.

ENTRENCH v. dig in, hole up.

ENTRUST v. crack to, spill to, buzz, lay the gaff, lay it on, let one in on, spring with the score, bend an ear.

ENUMERATE v. tick off, count heads, count noses, count the house, dope out, figure in, keep tabs, run down, take account of, tot, tot up, tote, tote up.

ENUMERATED adj. chapter and verse, by the numbers.

ENVIOUS adj. green-eyed, jelly, have big eyes for.

ENVIRONMENT n. hood, neck of the woods, stomping ground, territory, turf, ghetto, inner city, jungle, shanty town, skid row, slum, zoo. See NEIGHBORHOOD.

ENVIRONMENTALIST n. enviro, ecofreak, econut, tree hugger, guppy, eagle freak, earth muffin, birds and bunnies, duck squeezer, web-foot, greeny, true-blue green, sniffers, posy sniffers, banana (build absolutely nothing anywhere near anything).

ENVIRONS n.   hood, neck of the woods, stomping ground, territory, turf, ghetto, inner city, jungle, shanty town, skid row, slum, zoo. See NEIGHBORHOOD.

ENVOY n.   cookie pusher.

ENVY v.   turn green, eat one's heart out, to die over, I should have such luck.

EPAULETS n.   swab-downs (N.).

EPIDEMIC n.   what's going around.

EPILEPSY n.   falling sickness, wingding.

EPISODE n.   goings-on, hap, happening, happenso, scene, seg, cranking, doings, what's going down. See EVENT.

EPISODIC adj.   soap, soap opera, in segs.

EPISTLE n.   line, drop a line, Dear John, dear sir you cur, kite, cannonball, scratch, stiffo, sugar report (love), tab, tag, poison pen letter (malicious, Obsc., etc.), memo, thank-you note, get-well card, dead (not deliverable), FYI (for your information), invite.

EPSTEIN-BARR DISEASE n.   yuppie flu.

EQUAL adj.   look-alike, stack up with, horse-to-horse, double, like two peas in a pod, spit and image, spittin' image, opposite number, level playing field, six of one and half a dozen of the other, break even, even-steven, same difference. See also SAME.

EQUAL v.   hog-tie, push (bet), come up to. See also EMULATE.

EQUALITY n.   fair shake, fair practice, level playing field.

EQUALIZER n.   evener.

EQUATE v.   put two and two together, jive.

EQUIDISTANT adj.   betwixt and between, halfway in the middle, plump in the middle, smack in the middle, slap in the middle, smack dab in the middle.

EQUILIBRIUM n.   cool, keep one's cool, polish. See also CALM.

EQUIP v.   fit out, rag out, rag up, rig out, rig up, turn out, fix up, set up, warm up, gear up, psych oneself up, stake, heel (money), prep, ready up.

EQUIPMENT n.   stuff, kit and caboodle, outfit, contraption, setup, thing. See APPARATUS.

EQUITABLE adj.   square, square deal, fair shake, even-steven, fair-to-middling, level playing field, cricket. See FAIR.

EQUITY n.   blindfolded lady with scales, level playing field, square deal, piece.

EQUIVALENT n.   same difference, ditto, dead ringer, spitting image, carbon copy, six of one and half a dozen of the other, no matter how you slice it cut it or dice it. See SAME.

EQUIVOCATE v.   beg the question, CYA, cover your ass, pass the buck, blow hot and cold, flip-flop, shilly-shally, sit on the fence, waffle, hem and haw, cop out, cop a plea, shuck, jive, shuck and jive, fudge, jazz, bull, bullshit, BS, shovel the shit, con, con along, schmear, stonewall, cover up, run around, give one the runaround, double-talk, petti-fog, cloud the issue, blow smoke up one's ass, throw up a smoke screen, stall off, get around, beat around, beat around the bush, tell a little white lie, talk through one's hat, speak with forked tongue, nit pick, split hairs, make a big thing about, make a federal case out of, make a mountain out of a molehill, catch at straws. See also LIE.

EQUIVOCATION n.   copout, runaround, routine, stonewall, stall, con, cover, cover-up, terminological inexactitude, line of cheese, song, song and dance. See LIE.

ERADICATE v.   adios, trash, total, eighty-six, lose, deep-six (evidence), do away with, dog, ax, wipe off the map, wipe out, take out, stamp out, rub out, put out of the picture, knock out, KO, sanitize, sterilize, scrub, scratch, squash, dust, wash out, waste, waste one, put in the toilet, torpedo, mow down, shoot down, shoot down in flames, off, kibosh, put the kibosh on. See also KILL.

ERADICATED adj.   trashed, totaled, finished, done for, dead and done for, dog, down the drain, gone, had it, kaput, wiped out, stamped out, washed out, washed-up, all washed up, scratched, scrubbed, adiosed, eighty-sixed, offed, wasted. See also KILLED.

ERASE v.   blue-pencil, cut, trim, knock off, gut, launder, X out, scratch out, black out, blot out, stamp out, wipe out. See also CANCEL.

ERASER n.   rubber.

ERECT v.   whomp up, put up, throw up, fab, throw together, fudge together, knock together, cobble up, prefab.

ERECTION n.   hard, hard-on, rod-on, stiff-on, stiff stander, turned on, bone-on, boner, bone, charge, blue steeler, horn, have lead in one's pencil, heart, sport a woody, piss-hard, piss-proud, golden rivet, fuckstick, joystick, cunt stretcher, Irish toothache, wide-on (Fem.) (all Obsc.).

ERIE, PENNSYLVANIA   Dead City, Big E.

EROTIC adj.   steamy, dirty, blue, hot, hot stuff, kinky, purple, filthy, jerk-off, jerk-off material, jack-off material, psycho kick, off-base, off-color, out-of-line, raunchy, raw. See also OBSCENE.

EROTICA n.   peep show, porn, porno, hard porn, soft porn, skin flick, skin pix, smut, T and A (tits and ass), Tijuana

Bible, X-rated, triple X-rated, stag, hard core, soft core, hot stuff, jack-off material, jerk-off material.

ERR v. flub, fluff, muff, muff one's cue, fluff one's lines, blow, blow one's lines, blow it, blow it big time, queer, clinker, boot, bobble, boggle, blob, crumb, crumb up, juke, goof, goof up, gum up, gum up the works, hash up, louse up, screw up, foul up, fuck up, muck up, mung up, bitch, bitch up, ball up, bollix, bollix up, snarl up, slip up, bugger, bugger up, piss up, mess, mess up, make a mess of, mess and a half, make a boner, boo-boo, make a boo-boo, hash, make a hash of, cook, make a blooper, miss by a mile, screamer, floater, snafu, commfu (monumental), fubar, fubb, fumtu, janfu (joint army-navy fuck-up), tarfu, foozle, sink, dub, drop the ball, stumble, pull a blooper, pull a bloomer, pull a boner, pull a boo-boo, put one's foot in it, put one's foot in one's mouth, play the deuce with, play the devil with, play hell with, play merry hell with, play hob with, fall flat on one's face, fall flat on one's ass, donkey act, bark up the wrong tree, count one's chickens before they're hatched, shoot oneself in the foot, shoot down in flames, stub one's toe, go wrong, go at it ass backwards, jump out of the frying pan into the fire, drop a brick, bonehead into it, jim a deal.

ERRAND BOY n. gofer, gopher, leg man.

ERRATIC adj. flaky, kooky, oddball, queer potato, strange duck, bogus, blow hot and cold, up and down. See ECCENTRIC.

ERRATICALLY adv. willy-nilly, helter-skelter, higgledy-piggledy, herky-jerky, every which way, any which way, any old way, right and left, all over the shop, all over the lot, all over hell, here there and everywhere, hit-or-miss, fast-and-loose, by bits and pieces, by fits and starts, in dribs and drabs, do by halves, half-assed, slapdash, slapped out, slap-up, at one's own sweet will, blow hot or cold.

ERRONEOUS adj. all wet, way off, talking like a man with a paper ass, don't know one's ass from a hole in the ground, wrong number, out in left field, have another think coming. See WRONG.

ERROR n. boner, boo-boo, boot, bobble, goof-up, foul-up, fuck-up, screw-up, slip-up, typo, fool mistake. See MISTAKE.

ERUCT v. fart, crack a fart, rip, rip one, toot, fluff, let one go, let one rip, have the power, break wind, cut one, cut the cheese, leave one, let one fly, queef, step on a frog, backfire, nose closer, the butler's revenge (silent). See also BELCH.

ERUCTIVE adj. gassy, windy, farty, fart blossom, barking spiders (audible fart), nose-closer. See also BELCH.

ERUDITE adj. brainy, savvy, double-dig, highbrow, wised up, into, really into, in the know, wise to. See KNOWLEDGEABLE.

ERUPTION n. blowup, cat fit, conniption, conniption fit, duck fit, flare-up, wingding, shit hemorrhage. See also ANGER.

ESCAPADE n. high jinks, hi jinks, rib, gag, caper, hot one, monkeyshines, shenanigans, put-on. See also ADVENTURE.

ESCAPE n. 1. getaway, out, walk (escape punishment), powder, runout powder, break, breakout, crash-out, beat, fadeout, figary, mooch, mope, push, spring, tearaway, get, getaway route, getaway car, absquatulation, exfiltration. See also PRISON ESCAPE. 2. close call, close shave, close squeak, tight squeeze, squeaker, cliff-hanger, get out with one's eyeteeth. 3. kicker (one that negates work, contract, etc.), fine print, small fine print, escape hatch.

ESCAPE v. exfiltrate; walk, beat the rap (escape punishment); hook it, lam, take it on the lam, amscray, breeze, breeze-dust, fade out, heel, hop, vanish, vamoose, scram, smoke, rabbit-foot, spring, head for the hills, hightail, turn tail, jump, skip, skip out, cut out, split, bolt (quickly), blow, beat it, disappear, duck, dodge, shake, shake off, ditch, run for cover, lay low, fly the coop, go over the wall, mope, cop a mope, cop a plea, hide, hide out, crash out, break out, make a break for it, break away, take a powder, take a run-out powder, hoof it, steal away, get away, slip away, make a getaway, get while the going is good, get on one's bicycle, bob, weave, steer clear of, worm out of, wriggle out of, breathe easy, jink, jank (from enemy planes). See also PRISON ESCAPE.

ESCAPEE n. hot, lamster, lammister, on the lam, wanted, have smallpox.

ESCHEW v. duck, have no truck with, not touch with a ten-foot pole, give the go-by, give a miss to, steer clear of, cut dead. See AVOID.

ESCORT n. bird dog, alarm clock, date, gigolo, shag, tote, john, Johnny. See also BOY FRIEND.

ESCORT v. drag, take out, furp, squire, date.

ESPIONAGE TERMS fumigate, sweep (search for listening devices), toss (search a premises), lady (woman sent to compromise the opposition), legend (fictional cover story), lion tamer (one who deals with a former agent who threatens trouble), props (innocent players); music box, musician (wireless transmitter), naked (alone without help), biographic leverage (blackmail), black-bag job (bribery or burglary); demote maximally, terminate (purge by killing); BO, bug out (kill with toxic substance); BBs, L-pill (suicide pill), nasty (national security), cop (cover protection), phew (psychological warfare), run a wire (install tap or microphone); pest, pest control (hiring security), humint (human intelligence), sigint (electronic); wet operation, wet squad, wet work (involving shedding blood).

ESPOUSE v. go in for, take up, get into, back, stand behind. See also ENDORSE; APPROVE.

ESSAY n. 1. paper. 2. a go, crack, fling, header, lick, shot, stab, try, whack, one's all, one's damnedest, one's darnedest, one's level best, dry run, try on, tryout. See ATTEMPT.

ESSAY v. make a run at, take a stab at, take a whack at, have a shot at, have a go at, take on, try on for size, give it a go, do it or bust a gut. See ATTEMPT.

ESSENCE n. point, stuff, nub, key, bottom line, name of the game, nitty-gritty, nuts and bolts, heart, meat, punch line. See BASIC.

ESSENTIAL adj. key, nub, where it's at, coal and ice, cold, cold turkey, meat and potatoes, nitty-gritty, name of the game. See BASIC.

ESSENTIALS n. ABC's, brass tacks, nitty-gritty, nuts and bolts, groceries, guts, meat and potatoes, beginners, coal and ice, bottom line, rock bottom, at heart. See BASICS.

ESTABLISH v. ring in, set up, start the ball rolling, father. See also BEGIN.

ESTABLISHED adj. set, up-and-running, going concern, in place. See also PROVEN.

ESTABLISHMENT n. them, they, city hall, good old boys, Old Boy network, the Man. See also ADMINISTRATION, MANAGEMENT.

ESTEEMED adj. pop, drooly, okay people, touted, highly touted, score, big, large, large charge, BMOC, big man on campus, kimble (tries to be).

ESTIMABLE adj. big, big-name, big-time, big-league, major-league, bigwig, big-wigged, double-barreled, high-powered, in the limelight, name, not to be sneezed at. See IMPORTANT. See also CELEBRITY.

ESTIMATE n. guesstimate, ballpark figure, in the ballpark of, SWAG (slightly wild-assed guess).

ESTIMATE v. size, size up, dope, dope out, take account of, figger, figure, figure in, guesstimate, windshield appraisal (superficial, from a car), take an educated guess, take one's measure.

ESTRANGED adj. turned off, on the outs, in bad with, on one's shitlist, pfft, splits, at outs, at loggerheads, at sixes and sevens.

ET CETERA n. and like that, whatever, blah blah-blah.

ETERNALLY adv. for keeps, for ever so long, for a month of Sundays, till hell freezes over, till the cows come home, till shrimps learn to whistle. See ALWAYS.

ETERNITY n. wild blue yonder, kingdom come, upstairs, up there, the old bye and bye, great ad agency (any business) in the sky. See HEAVEN.

ETHICAL adj. true-blue, square, square shooter, straight, straight shooter, Christian, kosher, salt of the earth, fly right, nice guy, white, regular, scoutmaster, boy scout, clean as a hound's tooth.

ETIQUETTE n. P's and Q's, mind one's p's and q's.

ETYMOLOGIST n. jargonaut.

EULOGIZE v. give a bouquet, give a posy. See FLATTER.

EUNUCH n. capon.

EUNUCH, MAKE INTO A v. alter, deball, fix.

EUPHEMISMS doublespeak, doublespeech, weasel words.

EUPHORIC adj. blissed-out, orgasmic, gone, sent, dreamy, flying, floating, in the twilight zone. See ECSTATIC.

EUROPE n. abroad, across the drink, over there, the old country, Yurp.

EUROPEAN adj. Euro, Eurocrats (European community), Euro———(Eurokids, etc.).

EUROPEAN COMMON MARKET n. Euromart, EEC (European Economic Community).

EUTHANASIA n. mercy killing, pull the plug.

EVACUATE v. 1. cut out, bag ass, shag ass, ooze out, skin out, bail out, pull out, pack up, get git, skidoo, hightail, run for the hills, time to bail. See LEAVE. 2. shit, crap, dump, poop, poo-poo, take a shit, take a crap, take a dump, shake a few clinkers out, do one's business. See DEFECATE.

EVACUATION n. 1. walkout, powder, vanishing act, bow out. See also DEPART. 2. shit, crap, dump, caca, B.M., number two, nature's call, the shits, the runs, being regular, big one, business, aah-aah. See BOWEL MOVEMENT.

EVACUEE n. defector, boat people, D.P., displaced person.

EVADE v. 1. lay low, deek, stutter-step, shake and bake, blow off, give the slip, get on one's bicycle, get around, dodge. See AVOID. 2. give a miss to, not touch with a ten-foot pole, give the go-by, give a wide berth, give the slip, give the cold shoulder, chill, shine one on, freeze, pass the buck, buck-pass, pass up, stay shy of. 3. blow smoke, jive, shuck, shuck and jive, stonewall, waffle, fudge, gardening, hom-rim it, hedge one's bet, pussyfoot, cover your ass, CYA, beat around the bush. See HEDGE.

EVALUATE v. size, size up, peg, check, check out, price out, look over, windshield appraisal (superficial, from a car), read, take one's measure, dope out, take account of, figure, figure in, figure out, guesstimate.

EVALUATION n. guesstimation, take, the Fribbish scale (business).

EVASION n. copout, jive, stall, ditch, slip, dodge, routine, runaround, stonewall, fancy footwork, stutter-step. See also LIE.

EVASIVE adj. cagey, jivey, greasy, slippery, jukey, stonewalling.

EVEN adj. even-steven, dead even, break even, six of one half a dozen of the other, horse-to-horse, level playing field, halfway in the middle, plump in the middle, smack in the middle, smack dab in the middle, slap in the middle.

EVENING n. early black, dim, dark, black.

EVENT n. hap, happenso, happening, trip, real trip, thing, cranking, do, deal, big deal, scene, bit, piece, routine, come off, go down, goings-on, like it is, where it's at, the size of it, bummer, trial (bad). See also ACTION.

EVEN-TEMPERED adj. unflappable, cool, cool as a cucumber, keep one's cool, keep one's shirt on, not turn a hair, keep a stiff upper lip, roll with the punches. See IMPERTURBABLE.

EVENTIDE n. early black, black, dim, dark.

EVENTUAL adj. down the road, down the pike, in the cards. See FUTURE.

EVENTUALITY n. case, any case, hap, happenso, happening, go down, goings-on, come off, if the balloon goes up (the worst).

EVER adv. for keeps, till hell freezes over, till the cows come home, till you're blue in the face. See ALWAYS.

EVERYDAY adj. dime-a-dozen, garden, garden variety, vanilla, rum-dum, starch, mainstream, middle of the road, run of the alley, run of the mill, familiar tune. See ORDINARY.

EVERYTHING adj. the works, business, fixins', lock stock and barrel, whole enchilada, whole kit and caboodle, everything including the kitchen sink. See WHOLE. See also COMPLETELY.

EVERYWHERE adv. all over the map, all over creation, all over hell, to hell and gone, to hell and back, from hell to breakfast, from pole to pole, from here till Sunday.

EVICT v. bounce, kick out, boot out, drum out, freeze out, toss out on one's ear, throw one out on one's ear, throw out on the street, heave-ho, give one the heave-ho, adios one, French walk, send packing, show the door, give the gate, give the air, give one his walking papers, give one the bum's rush, give 'em the 1-2-3.

EVICTION n. boot, bounce, kicking out, old heave-ho, the gate, walking papers, walking ticket, rush, bum's rush.

EVICTOR n. bouncer, chucker, chucker-out, dude-heaver, boot-giver.

EVIDENCE n. dope, goods, info, smoking gun (crucial), clincher, cincher, grabber, clue, cue, hold water, the emess, gospel, flake (plant false). See FACTS.

EVIDENT adj. barefaced, plain as the nose on one's face, clear-cut, crystal-clear, open-and-shut, open-and-shut case, that's a fact Jack. See APPARENT.

EVIL adj. beastly, bad-assed, rat's ass, sleazeball, dank, stinking, murderous, poison, no good, N.G. See BAD.

EVILDOER n. shithead, heel, shitheel, sleazoid, creepo, turd, rat, mother, mofo, megabitch, hood, wrong'un. See SCOUNDREL.

EVIL EYE n. stink eye, whammy, double whammy.

EVIL-MINDED n. dirty, dirty old man, dirty-minded, mind in the gutter.

EVIL SPIRIT n. fiend, hellion, little devil. See DEVIL.

EVOKE v. worm out of one, worm something out of one, wring out, arm-twist, put the arm on. See ELICIT.

EXACT adj. dead on, on the button, on the numbers, on the money, on target, on the nose, on the noggin, right on, bull's-eye, a good eye, stone, dot the i's and cross the t's, draw it fine, cut it fine, hit the nail on the head, flat out, straight out, nailed-down, downright. See also CORRECT.

EXACT v. bleed, lean on, put the arm on, put the bite on, put the gorilla on, shake, put the shake on, squeeze, bite to death, make citizens. See ELICIT.

EXACTING adj. chickenshit, by the book, comma counter, nitpicker, picky, persnickety, smitty, stickler. See PRECISELY.

EXACTLY adv. on the button, on the money, on the nose, on the noggin, on the lemon, the ticket, the very thing, the checker, to a tee, Judy (I understand), cert, sure, why sure, sure thing, for sure, fer sure, fer shirr, surest thing you know, that's for sure, for a fact, you said it, no buts about it, no ifs ands or buts, and no mistake, exactamundo.

EXAGGERATE v. build up, boost, hike, hike up, jack up, jump up, put up, pyramid, up, overdo it, talk trash, loud talk, blarney, jolly, lay it on, lay it on thick, lay it on with a trowel, spread it on, spread it on thick, snow, give one a snow job, whitewash, doctor, cook, con, scam, put one on, B.S., b.s., BS, bs, bull, shit, bullshit, bulldog, bullskating (Af. Am.), throw the bull, shoot the bull, shoot the crap, shoot the shit, shovel the shit, sling the bull, shoot a line, hand one a line, blow, blow smoke, blow smoke up one's ass, fudge, throw one a curve, trump up, hoke up, phony up, fake, gammon, take it big, puff, ballyhoo, make out like, make a mountain out of a molehill, make a federal case out of something, make a big production.

EXAGGERATED adj. hammy, schmaltzy, tearjerking, seagoing, overkill, too-too. See also EXCESSIVE.

EXAGGERATION n. con, scam, jazz, jive, line, crap, crapola, shit, piece of shit, shitting, crock, crock of shit, bull, bull-pucky, bullshit, BS, horse shit, bullshitting, shit for the birds, bird turd, hocky, horse hockey, baloney, phony boloney, phonus bolonus, malarkey, marmalade, applesauce, borax, spiel, spinach, smoke, gas, garbage, guff, hogwash, riff, thick, thin, tripe, vanilla, whopper, hard sell, salve, snow job, blow job, cheese, line of cheese, yeast, fudge, build, buildup, the big lie (Pol.), cock-and-bull story, fish story, story, yarn, tall tale, tall story, big talk, tall talk, bunk flying, latrine rumor, full of hot air, full of beans, full of hops, full of prunes, song and dance, Mother Machree, Mother Macrea (story).

EXAGGERATOR n. shoveler, blowhard, bullshitter, bullshit artist. See also LIAR, BRAGGART.

EXAMINATION n. 1. physical, checkup, exam. 2. case, double-o, gunning over, gander, pike, eye, ex, hustle, eyeball examination. 3. third, third degree, grill, fishing expedition, legwork. 4. oral, orals, comp (comprehensive), final, prelim, cream (successful), bluebook, exam; drop quiz, flash quiz, shotgun quiz, pop quiz (all unannounced), PMS (pre-midterm exam stress).

EXAMINE v. 1. look-see, eye, gun, check, check out, case, scope, sweep, read, kick tires. See SEE. 2. give one the third, sweat it outta one, put one through the wringer, buzz, cat haul, cool out. See QUESTION. 3. frisk, pat down. 4. chew over, rap, confab, hash, rehash, hash over, kick around, knock around, let the daylight in, let the sunlight in. See ANALYZE. See also THINK.

EXAMPLE n. f'rinstance, for instance, excuse.

EXASPERATE v. brown off, piss one off, bitch one off, T off, get under one's skin, give one a hemorrhage, give one a shit hemorrhage, that grinds my gears, cop an attitude (Af. Am.), push one's key, hack, make waves, stick in one's craw, sound, sound off, burn one off, send one into a tailspin, drive one up the wall. See ANNOY.

EXASPERATED adj. bugged, hacked, blown-out, hacked-off, brassed-off, cheesed-off, aggro, pissed-off, peed-off, teed-off, burned-up, miffed, peeved, riled, rubbed the wrong way, driven up the wall, steamed. See ANNOYED.

EXASPERATING adj. pesky, pestiferous, bugs one, gives one a pain, pain in the ass, bitch, a bit much, too much, flea, from hell. See ANNOYING.

EXCAVATOR n. groundhog, sandhog.

EXCEEDINGLY adv. awfully, really, too much, stone (stone deaf), terribly, powerful. See VERY.

EXCEL v. shine, top, cap, wax, make it, got a hot hand, in the groove, on a roll, all the way live, large and in charge (Af. Am.), kick it live (Af. Am., do it well), all systems go, go to town, everything going for one, come through, come through with flying colors.

EXCELLENT adj. killer, ex, A, A-1, A-number one, A-plus, A-OK, okay, OK, aggro, 10, ten, sweet, tasty, ace, aces, ace high, ace of spades, in spades, bump'n', bitchin', twitchin', def, rad, fly, bomb, filthy, mint, cherry, deffest, dope, dual, fat, phat, fierce, fresh, fully on, fully, fully to the skull, epic, nitro, on the strength, raw, sick, filsh, stupid fresh, brutal, super, smashing, happenin', rattling, rocking, gnarly, megagnarly, awesome, it's to die for, dyno, dynamite, unreal, cool, coolsville, zero cool, cold, chill, daddy, lampin', terrific, terrible, down, wicked, evil, vicious, winner, choice, rad, radical, reet, gasser, a gas, Jake, ginchy, slammin', fabu, fab, fabulous, far out, funky, state-of-the-art, too much, cosmic, mongo, massive, key, major, master (Af. Am.), cranking, frantic, not half bad, stokin', wailing, whaling, dope on a rope, hype, stink, stone, stone groove, out-of-this-world, out-of-sight, gilt-edged, drooly, flash, like wow, not too shabby, something else, groovy, grooby, frantic, tough, tuff, tidy, tits, heavy, bad, baaadest, rat fuck, nose cone, marvy, best ever, top, tops, tiptop, topnotch, topflight, top-drawer, top-of-the-line, head-of-the-line, head-of-the-class, world-class, hundred-proof, first-class, first-chop, first-rate, star, boss, stunning, corking, corker, solid, solid sender, great, greatest, the most, the utmost, mostest, gonest, doozie, daisy, dilly, bo, boo, tickety-boo, deadly, deadly-boo, bong, sly, copacetic, kopasetic, the bee's knees, the cat's meow, the cat's whiskers, the cat's pajamas, the butterfly's book, the caterpillar's kimono, George, real George, good show, gear, golden, hard, hummer, humdinger, knockout, mad, mess, mezz, nasty, nifty, the nuts, the nerts, the end, endsville, hellacious, savage, solid gold, righteous, ripping, rip-snorter, sanitary, heavenly, bang-up, in fat city, in orbit, murder, neat, hunky-dory, all wool and a yard wide, jam-up, slap-up, dandy, fine and dandy, jim-dandy, crack, cracker-jack, peacherino, peach, peachy, ginger-peachy, peachy-keen, keen, salt of the earth, but good, strictly, super-duper, hooper-dooper, supercolossal, sweetheart, catch, find, plenty, zanzy, beautiful, cuspy, gimchy, check plus, stellar, dream, lollapaloosa, whiz, killer-diller, mean, ducky, hot, spiffy, nobby, delicious, scrumptious, swell, shirty, tawny, whale of a, world-beater, pip, pippin, lulu, darb, honey, beaut, mean, tubular, toast, this is some kinda ———, it's the berries, cracking, bully, sharp, the best, skull, brain, the end, the living end.

EXCEPTIONAL adj. world-class, job, primo, wizard, high cotton, splash, mother, motherfucker (Obsc.), muthah, muthahfuckah, mofo, skull, brain, grind.

EXCERPT n. quote, saying.

EXCESS n. overruns, overkill, the limit, he's the limit, too much.

EXCESSIVE adj. way out, worst-case scenario, overkill, glorkish, ultra-ultra, have ———-orexia (phone-orexia, study-orexia), out of all bounds, out of sight, too much, too-too, over the top, up the butt, up the ying-yang, everything but the kitchen sink. See EXTREME.

EXCESSIVELY adv. too much, too-too. See also EXTREMELY.

EXCHANGE n. network, net, LAN, Wall Street, the street, the Exchange, the Big Board, over-the-counter, OTC.

EXCHANGE v. 1. swap, swap horses, horse-trade, wash (even), See also NEGOTIATE. 2. put the cart before the horse, flip-flop, turn the tables. 3. have truck with, contact with, network, link up, hook up.

EXCISE v. blue-pencil, cut, trim, knock off, lop off, gut, launder, X out, scratch out, black out, blot out, stamp out, wipe out, scissor out.

EXCITABLE adj. high-strung, hot, hot-headed, hot around the collar, hot under the collar, have a short fuse. See also EMOTIONAL.

EXCITE v. jazz, jazz up, juice, juice up, send, zap, grab, hook, fuss, bug up, burn up, heat up, pep up, perk up, pick up, snap up, wake up, zip up, key up, fire up, get it up, steam up, stir up, work up, work up into a lather, work oneself into a stew, work oneself into a tizzy, work oneself into a pucker, wig out, adjy, flip, flip one's lid, egg on, turn on, whatever turns you on, whatever makes your boat float, turn one on, switch on, turn on the juice, turn on the heat, run a temperature, get hot under the collar, race one's motor, open one's nose, blow up, blow one's stack, blow one's top, blow a gasket, blow one away, go ballistic, fly off the handle, hit the ceiling, make waves, rabble-rouse, put the zingers in, get one's pratt, needle, put the needles in, throw wood on the fire, add fuel to the flames. See also DISTURB; STIR; ROUSE.

EXCITED adj. hyper, amped, charged, stoked, blow off, jacked, jaked, jazzed, wired, wired-up, revved, revved-up, juiced-up, zipped-up, zapped-up, fired-up, keyed-up, all keyed-up, steamed-up, hopped-up, hyped-up, pumped-up, worked-up, get all worked up, worked up into a lather, freaked out, flipped out, spazzed out, had a spaz attack, had a cow, switched on, turned on to, turned on, headin' up the mountain, horny (sexual), zonkers, stoned, high, high as a kite, fussed, shook, shook-up, all shook up, blow one's mind, mind-blowing, mind-bending, hot, hotheaded, hot as a firecracker, hot to trot, hots, hot stuff, hotter than a two-peckered mule, having the hots, hot and bothered, hot under the collar, warm around the collar, steamin' under one's silks, like crazy, like mad, have a fit, have kittens, cast a kitten, go up in the air, hit the ceiling, hog wild, shit in one's pants, have a shit hemorrhage, get one's bowels in an uproar, in a dither, in a lather, in a swivet, in a foofaraw, in a pucker, in a stew, in a tizzy, rooty, ready to cook, ready for Freddy, feel in one's guts, get to one. See also DISTURBED.

EXCITEMENT n. fireworks, up, upper, cloud nine land, heaven, high, buzz, charge, large charge, rush (get a rush), head rush, bang, kick, kicks, for kicks, big deal, big shit, turn-on, corker, circus, flash, flap, jollies, mess, razzle-dazzle, rowdydow, rowdy-dowdy.

EXCITING adj. frantic, wild, killer, cool, real cool, zero cool, far out, mega, megadual, marvy, nifty, spiffy, groove, in the groove, groovy, in the bubble, fab, boss, jazzy, sensay, sensaysh, big splash, jumping, mad, mean, the most, mostest, like wow, reet, reat, mind-blowing, mind-bending, out-of-this-world, out-of-sight, clean outta sight, turn on, turned on by, turned on to, kicky, wiggy, diddly-bop, a gas, gas up something, evil, knockout, all the way live (Stu.), live one, live wire, dolce vita, gone, real gone, barn burner, hot stuff, hairy, large, large charge, nervous, rootin'-tootin', snazzy, razzle-dazzle, glitzy, flashy, showy, smashing, bang-up, ace-high, swell, stunner, stunning, feel in one's guts, grabbed by, solid, solid sender, something, something else, something to shout about, something to write home about, swinging, fine, lush, sizzler, scorcher, one for the book, blood and thunder, chiller, cliff-hanger, cloak and dagger, page-turner, thriller. See also STIRRING.

EXCLAIM v. holler, holler out, blast, figure, beller, blow at, yawp.

EXCLAMATION n. yawp, holler, beller.

EXCLAMATION POINT n. dog's dick, dog's prick, dog's cock (all typesetter's, journalist's slang).

EXCLUDE v. pass by, pass up, pass on, shut out, cut out, ding, zing, cut, snip, drop, blackball, eighty-six, 86, kill, sidcline, ice out, hand one his walking papers, send one to the showers, dump, fluff off, give one the fluff, give one the cold shoulder, shoot down, dog, throw out, throw away, chuck, chuck out, turn thumbs down on, thumb down, adios it, heave-ho, nix, shit on, piss on, put down, shove it, stick it, stow it.

EXCLUDED adj. blackballed, cold-shouldered, out of the loop, left out in the cold, not in the picture, shut out, sidelined, baldhead, left on the outside looking in.

EXCLUSION n. ding, blackball.

EXCLUSIVE adj. high-hat, uppity. See SNOBBISH. See also ALOOF.

EXCLUSIVELY adv. onliest, one and only. See SINGULAR.

EX-CONVICT n. ex-con, jailbird, lag, lagger.

EXCRETE v. shit, crap, dump, squat, take a squat, drop a turd, shake a few clinkers out, make number two. See DEFECATE. 2. make number one, pee, pea, piss, leak, take a leak, make a pit stop, drain the dew, tap a kidney, go, go wee-wee, go pee-pee, tinkle, piddle. See URINATE. 3. break a sweat, sweat like a horse, sweat like a trooper, get all in a lather.

EXCRETION n. 1. shit, crap, dump, caca, BM, number two, poop, poot (gas), call, nature's call, turd, being regular, big one, boom-boom, business, poo-poo, aah-aah, the shits, the runs, trots, shits, GI's, GI shits, turistas, Montezuma's revenge. See also BOWEL MOVEMENT. 2. number one, piss, pee, pee-pee, piddle, pish, tinkle, wee, wee-wee. 3. buffalo chips, cow chips, cow flops, cow plops, cow pats, road apples, golden apples, hocky, horse hocky, shit, horseshit, lawn dressing, moose beans, moose pecans, moose nuggets.

EXCURSION n. Cook's tour, cruise, do Europe (or wherever), go on apex.

EXCUSE n. jive, shuck and jive, stall, song, song and dance, story, whitewash, coppin' deuces, have to see a man about a dog, off-time, cleanup, copout, cover, cover one's ass, cover-up, cover story, fish, fish story, fish tale, Mother Machree, Mother McCrea, routine, airtight alibi, the why and wherefore, the whyfor.

EXCUSE v. 1. cop a plea, cop out, crawl, square oneself, square a beef, square things, make up for, whitewash, alibi out of, crawl out of, worm out of, squirm out of. 2. let one off the hook, let one off this time, let one off easy, let it go, go easy on, wink at, write off. See ABSOLVE.

EXCUSED adj. let off, let go, walked, beat the rap, off the hook.

EXECUTE v. do the job, do the trick, turn the trick, do up brown, do a turn, do to a turn, do to a T, do oneself proud, break out with, bust out with (surprisingly or suddenly), pull off, pull it off, knock off, polish off, tear off, top, top off, make it, make out, be on, go on, as advertised, get to first base, earn one's wings, put across, put it over, put away, put it together, put over, one down, one down and two to go, sail through, take care of, deal with, come through, score, hit, perk, percolate, tick, do one's thing, get over, get there, ring the bell, sail through, go to town, hack it, hit the bull's-eye, fly, nail it, win one's spurs, squeak by (barely). T.C.B. (take care of business), come on like gangbusters (well), strut one's stuff, do one's stuff.

EXECUTED adj. 1. catch rope, dance, go through the trap, hoist, scrag, stretch, strung-up, swing, fried, burned. 2. buttoned-up, wrapped-up, mopped-up, dealt with, put over, wired, done to a T. See FINISHED.

EXECUTION n. 1. chops (talent), nuts and bolts, style. 2. necktie party, lynching bee, rub out, hit.

EXECUTIONER n. enforcer, torpedo, gorilla, gunsel, gun, gunman, piece man, hit man, trigger man. See KILLER.

EXECUTIVE n. C.E.O., CEO, C.O., exec, suit, pinstriper, vest, rainmaker, key player, A-number 1, chief, boss head, boss lady, mother, boss man, perkman, point man, old man, papa, super, skipper, czar, godfather, Don, governor, hot stuff, honcho, head honcho, head, head man, the man, lead-off man, general, hammer man, perc man, meal ticket, main squeeze, queen bee, the brass, brass hat, top brass, gold braid, rug rank (high), VIP, tycoon, baron, Mr. Big, Charlie, Mister Charlie (Af. Am.), Mr. Right, his nibs, big brother, big daddy, big gun, gun, big shot, big shit, big player, big boy, big number, big stuff, big noise, big ghee, big chew, big spud, apple, big apple, big weenie, big cheese, the whole cheese, big man, big name, wheel, big wheel, big-timer, big-time operator, BTO, wig, bigwigged, top, on top, topper, top hand, topkick, top drawer, top dog, the big bowwow, upstairs, man upstairs, exec suite, front office, higher-ups, high priest, king, kingfish, kingpin, king of the hill, cock, cook, chief cook and bottlewasher, bull of the woods, big league, shark, bread, brains, brain box, mastermind, guru, rishi, old man, old pro, pro, old warhorse, old hand, biggest hand, biggest frog in the pond, buddy seat, spark plug, juice, kicker, the force, powerhouse, upper hand, whip hand, hellmaster, straw boss, pusher, slave driver, Simon Legree, the say, the say-so, a lot to say about, a lot to do with, the word, righteous, geets, guts, string, ropes, avatar, wire, wire man, digger, fruit, oink (police), heavy stuff, heavy, weight, where the buck stops, cat bird, space cadet (young), hi-pot (young with potential), apparatchik (junior), mommy track (having children). See also COMMANDER.

EXECUTIVE BENEFITS n. golden parachute, perks, golden handcuffs (deferred).

EXECUTIVE RECRUITER n. headhunter.

EXECUTIVE SUITE n. front office, fast track, kiva, upstairs.

EXEMPLARY adj. neato, bueno, not too shabby, sweet, goodie, tuff, happenin', horror show, atsa nice, not bad, bootin' height, nasty, doin' a hundred, batting a thousand. See PRAISEWORTHY.

EXEMPT v. let one off the hook, clear, wipe the slate, go easy on, wink at, write off. See ABSOLVE.

EXERCISE n. daily dozen, constitutional, workout, aerobics, gym, warm-up, aerobicize, jazzercise.

EXERCISE n. gym, warm-up, jazzercise, workout, monkey drill.

EXERCISE v. aerobicize, lick into shape, put through the grind, put through the mill, pump iron, tune up, warm up, work out, work up a sweat, walk through, run through, hone, break, break in, dry run.

EXERCISE CLASS n. gym, workout.

EXERCISE SUIT n. body stocking, sweats, sweat suit.

EXERT v. sweat it, push, dig, plug, peg away, bust one's ass, in it to win it (Af. Am.), break one's heart, give it all one's got, give it one's best shot, put one's back into it, pour it on. See ATTEMPT.

EXHAUST v. 1. bleed white, suck dry. 2. fag, tucker, poop, poop out, conk out, burn out, fag out, tucker out, knock out, peter out.

EXHAUSTED adj. bushed, had it, blown out, crispy, creased, too pooped to pop, wiped out, wimped out, outta gas, outta juice, frazzled, worn to a frazzle, all-in, shot, fucked out, at the end of one's rope, bone-weary, dog-tired, hit the wall (marathon). See TIRED.

EXHAUSTING adj. heavy, hefty.

EXHAUSTION n. brain fag, burnout, hit the wall (marathon).

EXHAUSTIVE adv. to a fare-thee-well, do up brown, from A to Z, the works, not overlook a bet, leave no stone unturned. See THOROUGH.

EXHIBIT v. let it all hang out, showcase, show and tell, roll out, parade one's wares, wave it around. See DISPLAY.

EXHIBITION n. expo, exbo, exhib, exhibish, flash (gaudy merchandise or prize), frame-up, front, fireworks, an act, a scene, for show.

EXHIBITIONIST n. showboat, showoff, grandstander, grandstand player, hot dog, hotdogger, hotshot, streaker, flasher, troller, wand waver, weenie wagger, flasho, Flash Gordon.

EXHIBITOR n. exhib.

EXHILARATE v. send, turn on, jazz up, juice, juice up, pep up, perk up, pick up, snap up, zip up, jim-jam, put pep into, put zip into. See EXCITE.

EXHILARATED adj. flipped-out, high, blow one's mind, charged, hopped-up, jacked, jaked, jazzed, hyper, revved, revved-up, amped, turned-on. See EXCITED.

EXHILARATION adj. a rush (get a rush), head rush. See EXCITEMENT.

EXHORTATIVE adj. preachy, Bible-thumpin', fire-breathin', high-pressure.

EXIST v. get along, kick, just makin' it, get by.

EXISTENCE n. the big game, lifing, rat race, world, the real world, journey, hand (one is dealt).

EXISTING adj. alive and kicking, ticking, warm, here, in the lifestream, making it, hanging in there, still around.

EXIT v. haul ass, split, fuck off, flake off, move out, ooze out, get, git, color me gone, air out (Af. Am.), motorvate, motor, le-go, sko (let's go), bolt (quickly), blow, blow this joint, blow this pop stand, break camp, hoof it, hotfoot, jet, be-bop, roll out, I'm out, I'm outtie, I'm Audi 5000, absquatulate, get on (Af. Am.), do a vanishing act, I'm history, I'm outta here, I'm in the wind. See GO.

EXONERATE v. let off, let one off the hook, whitewash, sanitize, clear, wipe the slate clean. See ABSOLVE.

EXORBITANT adj. high, pricey, out of sight, cher, dear, steep, stiff, heavy sugar, big price tag, an arm and a leg, up to here (elbow), holdup, highway robbery, important. See EXPENSIVE.

EXOTIC adj. kinky, way out, far out, avant-garde, weird. See STRANGE. See also ALLURING.

EXPAND v. push the envelope, bulk up, beef up, soup up, hop up, heat up, pad, slap on, tack on, tag on, hitch on, pour it on, piggyback, hike, hike up, step up, jazz up, jack up, jump up, run up, up, build, build up, builder-upper, pyramid, spike, flesh out, spell out, spin out, string out, drag out, balloon, add bells and whistles, dump on, snow, snowball, sweeten, sweeten the pot, parlay, boost, press a bet, tish, join together, join up with, hook up with, hook on, plug into, add fuel to the fire.

EXPECT v. figure, in the cards, it's looking to, see it coming, be afraid, wait for the other shoe to drop. See ANTICIPATE. See also BELIEVE.

EXPECTANT adj. looking for, waitin' on, the noose is hanging, waiting for the other shoe to drop. See also HOPEFUL.

EXPECTED adj. as advertised, no big surprise, be just like one, be one all over, not put it past, figured in, figgered in. See ANTICIPATED.

EXPECTORATE v. let fly, hawk, spritz, squirt.

EXPEDIENT n. Band-Aid, quick fix, dodge, gimmick, trick, easy way out.

EXPEDITE v. cut red tape, hand-carry, hand-walk, walk it over, walk it through, go to the whip on, fast-track, railroad, grease the wheels, run interference for, run with the ball, handle personally. See SPEED.

EXPEDITION n. safari, snofari, swing, jaunt, cruise, trek, Cook's tour.

EXPEL v. 1. kick, kick out, can, fire, bump, bust, bounce, boot, give one his walking papers, give one the old heave-ho, give the bum's rush, give the hook, show the door, drum out, send packing, send to the showers. See DISCHARGE. 2. chuck out, adios one, French walk, bounce, boot out, give one the bum's rush, give one the heave-ho, throw one out on one's ear. See EJECT.

EXPEL GAS v. fart, break wind, crack a fart, rip, rip one, toot, fluff, let one go, let one rip, cut one, cut the cheese, leave one, let one fly, backfire, poot, the butler's revenge (silent), nose-closer. See ERUCT.

EXPELLED adj. washed-out, washed-up, all washed up, scratched, scrubbed, adiosed, eighty-sixed, offed, wasted. See also DISCHARGED.

EXPEND v. pay out, foot the bill, blow, dish it out, shell out, put out, fork out, spring for, throw money at. See PAY.

EXPENDED adj. down the tube, down the drain, down the spout, down the rathole, fell between the cracks, out the window, pissed away, diddled away, blown, petered out, shot, kiss it good-bye.

EXPENDITURE n. nut, bottom line, a throw, below the line, set one back, come to, to the tune of, hummer, highway mopery, payoff, cash on the nail, cash on the barrelhead, kickback, nickel and dime (minor), outlay.

EXPENSE n. nut, price tag, bite, bottom line, below the line, nickel and dime (minor), outlay, out of pocket, on one's own nickel, on one's own time and own dime. See COST.

EXPENSE ACCOUNT n. fall money, mad money, lulu, out-of-pocket, scandal sheet, swindle sheet, ICE (incidental company expenses: padding).

EXPENSES, CLEAR v. get off the gun, get off the nut, make the nut, out of the red. See also PROFIT.

EXPENSIVE adj. pricey, cher, dear, uptown, upscale, costing, big-ticket, steep, stiff, posh, executive, fancy, high, high-rent, plushy, swanky, ritzy, splendiferous, splendacious, heavy sugar, out of sight, out of bounds, important, high price tag, an arm and a leg, pretty penny, what the traffic will bear. up to here (elbow), holdup, highway robbery, highway mopery, paid through the nose, collectibles, worth its weight in gold, worth a king's ransom.

EXPERIENCE n. happening, happenso, hap, a trip, a real trip, cranking, been there, through the mill, been hit before; nightmare, bummer trails (bad). See EVENT.

EXPERIENCE v. be turned on to, feel in one's bones, feel in one's guts, get in touch, have a funny feeling, have heart, have a hunch, have vibes.

EXPERIENCED adj. 1. pro, vet, the right stuff, stuff, dynamite, fireball, one-man band, know one's stuff, something on the ball, a pistol. See SKILLED. 2. kicked around, been around, been around the block a few times, been there before, been through the mill, old hand, old-timer, old war-horse, sport, city slicker. See SOPHISTICATED.

EXPERIMENT n. R and D (research and development), trial run, try-on, tryout, fling at. See also TEST.

EXPERIMENT v. cut and try, fool around with, futz around, play around with, mess around, give a tryout, give a work out, give it a go, shake down, try on, try it on for size. See also TEST.

EXPERIMENTER n. numbers cruncher, mad doctor.

EXPERT adj. savvy, sharp, slick, there, crack, crackerjack, up one's alley, been there, have know-how, know one's onions, know one's stuff, big-league, enough ducks in a row. See SKILLFUL.

EXPERT n. shark, phenom, propeller head, guru, pro, old pro, ol' professor, old hand, maven, whiz, buff, trained seal, gnome, mean bean; bone man, heart man, big nose man (Medic. specialists); hotshot, checkbook witness (paid). See AUTHORITY.

EXPERTISE n. know-how, savvy, sharpness, goods, makings, stuff, chops, oil, one's thing, bag, dodge, line. See SKILL. See also KNOWLEDGE.

EXPIATE v. make up for, pay one's dues, square things. See COMPENSATE.

EXPIRE v. kick the bucket, go, buy it, croak, meet one's maker, give up the ghost, bite the dust, cash in one's chips, turn it in, deep-six, go to Davy Jones' locker (drown), fry, shove over, quit it, up and die, peg out, pass out, strike out, chalk out, flake out, head for a hearse, back gate, back-door parole, get a back-gate commute, one-way ticket, one-way ride, kayoed for keeps, trumped; dance, dance on air, dance on nothing, dance off (hang). See DIE.

EXPIRING adj. at the end of one's rope, done for, MFC (measure for coffin), on one's last legs, checking out, going down (Af. Am.), heading for the last roundup, one foot in the grave; one foot in the grave the other on a banana peel.

EXPLAIN v. spell out, lay out, lay it out for, lay down, break it down, beat it down (Af. Am.), decode, draw one a picture, show and tell, roll out, trot out, make one see daylight, let daylight in, let sunlight in, make clear, make perfectly clear, get across, put across, put one in the picture, paint a picture, put one straight, get over, open one's head, pull one's coat to, spotlight, limelight, highlight, give a for instance, give a f'instance.

EXPLANATION n. rundown, story, cover story, whatfor, whyfor, why and wherefore, the picture, the whole picture, the idea, the big idea, whole megillah.

EXPLETIVE: AGREEMENT absofuckinglutly!, crazy!, solid!, groovy!, works for me!, reet!, all reet!, right on!, hell yes!, what you say!, you said it!, you said a mouthful!, you just ain't whistling Dixie!, you bet!, you bet your life!, you bet your ass!, you bet your sweet ass!, you bet your boots!, you know it!, for sure!, fer sher!, fer shirr!, for dammed sure!, for darned sure!, for danged sure!, for a fact!, for a fact Jack!, thunderbird!

EXPLETIVE: ANGER shit!, oh shit!, merde!, son of a bitch!, SOB!, bitch!, bastard!, nuts!, hell!, oh hell!, God damn!, damn!, damn it!, darn!, darn it!, dad-blasted!, dad blast it!, dad blamed!, dad-burned!, doggoned!, dagnabbed!, gosh-darn!, gol-darned!, gol-dinged!, ding-blasted!, ding-dang!, dash it!, dash it all!, crap!, cripes!, crimus!, cripus!, crimony!, rats!, that bleeping thing!

EXPLETIVE: DISDAIN phooey!, eeyoo!, eeyuck!, yeeuck!, yeeuch!, phew!, pugh!, ugh!, feh!, pish!, hang it in your ear!

EXPLETIVE: HAPPY wow!, way!, way rad!, like wow!, wowie!, zowie!, man!, man-oh-man!, far out!, out of sight!, outta sight!, groovy!, sakes alive!, goody!, goody goody!, goody gumdrops!, boy oh boy!, hot dog!, hot diggety!, hot diggety dog!, hot ziggety!, keen-o!, keen-o peachy!, cowabonga!, cowabunga!, let the good times roll!, oowhee!, eeehaw!, yeehaw!, yahoo!

EXPLETIVE: HOSTILE asshole!, up yours!, up your ass!, up your wazoo!, shove it!, shove it up your ass!, stick it!, stick it up your ass!, kiss my ass!, bag your face!, bite me!, eat me!, eat shit!, drop dead!, nuts!, nerts!, bull!, bullshit!, horseshit!, baloney!, bury yourself!, big deal!, big shit!, T.T.!, tough titty!, T.S.!, tough shit!, fuck!, fuck it!, fuck you!, fuck off!, go fuck yourself!, crud you!, piss!, piss off!, piss on you!, mother!, motherfucker!, M.F.!, mofo!, muthuhfuckuh!, mother grabber!, mother clutcher!, mother jiver!, mother rucker!, lolla-lucka!, your mother!, your mama!, your mother's moustache!, your father's moustache!, says who!, says you!, sez you!, go soak yourself!, go soak your head!, for Pete's sake!, flip one the bird!, blow it out your barracks bag!, how do you like them apples?

EXPLETIVE: IGNORANCE it beats me!, beats me!, beats the shit outta me!, search me!, you got me!, damned if I know!, God only knows!, Lord knows!, heaven knows!, it's Greek to me!, I pass!, don't look at me!

EXPLETIVE: REJECTION forget you!, get bent!, kiss my ass!, bite me!, bite off!, bag that!, shove it!, shove it up your ass!, stick it!, stick it up your ass!, stick it in your ear!, stow it!, put it where the sun don't shine!, shine it!, you know what you can do with it!, nuts to you!, go to!, go to hell!, crud you!, fuck you!, fuck off!, big fucking deal!, BFD!

EXPLETIVE: SURPRISE no kidding!, oh yeah!, go on!, get out!, no shit!, shee-it!, holy Christ!, holy Christmas!, holy mackerel!, holy moley!, holy Moses!, holy smoke!, holy shit!, holy Toledo!, Jeez!, Jees!, Jeezy peezy!, jiggers!, jigs!, I'll be jig-swiggered!, I'll be jiggered!, what the fuck!, what the hey!, what in Sam Hill!, fuck a duck!, shoo fly!, twenty-three skidoo!, crazy!, search me!, wow!, like wow!, goodness gracious!, mercy!, whammo!, whamo!, for crying out loud!, for crying in a bucket!

EXPLETIVE: UNPLEASANT sheesh!, hairball!, eeyuk!, yeeuck!, yech!, yich!, yuk!, yucky!, eeoooh!, ick!, ugh!, ach!, bletch!, blechhh!, feh!, phew!, pugh!, phooey!

EXPLICATION n. why and wherefore, whatfor, whyfor, the picture, the whole picture, rundown, story, the idea, the big idea, megillah, whole megillah. See also DESCRIPTION.

EXPLICIT adj. all hanging out, on the nose, don't need no diagrams, no buts about it, no ifs ands or buts, adult (sexual). See also OBVIOUS.

EXPLODE v. go off, go blooey, go flooey, go flooie, kablooey, let go, va-voom, hit the fan.

EXPLODED adj. set off, blown, energetically disassembled.

EXPLOIT v. work (she worked the johns for tips), pick one's brains, mine, mining, get mileage out of. See also ADVANTAGE, TAKE.

EXPLOITER n. operator, carpetbagger, wire-puller, one on the make. See also CHEATER.

EXPLORE v. really get into, leave no stone unturned, turn inside out. See also SEARCH; INVESTIGATE.

EXPLOSION n. energetic disassembly, blowup.

EXPLOSIVE n. fireworks, pineapple, satchel charge, soup, power, dinah, grease, mulligan, Aunt Jemima, noise, peter, picric, shot, stew, string, booby trap, Bouncing Betsy.

EXPLOSIVES WORKER n. powder monkey, UXB.

EXPOSE v. dig, dig up, crack, leak, let the cat out of the bag, give away, give the show away, show up, spill, spill it, spill the beans, spill one's guts, blab, blabber, make noise, dump on, break, break it to one, tip, tip off, tip one's duke, tip one's hand, show one's hand, lay it on the stick, lay it on one, own up, come clean, come out, come out of the closet, bring it out into the daylight, out someone, let it all hang out, get it out of one's system, get it off one's chest, out with it, spit it out, open up, blow one's cover, spring, spring one's duke, spring with a crack, peach, burn (spy), debunk, do one dirt, drop a bomb, blow up, blow the lid off, blow sky high, blow the whistle, show, whip out, flash (also used in playing cards), moon (buttocks), B.A. (bare ass); hang a B.A. (expose buttocks), do a fruit salad (expose genitals), streak (run naked).

EXPOSED adj. caught with a hand in the cookie jar, caught with one's pants down, caught dead to rights, out on a limb, on the spot, got one's neck out. See CAUGHT. See also DEFENSELESS, NUDE.

EXPOSITION n. expo.

EXPOSURE n. handout, flashing, mooning, streaking. See also DISCLOSURE; REVELATION, PUBLICITY.

EXPRESS v. pop off, shoot off one's mouth, shoot one's wad, shoot one's bolt. See SPEAK.

EXPRESSIONLESS adj. deadpan, poker face, fish eye, straight-face, lead eyeballs, nobody home. See EMOTIONLESS.

EXPULSION n. brush, brush-off, rush, bum's rush, bounce, heave-ho, old heave-ho, the gate, Spanish walk.

EXPUNGE v. blue-pencil, cut, knock off, gut, launder, trim, scrub, X out, take out, zap, kayo, KO, nix, call off, call all bets off, kill, wipe out, blow the deal. See CANCEL. See also EDIT, DESTROY.

EXPUNGED adj. scrubbed, scratched, killed, offed, wasted, shot, shot down, shot down in flames, taken out, washed out, wiped out, all off, all bets off, kaput, zapped, blue-penciled, rubbed out.

EXPURGATE. v. bleep, bleep out, blue-pencil, clean up, cut, decontaminate, launder, sanitize, sterilize, scrub, squash. See REPRESS. See also SUPPRESS.

EX-SOLDIER n. vet, ex-GI, war horse, pro, old pro, old hand, old-timer, old salt, old sea dog, shellback, got his ruptured duck.

EXTEMPORANEOUS adj. improv, ginned up, ad lib, winging it, fake, off the cuff, off the top of one's head, toss off, toss out; jamming, taking it for a ride, thinking out loud. See IMPROMPTU.

EXTEND v. string out, stretch out, drag out, run on, stall, drag one's feet, pad, put some rubber into it, googly. See EXPAND.

EXTENSION n. buildup, boost, hike, up, upping, stretch, pad.

EXTENSIVE adj. across-the-board, wall-to-wall, big-time, in a big way.

EXTENT n. elbowroom, leeway, room to swing a cat, here to hell and gone.

EXTERMINATE v. erase, rub out, stamp out, blow away, knock off, kiss off, send to kingdom come. See KILL.

EXTERMINATED adj. offed, gone, down the drain, dusted, finished, kaput, popped-off. See KILLED.

EXTINCT adj. dead and gone, had it, passed on, checked out, went, goner, done for, dead as a dodo, dead duck. See DEAD.

EXTINGUISH v. kill (lights, fire, or cigarette), choke, douse, knock down, stamp out.

EXTOL v. puff up, hats off to, rave, root, hear it for, brag about, give a bouquet, give a posy, hand it to, have to hand it to, stroke, push, boost, give a boost to. See PRAISE.

EXTORT v. 1. hold up, skin, sting, clip, soak, stick, bleed, fleece, ice, make one pay through the nose, put the shake on, put the arm on, shake down, pull one's leg. 2. worm out of one, worm something out of one, wring out. See ELICIT.

EXTORTION n. payoff, payola, drugola, gayola, pressure, protection, shakedown, shake, squeeze, squeeze rates, arm, badger, bite, cooptation, leg pulling.

EXTORTIONIST n. shakedown artist, shake man, shakester, grafter, leech, vulture, shark, bloodsucker, badger, horseman, leg-puller, in line (paying sums to).

EXTRA adj. perks, option, all the options, golden parachute, tin parachute (nonmanagement employee), golden handcuffs (deferred), button, goodies, gravy, hat, ice, PM, spiff (salesman), sweetener, tip, fuss, gingerbread, gewgaws, bells and whistles, padding, spare tire, fifth wheel, widow, gash, lagniappe. See also BENEFIT, GRATUITY.

EXTRACT v. pull out, drag out, yank.

EXTRA-DURABLE adj. double-duty, heavy metal.

EXTRA, FILM n. penguin (formal wear), atmosphere.

EXTRAMARITAL SEX n. affair, fling, playing around, getting some on the side, carrying on, tip-out, extracurricular activity, extracurricular relations. See ADULTERY.

EXTRAORDINARY adj. killer, gnarly, mega-gnarly, zero cool, aggro, wicked, drop dead ———, nose cone, flash, like wow, primo, boss, mongo, like dynamite, Jake, ginchy, slammin', fabu, fab, in orbit, cosmic, major, cranking, tough, heavy. See EXCELLENT.

EXTRASENSORY PERCEPTION n. ESP, sixth sense, gut feeling.

EXTRATERRESTRIAL n. alien, ET, saucerman, spaceman, man from Mars, Martian, little green man.

EXTRAVAGANCE n. frill, frills, egg in one's beer, living high on the hog, icing on the cake.

EXTRAVAGANT adj. posh, steep, stiff, plush, ritzy, swank, swanky, like money was goin' outta style, spreading it around, fancy, high, high on the hog, out-of-bounds, out-of-sight, first-cabin.

EXTREME adj. far out, way out, gone, worst-case scenario, bitchen, boss, bodacious, radical (not political), over the top, up the butt, up the ying-yang, nose cone, ape, crazy, fancy, glorkish, all out, go all out, all get out, all get up, hell of a, hell-fired, all-fired, in spades, ultra-ultra, flaming, out-of-bounds, out-of-sight, out-of-this-world, throw out the baby with the bath water, KO, kayo punch, the chips are down, last straw, the straw that broke the camel's back, too-too, too much, everything but the kitchen sink, like carrying coals to Newcastle, like teaching one's grandmother to suck eggs, till hell freezes over, chichi, frou-frou, cushy, spiffy, flossy, high, steep, stiff, the end, bitter end, bad news, the pits, the dogs, the least, bottom out, jump off the deep end, short end of the stick, number ten (Korean War), one thou, one thousand (Vietnam War).

EXTREMELY adv. totally, fucking, too much, plenty, big-time, stone (stone deaf), terribly, terrifically, almighty, powerful. See VERY.

EXTRICATE v. bail one out, get out from under, save one's ass, save one's bacon, save one's neck, let go, let off. See FREE.

EXTROVERT n. showboat, character, Flash Gordon.

EXUBERANCE n. bounce, piss and vinegar, zip, zap, pep, juice, go juice, bounce, sock, pepper, get-up-and-go.

EXUBERANT adj. bouncy, chipper, zingy, zippy, zappy, feeling one's oats, full of piss and vinegar. See SPIRITED.

EXULTANT adj. hopped-up, set-up, blow one's mind, flipping, flying, high, turned-on, wowed. See ECSTATIC.

EXULTATION n. charge, large charge, do a Rocky, up, upper, high, bang, fireworks. See EXCITEMENT.

EYE v. clap eyes on, lay eyes on, set eyes on, give the eye, give the once over, give the OO, give the double O, take in, glom, check out, size up. See SEE.

EYE, GLASS n. gravel eye.

EYEGLASSES n. cheaters, glims, lamps, makeup, four-eyes, shades, specs, goggles, windows, mini-specs, sus-specs, nippers, gogs, granny glasses, professor (wearer). See GLASSES.

EYELIDS n. shutters.

EYES n. peepers, peekers, baby blues, blinkers, blinders, lamps, cheaters, lights, headlights, deadlights, gagers, gleeps, glims, glimmers, eyeballs, bugeyes, googly eyes, banjo eyes, popeyes, swivel eyes, saucer eyes, cockeyes, wall eyes, pies, mince pies, pincers, shutters, slanters, spotters.

EYESORE n. sight, dump, blot on the landscape. See also UGLY.

F

F n. Foxtrot, Fox.

FABLE n. 1. yarn, megillah, old chestnut, old saw, old touches, old wives' tale. See STORY. 2. whopper, fib, bunk, for the birds, crock, claptrap, fish story, cock-and-bull story, fairy tale, hogwash. See LIE.

FABRICATE v. 1. fab, prefab, throw together, throw up, knock together, whomp up, cobble up, whip up, fudge together. 2. take it off the top of one's head, brainstorm, head trip, spark, spitball, cook up, dream up, think up, make up. 3. make like, let on like, jive, shuck and jive, maple stick jive, bull, shit, fudge, goof on, talk trash, signify. See LIE.

FABRICATION n. jive, line of jive, jazz, fib, bull, shit, crap, crock of shit, yarn, cock and bull, smoke, line, 180 out (Mil.), hogwash, song and dance. See LIE.

FABULOUS adj. fab, fabu, Jake, ginchy, slammin', sweet, killer, it's to die for, rad, way rad, aggro, glor, froody, 10, ten, A, A-1, A-number one, A-plus A-OK, okay, OK, ace, aces, ace high, ace of spades, in spades, def, daddy, dyno, mongo, bump'n', evil, super, supercolossal, super-duper, hooper-dooper, smashing, brutal, cranking, massive, rattling, rocking, gnarly, mega-gnarly, lampin', happenin', unreal, rat fuck, cool, zero cool, cold, turn-on, wicked, mind-blowing, mind-bending, gone, real gone, cosmic, key, major, frantic, out-of-this-world, out-of-sight, stand-out, stick-out, sticks out like a sore thumb, nose cone, gilt-edged, drooly, oochie, not half bad, stokin', tubular, vicious, wailing, whaling, dope on a rope, hype, stink, stone, stone groove, flash, splash, like wow, best ever, primo, crack, crackerjack, peacherino, peachy, ginger-peachy, peachy-keen, keen, salt of the earth, top, tops, topnotch, topflight, top drawer, top of the line, tiptop, first-class, first-chop, first-rate, star, boss, stunning, corking, corker, solid, solid sender, great, greatest, dozer, doozie, daisy, dilly, bo, boo, tickety-boo, deadly, deadly-boo, bong, sly, copacetic, kopasetic, the bee's knees, the cat's meow, the cat's whiskers, the cat's pajamas, the butterfly's book, the caterpillar's kimono, George, real George, down, good show, gear, golden, solid gold, hard, hummer, humdinger, high-cotton, knockout, mad, mess, mezz, nasty, nifty, the nuts, the nerts, ripping, ripsnorter, sanitary, heavenly, bang-up, fat, in fat city, in orbit, murder, neat, kicky, hunky-dory, all wool and a yard wide, jam-up, slap-up, but good, strictly, sweetheart, catch, find, plenty, zanzy, beautiful, cuspy, check-plus, stellar, dream, lollapaloosa, whiz, killer-diller, mean, ducky, hot, spiffy, ripping, nobby, delicious, scrumptious, not too shabby, one for the book, something, something else, something to brag about, something to shout about, something to

write home about, groove, in the groove, groovy, tidy, tits, tough, tuff, heavy, bad, evil, terrible, terrific, marvy, winner, choice, reet, a gas, gas up something, gasser, dynamite, far-out, funky, state-of-the-art, too much, the most, the utmost, swell, savage, wild, jumping, shirty, tawny, whale of a, world-beater, pip, pippen, lulu (often Derog.), darb, honey, beaut, heller, hell of a note, helluva, some (some show), this is some kinda ———, it's the berries, cracking, bully, sharp, wizard, the best, man-sized, like all-get-out, like mad, like gangbusters, the end.

FACADE n. front, false front, show, window dressing, put-on, fake, plastic, phony. See PRETENSION.

FACE n. kisser, puss, map, mug, pan, grill, smacker, mush, phiz, phizog, biscuit, clock, dial, conk, Chevy Chase, gills, index, mask, potato, squash, deadpan, poker face, sourpuss, pickle puss, sugar puss.

FACE v. run into, face off, square off, face down, face to face, face the music, jam up, not take it lying down, take it, take it on the chin, bite the bullet, brace, cross, fly in the face of, fly in the teeth of, straighten out, put one's life on the line, eyeball, eyeball to eyeball, meet eyeball to eyeball, stick it out, stick to one's guns, stand up and be counted, one to one, go one on one, mano a mano, get real, get a life, get a clue, for real, take on, take out, take one on, take one up on, call one's bluff, knock the chip off one's shoulder, make something out of, step over the line, have a bone to pick, make my day, go on make my day, tell off. See also BRAVE, OPPOSE.

FACE POWDER n. flour, paint, makeup.

FACE REALITY v. face it, get real, get a life, get a clue, get with the program.

FACET n. angle, twist, switch.

FACE TREATMENT n. face-lift, facial, nose job, hamburger (mixture).

FACILE adj. 1. flip, fast talk, fast talker, thick-slung, slick, slicker, silky, smooth, smoothie, old smoothie, smooth apple, smooth operator, smooth article, gift of gab. 2. easy as pie, nothing to it, pushover, picnic, easy make, turkey shoot, breeze, walkover, child's play. See EASY.

FACILITATE v. grease the wheels, run interference for, open doors, walk through, hand-carry.

FACSIMILE n. 1. fax, dupe, xerox, clone, carbon, carbon copy, mimeo, stat, repro, knock-off, flimsy. 2. look-alike, work-alike, ringer, dead ringer, copycat, spitting image, chip off the old block, double, peas in a pod, twin, ———— compatible (PC compatible).

FACT n. brass tacks, no shit, straight shit, the real deal (Af. Am.), how it is, like it is, bottom line, emess. See TRUTH.

FACTION n. combination, combo, click, crowd, circle, insiders, the boys, Old Boy network. See ASSOCIATION.

FACTOR n. fixin's, makin's, part and parcel, board, plug-in.

FACTORY n. shop, sweatshop, salt mines.

FACTS n. dope, inside dope, goods, info, scoop, poop, poop sheet, hot skinny, score, story, whole story, brass tacks, chapter and verse, the know, picture, lowdown, no shit, like it is, the emess, the numbers, the goods, bottom line, meat and potatoes, gospel, nitty-gritty, what's what, the straight stuff, skinny, facts of life, from the horse's mouth, cue, clue, cold turkey. See also INFORMATION.

FACTUAL adj. for real, honest-to-God, kosher, legit, on the legit, on the level, card-carrying, the lowdown, the emess, all wool and a yard wide, righteous, straight from the horse's mouth.

FACULTY n. the right stuff, dynamite, has what it takes, know one's way around, up to snuff, up to the mark, a pistol. See SKILL. See also PROFESSOR; TEACHER.

FAD n. in, in thing, kick, newest wrinkle, the latest thing, the last word, wrinkle. See RAGE.

FADDIST n. freak, groupie, buff, hound, crazies, frenzie, trendoid, great one for, sucker for. See DEVOTEE.

FADE v. fag out, poop out, tucker out, peter out, peg out, fold, come apart at the seams, die on the vine. See TIRE.

FAIL v. 1. goof, goof up, gum up, gum up the works, hash up, bobble, boot, blow, get raked, eat it, flub, flub the dub, bugger, boo-boo, bugger up, ball up, screw up, foul up, crumb, crumb up, slip up, louse up, bitch, bitch up, muck up, trip up, crack up, piss up, fuck up, break, dump, pump up (gambling), mess up, mess and a half, make a mess of, make a hash of, make a boner, make a boo-boo, muff, muff one's cue, miss one's cue, fluff one's lines, miss by a mile, miss the boat, foozle, pratfall, brodie, brown off, take the heat, cool, hold the bag, hold the sack, clutch the gunny, take the gas, bomb, get creamed, bite the big one, blow off (to appear), blow it, blow the gig, blow it big-time, get blown out, get creamed, get dogged, get used, eat one's lunch, drop the ball, draw a blank, step in it, put one's foot in one's mouth, put one's foot in it, die, die on the vine, die standing up, die on one's feet, be on one's last legs, have one foot in the grave, have one foot in the grave and the other on a banana peel, go west, roll over, roll over and play dead, croak; flunk, flunk out, flush, flush it flag (test or course); bust out (expelled), tap out, conk out, peter out, poop out, flake out, veg out, wash out, peg out, fizzle out, fizz out, fink

out, turkey out, bilge out, ace out, crash and burn (romance), drawing dead, drop a brick, drop the ball, stub one's toe, trip up, come apart at the seams, come out on the short end of the stick, go soft, get hung up, get out of whack, get out of kilter, get out of commission, go on the blink, go on the fritz, go kaput, go tits up, go kerplunk, go wrong, go blooey, go flooey, go sour, go phut, go haywire, go to pieces, go down in flames, go down the chute, go down the tube, tanking (on purpose), go into the tank, go belly up, turn belly up, take the count, take it, take it on the chin, land on one's ass, fall flat on one's ass, fall flat on one's face, fall down on the job, fall down and go boom, bite the dust, lick the dust, jim a deal, pull a boner, pull a boo-boo, pull a bloomer, pull a blooper, go over like a lead balloon, not hack it, not make it, not work, not come off, not make the grade, not fill the bill, not get to first base, never pass Go, have a bad go at, left at the post (lose from the start), lose out, meet one's Waterloo; have a coral sandwich, get sucked up the face (surfing); be on the skids, stiff, stumble, flummox, flag, flag it, gleek it, tube it, come a-cropper, cave in, cut no ice, curdle, blob. 2. belly up, go toes up, toes, go bust, go chapter 11, fold, fold up, go broke, get raked, tap out, boff out, crap out, be cleaned out, be taken to the cleaners, go to the cleaners, take the knock, lose big, drop, drop a bundle (money), hooked, go under, go up, go to the wall, close one's doors. See also WEAKEN.

FAILED adj. blown out, blown out of the water, down the drain, flop, dead pigeon, turkey, in the dumper, never passed Go. See UNSUCCESSFUL.

FAILURE n. 1. turkey, deadbeat, beat, bum, good-for-nothing, moocher, loafer, bringdown, foul ball, has-been, nonstarter, also-ran, scrub, loser, out of luck, out of it, lumpy, never-wuz, a nobody, fall guy, stiff, stifferoo, booby, defeatee, squid, domo (downwardly mobile), duck, dues payer, down-and-outer, can't even get arrested, can't even write home for money, can't punch his way out of a paper bag, flash in the pan, flunkee. 2. flop, flopperoo, bomb, blank, bloomer, roof fell in (sudden), shellacking, stinkeroo, fluke, flummox, flookum, clambake, false alarm, dud, disaster, abortion, not work, not come off, that dog won't hunt, flunk, flunk out, crap out, strike out, down the drain, down the chute, down-and-out, down the toilet, in the toilet, washout, washed out, washed up, nowhere, A for effort, near miss, no dice, no go, back to the drawing board, phftt, skids, on the skids, hit the skids, on the rocks, on the ropes, totaled, total wipe, wipe out, gutted, wasteland, should have stood in bed, go under, cropper, pratfall muss-up, piss-up, fuck-up, foul-up, snafu, putdown, comedown, down for the count, wet smack, misfire, draw a blank, header, in over one's head, in deep water, flat failure, dull thud, brodie, total loss, rack and ruin, blue ruin, foozle, lamo, stinker, lead balloon (idea went over like a lead balloon), lemon, fizzle, frost, bagel, botch, clunker, dog, enema, hash, jumble, pancake, turd, turkey. 3. belly up, toes up, toes, chapter 7, chapter 11, chapter 13, foldo, bust, broke.

FAINT adj. rocky, woozy.

FAINT v. black out, go out like a light, keel over, pass out, freak out, flicker (also pretend).

FAIR adj. 1. regular, open, up front, right up front, on the up and up, on the level, even-steven, cricket, dinkum, sport, fair-to-middling, fair shake, square, square deal, square john, square shooter, real people, saint, straight, straight stuff, straight arrow, straight dope, straight out, straight shooter, straight from the shoulder, white, damn white, Christian, what you see is what you get, call 'em as one sees 'em, honest Injun (Derog.), Boy Scout, down home, fly right, Mr. Clean, third-rail, strictly union, level playing field, Sammy Smith concept, Susie Smith concept. 2. beaut, looker, honey, dishy, number, peach, knockout, easy on the eyes, tall dark and handsome. See BEAUTIFUL.

FAIRBANKS, ALASKA n. Bearflanks.

FAIT ACCOMPLI adj. done deal, wired, all set, fixed.

FAITH n. stock, store.

FAITHFUL adj. true blue, true believer, oncer, string along with, dyed in the wool, behind one, on one's side, ace in, ace through, come through, stand up for one, faithful but not blind.

FAITHLESS adj. two-faced, two-timing, cheater, double-crossing, chippy on one, step out on one, doggin', tip, witch. See UNFAITHFUL.

FAKE n. phony, actor, four-flusher, pseud, pseudo, put-on, bogue, bogus, bunco, bunko, bum, plastic, junque. See also COUNTERFEIT, ACT.

FAKE v. dive, take a dive, tank, go in the tank, put on, put on an act. See also PRETEND.

FAKERY adv. put-on, scam, flam, flimflam, shell game, skin game, spoof, whitewash job, front, window dressing, jiggery-pokery.

FALL n. header, spill, dive, nose dive, pratfall, belly buster, belly flop, belly whopper.

FALL v. land on one's ass, tip over, keel over, take a header, take a dive, take a belly whopper, spill, hit the dirt, nose-dive, lose it, do a pratfall, fall down and go boom, belly up, come a-cropper, go ass over teakettle.

FALLACIOUS adj. off, way off, bum, fishy, jivey, sincere (sarcasm), phony, fakey. See DECEPTIVE.

FALSE adj. 1.bogue, bogus, bogosity, autobogophobia, bogotified, bum, bone (street talk), bent, phony, queer, falsie, fake, faked, hokey, ersatz, wrong, wrong number, fishy, frame, framed, plant; planted, flaked (evidence); crock, crock of shit, slick, sincere, not kosher, not what it's cracked up to be, pirate goods, pirate labels, dirty work, no such animal, out in left field, soft shell, it won't fly, lame, stiffing it, gil, Hollywood, reach-me-down. 2. shady, sharp,

two-faced, gyp, snide, crooked, crooked stick, cheatin' heart, doberman (Af. Am.). See DECEITFUL.

FALSEHOOD n. whopper, line of jive, fib, balls, yarn, story, cock-and-bull story, cover-up, line of cheese, 180 out (Mil.), hogwash. See LIE.

FALSE MODESTY n. shit kick.

FALSIFICATION n. whopper, bogosity, crock of shit, hooey, story, cock-and-bull story, baloney, cover-up, song and dance. See also LIE.

FALSIFIER n. jive ass, jive turkey, phony, conner, con artist, con man, con merchant, crap merchant, oil merchant, promoter, quack, spieler, bullshitter, bullshit artist.

FALSIFY v. put on an act, put on a false front, con, promote, fake it, blow smoke up one's ass, frame up, play, trip, phony up, pencil-whip (documentation), cook the books, four-flush, salt, salt a mine. See LIE.

FALTER v. hem and haw, drop the ball, bobble, fluff one's lines, stub one's toe, trip up, come a-cropper. See FLOUNDER.

FAMILIAR adj. tight, buddy-buddy, palsy-walsy, chummy, thick, thick as thieves. See INTIMATE. 2. plugged-in, tuned-in, fly, grounded, with it, savvy, chilly, go go, rings a bell, been there, latched on, in the know, know one's stuff, kept posted. See KNOWLEDGEABLE. 3. cheeky, fresh, brassy, smart-aleck. See INSOLENT.

FAMILIARITY n. hands trouble, hand troubles, Roman hands and Russian fingers, flip, fresh, sassy, smart, smart-alecky, smart-ass, wise-ass, biggety, cocky, cheeky, crusty, gally, nervy, out of line, brassy, bold as brass, feeler, cop a feel.

FAMILIARIZE v. 1. get together, get with it, get buddy-buddy, break the ice, mix, let down one's hair. 2. post, put one in the picture, let next to, put on to, tip off. See ADVISE.

FAMILY n. folks, home folks, kinfolks; P's, peeps, rents (parents); shirttail relatives, kissin' cousins, insiders, bunch, click, crew, crowd, crush, gang, mob, outfit, ring, rack, off the same rack. See also GROUP.

FAMISHED adj. starving, starved, starved to death, empty, fly light, grits time, have a tapeworm, munchies, (after marijuana use), dog-hungry, could eat a horse, could eat the asshole out of a bear.

FAMOUS adj. w.k. (well known), celeb, star, name, numero uno, face, right up there, big number, biggie, monster. See CELEBRITY.

FAN n. wannabee, groupie, skeezer (hip-hop), junkie, buff, bug, freak, crazies, nut, trendoid, punker (punk rock), B-boy, B-girl (rap music), head banger (heavy metal), frenzie, crank, culture vulture, fiend, flip, hound, rooter, booster, alligator, gate, gates, gator, cat, hep cat, prophet, stargazer, blue farouq, flunky, stooge, eager beaver, great one for, demon, sucker for, filbert, fool, boo-bird (boos at games).

FANATIC n. fiend, demon, fan, freak, crank, crazies, nut, frenzie, fool.

FANATICAL adj. high on, turned-on, eat this shit, nuts for, freaked-out, bugged, flipped, got a wild hair up one's ass, wig out. See ENTHUSIASTIC.

FANCIER n. great one for, sucker for, buff, fan, freak, bug, crank, hound, nut, filbert, junkie, culture vulture, fiend, demon. See DEVOTEE.

FANCIFUL adj. flaky, kinky, fantasmo, offbeat, floating, floating on clouds, on cloud seven, on cloud nine, pipe dream, play with oneself, jack off, pie in the sky, castles in the air, blue sky.

FANCY adj. chichi, froufrou, spinach (excessive), cushy, spiffy, flossy. See also ORNATE.

FANCY n. 1. bag, groove, thing, turned on to, flash, weakness for, cup of tea, druthers, type, fool's paradise, pipe dream, pie in the sky. 2. big eyes, eyes for, hard-on for, wide-on (Fem.), jones for, itch, hot pants, lech, sweet tooth, yen, zazzle. See DESIRE. See also LOVE.

FANCY v. 1. yen for, have the hots for, lech for, itch for, fall for, spoil for, gone on, groove on, mad for, wild for, crazy about, have it bad. See LOVE. 2. dream up, make up, spark, spitball, head trip, take it off the top of one's head, think up, trump up. See CREATE.

FANTASIZE v. trip out, head trip, build castles in the air, moon, pipe dream, woolgather.

FANTASTIC adj. unreal, fantasmo, seven-ply gasser, mega-gnarly, rat fuck, out-of-this-world, out-of-sight, like wow, best ever, primo, first-class, Jake, ginchy, slammin', fabu, cranking, the cat's meow, hummer, zanzy, delicious, far-out. See FABULOUS.

FANTASY n. trip, head trip, mind trip, castle in the air, stare into the middle distance, fool's paradise, Disneyland, pipe dream, pie in the sky.

FAR adj. B.F.E., butt fucking Egypt, B.F.A., butt fucking Africa, clear to hell and gone, to hell and gone, bit, way, ways, good ways, a good long walk, piece, far piece, fer piece, spitting distance, stone's throw, just down the road, a hop skip and jump, Sunday run, tidy step, whoop, two whoops and a holler, a hoot and a holler, a shlep, sleeper jump, long chalk, sticks, boondocks, boonies, tullies, on the dance floor but can't hear the band, jumping-off place, godforsaken place, God knows where, middle of nowhere, back of beyond, end of the rainbow, almost over the county line, you can't get there from here.

FARCE n. pratfall comedy, camp, high camp, low camp, in-one-door-and-out-another comedy.

FARCICAL adj. camp, campy, joky, joshing, yokky, gagged up, for grins, in-the-door-out-the-door.

FARE v. make out, handle.

FAREWELL interj. bye-bye, G.B., see ya, I'll be seeing ya, ciao, so long, hasta, hasta la pasta, 'sko (let's go), later, catch you later, later tater, check you, gotta slide, I'm history, I'm outta here, goodby-ee, have a nice day, toodle-oo, Abyssinia, keep the faith baby, peace. See GOOD-BYE.

FAREWELL n. swan song, eighty-eights. See PARTING.

FARGO, NORTH DAKOTA Little Twins.

FARM n. egg orchard.

FARMER n. hayseed, country boy, clodhopper, apple knocker, plow jockey, hillbilly, Arkie, Oakie, Clem, cob, clay eater (So.), shit kicker, clover kicker, rube, gully-jumper, hay rube, briar hopper, Bill Shears, dirty neck, dust raiser, hay shaker, swamp angel, backwoods jockey, seed, woohat (Georgia), John Farmer, Alvin, Clyde.

FART v. break wind, cut one, cut the cheese, leave one, let one fly, backfire, poot, nose-closer, the butler's revenge (silent). See ERUCT.

FASCINATE v. hook, send, wow, slay, bait, turn on, come on, vamp, knock dead. See ATTRACT.

FASCINATED adj. sold on, hooked, wowed, turned-on, sent, gone on, tickled pink, tickled to death, head over heels in, pleased as Punch.

FASCINATION n. thing for, bug, hang-up, grabber. See OBSESSION.

FASHION v. whomp up, cook up, dream up, throw up, fab, throw together, knock together, fudge together, ad lib.

FASHIONABLE adj. faddy, trendy, stylin', mean, cosmo, corporate (Bus.), bust fresh, a go-go, in, in thing, latest thing, last word, mod, now, happenin', the rage, up to speed, chic. See STYLE. See also NEW.

FASHION MODEL n. Shirley.

FASHION TRENDS n. trendy, faddy, a go-go, in thing, the last word, latest thing, bust fresh, happenin', new wrinkle, newest wrinkle.

FAST adj. hot, scream, screamin', balls out, quickie, sizzler, speedball, fly, pronto, snap, snappy, spanking, barreling, chop-chop, on the double, on the double-quick, double time, double clutchin', get the lead out, get moving, get a move on, get going, get cracking, get with it, get a wiggle on, hop to it, move your tail, move your fanny, pretty damned quick, PDQ, right off the bat, toot sweet, book, book it, whip through, hubba-hubba, in a jiffy, wham-bam, in nothing flat, in jig time, in two shakes of a lamb's tail, in two shakes, in half a shake, before one can say Jack Robinson, horseback, don't spare the horses, step on it, snap to it, make it snappy, shake a leg, stir your stumps, bag ass, haul ass, barrel ass, cut ass, drag ass, shag ass, high-ball, peel rubber, burn rubber, really rolling, lickety-split, lickety-cut, pour it on, speed boy, speed merchant, storm out, hell-bent, hell-bent for election, hell-for-leather, hell to split, break neck, neck-breaking, like a shot, like a shot out of hell, like a house on fire, like sixty, like fury, like sin, like mad, like crazy, like all-get-out, like a blue streak, like a streak of lightning, like greased lightning, like a big-assed bird, like a BAB, like a scared rabbit, like a bat out of hell, like shit through a goose, going like a raped ape, gone in a cloud of sour owl shit (WWII), to beat the band, to beat the devil, to beat the Dutch, to beat the deuce, good hands, quick on the draw, quick on the trigger, hair-trigger, pack the mail, A.S.A.P. (as soon as possible), thick and fast (in large numbers).

FASTEN v. button, anchor, nail, freeze to, stay put, tack on, slap on, tag, tag on, hook on, hook up, hitch on, hitch up, stick like a barnacle.

FASTENED adj. anchored, nailed, hitched-up, hooked-up, locked, locked-in, buttoned-up, buttoned-down.

FASTIDIOUS adj. picky, picky-picky, nitpicker, stickler, ace, comma counter, fussbudget, fusspot, fancy pants, fuddy-duddy, granny, old woman, old maid, pernickety, persnickety. See also PARTICULAR.

FAT adj. fat-assed, fats, fatso, fatty, fat city, fat stuff, chubby, chubbo, bloater, candidate for pigginess, slob, fat slob, roly-poly, full-figured, loaf, roll, jelly-belly, tub, tubby, tubster, tub of guts, tub of lard, lardo, lard-ass, lard-assed, lard bucket, gutbucket, pus gut, blubber guts, spare tire, rubber tire, Dunlop syndrome, beerbelly, corporation, bay window, oinker, porker, hog, cow, beef, beef trust, walrus, whale, bikini whale (girl), hippo, baby elephant, heavy, horse-heavy, heavy cream, hefty, hippy, hipsters, love handles (hips and thighs), thunder thighs, chunky, chunky trunks, pleasingly plump, blimp, blimp boat, pig boat, bulge, battle of the bulge, butterball, bagels, Mr. Five by Five, Crisco (fat person), broad in the beam, man mountain, Bertha, judy (girl), two-ton Tessie, tun, tun of flesh, meat, meat show, solid suet, corn-fed, built for comfort, zaftig, avoirdupois, look like ten pounds of shit in a five-pound bag.

FATE n. Karma, break, handwriting on the wall, in the lap of the gods, Lady Luck. See DESTINY. See also LUCK.

FATED adj. in the cards, que sera sera, the way the ball bounces, the way the cookie crumbles, the way the beads read, the handwriting on the wall, kiss of death.

FATHER n. old man, O.M., pop duke, dad, daddy, big daddy, daddio, daddums, pa, papa, pappy, pap, pop, pops, poppa, padre, pater, governor, guv, gaffer, warden, zoo daddy (divorced).

FATIGUE n. brain fag, burnout.

FATIGUE v. fizzle, fizzle out, fade, fold, dust, fag, fag out, poop, poop out, tucker, tucker out, burn out, knock out, peter out, conk out.

FATIGUED adj. bushed, hung, pooped, dusted, beat, wimped out, out of gas, burned out, blown out, creased, crispy, played out, flaked out, wore out, fagged, zonked, ass in a sling, beatsville. See TIRED.

FAULT n. 1. boner, muff, bug, glitch, gremlin, boo-boo, boggle, goof, louse-up, muck-up, crumb, crumb-up, miscue, typo, fox pass, blow card, zit, catch. See MISTAKE. See also BLEMISH. 2. warts and all.

FAULTFINDER n. bitcher, griper, whiner, crab, crank, pill, 'plainer, sorehead. See COMPLAINER.

FAULTLESS adj. on target, right on, 10, ten, four-o, in the groove, textbook, to a fare-you-well. See PERFECT.

FAULTY adj. a few bugs, glitch, gremlins, seconds, lemon, rank. See IMPERFECT.

FAUX PAS n. boo-boo, fox paw, fox pass, fuck-up, mess up, goof, flub, flop. See MISTAKE.

FAVOR v. flash, pro, for, for it, go for it, go for, buck for, root for, groove, back, on one's side, be serious, tilt towards, turned on to, take to, take a liking to, take a fancy to, take a shine to, cotton to, hipped on, keen about, have a thing about, have it for one, have eyes for, eat this shit. See also PREFER, LIKE.

FAVORABLE adj. okay, okey-dokey, OK, ok, go, rave, puffy (exaggerated), sitting pretty, sitting in the driver's seat, sitting in the catbird seat.

FAVORED adj. pet, fair-haired boy, golden-haired boy, white-haired boy, blue-eyed boy, sweetheart deal, asshole buddy.

FAVORITE n. 1. pet, teacher's pet, main, main man, fave, fair-haired boy, golden-haired boy, blue-eyed boy, candy boy, evergreen, golden oldie, number one boy, pratt boy, chalk, asshole buddy. 2. front runner, shoo-in.

FAWN v. stroke, snow, massage, jolly, oil, lay it on, play up to, butter up, schmeer, suck ass, fall all over, kowtow, buddy up, carpet-bag, curry below the knee.

FEAR n. goose bumps, creeps, cold creeps, cold shivers, cold feet, buck fever, jitters, willies, fidgets, flap, fuss, lather, needles, pins and needles, stew, to-do, zingers, worriment, all-overs, chicken out, pucker, pucker-assed, asshole puckerin', asshole suckin' wind, stage fright.

FEARFUL adj. yellow, have cold feet, run scared, scared spitless, scared shitless, shit green, brick, shit a brick, rabbity, mousy, wimpy, wet rag, wet sock, weak-kneed, nebbish, candy-ass, asshole-puckerin', gutless, shake in one's boots, ague, creeps, heebie-jeebies, heebies, leaping heebies, the jams, the jims, the jim-jams, the jimmies, jittery, jumpy, shaky, shivery, quivery, in crisis mode, have butterflies in one's stomach, in a cold sweat, in a sweat, uptight, hung up, clutch up, D and D (deaf and dumb, afraid to testify), punk out, on the ragged edge. See AFRAID.

FEARLESS adj. ballsy, guts, gutsy, gutty, guttiness, gutsiness, gritty, cujo, game, hairy, nervy, chutzpahdik, I'm shakin' (response to threat, sarcasm), spunky, bodacious, brassy, bold as brass, chit, cheeky, crust, gally, fire-eater, cool hand, iceman, ice in one's veins, tough it out, ain't scared of shit, pizzazz, spetters, salty, come on strong, crusty, cocky, cock stuck up, puffed-up, chesty, sure, sure as shit, smart, smart-ass, smart-alecky, wise-ass, wise-guy, hot-shot, whippersnapper, too big for one's britches, biggety, crack, wisecrack, flip, fresh, lippy, sassy, hell of a, hell of a note, got the faith baby, racked, gamble on. See also DARING.

FEASIBLE adj. no sweat, no biggie, cinch, snap, push-over, doable, piece of cake, biscuit, setup, breeze, duck soup, pie, easy as pie, easy as falling off a log, simple as ABC. See EASY.

FEAST n. big feed, blow, blowout, movable feast.

FEAT n. stunt, mitzvah (good). See also ACTION.

FEATURE n. slant, twist, gimmick, angle, gag. See also ARTICLE, CHARACTERISTIC.

FECES n. shit, crap, dump, caca, B.M., BM, number two, turd; doggy-do, cow chips, road apples, horse hockey. See BOWEL MOVEMENT.

FECES, ANIMAL n. horse apples, alley apples, golden apples, horse hockey, bird turd, cow plops, dingleberries, doggy-do, dreck, hockey, hookey, moose beans, moose nuggets, moose pecans.

FEDERAL AGENCY BOND n. Fannie Mae, Ginnie Mae, Freddie Mac.

FEDERAL AGENT n. fed, federal, F.B., fibbie, feeb, feeble, G-man, T-man, tax man, Sam, narc, revenuer, hard John.

FEDERAL BUREAU OF INVESTIGATION n. FBI, F.B.I., Feeb, feeble, feeby, feebee, FIB, fibbie, G-men, the Feds, Foley Square, hard John, big department, gazers, spooks, monkey, prohy, whiskers.

FEDERAL COMMUNICATIONS COMMISSION n. FCC, Charlie, Big Charlie, Uncle Charlie, Big Double C, Candy Man, Friendly Candy Company, Funny Candy Company.

FEDERAL EMERGENCY MANAGEMENT AGENCY n. FEMA, Fema.

FEDERAL HOME LOAN MORTGAGE CORPORATION n. Freddie Mac.

FEDERAL NATIONAL MORTGAGE ASSOCIATION n. Fannie Mae.

FEDERAL RESERVE BOARD n. the Fed.

FEDERATION n. family, bunch, crew, crowd, gang, mob, outfit, ring, hookup, tie-up, tie-in, syndication, pool, tribe. See ASSOCIATION.

FEE n. 1. commish, ante, bite, chunk, cut, end, juice, piece, piece of the action, rake-off, click charge (metered charge), share, skig, slice, a little slack, a little something to sweeten the pot. See also CHARGE. 2. take, take-in, gravy, handle.

FEEBLE adj. 1. rocky, woozy, dopey, wishy-washy, out of gas, don't have the horses. 2. draddy, paper tiger, weak sister, wimp, herb, squid, basket case, chicken, nobody, clown, eightball, zero. See WEAK.

FEEBLEMINDED adj. feeb, exceptional, dork, megadork, dorf, droid, ditzo, yo-yo, beau, lunchbox, lunchsack, vacant lot, Z-head, nerd, nurdy, dickhead, lop, loser, winner, full hank, Fred, Barney, Wilma, biff (girl), assface, asswipe, McFly, lorg, gump, lamebrain, fuck-brained, beanbrain, birdbrain, rattlebrain, rattleweed, nebbish, out to lunch, lunch, lunchie, out of it, punter (easily defrauded), a coupla quarts low, jel, nobody home, light's on but nobody's home, jerk, lowbrow, dodo, dummy, dumbo, dum-dum, dumb bill, dumb bunny, dumb cluck, dumb Dora, dumb head, dumb ox, dumbfuck, dumbshit, mungshit, four-letter man (dumb), one doughnut shy of a dozen, elevator doesn't run to the top floor, a low-watt bulb, a few sandwiches short of picnic, one sandwich short of a picnic, belt does not go through all the loops, doesn't have both oars in the water, bonetop, boob, birk, box, oofus, twillie, ninny, nincompoop, Gumbyhead, algae head, air-head, bubblehead, balloonhead, meathead, musclehead, blockhead, pointyhead, buckethead, bullhead, bumhead, butthead, bananahead, squarehead, mushhead, cementhead, pumpkinhead, saphead, lunkhead, mutton-head, fathead, bonehead, knucklehead, shithead, doughhead, hammerhead, jughead, blubberhead, cheesehead, chickenhead chucklehead, mallethead, lardhead, peahead, pinhead, puddinghead, woodenhead, dunderhead, blunderhead, chowderhead, cabbagehead, potatohead, deadhead, flathead, rubblehead, rockhead, numbskull, numb-nut, numb-headed, numb-brained, knows from nothing, doesn't know from nothing, doesn't know the time of day, doesn't know from A to B, doesn't know A from izzard, doesn't know which way is up, doesn't know from straight up, doesn't know enough to come in out of the rain, dead-ass, gink, turkey, stupe, thick, loogan, schlemiel, schlamozzle, schlump, schlub, schmendrick, shmoe, schnook, schmuck, clod-pated, deadneck, dildo, dill, droop, dud, Elmer, gasser, gonus, good fellow, goofus, goofball, goon, goopus, got a hole in the head, jackass, knuckle, bloke, captain of the head, soft in the head, half-baked, nuthin' upstairs, boob, sap, mess, mutt, muttontop, meat mope, weak in the upper story, simp, lead-footed, marble dome, newt, dim-wit, nit-wit, nougat, one-eye, chump, clam, clock, cluck, cluckhead, clunk, dopey, dunce, dodunk, dub, fish, flub.

FEED v.   scarf, scoff, narf, trough out, grease one's chops, grease down, hoover, grind, munch out, nibble, snack, peck, pig out, fling a fang, feed one's face, tie on the feedbag, put on the feedbag. See EAT.

FEEL v.   1. be turned on to, feel in one's bones, feel in one's guts, have a funny feeling, have heart, have a hunch, have good vibes, have vibes, get vibes, get in touch, know where one is coming from. 2. frisk, feel up, put the feelers on one or something, grab ass.

FEELING n.   gut reaction, feel stuff, vibes, funky, emote, emoting (simulation), feel in one's bones, have a funny feeling, have a hunch, full up, get one's gage up, give out, where one is at, where one lives, shook, shook up, all torn up, all tore up, all shook up, fall apart, frantic, simpatico.

FEET n.   dogs, barking dogs (sore), bow-wows, tootsies, crunchers, tugboats, gunboats, canal boats, gondolas, canoes, clodhoppers, earth pads, flats, hocks, hoofs, hounds, pads, pups, barkers, boots, submarines, plates, platters, stompers, trotters, frito toes (smelly).

FEIGN v.   stonewall, put on, put on an act, put up a front, fake it, do a bit, blow smoke, phony up, put up a bluff, four-flush, play possum, salt a mine; wigger, poser, yo-boy (affect black mannerisms and speech). See PRETEND.

FEIGNED adj.   fake, faked, plastic, phony. See also COUNTERFEIT.

FEINT n.   stutter step, okey-doke, deek, juke.

FEINT v.   deek, juke, fish, flicker, hang one out to dry, shake and bake, stutter-step, put one in the cookie jar, sucker one, fake out, fake one out. See also PRETEND.

FELINE n.   puss, pussy, pussycat, kitty, kitty cat, Chessy cat, coon cat, meow-meow.

FELLATIO, PERFORM v.   suck, suck off, cocksuck, sucky-suck, scumsuck, blow, blow job, give one a perm, go down on, pearl-dive, head, give head, give cone, deep throat, talk to the mike, around the world, perform, give a knobber; give skull, slob the knob (Af. Am.); a shot upstairs, sixty-nine, bucket head, milk mouth, cannibal (one who performs), bananas and cream, French, French job, gobble, dickie lick, penilingism, peter puff, play the skin flute, cop a joint (all Obsc.).

FELLOW n.   dude, guy, hunk, beauhunk, tuna, Clydesdale (attractive), hoss (muscular), industrial, beefcake, man,

feller, pops, daddy, mac, stud, stallion, john, meat, boyo, boychick, punk, brother. See MAN.

FELON n.   yardbird, vic, ex-con, stir bird, brig rat, chain gang, fish, fresh one (new), jailbird, beast (sex offender), new blood, jice, new jice, lane, lifer, rock crusher, short, two-time loser, four-time loser. See also CRIMINAL.

FEMALE n.   mama, old woman, old lady (girl friend), broad, dame, filly, skirt, frail, tomato, tuna, duchess, she-stuff, he she, chichi, femme, fox, stone fox, 10, ten, dyno, beaut, beauty, my beauty, pinup, cheesecake, cupcake, cutie, squash blossom, babe, wren, jill, sis, kid, hell-cat, battle-ax, heifer, old bat, twat, piece. See WOMAN.

FEMININE adj.   twisty, she-stuff, chick.

FEMINISM n.   women's lib.

FEMINIST n.   libber, women's libber, bra burner (Derog.).

FENCE n.   swagman, swagsman.

FENTANYL n.   fen, China white.

FERMENT n.   stir, fuss, row, to-do, commo, dustup, flap, fuzzbuzzy, scene, hell broke loose, rhubarb, stink, rumble, fofarraw, foofooraw. See TURMOIL.

FERRET n.   monk.

FERRET OUT v.   smell out, nose out, smoke out, pick up on, be on to, have dead to rights.

FERRIS WHEEL n.   chump heister.

FERTILIZER n.   shit, bullshit, horseshit, batshit, cowshit, lawn dressing, buffalo chips, cow chips, cow flops, cow pats, golden apples, alley apples, road apples, turd.

FERVENT adj.   hot, hot for, hot to go, hot to trot, gung-ho, hopped up, go great guns, creaming to, full on, about to piss in one's pants, fall all over oneself, not let any grass grow under one's feet, ready for Freddie, dying to, gotta have. See also ENTHUSIASTIC.

FERVOR n.   jazz, oomph, pep talk, hot pants, weakness, turn-on. See also LOVE.

FESTIVE adj.   jumping, juiced up full, go-go, grooving, swinging, rocking, jazzed, upbeat, chipper, chirpy, perky, peppy, zippy, zingy, zappy, snappy, bouncy. See also HAPPY.

FESTIVITY n.   bash, clambake, shindig, blowout, shindy, hoopla, jamboree, whoopee, whooper-dooper, wingding, whinding, finger pop, do. See PARTY. See also REVEL.

FETCH v.   lug, pack, ride, piggyback, shlep, shlep along, tote, truck, back, birdie-back, buck, gun, heel, hump, jag, shoulder.

FIGURE   161

FETID adj.   lousy, rotten, stinking, gooky, stinko, stinky, strong, high, whiffy, nosy, gross, grody, pukey, pukoid, icky, yechy, yucky. See also FOUL.

FETTER v.   cuff, hang up, hog-tie, hold up, throw a monkey wrench into the works, drag one's foot. See HINDER.

FETTERS n.   darbies, derbies, cuffs, clinkers.

FEVER n.   the shakes, burning up, on fire, running a temperature.

FEVERISH adj.   1. burning up, the shakes, on fire, running a temperature. 2. driven, hyper, unglued, unzipped, unscrewed, hot, wired, keyed-up, fired-up, in a sweat, like crazy, like mad, mind-blowing. See EXCITED.

FEW n.   slim pickings. See also AMOUNT, SMALL.

FIANCÉ(E) n.   old lady, old man; bird, donah, donar; intended, steady, going steady, pinned, future.

FIASCO n.   flop, flopperoo, bomb, bobble, bonehead play, bonehead trick, boob stunt, dud, disaster, trouble in River City, mess, Edsel, abortion, tar baby, should have stood in bed, dumb thing to do, dumb trick. See FAILURE.

FIB n.   line of jive, jazz, bunk, bull, bullshit, BS, bullchitna (Esk.), horse hocky, shit for the birds, crock, yarn, story, fairy tale, spinach. See LIE.

FIB v.   jive, shuck and jive, shovel the shit, promote, plant, goof on, talk trash, tell a little white lie, speak with forked tongue. See LIE.

FIBBER n.   jive-ass, phony, con artist, promoter, quack, spieler. See LIAR.

FICKLE adj.   yo-yo, two-timer, double-crossing, cheat, cheat on, sneakin' deacon, witch. See UNFAITHFUL.

FICTION n.   1. yarn, book, clothesline, cliff-hanger, bodice-ripper (romance), splatterpunk (violent, lurid), potboiler, spyboiler, toughtec (mystery), old wives' tale. See STORY. 2. whopper, jazz, fib, shit, bullshit, BS, bullchitna (Esk.), bullskating (Af. Am.), crap, crock of shit, hooey, tall story, fish story, banana oil, smoke, 180 out (Mil.), terminological inexactitude. See LIE.

FICTITIOUS adj.   fake, faked, falsie, bogus, hyped-up, plastic, phony, queer, no such animal, made out of whole cloth.

FIDGETS n.   ants, ants in one's pants, antsy, antsy-pantsy, fantods.

FIDGETY adj.   jittery, jumpy, pissin', shittin', hyper, spooked, nervous wreck, wired-up, yantsy, antsy, antsy-pantsy, ants in one's pants, basket case, up the wall, on pins and needles, jumpy as a cat on a hot tin roof. See ANXIOUS.

FIELD n.   bag, cup of tea, strong suit, long suit, thing, weakness, racket. See OCCUPATION.

FIEND n.   hellion, hell-cat, little devil. See DEVIL.

FIERCE adj.   kill-crazy, blow-top, flipped, ape, gone ape, got a wild hair up one's ass, hitting out in all directions. See VIOLENT.

FIFTY CENTS n.   four bits, half a buck, half a rock, silver wing.

FIFTY DOLLARS n.   half a C, half a yard, half a bill, half bill.

FIFTY-FIVE MILES PER HOUR doing the fifty-five, double buffalo, double nickel, five-five, honest numbers, pair of fives, pair of nickels, holding in the reins, on the peg.

FIGHT v.   squab, brawl, pluggin', scruff-up, brannigan, brush, brush-off, rumble, roughhouse, dance, donnybrook, flap, gin, hassle, jihad, hey rube, rhubarb, hoedown, jump, mix-up, one-two, the old one-two, punch out, duke out, jackpot, jam, run-in, swindle, battle royal, go, a go at each other, knuckle buster, knuckle duster, rowdydow, rowdy-dowdy, row, rumpus, ruction, ruckus, stew, shindy, set-to, scrap, dustup, knockdown and drag-out, bone of contention, bone to pick, fuss, wrangle, beef, blowup, spat, tiff, words, romp, foofaraw, free-for-all, hell broke loose, raise Cain, raise sand, shivaree, socdolager, when push comes to shove. See also ARGUMENT, RIOT, BOXING.

FIGHT n.   buck, brawl, hassle, scrap, row, kick up a row, come out swinging, roughhouse, romp, slug, put the slug on one, blindside, smack, shuffle, give one a fat lip, put up a fight, put on the gloves, go a couple of rounds, mano a mano, take on, take one on, take a poke, tangle, tangle with, tangle ass with, bump heads with, bump titties, cross swords with, lock horns with, hook up with, knuckle up, knuckle with, shoot it out with, fly in the face of, fly in the teeth of, stand up to, set to, have at it, go toe to toe, go after each other, go up against, be agin, nix, bang heads, break the news (police), break it up, beat up, beat down, mix it up, knock one's brains out, duke, duke it out, put up one's dukes, open up, square up, square off, pitch a bitch, pitch into, sail into, light into, lay into, lay for one, sweat it, tummel, raise sand, pettifog, put up an argument, break with, you got four feet? (invitation to fight).

FIGHTER n.   mug, pug, lug, palooka, heavy, slugger, fancy Dan, punching bag, cauliflower ear, tanker, plug. See PRIZEFIGHTER.

FIGHT FOR v.   go to the wall, go to the mat, go after it. See also ATTEMPT.

FIGURE n.   shape, build, built, built like a brick shit-house, bod, chassis, classy chassis, classy chassy, frame, V-man.

FIGURE v.   tote, tote up, tot, tot up, keep tab, keep tabs, dope out, figure in, figure out, take account of, count heads, count noses, cut ice, cut some ice, run down, work out, get out the sharp pencil.

FIGUREHEAD n.   front, front man, stooge, straw boss, straw man, Charlie McCarthy, dummy.

FILAMENT n.   string.

FILCH v.   boost, hustle, scrounge, swipe, snitch, promote, appropriate, liberate, graze (steal and eat food in a supermarket), palm, bag, nick, rough off, snipe. See STEAL.

FILE n.   charts, shitlist, S list, crap list, sucker list, enemies list, hit list (punished or ostracized), briar. See DIRECTORY, DOSSIER.

FILIBUSTER n.   talkathon.

FILIPINO n.   goo-goo, gugu, gook, flip (WWII), moke (all Derog.).

FILL v.   jam, jam-pack, pack 'em in, pack like sardines, sardine, stuff, top, top off, paper (The.).

FILLED adj.   1. packed, jammed, jam-packed, packed like sardines, sardined, full up. 2. full house, fanny-bumper, filled to the rafters, standing room only, SRO, sold out; clean, gone clean (The.). 3. stuffed, stuffed to the gills, topped off, lousy with, crumbed up with, crummy with, stiff with, swagged up with, up to here, fit to bust, full as a tick.

FILM n.   flick, flickie, movie, talkie, remake, footage, rushes, dailies; porno flick, skin flick, nudie, beaver flick, fuck film (Obsc.); slasher flick, slice and dice (horror); chop socky (karate and kung fu), snuff film. See MOTION PICTURE.

FILM v.   lens, roll, shoot, turn, can, put in the can (complete).

FILM CREW n.   behind the camera, backlot, stagehands, gaffer, juicer, grip, best boy, props, dresser, lenser.

FILM DIRECTOR n.   megger, helmer, A.D. (Ass't.).

FILM EXTRA n.   penguin, number one (owns own dress suit), atmosphere.

FILM FESTIVAL n.   filmfest, expo.

FILM OPENING n.   preem, premiere, bow, opener, break in, first run, first round, first outing, first inning, getaway, unloading, unspooling.

FILM PRODUCTION n.   package, venture, project, deal.

FILM SHOWING n.   screening, unspooling, sneak (unscheduled test preview).

FILM TERMS   roll, roll 'em (go), cut (stop), track, truck, dolly (move), pan (move across), loosen (move camera back), tighten (move closer), zoom back (increase lens angle), zoom in (decrease lens angle), take, wrap, closeup, full shot, long shot, establishing shot, two-shot, over the shoulder, reverse angle, fade-in, fade-out, on location, cover (alternate plans), footage, dailies, rushes, key light, footage. See also MOTION PICTURE.

FILTH n.   scuz, smut, sleaze, dreck, crud.

FILTHY adj.   cruddy, crumb, crummy, crusty, grungy, scrungy, yecchy, scuzzy, sleazy. See DIRTY.

FINAL adj.   bottom-line, and that was all she wrote, curtains, curtains for, what you see is what you get, last hurrah, swan song, ass end, the end, bitter end. See ULTIMATE.

FINALE n.   closer, closing, when the fat lady sings, chaser, end piece, afterpiece, blow-off, button (last note of a musical), payoff, swan song. See also END.

FINALIZE v.   ice, put on ice, clinch, clinch the deal, tape. See CONSUMMATE.

FINALLY adv.   already, it's about time, long time coming.

FINANCE v.   angel, bankroll, grubstake, stake, back, greenback, juice, pick up the check, pick up the tab, knock (Af. Am.), lay on one, loan-shark, piece one off, prime the pump, go for, plow back into. See also GIVE.

FINANCEABLE adj.   bankable (film, business, etc.).

FINANCIAL ANALYST n.   numbers cruncher, bean counter, quant, quan.

FINANCIAL ASSISTANCE n.   bailout.

FINANCIAL DISTRICTS n.   Wall Street, the Street, the Curb, LaSalle Street, Threadneedle Street (London), the Bourse (Paris).

FINANCIAL TERMS   ITC (investment tax credit), takeover (merger); takeover artist, raider, slash-and-burn guys, bust-up artist, turnaround artist, bottom fisher (those dealing in junk bonds), ten-bagger (making ten times the investment), LBO (leveraged buyout), TBO (turnaround buyout), PIGs (passive income generators); white knight, white squire (friendly bidder in a takeover), gray knight (opportunistic second bidder); greenshoe, target (a vulnerable company), street sweep (buys entire block), porcupine provision (discourages takeover), shark (unfriendly financier forcing takeovers), smoking gun (error by a shark permitting the target to escape through an antitrust ruling); shark repellent, poison pill (takeover defense strategy), porcupine provisions (legal deterrents), feemail (legal fees), scorched earth (antitakeover measure), tin parachute (guarantees to employees in takeover), Pac-Man defense, Pac-Man counterattack, people pill, monkey points (net percentage), sweetener (added incentive), red herring (financial statement), straddle (put and call), tombstone (advertisement), zero out (not paying taxes); flipper, dolphin (buys new issue and sells as price rises), vulture fund (buys troubled companies for profit later), triple witching hour, megadink (young bankers).

FINANCIER n. the money, the bank, the bankroll, angel, backer, sponsor, fat cat, tycoon, butter-and-egg man, baron, robber baron, the one who signs the checks, meal ticket, sugar daddy, lady bountiful, fairy godmother, Santa Claus, stakeman, staker, grubstaker. See also BUSINESSMAN.

FIND v. hit upon, see the light, stumble on, collar, corral, smoke out, trip over, right under one's nose, dig up, uncover, strike (oil, gold). See DISCOVER.

FIND FAULT v. lint-pick, nit-pick, pick apart, henpeck, blow the whistle on, cap on, lay a bad trip on one, rap, bitch bitch bitch, peg, rip, bad-mouth, poor-mouth, trash, find the smoking gun. See CRITICIZE.

FINE adj. sweet, killer, aces, mean, gnarly, unreal, tasty, bump'n', cool, lampin', happenin', wicked, gilt-edged, crack, solid, great, cranking, hummer, neato, mean, spiffy, not too shabby. See EXCELLENT.

FINE n. rip.

FINE v. slap with a fine, hit with a fine, walk off fifteen yards, pay through the nose, throw the book at one, dock. See also SENTENCE.

FINESSE n. know-how, savvy, gamesmanship, one-upmanship, gimmick, grift, racket, con, runaround, the big stick.

FINESSE v. yank one, angle, finagle, faniggle, jockey, play games, pull strings, pull wires, operate, rig, wangle, wire-pull.

FINEST adj. killer, number one, world-class, greatest, hundred-proof, baaaadest, coolsville, all-time, master (Af. Am.), tops. See BEST. See also EXCELLENT.

FINGER n. feeler, claw, fang (musician), forks, hooks, fish hooks, lunch hooks, meat hooks, pinkie, poppers, stealers.

FINGERPRINT n. calling card, dab, print.

FINGERPRINT v. print.

FINICKY adj. choosy, comma counter, nitpicker, picky, picky-picky, ticky, stickler, fussbudget, fusspot, fuddyduddy, granny, old woman, old maid, pernickety, persnickety. See also PARTICULAR.

FINISH n. wrap, wrap-up, curtain, curtains, end of the line, when the balloon goes up, and that was all she wrote. See END.

FINISH v. wrap, wrap up, wrap it up, bag it, nuke, scrub, scrag, scratch, fold, fold up, wind up, break it up, mop up, round up, sew up, clinch, let up, cool it, tie it up, hang it up, tape, break the tape, shutter, close, close up, wipe up, wipe out, wash out, punch out, close out, close down, shut down, shoot down, shoot down in flames, wind down, ring down, drop, drop and go (dockworker use), drop the curtain, pull the pin, pull the plug, pull the big one, drop it, hold it, nip,

nip in the bud, put the lid on, kick, shake, cap, can, can it, cut, cut the shit, cut the crap, cut loose, cut it out, cut off, cut off one's water, turn off one's water, lay off, blow off, blow over, blow the whistle on, kiss off, sign off, zap, break off, break it off, break it up, call off, call all bets off, call it a day, call it quits, flag one, cold turkey, leave off, finish off, polish off, knock off, knock it off, turn it off, come off, come off it, come to a screeching halt, come to a screaming halt, come to a grinding halt, come to a shuddering halt, button up, clean up, slough a joint, wrap a joint up, get it under one's belt, get on the wagon, head for the barn, home-free, in the home stretch, see daylight, see the light at the end of the tunnel, chuck it, pack it in, roll in, put to bed, put the finisher on, put the kibosh on, put a cork in it, put on the brakes, drop anchor, kayo, KO, kill, be in at the kill, tune out, peter out, go the distance, go the route, that's all there is there ain't no more, deal coming down, jell, send one south, get down to the short strokes.

FINISHED adj. a wrap, wrapped-up, set, all set, fini, finished-up, wound-up, washed-up, buttoned-up, mopped-up, cleaned-up, tied-up, that's history, cashed, to a T, to a finish, to a frazzle, done to a T, done to a finish, done to a frazzle, done with, home, home-free, almost home (nearly), in the bag, nailed-down, on ice, open-and-shut, shot, wiped-out, under one's belt, all over but the shouting, you can turn off the lights, pow, pfft, kaput, signed sealed and delivered, when the fat lady sings, when the balloon goes up, yesterday's news.

FIRE n. rapid oxidation, up in smoke, hot spot, crown fire (treetop), fire running (spreading rapidly), bean pot (kitchen), build a parking lot (building burns to the ground).

FIRE v. can, kick out, lay off, hand one his walking papers, sack, give the bum's rush, pink slip, downsize, payroll adjustment, released resources, reshaping, rif (reduction in force), give the gate, cut loose (dockworker use), let one go. See DISCHARGE.

FIREARM n. blaster, piece, iron, rod, jammy (Af. Am.), snub nose, Saturday night special, equalizer, difference, speaker, persuader, convincer, hardware, tool, widow maker, zip gun, gat, six-shooter. See GUN.

FIRE AT v. blast, gun, zap, hemstitch (machine gun), grease, hose down (automatic fire), trigger, pull the trigger, squeeze one off, open up, shoot 'em up, let go with, let fly, throw lead, trade lead, turn on the heat, pop at, take a pop at, turkey shoot (from a helicopter in Vietnam), drop the hammer, fog away, bang away, give 'em both barrels, beat to the draw, get the drop on.

FIRECRACKER n. cherry bomb, dago bomb (Derog.), golf ball, squib, China cracker (Obs.), golf ball, torpedo.

FIRED adj. canned, laid off, written off, bounced, axed, pink-slipped, got the ax, got the gate, selected out. See DISCHARGED.

FIREFIGHTER n. fire-eater, smoke-eater, smoke jumper (airborne firefighter), winkie (volunteer), bakehead (R.R.), hazmaniac (handles hazardous materials), robomedic (paramedic), tillerator (tillerman who causes accident).

FIREFIGHTING TERMS blow up (sudden increase in fire intensity), cover (any vegetative material), crown fire (treetop), fire running (rapidly spreading), hot spot (particularly active area), mop-up, slash (debris left after logging or brush cutting).

FIRE HOSE n. spaghetti.

FIREMAN n. smoke-eater, fire-eater, winkie (volunteer), bakehead (R.R.).

FIRE STATION n. snake den.

FIRM adj. hang tough, set, dead set on, hard-nosed, stand-pat, set in concrete, Rock of Gibraltar, Rock of Gib. See STUBBORN.

FIRM n. megacorp, multinational, plunderbund, bunch, crew, crowd, gang, mob, outfit, ring. See also CORPORATION.

FIRMAMENT n. lid, the blue, the wild blue yonder.

FIRST adj. numero uno, number one, primo, A-number one, lead-off, first-off, first-class, top of the class, top of the list, at the head of the line, right up front, right off the bat.

FIRSTHAND adj. right from the horse's mouth, straight from the horse's mouth.

FISH n. bonehead (bonita), 'chovy, boils (school of anchovy), 'cuda (barracuda), dog (sea lion), flatties, barn doors (halibut), sandies (sand bass), tommy, tomcod, Malibu trout (croaker).

FISHING TERMS gig (spear), cattle boat (party-fishing), iron (metal lure).

FIST n. duke, dukes, grabbers, hams, paws, bunch of fives, bunch of knuckles, knuckle sandwich, lily whites, mitts, five-ouncers, club, deuce of clubs.

FIT adj. wrapped tight, click, fit as a fiddle, crunchy granola, up to snuff, up to the mark. See WELL. See also ABLE.

FIT n. blow, blow a fuse, blow a gasket, blow one's top, blow one's topper, blow one's stack, go ballistic, shit hemorrhage, wingding, cat fit, conniption, conniption fit, duck fit. See FRENZY.

FITFULLY adv. by bits and pieces, by fits and starts, in dribs and drabs, hit or miss, herky-jerky, right and left. See ERRATICALLY.

FITTING adj. on the button, on the nose, just what the doctor ordered, right on, that's the idea, that's the ticket. See also SUITABLE.

FIVE CENTS n. fish scale, buffalo, nickel, blip, flat.

FIVE DOLLARS n. fin, five, fiver, five case-note, five-spot, finif, pound, Abe, Lincoln.

FIVE HUNDRED DOLLARS n. D, five centuries, five C's, half a G, half a grand, small nickel.

FIVE THOUSAND DOLLARS n. big nickel, five grand, five dollars.

FIX v. 1. fix up, doctor, fiddle with, face-lift, retread, debug, red-line (Mil.). See also RESTORE. 2. freeze to, stay put, stick like a barnacle, anchor, nail down, put it in concrete.

FIXATION n. hang-up, have a thing about, have on the brain, tiger by the tail, bug up one's ass; case, crush (Rom.); chuck habit, chuck horrors (prison food). See OBSESSION.

FIXED adj. anchored, nailed, locked, locked-in, hitched-up, hooked-up.

FIXER n. doctor, little Miss Fixit, Mr. Fixit, trouble man, troubleshooter, efficiency expert.

FLABBERGASTED adj. blown away, put away, bowled down, bowled over, struck all of a heap, thrown off one's beam ends. See ASTONISHED.

FLABBY adj. soft, out of condition, out of shape, not what one used to be, run to seed, gone to seed, rusty, good and flabby.

FLAG n. Maggie's drawers, Old Glory, red white and blue, Stars and Stripes, Star-Spangled Banner, old Betsy, Jolly Roger, Stars and Bars (Confederate), screamer, monkey flag (Mil.), rag (semaphore), white (surrender), red (danger).

FLAGELLATION n. fladge.

FLAG, FOREIGN n. Maple Leaf (Canada), Tricolor (France), Meatball (Japan), Union Jack (Great Britain).

FLAGRANT adj. flashy, flaming, gross, grody, grody to the max, hanging out, hot shot, spot one like a lead dime, stick out like a sore thumb. See also CONSPICUOUS, GAUDY.

FLAIR n. pizzazz, dash, zip, glamour, presence, splash, splurge, have a bump for, have plenty on the ball, have something on the ball, shine at, shine in. See TALENTED.

FLAMBOYANT adj. flashy, flaky, jazzy, glamorous, gassy, highfalutin, purple, windy, sporting, sporty. See GAUDY.

FLAME n. rapid oxidation.

FLASHLIGHT n. flash, bull's eye, dimmer, glim, shiner.

FLAT adj. draggy, blah, dull as dishwater, ho-hum, vanilla, white bread, flat as a pancake, leaves one cold, go over like a lead balloon, lay an egg, bombed. See INSIPID.

FLAT n. condo, co-op, crash pad, dommy, pad, joint, walk-up, go-down (basement), place to lay your head and a few friends. See APARTMENT.

FLATTER v. stroke, snow, massage, massage one's ego, soft-soap, simonize, con, jolly, oil, dooze, blow smoke up one's ass, spread it on, lay it on, lay it on thick, lay it on with a trowel, get around, get next to, play up to, shine up to, make up to, act up to, butter up, soften up, schmeikle (Yid.), sweeten up, sweet talk, loud talk, dialogue one, honey, schmear, rub the right way, work on, work over; brown-nose, suck around, suck up to, suck off, suck ass, kiss butt, kiss ass, ass sucker, ass wipe, butt wipe, lick ass (Obsc.); bootlick, boost, pat on the back, build up, toss a bouquet, give a posy, give the man a big cigar, gold star, have to hand it to one, puff up, trade last, TL, blarney, buzz, charm, buck, contract, cream, bag-play, hand one a line, shoot a line, shoot the crap, shoot the bull, sling the bull, sling it, sell, shit, bullshit, pull one's leg, overdo it, string along, kid along, stooge, yes, be a yes man, fall over, fall all over, fish, play footsie, footsie-wootsie, footsie-footsie, handshake, heel, play Mr. Nice Guy, politic, run after, polish the apple, apple-polish, kowtow, caboodle, buddy up, carpet-bag, curry below the knee.

FLATTERER n. A.K., ass-kisser, ass-licker, brown-noser, fart sniffer, yes-man, simonizer, suck off, ear banger. See SYCOPHANT.

FLATTERY n. snow, snow job, stroke, strokes, jive, smoke, baked wind, a line, drip, abreaction route, hogwash, goo, hoke, hokum, hoky-poky, attaboy, bouquet, posy, shot in the arm, shot in the ass, trade last, TL, sweet talk, sweet nothings, eyewash, soap, soft soap, butter salve, grease, bullshit, con, short con, sell, build up, crap, schmear, promote, baloney, blarney, bunk, bunko, bunkum, shit, applesauce, balloon juice, oil, snake oil, banana oil, honey, horse feathers, hot air, malarkey.

FLAT TIRE n. blowout, flat, puncture.

FLATULENT adj. farty, fart blossom, barking spiders (audible fart), kweef (vaginal), gassy, windy, nose closer.

FLAUNT v. flash, sport, grandstand, showcase, streak, let it all hang out, roll out, trot out, break out, whip out, show off, show and tell, hot-dog, fan it, wave it around, style (Af. Am.), strut one's stuff, do one's stuff, go through one's paces, parade one's wares, make a scene, put on an act, hit one with, smack with, spring with, play to the gallery, take it big, come the heavy, do the heavy, throw one's weight around, chuck one's weight about.

FLAVOR v. hot it up, pep it up, zip it up, zap it up.

FLAVORFUL adj. delish, yummy, nummy, zesty.

FLAVORLESS adj. blah, dull as dishwater, flat, flat as a pancake, ho-hum, nothing, pablum, zero, draddy. See BORING.

FLAW n. bug, glitch, catch, Catch-22, gremlin, typo, slip-up, not come up to scratch, aggravation.

FLAWED adj. a lemon, rank, glitched, bugged, mucked-up, messed-up, loused-up. See IMPERFECT.

FLEDGLING n. boot, greenhorn, greenie, rookie, tenderfoot. See NOVICE.

FLEE v. split, blow, bolt (quickly), make tracks, take off, fuck off, scram, amscray, kick off, knock off, jump off, jump, hightail, hotfoot, rabbit-foot, run like a scared rabbit, step on it, step on the gas, cut and run, cut out, skin out, pull out, clear out, crush out, skip, skip out, fade, fade out, fade away, get small (from a crime), git, get, get git, get the hell out, get while the going is good, get away, make a getaway, make a break for it, make oneself scarce, beat it, bite moose, dog it, powder, take a powder, take a runout powder, shove, shove off, shove off for, vamoose, wail, fly the coop, lam, take it on the lam, exfiltrate, hook it, breeze, dust, smoke, spring, head for the hills, go over the wall, cop a mope, duck and run. See also ABSCOND, GO.

FLEECE v. rook, shaft, hose, jerk one around, dick, dick one around, fuck one over, run a game on, flimflam, burn, clip, gyp, take one to the cleaners. See CHEAT.

FLEECED adj. jived, suckered, skinned, set up, been had, been taken, taken for a bundle, get played (Af. Am.), clipped, aced-out, snookered, shafted. See CHEATED.

FLEET adj. screamin', speedball, barreling, on the double, in nothing flat, really rolling, like a house on fire, like greased lightning, like a big-assed bird, going like a raped ape. See FAST.

FLEETING adj. flash in the pan.

FLEXIBLE adj. all-around, go every which way, one who can do it all, ac/dc, AC/DC, acdac, cosplug, switch hitter, hang loose, roll with the punches, putty in one's hands, etched in sand, fungible.

FLICKERING adj. flicky.

FLIER n. flyboy, jet jockey, airplane driver, birdman, birdwoman; airdale, airedale (N.); barnstormer. See FLYER.

FLIGHT n. 1. hop, jump, helihop, 2. getaway, out, powder, runout powder, break, breakout, fadeout, get, beat, figary, mooch, mope, push, spring, tearaway, getaway route, getaway car, absquatulation, exfiltration.

FLIGHT ATTENDANT n. stew, cow pilot, stew zoo (quarters).

FLIGHTY adj. bubbleheaded, airhead, airedale, balloonhead, popcorn, spaz, dingbat, dingdong, ding-a-ling, rattlebrained, hare-brained, bird-brained, twit, chowderhead, chickenhead, gaga.

FLIMSY adj. Mickey Mouse, humpty-dumpty, tacky, ticky-tacky, sleazy, gimcracky, cheapjack, harum-scarum, slapdash, rocky, rickety, rinky-dink, held together by spit, held together by chewing gum, house of cards, cracker box (house), crappy, from hunger, el cheapo.

FLINCH v. blink.

FLING v. chuck, chunk, fire, heave, lob, peg, pitch, sling, toss, gollum (frisbee, wild throw).

FLIPPANT adj. fresh, flip, breezy, nervy, sassy, lippy, smart, smart-alecky, smart ass, wise ass, brassy, bold as brass. See INSOLENT.

FLIRT n. player, scrump queen, road whore, sleaze bucket, sleazebag, hosebag, swinger, vamp, gank, skeezer, operator, man trap, velvet trap, cruiser, gold digger, wolverine.

FLIRT v. hit on, crack on, put the rush on, put the move on, scam on, skeem on, come on, come on to, play on, lead on, go for it, make a pass, proposition, make one's move, move in on, coo, pitch, pick up, put it in cruise mode, lock it in cruise mode, do the street, window shop, check the block, troll, go for the cheese, swoop on one, throw drag on, tease, vamp, flam; gam, bus it (Af. Am.) eyeball, reckless eyeball, give one the eye, make eyes at, make goo-goo eyes at, make bedroom eyes at, bat one's eyes at, come hither, gold dig, look sweet upon, wolf-whistle, lollygag, dilly-dally, drop hairpins (homosexual conversation). See also DALLY.

FLIRTATION n. pickup, cruising, put the rush on, go for it, put it in cruise mode, do the street, check the block, troll, go for the cheese, beaver hunt, beaver patrol, tease, dropping hairpins (homosexual conversation).

FLOAT v. smooth along.

FLOG v. larrup, flax, wax, leather, paddle, whop, whomp, hide, tan one's hide, take it out of one's hide, belt, whip ass, beat the shit out of one. See HIT.

FLOGGING n. licking, larruping, walloping, whaling, buttwoopin' (Af. Am.), lathering, leathering, hiding, tanning, shellacking, waxing, paddling, lumps, get one's lumps, barrel punishment, dressing-down, strap oil, hazel oil, hickory oil, birch oil, dose of strap oil, dose of hazel oil, dose of birch oil, dose of hickory oil.

FLOOR n. boards, mat, canvas, deck.

FLOOR SHOW n. meat show, T and A, tits-and-ass show.

FLORIDA Bikini State, Everglades State, Peninsula State, Sunshine State.

FLORIDIAN n. alligator bait.

FLOUNCE v. swish, camp, nancy.

FLOUNDER v. flub, flub the dub, phumpher, go at it ass backwards, bobble, boot, blow, bugger, boo-boo, bugger up, crumb, crumb up, ball up, screw up, foul up, slip up, louse up, bitch, bitch up, muck up, trip up, crack, crack up, piss up, fuck up, snafu, mess up, make a mess of, make a hash of, muff, muff one's cue, miss one's cue, fluff one's lines, foozle, pratfall, brodie, crash, flop, lay an egg, lay a bomb, blow it, blow the gig, drop the ball, put one's foot in one's mouth, put one's foot in it, drop a brick, stub one's toe, trip up, come apart at the seams, get hung up, go to pieces, go tits up, land on one's ass, fall flat on one's ass, fall flat on one's face, fall down and go boom, bite the dust, lick the dust, be on the skids, stiff, stumble, flummox, flag, flag it, gleek it, come a-cropper, cave in, curdle, blob.

FLOURISH v. hit it big, get ahead, come along, on fire, hot, live high on the hog, have one's place in the sun, be on top of the heap, be fat dumb and happy. See SUCCEED.

FLOW v. smooth along.

FLOWERY adj. gassy, purple, windy, highfalutin.

FLUCTUATE v. yo-yo, blow hot and cold, shilly-shally, hem and haw. See VACILLATE.

FLUFF n. dust ball, kittens, pussies, dust kitty, ghost turds, beggar's velvet, slut's wool.

FLUID n. juice, bug juice, chaser, cooler, dope (heavy, such as sauce), goo, goop.

FLUSTER v. adjy, psych, spook, get to, flip, craze, bug, work up, make waves, stir up, discombobulate. See DISTURB. See also CONFUSE.

FLUSTERED adj. flustrated, in a flusteration, in a flustration, unglued, defrosted, discombobulated, shook up, bugged up, creeped out, farmisht, fertummeled, thrown, in the twilight zone, in a tizzy, in a flush, kerflumixed. See DISTURBED. See also CONFUSED.

FLUTE n. whiffer, stick whistle.

FLY v. jet out, jet over, helihop, take a hop, hop, wing, wing out, wing in, sky out, sky in, seagull (N., air travel), hedgehop (low), buzz, drive, drive an airplane, bend the throttle, whoosh, barnstorm, fly by the seat of one's pants, flat-hat.

FLYER n. flyboy, stick, jet jockey, airplane driver, throttle jockey, skyman, birdman, birdwoman, airdale, (N.), barnstormer, ace, empty kitchen (female), dodo (Stu.), blue suiter (A.F. test pilot), white suiter (civilian test pilot). See PILOT.

FOCUS v. home in, home in on, hone in, hone in on, zero in, zero in on, sharpen, sharpen up on, key on, move in, get one's head together, knuckle down, pour it on, skull-drag, sweat. See also THINK.

FOE v. oppo, opposish, opposite number, meat, bandit, bad guys, buddy (sarcastic), buddy-buddy, buddy fucker, crip, whose side are you on?, me and you, angries.

FOG n. ground clouds, London fog, soup, pea soup, pea souper, pea-soup fog, smaze, smog, visibility zero zero.

FOGGY adj. fogged-in, socked-in, closed-in, smazy, smoggy, soupy, pea-soupy, ceiling zero, zero zero.

FOIL v. 1. juke, shake, shake off, shuffle off, ditch, give the slip, jump, skip, skip out on, duck, dodge, get around, give the runaround, run circles around, run rings around. 2. hang up, foul up, fuck up, queer, crimp, cramp, stymie, crab, bollix, throw a monkey wrench into the works, upset one's apple cart, spike one's guns. See PREVENT. See also HINDER.

FOILED adj. stymied, hung up on, through the mill, up the wall, faked out, put away, skinned, queered, crabbed, fouled-up, fucked-up, bollixed-up, crimped, cramped, stonewalled, flummoxed, gridlocked. See also DEFLATED.

FOLD v. dog-ear.

FOLK SINGER n. folkie.

FOLLOW v. shadow, tail, trail, track, freeze, shag, on to, put a spot on, put a tail on, tail down, tailgate, hot on one's tail, on one's biscuit, on one's can, on one's pratt, on one's keister, on one's quiff (closely), on the prowl for, play catch up, run down, chase, go after, take out after, dog, dog one's heels, stick to, string along, tag after, tag along, schlep along, draft, spook.

FOLLOWER n. buff, fan, hanger-on, ho-dad, ho-daddy, skeezer (hip-hop), go in for, go out for, have a go at, plaster, shadow, echo, stooge, flunky, tail. See SUPPORTER. See also DEVOTEE.

FOLLOWING adj. next off. See also LATER.

FOLLY n. dumbo, dumb-de-dumb-dumb-dumb, dumb thing to do, dumb trick, fool trick, fool's trick. See also FOOLISHNESS.

FOND adj. soft on, big, big for, crazy for, crazy about, crazy over, lovey-dovey, mushy, nutty about, nutty over, all over one, partial to, heart in the right place.

FONDLE v. feel out, feel up, cop a feel, stroke, grope, grab ass, fool around, paw, play footsie, bear-hug, clutch, squeeze.

FOOD n. eats, grindage, grubbin, chow, bite, snack, feed, feedbag, grub, grub pile, groceries, wedge, take out, fast food, soul food, pharm food (natural), finger food, thousand on a plate (beans, Af. Am.), plastic cow (nondairy creamer), hots (hot meal, Mil.), be chow, be grub (satisfying), MREs (meals ready to eat, Gulf war; also, meals rejected by everyone), ribs, pogey, scoff, scoffings, cakes, go juice, chuck, slop, scuzz food (junk food), chewings, chop, chop-chop, chocker, movable feast, garbage, glop, blue plate, black plate (soul food); pecks, peckings (Af. Am.); natural, lump, dry lump, handout, set down, sticks to one's ribs, yum, yum-yum, vittles, grubbery, goodies, goonk, goulie, gubbins, grit, home cooking; punk, piss and punk, punk and white wine, gooby, chick (prison); peelings, swag, short order; kit food, meal kit (prepackaged).

FOOD, CANNED n. flipper, springer, sweller (spoiled).

FOOL n. dickhead, dork, dorf, asshole, ditz, penis wrinkle, quad, lop, lorg, gump, yutz, loser, winner, yo-yo, Fred, Barney, Wilma, dingbat, lamew, out to lunch, lunchie, nobody home, stark naked, jerk-off, beau, dodo, ninny, twillie, airedale, airhead, helium head, Gumbyhead, butthead, balloonhead, conehead, hamburger, jel, zombie, doesn't know from A to B, punter (easily defrauded), turkey, jive turkey, semolia (Af. Am.), schlemiel, schnook, half-baked, gerk (old). See STUPID.

FOOL v. kid, fox, outfox, geese, put on, jive, spoof, juke, deek, suck in, scam, con, snow, blow smoke up one's ass, diddle, fake out, pull a fast one, spoof, hornswoggle, put something over, put something across, slip one over on. See TRICK.

FOOLED adj. aced, aced out, foxed, outfoxed, deeked, juked, snowed, conned, jerked, jerked around, fucked over, sucked in, bamboozled, hornswoggled, flimflammed. See TRICKED.

FOOLHARDY adj. leave oneself wide open, go off the deep end, buy a pig in a poke, go out on a limb, devil-may-care. See CARELESS.

FOOLISH adj. screw-loose, jerky, nerdy, squirrely, harebrained, scatterbrained, rattlebrained, lamebrained, fuckbrained, birdbrained, cockeyed, dingy, dingy-dingy, weak in the upper story, goopy, flaky, kooky, dippy, punchy, punch-drunk, slappy, slap-happy, whip-silly, bubble-headed, foolheaded, goofus, gump, horse's ass, horse's collar, horse's neck, horse's tail, Mickey Mouse, sap, sappy, screwy, schlemiel, schloomp, schlub, schmendrick, shmoe, schnooky.

FOOLISHNESS n. dumb trick, fool trick, fool's trick, meatballism, poppycock, tommyrot, narrishkeit, fiddlesticks, twaddle, stuff and nonsense, bushwa, bushwah, booshwah, cheese, a line of cheese, claptrap, caca, cahcah, total cahcah, fiddle-faddle, flamdoodle, flapdoodle, fumadiddle, fermadiddle, balloon juice, horsefeathers, fudge. See also NONSENSE.

FOOTBALL n. leather, pigskin, pumpkin.

FOOTBALL KICK n. boot, hang time, coffin corner (out of bounds inside the five-yard line).

FOOTBALL PASS n. bomb (long), Hail Mary (a desperation long pass attempt to score), hook, jump pass, loop, looper, go up on top, take to the air, go to the air, go upstairs, go long, drop it down the chimney (looper), pitch out, pop (short pass), safety valve (short pass option), pump (feint), slant in, thread the needle (between defensive players), aerial, blind pass (without looking), button hook, comeback, comebacker, circle, circle pass, flare, down and in, down and out, right on the numbers, right on the money, rainbow (high arc), dump it off, dump off to, unload (get rid of the ball), complete, completion, incomplete, incompletion; pick, pick-off (interception), intercept, interception.

FOOTBALL PLAYER n. gridder, beefer, all-pro, all-star (honors), front line, suicide squad, scatback, scrambler, tailback (backfield), flankerback, nose guard, cornerman, rusher, ground gainer, runner-up, booter (kicker), monster, monster back, plugger, blitzer (linebacker), jitterbug (defensive back), safety man, reserve (substitute).

FOOTBALL PLAYS n. ground game, running game, smashball, smash-gut, up the gut (through the center), flying wedge, fire out (fast move off the ball), hand-off, hit the hole; hold, held (they held them from scoring); long gainer, muff, fumble, naked reverse, fake, fake-out, razzle-dazzle, fleaflicker (complex play), boomerooski (trick play), juke (feint), cut back, cut block, run to daylight (any opening), run double posts, run double corners, wide-open, drive (consecutive successful plays), shotgun, wishbone, wishbone T, fadeaway (quarterback move), rollout (quarterback move sideways to pass), slant, belly-back (ball carrier feint), buttonhook, keeper (quarterback keeps and runs with ball), belly series, Statue of Liberty play, sweep (a sweep around left), bootleg (hidden ball), break it (long gain), bump and run, carry, scramble (quarterback ball carry), eat the ball (quarterback has no option but to be tackled), cough up (lose ball during play), turnover (loss of possession of the ball); dog, red dog, blitz, blow in, check, chicken fight, (repeated blocks), jam, nickel defense, read (he read the handoff), safety blitz (by safety man), shut down (they shut down the offense), shut off (they shut off the short gain), audible (play change called verbally).

FOOTBALL RULES n. gridiron lawyer, chain (ten-yard measure), chain gang (officials positioning chain), clip (illegal block), crackback (blindside block, illegal), necessary line (gain needed for first down).

FOOTBALL, SCORE v. take it over, take it in, all the way, go all the way, go coast to coast (goal to goal), burn, convert, a conversion, safety, sit on a lead, sit on the ball, use the clock, yardage.

FOOTBALL SIGNALS n. call, the call, check off (change the call); audible, automatic (substitute play call), hike (start).

FOOTBALL TACKLE n. sack, dump (tackle the quarterback) bring down, nail, shoot the gap (get through to tackle), clothesline, horse collar, schmear, crawling (trying for more yardage after tackle, illegal).

FOOTBALL TERMS grid, gridiron, eleven, huddle, squad, taxi squad, bomb squad, suicide squad, kamikaze corps (special teams), flat (both sides behind the line), front four, red shirts (ineligible players), the pits (line of scrimmage), in the trenches (the line), wide open, bust it wide open, break it, break it open, the pocket (quarterback zone), snap, squib (onside kick), spike (he danced under the goal posts then spiked the ball), straightarm, uprights (goal posts), grind out (ground play); put it on the ground, put it on the carpet (fumble); whistle down, whistle dead (end the play by a whistle); hear footsteps (distraction, expecting a tackle), kill the clock (timeout), playing catch-up ball, run out the clock (stall), eat the clock, nutcracker (rough practice), skull practice, chalk talk (lecture session), wild card (makes playoffs), grandstand quarterback, Monday morning quarterback.

FOOT INSPECTION n. dog show (WWII).

FOOTLIGHTS n. foots.

FOOTWEAR n. clodhoppers, canal boats, gunboats, barkers, earth pads, ground grabbers, clunkers, bottoms. See SHOES.

FOP n. dude, flash, sport, swell, toff, snappy dresser, clotheshorse, Beau Brummell, Dapper Dan, macaroni.

FOR prep. pro.

FORBEARING adj. soft-shell, be big, live with, go easy on, go easy with.

FORBID v. cool, cool out, block, hog-tie, stymie, hang up, hold up, lock up, put the chill on, spike, ding, zing, nix, cut off one's water, shut down, freeze. See PROHIBIT.

FORBIDDEN adj. no-no, outta bounds, off-limits, closed, closed-down, closed-up.

FORBIDDING adj. hard-boiled, tough. See also UGLY.

FORCE n. 1. pow, sock, the force, beef, clout, punch, steam, the stuff, what it takes, the heavy artillery, full head of steam, an 800-pound gorilla. See POWER. See also COERCION. 2. troops, shop, crew, soldiers, horses.

FORCE v. pressure, high-pressure, strong-arm, twist one's arm, arm-twist, lean against, lean on, lean on it, hassle, push around, squeeze, bring in the heavy artillery, put the squeeze on, put the screws to, put the screws on, put the chill on, put the arm on, put the heat on, hold one's feet to the fire, put the scare on, gueril, put the gueril on, make it hot, walk heavy, crack down, clamp down, ram down one's throat, cram down one's throat, railroad, railroad through, steamroll, steamroller, roll over, bull in, bulldoze, muscle in, muscle out, take care of, throw one's weight around, throw a scare into, turn on the heat, make one an offer one can't refuse, sweat one, sweat it, rough up, roughhouse, move in on, chisel in, dump on, horn in, pour it on, go to town on, boost, work on, egg on, nag, jawbone, showboat, jackboat, bear down, bear down on it, put one's back into it, come at it from all sides.

FORCEFUL adj. punchy, gutsy, got the horses to do it, hoss, strong as an ox, bull, powerhouse, punch, go-getter, go-go, ball of fire, steamroller, come on strong, take over, take charge. See POWERFUL.

FORCEFULLY adv. by storm, slam-bang, turn on the heat, full on, all out, full tilt, full bore, in full swing, like gangbusters.

FORD CAR n. lizzie, tin lizzie, tin can, Model T, flying bedstead (1920), Henry, spider, sardine box, T-bone, Model A, deuce (1932).

FOREBODING n. sinking feeling, vibes (good or bad), feel in one's bones, funny feeling, wind change, handwriting on the wall, next week East Lynne. See PREMONITION.

FORECAST v. figure, figger, figger out, figure out, dope, dope out, call the turn, in the cards, it's looking to, telegraph, see it coming, see it in the stars. See PREDICT.

FOREFRONT n. leading edge, cutting edge, state of the art. See also NEW.

FOREFRONT, IN THE adj. on the line, in the thick of it, in the trenches.

FOREIGN adj. offshore.

FOREIGN CURRENCY n. P, pee, pea (pesos, piasters, etc.), forex (trading market).

FOREIGNER n. greenhorn, furriner, FOB (fresh off the boat), wetback, ginzo, guinzo, gringo, goum, greaseball, jaboney, jibone (all Derog.). See also ALIEN.

FOREKNOWLEDGE n. ESP, sixth sense.

FOREMAN n. head, headman, honcho, head honcho, Big Brother, boss, bosshead, pit boss, straw boss, gaffer, bull, bull of the woods, pusher, slave driver. See also EXECUTIVE.

FOREMOST adj. A-1, A-number 1, A per se, A1, number one, numero uno, primo, chief, hot stuff, hot shot, hot dog, hot shit, hot flash, hooper-dooper, the force, at the cutting edge, at the leading edge, heavy, heavyweight, heavy stuff, we're not talking about nutmeg here. See BEST.

FOREPLAY n. cat, tomcat, charge, chase, cruise, dark setting (Af. Am.), hit on, footsie-wootsie, fun and games, neck, pet, grovel, pitch woo, fling woo, spoon, smooch, eat face, face rape, suck heads, mesh, M.L.A. (major lip action), box tonsils, go for sushi, a little smacky, tease, cock tease, cop, cop a feel, feel, feel-up, bush patrol, muff-dive, butterfly kiss, boodle, finger-fuck, canoe, dry hump, group grope, get one's buns warmed, See AMOROUS PLAY.

FORESEE v. crystal-ball it, call the turn, dope out, psych it out, have a hunch, see it coming. See PREDICT.

FORESEEN adj. as advertised, no big surprise, it's what always happens, true to form, saw it coming, the handwriting was on the wall, it was in the cards, be just like one, be one all over, not put it past.

FORESHADOW v. telegraph, in the wind, the handwriting on the wall.

FORESKIN n. lace curtains (homosexual), end, sheath, Jewish nightcap, snapper, Rumpleforeskin.

FOREST n. big sticks.

FORESTALL v. cut 'em off at the pass, throw cold water on, spike one's guns, upset one's apple cart, knock the props from under one. See PREVENT.

FORETELL v. call it, call the turn, read, dope, dope out, figure, figure out, psych it out, crystal-ball it, make book, it's looking to, see it coming. See PREDICT.

FORETOLD adj. saw it coming, the handwriting was on the wall, as advertised, no big surprise, it's what always happens, true to form. See FORESEEN.

FOREVER adv. for keeps, till hell freezes over, till the cows come home, till you're blue in the face, when the donkey flies, since God was young, since the year one, since Hector was a pup. See ALWAYS.

FOREWARN v. tip, tip off, flag, wave a red flag, telegraph, cloud up, smell a rat, give the high sign, pull one's coat, put one wise, put a bug in one's ear, put a flea in one's ear.

FOREWARNING n. vibes (good or bad), vibrations, hunch, feel in one's bones, funny feeling, sinking feeling, tip-off, handwriting on the wall.

FORGE v. make like, fake, scratch, gammon, pirate, bite, hoke, hoke up, phony up, pencil-whip (documentation). See also COUNTERFEIT.

FORGE AHEAD v. plow ahead.

FORGED adj. phony, queer, bogus, pirate goods, pirate labels, fake, plastic, hokey, ersatz, scratch, bouncer, funny, funny paper, sour paper, hot paper, not what it's cracked up to be.

FORGED CHECKS, PASS v. bounce, bounce bum paper, bounce sour paper, hang paper, lay paper, lay sour paper, fly kites, hit one with, stiff, smash a stiff, push a stiff, push kites, push paper, smack with.

FORGED CHECKS, PASSER OF n. paperhanger, paper layer, paper pusher, sheet passer, shover, billposter, butterfly man, kiteman.

FORGER n. penman, scratcher, scratch man, one of a scratch mob, billposter; shoe, cobbler (forges passports). See COUNTERFEITER.

FORGERY n. carbon, carbon copy, lookalike, workalike, not what it's cracked up to be, twin, scrip, stiff. See also COUNTERFEIT.

FORGERY, CRIMINAL CHARGE OF n. paperhanging fall, scratch rap.

FORGET v. draw a blank, blow up, go up, go dry, balloon, clean forget, disremember, disrecollect, punt (someone or something) off, blow one's lines (The.).

FORGETFUL adj. out to lunch, popcorn-headed, airheaded, helium-headed, absentminded professor, Suzie (female), mooning, moony, pipe dreaming, woolgathering, goofing off, not on the job, asleep on the job, asleep at the switch, looking out the window, sloppy, would lose one's head if it wasn't tied on.

FORGETFULNESS n. blackout, block-out, blow, blow a line (The.), don't know if one's comin' or goin', go blank, lose one's marbles, brain fart, brain fade.

FORGIVE v. let off, let it go, let up on, let one off this time, let one off easy, wink at, blink at, write off, whitewash, launder, sanitize, bleach, clear, wipe it off, wipe the slate clean, go easy on, bury the hatchet, lifeboat, hand out clemo, commute, spring. See also CONCILIATE.

FORGIVEN adj. in from the cold, let off, let go.

FORGIVING adj. big, be big, live with. See COMPASSIONATE.

FORGO v. pass, pass on, pass up, sit out, swear off, blow off, take the oath, take the cure, go on the wagon, pack in, give in, give up. See ABSTAIN.

FORGOTTEN adj. 1. disremembered, disrecollected, draw a blank, clean forgot, clean forgotten, slipped one's mind, slipped between the cracks, fell between the cracks. 2. blown over, gone glimmering. See also PAST.

FORK n. spear.

FORLORN adj. godforsaken, destroyed, draggin' ass, down-and-out, in the dumps, blue, got the blue devils. See UNHAPPY.

FORM n. 1. layout, setup, sked, by the book, by the numbers, boilerplate, channels, ropes. 2. build, built, built like a brick shithouse, V-man, tuna. See BODY.

FORM v. whomp up, cook up, dream up, throw up, throw together, bring together, fudge together, knock together, knock out, knock off, dash off, pull off, polish off, come through, break out with, bust out with (surprisingly or suddenly), mount (The.).

FORMAL adj. straight-arrow, stiff, squaresville, Barbie and Ken, by the numbers, playing their game, granola head, stuffy. See CONVENTIONAL.

FORMAL ATTIRE n. tux, formal, tails, hammertails, white tie, black tie, bib and tucker, boiled shirt, soup 'n' fish, monkey suit.

FORMALITIES n. p's and q's, honors.

FORMER adj. onetime, ex, X.

FORMERLY adv. away back, back, back when, one shot, time was, olden days, water under the bridge, water over the dam, down memory lane, when Hector was a pup, when one was knee high to a grasshopper.

FORMIDABLE adj. hairy, murder, pisser, rough go, bitch, tough proposition, tall order, ball buster. See DIFFICULT.

FORMLESS adj. baggy, blobby.

FORNICATE v. fuck, screw, lay, hump, nail, ball, bang, boff, dork, bump, pump, boost, get together, get busy, get down, boogaloo, do the wild thing, do damage, get done, hoe-hoppin' (promiscuous, Af. Am.), knock boots with, make (someone) scream, maul, plug, ride the hobby horse, romp, rock (someone's) world, slam, square (someone's) circle, go the limit, get in, get it on, get some, get one's ashes hauled, get one's end wet, get laid, get it off together, jump in the sack, jump on one's bones, lay pipe, beat someone with an ugly stick, get beat with an ugly stick, rub the bacon, have one's ticket punched, trim, make out, put out (Fem.), go all the way (all Obsc.). See SEXUAL INTERCOURSE.

FORNICATION n. fuck, jazz, screw, lay, hump, boff, poke, bang, action, balling, laying pipe, beating someone with an ugly stick, getting beat with an ugly stick, bed and breakfast, parallel parking, fooling around, dork, jiggle, the dirty deed (all Obsc.). See SEXUAL INTERCOURSE.

FORSAKE v. take the oath, give up, drift away, kiss good-bye, wash one's hands of, change one's tune, change one's song, walk out on, run out on, leave flat, leave high and dry, leave holding the bag. See ABANDON.

FORSAKEN adj. godforsaken, thrown over, left in the lurch, left at the church.

FORTHRIGHT adj. up front, open, real people, the real deal (Af. Am.), like it is, no lie, straight shit, call a spade a spade. See SINCERE.

FORTHRIGHTLY adv. level, deal level, on the level, right up front, put it on the line, lay it on the line, straight, straight from the shoulder, talk turkey.

FORTIFY v. beef up, soup up, charge up, punch up, heat up, hot up, hop up, jazz up, juice up, build up, step up, pour it on, add fuel to the fire, needle, spike (drink).

FORTITUDE n. balls, guts, gutsiness, heart, nerve, stomach, grit, true grit, spunk, backbone, moxie, starch, clock, corazón, intestinal fortitude, hanging in there, staying power, what it takes; bottled courage, Dutch courage (intoxicated).

FORT LAUDERDALE, FLORIDA Beach City, Fort Liquordale, Spring Break.

FORTUITOUS adj. fluky, lucky dog, luck in, luck out, fall into the shithouse and come up with a five-dollar gold piece. See LUCKY.

FORTUNATE adj. hot, hot hand, on a roll, luck in, luck out, get the breaks, all the way live (Af. Am.), hold aces, strike it lucky, all systems go. See LUCKY.

FORTUNE n. 1. fighting chance, break, shot, whack, stab, fifty-fifty, toss up, flier. 2. karma, kismet, in the cards, the roll of the dice, that's the way the ball bounces, that's the way the cookie crumbles, everything's coming up roses, Dame Fortune. 3. scratch, lucky hit, lucky break, good break, run of luck, streak of luck, lucked out, luck into, hot, fluke; mazeltov (good), mazel (Yid.). See LUCK.

FORTUNETELLER n. mitt reader.

FORT WORTH, TEXAS Cow Town.

FORWARD adj. ballsy, pushy, fresh, in your face, nervy, smart ass, wise ass, brassy, aggro, come on strong. See AGGRESSIVE.

FOUL adj. 1. icky, yecchy, yucky, gagger, barfy, vomity, stinking, skank, raunchy, chili bowl (person), pigpen, barn, stable. See DIRTY. 2. bogus, below the belt, not cricket, raw deal.

FOULED-UP adj. fucked, fucked-up, all fucked up, snafu (situation normal all fouled up), commfu (complete monumental military foul-up), fubar (fouled up beyond all recognition), fumtu (fouled up more than usual), fubb (fouled up beyond belief), G.F.U. (general foul-up), imfu (imperial military foul-up), M.F.U. (military foul-up), janfu (joint army-navy foul-up), jaafu (joint Anglo-American foul-up), jacfu (joint American-Chinese foul-up), nabu (non-adjusting ball-up), sabu (self-adjusting ball-up), samfu (self-adjusting military foul-up), snefu (situation normal everything fouled up), snrafu (situation normal really all fouled up), tabu (typical Army ball-up), tafubar (things are fouled up beyond all recognition), T.C.C. fu (typical Coastal Command foul-up), tarfu (things are really fouled up), tuifu (the ultimate in foul-ups), sapfu (surpassing all previous foul-ups), susfu (situation unchanged still fouled up).

FOUND v. start up, start the ball rolling, father, ring in, get going. See also BEGIN.

FOUNDATION n. bottom line, rock bottom, ABC's, brass tacks, get down, get down to brass tacks, nitty-gritty, nuts and bolts, groceries, guts, meat and potatoes, begin-

ners, coal and ice, at heart, nub, bred in the bone, dyed in the wool.

FOUNDLING n. drop, fetch, guttersnipe, mudlark, rustle.

FOUNTAINHEAD n. horse's mouth, connection, tipster, tout.

FOUNTAIN PEN n. ball point, stick.

FOUR OF CLUBS n. bedpost, devil's bedpost.

FOUR-WHEEL-DRIVE TRUCK n. four by four, four-wheel drive.

FOWL n. banty, biddy, birdie, birdy, boid, chick, chickabiddy, chickadee, chicky.

FOYER n. squat pad.

FRACAS n. rumpus, brawl, row, flap, hassle, mix-up, run-in, rhubarb, ruckus, stew. See ARGUMENT.

FRACTION n. piece, bite, cut, slice, chunk, lion's share, bigger half, big end, halver, fifty-fifty, even-steven. See also SHARE.

FRACTIOUS adj. bitchy, cussed, mean, ornery, tetchy, thin-skinned, scrappy. See IRRITABLE.

FRAGMENT n. hunk, gob, lump, smithereen, bite, cut, slice, chunk.

FRAGRANT, BE v. smell well, smell good.

FRAIL adj. 1. weak sister, wishy-washy, wimp factor, wimpy, herb, sad sack, fish, poor fish, rocky, don't have the horses, what the cat dragged in. See WEAK. 2. humpty-dumpty, sleazy, tacky, ticky-tacky, rickety, rinky-dink, held together by spit, held together by chewing gum, house of cards. See FLIMSY.

FRAME n. Mr. Bones, cage.

FRANK adj. up front, right up front, open, like it is, call it like it is, lay it on the line; raw, whip it on (Af. Am.); on the level, on the up and up, come-at-able, straight, shoot straight from the shoulder, straight out, straight shit, true blue, talk like a Dutch uncle, call a spade a spade, put all one's cards on the table, make no bones about it, fly right, talk turkey. See SINCERE.

FRANKFURTER n. hotdog, hot dawg, frank, weenie, tube steak, balloon, beenie, bow-wow, bun pup, Concy Island pup, pimp stick, puppy, special, foot-long special.

FRANKLY adv. level, deal level, on the level, dead on the level, put it on the line, lay it on the line, whip it on (Af. Am.), straight, straight from the shoulder, talk turkey.

FRANTIC adj. unglued, unzipped, unscrewed, defrosted, hyper, grokked, gone, real gone, high, mad, wild, wicked, weird, weirded-out, far-out, out, wigged-out, hot, hot and bothered, hot under the collar, spazzed out, having a spazz attack, got a wild hair up one's ass, flipped-out, freaked-out, zonkers, wired, wired-up, keyed-up, all keyed up, shook-up, all shook up, steamed-up, fired-up, get all worked up, turned-on, in a stew, in a sweat, in a tizzy, in a panic, in a dither, in a lather, in a swivet, in a foofaraw, in a pucker, crazy, like crazy, like mad, hit the ceiling, shit in one's pants, have a fit, have kittens, cast a kitten, go up in the air, mind-blowing, mind-bending.

FRATERNITY n.   frat, Greeks, house.

FRATERNITY HOUSE n.   house, frat house, animal house, hut, tong.

FRATERNITY MEMBER n.   brother, rat, frat rat, frat dick, frat fag, frater, bagger, fratty bagger, Greek, legacy; pheeze, feeze (join); pledge (pending acceptance).

FRATERNIZE v.   mix, take down one's hair, break the ice, loosen up, warm up, open up, gang up, pal up, pal around, hang around with, tie up with, get with, run with, chum with, chum together, make the rounds, floss around.

FRAUD n.   1. con man, gyp, crook, mechanic, fourflusher, phony, double-dealer, doberman (Af. Am.), shark, horse trader, cheese eater, skunker, hoser; one had a pony, one used an airplane, equestrian (test cheating). See CHEATER. See also COUNTERFEIT. 2. hustle, con, sting, flimflam, scam, blow smoke up one's ass, pseud, fast shuffle, fast one, claptrap, line of cheese, borax, song, song and dance; ride-out, squat (fraudulent auto accident) churn and burn (investment), string, smoke, tripe, vanilla, bitch, skunk, cake cutter (circus), hanky-panky, hocus-pocus, huggermuggery, graft, grift, autograph, kiting checks, bucket shop, boiler room, Carrie Watsons, the engineer's daughter, double tray, dipsy doodle, shenanigans, monkeyshines, monkey business, funny business; limb, shit kicker, tap, tap game (advertising). See SWINDLER.

FREAK n.   geek (circus).

FRECKLE n.   daisy.

FREE adj.   1. comp, freebie, free ride, for free, for nothing, for love, do it for one's health, twofer, Annie Oakley, paper, paper the house, on the house, on the cuff, cuffo, on the arm, on the ice, hummer, free lunch (seems free but isn't), handout. 2. free-wheeling, on one's own, couldn't care less, don't give a damn, shoot the moon, fly kites, flake, free-spirited, break loose, cut loose, loose wig, down, get down, let down one's hair, go to town, up front, all hanging out, far out, stretched out. 3. freeloader, schnorrer, scab, deadhead, skip out.

FREE v.   let go, let off, let off the hook, kiss off, blow one off, spring, turn out, get a floater, get hours, get a twenty-four, put on the pavement, put on the sidewalk, put on the street, put on the bricks, bail one out, get out from under, save one's bacon, save one's neck. See also ABSOLVE.

FREED adj.   out, back on the street, beat the rap, walked, let off, let go.

FREEDOM n.   run, run of, free run of.

FREE PERIOD n.   float (no class, Stu.).

FREE TICKET n.   freebie, freeby, free ride, pass, free pass, comp, Annie Oakley, chit, paper, twofer, pigeon.

FREE TIME n.   off hours, good-off time, one's own sweet time, time to burn, time to kill.

FREE WILL n.   own hook, say-so, own say-so, own sweet way.

FREEZING adj.   freeze one's balls off, freeze one's ass off, freeze one's tits off, laying chilly, snappy, one-dog night, two-dog night, three-dog night. See COLD.

FREIGHTER n.   rust bucket, crock, tub, tramp.

FRENCH n.   frog, Froggy, frog eater, frog's legs (Fem.), tadpole (child), Frenchy (all Derog.).

FRENCH CANADIAN n.   Canuck, Pepsi (all Derog.).

FRENCH FRIED POTATOES n.   fries, shoestrings, matchsticks, steak fries, chips, f.f., fr.f.

FRENCH HORN n.   peck horn, pretzel.

FRENETIC adj.   unglued, unscrewed, hyper, weirded-out, wigged-out, spazzed-out, having a spazz attack, wired, wired-up, in a lather. See FRANTIC.

FRENZY n.   blow, blow a fuse, blow a gasket, blow one's top, blow one's topper, blow one's cap, blow one's stack, blow one's cork, blow one's wig, blow one's noggin, blow one's roof, blow one's lump, go ballistic, torqued, flip one's lid, cat fit, conniption, conniption fit, duck fit, shit hemorrhage, hell broke loose, all hell broke loose, every which way but up, free-for-all, rumpus, ruckus, ruction, dithers, allovers, flap, fuss, lather, needles, stew, to-do, zingers, fuzz-buzz (commotion), fuzz-buzzy, haroosh, foofaraw, fofarraw, wing-ding, rowdy-dow, stir, row, rumble.

FREQUENT v.   hang, hang out at, hang around, hang about, haunt, drop in, hit, play, give a play.

FRESH adj.   just out, the latest, mint, cherry, comer, now, state of the art, brand new, newie, what's happening, what's in. See NEW.

FRESHMAN n.   frosh, fresh, freshie, scrub, shmen, swench (female), dewdrop, rat, fish, crab, dog, frog, fox, green pea, redhead, hound, plebe (1920s); Mister Ducrot, Mister Dumbjohn, Mister Dumbguard (West Point), doolie, Mister Doolie (A.F. Acad.).

FRET v.   bleed, take on, eat one's heart out, stew, get into a stew, carry a heavy load, hassle, something is eating at one, something is beating down on one, get into a dither, work oneself into a lather, work oneself into a sweat, sweat it out.

FRETFUL adj. ornery, crabby, cranky, grouchy, mean, Mr. Coffee Nerves, wreck, got up on the wrong side of the bed. See PETULANT.

FRICTION n. flak, bone to pick, hassle, rhubarb, row, ruckus, rumpus, ruction, set-to, bad vibes, clinker, sour note. See DISCORD.

FRIDAY n. four and one, T.G.I.F., getaway day, fish day.

FRIED CHICKEN n. pigeon, yardbird (prison).

FRIED EGGS n. over, over easy, sunny side up.

FRIEND n. amigo, brother, little brother, brah, bra, bro, sister, homes, holmes (from home boy), homies, homeslice, homeskillet, dog, G, bud, buddy, bosom buddy, buddy boy, buddyroo, good buddy, asshole buddy, home biscuit, biscuit, road dog, chum buddy, chum, boogerhead, money, blood, skillet, slice, roomy, roommate, pard, pardner, partner, ace, spare, main man; main squeeze, hamma (girl); family, tribe, posse, crew (group); fella, B.F., guy, mellow (close), old man, old boy, cousin, kissing cousin, playmate, mate, matie, pal, bonded, sidekick, sidekicker, better half, Billy, captain, compadre, goombah, cut dub (reformatory), Jack, Jack at a pinch, lightning, go way back, cobber, bodo (1920), ghost (rarely seen), electric doughnut (known only by phone conversation), clutter buddy (helps get rid of clutter).

FRIENDLY adj. buddy-buddy, get buddy-buddy, clubby, down with, chummy, mellow, tight, pally, palsy-walsy, cozy, chuchala-muchala, right nice, right neighborly, downright neighborly, white, regular, square shooter, sucking around, kissy-kissy, kissing cousins, kissing up to, mix, get together, get with it, break the ice, let down one's hair, trade spit, swap spit, roommates, living in each other's pockets, sleepin' together, making it with.

FRIGHTEN v. spook, chill, chill off, put the chill on, scare shitless, scare stiff, scare the pants off one, scare hell out of, scare the shit out of, scare silly, scare the bejesus out of one, scare to death, throw a scare into, give one a turn, shit green, make one shit in one's pants, make one jump a mile, make one jump out of his skin, strike all of a heap, bowl down, bowl over, buffalo, bulldoze, chicken out, enforce, lean on, lean against, push around, whip one around (intellectually), showboat, walk heavy, put on the arm, put on the muscle, put the heat on, turn on the heat, put one through the wringer, bad eye, cuff, hang tough, goose, link back. See also STARTLE.

FRIGHTENED adj. up-tight, hung-up, clutched-up, in crisis mode, yellow, yellow-bellied, with a yellow streak, a yellow streak down one a yard wide, yellow streak down one's back, yellow stripe down one's back, have cold feet, have a fit, have kittens, 'fraidy cat, scaredy cat, run scared, scared stiff, scared witless, scared spitless, scared shitless, shit, shit green, crap out, shit a brick, shit in one's pants, fudge one's pants, fudge one's undies, pee in one's pants, piss in one's pants, push the panic button, jittery, jumpy, shaky, shivery, quivery, in a dither, in a sweat, in a cold sweat, have butterflies in one's stomach, have the willies, spooked, frozen, goose-bumpy, wimpy, rabbity, mousy, jellyfish, chicken, chicken out, chickenhearted, pigeonhearted, chicken-livered, white-livered, lily-livered, milk-livered, milksop, Milquetoast, Caspar Milquetoast, weak-kneed, weak sister, sissy, baby, big baby, nebbish, candy-ass, pucker, pucker-assed, asshole-puckerin', asshole suckin' wind, pecker-assed, gutless, shake in one's boots, ague, creeps, heebie-jeebies, leaping heebies, the jams, the jims, the jimjams, the jimmies, jumped a mile, jumped out of one's skin, give a jolt, bowled down, bowled over, struck all of a heap, D and D (deaf and dumb, afraid to testify), punk out, on the ragged edge.

FRIGHTENING adj. hairy, hellish, furry, hair-raising, white-knuckle, scary, spooky, grabber, chiller. See also STARTLING.

FRIGID adj. 1. colder 'n a witch's tit, colder than a well digger's ass, freeze one's ass off, snappy, three-dog night, icebox (place). See COLD. 2. cold tit, cold shoulder, tight-assed, butter wouldn't melt in his mouth, frosty, cool.

FRIGIDAIRE n. fridge, icebox.

FRILLS n. gingerbread, bells and whistles, fuss, gewgaws, gimcracks, garbage (food), dingbat, doodad, thing, fandangle, jazz, seagoing (large, absurd).

FRINGE BENEFITS n. fringes, perks, stuff, golden parachute, tin parachute (nonmanagement employee), golden handcuffs (deferred).

FRISBEE n. B.

FRISKY adj. jumpy, peppy, zippy, feeling one's oats, full of beans, full of piss and vinegar, full of ginger, goosy, trigger-happy. See SPIRITED.

FRITTER AWAY v. piss away, diddle away, run through, go through, blow, throw money around, pump up (gambling). See DISSIPATE.

FRIVOLOUS adj. hairbrained, airbrained.

FROG n. Dutch nightingale.

FROLIC v. let loose, cut loose, let go, go on a tear, go places and do things, fool around, kick up one's heels, whoop it up, raise hell. See REVEL.

FRONT n. put-on, false front, fake, plastic, phony.

FRONT PORCH n. stoop.

FRONT ROW n. bald-headed row.

FROWN n. dirty look, bad eye.

FROWN v. burn, burn up, do a slow burn, look daggers, give one a whammy, give one a dirty look, give one the evil eye, dog eye, bad eye, act the lion tamer, make a kisser, cloud up and rain on one.

FRUGAL adj. tight, tightwad, Scotch, nickel-nurser, penny-pincher, bog pocket, last of the big spenders. See STINGY.

FRUITLESS adj. spinning one's wheels, wild-goose chase. See USELESS.

FRUIT PICKER n. apple knocker, wetback, bracero.

FRUSTRATE v. cramp, cramp one's style, crimp, stymie, hang up, put one in a box, hold up, foul up, stump, give the runaround. See HINDER.

FRUSTRATED adj. hung up on, stymied, through the mill, up the wall, faked out, in a box, put away, skinned, queered, crabbed, fouled-up, fucked-up, bollixed-up, crimped, cramped, stonewalled, flummoxed, fuckstrated (sexual). See also DEFEATED.

FRUSTRATION n. letdown, setback, the old one-two, bitter pill, bitter pill to swallow, bummer, downer, drag, fizzle. See also HINDRANCE, DISAPPOINTED.

FRYING PAN n. spider.

FUEL n. alky, go juice, juice, motion lotion, motion potion, soup, synfuel (synthetic), diesel juice, caramel (nuclear reactor).

FUEL v. fill 'er up, gas 'er up, shoot 'em up.

FUEL ADDITIVE n. juice, pop.

FUGITIVE adj. hot, on the lam, lammister, wanted, have smallpox.

FUGITIVE-WANTED POSTER n. dodger, general, mugg on the board, reader, reader with a tail.

FULFILL v. fill the bill, hit the bull's-eye, score, be just the ticket, get one's jollies, got one's kicks, make the grade, make it. See SATISFY.

FULFILLMENT n. you got it, just name it, get off, get off on, kick, kicks, sure shock, just the ticket, just what the doctor ordered.

FULL adj. packed, jammed, jam-packed, filled to the rafters, full up, full as a tick, full house, standing room only, SRO, sold out; clean, gone clean (The.); stuffed, stuffed to the gills, topped off, lousy with, crumbed up with, crummy with, stiff with, swagged up with, up to here, fit to bust, fanny-bumper, packed like sardines, sardined. See also SATIATED.

FULLY adv. full on, all the way, all out, royal, from A to Z, from soup to nuts. See COMPLETELY.

FUMBLE v. phumpher, fluff, flub, couldn't get a handle on it, lost the handle. See ERR.

FUN n. ball, cold chillin', shits and giggles, laughs, lots of laughs, fun and games, grins, get some grins, just for grins, high old time, picnic, field day. See AMUSEMENT. See also ENTERTAINMENT.

FUNCTION v. move, make one's move, do one's thing, go to town, TCB (take care of business), get with it, boogie, time to boogie (time to get started), shit or get off the pot, percolate, cook, operate, move on (to something else), that dog'll hunt. See ACT.

FUNCTIONARY n. paper shuffler, buck passer, apparatchik, empty suit, cee gee, space cadet (young), lifer (Army), oink (police).

FUNCTIONING adj. hot, on track, on stream, on line, in place, going, a going concern, hit the ground running, percolating, ticking, clicking, in full swing, doing one's thing.

FUND v. pick up the check, pick up the tab, angel, bankroll, grubstake, stake, back, greenback, juice, knock (Af. Am.), lay on one, loan-shark, piece one off, prime the pump. See FINANCE. See also GIVE.

FUNDAMENTAL adj. bottom-line, coal and ice, cold turkey, meat and potatoes, nitty-gritty, key, nub, primo, name of the game, where it's at.

FUNDAMENTALIST CHRISTIANS n. fundies.

FUNDAMENTALS n. ABC's, brass tacks, get down, get down to brass tacks, nitty-gritty, nuts and bolts, groceries, guts, meat and potatoes, beginners, coal and ice, bottom line, rock bottom, at heart, bred in the bone, dyed in the wool.

FUND RAISING n. greentapping.

FUND RAISING, POLITICAL n. rainmaker; Emily, instacheck (quick donation), bagel (failed to collect), soft money (not counted in maximum limit).

FUNDS n. the bank, bankroll, nut, backing, budget, kitty, nest egg, stakes, pork barrel, space barrel (NASA), public crib, public till, public trough, rainmaker (fund raiser). See also ASSETS.

FUNERAL n. cold-meat party, planting, deep-six (sea).

FUNERAL WAGON n. Black Maria, bone box, dead wagon, glass wagon, meat wagon, last ride.

FUNNY adj. jokey, yokky, gas, for grins, had 'em in the aisles, hooper-dooper, hysterical, a scream, a zetser, laffer, knee-slapper, riot, laugh riot, humdinger, priceless, too funny for words. See AMUSING.

FUR n. dried barkers, skins, skin joint (shop).

FURBELOW n. bells and whistles, fuss, gewgaws, frou-frou, spinach (excessive), gingerbread, dingbat, doodad, thing, fandangle, jazz.

FURBISH v. doll up, gussy up, fix up, spruce up, deck out, put on the bells and whistles, put on the dog.

FURIOUS adj. browned-off, bent out of shape, blow, blow one's cool, bummed out, mad as a wet hen, hacked, steamed, get one's bowels in an uproar, have a conniption fit, fit to be tied, hopping mad, smoking. See ANGRY.

FURIOUSLY adv. like crazy, like mad, something fierce, something terrible, flaky, helter-skelter, holus-bolus, hurry-scurry, ramble-scramble. See also VIOLENTLY.

FURLOUGH n. orchid hunt (WAC), layoff, hiatus. See also LEAVE.

FURNISH v. feather one's nest, line one's nest (at the expense of others), heel (money), fix up. See also EQUIP.

FURNISHINGS n. turnout.

FUROR n. row, big stink, rhubarb, ruckus, commo, free-for-all, hell broke loose, raise Cain, raise sand, big scene.

FURTHER v. push, puff, ballyhoo, back up, give a boost to, go with, thump the tub for, take care of one for, open doors, lend a hand, bail out. See SUPPORT.

FURTIVE adj. under wraps, undercover, hush-hush, creep (mission), tref, triff. See SECRET.

FURTIVELY adv. on the q.t., on the quiet, on the sly, undercover, under wraps, hush-hush, strictly hush-hush, skunk works (secret manufacturing plant or laboratory), in a hole-and-corner way, in holes and corners.

FURY n. mad, sore, huff, dander, Irish, stew, storm, ruckus, wingding, slow burn, conniption, conniption fit, cat fit, duck fit, blowup, flare-up, boiling point, rise, more heat than light. See ANGER.

FUSS n. stink, to-do, commo, scene, flap, kick-up, wingding, fuzz-buzzy. See TURMOIL.

FUSSY adj. choosy, comma counter, nitpicker, picky, picky-picky, ticky, stickler, fussbudget, fusspot, fuddy-duddy, granny, old woman, old maid, pernickety, persnickety. See also PARTICULAR.

FUTILE adj. total shuck, goin' round in circles, on a treadmill, go fight City Hall, locking the barn after the horse is stolen, looking for a needle in a haystack, save one's breath. See USELESS.

FUTURE adj. down the road, down the pike, down the line, down the road a piece, in the cards, by and by, from now on in, from here in, from here on out, just around the corner.

FUZZ n. dust ball, kittens, pussies, dust kitty, ghost turds, beggar's velvet, slut's wool.

G

G n. Golf, George.

GAD v. traipse, bum, mooch, knock around, knock about, bat around, bat about, hit the road, hit the trail, walk the tracks, count ties. See WANDER.

GADFLY n. adjy, spark plug, pusher, operator, player, fireman, hatchet man, needle man, steam-up ghee, stormy petrel, wave maker.

GADGET n. gismo, contraption, sucker, bugger, mother, whatchamacallit, thigamajig, dojigger, dohickey, goofus. See APPARATUS.

GAFFE n. boo-boo, bloomer, clinker, howler, fox paw, fox pass, wrong riff, put one's foot in it, blow card. See MISTAKE.

GAG v. squelch, squash, put the lid on, keep the lid on, shut down on, bottle up, cork, cork up. See SILENCE.

GAIETY n. whooper-dooper, whoopee, wingding, shindig, brawl, grins. See also REVEL.

GAIN n. 1. gravy, payoff, take, velvet, peanuts (small), cush, in the black, rake-off. See INCOME. 2. buildup, boost, hike, up, upping.

GAIN v. 1. promote, clear, score, parlay, snowball, boost, pick up, rack up, build up, make a killing, feather one's nest. See GET. See also PROFIT. 2. beef up, hike up, jack up, jump up, put up, press up, press a bet, pyramid, builder-upper, sweeten the pot.

GAINFUL adj. going, going concern, paid-off, red, sweet, in the black.

GAINS n. bundle, harvest, package, skim, velvet, cream. See INCOME.

GAIT n. clip, getalong, lick.

GALA n. ball, bash, blast, brawl, bust, get-together, clambake, shindig, shindy, rub, belly rub (dance), hop, jump, prom, movable feast, blowout, stag, jag, jig, zig, jamboree, wingding, roast, donkey roast, drag party, do.

GALE n. big blow, chinook, mistral, Mister Hawkins, the hawk.

GALL n. guts, crust, nerve, cheek, chutspah, brass.

GALLANT adj. hairy, fire eater, stand tall, gritty, bigger 'n life.

GALLANT n. old man, Casanova, Don Juan, flame, Lothario, sugar daddy.

GALLERY n. peanut gallery, bloody-nose gallery, paradise; nigger heaven, Ethiopian paradise (Derog.); groot.

GALLEY n. crumb stash, bean gun (mobile, WWII).

GALLIVANT v. traipse, knock around, knock about, bat around, bat about, hit the road, hit the trail. See TRAVEL.

GALOSHES n. gunboats, goulashes, rubbers, pup tents.

GALVANIZE v. turn on, jazz up, pep up, perk up, snap up, zip up, put pep into it, put zip into it, zap. See STIMULATE.

GALVANIZER n. spark plug.

GAMBLE n. shot in the dark, spec, long shot, stab, have a fling at, irons in the fire, outside chance, toss-up, action. See WAGER.

GAMBLE v. get down, play, plunge, take the action, take a flyer, shoot the works, put one's money where one's mouth is, ball the jack. See WAGER.

GAMBLER n. high roller, plunger, dunker, player, big shot, big timer, dealer, wheeler-dealer, carder, cardsharp, card shark, punter, desperado, prof, tin horn, sharp, sharpie, sharper, sport, crap shooter, boneshaker, spec, gunslinger, Broadway boy (small-time), lame duck (stocks), scalper (ticket seller), K.G. (known gambler, police use), backer, the money, the bankroll, staker.

GAMBLING CASINO n. house, joint, shop, store, big store, toilet, trap, crib, flat, hell, bust-out joint, creep dive, creep joint.

GAMBLING TERMS action, skim, play it close to the vest, come, come again (repeat winner), fig (amount of money won or lost), salty (unlucky), copper on copper off; bust out, crap out (lose), black money (income), dead man's hand (aces and eights), trips (three of a kind), boat (full house), fold (go out), bump (raise), shill, ante up, feed the kitty, sandbag, under the gun (first player dealt to). See also DICE GAME TERMS, POKER TERMS.

GAMBOL v. horse around, fool around, kibitz around, carry on, make whoopee, cut loose, let loose, let go, whoop it up, kick up one's heels, cut, cut capers, cut a dido. See also REVEL.

GAMESMANSHIP n. psych out, give one the needle, one-upmanship.

GAME WARDEN n. possum sheriff.

176

GAMING HOUSE n. house, joint, shop, store, big store, toilet, trap, crib, flat, hell, bust-out joint, creep joint, creep dive.

GANG n. syndicate, outfit, tie-up, tie-in, mob, ring, clan, tribe, troupe, bunch, crowd, combination, combo, rat pack, zoo, hui (Hawaiian). See GROUP. See also CRIME, ORGANIZED.

GANG LEADER n. godfather, capo, war councillor.

GANG MEMBER n. gangbanger, cherry (new, inexperienced).

GANGSTER n. banger, gangbanger, geester, wiseguy, goodfella, godfather, mafioso, member of the family, goon, goonlet (young), gunsel, hit man, piece man, hood, hoodlum, hooligan, mo ghee, mob ghee, mobster, racketeer, soldier, cowboy, underboss (second in command), big juice, button man (Mafia), IBM (Italian Business Man, Derog.), pusher, dealer, digits dealer (numbers). See also CRIME, ORGANIZED.

GANGSTER'S GIRL n. squeeze, moll, gun moll, hairpin.

GAPE n. fish eye, gun.

GAPE v. eye, eyeball, get an eyeful, give the eye, eyeballs buggin' out like percolator tops, gawk, get a load of, size up, hold the glims on, take in, beam, pipe, pin, focus, lamp, rubber, gun. See also SEE.

GARAGE n. parking condo, barn, doghouse.

GARB n. threads, duds, rags, glad rags, feathers, Barbie and Ken (conventional), vine, weeds, rig, drapes, bib and tucker. See CLOTHING.

GARB v. turn out, fit out, rig out, rig up, rag out, rag up, tog, suit up, doll up, deck, deck out, dog out, dud, dude, dude up, dode (bad fit), drape.

GARBAGE n. gash, garbahge, dreck.

GARBAGE COLLECTOR n. san man, G-man, dirt bag (WWII).

GARBAGE TRUCK n. honey wagon.

GARBLED adj. ass backwards, bass ackwards, back asswards, double-talk, chewing gum.

GARGANTUAN adj. humongous, humungous, humongoid, humongo, mungo, monstro, honking, bonzai, big mother, biggy, butt-kicking, heavyweight, super-duper, supercolossal, jumbo, lolloping, whopping, thumper, thumping. See BIG.

GARISH adj. showy, glitzy, loud, screaming, gussied-up, kitschy, lit up like a Christmas tree. See GAUDY.

GARLIC n. stinking rose.

GARMENTS n. threads, duds, getup, feathers, vine, weeds, schmotte, sock frock, Barbie and Ken (conventional), honking brown (flashy), tailor-made, drapes, harness (leather, especially motorcycle). See CLOTHING.

GARNISH n. garbage (food), gingerbread, bells and whistles.

GARNISH v. doll up, fix up, gussy up, spruce up, put on the bells and whistles.

GARRET n. sky parlor.

GARRULOUS adj. yacky, gabby, gassy, long-winded, motormouth, blabbermouth, Chatty Cathy, spieler, flapjaw, gossipy. See TALKATIVE.

GARY, INDIANA Yellow Air, Yellow Breath, Bad Breath.

GAS CHAMBER n. dance hall, smogged (death).

GAS MASK n. chick (WWII, Army).

GASOLINE n. gas, juice, bug juice, go juice, ethyl.

GAS PEDAL n. gun, hammer.

GASTROINTESTINAL ORGANS n. guts, innards, inners, insides, inner man, inner works, inner workings, spaghetti, Department of the Interior.

GATE n. slammer.

GATHER v. bunch up, gang around, gang up, hang out, make the scene, round up, scare up, capture, corral, poke, punch.

GATHERING n. confab, clambake, meet, get-together, huddle, powwow, rap session, turnout. See MEETING.

GATHERING PLACE n. hangout, in spot, spot, place, in place, stamping ground, the grab.

GAUDY adj. showy, glitzy, ritzy, flossy, flashy, splashy, splurgy, loud, screaming, flaky, jazzy, snazzy, zappy, pizzazz, splendiferous, splendacious, chichi, frou-frou, spinach (excessive), gussied-up, kitschy, putting on the dog, putting on the Ritz, lit up like a Christmas tree, sporty. See also PRETENTIOUS.

GAUGE v. check, check out, dig it, eye, have one's number, look over, peg, size, size up, take one's measure, windshield appraisal (superficial, from a car), figure, figure in, dope out, take account of, guesstimate. See APPRAISE.

GAUNT adj. rattleboned, bag of bones, stack of bones, skin and bones, skeleton, peaked, peaky. See THIN.

GAY adj. bouncy, chirpy, chipper, zippy, feeling one's oats, full of beans, full of piss and vinegar. See also HAPPY.

GAZE n. fish eye, gun.

GAZE v. eye, eyeball, get an eyeful, give the eye, gawk, get a load of, size up, hold the glims on, take in, beam, pipe, pin, lamp, rubber. See also SEE.

GEAR n. 1. grandma (low gear, truck), Rachel (high gear). 2. stuff, kit and caboodle, outfit, contraption, setup, thing. See also APPARATUS. 3. drapery, feathers, toggery, togs, duds, threads, rags, glad rags. See also CLOTHING.

GEARSHIFT n. stick.

GELATIN n. nervous pudding.

GELD v. cut off one's balls, deball, fix, alter.

GELDED adj. altered, deballed, fixed.

GEM n. sparkler, spark, a girl's best friend, ice, cracked ice, stone, rock, rock candy, headlight, pennyweight, Simple Simon, glass (imitation).

GEMS n. stones, rocks, sparklers, ice, junk jewelry, Christmas, glass, hardware, pennyweight.

GENDERLESS adj. unisex.

GENERAL MANAGER v. G.M.

GENEROSITY n. heart, all heart.

GENEROUS adj. 1. big, bighearted, be big, softie, soft touch, have a heart, heart in the right place, loose, Santa Claus, good Joe, prince of a person, give one the shirt off one's back. 2. dime-a-dozen, aplenty, galore, no end, no end in sight, stink with. See PLENTY.

GENIAL adj. chipper, chirpy, corky, high, sunny, sunny side up, up, upbeat, upper, perky, Little Merry Sunshine, Little Mary Sunshine. See CHEERFUL.

GENITALIA n. family jewels, parts, private parts, privates, works, water works, apparatus, business, the business, one's business, equipment, unit, gadgets, tool box, machinery, moving parts; ass, pussy, cunt, purse, snatch, vige, twat, beaver, crack, hole, quiff, quim, crotch, snapper, snapping pussy, trim, box, fur, gash, nookie, poontang, tail, clam, bearded clam, cabbage, cookie, coochie (Af. Am.), love muscle, slash, fireplace, oven, Cape Horn, ace, ace of spades, coffee shop, mink, cuzzy, chacha, chocha, twelge, futy, gigi, jazz, jelly roll, nautch, notch, piece, cunny, honey pot, fruit cup, shaf, muffin, muff, receiving set, goldmine, moneymaker, puka, meat, dark meat, white meat, pink, the Y; cock, prick, dick, dork, pecker, peter, joint, middle leg, pencil, dummy, meat, burrito, lovesteak, wienie, stick, joystick, bone, enob, knob, joy knob, bishop, bicho, wang, thing, putz, schmeckel, schmuck, schwantz, pup, rod, pole, pego, pinga (Sp.), pud, dong, dang, dange, banana, shlong, dingus, staff, doodle, gun, head, tool, arm, jack, jimmy, jimbrowski, jock, Mr. Happy, thing, jigger, do-jigger, ding, hickey, fag, boo-boos, jang, jing-jang, ying-yang, tootsie roll, divining rod, snake, one-eyed monster, one-eyed wonder, shaft, jelly roll, meat whistle, skin flute, piccolo, rod of love,

root, worm, instrument, machine, nuts and bolts, basket, heart, hotchee, bug-fucker (small), hung (big), hung like a bull, hung like a chicken, hung like a rabbit (all Obsc.).

GENITALIA, FEMALE n. pussy, cunt, snatch, vige, twat, gash, beaver, crack, hole, quiff, quim, purse, beauty spot, trim, coochie (Af. Am.), nookie, box, muff, meat, the Y. See VAGINA.

GENITALIA, MALE n. cock, prick, dick, dork, pecker, peter, joint, wang, schlong, unit, tool, jelly roll, burrito, lovesteak, love muscle, bullets, chestnuts, clangers, gajoobies, hung (big), bug-fucker (small). See PENIS; TESTICLES.

GENITAL INSPECTION n. short-arm, short-arm drill, short-arm inspection (general or relaxed penis, originally Army use), long-arm inspection (erect penis).

GENIUS n. brain, brains, the brains, whiz kid, quiz kid, the goods, the stuff, the right stuff, candlepower, what it takes. See also INTELLIGENCE.

GENTILE n. WASP, goy, goyim, (Pl.), shegets (M.), shiksa (Fem., all Derog.).

GENTLE adj. laid-back, cool, mellow, tame.

GENTLEMAN n. 1. nice guy, good guy, good Joe, Joe Nice Guy, good egg, doll, pussycat, brick, trump, a real butt-kicker, stout fellow. See also MAN. 2. Brahmin, blueblood, lace curtain, silk stocking, swell, upper cruster. See ARISTOCRAT.

GENTLY, USE v. handle with care, don't bend the merchandise.

GENUINE adj. legit, open, for real, the real McCoy, genuine article, real people, kosher, up front, righteous, twenty-four-carat. See SINCERE.

GEOGRAPHIC DESIGNATIONS n. Coast, East, East Coast, West, West Coast, Pacific Rim, Wild West, Down East, Down Under, Down South, Down Home, Overseas, Seaside, the Shore, the Beach, the Carolinas, the Lower Forty-eight, the Old South, Solid South, Deep South, the Mountains, the Valley, the Walley (San Fernando), the Old Country, the Panhandle, Sun Belt, Snow Belt, Bible Belt, Borscht Belt, Rust Belt, Dust Bowl, the Islands.

GEOLOGIST n. sand smeller, rocksy, roxy.

GEORGIA n. Empire State of the South, Peach State.

GEORGIAN n. goober grabber, clay eater (Derog.).

GERM n. bug, cootie, crud, creeping crud, the plague, what's going around.

GERMAN n. Heinie, Kraut, Krauthead, sauerkraut, cabbagehead, hophead, limburger, Jerry, Boche, Fritz, turner, Dutchie, Dutcher, hun, pretzel; schatzi, schanzi (girl); bucket head, sausage (soldier) (all Derog.).

GERMANE adj.   kosher, legit, on the button, on the nose, right on, on target, that's the idea, that's the ticket. See APPLICABLE.

GESTATIONAL adj.   knocked up, expecting, infanticipating, in the family way, blessed eventing, expect a blessed event. See PREGNANT.

GESTURE n.   high sign, body language.

GET v.   clear, score, snag, bag, grab, snarf (with or without permission), hustle, wangle, promote, parlay, snowball, cash in on, clean up, pick up, scare up, lock up, rack up, snap up, build, build up, take up, buy up, buy off, buy out, buy into, make a buy, blow oneself to, make a good thing of, make a killing, make it big, make hay, make a haul, feather one's nest, line one's nest, catch, glom on to, get one's hands on, get hold of, latch on to, access, capture (computer data); cop, kipe, corral, boost, lift, liberate (steal).

GHOST n.   hant, haunt, haint, spook, things that go bump in the night.

GHOSTLY adj.   spooky, spookish, scary.

GHOSTWRITER n.   Grub, Streeter (also hack), spook, ghost, boo.

GIBBERISH n.   gubble, ubble-gubble, scat, double-talk, blah-blah.

GIBE n.   dump, putdown, rank-out, dig, dirty dig, crack, slam, swipe, jab, comeback, parting shot, brickbat, bazoo, raspberry.

GIDDY adj.   gaga, rocky, woozy, light-headed, bubble-headed, harebrained, punchy, slap-happy. See also DIZZY.

GIFT n.   handout, goodie, stake, giveaway (often prize), write-off, hand, helping hand, mitzvah, gifting, gash (unexpected), lump, poke out. See also DONATION.

GIFTED adj.   hot, hotshot, a lot of nifty, class act, mad, phenom, got it, shine at, shine in, have the smarts, have a bump for, have it on the ball, have plenty on the ball, have the goods. See INTELLIGENT.

GIGANTIC adj.   gross, humungous, humongoid, humongo, mungo, monstro, honking, butt-kicking, bonzai, moby, big mother, jumbo. See BIG.

GIGOLO n.   gash hound (Obsc.), lady-killer, heavy cake, blade, bun duster, candy kid, fancy Dan, fancy man. See LADIES' MAN.

GIN n.   panther piss, panther, white, bathtub gin, geneva, Gordon water (not common), gunpowder, jump steady, juniper juice, blue ruin, lightning, twankay.

GIN RUMMY TERMS   gin, blitz, schneider, a laydown.

GIRL n.   sis, beddy, betty, bet, nugget, nuggy, nectar, gooey nectar, necky, squash blossom, kid, kiddo, chick, chicklet, hip chick, Rita, freak mama, spring chicken, biddie, bird, broad, fly girl, wukka, zimmer, hammer, studette (man chaser), burger, double burger, triple burger with cheese, doll, babe, baby doll, talent, tenderoni (Af. Am.), destroyer (beautiful), boytoy, whistle bait, jail bait, San Quentin quail, pigeon, squab, canary, filet, bunny, cub, gadget, gidget, gaunch, ginch, wench, gumdrop, bimbette (young, sexy) muffy, fifi, Heather, foof (superficial, trendy) floozy, floogy, faloosie, frill, frail, frail eel, frame dame, cover, cupcake, cheese, cutie, skirt, miniskirt; cunt, pussy, gash, muff, bush, cou, couzie, quasar, hose, cock teaser, CT, (all Obsc.); queen, classis chassis, classy chassy, import, bag, baggage, package, jill, filly, heifer, teenybopper, bobbysoxer, bubble-gum rocker, kitten, kitty, hellcat, piece, sugar-wooga; tree (tall), cherry tree (tall virgin), granola (wears no makeup), brick house (big breasts), nun, cold tit (frigid), witch, battle; bikini whale, cow (fat); bat, boo hog, bama, barfola, paper-bag case, double-bagger, triple-bagger, pigmeat, sweat, hag, dog, beast, beat, lobo (all ugly); crock, jane, jellybean, jerry, moose (live-in, Korean War), klootch (Esk.), mort, mott, mouse, wren, rib, li'l mama, she-she, tomboy, twist, missy, little missy, slip, tomato, baby, eatin' stuff (Obsc.), butterfly, square broad, yuppie (young urban professional).

GIRL FRIEND n.   G.F., g-friend, old lady, squeeze, main squeeze, main queen, wrap, big moment, body and soul, hamma, mama, sweet mama, sweetie; main bitch, sweetback (Af. Am.), companion, constant companion, flame, nectar, gooey, gooey nectar, hookey, sugar, sugar pie, sugar bowl, jelly roll, kissing cousin, ace, ace lane, baby, total babe, love bird, turtle dove, oyster, armpiece, baby cake, cake, cakie, chick, gussie mollie (not common), patootie, hot patootie, sweet patootie, josan (Korean War), snoff, corn bread, home cooking, stone marten (beautiful), sponsored (has boy friend).

GIRLIE SHOW n.   T and A, tits and ass, jiggle, jiggly-wiggly, leg show, topless, burlesque, strip joint, a circus.

GIRL WATCH v.   pussy patrol (Obsc.), scope the local units, give one the eye, give one the cyclops, take in the sights, go for the cheese.

GIST n.   point, stuff, nub, bottom line, name of the game, nitty-gritty, nuts and bolts, the way of it, nature of the beast, drift, heart, meat, nub, score, punch line.

GIVE v.   gift, gift with, slip, give up, hand out, hand over, dish out, fork out, fork over, shell out, pony up, put up, put up or shut up, put out, put something in the pot, sweeten the pot, sweeten the kitty, feed the kitty, pass the hat, ante up, get it up, get it on, get it on the line, chip in, kick in, come through, come across, come across with, come down with, come down with the needful, plank down, plunk down, post, see, go, duke, weed, pass it on over, gimme, stake, put a buck one's way, throw, give away the store, run with the ball, do one's part.

GIVER n. angel, backer, Santa Claus, sugar daddy, fairy godmother, lady bountiful, heavy hitter, maxed-out (political limit).

GIVE UP v. give in, cave in, throw in the towel, cry uncle, fold, buckle under, drop, take the oath, flake, pull out, bail out, bow out, chicken out, walk out on, wash one's hands of, drop like a hot potato, back down. See ABANDON. See also SURRENDER.

GLAD adj. up, hopped-up, floating on air, pleased as Punch, tickled, tickled pink, tickled to death, can't complain. See HAPPY.

GLADIOLA n. glad.

GLAMOROUS adj. glam, ten, 10, dyno, boss, wukka, righteous, drooly, dishy, drop-dead gorgeous, glamour girl, hammer, stone, stone fox, foxy, nifty, biscuit, look like a million. See BEAUTIFUL.

GLAMOUR n. razzle-dazzle, animal magnetism, star quality.

GLANCE n. flash, gander, bad eye, the glad eye, eyeball, gun, hinge, glom, pike, slant, lamp, look-see, swivel.

GLANCE v. flash, pipe, eye, eyeball, get an eyeful, bat an eye at, give one the eye, give with the eyes, give it a thumb check, take in, take a gander, take a hinge, get a hinge, get a load of, check it out. See SEE.

GLARE n. dirty look, bad eye, dog eye.

GLARE v. look daggers, do a slow burn, give one a dirty look, dog-eye, bad-eye, act the lion tamer, cloud up and rain on one. See FROWN. See also SEE.

GLASS n. jigger, pony, snifter.

GLASSES n. specs, mini specs, nippers, shades, sunshades, sun specs, sus-specs, cheaters, frames, windows, rims, four-eyes, bop glasses, peepers, glims, googs, goggles, wraparounds, mask (sun), grannies, professor (wearer).

GLEAM n. flash, glitz, show, zap, glim, dimmer.

GLIB adj. flip, gift of gab, gabbo, fast talker, slick, smooth, smooth operator, spieler, all jaw, flap-jaw, big hot-air artist. See TALKATIVE.

GLIDE v. skate, smooth along.

GLIMPSE n. flash, gander, bad eye, the glad eye, eyeball, eyeball inspection, gun, hinge, glom, pike, slant, lamp, look-see, swivel.

GLIMPSE v. flash, pipe, eye, eyeball, get an eyeful, bat an eye at, give one the eye, give with the eyes, take in, take a gander, take a hinge, get a hinge, get a load of, check it out. See SEE.

GLISSANDO n. slurp, smear.

GLITTER n. flash, glitz, show, zap, tinsel.

GLOAT v. lick one's chops, rub one's nose in, horse-laugh, give one the horse laugh, hee-haw.

GLOBE n. apple, pellet, pill, sphere, big blue marble, real estate, spaceship earth.

GLOOMY adj. crumbed, dragged, low, blue funk, got the blue devils, in the dumper, down in the dumps, hang crepe, sad-sacky. See MELANCHOLY.

GLORIFY v. build up, hike, hike up, jack up, jump up, put up, put on a pedestal, boost. See also EXAGGERATE.

GLOSS v. soft-pedal, whitewash, cover up.

GLOVE COMPARTMENT n. hip pocket.

GLUE n. stickum, gunk, gummy, spit.

GLUM adj. down in the mouth, in the dumps, in the doleful dumps, crumbed, blue, in a blue funk. See MELANCHOLY.

GLUTINOUS adj. gooey, gloppy, globby, gook, gooky, goonk, gummy, gunk.

GLUTTED adj. full up, packed, lousy with, up to here in, up to one's ass in, coming out of one's ears. See FULL.

GLUTTON n. pig, porker, hog, oinker, belly god, mean scorfer, greedygut, greedyguts, hefty eater, husky eater, pelican, foodie, fresser, chocoholic (chocolate lover).

GLUTTONIZE v. gobble, gulp, bolt, gross out, munch out, blimp out, pork out, pig out, Mac out, trough out, scarf, scarf out, scarf back, throw back, scarf down, scorf down, narf, grease one's chops, grease down, hoover, pig down, bolt down, gobble down, gulp down, chow down, wolf, wolf down, put away, make a pig of oneself, make a hog of oneself, eat like a horse, eat one's head off, eat out of house and home, dispatch, dispose of, do oneself proud, get away with. See also EAT.

GNAT n. no-see-um, punkie, punky.

GNAW v. chaw, munch, chomp, gum, fling a fang into.

GO interj. fuck off, FO, stay out of my face, shove off, vamoose, scram, amscray, get, git, get the hell out, get outta here, get lost, gomer (get out of my emergency room, Medic.), blow, beat it, bug out, bug off, push off, buzz off, flake off, on your way, go chase yourself, bag ass, you're excused, split, hit the road Jack, hit the bricks, make yourself scarce, make like a tree and leave, make tracks, clear out, butt out, screw, shove, take a walk, take a powder, take a hike, skedaddle, cheese it, go chase yourself, scoot, up anchor, scat, get on your horse, go peddle your papers.

GO v. split, color me gone, air out (Af. Am.), motor, motorvate, get naked, sko, lesgo (let's go), jet, bolt (quickly), be-bop, blow, break camp, hoof it, beat it, fog, cruise, dedomicile, I'm history, I'm outta here, I'm out, I'm outtie 5000, I'm Audi 5000, I'm Audi, scram, amscray, trip, cut out, cut loose, cut and run, duck and run, cut ass, haul ass, bag ass, barrel ass, drag ass, shag ass, hit the road, hit the trail, hit the bricks, step off, jump off, hop off, bop off, push off, blast off, fuck off, flake off, knock off, nip, nip off, tear off, light off, kick off, slam off, roll out, bone out, move out, bow out, boo out, break out, ooze out, ease on, ease out, ease on out, faze out, flake out, walk out, run out, clear out, storm out, tear out, nix out, butt out, peel out, check out, opt out, catch out, dig out, skin out, bail out, kick out, push out, pull out, duck out, snake out, ship out, burn out, burn rubber, peel rubber, skip, skip out, bug out, bug off, light, light out, barge out, boogie, tool, tool along, vamoose, ankle, get on (Af. Am.), get away, get lost, get going, get, git, get-git, get the hell out, get the lead out, make oneself scarce, highball, dog it, blow, blow away, blow this pop stand, blow the joint, breeze, drift, drag, drag it, drag one's freight, pull one's freight, haul one's freight, take off, take off in a cloud, take off in a cloud of sour owl shit, take off like a big-ass bird, take off like a B.A.B., take the air, skidoo, skidoodle, skidaddle, skedaddle, hotfoot, play on down, scat, shove, shove off, shove in one's clutch, be getting along, trot along, toddle along, stagger along, ball the jack, perk, percolate, absquatulate, exfiltrate, roll, tick, hightail, make tracks, make a break for it, run like a scared rabbit, do a vanishing act, hop it, sashay off, buzz off, buzz along, wing it, powder, take a powder, take a run-out powder, sniff a powder, walk, take a walk, walk out on, run out on, ding, kiss good-bye, have to see a man about a dog, screw, slough, truck, truck on out, book, book it, time to book, time to bail, time to cruise, leg, leg it out of here, make it, fade, fade out, do a fade, fade away, get small (from a crime), drift away, duck, heel, bottle up and go, pull up stakes, up stakes, dust, plow ahead, fly the coop, scramble, scooch, scream, cheese it, step it, get to steppin', get off the dime, eat a worm, hat up, let the doorknob hit you, put it to the wind, slide, swoop, scratch gravel, collar a broom, cop a broom, quit the scene, quit cold, ditch, stay out of one's face, get out of one's sight, head for the barn (home), drift, drift away, leave flat, leave high and dry, take gypsy leave, take French leave, go A.W.O.L., go over the hill, go over the fence, go over the side, lam, take it on the lam, wail, mosey, mosey off, mosey along. See also DIE; ABSCOND.

GOAD v. goose, goose up, egg on, turn on, fire up, spark, key up, put up to, work up, work up into a lather, sound, trigger. See STIMULATE.

GOAL n. 1. gool. 2. zero, ground zero, surgical mission (precise target).

GOAT n. billy, billy goat, nanny, nanny goat.

GOATEE n. pez. See also BEARD.

GOD n. Dad, Head Knock, Man Upstairs, Lordy.

GODLY adj. born-again, got religion, Jesus freak, Holy Joe, Jesus lover, Jasper, knee blender, Mary, Christian, candy-ass, goody, goody-goody, goody two-shoes, scoutmaster. See also VIRTUOUS.

GO FREE v. beat the rap, walk, out, get away with murder, get off, let off, let go. See also PARDONED.

GO IN v. barge in, blow in, bust in, pop in, mooch in, ace in, breeze in, come breezing in, come barging in, come, come busting in, access, penetrate, break in, bum-rush.

GOLD n. yellow stuff, dust.

GOLF CLUB n. stick, shovel sticks, baffy, brassie, iron, wood, niblick, mashie.

GOLF CLUB BARROOM n. nineteenth hole.

GOLF COURSE n. prairie, back nine, blind hole, bunker, cheat sheet (course plan and yardage chart), dogleg, fat (wide part of green), front nine, home hole (final hole).

GOLF SCORE n. mulligan (extra shot, uncounted), halve (tie), hole (hole one), holeable, hole out, up (he was 3 up on Watson), ace (hole in one), birdie (one stroke under par), got a birdie, eagle (2 under par), bogey (one stroke over par), double bogey (2 over par), dormie (strokes ahead equal to the holes yet to play), gimme (short putt).

GOLF STROKE n. lay-up (intentionally short), foozle (clumsy), sandie (out of the trap in one), sclaff (divot digger), short game (approach and putt), slice (ball hit to right), banana ball (slice), hook (ball hit to left), duck hook (low), waggle (she waggled the club to relax), sink, back door (putt), borrow (putt, allow for slope), sidehiller (putt along the slope), yip (bad putt), approach shot, blast (from sand), carry (distance), chippie (approach shot that drops into hole), dub (hit poorly), whiff (miss), explosion shot, fat.

GOLF TERMS creep (slow round); can it, drain it (sink a putt); scratch player (plays at par), punk, pushover, dub, duffer, hooker (inferior player); Nassau (type of wager), rabbit (pro golf qualifier), away (ball farthest from hole), hole out (finish a hole), bunkered (in a hazard), lie (ball location), read the green, rim (the ball rimmed the hole and didn't drop), rub of the green (grain).

GONADS n. nads, nuts, rocks, balls, family jewels, diamonds, bag, ballocks, basket, cojones, boo-boos, ears.

GONE adj. petered out, dried-up, fall between the cracks, kiss (something) good-bye, out the window, down the tube, down the toilet, down the drain, down the spout, down the rathole. See also DEAD.

GONG n. gut hammer, hammer (usually iron triangle).

GONORRHEA n. V.D., clap, claps, dose, dose of clap, hammerhead clap, old clap, old dose (neglected case), the drip, the whites, pissing razor blades, head cold, caught a cold, picked up something, picked up a nail, lulu (painful case), burn, blue balls, social disease, old Joe.

GOOD adj. fresh, goodie, cool, sweet, bumpin' good; lookin' chilly, ace (Af. Am.); neato, def, fly, bomb, thicks, crazy, terriff, bueno, bad, down, real down, not too shabby, way, rad, way rad, beauteous maximus, Jake, ginchy, slammin', fabu, cherry, dual, fat, phat, straight, dope, nitro, sick, lampin', happenin', rattling, rocking, gnarly, nasty, a real butt-kicker, major, shimmy, cranking, righteous, stokin', tubular, vicious, wailing, whaling, dope on a rope, hype, stink, stone, stone groove, epic, genius, proper, doin' a hundred, batting a thousand, organic, up to snuff, up to speed, up to the mark, some (that's some doll), kind, some kind of. See PRAISEWORTHY, ADMIRABLE.

GOOD-BYE interj. bye-bye, G.B., see ya, so long, chow, ciao, hasta, hasta la pasta, 'sko (let's go), later, catch you later, later tater, check you, gotta slide, I'm history, I'm outta here, I'm audi 5000, I'm sideways, twist a braid, good-by-ee, after, while, adios, by now, ta-ta, see you, have a nice day, take it easy, dig ya later, see you later alligator, be good, happy landing, take care, toodle-oo, cheerio, cherro, cherry, thirty for now, that's thirty, don't take any wooden nickels, eighty-eights, good hunting, see you in church, Abyssinia, keep the faith baby, peace, it's been real, olive oil.

GOOD-BYE n. eighty-eights, swan song. See PARTING.

GOOD DEED n. mitzvah (Yid.), making brownie points.

GOOD-LOOKING adj. righteous, ten, 10, busting fresh, wukka, stud muffin, freak, freak mama, freak mommy, freak daddy, flygirl, fly guy, flyboy, down, brick house, hammer, burger, double burger, triple burger with cheese, drooly, dishy, beddy, nugget, nectar, gooey nectar, dyno, dreamboat, glam, phat chick, flavor (Af. Am.), living doll, schwing!, looker, good looker, hottie, ankle, tall dark and handsome, handsome thing, Adonis, lover boy, pretty boy, hotty (homosexual). See BEAUTIFUL.

GOOD-NATURED adj. Joe Nice Guy, Mr. Nice Guy, breezy, good scout, a real butt-kicker, sweet, a sweetie, a sweetheart, so sweet she can give you cavities, so sweet he can give you diabetes, softie, marshmallow. See also NICE.

GOOD NIGHT interj. night, nighty-night, sweet dreams, turn off the light and don't let the bedbugs bite, see you in dreamland.

GOODS n. the goods, material, stuff, jive (gaudy), seconds (flawed).

GOOD TIME n. ball, blast, cold chillin', picnic, rat fuck, high old time, panic.

GOOD WILL n. the good side of, the right side of.

GOOSEFLESH n. goose pimples, goose bumps, duck bumps.

GORGE v. gross out, blimp out, pork out, pig out, scarf back, throw back, gobble, narf, trough out, grease one's chops, grease down, hoover, mac out, pig down, make a pig of oneself, eat like a horse. See EAT.

GORGED adj. full up, fed up, fed to the teeth, fed to the gills, stuffed to the gills, packed, jammed, jam-packed, with a bellyful, with a skinful, with a snootful.

GORGEOUS adj. drop-dead gorgeous, lulu, dream puss, ten, 10, stone, stone fox, foxy, dyno, head rush, wukka, knock one's eyes out, beaut, easy on the eyes, living doll, centerfold. See BEAUTIFUL.

GOSSIP n. scuttlebutt, talk, grapevine, clothesline, leak, dirt, dish, back-fence talk, back-fence gossip, ear loft, earful, ear dust, slime, bibful, hash, blathergab, gam, latrine rumor, blowup, wire, hot wire, page-oner, vanilla, whispering campaign, black plague, nut cracking, rat fucking, dirty linen, dirty wash.

GOSSIP v. bad-mouth, dish, dish the dirt, rip on, rag on, pop junk, chew, chew the fat, cut up, cut one up and down, cut one into little pieces, cut one into ribbons, rap, gatemouth, rattle on, schmoose, schmoozle, wiggle-waggle, bend one's ear, ear duster, bat the chat, bat the breeze, bat one's gums, beat one's gums.

GOSSIPER n. sleaze monger, yenta (Yid.), ear-duster, polly, satch, gasser, gatemouth, load of wind, windbag, busybody, tabby, tattletale.

GOSSIPY adj. catty, all jaw, big-mouthed, evil, gabby, gassy, windy. See also TALKATIVE.

GO TO THE MOVIES v. flick it, take in a movie, catch a show.

GOUGE v. bleed, bleed white, screw, hold up, soak, stick, sting, clip, make pay through the nose, skin, fleece, fuck, fuck over. See OVERCHARGE.

GOURMAND n. greedygut, greedyguts, hog, pig, foodie, belly god, hefty eater, husky eater, pelican, mean scorfer, fresser, chocoholic (chocolate lover).

GOURMANDIZE v. gobble, gulp, bolt, gross out, munch out, blimp out, pork out, pig out, scarf, scarf out, scarf back, throw back, scarf down, scorf down, pig down, bolt down, gobble down, gulp down, chow down, wolf, wolf down, narf, trough out, grease one's chops, grease down, hoover, put away, make a pig of oneself, make a hog of oneself, eat like a horse, eat one's head off, eat out of house and home, dispatch, dispose of, do oneself proud, get away with. See also EAT.

GOVERN v. head, head up, run, run things, run the show, call the shots, call the signals, be in the driver's seat, pull the strings. See MANAGE.

GOVERNMENT n. Big Brother, the Feds, the Union, Uncle Sam, U.S., U.S.A., D.C., Washington, the mighty Dome, the digger.

GOVERNMENT AGENCIES n. alphabet soup.

GOVERNMENT AGENCY n. fed, Fed, feds, the Feds.

GOVERNMENT EMPLOYEE n. fed, Fed.

GOVERNMENT FUNDS n. pork barrel, space barrel (NASA), public crib, public till, public trough.

GOVERNMENT NATIONAL MORTGAGE ASSOCIATION n. Ginnie Mae.

GOVERNOR n. guv, head, headman, Big Brother, boss. See also EXECUTIVE.

GRAB v. snatch, snag, snarf (with or without permission), collar, corral, hook, land, nail, bag, nab, glom, glaum, glahm, glom onto, put the glom on, put the snatch on, put the snare on, clap hands on, get one's fingers on, get one's hands on. See also ARREST.

GRADE n. Brownie point, ten, 10, five-pointer (high). A: ace, four-pointer. B: three-pointer. C: hook. D: dog. E: eagle. F: fade (low or failing), flag, flunk.

GRADUATE n. grad, old grad, alum.

GRADUATE SCHOOL n. grad school.

GRADUATE STUDENT n. grad, doc, postdoc.

GRAFFITI n. bombing, spray bombing, buffing; tagger, writer, mobber, bomber (does graffiti).

GRAFT n. juice, payoff, payoff money, bad notes, payola, drugola, gayola, under the table, oil, on the take, contribution, padding, shake, skimming, squeeze, cream, boodle, hat. See also BRIBE; PROTECTION MONEY.

GRAFTER n. the juice man, flimflammer.

GRAND adj. fab, marvy, unreal, nifty, magnif, something else, smashing, super, super-duper, def, doozie, dynamite, man-sized, pip, solid gold, spiffy, bang-up, swell, stunning, out of this world. See IMPRESSIVE. See also DIGNIFIED; BIG.

GRANDEE n. upper cruster, blue-blood, lace curtain, silk-stocking, swell.

GRANDFATHER n. gramps, grandpa, grandpapa, grandpap, grandpappy, granddad, granddaddy, granddada, grampa, gramper, gramp, gramfer, granther, old man.

GRANDIOSE adj. splendacious, splendiferous, Flash Gordon, highfalutin, purple, showy, Mr. Big, Mr. Big Shot. See also MAGNIFICENT.

GRANDMOTHER n. grandma, grandmama, grandmammy, grandmaw, gramma, grammy, granman, grannam, granny, nana, nanny, big mama, gammer, gammy, safety, old woman; granny dumping, packed suitcase syndrome (abandonment).

GRAND RAPIDS, MICHIGAN Chair City.

GRANT n. handout, gifting, lump, pokeout.

GRANT v. 1. put out, drop, gift, gift with, stake, give with, come through, get it on. See GIVE. 2. bless, pass on, shake on, sign on, sign off on, yes one, go along with, give the nod, thumbs up, jibe. See also ALLOW. 3 come across, come around, give out, give in, give away the store, lie down and roll over for. See SURRENDER 4. like you say, you got it, sure thing, I'll drink to that, I hear you.

GRAPEFRUIT n. cannonball.

GRASP v. 1. snatch, snag, collar, corral, hook, land, nail, bag, nab, glom, glaum, glahm, glom onto, put the glom on, put the snatch on, put the snare on. 2. get, get the picture, get the hang of it, make, catch on, latch on, pick up, blow wise. See UNDERSTAND.

GRASS n. the green deck, carpet, rug.

GRASSHOPPER n. hopper, hoppergrass.

GRATIFICATION n. flash, kick, kicks, mess, hit, velvet, get off, get off on, sure shock, you got it, just name it.

GRATIFIED adj. 1. on cloud nine, in seventh heaven, have no kick coming, tickled pink, tickled to death, happy camper, hit the spot, just what the doctor ordered, pleased as Punch. See HAPPY. 2. fed to the teeth, fed to the gills, stuffed to the gills, skinful, snootful, bellyful, no more room.

GRATIFY v. fill the bill, score, hit the bull's-eye, make it, thanks I needed that, make a hit, hit the spot, do the trick, get one's jollies, get one's kicks, get off, get off on. See SATISFY.

GRATIFYING adj. kicks, for kicks, mellow, fine and mellow, lush, downhill, nervous, cool, cherry, wild.

GRATING n. waffle iron.

GRATIS adj. freebie, free ride, for love, on the house, Annie Oakley, cuffo. See FREE.

GRATUITY n. tip, toke (gambling), chip, cue, somethin', a little somethin', a little something to sweeten the pot, a little slack; subway, bus ride, one-way (5 or 10 cents); sweetener, grease, salve, palm oil, gravy, lagniappe, zukes, fringe benefit, goodies, perk, perks, button, hat, ice.

GRAVE adj. heavy, heavy number, strictly business, meaningful, serious talk, serious jelly, serious shit, no shit, no bird turdin', jelly, deadpan, not crack a smile, cold sober, sober as a judge. See SERIOUS.

GRAVE n. cold storage, dust bin, planted, daisy, pushing up daisies, deep-six, six, six feet under.

GRAVE-ROBBING n. body snatching.

GRAVEYARD n. boneyard, bone factory, bone orchard, marble orchard, marble town, headstone city, cold storage.

GRAVY n. dunk sauce, goo, gooey, goop, goopy, glob, globby, glop, gloppy, gop, gunk, gyppo, goozlum, gippo.

GREASE v. slick, slick on, grease the wheels, lube.

GREASING n. grease job, lube, schmear.

GREAT adj. 1. killer, A number one, aces, aggro, super-duper, def, deffest, mean, lampin', mega-gnarly, rat-fuck, zero cool, cold, chilly most, bump 'n', happenin', out-of-this-world, out-of-sight, a gas, Jake, ginchy, slammin', fabu, gonest, mostest, a doozy, like dynamite, dyno, nitro, brutal, fab, cherry, dope, dual, fat, fierce, fresh, fully on, fully, fully to the skull, epic, mint, on the strength, raw, sick, stupid fresh, tits, tough, heavy, major, cranking, frantic, rattling, rocking, rock, hellacious, bad. See EXCELLENT. 2. humongoid, humongous, humungous, mungo, mongo, monstro, butt-kicking, bonzai, moby, major-league, big-league, jumbo. See BIG. 3. monster, star, superstar, champ, lion, a somebody. See CELEBRITY.

GREAT BRITAIN Blighty, John Bull, Merry Old, Albion, Limeyland, Tight Little Island.

GREATCOAT n. car coat, Benny, binny, Benjamin, horse blanket.

GREATEST adj. baaadest, killer, gilt-edged, balls out, bitchin', twitchin', meanest, boss, cool, chilly most, terrible, gonest, hundred-proof, murder, stone. See also BEST, EXCELLENT.

GREAT FALLS, MONTANA High Water.

GREEDY adj. grabby, big-eye, poligot, greedyguts.

GREEK n. greaseball, grikola, marblehead (all Derog.).

GREEN BAY, WISCONSIN Title Town.

GREEN BEANS n. snaps (So.).

GREENWICH MEAN TIME n. zulu, G.M.T.

GREET v. highball, tumble, flag, shoulder, fly a sign (show a gang sign), whistle for, whistle down, flop, give one a flop, give one a toss, give one five, knock one some skin, give one the glad eye, give one the glad hand, give one the key to the city, roll out the red carpet.

GREETING interj. hi, hey, hey Homie, yo, 'sup?, ciao, checkin' in, gimme some skin, gimme five, gimme ten, slip me five, high five, low five, how do?, how's it happenin'?, what up?, what's up?, what's happenin'?, what it is?, what's the drill?, what's the scam?, what does it look like?, what's shakin'?, what do you know?, how's by you?, buzza, all right, what's going down?, what's coming down?, what's the skinny?, blood, cuh, cuz (Af. Am.). See HELLO.

GREETING n. a blow, tumble, rumble, high five, howdy, highball.

GREGARIOUS adj. clubby, clubbable. See also SOCIABLE.

GRENADE n. pineapple, apple, cookie, Chicago overcoat, potato masher.

GRENADE KILLING n. fragging.

GREYHOUND BUS n. big dog, dog, the hound.

GRIDDLECAKE n. flapjack, hotcake, blanket, saddle blankets, brown bucks, flats, manhole cover, tire patch, wheat, collision mat (WWII).

GRIDIRON n. field, grid.

GRIEF n. heartache, tsures (Yid.), blues. See MISERY. See also DISTRESS; MISFORTUNE.

GRIEVANCE n. stink, big stink, beef, where's the beef?, bitch, bellyache, grouse, gripe, the gripes, a hoo-ha, flack, a knock, mix, dido, hurting, pain, pain in the neck, pain in the ass, kick, blast, howl, holler, squawk, yell, roar, rumble, rap, rip, tsures (Yid.), CC (chief complaint), ax to grind.

GRIEVE v. carry on, eat one's heart out, sing the blues, take it big, take it hard, take on, cry me a river, hang crepe. See MOURN.

GRILL v. roast, go over, put through the third degree, third-degree, put on the grill, put the pressure on, put the screws on. See QUESTION.

GRIMACE v. make a face, mug.

GRIME n. gook, drek, gunk, prut, crud.

GRIMY adj. scuzzy, sleazy, cruddy.

GRIN v. crack a smile, grin from ear to ear, grin like a Cheshire cat, grin like a Chessy cat.

GRIP n. valpack, tote bag, jiffy bag, keister.

GRIP v. glom on to, clap a hand on, get one's fingers on, get one's hands on, nail.

GRIPE n. clutch, crunch, grab.

GRIPPE n. flu, bug.

GRISLY adj. sick, weird, grody, gross, yucky. See BAD.

GROGGY adj. dopey, punchy, punch-drunk, slap-happy, woozy, out of it. See DAZED. See also SLEEPY.

GROOM v. prep, ready, shape up, lick into shape, put through the grind, put through the mill. See TRAIN. See also PREPARE.

GROOMED adj. clean, flowered, ready, set, prepped, slotted.

GROOVE n. grind, daily grind, same old shit, SOS, S.O.S., same old same old (Af. Am.), rut, drill, sked, shtick, one's slot.

GROPE v. go at it ass backwards, phumpher, bonehead into it. See FLOUNDER.

GROSS adj. cheap, loud-mouthed, sleazy, raunchy. See VULGAR; UGLY.

GROTESQUE adj. grody, grody to the max, gross, weird, weirdo.

GROUCH n. sourpuss, lemon puss, bug, bug up one's ass, bug up one's nose. See COMPLAINER.

GROUND n. 1. dust, real estate, old sod, terra firma. 2. bottom line, nuts and bolts, rock bottom, nitty-gritty, meat and potatoes, beginners, coal and ice, ABC's, brass tacks, get down, get down to brass tacks.

GROUNDLESS adj. hot-air, bullshit, piss and wind, off-base, cockeyed, cockamamie, cahcah, coming from no-where, made up, made up out of whole cloth, who sez?, my eye, just talk, whataya talkin'?, talking through one's hat, you're talkin' like a man with a paper ass, where'd ya get that shit?

GROUND MEAT n. burger, beefburger, cheese-burger, hamburg, superburger, chewed fine, clean up the kitchen (order for hamburger, hash, or stew), Wimpy.

GROUNDS n. goods, info, dope, smoking gun (crucial), chapter and verse, the know, straight stuff, the emess, the numbers, gospel. See FACTS.

GROUP n. bunch, crowd, gang, posse (not necessarily a gang), click, crew, crush, mob, outfit, ring, circle, syndicate, hook up, tie up, tie in, tie in tie up, clan, insiders, family, ashram, groupie, skeezer (hip hop), pool, those one runs with, the boys, the boys uptown, tribe, troupe, troops, com-bination, combo; rat pack, yoot (teenage); beef squad (union toughs), clout (auto thieves), deb (girl gang member), Old Boy network, zoo, strange bedfellows (unlikely group). See also ASSOCIATION.

GROUP v. bunch up, gang around, gang up, hang out, make the scene, round up, scare up, corral, poke, punch.

GROUPING n. mixed bag, combo, everything but the kitchen sink, kludge (parts), mishmash.

GROUP SEX n. gang-bang, gang-shag, gang-shay, group grope, circle jerk, line up on, moresome (three or more), bunch punch, swinging, daisy chain, pull a train, choo-choo, chuga-chuga, club sandwich, fuckathon, team cream, Mazola party, Wesson party, party (two prostitutes, one customer); sugar and spice, vanilla chocolate and pecan (interracial); vanilla and chocolate (one black and one white prostitute, one customer), white meat turkey on pumper-nickel (two black prostitutes, one white customer) (all Obsc.).

GROUPS, SOCIAL n. 1. young upwardly mobile pro-fessional: YUP, yuppie, yumpie, Y-people, buppie (black upwardly mobile, Af. Am.), yavis (young attractive verbal intelligent successful), dewk (couple employed with kids) dinks, dinkies (double income, no kids), siks (single income, kids), dimps (double income, money problems), puppies (poor), yuffie (failure), guppies (gay), yummies (mommies), Yorkie (New York), chuppie (Chicano), juppies (Japanese), yucas (Cuban-American), PIB (people in black, artsy types), techno-brat (young media workers). 2. baby boomers (born 1946 through 1964), afterboomers, postie, post-boomers, baby busters, busters (born 1965 through 1974). 3. middle-aged: maffies (affluent), woofies (affluent over fifty), dump-ies (downwardly mobile professional). 4. older: woofs (well-off older folks), woopies (well-off older people).

GROVEL v. eat dirt, eat crow, suck up to, suck ass, kiss butt, kiss ass, lick ass, bootlick, stooge, yes, be a yes-man, fall over, fall all over, kowtow, curry below the knee. See also FLATTER.

GROW v. shoot up, snowball, mushroom, pyramid. See also EXPAND.

GROW OLD v. put mileage on, push, take hair off the dog, pull pages off the calendar.

GROW PLANTS v. green-thumb.

GROWTH n. buildup, beefing up, fleshing out, bulk-up, boost, hike, up, upping, sprawl (urban).

GRUDGE n. bone to pick, peeve, pet peeve.

GRUEL n. cush, grits, mush.

GRUELING adj. heavy, hellish, hairy, ass-busting. See DIFFICULT.

GRUESOME adj. sick, sicky, weird, gruesome two-some, grody, grody to the max, gross. See also UGLY.

GRUFF adj. snippy, snappy, short.

GRUMBLER n. bitcher, beefer, bellyacher, griper, grouse, crab, crank, crybaby. See COMPLAINER.

GUANTANAMO BAY, CUBA Gitmo.

GUARANTEE n. lock, a lock on, sure thing, fer shirr, sure as shooting, pipe, lead-pipe cinch, bet your ass, bet your bottom dollar. See CERTAINTY.

GUARANTEE v. stand up for one, get behind one, sign for, cosign, angel, back, greenback, bankroll, juice, grub-stake, pick up the check, pick up the tab, stake. See also ASSURE.

GUARANTEED adj. sure, sure enough, surefire, for damn sure, license to print money, for a fact, on ice, have a lock on. See CERTAIN.

GUARD n. screw, bouncer, chaser, eyes, hack, herder, hooligan, roach, roller, shields, sky, yard bull, stick, jaboney, jiboney, sidewinder, trigger man, lookout, bugster.

GUARD v. look out, shotgun, ride shotgun for, lay chickie; cover, cover up, cover one's ass, go to bat for, stonewall.

GUARD DUTY n. tour, watch, graveyard watch.

GUARDED adj. cagey, leery, on the lookout, with a weather eye open, with one's eyes peeled, handle with kid gloves, mind one's p's and q's.

GUARDHOUSE n. lockup, brig, clink, stockade. See also JAIL.

GUARDIAN n. sitter, babysitter, housesitter, cop, bird dog, alarm clock.

GUESS n. guesstimate, ball-park figure, in the ball park, hunch, shot, shot in the dark, stab, stab in the dark, sneaking suspicion, SWAG (slightly wild-assed guess).

GUESS v. figure, size up, guesstimate, go out on a limb, take a stab, take a shot. See SPECULATE.

GUEST n. company, out-of-towner, visiting fireman.

GUIDE n. 1. hot lead, lead, tip-off, telltale, print, bum steer (false), by the book, chapter and verse, no-no's, bible (authoritative book), by the numbers. 2. tour guide, bird dog, alarm clock.

GUIDE v. quarterback, mastermind, spearhead, trail-blaze, shepherd, have a handle on. See MANAGE.

GUIDELINE n. bible (TV), format.

GUILE n. gamesmanship, one-upmanship, runaround, dirty dealing, dirty work, dirty pool, dirty trick, double-cross, sellout, Judas kiss, stab in the back. See also TRICKERY.

GUILTY adj. caught in the act, caught red-handed, caught with one's hand in the cookie jar, dirty, hung up, hung up with, smoking gun, off-base, out-of-line, damned.

GUITAR n. belly fiddle, box, git, git fiddle, git box, gitter, guinea's harp (not common, Derog.), fuzz box (electronic hookup).

GUITARIST n. plunker, whanger, plink plunker, string whanger.

GULLET n. goozle, guzzle, gargle.

GULLIBLE adj. easy, mark, easy mark, believer, go for, fall for, tumble for, swallow, swallow whole, swallow hook line and sinker, eat up, lap up, bite, take the bait, be taken in, be a sucker, be a patsy, kid oneself, blue-eyed, wide-eyed, duck, yold, yo-yo, sucker, patsy, green.

GULP v. belt, chugalug, drop (drug), rock one back, swig, toss one back, throw back, scarf down, gorm, gorp, wolf, wolf down, inhale, gobble, bolt, dispatch, dispose, swabble. See SWALLOW.

GUN n. artillery, cannon, A.K., blaster, gage, gauge, (shotgun), shottie (shotgun), breakdown, burner, gat, piece, wheel gun, iron, rod, prop, jammy (Af. Am.), nine, junk guns, street sweeper, easy pieces, pound (.357 handgun), snubby, snub-nose, snub-noser, snub-nosed automatic, lug, Saturday night special, six-gun, six-shooter, bean shooter, peashooter, popper, pop, equalizer, difference, gong, speaker, Mr. Speaker, persuader, convincer, hardware, heater, heat, Betsy, patsy, Bolivar, Oscar, roscoe, mahoska, jerry, canister, canojerod, hog's leg, forty-five, deuce-deuce, double deuce (.22 pistol), deuce-five (.25 caliber), trey-eight, smokepole, smoke wagon; zip gun, Z, zip (homemade gun); slim, belly gun, snug, spud, potato, stick, boom stick, tool, noise tool, toy, works, business, blow, bark, barker, bow-wow, boom-boom (WWII), biscuit, pickle, prod, copper-dropper, crowd-pleaser (police), scatter gun, bear insurance; chopper, ugly guns, chatterbox, mack 10, Chicago piano, grease gun, burp gun (submachine); dumb gat, gagged gat, hush-hush, sissy rod (silencer); stun gun, taser (electric shock); hang (balance).

GUN, CARRY v. equalized, wired, carrying, carry the difference, totin', toting a gun, packing, packing a gun, packed, gat up, heeled, heeled-up, well-heeled, loaded, lugging iron, carry iron, lug, lug a rod, rodded-up, pack a rod, pack a heater, pack heat.

GUN COVER n. bloomers.

GUNFIGHT n. shoot-out, shoot-'em-up, cappin', fireworks, throwing slugs, Fourth of July, war.

GUNFIRE n. heat, give one the heat, cap, bust a cap, fireworks, gunplay, shootout.

GUNMAN n. hit man, gunsel, blaster, shootist, trigger, trigger man, piece man. See KILLER.

GUNNER n. guns.

GUNPLAY n. heat, give one the heat, cappin', fireworks, buckin' (Af. Am.), Uzi (use an assault weapon), gunplay, shoot-out, shoot-'em-up, throw slugs.

GUNSHOT WOUND n. hole in one.

GUSH v. rave, fall all over one, carry on over, make a to-do over, take on over, go on about, whoop it up for.

GUSHY adj. all over one, bubbling over.

GYMNASIUM n. gym, sweatshop, health club, spa.

GYMNASTICS n. tumbling, gym.

GYNECOLOGIST n. fingersmith.

GYPSY n. raghead, gyp, gip, jip (1890, Obs.), tinker (Derog.).

H

H n. Hotel, How.

HABIT n. thing, hang-up, one's bag, into, shot, kick, hook, Jones, monkey, monkey on one's back, grind, daily grind, groove. See also ROUTINE.

HABITAT n. 1. hood, neck of the woods, stomping ground, territory, turf. See NEIGHBORHOOD. 2. pad, box, cave, condo, den, domi, crib, digs, hole, home plate. See HOUSE.

HABITUAL adj. regular, SOS, same old shit. See also CUSTOMARY.

HABITUÉ OF THE STREET n. street person, bum, bag lady, skell.

HACK n. grind, greasy grind, Grub Street, pro, old pro, workhorse.

HACKNEYED adj. corny, hokey, tripe, old chestnut, old saw, familiar tune, run-of-the-mill, old hat, See TRITE.

HACKSAW n. briar.

HADES n. hell, the other place, down there, hot spot.

HAGGLE v. dicker, deal, hack out a deal, hammer out a deal, make a deal, work out a deal, hondle, Jew down (Derog.), knock down the price. See NEGOTIATE.

HAIL n. ice pebbles.

HAIL v. 1. flag, flag down, flop, give one a flop, give one a toss, highball, shoulder, tumble, holler, holler out, yawp, yoo-hoo, whistle for, whistle down. See also HELLO. 2. hear it for, root for. See ACCLAIM.

HAIR n. grass, pez, righteous moss, wig, wool, corn rows (braided hair, Af. Am.), nappy (kinky), pubehead (short, curly), frizzies (split ends), touch-up (dye).

HAIR BAND n. headache band.

HAIRCUT n. punk, crew, crew cut, butch, Mohawk, natural, afro, 'fro, bust, cameo, du, cut, trim, brush cut, chili bowl, Navajo, Caesar, California, Detroit, continental, Elvis, English, duck's ass, D.A., ducktail, cueball (just had a haircut), roach, feather cut, poodle cut, bandhouse clip, double-o, flattop, razor cut, fuzz cut, pachuco, dread locks, baldy (Army) white sidewalls (Marines). See also HAIR STYLE.

HAIRCUT, GET A v. get one's ears raised, get one's head scratched, get one's rug beat, mow the lawn.

HAIRDRESSER n. hair bender, crimper, hairburger (homosexual).

HAIR DRESSING n. axle grease, conk (Af. Am.), goo, gooey, goop, goup, goopy, glop, gloppy, glob, globby, gook, gooky, goonk, gunk, slickum.

HAIRLESS adj. baldie, baldy, chrome-dome, cueball, curly, egghead, skinhead, bald as a coot, bald as an egg, bald as an eagle.

HAIR STYLE n. 1. Women's: do, hairdo, blow-dry, punk, spiky, poodle cut, feather cut, pixie cut, pixie, gamin, pageboy, natural, beehive, rat's nest (1950s), pomp (WWII), high hair, streaked, roach, ponytail, horse tail, load of hay (long); banana curls, fried, konk (to straighten), made (straightened, Af. Am.); jap, strao, naps. 2. Men's: trim, cut, razor cut, fuzz cut, brush cut, crew cut, crew, butch, punk, cameo, continental, Caesar, California, Detroit, Elvis, English, duck's ass, D.A., ducktail, slave tail (boys), scone tail, bandhouse clip, double-o, buffalo, flattop, mohawk, Navajo, pachuco, chili bowl, cueball (just had a haircut); baldy (Army), wrap, skinhead, eggbeater, 3. Unisex: punk, punk wave, pubehead (short curly), Italian cut, atomic bomb, mushroom, crab meat, helmet head, spooged (sticks straight up), afro, 'fro, Jewfro, Isfro, righteous moss, corn rows (braided hair, Af. Am.), dreadlocks.

HAIR STYLIST n. hair bender, hairburger (homosexual).

HALE adj. alive and kicking, wrapped tight, chipper, fit as a fiddle, crunchy granola, in the pink, sound as a dollar. See HEALTHY.

HALF adj. halvers, halvies, half and half, even-steven, fifty-fifty.

HALFWAY adv. betwixt and between, halfway in the middle, plump in the middle, smack in the middle, slap in the middle, smack dab in the middle, middle of the road, over the hill, over the hump.

HALF-WIT n. dork, megadork, dorkmunder, dorf, numb-nut, lop, lump, loser, dickhead, dickweed, dimbo, dickwad, remo, sped, mouth breather, mental midget, ditzo, Fred, Barney, Wilma, beau, feeb, lorg, gump, yo-yo, out to lunch, lunchie, lunchbox, lunchsack, vacant lot, Z-head, McFly, lamebrain, beanbrain, birdbrain, fuckbrained, clambrain, rattlebrain, out to lunch, lunchie, assface, asswipe, jerk, jel, yutz, dumdum, four-letter man (dumb), squid, oofus, butthead, deadass, pointyhead. See STUPID.

HALL n. squat pad.

HALLUCINATE v. blow one's mind, freak out, trip, go on a trip, head-trip.

HALLUCINATING adj. tripping, head-tripping, devils's grandmother, seeing little men who aren't there, pink elephants.

HALLUCINATION n. trip, head trip, pipe dream, Disneyland, pink elephants.

HALLUCINOGENIC adj. mind bender, mind-bending, mind blower, mind-blowing.

HALLUCINOGENIC DRUG n. shroom (psychodelic), shroom dog (user). See also MARIJUANA, LYSERGIC ACID, DIETHYLAMIDE.

HALLWAY n. squat pad.

HALT adj. gimpy, gimp, game, crip, g'd up, geed up.

HALT n. freeze, break, break-off, cutoff, layoff, letup, screaming halt, shuddering halt, grinding halt, stoppage.

HALT v. cool it, can it, come to a screaming halt, come to a grinding halt, come to a shuddering halt, blow the whistle on, put a cork in it, drop anchor. See STOP.

HAM n. grunt, squeal, Noah's boy.

HAM AND EGGS n. cluck and grunt, ham and.

HAMBURGER n. burger, cheeseburger, beefburger, superburger, Big Mac, big boy, chewed fine, clean up the kitchen (order for hamburger, hash, or stew), hamburg, greaser, Wimpy, ground round, Salisbury steak.

HAMMOCK n. fleabag (N.).

HAMPER v. hang up, tie up, hold up, get in the way, stymie, cramp one's style, put one in a box, drag one's foot. See HINDER. See also PREVENT.

HAMPERED adj. stuck, stuck with, stung, snowed, hog-tied.

HAND n. mitt, paw, bunch of fives (fist), duke, fin, flipper, grabber, ham, hook, meat hook, biscuit hook, lily-white, potato grabber.

HAND v. fork over, drop, pass it on over, hand-carry, hand-walk, put on, put out, dish out, come across with, duke, weed, gimme.

HANDBAG n. bag, clutch, frame, hide, leather, jiffy bag, jitney bag, keister.

HANDBILL n. handout, literature, throwaway, flyer, dodger.

HANDCUFF v. cuff, put on the cuffs, put on the bracelets.

HANDCUFFS n. bracelets, cuffs, cufflinks, thumbs, darbies, derbies, irons, nippers, slave bracelets.

HANDGUN n. artillery, piece, iron, burner, snubby, Saturday night special, wheel gun, gat, pea shooter, equalizer, difference, hardware, roscoe; dumb gat, gagged gat, hush-hush (silencer). See GUN.

HANDICAP n. hang-up, baggage, psychological baggage, cap (racing).

HANDICAPPED adj. gimpy, gimp, hamstrung, hog-tied, taken out, sidelined, out of commission, crip, game, g'd up, geed up.

HANDKERCHIEF n. blower, duster, tear duster, sneezer, sniffer, snotrag, wipe.

HANDLE v. hack it, get a handle on something, cut the mustard, make out, make the grade, deal with, call the signals, run things. See MANAGE.

HANDLES n. ears.

HAND ORGAN n. hurdy-gurdy.

HANDSHAKE n. high five, high-fiving celebration (congratulations), the glad hand, gimme five, gimme ten, gimme some skin, give the man some.

HANDSHAKER n. glad-hander, duker, fin flipper, mitt glommer.

HANDSOME adj. tasty, hunk, beauhunk, tuna, stud muffin, Clydesdale, Adonis, Greek god, demigod, drool over, hoss (muscular), industrial, beefcake, beef-a-roni, crushman, mazeh (Yid.), freak daddy, fly guy, lover boy, pretty boy, G.Q. (Gentleman's Quarterly magazine), tall dark and handsome, handsome thing.

HANDSPRING n. flip, flip-flop.

HANDWRITING n. scrawl, scribble, chicken tracks, hen tracks, mark.

HANG v. stretch, stretch rope, string up, swing, catch rope, dance, go through the trap, hoist, scrag, top, be crooked.

HANGING n. necktie party, necktie social, necktie sociable, Texas cakewalk, hemp fever.

HANGMAN'S ROPE n. necktie, halter.

HANGOVER n. big head, morning after, hung, the shakes, DT's, crispy, cork flu, shot, under the weather, blown out, bottle fatigue, the feebles, the willies, crown fire, a hair of the dog (cure); roached (from marijuana).

HANKER v. yen for, cream for, have eyes for, have one's mouth fixed for, have a case on, partial to. See DESIRE.

HANKERING n. the urge, druthers, weakness, fire in the belly, the munchies (food), yen, zazzle. See DESIRE.

HAPHAZARDLY adv. any old way, willy-nilly, all over the map, higgledy-piggledy. See ERRATICALLY.

HAPLESS adj. jinxed, hoodooed, behind the eight ball, jonah, snake-bit, scrub, loser, a winner, sad sack, schlemiel (Yid.), dick in the dirt, poor fish. See UNFORTUNATE.

HAPPEN v. shake, smoke, what goes, come down, what's coming down, down, what's going down, action, what's happening, what cooks?, what's cooking?, cooking with gas. See OCCUR.

HAPPY adj. chipper, chirpy, jacked, jaked, jazzed corky, perky, upper, up, hopped-up, upbeat, lookin' good, stoked, flyin', flyin' high, float one's boat, floating, floating on air, walking on air, on a cloud, on cloud seven, on cloud nine, sunny, sunny side up, in seventh heaven, on a joy ride, joygerm fever, tea'd up, wowed, happy camper, pleased as Punch, happy as a clam, tickled, tickled pink, tickled to death, hummy, fat dumb and happy, high, high as a kite, can't complain, gassed, out of it, get one's grits, have no kick coming, blow one's mind, blowing one's roof, popping one's nuts, handsprings, backflips, flipping, hit the spot, just what the doctor ordered, Little Mary Sunshine, Little Merry Sunshine.

HARANGUE n. spiel, spouting, hassle, reading out, eating out. See SPEECH.

HARANGUE v. get on a soapbox, spiel, spout, chew the scenery, stump, go on about, blow off, dress down, yell one's head off. See ORATE.

HARASS v. bug, ride, eat, noodge, give a bad time to, give one a hard time, give one the needle, roust, work on, chew on, get to, utz (Yid.), chap, push one's key, dog, bulldog, rattle one's cage, hassle, jack one around. See ANNOY. See also INTIMIDATE.

HARASSED adj. hacked, tee'd off, browned off, catch shit, riled, spooked, hard put to it, picked on, torn down, steamed. See ANNOYED.

HARASSING, STOP v. fuck off, get a job, get off one's back, cut the shit, cut the comedy, unass one.

HARBOR SEDIMENT n. black mayonnaise.

HARD adj. 1. cold-blooded, cold fish, arctic, hard as nails, hard-boiled, tough, rhinoceros hide, thick-skinned, dead-ass, butter wouldn't melt in his mouth, got lead balls for eyes. See CALLOUS. 2. uphill, uphill battle, mean, heavy, hellish, hairy, murder, pisser, rough, bitch, tough proposition, dope, hard row of stumps, ballbreaker. See DIFFICULT.

HARDHEADED adj. bullheaded, pigheaded, hard-nosed, hang tough, tough nut, locked in, head in concrete, stand pat. See STUBBORN.

HARD-HITTING adj. punchy, socko, sockeroo.

HARDLY adv. by a hair, by the skin of one's teeth, pretty near, practically.

HARD-PRESSED adj. back to the wall, in the soup, at the end of one's rope, hard-up, up against it, up shit creek, up shit creek without a paddle, scraping the bottom of the barrel, fighting to keep one's head up, tryin' to stay alive, runnin' out of time, no more cards to play. See also DESPERATE.

HARDSHIP n. case, bad scene, hard knocks, nightmare, hard row to hoe, tough break, rum go, rainy day, tough luck, rotten luck, down on one's luck, up against it, on the skids, on one's uppers, gone to pot, gone to the dogs, bummer, downer, drag, grabber, can't even get arrested. See also ADVERSITY.

HARDTACK n. dog biscuit.

HARD TIMES n. bad times, bust, pull in one's belt, run for cover, shorten sail, batten down the hatches, rainy days, slack season, slump, crash, the big trouble.

HARDWARE STORE n. pig joint.

HARD, WORK v. work one's tail off, whiz, eager beaver, grind, greasy grind. See INDUSTRIOUS.

HARKEN v. listen up, pick up, tune in on, catch, get a load of, are you ready for this?, be all ears, knock on one's lobes. See LISTEN.

HARLEM Soul City, Soulville, Sugar Hill (elite section).

HARLOT n. hooker, call girl, hustler, ho, working girl, skeezer, model, pro, lot lizard (truck-stop parking lot), chippie, prosty, alley cat, roller (robs drunks), tart, bimbo, hostess, shady lady. See PROSTITUTE.

HARLOTRY n. in the life, the life, world's oldest profession, broad racket, the bottle, hustle, turning a trick, hitting the turf, stepping out, going out for a buck, on the turf, white slavery.

HARM v. 1. ding, wing, nick, tweak, total, take a hit, hit on, louse up, crumb, crumb up, mess up, muck up, ball up, rack up, hash up, get, zing, bend the goods. See DAMAGE. 2. dump on, put down, pooh-pooh, hit one where one lives, do a number on, lay a bad trip on one, get. See WOUND.

HARMLESS PERSON n. softie, paper tiger, pussycat.

HARMONICA n. mouth organ, harp, harpoon.

HARMONIOUS adj. simpatico, hit it off, mix, togetherness, good vibes, good vibrations, in sync, in tune with, on the same wavelength, kissing kin. See also FRIENDLY.

HARSH adj. hairy, hellish, hard-nosed, tough, wicked, bitchy, cussed, mean, hard-boiled, hard-shell. See STERN.

HARTFORD, CONNECTICUT Stag City.

HASH n. Irish turkey, gook, clean up the kitchen for one, the gentleman will take a chance (order), gooey (WWI), mystery, slumgudgeon, yesterday today and forever.

HASHISH n. hash, heesh, sheish, keef, candy, blond, blond hash, blond Lebanese, black Russian, carob chips, chocolate, fir, kif, Pakistan hash, sealing wax, shishi, soles, hash-head (user), hashover (hangover). See also MARIJUANA.

HASHISH (ALCOHOL EXTRACT) n. oil, black oil, hash oil, Indian oil, honey oil, cherry leb, son of one, the one.

HASTEN v. hustle, fog, shake a leg, make tracks, hotfoot it, barrel ass, snap shit, put the pedal to the metal, get the lead out of one's ass, get cracking, get a wiggle on. See SPEED.

HASTY adj. quickie, pronto, snappy, balls out, chop-chop, on the double, double-clutchin', pretty damned quick, PDQ, wham-bam, get cracking, in jig time, in nothing flat. See FAST.

HAT n. lid, topper, cap, boater, bowler, chimney, dip, skimmer, bugle warmer, opera (folding), straw, sailor, Panama, deer stalker, plug, plug hat, stove pipe, dicer, brim (Af. Am.), rim, sky, sky piece, Stetson, ten-gallon, sombrero, beaver, tit cap, tar bucket, brain bucket, hard hat, iron hat, tin hat, gimme cap, fore and aft (admiral), Detroiter (fur), go-to-hell cap (WWII, Army and Marines), crusher (1929).

HATCH v. cook up, dream up, trump up, whip up, frame up, come up with, throw together, spitball, breakout meeting (brainstorm session), brainstorm. See PLAN. See also SCHEME.

HATE v. have no use for, have an allergy to, grossed out on, allergic to, down on, have a hate on for, can't stand the guts of, hate one's guts, on one's shit list. See also DISLIKE.

HATEFUL adj. uncool, unhep, unhipped, awful, beastly, bitchy, cussed, mean, ornery; stanky, turbobitch (woman); gross, grody, grody to the max, pesky, pestiferous, funky (Af. Am.), act like one's shit doesn't stink. See also DESPICABLE.

HATRED n. no use for, allergy to.

HAUGHTY adj. biggety, sniffy, snooty, snotty, uppity, stuck-up, high-hat, on one's high horse, have one's glasses on (Af. Am.). See ARROGANT.

HAUL v. lug, pack, piggyback, ride, shlep, shlep along, tote, truck, back, birdie-back, buck, gun, heel, hump, jag, shoulder, move.

HAUNT n. hangout, the place, stamping ground, old stamping ground, stomping ground, ole stomping ground.

HAUNT v. hant, spook, voodoo, hoodoo. See also FREQUENT.

HAUNTED adj. spooked, spooky, hanted.

HAVE v. lock up, get hold of, bag, glom on to, latch on to, bogart, corner, corner the market, get a corner on, hog, get one's hands on, sit on.

HAWAII Aloha State, the Islands, Wahoo.

HAWKER n. candy man, pusher (drugs); travel agent (LSD), cheap jack, cheap john. See VENDOR.

HAZARD n. 1. long shot, hundred-to-one shot, go-at, stab, have a fling at, outside chance, snowball chance, toss-up. See WAGER. 2. that's the way the ball bounces, that's the way the cookie crumbles, that's the way (any number of things), lucky hit, lucky break, run of luck, luck into. See LUCK. 3. double trouble, thin ice, hot potato, dynamite, risky business.

HAZARD v. take a plunge, go for broke, skate on thin ice, go out on a limb. See RISK.

HAZARDOUS adj. hot, hairy, unhealthy, widow-maker, dicey, chancy, can get burned, in the tube, touchy. See DANGEROUS.

HAZE n. ground clouds, smaze, smog, soup.

HAZE v. needle, put on, rag, razz, rib, roast, yank one's crank, yank one's chain, jive, jolly, josh, kid, horse. See TEASE. See also JOKE.

HAZY adj. smoggy, smazy, muzzy, soupy.

HEAD n. 1. bean, old bean, noggin, noodle, noddle, dome, pate, attic, conk, conk piece, top story, upper story, upstairs, block, biscuit, cabbage head, calabash (Obs.), can, chimney (Af. Am.), cupola., coco, coconut, pimple, potato, poll, pumpkin, punkin, bonnet, cruller, knob, lemon, sconce, squash, thinker, think pot, box, think box, think tank, knowledge box, dream box, gray matter, little gray cells, wetware (brain), solid ivory, wig. 2. C.O., suit, bosshead, czar, godfather, head honcho, the man, Mister Charlie (Af. Am.), top dog, kingfish, lead-off man. See EXECUTIVE.

HEADACHE n. head, have a head, banger, bangeroo, hangover, a migraine.

HEADLIGHTS n. glim, glimmers, one-eye, eyeballs, quads (four), bright, dims (parking lights).

HEADQUARTERS n. ad building, tower of power, HQ, GHQ, CP, home office, puzzle palace (higher), Pentagon, toy factory (CA).

HEADQUARTERS ASSIGNMENT n. palace guard (police).

HEADSTRONG adj. bullheaded, hard-nosed, hard-core, hard-shell, mule, Turk, locked in, has one's Dutch up, murder (he's murder). See STUBBORN.

HEALTH, IN BAD adj. on one's last legs, poorly, one foot in the grave, one foot in the grave and the other on a banana peel, going down (Af. Am.), a walking disease, walking wounded. See ILL.

HEALTH SPA n. fat farm, milk farm.

HEALTHY adj. alive and kicking, wrapped tight, bright-eyed and bushy-tailed, crunchy granola, chipper, together, fit as a fiddle, full of beans, full of piss and vinegar, in fine feather, in fine whack, in high feather, in the pink, sound as a dollar, right, right as rain, solid as a rock, beefy, husky, strong as a horse, strong as a lion, strong as an ox.

HEAR v. listen up, pick up, catch, read, get, get a load of, are you ready for this?, be all ears, have one's ears to the ground, get an earful, hear tell, give ears, knock on one's lobes. See LISTEN.

HEARSAY n. scuttlebutt, talk, grapevine, clothesline, leak, ear loft, latrine rumor, wire, heard over the backyard fence. See GOSSIP.

HEARSE n. meat wagon, dead wagon, glass wagon, bone box, last ride, black Maria.

HEART n. 1. ticker, pump, clock, chimer, puffer, pumper, bad pump, bum clock, bum ticker. 2. bottom line, meat and potatoes, nitty-gritty, nub, key, nuts and bolts, groceries, coal and ice. See BASIC.

HEARTBEAT n. back beat, tick, tick-tock.

HEARTBROKEN adj. destroyed, sing the blues, cry the blues, hang crepe, bummed out, hurtin', hurting, in pain, in the pits, off one's feed, cracked up, cut up, tore up, all torn up, ripped. See UNHAPPY.

HEARTLESS adj. cold-blooded, cold fish, arctic, hard as nails, thick-skinned, dead-ass, butter wouldn't melt in his mouth, got lead balls for eyes. See CALLOUS.

HEAT WAVES n. witch-water (on the road, So.).

HEAVE v. peg, chuck, chunk, fire, lob, pitch, sling.

HEAVEN n. pearly gates, happy hunting ground, promised land, glory, kingdom come, upstairs, up there, blue, Blue Broadway, wild blue yonder, big skip, the old bye-and-bye, the great ballpark in the sky, the great ad (any business) agency in the sky.

HEAVY adj. hefty, lead-footed, tough, beefy, fatso, full-figured, two-ton Tessie, judy (girl), like lead. See also FAT.

HEAVYSET n. built, built like a brick shithouse, built for comfort, busty, curvy, zaftig, full-figured, fatty, chubbo, candidate for pigginess, See also FAT.

HECTIC adj. nutsy, jungle, zoo, banana factory, madhouse, all hell broke loose, to-do, hassle. See FRANTIC.

HEDGE v. cop out, cop a plea, jive, shuck, shuck and jive, stonewall, goof on, hem and haw, blow smoke, blow hot and cold, back and fill, flip-flop, shilly-shally, sit on the fence, waffle, fudge, gardening (political), hom-rim it, hedge one's bet, pussyfoot, beg the question, cover your ass, CYA, pass the buck, run around, give one the runaround, stall off, get around, beat around, beat around the bush.

HEED n. listen up, pop to, spotlight, tender loving care, TLC.

HEED v. 1. sit, baby-sit, keep tab, keep tabs on, ride herd on, mind the store, watch the store, watch over, not get off base, not get out of line, stay in line, toe the line, toe the mark, keep one's distance, keep a weather eye open, keep one's eye peeled, watch one's step, watch out, watch out for. 2. catch, get a load of, give ears, have one's ears on, knock on one's lobes, listen up, clue in, keg, pick up, dig, spot, give a ghee a toss, give a thing a toss, give a thing a play, rap, rumble, tumble.

HEEDLESS adj. out to lunch, asleep at the switch, goofing off, daydreaming, fast and loose, slapdash, sloppy. See CARELESS.

HEIGHTEN v. hop up, beef up, jazz up, punch up, soup up, heat up, hot up, add fuel to the fire, pour it on. See INTENSIFY.

HEINOUS adj. gross, grody to the max, beastly, raunchy, sucks, stinking, beat, godawful. See BAD.

HELICOPTER n. chopper, copter, whirlybird, bird, eggbeater, eye in the sky, telecopter (TV news, traffic), trafficopter, gunship, windmill; air bear, bear in the air, fling-wing, dustoff, smokey copter (police); Jolly Green Giant (Mil., double-rotor), Charlie copter (Govt.), Huey (Mil.), shithook (Mil., Chinook CH-47), snake (AH-1G Cobra), slick (Mil., unarmed), angel (N.); Jesus nut (rotor hub), rotorhead (pilot).

HELIUM n. balloon juice.

HELLO interj. hi, hey, hey there, hey homie, ciao, yo, checkin' in, how do?, look out, gimme some skin, gimme five, gimme ten, slip me five, high five, low five, buzza, cheerio, chorro, cherry, what up?, what's up?, 'sup?, you got it, what's going down?, what's coming down?, what gives?, what's shaking?, what's the drill?, what's the scam?, what's the skinny?, what's the lowdown?, what's the scoop?, what's the poop?, what's the rave?, what cooks?, what's cookin'?, what's cookin' good lookin'?, what it is, how's it happenin'?, what's happenin'?, what does it look like?, what do you know?, all right, hi-ya, howdy, howdy-do, how-de-do, how do ye do, how do?, hey now, say now, whatayasay?, well a hey, how you doing?, how's things?, how's by you?, how's tricks?, how goes it?, how's every little thing?, how's the world treating you?, hello Joe what do you know?, it's goin' on (response), long time no see.

HELMET n. brain bucket, hard hat, hat, iron hat, tin hat.

HELP v. 1. mayday. 2. buck up, boost, brace up, give a boost to, give a leg up, give a lift, lend a hand, plug, hype, push, hold a brief for, go with, go for, go to bat for, go to the mat for, go down the line for, go the route for, make a pitch for, beat the drum for, plump for, run interference for, grease the wheels for, thump the tub for, root for, stump for, front for, stand up for, stick up for, ride shotgun for, take care of one for, save one's bacon, put a flea in one's ear, put a bug in one's ear, open doors, hand out, splash, spot, throw the spotlight on, puff, ballyhoo, put on the map, press agent, up, back up, bail out, hold one's end up, straighten one out. 3. pick up the tab, angel, back, bankroll, grubstake, stake, go for. See FINANCE.

HELPER n. help, temp, sec, coffee bitch, girl Friday, gal, man Friday, gofer, hired hand, mother's helper, yard man, flunky, home guard, peon, savage, serf, slave, slavey. See ASSISTANT.

HELPLESS adj. handcuffed, with one's hands tied, pinned, basket case, over a barrel, tapped, tapped-out, up the creek, up the creek without a paddle, up shit creek, up shit creek without a paddle. See also DEFENSELESS.

HEMORRHOIDS n. grapes.

HEN n. banty, biddy, birdie, chick, chickabiddy, chicka-dee, chicky, gull, gump, sea gull, albatross (WWII).

HENCHMAN n. flunky, stooge, yes-man, goon, ass-hole buddy, ass kisser, brownnose, running dog, toad, ward heeler, heller.

HEN HOUSE n. egg orchard.

HERD v. round up, scare up, poke, punch, corral.

HERMAPHRODITE n. morph, morphodite.

HEROIC adj. stand tall, bigger 'n life, fire eater, gritty, gutsy, gutty, ballsy, hairy. See DARING.

HEROIN n. aitch, the big H, C, H, horse, snow, sugar, smeck, smack the beast, bag, Cadillac, piece, weight (ounce), fix, shit, goma, A-bomb, Aunt Hazel, dog food, Big Daddy, ca-ca, courage pills, dope, tootsie roll, downtown, peanut butter, ferry dust, foolish powder, gumball, globe trotter, gold dust, goods, Gulf P-funk, MPTP (synthetic), Henry, shag, scat, rock candy, nose candy, nose powder, the tragic magic, liquid sky (with sex), Lady H, yen shee, stuff, hard stuff, white, white lady, white stuff, China white, Chinese white, triangle stuff (Burma, Laos, Thailand), junk, hook, hot shot (overdose), pack, blanks, bones, boy, brother, brown, brown sugar, brown rine, Persian brown, Mexican brown, Mexican mud, carne (Mexican), tar, black tar, Chinese, Chinese red, Chinese rocks, red chicken, chiva, cobics, crap, doojee, dojee, doorjee, estuffa, first-degree, heroina, powder, joy powder, flea powder, polvo, scag, scar, scramble, tecaba, thing, bombita, dynamite, cold .45, Colt .45, schmee, antifreeze, caballo, deck, salt, his, him, hero, hero of the underworld, Harry, Big Harry, witch hazel, angel, noise, lemonade, poison, eye-opener (first of day), goldfinger (synthetic).

HEROIN ADDICT n. Scag Jones, smack slammer.

HEROIN AND COCAINE n. speedball, dynamite.

HEROIN AND MARIJUANA n. atom bomb.

HEROIN, USE v. chase the dragon, coast, cook, cook it, do up, pop it, jab a vein, sniff nose candy, snort dust, smacked back.

HEROIN USER n. smackhead, smack slammer, Scag Jones.

HERPES n. herpie, herped-up (infected).

HESITATE v. pussyfoot, pussyfoot around, hem and haw, straddle, fence-straddle, on the fence, sit on the fence, hang on the fence, run hot and cold, blow hot and cold, hedge, hedge off, shilly-shally, waffle, tic and twitch.

HETEROSEXUAL n. straight, right-handed, vanilla, breeder fish (lesbian use), jam (homosexual use).

HEX n. evil eye, stink eye, whammy, double whammy, horns, kibosh, hoodoo, voodoo, spook, kiss of death. See CURSE.

HEX v. cuss, damn, darn, jinx, spook, put the horns on, put the whammy on one, put the double whammy on one, give one a kine ahora (Yid.), hoodoo, hoodoo one, voodoo, voodoo one.

HIDDEN adj. covered-up, holed-up, put in the hole, planted, stashed, bagged, under wraps, under the fig leaf, doggo, incog, Q.T., hush-hush, hushed-up, skunk works (secret manufacturing plant or laboratory).

HIDE n. dried barkers, skins, skin joint (shop).

HIDE v. 1. stash, stash away, stache, ditch, duck, bag, plant, squirrel, squirrel away, hike, put in the hole, stick in the hole. 2. sweep under the rug, bury, cover, cover up, whitewash, duck, stonewall, blow smoke, finesse it, palm, paper over, hold out on, keep buttoned up, keep it under one's hat, keep under wraps, skim (income), unload, launder, white money (laundered). 3. hide out, hole up, play dead, lie doggo, lie low, lay low; on the down low, on the d.l. (Af. Am.); sit tight, plant, tunnel, cool off, duck outta sight, melt into the scenery, take it on the lam, do a crouch, flatten out, out, hit the shade, hit the mattresses.

HIDEOUS adj. sick, weird, animal, beast, beat, gross, plug (M.), plug-ugly, butt-ugly, ugly as sin, scag, grimbo, (Fem.), mud puppy, hagged-out, face would crack a mirror, pruneface. See UGLY.

HIDING PLACE n. fig leaf, cover, safehouse, hide-out, hideaway, getaway place, the scatter, hole, plant, shade, sneezer, stash, stache, drop, drop joint, drop off.

HIERARCHY n. pecking order, place, slot.

HIGH-FLOWN adj. highfalutin, high-hatted, high-nosed, high-toned, top-lofty, stuffed shirt, put on airs, dog it, purple, gassy, windy, cheesy, given to twenty-dollar words, bor-ring, over one's head. See also POMPOUS.

HIGHJACK v. jack, hijack, skyjack, heist.

HIGHLY adv. awful, awfully, real, really, but good, jolly, bloody, daisy, so much, mighty, plenty, too much, mucho, so, stone (stone-deaf), terribly, terrifically, almighty, powerful, right.

HIGH-MINDED adj. cocky, puffed-up, stuck-up, high-flown, high-nosed, have one's glasses on (Af. Am.), dog it, smarty-pants, smart-ass. See ARROGANT.

HIGH-PRICED adj. pricey, steep, upscale, uptown, executive, high, pretty penny, up to here (elbow), highway robbery, important, See EXPENSIVE.

HIGH SCHOOL n. hi, high.

HIGH SCHOOL STUDENT n. prep, preppy, preppie; freshie, frosh (first-year).

HIGH SOCIETY n. upper crust, hoity-toity, the big bucks, 400, high hat, rich bitch, jet set, mainliner, FFVs, Mr. and Mrs. Gotrocks. See ELITE.

HIGH-SPIRITED adj. 1.chipper, chirpy, corky, high, sunny, sunny side up, up, upbeat, upper, jazzed, perky, joy-germ fever, Little Merry Sunshine, Little Mary Sunshine. See HAPPY. 2. full of piss and vinegar, full of beans, full of prunes, full of hops. See SPIRITED.

HIGH-STRUNG adj. uptight, wired, wired up, hyper, jittery, jumpy, all shook up, clutched-up, on pins and needles, on the ragged edge, choked, zonkers. See NERVOUS.

HIGHWAY n. bricks, pavement, dragway, pike, rip strip, super slab, bowling alley, four-lane parking lot, world's longest parking lot. See ROAD.

HIGHWAY POLICE n. bear, Smokey, Smokey Bear, CHIPS (California).

HIKE n. legwork, constitutional, hump (Mil., with full equipment), schlep, traipse.

HIKE v. leg it, hoof it, ride shanks' mare, stump it, hit the road, hit the dirt, hit the grit. See WALK.

HILARIOUS adj. yokky, gagged-up, crack-up, gas, boffo, a scream, laffer, riot, priceless, screamingly funny, gut-busting, for grins. See AMUSING.

HINDER v. queer, crimp, cramp, put a crimp in, put one in a box, cramp one's style, stymie, get in the way, put a cork in it, skin, crab, hog-tie, tie up, pin, hang up, hold up, bring to a screaming halt, freeze, blow the whistle on, foul up, fuck up, louse up, snafu, bollix, gum, gum up the works, fake out, shut out, shut off, close out, close off, choke, choke off, stonewall, stall, flag one down, fix one's wagon, saddle with, drag one's feet, put on the brakes, weigh down, hang like a millstone round one's neck, flummox, stump, give one the business, sandbag, torpedo (a plan), throw a monkey wrench into the works, upset one's apple cart, spike one's guns, cut off one's water, turn off one's water, steal one's thunder, trash, take one down, take care of, take the wind out of one's sails, knock the bottom out of, knock the chocks from under one, knock the props from under one, down one, monkey with the buzz saw, monkey with, mix in. See also RESTRAIN; BURDEN.

HINDRANCE n. hang-up, baggage, excess baggage, psychological baggage, foot dragging, stumbling block, catch, Catch-22, glitch, joker, one small difficulty, a lock, jam-up, gridlock, bugaboo, crimp, crimp one's style, hump, stinger, monkey wrench, albatross, albatross around one's neck, ball and chain, millstone, schlepper, schlep along, get off my side, get off my case, get out of my life, whose side are you on?, with you as a friend I don't need an enemy.

HINDSIGHT adj. second-guess, Monday morning quarterback.

HINDU n. raghead (Derog.).

HINT n. tip-off, lead, hot lead, telltale, print, bum steer (false), flea in one's ear, sneaking suspicion.

HINT v. leak, spring, spring one's duke, tip one's duke, tip one's hand, let the cat out of the bag, put a flea in one's ear, drop hairpins (homosexual). See EXPOSE.

HINTERLAND n. boondock, boondocks, boonies, outback, sticks, stix, B.F.E., butt fucking Egypt, B.F.A., butt fucking Africa, woods, up country. See COUNTRY.

HIPPOPOTAMUS n. hippo.

HIRE v. sign on, sign up, take on, ink, pact, bring on board, come on board, truck with.

HIRED adj. on board, inked, signed, pacted.

HIRELING n. flunky, help, stiff, apparatchik, temp, pencil pusher, girl Friday, man Friday, white collar, pink collar, bright collar (intelligent, well-educated, young), blue collar, hard hat. See WORKER.

HISS n. Bronx cheer, raspberry, razz, the bird.

HISTRIONIC adj. hammy, schmaltzy, hokey, tearjerking, scenery chewing.

HIT n. belt, clout, cut, chop, whop, wham, whammy, biff, bash, bat, shot, swat, swipe, sock, slug, slog, zap, zetz, zinger, clip, lick, wallop, lollop, haymaker, bonk, dint, dozer, plunk, clump, one-two, one-two punch, one-two blow, roundhouse, roundhouse sidewinder, Sunday punch, the leather, blindside (unexpected).

HIT v. bash, trash, dog on, drub, flax, wax, lace, lather, larrup, leather, lambaste, blitz, cane, spank, paddle, work over, wham, bam, whop, whomp, whack, bushwhack, shellack, whip, whipsaw, wipe, hide, tan, tan one's hide, take it out of one's hide, take it out of one's skin, brain, bloop, bonk, conk, pop, bop, boff, biff, bean, belt, bat, bung, blind, K.O., kayo, chill, stretch, bust, dust, dust off, dot (precise blow), drop, deck, dump, dish, total, sock, slug, slog, smack, poke, powder, pepper, clout, clobber, cream, punk, jack, lump, lump up, clump, clunk, plunk, clonk, clock, crown, clip, flip, flatten, get, soak, zap, zetz, paste, waste, wing, measure, bump, jump, heel, mug, hurt, yerk, bust up, come at, have at, lay at, go for, pitch into, light into, sail into, wade into, lay into, crack down on, lean on, clean on, take one, take out, shot, take a shot, take a whack at, take one over the hurdles, take care of, take down, take one down, put down, slap down, smack down, shoot down, shoot down in flames, chop down, shut down, lay one out, lay one low, lay on sap, lay a glove on, wipe out, hand it to one, punch out, work out, knock, knock cold, knock dead, knock in, knock off, knock around, knock one out, knock the beholden out of one, knock the daylights out of one, knock the shit out of one, knock into the next county, knock one into next week, knock for a row of (anything), knock on the head, knock one on one's ass, knock one ass over teakettle, knock one on one's ear, knock one's block off, knock one for a loop, knock on one's biscuit, knock on one's can, knock on one's keister, knock on one's pratt, knock on one's quiff, knock one on one's wallet, deal a knockout blow to, wale the daylights out of one, wale, wallop, welt, blast, blast on, fire on, throw a punch, slough, slough around, put the slug on one, sock it to one, give one a fat lip, tangle ass with, go up against, let have it, dust one's jacket, give a deal to, give a dose of birch oil, give a dose of strap oil, give a dose of hickory oil, give a dose of hazel oil, floor one, banjax, plant one, down one, wheel and deal, ring one's bell, haul off on one, let one have it, land a haymaker, put the bee on one, boot, boot around, put the boots to, cold-cock, cold-pack, Chinese, floor one, dry-gulch, double-bank, give one the blanket, give one the works, put one in the hospital, going over, break one's face, hit a clip, go to town, kick one's cruller in, kick one's lemon in, kick one's sconce in.

HITCH n. catch, glitch, bug, hang-up, snafu, holdup, joker, one small difficulty. See DIFFICULTY.

HITCHHIKE v. hitch, hitch a ride, thumb, thumb a ride, thumb one's way, bum a ride, cadge a ride, hook a ride, long arm.

HITTER n. slugger, mugger, pile driver, knuckle-duster, lip-splitter. See also FIGHTER.

HOARD v. sock away, squirrel, stash, scrimp, skimp, put aside for a rainy day. See SAVE.

HOARDER n. hog.

HOAX n. 1. con, con game, hustle, sting, flimflam, scam, racket, dodge, fast shuffle, all hat and no cattle (Texas), total shuck; ride-out squat (fraudulent auto accident). See CHEAT. 2. crap, crock, fib, cock-and-bull story, whopper, bunco, hooey, banana oil, snow job, diddling. See LIE.

HOAX v. run a game on, blow smoke up one's ass, rook, fleece, sting, Murphy, pigeon-drop, play games with, suck in, pull one's leg, set up, frame up, fake out, goof on, humbug. See TRICK.

HOBBLE v. hang up, crimp, put a crimp in, cramp, cramp one's style; gimp. See also HINDER.

HOBBY n. thing, bag, kick, schtick, shot, go in for, be into, have a weakness for, do one's thing.

HOBO n. bum, stumblebum, king of the road, bo, stiff, stiffo, bindlestiff, bindleman, deadbeat, floater. See VAGRANT. See also BEGGAR.

HOCKEY PLAYER n. cement head, headhunter, iceman, sextet, anchorman, goalie.

HOCKEY PLAYS n. check, body check, stick check, assist, knee, kneeing, rag (keep possession of puck), shadow (guard closely), slap pass, slap shot, slapper, slash, steal, icing (illegal play), dipsy-doodle, play in traffic.

HOCKEY TERMS cannon (fast shot), wheels (speed), goalie's best friend (metal frame of goal), lingerie department (top of the net), lumber facial (hit to the face with stick), sin bin (penalty box), cage (goal), burn (score), deke (deceive), hat trick (3 goals by one player).

HODGEPODGE n. everything but the kitchen sink, mishmash, mishmosh, duke's mixture, mixed bag, goulash. See MIXTURE.

HOG n. porker, porkey, cob roller (young or small).

HOLD v. 1. stay put, cling like a burr, cling like ivy, freeze to, hold on like a bulldog, stick like a barnacle, stick like a leech, stick like a limpet, stick like a wet shirt. 2. lock up, bogart, hog, get hold of, glom on to, latch on to, corner, corner the market, get a corner on, get one's hands on, sit on. 3. swear up and down, swear on a stack of bibles, swear till one is blue in the face, cross one's heart and hope to die, say-so. See AFFIRM. 4. take as gospel truth, take stock in, set store by, swear by, okay, OK, buy, bet one's bottom dollar on, lay money on, lap up, have a hunch, have a sneaking suspicion. See BELIEVE. 5. cool off, cool down, hold down, hold off, keep the lid on, get one in a box, bottle up, cork up, lock up, put a lock on. See RESTRAIN. 6. sock away, squirrel, stash, scrimp, skimp, put aside for a rainy day. See SAVE.

HOLD BACK v. back off, dial back, go back on one's word, weasel out, worm one's way out, worm out of, fudge, welsh, renig, nig, backwater.

HOLIDAY n. two weeks with pay, liberty, layoff, a few days off, eyes to cool it, gone fishing.

HOLISTIC MEDICINE n. holismo (as a cure-all).

HOLLER v. blow, holler out, give a shout, hoot, squawk.

HOLLYWOOD n. Hollyweird, Filmdom, Glamour Town, Movieland, Movieville, moviedom, Tinsel City, Tinsel Town.

HOLY adj. Holy Joe, Jasper, knee bender, goody, goody-goody, goody two-shoes, scoutmaster.

HOME n. pad, crash pad, condo, joint, domi, flop, crib, digs, diggings; cradle, hat (Af. Am.); hole in the wall, hooch (Vietnam), castle, cave, home plate, turf, ole stomping grounds. See HOUSE. See also APARTMENT, NEIGHBORHOOD.

HOME ECONOMICS n. home ec.

HOME FOR THE AGED n. God's waiting room.

HOMELIKE adj. comfy, cushy, homey, folksy, downhome, haimish, snug as a bug in a rug.

HOMELY adj. plug-ugly, butt-ugly, pig, dogface, bowser, animal, beast, beat, limburger (girl no one will date), boo hog, barfola; paper-bag case, double-bagger, triple-bagger (all Fem.); gross, buttly, coyote ugly, fugly, piss-ugly, troll, eddie (M.), mud puppy. See UGLY.

HOMESICK adj. rhino.

HOMESPUN adj. folksy, homey, haimish (Yid.), vanilla, open-and-shut, meat-and-potatoes man, plain as an old shoe.

HOMICIDE n. bang job, big chill, offing, ride, wasting, bump-off erase, hit, rubout, scragging, the big M, the works, fragging (officer, Mil.). See KILLING.

HOMILY n. bromide, old saw, broken record, daffodil, cracker barrel, chew one's cabbage, chew one's tobacco.

HOMING PIGEON n. homer.

HOMOSEXUAL n. gay, homo, mo, faggot, fag, agfay, fruit, fruitcake, queer, fairy, pansy, lily, flower, loose in his loafers, Heblew, auntie, aunt (elderly), perv, prevert, nance, friend of Dorothy, butterfly, fly ball, bait, bronco (novice), mandrake, father fucker, out, out of the closet, gunsel, gazoonil, gazooney, gonif, swing the other way, lover, John; toy boy, aspro (prostitute); lacy, left-handed, lightfooted, Mary, mintie, mother, Nancy, bent, three-dollar bill, chicken, chicken delight (young), faunet, faunlet (preadolecent boy), chicken hawk, punk, government-inspected meat (Mil.), boy, capon, cocksucker, scumsucker, knobber, milk mouth, bucket head, flamer, fembo (male), drag queen, main queen, closet queen, flute, fluter, freak, frit, fooper, gobbler, yo-yo, girl, limp wrist, jocker, maricón, piccolo player, pix, peter puffer, swish, faygeleh, mintie, mola, pato (Sp.), paleface (White), pogey, bird taker, man's man, third sexer, eye doctor, cannibal, punk, jock, jocky, trapeze artist, tusk, wolf, ring tail, sod, angel, angela, angelina, baby, salesman, mason, male-oriented, identified, cake eater, sister, three-letter man (fag), four-letter man (homo), lamb, ma, nellie, skippy, rough trade (sadistic), truck driver (rough), twink, twinkie, willie, geep, fruit ma toot, cruiser, flinch bird, guzzler, muzzler, nibbler, snake charmer, joker, keister bandit, pug (Af. Am.), daddy, papa, uncle, prussian, short-arm bandit, short-arm heister, butt pirate, butt boy, butt shit, rumpranger, pile diver, booty bandit, turk, wheelman, apple pie, bender, bindle boy, brat, Mr. Brown, brownie-hound, dung-puncher, fudge packer, turd burglar, charity stuff, coozey, flap, floosie, flit ('30s); les, lez, dyke, bull dyke, diesel dyke, butch, bitch, boondagger, daisy, fairy lady, Amy, bird, gal officer, lesbine, lesbo, marge, lady lover, double-barreled broad, shemale, crunchies, lipsticks, fem, femme, finger artist, carpet chewer, rug muncher, donut bumper, douche bag, slut puppy, top sergeant (Fem.); flip, kid, half a man, chum-chum, catcher (all Derog and Obsc.).

HOMOSEXUAL, ABUSE OF n. gay bashing, fag busting (Derog.).

HOMOSEXUAL ACTIVIST n. Gay Lib, Gay Libber, Lesbyterian.

HOMOSEXUAL CLUB/BAR n. gay bar, fag joint (Derog.), meat market, fruit market, fruit stand, market, camp, gay hangout.

HOMOSEXUAL, FEMALE n. les, lez, lesbine, lesbie, lesbo, dyke, bull dyke, bull dagger, diesel dyke, butch, crested hen (butch), bitch, boondagger, daisy, fairy lady, Amy, bird, gal officer, marge, lady lover, female-identified, female-oriented, crunchies, lipsticks, fem, femme, finger artist, carpet chewer, rug muncher, donut bumper, douche bag, slut puppy, double-barreled broad, shemale, harpie, Jasper, sergeant, top sergeant (all Derog.).

HOMOSEXUAL GATHERING n. bird circuit, grab party, lavender convention, meat rack.

HOMOSEXUAL GRATIFICATION n. meat.

HOMOSEXUAL, MALE n. gay, fag, agfay, fairy, pansy, nance, boy, lily, capon, cocksucker, milk mouth, bucket head, flamer, aunt, scare queen, grey wolf (elderly), drag queen, main queen, closet queen, fembo, flute, fluter, freak, frit, gobbler, girl, limp wrist, jocker, knobber, maricón, piccolo player, pix, peter puffer, swish, sweet, faygeleh (Yid.), yo-yo, ass bandit, bent out of shape, chicken, chicken delight (young), chicken hawk, bronco (novice), left-handed mintie, mola, out, mandrake, paleface (white), pogey, bird taker; toy boy, aspro (prostitute); man's man, third sexer, eye doctor, cannibal, punk, jock, jocky, trapeze artist, tusk, wolf, ringtail, sod, angel, angela, angelina, baby, salesman, mason, male-oriented, identified, cake eater, sister, three-letter man ("fag"), four-letter man ("homo"), gunsel, gazoonil, lamb, ma, mother, nellie, skippy, rough trade (sadistic), truck driver (rough), twink, willie, geep, fruit ma toot, cruiser, flinch bird, guzzler, muzzler, nibbler, snake charmer, joker, keister bandit, daddy, papa, uncle, prussian, short-arm bandit, short arm-heister, butt pirate, butt boy, rump ranger, pile diver, booty bandit, bottoms, nic-nac, nick-nack, turk, wheelman, apple pie, bender, bindle boy, brat, Mr. Brown, brownie-hound, dung-puncher, fudge packer, turd burglar, Betty, Dyna, Gussie, Nancy, Miss Nancy, flip, kid, half a man, bitch, chum-chum, catcher, pug (Af. Am.); charity stuff, coozey, floosie, flit ('30s), fruit-picker (occasional); flap,; fag hag, fag bag (woman who dates homosexual men) (all Derog and Obsc.).

HOMOSEXUAL MOVEMENT n. Gay Lib, Gay Liberation.

HOMOSEXUAL REVELATION n. outing, come out, come out of the closet, drop beads, drop a hairpin, gadar (ability to recognize).

HOMOSEXUAL UNION, BE IN A v. be married, go shot for shot, play sixty-nine (Obsc.), swap stew for beans, swap spits, fag bag (woman married to a homosexual)., Derog.

HONEST adj. up front, right up front, open, going the hangout route, like it is, call it like it is, lay it on the line, on the up and up, on the level, the emess, no lie, what you see is what you get, WYSIWYG, honest to God, honest injun (Derog.), sure enough, twenty-four-carat, square, square John, square shooter, true blue, righteous, Christian, ko-sher, Boy Scout, down home, fly right, Mr. Clean, regular, legit, on the legit, raw, the real deal (Af. Am.), for real, real people, okay people, saint, spiffy, straight, straight arrow, shoot straight, straight shooter, straight from the shoulder, straight out, straight dope, straight stuff, straight shit, straight-up, third rail, talk like a Dutch uncle, call a spade a spade, white, damn white, put all one's cards on the table, make no bones about it, talk turkey, all wool and a yard wide, card-carrying, salt of the earth, clean as a hound's tooth. See also SINCERE.

HONESTLY adv. for real, honest to God, indeedy, not shit, no buts about it, no ifs ands or buts, real, really truly.

HONOR v. roll out the red carpet, give one the key to the city, give one the glad hand, give one the blue ribbon.

HOOD n. doghouse, sneeze guard (salad bar).

HOODLUM n. hood, con, wrong number, hooligan, crook, tough, toughie, punk, yoot (teenager), soldier, deuce (small-time), gorilla, goon, gun, gunsel, torpedo, wise guy. See CRIMINAL.

HOODWINK v. dick one around, run a game on, snake one in, blow smoke up one's ass, fleece, gas, clip, con, scam, stiff, sting, double-shuffle, skunk. See TRICK.

HOODWINKED adj. stung, taken for a sleigh ride, been taken, jobbed, fucked, fucked over, set up, sand-bagged, burned, fleeced, dicked, gaffled, boned, snowed, snowed in, snowed under. See TRICKED.

HOOLIGAN n. gorilla, pug, ape, strongarm, mug, goon, muscle, muscle man, hatchet man, hatchet boy, big boy, sleazeball, slimebucket, maggot, shower scum, heavy, hood, clipper, bad actor, tough, tough cookie, hellion, ter-ror, holy terror, sidewinder, roughneck, bruiser, mugger, ugly customer, plug-ugly. See also CRIMINAL.

HOOT v. howl, put up a howl, set up a howl, holler, give a shout, give one the Bronx cheer, give one the raspberry, give one a razzberry, give one the bird, boo.

HOPE n. bright side, fool's paradise, light at the end of the tunnel, pipe dream. See also PROSPECT.

HOPE v. sweat, sweat it, sweat it out, hang in, keep one's fingers crossed, look on the bright side.

HOPEFUL adj. bullish, on the make, glad-hander (overly), gung-ho, high, high on something, scoutmaster, keeping the faith, rosy, upbeat. See OPTIMISTIC.

HOPELESS adj. sunk, shot down, no-way, no-win sit-uation, can't win for losin', no more cards to play, gone, goner, gone goose, dead duck, one's ass is grass, bust, put the kibosh on it, at the end of one's rope, not a ghost of a chance, not a Chinaman's chance, not a prayer, not a snowball's chance in hell, not till hell freezes over, ass out, in the soup, in the toilet, in deep shit, up shit creek, up shit creek without a paddle, up the creek, up the creek without a paddle, hard-up, up against it, tryin' to stay alive, runnin' out of time, scrapin' the bottom of the barrel, got one's back to the wall, clutching at straws, spinning one's wheels, fight-ing to keep one's head up.

HORDE n. mob, push, turnout, blowout, crush, jam, jam up, everybody and his brother, everybody and his uncle, loaded to the rafters, wall-to-wall people. See CROWD.

HORN n. pretzel (French horn).

HORN BLOWING n. beep, honk, toot.

HOROSCOPE n. signs, scope, Big Zee.

HORRIBLE adj. awful, hellish, beastly, sickie, barfy, furry, hairy, skin-crawling, grim, scary. See BAD. See also DREADFUL.

HORRIFY v. chill off, scare shitless, scare the pants off one, scare the bejesus out of one, scare to death. See FRIGHTEN.

HORROR STORY n. chiller, chiller-diller, thriller, monster movie, blood and guts, spine tingler.

HORS D'OEUVRES n. finger food, dip, spread, munchies.

HORSE n. hoss, hack, nag, bronc, bronco, bangtail, broomtail (mare), old gray mare, old Nellie, pony, bushtail, bum, crab, crip (crippled), crowbait (ugly or mean), refuge from the glue factory (sick, thin), cayuse, daisy cutter, plug, paint horse, old paint, pinto, G.G., geegee, trotter, dobbin, hayburner, plater, jade, crock, crowbait, goat, stiff. See also RACEHORSE.

HORSE MANURE n. road apples, golden apples, alley apples, horse hocky, horse pucky.

HORSEPLAY n. monkeyshines, shenanigans, hijinks, fun and games. See also AMUSEMENT.

HORSEPLAY, INDULGE IN v. horse around, fuck around, screw around, roughhouse.

HORSEPOWER, ADD v. soup, soup up, souped-up, hop-up, hopped-up, juice up, juiced-up.

HORSE, RACE n. the ponies, pony, the g.g.'s, gee-gee, nag, bangtail, mudder, pig, plater, dark horse (unknown entry), stick-out (superior), maiden, chaser (steeplechase racer), claimer, bug (never won; apprentice jockey), beetle, cooler, lizard, getty up, gluepot, goat, hide; weanling, baby, juvenile (2-year-olds); lug in, lug out (rail), lugger, the parking lot (outside on the turn), side wheeler, skin, stiff (loser), tacky, stretch runner, breakdown (injury while racing), warm-blood (bred to produce jumpers).

HORSE RACE BETTING TERMS across the board (first, second, third), win, on the nose, place (second), show (third); exacta, trifecta (win, place, show pools); daily double, pick six, quinella, out of the money, also-ran, parlay, claim agent (bettor), the chalk (smart money), chalk eater (bookie), chalk favorite, hammered (heavily bet favorite), odds-on favorite, lobster (poorly bet favorite), longshot, layoff bet, if bet, hunch player, line, morning line (early odds), scratch sheet, tipster, tote board, odds board, tout, to tout (the tout touted me off number two), vigorish (track percentage share of betting pool), handle (total betting), OTB (Off Track Betting).

HORSE RACE CARE n. cooler (light horse blanket), cool out, exercise boy, hot walker, nerved (nerve block to hooves), put down (humane killing), bute (phenylbutazone, painkiller), swipe (a groom).

HORSE RACE, RIDING IN A adj. up, in the irons, acey-deucy (right stirrup shorter), win going away, hand-ride, scraping paint (tight on the rail), the parking lot (outside on the turn), near side (horse's left side), pinhead (bad jockey).

HORSE RACING TERMS also-ran, bear in, bear out, lug in, lug out, wear blinkers (restrict horse's side view), blowout (workout run), break (start from gate), the call, drive (he won under a drive), early foot (fast starter), speedball (fast horse), one-run horse, handily, breeze, the parking lot (outside on the turn), post time (starting time), photo (photo finish), scratch (withdraw entry); bat, gad (whip), caller (race announcer); fast, lightning fast, good, heavy, muddy, sloppy, slow, gumbo (track conditions), flat racing, give away weight (carry extra weight handicap), footing, maiden race, go, run, in the money; pilot, rider, hardboot (jockey); railbird (spectator), tack (equipment), the track, the charts, boat race, drugstore race (drugged or fixed); sweep (sweepstake); golf ball, soup, T, tea (drugs); produce race (unfoaled entries based on bloodlines), run for the Roses (Kentucky Derby); claimer, seller, selling race claiming race); starter (an entry), steal (lead all the way), wire to wire (start to finish), green (inexperienced horse), shipper (horse from another track), improving the breed (horse racing), dropping in class, dogs up (early morning workout).

HORSESHOES n. barnyard golf.

HOSE n. Georgia credit card (used for siphoning gasoline).

HOSPITABLE, BE v. roll out the red carpet, put out the welcome mat, give one the key to the city, break out the champagne, red-carpet treatment.

HOSPITAL n. bone factory, butcher shop, pogey (prison), alley (corridor); gomer (known drug addict, Get Out of My Emergency Room, Medic.).

HOSPITAL ZONE n. pill hill.

HOST v. do the honors, spread oneself, throw a party, pick up the check, pick up the tab. See also ENTERTAIN (SOCIAL).

HOSTELRY n. motel, airtel, aquatel, boatel, floatel, fleabag, chinch pad, flophouse, scratch crib.

HOSTILE adj. ornery, scrappy, snorky, bitchy, waspish, anti, be agin, allergic to, have a chip on one's shoulder, at outs, on the muscle. See ANTAGONISTIC.

HOTCAKE n. flapjack, blanket, brown bucks, flats, manhole cover, saddle blankets, tire patch, wheat, collision mat (WWII).

HOT CHOCOLATE n. hot cha, fifty-one, fifty-two (two cups).

HOT ROD n. bomb, bug (car and driver), can, rod, chopped (low chassis), low rider, hauler, hot iron, raked car. See also AUTOMOBILE.

HOT ROD TERMS nerf (push a car with a car), sandbag, shaved, speed shop, squirrel (weave from side to side, a novice driver), chicken (game), twin pots, wrinkle rod, fishtail, forked eight, bent eight.

HOT SPRINGS, ARKANSAS Hot Water City, Vapor City.

HOTEL n. motel, shortel (hourly rates), airtel, aquatel, boatel, floatel, chinch pad, flophouse, scratch crib.

HOTEL ROOM n. flop box.

HOT WEATHER n. broiler, roaster, scorcher, sizzler, swelterer, sticky, close, steamy, steam box, sweaty, one can fry eggs on the sidewalk, hotter than blue mud.

HOUND n. hound dog. See also DOG.

HOUND v. 1. dog, dog on (verbal), bulldog, penny dog, dog one's case, jump on one's case, on one's case, on one's back, hassle, bug, ride, be at, be on the back of, all right already, graum, yap at, on one's tail, tail, rag, rag on, crack on (Hum., Af. Am.), curdle. See ANNOY. 2. beat the bushes, bird-dog (scout), scout, scratch, scratch around, look all over hell, search high heaven, turn upside down, turn inside out, leave no stone unturned, take out after, track down. See also FOLLOW.

HOUNDED adj. dogged, picked-on, catch shit.

HOUR n. a chime, a coupla bells, straight up.

HOUSE n. pad, crash pad, crib, condo, co-op, coop, pied-a-terre, joint, cubbyhole, den, domi, dommy, setup, layout, flop, flophouse, kennel, digs, diggings, roof over one's head, hole, hole in the wall, pigpen, pigsty, shanty, lean-to, sty, dump, castle, box, cave, hi-lo (split level), railroad flat, homeplate, palace; cradle, hat (Af. Am.); rack, roost, turf, old stomping grounds, bullpen, dice house, hooch (Vietnam), yurt.

HOUSEBREAK n. caper, heist.

HOUSE OF PROSTITUTION n. house, cathouse, massage parlor, rap club, poontang palace, snake ranch, chicken ranch, hook shop, nautch joint, beaver base, service station. See BROTHEL.

HOUSE OF REPRESENTATIVES House, dark side of the moon.

HOUSEWORK n. shitwork, chickwork.

HOUSTON, TEXAS Astrodome City, Dome City.

HOVEL n. dump, hole, pigpen, pigsty, rattrap, rathole, stall.

HOVERCRAFT n. flying bathtub, flying crow's nest.

HOW ABOUT how's about.

HOWARD JOHNSON RESTAURANTS n. hojos.

HUBBUB n. hullabaloo, hubba-hubba, buzz-buzz, boom-boom, hoo-ha, rowdydow, hell broke loose, all hell broke loose, ruckus, fuss.

HUCKSTER n. pitchman, Arab (Derog.).

HUFF n. snit, miff, pet, stew, tiff. See PIQUE.

HUG v. grab, grab ass, clinch, clutch, bear-hug, squeeze, lock.

HUGE adj. humongous, humungous, humongoid, mungo, bahugen, gross, honking, monstro, butt-kicking, bonzai, king-size, big mother, supercolossal, jumbo, whopping. See BIG.

HUMAN BEING n. naked ape, human bean. See also PERSON.

HUMANITARIAN n. Robin Hood, bleeding heart, do-gooder, good scout, good Sam. See also BENEFACTOR, PHILANTHROPIST.

HUMBLE v. prick one's balloon, make one sing small, put one away, take down, take down a peg, take the starch out of, cut to the quick, put away. See HUMILIATE.

HUMBLED adj. crawling, in bad, in Dutch, in the doghouse, eat crow, eat dirt, eat humble pie, sing small, lost face, drummed out, took down, knocked from one's high horse. See HUMILIATED.

HUMDRUM adj. garden, garden variety, everyday, vanilla, dullsville, bromidic, dime-a-dozen, square John, L7, Clyde, meat-and-potatoes man. See BORING.

HUMID adj. steamy, close, boiler, steam bath, sweat box, sticky.

HUMILIATE v. tear down, shoot down, cut down to size, cut-rate, run down, put down, burn, burn down, burn one down, downplay, play down, take down, take down a peg, take down a peg or two, take the starch out of, take the shine out of, cap, cut to the quick, slice up, rip, rip on, pan, slam, smear, rag, rag on, bag on (Hum.), rank, shade, throw shade, squash, squelch, hit, blister, roast, scorch, rap, take a rap at, take a swipe at, take the shine out of, fluff off, brush off, dump on, shit on, do a number on, shred, mud-sling, needle, give one the needle, knock, knock down, poormouth, bad-mouth, bitter mouth, back cap, backbite, rip up the back, give a black eye, give one one's comeuppance, thumb one's nose at, pooh-pooh, rubbish, sour grapes, mark lousy, put the crimpers in, put the hooks in, put the needles in, put the zingers in, put away, put a tuck in one's tail, poke full of holes, shoot full of holes, prick one's balloon, puncture one's balloon, take the wind out of one's sails, blow sky-high, knock the bottom out of, knock the chocks out from under, knock the props out from under, knock one off his perch, make one sing small. See also EMBARRASS.

HUMILIATED adj. put-down, clowned, gone to bad, gone to the dogs, gone to hell, come out moldy, crawling, die, draw in one's horns, eat crow, eat dirt, eat humble pie, sing small, get one's comeuppance, burned, in bad, in Dutch, in the doghouse, faced, lost face, red-aced, drummed out, took down, comedown, cap, stumped, stymied, dumped on, egg on one's face, knocked from one's high horse, knocked off one's perch, tuck in one's tail.

HUMILIATION n. comeuppance, comedown, takedown, put-down, touche.

HUMORIST n. jokesmith, gagman, gagster, punster, quipster, wisecracker, stand-up comic, clown, cutup. See JOKER.

HUMOROUS adj. camp, campy, jokey, joshing, yokky, boffo, gagged-up, for grins, priceless, screaming, too funny for words. See AMUSING.

HUNCH, GET A v. have a funny feeling, feel in one's bones. See PREMONITION.

HUNDRED n. C, one C, century.

HUNGARIAN n. Hungry, goulash, Hunkie, Hunky, Bohunk (all Derog.).

HUNGER n. big eyes, eyes for, hard-on for, wide on (Fem.), jones for, itch, hot pants, lech, sweet tooth, yen, zazzle.

HUNGRY adj. dog-hungry, empty, fly light, grits time, have a tapeworm, munchies (following marijuana use), starving, starved, starved to death, chucks, chuckers, could eat a horse, could eat the asshole out of a bear.

HUNT v. beat the bushes, bird-dog (scout), scratch, scratch around, geek out (seek crumbs of cocaine), look all over hell, search high heaven, run down. See SEARCH.

HUNTING EXPEDITION n. snofari (snow).

HUNTSVILLE, ALABAMA Rocket City.

HURDLE RACE n. timber topper.

HURL v. chuck, chunk, fire, lob, heave, pitch, sling, fling, gun, peg.

HURRAH interj. rah, ray, yay, eehaw!, yeehaw!

HURRY v. hustle, fog, haul, shake a leg, make tracks, dust, roll, tool, hotfoot it, hump, barrel, tear ass, put on the afterburners, split the breeze, move, rip, get busy with. See SPEED.

HURRY UP interj. get the lead out, get the lead out of your ass, shake a leg, move, get moving, get going, get cracking, get with it, hop to it, hump along, move your tail, move your ass, move your fanny, get on the ball, don't spare the horses, get your ass in gear, get your motor running, shake it up, get a move on, get a wiggle on, step on it, snap shit, snap to it, make it snappy, chop-chop, stir your stumps, hubba-hubba, haba-haba (WWII).

HURT adj. 1. hurtin', bleedin', damaged, winged, nicked, zinged, cut, bunged-up, busted-up, burned, burned one's ass, put away, screwed-up, walking wounded, have to scrape one off the sidewalk. 2. all torn up, cut-up, hit where one lives, shook, shook-up, miffed, miffy, shot-down, have one's nose out of joint, sore, uptight.

HURT n. boo-boo (minor flesh wound), ouch, owy, chop, scratch, nick, graze, brand, jig cut, mark, rat mark, stool mark (knife), black-and-blue, down.

HURT v. 1. zing, lean on, put down, cap, hit one where one lives, lay a bad trip on one, give one a lefthanded compliment, thumb one's nose at, give one the finger, flip one the bone, give one the bone, burn, gross out. See WOUND. 2. mess up, rough up, shake up, total, wax, wing, nick, zing, cut up. See DAMAGE.

HUSBAND n. man, my man, old man, main man, on the hitch, ace lane, breadwinner, buffalo, better half.

HYDROGEN BOMB n. H-bomb, the bomb, mega-bomb, doomsday machine, nuke.

HYDROPLANE n. thunderboat, flying boat.

HYMEN n. maidenhead, cherry, bug (not common), bean, flower, an issue over tissue, big issue over a little tissue.

HYMN n. shout.

HYPERBOLE n. hype, ballyhoo, big talk, tall talk, lay it on, lay it on thick, lay it on with a trowel, make a mountain out of a molehill, puff, P.R. See EXAGGERATE.

HYPERSENSITIVE adj. thin-skinned, can't even look at one cross-eyed, tetchy, touchy, wired, wired-up, uptight. See SENSITIVE.

HYPOCHONDRIA n. medical student's disease, hypo.

HYPOCRISY n. soft soap, sweet talk, chicken, chicken-shit, goop, hooey, shit, spinach, chewing gum, crocodile tears. See INSINCERITY.

HYPOCRITE n. four-flusher, hook, fake, fraud, play actor, phony, smoothie, two-way ghee, two-faced, plastic, wishy-washy person, wolf in sheep's clothing, fluker, mission stiff, psalm-singing muzzler.

HYPOCRITICAL adj. fishy, two-faced, gil, Hollywood, reach-me-down, slick, plastic, sincere, snide, phony, fake, cry crocodile tears, touchy-funky, jivey, jive-assed.

HYPODERMIC INJECTION n. booster, booster shot, hypo, shot; bang, mainline bang, shot in the arm, trapdoor, trapdoor scab (injecting under a scab to hide needle marks), pop, skin pop, hit, fix, nip, dram (narcotics).

HYPODERMIC NEEDLE n. hypo, hype, hype stick, artillery, gun, hook, nail, point, spike, square needle, bayonet.

HYPOTHESIS n. guesstimate, SWAG (slightly wild-assed guess), hunch, shot, shot in the dark, sneaking suspicion, scenario, stab, stab in the dark. See also BASIS.

HYPOTHESIZE v. toss out, spitball, brainstorm, go out on a limb, take a shot, take a shot in the dark, take a stab, talk off the top of one's head. See also SPECULATE.

HYSTERICAL, GET v. flip, flip one's lid, blow a gasket, go ballistic, pop one's cork, come unglued, come apart, weirded out, have a short fuse, work oneself into a stew, work oneself into a lather, work oneself into a tizzy, work oneself into a pucker, get hot under the collar, run a temperature, race one's motor, blow up, blow one's stack, blow one's top, fly off the handle, hit the ceiling. See also DISTURBED.

I

I n. India, Item.

I pron. yours truly, number one, numero uno, Dudley, Ol' Uncle Dudley, big three (me, myself and I).

IBM n. Big Blue.

ICE n. diamonds, hail, Prudhoe Pineapple (bucket), hold the hail (no ice).

ICE CREAM n. ball (single scoop), pop (on a stick), Eskimo, mud pie, white (vanilla), geedunk, vanilla cow (vanilla soda, shake, malt), black (chocolate), black-and-white (soda, vanilla ice cream, chocolate sauce), black cow (root beer float, soda with vanilla ice cream), all-around chocolate, double chocolate (chocolate ice cream with chocolate sauce).

ICELANDER n. Goolie.

ICE, WITH adj. on the rocks.

ICE, WITHOUT adj. straight up, neat.

ICING n. glop, sugary glop, topping.

IDAHO Gem State.

IDEA n. child, brainchild, brainstorm, brain wave, spark, spark plug, flash, flash on it, bell-ringer, deep-think, flop, rumble, wig, I got it, it hit me, it just come to me, approach, big idea, slant, take, twist, wrinkle, new wrinkle, wienie, gimmick, angle, action, big play, scenario, scene, story, picture, big picture, pitch, proposition, setup, game plan, napkin notion, layout, bit, what's cookin', how one figures it, what's the action, bug in one's ear, bug up one's ass, bee, bee in one's bonnet, flea in one's nose, judgment call, op, say-so, two cents' worth, bad talk (radical), riff (musical), sneaking suspicion, booby trap, tune, the name of that tune.

IDEAL adj. outrageous righteous and relaxed, pie in the sky, never-never land, Shangri-la, have it all, fuck-you money. See also PERFECT.

IDEALIST n. stargazer, dreamer, scoutmaster.

IDEALIZE v. talk through one's hat, build castles in the air, look at the world through rose-colored glasses, gimme a drag on that before you throw it away.

IDENTICAL adj. double, look-alike, like two peas in a pod, spitting image, six of one and half a dozen of the other, xerox, carbon copy, dead ringer, ditto, same difference. See SAME.

IDENTIFICATION n. cookie cutter, button, buzzer, flash, potsy, shield, tin, white tin, yellow tin, dog tag, I.D., ID, logo, make, rap, papers, high sign.

IDENTIFICATION TAG n. tag, dog tag, dog tags (Armed Forces), bracelet, ident bracelet, I.D.

IDENTIFY v. make, card, peg, aim, put down for, tab, tag, button down, finger, put the finger on, put one's finger on something. See also CRIMINAL, IDENTIFY.

IDIOM n. jive, jive talk, lingo, street talk, weasel words, flash (thieves).

IDIOSYNCRASY n. shtick, bit, mishegoss. See CHARACTERISTIC.

IDIOSYNCRATIC adj. kooky, freaky, weirdo, strange one, off-the-wall, case, wacky, chirp, character, queer fish, rare bird, meshugena. See ECCENTRIC.

IDIOT n. dork, megadork, dorf, lop, yo-yo, twit, doyburger, kook, out-to-lunch, dumb ox, dickhead, dimbo (girl), simp, gink, meathead, fathead, pinhead, pointy head, butthead, feeb, lorg, gump, jel, numbskull, putz (Yid.), yutz, isn't playing with a full deck. See STUPID.

IDIOTIC adj. batty, daffy, gorked, dum-dum, exceptional, dingaling, jerk off, jackass, asshole, ass'ole, squirrely, hare-brained. See FOOLISH.

IDLE adj. on the shelf, on the bench, out of the rat race, out of action, out of the swim, down, closed-down. See UNEMPLOYED.

IDLE v. bum, bum around, veg, vegetate, hang out, hang around, goof around, fiddle around, fiddle-fart around, stick around, mooch around, scrounge around, jack around, bat around, mess around, hack around, knock around, monkey around, fool around, fuck around, futz around, poot around, fuck off, fake off, goof off, screw off, dork off, flub off, flub the dub, rat, R.F., rat fuck, fuck the dog, lurk, sit on one's ass, sit on one's butt, sit on one's duff, jelly, tool, tail, bail out, cat, warm a chair, press the bricks, lie down on the job, get no place fast, poke, poke around, poke along, mosey, toddle, schlep along, potchky (Yid.), featherbed, float. See also LINGER.

IDLENESS n. goof-off time, fuck-off time, time to burn, time to kill, one's own sweet time.

IDLER n. foot dragger, goof-off, fuck-off, goldbrick, schlepper, sleepyhead, beach bum, house plant, drugstore cowboy, cake-eater, couch potato, sofa spud, lounge lizard, lump, john, johnny, good-for-nothin', lazy good-for-nothin'.

IDOL n. dad, Head Knock.

IDOLIZE v. have a thing about, crazy over, nuts about, daffy about, wild about, wacky about, mad for, gone on. See ADMIRE.

IDOLIZED adj. 1. touted, highly touted, okay people, score, 2. gone, gone on, stuck on, hipped on, wild about, fell for, mad about, crazy about, nuts about, keen about, have a thing about, struck by lightning.

IGNORAMUS n. numbnut, asshole, butthole, doyburger, loser, winner, twit; biff, dimbo (girl); beau, lunchie, putz (Yid.), yutz, lowbrow, dodo, dummy, dumbo, dum-dum, dumb fuck, mental giant, mental midget, airhead, helium head, conehead, pointyhead, punter (easily defrauded), doesn't know the score, not know one's ass from one's elbow. See STUPID.

IGNORANCE n. meatballism.

IGNORANT adj. uncool, unhep, unhip, a narb, narbo, square, airhead, helium-headed, lowbrow, nerd, dope, lame, duck, lop, lophead, scrub, a mushroom, goaty, in the dark, out to lunch, out of it, blind as a bat, drowning, hard-head, bletcherous, half-assed, half-baked, half-cocked, wouldn't know it if it bit him in the ass, doesn't know from nothing, doesn't know one's ass from first base, doesn't know one's ass from a hole in the ground, a big know-it-all, damned if I know, search me, haven't the foggiest, not have a clue, not know the score, not know the time of day, not know one's ass from one's elbow, not know a rock from a hard place, not know shit from Shinola, not there, not getting it, not be with it, God knows, God only knows, Lord knows, Heaven knows, nobody knows, damned if I know, beats the shit outta me, it beats me, it has me guessing, it's got me guessing, it's Greek to me, search me, you've got me, I give up, I pass, I don't know what, how should I know?, who knows?, don't look at me.

IGNORE v. 1. ig, tune out, dial out, look the other way, let it go, let one off easy, let one off this time, wink at, live with, pay no mind, pay no never-mind, play past, pooh-pooh. 2. cut, cut dead, brush off, give one the brush, high hat, not give one the time of day, give the go-by, chili, chill, cool, play it cool, cold-shoulder, give one the cold shoulder, leave out in the cold, freeze, freeze on, ice, ice out, dog, shine one on, look right through. 3. be asleep at the switch, let go to pot, let slide, let ride, fall between the chairs, fall between the cracks.

ILK n. likes, likes of, lot, number, birds of a feather.

ILL adj. peaky, peaked, down, run-down, down with, got a bug, got the bug, rocky, punk, a wreck, rotten, feeling rotten, ratty, poorly, seedy, feeling awful, feeling something terrible, under the weather, below par, running a temperature, off-color, off one's feed, off one's feet, sick as a dog, on the sick list, bum, bummy, on the bum, on the blink, laid low, outta action, woozy, bunk fatigue (WWI), the trots, runs, burpy, barfy, pukish, puky, upchucking, green, green around the gills, blue around the gills, one foot in the grave, one foot in the grave and the other on a banana peel.

ILL-CONSIDERED adj. half-assed, half-baked, half-cocked, off the top of one's head.

ILLEGAL adj. crooked, heavy, off-base, out-of-line, racket, shady, dirty, hung up, hung up with, wildcat, under-the-counter, under-the-table, undocumented (illegal immigrant).

ILLEGAL CACHE n. drop, cover.

ILLEGAL ENTRY n. black-bag job.

ILLEGAL SEARCH n. bag job.

ILLEGITIMATE adj. 1. bastard, byblow, born on the wrong side of the blanket, come in though a side door, love child, whore's bird. 2. shady, racket, the rackets, under-the-table, under-the-counter, hanky-panky, heavy, off-base, out-of-line, wildcat.

ILL FORTUNE n. bummer, downer, bad scene, can of worms, crunch, deep shit, up shit creek without a paddle, tough shit, TS, drag, can't even get arrested, rainy day, double whammy, need it like a hole in the head. See ADVERSITY.

ILL-HUMORED adj. scrappy, salty, spiky, bitchy, cantankerous, cussed, mean, ornery, chip on one's shoulder, fire-eater, ugly customer. See IRRITABLE.

ILLICIT adj. crooked, heavy, off-base, out-of-line, racket, shady, dirty, hanky-panky, left handed, wildcat, under-the-counter, under-the-table. See also ADULTEROUS.

ILLINOIS Prairie State, Sucker State, Land o' Lincoln.

ILL-MANNERED adj. grody, grody to the max, bunk, loud, loud-mouthed, raunchy, mutant, raw, tacky, cheap, skank, dipshit, roughneck, galoot, gool, sleazeball. See also VULGAR.

ILL-NATURED adj. bitchy, cussed, dirty, mean, turbobitch, ornery. See IRRITABLE.

ILLNESS n. bug, crud, creeping crud, growth, the runs, trots, what's going around, the flu, the pip, dose, double scrudfantods, fascinoma (Medic.), burned (V.D.), willies (mythical).

ILLOGICAL adj. cockeyed, off the wall, off the beam, nuts, nutty, have another think coming, catch-22, pair of ducks. See WRONG.

ILL-TEMPERED adj. crabby, grouchy, grumpy, bitchy, touchy, cantankerous, ugly customer, short fuse, turbobitch, ticking bomb. See IRRITABLE.

ILLUMINATE v. hit with a light, hit with a spot, hit with a beam, spot, spotlight, limelight, highlight.

ILLUSION n. fool's paradise, pipe dream, Disneyland, trip, head trip.

ILLUSORY adj. blue-sky, float, pipe dream, play with oneself, castles in the air, Disneyland. See FANCIFUL.

ILLUSTRATE v. show and tell, get over, lay out, draw one a picture, open one's head, get across, spotlight, highlight, limelight, give a f'rinstance, roll out, trot out. See EXPLAIN.

ILLUSTRATION n. for instance, f'rinstance.

ILLUSTRIOUS adj. w.k. (well-known), celeb, star, superstar, name, monster, in the limelight, page-oner, big-league, knocker, heavy stuff. See CELEBRITY.

IMAGE n. dead ringer, spitting image, angel (radar), carbon, carbon copy. See COPY.

IMAGINARY adj. trumped-up, dreamed-up, Disneyland, pipe dream, fool's paradise.

IMAGINATION n. brainstorm, brainchild, brain wave, flash on it, wrinkle, new wrinkle, big idea, wienie, bell-ringer. See also IDEA.

IMAGINATIVE adj. head-tripping, brain wave, breaking new snow, way-out, weird-out, far-out, flaky, kinky, offbeat, avant-garde, floating on clouds, pipe dream, fantasmo, Disneyland, play with oneself, jack off, pie in the sky, castles in the air, blue sky.

IMAGINE v. makeup, cook up, dream up, trump up, come up with, take it off the top of one's head, brainstorm, breakout meeting (brainstorm session), spark, spitball. See CREATE.

IMBECILE n. lamebrain, birdie (teenage), biff (girl), lop, dork, dorf, droid, beau, dodo, dummy, dickhead, lorg, gump, lunchbox, vacant lot, Z-head, exceptional, butthead, pointyhead, dip, dipshit, one doughnut shy of a dozen, a low-watt bulb, a few sandwiches short of a picnic, jel, nuthin' upstairs. See STUPID.

IMBIBE v. put away, booze up, tank up, down, belt, chugalug, exercise the elbow, raise a few, pound, knock back, juice back, hang on a few, irrigate. See DRINK.

IMBIBER n. wino, boozer, lush, stew, rummy, brown bagger, shikker, soak, sponge, tosspot, elbow bender. See DRINKER.

IMBROGLIO n. 1. rhubarb, run-in, brawl, flack session, punch out, go, knockdown and drag-out. See ARGUMENT. 2. soap opera, can of worms, kettle of fish, the plot thickens, in the soup, it's your funeral.

IMBUE v. brainwash, fuck with one's head, break down, program.

IMITATE v. 1. knock off, dupe, xerox, carbon, clone, mimeo, ditto, stat. 2. act like, do, do like, go like, make like, chomp, mirror, take off as, do a take-off, put on, send up, play the ——— (affect a role). 3. borrow, pirate, fake, phony, bogus, knock off, steal, steal one's stuff, bite, lift, crib, take a leaf out of one's book.

IMITATION adj. ersatz, bogosity, bogotified, autobogophobia (fear of bogosity), bogue, plastic, not what it's cracked up to be, queer, fake, phony, hokey, soft-shell. See FALSE.

IMITATION n. 1. ditto, dupe, xerox, clone, carbon, carbon copy, mimeo, stat, repro, knock-off, flimsy. 2. look-alike, work-alike, ringer, dead ringer, copycat, spitting image, spit and image, chip off the old block, double, peas in a pod, twin, ——— compatible (PC compatible). 3. knock-off, phony, queer, bogue, bogus, bogotified, junque, pseud, pseudo, plastic, ersatz, pirate goods, pirate labels. See COUNTERFEIT. 4. cheese, takeoff, put-on.

IMITATOR n. copycat, double, stand-in, crock, crowk (radio use, animal).

IMMATERIAL adj. big deal, big shit, big whip, BFD, big fucking deal, no big deal, no biggie; ain't no thang, ain't no thing but a chicken wing (Af. Am.); don't mean shit, no biggie, flying fuck, no skin off one's nose, mox nix, not (used at end of a sentence), makes no never mind. See UNIMPORTANT.

IMMATURE adj. kid, kid stuff, baby, snotnose, sophomore, half-assed, half-baked, green, not dry behind the ears, a bit previous. See UNSOPHISTICATED.

IMMEASURABLE adj. no end of, no end to, more than you can shake a stick at, jillion, a jillion at least, zillion, bazillion, umpteen, umpteeenth, alive with, crawling with, thick as flies. See COUNTLESS.

IMMEDIATELY adv. like now, pronto, on the double, double time, move your ass, balls out, toot sweet, at the kickoff, off the pop, on the dot, in a New York minute, in half a mo, in jig time, in a jiffy, in half a jiffy, in a flash, in nothing flat, in a shake, in half a shake, in two shakes, in two shakes of a lamb's tail, like a shot, like a shot out of hell, like a big-ass bird, like a BAB, right off the bat, first crack out of the box, all of a sudden, PDQ, pretty damned quick, before one can say Jack Robinson, abracadabra.

IMMENSE adj. humongoid, humongous, humungous, honking, mungo, monstro, gross, butt-kicking, bonzai, king-size, moby, mother, motherfucker (Obsc.), big mother, major-league, super, jumbo, barn-door. See BIG.

IMMERSE v. dunk.

IMMERSED adj. up to here in, wrapped up in, into, really into, eat sleep and breathe something, turned-on, tied-up. See ENGROSSED.

IMMIGRANT n. greenhorn, greeny, F.O.B. (fresh off the boat); Hunk, Hunkie, Bohunk (Derog.), wetback, bracero, documented, undocumented, boat people, yacht people (affluent refugees from Hong Kong).

IMMINENT adj. in the cards, in the wind, at hand, see it coming, it's looking to, waiting on, the noose is hanging, handwriting is on the wall. See also ANTICIPATED.

IMMOBILE adj. anchored, nailed, nailed down, pat. See also STUBBORN.

IMMOBILIZE v. freeze, jack up, take one out, put a stopper in, throw a monkey wrench into, tie up, jam up, hang one up, gridlock.

IMMODERATE adj. too-too, too much, out-of-sight, like crazy, like mad, throw out the baby with the bath water. See EXTREME.

IMMODEST adj. biggety, cocky, showboat, blowhard, loudmouth, ego-tripping, swell-headed, stuck on oneself. See CONCEITED.

IMMORAL adj. 1. X-rated, blue. See DISSOLUTE. 2. open, wide-open, meat-eater, gone to bad, gone to hell, speedy, fast, fast-and-loose. See OBSCENE. See also DISHONEST.

IMMOVABLE adj. locked-in, hard-nosed, burly, tough nut to crack, set in concrete, standpat, dig in one's heels, stick to one's guns, mule-headed, dead set on, murder (he's murder). See STUBBORN.

IMMUNIZATION n. shot, shot in the arm, shot in the ass, booster, booster shot.

IMMUNIZE v. give a shot, shoot, give one the square needle.

IMMUNIZED adj. binged, got the hook, got the square needle, stabbed in the ass (WWII), jabbed in the ass.

IMP n. hellion, hellcat, fiend.

IMPACT n. crackup, crash, crunch, smash, smashup, kick, hit one, hit one like a ton of bricks.

IMPACT v. crack up, register, jolt, crash, smash, smash up, rack up, bang into, nerf, kick.

IMPACT SPORT n. contact sport.

IMPAIR v. ding, tweak, bend the goods, total, take a hit, rack up, goof up, gum up, hash up, rough up, snarl up, snafu, queer. See DAMAGE.

IMPAIRED adj. dinged, totaled, gone, down, on down time, on the blink, no-go, had it, busted, kaput, a few bugs, glitched, gremlins, on the fritz. See DAMAGED.

IMPARTIAL adj. call 'em as one sees 'em, on the fence, fence sitter, middle of the road, anythingarian, dawk (neither a dove or a hawk), even-steven, mugwumpian, mugwumpish.

IMPASSE n. standoff, Mexican standoff, catch-22, box, corner, dead end, gridlock, hole, damned if you do and damned if you don't, pickle.

IMPASSIONED adj. hot for, hot about, turned on, gone on, steamed-up, all hopped up about, worked up about, stoned, wild about, ape over, starry-eyed over, gaga over. See ENTHUSIASTIC.

IMPATIENT adj. antsy, antsy-pantsy, ants, ants in one's pants, about to piss in one's pants, itchy, ripe, keen, creaming to, dying to, on pins and needles, have a short fuse, work oneself into a stew, work oneself into a lather, work oneself into a tizzy, work oneself into a pucker, hot, hot for, hot to go, hot to trot, rarin' to go, full of get-up-and-go, go great guns, gung-ho, hopped-up, spark plug, self-starting, fall all over oneself, not let any grass grow under one's feet, ready for Freddie. See also ANXIOUS.

IMPECCABLE adj. A-okay, aces, 10, ten, on target, bump'n', apple pie, four-o, tiptop shape, outrageous righteous and relaxed. See PERFECT.

IMPEDE v. hang up, hold up, stymie, put one in a box, flag one, freeze, shut off, shut down, stonewall, close off, saddle with, cut off one's water, blow the whistle on, cramp one's style. See HINDER.

IMPEDIMENT n. hang-up, baggage, excess baggage, psychological baggage, ball and chain, catch, glitch, gridlock. See HINDRANCE.

IMPELLER n. blower, butter paddle, club, eggbeater, fan, pants stopper, prop, windmill.

IMPENETRABLE adj. bulletproof.

IMPENDING adj. in the cards, in the wind, at hand, see it coming, it's looking to, waiting to, the noose is hanging, the handwriting is on the wall.

IMPERATIVE adj. chips are down, hurry-up call, when you gotta go you gotta go, orders are orders, there's no turning back, matter of life and death. See URGENT.

IMPERFECT adj. 1. funky, lousy, seconds, crap, crappy, junk, shit, crud, cruddy, creep, creepy, clinker, cheap John, borax, dog, dreck, from hunger, G, garbage, dud, gummy, gook, ham, jelly-bean, jitney, lemon, Mickey Mouse, piece of shit, punk, rat's-ass, piss-poor, schlocky, rinky-dinky, abortion, turkey, bottom of the barrel, scrape the bottom of the barrel, sleazy, tripe, two-bit, ticky-tacky, slimpsy, minus, cheesy, grunge, grungy, below the mark, it sucks, sux, sucky, not up to scratch, not up to snuff, quick-and-dirty, plastic, cotton-pickin', low, rank, mucked-up, messed-up, loused-up. See also INADEQUATE, CHEAP. 2. a few bugs, a glitch, gremlins.

IMPERIL v. lay on the line, put on the spot, stick one's neck in the noose, stick one's neck out, play into one's hands, chance it.

IMPERILED adj. on the line, on the spot, out on a limb, got one's neck out, have one's ass out, caught with one's pants down.

IMPERIOUS adj. bossy, driver, pushy, whip-cracking, ass-kicking, crack the whip, high-and-mighty, on one's high horse, throw one's weight around, pull rank. See AUTOCRATIC. See also POWERFUL, MASTERFUL.

IMPERMANENT adj. temp, Band-Aid, quick fix, throwaway, here today gone tomorrow, fly-by-night.

IMPERSONAL adj. cool, cold, cold turkey, straight, strictly business.

IMPERSONATE v. make like, act like, go like, mirror, play the ——— (affect a role), ditto, do, do like, steal one's stuff, take off, take a leaf out of one's book, fake, hoke, hoke up.

IMPERTINENCE n. back talk, backchat, comeback, lip, sass, brass, crust, gall, guff, smart ass, wisecrack, wise guy, chutzpah.

IMPERTINENT adj. fresh, cheeky, sassy, smart-alecky, lippy, saucebox, chutzpadik, out of line, off-base. See INSOLENT.

IMPERTURBABLE adj. cool, cool as a cucumber, keep one's cool, keep one's shirt on, not turn a hair, not get one's balls in an uproar, not get oneself in an uproar, roll with the punches, unflappable, cold fish, hard as nails, rhinoceros hide, thick-skinned, dead-ass, without a nerve in one's body, keep a stiff upper lip. See also ASSURED.

IMPETUOUS adj. hopped-up, itchy, go off the deep end, go off half-cocked, jump the gun. See IMPULSIVE.

IMPLAUSIBLE adj. thick, thin, reachy, won't wash, won't hold water, fishy, for the birds, full of holes, too much, blow it out your ear, far-out. See UNBELIEVABLE.

IMPLEMENT n. contraption, can-opener (safe), Armstrong (requires strength). See APPARATUS.

IMPLEMENT v. phase in. See START.

IMPLICATE v. name, finger, point the finger at, hang something on, pin on, blow the whistle on one, frame, frame up, jacket, lay at one's door. See INCRIMINATE.

IMPORT n. bottom line, point, stuff, nub, name of the game, nitty-gritty, nuts and bolts, the way of it, nature of the beast, drift, heart, meat, nub, score, punch line.

IMPORTANT adj. 1. heavy, heavy number, power, meaningful, mean business, strictly business, get down to business, business end of, chill out, serious shit, serious jelly, cosmic, matter of life and death, something, something else, fab, fat, big-league, major-league, top-drawer, heavyweight, heavy stuff, the big picture, meat and potatoes, high-cotton, high-profile, buckle down, chips are down, hurry-up call, like all-get-out, no fooling, no shit, no bird turdin', bound and determined, dead set on, bent on, hell bent on, heat's on, hot flash, hot shit, fire in the belly, not playing around, not to be sneezed at, we're not talking about nutmeg here, money talks, walk heavy, walk tall, big deal, in, stand in with, cut ice, carry a lot of weight, throw a lot of weight, the juice, the force, underlined. 2. name, face card, big, biggie, big player, big chew, big boy, Mr. Big, big name, big one, gun, big gun, big man, big man on campus, B.M.O.C., big noise, big number, big shot, big shit, big timer, wheel, big wheel, wheeler-dealer, bigwig, big ghee, big spud, A-list, big butter-and-egg man, butter-and-egg man, big cheese, real cheese, whole cheese, apple, big apple, biggest frog in the pond, walk heavy, his nibs, honcho, magoo, main squeeze, movers and shakers, one who knows where the body's buried, kuhnocker, higher-ups, high muck-a-muck, high-muckety-muck, high monkey-monk, high pillow, hot shot, hot dog, top dog, topsider, suit, pinstriper, vest, tycoon, baron, brass, top brass, brass hat, VIP, V.I.P., visiting fireman, lion, connection, connection ghee, polly, wire, wire man, wire-puller, godfather, a somebody, hoohaw, double-barreled, in the limelight. See also CELEBRITY, EXECUTIVE.

IMPORTUNE v. work on, con, blarney, lay it on, lay it on thick, lay a rap, sell, shit, string along, egg one on, goose, caboodle, bone, hock one's charnik, noodge. See PERSUADE.

IMPOSE v. move in on, chisel in, horn in, muscle in, lay down the law, put one's foot down, read the riot act, dish it out, dish out, dump on, give it to one, stick it to one. See also FORCE.

IMPOSING adj. mind-blowing, mega, megadual, clean outta sight, one for the book, something else, something to write home about. See IMPRESSIVE.

IMPOSITION n. drag, pain in the ass, pain in the neck. See ANNOYANCE.

IMPOSSIBLE adj. it won't fly, that dog won't hunt, no-go, no way, im-fucking-possible, can't win for losin', no-win situation, not a prayer, not a ghost of a chance, not a Chinaman's chance, not a chance in hell, not a snowball's chance in hell, not till hell freezes over.

IMPOSTER n. faker, four-flusher, phony, pseud, actor, bogue. See QUACK.

IMPOTENT adj. 1. fire blanks, shoot blanks, blank cartridge, dud, no lead in the pencil, no toothpaste in the tube, can't get it up, don't have the horses, out of gas. 2. wimpy, gutless, nerdy, paper tiger, can't hack it, not have it, can't cut it, can't cut the mustard, can't make the grade. See WEAK.

IMPOVERISH v. bleed, bleed white, suck dry, wipe out, break, take for all one's got, clean one out, take one's last penny.

IMPOVERISHED adj. flat, flat broke, stony, truly needy, underdeveloped (nation or district), strapped, oofless, clean, tapped out, on the rocks, hurting, to the curb, have-nots, bag lady, piss-poor, on the rims. See DESTITUTE.

IMPRACTICABLE adj. no-go, it won't fly, that dog won't hunt, not a prayer, not a Chinaman's chance, not a chance in hell, not a snowball's chance in hell. See IMPOSSIBLE.

IMPRECATION n. whammy, double whammy, hoodoo, voodoo, jinx, cuss, cussword, dirty word, dirty name, four-letter word, no-no, swear word.

IMPRECISE adj. guesstimate, windshield appraisal (superficial, from a car), ball-park, ball-park figure, out in left field. See also WRONG.

IMPREGNABLE adj. bulletproof.

IMPREGNATE v. knock up, get in trouble, put in the family way.

IMPRESS v. register, blow away, blow one away, faze, move, score, kill, slay, grab, knock one's socks off, knock one out, knock one for a loop, hit like a ton of bricks, make one's teeth fall out, buffalo, bulldoze, enforce, lean on, push around, turn on the heat, walk heavy, showboat, show off, show-time, grandstand, hotdog, make a grandstand play, make a big splash, style (Af. Am.).

IMPRESSED adj. programmed, brainwashed, head-fucked, mind-fucked, boggled.

IMPRESSIVE adj. cool, real cool, zero cool, chilly most, killer, it's to die for, aggro, fab, far out, mean, mongo, mega, megadual, marvy, nifty, spiffy, frantic, unreal, major, dynamite, dyno, lampin', scandalous, in the groove, groovy, jazzy, jumping, mad, mean, brutal, evil, wicked, the most, mostest, like wow, reet, mind-blowing, mind-bending, out-of-this-world, turn on, kicky, diddly bop, a gas, live one, live wire, wild, dolce vita, gone, real gone, hot stuff, hairy, large, large charge, massive, nervous, rootin'-tootin', snazzy, solid, solid sender, one for the book, something, something else, something to shout about, something to write home about, daddy, cherry, deffest, dope, dual, fat, fierce, fresh, fully on, mint, nitro, on the strength, raw, sick, stupid fresh, swinging, fine, lush, sizzler, scorcher, big splash, out-of-sight, clean outta sight, razzle-dazzle, glitzy, flashy, showy, smashing, bang-up, brutal, ace-high, swell, stunner, stunning.

IMPRISON v. put away, hold, lock up, send up, ice, book, cool, cage. See JAIL.

IMPRISONED adj. boxed (after arrest), away, fell, go over, go up, up the river, in the slam, in the slammer, in the pokey, in the clink, in college, out of town, sent up, iced, put on ice, in the municipal farm, cooped, cooped up, jugged.

IMPROBABILITY n. very iffy, it don't figure, hundred-to-one shot, got two chances: slim and none, a nonstarter, not in the cards, not a chance in hell, not a Chinaman's chance, not a snowball's chance in hell, not a snowball's chance, outside chance, it won't fly.

IMPROMPTU adj. off the wall, off the cuff, off the top of the head, off the hip, shoot from the hip, improv, ginned-up, ad lib, wing it, vamp, fake, fake it, play by ear, dash off, strike off, knock off, throw off, toss off, toss out, whip up, spitball.

IMPROPER adj. bad form, off, way off, off-base, off-color, off-the-beam, not cricket, out of line, out in left field, wrong number, put one's foot in it, put one's foot in one's mouth, bend the law.

IMPROVE v. 1. upgrade, polish, sharpen, boost, sky-rocket, take off, make first rate, up, doll up, fix up, gussy up, pretty up, spruce up, dress up, look up, pick up, perk up, soup up. 2. step up, step up in class, shape up, get back in shape, get well (monetarily), be on the mend, pick up the pieces, brace up, take a brace, bounce back, come back, make a comeback, on the comeback trail, come from behind, come out of it, pull out of it, snap out of it, turn the corner, bottom out, be out of the woods, come around, come along, come alive. 3. clean up one's act, get one's act together, get with it, get on the ball, get real, get a life, get a clue, go straight, straighten out, straighten up and fly right, turn around, turn things around, turn over a new leaf.

IMPROVED adj. souped-up, sharpened, over the hump, out of the woods, on the comeback trail.

IMPROVEMENT n. uptick, upbeat, upgrade, retrofit.

IMPROVING adj. looking good, looking up, on the lift, on the rise, on the upbeat, on the upgrade, on the upswing, bottoming out.

IMPROVISATION n. ad lib, improv, blow room, blow session, hot lick, lick, riff, winging it, vamp, fake, off the wall, off the cuff, off the hip, off the top of one's head, shoot from the hip, spitball, play by ear, dash off, strike off, knock off, throw off, toss off, toss out, whip up, jamming, taking it for a ride.

IMPROVISE v. ad-lib, impro, improv, gin up, noodle around, play piano, brainstorm, breakout meeting (brainstorm session), head trip, spark, spitball, off the cuff, off the hip, shoot from the hip, off the top of one's head, wing it, fake, fake it, play it by ear, play it as it lays, jam, shuck, vamp, strike off, get off, throw off, throw out, toss off, toss out, knock off, knock out, dash off, bat out, slap out, slapdash, slap up, shove out, dream up, make up, whip up, cook up, think up, whomp up, trump up, up, mess around, noodle, noodle around, work something out, put together with spit and chicken wire.

IMPROVISED adj. ad lib, improv, ginned-up, off the cuff, off the top of the head, Band-Aid, quick fix, fly-by-night, hit-or-miss, Mickey Mouse, rinky-dink, slapdash. See IMPROMPTU.

IMPRUDENT adj. off the deep end, go off the deep end, step off the deep end, put one's foot in it, put one's foot in one's mouth, go to sea in a sieve, go out on a limb, go for broke, buy a pig in a poke, play with fire, leave oneself wide open. See also CARELESS.

IMPUDENCE n. back chat, backtalk, woof, brass, cheek, chutzpah, crust, face, gall, guff, lip, sauce, sass, smarts, smart-ass, the smarts, nerve, out-of-line, off-base.

IMPUDENT adj. brassy, get previous, flip, smart-ass, wise-ass, off-base, chutzpadik. See INSOLENT.

IMPUGN v. trash, slam, zing, zap, knock, rap, cap, put down, run down, burn down, burn one down, thumb down, rag, rag on, snappin' (Af. Am.), break, come down on, hit on, pin on, have something on, swipe at, throw the book at, skin alive, lay out, stick it to, cut to bits, cut to ribbons, blast, tar, smear.

IMPULSE n. flash, yen.

IMPULSIVE adj. flaky, mad, ad lib, blow hot and cold, up-and-down, winging it, off the wall, off the cuff, off the hip, off the top of one's head, shoot from the hip, spitball, play by ear, dash off, strike off, knock off, throw off, toss off, toss out, whip up, go off the deep end, step off the deep end, jump off the deep end, jump the gun, go off half cocked, at one's own sweet will. See also SPONTANEOUS.

IMPUTE v. hang something on, pin on, reference. See ASSIGN.

INACCESSIBLE adj. out-of-pocket, not got.

INACCURATE adj. off, way off, off the beam, off-base, all wet, that doesn't track, smoking your socks, have another think coming. See WRONG.

INACTIVE adj. dopey, draggy, drag-ass, blah, lox, sack artist, veg out, Stepin Fetchit, on the shelf, on the bench, on hold, in a holding pattern, in cold storage, out of the rat race, out of action, out of the swim, down, closed-down. See also UNEMPLOYED.

INACTIVE, BE v. sit on one's ass, sit on one's butt, sit one one's duff, sit on one's hands, cool one's heels, stand pat, stand by.

INADEQUATE adj. a few bugs, a glitch, gremlins, seconds, crap, crappy, junk, shit, cruddy, creepy, clinker, cheap John, budget, borax, dog, dreck, from hunger, funky, lousy, for the birds, G, gummy, gook, ham, jelly bean, jitney, lemon, Mickey Mouse, bush-league, piece of shit, punk, pile of shit, rat's ass, piss-poor, schlocky, bottom of the barrel, scrape the bottom of the barrel, sleazy, tripe, two-bit, ticky-tacky, slimpsy, minus, cheesy, grungy, bupkis, chickenshit, too little too late, zilch, below the mark, it sucks, sux, clown, bringdown, fuck-up, scrub, droob, drube, dag, loser, nerd, dexter, full hank, lop, narc, spud, squid, underachiever, twink, woofie, geek, geekoid, half-assed, half-baked, clunker, also-ran, no-good, loser, a real loser, a real winner, out to lunch, turkey, jive turkey, dip stick, squid, runt, outa gas, burned out, toast, cooked, low man on the totem pole, have nothing on, nothing on the ball, not up to scratch, not come up to scratch, not up to snuff, not hack it, not have it, not make it, not cut out for, not hold a candle to, quick and dirty, can't cut it, can't cut the mustard, can't fade that, can't make the grade, second-fiddle, second-string, dime-a-dozen, all thumbs, a menace, plastic, cotton-pickin', low, rank, gerk (old). See also INEFFECTIVE.

INANE adj. jerky, nerky, harebrained, lamebrained, birdbrained, ditzy, weak in the upper story, goopy, horse's ass, Mickey Mouse, sappy. See FOOLISH. See also INSIPID.

INAPPROPRIATE adj. off, way off, off-base, off-color, off the beam, out of line, out in left field, bad form, wrong number, humbug, put one's foot in it, put one's foot in one's mouth, bend the law, garbage.

INATTENTIVE adj. mooning, daydreaming, out-to-lunch, popcorn-headed, asleep at the switch, goofing off, looking out the window. See DISTRACTED.

INAUGURATE v. ring in, get things rolling, break the ice, break in, kick off, bow, fire up, cook up, dream up, make up, come up with. See BEGIN.

INCALCULABLE adj. jillion, zillion, bazillion, umpteen, umpteenth, more than you can shake a stick at, no end of, no end to, thick as flies, thick as hail. See COUNTLESS.

INCANTATION n. abracadabra, hocus-pocus, mumbo-jumbo, open sesame, ala kazam, hoodoo, voodoo.

INCAPABLE adj. uncool, fumble-fist, butterfingers, muff, muffer, duffer, slob, squid, a newt, lummox, lump, dub, yo-yo, can't hack it, scrub, loser, winner, turkey. See INADEQUATE.

INCAPACITATE v. hamstring, queer, take out, hog-tie, put out of commission, throw a monkey wrench into the works, spike one's guns, clip the wings of. See DISABLE.

INCAPACITATED adj. crip, gimp, gimpy, game, g'd up, geed up, hamstrung, hog-tied, taken out, sidelined, out of commission.

INCARCERATE v. put away, hold, lock up, send up, send up the river, ice, put on ice, book, throw the book at, cool, can, cage, lay the arm on, take one away, settle, slough, slough up, railroad.

INCARCERATED adj. iced, jugged, away, up the river, in the slammer, in college. See IMPRISONED.

INCAUTIOUS adj. devil-may-care, any old way, fast-and-loose, pay no mind, put one's foot in it, put one's foot in one's mouth, play with fire, stick one's neck out, leave oneself wide open, cowboy. See CARELESS.

INCENSE v. brown off, piss one off, bitch one off, T off, get under one's skin, get a rise out of one, fire up, egg on, ask for it, cop an attitude (Af. Am.), that grinds my gears, stick in one's craw. See ANGER.

INCENSED adj. bugged, hacked, blown-out, uptight, hacked-off, brassed-off, cheesed-off, aggro, pissed-off, peed-off, tee'd-off, browned-off, bummed-out, burned-up, hung-up, huffy, in one's hair, dogged, miffed, peeved, riled, rubbed the wrong way, spooked, all hot and bothered, at the end of one's rope, buffaloed, hard put to it, picked-on, driven up the wall, rousted, steamed. See also ANGRY.

INCESSANTLY adv. round the clock, day and night, for ever so long. See also ALWAYS.

INCIDENT n. happening, hap, happenso, trip, real trip, cranking, like it is, where it's at, the size of it, scene, go down, come off, goings-on. See EVENT.

INCISE v. chiv, shiv.

INCITE v. get to, push one's buttons, flip out, craze, jazz up, adjy, psych, spook, juice, send, blow up, trigger, bug, burn up, fire up, key up, kick up a row, put up to, work up, work up into a lather, egg on, turn on, make waves, make a scene, make a fuss, sound off, make it tough for all, put the zingers in, needle, give one the needle, put the needles in, ride, steam up, throw wood on the fire, add fuel to the flames, rabble-rouse, stir up, discombobulate, go on make my day, stick in one's craw, ask for it, get a rise out of one, turn one on, rile, get one's goat, get under one's skin, get in one's hair, brown off.

INCITER n. fireman, hatchet man, needle man, adjy, spark plug, pusher, steam-up ghee, stormy petrel, wave maker.

INCLINATION n. bag, groove, thing, natural at, handy at, shine in, take to something like a duck takes to water, have a bump for, turned on to, flash, weakness for, cup of tea, druthers, type, where one is at, head-set, mind-set, mind trip, tilt, big eyes, eyes for, hard-on for, jones for, itch, hot pants, lech, sweet tooth, yen, zazzle. See also DESIRE.

INCLUDE v. cut one in on, duke one in on, wrap into, hands on, sit in, get in the act.

INCLUSIVE adj. across-the-board, the whole ball of wax, wall to wall, all the options. See also WHOLE.

INCOGNITO adj. incog, bearding. See also ANONYMOUS.

INCOME n. net, velvet, pay, payoff, rake-off, gravy, bottom line, in the black, in the till, cush, cash flow, cash cow, revenue stream, bottom line, the big time, split, get, gate, handle, melon, peanuts (small), strength, sweetener, sweetening, what's in it for one, take, take-in, take-home, harvest, cream; brocas, cactus, dust, ends, bread, lace (large profits). See COMPENSATION.

INCOMMUNICADO adj. on ice, out of touch, out of pocket.

INCOMPATIBLE adj. poles apart, weird, diff, far cry, funky, offbeat, march to the beat of a different drummer, whale of a difference, like night and day.

INCOMPETENT adj. out to lunch, bringdown, that dog won't hunt, amateur night, amateur night in Dixie, can't hack it, can't cut it, can't cut the mustard, can't make the grade, can't fade that, not have it, not cut out for, uncool, Mickey Mouse, bush, bush-league, haywire, dead one, a newt, lame-brained, dub, flubdub, flub the dub, dud, fuddy-duddy, ham, half-assed, half-baked, helluva way to run a railroad, fumble-fist, butterfingers, muff, nowhere, out of one's depth, in over one's head, zilch.

INCOMPETENT n. asshole, assface, asswipe, fuck-up, nerd, jerk, full hank, yo-yo, droid, cheesehead, cheeseface, Captain Cheddar, turkey, clown, dipstick, runt, eightball, winner, real winner, loser, real loser, ham, bullstaller, schmendrick, schmo, muffer, duffer, slob, lummox, lump, gerk (old).

INCOMPREHENSIBLE adj. clear as mud, clear as dishwater, it beats me, beats the shit outta me, it's Greek to me, you've got me, I give up, I pass. See OBSCURE.

INCONCEIVABLE adj. 1. thick, thin, reachy, won't wash, fishy, phony, rings phony, in one's hat, pure bullshit, blow it out your car, not born yesterday. See UNBELIEVABLE. 2. no-go, it won't fly, no way, not a prayer, not a ghost of a chance, not a Chinaman's chance, not a chance in hell, nonstarter. See IMPOSSIBLE. 3. fantasmo, seven-ply gasser, gnarly, mega-gnarly, unreal, rat-fuck, cool, zero cool, cold, out of this world, out of sight, nose cone, like wow, stunning, mad, mess, mezz, fab, in orbit, murder, something, something else, dynamite, far out, funky, too much, the most, the utmost, hell of a note, this is some kinda ———, the end.

INCONSEQUENTIAL adj. 1. dinky, two-bit, big zero, big fucking deal, BFD, no biggie, no great shakes, entry level (job), bupkes. jerkwater (small town), 2. empty suit, herb, wimp, nebbish, squid, shrimp, runt, a nobody, small potatoes, small spuds, twirp. See UNIMPORTANT.

INCONSISTENCY n. pair of ducks, sometimesy, catch, catch-22.

INCONSPICUOUS adj. low-keyed, low-profile, soft-pedaled.

INCONSTANT adj. 1. wishy-washy, yo-yo, see-saw, picky, picky-picky. 2. two-faced, two-timer, dog one around, yard on, cheat on, chippy on one, step out on one. See UNFAITHFUL.

INCONTROVERTIBLE adj. surefire, sure as God made little green apples, sure as death and taxes, sure thing, sure as shootin', no two ways about it, absofuckinglutely, posolutely, absitively, nailed down, open-and-shut case, and no mistake. See CERTAIN.

INCONVENIENCE v. hang up, give one a bad time, give one a hard time, make it tough for, discombobulate, put in a hole, put in a spot, put on a spot, fuzzbuzz. See also TROUBLE.

INCORPORATE v. tie in, gang up, put together, pool, cross-dissolve (film), cue in (scripts, ms., songs); dub, hook in, marry (film), mix (recording). See ASSOCIATE.

INCORRECT adj. all wet, ass backwards, way off, off the beam, full of beans, smoking your socks, check that, that doesn't track, wrong number. See WRONG.

INCORRIGIBLE adj. stinking, gross, too much, beastly, a bit much, too far gone, wrong ghee, three-time loser, loser. See BAD.

INCREASE v. pad, pyramid, slap on, tack on, tag on, hitch on, pour it on, hook on, hook up with, piggyback, mushroom, up, beef up, soup up, hop up, ramp up, heat up, hike, hike up, step up, jazz up, jack up, pick up, jump up, shoot up, put up, run up, tish, build, build up, builder-upper, bring up, fetch up, goose up, spike, flesh out, spin out, string out, drag out, add bells and whistles, dump on, snow, snowball, sweeten, sweeten the pot, parlay, speed up, boost, press a bet, join up with, join together, plug into, add fuel to the fire.

INCREASED adj. beefed-up, hiked, hiked-up, jacked-up, upped, built-up, boosted, padded, spun-out, strung-out, dragged-out, run-out, pyramided.

INCREDIBLE adj. 1. fab, aggro, mongo, glor, superfly, outrageous, fantasmo, def, twitchin', piss-cutter, unreal, skrouk, a gas, seven-ply gasser. See FABULOUS. 2. thick, thin, reachy, won't wash, blow it out your ear, fishy, phony, rings phony.

INCRIMINATE v. finger, point the finger at, put the finger on, hang something on, pin on, pin it on one, blow the whistle on one, whistle-blow, name, frame, frame up, put up a job, aim, lay at one's door, jacket, front, front off, let one have it, stick it to one, find the smoking gun.

INCULCATE v. brainwash, head-fuck, mind-fuck, fuck with one's head, break down, program, shape up, work over. See also INSTRUCT.

INCURABLE adj. in the soup, had it, no more cards to play, nowhere to go, runnin' out of time, at the end of one's rope. See HOPELESS.

INDEBTED adj. into, on the tab, on the cuff, on the arm, on the nut, in hock, into the Shylock, into the Shy, hooked, in the red, on a string, owe one one, meet in the alley.

INDEBTEDNESS n. IOU, dues. See DEBT.

INDECENT adj. blue, X-rated, raunchy, raw, spark, stag, a circus, foul-mouthed, off-color, flaming (Obsc., computer conversations), dirty, filthy, flasher, do a fruit salad (expose genitals), wagger, rough. See OBSCENE.

INDECISIVE adj. pussyfoot, pussyfoot around, weenie, straddle, on the fence, hot-and-cold, back and fill, hedge off, shilly-shally, waffle, hem and haw. See UNDECIDED.

INDEED interj. no shit, indeedy, yes indeedy, amen, sure thing, you better believe it, you can say that again, for real, right rather. See ABSOLUTELY.

INDEFATIGABLE adj. dead set on, bent on, hell-bent on, nose to the grindstone, work one's tail off, bound, bound and determined, stick at nothing, ironclad. See INDUSTRIOUS.

INDEFINITELY adv. indef.

INDEPENDENT adj. free-wheeling, inde-goddamn-pendent, on one's own, on one's own hook, one's own sweet way, paddle one's own canoe, have fuck-you money, couldn't care less, look out for number one, don't give a damn, mugwumpian, mugwumpish, on the fence, indie (film). See also NONPARTISAN.

INDIAN n. red man, buck, brave; Injun, redskin (Derog.); apple, Uncle Tomahawk (white establishment-oriented).

INDIANA Hoosier State.

INDIANAPOLIS, INDIANA Indy, Naplus, Circle City, Speed Town.

INDIANAPOLIS SPEEDWAY n. Indy, brickyard.

INDIAN RESERVATION n. res.

INDICATE v. name, slot, tab, tag, make, peg, card, finger, lay one's finger on, put one's finger on, put the finger on, button down, pin down, pinpoint, put down for, make a noise, make noises, sign, high sign, signal, send a message, send a signal, flash.

INDICATION n. high sign, nod, wink. See also HINT.

INDICT v. finger, frame, frame up, put up a job, stick to one, stick it to one, stick one with. See also ACCUSE.

INDIFFERENT adj. unflappable, laid-back, iceberg, cold, cold fish, cool cat, cool, cool as a cucumber, keep one's cool, arctic, loose, no sweat, don't sweat it, keep one's shirt on, not turn a hair, could care less, blah, flat, tough, hard-boiled, hardhearted, hard as nails, rhinoceros hide, thick-skinned, dead-ass, don't give a shit, don't give spit, don't give a damn, don't give a darn, don't give diddly, don't give diddly-shit, don't give a fuck, don't give a flying fuck, don't give a hoot, phone it in, just going through the motions, walk through it, what's the diff?, what the hell, so what?, it's all the same to me, big deal, big fucking deal, BFD, that's your lookout, that's your pigeon, I should worry? See also ALOOF.

INDIFFERENT, BECOME v. chill, chill off, chill up on, ice, cool off, turn a cold shoulder.

INDIGENOUS adj. local, local yokel, home towner, landsman, paesano.

INDIGENT adj. flat, flat broke, busted, hard-up, strapped, oofless, wasted, tapped out, on the rocks, down-and-out, to the curb, piss-poor, bag lady, cold in hand (Af. Am.), on the rims, run on the rims, needy, truly needy, through the safety net. See DESTITUTE.

INDIGNANT adj. blown out, browned-off, pissy, pissed-off, p.o.'d, bent out of shape, bugged, steamed, ticked-off, tee'd-off, t.o.'d, miffed, burned-up, run a temperature, make one's blood boil. See ANGRY.

INDIGNATION n. slow burn, burning, mad, miff, huff, sore, rise, get a rise out of, put out, stew, dander, Irish, pet, more heat than light, boiling point. See also ANGER.

INDIGNITY n. put-down, cap, brickbat, backhanded compliment, left-handed compliment, dump, dump on, take down. See INSULT.

INDIRECT, BE v. go round the barn, went by way of, long way, long way home.

INDISCREET, BE v. put one's foot in it, fox paw, bad form.

INDISCRETION n. goof, misspeak, miscue, hash-up, louse-up, screw-up, foul-up, fuck-up, muck-up, bitch, bitch-up, slipup, fox paw, fox pass, gaff, blow card, bugger, bugger up, mess, mess-up, make a mess of, make a boner, fool mistake, dumb trick, boob stunt, boo-boo, make a boo-boo, bloomer, make a blooper, boot, bobble, drop the ball, stumble, pull a blooper, pull a bloomer, pull a boner, pull a boo-boo, diarrhea of the mouth, put one's foot in it, put one's foot in one's mouth, foot-in-the mouth disease, shoot oneself in the foot, stub one's toe, go at it ass backwards, jump out of the frying pan into the fire, drop a brick. See also LAPSE.

INDISPOSED adj. down, down with, got a bug, rocky, feeling rotten, poorly, under the weather, below par, on the sick list, outta action, laid-up, on the shelf. See ILL.

INDISPOSITION n. bug, crud, creeping crud, the runs, trots, what's going around, the flu, the pip, dose, fascinoma (Medic.), burned (V.D.). See ILLNESS.

INDISPUTABLE adj. open-and-shut, sure as shooting, sure as death and taxes, bet your ass, that's a fact Jack, no buts about it, checked and double-checked, and no mistake. See CERTAIN.

INDIVIDUAL n. unit, guy, dude, cat, bird, stud, joker, clown, head, ace (good), motherfucker, mofo, hairpin, number (hot number), boot (Af. Am.), poor fish. See PERSON.

INDIVIDUALIST n. an original, maverick, oddball, freak, crazy, weirdo, nature boy, offbeat, beatnik, hippie, yippie, square peg in a round hole. See ECCENTRIC.

INDIVIDUALISTIC adj. offbeat, diff, far cry, cool, funky, poles apart, far out, way out, out of sight, hip, hep, weird, whale of a difference, like night and day, march to the beat of a different drummer.

INDIVIDUAL RETIREMENT ACCOUNT n. IRA, Keogh.

INDOCTRINATE v. brainwash, mind-fuck, head-fuck, fuck with one's head, break down, program, work over. See also INSTRUCT.

INDOCTRINATED adj. programmed, brainwashed, head-fucked, mind-fucked. See also KNOWLEDGEABLE.

INDOLENT adj. dopey, draggy, blah, drag-ass, lox, veg out, sack artist, Stepin Fetchit, on the shelf, on the bench, out of the rat race, out of action, out of the swim, underachiever, down, closed down. See also LAZY.

INDORSE v. back, bless, boost, get behind, get on the bandwagon, go with, go for, hold with, buy, ditto, rubber stamp. See ENDORSE.

INDUBITABLE adj. sure as shooting, sure as I live and breathe, bet your ass, bet your life, fer sher, dead sure, absitively, for a fact, cold, lock-and-win situation, no ifs ands or buts, open-and-shut case, know damn well, rain or shine. See CERTAIN.

INDUCE v. promote, sell one on, soft-soap, sweet-talk, eat one's mind, duke in, iggle, goose, suck in, hold one's feet to the fire, twist one's arm, squeeze, steamroller. See PERSUADE.

INDUCEMENT n. come-on, leader, loss leader, con, bait, the Murphy, hook, sell, hard sell, soft soap, snow job, sweet talk, twist one's arm, shovelin' shit, goose, brainwash. See also BRIBE.

INDUCT v. sign on, sign up, swear in.

INDUCTEE n. boot, rookie, tenderfoot, draft bait (subject to conscription).

INDULGE v. 1. live it up, live high on the hog, live on the fat of the land, put on the dog, put on the Ritz. See INTEMPERATE. 2. look out for number one, take care of number one, be on an ego trip, ego trip, go on an ego trip. 3. spoil, spoil rotten, go along with, go easy with, go easy on.

INDULGED adj. spoiled, spoiled rotten, played up to, made over, stroked.

INDULGENT adj. soft-shell, be big, live with, go along with, go easy with, go easy on. See COMPASSIONATE.

INDUSTRIAL GROUPINGS n. smokestack industries, Sun Belt, Rust Belt, Silicon Valley, Pacific Rim, Motown, oil patch, Establishment, Northern Establishment.

INDUSTRIALIST n. fat cat, baron, robber baron, tycoon. See also BUSINESSMAN.

INDUSTRIOUS adj. hyper, grind, plugger, nose to the grindstone, springbutt, eager beaver, work one's tail off, whiz, ball of fire, chipper, burn, fireball, in full swing, jumping, on the go, perky. See also SPIRITED.

INDUSTRY n. megacorp, multinational, plunderbund, bunch, crew, crowd, gang, mob, outfit, ring. See also BUSINESS, CORPORATION.

INEBRIATED adj. tipsy, tight, bombed, stewed, stiff, stinking, plastered, pie-eyed, wasted, tanked-up, blind drunk, fried, smashed, polluted, loaded, wearing beer goggles, Coke bottle-eyed (all women look beautiful), DWI (driving while intoxicated), feeling no pain, embalmed, D.O.A., shikker, pickled, pissed, three sheets to the wind, have a skinful, in orbit, seeing pink elephants. See DRUNK.

INEFFECTIVE adj. wuss, nobody, empty suit, herb, nebbish, sad sack, shnook, wimp, limp dick, limp dishrag, clambake, false alarm, flash in the pan, deadbeat, bum, scrub, loser, out of luck, lumpy, never-wuz, total shuck, no great shakes, nothing to write home about, kaput, clown, dud, fuddy-duddy, flub the dub, good-for-nothing, bringdown, down-and-out, foul ball, eightball, half-assed, half-baked, that dog won't hunt, amateur night, amateur night in Dixie, ham, haywire, dead one, lame-brained, lame duck, piss-poor, Mickey Mouse, bullstaller, out of one's depth, in too deep, in over one's head, in a vicious circle, shooting blanks, zilch, go under, go hit your head against the wall, go fight city hall, go on a wild goose chase, looking for a needle in a haystack, locking the barn after the horse is stolen, no way, no dice, no go, nowhere, get nowhere, fall on one's face, fall on one's ass, fall down, fall down on the job, foldo, flop, down the drain, down the chute, down the toilet, in the toilet, washout, not come off, flunk, flunk out, crap out, strike out, on the skids, on the rocks, A for effort, near miss, back to the drawing board, out of it, out-to-lunch, missed the boat, can't even get arrested, can't even write home for money, can't punch his way out of a paper bag, should have stood in bed. See also INADEQUATE.

INEFFICIENT adj. can't hack it, can't cut the mustard, not cut out for, that dog won't hunt, Mickey Mouse, haywire, flubdub, dud, fuddy-duddy, half-baked, shooting blanks. See INCOMPETENT.

INEPT adj. all thumbs, butterfingers, fumble-fist, ham-fisted, ham-handed, bo, fuck up, yo-yo, scrub, a newt, loser, real loser, dingleberry, can't fade that, can't hack it, can't cut it, gerk (old). See INCOMPETENT.

INERT adj. down, closed down, on the shelf, on the bench, on ice, out of action.

INEVITABILITY n. shit happens, Karma, Kismet, in the cards, the beads, that's the way the beads read, that's the way the ball bounces, that's the way the cookie crumbles. See also CERTAINTY.

INEVITABLE adj. shit happens, sure as fate, sure as death, sure as death and taxes, for certain, on ice, cold, pat, all locked up, no buts about it, bet one's bottom dollar on, in the bag, the fix is in, name of the game. See CERTAIN.

INEXACT adj. bum, off, way off. See WRONG.

INEXHAUSTIBLE adj. more than you can shake a stick at, no end of, no end to, jillion, a jillion at least, zillion, bazillion, umpteen. See PLENTY.

INEXORABLE adj. locked, locked-in, no going back, like death and taxes, bound, bound and determined, stick to one's guns, stick at nothing, dead set on, bent on, hell-bent on, mean business, ironclad, set, sot, set in concrete, buried in concrete, chiseled in stone, Rocka Gibraltar, Rock of Gibraltar. See also STUBBORN.

INEXPENSIVE adj. dirt-cheap, cheapie, el cheapo, cheap as dirt, dog-cheap, steal, a real steal, buy, a real buy, low-budget, low-cost, cost nothing, cost next to nothing, more bang for the buck, bought for a song, cut-rate, low-tariff, dime-a-dozen, price is right.

INEXPENSIVELY adv. on the rims, nickel and dime it, cheap it out.

INEXPERIENCED adj. virgin, rookie, kid, green, green-ass, amateur night, amateur night in Dixie, gay cat, scut, spring chicken, don't know shit from Shinola, out of one's league, out of one's depth. See UNSOPHISTICATED.

INEXPRESSIVE adj. poker-faced, deadpan, straight face, fish-eye, lead eyeballs, wooden.

INFANT n. bambino, kid, babykins, cheese factory, toddler, nipper, papoose, preemie, bundle, little deduction. See BABY.

INFANTILE adj. kid stuff.

INFANTRYMAN n. GI Joe, G.I., crunchy, legos, dog-face, doughboy, footslogger, grunt, paddlefoot, gravel pounder, sad sack, leg (Vietnam). See SOLDIER.

INFATUATED adj. gone, far gone on, hipped on, stuck on, mad about, smitten, has a thing about, hooked. See LOVE, IN.

INFATUATION n. amore, mash, pash, weakness, case, crash, crush, yen, mad for, crazy for, wild for, spoiling for, itch for, hankering, partial to, shine, beaver fever, hot pants, turn-on, calf love, puppy love. See LOVE.

INFECTION n. bug, burned (V.D.), crud, creeping crud, runs, trots, what's going around.

INFER v. have a hunch, be afraid, figure, figger, add up to, boil down to, what one is saying is, read between the lines, read into, the way one sees it. See also BELIEF, SPECULATE.

INFERENCE n. guesstimate, subtext, hunch, shot, shot in the dark, sneaking suspicion, stab, stab in the dark.

INFERIOR adj. 1. second-fiddle, second-string, third-string, man Friday, pratt boy, peon, serf, droid, slave, slavey, girl Friday, bush-league, entry-level (employment), low man on the totem pole, bottom man on the totem pole, bottom rung, bottom man, bottom sawyer, back seat, yes man, poor man's something or somebody, hanger-on, flunky, furp, stiff, apparatchik, squeak, last hired first fired, minus, in one's power, in one's pocket, in one's clutches, under one's thumb, at one's mercy, at one's beck and call, at one's feet, a slave to, led by the nose, spear carrier, second banana, infra dig. See also INADEQUATE. 2. schlocky, sleazy, two-bit, cheesy, seconds, crap, crappy, gummy, junk, shit, budget, borax, dreck, lemon, gook, Mickey Mouse, punk, low-rent, low-ride, sad, not up to scratch. See IMPERFECT.

INFERNO n. hell, the other place, down there.

INFERTILE adj. shoot blanks, fire blanks, blank cartridge, dud, no lead in the pencil, no toothpaste in the tube.

INFIDELITY n. affair, carrying on, hanky-panky, playing around, two-timing, getting some on the side, working late at the office, extracurricular activity, cheat on, doggin', thing, your place or mine? See ADULTERY.

INFILTRATE v. penetrate, access, crack. See PENETRATE.

INFILTRATOR n. mole.

INFINITE adj. umpteen, jillion, a jillion at least, zillion, bazillion, more than you can shake a stick at, no end of, no end to, thick as flies, thick as hail. See COUNTLESS.

INFINITELY adv. for ever so long, for a coon's age, for a dog's age, for a month of Sundays, till hell freezes over, till you're blue in the face, till the cows come home, till shrimps learn to whistle.

INFIRM adj. rocky, laid low. See ILL.

INFIRMITY n. bug, crud, creeping crud, growth, the runs, trots, what's going around, the flu, the pip, dose, double scrudfantods, fascinoma (Medic.), burned (V.D.), willies (mythical). See ILLNESS.

INFLAME v. turn one on, heat up, steam up, jazz up, work up, switch on, turn on the heat, work up into a lather, fire up. See EXCITE.

INFLAMED adj. juiced-up, zipped-up, zapped-up, all fired up, worked-up, turned-on. See EXCITED.

INFLATE v. boost, balloon, hike, hike up, jack up, jump up, put up, build up, pyramid, up, beef up, flesh out, pad. See EXPAND.

INFLATION n. buildup, boost, hike, overheated economy, up, upping.

INFLEXIBLE adj. set, dead set on, stand one's ground, brick wall, solid as a rock, set in concrete, stuck in concrete, buried in concrete, chiseled in stone, bound and determined, do-or-die, hard-core, hard-line, stiff-necked, locked-in. See STUBBORN.

INFLICT v. move in on, chisel in, horn in, muscle in, lay down the law, put one's foot down, read the riot act, dish it out, dish out, dump on, give it to one, stick it to one. See also FORCE.

INFLUENCE n. juice, weight, string, ropes, drag, pull, yank, clout, access, fix, grease, alzo, contacts, channels, network, connection, hooks, license, nuts, wire, snow, suction, suck, a lot to do with, a lot to say about, in, inside track, wire-pulling, con, hook, sell, soft soap, sweet talk, twisting one's arm, body English, driver's seat. See also POWER.

INFLUENCE v. put a spin on, impact on, con, sell, snow, jawbone, lead by the nose, pull ropes, pull strings, pull wires, throw one's weight around, bring in the heavy artillery, whitewash, wire-pull, get one's hooks into, twist one's arm. See also PERSUADE.

INFLUENCE PEDDLER n. five percenter, fixer, logroller, wire-puller, connection.

INFLUENTIAL adj. major-league, name, big player, big chew, big gun, big noise, big wheel, main squeeze, movers and shakers, one who knows where the body's buried, hot dog, connection, wire. See IMPORTANT.

INFLUENZA n. flu, flue, bug, flu bug, virus, what's going around.

INFORM v. 1. tip, tip off, tip one's duke, spring one's duke, tout, steer, put hip, update, beat it down (Af. Am.), level, clue one in, share one up, do one up, crank one in, let in on, let in on the know, let next to, put next to, put it on the street, put in one's two cents, put one in the picture, put on to, put one wise, wise one up, put a bug in one's ear, put a flea in one's ear, fold an ear, show one the ropes, give one a tip, give one the word, give a pointer to, post, keep posted, touch base with, pull one's coat, break it to one, lace one's boots, lay it on one, lay it on the line, put it on the line, lay it out for, drum. See also INSTRUCT. 2. leak, blab, blabber, rat, squeal, squawk, stool, talk, verbalize, cop a plea, crack, peach, spit it out, spill, spill one's guts, spill the beans, give away, give with, give the show away, have a big bazoo, have a big mouth, let down one's hair, bring it out into the daylight, let it all hang out, let the cat out of the bag, sing, sing like a canary, chirp. 3. double-cross, deal, drop a dime on one, dime one out, fuck, fuck one's buddy, hose, screw, belch, narc (on one who uses drugs), split, knife, stab one in the back, finger, put the finger on, turn on, turn in, rat, rat on, eat cheese, fink, fink on, croon, sing, squeal, squeal on, stool, stool on, weasel on, holler, open up, buzz (in secret), blow, blow the whistle, blow the gaff, belch, sell out, let down, let down one's side, sell down the river, do one dirt, dump on, switch, snitch, dry snitch.

INFORMAL adj. folksy, down-home, haimish, homey, cas, cazh, laid-back, sporty, easygoing, let one's hair down, mellow, pokesy, throwaway, off-the-cuff, improv, cool, loose, loose as a goose. See CASUAL.

INFORMANT n. fink, nark, snitch, stoolie, canary, source, snout, blabbermouth, tattletale, whistle-blower, fat mouth, motor mouth, deep throat, tout. See INFORMER.

INFORMATION n. info, leak, update, network, tie-in, hookup, cue, clue, scoop, poop, hot poop, poop sheet, ammo, pipeline, boot snitch, score, skinny, hot skinny, low-down, dirt, dope, dope sheet, inside dope, medicine, inside wire, insider, tip, hot tip, hot poo, the know, picture, story, inside story, whole story, chapter and verse, goods, brass tacks, garbage, goulash (false), ear loft, break, beat, the latest, what's what, what's happenin', what's going down, chip, brush-up, earful, ear duster, hash, haymaker, hotshot, hot wire; kick in the ass, shot in the ass (bad); are you ready for this?, page oner. See also FACTS.

INFORMED adj. savvy, posted, hip, fly, with it, tuned in, chilly, into, been there, wise to, know the score, know what's what, on top of, kept posted. See KNOWLEDGEABLE.

INFORMER n. rat, rat fink, fink, yellow dog (gang), narc, finger, snitch, snitcher, squealer, stoolie, stool pigeon, snout, canary, chirper, songbird, nightingale, singer, yo-deler, source, weasel, blab, blabber, blabberer, blabbermouth, tattler, tattletale, telltale, whistle-blower, whistler, double-crosser, fat mouth, preacher, snake, snake in the grass, buddy fucker, beefer, copper, copperhearted, cheese bun, cheese-eater, bat carrier (1925), faded boogie (Af. Am.), geepo, cat, chalk hat, fork tongue, mouse, punk, ringtail, shamus, flip, deep throat, tout, noser, zuch, bird seed, loose link, cheese pride, cheesy rider.

INFRARED IMAGE CONVERTER n. snooper-scope.

INFRINGE v. 1. borrow, lift, steal, crib, bite, pick one's brains, pirate, rape. 2. chisel in, muscle in, butt in, crash, crash the gates, pirate. See ENCROACH. See also COPY.

INFURIATE v. brown off, burn up, rile, piss one off, bitch one off, T off, juice, that grinds my gears, blow one away, get under one's skin, whip up, fire up, steam up, put one's Irish up. See ANGER.

INFURIATED adj. blown out, pissy, pissed-off, p'd-off, cheesed-off, hacked-off, brassed-off, aerated, bent, pushed outta shape, aggro, bouncing, mad as a wet hen, hacked, steamed up, see red, bullshit, go apeshit, have a shit hemorrhage, hit the ceiling, burned up, smoking, hot, on the war path, yell bloody murder. See ANGRY.

INFURIATING adj. pesky, pestiferous, a bit much, too much.

INGENUOUS adj. 1. up front, open, call a spade a spade, make no bones about it, straight dope, straight shit, like it is, call it like it is, talk turkey. See FRANK. 2. babe in the woods, a narb, narbo, square, green, L7, mark, low-tech, uncool, wet behind the ears, shit kicker. See UNSOPHISTI-CATED.

INGEST n. wolf down, scarf, scoff, slurp, mow (mow a burger), gorp, graze, inhale, stuff one's face, tuck in, pack it away, put oneself outside of. See EAT.

INGRATIATE v. kiss butt, kiss ass, suck ass, suck up to, brown-nose, fall all over, apple-polish, bootlick, kowtow, hand one a line. See FLATTER.

INGRATIATING adj. smarmy, kissy-ass.

INGREDIENT n. fixin's, makin's, part and parcel.

INHABIT v. bunk, bunk out, hang out, crash, nest, perch, roost, squat, locate, park, hole up, hang up one's hat, hang up one's shingle.

INHALANT USE n. huffing, sniffing, huffer (user).

INHALE v. snort, sniff, pull, puff, drag.

INHARMONIOUS adj. sour, sour note, hit a sour note, clinker, hit a clinker, sound a clinker, sound a sour note.

INHIBIT v. hang up, hog-tie, stymie, faze, sandbag, cramp one's style, put one in a box, put on the brakes, drag one's foot. See HINDER.

INHIBITED adj. uptight, tight-assed, hung-up, a narb, narbo, square, iced, chilled, bottled-up, corked-up, hog-tied.

INITIALLY adv. right off the bat, for openers, for start-ers, devirginize (first time), break one's cherry, first crack out of the box.

INITIATE v. ring in, start the ball rolling, break the ice, kick off, intro, devirginize (first time), break one's cherry, trigger, rev up, fire up, cook up, dream up, make up, come out with, come up with. See BEGIN.

INITIATIVE n. gumption, spunk, drive, moxie, punch, push, steam, get-up-and-go.

INJECT v. 1. give a shot, shoot, shoot up, give one the square needle, joy pop, skin pop, trapdoor, trapdoor scab (injecting under a scab to hide needle marks), mainline, send it home. 2. fudge in, lug in, lug in by the heels, drag in, drag in by the heels, squeeze in, worm in, shoehorn it in.

INJECTED adj. binged, got the hook, got the square needle, stabbed in the ass.

INJECTION n. the needle, jab, shot, shot in the arm, shot in the ass, booster, booster shot, trapdoor, trapdoor scab (injecting under a scab to hide needle marks), hit, fix, nip, slug, bang, dram.

INJUDICIOUS, BE v. go off the deep end, put one's foot in it, put one's foot in one's mouth, go out on a limb, buy a pig in a poke, play with fire, leave oneself wide open. See RECKLESS.

INJURE v. 1. gotcha, rough up, shake up, hack up, total, wax, wing, ding, nick, zing, tweak, cut up, bend the goods. See DAMAGE. 2. do in, dump on, muck up, queer, hit on, hit one where one lives, lay a bad trip on one, give one a left-handed compliment, gross out. See WOUND.

INJURED adj. 1. hurtin', bleedin', damaged, winged, nicked, zinged, cut, bunged-up, busted-up, burned, burned one's ass, put away, screwed-up, walking wounded, have to scrape one off the sidewalk. 2. all torn up, cut-up, hit where one lives, shook, shook-up, miffed, miffy, shot-down, have one's nose out of joint, sore, uptight.

INJURY n. ouch, chop, scratch, nick, graze, gotcha, boo-boo (minor flesh wound), brand, jig cut, mark, rat mark, stool mark (knife), black-and-blue, down.

INJUSTICE n. raw deal, screwing, fucking, royal screwing, royal fucking, gurdy, hurdy, kick around, railroad, sellout, cheap shot, not cricket, hitting below the belt, dirty pool.

INK n. pen juice.

INKLING n. lead, hot lead, tipoff, tell-tale, flea in one's ear, sneaking suspicion, hunch, tip, straw in the wind.

INN n. B. and B., bed and breakfast, motel, airtel, aquatel, boatel, floatel, chinch pad, flophouse, scratch crib.

INNARDS n. guts, tripes, stuffings.

INNER adj. inner-space.

INNER CIRCLE n. insiders, click, circle, the loop, ring, gang, crew, crowd, bunch, the power curve, Old Boy network, in group, inside the Beltway (Washington, D.C.).

INNING n. one's move, one's say, go, go at, whack, one's turn, break, big break, shot, fling. See OPPORTUNITY.

INNOCENT adj. low-tech, uncool, green, wide-eyed, clean, lily white, softic, square, off-the-cob, search me. See UNSOPHISTICATED.

INNOCENT n. pussycat, greenhorn, kid, babe in the woods, hick, wimp, simp, schnook, Golden Bantam, eight-ball. See UNSOPHISTICATED.

INNOVATION n. leading edge, cutting edge, breaking new snow, breakout, avant-garde, last word, latest thing, latest wrinkle, new wrinkle, newie, newey, newfangled contraption, what's happening.

INNOVATIVE adj. state-of-the-art, leading edge, cutting edge, breaking new ground, contempo, fire-new, just out, avant-garde, newfangled. See NEW.

INNUMERABLE adj. jillion, zillion, bazillion, umpteen, umpteenth, more than you can shake a stick at, no end of, no end to, thick as flies, thick as hail, alive with, crawling with. See COUNTLESS.

INOCULATE v. give a shot, shoot, give one the square needle, stab in the ass.

INOCULATION n. shot, booster, booster shot, shot in the arm, shot in the ass.

INOFFENSIVE adj. clean, white-bread, vanilla.

INOPERABLE adj. no-go, crashed, down, go down, out of whack, out of kilter, out of order, out of commission, dusted, kaput, on the blink, on the fritz, haywire, conked-out, fouled-up, fucked-up. See DAMAGED.

INORDINATELY adv. too much, too-too. See also EXCESSIVE.

INQUIRE v. hit, hit up, knock, put out a feeler, feel out, test the waters, see which way the wind blows, send up a trial balloon, grill, roast, put the screws on, go over. See QUESTION. See also INVESTIGATE.

INQUIRY n. fishing expedition, third, third degree, what's happening?, what's cooking?, what cooks?, what's with one or something, witch hunt, Q. and A., wringer, legwork, feeler, trial balloon, poll. See also INVESTIGATION.

INQUISITION n. witch hunt, third, third degree, wringer.

INQUISITIVE adj. snoopy, nosy, nosy Parker, in one's crack, rubbernecking, lookie lou, gawker, gawker's block (freeway slowdown at the scene of an accident), playing the bird with the long neck, on the earie, on the gun, on the i.c. (eye see), on the lake, on the mooch, on the pike, on the prowl, on the squint.

INSANE adj. wacko, unglued, unzipped, unscrewed, bent, head-case, screwy, schitzy, schizzed-out, psycho, psyched-out, freaked-out, flipped one's lid, half-deck, totally baked, out of one's gourd, out of one's tree, out of one's bird, off one's chump, in the ozone, crackers, bonkers, bananas, gone ape, have a lugnut loose, nutter, nutted up, nuts, nutty as a fruitcake, wacked out, off one's rocker, lost one's marbles, cutting out paper dolls, section 8, gonzo, gonzoitis. See CRAZY.

INSANE ASYLUM n. booby hatch, funny farm, loony bin, bughouse, nuthouse, crazy house, bat house, funny house, warehouse, rubber room, soft walls, cracker factory, acorn academy, college, nut college, nut factory, nut farm, nut hatch, zoo, ding tank (holding cell).

INSANE ASYLUM, COMMIT TO v. drop the net on, bug, lag; make the bughouse, get the straw hat and the red tie (be committed).

INSANE, GO v. crack up, blow, blow a fuse, blow one's top, blow one's cap, blow one's cork, blow one's noggin, blow a gasket, blow one's roof, blow one's stack, blow one's mind, flip, flip out, flip one's lid, flip one's stack, pop one's cork, go ape, go apeshit, go ballistic, go bananas, go bonkers, go nuts, nut up (Stu.), go crackers, go bugs, go coo-coo, go daffy, lose one's taffy, go off one's head, go off one's nut, go off one's rocker, go off one's base, go off the track, go off the trolley, slip one's trolley, go out of one's skull, go round the bend, go for soft-wall treatment, head for the funny farm, come unglued, come unzipped, come off the wall, flake out, schitz out, schizz out, psych out, freak out, snap, lose all one's buttons, lose all one's marbles, cut out paper dolls.

INSCRUTABLE adj. clear as mud, it beats me, you've got me, it's Greek to me, deep. See OBSCURE.

INSECTICIDE n. bug bomb.

INSECTS n. crabs, crum, crumb, grayback, seam squirrel, shimmy lizard; crumby, crummy, cooties, lousy (afflicted with).

INSECURE adj. shaky, choked, jumpy, touchy, uptight, touch-and-go, on slippery ground, on thin ice, hanging by a thread.

INSENSITIVE adj. hard as nails, hardhearted, cold fish, rhinoceros hide, thick-skinned, dead ass, has lead balls for eyes, tough. See CALLOUS.

INSERT v. stick in, shove it in, shoehorn it in, cut it in, drag in, drag in by the heels, lug in, lug in by the heels, squeeze in, fudge in, worm in.

INSIDE adj. inner-space.

INSIDIOUS adj. snake, snake-in-the-grass, worm. See DECEITFUL.

INSIGHT n. aha reaction, savvy, hep to, wise to, see the light, flash on it, get one's drift, on the same wavelength, I got it, it hit me, it just come to me.

INSIGNIA n. hardware, hash mark, hash stripe, Hershey bar, fruit salad, ruptured duck, brag rag, chest hardware, jack (Cavalry), monkey flag, track, railroad track, Spam cluster, one-striper, two-striper, three-striper, two-and-a-half-striper, travel bar, diag (gold braid, Annapolis), didie pin (2d Lieutenant, gold bar), homing pigeon, hook (chevron), the bird (eagle, Army Colonel, N. Captain), gold bar (2d Lieutenant), R.R. track (Army Captain), buzzard (Army, N.), chicken guts (trimmings), scrambled eggs, fried egg, costume jewelry (WAC), chevron, strip, crow.

INSIGNIFICANT adj. 1. no big deal, no biggie; ain't no thang (Af. Am.), ain't no thang but a chicken wing (Af. Am.); flying fuck, Podunk, entry level (job), bottom-rung, lower-rung, not worth a hill of beans, not worth the powder to blow it to hell. 2. small-time, gadget, geekoid, spear carrier, Mr. Ducrot (West Point), small fry, small beer, small change, small pot, a lightweight, fly speck, flea, a hump, underwhelming, nickel and dime, penny ante, peanuts, pokerino, shot, scratch, skag, jerkwater (small town). See UNIMPORTANT.

INSINCERE adj. fishy, jivey, jive-assed, shuckin' and jivin', two-faced, gil, Hollywood, reach-me-down, put on, slick, sincere, snide, phony, fake, plastic, cry crocodile tears. See also DISHONEST.

INSINCERITY n. jazz, jive, chicken, chickenshit, shit, bull, bullshit, throw the bull, shoot the bull, shoot the shit, bullshit artist, bull shooter, bull shot, bull skate, horseshit, piece of shit, pile of shit, crock of shit, chewing gum, goop, hooey, spinach, put-on, blow smoke up one's ass, crocodile tears, soft soap, sweet talk, fast talk, con, hoke, hokum, hoky, hoky-poky, double-dealing, lay it on thick, do a number on one.

INSIPID adj. blah, beige, draggy, draddy, dull as dishwater, cheesy, ho-hum, bor-ring, bore one stiff, nebbish, rundown, a yawn, big yawn, dead, diddly-bop, gasser, gummy, grunch, grungy, icky, the least, nowhere, Noplaceville, Nadaville, Dullsville, nothing, nothing doing, tired, wiped out, a snooze, flat, flat tire, flat as a pancake, pablum, zero, big zero, squid, big deal, no big deal, no biggie; ain't no thang, ain't no thing but a chicken wing (Af. Am.); animal (political campaign), big shit, no big shit, winner, real winner, scrub, loser, real loser, downer, dog, go over like a lead balloon, lay an egg, bombed.

INSOLENCE n. backtalk, brass, cheek, chutzpah, gall, guff, lip, sass.

INSOLENT adj. get previous, flip, fly, jazzy, fresh, breezy, nervy, cheeky, sassy, smart, smarty, smarty pants, smart-alecky, smart-ass, wise-ass, wise guy, wiseacre, wisenheimer, brassy, bold as brass, whippersnapper, puppy, barefaced, lippy, minx, hussy, saucebox, gally, biggety, put down, run down, chutzpadik, cocky, crusty, out of line, off-base, give one the business.

INSOLVENCY n. belly up, go belly up, go toes up, go toes, go under, chapter 7, chapter 11, chapter 13, close the doors, in the toilet, in the tub, take a bath. See BANKRUPTCY.

INSOLVENT adj. flat broke, stone broke, strapped, clean, tapped out, on one's ass, on the rocks, down to one's last penny, seen better days, piss-poor. See DESTITUTE.

INSPECT v. flash, flash on, scope, clock, lamp, pipe, eye, eyeball, look-see, bus it (Af. Am.), scout, give the once-over, double O, case, check, check out, kick the tires, candle (investigate a company or department), See SEE.

INSPECTION n. Cook's tour, double O, once-over, check, frisk, read, flash, eyeball inspection, eyeball examination, look-see, squawk (WWII).

INSPECTION STATION n. checkpoint, Checkpoint Charlie.

INSPIRATION n. brainchild, brainstorm, brain wave, spark plug, spark, flash, bell-ringer, deep think, rumble, rah-rah, I got it, it hit me, it just come to me, approach, big idea. See IDEA.

INSPIRE v. jazz up, juice, juice up, fire up, work up, spark, turn on, trigger, zap, give a lift, put one on top of the world, put one on cloud nine. See SUPPORT.

INSPIRED adj. pumped-up, fired-up, sparked, fire in the belly, turned-on, juiced, juiced-up, zapped, get a lift.

INSPIRED EFFORT n. heads-up play, play over one's head, knock oneself out.

INSTALLMENT PLAN, USE v. buy jawbone, buy on time.

INSTANT n. sec, split second, mo, half a mo, tick, half a tick, bat of an eye, jiffy, jiff, half a jiffy, shake, half a shake, two shakes, two shakes of a lamb's tail, nothing flat.

INSTANTLY adv. like now, pronto, balls out, double time, in jig time, move your ass, in half a mo, like a shot, pretty dammed quick, PDQ, before one can say Jack Robinson. See IMMEDIATELY.

INSTIGATE v. fire up, put up to, work up, egg on, turn on, make waves, adjy, needle, steam up, throw wood on the fire, add fuel to the flames, rabble-rouse, stir up, turn one on. See STIMULATE.

INSTIGATOR n. spark plug, adjy, pusher, fireman, hatchet man, needle man, steam-up ghee, stormy petrel, wave maker.

INSTILL v. brainwash, fuck with one's head, mindfuck, program.

INSTINCT n. hang, hang of it, know-how, savvy, nose for, nose, good nose, by the seat of one's pants, flying by the seat of one's pants, feel in one's bones, have a funny feeling, have a hunch. See also INCLINATION.

INSTINCTIVE adj. knee-jerk reaction, by the seat of one's pants.

INSTITUTE v. intro, ring in, start the ball rolling, get things rolling, break the ice, break in, kick it, kick off, bow, open, open up, rev, rev up, fire up, cook up, dream up, make up, come out with, come up with. See BEGIN.

INSTRUCT v. brainwash, break, break in, let in on the know, let next to, put next to, put hip, put hep, put through the grind, put through the mill, put in one's two cents, put one in the picture, put on to, put one wise, wise one up, show one the ropes, update, level, clue one in, fold an ear, put a bug in one's ear, put a bug up one's ass, put a flea in one's ear, tip, tip off, tout, steer, give one a tip, give one the word, give a pointer to, post, keep posted, pull one's coat, break it to one, lace one's boots, lay it on one, lay it out for, lay it on the line, beat it down (Af. Am.), drum, drum into.

INSTRUCTED adj. plugged-in, tuned-in, grounded, savvy, sharp, wise to, into, really into, go-go, all woke up, in the know, know one's business. See KNOWLEDGEABLE.

INSTRUCTION n. 1. chalk talk, skull session. See also ADVISE. 2. dope sheet, poop sheet, DWIM (do what I mean), DTRT (do the right thing).

INSTRUCTOR n. prof, teach, baby-sitter, Dr. Nytol (boring), grind, gun, slave driver. See also PROFESSOR.

INSTRUMENT n. tool, ax, gismo, doodad, thigamajig, thigamabob. See also APPARATUS.

INSUBSTANTIAL adj. 1. cheap-jack. 2. without a leg to stand on, pipe dream, pie in the sky, castles in the air, blue sky, fly-by-night.

INSUFFICIENT adj. half-assed, half-baked, bupkis, chickenshit, too little too late, minus, short. See also INADEQUATE.

INSUFFICIENT FUNDS n. shortfall, light, short.

INSULT n. single-digit salute, the finger, cap, put-down, take-down, zinger, brickbat, cheap shot, rap, slam, black eye, hit, dirty dig, dump, dump on, dozens, dirty dozens, woofing, back-handed compliment, left-handed compliment, slap in the face, low rent, bazoo, raspberry.

INSULT v. put down, diss, dump on, hit on, rag, rag on, pop junk, single-digit salute, bag (Af. Am.), give one the finger, give one five fingers, flip one the finger, flip one the bone, give one the bone, chop, blister, roast, scorch, burn, wing, nick, cut up, zing, give one a zinger, give one the cold shoulder, give one a backhanded compliment, give one a left-handed compliment, thumb one's nose at, slap in the face, hurl brickbats at, play dirty dozens, sound dozens, sound, signify, signifying shucking and jiving, S'ing'n' J'ing, woofing, eighty-six, hurt one where he lives, hit one where he lives, blow off, chop, cut, cut to the quick.

INSULTED adj. dissed, put down, cut up, blown off, shucked and jived, miffed, miffy, bleeding, on one's ear, get up on one's ear. See also OFFENDED.

INSULTING adj. sassy, flip, fresh, smart, smart-alecky, smart-ass, wise-ass, biggety, cocky, cheeky, crusty, base, gally, nervy, out-of-line, hell of a note, helluva note. See INSOLENT.

INSURANCE POLICY n. floater, coverage, rain insurance (travel).

INSURANCE RACKETEER n. flopper, repeater, twister.

INSURE n. cover one's ass, hedge, hedge one's bet, lay off. See also ASSURE.

INSURMOUNTABLE adj. no-go, no way, no-win situation, can't win for losing, it won't fly, nonstarter, not a prayer, not a ghost of a chance, not a Chinaman's chance, not a chance in hell, not a snowball's chance in hell, not till hell freezes over, f'get it, forget it.

INTEGRAL n. fixings, makings, part and parcel, nuts and bolts, meat and potatoes, kit and kaboodle, the whole ball of wax. See also WHOLE.

INTEGRATE v. get together, throw in together, come together, meld with, interface. See ASSOCIATE. See also BLEND.

INTELLECT n. savvy, smarts, brains, candlepower, the goods, good head, the stuff, the right stuff, what it takes. See also BRAIN.

INTELLECTUAL n. genius, nerd, the brain, propeller head, egghead, hard-boiled egghead (tough-minded), scrambled egghead (fuzzy-minded), gasser, gray matter, whiz, wizard, avant-garde, beard, big think, double-dome, ivory dome, highbrow, long-hair, full hank, pointy head, conehead, good head, pundit, skull, thumbsucker, wig, Einstein. See also INTELLIGENT.

INTELLIGENCE n. 1. I.Q. smarts, candlepower, savvy, fly, stuff, the right stuff, what it takes, with it, have something on the ball, plenty on the ball, have a bump for, green thumb, meal ticket, the goods. 2. info, leak, inside dope, insider, hot tip, hot skinny, picture, lowdown, dirt, clue, brush up, let one in on, poop sheet, inside story, what's going down. See INFORMATION. See also FACTS.

INTELLIGENCE AGENT n. spook, mole, agent, operative, Mexican infantry (Mil.), sheep dip (Mil., disguised as civilian); company brown-nose, keek (industrial). Enemy: ac-op (active opposition), barbarians, Indians, visiting team, wad agent (hired assassin). See SPY.

INTELLIGENCE QUOTIENT n. I.Q.

INTELLIGENCE TEST n. I.Q., bug test.

INTELLIGENT adj. brain, brainy, propeller head, egghead, technotrash (social idiot), got the smarts, have savvy, have the smarts, have gray matter, sharp as a tack, tack, smart as a whip, whiz, whiz kid, bright, brill, have a good head on one's shoulders, have a head on one's shoulders, have one's head screwed on right, have all one's marbles, nobody's fool, no dumbbell, not born yesterday, not so dumb, on the ball, have plenty on the ball, have the goods, have the stuff, have the right stuff, have what it takes, rocket scientist, beard, big think, deep, double-dome, ivory dome, heavy, highbrow, long-hair, long-haired, pointy-headed, pundit, skull, thumbsucker, wig, IQ, quick on the trigger, nifty, a lot of nifty, together, all together, got it, got it all together, got it up here, quick on the draw, quick on the uptake, commonsensical, got one's boots on, have horse sense, Philadelphia lawyer, genius, gasser, wizard, Einstein.

INTEMPERANCE n. life in the fast lane, drive in the fast lane with no brakes, live in the fast lane, high living, burn one's candle at both ends, go to hell, hellbent, go to hell in a handbasket.

INTEMPERATE adj. 1. on a tear, raising a rumpus, raising a ruckus, kicking up a row, kicking up a shindy, kicking up one's heels. 2. off-base, out-of-line, out-of-order, burn one's candle at both ends, live in the fast lane, drive in the fast lane, drive in the fast lane with no brakes, go to hell in a handbasket.

INTENDED n. steady, going steady, pinned, bird, asked-for; donah, donar; future, set, setup, accidentally on purpose.

INTENSIFY v. soup up, beef up, step up, jazz up, hop up, heat up, hot up, punch up, build up, add bells and whistles, add fuel to the fire, jump out of the frying pan into the fire, pour it on, full on, spike (Usu. drink).

INTENT n. point, stuff, nub, key, bottom line, name of the game, nitty-gritty, nuts and bolts, the way of it, nature of the beast, drift, heart, meat; score, punch line.

INTENTION n. game plan, gimmick, angle, action, setup, scenario, how one figures it, where one's heading. See PLAN.

INTER v. adios it, cover up, plant, deep-six, put six feet under.

INTERACT v. relate, contact, interface, network, connect, mesh, give tit for tat, touch, touch base, keep in touch, reach out, reach out and touch someone, have truck with, get across, get the message, grok, back-channel (secretly).

INTERACTION n. teamwork, team play, networking, mesh, tit for tat.

INTERCEDE v. butt in, barge in, stick one's nose in, throw a monkey wrench in, monkey with, mix in. See INTERFERE. See also INTRUDE, MEDIATE.

INTERCEPT v. bug, shortstop, cut off, cut off at the pass, cut in.

INTERCHANGE v. interact, interface, contact, network, relate, connect, mesh, give tit for tat, keep in touch, grok, back-channel (secretly). See COMMUNICATE.

INTERCHANGEABLE adj. six of one and half a dozen of the other, compatible, work-alike.

INTERCOMMUNICATOR n. intercom, chatterbox, squawk box, growler.

INTERCOURSE n. 1. teamwork, team play, networking, mesh. 2. fuck, jazz, screw, lay, lay pipe, hump, bump, boff, boogaloo, do the wild thing, nookie, action, balling, meat injection, rubbing the bacon, the dirty deed, oil change, parallel parking, bed and breakfast, fooling around. See SEXUAL INTERCOURSE.

INTEREST n. 1. vig, vigorish, juice, flipping (interest on interest), front-end loading, points, commish, drag. See also PERCENTAGE, SHARE. 2. racket, thing, bag, game, into, lookout, fish to fry.

INTEREST v. turn on, turn one on, grab, hook. See INTRIGUE.

INTERESTED adj. buy it, caught, hooked, on the case, sold, into, really into, gone, turned on, up to here in, eat sleep and breathe something. See ENGROSSED.

INTERESTING adj. grabber, turn-on. jazzy, jazzed-up, See also EXCITING.

INTERFERE v. mix in, barge in, butt in, chisel in, horn in, muscle in, stick one's nose in, poke one's nose in, jam, hang up, hold up, kibitz, put in one's oar, put one's two cents in, fool with, fool around with, mess with, mess around with, mess over, monkey with, monkey around with, monkey with the buzz saw, throw a monkey wrench into the works, cramp one's style, drag one's foot.

INTERFERE, DON'T interj. butt out, keep your nose out of, mind your own business, mind your own beeswax, don't mix in, buzz off, fuck off, hands off (Usu. management).

INTERFERENCE n. background, flitter (radar), buckshot, breaking up, covered up (radio).

INTERIM n. breather, breathing spell, break, break-off, coffee break, downtime, letup, five, ten, time, time-out, freeze, cutoff, layoff.

INTERIOR adj. in-house, inner-space.

INTERJECT v. stick one's nose in, poke one's nose in, put in one's oar, put one's two cents in, shove in one's oar, fudge in, lug in, lug in by the heels, squeeze in, worm in. See INTERFERE.

INTERLOPER n. buttinski, buttinsky, crasher, gate crasher.

INTERMEDIARY n. connection, go-between, cutout (secret), fixer. See also INFLUENCE.

INTERMENT n. cold-meat party, planting, deep six.

INTERMINABLE adj. on a treadmill, looped, no end of, no end to, and then and then, spun out, strung out, dragged out, day and night.

INTERMINABLY adv. round the clock, for ever so long, forever and a day, for a coon's age, for a dog's age, for a month of Sundays, till hell freezes over, till you're blue in the face, till the cows come home, till shrimps learn to whistle.

INTERMINGLE v. network, mesh, pool, swing in with, throw in with, throw together, come together. See ASSOCIATE.

INTERMISSION n. break, break-off, five, ten, time-out, breather, breathing spell, letup, layoff, downtime.

INTERMITTENT adj. herky-jerky, by bits and pieces, by fits and starts, hit or miss, in dribs and drabs, willy-nilly. See ERRATICALLY.

INTERNAL adj. in-house.

INTERNAL ORGANS n. guts, innards, insides, inners, works, inner works, inner workings, inner man, spaghetti, kishkes, stuffings, plumbing, department of the interior.

INTERNATIONAL BUSINESS MACHINES n. IBM, Big Blue.

INTERNATIONAL CRIMINAL POLICE ORGANIZATION n. Interpol.

INTERNE n. tern (Medic.).

INTERNIST n. flea (Medic.).

INTERPOSE v. mix in, butt in, horn in, muscle in, poke one's nose in, drag in, fudge in, squeeze in, worm in. See INTERFERE.

INTERROGATE v. work over, go over, grill, roast, sweat out, give one the third, put one through the wringer, put the screws on, hit up, knock. See QUESTION.

INTERROGATION n. third, third degree.

INTERRUPT v. cut off, step on one's lines, shortstop, break, break break, breaker breaker, break in, butt in, bust in, barge in, chime in, chip in, cut in, horn in, lean in, close down. See also INTRUDE.

INTERRUPTION n. break, break-off, cutoff, layoff, letup, shortstop, blackout.

INTERSECTION n. mixmaster (highway cloverleaf), cross street.

INTERSTATE COMMERCE COMMISSION n. ICC, I Can Catch (truck driver use).

INTERTWINE v. connect, network, mesh, relate. See ASSOCIATE.

INTERVAL n. breathing spell, break, downtime, layoff, letup, five, ten, time-out.

INTERVENE v. mix in, barge in, butt in, chisel in, horn in, muscle in, stick one's nose in, kibitz, put one's two cents in. See INTRUDE.

INTERVIEW n.   1. call, callback, cattle call (The.). 2. phoner (radio).

INTESTINAL ORGANS n.   guts, innards, inners, insides, inner man, inner works, inner workings, spaghetti, department of the interior.

INTESTINES n.   insides, guts, tripes, stuffings, spaghetti, kishkes.

INTIMATE adj.   buddy-buddy, get buddy-buddy, clubby, mellow, tight, pally, palsy, palsy-walsy, cozy, down with, chuchala-muchala, right nice, right neighborly, downright neighborly, white, regular, square shooter, sucking around, kissing up to, mix, get together, get with it, break the ice, let down one's hair, trade spit, swap spit, roommates, sleepin' together, making it with.

INTIMATE n.   amigo, brother, little brother, brah, sister, bud, buddy, bosom buddy, buddy boy, buddyroo, good buddy, asshole buddy, home biscuit, biscuit, road dog, boogerhead, money, tribe; posse, crew (group); roomy, main man; wrap, chum, main squeeze (girl); sweetback (Af. Am.), family, kissing cousin, pal. See FRIEND.

INTIMATE v.   spring, spring one's duke, spring with a crack, tip one's duke, tip one's hand, leak, let the cat out of the bag, spill the beans, peach, make noise, put a flea in one's ear. See EXPOSE.

INTIMATION n.   1. sinking feeling, sneaking suspicion, feel in one's bones, hunch, have a funny feeling, have a hunch, vibes, vibrations. 2. lead, hot lead, tip-off, telltale, flea in one's ear, bug in one's ear.

INTIMIDATE v.   chill, chill off, put the chill on, spook, scare shitless, scare stiff, scare the pants off, scare hell out of, scare the shit out of, scare silly, scare the bejesus out of, scare to death, throw a scare into, shine one on, nut on one, woof, give one a turn, make one shit in one's pants, make one jump a mile, make one jump out of his skin, strike all of a heap, bowl down, bowl over, buffalo, bulldoze, chicken out, enforce, lean on, lean against, push around, whip one around (intellectually), showboat, walk heavy, put on the arm, put on the muscle, put the heat on, turn on the heat, put one through the wringer, bad-eye, cuff, hang tough, goose, jackboot, full-court press, fat nuts (Af. Am.).

INTIMIDATED adj.   scared stiff, scared shitless, have cold feet, clutched up, bufflaloed, D and D (deaf and dumb, afraid to testify), bowled down, bowled over, feel the heat. See FRIGHTENED.

INTOLERABLE adj.   too much, a bit much, enough already, last straw, straw that broke the camel's back, that's it, that blows it, that tears it.

INTOLERANT adj.   have a short fuse, agin, one-sided, down on, tilted, weighted, red-neck, red-baiter, Jew-baiter, black-baiter, Archie Bunker, a regular Archie Bunker, jingoist, male chauvinist pig, MCP, pig, good old boys, good old boys network, McCarthyite. See also PREJUDICED; STUBBORN.

INTOXICANT n.   hooch, booze, red-eye, sauce, medicine, mouthwash, poison, idiot oil, firewater, fog cutter, likker, panther piss, rotgut, alky, embalming fluid, kickapoo joy juice. See LIQUOR.

INTOXICATE v.   turn on, whip up, get high, get schnokkered, get a snootful, get pissed, get pissy-eyed, get cockeyed, liquor up, booze up, beer up, gin up, hit the sauce, hit the booze, hit the red-eye, go on a drunk, crack a six-pack (beer), belt the grape, get a bun on, get a buzz on, fight a bottle, hang a few on, hang on a few.

INTOXICATED adj.   1. tight, tipsy, bombed, stewed, stinking, plastered, wearing beer goggles, Coke bottle-eyed (all women look beautiful), looped, DWI (driving while intoxicated), high as a kite, blind, blotto, juiced up, stoned, tanked up, D.O.A., dead drunk, fried, smashed, swacked, tied one on, feeling no pain, on a bat, shikker, schnokkered, stewed to the gills, sloshed, seeing double, Kentucky fried. See DRUNK. 2. stoned, high, zerked-out. See DRUG USE.

INTRACTABLE adj.   hard-core, hang tough, tough nut, tough nut to crack, burly, locked, locked-in, rock-ribbed, pat, stand-pat, hardheaded. See STUBBORN.

INTRAMURAL adj.   in-house.

INTRANSIGENT adj.   locked, locked-in, hang tough, tough nut, tough nut to crack, burly, head in concrete, chiseled in stone, Rock of Gibraltar, pat, stand-pat. See STUBBORN.

INTRAUTERINE DEVICE n.   IUD, Copper T, pussy butterfly.

INTRAVENOUS RACK n.   ivy pole.

INTREPID adj.   ballsy, gutsy, gutty, gritty, spunky, I'm shakin' (sarcastic response to threat), bodacious, iceman, ice in one's veins. See FEARLESS.

INTRICATE adj.   mega-factor, Rube Goldberg, hi-tech, can of worms, gasser, rat's nest, snake pit, wheels within wheels.

INTRIGUE n.   game, little game, fix, frame, frameup, hookup, Barney (fixed), put-up job. See SCHEME.

INTRIGUE v.   1. cook up, finagle, frame up, operate, promote, angle, set up, be in cahoots with, work hand in glove with. See SCHEME. 2. grab, turn on, turn one on, hook, pull, send, wow, draw, bait, mousetrap, vamp, shill, steer, tout, lead one on, give one the come-on, give one a come-hither look, make a hit with, sweep off one's feet, knock dead, knock out, bat one's eyes at, suck in, rope in, humbug, con, lead up the garden path.

INTRIGUED adj. caught, on the hook, hooked, on the case, sold, sold on, buy it, into, really into, gone, turned-on. See also BEWITCHED.

INTRIGUER n. finagler, operator, wangler, wire-puller, mastermind, brain.

INTRODUCE v. intro, knock down, give a knock-down, do the honors, break the ice, open up, get things rolling, start the ball rolling, kick it, kick off, boot, bring out, come out with, fix up, get together, spring with. See also ORIGINATE.

INTRODUCTION n. intro, blind date, knockdown, preem.

INTROVERT n. loner, creep, creepy, bent, drip, dolo, oddball, weirdo, wet blanket, gool, wimp, mince, nerd.

INTRUDE v. mix in, barge in, butt in, chisel in, horn in, muscle in, stick one's nose in, poke one's nose in, hang up, hold up, kibitz, put in one's oar, put one's two cents in.

INTRUDER n. buttinsky, crasher, gate-crasher.

INTRUSIVE adj. nosy, pushy, snoopy.

INTUIT v. have a hunch, get vibes, have vibes, feel in one's bones, feel in one's guts, have a funny feeling, get in touch, figure, be turned on to.

INTUITION n. sixth sense, ESP, hunch, have a hunch, aha reaction, gut reaction, feel in one's bones, have a funny feeling, a nose, a nose for, a good nose, seat of one's pants, by the seat of one's pants, flying by the seat of one's pants.

INUNDATE v. snow, snow under, dunk, flood with, swamp.

INVADE v. barge in, bust in, horn in, muscle in, go in, access, bum-rush, penetrate (secret agent), crash, crash the gates. See also RAID.

INVALID adj. peaky, peaked, below par, down, poorly, run-down, laid low, outta action, on the sick list. See also ILL.

INVALIDATE v. blow sky high, knock the bottom out of, knock the chocks out from under, knock the props out from under, poke full of holes, shoot full of holes, not (used at end of a sentence), nix, X out. See CANCEL.

INVEIGH v. blister, roast, scorch, blast, lambaste, trash, jump on, jump on one's case, jump down one's throat, work over, lay out, read one out, go after, go for, go to town on, have at, lay at, crack down on, come down on, come down hard on one, give 'em hell, give one both barrels, let one have it with both barrels, let one have it, give one the blanket, give one the works, sock it to one, land all over one, get on a soapbox, soapbox, spiel, spout, stump, blow, lay it on, lay a rap, skin alive, lace, lace into, lay into, pitch into, light into, sail into, wade into, rip into, rip up, rip up one side

and down the other, slap down, take on, pepper, take one over the hurdles, blitz, fly in the teeth of.

INVEIGLE v. stroke, snow, massage, soap, soft-soap, jolly, oil, spread it on, lay it on, lay it on thick, lay it on with a trowel, get around, play up to, butter, butter up, soften up, sweeten up, sweet-talk, honey, schmear, work on, work over, get around, buzz, charm, hook, give a come-hither look, come on, bat the eyes at, rope in, suck in, buck, contract, cream, bag-play, hand one a line, shoot a line, shoot the crap, shoot the bull, sling the bull, sling it, pull one's leg, overdo it, string along, egg one on, goose, kid along, blarney, caboodle. See also ATTRACT, FLATTER.

INVENT v. 1. think up, hatch, come up with, cook up, cobble up, dream up. 2. improv, ginned up, ad lib, off the cuff, off the hip, off the top of one's head, fake, fake it, jam, shuck, knock off, toss off. See CREATE.

INVENTION n. gismo, black box, dealie bob, mother-grabber, grabber, gimmick, doodad, doowillie, frobnitzem, coil. See APPARATUS.

INVENTIVE adj. breaking new snow, avant-garde. See IMAGINATIVE.

INVENTORIED adj. by the numbers, chapter and verse.

INVERT v. turn the tables, double back, back track, put the cart before the horse, renig, flip-flop, put assbackwards, put bassackwards, put ackbasswards.

INVEST v. buy in, sink money in, get into, plow back into, go in for, angel, back, bankroll, juice, grubstake, plunge, pick up the check, pick up the tab, stake. See FINANCE.

INVESTED adj. in, bought-in, tax-sheltered.

INVESTIGATE v. tune in on, bug, tap, wiretap, body mike, slurp, buzz, check, check out, check it out, check over, check up, cool out, feel out, eyeball it, bus it (Af. Am.), give it the once over, give it the double O, give it the OO, double O, OO, kick tires, run it down, nose around, scrounge around, candle, case, frisk, look-see, read, scout it out, spy out, stake out, squack, listen in, be all ears, ears into, Erie, on the Erie. See also SEARCH, QUESTION, RECONNOITER.

INVESTIGATION n. ex, hustle, case, double O, gunning over, gander, pike, eyeball examination, fishing expedition, witch hunt, out for bear, legwork. See also INQUIRY.

INVESTIGATOR n. bugger, plumber, sleeper (M.) little pitcher with big ears. See DETECTIVE.

INVESTMENT n. right money, smart money, flyer, flier, backing, in on the ground floor, inside, piece, plunge, spec, stab, flutter, hunch, shot, shot in the dark, melon (dividend); bear market, bearish market (low); bull market, bullish market (high). See also STOCKS, BONDS.

INVESTMENT FUND n.　go-go, go-go fund, money market.

INVESTMENT TERMS　ITC (investment tax credit), takeover (merger); takeover artist, raider, slash-and-burn guys, churn and burn, up artist, turnaround artist, bottom fisher (those dealing in junk); tenbagger (making ten times the investment), LBO (leveraged buyout), TBO (turn-around buyout), PIGs (passive income generators); white knight, white squire (friendly bidder in a takeover), gray knight (opportunistic second bidder); greenmail (payment to thwart takeover), target (a vulnerable company), shark (unfriendly financier forcing takeovers), smoking gun (error by a shark permitting the target to escape through an anti-trust ruling); shark repellent, poison pill, (takeover defense strategy), porcupine provisions (legal deterrents), scorched earth (antitakeover measure), Chinese wall (protective measure), monkey points (net percentage), sweetener (added incentive), red herring (financial statement), straddle (put and call), vulture fund (buys troubled companies for profit later), tombstone (advertisement), repo, uptick, gorilla (bond trader), parking (holding stocks to hide investment).

INVESTOR n.　backer, angel (The.), the money, the bank, the bankroll, the one who signs the checks, staker, gunslinger, lame duck (stocks), lamb (new), plunger, scalper (ticket seller), spec. See also FINANCIER.

INVIGORATE v.　jazz up, perk up, pick up, chirk up, snap up, zip up, put zip into, pep up, put pep into, juice up, turn on the juice, zap, trigger, turn on. See STIMULATE.

INVIGORATED adj.　high, hyper, charged, flipped-out, jacked, jaked, jazzed, turned-on, get a lift, revved, revved-up, stoked, juiced-up, hopped-up, pepped-up, zipped-up, zapped up.

INVINCIBLE adj.　bulletproof.

INVITATION n.　bid, invite, stiff card, pass, paper, rain check (for another time), come-on, give one the eye, wolf whistle, come-hither, feeler, proposition, pass, hit. See also LURE.

INVITE v.　hit on, rope in, come on to, give one the come on, suck in, bat one's eyes at, give one a come-hither look, do you want an engraved invitation?, sweep off one's feet, vamp. See ATTRACT.

INVOCATION n.　abracadabra, hocus-pocus, mumbo-jumbo, hoodoo, voodoo, open sesame.

INVOLUNTARY adj.　knee-jerk reaction.

INVOLVE v.　get around, charm, hook, contract, bag, turn on, duke in, rope in, suck in, swindle in, swindle up, foozle, embrangle, set up, frame, frame up, finger, hang something on, put up a job. See also INCRIMINATE.

INVOLVED adj.　1. into, really into, hooked into, sucked into, heavily into, up to here in, knee deep in, up to one's ass, wrapped up in, eat sleep and breathe (something). See ENGROSSED. 2. hi-tech, can of worms, gasser, rat's nest, snake pit, wheels within wheels, Rube Goldberg.

INVOLVEMENT n.　hands on, sit-in, get in the act, behind, get behind (a person or idea).

INVULNERABLE adj.　bulletproof, Teflon.

IOTA n.　itsy-bitsy pieces, chewed fine.

IOWA　Hawkeye State, where the tall corn grows.

IRASCIBLE adj.　cantankerous, feisty, grouchy, snappish, bear, ogre, bad-assed, uptight, thin-skinned, ready to fly off the handle, edgy. See IRRITABLE.

IRATE adj.　blown out, pissy, pissed off, p'd off, p.o.'d, aerated, aggro, bent out of shape, blow a gasket, blow one's stack, bummed out, steamed, ticked off, tee'd off, t'd off, bullshit, apeshit, hopping mad. See ANGRY.

IRE n.　slow burn, conniption, conniption fit, cat fit, blowup, boiling point, more heat than light. See ANGER.

IRISH n.　Mick, Micky, Mike, Pat, paddy, donkey, Harp, Irisher, spud, Mulligan, lace-curtain Irish (prosperous), shanty Irish (poor), Greek, sham, shamrock, bog hopper, bog trotter, turf cutter, terrier (all Derog.).

IRISH REVOLUTION n.　troubles, the troubles, the Troubles, the throubles.

IRK v.　be at, eat, noodge, piss one off, bitch one off, make waves, give one a hard time, fuck with one's head, get to, cop an attitude (Af. Am.), that grinds my gears, all right already. See ANNOY.

IRKSOME adj.　tough, pushy, noodgey, nitpicking, humdrum.

IRRATIONAL adj.　flaky, freaky, kooky, cockamamie, wacky, loony, out to lunch, off the wall, nut job, have a lug nut loose, throw out the baby with the bath water. See CRAZY.

IRREFUTABLE adj.　checked and double-checked, for a fact Jack, cold lay, no ifs ands or buts, bet your ass, absitively, dead to rights, set, right on, odds-on, bet on, bet one's gospel truth, ironclad contract. See CERTAIN.

IRREGULAR adj.　herky-jerky, by bits and pieces, hit or miss, in dribs and drabs, willy-nilly, cockeyed.

IRREPRESSIBLE adj.　scoutmaster, Pollyanna, ray of sunshine, eager-beaver, beaver. See also UNRESTRAINED.

IRRESISTIBLE adj.　drooly, traffic stopper, glamour girl, schwing!, looker, sex kitten, mink, stone, stone fox, foxy, head rush, scrumptious, stunner, stunning, zimmer, oh yeah. See BEAUTIFUL.

IRRESOLUTE adj.　wimpy, wishy-washy, fence hanger, on the fence, run hot and cold, back and fill, shilly-shally, waffly, pussyfooting, pussyfooting around. See UN-DECIDED.

IRRESPONSIBLE adj. devil-may-care, let George do it, pass the buck, no account, don't give a shit. See also RECKLESS.

IRREVERENT adj. flip, fresh, sassy, smart-ass, wise-ass, cocky, cheeky, crusty, out-of-line, off-base, off-color. See INSOLENT.

IRRITABLE adj. bitchy, bad-ass, mean, ornery, dank, stanky (Fem.), tetchy, cantankerous, cussed, grouchy, grumpy, beefing, bellyaching, bitching, crabby, cranky, grousing, snappish, waspish, scrappy, salty, spikey, bear, ogre, ugly, ugly customer, turd poodle, uptight, sucking eggs, thin-skinned, hotheaded, fire-eater, blow-top, firecracker, short fuse, ticking bomb, ready to fly off the handle, not a happy camper, edgy, on the ragged edge, wreck, a bundle of nerves, Mr. Coffee Nerves, pushing out one's lips, outta sorts, got up on the wrong side of the bed.

IRRITATE v. bug, give a bad time to, give one the business, fuck with one's head, get, get under one's skin, drive one up a tree, rile, chap, push one's key, rattle one's cage. See ANNOY.

IRRITATED adj. blown-out, browned-off, pissed-off, pushed outta shape, uptight, aggro, drove, way drove, lose it, defrosted, blow, blow one's cool, blow it out, bouncing, bugged, bummed-out, driven up the wall, all hot and bothered. See ANGRY.

IRRITATING adj. rub the wrong way, spiky, from hell, pesky, pestiferous, a bit much, too much. See ANNOYING.

IRRITATION n. drag, a pain, pain in the ass, pain in the neck, wet blanket, headache, dead wood, blister, botheration, worriment. See ANNOYANCE.

ISOBUTYL NITRITE n. popper.

ISOLATED adj. far out, out of it, cool, play it cool, spaced out, out in left field. See also ALONE.

ISOLATION n. the cold, salt mines, back to the salt mines; the hole, solitary, blue room (prison), bubble.

ISSUE n. offspring, get (animal). See also CHILD.

ISTHMUS n. choke point, bottleneck.

ITALIAN n. wop, dago, pizza man, pizza head, macaroni, spic, spig, spiggoty, spaghetti, spaghetti bender, Eyetalian, Eytie, ringtail, dingbat, dino (laborer), ginzo, guinzola, guinea, ginney, greaseball, meatball, pizon (all Derog.).

ITEM n. piece, think piece, column, scoop, blurb, write-up, story, bit, scrap.

ITEMIZE v. spell out, lay out, take it line by line, cross the T's and dot the I's, sweat the details, quote chapter and verse, get down to brass tacks, get down to cases. See also CATALOGUE.

ITEMIZED adj. by the numbers, chapter and verse.

ITERATE v. say again, again, come again, ditto, echo, one more time, una mas, run that by me once more, chew one's cabbage twice, do, do like, go like, make like. See REPEAT.

ITINERANT WORKER n. Okie, wetback, floater.

ITINERARY n. the bricks (hobo, police, union), beat, run.

IVY LEAGUE n. Kee, Key.

IVY LEAGUE STUDENT n. shoe, white shoe, key, white buck, white bucks.

IWW n. Wobbly, Wob, clear (member, Obs.), dehorn (leave IWW).

J

J n. Juliette, Jig.

JABBER n. hot air, gab, gas, yak, yakkety-yak, talkee-talkee, guff, blah-blah, bibble-babble. See also SPEECH.

JABBER v. gas, gab, jaw, yak, yakkety-yak, go on, go on and on, run on, run off at the mouth, have diarrhea of the mouth, shoot off one's mouth, shoot off one's face, shoot the breeze, bat the breeze, bat the chat, beat one's gums, talk through one's hat, bull, bullshit, BS, throw the bull, bibble-babble, twiddle. See also SPEAK.

JACKASS n. Rocky Mountain canary.

JACKET n. threads, sack (Af. Am.), flogger, peacoat, Eisenhower, Mao.

JACKSON, MISSISSIPPI Capital J.

JACKSONVILLE, FLORIDA Jax.

JADED adj. fed-up, full-up, done it all, been around twice, cool, laid-back, mellow, blah, up to here, had it up to here, ho-hum, so what else is new. See also INDIFFERENT.

JAGUAR n. cat, Jag (auto).

JAIL n. jug, slam, slammer, stir, pen, can, pokey, clink, hoosegow, joint, Club Fed, G. joint (federal), lockup, coop, cooler, bull pen, cage, big cage, gulag, booby hatch, chokey, choky, caboose, cally, calaboose, brig, guardhouse (Mil.), dump, eighty-four (N.), icebox, maxi (maximum security), the rack, inside, Camp Adirondack, playhouse (small), gladiator school, pink clink, right joint, mill, crossbar hotel, graybar hotel, crowbar hotel, county hotel, bastille, college, graystone college, hook, hospital, municipal farm, jam, lag, limbo, prod, soak, tough can, jook joint, quad, quod, quads, campus, refrigerator, big joint, big house, sugar house, bug house, iron house, up the river, locked down, statesville, doing time, school, big school, boob, freezer, squeezer, band box, coop, Disneyland, hen pen, iron pile, poogie, Q (San Quentin), sent up; solitary, the hole (solitary confinement); crate, bandbox, bandhouse, tank, bucket, fish bowl, pokery, wire city, the bricks (outside).

JAIL v. put away, hold, lock up, send up, send up the river, ice, put on ice, book, put one away, throw the book at, cool, can, cage, lay the arm on, take one away, settle, slough, slough up, railroad.

JAIL CELL n. tank, fish tank, drunk tank, bull pen, coop, cage, hard room, lockup. alley, boxcar, bug trap, can, crib, cement tomb, drum, junk tank (alcoholics, addicts), tiger cage, house, hut.

JAILED adj. away, boxed (after arrest), up the river, in the slammer, in the clink, in college, out-of-town, iced, put on ice, cooped, cooped up, jugged. See IMPRISONED.

JAILER n. screw, chaser, eyes, hack, herder, hooligan, roach, roller, slave driver, sky, yard bull, horse (corrupt, smuggles in dope, etc.). See also WARDEN.

JAIL SENTENCE n. bid (Af. Am.).

JAIL, TRANSFER TO ANOTHER v. go round the horn.

JAMAICA GINGER n. jake.

JAMMED adj. jam-packed, sardined, standing room only, SRO, up to the rafters, mobbed, gridlocked, fanny-bumper, full as a tick. See CROWDED.

JAMMING n. background, buckshot, covered-up (radio).

JANGLE v. hit a clinker, hit a sour note, sound a sour note.

JANITOR n. super, sitter, house sitter, swamper, crumb boss (hobo, logger).

JANUARY n. first thirty.

JAPANESE n. Jap, Nip, gook, slant-eye, yellow peril, Tojo (soldier), skippy (woman or prostitute), Jerkanese (all Derog.), banana (sympathetic to whites).

JAR v. hit a clinker, hit a sour note, sound a sour note.

JARGON n. jive, jive talk, street talk, doublespeak, hillspeak, bafflegab, bunkum, buzzwords, federalese, officialese, gobbledygook, lingo, mumbo-jumbo, weasel words, flash (thieves). See also VERNACULAR.

JAUNT n. Cook's tour, cruise (pleasure trips). See TRAVEL.

JAUNT v. hit the road, hit the dirt, hit the grit, joyride. See TRAVEL.

JAUNTY adj. 1. feel-good, high wide and handsome, bouncy, chirpy, chipper, feeling one's oats, full of beans, full of piss and vinegar, zippy. See CHEERFUL. 2. trendy, in, in thing, now, really now, mean, captain hipness, ragging, sharp, spiffy, nifty, natty, reet, sharpie, swanky, ritzy, dressed to kill, go-go, hip, mod, mellow back (Af. Am.), snazzy, cat's meow, chichi, chic, fashion plate, knock one's eye out, doggy, jazzbo, dap, high-powered, toney.

JAW n. clam shells, button, chops, glass jaw, point.

JAZZ n. jive, blues, swing, soul music, blue-eyed soul, progressive, pop, Dixieland, bop, bebop, rebop, boogie-woogie, rag, ragtime, race music, barrelhouse, cat house, back alley, jam, jam session, riff, gut bucket, carrying weight (blues), down-home (New Orleans), electric, funk, funky, gully low, low-down dirty, low-down and dirty, slurred gut-bucket, smooth and mellow, tailgate, blaring tailgate, cool jazz, far out, way out, light (sympathetic to), swinging like a gate, long underwear, meet (jam), mellow, mop-mop.

JAZZ MUSICIAN n. sideman, cat, cool cat, hep cat, gay cat, blowing cat, blue blower, alligator (white), gate, gator, in orbit (avant-garde), lip-splitter, satchel, sender, solid sender, swinging gate, wig, iron man, band man, paper man, rag man; ear man, faker (musically illiterate); rocker, monster (popular).

JAZZ TERMS jam, jam session, riff, jive, blow, blow the blues, blow up a storm, send, sending, combo, grooving, coon shouting, lick, break, coast, flare-up, lumpy (played badly), the Man (leader), get off (solo), push, strictly union.

JEALOUS adj. green-eyed, jelly, turn green.

JEALOUSY n. green-eyed monster, sour grapes, eat one's heart out.

JEER n. put down, put on, rank out, dump, dig, dirty dig, crack, slam, swipe, jab, comeback, parting shot, brickbat, bazoo, raspberry.

JEFFERSON CITY, MISSOURI Jeff City.

JELL-O n. nervous pudding, shivering Liz.

JELLY n. red lead, nervous pudding.

JEOPARDIZE v. lay it on the line, put on the spot, stick one's neck in the noose, stick one's neck out, play into one's hands, chance it, go out on a limb, fail to cover one's ass.

JEOPARDIZED adj. on the line, on the spot, out on a limb, got one's neck out, have one's ass out, caught with one's pants down.

JEOPARDY n. double trouble, out on a limb, on the line, on the spot.

JERK n. yank, yerk.

JERKY adj. herky-jerky, by fits and starts, by bits and pieces, in dribs and drabs, higgledy-piggledy.

JEST n. gag, laugh, one-liner, a funny, nifty, rib, rib-tickler, spoof, jive, crack, wisecrack. See JOKE.

JEST v. jive, kid, put on, spoof, needle, rib, rag, razz, roast, josh, jolly, pull one's leg, funnin', who you jivin'?, make a funny. See JOKE.

JESTER n. clown, Bozo, Joey, paleface, cutup, life of the party, madcap, trickster, card, kibitzer, funster, quipster. See JOKER. See also BANTERER.

JESUIT n. Jebby.

JESUS CHRIST J.C., Head Knock, Jeeze, Hay-Soose, Jerusalem Slim, Jesus H. Christ, Jesus Mariah Christ, One Of Our Boys (Yid.) (all Derog.).

JET n. spritz.

JET ENGINE STALL n. burnout, flameout.

JET FUEL n. zip fuel.

JET PLANE n. jet, ramjet, scramjet, air breather, flamethrower, fizz, job, blowtorch, flying blowtorch, heat can, squirt, stovepipe, whale, lightning rod (fighter), knee-cap (NEACP plane). See also AIRPLANE.

JETTISON v. deep-six. See also DISCARD.

JEW n. Jew boy, Hebe, kike, Yid, rabbi, bagel bender, sheeny, mocky, motzy, cloak and suiter, eagle beak, hook nose, Abe, Abie, Ike, Ikie, Izzie, Rachel, porker, kosher, sammy, Yehuda, Goldberg, Hymie, Jewish American Princess, JAP, fruppie (upwardly mobile, religiously observant), member of the tribe, M.O.T., skid, lid, yit, geese, clip, clip-cock, clipped dick, kosher pickle (all Derog.).

JEWELRY n. junk jewelry, brass (cheap or fake), stones, rocks, sparklers, ice, glass, Christmas, hardware, pennyweight, gullion.

JEWELRY STORE n. icehouse, ice palace, slum joint, stone joint, gullion joint.

JIGGLE v. jigger, jigget.

JILT v. drop, dump, ditch, give one the air, give one the gate, give one the wind, give back one's ring, leave, leave at the church, leave at the altar, leave flat, hand one one's walking papers, throw over, break it off. See also ABANDON, REJECT.

JILTED adj. left at the church, thrown over, ditched, dumped, out, on the rebound. See also REJECTED.

JIMSON WEED n. devil's trumpet.

JINX n. whammy, double whammy, kibosh, hoodoo, voodoo, kiss of death.

JINX v. cuss, damn, darn, spook, put the horns on, put the whammy on one, put the double whammy on one, give one a kineahora (Yid.), hoodoo, hoodoo one, voodoo, voodoo one.

JOB n. gig, J.O., nine-to-five shit, rat race, grind, racket, swindle, shitwork, McJob (service). See WORK.

JOBBER n. middleman.

JOBLESS adj. out of action, on layoff, on the dole, down, closed-down, cut loose (dockworker), in short pants. See UNEMPLOYED.

JOCKSTRAP n. jock, cup, hector protector.

JOCULAR adj. camp, campy, jokey, joshing, yokky, boffo, gagged-up, for grins, flaky, wacky, crazy, daffy, tomfool, fool around. See also AMUSING, WITTY, CHEERFUL.

JOIN v. 1. team up, tie up with, turn, throw in together, get in with, join together, join up with, sign on, come aboard, marry, plug into. See ASSOCIATE. 2. tag on, tack on, slap on, hitch on. See also FASTEN.

JOKE n. gag, laugh, one-liner, throwaway, topper, payoff, boff, boffo, boffola, yak, yock, yuck, funny, a ha-ha, horse, horseplay, howl, hot one, needle, nifty, rib, rib-tickler, sizzler, spoof, shtick, story, location joke (you had to be there), button (punch line), whiz-bang, jive, crack, smart crack, wisecrack, chestnut, old chestnut, wheeze, old wheeze, old saw, old turkey, oldie, joke with whiskers, warmed-over cabbage, bark, bromide, corn, knee-slapper; an egg, an omelette, a bomb, bombed out, laid there, laid an egg (unfunny).

JOKE v. jive, kid, put on, spoof, needle, rib, rag, razz, roast, josh, jolly, ride, kibitz, kibitz around, kid around, horse around, horseplay, goof on, pull one's leg, funnin', who you jivin'?, wisecrack, crack wise, make a funny, get off a joke.

JOKE LINE n. punch line, straight line, feed, feed line, setup, setup line, beat, snapper, zinger, wisecrack, comeback.

JOKER n. stand-up comic, baggy-pants comic, hokum comic, straight man, roaster, stooge, banana, top banana, second banana, clown, Bozo, Joey, paleface, cutup, life of the party, madcap, trickster, card, a million laughs, kibitzer, booger, bugger, jokesmith, gagman, gagster, funster, punster, quipster, wisecracker. See also BANTERER.

JOLLITY n. laughs, lots of laughs, grins, get some grins, action, ball, fun and games, cold chillin', big time, high time, high old time, hoopla, picnic, whoopee, whooper-dooper, wingding, shindig, brawl. See AMUSEMENT, PARTY.

JOLLY adj. jokey, joshing, for grins, daffy, lots of laughs, bouncy, chirpy, chipper, zippy. See JOVIAL.

JOLT n. kick in the ass, shot, shot in the ass, whammy, double whammy, from out in left field. See SURPRISE.

JOLT v. rock, gork, floor, shake one up, give one a shot, bowl over, spring something on one, knock one over, knock for a row of pins. See SURPRISE.

JOLTED adj. shook, shook-up, rocked, defrosted, gorked, slaphappy, hit like a ton of bricks. See SURPRISED.

JOSH v. jive, kid, put on, spoof, needle, rib, ride, kibitz, kibitz around, wisecrack, crack wise, make a funny, get off a joke. See TEASE, JOKE.

JOSTLE v. push around, bang into, nerf, crash, rowdy-dowdy, rough and tumble, tumul, bump heads.

JOURNAL n. daily, rag, scandal sheet, sheet, bladder, blat, bulldog (earliest edition), chroniker, extra, fish wrapper, snitch sheet, toilet paper. See also MAGAZINE. 2. comic book, funny book. 3. swindle sheet.

JOURNALISM n. gee whiz journalism (sensational), gonzo journalism (mixed fact and fiction), checkbook journalism (paid interview).

JOURNALIST n. scribe, scrivener, columnist, jib-rat (reports war from distance), stringer, leg man, news hen, news hound, cub, pen driver, pen pusher, pencil driver, pencil pusher, scratcher, ink slinger. See also WRITER.

JOURNEY n. hop, swing, jaunt, cruise, junket, trek, overnight, weekend, Cook's tour. See TRAVEL.

JOURNEY v. jet, jet around, knock about, bat around, go places, country-hop, globe-trot, cruise, on the move, junket. See TRAVEL.

JOVIAL adj. jokey, joshing, yokky, boffo, gagged up, for grins, loony, off-the-wall, crazy, daffy, nutty, dippy, dizzy, lots of laughs, do the crazy act, do the crazy bit, do the crazy shtick, tomfool, fool around, make a monkey of oneself, fool, foolheaded, bouncy, chirpy, chipper, zippy. See also CHEERFUL.

JOYFUL adj. flyin', flyin' high, on a joy ride, high, high as a kite, blow one's mind, flipping, Little Mary Sunshine. See HAPPY.

JOYLESS adj. dragged, low, down in the mouth, in the pits, have the blahs, clanked, droopy, mopey. See UNHAPPY.

JOYOUS adj. upbeat, flyin', sunny, sunny side up, tea'd up, joygerm fever, popping one's nuts, doing handsprings, doing backflips. See HAPPY.

JUBILANT adj. set-up, hopped-up, joygerm fever, backflips, flipping, pleased as Punch, flying, sold on, tickled, tickled to death. See ECSTATIC.

JUBILATION n. large charge, big deal, big shit, upper, cloud nine land, high, buzz, circus, fireworks, flash. See EXCITEMENT.

JUDGE n. 1. hizzoner, beagle, beak, bench nibs, Blackstone, Father Time, tough ghee with too much time, ghee with plenty of numbers, gavel jockey, hanging judge, hard rapper, monk, wig, rent-a-judge (retired). 2. aisle sitter, Monday morning quarterback, nitpicker, zapper, crix (Pl.).

JUDGE v. 1. throw the book at one, let one have it, let one have plenty of numbers, jump all over one, lay on a hard rap, jump down one's throat, knock, lower the boom, lay on, come down on, come down hard on, land on. See also CRITICIZE. 2. size, size up, take one's measure, make the call, take a decision, the way one sees it, run it up the flagpole, run it by one again. See also APPRAISE.

JUDGMENT n. 1. call-down, put-down, rap, rap on the knuckles, slap on the wrist, fall, cut, cutting, flak, hit, knock. See also CRITICISM. 2. notice, write-up, paper. 3. value judgment, judgment call. See also OPINION, SENTENCE. 4. the riot act, say, the word.

JUDO n. black belt (expert), white belt (novice).

JUG n. bucket, hooker, tub, growler (large for beer), rush the growler.

JUKEBOX n. juke, goola box (Af. Am.).

JUMBLE n. goulash, garbage, mishmash, mishmosh.

JUMP v. barge, sky.

JUNCTION n. hookup, tie-in, tie-up, plug-in, interface.

JUNGLE n. zoo.

JUNIOR COLLEGE n. J.C., jaycee, juco.

JUNIOR HIGH SCHOOL n. junior hi, junior high.

JUNK n. gash, hogwash, garbage.

JUNKET n. g'dong, gedunk, glop, goop, pud. See also TRAVEL.

JURISDICTION n. territory, turf, stomping grounds, one's neck of the woods, slot, wing. See also CONTROL.

JURIST n. 1. beagle, beak, bench nibs, Blackstone, Father Time, gavel jockey, hanging judge, hard rapper, monk, wig. 2. mouthpiece, shyster, ambulance chaser, legal eagle, lip, the L.A., Philadelphia lawyer, bomber (divorce). See ATTORNEY.

JUSTICE n. 1. beagle, beak, bench nibs, Blackstone, Father Time, gavel jockey, hanging judge, hard rapper, monk, wig, old man. 2. blindfolded lady with scales, square deal, straight.

JUSTICE OF THE PEACE n. JP.

JUSTIFICATION n. song and dance, story, the idea, the big idea, the whole idea, the what-for, the why and wherefore, the why-for. See EXCUSE.

JUSTIFY v. alibi, alibi out of, crawl out of, squirm out of, worm out of, cry sour grapes, crawl, square oneself, square things, cop out, cop a plea, make up for, whitewash, put the best face on, get down on one's marrowbones.

JUT v. stick out, pop out, bug out, googly.

JUVENILE adj. kid stuff.

JUVENILE n. juve, punk, yoot, bobby-soxer, chicken, San Quentin quail, jailbait (Fem.). See also BOY, GIRL, YOUNG MAN, YOUNG WOMAN, YOUTH, TEENAGER.

JUVENILE COURT n. short-pants division.

JUVENILE DELINQUENT n. J.D., juvie, juvey, minor, yoot, diaper-rashed punk.

K

K n. Kilo, King.

KALAMAZOO, MICHIGAN Zoo Town, Guitar City.

KANSAN n. Jayhawker.

KANSAS Sunflower State.

KANSAS CITY, KANSAS Casey, Kasey, K.C., K.C.K., Kaw Town.

KANSAS CITY, MISSOURI Beef City.

KARAOKE n. croaky.

KARATE GRADE n. black belt (advanced), white belt (novice).

KEEN adj. 1. sharp, whiz, whiz kid, Einstein, quick on the trigger, quick on the uptake, smart as a whip, sharp as a tack, nobody's fool, no dumbbell. See INTELLIGENT. 2. creaming to, dying to, gotta have. See IMPATIENT.

KENTUCKIAN n. colonel.

KENTUCKY Blue Grass State.

KERNEL n. bottom line, heart, meat and potatoes, nitty-gritty, nub.

KETCHUP n. red lead, red paint, kid stuff.

KEY n. hog eye (skeleton), screw, twister.

KEYBOARD n. eighty-eights, ivories.

KICK v. boot, kick ass, jack up, rack up, give him an ass full of leather, give one a tokus full of toes, kick the bejesus out of one, kick the beholden out of one, kick the shit outta, kick the daylights out of one, give one the foot.

KIDNAP v. grab, shanghai, snatch, put the bag on one, put the snatch on one, sneeze, hijack, skyjack, carjack, dognap (dog abduction).

KIDNAPPER n. snatch man, sneezer, snatcher, body snatcher, hijacker, highjacker, skyjacker, carjacker.

KIDNAPPING n. snatch, the snatch, body snatch, grab, put the snatch on, sneeze, hijacking, highjacking, skyjacking.

KILL v. liquidate, neutralize, waste, compromise (espionage), smoke, get a body, take out of the box, do, do in, do away with, hit, get, snuff, croak, dust, whack, wax, zap, burn, cook, chill, ice, off, total, fry, cool, go cool, cool out, cool off, wipe off the map, wipe out, X out, take out, knock out, KO, blot out, stamp out, lay out, rub out, erase, top, top off, iron out, lay one out, wash out, whack out, drop, bop, pop, pop one, pop one off, pay off, bump off, blip off, kiss off, knock off, finish off, polish off, push, push off, push across, put away, put to sleep, put down, put out of one's misery, put out a contract, put on ice, pull the plug, plug, punch one's ticket, blast, blow one's brains out, blow away, do away with, executive fallout (Bus.), frag (usually hand grenade), scrag, smear, grease, score, fix, dump, drill, gun down, mow down, shoot down, dry-gulch, fog, guzzle, buy one concrete galoshes, clip, cream, take care of, take for an airing, take the wind out of, take one's wind, take for a ride, give the business, give the works, give one a wood overcoat, lynch (Af. Am.), pickle, let one have it, set over, settle, make one disappear, send to kingdom come; bug out, BO (kill with toxic).

KILLED adj. iced, wasted, offed, bumped-off, knocked-off, cooled-off, chilled, greased (Mil.), totaled, piffed, pifted, wiped-out, stamped-out, liquidated, neutralized, finished, disappeared, cooked, rubbed-out, snuffed, snuffed-out, stonkered, dead and done for, done for, done in, down the drain, down the tube, tubed, sunk, gone, had it, hashed-up, kaput, fragged, offed.

KILLER n. hit man, trigger, trigger man, piece man, torpedo, enforcer, exterminator, terminator, gorilla, gun, gunman, gunsel, bump man, button man, hatchet man, bang man, iceman, apache, shootist, clipper, plugger, soldier, troop, butcher, blaster, knock-off ghee, red-hot, hired gun, dropper (hired).

KILLING n. off, offing, knock-off, wasting, hit, erase, rub out, taking out, the big M, cool, chill, big chill, bump-off, a ride, croaking, bang job, cut down, fragging (officer, Mil.), scragging, the works, dying of the measles (spy, looks like natural causes), liquidation, neutralization, kiss-off.

KILL, INTEND TO v. gun for, lug a chiv, lug iron for, pack a chiv for, pack a rod for, have a contract on, set up for a hit.

KILLJOY n. party pooper, buzz crusher, buzz killer, drag, drip, wet blanket, crepe hanger, sourpuss, sourbelly, sourball, gloomy Gus, downer, worry wart, Calamity Jane, stick-in-the-mud, moldy fig.

KILOMETER n. click, klick, klik.

KIND adj. big, all heart (Derog.), bleeding heart, heart in the right place, softhearted, old softie.

KIND n. likes, likes of, lot, number.

KINDLE v. fire up, burn up, key up, egg on, turn on, work up, get smoking. See INCITE.

KINDLY adj. cool, mellow.

KINDNESS n. heart, mitzvah.

KINSMAN n. folks, homefolks, kinfolk; P's. peeps, rents (parents); kissin' cousin, kissing cousin, shirttail kin, blood.

KISMET n. karma, in the cards, the beads, that's the way the beads read, that's the way the ball bounces, that's the way the cookie crumbles. See DESTINY.

KISS n. peck, smack, smooch, X, buss, face rape, M.L.A. (major lip action), tonsil hockey, slobbin', mush, muzzle, sugar, soul kiss, butterfly kiss, French kiss, fish-kiss (puckered lips), lay one on the lips, mouth music.

KISS v. pucker up, peck, smack, smash, smooch, eat face, chew face, do face time, suck face, suck heads, mesh, swap slops, swap spit, buss, French kiss, soul kiss, box tonsils, give a tonsillectomy, play tonsil hockey, go for sushi, a little smacky, tongue-wrestle, scoop, smash mouth, butterfly kiss, spark, buzz, X, mush, muzzle, sugar, lay one on the lips, mouth music, maw (and pet), mouth-to-mouth resuscitation.

KITCHEN n. crumb stash, bean gun (mobile, WWII).

KITTEN n. kitty, kitty cat, puss, pussy, pussycat.

KLAXON n. beeper, honker, tooter.

KLEPTOMANIA n. light fingers, sticky fingers, taking ways.

KLEPTOMANIAC n. klepto. See also THIEF.

KNACK n. hang, hang of it, know-how, savvy, good hands. See SKILL.

KNEE n. knob, duke, deuce of benders (Pl.), prayer bone, prayer handle.

KNIFE n. blade, shiv, chiv, chib, edge (Af. Am.), switch, switchblade, bill (Af. Am.), Arkansas toothpick, Harlem toothpick, Tennessee toothpick, bylow (Barlow), stick, pig sticker, frog sticker, flick, ripper, steel, shank.

KNIFE v. slice, stick, cut, cut a new kisser for, chiv, shiv, brand, open up, chop down, clip, carve, carve initials in one, jag, chop, shank. See also WOUND.

KNOCK DOWN v. drop, deck, flatten, flip, floor one, down one, take down, take one down, put down, smack down, shoot down, shoot down in flames, lay one out, lay one low, wipe up the floor with, wipe up the place with, knock one on one's ass, knock one ass over teakettle, knock one on one's ear, knock on one's biscuit, knock on one's can, knock on one's keister, knock on one's pratt, knock on one's quiff, knock one on one's wallet, knock one into next week. See also HIT.

KNOCK OUT v. KO, K.O., kayo, deck, hit the deck, hit the mat, hit the canvas, kiss the canvas, total, waste, erase, flatten, floor, smear, lay one out, punch one out, knock cold, knock one out, knock on the head, knock one for a loop, lower the boom, deal a knockout blow to, put away, put the slug on one, ring one's bell, land a haymaker, cold-cock, cold-pack, curtains for, hearts and flowers, Chinese, dry-gulch. See also HIT.

KNOW v. into, got it, getya, gotya, get the idea, get the point, on top of, catch on, booted on, blow wise, have down cold, know one's onions, know the score, collar the jive. See UNDERSTAND.

KNOWING adj. wised-up, cool, sharp, have smarts, street smarts, tuned-in, into, really into, all woke up, crack, crackerjack, have savvy, not born yesterday, foxy, crazy like a fox, phenom, pro, whiz kid, enough ducks in a row. See SHREWD. See also INTELLIGENT.

KNOWLEDGE n. the know, poop, picture, dirt, dope, inside dope, inside story, goulash (false), what's happenin', what's what, what's going down. See INFORMATION.

KNOWLEDGEABLE adj. cool, posted, fly, hip, hep, hipped, hipster, hepster, hep cat, hip to the jive, brains, brainy, brill, technotrash (social idiot), sharp, have savvy, groovy, go-go, with it, chilly, all woke up, been there, tuned in, in the picture, booted on, on to, into, really into, plugged in, wise to, wised up, inside, on the inside, have the inside track, have the smarts, book smart, have a good head on one's shoulders, have a head on one's shoulder, have one's head screwed on right, have one's ships in a row, smart as a whip, sharp as a tack, not born yesterday, tool, power tool, cereb, IQ, together, got it all together, got it up here, commonsensical, got one's boots on, have horse sense, gray matter, wizard, highbrow, in the know, know-how, know damn well, be up on, have down pat, have down cold, know one's onions, know the score, know the ropes, know all the ins and outs, know it all, know all the answers, know what's what, know one's stuff, know one's business, know one's p's and q's, on, on top of, the smart money, ear to the ground, grounded, on the beam, double digs, hear tell of, hear say, kept posted, nobody's fool, not so dumb, no dumbbell, Philadelphia lawyer. See also ALERT, SKILLED.

KNOXVILLE, TENNESSEE K Town.

KOREAN (SOUTH) n. gook (Derog.), katusa (Korean attached to U.S. Army), ROK.

KOWTOW v. lie down and roll over for, roll over and play dead, go social, toe the mark, play ball, fold, give in, give up, go along with, cave in, cry uncle, say uncle, knuckle under, knuckle to. See also FLATTER.

KUDOS n. strokes, raves, plum, Dr. Spocking the help, pat on the back, pat on the head, PR, puff, puffing up, pumping up, low profile (avoid). See also FLATTERY.

L

L n. Lima, Love.

LABEL n. logo. See also NAME.

LABOR n. grind, daily grind, the salt mines, donkey-work, gruntwork (army), hemo jo (hard labor), shitwork, day gig, moonlight, rank and file, blue collar. See WORK.

LABOR v. scratch, sweat and slave, plug away, plug along, pour it on, beat one's brains out, bust one's buns, work one's head off, bear down on it, dog it (inferior), mouse milking (maximum time for minimum return). See WORK.

LABORATORY n. lab, chem lab, photo lab, JPL (Jet Propulsion Lab, Pasadena), think tank, skunk works (usually secret, originally Lockheed).

LABORER n. working stiff, help, hard hat, blue collar, blue-collar worker, dirty neck, breadwinner, workhorse, dinner-pailer, prentice, come-along (temporary, inexperienced), floater. See WORKER.

LABORIOUS adj. uphill battle, wicked, hairy, bitch, tough one, tough proposition, tough job, rough go, hard pull, hard row to hoe, hard row of stumps, ballbreaker, ballbuster, backbreaker. See DIFFICULT.

LACK v. no-got, minus, 86, eighty-six, out, hurting for, come up short, too little too late, half-assed, half-baked.

LACKADAISICAL adj. laid-back, cas, cazh, spring fever, moony, daydreaming. See LANGUID.

LACKEY n. stooge, yes-man, flunky, brownnose, ass-kisser, asshole buddy, goon, ward heeler, running dog, toad. See INFERIOR.

LACKING adj. minus, not come up to scratch, not hack it, not make it, can't cut it, can't cut the mustard, short, come up short. See INADEQUATE.

LACKLUSTER adj. draggy, blah, dull as dishwater, vanilla, flat, flat as a pancake, whitebread, ho-hum, nothing, pablum, zero, phoned-in, laid-back. See INSIPID.

LAD n. tad, kid, kiddo, shemp, punk kid, bub, buddy, runt, half-pint, little shaver, yupster, bugger, chicken, wet behind the ears, boyo, boychik. See BOY. See also YOUNG MAN, YOUTH.

LADDER n. big stick (firefighter).

LADIES' MAN n. chaser, wolf, gash hound, make-out artist, killer, lady-killer, heavy cake, heavy hitter, blade, parlor snake, poodle faker, prom trotter, sailor, lounge lizard, good-time Charlie, cake-eater, bun duster, candy kid, campus butcher, fancy Dan, fancy man, furper (1930), gay cat, tea hound, stick daddy (police).

LADLE n. bug (industrial or baker's).

LADY n. broad, dame, doll, mama, queen, queen bee, granola (wears no makeup), frail, frail eel, butterfly, fine fryer, stewer (old), biddy, bag, old bag, doe (alone), mare, harpy, bitch (all Derog.). See WOMAN.

LAG v. schlep along, get no place fast, toddle, jelly, tool, tail. See LINGER.

LAGGARD n. slowpoke, foot-dragger, stick in the mud, goof-off, fuck-off, house plant, goldbrick, schlepper. See DAWDLER.

LAME adj. gimpy, gimp, crip, game, g'd-up, geed-up, hamstrung, hog-tied, sidelined, out of commission.

LAMENT v. bleed, hurt, blubber, boo-hoo, eat one's heart out, take it big, take it hard, sing, sing the blues, cry the blues, cry me a river, cry over spilled milk, go for a crying towel, get out the crying towel, kick one's self, beat one's breast, rain, carry on, take on, howl, raise a howl.

LAMENTABLE adj. awful, dirty, godawful, goshawful, grim, lousy, hurting, rotten, stinking, shitty, tough shit, TS. See also BAD, SAD.

LAMP n. bug, bug torch, dimmer, glim, bitch, bitch lamp (hobo), gump light (miner), kenten (for opium), bird-cage, hay burner.

LAMPOON n. takeoff, roast, put-on, take-down. See RIDICULE.

LAND n. real estate, terra firma, old sod.

LAND v. touch down, come in, set her down, put her down, make a three-pointer, splashdown, grease it in, grease job (smooth), go in, ditch, splash, pancake, thump in. See also ARRIVE.

LANDING n. touchdown, three-point, three-pointer, touch-and-go (practice), dead stick, splash, splashdown, power off; pancake, ditch (crash).

LANDING FIELD n. runway, strip, air-strip, landing strip, home plate (A.F.). See AIRPORT.

LANDLORD n. landprop, saw, slumlord.

LANDSMAN n. landlubber, ground gripper.

LANGUAGE n. lingo, bafflegab, doublespeak, double-talk, gobbledygookese; Hillspeak, Washingtonese (Washington, D.C.), officialese, federalese; psychobabble, Urbabble (city Govt.), ecobabble, Yerkish (artificial), Yinglish (English using many Yiddish words), Franglish (French using English words), jive talk, street talk, talkin' white (Af. Am.), flash (among thieves).

LANGUID adj. laid-back, blah, blahs, dopey, drippy, draggy, nebbish, wimpy, moony, sleepyhead, on the nod, snoozy, stretchy, out of it, have spring fever, June around.

LANGUISH v. fizzle out, fade, fag, fag out, poop, poop out, tucker, tucker out, burn out, knock out, peter out, conk out, peg out, go soft, go to pieces, come apart at the seams, die on the vine. See DETERIORATE.

LANGUOROUS adj. laid-back, loose, hang loose, dopey, moony, stretchy. See LANGUID.

LANKY adj. twiggy, beanpole, beanstalk, stilt, long drink of water, hatrack, broomstick, clothes pole, gangly, spindleshanks. See THIN.

LANTERN n. dimmer, glim, bird cage, bug, bug torch, hay burner, bitch, bitch lamp (hobo), gump light (miner), kenten (for opium).

LAPSE n. flub, fluff, muff, boner, boo-boo, blooper, goof, goof-up, screw-up, gum-up, miscue, slip-up, clinker, flap (social), fox paw, fox pass, gaff, klong, bonehead play, fool mistake. See MISTAKE.

LARGE adj. humongous, humungous, humongoid, humongo, mungo, gross, honking, monstro, bonzai, king-size, big mother, biggy, seagoing, jumbo, man-sized, lunker, blimp, barn door, whopping, thumping, would choke a horse. See BIG.

LARGESS n. gravy, grease, palm oil, salve, sweetener, zukes, tip, toke (gambling), chip, cue, somethin', a little somethin'.

LARK n. 1. binge, ball, bash, bust, caper, tear, blowout, wingding, shindig, carousing, hell-around, hell-bender, high old time, high jinks, field day. See REVEL. See also PARTY. 2. gag, rib, put-on, hotfoot, hot one, monkeyshines, shenanigans.

LARYNX n. pipes.

LASCIVIOUS adj. filthy, dirty, nasty, blue, X-rated, raunchy, raw, hard-core, soft-core, stag, steamy, hot, heavy, hot and heavy, hot for, hot stuff, flaming (Obsc. computer conversations), rough, rough stuff, evilminded, foul-mouthed, salty, off-color, low-down, low-down and dirty, in the gutter, turned on, horny, rammy, cream jeans, hot pants, lechy, a lech on, letchin'.

LASS n. sis, kid, chick, chicklet, studette (man chaser), bird, doll, jill, filly, heifer, teenybopper, bobby-soxer, bubble-gum rocker, jellybean, li'l mama, little missy, jailbait, San Quentin quail, Gidget. See GIRL.

LAST adj. ass-end, the end, bitter end, tail ass (A.F.), case (cards), the chips are down, curtains, curtains for, last hurrah, swan song. See ULTIMATE.

LASTING adj. in for the long haul, forever and a day, for a coon's age, for a month of Sundays, time out of mind, till hell freezes over, till shrimps learn to whistle, till the cows come home. See PERMANENT.

LAST MINUTE n. the nick of time, eleventh hour.

LAST RESORT n. bottom of the barrel, scrape the bottom of the barrel.

LAS VEGAS, NEVADA Vegas, Lost Wages, Sin City, Dice City, Divorce City, Glitter Gulch (downtown).

LATE adj. hung-up, held-up, in a bind, jammed, jammed-up, strapped for time, burn the midnight oil, snooze you lose.

LATE, TOO adj. left at the starting gate, left at the post, gone, blew it, blew one's chance, out of luck, a day late and a dollar short, missed the boat, the boat has sailed, let slip through one's fingers, lock the barn door after the horse is stolen.

LATER adv. by and by, come Sunday, down the line, downstream, down the pike, down the road a piece.

LATEST n. faddy, trendy, state of the art, bust fresh, in, in-thing, the thing, latest thing, latest wrinkle, last word, happenin', mod, now, really now, up to speed, up to the minute. See STYLISH.

LATIN AMERICAN n. Latino, Chicano, Chicana; greaser, wetback, spic, dago (working class), coconut (white attitudes), spaghetti, spig, spick, spiggoty (all Derog.). See also MEXICAN.

LATITUDE n. elbowroom, leeway, run, run of, space, room to swing a cat.

LATRINE n. can, john, head, facilities, amenities, terlit, piss house, shithouse, shitter, crapper, chamber of commerce, altar room, throne room, showers, where the dicks hang out, old soldiers' home. See also TOILET.

LAUD v. build up, stroke, boost, pat on the back, toss a bouquet, give a posy, give the man a big cigar, have to hand it to, hats off to. See FLATTER.

LAUDABLE adj. neato, keen, pink, stellar, sweet, terriff, not bad, not too shabby, gnarly, slick, lookin' chilly (Af. Am.), nasty, horror show, real mean, beaut, atsa nice, bootin' height, organic, check-plus. See PRAISEWORTHY.

LAUGH n. crack-up, yok, yock, yak, yack, yuk, yuck, howl, scream, boff, boffo, boffola, buffola, belly laugh, guffaw.

LAUGH v. crack up, break up, bust up, fracture, die, die laughing, boff, howl, scream, roll in the aisles, tear one apart, snap, split, split one's sides, blow a gut, laugh it up, laugh fit to die, laugh fit to bust, laugh fit to burst, bust a gut laughing, pee in one's pants laughing, fall out laughing, be in stitches, show some teeth.

LAUGHABLE adj. jokey, yok, yokky, gagged-up, for grins, camp, campy, joshing, boffo, break one up, tear one apart, lay 'em in the aisles, scream, zetser, laffer, har-har, riot. See AMUSING.

LAUNCH v. kick off, bow, start the ball rolling, get things rolling, get the show on the road, begin the beguine, break the ice, break the seal. See BEGIN.

LAUNDER v. dobee, doby (by hand), button chop; wash, smurfing (money, title). See also CLEAN.

LAUNDROMAT n. slosh-and-wash, washing emporium.

LAUNDRY n. button chopper, Chinks (Derog.).

LAUNDRYMAN n. button chopper, button hopper (WWII), Chinaman (ship).

LAUREL n. the cookies, feather in one's cap, gold star, the gold, Oscar, blue ribbon.

LAVATORY n. can, john, powder room, reading room, library, head, facilities, terlit, piss house, shithouse, sandbox, biffie, chamber of commerce, holy of holies, his, hers, little girls' room, little boys' room, pissoir. See TOILET.

LAVISH adj. posh, plush, plushy, ritzy, swanky, splendiferous, splendacious, like money was goin' outta style, spreading it around, fancy, high, high on the hog, too much, bodacious, ultra-ultra, far out, way out, out of this world, out of bounds, out of sight, no end, no end in sight, stink with, crawling with, up to one's ass in, first-cabin.

LAVISH v. go for a meg, throw money at, throw money around, piss it away, run through, go through, live high on the hog, spend money like water, spend money like it was going out of style. See SQUANDER. See also GIVE.

LAW n. reg.

LAW-ABIDING adj. legit, on the legit, on the level, up to code, straight, straight-arrow. See also VIRTUOUS.

LAWBREAKER n. crook, hood, con, heavy, hustler, racketeer, inside man, wrong number, mobster, hoodlum, goon, gun, gunsel, trigger man, repeater. See CRIMINAL.

LAWFUL adj. legit, kosher, card-carrying, on the legit, on the level, on the up and up, hold water, hold together, hold up in the wash, wash. See LEGAL.

LAWYER n. mouthpiece, shyster, ambulance chaser, ack-ack, legal eagle, beagle, the L.A., pleader, pelican (appellate), fixer, bomber (divorce), noodleman, dumptruck (prison term), ghost (writes briefs), cutter (prosecutor). See ATTORNEY.

LAX adj. sloppy, any old way, any which way, devil-may-care, leave oneself wide open, goofing off, pay no mind, looking out the window, out to lunch, asleep on the job. See CARELESS.

LAXATIVE n. cc pills.

LAZY adj. dopey, out of it, sleepyhead, snoozy, on the nod, stretchy, drag-ass, underachiever, Stepin Fetchit, lox, lump, sack artist, bum, no good bum, slug, blanket presser, couch potato, sofa spud, larking lounge lizard. See also INDOLENT.

LEAD n. edge, bulge, ahead, over, top, on top, spark. See ADVANTAGE.

LEAD v. head, helm, shepherd, run things, call the shots, call the signals, quarterback, mastermind, get the jump on, go out in front, spearhead, trail-blaze. See MANAGE.

LEADER n. front runner, chief, C.O., exec, suit, boss lady, boss man, godfather, head honcho, queen bee, top, on top, topper, topkick, kingpin, king of the hill, lead-off man, guru, juice. See EXECUTIVE.

LEADING adj. number one, numero uno, primo, A-number one, tops, top of the class, top of the list, top-drawer, at the head of the line, first off, key, right up front. See BEST.

LEAFLET n. broadside, flyer, handout, literature, zap art (for a cause).

LEAGUE n. crew, bunch, crowd, gang, mob, outfit, ring, hookup, tie-up, circle. See ASSOCIATION.

LEAN adj. skinny, stick, twiggy, shadow, bag of bones, beanpole, stilt, hatrack, clothes pole, cadaver, long drink of water, gangling, gangly. See THIN.

LEANING n. bag, groove, thing, cup of tea, mindset, where one is at, weakness for. See INCLINATION.

LEAN ON v. bank on, bank upon, bet on, bet one's bottom dollar on, gamble on, lay money on, use as a crutch, ride on one's coattails.

LEAP v. go up the ladder (leap upward), hippety-hop, cut, pass up.

LEARN v. 1. get down, get down pat, get down cold, get hold of, get into one's head, get the hang of, get the knack of, pick up, pick up on, learn the ropes, learn backwards and forwards, go through the school of hard knocks, dig up, uncover, smoke out, stumble upon, suss out, trip over, thread the needle. 2. crack the books, megastudy, grind, cram, skull practice, skull drag, dig, bag some food for the brain, cruise a subject, hard-wire (by rote). See STUDY.

LEARNED adj. brain, brainy, sharp, posted, fly, hip, hep, with it, book-smart, all woke up, in the picture, booted on, in the know, know all the answers, technotrash (social idiot), double digs. See KNOWLEDGEABLE.

LEAST adv. at the bottom of the heap, short end of the stick, sticky end of the stick, entry level, low man on the totem pole, low in the pecking order, second fiddle, third stringer, in the gutter. See also LOWEST.

LEAVE interj. fuck off, stay out of my face, shove off, forget you, vamoose, scram, get lost, blow, bite moose, beat it, bug off, make yourself scarce, make like a tree and leave, make tracks, clear out, butt out, screw, shove, take a walk, gomer (get out of my emergency room, Medic.), go chase yourself, scat, go peddle your papers. See GO, INTERJ.

LEAVE n. 1. layoff, eyes to cool it, liberty. See also FURLOUGH. 2. go-ahead, green light, okay, OK. See CONSENT.

LEAVE v. split, I'm history, I'm outta here, I'm out, I'm outtie 5,000, I'm Audi 5000, I'm Audi, color me gone; get on, bread wide, slide (Af. Am.); bolt (quickly), air out, motor, motorvate, sko, le-go (let's go), jet, be-bop, let's blaze, bus one, dip, flex, jamit, do a train, do a ghost, beat it, raise, scram, haul ass, bag ass, barrel ass, cut ass, drag ass, shag ass, trip, hit the road, bop off, fuck off, roll out, bone out, move out, check out, bail out, light out, get lost, get going, git, get git, blow, blow this joint, blow this pop stand, skedaddle, break camp, hoof it, hotfoot, shove off, step off, fade, time to cruise, percolate, make tracks, let the doorknob hit you. See GO.

LEAVETAKING n. swan song.

LEAVINGS n. leftovers, broken arm (table scraps).

LECHER n. letch, lech, old letch, Chester Molester, poon hound, heavy hitter, heavy cake, playboy, player, high liver, nighthawk, night owl, dude, operator, speed, mother, cruiser, smoothie, lookin' to get lucky, lookin' to score, campus butcher, old goat, dirty old man, troll (old), beastmaster (dates ugly women), Mr. Groin, wolf, tomcat, cat, sharp cat, gay cat, alley cat, sport, C.S.P. (casual sex partner), swinger, rake, lover boy, killer, lady-killer, ladies' man, man on the make, on one's tit, make-out artist, chaser, broad chaser, woman chaser, skirt chaser, cunt chaser, tail chaser, cocksman, stick daddy (police), poodle faker, masher, rip, rounder, gay deceiver, gay dog, blade, gay blade, good-time Charlie, hound, whorehound, gash hound, prom trotter, tea hound, bun duster, sailor, Lothario, Don Juan, Casanova, lounge lizard, parlor snake, cake-eater, candy kid, fancy dan, furper, drugstore cowboy.

LECHEROUS adj. raunchy, low-down and dirty, horny, rammy, hot and heavy, cream jeans, a lech on, lechin's, letchin'. See LASCIVIOUS.

LECTURE n. chalk talk, pep talk, pitch, spiel, soapbox oration, skull session. See SPEECH.

LECTURE v. get on a soapbox, spiel, spout. See SPEAK.

LECTURE TOUR n. rubber-chicken circuit, mashed-potato circuit.

LEECH n. freeloader, beat, deadbeat, hanger-on, hose, schnorrer, scab, sponge, sponger. See PARASITE.

LEEWAY n. elbowroom, room to swing a cat.

LEFT-HANDED adj. lefty, leftie, southpaw, portsider, side wheeler.

LEFT LANE n. side door, lane one.

LEGAL adj. legit, kosher, card-carrying, sure enough, honest-to-God, twenty-four carat, all wool and a yard wide, on the legit, on the level, on the up and up, stand up, hold up, hold water, hold together, hang together, hold up in the wash, wash, go, fly, for real, okayed.

LEGAL ACTION n. heat, Twinkie defense (impairment due to eating sweets), rocket docket (fast track for cases).

LEGAL ALIEN n. Green Card, documented.

LEGAL DOCUMENT n. papers.

LEGALIZE v. launder, wash, white money, smurfing (money, title), clean up.

LEGGINGS n. chaps, chaquata (plus jacket).

LEG IRONS n. anklets, boot, bull chain, clinker, Oregon boot, rat shackle, rattler, tracer chain.

LEGISLATE v. put through; jam through, railroad, railroad through, steamroller through (forced).

LEGISLATURE n. House.

LEGITIMATE adj. legit, kosher, on the legit, on the level, on the up and up, front-door, twenty-four-carat, for real, hold up in the wash, honest-to-God. See LEGAL.

LEGITIMIZE v. launder, wash, smurfing (money, title), clean up.

LEGLESS adj. halfy.

LEGS n. gams, gambs, hams, pins, pegs, stems, benders, choppers, drumsticks, hinders, pillars, props, shafts, stilts, sticks, trotters, underpinnings, uprights, hind legs, stumps, wheels, bad wheels (injured or ugly).

LEISURE n. kickback time, chill-out time, goof-off time, fuck-off time, time to burn, time to kill, one's own sweet time. See also REST.

LEMONADE n. lemo, forty-one.

LEND v. knock (Af. Am.), lay on one, shark, loan shark, piece one off, stake. See LOAN.

LENDER n. shark, loan shark, shylock, shy, soft touch, uncle (pawnbroker).

LENDING INSTITUTION n. damper, jay, jug.

LENGTHEN v. drag out, drag one's feet, spin out, stretch out, put some rubber in it. See also EXPAND.

LENIENT adj.   go easy with, go easy on, be big, live with, soft-shell. See COMPASSIONATE.

LEOPARD n.   cat, spots.

LESBIAN n.   les, lez, lezzie, lesbine, lesbie, lesbo, dyke, bull dyke, bull dagger, diesel dyke, butch, crested hen (butch), bitch, boondagger, daisy, fairy lady, Amy, bird, gal officer, marge, lady lover, female-identified, female-oriented, crunchies, lipsticks, fem, femme, finger artist, rug muncher, double-barreled broad, shemale, harpie, Jasper, sergeant, top sergeant (all Derog.).

LESSEN v.   cut back, roll back, downsize, leblang (theater ticket price), soft-pedal, take the bite out, take the edge off, take the sting out. See REDUCE.

LESSER adj.   bush-league, low in the pecking order, low man on the totem pole, bottom man on the totem pole, bottom man, bottom sawyer, second-fiddle, second-string, third-string, a notch under. See INFERIOR.

LESSON n.   chalk talk, skull session.

LET v.   sit still for, give the go-ahead, give the green light, okay, OK, be big, hear of, live with, suck it up, free up. See PERMIT.

LETHARGIC adj.   laid-back, blah, blahs, dopey, drippy, draggy, nebbish, wimpy, moony, sleepyhead, on the nod, snoozy, stretchy, out of it, have spring fever, June around. See LANGUID.

LETTER n.   line, memo, junk mail, drop a line, thank-you note, Dear John, dead (not deliverable), kite, cannonball, scratch, stiffo, sugar report (love), mash note, tab, tag, poison-pen letter (malicious, obscene, etc.).

LETTER WRITER n.   pen pal.

LETTUCE n.   rabbit food, grass, leaves, keep off the grass (no lettuce).

LEVELHEADED adj.   together, got it together, cool, cool as a cucumber, have horse sense, commonsensical, all there, in one's right mind, got all one's marbles.

LEVERAGE n.   edge, break, juice, clout, drag, pull, suction, ropes, weight, bring in the heavy artillery, have a jump on, have a leg up on, bargaining chip, ace in the hole, fix, grease, wire, loose change (temporary). See ADVANTAGE. See also INFLUENCE.

LEVITY n.   grins, laughs, lots of laughs, high old time, picnic, hoopla, whoopee. See also AMUSEMENT.

LEWD adj.   filthy, dirty, blue, X-rated, raw, hard-core, soft-core, stag, hot, hot stuff, rough, evil-minded, foul-mouthed, flaming (Obsc., computer conversations), off-color, low-down and dirty, purple; hot pants. See OBSCENE.

LIABILITY n.   tab, bad news, damage, bite, chit, IOU, in the red, nut, below the line, baggage. See DEBT.

LIAISON n.   go-between, cutout (secret intermediary), fixer, connection, in, interface.

LIAR n.   jive-ass, jive turkey, phony, long nose, shady, promoter, con artist, con man, con merchant, conner, crap merchant, oil merchant, bullshitter, bullshit artist, burn notice (warning that a person is a liar).

LIBEL v.   give one a black eye, blister, roast, scorch, crack, knock, mark lousy, mark wrong, bad-mouth, do one dirt, put the hooks in, put the needles in, put the zingers in, slag, drag one's name through the mud, sizzle. See SLANDER.

LIBELER n.   knocker, mudslinger, backbiter.

LIBERAL adj.   1. big, be big, bighearted, have a heart, heart in the right place, softie, soft touch, loose, Santa Claus, good Joe, prince of a person, free-and-easy, casual. 2. dime a dozen, aplenty, galore, no end, no end in sight, stink with. See PLENTY. 3. left of center, L-word, left, lefty, lefto, left-winger, New Left, Old Left, pink, pinko, parlor pink, radish, fellow traveler, linky dink, bleeding heart, do-good-er, innocent (Af. Am.), knee-jerk reaction, commie, com-symp, hippie, yippie, radiclib, red, rim, underground, Wobbly.

LIBERATE v.   free up, bail one out, get out from under, save one's bacon, save one's neck, save one's ass. See FREE.

LIBERTINE n.   1. playboy, player, poon hound, night-hawk, cruiser, letch, wolf, hound tomcat, alley cat, cunt chaser, cocksman, rounder, sailor. 2. pushover, round heels, easy woman, scrump queen, road whore, sleaze bucket, sleazebag, hosebag, chippy, floozy, tramp, slut, charity girl, run-around, floss-around, piece of trade, pigmeat (old). See LECHER.

LIBERTY n.   run, run of, free run of.

LIBIDINOUS adj.   heavy, horny, hot, hot and heavy, rammy, lechy, a lech on. See LASCIVIOUS.

LIBRARY n.   zoo (Stu.), lib, libe, Phi Beta House.

LIBRETTO n.   book.

LICE n.   cooties, bugs, crabs, crotch pheasants, walking dandruff, bugs in the rug (pubic), seam squirrel.

LICENSE n.   1. go-ahead, green light, okay, OK. 2. ticket (maritime). See CONSENT.

LICENSE PLATE n.   plates, pad, pads, marker, tags.

LICENTIOUS adj.   fast, fast and loose, fast and loose with, drive in the fast lane with no brakes, high-living, speedy, high liver, swinger. See DISSOLUTE.

LIE n.   jive, line of jive, jazz, fib, whopper, bunk, bull, shit, pile of shit, piece of shit, bullshit, BS, bullchitna (Esk.), bulldog, horseshit, horse manure, horse hocky, hocky, shit for the birds, crap, crapola, crock, crock of shit, lip gloss, 180 out (Mil.), claptrap, hooey, hokum, balls, yarn, story, tall story, fish story, cock-and-bull story, cock and bull, tall tale, fairy tale, baloney, malarkey, banana oil, ball, thick, thin, con, cover, cover-up, smoke, string, line, line of cheese, marmalade, spinach, applesauce, tripe, vanilla, garbage, hogwash, doesn't wash, taradiddle, dirty lie, terminological inexactitude, borax, dog it, song, song and dance, no such animal, the big lie (Pol.).

LIE v. scam, jive, shuck and jive, maple stick jive, bull, shit, bullshit, shovel the shit, string along, soft-soap, snow, fudge, jazz, con, play, trip, promote, blow smoke up one's ass, schmear, queer, goof on, jeffin', talking out of one's neck, lead up the garden path, put on, put on an act, frontin', put up a front, put on a false front, fake, fake it, hoke up, frame, frame up, plant, phony up, put up a bluff, four-flush, lie through one's teeth, make believe, make like, let on, let on like, play possum, talk trash, build up, pass, signify, gammon, tell a little white lie, talk through one's hat, speak with forked tongue, cram, doctor, cook, deacon, duff, flaking, load, salt, salt a mine.

LIE DETECTOR n. flutterer, go on the box (take test).

LIEUTENANT (ARMY) n. looie, looey, loot, lieut, lute, shavetail, gold brick, jeeter, john, first john, second john, 1st looie, 1st looey, 2nd looie, 2nd looey, ninety-day wonder, tent Johnny.

LIEUTENANT COLONEL n. light colonel.

LIEUTENANT JG (NAVY) n. first luff, one-and-a-half striper, two-striper.

LIFE n. rat race, the big game, world, the real world, journey, hand (one is dealt).

LIFE JACKET n. Mae West.

LIFELESS adj. draggy, blah, dull as dishwater, flat, flat as a pancake, ho-hum, nothing, pablum, zero. See INSIPID. See also DEAD.

LIFE PRESERVER n. Mae West, water wings.

LIFETIME n. all one's born days, womb to tomb, cradle to the grave.

LIFT n. leg, leg up, boost. See SUPPORT.

LIFT v. bring up, build up, fetch up, boost, goose, goose up, hike, hike up, jack up, jump up, put up. See ASSIST.

LIFT WEIGHTS v. pump iron, press, press weights, bench-press.

LIGHT adj. perky, chipper, chirpy, corky, lite up, upbeat, upper, high, sunny, sunny side up. See CHEERFUL.

LIGHT n. 1. dimmer, glim; foots, jewelry, spot, juniors, babies, kliegs (Pl.). 2. flash, bitch, bitch lamp (hobo), gump light (miner), birdcage, bug, bug torch, hay burner (R.R.).

LIGHT v. hit with a spot, hit with a light, hit with a beam, spot, spotlight, limelight, highlight.

LIGHTEN v. take a load off, take a load off one's mind, take a load off one's chest.

LIGHTHEADED adj. rocky, gaga, woozy, punchy, the room going around.

LIGHTHEARTED adj. laid-back, feel-good, high wide and handsome. See BUOYANT.

LIKABLE PERSON n. ace, Mr. Nice, nice guy, right guy, good dude, good head, good egg, good Joe, Joe Nice Guy, one-way ghee, sweet, sweetheart, sweetie, sweetie pie, pussycat, prince, prince of a fellow, regular fellow, a real butt-kicker, after one's own heart, salt of the earth.

LIKE adj. double, look-alike, like two peas in a pod, six of one and half a dozen of the other, spit and image, spittin' image. See SAME.

LIKE v. 1. go for, fall for, be sprung on, goof on, have eyes for, big eyes for, have a thing about, stuck on, have a case on, take to, take a liking to, take a shine to, cotton to, partial to, hit it off. See LOVE. See also DESIRE; FAVOR. 2. groove on, balling, grok, dig the most, rat fuck, R.F., get some grins, get off on, get high on, flip for, drop the bomb. See ENJOY.

LIKED adj. okay people, touted, highly touted, score, make it with one, rate with one, regular, regular guy, one's kind of guy, one of the boys, babelonia (girl). See also POPULAR.

LIKELIHOOD n. even break, fair shake, fighting chance, fifty-fifty, a coin flip, toss-up, near as one can tell, level playing field, have a shot at, long shot, hundred-to-one shot, outside chance, not a chance in hell, dollars to doughnuts. See POSSIBILITY.

LIKELY adj. like as not, like enough, dollars to doughnuts, a lead-pipe cinch, bet the ranch on it, bet the house on it, bet the rent on it.

LIKEMINDEDNESS n. groupthink.

LIKENESS n. look-alike, work-alike, likes of, ditto, knock-off, xerox, clone, carbon, carbon copy, dead ringer, double, spitting image, peas in a pod, two of a kind, angel (radar), birds of a feather. See COPY.

LIMBO n. nowhere, Siberia, there's no there there (originally said of Oakland, CA), no-man's-land, out there, left field, cold storage, Erewhon, Yemensville, Lower Slobbovia, hell and back.

LIMBS n. gams, pins, stems, drumsticks, hind legs, wheels, bad wheels (injured or ugly). See LEGS.

LIMELIGHT n. center stage. See also CELEBRITY.

LIMIT n. the max, ape, far out, the most, tops, bottom line, bottom out (lower limit), cap, fence.

LIMIT v. ice, cap, keep the lid on, bottle up, cork, cork up, draw the line, hog-tie. See RESTRAIN.

LIMITED OBJECTIVE n. surgical mission.

LIMITLESS adj. wide-open, no end of, no end to, no strings, no holds barred, no joker, no ifs ands or buts, more than you can shake a stick at. See UNLIMITED. See also COUNTLESS.

LIMP n. bad wheels, floppy, gimp, loose, hitch in one's get-along.

LIMP v. gimp.

LINCOLN (CAR) n. boat, pap.

LINEAR adj. on the beam, beeline, as the crow flies, down the alley, down the pipe, in the groove, slam-bang.

LINGER v. hang around, hang out, hang in, hang on, hang about, stick around, monkey around, fool around, fuck around, fuck off, fake off, goof around, goof off, screw off, flub off, flub the dub, rat fuck, R.F., fuck the dog, cool it, cool one's heels, sit on one's ass, sit on one's butt, sit on one's duff, jelly, tool, stall, warm a chair, get noplace fast, poke around, poke along, mosey, toddle, schlep along, potchky (Yid.), piddle-diddle (So.), put on hold. See also DAWDLE.

LINGERER n. hanger-on, foot-dragger, slowpoke, stick-in-the-mud, schlep.

LINGERIE n. briefs, undies, underthings, unmentionables, bra, panties, teddy, nightie, jammies, PJ's. See UNDERWEAR.

LINK n. network, tie-in, in, interface, hookup, contact, connection, channel.

LINK v. 1. network with, interface, plug into, hook up, throw in with, team up with, go in partners, meld with, swing in with, tie in with, mob up. See ASSOCIATE. 2. tack on, tag on, tag along, slap on, hitch on.

LINT n. dust ball, kittens, pussies, dust kitty, dust bunnies, ghost turds, beggar's velvet, slut's wool.

LION n. Leo, big cat.

LIPS n. kisser, chops, rubies.

LIQUID n. juice, bug juice, goo, goop, dope (heavy, such as sauce).

LIQUIDATE v. cash in, cash out. See also KILL.

LIQUID OXYGEN n. lox.

LIQUOR n. hootch, hooch, booze, idiot oil, hard liquor, likker, brown bag (concealed), alky, doctor, antifreeze, squeeze, corn, corn likker, cave corn, moonshine, moon, mountain dew, prairie dew, squirrel dew, red-eye, sauce, rotgut, slop, white, white line, white lightning, chain lightning, Jersey lightning, gray mule, white mule, white horse, potato water, tiger milk, panther, panther piss, panther sweat, tiger sweat, pig sweat, pig iron, scrap iron, gas, drop, wee drop, neat, straight up, on the rocks, medicine, snake medicine, poison, snake poison, rat poison, nightcap, swill, ball, bat and ball, jug, firewater, fogmatic, fog cutter, gargle, mouthwash, short dog (cheap wine in a brown paper bag), dog's nose, hair of the dog, hair of the dog that bit one, pickup, pick-me-up, eye-opener, corpse reviver, donk, heel tap, Kong, King Kong, rerun, smoke, canned heat, third rail, hall, John Hall, high wine (with Coca-Cola), gage, hardware, scat, magic, hospital alcohol, formaldehyde, fluid, embalming fluid, paint remover, varnish remover, shellac, coffin varnish, brush whiskey, bathtub gin, home brew, homespun, nigger pot (Derog.), cooler, juice, A-bomb juice, bug juice, cactus juice, happy juice, joy juice, kick-a-poo joy juice, kick-a-poo juice, torpedo juice, caper juice, Kool-Aid, spot, scrap iron, sheep dip, dehorn, swamp root, blue blazer, boilermaker's delight, bourbon poultice, oil of joy, bottle, boxcar, budge, busthead, conk buster (Af. Am.), forty-rod, boldface, paleface, rumpot, sap, seafood, shine, sneaky pete, stuff, screech, steam, belly wash, catgut, blind tiger, blue run, angel teat, gee, glue, whoopee, giggle bottle, giggle water, giggle-soup (So.), goat hair, google eye, hard stuff, hardware, hop toad, load, popskull (homemade), stiffener, dirty bird (Old Crow), powder ('20s), serum, zombie, finger (amount).

LIQUOR GLASS n. jigger, shot glass, snifter.

LIQUOR STORE n. corn cellar, happy shop, LQ, leeky store (Af. Am.).

LIST n. lineup, drop-dead list (fired, expelled, excluded), laundry list (agenda), enemies list, shitlist, S list, hit list, pap (Annapolis), loop (distribution list). See DIRECTORY.

LIST v. spell out, type-cast, tab, peg, chart, button down, put down as, put down for.

LISTEN v. catch, listen up, pick up, pick up on, tune on, get, get a load of this, get a load of that, are you ready for this?, have an ear cocked, be all ears, give ears, have one's ears on, knock on one's lobes, hear tell. See also OVERHEAR, EAVESDROP.

LISTENING adj. on the earie, on the lake, sails are flapping.

LISTLESS adj. laid-back, blah, blahs, dopey, drippy, draggy, nebbish, wimpy, moony, sleepyhead, on the nod, snoozy, stretchy, out of it, have spring fever, have tired blood, June around.

LITERATURE n. lit, lit course, shrink lits (condensed classics).

LITHUANIAN n. Litvak, Lit, Lugan, Bohawk, Hunk, Hunky (all Derog.).

LITIGATE v. have the law on, law, take the law on, haul into court, drag into court, drag one's ass into court, see one in court, have up.

LITTERER n. litterbug.

LITTLE adj. teeny, teensy-weensy, itsy-bitsy, junior, shrimp, peanut, runt, dinky, two-by-four, half-pint, tad, titch. See SMALL.

LITTLE ROCK, ARKANSAS Rock City, the Rock.

LIVE v. 1. get along, just makin' it, get by. 2. bunk, bunk out, hang out, crash, nest, perch, roost, squat, hang up one's hat, hang up one's shingle, hole up, locate, park. See INHABIT. 3. shack up, shack up with.

LIVELIHOOD n. what one is into, thing, nine-to-five shit, rat race, day gig, beeswax, game, dodge, slot, grind, racket, swindle, grift. See OCCUPATION.

LIVELY adj. jazzed, jacked, jaked, perky, bouncy, chipper, zingy, jumping, hyper, snappy, juiced-up, ball of fire, go-go, full of beans, full of piss and vinegar. See SPIRITED.

LIVEN v. spice, spice up, zip up, zap up, perk up, pep up, juice up, snap up. See ENLIVEN.

LIVER n. sugar factory.

LIVESTOCK n. dogie, longhorn, moo cow, shorthorn, whiteface, stray, dinge (substandard, unbranded). See also COW, BULL.

LIVE TOGETHER v. shack up, shack up with, LT, LTR.

LIVE WELL v. piss on ice, eat high on the hog, on velvet, on a bed of roses, loving life, loving it, live off the fat of the land, have it made.

LIVING adj. alive and kicking, ticking, warm, in the lifestream.

LIVING QUARTERS n. pad, condo, co-op, domi, dommy; cradle, hat (Af. Am.); roof over one's head, hole in the wall, dump, homeplate, turf. See HOUSE.

LIVING TOGETHER, PERSONS n. apartmates, convivante, mingles, LTR.

LOAD n. albatross, albatross around one's neck, excess baggage, schlepper, ball and chain. See HINDRANCE.

LOAD v. top, top off, onload, pile it on, heap on, weigh down, chock, jam-pack, ram in.

LOAF v. bum, bum around, hang out, goof around, knock around, fool around, fuck around, futz around, fuck off, fake off, goof off, rat fuck, R.F., fuck the dog, sit on one's butt, lie down on the job, drag one's ass, drag one's tail, featherbed. See IDLE.

LOAFER n. goof-off, fuck-off, veg, vegetate, slug, house plant, goldbrick, lump, beach bum, drugstore cowboy, good-for-nothin', lazy good-for-nothin'. See IDLER.

LOAN n. on the cuff, on the muscle, on pump, on the arm, on tick, tick, extension (maximum), angel dust, bite, floater, juice (usurious interest), balloon payment (final).

LOAN v. lay on one, piece one off, loan-shark, score, touch, scratch, take (secure a), stake, grubstake, knock (Af. Am.), front-end loading, jawbone, loan out (often refers to film and TV talent under contract).

LOAN COLLECTOR n. juice man, skip tracer.

LOATHE v. have an allergy to, have no use for, allergic to, down on, grossed out on. See DISLIKE.

LOATHSOME adj. sleazy, sleazeball, stinker, sludgeball, wimpy, spastic, funky (Af. Am.), lousy, bad case of the uglies, mutant, gummy, gross, bunk, pail, bucket, cocksucking, it rots, poxy, scurvy, scuzzo, scuzzy, shitsky, shitburger, skewy, shower scum, grody, grody to the max, beastly, slime bucket, maggoty, creepy-crawly, uncool, in one's hat, for the birds, gives one a pain, gives one a pain in the neck, gives one a pain in the ass, pesky, pestiferous, bitchy. See also DESPICABLE.

LOBBY n. squat pad.

LOBBY v. hype, plug, push, sell, hard-sell, high-pressure, soft-sell, sell one on, sweet-talk, soft-soap, pitch, make a pitch for, drum, beat the drum for, thump the tub for, goose, juice, juice up, build up, puff, splash, spot, throw the spotlight on, press agent, ballyhoo, bill, billboard, boost, root for, buttonhole, politick, get behind, egg one on, knock on doors, work on, work over, lean on, hold one's feet to the fire, twist one's arm, put the screws on, put the bee on, put the squeeze on, put on the spot, put on the map, bug, jawbone.

LOBBYIST n. five percenter, hired gun, knife thrower, rainmaker, duck, ollies (oil industry).

LOCAL n. branch, branch house, affil (TV), offshoot; milk run, meat run (trains).

LOCALE n. turf, scene, spot, X marks the spot, neck of the woods, hole, zone.

LOCATE v. 1. pinpoint, scare up, hook, read (radar), zero in, pick up on, hit upon, stumble on, trip over, right under one's nose, uncover, strike (oil, gold), spot, smoke out, smell out, nose out. 2. hang up one's hat, hang up one's shingle, park, dig in.

LOCATION n. spot, X marks the spot, scene, zone, turf, fix, hole, how the land lies, the lay of the land, neck of the woods, pit (racing, gambling).

LOCK v. button, button up, slough, slough up. See also CLOSE.

LOCOMOTIVE n. choo-choo, hog, bull engine, goat (switch), battleship (heavy duty), battlewagon (tender), kettle (small), yard goat. See RAILROAD LOCOMOTIVE.

LODGE v. bunk, bunk out, hang out, crash, nest, perch, roost, squat, hang up one's hat, hang up one's shingle, hole up, locate, park. See INHABIT.

LODGING n. crash pad, digs, crib, diggings, pad; cradle, hat (Af. Am.); roof over one's head, castle, palace, bed and breakfast, dorm, fratority, sorenity, birdcage, bullpen, bullypen, frau shack, henranch, hencoop, quail roost, zoo; motel, shortel (hourly rates), airtel, aquatel, boatel, floatel, chinch pad, flophouse, hooch (Vietnam), scratch crib. See also HOUSE.

LOFT n. sky parlor.

LOFTY adj. high-rise. See also ARROGANT.

LOG n. comic book, funny book, swindle sheet; load of sticks (Pl.).

LOGICAL adj. commonsensical, resonate (that resonates), smitty, hold up, hold water, hold together, hang together, hold up in the wash, wash, fly, legit, kosher, signify, stand up, go, all there.

LOGOTYPE n. logo.

LOITER v. hang around, goof around, jack around, monkey around, rat fuck, R.F., get noplace fast, poke around, patrolling (indecisively, aimlessly). See IDLE.

LOITERER n. goof-off, fuck-off, house plant, goldbrick, slug, schlepper, sleepyhead, beach bum, drugstore cowboy, cake-eater, lounge lizard, couch potato, sofa spud, john, johnny, good-for-nothin', lazy good-for-nothin', stick-in-the-mud. See also DAWDLER.

LOLLIPOP n. sucker, all-day sucker (large).

LONE adj. onliest, stag, solo. See ALONE.

LONELY adj. godforsaken, down, bummed out.

LONG adj. king-size, stretch (car, limo, airplane). See also PROLONGED.

LONG v. yen for, cream for, itch for, hanker for, spoil for, give one's eyeteeth for, wild to, have a case on. See DESIRE.

LONG DISTANCE n. way, ways, far piece, long chalk, a sleeper jump, overland route, clear to hell and gone. See FAR.

LONGEVITY n. in for the long haul, golden age, gray power, the dwindles. See also AGED.

LONGING n. hots, itch, lech, nasties, the urge, sweet tooth, fire in the belly, yen, zazzle. See DESIRE.

LONGSHOREMAN n. dock walloper, roustabout.

LOOK n. flash, gander, gun, gunning over, case, pike, hinge, glom, once-over, the OO, the double O, the eye, squint, slant, lamp, look-see, eyeball inspection, pike, swivel, come-hither look, bedroom eyes, the glad eye, bad eye, whammy, a murder-one look.

LOOK v. flash on, read, lamp, focus, eye, eyeball, lay one's glims on, get a hinge, look-see, scout, put it in cruise mode, give one the eye, give one the cyclops, tumble, rubberneck, give a thing a toss, give it a thumb check, check this out, bus it (Af. Am.), look one up and down, look at one cross-eyed, go slumming, slum, take in the sights. See SEE.

LOOKING GLASS n. gaper.

LOOKOUT n. 1. weather eye, peeled eye, eagle eye, gapper, hawk, spotter, tip, anchor, case, gap, jigger, jigger guy, jigger man, outside man, zex man, lay zex, lay butzo, lay jiggers, lay chickie, gander (criminal, not common). 2. O.P. (observation post), catbird seat. See also GUARD.

LOOK OUT v. 1. gun, peg, scope, spot, spy, eagle-eye, take a hinge, look-see, check out, check something out, case, size up, keep tab, keep tabs on. 2. keep one's eyes peeled, keep a weather eye peeled, peel one's eyeballs, pick up on, ride shotgun for, shotgun, burn up. See SEE.

LOOKS n. cut of one's jib, phiz. See COUNTENANCE.

LOOMING adj. in the cards, in the wind, at hand, see it coming, looking to, the noose is hanging, the handwriting is on the wall.

LOOPHOLE n. fine print, small fine print, small fine print at the bottom, out, kicker (one that negates work, contract, etc.).

LOOSE adj. 1. out of control. See DISSOLUTE. 2. high liver, nighthawk, night owl, playboy, player, swinger, C.S.P. (casual sex partner), slag, slagheap, hank, operator, speed.

LOOT n. goods, hot goods, hot items, take, graft, swag, squeeze, boodle, make, pickings, flapjacks (somoli).

LOOT v. grab, smash and grab, rip, rip off, boost, lift, loft, kipe, touch, take a five-finger discount (shoplift), snatch, snitch, swipe, salvage, appropriate, liberate, requisition, moonlight requisition, buzz, crab, make, rough off, take, tip over.

LOQUACIOUS adj. long-winded, great talker, yacker, gift of gab, shoots the gab, windjammer, ear-bender, all jaw, flapjaw, motormouth, have verbal diarrhea, diarrhea of the mouth. See TALKATIVE.

LORD n. Dad, Head Knock, Lordy, Man Upstairs.

LORDLY adj. bossy, crack the whip, high and mighty, on one's high horse, throw one's weight around. See ARROGANT.

LOS ANGELES, CALIFORNIA L.A., Ellay, Los, LaLa Land, Lotusland, City of the Angels, Angel City, Shaky

City, Dodger Town, 40 suburbs in search of a city (1950), the Coast.

LOS ANGELES RESIDENT n. Angeleno, Angelena, Angelino, Angelina, Angel.

LOSE v. take the gas, bomb, get creamed, bite the big one, blow it, get blown out, get dogged, get used, crap out, boff out, lose out, be taken to the cleaners, drop, drop a bundle (money), go tits up, bite the dust, take the count, take a bath, take a splash, blow, kiss good-bye, pump up (gambling), drawing dead, come out on the short end of the stick, come out with the short end of the stick, take the heat, be bumped (reservation). See FAIL.

LOSE CONSCIOUSNESS v. pass out, conk out, zonk out, keel over, black out, go out like a light.

LOSE CONTROL v. lose it, come unglued, come unzipped, schiz out, psych out, flip, flip out, go ape, go bananas, go to pieces, come apart, freak out, spazz, spazz out, blow a hype, blow one's cool, have a fit, have a hemorrhage, have a shit hemorrhage, hit the panic button, push the panic button. See also CRAZY, GO.

LOSE ONE'S NERVE v. choke, choke up, psyched out.

LOSER n. also-ran, neverwuz, fall guy, deadbeat, jive turkey, turkey, down-and-outer, caught the brass ring, can't even get arrested, can't even write home for money, can't punch his way out of a paper bag, scrub, dag, flunkee. See FAILURE.

LOSING adj. hurting, cold, dumping, in, into, in for, pump up, wicked, down.

LOSS n. 1. red ink, fall, beating, trimming, shellacking, trashing, clobbering, walloping, shutout, disaster, roof fell in (sudden), flunk, get one's lumps, shuck, total shuck, total loss, come down. See DEFEAT. 2. skunk costs, bundle, package, in the red, red ink (all Pl.).

LOST adj. 1. bushed (in forest), going in circles, don't know which way is up, running by the seat of one's pants. 2. out the window, down the tube, down the toilet, down the drain, down the spout, down the rathole, kiss something good-bye, fall between the cracks.

LOT n. break, breaks, karma, in the cards, the beads, that's the way the beads read, that's the way the cookie crumbles, shit happens, run of luck, hand (one is dealt). See DESTINY.

LOTTERY n. the numbers, the numbers game.

LOUD adj. leather-lunged, booming, cranked, turned up, ear-splitting, ear-poppin', wake up the dead, can't hear oneself think, jumpin', yakky, pump it up (turn up the volume).

LOUDSPEAKER n. P.A., speaker, tweeter, woofer, squawk box, hog caller.

LOUISIANA Lousy Anne, Creole State, Pelican State, Sugar State.

LOUISIANAN n. Pelican.

LOUISVILLE, KENTUCKY Derbyville, Derby Town.

LOUNGE n. 1. squat pad. 2. dive, spot, joint, juke joint, juice joint, after-hours joint, snake ranch, fleshpot, gargle factory, meat market (singles bar), taproom; meat rack, gay bar (homosexual); water hole, beaver palace, candy store, fern bar, fernie, fillmill, grog mill, guzzery, guzzlery, hideaway, room, rum room. See also BAR.

LOUSE n. cootie, cutie, grayback, seam squirrel, cootie garage (hair puffs in which louse lives).

LOVE n. amore, mash, pash, weakness, case, crash, crush, yen, mad pash, mad for, crazy for, wild for, spoiling for, itch for, hankering, partial to, shine, beaver fever, hot pants, the hots, turn on, calf love, puppy love.

LOVE v. gone on, far gone on, sprung on, groove on, get high on, goof on, freak out on, hipped on, mad on, mad for, mad about, daffy about, wild to, wild for, wild about, crazy about, crazy over, crazy for, queer for, letch, letch for, nuts about, keen, keen on, keen about, have a thing about, wacky about, for, moon for, die over, sweet tooth, sweet on, stuck on, have a case on, have a crush on, have a mash on, have eyes for, have it bad, got it bad, have it for one, be serious, be smitten, that way, carry the torch for, torching, take to, take a liking to, take a shine to, cotton to, partial to, hit it off, wrapped up in, nose open, rings my bell, go for, hot for, have the hots for, have hot pants for, hard-on for, jones for, wide-on (female), cream for, yen, yen for, itch, itch for, hanker for, fall for, big eyes for, spoil for, give a shit for, give one's kingdom in hell for, give one's eyeteeth for, have one's mouth fixed for, struck by lightning.

LOVE AFFAIR n. 1. affair, a relationship, Roman spring (late in life), thing. 2. hanky-panky, nooner, matinee, tip, tip-out, extracurricular activity, extracurricular sex, extracurricular relations, your place or mine? See also AFFAIR.

LOVE, IN adv. gone, gone on, far gone on, sprung on, hipped on, stuck on, sweet on, wild about, mad about, crazy about, nuts about, gaga about, keen about, struck by lightning, moonstruck, took a fancy to, took a shine to, cottoned to, goofy, goofy about, wrapped up in, smitten, fell for, has a thing about, has a thing for, has one's nose open, head over heels, hooked.

LOVE LETTER n. mash note, Billy-do.

LOVELY adj. drooly, dishy, drop-dead gorgeous, whistle bait, daisy, mink, stone, stone fox, foxy, head rush, scrumptious, stunner, delicious, beaut, living doll, knockout, picture. See BEAUTIFUL.

LOVE POTION n. love drug, popper, Spanish fly, turn-on, wampole.

LOVER n. old lady, squeeze, main squeeze, main dude, main man, scam, ace lane, hamma, wrap, mama, sweet mama, sweet papa, sweet back (Af. Am), daddy, significant other, nectar, gooey nectar, jelly roll, total babe, back-door man, armpiece. See SWEETHEART.

LOW adj. 1. dragged, ass in a sling, dick in the dirt, blue, down, down in the dumps, down and out, down in the mouth, low-down, singing the blues, buggin', in the pits, mopey, sad-sacky. See DEPRESSED. 2. gross, grody, grody to the max, crumb, creep, turd, heel, shitheel. See OFFENSIVE. 3. blue, off-color, off time. See OBSCENE.

LOWBROW adj. from hunger, galout, ignoramus, peasant.

LOWER adj. bush-league, not hold a candle to, low in the pecking order, low man on the totem pole, second-fiddle, second-string, poor man's something or one, lower-rung. See INFERIOR.

LOWER v. cut back, roll back, downsize, low-ball, leblang (ticket price, The.). See REDUCE. See also DEMOTE, BELITTLE.

LOWER CLASS n. peasants, lower cut, the great unwashed, riffraff.

LOWEST adj. the pits, cellar, bottom dollar, bottom rung, bottom man, rock bottom, entry level (job), low man on the totem pole, scraping the bottom of the barrel. See also LEAST.

LOW-FIDELITY adj. low-fi.

LOW LIFE n. sleazeball, crud, gone to bad, gone to the dogs, gone to hell. See VILLAIN.

LOW-MINDED adj. dirty, dirty-minded, dirty old man, mind in the gutter. See also VULGAR.

LOW PRICED adj. low-cost, low-budget, buy, steal, real steal, cost nothing, cost next to nothing, dirt cheap, cheap as dirt, dog cheap, cheapie, el cheapo, cut-rate, low-tariff, dime-a-dozen, price is right, more bang for the buck, bought for a song.

LOYAL adj. on one's side, true blue, true believer, oncer, string along with, yellow dog, dyed in the wool, behind one, ace in, ace through, come through, stand up for one, faithful but not blind.

LSD n. acid, acido, the chief, big chief, cresto, tru, pellet, paper, vitamin A, animal crackers, luggage, cid, sid, delysid, outer, Raggedy Ann, T, tee, the hawk, candy, cube, trip, ticket, LSD-25, 25, cap, flight, big D, coffee, instant Zen, Zen, peace, sugar, sugar lump, sunshine, California sunshine, Hawaiian sunshine, sunshine pill, orange, orange mushroom, orange wedges, wedges, orange sunshine, yel-low sunshine, yellow, mellow yellow, pink, pink swirl, purple flats, purple haze, purple microdots, blue acid, blue cheer, blue splash, royal blue, blue flag, blue heaven, blue mist, strawberry fields, gelatin, white lightning, clear light, haze, contact lens, Owsley's, Owsley acid, paper acid, flake acid, domes, dots, microdots, brown dots, cherry top, chocolate chips, flats, Lucy in the Sky with Diamonds, pearly gate, barrels, blotters, frogs, lids, windowpanes, tab.

LSD, USE v. baby sit, copilot, guide (guide one on a trip); experience, trip, head trip; echoes (lingering effect).

LUBRICATE v. grease the wheels, lube, slick, slick on.

LUBRICATION n. grease job, lube, lube job.

LUCID adj. all there, cool, together, got one's head together, in one's right mind. See REASONABLE.

LUCIFER n. the debbil, the Deuce, the Dickens, Old Harry, Old Nick, Old Ned, Old Horny, Old Scratch, Old Gooseberry, Old Bendy, Old Clootie, Old Poker, the Old Gentleman.

LUCK n. Dame Fortune, Lady Luck, run of luck, streak of luck, luck out, lucked out, luck into, lucky strike, lucky scratch, lucky hit, lucky break, break, breaks, big break, good break, mojo (Af. Am.), fluke, mazel, mazeltov (good), snowball chance, fifty-fifty, toss-up, shit happens, karma, the beads, in the cards, in the lap of the gods, that's the way the ball bounces, that's the way the cookie crumbles, that's the way (any number of things).

LUCK, BAD n. tough luck, rotten luck, snakebit, shit out of luck, S.O.L., tough shit, TS, shit happens, can't even get arrested, up against it, payin' dues, up shit creek, double whammy, bad break, bugaboo. See ADVERSITY.

LUCKY adj. hot, hot hand, on a roll, on a streak; all the way live, mojo (Af. Am.); jammy, luck in, luck out, fall into the shithouse and come up with a five-dollar gold piece, get a break, get the breaks, hold aces, turn up trumps, strike oil, strike it rich, strike it lucky, make a lucky strike, golden, hit it, hit it big, lucky dog, all systems go, in the groove, everything's coming up roses, everything going for one; greasing it out, sleazeball, sleazing (tennis shots); door sign, into something.

LUCRATIVE adj. sweet, cash cow, in the black, paid off, off the nut, cost-effective.

LUGGAGE n. bags, carry-on, fortnighter, gear, two-suiter, garment bag, duffle, duffle bag, jiffy bag, keister, valpack, tote, tote bag, meter, peter, slough, swag bag, A & P suitcase (grocery bag used to hold clothing), turkey, things.

LULL n. break, coffee break, break-off, breather, breathing spell, downtime, letup, time out, layoff.

LULL v. cool, cool out, cool it, cool off, stroke, pour oil on troubled waters, take the edge off, take the bite out, take the sting out of, take it easy, lay back, soft-pedal, put the lid on. See PACIFY.

LUMBER n. load of sticks.

LUMBERING adj. clunky, clunker, two left hands, two left feet, clodhopper, stumblebum, galoot, goaty (Army), goof ball, lead-footed, walrus, klutz, klutzy. See CLUMSY.

LUMINAL PILL n. purple heart.

LUMP n. chunk, gob, goose egg, hickey, hump, hunk, knot, konk.

LUNAR MODULE n. LEM, LM.

LUNAR ROVER n. lunar limo, rover, moon car, moon crawler.

LUNATIC n. dingaling, kook, zip, flake, whacko, screwball, head case, screwloose, schitzo, psycho, freak, nut, nutsy Fagan, have a lug nut loose, nutcake, fruitcake, banana truck, crackpot, crazy old coot, loon, cuckoo, meshuga, meshugana, squirrel, yo-yo, goof, scatterbrain, lamebrain, a case, snap case, sickie, section 8.

LUNATIC adj. dippy, dingy, kooky, flaky, wacko, bent, loco, loc, screwy, schitzy, schizzed-out, schitzoid, psycho, psyched-out, freaked-out, flipped-out, out of one's tree, baked, totally baked, bananas, bonkers, gone ape, off one's rocker, missing a few buttons, lost one's marbles, batty, crazier than a bedbug. See CRAZY.

LUNATIC ASYLUM n. booby hatch, funny farm, nuthouse, rubber room, soft walk. See INSANE ASYLUM.

LUNCH v. do lunch, do the lunch thing, brown-bag it, grab a bite, take a break, put on the feedbag, brunch (late morning); power lunch, working lunch (Bus.).

LUNCH BOX n. nose bag, brown bag.

LUNCH COUNTER n. fast food, quick and dirty, short order, Coney Island. See also RESTAURANT.

LUNGS n. air bags, wind bags.

LURE n. draw, bait, mousetrap, shill, tout, B girl, come-on, come-on man, deek, nark, plant, sitting duck, vamp, hook, sweetening, sweetener, puffer, humbug. See also INVITATION, BRIBE.

LURE v. pull, grab, draw, bait, mousetrap, shill, steer, tout, drag, turn on, turn one on, hit on, sound on, come on, deek, plant, come on to one, give one the come-on, give one a come-hither look, make a hit with, sweep off one's feet, vamp, hook, bat one's eyes at, bat the eyes at, make with bedroom eyes, suck in, rope in, humbug, chum (fishing).

LURID adj. blue, dirty, purple, low-down, and dirty, off-color, rough, salty, raunchy. See OBSCENE.

LUSCIOUS adj. delish, grinds, yummy, yummy in the tummy, nummy, divine, heavenly, scrumptious.

LUST n. hots, hot pants, bag, itch, in heat, lech, nasties, the urge, yen, yen-yen, big eyes, zazzle, weakness, fire in the belly, the munchies (food). See DESIRE.

LUSTFUL adj. horny, heavy, hot, hot and heavy, hot pants, turned-on, cream jeans, a lech on, letchin'; hot stuff, filthy, dirty, raunchy, raw, evil-minded, low-down. See LASCIVIOUS.

LUXURIATE v. live high on the hog, live off the fat of the land, live it up, live on easy street, put on the dog, put on the Ritz.

LUXURIOUS adj. luxo, plush, plushy, posh, uptown, upscale, ritzy, swanky, fancy, first-cabin, ultra-ultra, far out, way out, too much, too-too, high, high on the hog, with all the extras, splendiferous, splendacious, done to the nines. See also WEALTHY, LAVISH, MAGNIFICENT.

LUXURY n. lap of luxury, velvet, bed of roses, clover, the life of Riley, Easy Street, high on the hog, living high on the hog, on top of the heap, egg in one's beer, frill, frills, icing on the cake.

LYING adj. double-crossing, snake in the grass, two-faced, two-timing jive-assed, sincere, cry crocodile tears.

LYNCH v. stretch, string up, swing, catch rope, dance, go through the trap, hoist, scrag, top, be crooked.

LYNCHING n. necktie party, necktie social, necktie sociable, Texas cakewalk, hemp fever.

LYSERGIC ACID DIETHYLAMIDE n. acid, candy, cube, trip, ticket, LSD, LSD-25, 25, cap, flight, big D, coffee, instant Zen, Zen, peace, sugar, sugar lump, i.acido, the chief, big chief. See LSD.

LYSERGIC ACID, USE v. trip, head trip, fly, experience, on a ride, blow one's mind; guide (guide one on a trip), copilot, baby-sit, trip-sit; free trip, echoes (lingering effect).

LYSERGIC ACID USER n. acidhead, acid dropper, acid user, cubehead, Explorer's Club.

M

M n. Mike.

MACABRE adj. spooky, spookish, scary.

MACARONI n. worms, makko, dago (Derog.).

MACHIAVELLIAN adj. smooth, smarts, street smarts, streetwise, foxy, crazy like a fox, cagey, fancy footwork, full of fancy footwork, slick, slippery, a little gamesmanship, one-upmanship, sly-boots. See also SHREWD.

MACHINATE v. trump up, frame up, come up with, hatch, mastermind, finagle, promote, wangle, yank one, play games, pull strings, pull wires. See SCHEME.

MACHINATION n. hanky-panky, monkey business, gamesmanship, one-upmanship, song and dance, skulduggery, on the make, dirty work, sellout, double shuffle. See also SCHEME.

MACHINATOR n. operator, mastermind, brain, pusher, driver, finagler, wangler, wire-puller, carpetbagger, velcroid (sticks to important people).

MACHINE n. contraption, gadget, widget, job, jobby, dealie bob, sucker, mother, motherfucker, thingumabob, gasser, hootenanny, wingding, coil, clunker. See APPARATUS.

MACHINE GUN n. Uzi, tommy, tommy gun, chopper, ack-ack, mack 10, chatterbox, grease gun (submachine gun), lead typer, Chicago piano (Thompson), typewriter, Remington.

MACHINE-GUN BULLET n. hemstitch, B.B., beebee.

MACHINE GUNNER n. tommy, tommy man, MG.

MACHINERY n. hardware.

MACKINTOSH n. mack, Fog, slicker.

MAD adj. ding-a-ling, kooky, flaky, whacko, head-case, screwball, screwloose, schitzy, schizzed out, schitzoid, bent, psycho, psyched-out, flipped one's wig, crackers, nuts, nutsy Fagan, have a lug nut loose, tetched, cutting out paper dolls. See CRAZY.

MADAM n. aunt, Aunt (brothel).

MADDENING adj. 1. uncool, bugs one, weenie, pain in the neck, pain in the ass, too much, from hell, pesky. See ANNOYING. 2. frantic, wild, cool, real cool, zero cool, mean, mind-blowing, mind-bending, gone, real gone. See EXCITING.

MADHOUSE n. booby hatch, banana factory, funny farm, loony bin, bughouse, nuthouse, crazy house, warehouse, nut college, nut farm, zoo. See LUNATIC ASYLUM.

MADLY adv. like crazy, like mad, something fierce, something terrible, flaky, helter-skelter, holus-bolus, hurry-scurry, ramble scramble.

MAFIA n. mob, family, famiglia, Cosa Nostra, mafiosi, mafioso, IBM (Italian Business Man), goombahs, outfit, syndicate, gang, Black Hand, wiseguys, goodfellas, made members (members). See also GANGSTER.

MAGAZINE n. mag, zine, fan mag, fanzine (fan magazine), teenzine, slick, glossy, pulp, joint, limb joint, sheet, rag, throwaway, fag mag, stag mag, skin mag, magalog.

MAGIC n. hocus-pocus, mumbo-jumbo, hoodoo, voodoo, evil eye, stink-eye, go, jinx, whack, whammy, abracadabra.

MAGISTRATE n. beagle, beak, bench nibs, Blackstone, Father Time, gavel jockey, hard rapper, monk, wig, hanging judge.

MAGNANIMITY n. heart, all heart.

MAGNANIMOUS adj. softie, soft touch, big, be big, all heart, bighearted, have a heart, heart in the right place, loose, Santa Claus, good Joe, prince of a person.

MAGNATE n. tycoon, fat cat, the money, big butter-and-egg man, baron, robber baron. See also BUSINESSMAN.

MAGNIFICENT adj. killer, it's to die for, magnif, magnifico, mean, splendiferous, splendacious, aggro, def, plush, posh, swanky, sooper-dooper, splashy, splurgy, super, super-duper, supercolossal, fab, fat, mongo, lampin', cool, chilly most, cherry, deffest, dope, dual, fat, fierce, fresh, stupid fresh, a gas, fully on, fully, fully to the skull, epic, mint, nitro, on the strength, raw, sick, marvy, unreal, nifty, something, something else, smashing, doozie, dyno, dynamite, mad, man-sized, evil, wicked, pip, solid gold, tidy, tits, tuff, spiffy, bang-up, ace-high, swell, stunning, out-of-sight, out of this world, like all-get-out.

MAGNIFY v. beef up, pad, pyramid, boost, figure in, hike, hike up, step up, jack up, jump up, run up, up, build up, puff up, blow up, make a federal case out of, snowball, sweeten, sweeten the pot, add fuel to the fire.

MAID n. cleaning lady, cleaning woman, woman, girl, help, live-in, tweeny, pillow puncher, biddy, slavey, cabin girl (chambermaid).

MAIDEN n. 1. cherry, canned goods, bug. 2. chick, chicklet, spring chicken, bird, broad, studette (man chaser), doll, jailbait, San Quentin quail, frill, frail, cupcake, granola (wears no makeup), filly, slip, babe, baby. See GIRL.

MAIL CAR n. blind, blind baggage.

MAIL CLERK n. intermodalist (business).

MAIMED adj. gimp, gimpy, crip, game, g'd up, geed up, hamstrung, hogtied.

MAINE Pine Tree State.

MAINE RESIDENT n. Mainiac, Mainer, Down Easter.

MAIN OFFICE n. HQ, GHQ, CP. See also HEAD-QUARTERS.

MAINSTAY n. good right arm, right-hand man, main man, old standby, standby, linchpin.

MAIN STREET n. main artery, main stem, funky Broadway.

MAINTENANCE n. the wherewithal, keep, bread, bread and butter, the bacon, the necessary.

MAJESTIC adj. stunning, killer, cool, fab, marvy, mind-blowing, out-of-sight, clean outta sight, out of this world, smashing, bang-up, ace-high, big splash. See also DIGNIFIED.

MAJOR adj. heavyweight, meaningful, serious shit, serious jelly, matter of life and death, major-league, we're not talking about nutmeg here. 2. major-league, biggie, big player, big chew, big wheel, movers and shakers, top dog, a somebody. See IMPORTANT.

MAJOR n. leaf (Army or A.F.), star.

MAJORITY n. 1. prime, prime of life, dry behind the ears, ripe age, age of consent, drinking age. See MATURITY. 2. big end, big half, lion's share, big end of the stick, max, maxi, the most, the mostest.

MAJOR ROLE n. fat part, lead, star, mover and shaker, key player.

MAKE v. 1. whip up, whip out, whomp up, cook up, dream up, throw up, fab, throw together, fudge together, knock together, knock out, knock off, dash off, tear off. 2. drag down, make a buck, pull, pull down, clear, hustle, rate, sock, turn, bring home the bacon, bring home the groceries, cop, get along, keep the wolf from the door, pay one's dues, be in line for.

MAKE LOVE v. make it, make out, coo, lallygag, lollygag, rock, roll, rock and roll, date, go all the way, juice, juke, bump, bootie, bootie drought (lack of), fuckstrated (frustrated sexually), cook-up with, get down, grab, grab on, grease, hound, fool around, a little heavy breathing, he'n and she'n, fun and games, do it, do the dirty deed, go to bed with, go the limit, get it on, get it off together. See also SEXUAL INTERCOURSE.

MAKESHIFT adj. slapdash, Band-Aid, temp, quick fix, fly-by-night, hit-or-miss, Mickey Mouse, rinky-dink, dink, hugger-mugger, throwaway.

MAKEUP n. drugstore complexion, paint, war paint.

MAKE UP v. 1. ad-lib, play it by ear, impro, improv, gin up, wing it, fake it, off the cuff, dash off, strike off, knock off, toss off, whip up, cook up, whomp up, fudge together. See IMPROVISE. 2. put on one's face, put on one's war paint, powder one's nose, fix up, freshen up.

MAKEUP MAN n. grease pusher.

MALADROIT adj. klutzy, clunky, all thumbs, bogus, ham-fisted, ham-handed, two left hands, two left feet, stumblebum, garbage time. See CLUMSY.

MALADY n. bug, crud, creeping crud, growth, the flu, virus, the runs, what's going around, the pip, willies (mythical), dose, double scrudfantods, fascinoma (rare, Medic.), blue flu (faking it), Asian flu, summer flu, 24-hour flu, 24-hour virus.

MALCONTENT n. bitcher, bellyacher, kvetch, whiner, crab, crank, pill, plainer, sorehead, unhappy camper, nitpicker. See COMPLAINER.

MALE n. dude, nail, pops (Af. Am.), hunk, beauhunk, tuna, Clydesdale (attractive), hoss (muscular), beefcake, man, big man, beef-a-roni, Greek god, demigod, drool over, crushman, papa, macho, jock, caveman, ape, butch, stud, wolf, john, goon, he-man, hombre, shemp (young), animal, bruiser, bozo, tiger. See MAN.

MALEDICTION n. whammy, double whammy, jinx, cuss, cussword, dirty word, dirty name, four-letter word, no-no, swearword, kibosh, hoodoo.

MALEFACTOR n. gorilla, crook, hood, heel, mug, doberman (Af. Am.), bad actor, bad egg, fagin, wrong number, hooligan, strong-arm man, goon, hatchet man. See CRIMINAL.

MALE PARENT n. old man, O.M., dad, daddy, big daddy, daddio, daddums, pa, papa, pappy, pap, pop, pops, poppa, padre, pater, governor, guv, warden.

MALEVOLENT adj. bad-assed, dirty, dank, rough, tough, poison, bum, lousy, murder, murderous, kill-crazy, catty, evil, waspish, snake in the grass, doin' dirt, eighteen-carat, hellish. See MALICIOUS.

MALFUNCTION n. glitch, bug, gremlins.

MALIBU Bu, Maliboo-boo.

MALICIOUS adj. uncool, unhep, unhipped, awful, beastly, bitchy, cussed, mean, ornery, low blow, gross, grody, grody to the max, pesky, pestiferous, funky (Af. Am.), accidentally on purpose, do one dirt, give one a raw deal. See also MEAN.

MALIGN v. smear, roast, rap, take a swipe at, do a number on, mud-sling, run down, run into the ground, rag, rag on, rip on, pop junk, poor-mouth, bad-mouth, peg, slag, rip up the back, give a black eye. See SLANDER.

MALINGER v. fuck off, fake off, goof off, fluff off, flub off, flub, flub the dub, goldbrick, blow off, dog, dog it, fuck the dog, featherbed, lie down on the job, look busy, find Rover (work).

MALINGERER n. fuck-off, goof-off, goldbrick, dog, deadwood, buck passer, clock-watcher, coffee cooler, featherbedder, skimper.

MALL n. strip, podmall (small); mall brat, mall rat (teenager).

MALLEABLE adj. putty in one's hands, go with the flow, roll with the punches, wimpy, wet rag, wet sock, wet noodle. See also SUBMISSIVE.

MALODOROUS adj. rotten, stinky, stinko, strong, high, whiffy, funky, phooey, nosey, lousy, gooky, yechy.

MAN n. dude, guy, nail (Af. Am.), hunk, beauhunk, tuna, Clydesdale (attractive), hoss (muscular), beefcake, industrial, man, big man, beef-a-roni, Greek god, demigod, drool over, crushman, feller, pops, papa, cool papa, daddy, daddio, big daddy, sugar daddy, gent, macho, diesel, jock, caveman, cat, cap, mac, ape, monkey, fox, bub, buster, butch, chap, chappie, animal, stud, stallion, cock, cocksucker (Obsc.), cocksman, rooster, ass man, big lug, jelly roll, wolf, rake, ladies' man, Don Juan, Casanova, Joe, Jack, Joe Blow, Joe Doakes, Joe Zilch, john, poor john (less fortunate), John Doe, Richard Roe, Herman, lounge lizard, cake-eater, cowboy, bucker, buckaroo, clown, cookie, hipster, digger, gate, old softie, old smoothie, customer, goon, mug, colt, duck, gee, hard-leg, hairy, he-man, hombre, two-fisted, crud, cuss, dog, dirty dog, bastard, sidewinder, stiff, storch, wise guy, bum, bummer, bugger, bommer (1930), boilermaker, bruiser, bozo, tiger, apple, applehead, Arab, geezer, geezle, gazebo, ginzo, hairpin, meat, pants, lad, boy, boyo, big boy, Broadway boy (gambler), bo, blade, gay blade, bloke, blood (Af. Am.) bird, brother, prune, cracker, hick (So.), huckleberry, joker, jasper, party, character.

MANACLE v. cuff, put on the cuffs, put on the bracelets.

MANACLES n. bracelets, cuffs, cufflinks, thumbs, darbies, derbies, irons, nippers, slave bracelets.

MANAGE v. 1. fix, finagle, spin, spin control (manage opinion), wangle, yank one, push around, mind-fuck, rig, doctor, cook, plant, con, scam, upstage, jockey, play games, pull strings, pull wires, wire-pull, swing, work, put one on, put one over, put over. 2. head, head up, boss, captain, skipper, helm, herd, shepherd, ride herd on, sit on top of, run, run things, run the show, hold the reins, pull the strings, push the buttons, kick ass, kick butt, mastermind, quarterback, call the shots, call the signals, call the tune, call the play, lay down the law, be in the driver's seat, be in the saddle, pull the strings, pull the wires, pull things together, take over, take the conn, walk heavy, crack the whip, throw one's weight around, have the say, have the say-so, rule the roost, wear the pants, keep under one's thumb, twist around one's little finger, wind around one's little finger. 3. get a handle on something, hack, hack it, get on, get along, come on, come along, cut the mustard, make it, make out, make the grade, make a go of it, live with, truck with, cool down, cool off, handle, deal, deal with, shape up, straighten up, handle.

MANAGEMENT n. front office, execs, executive suite, man upstairs, people upstairs, people in the front office, micromanagement (petty), mainframe management, brass, top brass, head, big brother, bosses, boss class ('30s), shakeup (change). See also EXECUTIVE, ADMINISTRATION.

MANAGER n. head man, old man, boss, suit, top dog, top hand, topkick, digger, the man, boss man, boss lady, straw boss, slavedriver, zookeeper. See EXECUTIVE.

MANDATE n. blank check, carte blanche, go-ahead, green light.

MANDRAKE n. devil's testicle, Satan's apple.

MANEUVER n. fancy footwork, fast shuffle, stunt, angle, play, game, plant, one-upmanship, curve ball, shenanigans. See STRATAGEM.

MANEUVER v. rig, angle, wangle, work, come up with, upstage, doctor, cook, plant, con, scam, mind-fuck, put one on, put one over, jockey, jockey for position, scramble for, yank one, push around, leave holding the bag, operate, play games, pull strings, pull wires, wire-pull, finagle, back and fill, fence. See also PLAN, SCHEME.

MANEUVERABLE REENTRY VEHICLE n. MRV, MERV.

MANIA n. hang-up, jones, have a thing about, have on the brain, grabber, tiger, tiger by the tail, bee, bee in one's bonnet, bug, bug in one's ear, bug up one's ass, bag, ax to grind. See OBSESSION.

MANIAC n. zip, kook, flake, wacko, screwball, schizo, schizoid, psycho, head case, nut, fruitcake, banana truck, crackpot, cuckoo, sickie, section 8. See LUNATIC.

MANIACAL adj. psycho, psyched-out, freaked-out, flipped, out of one's mind, in the ozone, nutty as a fruitcake, off one's trolley, snakes in one's head, non compos mentis, bughouse. See CRAZY.

MANIC adj. high, up, hopped-up, turned-on, freaky, freaked-out, flipped, flipped-out, worked up into a lather. See EXCITED. See also CRAZY.

MANIFEST adj. clear-cut, crystal clear, big as life, open-and-shut, if it were a snake it would bite you, goes without saying, cheesecloth (person), commando (sex), jazzy. See APPARENT.

MANIFEST v. let it all hang out, flash, sport, showcase, show and tell, parade one's wares, strut one's stuff, wave it around. See DISPLAY.

MANIPULATE v. spin control (opinion), mind-fuck, finagle, message, push around, upstage, jockey, play games, pull strings, pull wires, yank one, wind around one's little finger. See MANAGE.

MANLY adj. macho, he-man, hunk, beauhunk, industrial, Cholo, Diesel, Clydesdale (attractive), hoss (muscular), beefcake, stud, beef-a-roni, Greek god, demigod, drool over, crushman, jock, jockstrap, two-fisted, caveman, bucko, hairy, jelly roll, tiger, colt, chrismo, chismo. See FEARLESS. See also MAN.

MANNERED adj. campy, camp around, frontin' (Af. Am.), artsy, artsy-crafty, artsy-fartsy, chichi, putting on the dog, putting on the ritz, ritzy, stuck up, airish, crooker, pinky crooker, highfalutin, ham, gone Hollywood, play the ———, put the hat on. See PRETENTIOUS.

MANNERS n. P's and Q's, minding one's p's and q's.

MAN OF ACTION n. go-getter, hustler, ball of fire, live wire, powerhouse, workaholic, beaver, eager beaver, operator, big-time operator, BTO, wheeler-dealer, new broom, take-charge guy, spark plug, mover and shaker, human dynamo, busy bee.

MANSERVANT n. man, man Friday, boy, number one boy, pratt boy, flunky, houseman, houseboy. See also SERVANT.

MANUAL n. bible, cookbook (chem lab).

MANUAL LABOR n. grind, daily grind, grindstone, the salt mines, gruntwork (Army), scutwork, donkeywork, hemo jo (hard labor), shitwork, chickwork (household), elbow grease; rank and file, blue collar. See WORK.

MANUFACTURE v. throw together, knock together, fudge together, fab, prefab, cobble up, cook up, trump up, whomp up, throw up, knock up, whip up, put out.

MANUFACTURER n. garmento (clothing).

MANURE n. shit, horseshit, cowshit, lawn dressing, meadow muffins, road apples, alley apples, golden apples, buffalo chips, cow chips, cow flops, cow pats, turd, moose beans, moose nuggets, moose pecans.

MANUSCRIPT n. ms., script, pages.

MANY adj. umpteen, jillion, loads, rafts, whole slew, gobs, scads, mess, heaps, bags of, oodles, lousy with, no end of, bokoo, boku. See AMOUNT, LARGE.

MAPLE SYRUP n. alamagoozlum.

MAR v. ding, tweak, bend the goods, fuck up, foul up, mess up, rough up, shake up, screw up, louse up, hash up, muck up, crumb, crumb up, queer. See DAMAGE.

MARBLES n. migs, mibs, cat's eye, aggies, canicks, shooters, commy (cheap glass), immies, peewees, pottrie, purey, real.

MARCH v. hoof it, drill, boot, boot it, stomp, pound the pavement, move out, stump it, traipse, traipse around, strut one's stuff. See WALK.

MARGARINE n. marge, oleo, hard oil.

MARGIN n. elbowroom, leeway.

MARGINAL adj. on the bubble.

MARIJUANA n. pot, grass, joint, reefer, endo, boom, skunk, chocolate tide, indigo, tropicana, chronic, blunt (hollowed out cigar filled with marijuana), reefer weed, weed, lone weed, bud, chronic, Budd, Ty bud, endica bud, trom (student use), viper's weed, ragweed, killer weed, organic stuff, hash, shit, hooch, hemp, jay, roach, Mary, Mary Jane, Mary Anne, Mary Wanna, Mary Warner, Mary and Johnnie, discipline, greefo, griefo, grefa, grafa, greapha, ganga, gangi, gank (Af. Am.), sinsemilla, sinse, sense, sense bud, hay, Indian hay, alfalfa, mezz, the mighty mezz, cheese, Thai stick, Mexican red, Mexican brown, Cam, Cambodian red, Panamanian red, Panama red, Colombian red, Colombian, Colombian gold, Acapulco gold, Panama gold, Santa Marta gold, African black, Jersey green, golden leaf, Maui-wowee, A-bomb, love blow, bambalacha, Margarita, Marjorie, bammy, Michoacán, black gungeon, black gunny, black mo, black moat, brick, broccoli, tosca, charas, yedo, jeeba, Durban poison (So. Africa), dirt grass, Hawaiian, iceberg, icepack, kickstick, mess, laughing grass, lobo, locowced, diambesta, M, light green, bone, smokables, oregano, boot, bule, collyweed, corn, cranny, early girl, stinkweed, tripweed, wacky weed, wisdom weed, ses weed, food, hooter, ily, maroochie, ned, chub, red hair, wacky-backy, wacky-tabbacky, primo (best), skonk (bad-smelling), straw, stuff, beetle, belt, birdwood, bomber, belt, drag, hit, bush, charge, beat, dynamite, fu, gauge, gage, stick, stick of gage, herb, goofball, spliff, spleef, splim, ja, jadja, Indian hemp, smoke, joy smoke, giggle smoke, giggle weed, juane, kef, keef, kif, kief, moocah, mota, musta, mutah, mutha, muggles, pod, Texas tea, splay, red dirt marijuana, salt and pepper, stuff, snap, boo, gungeon, gunion, black gunion, jabooby, Lipton's (fake), weed tea, yesca, yeska, Alice B. Toklas brownies, Jimmy dog, James Earl dog, hootchdog, Jim Jones (marijuana laced with cocaine dipped in PCP), frios, lovlies (dipped in PCP), bush, mootah, mu, panatella, dope, rope, seed, baby, blue sage, dagga, 13, 13-M, thirteen, love blow, bo-bo, pukalolo, dew, bar, gold leaf, manicure, sweet Lucy, baby, Banji, bhang, catnip, Coli, sativa, ace, cheeba, cheeo (seed to be chewed).

MARIJUANA ADDICT n. hash head, viper, grass-hopper, pothead, burnout, deadhead, slug brother, marijuana mush mind.

MARIJUANA AMOUNT n. bag, tray ($3), dime bag, nickel bag, bag up (divide into one-ounce amounts), eighth (one-eighth oz.), dime's worth, cap; matchbox, stick (cigarette); quarter bag, can, sandwich bag ($40 worth), lid, O.Z., weight (oz.); elbow (lb.); key, kee, ki (kilo); brick (compressed kilo), cop (to purchase).

MARIJUANA CIGARETTE n. joint, reefer, J., jay, J. smoke, joy smoke, J-bo, discipline, coca puff, mezz, mighty mezz, stick, stick of T, stick of tea, weed, hooch, hooch dog, Jimmy dog, dream stick, tea stick, joy stick, J-stick, jive stick, happy stick, kick stick, giggle stick, Buddha stick, dope stick, hop stick, hot stick, thumbs, drag, gage, stick of gage, gage butt, giggle smoke, good butt, goof butt, gow, greefa, griffa, goifa, greeta, bomber, hooter, jolt, gyve, jive, gangster, hemp, juju, killer, pin, Mary Jane, Mary Ann, funny cigarette, left-handed cigarette, bomb, bib bomber, bone, fatty, nail, number, rainy-day woman, root, mig, miggies, mooter, moota, mootie, muggles, number, reefer weed, rope, sausage, seed, snipe, spleef, spliff, stencil, torpedo, birdwood, ace, cocktail, doobie, doobage, dube, dubby, belt, bazooka, rocket, cone joint, twist, mezzrole; spliff, straight slim, square (half tobacco); blunt (rolled in a cigar), primo (contains cocaine), A-bomb (contains heroin or opium), banana with cheese, burnies (shared), roach (butt), sherm (dip), Zig-Zags (paper used to roll), Charlie (water pipe).

MARIJUANA PARAPHERNALIA n. roach clip, airplane, Jefferson airplane, crutch, snap (holder); bong (pipe), toker (water pipe), marygin (seed remover), icer (increases potency), stash bag, stash box, stash jar, Woodstock emergency pipe (aluminum foil).

MARIJUANA SELLER n. reefer man, viper, pad (sales place), cap (buy).

MARIJUANA SMOKING SITE n. balloon room, ballroom, head shop, parachute, spot.

MARIJUANA USE v. drag, hit, toke, smoke a toke, smoke out, smoke a bowl, blow smoke, blow gage, blow weed, blow major jaw (smoke buds), blow a stick, blow hay, blow jive, blow tea, blunted, zoom, blast, blazed, bogart, buzz (effect), catch a buzz, doobious (feeling the effect of), baked, trip, trip out, freak out, flip out, X out, turn on, get there, get small, gage, get high, get some discipline, bent out of shape, irie, smash some buds, kick the gong around, bang, take bong hits, mainline, hit the mainline, shoot the pin, take a shot, sent, tead up, tea pad, tea party, Franch-fried.

MARIJUANA USER n. head, pothead, user, stoner, fiend, tripper, doper, reefer, freak, junkie, burner, grasshopper, grasshead, mugglehead, weedhead, tea head, tea hound, hay burner, hay head, bushwhacker, griefer, motter,

tea blower, tea man, Cap'n Toke, tea toker, Alice B. Toklas, Toklas, viper, belongs to M.J.; English Channel eyes (bloodshot from smoking).

MARIMBA n. woodpile.

MARINE n. gyrene, leatherneck, jarhead, seagoing bellhop, skinhead (recruit), devil dog, bullet bait (untrained), cannon fodder.

MARINE BASE n. green machine.

MARINE CORPS n. the crotch.

MARINER n. mate, shipmate, sea dog, gob, swab, bluejacket, salt, old salt, yachtie.

MARK n. logo, brand, X, autograph, sig, fist, ink, John Hancock, John Henry, on the dotted line.

MARK v. brand, X, autograph, sig, ink, put your John Hancock on the dotted line, pinpoint, pin, spot, spotlight, limelight, button down, finger, put the finger on, put one's finger on something, make, peg, put down for, tab, tag. See also INDICATE.

MARKET n. 1. Wall Street, contact, truck, the Exchange, the Big Board, over the counter. 2. bridge market (inexpensive designer clothing), bridge line (designer clothes for half price). 3. supermarket, superette, super, deli, stand, co-op, bodega (liquor or N.Y.C. grocery), down to the corner for a bottle. See STORE.

MARKETABLE adj. bankable, hotcake, hot item, hot property, hot ticket.

MARKET, ILLEGAL n. black market, under the counter, the street.

MARRED adj. dinged, fucked-up. See DAMAGED.

MARRIAGE n. bells, wedding bells, shotgun wedding, hook.

MARRIAGE BROKER n. matchmaker, schatchen, shotgun.

MARRIED adj. hitched, hooked, tied, wear a hat, have a hat, have papers (Af. Am.).

MARRIED MAN n. old man, O.M., better half, brown bagger, breadwinner, goonie, shack man, on the hitch.

MARRIED WOMAN n. old lady, O.L., better half, little woman, wiff, roommate, ball and chain, block and tackle, grass widow, glass widow (husband is alcoholic), War Department. See WIFE.

MARRY v. hitch, get hitched, hitch up, splice, get spliced, hook, tie the knot, merge, middle-aisle it, walk down the aisle, put the clamps on, rob the cradle, cradle-snatch, tie down, land, wedding-bell it, snap on the ol' ball and chain, take the plunge, jump off the deep end, jump the hurdle, step off, step off the carpet, settle down.

MARSHAL n. cop, fuzz, copper, shamus, flic, cossack, arm, dick, pig, oink, clown (rural), the man, badge, Big Brother, boy scouts, county Joe, county mounty, county mountie, hick dick, law, local yard, local yokel, local boy. See POLICE OFFICER.

MART n. 1. discount house, superette, supermarket, the grab, schlock joint, chain store, outlet store, co-op. See STORE. 2. Wall Street, the Exchange, the Big Board, over the counter.

MARTIAL ARTS n. chucks, nunchucks (weapons).

MARTINI n. martooni, teen, teenie, see-through.

MARVEL n. one for the book, something else, something to shout about, something to write home about, stunner.

MARVELOUS adj. marvy, aggro, fab, fantasmo, def, super, super-duper, it's to die for, bad, evil, terrible, grimy, frantic, mongo, solid, solid sender, solid gold, outrageous, out of this world, the greatest, boss, skrouk. See FABULOUS.

MARYLAND Free State, Old Line State, Terrapin State.

MASCULINE adj. hunk, beauhunk, tuna, Clydesdale (attractive), hoss (muscular), beefcake, beef-a-roni, Greek god, demigod, daddio, macho, nail (Af. Am.), jock, caveman, ape, stud, industrial, stallion, cock, hairy, he-man, hombre, two-fisted, bruiser, bo, blood (Af. Am.). See MAN.

MASH v. scrunch, squish.

MASK n. fig leaf, cover, cover-up, front, beard.

MASK v. cover, cover up, front (usually illegal activities); beard. See also COVER UP.

MASOCHISM n. leather, into leather, M, SM, into SM, bondage, endo.

MASOCHIST n. glutton for punishment.

MASQUERADER n. fake, faker, four-flusher, fraud, gouge, phony, all front, a put-on. See also CHEATER.

MASS n. goose egg, hickey, hump, knot, konk, hunk, chunk, gob. See also AMOUNT, LARGE.

MASSACHUSETTS Bay State, Old Colony.

MASSACHUSETTS RESIDENTS Massholes.

MASSAGE n. beating, rub, Rolfe.

MASSAGE v. rub down, Rolfe.

MASSAGE PARLOR n. rap club, rap parlor. See also BROTHEL.

MASSES n. the mob, the great unwashed, the public, John Q. Public, Billy Sixpack, Joe Lunchbucket, hoi polloi.

MASSIVE adj. humongous, humungous, humongo, mungo, gross, honking, monstro, butt-kicking, bonzai, doby, big mother, colossal, blimp, barn-door, walloping, whopping, whopper. See BIG.

MAST n. pole, stick, tree.

MASTECTOMY n. boob job.

MASTER n. 1. pro, real pro, old pro, ol' professor, old hand, old war-horse, mavin, trained seal, whiz, whiz-bang, wizard, buff. See AUTHORITY. 2. numero uno, chief, head man, skipper, general, Mister Charlie (Af. Am.), big player, big gun, wheel, big cheese, top hand, topkick, top dog, avatar, pro, old man, spark plug, whip hand, slavedriver. See EXECUTIVE.

MASTER v. 1. break, break in, bust, gentle, run the show, call the shots, ride herd on, henpeck, crack the whip, pussywhip (Fem.), rule the roost, serve, kick ass, kick butt, keep under one's thumb, lead by the nose, have the upper hand, have it covered, have the say, have the say so, hold the reins, pull the ropes, pull the strings, pull the wires, reel one back in, bring to heel, box in, get one in a box, get one's hooks into, sit on top of. See MANAGE. 2. beat the game, beat the system, run away with, win out, put on ice, blow 'em away, swamp, sink the opposition, make a payday. See WIN. 3. hit the books, megastudy, power study, grind, plug, pour it on, bone up, bury oneself in, cram, skull-drag, hard-wire (by rote). See STUDY. 4. get down, get down pat, get down cold, get hold of, get into one's head, get the hang of, get the knack of, pick up, learn backwards and forwards, learn the ropes.

MASTERFUL adj. bossy, crack the whip, high-and-mighty, on one's high horse, throw one's weight around, dealing with, got a handle on it, iceman, in charge, in the driver's seat. See also IMPERIOUS; POWERFUL.

MASTER OF CEREMONIES n. emcee, MC, femcee, the chair.

MASTICATE v. fling a fang into, chaw, munch, chomp, gum.

MASTURBATE v. bop, she-bop, bop one's baloney, jack off, jerk off, beat off, beat the dummy, beat one's meat, pull one's pud, pound one's pud, play with oneself, beat the bishop, wack, whack the weasel, whack the bishop, whack one's willie, flog the hog, flog the log, flog the dummy, flog the sausage, flog one's dong, slap the salami, milk, milk the mamba, milk the chicken, milk the lizard, choke the chicken, paddle the pickle, jerk the gherkin, pull the chain, yank the crank, fist-fuck, fuck Mary Fist, jerk, frig, diddle (female), wank off, screw off, fuck off, fingerfuck, spank, spank the monkey, give a hand job, hand jive, play pocket pool, ream, sew, stroke, circle jerk (group) (all Obsc.).

MASTURBATION n. hand job, hand jive, jerking off, bananas and cream, bishop beating, pocket pool, dong flogging, hog flogging, fist fuck, gherkin jerking, chicken milking, lizard milking, Mary Fist, pickle paddling, Yankee, pulling the wire, shucking your corn, shredding your wheat, stroke the salami, having yourself, circle jerk (group) (all Obsc.).

MASTURBATOR n. diddler, jerk, jerk-off, hog flogger, chicken choker, wanker.

MATCH n. 1. light, Lucifer, snapper, fire. 2. go.

MATCH v. 1. put two and two together, jive, click. See also EQUAL. 2. lip-sync, sync, sync up.

MATCHED adj. in sync.

MATCHMAKER n. schatchen, shotgun.

MATE n. 1. old man, O.M., old lady, O.L., bread winner, better half, roommate, ball and chain, block and tackle, front office. See SPOUSE. 2. amigo, brother, sister, buddy, asshole buddy, chum, roomie, room mate, pard, home biscuit, playmate, matie, pal, sidekick. See FRIEND. 3. the like of, the likes of, look-alikes, peas in a pod, two of a kind.

MATE v. 1. get hitched, get spliced, tie the knot, merge, middle-aisle it, land, snap on the ol' ball and chain. See MARRY. 2. fuck, screw, lay, lay pipe, nail, hump, ball, bang, boff, jazz, dork, ride, do the deed, do the dirty deed, rubbing the bacon, jump in the sack, bed down, go to bed with, go the limit, get it off together. See SEXUAL INTERCOURSE.

MATHEMATICS n. math, number crunching.

MATING n. fuck, screw, lay, boff, plowin', bang, action, balling, shot, roll in the hay, score, boogaloo, do damage, get done, get down, the business, meat injection, night baseball, bed and breakfast, fooling around, bush patrol, he'n and she'n, she'n and she'n, he'n and he'n, fun and games. See SEXUAL INTERCOURSE.

MATRIMONY n. bells, wedding bells, shotgun wedding, hook.

MATTER n. goings-on, bag, job, lookout, nub, thing. See also SUBSTANCE; PREDICAMENT.

MATTER v. cut ice, cut some ice, carry weight.

MATTRESS n. fleabag, donkey's breakfast (straw).

MATURE v. 1. arrive, get hip, grow up, comin' up, cut one's eyeteeth, cut one's wisdom teeth, have sown one's wild oats, settle down. 2. shoot up, snowball, mushroom, blossom.

MATURITY n. prime, prime of life, dry behind the ears, ripe age, age of consent, drinking age, grumpies (grown-up mature people).

MAUDLIN adj. syrupy, drippy, soap, soapy, slush, teary, cornball, mushy, schmalzy. See SENTIMENTAL.

MAUL v. work over, wax, skin, take it out of one's hide, take it out of one's skin, muscle, mug, paw, bash, bung, bung up, paste, hurt, kick ass, whip ass, lean on, clean on, take care of, wipe up the floor with, wipe up the place with, make mincemeat out of, make hamburger out of, punch one out, knock around, jump all over, let one have it, put one in the hospital, go over, break one's face. See also HIT, WOUND.

MAWKISH adj. sticky, icky, gooey, sappy, sloppy, gushing, teary, beery, namby-pamby. See SENTIMENTAL.

MAXIM n. daffodil.

MAXIMUM adj. maxi, max, the most, the mostest, the end, the livin' end. See also SUPERLATIVE.

MAYONNAISE n. mayo.

MAYOR n. city father, hizzoner.

McDONALD'S n. McDuck's, McD's, Mickey D's.

MDA n. Ecstasy, E., Epsom salts, adam, X.

ME pron. yours truly, big three (me, myself, and I) number one, numero uno, this body, Dudley, Uncle Dudley, Ol' Uncle Dudley.

MEADOW n. green deck, carpet, rug.

MEAGER adj. 1. bupkis, chickenshit, too little too late, zilch. See NOTHING. See also SCANT. 2. skinny, gangling, gangly, twiggy, rattleboned, bag of bones, stack of bones, skin-and-bones, gangleshanks, beanpole, beanstalk, broomstick. See THIN.

MEAL n. eats, chow, chow time, finger food, feed, feedbag, nosebag, grub, grub pile, MREs (meals ready to eat, Gulf war; also, meals rejected by everyone), ribs, cookout, brunch, din-din, squares, square meal, mess, hots (hot meal, Mil.), blue plate, black plate (soul food); pecks, peckings (Af. Am.), pot luck; power lunch, power breakfast, working breakfast (Bus.); hot (hobo). See also FOOD.

MEAL TICKET n. grazing ticket.

MEAN adj. dirty, low-down and dirty, low-down no-good, meanie, down, lousy, louse, rat, bitchy, turbobitch, son of a bitch, SOB, so-and-so, son of a so-and-so, son of a gun, chickenshit, hard, hard-nosed, snide, the lowest, stinker, stinkeroo, stinking, schtoonk, sucks eggs. See DESPICABLE.n

MEAN v. talking (I'm talking big bucks), cut ice, cut some ice, go into one's dance (The.). See also INFER.

MEANDER v. get sidetracked, all over the map. See WANDER.

MEANING n. point, stuff, key, bottom line, name of the game, nitty-gritty, nuts and bolts, the way of it, nature of the beast, drift, heart, meat, nub, score, punch line, kicker (point of a story, joke, etc.).

MEANINGFUL adj. heavy, deep. See IMPORTANT.

MEANINGLESS adj. double-talk, doublespeak hot air, piss and wind, that doesn't chop any wood, that doesn't cut any ice, big zero, nothing, makes no never mind, nutmeg. See UNIMPORTANT.

MEANS n. 1. bankroll, nut, nest egg, rainy day, sock, mattress full, kitty, stake, backing, budget, ace in the hole, ace up one's sleeve (hidden), stuff, 2. Band-Aid, dodge, gimmick, trick.

MEASURE n. hit, shot, fix, nip, slug, bang, dram.

MEASURE v. size, size up, peg, check, check out, dig it, eye, look over, read, have one's number, take one's measure, dope out, take account of, windshield appraisal (superficial, from a car), figure, figure in, guesstimate.

MEAT LOAF n. mystery, rubber heels, death loaf, monkey nuts (meatballs).

MECHANIC n. grease monkey, wrench.

MECHANICAL adj. 1. by the numbers, go through the motions, phone it in, walk through it. 2. ticky.

MECHANICAL BREAKDOWN n. down, downtime, on the fritz, on the blink. See DAMAGED.

MECHANICS n. nuts and bolts.

MECHANISM n. idiot box, black box, job, jobby, dealie bob, gimmick, thingamajig, dohinkey, dingus, wingding, coil.

MEDALS n. fruit salad, brag rags, chest hardware, chicken guts (trimmings), gong, gonger, hardware; purple hurt, bolo badge (purple heart), no-clap medal (good conduct), the gold, jockstrap medal (CIA, secretly awarded).

MEDDLE v. mix in, butt in, horn in, stick one's nose in, kibitz, get on one's case, put one's two cents in, monkey with, fuck around with, futz around with. See INTERFERE.

MEDDLER n. buttinsky, kibitzer, snoop, yenta, backseat driver, nosy Parker, Paul Pry, crasher, gate crasher.

MEDDLESOME adj. nosy, pushy, snoopy.

MEDIATE v. make a deal, meet halfway, strike a happy medium, go fifty-fifty, can't fight 'em join 'em, come to school, trade off, settle.

MEDIATOR n. rent-a-judge, umpire, ref, go-between, fixer, middleman.

MEDICAL ATTENDANT n. candy striper, medic, bedpan commando (WWII), titless nurse (Medic. corpsman).

MEDICAL BILL FRAUD n. Ping-Pong.

MEDICAL EXAMINATION n. checkup, physical, exam.

MEDICAL PATIENT n. crock, gomer (drug addict), player (complainer), train wreck (several problems), albatross (chronically ill), banana (jaundiced), crunch (bad accident), crispy critter (burn), space cadet (overmedicated), looney tunes, not with the program, out to lunch (confused), to poot, go poopoo, to crump (take a turn for the worst), hit (assigned to resident).

MEDICAL STUDENT n. med, pre-med.

MEDICAL TERMS gomer (drug addict), goomer (get out of my emergency room); buff cap, buffalo cap (intermittent I.V.), MI (myocardial infarction), strepto (administer streptokinaise), hose one (pump stomach), the unit, ICU, Expensive Care Unit, Insensitive Care Unit (intensive care unit), ECU (eternal care unit, heaven), red pipe (artery), blue pipe (vein), ——— drip (administering intravenously), rose garden (room for comatose patients), horrenderoma (large tumor), gork (brain dead), boxed on the table (died in surgery), code brown (messy bowel movement), code yellow (incontinence), code blue (cardiac arrest), code 99 (emergency); hepatic rounds, liver rounds, fluids & electrolytes conference (party in hospital); docs in a box (nonhospital emergency room), school's out (unsuccessful treatment), vitamin P (sex), Peter Rabbit ward (pediatric), kangaroo care (infant care), AMA (against medical advice).

MEDICATE v. doctor, dope, dope up, dose, dose up.

MEDICATION n. shotgun remedy (drug combination), liquid cork (for diarrhea), OTC (over-the-counter drug).

MEDIOCRE adj. so-so, fair, fair to middling, run of the alley, run-of-the-mill, no great shakes, strictly union, humdrum, mainstream, vanilla, starch. See AVERAGE.

MEDIOCRITY n. meatballism, hamfat.

MEDITATE v. woolgather, moon, head trip, noodle, noodle it around, put on one's thinking cap, figger, crunch, chew the cud, track, blow change. See THINK.

MEDLEY n. mixed bag, combo, duke's mixture, mishmash, mishmosh, everything but the kitchen sink.

MEEK adj. weak sister, Milquetoast, Caspar Milquetoast, wishy-washy, tail between one's legs, schnook, pablum, zero. See also SUBMISSION.

MEET v. bump into, run into, run up against, come up against, go up against, meet face to face, meet eyeball to eyeball, meet up with, make a meet, take a meet, have a meet, dig up, pop upon, rub eyeballs, run smack into, strike, rendezvous with, get together, show. See also ASSEMBLE, FACE, QUALIFY, SUFFICE.

MEETING n. 1. confab, one on one, clambake, affair, meet, rally, pep rally, gang, bunch, crowd, get-together, barbeque, huddle, call, cattle call, powwow, session, buzz session, rap, rap session, bull session, bitch session, jam session, gig, sit-in, turnout, ashram, groupie, mob, mess, flap (urgent), showdown, gam; triff, tref (clandestine); put heads together. 2. date, heavy date, blind date, love nest, matinee, noonie, one-night stand, quickie, rendezvous, meet.

MEETINGHOUSE n. aud, Amen Corner, dirge factory, God box.

MEETING PLACE n. hangout, place, in-place, spot, stamping ground, the grab, big store, dinghe, hideout, hole, jungle, meet, plant, scatter, shebang, spot, stash (U.).

MEET REQUIREMENTS v. come up to snuff, cut it, cut the mustard, check out, make the cut, get by, score, fill the bill, make it, make the grade, pass, pass muster.

MEGRIM n. head, have a head, hangover, migraine.

MELANCHOLIA n. blahs, blah-blahs, blues, blue devils, blue funk, funk, bummer, downer, down trip, letdown, dolefuls, dismals, dumps, mumps, mopes, mokers, mulligrubs.

MELANCHOLY adj. dragged, ripped, crumbed, low, destroyed, dragging ass, have one's ass in a sling, dick in the dirt, blue, in a blue funk, funky, grim, got the blue devils, in the toilet, in the dumper, in the dumps, down, on a downer, let down, taken down, taken down a peg, down in the dumps, in the doleful dumps, down and out, down in the mouth, downbeat (movie, song, etc.), low-down, crummy, cleek, sob story, sob stuff, tear-jerker, weeper, tear-drop special, make like an alligator, nightmare, have the blues, singing the blues, crying the blues, hang crepe, on a bummer, bummed out, flaked out, put away, carry the torch, hurtin', bleeding, in pain, in the pits, shook, shot down, should have stood in bed, carry a heavy load, off one's feed, rhino, have the mulligrubs, have the dolefuls, have the blahs, clanked, clanked-up, cracked-up, tore-up, all torn up, droopy, mopey, moony, gloomy Gus, wet blanket, raining on one's parade, sad-sacky, killjoy, prune-faced, sourpuss, spring fever. See also DESPAIRING.

MELANCHOLY n. blahs, blah-blahs, blues, blue devils, blue funk, funk, crumbed, bummer, downer, down trip, letdown, nightmare, dolefuls, dismals, dumps, mumps, mopes, mokers, mulligrubs.

MELANGE n. everything but the kitchen sink, mishmash, mishmosh, mixed bag, combo, duke's mixture (strange), stew, soup (liquid), lorelei.

MELD v. feather in, interface, camouflage, marry; dissolve, cross-dissolve (film). See also ASSOCIATE.

MELIORATE v. 1. upgrade, polish, make first-rate, up, doll up, pick up. 2. step up, shape up, turn the corner, be out of the woods, come along. 3. get one's act together, get with it, get on the ball, straighten up and fly right, turn things around. See IMPROVE.

MELLOW v. arrive, get hip, grow up, cut one's eye-teeth, cut one's wisdom teeth, have sown one's wild oats, settle down. See also SOFTEN.

MELODRAMA n. meller, melo, chiller, thriller, cliff-hanger, barn-burner, corn, cornball, hoke, grabber, penny dreadful, potboiler, Tom show. See also PLAY.

MELODRAMATIC adj. hammy, hokey, blood and thunder, cliff-hanging, cloak-and-dagger, ham.

MEMBER n. 1. branch, branch house, affil (TV), offshoot. 2. clubber, joiner, blood, blood brother, brother, sister.

MEMORABLE adj. heavy, heavyweight, heavy number, heavy stuff, meaningful, a gas, splash, standout, cosmic, super, super-duper, terrible, terrific, doozie, the most, the utmost, too much, hooper-dooper, the end, far out, mind-blowing, like wow, boss, bitchin', twitchin', lampin', cool, murder, neat, nose cone, some (some show), like dynamite, daisy, dilly, A, A-1, ace of spades, bang-up, cold, corker, corking, cracking, crackerjack, chill out, serious shit, serious jelly, matter of life and death, something, something else, big-league, major-league, top-drawer, hot shit, underlined.

MEMORANDUM n. memo, chit, note.

MEMORIZE v. get it through one's head, get down, get down cold, learned by heart, get by heart, get letter-perfect.

MEMORY n. flashback, flash on.

MEMORY LOSS n. blackout, block out, brain fart, blow, blow a line (The.), don't know if one's comin' or goin', go blank, lose one's marbles, brain fade.

MEMPHIS, TENNESSEE Big M.

MENACE v. lean on, make one an offer one can't refuse, push around, whip one around (intellectually), put on the arm, put on the muscle, put the heat on, bad eye, spook, chill, scare hell out of, scare the shit out of. See INTIMIDATE.

MENACED adj. spooked, frozen, feel the heat, heat's on, hot, goose-bumpy, panicked, run scared, shake in one's boots, given a turn, given a jar, given a jolt. See also FRIGHTENED.

MEND v. fix up, doctor, fiddle with.

MENDACITY n. crock of shit, bull, hocky, crap, claptrap, thick, thin, con, cover, cover-up, smoke, string, line, line of cheese, doesn't wash, dirty lie, terminological inexactitude. See LIE.

MENDICANT n. bum, stumblebum, moocher, panhandler, promoter, bag lady, bag woman, stiff, guttersnipe. See BEGGAR.

MENIAL n. live in, help, girl, woman, man, boy, houseman, houseboy, biddy, furp, peon, serf, slave, slavey, pancake (Uncle Tom). See SERVANT.

MENOPAUSE n. change of life, hot flashes, the change.

MENSTRUATE v. get the curse, have one's period, have the rag on, on the rag, O.T.R., on the stick (uses tampon), unwell, under the weather, have the monthlies, get the monthly bill, fall off the roof, having a visitor, got the painters in, little sister's here, come around (late), flagging it, flying the flag, flying the red flag, the red flag is up, Baker flying, the Red Sea's in, wear a red camellia, visit Red Bank.

MENSTRUATION n. curse, curse of Eve, period, Aunt Flo, have the rag on, on the rag, O.T.R., raggin', ragtime, unwell, under the weather, monthlies, the monthly bill, that time, that time of the month, holy week, wet season, fall off the roof, having a visitor, friend, got the painters in, little sister's here, country cousin, come around (late), dog days, flagging it, flying the flag, flying the red flag, the red flag is up, flag is up, Baker flying, high tide, the Red Sea's in, red camellia.

MENTAL adj. brainy, got the smarts, have savvy, have the smarts, big think, deep, double-dome, heavy, gasser, gray matter. See INTELLECTUAL. See also INTELLIGENT.

MENTAL ATTITUDE n. tude, cop a tude (bad), head-set, mind-set, mind trip, routine, where one is at, where it's at, where one's head is.

MENTAL BLOCK n. hang-up, hung, hung up, up-tight.

MENTAL FATIGUE n. burnout.

MENTAL HOSPITAL n. booby hatch, funny farm, loony bin, bughouse, nuthouse, warehouse, soft walls, acorn academy, laughing academy, college, nut college, nut factory, nut farm, zoo, cracker factory. See INSANE ASYLUM.

MENTAL LAPSE n. brain fade, brain fart.

MENTALLY DEFECTIVE adj. retardo, one-eye. See also RETARDED.

MENTALLY ILL adj. in the ozone, dingy, loco, loc, unglued, unzipped, unscrewed, screw loose, schizy, schizzed-out, schizoid, psycho, psyched-out, freaked-out, nobody home, light's on but nobody's home, out to lunch, out of one's tree, baked, totally baked, bent, ape, nerts, not have all one's buttons, have a lug nut loose, batty, loony, haywire, potty, cuckoo, mental job. See CRAZY.

MERCEDES-BENZ n. MBZ, Benzo.

MERCENARY adj. go with the money, flow with the dough, gold digger, money talks bullshit walks, grabby, poligot, greedyguts.

MERCENARY n. soldier of fortune, merc.

MERCHANDISE n. the goods, material, stuff, hot number, jive (gaudy), seconds.

MERCHANDISE, DAMAGED n. ninety-nine.

MERCHANT n. big-time operator, BTO, big wheel, wheeler-dealer, dealer, middleman, tycoon, cockroach (small), nickel-and-dime operator, small potatoes, trade-ster, robber baron, big butter-and-egg man. See TRADER.

MERCI BEAUCOUP interj. messy bucket, murky bucket, mercy buckup.

MERCIFUL adj. softhearted, all heart, bleeding heart (Derog.), old softie, heart in the right place; live with, soft-shell, go easy with, go easy on.

MERCILESS adj. cutthroat, go for the jugular, killer instinct, mean machine, dog-eat-dog, hatchet job, take no prisoners. See also CALLOUS.

MERCURIAL adj. up-and-down, yo-yo, bubble-headed, gaga, flaky, mad, ad lib, blow hot and cold, race one's motor, have a short fuse, in a stew, in a lather, in a tizzy, in a pucker, hot under the collar, run a temperature, blow up, blow one's stack, blow one's top, blow a gasket, flip, flip one's lid, fly off the handle, go ballistic, hit the ceiling.

MERCURY n. Merc (auto).

MERCY n. lifesaver, clemo.

MERGE v. 1. tie in, pool, come aboard, throw in together, deal one in, plug into, go partners, interface, mob up, join up with, hook up with, line up with, swing in with, meld with, team up with, network with. See ASSOCIATE. 2. hook up, hook on, tag, tag on, tack on, slap on, hitch on. 3. cross-dissolve (film), cue in (scripts, ms., songs), dub, hook in, marry (film), mix (recording).

MERGER n. takeover, tie-up, tie-in tie-up, hookup, ca-hoots, lineup; white knight, white squire (friendly bidder in a takeover), gray knight (opportunistic second bidder); target (vulnerable company), shark (unfriendly financier forcing takeovers), smoking gun (error by a shark permitting the target to escape through an antitrust ruling), shark repellant, poison pill (takeover defense strategy), porcupine provisions (legal deterrents), scorched earth (antitakeover measure).

MERGER TERMS takeover, hostile takeover, acquisitions, Pac-Man, raider, sugar pill, lollipop, poison pill (takeover defense strategy), greenmail, golden parachute, golden handcuffs (deferred payment), junk bond, crown jewel option, shark repellant, arbs (arbitrageurs), garbitageur (manipulates deals); white knight, white squire (friendly bidder in a takeover), gray knight (opportunistic second bidder); target (a vulnerable company), shark (unfriendly financier forcing takeovers), smoking gun (error by a shark permitting the target to escape through an antitrust ruling), porcupine provisions (legal deterrents), scorched earth (antitakeover measure), killer bees (help fight takeovers, law firms, etc.).

MERINGUE n. calf slobber.

MERIT v. rate, be in line for, what is coming to one, what one has coming, get one's comeuppance.

MERITORIOUS adj. mega-gnarly, 10, ten, winner, choice, rad, top-drawer, first-chop, boss, good show, golden, hummer, mad, mess, mezz, nasty, nifty, bang-up, world-beater. See EXCELLENT.

MERRIMENT n. grins, laughs, lots of laughs, high old time, picnic, hoopla, whoopee. See AMUSEMENT.

MERRY adj. jumping, go-go, grooving, rocking, jazzed, perky, zippy, zingy, zappy, bouncy, full of go, full tilt, in full swing, swingle, feeling one's oats. See CHEERFUL.

MERRY-GO-ROUND n. whirligig, goofus, flying ginny (not common).

MERRYMAKING n. grins, laughs, lots of laughs, high old time, picnic, wingding, shindig, brawl, cold chillin', whoopee, whooper-dooper, hoopla, fun and games. See also REVEL.

MESCALINE n. pumpkin seed, big chief, mesc, bean, button, mescal, moon, shroom (psychodelic), shroom dog (user).

MESS n. bloody mess, holy mess, unholy mess, rat's nest, looks lived in, arsy-varsy, every which way, galley west, hectic, all over hell, all over the shop, discombooberation. See CONFUSION.

MESSAGE n. news, poop, dope, earful, blitz (electronic mail), hot wire; kick in the ass, shot in the ass (bad), cannonball. See also INFORMATION.

MESSENGER n. boy, shlepper, bag man, mule, runner, speedy, gofer, gopher, smurf (carries illegal money for laundering).

MESS HALL n. ptomaine palace, ptomaine domain.

MESS SERGEANT n. bean, cookie, B-boy.

METAL DETECTOR (WALK-THROUGH) n. mechanical stoolie, mechanical stool pigeon.

METER n. beat.

METHADONE n. meth, biscuits, medicine, dolls, dollies, Finnegans (boosts effectiveness).

METHAMPHETAMINE n. tweak, go-fast medicine, ice (extra potent smokable form), crystals, Cris, Cristine, crank, elephant, elephant tranquilizer, dynamite, speed.

METHANOL n. alky.

METHAQUALONE n. pillow, soap, soaper.

METHEDRINE n. crystals, love drug.

METHEDRINE PILL n. businessman's trip, crystal, meth, speed.

METHOD n. channels, red tape, by the numbers, by the book, wrinkle, new wrinkle, nuts and bolts, style, mechanism. See also PLAN.

METHODICAL adj. in a groove, grooved, by the numbers, by the book, cut and dry, set-up, fixed, framed, glued (antonym: unglued), together, all together, have all the pieces in place, have one's act together, have one's shit together, have one's head together, have one's head screwed on right, laid on. See also NEAT, ORDERLY.

METHYLENEDIOXYAMPHETAMINE n. Ecstasy, MDA.

METHYL FENTANYL n. China white.

METICULOUS adj. picky, smitty, nitpicker, stickler, dot the i's and cross the t's, fussbudget, fusspot, Felix, persnickety, chickenshit, by the numbers. See PARTICULAR.

METROPOLIS n. urb, burg, apple, Big Town, Big Time, boomer, boomtown, right tank, slab, two-stemmer, tough town, wide-open joint, dump, wrong tank.

METTLE n. backbone, grit, guts, moxie, nerve, spunk, heart, starch. See COURAGE.

MEXICAN n. Cholo, bean, beaner, bean eater, Mex, Chili, chili eater, frito, tostado, taco head, taco bender, tamale, padre, wetback; bracero, dino (laborer); greaser, grease gut, oiler, hombre, peon, pepper, pepper belly, spic, spig, spiggoty, Tio Taco (Mexican American) (all Derog.); Latino, Chicano, Chicana.

MEXICAN CUISINE n. Tex Mex, gringo food, Montezuma's revenge, Mexican heartburn, Mexican two-step (the day after).

MEXICO CITY Makesicko City.

MICHIGAN Wolverine State, Auto State, Lady of the Lakes, Lake State.

MICHIGAN RESIDENT n. Michigander.

MICROBE n. bug, crud, creeping crud, the plague, what's going around.

MICROCOMPUTER n. P.C., micro.

MICROGRAM n. mike (drug).

MICROMETER n. mick.

MICROPHONE n. mike, bug, lollipop.

MICROSCOPE n. mike.

MICROWAVE v. nuke it, microblast.

MICROWAVE OVEN n. zapper, nuker, microblaster.

MIDDLE adj. mainstream, middle-of-the-road, betwixt and between, halfway in the middle, plump in the middle, smack in the middle, slap in the middle, smack dab in the middle, straddle the fence.

MIDDLE-AGED PEOPLE n. maffies (affluent), woofies (affluent over fifty), dumpies (downwardly mobile professional).

MIDDLE-CLASS adj. plastic, white-bread.

MIDDLE CLASS n. Main Street, Middle America, suburbia, boorjoisie, MODS (teen age).

MIDDLE EASTERN PEOPLE n. sand niggers, ragheads (Derog.).

MIDDLE FINGER n. the finger, give one the finger, flip one the finger, single-digit salute, stink finger, the bird, fuck finger, fuck you, give one the bird.

MIDDLEMAN n. connection, go-between, fixer. See also INFLUENCE.

MIDGET n. little people, trial size, shorty, shrimp, runt, peanut, peewee, squirt, bantam, sawed-off, half-pint, half portion, short pint, shortish, dusty butt, knee-high, knee-high to a grasshopper.

MIDRIFF n. midsection, gut, spare tire, Dunlop syndrome. See also STOMACH.

MIDSHIPMAN n. middy (Naval Acad.).

MIDSUMMER n. dog days.

MIDWAY adj. betwixt and between, halfway in the middle, plump in the middle, smack in the middle, slap in the middle, smack dab in the middle, middle-of-the-road, over-the-hill, over-the-hump.

MIDWIFE n. granny-woman (So.).

MIEN n. cut of one's jib, image, style, act, front.

MIGHT n. the force, zap, sock, beef, clout, might and main, moxie, punch, steam, powerhouse, the stuff, get-up-and-go. See POWER.

MIGHTY adj. got the horses to do it, hoss, strong as a horse, strong as a lion, strong as an ox, the heavy artillery, powerhouse, steamroller. See POWERFUL.

MIGRAINE n. head, have a head.

MIGRATION n. brain drain, brawn drain.

MIGRATORY WORKER n. wetback, bracero, Okie, short staker, shuffler, stiff.

MILD adj. cool, mellow, vanilla, blah, draddy, flat, ho-hum, nothing, nothing much, pablum, weak sister, Milquetoast, Caspar Milquetoast, schnook. See also INSIPID.

MILIEU n. scene, bag, thing, space, place, environment, nabe, turf. See also ATMOSPHERE.

MILITARIST n. hawk, Dr. Strangelove, Strangelove.

MILITARISTIC adj. hawkish.

MILITARY DISCHARGE n. ruptured duck (WWII), section 8 (mental).

MILITARY OFFICERS n. brass, top brass, brass collar, brass hat, C.O., CINC, CINCPAC (commander in chief Pacific), Joint Chiefs, exec, feather merchant (Naval Reserve), ripple (noncom, Waves), Sam Brown, NCO (noncom) purple suiters (top brass), rug rank (high-ranking), elephant (boss), horse-holder (serves senior officer).

MILITARY POLICE n. MP, M.P., snowdrop.

MILITARY TERMS AWACS (Airborne Warning and Control Systems), CASH (Combat Support Hospital), DEAF SMACK (Defense Special Missile and Aeronautics Center), HARM (High-Radiation Anti-Radar Missile), FLIR (Forward-Looking Infrared System), SAM (Surface-to-Air Missile), SLAM (Stand-off Land Attack Missile), the beach (Saudi desert), bush (jungle), cammies (camouflage clothing), quartermaster material (dead); glad bag, mummy sack, body bag (all Vietnam war); chairborne (bureaucrat), chicken guts (gold braid), the Gold Room (Joint Chiefs' conference room), hitch (period of enlistment), humping (marching); ptomaine domain, ptomaine palace (mess hall); repple-depple (replacement depot); newby, newfer (replacements); sitmap (situation map), the tank.

MILITARY VEHICLE n. Hummer, Humvee (High-Mobility Multiwheeled Vehicle), blitz buggy, half-track, jeep, leapin' lena, puddle jumper, weapons carrier.

MILITARY WEAPONS n. hardware, hog-60 (M-60 machine gun), K-Bar (Mil. knife), toadsticker (bayonet), zippo (flame-thrower), palm (napalm), grease, HARM (High-Radiation Anti-Radar Missile), SAM (Surface-to-Air Missile), SLAM (Stand-off Land Attack Missile), slickum (SLCM, Sea-Launched Cruise Missile), glockem (ALCM, Air-Launched Cruise Missile).

MILK n. cow juice, cow, moo juice, laiche, cat beer, bovine extract, chalk, Jersey highball, sweet Alice, five, forty-one; armored cow, armored heifer, city cow, canned cow, tin cow, sea cow (canned milk); black cow (chocolate), drive the cow down (pass the milk).

MILK A COW v. juice.

MILKSOP n. jellyfish, chicken heart, candy ass, pecker ass, weak sister, big baby, gutless wonder, nerd, turkey. See EFFEMINATE. See also COWARD.

MILK TOAST n. graveyard stew.

MILL n. sweatshop, shop.

MILLION DOLLARS n. megabucks, bar.

MILWAUKEE, WISCONSIN Beer City, Beer Town.

MIMIC n. copycat; crock, crowk (radio use, animal imitations).

MIMIC v. do, do like, make like, go like, mirror, ditto, ape, take a leaf out of one's book, fake, play the ——— (affect a role). See IMITATE.

MINCE v. whack, hack.

MIND n. brain, box, think box, think pad, clockwork, wig. See also INTELLECT.

MIND v. 1. sit, baby-sit, ride herd on, mind the store, toe the line, watch one's step, watch out. 2. get a load of this, get a load of that, are you ready for this?, give ears, clue in, knock on one's lobes, listen up, dig. See HEED.

MINDFUL adj. 1. hep, on to, hip, in the know, be up on, know all the answers, know all the ins and outs, wake up and smell the coffee, plugged-in, tuned-in. See KNOWLEDGEABLE. 2. cagey, handle with kid gloves, leery, on the ball, on the job, on one's toes, with one's eyes peeled. See CAUTIOUS.

MINDLESS adj. out, out to lunch, out of it, spaced-out, veged-out, mooning, moony, pipe-dreaming, daydreaming, woolgathering. See UNAWARE.

MINE n. booby trap, bouncing betsy, egg (N.).

MINER n. groundhog, sandhog, desert rat, hard rocker, sourdough, hard ankle.

MINERAL WATER n. mixer, seltzer, soda back (on the side), penny plain, two cents plain.

MINGLE v. pool, tie in, gang up, network; work the fence, work the room (Pol.). See ASSOCIATE.

MINIATURE adj. mini, minny, teensy, teensy-weensy, itsy-bitsy, mite, pint-sized. See SMALL.

MINIMIZE v. downplay, play down, put down, cut down to size, cut-rate, pooh-pooh, knock, knock down, pan, poor-mouth. See BELITTLE. See also UNDERPLAY.

MINION n. ass-kisser, ass-licker, tukis licker, brownie, those aren't freckles on his nose, yes-man, nod guy, flunkey, flunkey-stooge, stooge, hanger-on, waterboy, waterman, lackey, sideman. See SYCOPHANT.

MINISTER n. padre, the rev, sky pilot, Bible-beater, gospel pusher, preacher man, sin hound, shepherd, glory roader. See CLERGYMAN.

MINISTER v. 1. do for, watch over. 2. ride herd on, run, run the show, head up, sit on top of, be in the driver's seat, boss, hold the reins. See MANAGE.

MINNEAPOLIS, MINNESOTA Big Twin, Minnie, Twin City, Mill City, Flour City.

MINNEAPOLIS-ST. PAUL Twin Cities.

MINNESOTA Gopher State, North Star State.

MINNOW n. minny.

MINOR adj. two-bit, ticky-tacky, slimpsy, minus, below the mark, not up to scratch, not up to snuff, plastic, cotton pickin', low, bush-league, low man on the totem pole, poor man's something or one. See also INFERIOR.

MINOR n. juve, punk, yoot, jailbait, San Quentin quail (Fem.).

MINSTREL SHOW TERMS Bones, Mr. Bones, Mr. Interlocutor (end man), jig show (Derog.), plant show, cork opera.

MINUTE adj. teeny, teeny-weeny, eentsy-weentsy, itsy-bitsy, titch, piddling. See SMALL.

MINUTE n. mo, half a mo, min, tick, shake, half a shake, two shakes, two shakes of a lamb's tail, sec, split second, bat of an eye, jiff, jiffy, half a jiffy, nothing flat, mick (Mil.).

MIRACULOUS adj. fantasmo, too much, the utmost, unreal, heavy, gas, seven-ply gasser, far-out, one for the book, something to write home about. See FABULOUS.

MIRAGE n. witch-water (heat waves on the road, So.).

MIRE n. goo, gooey, glop, gloppy, Mississippi mud, gunk.

MIRROR n. gaper.

MIRROR v. act like, do, do like, go like, make like, take off as, do a takeoff, chomp, play the ———(affect a role).

MIRTH n. grins, laughs, kicks, whoopee. See AMUSEMENT.

MIRTHFUL adj. jokey, joshing, yokked-up, crack-up, ball, fun, gas, for grins, laffer, riot, priceless, screaming, screamingly funny, gut-busting, side-splitting, million laughs. See AMUSING.

MISBEHAVE v. cut up, act up, horse around, fool around, carry on, carry on something awful, cut up rough, roughhouse, go wrong, sow one's wild oats, bend the law.

MISBEHAVING adj. off-base, out-of-line, out-of-order, trouble-making. See also ROWDY.

MISCALCULATE v. screw up, fuck up, slip up, piss up, mess up, blow, cook, that dog won't hunt, make a blooper, miss by a mile, drop the ball, stumble, pull a blooper, pull a bloomer, pull a boner, pull a boo-boo, put one's foot in it, shoot oneself in the foot, stub one's toe, get one's signals mixed, misread. See ERR.

MISCALCULATION n. boner, blooper, goof, megamistake (big), hash, hash-up, fool mistake, miss by a mile, have another think coming. See MISTAKE.

MISCELLANY n. mixed bag, combo, kludge (parts), everything but the kitchen sink, mishmash, mishmosh, garbage.

MISCHIEF n. dirty trick, rib, gag, high jinks, shenanigans.

MISCHIEVOUS PERSON n. holy terror, little dickens.

MISCREANT n. shit, shithead, shitheel, louse, motherfucker, buddy fucker, lolla-lucka, rat, rat fink, fink, stinker, hairball, sleazeball, shower scum, bad egg, bad 'un, wrong 'un, black sheep, bastard, son of a bitch, SOB. See SCOUNDREL.

MISDEED n. dirt, dirty pool, dirty deed, miscue, slip-up. See also CRIME.

MISDIRECTION n. bum steer, double-cross, double-talk, runaround, jive. See also CHEAT.

MISER n. skinflint, piker, cheapskate, hard man with a buck, Scrooge, pinchfist, pinchgut, penny-pincher, nickel-nurser, sticky-fingered one.

MISERABLE adj. hurting, on a downer, on a bummer, destroyed, put away, ass in a sling, godforsaken, dick in the dirt, got the blue devils. See UNHAPPY.

MISERLY adj. stingy, cheapskate, close, tight, last of the big spenders, last of the big-time spenders, fast man with a buck, skinflint, screw. See STINGY.

MISERY n. heartache, headache, hurting, grabbing, blues, worriment, tsures, stew, all-overs, cliff-hanging, pins and needles, who needs it, this I need yet, need it like a hole in the head, pain in the ass, pain in the neck, bad news, stab in the ———, making like the anvil chorus in one's skull, next week East Lynne.

MISFIT n. zoid, fish out of water, oddball, square peg in a round hole. See also DISSOLUTE.

MISFORTUNE n. rough, tough, tough luck, rotten luck, downside, bad news, rainin', deep shit, shit hit the fan, total shuck, can't even get arrested, on the skids, bad break, tit in the wringer, tsuris, crunch. See ADVERSITY.

MISGUIDE v. jerk around, stonewall, low ball, shuck and jive, disinform, goof on, bum steer, give one a bum steer, shine one on, lead one up the garden path, mousetrap, throw one a curve, talk trash, double-talk, double-speak, fake it, beard, put up a smokescreen. See MISLEAD.

MISHANDLE v. goof up, flub, blow, bobble, make a mess of, put one's foot in it, shoot oneself in the foot, juke, go at it ass backwards. See ERR.

MISINFORM v. cover up, signify, bait and switch, low-ball, shine one on, disinform, mousetrap, put on, string one along, wrong steer, double-talk, double-speak, put on a false front, put up a smokescreen, put on an act, let on like, four-flush. See MISLEAD.

MISINFORMED adj. all wet, nuts, out in left field, smoking your socks, off, way off, off base, off the beam. See also WRONG.

MISJUDGE v. miss by a mile, drop the ball, stumble, pull a boner, put one's foot in it, bark up the wrong tree, count one's chickens before they're hatched, go at it ass backwards, bonehead into it, jim a deal. See ERR.

MISLEAD v. rip off, jerk one off, jerk one around, rook, screw, shaft, frig, fudge, hose, hump, pratt, job, rim, dick, dick one around, fuck one over, low-ball, blow smoke, blow smoke up one's ass, jive, shuck, shuck and jive, frontin', goof on, run a game on, shine one on, snake one in, trip, rope in, do a number, do a number on, disinform, stonewall, cover up, whitewash, pass, sell wolf cookies, signify, bull, throw the bull, bullshit, bull-pucky, bunco, cheek it, fake it, fake one out, four-flush, cross up, cross one up, double-cross, XX, double-clock, two time, caboodle, gammon, talk trash, double-talk, double-speak, fast-talk, fleece, gas, gum, flam, flim-flam, stick, burn, beat, bleed, bleed white, bilk, clip, con, chisel, gouge, gyp, scam, sting, sandbag, mousetrap, bait and switch, throw one a curve, give one a bum steer, give one a gurdy, hurdy, give one the runaround, Murphy, pigeon-drop, ike, pluck, take, take one to the cleaners, take one for a ride, take for a sucker, play games with, play the nine of hearts, play for a sucker, sucker, suck in, sucker into, cream, pull something on one, pull one's leg, pull a quickie, pull up a bluff, put up a bluff, pull a fast one, pull a fast shuffle, double-shuffle, double-deal, second-deal, give one a raw deal, bottom-deal, deal from the bottom, set up, doctor, cook, cook up, deacon, duff, hoke up, frame, frame up, load, salt, salt a mine, plant, phony up, queer, promote, string, string along, string one along, sleighride, snow, snow job, snow under, cold haul, cold deck, buffalo, bamboozle, gazoozle, hocus, slip one over on, wear cheaters, slap on some glims, flash the gogs, throw on a makeup, phony up one's getup, beard, put something over, put something across, put one over on, put on, put on the check, put a different face on, put up a front, put on a front, put up a smokescreen, put on an act, make like, let on, play possum, pussyfoot, hype, soak, sell one a bill of goods, sell gold bricks, chouse, chouse out of, fake out, bust out, kiss out, psych out, outfox, fox, kid, pull the wool over one's eyes, have, humbug, hornswoggle, ice, grift, rinky-dink, score, shag, single-o, ride a pony, diddle, vamp, hook, gaff, lead one up the garden path, they're peeing on us and telling us it's raining, go South.

MISMANAGE v. goof, goof up, gum up the works, make a mess of, make a hash of, count one's chickens before they're hatched, shoot oneself in the foot, juke, go at it ass backwards. See ERR.

MISREPRESENT v. shuck and jive, maple stick jive, con, promote, blarney, jolly, goof on, play, trip, lay it on, lay it on thick, lay it on with a trowel, spread it on, snow, give one a snow job, pirate, phony up one's getup, wear cheaters, slap on some glims, flash the gogs, throw on a makeup, beard, cover up, put up a bluff, blow, blow smoke, blow smoke up one's ass, bunk flying, cheese, a line of cheese, yeast, throw one a curve, build up, take it big, puff, ballyhoo. See LIE.

MISREPRESENTATION n. line, line of jive, jive, fig leaf, cover-up, hokum, phony boloney, the big lie (Pol.), fairy tale. See LIE.

MISS v. 1. fall between the chairs, fall between the cracks, close but no cigar, cut, pay no mind, let slide. 2. flub the dub, blow, miss one's cue, miss by a mile, miss the boat, drop a brick, drop the ball, trip up, fall flat on one's ass, fall flat on one's face, come a-cropper.

MISS A CUE v. fluff, flub, go up, go up in the air, blow it.

MISS A MEAL v. fly light.

MISSED adj. close but no cigar, cut, passed-up.

MISSILE n. bird, bat bomb, dingbat (stone or wood), egg, beast (Army), SAM, telephone pole (SAM), MX, cruise, scud, spud (scud), Silkworm, Popeye (Israeli), slow flyer (cruise), stealth, MIRV, MARV.

MISSING adj. short, M.A. (not knowing a person's whereabouts), awol, AWOL, a.w.o.l., A.W.O.L. See ABSENT.

MISSION n. 1. fishery (Rel.). 2. box-top mission, milk run, scramble (A.F.).

MISSIONARY n. padre, Holy Joe, Bible beater, Bible thumper, Bible basher, Bible puncher, devil driver, fire insurance agent, gospel pusher, salvation rancher, preacher man, sin hound, glory roader. See CLERGYMAN.

MISSISSIPPI Bayou State, Magnolia State.

MISSISSIPPI RIVER n. Old Man River, old man river, old muddy, Old Al, Old Big Strong.

MISSIVE n. line, memo, junk mail, drop a line, thank-you note, kite, cannonball, scratch, stiffo, sugar report (love), tab, tag, poison-pen letter (malicious, obscene, etc.).

MISSOURI Show-Me State, Puke State (19th-cent.).

MISSPEND v. blow, diddle away, piss away, splurge on the line, run through, go through, spend money like water, spend like it was going out of style. See SQUANDER.

MISSPENT adj. blown, blown-out, diddled away, down the drain, down the toilet, down the rathole, down the spout, down the tube, pissed away.

MIST n. ground clouds, soup, visibility zero zero.

MISTAKE n. boner, flub, fluff, muff, bug, glitch, fudge factor, gremlin, megamistake (big), boo-boo, blooper, bloomer, bust, butch, botch up, boot, crumb, crumb up, bobble, boggle, goof, goof-up, foul-up, fuck-up, louse-up, muck-up, screw-up, gum-up, hash-up, slip-up, blow it, blow it big-time, snafu, commfu (monumental), tarfu, tuifu, tofu, plumb (serious), clinker, dumbo, fungo, typo, etaoin shrdlu, howler, screamer, flap (social), foozle, fox paw, fox pass, gaff, hummer, klong, brodie, blob, fathead, floater, bonehead play, bonehead trick, boob stunt, donkey act, dumb trick,

dumb thing to do, fool mistake, fool trick, pratfall, wrong riff, go wrong, bark up the wrong tree, miss by a mile, mess up, mess and a half, have another think coming, count one's chickens before they're hatched, put one's foot in it, blow card.

MISTAKEN adj. goofed, boo-booed, smokin', blowing smoke, smoking your socks, fooled out, all wet, way off, off the beam, talking like a man with a paper ass, wrong number, bark up the wrong tree. See WRONG.

MISTREAT v. 1. mess up, manhandle, roughhouse, rough up, bend the goods, bung, bung up, cut up, shake up, total, wax, hose, hump. 2. do a number on, dump on, play dirty dozens, give a black eye, trash, bash, back-cap, backbite, rip up the back, punk, jack, chop, do one wrong, break one's balls, push around, kick one around, screw, take over the hurdles. See ABUSE. See also WOUND.

MISTRESS n. old lady, ol' lady, main squeeze, wrap, best girl, girl friend, G.F., nectar, gooey nectar, sugar, sweetie, sweet back (Af. Am.), roommate, moll, ball and chain, kept woman, keptie, shack, shack job, skibby, dream girl. See also GIRL FRIEND.

MISTRESS OF CEREMONIES n. femcee, the chair.

MISTRUSTFUL adj. cagey, leery, pussyfoot, walk on eggs, handle with kid gloves, think twice, watch one's step, keep on one's toes, play safe, not born yesterday, walk wide, on the lookout. See CAUTIOUS.

MISTY adj. fogged in, socked in, closed in, pea-soupy, soupy.

MISUNDERSTAND v. get one's signals mixed, misread.

MISUNDERSTANDING n. spat, tiff, beef, fuss, words, bad vibes, falling out, crossed wires, sour note, blowup, set-to, run-in. See DISCORD. See also ARGUMENT.

MISUSE v. 1. diddle away, piss away, blow, run through, go through, spend money like water, throw out the baby with the bath water, kill the goose that lays the golden egg. 2. mess up, manhandle, roughhouse, rough up, bung, bung up, cut up, shake up, total, wax, hose, hump. 3. bad-mouth, trash, bash, peg, rip up the back, do a number on, dog on (verbal), crack on (Hum., Af. Am.), pick on, dump on, rag on, tool on, punk, jack, knock, put down, run down, tear down, do one wrong, kick one around. See ABUSE.

MITIGATE v. cool, cool it, cool out, make it up, come together, meet halfway, pour oil on troubled waters, take the edge off. See SOFTEN. See also EXCUSE; PACIFY.

MIXTURE n. everything but the kitchen sink, mishmash, mishmosh, mixed bag, combo, duke's mixture (strange), stew, goulash, soup (liquid), lorelei.

MOBILE HOME n. wheel estate, condo on wheels, condominium on wheels, tin can on wheels, land yacht.

MOCK adj. bogue, bunco, bunko, bum, junque, phony, pseud, pseudo, put-on, ersatz, hokey, plastic, soft-shell. See COUNTERFEIT.

MOCK v. 1. jive, needle, do a number on, kid, kid around, goof on, razz, rib, thumb one's nose at one, give five fingers to one. See RIDICULE. 2. mirror, make like, play the ———— (affect a role), ditto, do, do like, go like, steal one's stuff, take a leaf out of one's book, fake, hoke, hoke up.

MOCK COURT n. kangaroo court, moot court.

MODE n. 1. the thing, latest thing, latest wrinkle, new wrinkle, newest wrinkle, last word, fad, mainstream, in-thing, mod, now, really now, the rage, up-to-speed. See also NEW. 2. mechanism, channels, the numbers, the book, wrinkle, new wrinkle, nuts and bolts.

MODEL n. 1. mock-up, setup, layout, paste-up, visual, dummy, game plan, picture, paper doll. 2. ringer, dead ringer, look-alike, work-alike, ditto, knockoff, clone, copycat, spitting image, spit and image. 3. Shirley (fashion).

MODEL A FORD n. tin lizzie, Model A, A-bone.

MODERATE adj. cool, mellow, mainstream, middle-of-the-road, straddle the fence.

MODERATE v. soft-pedal, coast, cool out, get together on, meet halfway, take the sting out. See PACIFY.

MODERATOR n. ref, umpire, the chair, M.C., emcee, femcee, toastmaster, rent-a-judge. See also ARBITRATOR.

MODERN adj. state-of-the-art, the leading edge, the cutting edge, at the cutting edge, now, today, contempo, avant-garde, up to speed, last word, po-mo (postmodern). See NEW.

MODIFICATION n. custom job, special, customized, about-face, flip-flop, mid-course correction, switch, switch-over, quantum leap (major), transmogrification, demon tweak.

MODIFY v. doctor, customize, switch over, shift gears, take it in a little, midcourse correction, transmogrify, tweak, turn over a new leaf, turn the corner, turn one around, turn the tables. See CHANGE.

MODISH adj. faddy, trendy, cosmo, bust fresh, in, in-thing, the thing, latest thing, latest wrinkle, last word, now, up to speed, happenin', the rage. See STYLISH.

MODULATE v. give it a tweek (small), fine-tune, take it in a little, monkey around with, bottom out, revamp, transmogrify, do up, switch, switch over, yo-yo. See CHANGE.

MOGADISHU The Dish, Bermuda Triangle (bandit-infested area).

MOGUL. n. tycoon, key player, big chew, czar, top brass, big shit, big gun, kingpin, suit, pinstriper, vest, beef. See EXECUTIVE.

MOLD v. shape up, fudge together, whomp up.

MOLE n. beauty mark, beauty spot.

MOLESTER, CHILD n. chicken hawk, short, short eyes, cho-mo, Chester the Molester, diddler, Pamper pirate, Pamper sniffer.

MOLINE, ILLINOIS Quad City.

MOLLIFY v. cool, cool out, fix up, make matters up, patch things up, pour oil on troubled waters, take the sting out. See PACIFY.

MOLTEN METAL n. soup.

MOMENT n. mo, half a mo, tick, sec, split second, shake, half a shake, two shakes, two shakes of a lamb's tail, jiff, half a jiff, jiffy, nothing flat.

MOMENTOUS adj. heavy, heavy number, power, serious shit, serious jelly, cosmic, chips are down, we're not talking about nutmeg here. See IMPORTANT.

MONAURAL adj. mono.

MONEY n. cold cash, hard cash, spot cash, bucks, big bucks, megabucks, hard coin, important money, notes, snaps, bread, long bread, cake, heavy money, dough, heavy dough, oday, do-re-mi, grip, duckets, ends (Af. Am.), almighty dollar, petrodollars, petrobillions, dinero, spent (cash), the ready, ready cash, caish, scudi, the wherewithal, the necessary, needful, mazuma, mazulla, mon, moolah, loot, lucre, filthy lucre, skins, eagle shit, scratch, gelt, gold, ocher, green, green money, green stamps, greenbacks, greenery, green stuff, mean green (Af. Am.), green folding, folding, folding green, long green, folding dough, folding money, lettuce, folding lettuce, folding cabbage, cabbage, happy cabbage, kale, kale seed, roll, bank, bankroll, the bank, glory roll, Michigan roll, Philadelphia bankroll, wad, paper, bills, billies, crazy bills, soft money, happy money, mad money, smackers, dividends, frog hair, frogskin, gee, geech, geetis, geets, geedus, greedus, gingerbread, glue, gravy, bundle, change, feed, chickenfeed, chicken money, birdseed, hard money, hard stuff, hardtack, coin, iron (silver coin), hay, jangle, jingle-jangle, hunk of change, piece of change, piece of jack, juice, hip gee, ice, kick, laydown, line, grift, handsome ransom, lumps, Maine line, mezonny, mint, mint leaves, mopus, morphine, offtish, oil of palms, ointment, oof, ooks, oofus, ookus, package, pazoza, peanuts, poke, color, cookies, corn, cush, darby, dead president, dibs, dingbat, dust, dirt, fews and twos, rags, rhino, rivets, rocks, salve, scrip, sheets, shekels, bad notes, payola, pretty penny, black money (illegal), white money (laundered), blunt, bob, bomb, bones, boodle, brass, buttons, sugar, candy, chump change, chips, clinks, China, shinplaster, shortbread, shorts, small bread, small potatoes, simoleons, silk, velvet, sleeper, soap, soft, the soft, spending snaps, spinach, trading stamps, wampum, adobe dollar, alfalfa, bait, ballast, bark, bat hides (paper), beans, beater, bees and honey, beewy, berries, bird (gold coin), biscuit, bite, spon, spondoolicks, spondulix, taw, tin, tough bud, tusherony, tucheroon, the mother's milk of politics.

MONEY: CENT n.   red cent, Indian head, peanuts, copper, brown, brown Abe, brownie, red, silver, throw money, wampum, washers.

MONEY: FIVE CENTS n.   nickel, blip, buffalo head, fish scale, flat.

MONEY: TEN CENTS n.   dime, thin dime, thin, thin one, thin man, deece, deemar, deemer, demon, dimmer, jit, jitney, liberty, saw, silver Jeff, tenth part of a dollar.

MONEY: TWENTY-FIVE CENTS n.   quarter, two bits, cuter, kyuter, quetor, big George, squirt, gas meter, meter, ruff, shinplaster (bill), silver Jeff, light piece (silver).

MONEY: FIFTY CENTS n.   four bits, half a buck, silver wing.

MONEY: SEVENTY-FIVE CENTS n.   six bits.

MONEY: DOLLAR n.   bill, billies, buck, single, clam, one, potato, simoleon, slug, skin, greenback, smack, smacker, smackeroo, ace, peso, berry, bob, boffo, bone, case, case buck, case dough, case note, check, clacker dollar, cholly, coconut, cucumber, fish, frog, frogskin, bumblebee, lizard, man, plaster, plunk, rag, rock, rutabaga, scrip, Simon, year, hog, hogs, iron man, Jewish flag (Derog.), last dollar.

MONEY: SILVER DOLLAR n.   iron man, cartwheel, wheel, ball, bullet, copek, D, hardtack, plug, shekel, shiner, sinker.

MONEY: TWO DOLLARS n.   two-spot, deuce, deucer, deuce spot, two-case note, two cents.

MONEY: FIVE DOLLARS n.   five, fiver, five-spot, fin, finif, finiff, finski, Abe, Lincoln, nickel, nickel note, Abe's Cabe; half eagle, bean (gold coin).

MONEY: TEN DOLLARS n.   tenner, ten-spot, ten, sawbuck, saw, dews, dime note, dix, eagle (gold coin).

MONEY: TWENTY DOLLARS n.   double sawbuck, double eagle (gold coin), twenty, twenty cents.

MONEY: TWENTY-FIVE DOLLARS n.   squirt.

MONEY: FIFTY DOLLARS n.   half a C.

MONEY: ONE HUNDRED DOLLARS n.   C,   C note, century, century note, one bill, yard, hun, dollar, hollow note.

MONEY: FIVE HUNDRED DOLLARS n.   D, five centuries, five C's, half G, half a grand, nickel, small nickel.

MONEY: ONE THOUSAND DOLLARS n.   G, G note, grand, dollar, thou, yard, big one, dime, horse, kilobuck.

MONEY: FIVE THOUSAND DOLLARS n.   big nickel, five dollars.

MONEY: ONE MILLION DOLLARS n.   megabuck, mill, bar.

MONEY: ONE BILLION DOLLARS n.   yard.

MONEY BAG n.   grouch bag.

MONEY BELT n.   boodle belt, skin plaster.

MONEY, BRIBE n.   payoff, bad notes, payola, drugola, gayola, take, contribution, under-the-table, fix, juice, schmear, sugar, mordida; laying pipes, Abscam (political). See BRIBE.

MONEY, COUNTERFEIT n.   bogus, paper, queer, funny money, phony money, wallpaper, boodle, green goods, gypsy bankroll, long green, plug, sourdough. See COUNTERFEIT MONEY.

MONEYED adj.   loaded, in the chips, stinking rich, well-heeled, have a mint, coupon clipper, well-to-do, fat cat, the haves, the leisure class, got a buck or two, oofy, uptown, upscale. See WEALTHY.

MONEY LENDER n.   shark, loan shark, shylock, shy, uncle, softie.

MONEYLESS adj.   stone broke, flat, busted, blasted, hard-up, strapped, clean, tapped-out, on one's uppers, down to one's last cent, down to one's last penny, down-at-the-heel, not have one dollar to rub against another, not have one dime to rub against another. See DESTITUTE.

MONEY POOL n.   chips, kitty, pot.

MONEY, STOLEN n.   swag, take, knockdown, loot, make, mark, sting.

MONGREL n.   mutt, pooch, Heinz, Heinz 57, Heinz 57 varieties, fleabag, flea hotel. See DOG.

MONITOR v.   track.

MONKEY n.   monk, monkee.

MONOGRAM n.   mono, chop.

MONOLOGUE n.   mono, one-man show, one-woman show, stand-up bit.

MONOMANIA n.   one-track mind.

MONONUCLEOSIS n.   mono, kissing disease, yuppie flu.

MONOPOLIZE v.   corner, corner the market, get a corner on, bogart, hog, take over, lock up, sit on.

MONOTONOUS adj. flat, flat as a pancake, blah, draddy, dull as dishwater, ho-hum, nothing, put one to sleep. See BORING.

MONSTER n. Frankenstein, hellion, hellcat, little devil.

MONSTER adj. humongous, humungous, humongoid, mungo, monstro, honking, king-size, butt-kicking, bonzai, moby, big mother, biggy, big-ass, supercolossal, jumbo, lunker, hoss, whacking, whopping, thumping. See BIG.

MONTANA Treasure State, big sky.

MONTGOMERY, ALABAMA Monkey City, Monkey Town.

MONTGOMERY WARD n. Monkey Ward.

MONTH n. deano (thief use), moon.

MONTREAL, CANADA Moreal.

MOOD n. one's bag, bit, in the groove, scene, soul, color. See TEMPER.

MOODY adj. moony, up-and-down, yo-yo, blow hot and cold, have spring fever, let-down, out of sorts. See MELANCHOLY.

MOON n. pumpkin, green cheese.

MOONSHINE n. mountain dew, corn, cane corn, white mule, white lightning, jug whiskey, See also LIQUOR.

MOPE n. nerd, wimp, herb, wet blanket, cheeseman, cheesebag, cheesehead, cheeseface, Captain Cheddar, dingleberry, crepe-hanger, drag, sourpuss, sourbelly, downer.

MOPE v. bleed, eat one's heart out, stew over, sweat over, chew the cud.

MORAL adj. regular, square, square shooter, straight, straight shooter, true blue, Christian, kosher, salt of the earth, fly right, nice guy, white, scoutmaster, boy scout, clean as a hound's tooth.

MORBID adj. sick, sick sick sick, sicky.

MORGUE n. icebox, slab, ward X (Medic.), chop shop, greenhouse (prison).

MORMON n. carrot-eater, carrot snapper (Derog.).

MORNING n. crack of dawn, day peep, sunup, bright, early bright, early beam, early yawning, early yawning hours, foreday.

MORNING GLORY SEED n. flying saucer, heavenly blue, blue star, glory seeds, pearly gate, pearly whites, summer skies.

MORON n. dickhead, feeb, droid, dogburger, dorf, dork, megadork, ditzo, fred, Barney, Wilma, beau, lunchbox, lunchsack, vacant lot, Z-head, nerd, full hank, lop, loser, algae head, McFly, lorg, gump, hamburger, jel, lamebrain, a coupla quarts low, four-letter man (dumb), dumbo, mo-mo, cheesehead, cheeseface, Captain Cheddar, butthead, gink, numbskull, doesn't know enough to come in out of the rain, stoop, simp, dimwit. See FEEBLEMINDED.

MOROSE adj. down in the mouth, down in the dumps, blue, in a blue funk, singing the blues, got the blue devils, have the blahs. See MELANCHOLY.

MORPHINE n. M, morph, morf, cube juice, dime's worth, dreamer, medicine, God's own medicine, God's drug, soldier's drug, happy dust, Ixey, joy powder, Miss Emma, Em, Aunt Emma, emsel, coby, dope, junk, gunk, first line, glad stuff, stuff, happy stuff, happy powder, lent, reffi, hocus, unkie, sweet Jesus, red cross, sugar, snow, blue happiness, white stuff, white dust, white nurse, mojo, whizbang (mixed with cocaine).

MORSEL n. smithereen, chaw, chomp, chunk, gob, hunk, lump, bite, cut, slice, chunk, gob.

MORTAL n. human bean, naked ape. See also PERSON.

MORTAR n. mud.

MORTGAGE n. Daddy MAC (shared equity mortgage); first, second (I have a first on my home but not a second); GPM (graduated-payment), ARM (adjustable-rate), GPARM (graduated-payment adjustable-rate), IRMA (individual retirement mortgage account), Maggie Mae (Mortgage Guaranty Insurance Corporation), monkey, monkey on the house, monkey with a long tail.

MORTIFICATION n. boo-boo, goof, drop a brick, hot potato, could have sunk into the floor, wished the floor would open up, egg on one's face, shoot oneself in the foot, cap, takedown, put-down, bazoo, zerbert, raspberry.

MORTIFIED, BE v. die, have egg on one's face, lose face, crawl, come out moldy, come up moldy, draw in one's horns, eat crow, eat dirt, eat humble pie, sing small. See HUMILIATED.

MORTIFY v. put away, shred, put down, take down, shoot one down, burn down, burn one down, prick one's balloon, get one's comeuppance, take the wind out of one's sails, lay one out, let one have it. See HUMILIATE.

MORTUARY n. Ward X (Medic.), greenhouse (prison), icebox.

MOSQUITO n. skeeter, Alaskan state bird.

MOST n. lion's share, bigger half, big end, big end of the stick, max, maxi, the most.

MOTEL n. shortel (used for assignation). See also HOTEL.

MOTEL ROOM n. flop box, nap trap.

MOTHER n. mama, mammy, mam, mater, ma, maw, mom, moms, mommy, mootie, mom duke, motherkin, motherkins, mumsy, mimsy, mummy, muzzy, old lady, old woman, warden.

MOTHER-IN-LAW n. battle-ax.

MOTION n. body English, high sign.

MOTION, IN adj. on the go, on the move, movin', moving out, coming down, in full swing.

MOTION PICTURE n. movie, the movies, film, pictures, picture show, big screen, pic, pix, flick, flickie, flickers, slasher flick, talkie; horse opera, oater, western, spaghetti western, sagebrusher (western movie); chop socky (karate and kung fu), splatter (blood and gore), weeper, boom-boom, bang-bang, slice and dice, clacker, remake, sequel, prequel, A, B; deepie, depthie, 3-D (three-dimensional), low-budget, cheapie, quickie, short, doc, Mickey Mouse (Army training or VD information film), trailer; pornoflick, skin flick, beaver flick, snuff, nudie, smoker, stag film, fuck film; E-ticket (best); locomotive, tent pole, has legs, blockbuster, hit (all box-office success).

MOTION PICTURE CAMERA n. wobblyscope (hand-held).

MOTION PICTURE INDUSTRY n. Hollywood, dream factory, filmdom, moviedom, the industry, the movies. See also FILM TERMS.

MOTION PICTURE STUDIO n. dream factory, lot, back lot, studio, set.

MOTION PICTURE THEATER n. movie house, house, movie, the movies, pictures, picture show, movie theater, cave, hall, hard top; drive-in, ozoner (drive-in theater), flick, flickers, nickelodeon, bug house, grind house, fleabag, passion pit, screen, big screen, silver screen; skin house, stroke house, porno palace, adult movie, adult theater (pornographic).

MOTION, SLOW n. slo mo, slomo.

MOTIVATE v. goose, goose up, egg on, spark, sound. See PERSUADE. See also STIMULATE.

MOTIVATION n. fire in the belly, push, goose, kick in the ass, right stuff, get-up-and-go, action, gimmick, angle.

MOTIVATOR n. trigger, spark plug, the driver, the igniter, mover and shaker.

MOTOR n. horses, power plant, under the hood, barrel (cylinder), maud, pot, putt-putt, rubber band, eggbeater.

MOTOR BOAT n. stinkpot, outboard, yach, yachet, putt-putt.

MOTORCYCLE n. chopper, bike, cycle, hog, pig, trike, shovel, horse, grid, heap, iron, iron pony, motocycle, motorbike, road bike, dirt bike, minibike, microbike, ass-hammer, garlic burner (Italian), rice burner (Jap.), hornet, scrambler,

trumpet, wasp, bumblebee, cyclone cycle; bathtub, buddy seat (sidecar), ape hangers (long steering handles).

MOTORCYCLE CLOTHES n. harness (leather clothes and accessories); gourd guard, hat, skid lid (helmet).

MOTORCYCLE POLICEMAN n. Evel Knievel, chopper copper.

MOTOR HOME n. camper, RV, moho.

MOUNTAIN n. hump.

MOUNTAIN CLIMBER n. rock jock.

MOUNTAINEER n. ridge runner.

MOURN v. bleed, hurt, blubber, boo-hoo, rain, carry on, eat one's heart out, go for a crying towel, get out the crying towel, cry me a river, cry the blues, sing the blues, take it big, take it hard, take on, beat one's breast, crepe-hang, hang crepe.

MOUTH n. kisser, trap, chops, bazoo, mush, yap, beak, box, gob, clam, clam shells, clam trap, fish trap, fly trap, potato trap, kissing trap, talk trap, satchel mouth, puke hole, funnel, dipper, gab, gap, jap, gash, gills, hatch, head, mug, box of dominoes.

MOUTHFUL n. chaw, chomp, gob.

MOVE v. 1. dedomicile, up stakes, pull up stakes, truck, move out. 2. beat it, scram, split; slide, air out (Af. Am.), color me gone, motor, motorvate; le-go, sko (let's go), bolt (quickly), blow, blow this joint, blow this pop stand, brake camp, hoof it, haul ass, barrel ass, cut ass, drag ass, shag ass, hit the road, jet, roll out, move out, clear out, check out, dig out, ship out, skip out, get the hell out, shove off, be-bop, drift away, hat up, quit the scene. See GO. See also ACT, EXCITE, AROUSE, PERSUADE, REMOVE.

MOVED adj. turned on by, turned on to, feel in one's guts, feel for, get to one, grabbed. See also EXCITED.

MOVER n. 1. drifter, grifter, bo, bum, floater, bindlestiff, gad, gadabout, jet-setter, globe-trotter, rod rider. 2. operator, spark plug, mover and shaker, catalyst, wire-puller, trigger, driver.

MOVING adj. on the move, cool, real cool, zero cool, fab, far out, mega, megadual, marvy, like wow, reet, mind-blowing, mind-bending, out of this world, turn on, turned on by, turned on to, gone, real gone, hot stuff, hairy, large, large charge, nervous, rootin'-tootin', solid, solid sender, one for the book, something, something else, something to shout about, something to write home about, stunner, stunning, feel in one's guts, grabbed by.

MUCH adj. mega (stu.), up to one's ass in, up the ying yang in, loads, galore, scads, mucho, mucho-mucho, lotsa, heaps, mongo, plate is full. See PLENTY.

MUCILAGE n. stickum, gunk, spit, gummy.

MUCILAGINOUS adj. gooey, gloppy, globby, gook, gooky, goonk, gummy, gunk.

MUCK n. goo, gooey, glop, gloppy, Mississippi mud, gunk, scrunge.

MUCKRAKER n. knocker, mudslinger, sleazemonger, yellow journalist, whistle-blower.

MUCUS n. boggie, bugger, booger; skeet, skeet shooting (blowing one's nose into the air), goob, snot, cream.

MUD n. goo, gooey, glop, gloppy, Mississippi mud, gunk, gumbo.

MUDDLE n. mess, mess and a half, rat's nest, foul-up, fuck-up, screw-up, snarl-up, mishmosh, can of worms, every which way but up. See CONFUSION.

MUDDLE v. discombobulate, ball up, louse up, blow it, blow it big-time, rattle, throw, psych out, fuck with one's head, put one on a crosstown bus. See CONFUSE.

MUDDLED adj. unglued, discombobulated, in the twilight zone, slap-happy, punchy, bollixed up, fussed, fried, rattled, rattlebrained, higgledy-piggledy, ass backwards, bassackwards. See CONFUSED.

MUDDY adj. greasy, gummy, gunky.

MUFFIN n. dingbat, garbo.

MUFFLE v. gag, hush, ice, muzzle, shut down on, put the lid on, sit down on. See SILENCE.

MUFTI n. civvies, cits, street clothes.

MULATTO n. banana, hi yalla, high yella, high yellow, high yeller, yellow-back, lemon, bird's-eye maple, poontang, yellow girl, pinky, pink toes, red bone (woman), bright, kelt, keltch, tush, beige, black-and-tan, brown-and-tan, bleached ebony, mahogany, sepe, sepia, tan, white nigger, zebra (all Derog.). See also AFRICAN AMERICAN.

MULE n. hay burner, jar head, jug head, hardtail (Army).

MULE DRIVER n. skinner, mule skinner.

MULL v. stew over, sweat over, figger, moon, pipe dream, crunch, rack one's brains, crack one's brains, cudgel one's brains, hammer, hammer away at, put on one's thinking cap, chew the cud, woolgather. See also THINK.

MULTIPLE INDEPENDENTLY TARGETED REENTRY VEHICLE n. MIRV.

MULTIPLE ORBIT BOMBARDMENT SYSTEM n. MOBS.

MULTIPLE SCLEROSIS n. MS.

MULTITUDE n. mob, push, turnout, blowout, crush, jam, jam up, everybody and his brother, everybody and his uncle, loaded to the rafters, wall-to-wall people. See CROWD.

MULTITUDINOUS adj. umpteen, zillion, jillion, bazillion, mucho, eleventeen, whole slew, wads, gobs, scads, heaps, piles, oodles, bokoo, boku, more than one can shake a stick at. See AMOUNT, LARGE.

MUNICIPAL ASSISTANCE CORPORATION n. Big Mac.

MUNICIPALITY n. urb, burg, apple, Big Town, big time, boomer, boomtown, dump, slab, two-stemmer, tough town, wide open joint, wrong tank, right tank.

MUNIFICENT adj. big, bighearted, be big, softie, soft touch, have a heart, heart in the right place, loose, good Joe, prince of a person, Santa Claus.

MURDER n. off, offing, wasting, hit, taking out, the big M, big chill, liquidation, measles (spy, looks like natural causes), kiss-off. See KILLING.

MURDER v. off, snuff, ice, chill, waste, hit, grease, get a body, liquidate, get, fog, smoke, take out, rub out, do in, bump off, blow away, compromise (espionage use), kiss-off. See KILL.

MURDERED adj. wasted, offed, cooled off, knocked off, rubbed out, snuffed, compromised (espionage use), liquidated. See KILLED.

MURDERER n. hit man, trigger man, piece man, torpedo, enforcer, gunsel, bumpman, soldier. See KILLER.

MURMUR v. buzz, sotto.

MUSCLES n. guns, cows, abs (abdominal), delts (deltoid); pecks, pects (pectoral); lats (back), six-packs (stomach).

MUSCULAR adj. hunk, hulk, hoss (muscular), gorilla, buffed, Clydesdale (attractive), ripped, husky, hefty, beefy, beefcake, beef-a-roni, beauhunk, crushman, bruiser, big bruiser, bone crusher, tiger, Turk, wicked, down, tough, tough guy, puffed-out, pumped-up, strong-arm, muscle, muscle man, he-man, industrial, powerhouse, strong as a lion, strong as a horse, strong as an ox, sturdy as an ox, built like a brick shithouse, Clark Kent (wears suit and glasses), float (shows off muscular body), coon (stupid).

MUSE v. feel, moon, percolate, float, sweat over, cool something over, skull-drag, chew over, chew the cud, woolgather, pipe dream, build castles in the air. See THINK.

MUSEUM UNIVERSITY DATA PROCESSING INFORMATION EXCHANGE n. MUDPIE.

MUSHROOM n. shroom (psychedelic), shroom dog (user).

MUSICAL ACCOMPANIMENT n. backup singers, back, backing.

MUSICAL COMEDY n. tuner, musical, song-and-dance show.

MUSICALE n. hootenanny, folk sing, sing, sing-in.

MUSICAL ENSEMBLE n. combo, group, rock group, heavy metal, big band, jazz band, jump band, swing band.

MUSICAL INSTRUMENT n. ax, money number.

MUSICAL NOTE n. bent note, biff, biffer (unsuccessful brass high note); blue note, blow for canines (high, trumpet); clam, clinker (sour or wrong); scooping pitch, slurred note, spots, sting.

MUSICAL PERFORMANCE n. gig, rave (techno concert with drugs), action, phat flavor (good), blow, funky, ride, moan, jive, jam, bumpin' (good, Af. Am.), tickle the ivories (piano), burning (play wonderfully), groove, groovy, in the groove, date it (play badly), lumpy (jazz played badly), put it in the alley, jammin', partying, pump it up (louder); jerk off, masturbate (indulge in long solos).

MUSICAL TERMS strictly union (corny), rockumentary (rock music documentary film), music video (rock tape), sounds, spots (notes), cornfed (plays or appreciates classical); corny, cornball (country, hillbilly), take it from the edge (begin), chops (ability, technique), go man go, groove, in the groove, ickie (unappreciative); charts, maps (sheet music); rideout, ride (improvise jazz), hit a lick (emphasize), scat, set, book, roadie (travels with band).

MUSICAL WORK n. comp, getup, piece, setup, tune, arrangement, number.

MUSIC DEVOTEE n. rocker, head banger (hard-rock fan), metal head; b-girl, b-boy (rap music), sender, solid sender, cat, hepcat, hipster, groupie, bubblegum groupie, skeezer (hip-hop), wannabee, alligator, gate, swinging gate, gator, jitterbug, moldy fig, ragger, rug cutter, sharpie, sweet, with it, woof hound, music buff.

MUSIC FORMS n. fusion, rap, rock, rock and roll, rock n' roll, R. & R., hard rock, soft rock, acid rock, shock rock, heavy rock, AOR (album-oriented rock), white rock, scum rock, skronk, noise rock, heavy metal; glam, metal funk, speed metal, thrash (forms of heavy metal); ragarock, rockabilly, pop rock, rock steady, soft rock, blue-eyed soul (soft rock), folk rock, alternative rock, techno, synthpop, hip-hop, jungle jive (black rap), new ro (new romantic), doo wop, punk, punk funk, punk rock, hard-core, alternative, new wave, power pop, New Jack Swing, bop, bebop, rebop, riba, hard bop, house music, western, country, country western, bluegrass, ranchera, garage pop, disco, industrial disco, dancecore, Euro-body music, jazz, Chicago jazz, New Orleans jazz blues, zydeco (southern blues style), barrelhouse, gutbucket, Dixie, Dixieland, soul music, rag, ragtime, honky-tonk, pop, swing, big beat, rhythm & blues, R. & B., boogie, boogie-woogie, bounce, businessman's bounce, society music, jump, ear candy, bubblegum, bubblegum and popcorn music, heavenly metal, evangelical pop, Christian pop, sandwich music (jazz and rock), Motown, reggae, dub, ska, salsa, chaser, runoff, chestnut (old), classical, long underwear, longhair, longhair juke, ricky-tick, scat, shout, whorehouse piano, piano bar, Muzak, elevator music.

MUSICIAN n. longhair, long underwear, studio, cat, cool cat, blowing cat, gay cat, alligator (white), gate, gator, in orbit (avant-garde), lip-splitter, satchel, sender, solid sender, swinging gate; wig, loose wig (inspired); muso (superb), sideman, iron man, metallurgist (heavy metal), band man, paper man, rag man; ear man, faker (musically illiterate); rocker, monster (popular), slut (eager to play), jazz fag (very sophisticated).

MUSTACHE n. brush, soup strainer, tickler, toothbrush, handlebars, lip fuzz, pez, stash, stache, foxtail (Navy, WWI).

MUSTANG (CAR) n. horse.

MUSTARD n. Coney Island butter, baby shit.

MUSTER n. head count, nose count, call-up, draft.

MUSTER OUT v. demob, get the ruptured duck (WWII).

MUTE v. gag, hush, keep it down, pipe down, decrease the volume, muzzle, put the damper on, put the lid on, bottle up, cork up, put a cork in it. See SILENCE.

MUTILATE v. bugger, bugger up, queer, mess up, hash up. See also DAMAGE.

MUTINY v. kick over the traces.

MUTTON n. Aussie steak (WWII), billy goat.

MUTUALLY ASSURED DESTRUCTION n. MAD.

MUZZLE v. squelch, squash, gag, ice, dummy up, dry up, shut one's face, bottle up, put the damper on, put the lid on, cork up, shut down on, crack down on, clamp down on. See SILENCE.

MY EYES GLAZE OVER MEGO.

MYRIAD adj. loads, raft, slew, gobs, scads, mint, heap, oodles, stacks, bokoo, boku, no end of. See COUNTLESS.

MYSELF pron. this body, big three (me, myself, and I), number one, numero uno, yours truly, Dudley, Uncle Dudley, Ol' Uncle Dudley.

MYSTERY n. 1. chiller, thriller, chiller-diller, whodunit, who-done-it, cliff-hanger, spyboiler, grabber. 2. sixty-four-dollar question, twister, teaser, sticker, mind-boggler, stumper, burly, hard nut to crack, tough nut to crack.

MYSTIFIED adj. stuck, stumped, floored, thrown, flummoxed, kerflumixed, bamboozled, buffaloed, beat, licked, foggy, in a fog, wandering around in a fog. See PUZZLED.

MYSTIFY v. buffalo, put one on a crosstown bus, muddy the waters, stump, floor, put off, get to, rattle, throw, flummox. See PUZZLE.

N

N n. November, Nan.

NADIR n. the pits, cellar, bottom rung, rock bottom, bottom out, dick in the dirt.

NAG v. bug, hound, be at, be on the back of, eat, noodge, nudge, nudzh, give one hemorrhoids, push one's key, push one's buttons, work on, hit on, chap, penny-dog, worry, hock a charnik, pick at. See ANNOY.

NAIVE adj. wide-eyed, blue-eyed, babe in the woods, a narb, narbo, cube, square, L7, duck, lamb, sucker, patsy, virgin, don't know from nothin', don't know crossways from crosswise, search me. See UNSOPHISTICATED.

NAKED adj. bare-assed, bald, nudie, in the altogether, in the buff, buffo, in the raw, au naturel, skinny, starkers. See NUDE.

NAME n. handle, handle to one's name (title), John Doe, John D., John Hancock, John Henry, moniker, tag, what's-his-name, what's-his-face, brand, flag (assumed), front name, label, tab.

NAME v. finger, lay one's finger on, put one's finger on, put one's finger on something, put the finger on, slot, tab, tag, make, peg, aim, button down, pin down, put down for.

NAMELESS adj. incog, a certain person, John Doe, X, George Spelvin, whatchamacallit, what-d'ye-call-'em, what's-his-face, bearding, I'll never forget what's-his-name. See ANONYMOUS.

NAP n. catnap, forty winks, microsleep, snooze, a few Z's, the nod, spot, rack duty, rack time, bye-bye. See SLEEP.

NAP v. snooze, zizz, grab a few Z's, bag some Z's, cop some Z's, log some Z's, blow Z's, rack time, saw logs, catnap, doss, dozz, doz, rack, grab some shut-eye, knock a nod, cop a nod, dig oneself a nod, collar a nod, catch a wink, take forty winks. See SLEEP.

NAPE n. kitchen (Af. Am.).

NAPKIN n. bib.

NARCOTIC CAPSULE n. cap, doll.

NARCOTICS n. junk, shit, controlled substance, narky, uppers, downers, stuff, hard stuff, hard drugs, cement, goods, Jones, starch, hocus, merchandise, happenings, fix, needle candy, bang, cotics, ice cream (crystal), ammunition, God's medicine, hype, death boy, fruit salad (mixture). See DRUGS. See also AMPHETAMINE, AMYL NITRITE, BARBITURATE, BENZEDRINE, BIPHETAMINE, CHLORAL HYDRATE, COCAINE, COCAINE AND HEROIN, DEXAMYL, DEXEDRINE, DEXTROAMPHETAMINE, DIMETHYLTRYPTAMINE, DIPROPYLTRYPTAMINE, FENTANYL, HASHISH, HEROIN, HEROIN AND COCAINE, HEROIN AND MARIJUANA, ISOBUTYL NITRITE, JIMSON WEED, LSD, LUMINAL PILL, MANDRAKE, MARIJUANA, MDMA, MESCALINE, METHADONE, METHAMPHETAMINE, METHAQUALONE, METHEDRINE, METHYLENEDIOXYAMPHETAMINE, METHYL FENTANYL, MORNING GLORY SEED, MORPHINE, NEMBUTAL, NEMBUTAL AND MORPHINE, OPIUM, PAREGORIC, PEYOTE, PHENCYCLIDINE, QUAALUDE, SECONAL, TUINAL, VALIUM.

NARCOTICS ADDICT n. A-head, head, A.D. See ADDICT.

NARCOTICS ADDICTION n. habit, hook, Jones, jones, sweet tooth, garbage habit (mixture), monkey, monkey on one's back, hooked. See DRUG ADDICTION.

NARCOTICS AGENT n. narc, narco, dope bull, owl, Big John, Fed, Federal, gazer, people, Sam, uncle, Uncle Sam, whisker.

NARCOTICS BUY n. bag, dime bag, nickel bag, paper, dime's worth, ten cents, foil, cap; matchbox, stick (cigarette); quarter bag, can, lid, O.Z., weight (oz.); key, kee, ki (kilo); half a load (15 bags), brick (compressed kilo), bird's-eye.

NARCOTICS, BUY v. make a buy, score, score some, keep the meet, cop, hit, re-up, sail, ten cents, trey, turn.

NARCOTICS DOCTOR n. ice-tong doctor, right rocker.

NARCOTICS HABIT, CURE v. take the cure, kick the habit, kick, cold turkey, go normie, get the monkey off, get the monkey off one's back, off the habit, get straight, clear up, kill the Chinaman.

NARCOTICS MARKETPLACE n. stach house, rock house (fortified), Alphabet Town (N.Y.C.), Sherm Alley (L.A.), head shop, smoke shop.

NARCOTICS OVERDOSE n. OD, oh dee, overjolt, overvamp, overamp, overcharge, burn out, freak out, jazz out, rock out, zone out, zonk out.

NARCOTICS PARAPHERNALIA n. works, toys, spike, point, head kit, kit, fit, outfit, the business, joint (total equipment), flake spoon, cooker, gun, hook, ken ten (lamp for opium), artillery, banger, hype stick, light artillery, needle, pin, quill (matchbook cover), bong (pipe), mary-gin (seed remover), roach clip, Woodstock emergency pipe (aluminum foil); stash bag, stash box, stash jar (marijuana).

NARCOTICS, SELL v. peddle, push, slangin' 'caine, clocking (selling crack), scag trade.

NARCOTICS SELLER n. dealer, pusher, connection, kilo connection (wholesaler), ounce man, the people, peddler, dope peddler, source, one who's holding, hyp, hype, hipe, mother, mule, junker, shover, viper, the Man, heavy man, tea man, reefer man, candy man, swing man, bagman, Big man, scag man, bingles, bingler, broker, house connections, juggler, missionary, operator, trafficker, travel agent (LSD), beat artist, fixer.

NARCOTICS TERMS cut, doctor, phony up (adulterate), cut deck (adulterated), charge, load-load plane (carries narcotics), skinful, shot, hit, piece, can, deck, phony bingle, carrying (possession); scag trade, golden triangle (opium poppy growing area of Siam), factory, underground factory, basement lab, tracks (needle scars).

NARCOTICS adj. up, on the needle, strung-out, skagged-out, mellowed-out, dusted (high on PCP), wiped-out, junked-up, teaed-up, hopped-up, gonged, goofed, kick, charge, maxed, flying, tripping-out, high, wrecked, flight, on the nod, in the ozone, in the zone, wired, snowstorm (party), whistling (no money for a fix), chemical dependency, habit, ice cream habit, chipping (occasional use). See DRUG.

NARCOTICS, USE v. shoot, shoot up, drop, pop, use, space out, nod, fix, take a fix, waste, take a drag, hit, hit the dope, toke, blow major jaw (smoke buds), smoke a toke, smoke a bowl, get high, trip, get off, go on out, get behind, get down, go up, sniff, snort, blow, mainline, freebase, bang, bomb, jolt, joy pop, skin pop, trapdoor, trapdoor scab (injecting under a scab to hide needle marks), geeze, jack up, do drugs, string out, tie up, ping-wing, pin-shot (injected), whistling (no money for a fix). See DRUG USE.

NARCOTICS USE SITE n. head shop, gallery, shooting gallery, ballroom, balloon room, kick pad (detoxification site), parachute, spot.

NARCOTICS USER n. A-head, junkie, user, doper, chipping (occasional use), Cap'n Toke, mainliner, freak, head, hophead, drughead, toxic waste dump, coke head, basehead (freebase), acid head, pillhead, garbage head (mixture), fiend, stoner, needle man, smack slammer, tripper, cokie, Skag Jones, snowbird, goofball. See DRUG USER.

NARCOTICS WITHDRAWAL n. kick the habit, dry out, sweating it out, whistling (no money for a fix), take the cure, clear up, shakes, wet-dog shakes, bogue, cold turkey, become Mr. Fink.

NARRATIVE n. yarn, line, clothesline, long and the short of it, potboiler, old chestnut, old wives' tale, book. See STORY.

NARROWLY adv. by a hair, squeak by, by the skin of one's teeth, pretty near, close shave, practically.

NARROWS n. bottleneck, choke point.

NASHVILLE, TENNESSEE Guitar Town, Nastyvilly, Opryland.

NASTY adj. grody, grody to the max, mung, bunk, gross, beastly, bad-assed, funky (Af. Am.), barfy, pukey, pukoid, scurvy, skewy, bitchy, turbobitch, mean, ornery, cussed, grungy, raunchy, rough, stinking, stanky (Fem.), tough, eighteen-carat, fierce, something fierce, awful, godawful, icky, yucky, lousy, murder, murderous, nuts, poison, bum, doin' dirt, hellish, hell of a note, hipper-dipper. See also UNSAVORY.

NATIONAL AERONAUTICS AND SPACE ADMINISTRATION n. NASA.

NATIONAL ASSOCIATION OF SECURITIES DEALERS AUTOMATED QUOTATIONS n. NASDAQ.

NATIONAL BROADCASTING COMPANY n. NBC, peacock network.

NATIONALIST n. arm waver, flag waver (super), hard hat, hundred percenter, hundred percent 'Merkin, jingoist, patrioteer, scoutmaster.

NATIONAL LEAGUE n. senior circuit (baseball).

NATIONAL ORGANIZATION FOR WOMEN n. NOW, N.O.W.

NATIONAL RAILROAD PASSENGER CORPORATION n. AMTRAK.

NATIONAL SECURITY AGENCY n. NSA, Never Say Anything (denies it even exists), puzzle palace.

NATIVE n. home towner, local, local yokel, landsman, paesano.

NATIVE AMERICAN n. Injun, redskin, buck, brave, red man (all Derog.); redskin apple, Uncle Tomahawk (white establishment-oriented).

NATIVE, PACIFIC ISLANDS n. Guinea, Ginny; Geechie, Cheeckee, goo-goo, gu-gu, gook (WWII, all Derog.).

NATURAL adj. 1. on the natch, go organic. 2. folksy, haimish, homey, with the bark on, all hanging out, up front, free-spirited, down, get down, let down one's hair, break loose, cut loose, loose wig, stretched-out, laid-back. See also PLAIN.

NATURALIST n. bug hunter, bugologist.

NATURALLY adv. natch, but of course.

NATURE n. 1. thing, one's thing, like, likes of, one's way, the way of it, way it is, that's one all over, just like one, where one's at, bag, one's bag, the name of that tune, nature of the beast. See also CHARACTERISTIC. 2. heart, point, key, stuff, nub, drift, meat, score, bottom line, name of the game, nitty-gritty, nuts and bolts, punch line, nature of the beast.

NAUGHT n. zero, big zero, zip, zippo, zip city, zot, zilch, cipher, scratch, squat, diddly, diddly-squat, doodly-squat, egg, duck egg, goose egg, bagel, beans, borscht, shut out, empty, harlot's hello, horse collar, nit, nada, 86. See NOTHING.

NAUGHTY adj. 1. bad-assed, barfy, bum, doin' dirt, raunchy, rough, tough, tough nuggies, tripe, eighteen-carat, hellish, hell of a note, hipper-dipper. 2. holy terror, little dickens. 3. adult, purple, blue, dirty, hot, porn, porno, steamy, low-down and dirty, off-color, rough, salty, raunchy, fast, fast and loose, loose, speedy. See OBSCENE.

NAUSEATED adj. barfy, pukes, pukish, puky, rocky, sick as a dog. See also VOMIT.

NAUTICAL adj. salty, seagoing.

NAVAL LIEUTENANT COMMANDER n. two-and-a-half striper, two-and-one-half striper.

NAVAL OFFICERS n. gold braid, crow.

NAVEL n. belly button.

NAVIGATIONAL DATA n. fix, on track.

NAVIGATOR n. clerk, pencil pusher, Magellan (aircraft).

NAVY PERSONNEL n. mate, shipmate, gob, blue jacket, tar, Jack Tar (Obs.), hack driver (chief petty officer); snipe, black shoe, mule (flight deck handler).

NAVY UNIFORM n. blues, dress blues, whites, dress whites, bell bottoms, peacoat.

NEAR adv. around, along toward, on the bubble (borderline), screwdriver turn away, warm, hot, burning, whoop, within a whoop and a holler, within two whoops and a holler, within a stone's throw, in spitting distance, in the vicinity of, in the neighborhood of, in the ball park, upwards of, pretty near, hair's breath, give or take a little, practically, on one's heels, close by, close shave, slicing it thin, near miss, close but no cigar (miss).

NEARLY adv. practically, craptically, around, pretty near, on the bubble (borderline), something like, give or take a little, ballpark figure, in the ballpark of, in the neighborhood of, upwards of, by the skin of one's teeth, close but no cigar (miss).

NEAT adj. apple-pie, apple-pie order, tacked down (Af. Am., neatly dressed), neat as a button, neat as a pin, Bonnie Brillo (neat person), slick, to rights, all policed up, in good shape, shipshape. See also ORDERLY, METHODICAL.

NEBRASKA Beef State, Cornhusker State, Tree Planter State.

NECESSARY adj. bottom-line, key, plain vanilla, nitty-gritty, where it's at, name, name of the game, cold, cold turkey, nub, meat and potatoes, coal and ice. See also VITAL.

NECK n. stretcher.

NECKBAND n. choker, dog collar, (priest), horse collar (protective).

NECKLACE n. choker, chocker, ice.

NECKTIE n. choker, chocker, noose, stretcher.

NECROPHILE n. necro, table hopper, table topper, cadaver cadet, slab boy.

NECROPHILIA n. raiding the icebox, frig frigging, slabbing, table hopping, table topping, getting some cold comfort, having a stiff one on the rocks.

NEED n. itch, the urge, have one's tongue hanging out for, weakness, fire in the belly, the munchies (food). See DESIRE.

NEED v. ache for, drive for, yen for, die for, letch for, hurting for.

NEEDY adj. have-nots, truly needy, disadvantaged, deprived, underdeveloped (nation or district), the poor, piss-poor, flat, dead broke, bag lady, oofless, on the rocks, down-and-out, down to one's last cent, down-at-the-heel, seen better days. See DESTITUTE.

NEGATE v. be agin, kill, ding, zing, cap, splash, put down, pass on, not (used at end of a positive sentence), nix, blackball, break with, buck, dump, turn down, turn thumbs down, stuff it, stick it, shove it, cram it up one's ass, stick it up one's ass, shove it up one's ass, stick it in one's ear, fly in the face of; plead a five, take the fifth (plead the fifth amendment); stonewall. See also CANCEL.

NEGATION n. N.O., nix, no way, November Foxtrot Whiskey (no fucking way), no way José, no sale, bump that, forget it, fat chance, stonewall, negatory, like fun, like hell. See DENIAL.

NEGATIVE adj. not (used at end of a positive sentence), anti, agin, con, ornery, stuffy, draw a blank, not so hot, no-go, Velveeta, Cap'n Chedda, nasty, sick, debit side, on the debit side, on the down side, the bad news, nix, have no use for.

NEGLECT v. ig, let it go, tune out, fuck off, goof off, dog, dog it, live with, pay no mind, pay no never mind, let go to pot, let slide.

NEGLIGENT adj. asleep at the switch, pay no mind, slapdash, sloppy, by halves, leave oneself wide open. See CARELESS.

NEGLIGENTLY adv. any old way, any which way, do by halves, knock off, knock out, bat out, shove out, slap out, slap up, slapdash, throw off, toss off, toss out, mess around, fast and loose, half-assed, helter-skelter, higgledy-piggledy.

NEGOTIATE v. 1. dicker, deal, cut a deal, done deal, hack out a deal, hammer out a deal, make a deal, work out a deal, hondle, horse trade, wash (without gain), swap, swap horses, Jew down (Derog.), knock down the price, come across with, dish out, drop, fork over, network with, connect with, have truck with. 2. make it, make the grade, make out, pull off, pull it off, do the trick, turn the trick, do the job, put it over; break out with, bust out with (surprisingly or suddenly), deal with, get there, hack it, squeak by (barely).

NEGOTIATOR n. go-between, fixer.

NEGRO n. brother, sister, blo, blood, bro, soul; nigger, member, moolie, spade, smoke, coon, darkie, buck, boogie, shine, spook, splib, eightball, geechee, shvartzeh (Yid.), jigaboo, zigaboo, handerkerchief head (all Derog.). See AFRICAN AMERICAN.

NEGRO, FEMALE n. sister, soul sister; band, bantam, barbeque, covess dinge, dange broad, black and tan, banana, bird's eye maple, high yella, high yeller, high yellow, lemon, poontang (sexual Derog.), Aunt, auntie, Aunt Jane, Aunt Jemima, Aunt Tom, Sapphire (all Derog.).

NEGROPHILE n. nigger lover (Derog.), Crow Jimism.

NEIGHBOR n. homeboy (Af. Am.), homey.

NEIGHBORHOOD n. nabe, hood, the block, the blot, the street, neck of the woods, stamping ground, stomping ground, old stomping grounds, territory, turf, ghetto, inner city, slurb, shanty town, skid row, slum, jungle, zoo. See also DISTRICTS.

NEIGHBORING adj. around, whoop and a holler, stone's throw, spitting distance, pretty near, close by, just down the road, just down the pike. See NEAR.

NEMBUTAL n. purple heart, yellow, yellow angel, yellow bullet, yellow jacket, blockbuster, pill, nebbie, nem, nemish, nemmie, nimby, abbot.

NEMBUTAL AND MORPHINE n. purple heart.

NEMESIS n. bugaboo, dues. See also PUNISHMENT.

NEO-CONSERVATIVE n. neo-con.

NEOPHYTE n. rookie, newie, newbie, greeny, punk, boot, new kid on the block, fish, tenderfoot, jice, new jice. See NOVICE.

NERVE n. balls, guts, heart, stomach, what it takes, grit, spunk, starch, chutzpah, intestinal fortitude, Dutch courage (intoxicated). See COURAGE.

NERVOUS adj. wired, wired up, uptight, hung-up, in crisis mode, basket case, hyper, defrosted, horny (sexual), creeped out, jittery, jumpy, pissin', shittin', agita, butterflies, goosy, shaky, shivery, quivery, charged, high, spazzed-out, flipped-out, freaked-out, shook-up, all shook up, worked-up, all worked up, clutched, clutched-up, tightened-up, hopped-up, all keyed up, keyed-up, steamed-up, strung-out, high-strung, trigger-happy, on pins and needles, on tenter-

hooks, on the ragged edge, don't trip, all hot and bothered, choked, yantsy, zonkers, twitty, have one's teeth on edge, wreck, nervous wreck, bundle of nerves, nervy, all-overish, jumpy as a cat on a hot tin roof, shot to pieces, fall apart, sweaty, have kittens, cast a kitten, the screaming meemies, the meemies, heebie-jeebies, the jams, the jims, jimjams, the jumps, jitters, on the gog, spooked, got a wild hair up one's ass, in a sweat, in a cold sweat, sweating bullets, shaking in one's boots, in a lather, in a dither, in a swivet, in a tizzy, in a foofaraw, in a pucker, have a short fuse, have the leaps, have butterflies in one's stomach, work oneself into a stew, work oneself into a lather, work oneself into a tizzy, work oneself into a pucker, get hot under the collar, run a temperature, race one's motor, shit in one's pants, fuzzbuzzy.

NERVOUS BREAKDOWN n. basket case, crackup, schizzed out, psyched out, breakdown, come apart at the seams, conk out, strung out.

NERVOUSNESS n. creeps, cold creeps, shivers, cold shivers, sweat, cold sweat, fidgets, jitters, willies, heebie-jeebies, jimjams, jumps, shakes, quivers, trembles, dithers, butterflies, all-overs, flap, fuss, lather, needles, stew, to do, zingers, pucker, swivet, tizzy, goose bumps, stage fright, buck fever. See also ANXIETY.

NETHER WORLD n. hell, hot spot, other place, down there.

NETTLE n. 1. sticker. 2. tiff, miff, pet, stew, snit. See ANNOYANCE.

NETWORK n. hookup, net, LAN (local area network, computer), coast-to-coast hookup.

NETWORK, BROADCAST n. web, net.

NEUROTIC adj. screwed-up, hung-up, uptight, tightened-up, clutched, clutched-up, wired, wired-up, choked, yantsy, zonkers, spooked, sick, sickie, wreck, nervous wreck, shot, shot to pieces, basket case, bundle of nerves, on the ragged edge, on the gog. See also NERVOUS.

NEUTRAL adj. vanilla, flat, copout, straddle, nothingarian, anythingarian, dawk (neither a dove or a hawk), neither fish nor fowl, play it cool, could care less, don't care one way or another, don't care one way or t'other, don't give a shit, don't give a damm, don't give a hoot, what's the diff?, what the hell, so what?, it's all the same to me, call 'em as one sees 'em, the middle ground, middle of the road, on the fence, fence-sitter, even-steven, no-man's-land, mugwumpian, mugwumpish.

NEUTRON BOMB n. cookie cutter, Enhanced Radiation Device, ERD, Wall Street weapon.

NEVADA Battle-Born State, Divorce State, Sagebrush State, Silver State.

NEVER adv. no way, forget it, fuck that noise, not on your life, not on your tintype, bump that, yank on that, you should live so long, don't hold your breath, in a pig's eye, it'll be a cold day in July, it'll be a cold day in hell, till hell freezes over, tomorrow, manana, one o' these days, any day now, on the 31st of February.

NEW adj. state-of-the-art, the leading edge, the cutting edge, at the cutting edge, po-mo (postmodern), avant-garde, fly, now, the now generation, today, with it, chilly, what's happening, breaking new snow, breaking new ground, what's in, the in-thing, contempo, mint, cherry, newey, brand-new, spanking new, brand spanking new, fire new, hot off the fire, hot off the griddle, hot off the spit, hot off the press, just out, up-to-date, up-to-the-minute, last word, the latest, latest thing, latest wrinkle, new wrinkle, newfangled, newfangled contraption, comer, young Turk, new blood, new boy on the block, new kid on the block.

NEWCOMER adj. new kid on the block, young Turk, turkey, blow in, rook, rookie, new blood, wetback, bracero, cheechako, chukoko, Johnny-come-lately, fish, tenderfoot, greenhorn, greenie; Hunk, Hunkie, bohunk, Bohunk (Derog.). See also NOVICE.

NEW ENGLAND down east, Yankee Land, Chag, (New Englander).

NEW ENGLAND COLLEGES n. Ivy League, Halls of Ivy.

NEWFOUNDLANDER n. Newfig, Newfie.

NEW GUINEA NATIVE n. Guinea, guinea, Ginney, ginney, Ginnee, ginee, guinie (all Derog.).

NEW HAMPSHIRE Granite State, White Mountain State.

NEW JERSEY Clam State, Garden State, Jersey Blue State, Mosquito State, New Spain.

NEW MEXICO Cactus State, Land of Enchantment, Spanish State, Sunshine State.

NEW ORLEANS, LOUISIANA Dixie Town, Craw Town, Fun City, Jazz City, Crescent City, Orleans, Mardi Gras City, the Big Easy.

NEWS n. info, infotainment (TV), slime-time (TV talk show), leak, network, tie-in, hookup, cue, clue, flash, scoop, poop, hot poop, poop sheet, ammo, pipeline, boot snitch, score, skinny, hot skinny, lowdown, dirt, dope, dope sheet, medicine, inside dope, inside wire, insider, tip, hot tip, the know, picture, chip, handout, squib, whole story chapter and verse, goods, brass tacks, garbage, goulash (false), ear loft, break, breaking story, beat, the latest, what's happenin', what's going down, chip, brush-up, earful, ear duster, hash, haymaker, hotshot, hot wire; kick in the ass, shot in the ass (bad); are you ready for this?, let one in on, page-oner, gone cold (old). See also REPORT.

NEWSMONGER n. sleazemonger, yenta, catty, polly, satch, gasser, load of wind, windbag, busybody, tabby, tattletale.

NEWSPAPER n. daily, rag, scandal sheet, sheet, bladder, blat, bulldog (earliest edition), chroniker, extra, fish wrapper, snitch sheet, toilet paper, reefer (reference to inside story).

NEWSPAPERMAN n. animal (political campaign), scribe, scrivener, columnist, stringer, leg man, newshen, cub, pen driver, pen pusher, pencil driver, pencil pusher, scratcher, ink slinger. See also WRITER.

NEWSPAPER OPINION SECTION n. op-ed page.

NEWSPAPER SELLER n. newsie, newsy, newspaper boy, newspaperman.

NEWS TERMS (TV) b-roll, background roll (establishing shot); shooter (camera operator), cutter (editor), sound bite, TRT (total running time).

NEWSWORTHY adj. newsy, splash, break, hot item.

NEW YORK Empire State.

NEW YORK CITY Big A, Big Apple, Gotham, Big Lady, Fun City; Hymie Town, Jew York (Derog.); N.Y., NYC, Noo York, the Big Smear, the Big Onion, the City.

NEW YORK RESIDENT n. Gothamite, Madhattaner, Noo Yawker.

NEW ZEALAND Down Under.

NEW ZEALANDER n. kiwi, Anzac.

NEXT adv. next off, coming up.

NIBBLE v. munch, munch on, nab at, snack, peck, peck at, graze, nosh, eat like a bird. See EAT.

NICE adj. all reet, rightee, ducky, Joe Nice Guy, Mister Nice Guy, Mr. Nice Guy, good joe, sweet, a sweetie, a sweetheart, so sweet she can give you cavities, so sweet he can give you diabetes (too nice), pussycat, a real butt-kicker, not half bad, coolville, chilly most, copacetic, okay, fucking-A, okey-doke, hunky-dory, fine and dandy, Jake, peachy, swell, fat, neato, nifty, orgasmic, home cooking, gasser, groovy. See AGREEABLE.

NIGGARDLY adj. cheap, close, tight, last of the big-time spenders, skinflint, screw, Scrooge, Scotch, squeezing the eagle, piker. See STINGY.

NIGH adj. round, warm, hot, burning, within a whoop and a holler, within a stone's throw, in spitting distance, pretty near, hair's breadth, close by. See NEAR.

NIGHT n. black, dim, after dark, after hours.

NIGHTCLOTHES n. nightie, shortie, baby dolls, jams, jammies, jam jams, P.J.'s, peejays, pygies, sleepers, sleeping suit.

NIGHTCLUB n. night spot, nitery, club, disco, saloon, joint, after-hours joint, juke joint, juice joint, hop joint, rub joint, right joint, scatter, scatter joint, clip joint, gyp joint, trap, boob trap, drum, dump, dive, toilet, spot, hot spot, shine box, honky-tonk, speakeasy, blind pig, blind tiger, crib, fleshpot, frolic pad, free-and-easy, hideaway, room, rum room.

NIGHTCLUB ACT n. floor show, peep show, girlie show, topless, T and A, tits and ass.

NIGHTCLUB SECURITY n. bouncer.

NIGHTFALL n. black, dim.

NIGHTGOWN n. nightie, shortie, baby dolls. See also NIGHTCLOTHES.

NIGHT-ORIENTED PERSON n. night owl, night people, swing shifter, graveyard shifter.

NIGHTTIME n. black, dim.

NIGHT WATCHMAN n. Charley, stick.

NINCOMPOOP n. dork, dorf, dickhead, dickweed, dickwad, simp, dimbo (girl), yutz, lop, doyburger, feeb, lorg, gump, hamburger, jel, nobody home, dumdum, bonetop, ninny, airedale, musclehead, butthead, blockhead, pointyhead, pinhead, saphead, puddinghead, potato head, numbskull, knows from nothing, doesn't know enough to come in out of the rain, one sandwich short of a picnic, belt does not go through all the loops, doesn't have both oars in the water, stoop, deadass, gink, nuthin' upstairs, nitwit, dope. See STUPID.

NINE n. niner, niner from Caroliner, Nina from Carolina.

NINETEEN-TWENTIES n. roaring twenties, golden twenties, jazz age, age of the red-hot mamas, mad decade.

NIP v. nab at, sink one's teeth into, take a chunk out of, chaw on.

NIPPLES n. nips; razzberries, rosebuds (Fem.); bee bites (M.).

NITROGLYCERINE n. nitro, dinah, dine, grease, juice, noise, soap, pete, stew.

NITROMETHANE n. juice, pop, nitro.

NITROUS OXIDE n. laughing gas.

NITWIT n. nerd, numbnut, ditzo, dorf, megadork, dorkmunder, dickhead, dickweed, dickwad, cheese dong, goob, lump, subhuman, mouth breather, mental giant, mental midget, beau, lunchbox, lunchsack, vacant lot, Z-head, feeb, lorg, gump, jel, lamebrain, birdie (teenage), clambrain, fuckbrained, scatterbrain, rattleweed, dumdum, four-letter man (dumb), McFly, hamburger, boob, airedale, airhead, helium head, butthead, balloonhead, conehead, meathead, pointyhead, broomhead, zombie, numbskull, stupe, thick, gink, goofus, Barbie and Ken, leak in the think tank, dunce, dead ass. See STUPID.

NO adv. no way, N.O., nix, November Foxtrot Whiskey (no fucking way), no dice, no-go, nope, naw, no siree, no way José, no can do, no sale, no soap, not (used at end of a positive sentence), frig it, fuck that noise, bump that, yank on that, bite my clit, not on your life, nothing doing, negatory, go jump in the lake, take a hike, like hell, shove it, shove it up your ass, stick it up one's ass, stow it. See DENIAL.

NOBLE adj. 1. big, live with, a mensch. See also VIRTUOUS. 2. blueblood, silk-stocking, ritzy.

NOBLE n. blueblood, silk stocking.

NOBLEMAN n. blueblood, lace curtain, silk stocking, swell, upper cruster.

NOBODY n. empty suit, herb, wimp, squid, wuss, little guy, lop, semi-dork, nebbish, squirt, small potato, nobody, Mr. and Mrs. Nobody, Tom Dick and Harry, zilch, zero, zip, zippo, zip city. See UNIMPORTANT.

NOISE n. jam, ruckus, fuss, buzz-buzz, hoo-ha, clinker, rowdydow, hubba-hubba, hullabaloo, fireworks.

NOISE, MAKE v. squawk, squack, put up a squawk, holler, beef, howl, raise a howl, put up a howl, raise Cain, raise a ruckus.

NOISY adj. ear-poppin', ear-splitting, wall-shaking, booming, turned-up, cranked, can't hear yourself think, raising the roof, screaming, jumpin', loudmouth, leather-lunged, yakky, raising Cain, raising hell, rambunctious, rootin'-tootin', rowdy-dowdy, ziggy.

NOMINAL adj. all there, as advertised, right on.

NOMINATE v. tab, tag, peg, put down for, name, slot, slate.

NONADDICTIVE DRUG n. soft drug.

NONAPPEARANCE n. no-show, break a date, stand one up.

NONCHALANCE n. cool, keeping one's cool, polish.

NONCHALANT adj. cas, cazh, cool cat, cool, unflappable, laid-back, breezy, mellow, loose, hang loose, not turn a hair, go with the flow, poker-faced, phone it in. See INDIFFERENT.

NONCOMMISSIONED OFFICER n. NCO, non-com, sarge, topkick, tech sarge; ripper, ripple (WAVE); Hollywood corporal, zebra.

NONCOMMITTAL adj. 1. middle-of-the-road, on the fence, fence-sitter, play it cool, it's all the same to me, the middle ground, even-steven, no-man's-land, mugwumpian, mugwumpish. See NEUTRAL. 2. buttoned-up, clam, clam up, hush-hush, zip one's lips, button up one's lip, between one and the lamppost, tight chops, play it cool.

NONCONFORMING adj. anti, agin, con, beat, beatnik, beat generation, offbeat, off the beaten track, off the beaten path, dudical, radical dude, cool, far out, way out, avant-garde, flake, flakey, fringy, kinky, bent, weird, weirdo, coo-coo, cooky, kook, kooky, off the wall, out in left field, zoid, trippy, off base, out of line, march to a different drummer. See also ECCENTRIC.

NONCONFORMIST adj. maverick, oddball, swinger, bohemian, an original, offbeat, beatnik, hippie, yippie, dropout, freak, flower child, nature boy, street people, night people, crazy, weirdo, weirdie, fish out of water, square peg in a round hole.

NONCONFORMIST, BE A v. drop-out, opt out, cop out, get out of line, rock the boat, make waves, leave the beaten path, kick over the traces. See also DISAGREE.

NONDRINKER n. A.A., teetotaler, on the wagon, on the water wagon, Christer.

NONE n. zip, zippo, zip city, zilch, goose eggs, shit-all. See also NOTHING.

NONENTITY n. empty suit, herb, wimp, little guy, squid, nebbish, pipsqueak, small potato, jackstraw, nobody, zilch, zero, zip, zippo, zip city. See UNIMPORTANT.

NONESSENTIAL adj. deadwood, excess baggage, Mickey Mouse, need it like a hole in the head, this I need?, who needs it. See also UNIMPORTANT.

NONFUNCTIONAL adj. crashed, down, go down, on downtime, no go, busted, dusted, out of commission, on the blink, on the fritz, kaput, freeze up, frozen, haywire. See DAMAGED.

NONINTERVENTION n. butt out, not butt in, cool one's heels, sit on one's ass, sit on one's butt, sit on one's duff, sit on one's hands, mind your own beeswax, hands off (usually management), peanut policy (Pol.).

NON-JEW n. goy, goyim, shegets, shiksa (all Derog.).

NONPAREIL adj. world-class, 10, ten, A number one, ace high, mega-gnarly, zero cool, chilly most, aggro, rad, Jake, ginchy, slammin', fabu, fab, dyno, dynamite, state-of-the-art, flash, tops, first-class, first-chop, stellar, daddy, cherry, deffest, dope, dual, fat, fierce, fresh, fully on, fully, mint, nitro, on the strength, raw, sick, stupid fresh, lampin', happenin', evil, wicked, boss. See BEST.

NONPARTICIPANT n. nonstarter, along for the ride.

NONPARTICIPATION n. peanut policy (Pol.), butt out, not butt in, cool one's heels, sit on one's ass, sit on one's butt, sit on one's duff, sit on one's hands, hands off (usually management), mind your own beeswax.

NONPARTISAN adj. free-wheeling, on one's own, nothingarian, anythingarian, dawk (neither a dove or a hawk), play it cool, middle-of-the-road, on the fence, mugwumpian, mugwumpish. See NEUTRAL

NONPAYER n. deadbeat, deadhead, welcher, welsher, freeloader, load of hay (group), rabbit, stiff, desperado, skipper, skedaddler, schnorrer, no-show, behind.

NON-PAYING adj. skip out, shoot the moon, fly kites.

NONPLUS v. rattle, rattle one's cage, bug, throw, throw into a tizzy, buffalo, fuck with one's head, mess with one's head, play hob with, floor, flummox. See PUZZLE.

NONPLUSSED adj. unglued, discombobulated, defrosted, shook-up, balled-up, hung-up, floored, stunned, struck dumb, thrown, rattled, in a fog, in the twilight zone, bamboozled, buffaloed. See PUZZLED.

NONPROFESSIONAL n. nonpro, am, ammie, ham, bush, bush league, jackleg, Sunday———(e.g., Sunday driver). See AMATEUR.

NONRESISTANT adj. pushover, go along for the ride, go with the flow, wimpy, blah. See also SUBMISSIVE.

NONSAILOR n. landlubber, ground gripper.

NONSENSE n. jazz, jive, bafflegab, double-talk, gobbledygook, hoke, hokum, hoky, hoky-poky, hop, bub, noise, applesauce, poppycock, tommyrot, rot, narrishkeit, fiddlesticks, twaddle, bunch of baloney, baloney, phoney boloney, globaloney, phonus bolonus, spinach, gas, wind, song and dance, bunk, bunko, bunkum, bull, bull-pucky, shit, bullshit, BS, horseshit, pile of shit, crap, crapola, ap-cray, shit for the birds, bird turd, stuff and nonsense, blah, blah-blah, bushwah, boushwah, bosh, banana oil, blarney, chicken, cheese, a line of cheese, claptrap, tripe, pshaw, caca, total cahcah, guff, scat, bop, drool, bilge, piffle, moonshine, fiddle-faddle, flamdoodle, flapdoodle, flumadiddle, balloon juice, hot air, piss and wind, horsefeathers, hooey, fudge, slush, hogwash, garbage, malarkey, full of beans, full of hops, full of hot air, full of prunes, talk through one's hat, talk like a man with a paper ass, tell it to the marines, crackpot, crackers cockamamie, cockeyed, bughouse, off the wall, wacky, wacko, loco, loc, blue loco, loony, loopy, loose, screwloose, screwy, screwball, squirrely, birdie (teenage), skag, jerky, batty, sappy, goofy, daffy, kooky, potty, dotty, ding-a-ling, dingy, dippy, dumbo, dumb-de-dumb-dumb-dumb, dumb thing to do, dumb trick, fool trick, fool's trick, foolheaded, meatballism, goofy, goo-goo, gaga, cuckoo, meshuga, meshugana, fruity, fruitcakey, nutty as a fruitcake, nutty, nutsy Fagan, nuts, just plain nuts, nerts, dizzy, bananas, goofus, bonkers, barmy, beany, buggy, bugs, round the bend, snap case, do the crazy act, do the crazy bit, do the crazy shtick.

NONSUPPORTIVE adj. off the reservation.

NONTIPPER n. deadbeat, flathead, stiff, clutch, George, Eddy, load of hay (party).

NONUNION WORKER n. scab (strikebreaker), red apple, papoose, scissorbill, free rider.

NONWHITE n. breed, generic, off-brand (Derog.).

NO PARKING red zone.

NOOSE n. rope, hemp, the hemp, hemp four-in-hand, hemp bridle, hemp collar, hemp necktie.

NORFOLK, VIRGINIA Sailor City.

NORMAL adj. together, all there, glued (antonym: unglued), as advertised, right, right in the head, in one's right mind, have all one's buttons, have all one's marbles, have both oars in the water, up to par. See also AVERAGE.

NORTH AMERICAN DEFENSE COMMAND n. NORAD.

NORTH ATLANTIC TREATY ORGANIZATION n. NATO.

NORTH CAROLINA Old North State, Tar Heel State.

NORTH DAKOTA Flickertail State, Sioux State.

NORTHERN CALIFORNIA No Cool, Nor-Cal.

NOSE n. smeller, schnoz, schnozzola, schnozzle, bazoo, beak, bugle, horn, honker, honk-honk, hooter, snoot, nozzle, banana, bill, beezer, boke, boko, conk, handle, sniffer, snuffer, whiffer.

NOSTALGIA n. schmaltz, goo, mush, slop, glop, slush, sob story, tear-jerker, hearts and flowers.

NOSTALGIC adj. 1. syrupy, drippy, soppy, tear-jerker, beery, sticky, sappy, sloppy, gushing, hearts and flowers, cornball, mushy, shmaltz, schmalzy. See SENTIMENTAL. 2. down memory lane, strike a note, like it was yesterday, old hat, rhino.

NOSTRUM n. fix, quick fix.

NOT adv. N.O., nix, ixnay, no way, no dice, nope, unh-unh, uh-uh, ugh ugh, nah, naw, no siree, no way José, no can do, no sale, no soap, ask me another, frig it, forget it, forget you, who me?, not on your life, not by a long shot, not by a long chalk, not by a long sight, not by a damm sight, not a bit of it, not a chance, not a Chinaman's chance.

NOTABLE adj. heavy, heavy stuff, serious shit, something else, big-league, major-league, top-drawer, high-profile, hot flash, underlined. See IMPORTANT.

NOTABLE n. name, biggie, big name, big gun, big man on campus, B.M.O.C., big cheese, magoo, high up, high pillow, face card, hot dog, V.I.P., visiting fireman, lion, a somebody, in the limelight. See IMPORTANT. See also CELEBRITY, EXECUTIVE.

NOTE n. 1. memo, line, thank-you note, scratch, reminder. See also LETTER. 2. football (Mus., whole note), lick (music).

NOTE v. flash on, dig, spot, clock, take in, tumble, take a tumble, catch, get an eyeful of, get a load of, pick up on. See SEE.

NOTEBOOK n. little black book.

NOTED adj. celeb, star, name, number 1, number one, numero uno, a somebody, w.k. (well-known), face, lion, page-oner, hot dog. See CELEBRITY.

NOTEPAPER n. scratch pad.

NOTEWORTHY adj. heavy, meaningful, splash, stand-out, super-duper, dag, terrific, the utmost, the end, mind-blowing, boss, bitchin', cool, chilly most, murder, serious jelly, something else, big-league, major-league, high-profile, hot shit, we're not talking about nutmeg here, underlined. See IMPORTANT.

NOTHING n. 1. zero, big zero, zip, zippo, zip city, zot, zilch, nix, cipher, goose egg, duck egg, egg, shutout, empty, horse collar, nit, a collar, nada, 86, scratch, squat, diddly, diddly-squat, diddly-poo, shit, diddly-shit, doodly-squat, dunnage (dockworker use), beans, Jack, jack shit, borscht, fly speck, flea, chit, chirp, a chromosome, crumb, drip, dinky, measly, minimal to the max, from nothing. 2. chickenfeed, chickenshit, Mickey Mouse, gadget, rinky-dink, nutmeg, two by four, two-bit, nickel and dime, penny ante, peanuts, pissy-tailed, big deal, no big deal, big shit, no big shit, no biggie, no big thing, no skin off one's nose, never mind, no matter; ain't no thang, ain't no thing but a chicken wing (Af. Am.), bupkes, a hump, shot, tinhorn, entry level (job), bottom rung, lower rung, small potatoes, small spuds, small beer, small change, small time, small pot, pokerino, pinchy, one-horse, jerkwater (small town), nowhere, drop in the bucket, drop in the ocean, sucking wind, little go, macht nichts, mox nix, makes no never mind, no great shakes, mere bagatelle, flying fuck, frig it, chuck it, drop it, forget it, let it pass, skip it, not worth a hill of beans, not worth a row of beans, row of buttons, row of pins, damn, darn, tinker's dam, a hoot, got other fish to fry, other fish in the sea, other pebbles on the beach, raggedy act, harlot's hello. 3. asshole, assface, wuss, wimp, empty suit, herb, jerk, lop, penis wrinkle, semi-dork, sad sack, nebbish, squirt, twerp, shrimp, scrub, runt, squid, little guy, small pototoes, small fry, cipher, zero, nobody, Mr. and Mrs. Nobody, Brown Jones and Robinson, John Doe and Mary Roe, John Doe and Richard Roe, Tom Dick and Harry, pushover, winner, real winner, dog, scrub, dag, loser, real loser, punk, tinhorn, flat tire, dud, skag, pipsqueak, whippersnapper, whiffet, flash in the pan, jackstraw, man of straw, gerk (old).

NOTICE n. info, tip, score, picture, lowdown, know, goods, cue, clue, dope, dope sheet, poop, poop sheet, squib, write-up, story, whole story. See NEWS. See also ADVERTISEMENT.

NOTICE v. flash on, dig, spot, clock, take in, tumble, catch, get an eyeful of, get a load of, pick up on, rap, rumble. See SEE.

NOTICEABLE adj. big as life, one can't miss it, open-and-shut, open-and-shut case, under one's nose, if it was a snake it would bite you. See APPARENT.

NOTIFICATION n. tip, hot tip, info, score, lowdown, goods, cue, clue, dope sheet, poop sheet, let one in on. See INFORMATION.

NOTION n. weenie, spark, flash, flash on it, approach, slant, take, twist, wrinkle, angle, how one figures it. See IDEA.

NOTORIETY n. 1. flak, ballyhoo, splash, big noise, ink, noise about, pitch, scratch, spread, bell, make a big splash, get ink. 2. flash in the pan, on center stage, in the spotlight.

NOTORIOUS, BE v. live in a glass house, hanging out, spot one like a lead dime, stick out like a sore thumb, make a splash, page-oner, wanted, candy, candy kid, duded up, belled. See CELEBRITY.

NOUGHT n. zero, big zero, zip, zippo, zip city. See NAUGHT.

NOURISHING adj. sticks to one's ribs.

NOURISHMENT n. eats, feed, grub, go juice, lump, finger food, sticks to one's ribs, vittles, grubbery, hots (hot meal, Mil.), home cooking. See FOOD.

NOVEL adj. offbeat, dif, diff, far cry, funky, at the cutting edge, breaking new snow, avant-garde, now, contempo, fire new, just out, newfangled. See NEW.

NOVEL n. book, yarn, clothesline, cliff-hanger, stroke book (Porno.), bodice-ripper (romance), splatterpunk (violent, lurid), potboiler, spyboiler. See STORY.

NOVELTY n. an original, crazy, oddball, weird, last word, fire-new, new fangled contraption. See NEW.

NOVICE n. rook, rookie, newie, newbie, greeny, gremlin, gremmie, freshie, turkey, punk, boot, starter, new blood, new boy, new boy on the block, new kid on the block, break in, gazooney (maritime), fish, greenhorn, student, tenderfoot, heel, heeler (reporter), peg boy, pratt boy, buckwheater, cheechako, chukoko, dub, jice, new jice, john, mark, know from nothing, not know the score, not be with it, not know one's ass from one's elbow, not have the foggiest, first of May. See also APPRENTICE, RECRUIT, BEGINNER.

NOW adv. pronto, on the double, double time, like now, balls out, toot sweet, off the pop, in jig time, in nothing flat, pretty damned quick, PDQ. See IMMEDIATELY.

NUB n. bottom line, heart, meat and potatoes, nitty-gritty. See BASIC.

NUCLEAR ACCIDENT n. event, meltdown, China syndrome, broken arrow.

NUCLEAR PARTICLES n. fallout, zoo.

NUCLEAR POWER n. glowboy (plant employee).

NUCLEAR TERMS nuclear football (electronic controls carried by head of state), soft (vulnerable target).

NUCLEAR WEAPON n. nuke, mininuke, backpack nuke, doomsday machine, physics package, special stores (N.).

NUCLEAR WEAPONS SYSTEMS n. MX, Cruise, Stealth, Honest Johns, MARv, MIRv, Goloshes, Scuds, Frogs, Scapegoats, Aphids, Sparrows, Kangaroos, Kitchens, Walleyes, Fishpots, Tweets, Aardvarks.

NUDE adj. bare-assed, B.A., peeled, bald, buck naked, naked as a jaybird, nudie, in one's birthday suit, in the altogether, buff, buffo, in the buff, native buff, stripped to the buff, raw, in the raw, without a stitch, an naturel, skin, wear a smile.

NUISANCE n. headache, drag, pain, pain in the ass, pain in the neck, blister, buzz crusher, nudzh, noodge, nudge, nag, bummer, creep, pill, drip, kibitzer, flat tire. See ANNOYANCE. See also BORE.

NULLIFY v. zap, scrub, kill, trash, cream, torpedo, ax, crab, squash, dial back, forget it, knock out, call all bets off, scratch, blow off, blue-pencil, dust, wash out, wipe out, stamp out, take out, renig, nig. See CANCEL.

NUMBER v. count noses, count heads, count off, tick off, cut ice, cut some ice, dope out, figure in, keep tabs, run down, take account of, tote, tote up.

NUMBERLESS adj. umpteen, zillion, jillion, bazillion, eleventeen, rafts, gobs, heaps, bags of, bokoo, boku, no end of, no end to. See COUNTLESS.

NUMBERS, LARGE n. zillion, skillion, gillion, jillion, stillion, bazillion, eleventeen, forty-'leven, skaty-eight, umpteen, umpteenth, umpty, umpty-umpth, steen, flock of, googol, googolplex, slew, whole slew of, a boodle, whole kit and boodle, caboodle, whole kit and caboodle, everybody and his brother, everyone and his uncle. See also AMOUNT, LARGE.

NUMBERS RACKETEER n. digits dealer.

NUMBERS, SMALL n. buttons, peanuts, nothing, bupkis, next to nothing, practically nothing, no one, practically no one. See also AMOUNT, SMALL.

NUMEROUS adj. umpteen, zillion, jillion, bazillion, mucho, gobs, scads, heaps, lousy with, bokoo, boku, stacks. See AMOUNT, LARGE.

NUN n. hood.

NURSE n. sitter, baby-sitter, white cap, death crew (overnight shift), nanny, mammy.

NURSE v. sit, baby-sit, watch over, watch out for, keep an eye on, keep tabs on, ride herd on.

NURSEMAID n. sitter, baby-sitter, nanny sitter, mammy, nanny.

NURTURE v. bring up, fetch up, drag up.

NUTRITIOUS adj. sticks to one's ribs.

NYMPHET n. nymph, nympho, sex job, Lolita, jail-bait, San Quentin quail.

NYMPHOMANIAC n. hose monster, broad, nymph, nympho, fast, swinging, bone addict, sleep around, C.S.P. (casual sex partner), pushover, round heels, helium heels, stanky tuna, easy lay, easy woman, loose, loose woman, woman of easy virtue, mink, chippie, chippy, floozy, punch-board, alley cat, scrump queen, hosebag, for free, tramp, bum, slut, dog, frail, frail sister, blimp, bombshell, charity girl, chaser, run around, floss around, cuddle bunny, fruit, town pump, piece of trade, pigmeat (old), sex job, ginch.

O

O n. Oscar, Oboe.

OAF n. boob, numbnut, asshole, droob, drube, loser, winner, lamebrain, birdie (teenage), birdbrain, clambrain, ditzo, dorf, dork, dorkmunder, mutant, dimbo (Fem.), doofus, lump, remo, subhuman, mouth breather, mental giant, mental midget, dickhead, Fred, Barney, Wilma, biff (girl), beau, penis wrinkle, feeb, out to lunch, lunchie, lunchbox, lunchsack, vacant lot, Z-head, dip, gink, lorg, gump, hamburger, dodo, dummy, dumbo, dum-dum, dumb Dora, dumb head, dumb ox, twillie, four-letter man (dumb), gerk (old). See STUPID.

OAKLAND, CALIFORNIA Big Oak, Oaktown.

OATH n. four-letter word, cuss, cuss word, dirty word, dirty name, no-no, swear word. See also EXPLETIVE.

OATMEAL n. grits, cush, mush.

OBDURATE adj. 1. thick-skinned, cold fish, cold-blooded, mean, rhinoceros hide, dead ass. See CALLOUS. 2. hard-nosed, hang tough, tough nut to crack, take no prisoners, head in concrete, set in concrete, rock-ribbed, hard-headed, burly, bullhead, stubborn as a mule. See STUBBORN.

OBEDIENT adj. in one's power, in one's pocket, in one's clutches, under one's thumb, at one's mercy, at one's beck and call, at one's feet, a slave to, on a string, on a leash, yes-man, ass-kisser, pussy-whipped, led by the nose, tied to one's apron's strings, dance to one's tune, putty in one's hands. See also SUBMISSIVE.

OBESE adj. fatso, fat city, whale, hippo, baby elephant, oinker, heavy, blimp, crisco, butterball, full-figured, judy (girl), two-ton tessie, avoirdupois. See FAT.

OBEY v. knuckle under, go by the book, go by the numbers, stay in line, not get out of line, toe the line, toe the mark, lie down and roll over for, go along with, give in, don't make waves, don't rock the boat, go with the flow, go social. See COMPLY.

OBFUSCATE v. con, diddle, double-talk, sell wolf cookies, muddy the waters, stir the waters, pettifog, cloud the issue, throw up a smokescreen, blow smoke, blow smoke up one's ass, stonewall, cover up, fuzz (words). See CONFUSE.

OBITUARY n. obit.

OBJECT n. 1. jobby, dealie bob, motherfucker, mofo, mother grabber, gimmick, gismo, widget, do hinkey, shtick, dingus, whatchamacallit, whatzis, frobnitzem. See APPARATUS. 2. ground zero, surgical mission (precise target), zero.

OBJECT v. 1. bitch, beef, get off my case, get outta town, give me a break, don't sweat me (Af. Am.), cut me some slack, make a stink, gripe, sound off, gritch, squawk, crab, grouse, kick. See COMPLAIN. 2. be agin, buck, take on, mix it up with, tangle with, cross, go one on one. See OPPOSE.

OBJECTION n. bellyache, beef, where's the beef?, bitch, kick, squawk, stink, gripe, blackball. See GRIEVANCE. See also DISAPPROVAL; CRITICISM.

OBJECTIONABLE adj. it sucks, sux, sucky, beat, bummer, take down, downside, bad news, bad scene, godawful, murder, poison, lousy. See UNDESIRABLE. See also OBNOXIOUS.

OBJECTIONABLE PERSON n. asshole, assface, barney, geek, geekoid, scrounge, nightie (nightmare), smack (overachieving geek), wanker, bub, cull, turkey, toad, phrog (person), creep, barf bag, jerk, drip, chirp, chit, nerd, dexter, full hank, lop, narc, spud, squid, twink, woofie, penis wrinkle, wet blanket, stinky, twerp, gives one a pain, gives one a pain in the neck, gives one a pain in the ass, gripes one. See UNDESIRABLE PERSON.

OBJECTIVE adj. like it is, call 'em as one sees 'em, cool, cold, cold turkey, strictly business, straight, straight from the shoulder, the emess, no shit, no bull, no bullshit, no bullshitting, on the square, warts and all. See also FAIR, UNEMOTIONAL.

OBJECTIVE n. ground zero, surgical mission (precise target), zero.

OBLIGATED adj. hooked, into, on the tab, in hock, on a string, owe one one.

OBLIGATION n. IOU, in debt, in the red, in hock, on the nut, hooked, chit, due bill, dues. See DEBT. See also RESPONSIBILITY.

OBLIGE v. fit in, fill the bill, be just what the doctor ordered, be just the ticket, make room, meet halfway, go fifty-fifty, find the middle ground, don't rock the boat, don't make waves, roll with the punches, swim with the tide, if you can't beat 'em join 'em, when in Rome do as the Romans do, toe the mark, grin and bear it, take it, come around, come over, move over, bend over backwards, lean over backwards, make a deal.

OBLITERATE v. blue-pencil, scrub, nix, kill, cut, X out, ax, zap, trash, total, cream, torpedo, do in, dial back, waste, off, finish, finish off, knock off, knock out, kayo, KO, sink, bog, squash, smash, smash up, bitch up, scratch, shoot down, shoot down in flames, put the kibosh on, wash out, wipe out, wipe off the map, take out, take apart, tear down, stamp out, rub out, blue ruin, blow sky high, fix, fix one's wagon, come down on, cook, cook one's goose, destabilize, deep-six (evidence). See also CANCEL, KILL.

OBLITERATED adj. scrubbed, killed, offed, wasted, shot, shot down, shot down in flames, washed out, wiped out, all bets off, all off, kaput, zapped, totaled, nixed, scratched, blue-penciled, rubbed out. See also KILLED.

OBLIVION n. no-man's-land, out there, gone, nowhere.

OBLIVIOUS adj. gorked, gone, zonked, spacey, out to lunch, strung out, not all there, not with it, zoned out, z-head. See UNCONSCIOUS.

OBNOXIOUS adj. rotten, gross, awful, beastly, stinking, stanky (Fem.), chopped, hane, scoob, goob, goober, goobatron, yernt, barney, geek, geekoid, scrounge, nightie (nightmare), smack (overachieving geek), obno, obnoc, nob, social zero, nothing burger, cheesehead, cheeseface, Captain Cheddar, hodad, hodaddy, bunk, pail, bucket, it rots, poxy, skewy, grody, grody to the max, pesky, pestiferous, bitchy, cussed, mean, ornery, funky (Af. Am.), chromo, crumb, creep, turd, nerd, nudnick, pill, heel, shitheel, shit hook, scumsucker, big mouth, gives one a pain, pain in the ass, pain in the neck, hunk of cheese, blue, off-color, off time, zod.

OBOE n. thermometer, snake charmer, ill wind.

OBSCENE adj. filthy, feelthy, dirty, blue, X-rated, adult, porn, porno, porny, raunchy, raw, mature, hard-core, soft-core, hot, heavy, hot and heavy, hot stuff, jack-off material, jerk-off material, steamy, rough, rough stuff, evil-minded, foul-mouth, foul-mouthed, salty, off-color, off-base, out-of-line, low down, low-down and dirty, smutty, flaming (Obsc., computer conversations), jiggly, purple, in the gutter, horny, cream jeans, C.F.M. (come fuck me: sexually suggestive clothing), hot pants, a lech on, lechin's.

OBSCENITY n. scuz, smut, sleaze, cuss, cuss word, dirty word, dirty name, four-letter word, no-no, swear word, porn, porno, soft porn, hard porn, soft core, hard core, skin flic, skin pix, snuff, T and A, Tijuana Bible, X-rated, triple X-rated, hot stuff, jack-off material, jerk-off material, peep show.

OBSCURE adj. clear as mud, clear as dishwater, clear as ditch water, heavy, fuzzy, mumbo-jumbo, Greek, it's Greek to me, Choctaw, double-Dutch, tough, tough nut to crack, mind-bending, it beats me, beats the shit outta me, you've got me, you got me, I pass, I give up, too much, too deep for one, over one's head.

OBSCURE v. con, diddle, double-talk, muddy the waters, stir the waters, pettifog, cloud the issue, throw up a smoke screen, blow smoke, blow smoke up one's ass, stonewall, cover up. See also EQUIVOCATE; CONFUSE.

OBSERVANT adj. on the ball, on the job, on one's toes, on the lookout, on the qui vive, not miss a trick, not overlook a bet, see to. See ATTENTIVE.

OBSERVATION n. saying, catchphrase, crack, wisecrack, say-so, comeback, mouthful (you said a mouthful).

OBSERVATION POST n. O.P., catbird seat.

OBSERVE v. 1. flash, flash on, beam, spot, spy, dig, read, lamp, catch, eagle-eye, eyeball, take in, get an eyeful of, get a load of, check this out, bus it (Af. Am.), pick up on. See SEE. 2. go slumming, slum, take in the sights, gap, jap (crime). 3. mouth off, crack, wisecrack, spring with a crack.

OBSERVER n. kibitzer, nark, sidewalk superintendent, watcher, gaper. See also AUDIENCE.

OBSESSED adj. fiendish, gone, hung up, bugged, hooked, taken over by, into, really into, heavily into, up to here in, head over heels in, all wound up in, wrapped up in, eat sleep and breathe something, turned on, tied up, have a bee in one's bonnet, have a bug in one's ear, have a bug up one's ass, have an ax to grind, have a thing about, have a tiger by the tail.

OBSESSION n. hang-up, jones, monkey, a must, have a thing about, have on the brain, bug, bug up one's ass, bug in one's ear, bag, ax to grind, bee, bee in one's bonnet, head in concrete, set in concrete, one-track mind, tiger, tiger by the tail, case, crush (romantic).

OBSOLETE adj. out, gone, had it, out of it, dust, has-been, old-hat, dinosaur, fossil, horse-and-buggy, icky, back number, of the old school, dead as a dodo, dead and done for, done for, moldy fig, played-out, kaput. See also DEAD.

OBSTACLE n. catch, joker, Catch-22, hang-up, psychological baggage, stumbling block, monkey wrench, booby trap. See HINDRANCE.

OBSTETRICIAN n. baby catcher.

OBSTINATE adj. hard-shell, hang in there, hang tough, locked-in, head in concrete, set in concrete, chiseled in stone, solid as a rock, brick wall, stand one's ground, dig in one's heels, stick to one's guns, pigheaded, dead set on, have one's Dutch up. See STUBBORN.

OBSTINATE, BE v. hang in, hang in there, hang tough, hang on, hang on for dear life, hang on like a bulldog, hang on like a leech, stick it, stick it out, stick to it, stick with it, stick to one's guns, go the whole hog, go all out, go through hell and high water, go for broke, go for it, not give up the ship.

OBSTREPEROUS adj. rambunctious, raising a riot, raising a ruction, raising a rumpus, kicking up a row, out of order, out of line. See also NOISY.

OBSTRUCT v. hang up, hold up, foul up, fuck up, queer, stymie, crab, put one in a box, gum up the works, stonewall, blow smoke, stall, weigh down, drag one's foot, hang like a millstone round one's neck, sandbag, monkey with the buzz saw, monkey with, mix in. See HINDER. See also PREVENT.

OBSTRUCTION n. stumbling block, one small difficulty, a lock, jam-up, monkey wrench, booby trap, gridlock. See HINDRANCE.

OBTAIN v. snag, grab, cop, kipe, kype, corral, wangle, promote, latch on to, scare up, snap up, buy up, blow oneself to, access, capture (computer data). See GET.

OBTAINABLE adj. on tap, on deck, in stock, push-over, come-at-able, getable, get-in-able, no sweat, no problem, no biggie, duck soup, cherry pie, piece of cake, can o' corn, ready willing and able, there for the taking, ready to be plucked, ready to be taken. See also EASY.

OBTUSE adj. nerky, lamebrained, birdbrained, four-letter man (dumb), thick, clodpated, blockheaded, pointyheaded, woodenheaded, deadheaded, flat tire, numbskulled, doesn't know which way is up, doesn't know enough to come in out of the rain, wouldn't know it if it bit him in the ass, dope, dead-ass, dub, drip, farmer, Barbie and Ken, slow on the uptake, slow on the draw. See STUPID.

OBVIOUS adj. ob, barefaced, plain as the nose on one's face, crystal-clear, big as life, open-and-shut, open-and-shut case, goes without saying, you know it, cheesecloth (person). See APPARENT.

OCARINA n. sweet potato.

OCCASION n. hap, happening, happenso, scene, goings-on, go down, come off, cranking, time. See EVENT.

OCCASIONALLY adv. once in a blue moon, once in a coon's age, every now and then, every once in a while, every so often.

OCCIDENTAL n. round-eye (Derog.).

OCCUPATION n. gig, day gig, rig gig (truck driving), bag, beeswax, biz, schmear, game, gesheft, line, line of business, number, go, do, dodge, wheelin' & dealin', what one is into, thing, hang, nine-to-five shit, rat race, slot, setup, grind, daily grind, grindstone, lick, moonlight, the salt mines, play, racket, swindle, grift, gyppo, jippo, hemo jo, shitwork, chickwork (household), scutwork, donkeywork, coffee-and-cake job. See also WORK.

OCCUPATIONAL SAFETY AND HEALTH ADMINISTRATION n. OSHA.

OCCUPIED adj. at warp one, clocked up, busy as a bee, busier than a one-armed paperhanger, tied up, head over heels in, enough on one's plate. See BUSY.

OCCUR v. gel, jell, shake, smoke, what goes, what's coming down, what's going down, action, where's the action?, what's happening, cook, cook up a storm, what cooks?, what's cooking?, cooking with gas.

OCCURRENCE n. happening, hap, happenso, go down, come off, cranking, trip, real trip, like it is, where it's at, the size of it, scene, bit, piece, routine, shtick, spot, goings-on, if the balloon goes up (the worst). See EVENT.

OCEAN n. drink, big drink, the pond, big pond, bounding main, deep, the briny, briny deep, Davy Jones' locker, sink, splash.

ODD adj. funky, kooky, offbeat, funny, weirdo, weirdie, bogus, melba, oddball, foul ball, avant-garde, fringy, kinky, geeky, flaky, quirky, far out, way out, crazy, off the wall, not wrapped real tight, character, spacey. See ECCENTRIC.

ODIOUS adj. ornery, mean, stanky (Fem.), chromo, crumb, barf bag, creep, turd, heel, shitheel, scumsucker, pain in the ass, pain in the neck. See OBNOXIOUS.

ODOROUS adj. stinko, stinky, stinking, whiffy, nosy, strong, loud (strong).

OF prep. a (piece a cake).

OFFEND v. zing, turn off, diss, cool, chop, cut up, sound dozens, lay a bad trip on one, flip one the finger, flip one the bone, give one the bone, burn, give five fingers to one, hit one where one lives, do a number on one, kick one around. See INSULT.

OFFENDED adj. dissed, burnt-up, browned-off, bleeding, sore, all torn up, cut-up, miffed, miffy, hit where one lives, shook, shook-up, shot down, peeved, uptight, have one's nose out of joint. See also INSULTED.

OFFENSE n. 1. put-down, zinger, rap, cap, slam, black eye, hit, dirty dig, left-handed compliment, slap in the face, low rent, bazoo, raspberry. See INSULT. 2. blitz, blitzkrieg, push, mugging. 3. blot on the landscape, sight, dump.

OFFENSIVE adj. rotten, gross, stinking, grody, chromo, crumb, turd, blue, off-color, off-time. See OBNOXIOUS.

OFFER n. feeler, hit, proposish, proposition, pass, pitch, action.

OFFER v. hit on, proposition, make a pitch, put a feeler out, pop the question.

OFFHAND adj. laid-back, cool, mellow, cas, cazh, breezy, easygoing, down home, homey, haimish, folksy, pokesy, sporty, let one's hair down. See CASUAL. 2. throwaway, ad lib, off the cuff, off the hip, off the top of one's head, shoot from the hip. See IMPROVISE.

OFFICE n. workstation, cave, foundry, salt mines, front office, kiva, shop, store, setup, electronic cottage (home worker).

OFFICEHOLDER n. pol, politico, glad-hander, handshaker, hack, party hack, satch, war-horse, wheeler-dealer, logroller, boss, man higher up, baby kisser, bell-ringer. See POLITICIAN.

OFFICER n. cop, slime, bucket (Derog.); arm, narc (narcotics), the man, bubblegum man, black-and-white, badge, city kitty, Snow White, county mounty, flatfoot, fly cop, fly dick, shamus. See POLICE OFFICER.

OFFICER'S CLUB n. henhouse.

OFFICE WORK n. nine-to-five, nine-to-five shit, white collar, pink collar, desk jockey, catching (police duty), day gig, shitwork, salt mines.

OFFICIAL n. CEO, exec, exec suite, big shot, upstairs, man upstairs, front office, boss, suit, kingpin, brains, head, headman, old man, papa, Big Daddy, Big Brother, brass, top brass, brass hat, gold braid, the topper, the top, on top, top dog, top drawer, higher-ups, perkman, space cadet (young), apparatchik (junior), rug rank (high), cee gee, killjoy, S.O.P., buck passer. See also EXECUTIVE, POLITICIAN, POLICE OFFICER.

OFFICIALDOM n. pecking order. See also ADMINISTRATION, BUREAUCRACY, ESTABLISHMENT, MANAGEMENT.

OFFICIALISM n. red tape, red tapism, red tapery, foolocracy, gunocracy, mediocracy, moneyocracy.

OFFICIAL LANGUAGE n. officialese, legalese, federalese, bafflegab.

OFFICIAL PAPERS n. ticket.

OFFICIATE v. do the honors, boss, chair, ride herd on, run, handle. See also MANAGE.

OFF-KEY adj. clinker, hit a clinker, sour, hit a sour note, sour note.

OFF SEASON n. fifth season, slack season, pinochle season (clothing industry).

OFFSPRING n. kid, sprout, bambino, nipper, pup, cub, chip off the ole block, little shaver, little bugger. See CHILD.

OGLE v. gun, gawk, glom, hold the glims on, lamp, pipe, get a load of, get an eyeful of, give the double O, smoke, rubber, rubberneck, 87 1/2 (look at a girl, restaurant), give the eye, give a thing a play. See SEE.

OGLER n. girl-watcher, drugstore cowboy, rubberneck, rubbernecker. See also FLIRT.

OHIO Buckeye State.

OIL n. devil's tar, liquid gold, mud, oil patch (oil-producing area).

OIL v. grease the wheels, lube, slick, slick on.

OIL-FIELD WORKER n. roughneck, sloper (Alaska).

OILING v. grease job, lube.

OILSKIN n. slicker, mack, fog.

OIL-WELL INVESTOR n. oilie.

OKAY interj. OK, O.K., A-OK, A-O.K., A-okay, okey-dokey, okey-doke, four, ten-four, four-ten (emphatic), easy, I can live with that, you got it, it's going on, shoot, that'll work, that works for me, not half bad, ding-ho, ding-how, ding-hau, ding-hao, no slouch, all reet, reat, right, all right, solid, aces, aljoe, alzo, swell, dory, oky-dory, hunky-dory, ducky, just ducky, peachy, peachy-keen, copacetic, twenty-two-carat, goods, jake, keen, keeno, kosher, McCoy, nuts, pat, patsy. See also ACCEPTABLE.

OKINAWAN n. Okie (Army use, Derog.).

OKLAHOMA Sooner State.

OKLAHOMA CITY, OKLAHOMA Okie (Derog.).

OKLAHOMAN n. Okie (Derog.).

OLD adj. 1. rusty, moth-eaten, a lot of mileage, been around, bent, gone, hairy, passé, oldie, old as the hills, tired, worse for wear, back number, fossil, antique, relic, piece, from way back, shot. See also DATED. 2. senior, senior, citizen, pop, gray, gray-haired, blue-haired, older than dirt, old fart, old-timer, wrinklie, no spring chicken, got a few miles on one, on one's last legs, over the hill, older than God, gerk (fool), opal (older person with active lifestyle). See AGED.

OLD AGE n. golden years, golden age, gray power, the dwindles. See also AGED.

OLD-FASHIONED adj. funky, lame, played-out (Af. Am.), tired, out, old hat, passé, back number, moth-eaten, crunchy granola (still living in the sixties), square, corny, horse-and-buggy, of the old school. See DATED.

OLD MAN n. oldster, O.M., old boy, golden ager, senior citizen, senior, gray, gray-haired, pop, pops, dad, gramps, grampa, grandpa, granddad, creak, creaker, back number, antique, relic, fossil, old fossil, geezer, old geezer, dodo, old dodo, duffer, old duffer, gaffer, codger, old codger, coot, old coot, fogy, old fogy, regular old fogey, old fart, old poop, old crock, old-timer, old goat, old bat, old gent, old chap, old cuss, old dog, A.K., alte kocker, alter cocker, baldie, baldy, chrome-dome, buzzard, desert rat, duddy, fuddy-duddy, ager, raisin, upper plates, gink, gummer, pappy guy, foozle, mossback, gerk (fool). See also AGED.

OLD PERSON n. golden ager, senior citizen, no spring chicken, moth-eaten, a lot of mileage, been around, wrinklie, old fossil, old coot, duffer, gerk (fool). See AGED.

OLD WOMAN n. old lady, old girl, oldster, golden ager, senior citizen, senior; P., peep (parent); grandma, gramma, gramms, granny, old granny, old bag, haybag, old haybag, hag, old hag, old dame, old hen, old battle-ax, war-horse, old frump, biddy, biddie, back number, creak, creaker, antique, relic, fossil, old fossil, dodo, old dodo, old folks, old crock, old-timer, old bat, buzzard, ager, raisin, upper plates, gummer, foozle. See also AGED.

OLEOMARGARINE n. margarine, oleo, hard oil.

OLIVE DRAB adj. O.D.

OMAHA, NEBRASKA Beef City, Big O.

OMAHA RESIDENT n. Omahog.

OMBUDSMAN n. troubleshooter, fireman, fixer.

OMIT v. cut, snip, pass up, drop, X out, trim, knock off, See also EDIT, EXCLUDE, FORGET.

ONCE adv. back, back when, away back, time was, in the olden days.

ONE n. uno, numero uno, ace (restaurant), uh.

ONE pron. me myself and I, big three (me, myself and I), number one, numero uno, yours truly, a dude, cat, a ghee.

ONEROUS adj. heavy, hefty, tough, tough proposition, large order, tall order, backbreaker, ballbreaker, ballbuster, rough go, heavy sledding, bitch, headache, beyond the pale, can of worms, it's your funeral. See DIFFICULT. See also TROUBLESOME.

ONESELF pron. yours truly, big three (me, myself, and I), number one, numero uno.

ONE-TIME adj. one-shot, one-shot deal, once in a lifetime.

ONION n. breath, skunk egg, stinker, tear gas, rose.

ONION ROLL n. bialystok, bialy, tsibilah (Yid.).

ONLOOKER n. kibitzer, nark, sidewalk superintendent, watcher, rubbernecker, gaper.

ONLY adj. one-shot, onliest, once in a lifetime.

ONSTAGE adv. on.

OOZE n. goo, gook, gooey, glop, gloppy, Mississippi mud, gunk.

OPEN adj. 1. up front, mellow, call it like it is, lay it on the line, on the level, straight from the shoulder, straight arrow, talk like a Dutch uncle, call a spade a spade, talk turkey. See FRANK. See also FREE, SINCERE, TALKATIVE. 2. folksy, homey, haimish, vanilla, meat-and-potatoes man. 3. come-at-able, get-in-able, getable, reachable, on tap, on deck. 4. open-and-shut, clear as the nose on one's face.

OPEN v. 1. crack, crack open, break out, break in, bust in, kick in, jimmy. See also BREACH, PENETRATE. 2. kick off, ring in, bow, preem, start the ball rolling, get things rolling, raise the curtain on. See BEGIN.

OPENER n. church key (beer).

OPENING n. 1. opener, curtain-raiser, bow, preem, coming out, coming-out party. See also BEGINNING. 2. break, big break, shot, get a shot at, go, go at, a fling at, whack, whack at, cut, cut at, a run at, in the hunt, in the running, iron in the fire, connection. See OPPORTUNITY.

OPENLY adv. in broad daylight, under one's nose, warts and all. See also FRANKLY.

OPERA n. uproar, grand uproar.

OPERATE v. 1. percolate, perk, tick, click, hum, cook, it cooks, whittle, that dog'll hunt, cut (surgical). 2. move, make one's move, move on (to something else), break out with, bust out with (surprisingly or suddenly), do a number, go to town, TCB (take care of business), pull off, get in there, run with the ball. See ACT. 3. head up, sit on top of, run, run things, run the show, large and in charge (Af. Am.), call the signals, call the play, be in the driver's seat, be in the saddle, hold the reins, pull the strings, pull the wires, handle. See MANAGE.

OPERATING adj. hot, on track, on stream, on line, all systems go, hit the ground running, going, in full swing, with a full head of steam, doing one's thing, percolating, cooking, cooking on all burners, ticking, clicking.

OPERATING EXPENSE n. nut, outlay.

OPERATING ROOM n. OR, the pit.

OPERATION n. 1. ball game, scene, trip, where the action is, goin' down, happening, movin' out, plan, stunt, bit, deal. See ACTION. 2. going concern. See BUSINESS.

OPERATION RESTORE HOPE The Tar Baby; N G Os, tree huggers, Birkenstocks (relief workers); flapjacks (looters), rice bandits (steal food shipments).

OPERATIVE n. agent, op, spook, mole, beekie, buddy fucker, humint, plant, rug merchant, sheep dip (Mil. disguised as civilian); enemy: ac-op (active opposition), barbarians, Indians, visiting team, sleeper; company brownnose, keek (industrial), dick, shamus, flatfoot, tec, private eye, P, eye, narc, man, G-man, T-man, revenuer, Federal, fed, FBI; Pinkerton, Pink, Pinkie, the Eye, the eye (Pinkerton detective or Pinkerton National Detective Agency); shoe, gumshoe, gumboot, gumheel, rubber heel, brain, deek, elbow, fink, plumber, sleeper (M.), bird dog, nab, peeper, eagle eye, house dick, door knocker, shadow, shagger, slewfoot, stag, star, tail, pounder, bear tracker (plainclothes), Hawkshaw, sleuth, sleuth-hound, beagle, skip tracer, spotter, cutout (secret intermediary).

OPINION n. take, judgment call, value judgment, op, say-so, slant, two-cents' worth, one's two-cents' worth, vox pop, another country heard from. See also ATTITUDE.

OPINIONATED adj. tilted, weighted, one-sided, cold deck, hard-line, locked-in, head in concrete, stick to one's guns, hardheaded, stuffy, set on, bitter ender, puffed-up, chesty, cocky, bossy. See STUBBORN. See also CON-CEITED.

OPIUM n. O, big O, pop, poppy, pox, grease, pill, Chinese tabacco, gow, ghow, gom, goma, hop, hops, mud, tar, gee, stem, yen, yen shee, pen yan, pen yen, bird's eye, high hat, fire plug, black stuff, black pills, black silk, black smoke, brick, brick gum, dopium, gong, gonger, poppy train, dream beads, dream wax, dream gum, dreams, God's own medicine, midnight oil, yam-yam, smoke.

OPIUM PIPE n. dream stick, joy stick, hop stick, gee stick, saxophone, Chinese saxophone, gong, gongola, bamboo, stem, water pipe, yen hook, stem.

OPIUM, USE v. burn the midnight oil, kick the engine around, kick the gong around, beat the gong, hit the gong, hitting the pipe, lamp habit, ken ten (lamp), lay down, lay up, laying on the hip, lie down, suck bamboo, on the gonger, on the three taps; pill pad, hop joint (den); ice-cream man (dealer).

OPIUM USER n. campfire boy, gongbeater, gong kicker, bowler, gowster, hip layer, pipe hitter, lobby gow, chef, cook (prepares), sick (needs injection).

OPPONENT n. opposish, oppo, opposite number, bad guy, bandit, buddy-buddy (sarcasm), buddy fucker, crip, meat, me and you, angries, dark horse (unknown). See also PRIZEFIGHTER.

OPPORTUNIST n. hustler, finagler, carpetbagger, on the make, operator, wire-puller, bird dog, one on the make, velcroid (sticks to important people).

OPPORTUNITY n. 1. break, breaks, big break, even break, one's move, one's say, one's turn, shot, shot at, get a shot at, whack, whack at, go, go at, stab, stab at, cut, cut at, have a fling at, run at, in the running, in the hunt, opps, prayer, irons in the fire, connection, fair shake, fighting chance, outside chance, fifty-fifty, toss up, level playing field, flier, flyer, plunge, play, action, a find. 2. lucky strike, lucky scratch, lucky hit, lucky break, good break, run of luck, luck out, luck into, a fluke. See LUCK.

OPPORTUNITY, LOSE THE v. blow it, goof, boot, boot it, muff, muff it, bobble it, drop the ball, miss the boat, miss the bus, lock the stable door after the horse is stolen.

OPPOSE v. be agin, go agin, buck, sass, backtalk, top, take on, take out, mix it up with, tangle with, break with, ain't with that (Af. Am.), bump heads with, cross, cross swords with, lock horns with, tell off, square off, face off, face down, put down, jam up, push out your lips at one, go one on one, one to one, mano a mano, have a bone to pick, hold no brief for, hit, take a dim view of, zap, nix, blackball, turn thumbs down on, fly in the face of, put the blocks to, put up a fight, put up a struggle, pan, knock, knock the chip off one's shoulder, straighten out. See also DISAGREE, RESIST, FIGHT, BRAVE.

OPPOSED adj. agin, anti, con, allergic to, down on, ran into a buzz saw (unexpected), have a bone to pick, have no use for, turned off by, copper a tip (act against advice). See also CONTRARY.

OPPOSITE adj. anti, agin, con, other side of the coin, flip side, ass-backwards, bass-ackwards, topsy-turvy, copper a tip (act against advice), ornery, stuffy. See also CONTRARY.

OPPOSITION n. oppo, opposish, opposite number, ran into a buzz saw (unexpected), bad guy, the bad guys, angries.

OPPRESS v. bug, ride, pick on, put the squeeze on, put the screws on, put the heat on, put one through the wringer, on one's back, on one's case, dog, dog one's case, drive one up the wall. See also FORCE, DOMINEER, DEPRESS.

OPPRESSIVE adj. 1. heavy, hefty, mean, heavy-handed, tough, tough proposition, backbreaker, ballbreaker, ballbuster, rough go, heavy sledding, bitch, headache. 2. close, sticky, steam bath, steamy, sweatbox.

OPPRESSOR n. a Hitler, Simon Legree, slavedriver, czar, cossack.

OPTIMAL adj. top-flight, ace-hi, world-class, greatest, gonest, hundred-proof, baaaadest, coolville, gilt-edge, solid gold. See BEST. See also EXCELLENT.

OPTIMIST n. scoutmaster, Pollyanna, ray of sunshine, cheerleader.

OPTIMISTIC adj. rosy, upbeat, bullish, high, high on something, Pollyannaish, sunny, ray of sunshine, keeping the faith, looking at the world through rose-colored glasses, looking at something through rose-colored glasses, looking at the bright side, the game ain't over till the last man is out, one can dream can't one?

OPTION n. flip side, pickup, take it or leave it, other side of the coin, other fish to fry, other fish in the sea, other pebbles on the beach. See also CHOICE.

OPULENCE n. lap of luxury, velvet, bed of roses, high on the hog, living high on the hog, on top of the heap, clover, the life of Riley, Easy Street, frill, frills, icing on the cake. See also PLENTY.

ORAL SEX n. blow job, perm, head, skull (Af. Am.), face, face man, face job, hat job, French, French job, French way, box lunch, fruit cup, fur burger, muff dive, seafood, sugar bowl pie, tongue wash, tuna taco, yodeling in the gully, eating at the Y, blow job, suck, deep throat, shot upstairs, sixty-nine, bananas and cream, penilingism, peter puff (all Obsc.).

ORAL SEX, DO v. eat it, eat out, eat pussy, eat at the Y, French, French kiss, give a face job, give face, give head, give skull (Af. Am.), give cone, go down on, go around the world, have hair pie, muff dive, perform, sit on one's face, sixty-nine, suck, go for sushi, cocksuck, sucky-suck, suck off, blow, blow job, give a blow job, give one a perm, head, deep throat, slob the knob (Af. Am.), cannibal (one who performs), gobble, peter puff, play the skin flute, cop a joint (all Obsc.). See also CUNNILINGUS, DO; FELLATIO, DO.

ORANGEADE n. forty-one (Rest.).

ORANGE JUICE n. OJ, squeeze one.

ORATE v. pitch, spiel, spout, stump, soapbox, get on a soapbox, chew the scenery, blow, blow hot air, lay it on, lay it on with a trowel, lay it on thick, pile it on, talk big, talk tall, talk highfalutin. See also SPEAK.

ORATION n. stem winder (excellent), soapbox oration, pitch, spiel, chalk talk, pep talk. See SPEECH.

ORATOR n. chalk talker, jawsmith, soapboxer, soapbox orator, spieler, spouter, stumper, tub thumper.

ORCHESTRA n. ork, orc, orch, combo, group, sidemen, backup, big band, jump band, swing band, jazz band, jazz blowers, blue blowers.

ORCHESTRA LEADER n. professor, monkey.

ORCHESTRATION n. charts.

ORDAIN v. call the play, call the signals, call the tune, lay down the law, deal, deal with, put one's foot down, read the riot act, walk heavy, bulldoze. See COMMAND.

ORDER n. pecking order, down the line, place, slot. See also SEQUENCE.

ORDER v. 1. lay down the law, pull the strings, call the shots, call the signals, call the tune, crack the whip, rule the roost. See MANAGE. 2. blow oneself to, cop, make a buy, buy off, buy out.

ORDERLY adj. together, all together, glued (antonym: unglued), have all the pieces in place, have one's act together, have one's shit together, have one's head together, have one's head screwed on right, apple pie, apple pie order, neat as a button, neat as a pin, Bonnie Brillo (neat person), slick, to rights, in shape, in good shape, shipshape, all policed up, set-up, fixed, framed, it is laid on. See also METHODICAL.

ORDERLY n. dog robber (WWI).

ORDINANCE n. reg, up to code.

ORDINARINESS n. meatballism, hamfat.

ORDINARY adj. everyday, generic, garden variety, plastic, no great shakes, so-so, strictly union, vanilla, whitebread, rumdum, run of the mill. See AVERAGE.

OREGON Beaver State, Sunset State, Webfoot State.

ORGAN n. 1. god box, wind box, Mighty Wurlitzer. 2. org, insides, guts, parts, nuts and bolts, family jewels.

ORGANIST n. monkey grinder.

ORGANIZATION n. the Company, the Establishment, the Man, syndicate, outfit, T.O., dotted-line responsibility, pecking order, jungle, zoo, org, tie-up, tie-in, tie-in tie-up, hookup, gang, mob, ring, clan, tribe, troupe, combination, combo. See also ASSOCIATION.

ORGANIZATION OF PETROLEUM EXPORTING COUNTRIES n. OPEC.

ORGANIZATION TABLE n. dotted-line responsibility, T.O.

ORGANIZE v. 1. put in shape, clear the decks, button down, tailor, work out a deal, get one's act together, get one's ducks together, pull things together, team up. See ARRANGE. 2. line up, set up, lay out, get set for, frame, mastermind, fix to. See PLAN.

ORGANIZED adj. 1. together, all together, glued (antonym: unglued), have all the pieces in place, have one's act together, have one's shit together, have one's head together, have one's head screwed on right, cut and dried. 2. all lined up, by the numbers, apple pie, apple pie order, slick, to rights, in shape, in good shape, shipshape, set-up, jumped-up (hastily), fixed, framed, it is laid on. See also PLANNED.

ORGANIZED CRIME n. Mafia, Cosa Nostra, the famiglia, the family, syndicate, the organization, our organization, our outfit, our thing, IBM (Italian Business Man), the rackets, the people, the arm, the commission, crime cartel, dope ring, black market, Black Hand.

ORGASM n. get it off, get off, get one's rocks off, come, blow, shoot, shoot one's wad. See SEXUAL CLIMAX, ATTAIN.

ORGY n. bender, bat, binge, tear, toot, wing-ding, bust; circle jerk, circus, circus love, gang bang (all Obsc.). See also PARTY; REVEL.

ORIENTAL n. dink, slope, slant-eye, gook, banana (favors whites, yellow on the outside white inside), gooney, gooney bird, moose (Fem.), rice burger, rice grinder, skibby (all Derog.).

ORIENTATION n. 1. backgrounder, breaking-in. 2. fix, how it is, how the land lies, the lay of the land.

ORIGIN n. 1. opener, square one, day 1, day one, first crack out of the box, from the gate, from the word go, git-go, blast-off. See BEGINNING. 2. horse's mouth, connection, tipster, tout.

ORIGINAL adj. breaking new snow, avant-garde, pomo (postmodern), cherry, O.G. See also NEW.

ORIGINATE v. intro, father, break the ice, open up, think up, come up with, spark, spitball. See CAUSE, INNOVATE.

ORNAMENT n.   gingerbread, bells and whistles, fuss, gewgaws, gimcracks, spinach (excessive), froufrou, dingbat, do-dad, doodad, thing, fandangle, jazz, garbage (food).

ORNAMENT v.   doll up, fix up, gussy up, spruce up, pretty up, ungepotch (Yid.).

ORNATE adj.   showy, glitzy, flashy, splashy, cushy, spiffy, splendiferous, splendacious, chichi, froufrou, lit up like a Christmas tree. See GAUDY. See also ELEGANT; EMBELLISHMENT.

ORPHAN n.   drop, fetch, guttersnipe, mudlark, rustle.

ORTHODOX adj.   straight, straight-arrow, Barbie and Ken, narb, square, by the numbers, in line, in the groove, according to the book. See CONVENTIONAL.

OSCILLATE v.   fishtail.

OSCILLATION n.   judder, pitch, chatter.

OSCULATE v.   swap slops, swap spit, peck, pucker up, smack, smash, smooch, eat face, suck face, face-rape, suck heads, mesh, M.L.A. (major lip action), box tonsils, give a tonsillectomy, play tonsil hockey, go for sushi, a little smacky, buss, French kiss, butterfly kiss, spark, buzz, X, mush, muzzle, sugar, lay one on the lips, mouth music.

OSCULATION n.   mouth music, peck, smack, smooch, X, buss, mush, muzzle, soul kiss, sugar, butterfly kiss, French kiss, lay one on the lips.

OSSINING, NEW YORK   Stirville, Sing Sing.

OSTENTATION n.   shine, splash, splurge, grandstand play, showboat, showoff, show, showing out, for show, false front, put on, put on the dog, flash, Christmas (clothes and jewelry), neon ribbons. See PRETENSION.

OSTENTATIOUS adj.   flashy, splashy, showy, gold-card, uptown, highfalutin, tony, classy, splurgy, duded up. See PRETENTIOUS.

OSTRACIZE v.   blackball, ding, cut, drop, ice out, shut out, turn thumbs down on, leave out in the cold. See EXCLUDE. See also BANISH.

OTHERWISE adv.   or else.

OUST v.   boot out, kick out, bounce, adios one, give one the old heave-ho, give the bum's rush, give 'em the 1-2-3, throw out on one's ear, send packing. See EVICT. 2. give the gate, pink-slip, can, fire, lay off, ax, give the ax, give the air, hand one his walking papers, sack, cut loose (dockworker use), downsize, let one go. See DISCHARGE.

OUSTED adj.   unfrocked (any profession), canned, drummed-out, turned-off, sent packing.

OUSTER n.   ax, sack, boot, the gate, door, bounce, grand bounce, golden handshake (rich bonus guarantee), layoff, rif (reduction in force), early retirement, walking papers, the bullet, bum's rush, old heave-ho. See DISMISSAL.

OUTBOARD MOTOR n.   eggbeater, kicker, putt-putt.

OUTBURST n.   blow, blowup, cat fit, duck fit, conniption, conniption fit, flare-up, wing-ding, shit hemorrhage. See also ANGER.

OUTCAST adj.   iced, blackballed, cold-shouldered, out of the loop, left out in the cold, not in the picture, baldhead, shut out.

OUTCOME n.   upshot, reaction, chain reaction, flak (bad), score, blowoff, payoff, fallout, verdict isn't in on that. See RESULT.

OUTCRY n.   hullabaloo, hoo-ha, flack, hubba-hubba.

OUTDATED adj.   tired, out, played-out (Af. Am.), not with it, old hat, passé, back-number, moth-eaten, has-been, crunchy granola (still living in the sixties), square, ricky-tick. See DATED.

OUTDISTANCE v.   run away, lap, blow out, break out.

OUTDO v.   1. ace, ace out, outgun, beat one's time, top, outfox, end-run, fake out, juke, deek, cop a heel on, cop a sneak on, pull a quickie on, pull a fast one. 2. bury, blank, cook, trim, fix one's wagon, shave, bulldoze, torpedo, tube, trash, cream, do in, lick, snow under, blow out, blow off, blow one out of the water, pin one's ears back, have it all over, bring home the bacon, take the cake, put one's nose out of joint, run rings around, run circles around, clean on. See DEFEAT.

OUTDONE adj.   aced out, blanked, creamed, clobbered, hosed, topped, murdered, skinned, done in, done for, shut down, shut off, flameout, get one's lumps, cry uncle, say uncle. See DEFEATED.

OUTFIT v.   fit out, rig out, rig up, rag out, rag up, turn out, doll up, dog out, dud, dude up, dode (bad fit), suit up, tog, drape, deck, deck out.

OUTHOUSE n.   closet, shithouse, johnny house, necessary, Chic Sale, one-holer, two-holer. See also TOILET.

OUTLANDER n.   floater, blow-in, bum face, geepo, weed, strange weed. See also ALIEN.

OUTLAW n.   crook, hood, con, ex-con, mug, bad actor, bad guy, jailbird, racketeer, wrong number, gang banger, carjacker, gangster, mobster, drifter, saddle tramp, desperado, hoodlum, hooligan. See CRIMINAL.

OUTLAY n.   price tag, bad news, damage, score, tab, bite, nut, bottom line, a throw, below the line, set one back, come to, to the tune of, hummer, highway mopery. See also EXPENSE.

OUTLOOK n. head-set, mind-set, mind-trip, routine, where one's head is, where one is at, where it's at, like it is, the size of it.

OUTMANEUVER v. outfox, ace, ace out, beat one's time, con, end-run, fake out, juke, cop a heel on, pull a fast one. See OUTWIT.

OUTMODED adj. tired, out, played-out (Af. Am.), old hat, bent, back-number, moth-eaten, has-been, dinosaur, horse-and-buggy. See DATED.

OUT-OF-STOCK adj. 86, smack out, clean out, gone clean (The., tickets).

OUTRAGE n. mad, huff, stew, storm, ruckus, conniption, conniption fit, cat fit, duck fit, blowup, flare-up, boiling point. See ANGER.

OUTRAGE v. burn up, whip up, fire up, kick up a row, raise Cain, raise hell, raise the devil, hit the ceiling, reach boiling point, boil over. See ANGER.

OUTRAGEOUS adj. ape, crazy, glorkish, out of all bounds, over the top, worst-case scenerio, last straw, too much, bitter end, the pits. See EXTREME. See also BAD; EXPENSIVE; UNBELIEVABLE.

OUTSIDER n. blow-in, bum face, floater, geepo, weed, strange weed. See also ALIEN.

OUTSKIRTS n. slub, slurb, burb, spread city, bedroom community, sticks, stix.

OUTSMART v. ace, ace out, fox, outfox, pull a quickie on, pull a fast one, finagle, work one's points, put one in the cookie jar, put one in the popcorn machine. See OUTWIT.

OUTSPOKEN adj. up front, lay it on the line, talk like a Dutch uncle, call a spade a spade, make no bones about it, talk turkey. See FRANK.

OUTSTANDING adj. killer, A, A-1, A-number 1, A-number one, A-one, number one, numero uno, primo, ten, 10, ace, ace-hi, aces, def, a gas, world-class, classic, greatest, bump'n', out-of-sight, out-of-this-world, far out, gonest, hundred-proof, mostest, baaaadest, bad, bitchin', twitchin', daddy, lampin', boss, cool, zero cool, coolsville, chilly most, cherry, deffest, dope, dual, fat, fierce, fresh, fully on, fully, mint, nitro, dyno, on the strength, raw, sick, stupid fresh, master (Af. Am.), brutal, evil, wicked, crack, murder, first chop, super; mother, motherfucker, muthah, muthahfuckah, mofo (all Obsc.); key, gilt-edged, splash, wizard, high-cotton, all-time, Sunday best, stone, terrible, terrific, skull, brain, grind, tops, top-of-the-line, top-dog, top-drawer, topflight, top-notch, righteous, tiptop, the most, the end, endsville, savage, solid gold, winner, champ, king o' the hill, white hope, white knight.

OUTWIT v. ace, ace out, beat one's time, cap, top, fox, outfox, goose, con, short con, gyp, jip, end-run, fake out, juke, cop a heel on, cop a sneak on, pull a quickie on, pull a fast one, finagle, work one's points, put one in the cookie jar, put one in the popcorn machine.

OVATION n. hand, big hand, O., standing O., bring down the house, have 'em on their feet, mitt-pound.

OVER adj. hyper.

OVERACT v. ham, ham it up, mug, milk a scene, chew up the scenery. See also OVERDO; DRAMATIZE.

OVERALLS n. Levi's, leaves, coveralls.

OVERAWE v. blow one away, knock one's socks off, hit like a ton of bricks, score big, snow, do a snow job, highbrow, cut you a swath, fold one's ears back (talk). See IMPRESS.

OVERBEARING adj. cocky, bossy, sniffy, snotty, snotnose, smart-ass, uppity, king shit, high-and-mighty, hoity-toity. See ARROGANT.

OVERBLOWN adj. hyped-up, puffed-up. See also AGED.

OVERCHARGE v. rip off, jerk one off, rook, screw, hose, stick, burn, beat, bleed, bleed white, bilk, clip, con, chisel, gouge, gyp, scam, stiff, sting, pluck, take one to the cleaners, take one for a ride, take for a sucker, cream, milk, give one a raw deal, strip bare, skin, hold up, hype, soak, sell one a bill of goods, do in, do out of, chouse, chouse out of, hornswoggle, hook, throw the hooks into. See also CHEAT.

OVERCHARGED adj. been had, been taken, been took, clipped, jobbed, fucked, screwed, stung, hosed, get hosed, stuck, stuck with, fleeced, iced, rooked. See also CHEATED.

OVERCOAT n. greatcoat, car coat, horse blanket, benny, binny, Benjamin, threads, flogger; lead sheet, orchestration (Af. Am.).

OVERCOME adj. blown away, blown out of the water, run over, buried, taken, taken down, swamped. See DEFEATED.

OVERCOME v. 1. kick, kick the bug, kick the habit, kick the illness, normie, get straight, clear up, hit the burner (a crisis). 2. get around, ban-jax, flip, blow away, blow one out, blow one's mind, blow one out of the water, snow, snow under, hit, knock one's socks off. See also DEFEAT, TRIUMPH.

OVERCONFIDENT adj. know-it-all, wise-ass, wise-guy, smarty, smarty-pants, smart-ass, smart-guy, smart-aleck. See also ARROGANT; CERTAIN.

OVERDO v. lay it on, lay it on thick, lay it on with a trowel, puff, hype, ballyhoo, talk big, take it big, blow up something, make a big production of something, make a federal case out of, make a mountain out of a molehill, drive it into the ground, go whole hog, go all out, get carried away, flip, flip out, wig out, bust one's nuts, break one's balls, break one's back, break one's ass, bust one's balls, bust one's back, bust one's ass, gweep (one who is overworked), pressure, push; mug, ham it up, chew up the scenery (The.). See also EXAGGERATE, DRAMATIZE.

OVERDOSE v. overjolt, overvamp, overamp, overcharge, OD, oh dee, burn out, freak out, jazz out, rock out, zone out, zonk out.

OVERDRESSED adj. jellybean, sharpie.

OVERDUE adj. held-up, hung-up, jammed.

OVEREAT v. gross out, blimp out, pork out, pig out, mac out, scarf out, pig down, wolf, narf, trough out, grease down, hoover, make a pig of oneself, eat out of house and home. See GLUTTONIZE. See also EAT.

OVERENTHUSIASTIC adj. freaked-out, overboard, steamed-up, flipped, rarin' to go, throw out the baby with the bathwater. See ENTHUSIASTIC.

OVEREXCITED adj. hyper, wired-up, fire-up, revved, revved-up, amped, spazzed-out, freaked-out, zonkers, like crazy, like mad, hit the ceiling, hog-wild, have a shit hemorrhage. See EXCITED.

OVEREXERT v. go all out, break one's balls, break one's back, break one's ass, bust one's hump. See OVERDO.

OVEREXTENDED adj. in too deep, out of one's depth, over one's head, bit off more than one can chew, too many irons in the fire, too many balls in the air, don't write a check your ass can't cash.

OVERHAUL n. facelift, retread, fix up, doctor, fiddle with, debug, redline (Mil.).

OVERHEAD n. nut, outlay.

OVERHEAR v. catch, get, read, be all ears, get an earful, hear tell. See also LISTEN; EAVESDROP.

OVERHEAT TIRES v. fry the tires.

OVERINDULGE v. go whole hog, go big time, get carried away. See OVERDO. See also EAT.

OVERINDULGED adj. spoiled rotten.

OVERLOOK v. 1. look the other way, ig, tune out, live with, pay no mind, pay no never mind, play past, pooh-pooh, go along with, be big, handle, put up with, suck it up, stomach something, grin and bear it, string along with, roll with the punches, play the game, swim with the tide, bear with, stand for, take. 2. wipe the slate clean, whitewash, let off, let go, let it go, wipe it off, write off, let one off easy, let one off this time, wink at, blink at. See ABSOLVE. See also FORGIVE. 3. be asleep at the switch, let go to pot, let ride, let slide, fall between the chairs, fall between the cracks.

OVERLY adv. too much, too-too.

OVERNICE adj. nicey-nice, sticky, so sweet she can give you cavities, so sweet he can give you diabetes (too nice),

OVERPAY v. pay through the nose.

OVERPLAY v. lay it on thick, blow up something, make a mountain out of a molehill, get carried away; mug, ham it up, chew up the scenery (The.). See OVERDO.

OVERPOWER v. clobber, trash, drub, kayo, total, cream, waste, take out, take care of, lay one out. 2. bury, blank, murder, trounce, swamp, smoke, shellack, bulldoze, roll over, torpedo, tube, meat-ball, make one say uncle, beat all hollow, shut off, blow away, put away. See DEFEAT.

OVERPOWERED adj. blanked, creamed, clobbered, topped, trimmed, trounced, murdered, snowed, snowed under, shut down, blown away, blown out, have one's ass in a sling. See DEFEATED.

OVERPRAISE v. spread it on, lay it on, lay it on thick, lay it on with a trowel, snow, work over, suck ass, kiss ass, kiss butt, ballyhoo, phony up, puff up, bullshit, bullskating (Af. Am.), shoot a line, fall all over. See FLATTER.

OVERPRICE v. rip off, jerk one off, run a game on, rope in, flimflam, stick, burn, bleed, bleed white, bilk, clip, con, chisel, gouge, gyp, stiff, sting, take, take one to the cleaners, give one a raw deal, skin, hold up. See OVERCHARGE.

OVERPRICED adj. paid through the nose, out-of-sight, steep, stiff, heavy sugar, holdup, highway robbery, highway mopery. See EXPENSIVE.

OVERREACH v. bite off more than one can chew, write a check your ass can't cash, have too many irons in the fire, have too many balls in the air.

OVERREACT v. freak out, spazz, spazz out, blow a hype, take it big, flip, flip out, wig out, get carried away, drive it into the ground, go whole hog, make a mountain out of a molehill; mug, ham it up, chew up the scenery (The.). See also REACT.

OVERRIPE adj. bum, bummy.

OVERSEE v. captain, skipper, herd, shepherd, ride herd on, baby-sit, sit on top of, run the show, call the shots, be in the driver's seat. See MANAGE.

OVERSEER n. boss, big brother, head, head honcho, bosshead, super, suit, skipper, old man, top hand, digger, the man, pit boss, kingpin, bull, straw boss, slavedriver, pusher. See EXECUTIVE.

OVERSENSITIVE adj. hyper, wired-up, uptight, hung-up, wreck, nervous wreck, shot to pieces, thin-skinned, can't even look at him cross-eyed. See SENSITIVE.

OVERSHOES n. galoshes, goloshes, rubbers, gunboats, pup tents. See also SHOES.

OVERSIGHT n. slip-up, goof, boot, dumb trick, mis-cue, fool mistake. See MISTAKE.

OVERSIGHT FUNCTION n. watchdog.

OVERSLEEP v. sleep in. See also SLEEP.

OVERSTATE v. talk trash, lay it on, snow, give one a snow job, cook, shovel the shit, puff, ballyhoo, overdo it, hit too hard, make a mountain out of a molehill, make a federal case out of something. See EXAGGERATE.

OVERSTATEMENT n. baloney, malarkey, jazz, jive, hype, line, bullshit, bullskating (Af. Am.), that dog won't hunt, thick, whopper, snow job, blow job, build up, the big lie (Pol.), tall tale, big talk. See EXAGGERATION.

OVERTALKATIVE adj. big-mouthed, all jaw, gabby, gassy, windy. See TALKATIVE.

OVERTAX v. run into the ground, drive it into the ground, bust one's nuts, gweep (one who is overworked), pressure, push. See OVERDO.

OVERTHROW v. destabilize (espionage use).

OVERTIME n. golden time, runover, time and a half, double time, triple time, burn the midnight oil, pull an all-nighter.

OVERTIRED adj. bushed, wiped out, blown out, wrung out, wore out, draggin' ass, worn to a frazzle, nearly dead, done in, all in, bone-tired, bone-weary, dog-tired. See TIRED.

OVERTLY adv. under one's nose, in broad daylight.

OVERTURE n. openers, feeler, pitch, proposition, proposish, big idea (unwelcome).

OVERWEIGHT adj. fatty, tubby, spare tire, biggums, Dunlop syndrome, chubby, chubbo, heavy, heavy cream, hefty, Bertha, zaftig. See FAT.

OVERWHELM v. 1. bury, steamroller, blank, kill, swamp, bulldoze, roll over, torpedo, tube, meatball, make one say uncle, do in, beat all hollow, snow, snow under, finish off, blow one out of the water, run rings around, run circles around, clean on. See also ASTONISH 2. take out, shut out, wipe out, wipe off the map, total, knock the props out from under. See DEFEAT.

OVERWHELMED adj. aced-out, blanked, burned, bit the dust, creamed, clobbered, hosed, topped, murdered, snowed, snowed under, done in, blown away, blown-out, in too deep, out of one's depth, over one's head, up to one's ass in, wrote a check your ass can't cash, bit off more than one can chew, too many irons in the fire. See DEFEATED. See also ASTONISHED.

OVERWORK v. drive it into the ground, go whole hog, get carried away, bust one's nuts, gweep (one who is over-worked), pressure, push. See OVERDO.

OVERWROUGHT adj. spazzed-out, creeped-out, wired-up, hyper, keyed-up, defrosted, hissy, all shook up, hopped-up, steamed-up, fired-up, got a wild hair up one's ass, flipped-out, freaked-out, high, stoned, zonkers, hot-and-bothered, hot under the collar, like crazy. See EXCITED.

OVERZEALOUS adj. off the deep end, go off the deep end, step off the deep end, throw out the baby with the bathwater. See ZEALOUS. See also EAGER.

OWE v. be into one for, behind, ducking one, on the cuff, on the tab, on the tick, in hock.

OWED adj. comeuppance, what is coming to one, what one has coming.

OWNED AND OPERATED adj. O and O.

OWNER n. landprop, saw, slumlord, governor.

OWNERSHIP n. piece, piece of a joint, cut, end, slice, make a grab, muscle in, push in, take over, unfriendly takeover (by coercion).

OX n. bull (logger).

OXFORD ENGLISH DICTIONARY n. O.E.D.

OXYGEN n. oxy, gox (gaseous), lox (liquid).

OXYGEN MASK n. bag.

OZONE LAYER n. Antarctic doughnuts (hole).

P

P n. Papa, Peter.

PACE n. 1. clip, lick, getalong. 2. beat, bounce, downbeat, brown-off (break).

PACIFIC OCEAN n. Big Drink.

PACIFIER n. trank, tranx, backwards, dope, goofball, knockout drop, Mickey Finn, gig, gigi, gee-gee.

PACIFIST n. dove, dove of peace, peacenik.

PACIFY v. cool, cool out, cool it, cool off, stroke, con, schmear, butter up, grease, pour oil on troubled waters, take the edge off, take the bite out, take the sting out of, take it easy, lay back, soft-pedal, put the lid on, square, fix up, bury the hatchet, kiss and make up, make up, make it up, make nice, patch things up, play up to, get together on, come together, meet halfway.

PACK n. gang, bunch, crowd, mob, circle.

PACK v. 1. jam, jam-pack, pack 'em in, pack like sardines, sardine, ram in, chock, chockablock, stuff, top off. 2. lug, tote, truck, piggyback, ride, shlep, shlep along, birdie back, buck, gun, heel, hump, jag, shoulder.

PACKAGE n. roll, biddle, bindle, load.

PACKED adj. jam-packed, mobbed, sardined, packed like sardines, up to the hilt, up to the rafters, right to the roof, chock, chock full, full as a tick, full to bursting, fanny-bumper, wall-to-wall people.

PACT n. deal, dicker, ticket, paper, piece of paper. See AGREEMENT.

PAD n. scratch, scratch pad.

PADDLE v. sky an oar.

PAGE v. beep.

PAGER n. beeper.

PAID FOR BY adv. on (it's on me), popped for, taken care of, handled, put on the line for, laid out.

PAIL n. gutbucket, billycan, growler.

PAIN v. do a number on, dump on, hit one where one lives, lay a bad trip on one, gross out, mess up, nick, zing. See WOUND.

PAINFUL adj. hurting, grabbing, stab in the ——, making like the anvil chorus in one's skull, take some hide and hair.

PAINKILLER n. shot, dope, knockout drop.

PAINSTAKING adj. picky, smitty, stickler, dot the i's and cross the t's, fussbudget, fusspot, fuddy-duddy, pernickety, persnickety, chickenshit, by the book, by the numbers. See PARTICULAR.

PAINT v. slap on, slop on, slather on, slather with, cover up, put on a couple of coats, daub, decorate, orange-peel (texture).

PAIR n. team, twosome, gruesome twosome, spic and span (Puerto Rican and Af. Am, Derog.).

PAJAMAS n. jams, jammies, jam-jams, P.J.'s, peejays, pygies, baby dolls, sleepers, sleeping suit.

PAKISTANI n. Paki, Packie, dot head (all Derog.).

PAL n. amigo, brother, brah, bro, blo, home biscuit, bud, buddyroo, good buddy, asshole buddy, chum, old man, old boy, mate, sidekick, tribe (group), crew (group), ghost (rarely seen) blood, cuh, cuz (Af. Am.). See FRIEND.

PALATABLE adj. 1. delish, grinds, yummy, nummy, divine, heavenly, scrumptious, sweetened, sugar-coated. 2. cool, A-OK, copacetic, hunky-dory, jake, peachy, slide by easy, groovy, home cooking. See ACCEPTABLE.

PALAVER v. rap, mack (Af. Am.), yak, jaw, gab, schmoose, chin, chew the fat, bat the chat, shoot the breeze, shoot the shit, bend one's ear, run one's mouth, have diarrhea of the mouth, rattle on. See SPEAK.

PALLIATIVE n. fix, quick fix, Band-Aid.

PALMIST n. mitt reader.

PALPITATE v. go pitapat.

PALPITATION n. pitapation.

PAMPERED adj. spoiled, spoiled rotten, played up to, made over, stroked.

PAMPHLET n. broadside, flyer, handout.

PANAMA CANAL n. Big Ditch.

PANCAKE n. flapjack, hotcake, blanket, saddle blankets, flats, brown bucks, manhole cover, tire patch, wheat, collision mat (WWII).

PANDEMONIUM n. all hell broke loose, rumpus, ruckus, bloody mess, hassle. See BEDLAM.

PANDER v. 1. suck, suck around, suck up to, kiss butt, kiss ass, brown-nose, play up to, fall all over, play footsie, play Mr. Nice Guy, politic, stroke, massage, snow, soften up, soap, lay it on, spook, fish. See CAJOLE. 2. have a string of hustlers, run a stable, have a sister-in-law, steer, tout. See also PIMP.

PANDERER n. mack, macko man, mackman, hard Mack (violent), dude, hustler, Johnny Ponce, pee eye, P, ponce, player, honey man. See PIMP.

PANIC n. crisis mode, crash, bust, slump, rainy days. See also DEPRESSION.

PANIC v. crap out, shit, shit in one's pants, shit green, pee in one's pants, piss in one's pants, pucker-assed, asshole-puckerin', asshole suckin' wind (Obsc.), push the panic button, hit the panic button, in crisis mode, run scared, have cold feet, have a fit, have kittens, chicken out, pucker, shake in one's boots, clutch up, punk out, come apart, freeze up. See also FRIGHTENED.

PANTS n. slacks, jeans, jeans and docs (Doc Martin's boots), Levi's, denims, cords, ducks, whites, bell bottoms, bells, hip huggers, pedal pushers, Capris, clam diggers, hot pants, shorts, Bermudas, kneebusters, baggies, jammies, chinos, chaps, gaucho pants, dungarees, pegs, striders, strides, britches, high-water pants, pistols (pegged), fat-boy pants (down), plus fours (1930), knickers, bloomers, drawers, longies, bags, trousers with the reet pleat.

PAP n. pablum.

PAPER BAG n. jiffy bag, brown bag.

PARACHUTE n. chute, silk, overcoat, umbrella, skyhook.

PARACHUTE v. hit the silk, jump, bail out, hang out the laundry (WWII).

PARACHUTIST n. chuter, chutist, jumper, smoke jumper, paratrooper (Mil.).

PARADE n. rat race.

PARADE GROUND n. grinder.

PARADISE n. 1. pearly gates, kingdom come, happy hunting ground, promised land, upstairs, up there, the great ballpark in the sky. 2. pie in the sky, Nadaville, cloud seven, cloud nine, seventh heaven, fat city, hog heaven. See HEAVEN.

PARADOX n. pair of ducks, Catch-22, catch.

PARAGRAPH n. squib, graph.

PARANOID adj. noid.

PARASITE n. deadbeat, freeloader, beat, gremlin, gremmie, hanger-on, leaner, schnorrer, scab, sponge, sponger, hose, ass-kisser, A.K., bun duster, groupie, taker, waterboy, waterman, yes-man, nod guy, sideman, suck, cocksucker, brownie, brownnose, fart sniffer (Obsc.), bootlick, bootlicker, flunky, stooge, flunky-stooge, lackey.

PARASITIC adj. on one's back, on one's coattails, tripping on one, velcroid, carrying one.

PARATROOPER n. bloomer boy, airborne, chutist, chuter, jumper.

PARCEL n. 1. load, bindle, biddle. 2. piece, bite, cut, slice, chunk, piece of the action, piece of the pie, rake-off, halver, lion's share, bigger half, big end, fifty-fifty, even-steven.

PARCEL v. divvy, divvy up, split up, cut up, cut in, cut the melon, slice up, slice the pie. See DIVIDE.

PARCHED adj. dry as dust, cotton-mouth.

PARDON n. lifeboat, clemo, commute, spring, lifesaver, anchor.

PARDON v. let off, let one off this time, let one off easy, wink at, blink at, write off, wipe the slate clean, bury the hatchet, lifeboat, hand out clemo, spring. See ABSOLVE.

PARDONED adj. beat the rap, walked, let off, let go, off the hook, in from the cold.

PARE n. knock off, shave.

PAREGORIC n. blue velvet, black jack.

PARENT n. P., peep, unit, rent, rental, fossil, OM, old man, old lady, folks, old folks, raise (Af. Am.), foozle, toad, sandwich parent (cares for parents and children).

PARENTHOOD n. parenting, gayby boom (increased adoptions by gays and lesbians).

PARLANCE n. lingo, bafflegab, doublespeak, doubletalk, gobbledygookese, officialese, psychobabble, Urbabble (city Govt.). See LANGUAGE.

PARLEY n. confab, meet, get-together, groupthink, powwow, clambake. See MEETING.

PARLEY v. confab, give a meeting, take a meeting, have a meet, hold a meet, brainstorm, breakout meeting (brainstorm session), toss some ideas around, put in the loop, put in the know, kick some ideas around, groupthink, get heads together, huddle, go into a huddle, pick one's brains, rap, chew the fat. See CONFER. See also SPEAK.

PARODY n. takeoff, play on.

PARODY v. put on, send up, sheik, take off.

PAROLE n. clemo.

PAROLE v. spring, put out on the street, put out on the bricks, put out on the pavement, get your ticket punched (parole rejected).

PARSIMONIOUS adj. stingy, penny-pinching, close, tight, tightwad, tight-fisted, last of the big-time spenders, a regular Jack Benny, skinflint, screw, Scotch, squeezing the eagle, chintzy. See STINGY.

PARSON n. padre, reverend, Holy Joe, sky pilot, Bible beater, Bible basher, Bible puncher, devil driver, fire escape, fire insurance agent, salvation rancher, buck, preacher man. See CLERGYMAN.

PART n. 1. hunk, chunk, gob, glob, lump, smithereen. 2. piece, piece of the action, bite, cut, cut in, divvy, lion's share, big end, drag, slice, slice of the pie. See SHARE. 3. stint (role), lead, bit, extra, walk-on, spear carrier. 4. makin's, making, fixings, fixin's, spares.

PART v. 1. blow one off (in anger), ding, split, split up, break, break off, break up, kiss off, wash up, rat-fuck, couldn't make it, dedomicile, go pffft. 2. split, beat it, jet, fog, cut out, cut and run, cut ass, haul ass, color me gone, air out (Af. Am.), motor, motorvate, le-go, sko (let's go), bolt (quickly), blow, blow this joint, blow this pop stand, break camp, hoof it, be-bop, roll out, I'm out, I'm outtie 5,000, hit the road, push off, bow out, ooze out, ease on, ease out, clear out, pull out, ship out, haul one's freight, shove, shove off, quit the scene, fly the coop, leave flat, run out on, walk out on. See GO.

PARTAKE v. make the scene, do (do drugs), be into, be in on, sit in, sit in on, have a finger in, have a finger in the pie, get in the act, latch on, tune in, give with the eyes. See also EAT.

PARTIALITY n. bag, cup of tea, dish, dish of tea, druthers, flash, thing, type, turned on to, weakness for. See INCLINATION.

PARTICIPANT n. player, in.

PARTICIPATE v. do (do drugs), make the scene, be into, be in on, sit in, sit in on, have a finger in, have a finger in the pie, get into the act, latch on, tune in.

PARTICIPATION n. getting in the act, hands on, sitting in.

PARTICLE n. smithereen; itsy-bitsy pieces, chewed fine (Pl.).

PARTICULAR adj. choosy, choicy, comma counter, nitpicker, picky, picky-picky, ticky, smitty, stickler, stiff, ace, tough, rough, cut it fine, draw it fine, dot the I's and cross the T's, mind one's P's and Q's, watch one's step, bend over backwards, handle with kid gloves, fussbudget, fusspot, fuddy-duddy, granny, old woman, old maid, pernickety, persnickety, crab, chickenshit, according to Hoyle, hardliner, by the book, by the numbers.

PARTICULAR n. the case, what's what, where it's at, chapter and verse, spelled out, nitty-gritty. See DETAIL.

PARTICULARIZE v. spell out, lay out, take it line by line, fly-speck, sweat the details, get down to brass tacks, paint a picture, get down to cases, fine tune. See SPECIFY.

PARTICULARS n. 1. ABC's, ABC of it, blow by blow, rundown, spelled out, like it is, make, picture, the numbers, the goods, bottom line, meat and potatoes, chapter and verse, gospel, megillah, scud, scut, nitty-gritty, nuts and bolts. 2. the straight stuff, what's what, know, facts of life, from the horse's mouth, cue, clue, dope, inside dope, scoop, score, skinny, story, whole story, lowdown, brass tacks, no shit, the emess, cold turkey. See FACTS.

PARTING n. break, breakup, come to a parting of the ways, on the rocks, on the out and out, phfft, pfft, Renovating, split-up, splitsville, washed up, eighty-eights, swan song.

PARTITION v. divvy, divvy up, go halfies, go halvers, go fifty-fifty, go even-steven, slice up, cut the pie, cut the melon, slice the melon, slice the pie, slice, split, split up, crack, cut, cut up, cut in, cut into, cut one in, duke one in, cut up the touches, cut up the pipes, cut up the jackpot, piece up, whack up, bump into, size into (chips), buck it over.

PARTNER n. buddy, buddy-buddy, pard, pardner, sidekick, playmate, date. See also WIFE, HUSBAND, FRIEND.

PARTNERSHIP n. hookup, tie-in, tie-up, gang, mob, ring, clan, outfit, syndicate, go partners, in cahoots with, get together, team up with, throw in together, throw in with, join up with, line up with. See also ASSOCIATION.

PARTNERSHIP, ACCEPT v. count one in, fill, shake on it.

PARTURITION n. blessed event, producing, visit from the stork, drop one.

PARTY n. rage, clubbing, ball, bash, bat, binge, bender, blast, brawl, bust, beer bust, kegger, bow, opener, coming-out, coming-out party, tailgating, get-together, carousing, clambake, crush, brannigan, shindig, blast party (marijuana), rub, belly rub (dance), hop, jump, boogie, mingle, prom, movable feast, BBQ, barbecue, camp it up, blowout, hen party, stag, jag, jig, zig, hullabaloo, rat race, rent party, skiffle, scramble, shag, set, coffee klatch, smoker, shindy, drunk, drunken brawl, hoopla, jamboree, merry-go-round, on the town, paint the town red, rip, tear, toot, whoopee, whooper-dooper, wing-ding, finger pop, boogaloo, racket, belling, horning, jam, roast, donkey roast, drag party, drag-out, do, fight, freeload, flap, gas, gig, hoedown, hoedig, hoodang, hog wrestle, scene, serenade, shivaree, skimmelton. See also REVEL.

PASADENA, CALIFORNIA Pass the doughnuts.

PASS n. freebie, free ride, Annie Oakley, chit, paper, twofer, pigeon, comp.

PASS v. duke, weed, gimme, give the go-by, pass up, pass on, pass it on over, buck it over, pass in the dark, masquerade, blow over. See also QUALIFY, APPROVE.

PASS BAD CHECKS v. paper-hang, down paper, kite.

PASSBOOK n. damper pad.

PASS COUNTERFEIT MONEY v. lay paper, paper, push, hit one, smack with, pass, pass the queer, shove, shove the queer.

PASSÉ adj. out, out of it, old-hat, played-out (Af. Am.), back-number, has-been, yesterday, of the old school. See DATED.

PASSENGER n. line load (taxi), deadhead (free), drop, seat cover, PAX, dogs, hawk.

PASSION n. 1. amore, mash, pash, weakness, case, crash, crush, yen, the hots; emote, emoting (simulate). See LOVE. 2. oomph, jazz, pep talk, where one is at, drive.

PASSIONATE adj. 1. hot, hot for, horny, turned-on, pash, sexy, hot baby, hot number, hot pants, hot patootie, rammy, heavy, heavy-breathing, hot-and-heavy. See AMOROUS. 2. all torn up, all tore up, all shook up, feel stuff, fall apart, frantic, full up, funky, get one's gage up, give out, gutty, hopped-up, shook, shook-up, shot down. See also ENTHUSIASTIC.

PASSIONLESS adj. cold, cold tit, cold shoulder, cold-blooded, tight-assed. See also EMOTIONLESS.

PASSIVE adj. laid-back, flat, moony, cool, unflappable, cas, cazh, go with the flow, dead-ass, poker-faced, phone it in, just going through the motions, walk through it. See INDIFFERENT.

PASSIVE, BE cool one's heels, sit on one's ass, sit on one's butt, sit on one's duff, sit on one's hands, stand pat.

PASSPORT n. shoe (forged).

PAST adj. ancient history, good old days, olden days, olden daze, olden times, stone age, away back, from way back, way back when, back when, behind one, time was, ages ago, since God knows when, water under the bridge, water over the dam, down memory lane, since Hector was a pup, when one was knee high to a grasshopper.

PASTE n. stickum, gunk, gummy, spit.

PASTIME n. fun and games, rec.

PASTOR n. padre, the rev, Holy Joe, sky pilot, Bible beater, Bible puncher, devil driver, fire escape, fire insurance agent, preacher man, right buck, buck, shepherd, glory roader. See CLERGYMAN.

PASTRY n. fat pill.

PASTURE n. the green deck, carpet, rug.

PATCH n. blob, chunk, hunk, fix, Band-Aid.

PATCH v. fix up, doctor, fiddle with, retread.

PATE n. bean, noggin, noodle, dome, attic, upper story, chimney (Af. Am.), coco, knob, think pot, dream box. See HEAD.

PATENT adj. barefaced, plain as the nose on one's face, clear-cut, crystal-clear, open-and-shut, is the Pope Catholic? See APPARENT.

PATENT MEDICINE n. snake oil, punk.

PATH n. 1. rut, groove; lane, track (Stu.). 2. aisle, byway, stroll, rail.

PATIENCE n. backbone, grit, guts, gutsiness, heart, moxie, starch, cool, hanging in there, hang tough, legs, intestinal fortitude, staying power, sitzfleisch, stick-to-itive-ness.

PATIENT n. crock, gomer, player (complainer), train wreck (several problems), albatross (chronically ill), banana (jaundiced).

PATIENT, BE v. keep one's shirt on, not hold one's breath, hang in, keep one's cool, cool it, cool one's heels, sit tight.

PATRICIAN n. blue-blood, silk-stocking, lace curtain, swell, upper-cruster.

PATRIOT n. arm-waver, flag-waver (super), hundred percenter, jingoist, patrioteer, scoutmaster, pastel patriot (weak).

PATRIOTIC adj. flag-waving, wrap oneself in the flag.

PATROL v. ride shotgun for, shotgun. See also WATCH.

PATROL CAR n. fuzzmobile, black-and-white, skunk wagon, bear car, bearmobile, buzz, buzzer, screaming gasser, whistler, catch car; brown bag, plain wrap (unmarked); cherries (flashing lights), buggy whip (transmitter).

PATROL WAGON n. battlewagon, paddywagon, Black Maria, Maria, fuzzmobile, black-and-white, booby hatch, go-long, milk wagon, piewagon.

PATRON n. the money, angel, sponsor, backer, greenback, sugar daddy, rabbi, Chinaman, fairy godmother, lady bountiful, meal ticket, Santa Claus, staker, grubstaker, pigeon, grape (waiting to be squeezed), live one, mark, believer, front, head, fan.

PATRONAGE n. pork barrel.

PATRONIZE v. toss a few crumbs, act like one of the boys, go along with, high-hat, look down one's nose at, look down on.

PATRONIZING adj. biggety, dicty, sidity, siditity, sniffy, snippy, snooty, uppish, uppity, upstage, ego-tripping, high-toned. See ARROGANT.

PAUNCH n. beer belly, spare tire, rubber tire, bulge, battle of the bulge, corporation, bay window, tub of guts, gutbucket, pus gut, blimp. See FAT.

PAUPER n. bum, bummer, stumblebum, slum bum, rubber bum, ragbag, bag lady, bag woman, in the gutter, bo, weed. See also DESTITUTE.

PAUPERIZE v. bleed, bleed white, suck dry, wipe out, break, take one for all one's got, clean one out, take one's last penny.

PAUPERIZED adj. stone broke, truly needy, oofless, on one's ass, on the rocks, on the edge, down-and-out, down to one's last cent, down to one's last penny, disadvantaged, deprived, have-nots, not have one dollar to rub against another, not have one dime to rub against another, bag lady, in dire straits, piss-poor, dirt-poor. See DESTITUTE.

PAUSE n. break, coffee break, break-off, breather, breathing spell, downtime, letup, five, ten, time out, freeze, cutoff, layoff, letup; happy hour, attitude adjustment hour (cocktail hour). See DELAY.

PAUSE v. put on hold, call time, come up for air, take a break, take five, take ten, take a smoke, break it off, break it up, drop, drop it, pigeonhole, shake, sideline.

PAVEMENT n. the bricks.

PAWN n. patsy, cat's paw, mark, believer, pigeon, stooge.

PAWN v. hook, soak, hock, put in hock, see Uncle.

PAWNBROKER n. loan shark, Shylock, soft touch, Uncle.

PAWNSHOP n. hockshop, three balls, Uncle's, spout.

PAY n. bread, bacon, scale, take-home, eagle shit; peanuts, coffee and cakes (small); double dipping (compensation from two government agencies), See COMPENSATION.

PAY v. 1. pay up, pay off, pay out, pay down, put down (begin to pay), pay-go (pay as you go), pay to the tune of, pay through the nose, foot the bill, pick up the check, pick up the tab, kick in, chip in, cough up, pony up, ante up, come through, come across, come down with, come down with the needful, come up with the necessary, blow, blow out, plank out, plank up, plank down, plunk down, clunk, clunk down, cash out, dish it out, shell out, put out, lay out, fork out, fork over, fork up, hand over, spring for, make good, lay on one, lay it on the line, put it on the line, put one's money on the line, throw money at, throw money around, piss it away, iron off, post, go for a meg, go Dutch, Dutch treat. 2. buy, buy off, swing for bread, comp, square, square things, square up, square the beef, make up for, sugar coat, stroke, sweeten, sweeten the pot, tickle the palm, pay the piper, pay one's dues, pay through the nose, slip one a buck, take an envelope, grass eater (police officer who will take), meat eater (police officer who demands), take care of, take a chicken, schmear, grease, grease one's palm, oil, oil one's palm, barry (hiring boss), fix, fix the alzo, put in the fix, piece one off, gaff, fit the mitt, put in the bag, put in the zingers, buzz, crack business, do business, see, see the cops, reach, get at, get to. See also BRIBE, SQUANDER.

PAY BACK v. square, square things, square a beef, make up for, pay one's dues, you scratch mine and I'll scratch yours. See also PAY; REVENGE.

PAYDAY n. day, eagle day, day the eagle shits, day the eagle flies, day the eagle screams, when the eagle flies, four and one.

PAY EXTORTION v. pay off, buy off, pay through the nose, pay off on the moosh, kick in on the squash.

PAY FOR v. blow one to, blow, on one, on the house, I'll get it (pay the check), I'm buyin', pick up the check, pick up the tab, pop, pop for, spring for, stand for, set up, stake.

PAYING adj. in the black, going, going concern, paying off, cashing in, red, sweet.

PAYMENT n. payoff, drop, kickback, bad notes, payola, drugola, gayola, juice, ante, bite, chunk, end, cut, slice, share, piece, piece of the action, rake-off, commish, skig, cash on the line, cash on the nail, cash on the barrelhead, out of pocket, outlay, the wherewithal, the necessary, vig, vigorish, flipping (interest on interest), front-end loading, balloon (final), points. See also BRIBE; COMPENSATION.

PAYROLL n. payoff, payola, scandal sheet.

PAYROLL TIMEKEEPER n. biscuit.

PCP n. angel dust, P.C.P., water, Sherms (cigarette), P-stuff, busy bee, crystal, elephant, elephant tranquilizer, embalming fluid, dust, rock dust, T dust, magic dust, monkey dust, fairy dust, devil dust, dummy dust, stardust, white dust, angel mist, mist, magic mist, black whack, cozmos, Detroit pink, herms, hog, horse trank, jet fuel, kaps, kools, puffy, scuffle, skuffle, skaffle, killer weed, peace pill, rocket fuel, cannabinol, lovely, tic, animal, pig killer, cadillac, C.J., K.J., goon, sheets, hog, mint, monkey, snorts, Aurora Borealis, dummy, ozone, soma, cyclone, horse, new magic; super joint, super grass (marijuana sprinkled with PCP), squeeze, Mr. Whipple, bomb (mixed with embalming fluid).

PEACE ADVOCATE n. peacenik, dove, dove of peace.

PEACEFUL adj. level vibes, smooth, mellow, all quiet on the Potomac, all quiet on the Western front.

PEACE, MAKE v. bury the hatchet, kiss and make up, make up, offer an olive branch. See PACIFY.

PEACE OFFICER n. cop, fuzz, copper, bubble-gum man, shamus, flic, dick, diaper dick (handles children), narc (narcotics), pig, oink, black-and-white, badge, buttons, bluecoat, bluebird (Af. Am.), flatfoot, harness bull, law, Kojak, Smokey, Smokey the Bear. See POLICE OFFICER.

PEAK adj. in full swing, tops, in top form, the greatest, level best, all-out, world-class. See BEST.

PEAK n. 1. hump. 2. spike (Elec.).

PEANUT n. goober.

PEANUT BUTTER n. goober grease.

PEARLS n. tears, teardrops, oyster berries.

PEAS n. bullets, sheep shit.

PECTORAL adj. pec.

PECULIAR adj. freaky, kooky, beat, bent, weirdie, oddball, bogus, fringy, kinky, geeky, glick, flaky, far out, way out, off the wall, wombat, quirky, not wrapped real tight, fly-ball, aired out, character, creep, whacky, spacey. See ECCENTRIC.

PECULIARITY n. shtick, slant, twist, gimmick, bit, mishagoss. See CHARACTERISTIC.

PEDANT n. egghead, hardboiled egghead (tough-minded), scrambled egghead (fuzzy-minded), brain, cereb, mc squared, gnurd, gnome, grind, auger, comma counter, pencil geek, throat, bookworm, grub, ink squirter, spider, squid, weenie, poler, wig, wonk, moldy fig.

PEDDLER n. Arab, bag guy (balloon), butch, butcher, hawker, pitchman; candy man, pusher, travel agent (LSD), dealer (drugs); cheap jack, cheap john. See VENDOR.

PEDESTRIAN n. boot jockey, gumshoe, jaywalker.

PEEP n. free show, peeping Tom, flash, keek.

PEEP v. flash, flash on, spy, catch, eyeball, take in, check this out, bus it (Af. Am.), get a load of, get an eyeful of, take a squint, have a look-see. See SEE.

PEER n. blue-blood, lace curtain, silk-stocking, swell, upper-cruster.

PEER v. glom, glim, gun, gawk, beam, focus, eye, eagle-eye, eyeball, pin, rubber, rubberneck, get a load of, put the squint on, gap. See SEE.

PEERLESS adj. world-class, greatest, out-of-sight, out of this world, bump'n, gonest, aces, mostest, baaaadest, first-chop, super, gilt-edge, all-time, tops, key, solid gold, champ. See EXCELLENT.

PEEVED adj. bugged, hacked, hissy, hacked off, brassed off, cheesed off, pissed off, peed off, aggro, push one's key, bummed out, burned-up, miffed, rubbed the wrong way, all hot and bothered, driven up the wall, steamed. See ANNOYED. See also ANGRY.

PEEVISH adj. bitchy, mean, ornery, tetchy, out of sorts, cantankerous, cussed, grouchy, grumpy, beefing, bellyaching, bitching, crabbing, crabby, cranky, grousing, griping, kicking, snappish, scrappy, kvetchy, bear, ogre, ugly, ugly customer, turd poodle, bad-assed, uptight, thin-skinned, not a happy camper, pushing out one's lips, ready to fly off the handle, edgy, on the ragged edge, got up on the wrong side of the bed.

PELT n. dried barkers, skins, skin joint (shop).

PEN n. stick, ink stick, ball-point, nerd pack (plastic pocket protector for pens).

PENALIZE v. dock, slap with a fine, hit with a fine, walk off fifteen yards, pay through the nose, throw the book at one. See also SENTENCE.

PENALTY n. hell to pay, rap, fall, pay dues, rip.

PENCHANT n. a thing for, weakness for, turned on to, druthers, tilt, big eyes, eyes for, itch, sweet tooth, yen, zazzle. See INCLINATION.

PENCIL n. stick.

PENDING adj. in the works, in line, on the board, on the fire, on line.

PENETRATE v. 1. barge in, break in, blow in, bust in, mooch in, come barging in, come, come busting in, access, crack, crack a safe. 2. get over, put over, get across, sink in, soak in, work one's points, ace in.

PENILINGUS n. blow, blow job, head job, job, knob job, pipe job, suck, suck-off, sucky-fucky, tongue fuck.

PENIS n. cock, prick, dick, dork, lob, pecker, peter, pee-pee, pisser, pistol, joint, horn, hose, tail, tubesteak, big daddy, bone phone, chicken, bazooka, affair, business, agate (small), middle leg, third leg, pencil, dummy, meat, weenie, peenie, burrito, lovesteak, love pump, love muscle, heat-seeking muscle, stick, joystick, cream stick, dipstick, licorice stick, swizzle stick, bat, bone, enob, knob, joy knob, dinosaur, bishop, bicho, wang, flying wang, it, thing; putz, schmeckel, schmuck, schwantz (Yid.); pup, rod, hot rod, humpmobile, pole, pego, percy, oscar, long John, Johnnie, Willy, master of ceremonies, pinga (Sp.), pud, pood, dong, dang, dagger, banana, cucumber, kosher pickle (circumcised), baloney, sausage, salami, frankfurter, wurst, pork, hambone, peppermint stick, magnum, shlong, dink, dinger, dingus, weeder, staff, doodle, dodad, gun, weapon, head, tool, screwdriver, plunger, fountain pen, trouser snake, arm, short arm, jack, blackjack, jimmy, jimbrowski, jock, big Ben, Mr. Happy, John Thomas, John Henry, Johnson, jones (Af. Am.), junior, redcap, Rumpleforeskin, jigger, frigamajig, ding, hickey, fag, booboos, yang, ying-yang, jang, jing-jang, tootsie roll, divining rod, pike, piston, prod, serpent, snake, lizard, one-eyed monster, one eyed wonder, one-eyed brother, one-eyed milkman, one-eyed rocket, stalk, corn on the cob, shaft, prong, spear, sword, jelly roll, meat whistle, skin flute, piccolo, love muscle, rod of love, root, roto rooter, girlometer, whammer, worm, instrument, machine, baby maker, nuts and bolts, banger, poker, hammer, rammer, ramrod, battering ram, family organ, chimney brush, paint brush, charger, stretcher, cunt stretcher, peace maker, cherry picker, basket, heart, hotchee, hootchee, log, maypole, pole, pylon, eleventh finger, hung (big), hung like a bull, hung like a chicken, hung like a rabbit, stub, bugfucker; needle dick, pencil dick (small); pimple, wick, dangling participle; meat and two vegetables, Dickie and the boys (penis and testicles) (all Obsc.); lace curtains (homosexual), end, sheath, Jewish nightcap, kosher meat, snapper, Roger, Jolly Roger, lollipop, thing, bald-headed mouse, crackhunter, hard-nosed (erect).

PENITENTIARY n. pen, hard pen (tough), joint, right joint, big joint, big house, slam, slammer, up the river, statesville, Q (San Quentin), Sing Sing, sent up, maxi (maximum security), inside, school, big school, campus, college, greystone college, graybar hotel, crossbar hotel, crowbar hotel, bastille, municipal farm, lag, Club Fed, G. joint (federal). See also JAIL.

PENMANSHIP n. chicken tracks, hen tracks, mark, scrawl, scribble.

PENNANT n. screamer, streamer, flag (Bsbl.), bean rag (N.).

PENNILESS adj. broke, flat broke, dead broke, flat, stony, strapped, clean, tapped out, tap city, on one's ass, on one's uppers, to the curb, down to one's last cent, down to one's last penny, not have one dollar to rub against another, not have one dime to rub against another, over a barrel, piss-poor, dirt-poor, on the rims. See DESTITUTE.

PENNSYLVANIA Coal State, Keystone State, Oil State, Pennsy, Quaker State, Steel State.

PENNSYLVANIA RAILROAD n. Pennsy.

PENSIONER n. senior, senior citizen, wrinklie, on the shelf, out of circulation, over the hill, passed it, a once-was, has-been, hung up one's spurs, ———— years young, old timer, gerk (fool). See also AGED.

PENTAGON n. Puzzle Palace, Fort Fumble, Fudge Factory, Five-Sided Wailing Wall, D.O.D., ground zero, target A, purple suiters (top brass), elephant (boss), horseholder (serves senior officer).

PENULTIMATE adj. down to the short strokes.

PENURIOUS adj. cheap, cheapskate, close, stingy, tight, skinflint, skin, screw, Scotch, sticky-fingered, squeezing the eagle, piker, scrimpy, skimpy, pinch-fisted. See STINGY.

PEOPLE n. bodies, cats, dudes, heads, hoi polloi, the public, John Q., John Q. Public, Billy Sixpack, Joe Lunchbucket, Tom Dick and Harry, Brown Jones and Robinson, booboisie, the little guy.

PEOPLE MAGAZINE n. Peephole.

PEPPER n. dirt (Army), hot it up.

PEPPERY adj. shotgun.

PERCEIVE v. 1. flash on, spot, spy, dig, lamp, eyeball, get a load of, take a hinge, have a look-see. See SEE. 2. get it, get the picture, flash on, blow wise, track, feature, dig, pin, copy, read, get the message. See UNDERSTAND.

PERCEIVED adj. hep to, on to, pat, down pat, wise to, pegged, got, got the picture, dug, know where one is coming from, picked up on, dawned on one, light dawned. See also APPARENT.

PERCENTAGE n. cut, piece, piece of the action, points, end, rake-off, share, commish, vig, vigorish, bite, chunk, juice, skig, slice, cut in, cut up, cut a melon (profits), piece of the pie, drag, P.C., taste. See also INTEREST; SHARE.

PERCEPTION n. brain wave, brainchild, approach, big idea, picture, flash on it, take, see the light, the light. See IDEA. See also PLAN.

PERCEPTIVE adj. hip, hep, hip to the jive, hep to the jive, a brain, brains, brainy, sharp, sharp as a tack, tack, savvy, fly, with it, chilly, been there, all woke up, tuned in, booted on, wise to, know one's onions, know what's what, know one's stuff, on top of, the smart money, ear to the ground, on the beam, got good antenna. See also AWARE.

PERDITION n. 1. hell, the other place. 2. blue ruin, rack and ruin, totaled, total wipe, wipeout.

PERFECT adj. A-O.K., A-okay, aces, right on, 10, ten, out of this world, clean, crisp, bull's-eye, on target, on the button, on the numbers, on the money, dead on, dead nuts, gig, bump'n', fully, fully on, apple pie, four-o, in the groove, outrageous righteous and relaxed, textbook, tiptop shape, to a T, to a turn, to a frazzle, to a fare-thee-well, done up brown, down to the ground, not do by halves. See also CORRECT.

PERFECTIONIST adj. picky, picky-picky, smitty, stickler, dot the i's and cross the t's, fussbudget, fusspot, pernickety, persnickety, according to Hoyle, by the book, by the numbers. See PARTICULAR.

PERFECT SCORE n. ace, par, scratch (golf).

PERFIDIOUS adj. double-crossing, snake in the grass, two-faced, two-timing, low-down and dirty, dirty work, cheatin' heart, slick, slippery, speak with forked tongue. See DECEITFUL.

PERFORATE v. poke full of holes, shoot full of holes.

PERFORM v. 1. be on, go on, do a turn, do a number, strut one's stuff, play one's gig, go into one's song and dance, chew the scenery, ham, ham it up, tread the boards, emote, bring down the house, 2. go that route, go to town, move, make one's move, move on (to something else), do one's thing, kick it live (Af. Am., do it well), TCB (take care of business), take a flier (impulsively), pull off, shit or get off the pot, perk, percolate, tick, operate, run with the ball, come on like, do one's stuff, deliver the goods. See ACT.

PERFORMANCE n. 1. gig, stunt, perf, set (musical), cut (recording), dumb act (without words), high jinks, hi jinks; exhebeesh, exhibicion (sex acts). See also ACT. 2. track record.

PERFORMER n. ham, hambone, star, trouper, legiter, lead, bit player, thesp, straight man, stooge, mugger, baddie, talent, heat (box office power). See ACTOR.

PERFUME n. smell well, smell good.

PERFUNCTORY adj. laid-back, loose, could care less, don't give shit, don't give a shit, phone it in, just going through the motions, walk through it, asleep at the switch. See INDIFFERENT. See also CARELESS.

PERIL n. double trouble, deep shit, risky business.

PERILOUS adj. hot, hairy, hellish, loaded, dynamite, unhealthy, widow maker, jungle, zoo, rugged, dicey, chancy, risky business, in the tube, play with fire, hot potato, play Russian roulette, on thin ice, touch-and-go. See DANGEROUS.

PERIODICAL n. mag, pulp, sheet, slick, rag, throwaway, fan mag; joint, limb joint (nonexistent). See also NEWSPAPER.

PERISCOPE n. scope.

PERISH v. go, kick off, kick the bucket, buy the farm, pass away, croak, give up the ghost, OD, pull the plug, bite the dust, kiss off, cash in one's chips, check out, turn it in, one-way ticket. See DIE.

PERISHED adj. stone cold, bought the farm, had it, offed, dead meat, quartermaster material (Mil.), stiff, belly up, kicked the bucket, croaked, gone west, gone to that great (whatever) in the sky, on a slab, out-of-range, boxed. See DEAD.

PERMANENT adj. set, set in concrete, in for the long haul, forever and a day, for keeps, for a coon's age, for a month of Sundays, ever so long, time out of mind, till hell freezes over, till one's blue in the face, till shrimps learn to whistle, till the cows come home.

PERMISSIBLE adj. legit, kosher, on the up and up, on the legit. See LEGAL. See also ACCEPTABLE.

PERMISSION n. go-ahead, green light, okay, OK, stamp of approval. See CONSENT.

PERMIT v. bless, buy, okay, OK, sign, sign off on, pass, pass on, shake on, thumbs up, put one's John Hancock on, boost, get behind, go for, give the nod, give the go-ahead, give the green light, it's a deal, done deal, like you say, you got it, take kindly to, give the stamp of approval, rubber-stamp, cave in, bear with, live with, hold with, go along with, string along with, put up with, be big, hear of, stand for, sit still for, lump it and like it, stomach something, grin and bear it, face it. See also ALLOW.

PERMITTED adj. legit, kosher, on the legit, on the level, on the up-and-up, card-carrying. See ACCEPTED.

PERPETRATOR n. perp.

PERPETUALLY adv. for ever so long, for a coon's age, for a dog's age, for a month of Sundays, till hell freezes over, till you're blue in the face, till the cows come home, till shrimps learn to whistle, when a donkey flies.

PERPLEX v. mess with one's head, get to, discomboberate, discombobulate, rattle, rattle one's cage, buffalo, fuddle, put one on a crosstown bus, muddy the waters, snow, stum, flummox. See PUZZLE.

PERPLEXED adj. unglued, shook-up, all balled up, bugged-up, bollixed, bollixed-up, hung, hung-up, mixed-up, messed-up attic, floored, in a fog, in the twilight zone, don't know from nothing, don't know which way is up. See PUZZLED.

PERQUISITE n. fringe benefit, goodies, gravy, perk, perks, golden handcuffs, golden parachute, swindle sheet. See also EXTRA.

PERSECUTE v. bug, ride, pick on, put the squeeze on, put the screws on, put the heat on, put one through the wringer, on one's back, on one's case, dog, dog one's case, drive one up the wall. See also ANNOY.

PERSECUTED adj. picked-on, dogged, catch shit.

PERSECUTION n. witch hunting, red-baiting, fishing expedition.

PERSEVERANCE n. backbone, drive, moxie, spunk, gits, grit, guts, cool, keep on keeping on, sitzfleisch, stick-to-itiveness, never say die.

PERSEVERE v. hang tough, hang in, hang in there, stick it, stick it out, stick with it, go for it, go for broke, see it through, leave no stone unturned, stay the course, never say die. See PERSIST.

PERSEVERING adj. mulish, stiff-necked, the game ain't over till the last man is out, tough, game, dead set on, bound, bound and determined, going the whole hog, hanging in, going for broke. See STUBBORN. See also DETERMINED.

PERSIAN GULF WAR TERMS Big Red (sun), BMO, black moving object, Ninja woman (Arab woman), bolo badge (Purple Heart medal), dog one out (criticize), grease (food), heat tab (sun), homey (friend), KTO (Kuwaiti Theater of Operations), lost-and-found badges (I.D. tags), M.R.E.s (meals ready to eat, also meals rejected by everyone), Saudi champagne (apple juice and Perrier).

PERSIST v. hang tough, hang in, hang in there, hang on for dear life, hold on like a bulldog, hang on like a leech, stick like a leech, stick like a barnacle, stick like a limpet, stick like a wet shirt, stick it, stick it out, stick to it, stick with it, stick to one's guns, tough it out, stay put, go for it, go for broke, go the whole hog, go the limit, go on with the show, go all the way, go to any length, go through fire and water, go through hell and high water, go through with, see through, see it through, carry through, leave no stone unturned, leave no avenue unexplored, follow up, follow through, get on with it, let it ride, plug along, plug away, peg away, stay the course, dig, grind, hammer, move heaven and earth, not give up the ship, never say die, hold the fort. See also ENDURE.

PERSISTENCE n. staying power, hanging in there, hanging tough, stick-to-itiveness, sitzfleisch, cool. See also TENACITY.

PERSISTENT adj. bound, bound and determined, keeps coming back for more, in for the long haul, like a bad penny, always turning up like a bad penny, sticky, hang tough, murder (he's murder), never say die. See DETERMINED. See also STUBBORN.

PERSON n. unit, guy, dude, cat, feller, lad, chap, bird, duck, stud, joker, character, clown, jasper, bugger, bastard, customer, party, certain party, head, ace (good), bad news, type; motherfucker, mofo, M.F., mothafucka, mother clutcher, mother grabber (all Obsc.); bod, warm body, face, hairpin, job, number (hot number), boogie bear (ugly), boot (Af. Am.), cake, poor fish, skin, geezer, so-and-so, ghee, hip ghee, mickey, stiff, fly horse, gapper.

PERSONABLE adj. ace, aces, O.K. guy, good Joe, right guy, all right guy, good guy, nice guy, one's kinda guy, a sweetheart, a prince, white hat, good egg, hipster, sport, big deal, softy, old softy, old smoothy, easygoing, all heart, brick, crackerjack, cutie, got that certain something, snuggle bunny, cher, daisy, doozie, honey, hot stuff, one after one's own heart, true blue, solid citizen, good apple. See also BEAUTIFUL; CHARISMA; PERSUASIVE.

PERSONAGE n. celeb, star, superstar, monster, name, numero uno, V.I.P., w.k. (well known), face, page-oner, prima donna, right up there, hot shot, big, big noise, big cheese, knocker, large charge, visiting fireman, gun. See CELEBRITY.

PERSONAL APPEARANCE n. PA, flesh show.

PERSON, DISLIKED n. shit, shitheel, piece of shit, cocksucker, prick, cunt, twat, ass, asshole, jackass, bad ass, shithead, bad medicine, bad news, bad guy, bad actor, bad hat, black hat, bad egg, bad shit, son of a bitch, S.O.B., penis wrinkle, mother, motherfucker, M.F., mofo, mothuh-fuckuh, mother-humper, mother-jumper, mother-jammer, mammy-jammer, mother-lover, mother-rucker, mother-grabber, grabber, mother's cunt (all Obsc.); hairball, hodad, hodaddy, barney, geek, scrounge, nightie (nightmare), smack (overachieving geek), bub, elrod, scoob, goob, goober, goobatron, yernt, social zero, nothingburger, turkey, animal, beast, barfbag, scumbag, scum, scumsucker, gross,

stinker, stink pot, skunk, louse, crud, scrub, scuzzo, scuzzy, shitsky, shitburger, scurvy, cull, dag, loser, real winner, a nothing, creep, drip, fink, rat fink, rat, bastard, rat bastard, fuckface, heel, hood, hit man, finger man, hatchet man, snitch, snake, ballbreaker, ballbuster, low-life, double-dealer, double-crosser, wrong ghee, bum, crumb bum, crumb, stumblebum, yo-yo, zombie, banana, dumb cluck, cluck, dumbo, mince, simp, spastic, weenie, wimp, worm, bad case of the uglies, Arkansas lizard, won't give one the time of day, lame, rum-dum, low rider, nic-nac, punk, gunsel, gerk (old).

PERSON, IN adj. in the flesh, live.

PERSONNEL n. troops, shop, crew.

PERSPECTIVE n. head set, mind set, mind trip, where one's head is, where one is at, where it's at, like it is, the size of it, take, P.O.V. (point of view), angle.

PERSPIRATION ODOR n. BO, B.O.

PERSPIRE v. break a sweat, sweat like a horse, sweat like a trooper, get all in a lather.

PERSUADE v. work on, work over, soften up, soft-soap, sweet-talk, stroke, dooze, lay it on, lay it on thick, lay it on with a trowel, lay a rap, schmear, schmeikle, butter, butter up, honey, soap, oil, kid along, play up to, give a come-hither look, come on, bat the eyes at, give with bedroom eyes, get around, turn one's head around, brainwash, eat one's mind, crack one or something, put across, con, duke in, promote, spark, sound, rope in, swindle in, sell, sell one on, hard sell, soft sell, fast-talk, snow, snow under, push, goose, goose up, jolly, blarney, caboodle, fire up, key up, suck in, hand one a line, hook, hook in, nag, twist one's arm, egg one on, iggle, lobby, bug, buttonhole, jawbone, hold one's feet to the fire, put the screws on, put the bee on, lean on, make it hot for, put the squeeze on, put up to, push around, break one's arm, break one's finger, break one's leg, make a believer out of, cream, twist one's arm, sweat one, put on the spot, throw one's weight around, cram down one's throat, ram down one's throat, come at from all sides, high-pressure, squeeze, juice, steamroller, bulldoze, knock on doors, politick.

PERSUADED adj. satisfied, bought, sold.

PERSUASION n. sell, hard sell, soft soap, snow job, sweet talk, blow job, shovelin' shit, con, hook, arm-twist, working over, goose, brainwash, promote, squeeze, juice. See also BELIEF.

PERSUASIVE adj. fast talker, gift of gab, slick, smooth, smoothie, old smoothie, smooth article, smooth apple, smooth operator, slicker, silky, spieler.

PERT adj. flip, fresh, breezy, nervy, sassy, smart, smart-alecky, smart-ass, wise-ass, brassy, bold as brass, have a mouth. See also CHEERFUL, INSOLENT.

PERTINENT adj. on the button, on the nose, on target, right on, kosher, legit, that's the idea, that's the ticket, just what the doctor ordered.

PERTURB v. get to, adjy, spook, bug, chap, make waves, make a scene, needle, rabble-rouse, stir up. See DISTURB. See also CONFUSE; DISTRESS.

PERTURBED adj. discombobulated, all shook up, bugged, defrosted, hissy, in a stew, in a lather, fussed, have kittens, wreck, shot to pieces, in a botheration. See DISTURBED. See also CONFUSED; DISTRESSED.

PERVASIVE adj. wall-to-wall, all over the place, all over the lot, stinking with, can't get away from it.

PERVERSE adj. bitchy, ornery, hard-nosed, locked in, stuck in concrete, brick wall, pat, stand-pat, mulish, mule, stubborn as a mule, horse, stiff-necked, sticky, bitter ender. See STUBBORN. See also IRRITABLE.

PERVERT n. gooner, freak, geek, panty thief, perv, pervo, prevert, queer.

PERVERT v. 1. doctor, doctor up, spike, water, water down, cut, load, salt, salt a mine, fudge, plant, fake, phony up, queer. 2. lead one down the primrose path, brain wash, get one hooked, hook.

PERVERTED adj. kinky, queer. See also CORRUPT, VICIOUS.

PESO n. adobe dollar, p, pa.

PESSIMISM n. dim view, dark side.

PESSIMIST n. drag, buzz crusher, buzz killer, wet blanket, killjoy, crepe hanger, gloomy Gus, downer, sourpuss, sourbelly, sourball, drip, party pooper, dog in the manger, worry wart, Calamity Jane, calamity howler.

PEST n. 1. headache, drag, pain, pain in the ass, pain in the neck, blister, nudge, nudzh, noodge, nag, buzz crusher, bummer, creep, pill, drip, kibitzer, flat tire, wet blanket, crashing bore. 2. crabs (Pl.), crum, crumb, grayback, seam squirrel, shimmy lizard; crumby, crummy, lousy (afflicted with pests).

PESTER v. bug, ride, be at, noodge, nudge, give one hemorrhoids, sweat, hassle, work on, get in one's hair, chap, push one's key, hound, dog, bulldog, nag, worry, hock a charnik, mess with, graum, get on one's nerves. See ANNOY.

PESTICIDE n. bug bomb.

PET n. 1. animal companion (politically correct). 2. fair-haired boy, blue-eyed boy, candy boy, number one boy, pratt boy, evergreen, fave.

PET v. grab ass, ball, make out, grovel, smooch, mesh, box tonsils, go for sushi, a little smacky, spoon, perch, pitch woo, fling woo, feel up. See also AMOROUS PLAY.

PETITION v. put in for. See REQUEST.

PETRIFIED adj. scared stiff, scared witless, scared shitless, shit green, brick, shit a brick, push the panic button, frozen, pucker-assed, asshole suckin' wind, shake in one's boots, struck all of a heap. See FRIGHTENED.

PETRIFY v. chill, chill off, put the chill on, spook, scare shitless, scare stiff, scare silly, strike all of a heap. See FRIGHTEN.

PETROL n. gas, bug juice, juice, go juice, Ethyl.

PETROLEUM n. gas, black gold.

PETROLEUM WORKER n. oilie.

PETTY adj. dinky, measly, two-bit, big zero, no big deal, no biggie, no great shakes, ain't no thang, ain't no thing but a chicken wing (Af. Am.), pissy-tailed, tinhorn, chickenshit, flying fuck, frig it, not worth a hill of beans, nickel-and-dime, penny ante, peanuts, pokerino, shot, scratch, skag. See UNIMPORTANT. See also SELFISH.

PETULANCE n. miff, pet, stew, tiff, snit.

PETULANT adj. bitchy, mean, tetchy, crabby, cranky, kvetchy, whiny, snappish, crybaby, pill, plainer, rapper, sorehead, uptight, thin-skinned, pushing out one's lips, got up on the wrong side of the bed. See PEEVISH.

PEYOTE n. mescal, button, biscuits, dog biscuits, legume, plants, magic pumpkin.

PEYOTE CACTUS n. shroom (psychodelic), shroom dog (user).

PHALLUS n. cock, prick, dick, dork, pecker, peter, joint, pencil, meat, burrito, lovesteak, weenie, joystick, bone, knob, joy knob, bishop, wang, thing, putz, schmuck, dong, shlong, dingus, tool, one-eyed monster, one-eyed wonder, hung (big) (all Obsc.). See PENIS.

PHANTOM n. haint, hant, spook, things that go bump in the night.

PHENCYCLIDINE n. PCP, P.C.P., water, angel dust. See PCP.

PHENOMENON n. one for the book, something else, something to write home about, stunner.

PHI BETA KAPPA n. Phi Bete, fly bait.

PHILADELPHIA, PENNSYLVANIA Philly, Phillie, Philly Town, City of Brotherly Love, Big Brother, Liberty City, Quacker City, Big Pretzel.

PHILANDER v. dilly-dally, two-time, monkey, monkey around, horse around, mess around, kid around, muck around, fart around, fool around, fuck around, play around, screw around, lollygag, jerk off, fool with, play games with.

PHILANDERER n. playboy, player, nighthawk, poon hound, dude, operator, cruiser, heavy cake, C.S.P. (casual sex partner), letch, wolf, hound, tomcat, alley cat, swinger, lover boy, lady-killer, man on the make, on one's tit, chaser, skirt chaser, tail chaser, beastmaster (dates ugly women), rounder, whorehound, Don Juan, good-time Charlie. See LECHER.

PHILANDERING adj. two-timing, moonlighting, cheat, cheater, cheating, cheat on, doggin', playing around, fooling around, extracurricular activities, double-crossing, sneakin' deacon, step out on one, chippy on one, tip, two-faced, witch, yard, hanky-panky.

PHILANTHROPIST n. do-gooder, bleeding heart, good scout, angel, fairy godmother, lady bountiful, Robin Hood, Santa Claus, sugar daddy. See also BENEFACTOR.

PHILIPPINE n. chico, Filipino, Philippino, moke (all Derog.).

PHILOSOPHICAL adj. cool, cool as a cucumber, keep one's cool, keep one's shirt on, keep a stiff upper lip, not turn a hair, roll with the punches, unflappable, commonsensical, ah-ah head.

PHILOSOPHY n. phil.

PHLEGM n. snot, ginder, green ginder, green one, gob, goober, green goober, glob, globber, honker, hawker, wad.

PHLEGMATIC adj. mopey, dopey, blah, flat, drippy, nebbish, wimpy, what the hell, it's all the same to me, could care less, draggy. See LANGUID. See also INDIFFERENT.

PHOBIA n. bug, bug in one's ear, bug up one's ass, have a thing about, have on the brain, hang-up, tiger, tiger by the tail, bee, bee in one's bonnet, bag, grabber, ax to grind; chuck habit, chuck horrors (prison food).

PHOENIX, ARIZONA Sun City.

PHONOGRAPH n. hi-fi, stereo, boom, boom box, thunderbox, box, jukebox (commercial), low-fi (Hum.), noisola, phono, pick, playback.

PHONOGRAPH RECORD n. platter, album, disc, licorice pizza, single, sides, wax, acetate, manhole cover.

PHOTOGRAPH n. pic, pix, shot, photo, photops (photo opportunities), snap, art (News., criminal), beefcake (M.), cheesecake (Fem.), blowup, mug, mug shot, pinup, Aunt Minnie (tourist photo of strategic intelligence location), atta-boy shot (TV sports closeup), French post card (porno), gow, centerfold (nude), eight-by-ten glossy, 8×10 glossy, picture gallery (file).

PHOTOGRAPH v. film, lens, shoot, roll, turn, gun, flash, burn, pop, long shot, closeup, mug, snap, get, can.

PHOTOGRAPHER n. fotog, photog, lenser, shutterbug, camerabug, glowworm, mugger, paparazzo, paparazzi.

PHOTOGRAPH GALLERY n. mug joint.

PHYSIC n. cc pills.

PHYSICAL EDUCATION n. phys ed, gym.

PHYSICALLY FIT adj. in the pink, wrapped tight, crunchy granola, fit as a fiddle, 1A (Mil. draft).

PHYSICALLY UNFIT adj. out of shape, run down, good and flabby, let oneself go, 4F (Mil. draft).

PHYSICAL THERAPY n. rolfing, workout.

PHYSICIAN n. M.D., medico, medic, doc, quack, bones, sawbones, pill pusher, pill slinger, big eye man, big nose man, big heart man, bone bender, Dr. Feelgood, shrink, head shrinker, ice-tong doctor, script writer (prescribing drugs illegally), back-alley abortionist. See DOCTOR.

PHYSIOGNOMY n. kisser, puss, map, mug, pan, mush, moosh, phiz, phizog, biscuit, clock, dial, conk, Chevy Chase, gills, index, mask, potato, squash, deadpan, poker face, sourpuss, picklepuss, sugarpuss.

PHYSIQUE n. bod, build, built, shape, shaft, chassis, classy chassis, beefcake, muscle man, muscles, stacked, V man, built like a brick shithouse, cream puff (small, weak), frame, Coke frame (Fem.), anatomy, corpus, bag of bones, booty.

PIANIST n. fingers, ivory tickler, ivory thumper, itches a mean ivory, tickles the ivories, thumper, piano kid, professor.

PIANO n. ivories, box, tinkle box, eighty-eight, 88, goola, grand, upright, studio.

PIANO KEYS n. eighty-eights, ivories, goola.

PIAZZA n. gallery, front stoop, stoop.

PICAYUNE adj. chicken, chickenshit, nitpicking, picky, picky-picky, small, small-time, tinhorn, measly, two-bit, punk, one-horse, two-by-four, jerkwater. See UNIMPORTANT.

PICK n. bag, cup of tea, druthers, turned on to, weakness for. See CHOICE.

PICK v. opt, tap, finger, name, aim, tab, tag, slot, go down the line, say so, take it or leave it. See SELECT.

PICKAX n. anchor.

PICKET v. hit the bricks, walk out. See STRIKE.

PICKPOCKET n. dip, cannon, tool, wire, mechanic, Catholic, cutpurse, digger, fanner (locates victim), file, forks, five fingers, finger, fingersmith, front gee, gavar, gee, gee whiz (armed), greasy finger, gun, knucker, knucksman, moll buzzer, shot, picks, friskers, hooks, spitter, wise, jostle, jostler, clipper.

PICK POCKETS v. dive, lift, dip, beat, boost, dig, make, make a mark, make a poke, drop the duke, put the duke down, kiss the dog, reef, riffle, whiz, wiz, work the get-ons, work the put-offs, work a short, work a spill, work a tip, work the breaks, out on the shorts, jostle, rooting on the cannon.

PICKPOCKET'S ASSISTANT n. bumper, nudger, stall, stick, squealer (infant used as a distraction).

PICTURE n. 1. art (News.), doodle (meaningless pattern), snap (Photo.). 2. angel (radar). 3. dead ringer, spitting image.

PIE n. chocker (large), magoo (custard pie for throwing).

PIECE n. chunk, gob, hunk, lump, shtick, smithereen, bite, chaw, chomp, cut, slice, halver. See also INTEREST, SHARE.

PIERCE v. crack, crack open, break in, jimmy.

PIG n. porker, porky, cob roller (young or small).

PILE n. 1. buildup. 2. chunk, gob, hunk.

PILFER v. rip off, appropriate, boost, scrounge, pinch, promote, buzz, cop, kipe, liberate, graze (steal and eat food in a supermarket), take a five-finger discount (shoplift), lift, moonlight requisition, touch, snatch, snitch, swipe, snipe, scoff, glom, glaum, glahm, glue, burn, annex, borrow, palm, bag, nip, snare, rough off, pluck. See also STEAL, APPROPRIATE.

PILFERED adj. lifted, bent, kyped, moonlight requisitioned, liberated. hot, hot stuff, hot ice, hot paper, kinky, sizzling, swag (without a gun).

PILL n. doll, jelly bean, amp, bombita, cockleburr (pep), downer, Finn, fruit salad (mixture), 'lude, Mickey Finn, peter, popper, upper; dizzy wizzy, goofball (nonnarcotic), G.B.

PILOT n. flyboy, stick, jockey, jet jockey, throttle jockey, airplane driver, bird legs, birdman, birdwoman, empty kitchen (Fem.), goofer, dodo (Stu.), eagle, rotorhead (helicopter), blue suiter (A.F. test pilot), white suiter (civilian test pilot). See FLYER.

PILOT HOUSE n. brain box (river towboat).

PIMP n. mack, mackman, macko man, hard mack (violent), sweet mack, mac, mackeral, maggot, dude, flesh peddler, hustler, Johnny Ponce, king bung, missionary, outlaw, pee eye, P, ponce, brother-in-law, husband, daddy, Mr. McGimp, McGimper, player, rack salesman, skirt man, honey man, sweet man, fancy man, old man, bull bitch, butch pimp, cadet, driver, easy rider, low rider.

PIMP v. run a stable, have a string of hustlers, have a sister-in-law, steer, tout.

PIMPLE n. hickey, zit, gone, gone under, goob, goober, goophead, pip, beauty spot, bloom, doohickey, dohinky, blem.

PIMPLY adj. crater-face, pizza-face.

PINBALL MACHINE n. whiffle board.

PINCE-NEZ n. nippers.

PINCH n. crunch, clutch, box, tight spot, tight squeeze, between a rock and a hard place. See DIFFICULTY.

PINCHED adj. at the end of one's rope, hard up, up against it. See DESTITUTE.

PINE v. carry a torch, hanker for, itch for, yen for, have a yen for, spoil for, give one's kingdom in hell for, give one's eyeteeth for, eat one's heart out. See DESIRE. See also MOURN.

PINEAPPLE SUNDAE n. Chicago (also soda).

PINNACLE n. the greatest, the most, the max, tops, in top form, in full swing, ape. See BEST.

PIONEER v. trail-blaze, spearhead, get the jump on, go out in front. See also BEGIN.

PIOUS adj. born-again, got religion, Jesus freak, Holy Joe, Jesus lover, Jasper, knee bender, Mary, goody, goody-goody, goody two-shoes, scoutmaster.

PIPE n. stove, hay burner, bug juice (residue).

PIQUANCY n. guts, kick, zip.

PIQUE n. miff, pet, stew, rise, get a rise out of, tiff, snit, peeve, pet peeve, sore, huff, dander, Irish, miff, storm, ruckus, wing-ding, slow burn, conniption, conniption fit, cat fit, duck fit, blowup, flareup, bone to pick.

PIQUE v. 1. piss one off, bug, cop an attitude (Af. Am.), turn one off, get off my case, get outta town, give me a break, cut me some slack, don't sweat me (Af. Am.), chew on, make waves, chap, give a bad time to, give one a hard time, give one the business, give one the needle, hit on, fuck with one's head, get a rise out of one, get one's dander up, get under one's skin. See ANNOY. 2. goose, goose up, grab, egg on, turn on, fire up, key up, put up to, work up, hook trigger, pressure, push. See INTRIGUE.

PISTOL n. artillery, cannon, blaster, burner, gat, piece, iron, rod, jammy (Af. Am.), snubby, snub nose, Saturday night special, bean shooter, peashooter, popper, pop, equalizer, difference, speaker, Mr. Speaker, persuader, convincer, hardware, heater, heat, Betsey, roscoe, forty-five, zip gun, slim, belly gun, snug, spud, potato, tool. See GUN.

PIT AREA n. zoo (racing).

PITCH v. chuck, chunk, fire, lob, heave, sling, fling, gun, peg, toss.

PITCHER n. growler (large, for beer).

PITCHMAN n. barker, booster, plugger, huckster, hucksterer, ad man, ad writer, adsmith, blurbist, ballyhooer, ballyhoo man, grifter, grinder, spieler. See also ADVERTISING MAN, PUBLICIST.

PITFALL n. catch, Catch-22, booby trap, bag, hook, swindle, box, setup, come-on.

PITH n. bottom line, heart, meat and potatoes, nitty-gritty, nub.

PITIFUL adj. wimpy, fish, poor fish, what the cat dragged in, nebbish. See also UNHAPPY.

PITILESS adj. cutthroat, go for the jugular, killer instinct, mean machine, dog-eat-dog, hatchet job, take no prisoners. See also CALLOUS.

PITTSBURGH, PENNSYLVANIA Steel City.

PIZZA n. tza, za, garbage pizza (everything on it), New York (thick crust), Chicago (stuffed).

PLACATE v. cool, stroke, pour oil on troubled waters, take the edge off, soft-pedal, fix up, make matters up, make nice, play up to. See PACIFY.

PLACE n. 1. hangout, joint, lay, layout, plant, dump, hooch (Vietnam), digs, scene, fix, hole, spot, X marks the spot, pad, crib, cradle, hat (Af. Am.), crash pad, roof over one's head, barf city, the pits, armpit (undesirable), office, neck of the woods, zone, turf, cloud-cuckoo-land. 2. where one is at, slot, pecking order, down the line.

PLACE v. park, peg, nail, spot, finger, plank, plank down, plunk, plop. See also INDICATE.

PLACED adj. set-up, fixed, framed, laid-on.

PLACID adj. cool, cool as a cucumber, ah-ah head, unflappable, level vibes. See CALM.

PLAGIARIST n. pirate.

PLAGIARIZE v. pirate, lift, bite, steal, borrow, crib, pick one's brains, rape.

PLAIN adj. 1. unvarnished, vanilla, stripped-down, clean, barebones, white-bread, with the bark on. 2. folksy, homey, haimish, meat-and-potatoes man. 3. big as life, open-and-shut, open-and-shut case, under one's nose, if it were a snake it would bite you, makes no bones about it, call a spade a spade, what you see is what you get, plain as the nose on one's face, talk turkey. See APPARENT. 4. plain as a mud fence, plain enough to stop a clock, barefaced, hard on the eyes, short on looks.

PLAINSPOKEN adj. up front, right up front, call it like it is, straight, shoot straight, talk like a Dutch uncle, call a spade a spade, put all one's cards on the table, make no bones about it. See FRANK.

PLAINTIVE adj. bitchy, out of sorts, not a happy camper, cantankerous, grumpy, beefing, bellyaching, bitching, crabby, cranky, grousing, ugly customer. See PEEVISH. See also UNHAPPY.

PLAN n. game, game plan, layout, have all the pieces in place, gimmick, angle, action, big picture, picture, pitch, proposition, proposish, dodge, setup, play, scenario, scene, story, bit, child, brain child, slant, take, trick, twist, switch, hidden agenda (secret), booby trap, lay of the land, what's cookin', how one figures it, what's the action, where one's heading. See also SCHEME.

PLAN v. hatch, mastermind, quarterback, brainstorm, spitball, craft, line up, ready up, set up, cook up, dream up, trump up, frame up, whip up, come up with, up, throw together, get one's act together, lay out, work something out, block out, get set for, fix to. See also SCHEME.

PLANE n. jet, ramjet, crate, boxcar, ship, can, big iron (multiengine), cloud buster, bird, wind wagon, bug smasher, Indian zoo, animal (press), dumbo (rescue sea plane), kneecap (NEACP plane). See AIRPLANE.

PLANET n. apple, big blue marble, real estate, spaceship earth.

PLANKS n. load of sticks.

PLANNED adj. fixed, wired, rigged, framed, packed, stacked, put-up, set-up, cooked-up, gimmicked-up, sewed-up, in the bag, on ice, cinched, that dog'll hunt, cut and dry, bagged, gaffed, sacked, spike, square, had zingers put in. See also PREARRANGED.

PLANNER n. brain, mastermind. See also CONSPIRATOR.

PLASTIC CARD n. loid (used to open locks).

PLASTIC COVER n. blister (aircraft).

PLASTIC EXPLOSIVE n. Aunt Jemima.

PLASTIC SURGERY n. facelift, nose job, eye job, tummy tuck, body-and-fender man (surgeon).

PLATE n. manhole cover.

PLATFORM n. soapbox, stump, bally stand (circus).

PLATITUDE n. buzzword, boiler plate, high camp, hokum, corn, familiar tune, chestnut, old chestnut, saw, old saw, old song, old story, potboiler.

PLATTER n. manhole cover.

PLAUSIBLE adj. like as not, like enough, very likely. See also BELIEVABLE, LOGICAL.

PLAY n. legiter, legit, piece, potboiler, one-acter, book show, dromedy (dramatic comedy), curtain-raiser, meller, minstrel show, cork opera, dumb show, toby show; hit, smash, smash hit, boff (success); turkey, flop (failure) (these also refer to TV, books, radio, movies, etc.).

PLAY v. carry on, horse around, mess around, clown, kibitz, let go, let loose, kick up one's heels, cut up, cut up a few touches, go places and do things, go on a spree. See REVEL. 2. do a turn, do one's bit, strut one's stuff, play one's gig, chew the scenery, ham, ham it up, tread the boards, come on like gangbusters (well); blow, lay a bomb, lay an egg, go into the toilet (badly). See ACT.

PLAYBOY n. player, high liver, night owl, operator, speed, heavy hitter, C.S.P. (casual sex partner), wolf, hound, poon hound, tomcat, cat, alley cat, beastmaster (dates ugly women), sport, swinger, lover boy, killer, man on the make, make-out artist, on one's tit, chaser, rounder, gay dog, whorehound, good-time Charlie. See LECHER.

PLAYER n. 1. trouper, ham, hambone, legiter, thesp, lead, star, bit player, stand-in, scene sweller, spear carrier, talent, moppet (child). See ACTOR. 2. jock, animal, ape, gorilla, V man, muscle man, meathead, speed merchant, superjock. See ATHLETE. 3. plunger, piker, tinhorn, tinhorn gambler, two-dollar better, chalk player, sharp, sharper, sharpie, crap shooter, boneshaker. See GAMBLER. 4. rocker, monster (popular), cool cat, long hair, long underwear, lip-splitter, sender, solid sender, swinging gate, wig. See MUSICIAN.

PLAYFUL adj. zippy, zappy, snappy, peppy, full of pep, full of piss and vinegar, full of beans, full of hops, feeling one's oats, go-go, have lead in one's pencil. See SPIRITED.

PLAYGOER n. fan, house, showcase, standee, theater-goer, turnout (Pl.). See AUDIENCE.

PLAYHOUSE n. house, four walls, black box, deluxer, legiter, legit, opera house, barn, boards, garlic opera (old, cheap), grind house, mousetrap. See THEATER.

PLAYING-CARD HOLDER n. shoe.

PLAYING CARDS, MARKED n. readers, coolers, paper, hot paper, humps, strippers, low-belly strippers, edgework, lacework, pinwork, greasy aces, B-backs, fish backs, slick backs, broads with ears; shaved deck, cheater, sorts (marked or stacked decks).

PLAYING-CARD TERMS bullet (ace), deuce (two), trey (three); fever, nickel (five); sevener; eighter, eighter from Decatur (eight); niner, niner from Carolina, Nina from Carolina (nine); tension (ten); hook, John, Johnny (jack); girl bitch, lady (queen); cowboy (king); bug, cuter, cutter (joker); wash (shuffle), deck, California bible, California prayer book (1855), boards; cold deck, shaved deck, stacked deck, cheater (marked or prearranged), player; card sharp, card shark, sit in on a hand, bumblepuppy, goulash (unusual hand); Yarborough, lollapaloser (poor hand); low belly strippers, boards, pasteboard, paint, picture, one-eyed Jacks, wild card (joker or any designated card), puppy dog feet (clubs); duke, mitt (hand); rag, riffle (shuffle), ups and downs, wedges.

PLAY MUSIC v. wail, jam, jazz, jive, blast, blow, lip, rag, tootle, wig, blow one's ass off, blow the roof off (loud), blow up a breeze, blow up a storm, get off (swing), kick it (jazz), hit it up, scratching (records).

PLEA n. copout, jive, song, song and dance, whitewash, cleanup, story, fish, fish story, fish tale, have to see a man about a dog, off time. See EXCUSE.

PLEA-BARGAIN v. cop a plea, cop out, do business, discount justice.

PLEAD v. cop a plea, cop out, crawl, square oneself, square a beef, square things, make up for, get down on one's marrowbones. See also BEG; APPEAL.

PLEAD GUILTY v. ride a beef, cop a plea, cop out, plea-bargain.

PLEAD POVERTY v. poor-mouth.

PLEASANT adj. all reet, all righty, coolville, copacetic, fine and mellow, home cooking, all to the mustard, hotsie-totsie, Joe Nice Guy, Mr. Nice Guy. See AGREEABLE.

PLEASE v. slay, score, wow, grab, kill, turn on, go over big, hit the spot, hit the bull's-eye, fill the bill, sell, sell one on, be just the ticket, just what the doctor ordered, make the grade, make it, sweep off one's feet, thanks I needed that. See also OBLIGE.

PLEASED adj. up, upbeat, flyin', flyin' high, floating on air, in seventh heaven, pleased as Punch, tickled pink, gassed. See HAPPY.

PLEASING adj. orgasmic, cool beans.

PLEASURABLE adj. kicks, for kicks, mellow, fine and mellow, lush, nervous, cool, wild, downhill, just for grins, fun (fun party), clear sailing.

PLEASURE n. turn-on, flash, kick, kicks, knocks, mess, velvet, buzz, get off, get off on, get naked. See also AMUSE-MENT; DESIRE; CHOICE.

PLEAT n. reet pleat.

PLEBE n. dumbjohn, ducrot, Mister Dumbjohn, Mister Ducrot, Mister Dumbguard (all West Point).

PLEBEIAN n. boojy, pleb, Billy Sixpack, Joe Lunchbucket.

PLEDGE v. 1. hock, put in hock, hook, soak. 2. feeze, pheeze (fraternity).

PLEDGED adj. 1. steady, going steady, pinned, bird, donah, donar, future, intended. 2. in the bag, nailed down, on ice, cinched. See also AGREED; DETERMINED.

PLENTY adj. no end, no end of, no end to, mega——— (prefix, as in megabucks, megawork), up to one's ass in, up the ying-yang in, up to one's ears with, lousy with, filthy with, stink with, stinking with, crawling with, alive with, thick with, thick as flies, thick as hail, thick as fleas on a hound dog, a dime a dozen, a mess, loaded, loads, loads of, plate is full, enough on one's plate, drug on the market, galore, money to burn, scads, rolling in, coming out of one's ears, all over the place, a ton, mucho, mucho mucho, heavy, a raft of, bags of, lots of, lotsa, oodles, oodles and oodles, mongo, beaucoup, bocoop, bocoo, boocoo, umpteen, eleventeen, jillion, zillion, bazillion, knee-deep in, sockful, shithouseful, shit load, wad, more than one can shake a stick at, coals to Newcastle, egg in one's beer, heap, heaps, passel, flock, aplenty, fat, good 'n' plenty.

PLIANT adj. go with the flow, putty in one's hands, hang loose, roll with the punches, wimpy, wet rag, wet sock, See also SUBMISSIVE.

PLIGHT n. shit, deep shit, serious shit, serious jelly, one's ass is grass, bad news, downside, double trouble, in deep doo-doo, fix, jam. See PREDICAMENT.

PLOD v. plug, plug along, plug away, dig, grind, hammer, peg along, peg away, buckle down, knuckle down, put one's nose to the grindstone, slave, sweat, sweat and slave, back to the salt mines, dog it (inferior), mess around, heel (Stu.), scratch, bear down on it, schlep. See also WALK.

PLODDER n. grind, greasy grind, nose to the grindstone, workhorse, workaholic.

PLOT n. 1. line, story, story line, picture, scenario, scene, weenie. 2. fix, frame, frame-up, booby trap, game, little game, setup, scam, lay of the land, put-up job. See SCHEME. See also PLAN.

PLOT v. cook up, finagle, angle, frame, frame up, operate, promote, wangle, wire, put out a contract. See SCHEME. See also PLAN.

PLOTTER n. finagler, operator, brain, mastermind, wire-puller.

PLUCK n. guts, gutsiness, grit, backbone, heart, intestinal fortitude, starch, moxie, nerve, spunk. See COURAGE.

PLUCK v. slap (bass viol strings).

PLUCKY adj. gutsy, gutty, gritty, nervy, spunky, game, tough, I'm shakin' (sarcastic response to threat), cool hand. See FEARLESS. See also DARING.

PLUMP adj. roly-poly, pleasingly plump, heavy cream, hefty, hippy, chunky, battle of the bulge, butterball, built for comfort, zaftig. See FAT.

PLUNDER n. goods, hot goods, hot items, pickings, take, squeeze, make, swag, boodle, graft.

PLUNDER v. grab, smash and grab, lift, loft, kipe, snatch, salvage, appropriate, take a five-finger discount (shoplift), liberate, requisition, moonlight requisition. See LOOT.

PLUNGE n. header, nose-dive, belly buster, belly flop, belly whopper.

PLUNGE v. 1. take a belly whopper, take a header, dunk, nose-dive, belly-flop. 2. take a header, go the limit, go big time, go whole hog, shoot one's wad, shoot the works, take a flyer. See WAGER.

PNEUMOCONIOSIS n. black lung.

POCATELLO, IDAHO Poca, Pocaloo.

POCKET n. coffee bag, poke, binny (large, for shoplifters), frame, hideaway, keister, kick, mouse, prat kick, rathole.

POCKETBOOK n. shoulder bag, bag, clutch, tote, jiffy bag, jitney bag, keister, frame, hide, leather.

PODIUM n. soapbox, stump.

POINT n. bottom line, nub, name of the game, nittygritty, nuts and bolts, the way of it, drift, heart, meat, stuff, score, punch line, kicker (point of a story, joke, etc.).

POINT v. name, tab, tag, make, peg, finger, lay one's finger on, put one's finger on, put the finger on, button down, pin down, put down for.

POINTLESS adj. goin' round in circles, in a vicious circle, on a treadmill, going nowhere, wombat (waste of money, brains and time), locking the barn after the horse is stolen, looking for a needle in a haystack. See USELESS.

POINT OF VIEW n. POV, P.O.V., angle, slant, take, where one is at, as one sees it, from where one's sitting.

POINT, TO THE adj. 1. on the button, on the nose, right on, kosher, legit, that's the idea, that's the ticket, just what the doctor ordered. 2. in a nutshell, short and sweet, get right to it, make a long story short, boiled down, drawing one a picture, laying it on the line, make no bones about it, call a spade a spade, talk turkey.

POISE n. cool, keep one's cool, polish.

POKE n. shot, sock, zetz, goose.

POKE v. 1. give one the elbow, goose, give one the goose. 2. mosey, schlep long, get no place fast, toddle. See also IDLE.

POKER CARDS AND HANDS n. deuce (two), trey (three), nickel (five), sevener (seven); eighter, eighter from Decateur (eight); niner, niner from Carolina, Nina from Carolina (nine), tension (ten); boy hook, John, Johnny (jack); lady, girl bitch (queen), cowboy (king), bullet (ace); bug, cuter, cutter (wild card), case (last of a number), case ace (last ace), fourth street (fourth card), fifth street (fifth card), ladies (two queens), oldsmobile (pair of eights), ace in the hole, ace-high, dead man's hand (two pair, aces and eights), Hart Schaffner and Marx (three jacks), trips (three of a kind); back-door flush, back-door straight (acquired on last card), made a run (consecutive cards), wired (hidden pair), split week, straight, tiger (lowest hand), kicker (unpaired high card), off suit (two cards, different suits); the flop, on board (face-up cards), suited (two or more cards, same suit), open-ended straight, pat hand (no more cards are needed), hole cards (down cards), door card (first card exposed in stud), crowded cabin (full house), lock (can't be beaten).

POKER CHIPS n. barber pole, buy in, checks, blacks ($100); greens, quarters ($25); reds, nickel ($5), stack, bingle (one chip).

POKER PLAYER n. the gun (dealer), under the gun (first player left of dealer), four-flusher (bluffer with four cards of a flush showing).

POKER PLAYS n. gut shot (draw to an inside straight), burn a card (discard the top card of the deck), fill, fill up (make a full house), drop, over, fold, chase (call a better hand than yours), check (player under the gun doesn't bet).

POKER TERMS crank the wheel (deal), door card (first exposed card in stud), marker (player's I.O.U.), drop, over, fold, bug (wild card), cut, bingle (chip), case (last of a number) case ace (last ace), ace in the hole, ace high, ante up, feed the kitty, stand pat, stay, ride 'em, play 'em close to the vest (conservative), pot (bets made), see, blind, sandbag, bump (raise), slow play (bluffing), put one on (guess opponent's hand), the gun (dealer), under the gun (first player left of the dealer); the flop, on board (face-up cards), lock, nuts (certain to win); sit out, deal one out (skip a hand), sucker bet, limit (maximum bet), call (matched bet), takeout (money brought to game), house (host).

POLE n. Polack, Pollack, Pollock, Stash, Stella, Bohunk, Hunky, Hunkie (all Derog.).

POLICE AIRCRAFT n. air bear, chopper copper, copper chopper, eye in the sky, pie in the sky.

POLICE CAR n. skunk wagon, black-and-white, bubble-gum machine, popcorn machine, fuzzmobile, bear car, bearmobile, pigmobile, buzz, buzzer, catch car, Tijuana taxi, prowl car, cherry top, screaming gasser, whistler; brown bag, plain wrap (unmarked); buggy whip (transmitter), cherries (flashing lights), bubs (blue lights), gumball (lights).

POLICE CLUB n. billy, sap stick, stick, nightstick, business, conk buster, conk crusher, convincer, duffy silencer, persuader, rosewood, rosh, works, shill.

POLICE FORCE n. boys in blue, fuzz, five-O (Af. Am.), goon squad, heat, John Law, long arm of the law, New York's finest, the force, the law, pigs, boy scouts, Babylon (Af. Am.).

POLICE HELICOPTER n. bear in the air, eye in the sky, chopper copper, copper chopper.

POLICE LEDGER n. blotter, sheet, rap sheet, fuzzbiz.

POLICE LIEUTENANT n. boss, lieu, lou.

POLICEMAN'S BADGE n. buzzer, button, cookie cutter, flash, tin, white tin, yellow tin.

POLICE OFFICER n. cop, fuzz, fuzzy, copper, fur, slime, slime bucket, bull, shamus, heat, flic, cossack, arm, dick, diaper dick (handles children), narc (narcotics), pig, oink, lard bacon, Uncle Nab (Af. Am.), clown (rural), the man, the men, bubble-gum man, wiggy man, black-and-white, badge, badge bandit, bike (motorcycle), onetime, the boys, boys in blue, blue man, bluecoat, bluebird (Af. Am.), big brother, boy scouts, jakes, mallet, city kitty, C.O. (corrections officer), county Joe, county mounty, flathead, flatie, flaty, flatty, flatfoot, harness bull, harness dick, harness cop, Keystone Kop, sparrow cop, Evel Knievel, hick dick, law, John Law, Johnny Law, long arm, long arm of the law, Kojak, bear, Smokey, Smokey the Bear, lady bear, girlie bear, mama bear, mama Smokey, baby bear (rookie), Goldie Locks, little bear (local), local bear, local yard, local yokel; CHP, CHIPS (California Highway Patrol), bearded buddy; yard bull, cinderbull (railroad); deputy dog, goobie (campus), grasshopper (accepts bribes); grasseater, meat-eater (corrupt); local boy, mafia, nightcrawler, savage, slewfoot, road ranger, buttons, collar, finger, elbow, fink, cookie cutter, geerus, goms, goon squad, jade squad (deals with Asian crime), gum foot, gumshoe, headbeater, occifer, ossifer, popo, Mulligan, nab, penny, roach; Dirty Harriet, Jane Wayne (women who overreact); Charley Goon, Charlie Nebs, Dan O'Leary, claw, fly, fly ball, fly bob, fly bull, fly cop, fly dick, fly mug, shoo fly, sky, grumbler (chief), pounder, sham, shammus, roller, slough, snake, snatcher, stick, stool, geepo, boogle man, foot soldier, hat rack (traffic), infantry, paper hanger, Peter Rabbit, the man with the headache stick, the brass, brass hat, five-0. See also DETECTIVE.

POLICE PATROL WAGON n. battlewagon, paddywagon, black-and-white, Maria, Black Maria, Black Annie (So.), fuzzmobile, booby hatch, go-long, milk wagon, piewagon.

POLICE RECORD n. pedigree, prior, rap sheet, fuzzbiz.

POLICE SERGEANT n. sarge, desk sarge, boss.

POLICE SPY n. plant, fly, nose, narc (narcotics).

POLICE STATION n. station, station house, glass house, can, cop shop, front office, bear cage, bear cave, lock-'em-up, lockup, piss-house, graybar Hilton, cally (hobo).

POLICE TERMS buzzer, cookie cutter, tin, gold tin (badge); smell the bacon (police present), box (telephone operator), the company (metropolitan force), swoop (raid), O.P. (observation post), U.C. (undercover unit); make, make one (recognize); taking pictures (radar), stake, stakeout, 85 (girlfriend), hog (uniform).

POLICEWOMAN n. Dickless Tracy, meter maid, Min, lady bear, girlie bear, mama bear, city kitty, sow.

POLICY n. channels, red tape, by the numbers, by the book. See also PLAN.

POLICY NUMBERS LOTTERY n. numbers, policy game, bank, banker, number baron, number man, payoff ghee (boss of), play the numbers (make a bet), hit, hit the numbers (win), comptroller, runner (subordinate).

POLIOMYELITIS n. polio.

POLISH adj. Polack, Pollack, Pollock, Hunkie, Hunky, Bohunk, lock, blitz (WWII) (all Derog.).

POLISH v. buff up, shine.

POLITIC adj. cool, sharp, tuned-in, play it cool, handle with kid gloves, mind one's p's and q's, on the lookout. See also DISCREET.

POLITICAL ACTION COMMITTEE n. PAC.

POLITICAL CAMPAIGN n. politicking, rubber-chicken tour, on the stump, stumping the hustings, off kissing babies, pressing the flesh (shaking hands), Super Tuesday (primary), blowout (landslide), rainmaker (fundraiser), October surprise (damaging bombshell).

POLITICAL CONVENTION n. powwow, quadrennial circus.

POLITICAL FUND-RAISING TERMS rainmaker, Emily, Emily's list (Early Money Is Like Yeast), instacheck (quick donation), bundling (employer coerces employees to contribute, individual contributions are bundled to avoid maximum limit), bagel (failed to collect), soft money (not counted in maximum limit).

POLITICAL HOLDOVER n. lame duck.

POLITICAL JARGON n. bafflegab, bunkum, federalese, gobbledygook, officialese, Washingtonese, hillspeak, fuzzwords.

POLITICALLY CORRECT adj. P.C., poco.

POLITICAL OPPONENTS n. opposish, enemies list, hit list, shit list.

POLITICAL ORGANIZER n. ward heeler, one of the troops, rainmaker (fund raiser).

POLITICAL SCIENCE n. poli sci.

POLITICAL TERMS wedge issue (divisive), bullet vote (single issue voter), switcher issue (single subject), smoked-filled room, animal (political campaign), zoo plane (carries press).

POLITICIAN n. pol, politico, two-bit politician, peanut politician, jackleg politician, pork-barrel politician, boys in the backroom, the boys uptown, dark horse (candidate), boodler (corrupt), glad-hander, grandstander, handshaker, hack, party hack, satch, warhorse, wheeler-dealer, logroller, boss, man higher up, ward heeler, flesh presser, party boss, party chieftain, stumper, stump speaker, stump orator, whistle-stopper, baby-kisser, bell-ringer, plum (political), prune (appointee with experience), policy wonk, strange bedfellows, velcroid (sticks to important people).

POLITICS n. art of the possible, smoke-filled room, backroom politics, jungle, zoo, bossism, peanut politics, kid-glove politics, silk-stocking politics, hotairistocracy.

POLL v. polling the nabes (family and friends), polling the horn-rims (staff intellectuals), polling the wiz (computer), trying it out on the dog (public), put out a feeler, test the waters, see which way the wind blows, send up a trial balloon.

POLL TAKER n. numbers cruncher, pollster, pulse-taker.

POLLUTED adj. dirty, exposed, cooked (radiation), mucked-up.

POLLUTION n. smaze, smog, vog (volcanic).

POLYGRAPH TEST n. fourth degree, flutter (administer), fluttering (take test).

POLYSYLLABIC adj. jawbreaking.

POMADE n. axle grease, conk.

POMPOUS adj. biggety, bossy, dicty, sidity, puffed up, uppity, gold card, stuck on oneself, chesty, high-and-mighty, high-hat, high-flown, highfalutin, put on airs, have one's glasses on (Af. Am.), stuffed shirt, windbag, windy, full of hot air, gassy, top-lofty. See CONCEITED.

POND n. splash.

PONDER v. figger, moon, noodle it around, crunch, put on one's thinking cap, chew the cud, woolgather, pipedream, build castles in the air. See THINK.

PONDEROUS adj. heavy, hefty, deadly, cheesy, borring. See also CLUMSY, TROUBLESOME.

PONTIFF n. papa.

POOL OF MONEY n. kitty, pot.

POOL TERMS crip, eight ball, pool parlor, ham joint, scratch (miss), rack 'em up, run 'em (sink all the balls), English, bridge shot, the break, ringer, hustler.

POOR adj. needy, truly needy, disadvantaged, deprived, underdeveloped (nation or district), hard-up, tapped, played out, on one's ass, on the rocks, down and out, have-nots, seen better days, bag lady, piss-poor, dirt-poor, the poor, poor as a church mouse. See DESTITUTE.

POPCORN n. old maids (unpopped kernels).

POPE n. papa.

POPSICLE n. pop.

POPULACE n. bodies, cats, dudes, heads, hoi polloi, the public, John Q., John Q. Public, Billy Sixpack, Joe Lunchbucket, the mob, riffraff, cattle, the great unwashed. See PUBLIC.

POPULAR adj. selling, selling like hotcakes, sizzler, tuff, hip, hep, mod, cosmo, trendy, flavor-of-the-month, up to speed, in the swim, in the mainstream, in, in-thing, the thing, in there, happenin', mod, now, really now, the rage, spinach, trendy, faddy, up-to-the-minute, fashion plate, go-go, hip, hep, mellow back, catch on, caught on, in-spot, happening place, groovy hangout, hot spot, masscult, crazy, gas, a gas, gasser, in the groove, groovy, off the chart, far out, home cooking, hotsie-totsie, ice, sharp. See also NEW; STYLISH.

POPULAR CONCERT n. pop concert, pops.

POPULAR MUSIC RATINGS n. the charts, top ten, hit parade.

POPULAR PERSON n. lulu, one of the boys, big man on campus, BMOC, prom trotter, kimble (tries to be), crowd-pleaser, right guy, okay people, regular big with, babelonia (girl). See also LIKED.

PORCH n. stoop, front stoop, gallery.

PORCUPINE n. quill pig.

PORK n. sow belly (bacon, salt pork), squeal, piano (spare ribs), Cincinnati cracklings (scraps), Cincinnati oysters (pigs' feet), Cincinnati quail (fatback).

PORNOGRAPHIC adj. X-rated, adult, purple, blue, dirty, hot, porn, porno, porny, stag, steamy, low-down and dirty, off-color, flaming (Obsc., computer conversations). rough, salty, raunchy. See OBSCENE.

PORNOGRAPHIC BOOKSTORE n. adult bookstore, emporium, sex shoppe.

PORNOGRAPHIC FILM n. nudie, X-rated, porn, porno, pornoflick, soft porn, hard porn, skin flick, beaver flick, flesh flick, slasher flick, fuck film, adult film, snuff film, stag film, eroduction.

PORNOGRAPHIC PUBLICATION n. adult magazine, skin magazine, nudie, Tijuana Bible, fuck book, stroke book (novel).

PORNOGRAPHY n. hot stuff, hard-core, soft-core, flaming (obscene computer conversations). jack-off material, jerk-off material, porn, hard porn, soft porn, X-rated, triple X-rated. See OBSCENITY.

PORRIDGE n. cush, grits, mush.

PORTEND v. call it, call the turn, call one's shots, read, have a hunch, in the cards, it's looking to, see it coming, crystal-ball it, psych it out. See PREDICT.

PORTENT n. hunch, vibes (good or bad), feel in one's bones, funny feeling, sinking feeling, in the wind, handwriting on the wall. See PREMONITION.

PORTER n. sky cap, red cap, baggage smasher, baggage masher, flunky, grip gorilla, pack rat, punk, razorback, swamper.

PORTION n. 1. hit, shot, fix, slug, bang, dram, chunk, gob, glob, hunk, lump, smithereen. 2. P.C., piece, piece of the action, bite, cut, divvy, lagniappe, plum, taste, lion's share, bigger half, drag. See SHARE.

PORTLAND, OREGON Big Port.

PORTLY adj. beerbelly, bay window, corporation, spare tire, rubber tire, Dunlop syndrome, hefty, hippy, broad in the beam, corn-fed, built for comfort, avoirdupois. See FAT.

PORTUGUESE n. don; gese, Portugoose, Portugee, Portergee (Derog.).

POSE v. play-act, put up a front, do a bit, fake, lay it on thick, make out like, put on, take off as. See POSTURE. See also PRETEND.

POSITION n. 1. the scene, spot, fix (stationary), where it's at, where one is at, X marks the spot, how the land lies, lay of the land. 2. day gig, bag, do, dodge, gig, go, hang, nine-to-five shit, rat race, slot. See OCCUPATION. 3. situash, spot, happenin', like it is, the size of it, the way it shapes up, how things stack up, ball game. See CONDITION. See also BASIS, OPINION, ATTITUDE.

POSITIVE adj. absofuckinglutely, posolutely, absitively, sure as I live and breathe, cocksure, dead sure, surefire, on ice, cold, no buts about it, checked and double-checked. See CERTAIN.

POSITIVELY adv. flat, flat out, flat-ass, come hell or high water, cert, amen, sure, why sure, sure thing, fer sure, sure as God made little green apples, absofuckinglutely, absitively, posolutely, you know, you know it, you better believe it, you betcha, you betcher life, you bet, you said it, you said a mouthful, you can say that again, you're not kidding, you're darn tootin', straight out, no strings attached, no holds barred, no catch, no kicker, no buts about it, no ifs ands or buts, with knobs on, with tits on, in a handbasket, the real McCoy, I'll tell the world, I'll tell the cockeyed world, in spades, check, with bells on, on the button, on the money, on the nose, the ticket, the very thing, the checker, to a tee, Judy (I understand), on the lemon, on the noggin, it, is the Pope Catholic?, does a bear shit in the woods?, is a bear Catholic?, does the Pope shit in the woods?, honest to God, indeedy, yes indeedy, for a fact, for a fact, Jack, real, for real, really truly, righto, right on, right as rain, right you are, rather, in a heartbeat, woofing.

POSSESS v. lock up, get hold of, bag, glom on to, latch on to, grab, bogart, corner, corner the market, get a corner on, hog, get one's hands on, sit on.

POSSESSED adj. fiendish, gone, hooked, taken over, into, really into, eat sleep and breathe something. See OBSESSED.

POSSIBILITY n. break, breaks, big break, even break, shot, shot at, get a shot at, have a shot at, long shot, hundred-to-one shot, whack, whack at, go, go at, stab, stab at, have a fling at, opps, prayer, in the running, irons in the fire, fair shake, fighting chance, outside chance, near as one can tell, level playing field, dollars to doughnuts, a Chinaman's chance, as much chance as a snowball in hell, snowball chance, fifty-fifty, toss-up, play, action, maximax (big return, big loss), maximin (small return, big loss), minimax (safe), fluke.

POSSIBLE adj. no sweat, no biggie, cinch, can-do, snap, pushover, piece of cake, setup, doable, breeze, duck soup, easy as pie, easy as falling off a log, simple as ABC. See EASY.

POST BILLBOARDS v. snipe.

POST EXCHANGE n. PX.

POSTMODERN adj. po-mo.

POSTAGE STAMP n. sticker, hot sticker (counterfeit).

POSTER n. three-sheet, twenty-four sheet.

POSTERIOR n. buns, fanny, ass, behind, backside, bottom, butt, bubblebutt (large and rounded), can, cheeks, moon, tail, derriere, pratt, rear end, tush, tuchis, tokus, duff. See BUTTOCKS.

POSTGRADUATE n. postgrad.

POST OFFICE n. P.O., APO (Mil.).

POSTPONE v. shelve, put on the back burner, put on hold, hang fire, pigeonhole, cool it, give one a rain check. See DELAY.

POSTPONED adj. 1. hung-up, held-up, scrubbed, slowed-up, tied-up, pigeonholed, stabbed, buttonholed, shelved, put on the shelf, put on hold, put on the back burner. 2. in a bind, jammed, jammed-up, strapped for time.

POSTURE n. brace, brush (Army). See also ATTITUDE, OPINION.

POSTURE v. do a bit, fake, lay it on thick, make out like, play-act, put up a front, fake it. See also PRETEND.

POTATO n. spud, murphy, mickey, tater, earth apple, Irish grape, fries.

POTENCY n. juice, snap, zap, zing, zip, sock, kick, moxie, punch, steam, what it takes, piss and vinegar. See POWER.

POTENT adj. zippy, zappy, got the horses to do it, powerhouse, go-getter, on the ball, ball of fire, spanking, punchy, gutsy, have lead in one's pencil. See POWERFUL.

POTPOURRI n. everything but the kitchen sink, mishmash, mishmosh, mixed bag, combo, duke's mixture (strange), stew, goulash, soup (liquid), lorelei.

POVERTY-STRICKEN adj. on the rims, run on the rims, under the safety net, through the safety net.

POWER n. 1. juice, go juice, bounce, snap, zap, zing, zip, zippo, ginger, pow, sock, kick, kicker, pizzazz, dash, splash, the force, beef, clout, might and main, moxie, punch, steam, powerhouse, heavy artillery, poop, hustle, the stuff, the goods, the word, what it takes, grease, alzo, connection, hooks, in, license, wire, a lot to do with, a lot to say about, inside track, wire-pulling, vim, pep, pepper, pepper-upper, picker-upper, pick-me-up, pop, get-up-and-go, piss and vinegar, full head of steam, steamroller. See also INFLUENCE. 2. boss, suit, czar, rug rank (high), big shot, big shit, big cheese, top dog, high-up, kingpin, bull of the woods, head, a lot to say about, the say, the say-so, a lot to do with. See EXECUTIVE.

POWERFUL adj. 1. wicked, husky, buffed, industrial, hefty, beefy, gutty, gutsy, got the horses to do it, hoss, powerhouse, hyper, hypercharged, bull, push, punch, go-getter, go-go, play hard ball, ball of fire, hotshot, steamroller, get up a head of steam, Norwegian steam, spanking, punchy, zippy, zappy, snappy, peppy, live, full of beans, double-barreled, mover and shaker, heavy artillery, wave maker, have lead in one's pencil, the juice, the force, money talks, pull, in, connected, connections, stand in with, cut ice, throw a lot of weight, carry a lot of weight, sit fat, built like a brick shithouse, sturdy as an ox, strong as a lion, strong as an ox, strong as a horse, come on strong, magnum force, gorilla, bruiser, bone-crusher, beefcake, beef-a-roni, crushman, strong-arm, muscle man, he-man, hulk, hunk, tiger, Turk, big bruiser, tough, tough guy, come on like gangbusters, walk heavy, walk tall, takeover, take charge, bossy, fair hell, high-cotton, hot flash, hot shit, we're not talking about nutmeg here. 2. big, biggie, Mr. Big, big-name, name, big-time, big-time operator, B.T.O., big-timer, big-player, big wheel, wheeler-dealer, big man, big man on campus, B.M.O.C., big boy, big number, big one, big shit, big shot, hotshot, hotdog, top dog, A-list, face card, gun, big gun, big noise, big chew, bigwig, big-wigged, big butter-and-egg man, big ghee, big spud, big-league, major-league, rainmaker, big deal, big stuff, heavy stuff, heavy, 800-pound gorilla, V.I.P., apple, big apple, big cheese, big piece of cheese, real cheese, whole cheese, biggest frog in the pond, walk heavy, his nibs, honcho, hooper-dooper, higher-ups, the high-rise boys, high-profile, in the limelight, high muck-a-muck, high muckety-muck, high monkey-monk, high pillow, lion, knocker, kuhnocker, connection, connection ghee, magoo, main squeeze, one who knows where the body's buried, polly, wire, wire man, wire-puller, a hook (police), godfather, czar, tycoon, baron, brass, top brass, brass hat, topsider, a somebody, something.

POWERLESS adj. 1. paper tiger, weak sister, wishy-washy, wimp, chicken, gutless, nerd, putty in one's hands, can't hack it, not have it, can't cut it, can't cut the mustard, can't make the grade, can't fade that, 2. dud, no lead in the pencil, no toothpaste in the tube, fire blanks, shoot blanks, blank cartridge, can't get it up, don't have the horses, out of gas, over a barrel, tapped, tapped out. See WEAK.

PRACTICAL adj. commonsensical, resonate (that resonates), hardheaded, nuts-and-bolts. See also LAZY.

PRACTICE v. hone, tune up, warm up, work out, dry run, call, shake down, shakedown cruise, tryout, dress, walk through, run through; lick into shape, put through the grind, put through the mill.

PRAGMATIC adj. commonsensical, hardheaded.

PRAISE n. warm fuzzies, pat on the back, pat on the head, PR, puff, puffing up, pumping up, rave, strokes, stroking, abreaction route, commercial, cow sociology, Dr. Spocking the help, opening up. See also FLATTERY.

PRAISE v. hear it for, kudos, rave, root, root for, beat one's skin for, stroke, boost, push, puff up, build, build up, brag about, toss a bouquet, give a bouquet, give a posy, give the man a big cigar, hand it to, have to hand it to, pat on the back, hats off to, gold star, trade last, TL.

PRAISEWORTHY adj. fresh, goodic, cool; sweet bumpin', lookin' chilly, ace (Af. Am.), stellar, cas, cazh, major, neato, keen, terriff, yummy, bad, not bad, not too shabby, rattling, rocking, gnarly, bueno, slick, chilly most, lampin', happenin', nasty, cranking, doin' a hundred, batting a thousand, tuff, tough, horror show, real mean, beaut, atsa nice, bootin' height, cuspy, Jesus bread, mitzvoh, organic, fat city, gone, reet, check-plus, swell, a prince of a fellow, Christian, true Christian, pillar of the church, salt of the earth. See also ADMIRABLE.

PRANK n. rib, gag, put-on, caper, spoof, high-jinks, hi-jinks, hot foot, hot one, monkeyshines, shenanigans, pull one's leg.

PRANKSTER n. card, cutup.

PRATTLE v. yackety-yak, yap, natter, patter, beat one's chops, beat one's gums, bat the breeze, jibber-jabber, run off at the mouth, run one's mouth, rattle, rattle on. See SPEAK.

PREACH v. get on a soapbox, blow, lay it on, lay it on with a trowel, lay it on thick, pile it on, talk big, talk highfalutin, talk tall.

PREACHER n. padre, Holy Joe, sky pilot, Bible thumper, Bible basher, fire escape, fire insurance agent, gospel pusher, devil driver, devil dodger, preacher man, glory roader, jackleg preacher (lay). See CLERGYMAN.

PREADOLESCENT n. weeny bopper, teenybopper, bobby-soxer. See also GIRL.

PREAMPLIFIER n. preamp.

PREARRANGE v. fix, frame, frame up, wire, cook, cook up, sew up, set up, rig, pack, slant, stack the cards, pack the deal, load the dice, put in the bag, put on ice, rig the jury, satchel. See PREPARE. See also PLAN; SCHEME.

PREARRANGED adj. wired, bagged, fixed, gaffed, planted, rigged, sacked, stacked, stacked deck, packed, packed deal, packed jury, rigged jury, put-up job, cut-and-dry. See PREPARED.

PRECARIOUS adj. hot, hairy, hellish, loaded, dynamite, unhealthy, rugged, dicey, iffy, chancy, too hot to handle, on thin ice, on slippery ground, out on a limb, in the tube, touch-and-go, hanging by a thread. See DANGEROUS. See also DOUBTFUL.

PRECEDING adj. onetime, ex, X.

PRECIOUS adj. worth its weight in gold, worth a king's ransom, worth one's eyeteeth, collectibles, would give one's eyeteeth for.

PRECIPITATE adj. off the hip, jump the gun, go off half-cocked, off the top of one's head, shoot from the hip. See IMPULSIVE.

PRECIPITATION n. wet stuff, heavy dew, precip, window washer, gully washer, cloud juice, deep water (heavy), drownder. See RAIN.

PRECIPITOUSLY adv. early on, jump the gun. See also IMPULSIVE.

PRECISE adj. on the button, on the nose, choosy, comma counter, nitpicker, picky, picky-picky, ticky, stickler, pernickety, persnickety, smitty, dot the i's and cross the t's. See EXACT.

PRECISELY adv. on the button, on the money, on the nose, on the noggin, on the lemon, the ticket, the very thing, the checker, to a tee, Judy (I understand), hit the nail on the head, cert, sure, why sure, sure thing, for sure, fer sure, fer sher, fer shirr, surest thing you know, that's for sure, for a fact, you said it, no buts about it, no ifs ands or buts, and no mistake.

PRECISIONIST adj. comma counter, nitpicker, ace, picky, picky-picky, pernickety, persnickety, stickler, fuss-budget, fusspot, fuddy-duddy, granny, old woman, old maid. See also PARTICULAR.

PRECOCIOUS adj. pushy, cheeky, cocky, flip, fresh, crusty, gally, nervy, chutzpadik, biggety, sassy, smart, smart-alecky, smart-ass, wise-ass, brassy, bold as brass, the cutes. See also AGGRESSIVE.

PRECOGNIZE v. have a hunch, get vibes, feel in one's bones, have a funny feeling. See SENSE.

PREDETERMINED adj. wired, fixed. See PREARRANGED.

PREDICAMENT n. shit, deep shit, serious jelly, serious shit, bad news, bad scene, downside, clutch, hang-up, drag, bind, double bind, one's ass is grass, tall order, large order, rough go, heavy sledding, rainin', ticklish spot, tight spot, tight squeeze, trouble in River City, lose-lose situation, no-win situation, tar baby, gasser, pisser, rat's nest, snake pit, box, crunch, catch, Catch-22, bitch, handful, headache, bummer, downer, worriment, botheration, grabber, hooker, double trouble, behind the eight ball, boxed in, in a box, in a crack, in deep doo-doo, in a fix, in a hole, snafu, jam, in a jam, in a clutch, in a mess, in a pickle, scrape, in a scrape, in a spot, in a tight spot, in a hot spot, on the hot seat, hot water, in deep water, in heavy water, ass out, in a stew, in over one's head, up a tree, up the creek, up the creek without a paddle, up shit creek, up shit creek without a paddle, pain in the ass, pain in the neck, between a rock and a hard place, tail in a gate, tit in a wringer, mix, mess, holy mess, unholy mess, nightmare, kettle of fish, fine kettle of fish, a fine mess you've got us into, fine how-do-you-do, hobble, pickle, pretty pickle, pretty pass, squeeze, sticky wicket, hard row to hoe, hard row of stumps, hard time, hard pull, heat's on, a mountain out of a molehill, heavy load to haul, the devil to pay, hell to pay, bug, glitch, puzzler, can of peas, can of worms, Pandora's box, green hornet (Mil.), honey, hot potato, stinker, tsuris, tumul, what's with, sixty-four-dollar question, twister, teaser, sticker, floorer, stumper, bugaboo, crimp, crimp one's style, hump, stinger, hot grease, jackpot, mess up, screw up, need it like a hole in the head, next week East Lynne, rub, push comes to shove, when things get tough, toughie, tough proposition, tough to buck, tough nut to crack, tough going, hard going, joker, scuffle, put on the spot, hit a snag, a holdup, come a-cropper, one small difficulty.

PREDICT v. dope, dope out, figure, figger, figger out, figure out, size up, call it, call the turn, call one's shots, call the shots, read, make book, have a hunch, in the cards, it's looking to, telegraph, see it coming, see the handwriting on the wall, crystal-ball it, psych it out, be afraid, wait for the other shoe to drop.

PREDICTION n. scenario, indicator, dope, tip.

PREDICTOR n. dopester, tipster, tout, touter, oddsmaker.

PREDILECTION n. bag, dish, dish of tea, cup of tea, thing, a thing for, weakness for, turned onto, druthers, flash, groove, type, mind-set, where one is at. See INCLINATION.

PREDISPOSITION n. bag, dish, dish of tea, cup of tea, druthers, flash, groove, thing, turned on to, type, weakness for. See also INCLINATION.

PREEMPT v. bump.

PREFABRICATE v. prefab.

PREFABRICATED adj. ready-made, prefabbed, off-the-rack.

PREFER v. opt, tag, tap, finger, go down the line, partial to, thing for, turned on to. See also SELECT, DESIRE.

PREFERENCE n. bag, cup of tea, druthers, go down the line, flash, groove, turned on to, weakness for, say-so, take it or leave it, other side of the coin, other fish to fry, other fish in the sea, other pebbles on the beach. See also INCLINATION, DESIRE.

PREGNANT adj. knocked up, preggie, preggy, expecting, expecting a blessed event, blessed eventing, in a family way, in a delicate condition, on the nest, got one in the oven, got a bun in the oven, have a cake in the oven, bumped, infanticipating, heir-apparenting, fragrant, full of heir, have one, bagged, belly-up, storked, family development project, join the club, swallow a watermelon seed, watermelon on the vine, stick test (home pregnancy test).

PREGNANT, MAKE v. knock up.

PREJUDICE n. head-set, mind-set, mind trip, 'tude, tilt, where one is at, cold deck, down on, flash, glass ceiling (invisible barrier to promotion), Jim Crow, Jim Crowism, Jane Crow (against women), feel a draft (recognition of).

PREJUDICED adj. agin, down on, one-sided, tilted, weighted, cold deck, flash, red-neck, red-baiter, Jew-baiter, black-baiter, Jim Crow, Jane Crow (against women), a regular Archie Bunker, homer (umpire favoring home team). See also INTOLERANT.

PRELUDIN n. ludens, ludins.

PREMATURE adj. a bit previous, early on, half-assed, half-baked, half-cocked, jump the gun.

PREMATURE BABY n. preemie, preemy.

PREMATURELY adv. previous, a bit previous, bright and early, early bird, early on.

PREMEDICAL adj. pre-med.

PREMEDITATE v. set up, fix, frame up, rig, lay out, put in the bag, sew up, pack the deal, stack the cards, stack the deck. See PLAN.

PREMIERE n. preem, opening. See also BEGINNING.

PREMISES n. hangout, joint, lay, layout, plant, dump, digs, scene, fix, hole, spot, X marks the spot, pad, crib, crash pad, roof over one's head; barf city, the pits, armpit (undesirable), office, neck of the woods, zone, turf. See also HOUSE, OFFICE.

PREMIUM n. gravy, spiff, P.M., button (salesman's reward). See also EXTRA.

PREMONITION n. hunch, vibes (good or bad), vibrations, feel in one's bones, funny feeling, sinking feeling, worriment, batten down the hatches, winds, in the wind, winds of change, wind change, handwriting on the wall, no light at the end of the tunnel, next week East Lynne.

PREOCCUPATION n. hang-up, have a thing about, have on the brain, have on the mind, bee, bee in one's bonnet, bug, bug in one's ear, bug up one's ass, bag, ax to grind, grabber, tiger, tiger by the tail. See also OBSESSION.

PREOCCUPIED adj. mooning, moony, pipe-dreaming, daydreaming, woolgathering, out to lunch, spaced out, popcorn-headed, airheaded, absentminded professor, Suzie (Fem.), have on the brain, have on one's mind, have a thing about, hung up, have a bee in one's bonnet, have a bug in one's ear, have a bug up one's ass, bugged, asleep at the switch, asleep on the job, not on the job, goofing off, looking out the window, pay no mind. See also OBSESSED.

PREORDAINED adj. in the cards, so it goes, the way the deck is stacked, the handwriting on the wall.

PREPARATION n. prep, prepping, have all the pieces in place, readying, readying up, lead time, breaking in, dry run, runthrough, shakedown, shakedown cruise, tryout, workout; rundown, backgrounder, briefing.

PREPARATORY SCHOOL n. prep school.

PREPARATORY SCHOOL STUDENT n. preppie, preppy, prep, prep scholar.

PREPARE v. 1. prep, warm up, ready, ready up, red up, gear up, line up, psych oneself up, set up, get set for, get the juices flowing, loosen up, shape up, sharpen, work over, work up, whip into shape, lick into shape, toughen up, build up, fix to, clear the decks, pave the way, cram, do one's homework, lay out, work something out, pack, stack the cards, pack the deal, put through the grind, put through the mill. See also TRAIN. 2. fill in, fill one in, brief, put on to, put one in the picture, wise up, give a pointer to, let in on the know, keep one posted, frame, frame up, rig, rig up.

PREPARED adj. prepped, have all the pieces in place, wired, bagged, fixed, down, gaffed, gimmicked-up, rigged, sacked, framed, square, squared away, had zingers put in, packed, stacked, up, set-up, put-up, up on, psyched-up, cooked-up, sewed-up, in the bag, on ice, cinched, cut-and-dry, got it covered, all bases covered, looking to, looking for, waitin' on, the noose is hanging, ready for prime time, at the ready, loaded for bear, have one's ducks in a row.

PREPAYMENT n. front money, up front, in front, in the blue, front-end loading (loan interest).

PREPONDERANCE n. lion's share, big half, bigger half, big end, max, maxi, the most, mostest.

PREPOSTEROUS adj. ass backwards, bass ackwards, back asswards, harebrained, lamebrained, thick, reachy, pure bullshit, over the top, too much, bubbleheaded, horse's ass, far-out, takes the cake. See UNBELIEVABLE.

PREPUCE n. lace curtain (homosexual use).

PRESCRIPTION n. scrip, script, reader, OTC (over-the-counter drug).

PRESENT adj. yo, check, dig, made the scene, on board, on deck, on hand, show, show up, there with bells on, there with knobs on, there with tits on.

PRESENT n. goodie, stake, giveaway (often prize), writeoff, handout, mitzvah, gifting, gash (unexpected), lump, poke out. See also GIFT, MODERN.

PRESENT v. 1. do the honors, give a knockdown, knock down, fix up, get together, intro. See INTRODUCE. 2. pitch, make a pitch, speak one's piece, put on, roll out, trot out, hit, lay down, lay out, pop the question, proposition. 3. get it up, kick in, gift, give with, gift with, come up with, get it on, lay on, put something in the pot, sweeten the kitty. See GIVE. 4. bring out, come out with, boot, spring with.

PRESENTATION n. pitch, sales pitch, dog-and-pony show, intro, knockdown.

PRESENTIMENT adj. hunch, vibes (good or bad), feel in one's bones, funny feeling, sinking feeling, worriment, in the wind, handwriting on the wall, no light at the end of the tunnel. See PREMONITION.

PRESENTLY adv. by 'n' by, come Sunday, down the line, down the road, coming down the pike, in a short, short-short, before you know it.

PRESERVATIONIST n. eagle freak, ecofreak, econut, guppy, greeny.

PRESIDE v. run, run the show, head, head up, sit on top of, do the honors, call the shots, call the signals, be in the driver's seat, pull the strings. See also MANAGE.

PRESIDENCY n. White House, Oval Office, top job, bully pulpit.

PRESIDENT n. Pres, Prez, prex, prexy (Usu. college), Great White Father (U.S.), POTUS (President of the U.S.). CINC, C.O., exec, key player, A-number 1, chief, bosshead, head, head honcho, head man, where the buck stops. See also EXECUTIVE.

PRESIDENT OF THE UNITED STATES n. Great White Father, Chief, CINC, POTUS, Prez, Pres.

PRESIDENT'S BLACK BOX n. football.

PRESS n. Fourth Estate, media.

PRESS v. 1. scrunch, squish. 2. squeeze, put the squeeze on, railroad through, buttonhole, sell, work on, lean on, put the bee on, come at from all sides. See PERSUADE. See also FORCE. 3. bear down on, get cracking after, shag ass, not spare the horses.

PRESS AGENT n. puffer, drum beater, PA, PR, flack, space bandit. See PUBLICIST.

PRESS BRIEFING n. Aesop's fables (White House daily briefing).

PRESSING adj. chips are down, fire in the belly, heat's on, fat's in the fire, hurry-up call, matter of life and death. See URGENT.

PRESS PLANE n. zoo, animal.

PRESSURE n. 1. crisis mode, clutch, crunch, heat, if one can't stand the heat get out of the kitchen, pressure cooker, full-court press, albatross around one's neck, choke (react to), get off my case, cut me some slack, don't sweat me (Af. Am.), get outta town, give me a break. See also FORCE, COERCION. 2. juice, drag, pull, clout, string, ropes, weight, a lot to do with, a lot to say about, inside track. 3. suction, suck.

PRESSURE v. 1. keep the lid on, bottle up, cork, cork up, hog-tie, hold down, put a half nelson on. 2. sell, high-pressure, squeeze, work over, lean on, twist one's arm, bring in the heavy artillery, put the screws on, push around, come at from all sides, make it hot for, hold one's feet to the fire, throw one's weight around, knock on doors, politick. See PERSUADE. See also FORCE.

PRESSURED adj. in crisis mode, stressed-out, get off my case, get outta town, give me a break, cut me some slack, choke, in a pressure cooker.

PRESUME v. be afraid, figure, go off half-cocked, jump the gun, it's looking too. See SPECULATE. See also BELIEVE.

PRESUMPTION n. shot, shot in the dark, stab, sneaking suspicion.

PRETEND v. jive, shuck and jive, maple stick jive, shovel the shit, shit, fudge, stonewall, whitewash, jazz, goof on, put on, put on an act, put up a front, put on a false front, fake, fake it, fake out, fake one out, wigger, poser, yo-boy (affects Af. Am. mannerisms and speech), deek, juke, fish, flicker, hang one out to dry, shake and bake, stutter step, sucker one, do a number, do a bit, lay it on thick, chuck a dummy, frame, frame up, plant, phony up, put up a bluff, four-flush, make believe, make like, let on, let on like, play possum, talk trash, pass, signify gammon, flaking, load, salt, salt a mine.

PRETENDER n. fake, faker, fraud, four-flusher, phony, playactor, wannabe, gouge. See QUACK.

PRETENSE n. routine, shtick, gag, shuck and jive, stall, put-on, stunt, bit, false front, fake, phony, crocodile tears,

soft soap, sweet talk, dumb act (without words), hoke act, okey-doke (feint). See also EXCUSE.

PRETENSION n. front, false front, fake, phony, put-on, put on the dog, put on the Ritz, big talk, tall talk, show, for show, showboat, showoff, showing out, big shot, splash, flash, Flash Gordon, go Hollywood, live it up, lay it on thick, drag, Christmas (clothes and jewelry), dog, dozer, fofarraw, foofooraw, neon ribbons.

PRETENTIOUS adj. flashy, jazzy, splashy, make a big splash, showy, frontin' (Af. Am.), artsy, artsy-crafty, artsy-fartsy, art fag, chichi, kitschy, campy, camp around, uptown, putting on the dog, putting on the Ritz, ritzy, gold-card, stuck-up, airish, crooker, pinky crooker, ham, stuffed shirt, highfalutin, splendiferous, splendacious, high-toned, toney, classy, splurgy, candy, flossy, belled, duded-up, hanging-out, gone Hollywood, play the ———, live in a glass house, hotshot, spot one like a lead dime; stick out like a sore thumb, a somebody.

PRETEXT n. cover, cover-up, cover story, fig leaf, clean up, copout, fish tale, fish story, Mother Machree, Mother McCrea, routine, song and dance, stall. See EXCUSE.

PRETTIFY v. doll up, fix up, gussy up, pretty up, spruce up.

PRETTY adj. dishy, ten, 10, dyno, boss, lulu, cher, dreamboat, schwing!, looker, mink, wukka, stone, stone fox, foxy, head rush, cute, oochie, number, eyeful, living doll, hottie, freak, fly-girl, picture. See BEAUTIFUL.

PREVAIL v. 1. get well, get fat, get there, go places, go great guns, make it, make out, ring the bell, take off, move out, strike oil, hit pay dirt, sail through, luck in, luck out, home free, come out on top of the heap. See SUCCEED. See also TRIUMPH. 2. get around, eat one's mind, crack one or something, put across, promote, sell one on, suck in, cram down one's throat, ram down one's throat. See PERSUADE.

PREVAILING adj. regular, by the numbers, SOS, same old shit, according to the book, according to Hoyle, playing it safe, in the groove, in a rut, chicken, chickenshit. See also BEST.

PREVALENT adj. trendy, faddy, fly, hip, mod, now, ongoing, state-of-the-art, the latest, last word, latest word, latest wrinkle, the leading edge, up to date, up-to-the-minute, up-to-the-moment, what's happening, with it, on the front burner, swinging, in the swim, in line. See also NEW; STYLISH.

PREVARICATE v. scam, jive, bullshit, shit, con, blow smoke up one's ass, put on, phony up, tell a white lie, jeffin', talking out of one's neck, play, trip, speak with forked tongue. See LIE.

PREVARICATION n. jive, line of jive, fib, BS, bullchitna (Esk.), horse manure, horse hocky, shit for the birds, story, tall story, fish story, baloney, smoke, line, lip gloss, hogwash, 180 out (Mil.), terminological inexactitude. See LIE.

PREVARICATOR n. con artist, con man, con merchant, conner, jive ass, jive turkey, phony, promoter, quack, spieler, bullshitter, bullshit artist, crap merchant, oil merchant.

PREVENT v. 1. cool, cool off, cool out, chill, chill off, faze, keep the lid on, block, bottle up, cork up, box in, get one in a box, hog-tie, tie up, jam up, gridlock, lock up, put a lock on, put a stopper in, bring to a screaming halt, put a half nelson on, put the chill on, kill, spike, throw cold water on, throw a wet blanket on, act like a wet blanket, put a damper on, cut off one's water, turn off one's water, put off, turn off, hold (hold the mayo), hold down, strong-arm, put the arm on, twist one's arm, put down, run down, play down, shut down on, sit on, sit down on, take care of, cross up, double-cross, kid out of, talk out of, hedge in. 2. put a crimp in, queer, stymie, snooker, put a cork in it, crab, hang up, hold up, foul up, fuck up, louse up, snafu, box in, get one in a box, freeze, shut off, stall, flummox, torpedo (a plan), throw a monkey wrench into the works, upset one's apple cart, spike one's guns, take the play away from, knock the bottom out of, blow the whistle on. See also HINDER.

PREVIEW n. sneak.

PREVIOUS adj. onetime, ex, X.

PREVIOUSLY adv. away back, back, back when, priors (criminal records), one-shot, time was.

PRICE n. price tag, list, bad news, damage, score, tab, bite, nut, nick, dues, tick, ticket, squeeze, come to, what's it come to?, to the tune of, tidy sum, bottom line, outlay, what the traffic will bear. See COST.

PRICELESS adj. out-of-sight, out-of-bounds, out of all bounds, collectible, worth its weight in gold, worth a king's ransom.

PRICE SUPPORTS n. pump priming.

PRIDE n. ego trip, face.

PRIEST n. padre, Holy Joe, sky pilot, abbey, fireproofer, bish, devil driver, fire escape, fire insurance agent, gospel pusher, sin hound, buck, turn-around collar. See CLERGYMAN.

PRIG n. bluenose, goody-goody, goody two-shoes, old maid, Miss Priss, Holy Joe. See also STRAITLACED.

PRIM adj. uptight, straight, tight-assed, short haircut, Jesus freak, bluenose, old-maidish, stuffy, choosy, comma counter, nitpicker, smitty, picky, ticky, stickler, pernickety, persnickety, dot the i's and cross the t's, draw it fine, cut it fine, goodie, goody-goody, goody two-shoes, Miss Priss, Holy Joe. See also STRAITLACED.

PRIMA DONNA n. prim.

PRIMARY adj. primo, meat and potatoes, ABC's, three R's, basics, right off the bat, first off, numero uno. See also BASIC.

PRIME adj. 10, ten, A-number one, number one, A-plus, super-duper, mega-gnarly, zero cool, endsville, crackerjack, top-of-the-line, first-class, world-class, first-chop, stellar, mean, gonest, baaaadest, Jake, ginchy, slammin', fabu, fab, hot, tough, heavy, cherry, deffest, dope, dual, fat, fierce, fresh, fully on, fully, fully to the skull, epic, mint, nitro, on the strength, raw, sick, stupid-fresh, chilly most, lampin', happenin', master (Af. Am.), cranking, righteous, state-of-the-art. See EXCELLENT.

PRIME v. ready, prep, cram, put through the grind, put through the mill. See PREPARE.

PRIMED adj. wired, bagged, revved, revved-up, rigged, sacked, packed, stacked, have all the pieces in place, set up, down, psyched-up, on ice, cut-and-dry, got it covered, loaded for bear. See PREPARED.

PRINCIPAL n. CEO, C.O., exec, key player, chief, head, head honcho, head man, queen bee, Mr. Big, high priest, bread, guru, old man. See EXECUTIVE.

PRINCIPLED adj. true blue, square, square shooter, straight, straight shooter, Christian, kosher, salt of the earth, fly right, a narb, nice guy, Joe Nice Guy, white, regular, clean as a hound's tooth, boy scout, scoutmaster.

PRINTER'S ERROR n. typo, PE, etaoin shrdlu.

PRIORITIES n. laundry list, shopping list.

PRIORITY n. crash program, crash project, on line.

PRISON n. slam, slammer, pen, can, joint, G. joint (Federal), Club Fed, walls, big cage, maxi (maximum security), gladiator school, pink clink, hen pen, mill, crossbar hotel, graybar hotel, crowbar hotel, bastille, college, greystone college, municipal farm, hospital, campus, gulag, big house, big joint, up the river, statesville, big school, boob, freezer, squeezer, band box, coop, Disneyland, iron pile, poogie, Q (San Quentin), Sing Sing, keep, sent up, dancehall (execution chamber). See JAIL.

PRISON CELL n. cage, birdcage, monkey cage, lockup, cooler, bullpen, coop, clink, calaboose, brig, bing, drum, tank, drunk tank, fish tank, alley, boxcar, bug trap, can, crib, junk tank (alcoholics, addicts), tiger cage, house, hut, daddy tank (lesbian); hard room, cement tomb, bank, hole, box, icebox, iso, izo, klondike, P & Q (peace and quiet); seclusion, solitary, stretch sol (solitary confinement), bing, black lock, black lockup, damper, digger, on the shelf, going to the Bahamas, the C.C.'s, dancehall (death house or row).

PRISON CHAPLAIN n. Bible back, buck, frocker, goody, psalmer, the church.

PRISON DEATH CHAMBER n. up back, in the back, in the backroom, dancehall, schweiner; last mile, last waltz, trip up back (walk to); baker, juice ghee (death chair switch operator).

PRISON DISCHARGED n. spring, check out, cut out, kick out, go, go home, hit the bricks, hit the pavement, hit the sidewalk, hit the street, leave one the bucket.

PRISON DISCIPLINE n. lockup, lock in, double-lock, deadlock, keep locked, jam-up, standup, sweat box, barrel, boat, spot, bury, chalk in, walking the line (harsh), get one right, pencil, take one's number, put in a beef, put in a pinch, hang a rap on, hang a shingle on, hit with a tin, sting.

PRISONER n. jailbird, con, vic, ex-con, lifer, two-time loser, yardbird, schoolmate (fellow convict), chain gang, rock crusher, PW, stir bird, rat, brig rat, goodie, hog, lag, Robuck (bully), SD (troublemaker), politician (privileged), merchant, eel, slippery eel, center man, real man, right guy, gee, geezo, gorilla, tough, punk, hipster, spear chicken, apple knocker; home boy, homie, homes, home slice, home dirt (from same city or state); pahtner, roadie, road dog, money, my gun (friend), highbinder; rah-rah, featherwood (Fem.); button (lookout), lane, kazoonie, chump (homosexual), square John; fish, fish number, fresh one, fresh meat, hoosier, butterfly, jice, new jice, cherry (new, no experience); hide-out (escapist); short, short eyes, cho-mo, Chester the Molester, diddler, pamper pirate, pamper sniffer, (child molester); beast, asocial, A-Soc (sex offender); tree jumper, rape-o (rapist), walkie-talkie; hangin' on the leg, leg hanger (fraternizes with prison staff), out of the pocket (abnormal), slick leg (innocent), accelerator (arsonist).

PRISONER OF WAR n. POW, P.O.W., Kriegie (American in German prison).

PRISON ESCAPE n. break, getaway, over the wall, lam, beat, blow, clemo, crush, crush out, gut, have the measles, on the bush, bush patrol, jackrabbit parole, map a get (plan), mope, mouse; Big Ben, beat whistle, lam whistle (siren); barspreader, blade, briars, chopper, John Sperl (tools).

PRISON, ESCAPE FROM v. break, break out, crush out, heel, go over the hill, go over the wall, beat, beat a joint, beat a stir, blow stir, chop a bar, make a break, hang it, lam, lam the joint, take it on the lam, cop a mope, take a mope, make bush, hit the hump, walk (escape punishment).

PRISON GANGS n. rounder (member), tip, Mau Mau (Af. Am.), outfit (Italian), gangster (use force); political tats, rags, colors (tattoos or insignia).

PRISON GUARD n. chaser, screw, eyes, hack, herder, hooligan, roach, roller, slavedriver, sky, yardbull horse (corrupt, smuggles in dope, etc.).

PRISON INFORMER n. noser, zuch, birdseed, loose link, cheese eater, cheese pride, cheesy rider.

PRISON SENTENCE n. time, hitch, skid-bid, stretch, do a stretch, term, up, up the river, trick, knock, rap, jolt, icebox, fall, good time, hard time, down, behind the door, do bird, dropped in the bucket, hit the pit, on ice, out to pasture, big pasture, getup, make little ones out of big ones, throw the book at one, sleep, vacation, curtains for; big bit, long bit, flat bit, flat time, bad rap, buried (long); all, do it all, all day, the clock, the book, natural life (life); stacked, bowlegged (multiple sentences); wino time, sleeping time (short), newspaper, magazine, calendar; boppo, boffo, bullet (one-year); ace, spot (year; one-spot, two-spot), deuce (two-year), deuce and a quarter (two- to twenty-five-year); three deuces jammed, three deuces running wild (three two-year, concurrent), trey (three-year); fistful, handful, five, nickel (five-year), nickel to a dime (five- to ten-year); both hands, dime, tenner, ten-spot (ten-year), do a quarter (twenty-five-year), yard (one-hundred-year), break (reduction), butt (remainder), bid (Af. Am.), bit, dipsey, lag, life on the installment plan (indeterminate sentence), B.O.T. (balance of time), lifeboat (commuted), walk (escape punishment), kiss the baby (sentence guaranteed), copper time (time off for good behavior), jump street (beginning), skid-bid (time served).

PRISON TRUSTY n. big ghee, biggie, big number, big shot, con turnkey, dep, dep's man, outside man, P.K.'s man, state man, warden's man, right ghee, number, trusty, stockholder.

PRISON UNIFORM n. state-o.

PRISON WARDEN n. king, main ghee, man, the man, skipper, belly robber, gut robber, big noise, big shot, big spud, strib, screw.

PRISSY adj. tight-assed, old-maidish, picky, ticky, stickler, pernickety, persnickety, goody-goody, goody two-shoes, Miss Priss, Holy Joe. See PRIM.

PRIVACY n. one's space. See also RETREAT.

PRIVACY, LACK v. live in a goldfish bowl, live in a glass house, in the spotlight, in the limelight.

PRIVATE adj. hush-hush, inside, eyes only, under one's hat, close to one's chest. See SECRET.

PRIVATE INVESTIGATOR n. dick, shamus, flatfoot, private eye, P.I., eye, gumshoe, door knocker, sleuth. See DETECTIVE.

PRIVATE SCHOOL n. hen pen (girls).

PRIVILEGED adj. 1. okayed, OK'd, kosher, legit. 2. inside, inside info, top secret, for your eyes only, under one's hat, on the QT. See SECRET.

PRIVY n. one-holer, two-holer, Andy Gump, out back, Chic Sale, chic sale, pisshouse, shithouse, shitter, crapper, can, john, necessary. See TOILET.

PRIZE n. the gold, gold star, the cookies, feather in one's cap, strokes, brownie button (Hum.), plum, sweetening, sweetener, what's in it for one.

PRIZEFIGHT n. bout, go, match.

PRIZEFIGHTER n. mug, pug, lug, palooka, heavy, slugger, scrapper, champ, fancy Dan, knuckle duster, dukester, lip-splitter, tiger, brawler, glass jaw, punching bag, bag puncher, powder puff (cautious), stiff (loser), canvasback, caveman, cavalier; stumblebum, bum (unemployed); cauliflower ear, cutie, cutey, dancer (coward), foul ball, ham and egger, hamburger, catcher (untalented), gladiator, sausage, tanker, loogan, round heels, plug, plug-ugly, water bag (inferior), white hope.

PROBABILITY n. prayer, shot, have a shot at, outside chance, toss-up, near as one can tell, like as not, snowball chance. See POSSIBILITY.

PROBABLY adv. dollars to doughnuts, like as not, like enough.

PROBATION n. pro.

PROBATIONER n. probe.

PROBE n. fishing expedition, legwork, third, third degree.

PROBE v. check, check out, check over, check up, looksee, double O, double oo, eye, glim, kick tires. See INVESTIGATE.

PROBLEM n. 1. shit, deep shit, box, crunch, downside, headache, damage, hitch, worriment, botheration, between a rock and a hard place, trouble in River City, scrape, tail in a gate, tit in a wringer, mess, holy mess, hot water, pickle, squeeze, white elephant (possession), can of peas, can of worms, hot potato, tsuris, your court (your problem), it's your funeral, tough nut to crack, tar baby. See PREDICAMENT. 2. cliff-hanger, grabber, sixty-four-dollar question, twister, teaser, sticker, floorer, stumper, white elephant (possession), mind boggler, hard nut to crack, tough nut to crack, tough proposition.

PROBLEMATIC adj. chancy, iffy, burly, up for grabs, leery, don't hold your breath. See DOUBTFUL.

PROBOSCIS n. smeller, schnoz, schnozzola, schnozzle, bazoo, beak, bugle, hooter, horn, honker, snoot, nozzle, banana, bill, beezer, boke, boko, conk, handle, sniffer, snuffer.

PROCEDURE n. grind, daily grind, shtick, sked, channels, back channels (secret), red tape, by the numbers, by the book, game plan, same old shit, SOS, layout, setup, gimmick, action, how one figures it, nuts and bolts.

PROCEED v. move on (to something else), get the green light, get the go-ahead, move out. See also ACT, GO.

PROCEEDING n. goings-on, go down, come off, hap, happening, happenso, cranking, come off, through channels, red tape, by the numbers, by the book. See also ACTION.

PROCEEDS n. the take, handle, in the till, split, gate. See INCOME.

PROCESS n. channels, red tape, by the numbers, by the book. See also PROCEDURE.

PROCESS, IN adj. in the hopper, in the pipeline, in the works.

PROCESSING SOLUTION n. hypo, soup.

PROCLAIM v. sound off, pop off, spout, spiel, call, blast, trumpet, drum, stump, get on a soapbox, spread it around, pass the word, lay down the law, put one's foot down, read the riot act, chew the scenery, run off at the mouth, shoot off one's mouth. See DECLARE. See also ASSERT, PROMULGATE.

PROCLIVITY n. thing, a thing for, weakness for, turned on to, bag, cup of tea, dish of tea, druthers, flash, groove, type. See INCLINATION.

PROCRASTINATE v. hold off, hang fire, cool, goldbrick, shilly-shally, sit on one's ass, blow things off, give one the runaround (repeatedly), drag one's heels, stooge around, let slide, piddle-diddle (So.). See DELAY.

PROCRASTINATOR n. goof-off, blow-off, goldbrick, putter-offer.

PROCTOLOGIST n. rear admiral, goldfinger, silver goose (proctoscope).

PROCURE v. 1. score, grab, snarf (with or without permission), cop, kipe, kype, corral, wangle, promote, buy up, buy out, make a haul, glom onto, get one's hands on, latch on to. See GET. 2. fix up, pimp, run a stable, have a string of hustlers, have a sister-in-law, steer, tout.

PROCURER n. mack, mackman, macko man, hard mack (violent), sweet mack, mackerel, dude, flesh peddler, hustler, Johnny Ponce, ponce, brother-in-law, rack salesman. See PIMP.

PROD v. goose, goose up, egg on, spark, sound, turn on, trigger.

PRODIGAL n. deep pockets, big-time spender, last of the big-time, spenders, good-time Charlie, sport, big sport.

PRODIGIOUS adj. 1. humongous, monstro, mongo, gross, honking, king-size, moby, biggy, big-ass, super-colossal, jumbo, butt-kicking, thumping. See BIG. 2. unreal, mega-gnarly, heavy, bad, evil, marvy, fab, state-of-the-art, the utmost, it's to die for, rat-fuck, out of this world. See FABULOUS.

PRODIGY n. child wonder, wonder child, wonderkind, boy wonder, natural.

PRODUCE v. 1. whip up, whomp up, cook up, dream up, throw together, fudge together, knock together, knock out, knock up, dash off, tear off. See CREATE. 2. perk, percolate, tick, put out, do the job, do a number, do the trick, break out with, bust out with (surprisingly or suddenly), pull off, come through, T.C.B. (take care of business), make it, make it big. See ACT. 3. mount (The.).

PRODUCT GROUP n. brand, line.

PRODUCTION, IN adj. in the works, in the pipeline.

PROFANE v. trash, tar, mud-sling, cuss, damn, darn, drat, flame, put the horns on, put the whammy on one, put the double whammy on one, hoodoo one, voodoo one, talk dirty.

PROFANITY n. cuss, cussing, cuss word, no-no, four-letter word, swearword, dirty word, dirty language, dirty talk, dirty name, French, pardon my French.

PROFESS v. 1. swear up and down, swear on a stack of bibles, swear till one is blue in the face, swear on one's mother, swear on one's mother's grave, cross one's heart and hope to die, say so. 2. come out of the closet, fess, fess up, get it out of one's system, out with it, open up, own up to, get it off one's chest, sing, croon, let it all hang out. 3. get on a soapbox, soapbox, spiel, spout, chew the scenery, stump, blow, blow hot air, lay it on, lay it on with a trowel, lay it on thick, lay a rap, pile it on, talk big, talk highfalutin, talk tall. See also PROCLAIM.

PROFESSION n. line, line of business, bag, biz, game, gesheft, dodge, what one is into, thing, hang, rat race, slot. See OCCUPATION.

PROFESSIONAL adj. sharp, slick, there, crack, crackerjack, on the ball, on the beam, up to speed, have know how, know one's onions, know one's stuff, enough ducks in a row. See SKILLFUL.

PROFESSIONAL n. pro, real pro, old pro, ol' professor, old hand, old war-horse, ringer, whiz, whiz bang, whiz kid, wizard, maven, shark, phenom, pundit, egghead, ivory dome, brain, star, superstar, hotshot, topper, top hand, powerhouse, Y-people, YAP (young American professional), yuppie (young urban professional), bubbie (black urban professional), yupfie (young urban professional failure), yumpie (young upwardly mobile professional), yavis (young attractive verbal intelligent successful). See also AUTHORITY.

PROFESSOR n. prof, teach, guru, brain, pundit, egghead, hard-boiled egghead (tough-minded), scrambled egghead (fuzzy-minded), nerdmeister, ivory dome, maven, Dr. Nytol (boring), quant, rocket scientist. See also SCHOLAR.

PROFFER n. feeler, hit, proposish, proposition, pass, pitch, action.

PROFFER v. 1. hit on, proposition, make a pitch, put a feeler out, pop the question. 2. gift, gift with. See GIVE.

PROFICIENCY n. know-how, the formula, savvy, goods, makings, stuff, the right stuff, what it takes, on the ball, something on the ball, up one's alley, chops, moxie, oil, meal ticket, green thumb. See SKILL.

PROFICIENT adj. sharp, savvy, hep, go-go, with it, all woke up, a lot of nifty, slick, crack, crakerjack, no slouch, on the ball, on the beam, up to speed, phenom, pro, whiz, know one's stuff, know one's business. See SKILLED.

PROFIT n. velvet, net, payoff, gravy, bottom line, in the black, split, melon, license to print money, harvest, turkey shoot (easy), skim; brocas, cactus, dust, ends, bread, lace (large profits). See INCOME.

PROFIT v. pay, pay off, pay the rent, clean up, clear, score, cash in on, make a good thing of, make a killing, make it, make it big, make hay, make a haul, turkey-shoot (easy), line one's nest, feather one's nest, do the trick, fill the bill, get mileage out of. See also EARN.

PROFITABLE adj. cash cow, going, going concern, license to print money, paid off, off the nut, sweet, turkey-shoot (easy), in the black, cost-effective.

PROFLIGACY n. high living, life in the fast lane, burn one's candle at both ends, hell-bent, gone to the dogs. See DISSIPATION.

PROFLIGATE n. speed, sport, big-time spender, last of the big-time spenders, high liver, playboy, C.S.P. (casual sex partner), swinger, operator, nighthawk, letch, dirty old man, wolf, beastmaster (dates ugly women), chaser, make-out artist, old goat, hound, poon hound, whorehound, alley cat, tomcat. See LIBERTINE.

PROFOUND adj. heavy, deep, power, talking serious shit.

PROFUSE adj. no end, galore, aplenty, dime-a-dozen, drug on the market, alive with, crawling with, thick with, thick as flies, thick as hail. See PLENTY.

PROFUSION n. scads, a ton, mucho, mucho mucho, heavy, stinking with, oodles, oodles and oodles, beaucoup, fat, spreading it around. See PLENTY.

PROGENY n. offspring, get (animal). See CHILD.

PROGNOSTICATE v. dope out, figure out, call it, read, make book, have a hunch, in the cards, see it coming, crystal-ball it. See PREDICT.

PROGNOSTICATOR n. dopester, tipster, tout, touter.

PROGRAM n. lineup. See also PLAN.

PROGRAM v. line up, get on line, pencil in, set, set up.

PROGRAMMER, COMPUTER n. hacker (illegal), gearhead, bit fiddler, bit tweeker, tweeker.

PROGRESS n. breakthrough, break, boost, buildup, go-ahead, hike, kick upstairs. See ADVANCE.

PROGRESS v. clean up one's act, get with it, turn over a new leaf, get on the ball, truck, straighten up and fly right, shape up, boost, upgrade, make first-rate, mat down, See IMPROVE. See also ADVANCE.

PROGRESS, IN adj. in the hopper, in the pipeline, in the works.

PROGRESSING adj. looking good, looking up, look up, making it, rolling, up, upping, uptick, upbeat, on the upbeat, on the upswing, on the upgrade, on the rise, on the lift, come along, perk up, pick up, skyrocket, take off, getting along, getting there.

PROGRESSIVE adj. bleeding-heart, do-gooder, left, lefty, left of center, new left, linky-dink, pink, pinko, parlor pink, radish, fellow traveler, innocent (Af. Am.). See LIBERAL.

PROHIBIT v. keep the lid on, bottle up, cool, cool off, cool out, cork, cork up, block, box in, get one in a box, hog-tie, tie up, jam up, gridlock, stymie, hang up, hold up, lock up, put a lock on, put a cork in it, put a stopper in, bring to a screaming halt, put a half nelson on, put the chill on, kill, spike, ding, zing, put the zinger in, nix, put down, pass on, throw cold water on, throw a wet blanket on, cut off one's water, turn off one's water, put off, turn off, put on hold, hold (hold everything), hold down, strong-arm, put the arm on, shut down on, sit on, sit down on, take care of, hedge in, bring to a screaming halt, flag one, freeze, shut out, shut off, close out, throw a monkey wrench into the works, spike one's guns, take one down, take the wind out of one's sails, knock the bottom out of, knock the chocks from under one, knock the props from under one, cramp one's style.

PROHIBITED adj. no-no, out of bounds, off-limits, off-base, out-of-line, crooked, heavy, shady, wildcat, close-down. See also BANNED.

PROHIBITION n. a don't, no-no, off-limits, out-of-bounds, bleeper, blankety-blank (word or expression).

PROHIBITION AGENT n. revenuer, revenooer, prohi.

PROHIBITION ERA TERMS speak, speakeasy; bootleg, bootlegger, moonshine, moonshiner, rum runner; bathtub gin, hooch, home brew; wet, dry; Fed, feds (enforcement officer).

PROHIBITIONIST n. dry, Volstead actor, Volstead baby, WCTU, blue nose.

PROJECT n. baby, bag, bag one's into, thing, thing one's into, biggie (major), deal, pet project, proposition, setup.

PROJECT v. pop-out, bug out, googly. See also PREDICT.

PROLETARIAT n. the mob, riffraff, cattle, ragtag, ragtag and bobtail, the great unwashed.

PROLONG v. stretch, stretch out, get on with it, let it ride, hold up, pad, stall, vamp, drag one's feet, drag out, drag on, spin out. See DELAY.

PROLONGED adj. spun-out, strung-out, dragged-out, dragged-on, dragged on and on, run out, held off, boosted, padded, in for the long haul.

PROMENADE v. ankle, ank, toddle, sashay, cruise, traipse, trapse, traipse around, ooze, mooch, boogie, air out, beat the rocks, diddy-bop, truck, percolate. See WALK.

PROMINENT adj. 1. flashy, candy, candy kid, duded-up, hanging out. 2. live in a glass house, spot one like a lead dime, stick out like a sore thumb. 3. world-class, big-league, major-league, high-cotton, high-profile, throw a lot of weight, the juice, the force, A-list, underlined. 4. in the limelight, biggie, big name, big noise, big shot, big-timer, big-league, major-league, face card, knocker, hot-dog, VIP, a somebody. See IMPORTANT.

PROMISCUOUS adj. fast, swinging, swinger, on the make, slag, slagheap, bone addict, chippy around, run around, floss around, sleep around, C.S.P. (casual sex partner), musical beds, two-time, stretch the rubber, put out, put the horns on, pushover, round-heels, helium heels, stanky tuna, easy lay, easy make, cheap, loose, loose woman, brownie, hobbler, punchboard, alley cat, scrump queen, road whore, sleaze bucket, sleazebag, hosebag, hose monster, dishy, hank, skank, for free, bum, tramp, slut, dog, frail, blimp, broad, mink, bombshell, hootie-mama, chippie, chaser, trick, naga, fruit, office bike, town bike, town pump, cuddle bunny, charity girl, piece of trade, pigmeat (old), sex job, ginch, no better than she should be.

PROMISE v. 1. string, string one along, jerk one along, jerk one around. 2. swear up and down, swear on a stack of bibles, swear till one is blue in the face, cross one's heart and hope to die, say so.

PROMISED adj. nailed down, on ice, cinched, in the bag.

PROMISED n. donah, donar, steady, going steady, pinned, bird, future, intended.

PROMISSORY NOTE n. IOU, marker, paper, tab, dog.

PROMOTE v. 1. hype, plug, push, hard-sell, make a pitch for, beat the drum for, build up, throw the spotlight on, press agent, ballyhoo, billboard, boost, get behind, put on the map. See ADVERTISE. 2. kick upstairs, win one's wings, up, deadhead (bypass a senior), up one's pay, boost one's pay. See also ADVANCE.

PROMOTER n. 1. player, operator, con, con man, tout, touter. 2. PR man, flack, plugger, puffer, huckster, ballyhoo man, space bandit, space peddler, booster. See PUBLICIST.

PROMOTION n. 1. boost, buildup, bump, jump, jump up, move up, step up, break, breakthrough, go-ahead, hike, Mexican raise (promote without raise in pay), kick upstairs. 2. buildup, PR, hype, pitch, promo, hard sell, ballyhoo, hoopla, plug, puff, puffery, pizzazz, squib, screamer, spread, blurb, dynamiting, blasting, bulldogging, Mad Avenue, pluggery; low profile (avoid). See also PUBLICITY.

PROMPT adj. on the ball, on the button, on the dot, on the nose.

PROMPTLY adv. pronto, on the double, move your ass, like now, off the pop, in nothing flat, in jig time, like a shot, pretty damned quick, PDQ. See IMMEDIATELY.

PROMULGATE v. spread it around, pass the word, drum, call, trumpet, call the play, call the signals, call the tune. See also PROCLAIM; DECLARE.

PRONE adj. bag, thing, head-set, mind-set, mind-rip, flash, groove, tilt, type, where one is at, cup of tea, druthers, turned on to, weakness for.

PRONOUNCE v. verbalize, mouth, sound off, blast, spread it around, drum, trumpet, call. See also PROCLAIM, DECLARE, SPEAK.

PROOF n. info, dope, goods, smoking gun (crucial), clincher, cincher, grabber, paper trail, clue, cue, skinny, scoop, score, chapter and verse, the know, picture, hold water, straightstuff, from the horse's mouth, lowdown, like it is, the emess, the numbers, gospel, nitty-gritty.

PROPAGANDA n. agitprop, infomercial, advertorial, hogwash, disinformation, Prop Art.

PROPELLER n. eggbeater, prop, windmill, fan, blower, butter paddle, club, pants stopper.

PROPENSITY n. thing, turned on to, flash, weakness for, where one is at, tilt, eyes for, itch, sweet tooth, yen. See INCLINATION.

PROPER adj. 1. chickenshit, according to Hoyle, according to the book, by the book, by the numbers, in line, kosher. See STRAITLACED. 2. solid, stone, a narb, narbo, straight, straight-arrow, straightedge, square, squaresville, L7, cubular, granola head, spiffy, stuffy. 3. on the ball, on target, on the right track, righteous, right you are, right as rain, reet, just what the doctor ordered, on the button, on the nose, that's the idea, that's the ticket. See also CORRECT, SUITABLE.

PROPERTY n. prop, props.

PROPHESY v. crystal-ball it, psych it out, call it, call the turn, call the shots, read, make book, have a hunch, see it coming. See PREDICT.

PROPHYLACTIC n. pro, prophy, pro pack, rubber, safety, nightcap, bag, scumbag, Trojan, armor, skin, fish skin, French letter, Frenchy, purse. See CONTRACEPTIVE.

PROPOSAL n. feeler, pitch, proposition, proposish, pass, game plan, setup, layout, angle, big idea (unwelcome), picture, scenario, brainchild. See PLAN.

PROPOSE v. hit on, proposition, come up with, I'm talking ———, make a pitch, pop the question, speak one's piece, kibitz, put a flea in one's ear, spitball, try it on for size.

PROPRIETOR n. front office, meal ticket, gyppo, jippo (piecework), landprop, saw, slumlord.

PROSAIC adj. everyday, garden variety, vanilla, white-bread, nothing, nowhere, clean, square, L7, blah, draddy, draggy, ho-hum, dull as dishwater, yawn, big yawn, dead, diddly-bop, dullsville, gummy, flat, flat as a pancake, flat tire, pablum, zero, the least, corny, bromidic, old hat, folksy, homey, haimish, dime-a-dozen, gasser, noplaceville, square John, Clyde, meat-and-potatoes man.

PROSECUTE v. drag into court, haul into court, see one in court, have up, have the law on, law, take the law on, put one away, pull up, take out after, turn on the heat, burn one's ass.

PROSECUTION n. heat.

PROSECUTOR n. cuter, D.A., beak, beagle, legal eagle. See also ATTORNEY.

PROSELYTIZATION n. agitprop, infomercial, advertorial, hogwash.

PROSPECT n. irons in the fire, by and by, from now on in, from here in, from here out, just around the corner, in the cards, in the lap of the gods, mark, believer, sucker, white hope. See also CUSTOMER, HOPE, FUTURE.

PROSPECTOR n. desert rat, hard rocker, sourdough.

PROSPER v. get fat, get there, go places, go to town, make it, make a killing, strike it rich, hit it big, hit the jackpot, score, kick it live (Af. Am., do it well), bring home the bacon, arrive, do a land-office business, live off the fat of the land. See SUCCEED.

PROSPERITY n. good times, boom, gravy train, land-office business, high on the hog, on top of the heap, bed of roses, clover, Easy Street, lap of luxury, the life of Riley, velvet.

PROSPEROUS adj. the haves, have it made, on top of the heap, high on the hog, large, up in the bucks, in the chips, money to burn, lousy rich, bifftad, well-heeled, well-fixed, livin' large, clockin', sitting pretty, fat city, fat cat, upper-class, main-line, uptown, piss on ice. See WEALTHY.

PROSTATE CANCER n. PSA (test).

PROSTITUTE n. hooker, call girl, hustler, ho, working broad, working chick, working girl, nok, model, pro, floozie, skeezer, chippy, prosty, streetwalker, tart, bag, baggage, B-girl, bimbo, bimbette (young, sexy), slag, slagheap, broad, chicken, chicken rancher, pavement princess, lot lizard (truckstop parking lot), bangster, bat, beast, bitch, blister, blower, bawd, bum, cat, alley cat, moll, cement mixer, coffee grinder, chile whore, chacha, fallen woman, dog, fish, gull, forty-four, gooh, piccolo player, piece of trade, biscuit, strawberry (receives dope as payment), blouser, flesh peddler, ass peddler, snatch peddler, coozy, merchandise, zook (U.), Hershey bar (WWII), moose (Korean War), dress for sale, flatbacker, quiff, puta, squaw, schatzi, schanzi, wet deck, white slave, creeper, panel worker (thief), chick on the block, orphan (without a pimp), free-lancer, hole, hostess, lady, shady lady, stick, vegetarian (won't perform fellatio); pig, pig meat, bunter, cruiser, fruitwoman, trull, biff (homely), dow, yes-girl, mixer, sitter, taxi drinker (bars), roller (robs drunks), jade, easy woman, easy lay, woman of easy virtue, frail sister, sidewalk socialite, ginch, sex worker, nympho.

PROSTITUTE, MALE n. midnight cowboy, cocksman, pink pants, pratt boy, toy boy, aspro, snatch peddler, stern wheeler, Mr. Brown, chicken.

PROSTITUTE'S CUSTOMER n. John, trick.

PROSTITUTION n. in the life, the life, world's oldest profession, broad racket, the bottle, hustle, turning a trick, hitting the turf, working the street, stepping out, going out for a buck, on the turf, white slavery.

PROTECT v. cover, cover up, cover one's ass, cover all bases, go to bat for, go to the mat for, ride shotgun for, shotgun, stonewall, hedge, hedge one's bet, gardening, homrim it, lay off.

PROTECTION n. umbrella, insurance, fix, hat, props (weapons or bodyguards), bubble (especially president).

PROTECTION MONEY n. payoff, the envelope, payola, drugola, gayola, kickback, ice, take, on the take, under the table, protection, the fix, juice, graft, gravy, perk, perks, fringe benefit, contribution, goodies, cream, hush money, grease, schmear, smear, salve, palm oil, soap, shake, cough syrup, sugar, sweetener, hat, a chicken, mordida, boodle, pound, chop, freight, slush, slush fund, nut, contract, cush, boksheesh, touch, street money, walking-around money, chop, fall dough, freight.

PROTÉGÉ n. candy kid, fair-haired boy.

PROTEST n. 1. stink, big stink, beef, where's the beef?, bitch, blow at, holler, howl, kick, squawk, flak, knock, nix, not (used at end of a positive sentence), gripe, grouse, bellyache, blackball. See GRIEVANCE. 2. demo, march, teach-in, sit-in.

PROTEST v. 1. make a stink, bitch, beef, pop off, sound off, squawk, blast, holler, howl. See COMPLAIN. 2. be agin, go agin, buck, back-talk, blackball, thumbs down, put up a fight. See OPPOSE.

PROTESTANT n. WASP, Wasp, left foot.

PROTESTER n. angries, marcher, beatnik, yippie, freak, offbeat, Bohemian, weirdo, oddball. See DISSENTER.

PROTOCOL n. P's and Q's, p's and q's.

PROTRACT v. stretch, stretch out, let it ride, hold up, hold off, blow things off, put off, put something on hold, cool, cool it, put some rubber in it, pad, stall, vamp, drag out, drag on, spin out, piddle-diddle (So.), tish. See DELAY. See also DEFER, LENGTHEN.

PROTRACTED adj. spun-out, strung-out, dragged-out, in for the long haul, dragged-on, dragged on and on, run-out, held-off, boosted, padded.

PROTRUDE v. pop out, bug out, googly.

PROUD adj. cool, cocky, biggety, dicty, sidity, sniffy, puffed-up, chesty, high-and-mighty, high-toned, high-nosed, standing tall, that's my boy (girl, etc.). See ARROGANT.

PROVE v. add up, check out, check up, check up on, double-check, crack on one or something, debunk (prove false), pan out, stand up, hold one up. See also TEST, CONFIRM.

PROVEN adj. sure, sure as shit, sure enough, sure as fate, sure as shooting, sure as God made little green apples, sure as hell, sure as the devil, sure as I live and breathe, dead sure, dead to rights, sure as death, sure as death and taxes, sure as can be, sure thing, surest thing you know, surefire, for sure, fer sher, that's for sure, for damn sure, for danged sure, for a fact, for certain, cold, have down cold, pat, down pat, have down pat, nailed down, have a lock on, lock-and-win situation, all locked up, no buts about it, no ifs ands or buts, on ice, open-and-shut, set, odds-on, bet on, bet one's bottom dollar on, checked and double-checked, lead-pipe cinch, cinched, clinched, come hell or high water, in the bag, racked, that's death and no mistake, know damn well, know darn well, is the Pope Catholic?, does a bear shit in the woods?, do they grow corn in Iowa?

PROVERB n. daffodil.

PROVIDE v. feather one's nest, line one's nest (at the expense of others), heel (money), stake, grubstake, fix up, fix up with. See GIVE.

PROVIDENCE, RHODE ISLAND Ivy Town.

PROVIDENT adj. tight, tightwad, Scotch, nickel-nurser, penny-pincher, last of the big spenders. See THRIFTY. See also CAUTIOUS.

PROVIDER n. fairy godmother, lady bountiful, angel, Santa Claus, greenback, sugar daddy, giver, heavy hitter. 2. dealer, middleman, tycoon, cockroach (small), nickel-and-dime operator, tradester, robber baron, big butter-and-egg man.

PROVISION n. joker, kicker, catch, Catch-22, string, string to it, a string attached to it, small print, fine print, fine print at the bottom, small fine print, small fine print at the bottom.

PROVISIONALLY adv. with a catch to it, with a grain of salt, with a joker to it, with a kicker to it, with a string attached, with a string to it.

PROVISO n. string, string to it, a string attached to it, catch, Catch-22, joker, kicker, small print, fine print, fine print at the bottom, small fine print, small fine print at the bottom.

PROVOCATION n. defi, defy, brickbat, put-down, grabber. See also INSULT.

PROVOKE v. get in one's face, go on make my day, make waves, burn, trigger, ride, fire up, key up, put up to, work up, work up into a lather, flip one the finger, flip one the bone, give one the bone, give one the finger, give one five fingers, give one a backhanded compliment, give one a left-handed compliment, cap, dump on, hit one where he lives, get under one's skin, get in one's space, rile, nag, thumb one's nose at, hurl brickbats at. See ANNOY.

PROVOKED adj. hacked, hacked-off, brassed-off, cheesed-off, pissed-off, aggro, riled, rubbed the wrong way, at the end of one's rope, hard put to it, driven up the wall, rousted, steamed. See ANNOYED.

PROWESS n. balls, guts, heart, nerve, stomach, stuff, the right stuff, grit, true grit, spunk, backbone, moxie, starch, clock, corazón, Dutch courage (intoxicated), what it takes. See COURAGE. See also SKILL.

PROWL v. gumshoe, pussyfoot, snake, mooch around, mooch in, mooch out.

PROWL CAR n. fuzzmobile, black-and-white, skunk wagon, bear car, bearmobile, buzz, buzzer, screaming gasser, whistler, catch car; brown bag, plain wrap (unmarked), cherries (flashing lights).

PROXIMATE adj. warm, hot, burning, around, along toward, within a stone's throw, in spitting distance, pretty near. See NEAR.

PROXY n. sub, backup, bench warmer, dog chaser, fill-in, pinch hitter, pinch runner, ringer, stand-in, front, beard.

PRUDE n. a stick, stick-in-the-mud, blue-nose, a narb, narbo, cube, square, straight, wet blanket, moldy fig, Christer, nice Nellie, prune, goody-goody, goody two-shoes, old maid, crabapple Annie. See also PRIM.

PRUDENT adj. leery, play it cool, play safe, keep on one's toes, think twice, hedge one's bets, not go out on a limb. See CAUTIOUS.

PRUDISH adj. uptight, square, tight-assed, stuffy, straight, short haircut, Jesus freak, bluenose. See also PRIM.

PRUNE v. knock off, chop, cut, gut.

PRUNES n. strawberries, army strawberries, nigger-heads (Derog.).

PRURIENT adj. dirty, blue, X-rated, raunchy, raw, hard-core, soft-core, off-color, stag, low-down and dirty, flaming (Obsc., computer conversations), jack-off material, smutty. See OBSCENE.

PRY v. nose around for, nose out, bug, tap, wiretap, be all ears, ears into, really get into, listen in, tune in on, Erie, on the Erie, slurp.

PRYING adj. nosy, snoopy, in one's crack.

PSALM n. shout.

PSEUDO adj. not kosher, not what it's cracked up to be, bogue, bogus, phony, queer, falsie, fake, ersatz, plastic, pirate goods, pirate labels. See FALSE.

PSEUDONYM n. nickname, AKA, A.K.A., handle, summer name.

PSYCHIATRIST n. shrink, headshrinker, shrinker, couch doctor, dome-doctor, guy with the net, guy in the white coat, head peeper, guru, wig picker, squirrel, nut doctor, bug doctor (prison).

PSYCHOANALYSIS n. the couch.

PSYCHOANALYST n. shrink, headshrinker, shrinker, couch doctor, nut doctor, dome-doctor, guy with the net, guy in the white coat, guru, squirrel.

PSYCHOLOGICAL BLOCK n. hang-up, hung, hung up, uptight.

PSYCHOLOGICAL OPERATIONS n. psy ops.

PSYCHOLOGICAL PROBLEM n. hang-up, thing about, block.

PSYCHOLOGICAL TEST n. bug test, I.Q.

PSYCHOLOGICAL WARFARE n. psyop (action), psywar, the Bell Telephone Hour.

PSYCHOLOGIST n. shrink, head shrinker, shrinker, couch doctor, guy with the net, guy in the white coat, dome-doctor, nut doctor, bug doctor (prison), guru, wig picker, squirrel.

PSYCHOLOGY n. psych, where one is at, where one's head is at.

PSYCHOPATH n. psycho, section 8, wrong number, schizo, schizoid, hospital H.

PSYCHOPATHIC WARD n. flight deck, psycho ward.

PSYCHOTHERAPIST n. shrink, head shrinker, shrinker, couch doctor, nut doctor, guy with the net, guy in the white coat, dome doctor, bug doctor (prison), guru, squirrel.

PSYCHOTIC adj. psycho, sick, sick sick, sickie, schizzed out, schizo, schizy, flippo, over the edge, nutsy fagin, nuts.

PUB n. joint, after-hours joint, juice joint, beer joint, taproom, bucket shop, suds shop, gashouse, alehouse, beer house, mug house, ginmill. See BAR.

PUBIC HAIR n. beaver, beard, muff, mink, bush, short hairs, brush, beehive, moss, bird's nest, patch, arbor, forest, fleece, fur, rug, shaving brush, cotton (Fem.), grass, hat, pubes, merkin (wig).

PUBLIC n. bodies, cats, dudes, heads, hoi polloi, the man in the street, the guy next door, John Doe, Jane Doe, John Q., John Q. Public, Billy Sixpack, Joe Lunchbucket, Joe Dookes, the average Joe, Mr. and Mrs. America, Tom Dick and Harry, Brown Jones and Robinson, booboisic, the little guy, the mob, riffraff, cattle, ragtag, ragtag and bobtail, the great unwashed.

PUBLIC ADDRESS SYSTEM n. P.A., bullhorn, squack box, bitch box, growler, hog caller.

PUBLIC DEFENDER n. dump truck (prison term).

PUBLIC FUNDS n. pork barrel, space barrel (NASA), John Q's pocket, deep pockets, public crib, public trough, public till, public purse.

PUBLIC IMAGE n. front, pose, act, rep.

PUBLICIST n. PR man, spin meister, spin doctor, flack, plugger, puffer, huckster, ballyhooer, booster, DINFO (Pentagon), space bandit, booster, blurbist, pluggery (firm), gas man. See also ADVERTISING.

PUBLICITY n. puff, puffery, hype, plug, PR, P.R., pub, photops (photo opportunity), promo, spin, blurb, build up, hoopla, flack, flackery, ballyhoo, big noise, ink, get ink, handout (release), noise about, pitch, scratch, spread, fallout (adverse), low profile (avoid), mention, shot. See also ADVERTISING.

PUBLICITY SEEKER n. hot dogger, publicity hound, showoff.

PUBLICIZE v. promote, hype, plug, push, pitch, splash, spot, boost, build up, puff, ballyhoo, press agent, throw the spotlight on, put on the map, make a pitch for, drum, beat the drum for, tub-thump, thump the tub for, hard-sell, soft-sell, bill, billboard. See ADVERTISING.

PUBLICLY adv. openly, in front of God and everybody, go public, in the limelight, in the spotlight.

PUBLIC OFFICIAL n. paper shuffler, buck passer, apparatchik (minor).

PUBLIC RELATIONS n. puffery, hype, spin, plug, PR, P.R., pub, promo, flack, flackery, ballyhoo, big noise, low profile (avoid). See PUBLICITY.

PUBLIC SPEAKER n. soapboxer, soapbox orator, spieler, spouter, stumper, jawsmith, tub thumper, chalk talker.

PUBLIC TREASURY n. pork barrel, space barrel (NASA), John Q's pocket, deep pockets, public crib, public trough, public till, public purse.

PUBLISH v. put to bed, go to bed, roll the presses, go public, get the word around, spread it around, pass the word, drum, call, trumpet.

PUBLISHER n. pub, pubbery.

PUBLISHING TERMS AA (author's alteration), EA (editor's alteration), PE (printer's error).

PUDDING n. g'dong, gedunk, glop, goop, pud.

PUDDLE n. loblolly.

PUDENDUM n. pussy, cunt, snatch, twat, vige, beaver, crack, hole, quim, snapper, box, clam, coochie (Af. Am.), nookie, love muscle, oven, piece, cunny, honey pot, muff, the Y. See VAGINA. See also GENITALIA, MALE.

PUDGY n. roly-poly, tubby, tubster, heavy cream, hefty, love handles (hips and thighs), butterball, Bertha, zaftig. See FAT.

PUERILE adj. kid-stuff.

PUERTO RICAN n. Rican; Nuyorican, spic, spick, spig, spiggoty, spic and span, chico, greaseball, Pedro, spill (racially mixed), hatchet thrower, hick, parakeet (all Derog.).

PUGILIST n. mug, pug, palooka, slugger, fancy Dan, punching bag, glass jaw, bag puncher, cauliflower ear, loogan, plug, plug-ugly, white hope. See PRIZEFIGHTER.

PUGNACIOUS adj. scrappy, snorky, salty, spiky, cantankerous, dukes up, out for a rep, have a bone to pick, have a chip on one's shoulder. See BELLIGERENT.

PULITZER PRIZE n. Pullet Surprise, Putziler Prize (for mediocrity).

PULL v. pull out, yank, yerk, lug, schlep, shlep, shlep along, truck.

PULLMAN PORTER n. George, bedbug.

PULSATE v. go pitapat, tick.

PULSE n. pitapation.

PUNCH n. belt, shot, sock, slug, bash, zap, zinger, clip, lollop, plunk, one-two, one-two punch, Sunday punch. See HIT.

PUNCH v. punch out, punch one out, throw a punch, bash, bonk, conk, belt, sock, slug, smack, poke, clip, zap, paste, plant one. See HIT.

PUNCTILIOUS adj. on the button, on the numbers, on the money, on target, on the nose, on the noggin, right on, dead on, bull's-eye, a good eye, chickenshit, by the book, persnickety. See PARTICULAR.

PUNCTUAL adj. on the dot, on the button, on the nose, on the ball.

PUNCTURE v. poke full of holes, shoot full of holes, blow sky-high, knock the bottom out of, knock the chocks from under, knock the props from under.

PUNDIT n. prof, teach, guru, brain, egghead, hard-boiled egghead (tough-minded), scrambled egghead (fuzzy-minded), Dr. Nytol (boring), ivory dome, gnurd, gnome, grind, auger, tool, power tool, throat, cutthroat, wonk, bookworm, cereb, pencil geek, ink squirter, spider, squid, trained seal, grub, weenie, maven.

PUNGENT adj. stinko, stinking, stinky, whiffy, nosy, strong, loud (strong), salty, high, pfui, phooey, peeyooey.

PUNISH v. can, carry the can, tie the can on one, bust, knock, drop the boom, lower the boom, rap, rap one's knuckles, slap on the wrist, put the slug on one, sock it to one, stick it to one, go upside one's haid (Af. Am.), cloud up and rain on one, let one have it, let fly, fix, fix one's clock, skin, skin alive, scorch, blister, roast, fry, clobber, tear into, draw the line, lambaste, mop up the floor with, wipe up the floor with, jack up, hoist, rag, dig at, jaw, jawbone, kick ass and take names, have someone's ass, chew, chew ass, fire on, rip on, chew out, eat out, eat out one's ass, ball out, bawl out, ream, ream out, ream ass, read one out, cuss out, go after, rip, zap, cap on, lay into, lay out, rank out, straighten out, serve one out, pay, pay out, sound off, lean on, sit on, jump on, jump all over, jump down one's throat, jump on one's shit, climb, climb all over, climb one's frame, light into, land on, rake, rake up one side and down the other, rake over the coals, haul over the coals, trim, have one on the carpet, have one on the mat, call on the carpet, put one on the carpet, dance the carpet, call to task, smack down, slap down, call down, dress down, put down, come down on, come down on hard, take down, take down a peg, downmouth, ding, gig, growl, glue, read the riot act, throw the book at one, speak to, talk to, tell a thing or two, tell off, tell where to get off, tee off on one, attend to, give it to, give what for, give a bawling out, give a going over, give a bit of one's mind, give a piece of one's mind, give one the business, give one both barrels, give one the deuce, give one the devil, give one the dickens, give one hell, give one hail Columbia, give one his lumps, give one his comeuppance, settle, settle one's hash, settle the score, campus, nail to the wall, nail to the cross.

PUNISHMENT n. bawling out, chewing out, cussing out, speaking to, talking to, going over, catch, catch it, catch hell, hell to pay, pay through the nose, get yours, get hers, get his, get what is coming to one, get it in the neck, what one was asking for, piece of one's mind, bit of one's mind, rap on the knuckles, slap on the wrist, calling-down, dressing, dressing-down, set-down, lumps, take one's lumps, take one's medicine, what for, for it, jacking up, comeuppance, walk (escape punishment).

PUNSTER n. cutup, gagman, gagster, jokesmith, madcap, wisecracker. See also JOKER.

PUNY adj. 1. shrimp, squid, wee, peewee, peanut, runt, short, small fry, small-time, dinky, measly, tomtit, shit, chickenshit, chippie, button, wart, mite, piddling, two-bit, two-by-four, pint-sized, half-pint. See SMALL. 2. wimpy, wimp, empty suit, neb, nebbish, nothing, zero, zilch, wishy-washy, don't have the horses.

PUPIL n. undergrad, grad, doc, prep, preppie, preppy, brain, skull, tool, mc squared, grind (bookworm), greasy grind, dig, bookbuster, wonk, corndog, bone, boner. See STUDENT.

PUPPET n. 1. stooge, tool, yuld, yold, yo-yo, cat's paw, apple, patsy, pushover, vic, mom, chump, soft touch, fall guy, babe in the woods, boob, schlemiel, jack, duck, goofus, gopher, jay, lobster, prize sap. 2. muppet, Charlie McCarthy.

PURCHASE v. make a buy, blow oneself to, take up, buy out, buy off, buy into, cop.

PURCHASER n. pigeon, float, head, mark, believer, grape (waiting to be squeezed), walk-in, live one.

PURE adj. all wool and a yard wide, Christian, kosher, twenty-four-carat, wide-eyed, wet behind the ears, cherry, babe in the woods, Bambi, blue-eyed, baby blue eyes, clean, kid, lily-white, look as if butter wouldn't melt in one's mouth. See also UNSOPHISTICATED, UNADULTERATED, VIRTUOUS.

PURGATIVE n. cc pills.

PURGE v. liquidate, do away with, executive fallout (Bus.), unload the dead wood, wipe off the map, wipe out, clean out, shake out. See KILL.

PURGED adj. liquidated, unfrocked (any profession), drummed-out, turned-off.

PURITAN n. a narb, narbo, cube, square, straight, buzz killer, short haircut, goody-goody, goody two-shoes, bluenose, Christer, nice Nellie, Crabapple Annie, prune. See STRAITLACED.

PURPLE HEART MEDAL n. Bolo Badge (Persian Gulf War), purple hurt, heart.

PURPORT n. drift, point, heart, meat, nub, score, stuff, bottom line, name of the game, nitty-gritty, nuts and bolts, the way of it, nature of the beast, punch line, kicker (point of a story, joke, etc.).

PURPOSE n. where one's heading, drift, the big idea, idea, the what-for, the whole idea, the why and wherefore, the why-for.

PURPOSEFUL adj. dead set on, bent on, hell bent on, mean business, be out for blood, playing hard ball. See DETERMINED.

PURSE n. grouch bag, leather, lizard, pocket, bag, shoulder bag, tote, poke, frame, hide, clutch.

PURSE-SNATCH v. glom a leather, make a poke, bushwhack, buzz, moll-buzz.

PURSE SNATCHER n. bushwhacker, buzzer, leather glommer, moll buzzer.

PURSUE v. 1. tail, trail, play catch-up, run down, run to ground, go after, take out after, tag after. See FOLLOW. 2. bird-dog (scout), scout, beat the bushes, search high heaven, leave no stone unturned, track down. See SEARCH. 3. dog, dog one's case, bug, on one's back, on one's case, put the squeeze on, put one through the wringer, put the screws on, put the heat on, turn on the heat, burn one's ass, drag into court, haul into court, have the law on, have up, law, put one away, pull up, drive one up the wall, take out after, set one's cap for. 4. go in for, go out for, have a go at, get it on with. 5. date, chase, rush, go for, go after, go steady, play up to, hit on, crack on, put the move on, put the rush on, scam on, go for the cheese, make eyes at. See COURT.

PURSUIT n. biz, beeswax, game, gesheft, line, go, do, dodge, bag, what one is into, thing, hang, racket, swindle, grift. See OCCUPATION.

PUSH n. gumption, spunk, drive, guts, get-up-and-go.

PUSH v. 1. lean on, push around, bear down, pressure, high-pressure, strong-arm, squeeze, put the screws on, put the arm on, railroad through, steamroll, muscle in, muscle out, throw one's weight around, move in on, pour it on, go to town on. See FORCE. 2. fire up, key up, put up to, turn on, egg one on, goose, sell one on, jolly, kid along, lay it on. See URGE.

PUSILLANIMOUS adj. wimpy, nerdy, gutless, candy-ass, pucker-assed, paper tiger, jellyfish, turkey, weak sister, big baby, yellow-bellied. See COWARDLY.

PUSTULE n. zit, hickey, goob, goober, goophead, pip, beauty spot, bloom, doohickey, dohinky.

PUT v. plank, plank down, plunk, plunk down, park, peg, nail, plop.

PUTRID adj. strong, high.

PUTTER v. mess around; potchky, potchky around (Yid.). See DABBLE.

PUZZLE v. bamboozle, get, get to, beat, lick, bug, psych out, gross out, take one's mind, fuck with one's head, mess with one's head, mess with one's mind, make a mess of, fuddle, stump, buffalo, ball up, profundicate, synomaniac (one who complicates), muddy the waters, stir the waters, rattle, rattle one's cage, throw, throw a monkey wrench into the works, play hob with, put one on a crosstown bus, make waves, open up a can of worms, make hash out of, snow, floor, put off, flummox.

PUZZLED adj. all balled up, balled-up, spaced out, hung, hung-up, mixed-up, blaaed-up, gummixed-up, gummoxed-up, unglued, unzipped, unscrewed, come unglued, come unzipped, come apart, come apart at the seams, discombobulated, discombooberated, mind is blown, shook, shook-up, fouled-up, fucked-up, loused-up, messed-up, mucked-up, mussed-up, screwed-up, bugged-up, bollixed, bollixed-up, messed-up attic, floored, flipped out, farmisht, fertummeled, farshimmelt, woozy, thrown, dopey, lost one's cool, fussed, rattled, rattlebrained, foggy, wandering around in a fog, in a fog, in the twilight zone, in a botheration, like a chicken with its head cut off, out to lunch, psyched out, kerflumixed, licked, stuck, stumped, double Dutch, boogily-woogily, drowning, hugger-mugger, bamboozled, buffaloed, bowled over, bowled down, struck all of a heap, thrown off one's beam ends. See also DISTURBED.

PUZZLER n. sticker, stumper, teaser, twister, floorer, sixty-four-dollar question, hard nut to crack, tough nut to crack, tough proposition.

PYROMANIAC n. firebug, torch. See ARSONIST.

Q

Q n. Quebec, Queen.

QUAALUDE n. lude, quad, quas, quacks, sopor, pillows, vitamin Q, Canadian quail.

QUACK n. fake, faker, fraud, four-flusher, phony, pseud, pseudo, put-on, actor, play-actor, bogue, diddler, S.L.O.B. (silver-lipped operator of bullshit), con man, con artist, clip artist, sharpie, flimflammer, flimflam man, bunco, bunco artist, whip, bum, shark, sharp, jackleg, slicker, boogerboo, shiever, hoser.

QUADRANGLE n. quad.

QUADRIPLEGIC n. quad, curly fingers, gimp, crip, blinker, basket case.

QUAINT adj. offbeat, off the beaten track, funky, weird, weirdo, weirdie, strange one, oddball, goofball, special, cozy, funny, funny-looking, rare bird.

QUAKE v. jitter, shake, shiver.

QUAKING n. shakes, shivers, cold shivers, teeth chattering, heebie-jeebies.

QUALIFICATION n. goods, makings, stuff, what it takes. See SKILL.

QUALIFIED adj. up to speed, up to the mark, up to snuff, up to code, pro, vet, warhorse, paid one's dues, won one's spurs, one of the old school, old-timer, been through the mill, have one's ticket punched, have know-how, know one's onions, know one's stuff, know one's business, know one's oats, know one's beans, know one's bananas, know one's fruit, know one's groceries, know one's oil, know one's goods, all-around, wasn't born yesterday, didn't come into town on a load of wood, from way back. See also CAPABLE, SKILLFUL.

QUALIFY v. make it, make the cut, make the grade, score, cut it, cut the mustard, come up to snuff, check out, earn one's wings, hack it, pass, pass muster, pass in the dark, fill the bill, get by. See also SUFFICE.

QUALITY n. nature of the beast, the way of it, name of that tune, what you see is what you get. See also NATURE.

QUALITY, HIGH adj. ace-high, prime, killer, 10, ten, A-number one, uptown, righteous, gnarly, mega-gnarly, zero cool, winner, choice state-of-the-art, top-of-the-line, first-class, happenin', greatest, up to snuff, this is some kinda ———, the best. See EXCELLENT.

QUALITY, POOR adj. cheesy, drek (Yid.), piece of shit, rinky-dinky ratty-tatty, shitbox, shitbag, shitburger, ain't worth diddly-shit, ain't worth a plugged nickel, el cheapo, cotton-pickin', piss-assed, garbage, junk, lousy, not worth a hill of beans, lemon, dud, white elephant, jeasley, bogus, punk, turkey, abortion, bum, cracker-box (house), tinhorn, Mickey Mouse, humpty-dumpty, tacky, ticky-tacky, cheapjack, held together by spit, held together by chewing gum, house of cards. See CHEAP.

QUANDARY n. clutch, hang-up, bind, spot, box, crisis mode, Catch-22, double trouble, in a box, in a pickle, burly, up a tree, between a rock and a hard place, fine how-do-you-do, tough nut to crack. See PREDICAMENT.

QUANTIFY v. size, size up, peg, check, check out, dig it, eye, look over, have one's number, take one's measure, dope out, take account of, figure, figure in, guesstimate.

QUANTITATIVE ANALYSIS n. quant, quan.

QUANTITY n. 1. mega——— (prefix, as in megabucks, mega-bitch), heap, loads, buttloads, lots, bags, peck, passel, flock, whole slew, scads, zillion, bazillion, umpteen, kind (that kind of money, both small or large amount), bundle, oodles, crawling with, no end of, no end to. See AMOUNT, LARGE. 2. titch, smidge, skoshe, taste, weenchy, teensy-weensy, bite, cut, nip, slice, smithereen. See AMOUNT, SMALL.

QUARREL n. blowup, hassle, spat, tiff, words, run-in, scene, flack session, rhubarb, wrangle, fireworks. See ARGUMENT.

QUARREL v. take on, lock horns, set-to, hassle, row, scrap, bump heads, cross swords, have at it, pick a bone, tangle with, tangle ass with, go up against, pitch a bitch, put up a fight, beat a dead horse, go round and round. See ARGUE.

QUARRELSOME adj. ornery, scrappy, snorky, bitchy, cussed, tetchy, salty, spiky, limber, cantankerous, have a bone to pick, have a chip on one's shoulder, at loggerheads. See BELLIGERENT.

QUARTER n. 1. territory, turf, hood, neck of the woods, stomping ground, old town, ghetto, inner city, slurb, slum, zoo, garment district, skid row. 2. Shubert Alley, Tin Pan Alley, Broadway, the Great White Way (The.), West End, Wall Street, Las Vegas Strip, Sunset Strip, SoHo. See DISTRICTS.

QUARTERS n. dorm, fratority, sorenity, birdcage, bull pen, bullypen, frau shack, hen ranch, hen coop, quail roost, zoo. See HOUSE.

QUASH v. 1. black out, shut down, kill, queer, squelch, hush up, put the lid on, put the damper on, crack down on, clamp down on, cork up, bottle up. 2. snow under, squash, squish, scrunch, trash. See REPRESS.

QUEASY adj. barfy, pukish, pukey, rocky, sick as a dog, under the weather. See ILL.

QUEER adj. flaky, freaky, kooky, offbeat, bogus, weird, weirdo, grody, bunk, oddball, fringy, funky, kinky, geeky, off the wall, trippy, wombat, quirky, not wrapped real tight, flyball, queer duck, rare bird, aired out, jell brain, jelled, character, wacky, yo-yo. See ECCENTRIC.

QUELL v. shut down, pour oil on troubled waters, black out, torpedo, kill, queer, squelch, hush up, sit on, put the lid on, crack down on, ding, zing. See REPRESS. See also PACIFY.

QUENCH v. kill (fire or cigarette), choke, douse, knock down, stamp out.

QUERULOUS adj. bitchy, out of sorts, cantankerous, grouchy, grousing, scrappy, bearish, uptight, thin-skinned, whiny, ready to fly off the handle, edgy. See PEEVISH.

QUERY v. hit up, knock, put out a feeler, test the waters, see which way the wind blows, so?, cool out, P. (Suff., beer-p? = Want a beer?), what's with one or something?, what's going down?, what gives? See QUESTION.

QUESTION n. Q. and A., wringer, sixty-four-dollar question, poll, third, third-degree. See also INQUIRY.

QUESTION v. hit, hit up, hold out for, knock, pop the question, toss, whistle for (but won't get), sweat, sweat it out of one, sweat out, third degree, give one the third, give one the third degree, put through the third degree, put one through the wringer, put the heat on one, put on the grill, grill, roast, put the screws on, put the screws to, go over, work over, flutter (give one a lie detector test), pick one's brains, so?, buzz, cat haul, cook, P. (Suff., beer-p? = Want a beer?), yeah?, what's with one or something?, what's going down?, what gives?

QUESTIONABLE adj. chancy, iffy, dicey, touch-and-go, hanging by a thread, fishy, been hit before, you should live so long, the jury's out. See DOUBTFUL.

QUESTIONS AND ANSWERS n. Q. and A.

QUIBBLE v. nitpick, lint-pick, split hairs, make a big thing about, make a mountain out of a molehill, catch at straws, blow hot and cold, flip-flop, shilly-shally, waffle, hem and haw, hassle, set to, talk back, have at it, pick a bone, put up an argument, pettifog. See also EQUIVOCATE.

QUIBBLER n. nitpicker, hair splitter.

QUICK adj. on the double, quickie, ASAP, pronto, balls out, snappy, double-time, in jig time, Jim quick, get the lead out, move it, get a move on, get going, get on your motorcycle, get on your bicycle, get on your horse, step on it, step lively, shake a leg, haul ass, barrel ass, cut ass, drag ass, shag ass, like a bat out of hell, like shit through a goose. See FAST.

QUICK-WITTED adj. sharp, wired, gasser, whiz, whiz kid, Einstein, have smarts, have savvy, on the ball, quick on the trigger, quick on the uptake, quick on the draw, smart as a whip, smart as a tack, sharp as a tack. See INTELLIGENT.

QUIESCENT adj. out of action, on the shelf, on the bench, out of the rat race, out of the swim, closed down, down.

QUIET adj. clammed-up, buttoned-up, iced, keep one's trap shut, not say boo, saved one's breath, dummied-up, garbo, could hear a pin drop, ah-ah head. See SILENT.

QUIET interj. shut up, knock it off, hold it down, take it down a thousand, can it, clam up, dummy up, cool it, drop it, come off it, shush, hush, shut your trap, shut your tater trap, shut your face, shut your mouth, blow your nose, fold up. See SILENCE.

QUIET n. dead air.

QUIET v. 1. gag, ice, muzzle, squelch, squash, shut up, cool it, can it, soft-pedal, dummy up, clam up, hold it down, take it down a thousand, button one's lip. See SILENCE. 2. cool, cool out, cool it, cool off, stroke, fix up, make matters up, patch things up, square, take the bite out. See PACIFY.

QUIET, BE v. shut up, shut one's trap, shut one's head, shut one's face, shut one's mouth, hush one's mouth, put up or shut up, pipe down, bite one's tongue, hold one's tongue, cut it out, clam up, close up, hang up, dummy up, fold up, dry up, choke in, choke up, drag in one's rope, pull in one's ears, rest one's jaw, sign off, ring off, lay off, roll up one's flaps, stow it, save it, chuck it, can it, stifle it, take it down a thousand, step on it, put a lid on it, button one's lip, zip one's lip, bag one's lip, bag it, bag your face, bag one's head, beat it, go away, be cool, cool one's chops, drink one's beer.

QUINTESSENTIAL adj. greatest, ten, 10, aces, world-class, gonest, hundred-proof, mostest, drop dead ——— (anything), bump'n', ain't half steppin' (Af. Am.), coolsville, gilt-edge, balls out, all-time, the most, endsville, solid gold. See BEST.

QUINTUPLET n. quint.

QUIPSTER n. clown, cutup, life of the party, madcap, trickster, card, a million laughs, kibitzer, booger, bugger, jokesmith, gagman, gagster, funster, punster, wisecracker.

QUIT v. 1. wind up, wrap up, sew up, pack in, pull the pin, kick over, kick the habit, take the cure, drop and go (dockworker use), knock off, break off, go normie, get straight, cut it out, chicken out, call all bets off, call it a day, call it quits, quit cold, quit cold turkey, leave flat, ding, run out on, want out, drop out, get on the wagon, put the finisher on, hang it up. See STOP. 2. cut out, cut ass, bag ass, drag ass, drag it, push off, bow out, ooze out, faze out, nix out, check out, drop, drop out, catch out, pull out, get the hell out, take a walk, book, time to book, break out (Af. Am.), time to bail, hang it up, run out on, walk out on. See GO.

QUITTER n.   deuce, slacker, welsher.

QUIVER v.   jitter, shake, shiver.

QUIVERING n.   shakes, shivers, cold shivers, heebie-jeebies.

QUIZ n.   exam, cream (successful), blue book, Bluebook; drop quiz, shotgun quiz, pop quiz (unannounced).

QUIZ v.   pick one's brains.

QUOTA n.   piece, a piece of the action, cut, bite, slice, chunk, split, end, divvy, cut of the pie, cut of the melon, slice of the pie, slice of the melon. See also SHARE.

QUOTATION n.   saying, quote.

QUOTATION MARK n.   quote, rabbit ears (Pl.).

QUOTE v.   reference.

R

R n. Romeo, Roger.

RABBI n. Reb, sky pilot, sky scout, sky merchant.

RABBLE n. mob, riffraff, cattle, ragtag, ragtag and bobtail, the great unwashed, turnout, blowout, crush, everybody and his brother, everybody and his uncle, loaded to the rafters, wall-to-wall people, jam, jam-up, push. See also POPULACE.

RABID adj. 1. freaked out, bugs on, hot, hot for, nutty about, overboard, stoned, bugged, steamed-up, flipped, worked up about, jacked-up. See ENTHUSIASTIC. 2. ranting and raving, raving mad, roaring mad, hopping mad, good and mad, mad as a hornet, mad as a wet hen, hacked, steamed-up, at the boiling point, boiling over, see red, shit blue, go ape-shit, have a conniption, hit the ceiling, sizzling, smoking. See ANGRY.

RACE n. competish, go, run.

RACE, FIXED n. dead cert, boat race (horse racing).

RACEHORSE n. the ponies, pony, nag, the g.g.'s, gee-gee, bangtail, mudder, pig, plater, dark horse (unknown entry), stick out (superior), chaser (steeplechase racer), claimer; maiden, bug (never won); beetle, cooler, dog, jobbie, lob, meat eater, muncher, oat burner, oil burner, plater, plodder, beagle, big horse, big train (favorite), lizard, getty-up, glue pot, goat, hide; weanling, baby, juvenile (two-year-old); lug in, lug out (rail), lugger, side wheeler, skin, stiff (loser), tacky, stretch runner, breakdown (injury while racing). See also HORSE.

RACEHORSE RIDER n. jock, jockette (Fem.), up, bug boy (apprentice), big boy, punk, rider, postboy.

RACEHORSE TERMS also-ran, bear in, bear out, lug in, lug out, wear blinkers (restrict horse's side view), blowout (workout run), break (start from gate), the call, drive (he won under a drive), early foot (fast starter), handily, breeze, post time (starting time), photo (photo finish), scratch (withdraw entry), bat, gad (whip); caller (race announcer), claimer; fast, good, heavy, muddy, sloppy, slow, gumbo (track conditions); flat racing, give away weight (carry extra weight handicap), footing, maiden race, go, run, in the money; pilot, rider (jockey); railbird (spectator), tack (equipment), the ponies, the track, the g.g.'s, charts, dark horse (unknown entry); maiden, bug (horse who has never won); boat race; drugstore race, drugstore handicap, hophead, dust a horse, (drugged or fixed); sweep (sweepstake); golf ball, soup, T, tea (drugs); produce race (unfoaled entries based on bloodlines), Run for the Roses (Kentucky Derby);

seller, selling race (claiming race), starter (an entry), steal (lead all the way), wire-to-wire (start to finish), cooler (light horse blanket), cool out, exercise boy, hot walker, nerved (nerve block to hooves), put down (humane killing), bute (phenylbutazone, painkiller), swipe (a groom).

RACING CAR n. Indy car, stock, stocker, formula car, formula A, formula B, formula C, formula F (Ford), formula 5000, formula I, formula II, formula III, formula VEE, blown formula Super VEE (supercharged), funny car, hobby car, mule (practice car), pace car, clean (smooth, aerodynamic body).

RACING CAR DRIVER n. foot, hot shoe (star driver), ride (got a ride).

RACING CAR MAINTENANCE n. blip, gun (race engine briefly), blueprint (rebuild engine to exact stock specifications), prodify (modify a production car), methanol, nitro (nitromethane); wrench (mechanic).

RACING CAR PARTS n. crash box (transmission), footprint, nerf bar (kind of bumper), roll bar, roll cage, pot, scattershield (safety flywheel and clutch housing), scuff (used tire), slicks (treadless tires).

RACING CAR TERMS boondocks (off the course), bull ring (short dirt-racing track), chute (straightaway), honking (top speed), Indy (Indianapolis 500), June bug, water, push one's key, bug (Indianapolis racing car), brain bucket (helmet).

RACING FORM n. sheet, scratch sheet, dope sheet, form.

RACISM n. feel a draft (recognition of), glass ceiling (invisible barrier to promotion), Jim Crow, Jim Crowism, Jane Crow (against women).

RACKET n. ruckus, ruction, fuss, fuzz-buzz, hoo-ha, rowdydow, hubba-hubba, hullabaloo, brouhaha. See also COMMOTION; NOISE.

RACKETEER n. hood, hoodlum, hooligan, mo ghee, mob ghee, mobster, big juice, member of the family, goon, underboss (second in command), pusher, dealer, digits dealer (numbers). See GANGSTER. See also CRIMINAL; MAFIA.

RADAR DETECTOR n. brownie (unit), camera (police), electric teeth, fuzzbuster (auto), huff duff (H.F.D.F.), Kodak, picture box, Polaroid, X-ray machine.

RADAR IMAGE n. blip, angel (echo), bogie, skunk (unidentified or hostile), clutter, flitter (static).

RADAR OPERATOR n. scopehead.

RADICAL adj. far out, way out, gone, left field, flaming, out of all bounds, all-get-out, too much, ultra ultra, over the top, knee-jerk reaction. See EXTREME.

RADICAL n. lunatic fringe, linky-dink, innocent (Af. Am.), underground.

RADICAL, LEFT n. bleeding heart, do-gooder, commie, comsymp, fellow traveler, flamer, knee-jerk lefty, left, left winger, lefty, leftie, leftist, lefto, New Left, Old Left, left of center, pink, pinko, parlor pink, linky-dink, red, radish, hippie, yippie, radiclib, rim, Wobbly.

RADICAL, RIGHT n. right-winger, right, right wing, extreme right, far right radical right, New Right, stand pat, stand-patter, skinhead, Bircher, Birchite, John Bircher, Black Shirt, Brown Shirt, diehard, hard-hat, Klu Kluxer, McCarthyism, old line, Posse Comitatus, red-baiter, redneck, storm trooper, witch hunter.

RADIO n. boom box, boom, box, stereo, hi-fi, jambox, boogie box, ghetto buster, ghetto blaster, ghetto box, thunderbox, third world attaché case (portable with tape player), third world briefcase, walkman, joy box, portable, tube gear, beeper.

RADIOACTIVE adj. dirty, hot.

RADIOACTIVE PARTICLES n. fallout.

RADIO AUDIENCE n. listener, drive-time audience (listener in a car).

RADIO OPERATOR n. ham, ham operator, sparks, dit-da artist, dit-da jockey, dit-da monkey, brass pounder (1925).

RADIO OPERATOR'S ROOM n. shack, radio shack.

RADIO RECEIVER n. boom box, boom, box, thunderbox, ghetto blaster, third world attaché case, Walkman, stereo, hi-fi, joy box, tube gear.

RADIO SHOW HOST n. D.J., deejay, disc jockey, platter pusher, anchor.

RADIO STATION n. antenna farm, ozoner.

RADIOTELEPHONE n. cellular phone, port-o-phone, remote, cordless, rig, squawkie-talkie, walkie-talkie.

RADIO TRANSMITTER n. squawkie-talkie, walkie-talkie, Gibson Girl (WWII), tower.

RAFFLE n. the numbers, the numbers game.

RAGE n. 1. mad, huff, dander, storm, wingding, conniption fit, shit hemorrhage, blowup, push one's key, tearing up the pea patch. See ANGER. 2. cosmo, faddy, trendy, happenin', bust fresh, in, in-thing, the thing, latest thing, latest wrinkle, new wrinkle, newest wrinkle, last word, now, really now, the rage, up to the minute, go-go, hip, hep, mellow back, in-spot, happening place, groovy hangout, hot spot, masscult.

RAGE v. burn up, blow up, blow one's top, blow one's topper, blow one's stack, blow a fuse, blow a gasket, blow one's cap, blow one's cork, blow one's wig, blow one's noggin, blow one's roof, blow one's lump, flip, flip out, flip one's lid, fly off the handle, go ballistic, go apeshit, get sore, see red, get hot under the collar, sizzle, get into a dither, get into a stew, get one's dander up, get one's Irish up, get one's mad up, work oneself into a lather, work oneself into a sweat, have a hemorrhage, have a shit hemorrhage, have a bug on, sport a bug on, bug up, pop off, sound off, raise Cain, raise hell, raise the devil, raise the roof, hit the ceiling, sound off, boiling point, boil over, steam up, tear, tear up the pea patch, go into a tailspin.

RAGGED adj. ratty-tatty, beat-up, tacky, frowzy, sleazy, dog-eared.

RAGING adj. bent out of shape, blowing one's cool, blowing a fuse, blowing a gasket, blowing one's stack, blowing one's top, blowing the roof, mad as a hornet, mad as a wet hen, torqued, at the boiling point, boiling over, see red, shit blue, go apeshit, having a shit hemorrhage, throwing a fit, on the warpath, raising hell, ranting and raving, raving mad, roaring mad. See ANGRY.

RAGOUT n. mulligan, salmagundi, slumgullion, coll, Black Mike (hobo), lorelei.

RAID v. knock off, knock over, tip over, heat, storm, pull a joint, slough, slough up, slough a joint, lean against, lean on. See also INVADE; LOOT.

RAILROAD BRAKEMAN n. brakie, baby lifter, car catcher, club winder, hind hook, shack stinger, groundhog.

RAILROAD COACH n. ding-dong, rubberneck (observation), sleeper, the cushions (first-class passenger car).

RAILROAD CONDUCTOR n. dude, drummer, grabber, kayducer, captain, skipper, big O, big ox, brains, chopper, con.

RAILROAD CREW n. hat; hogger, hog head, hog jockey, hog, eagle-eye (engineer); piglet (training to be engineer), bell ringer, clinker, diamond cracker, diamond pusher, diamond thrower, ash can, dust raiser; smoke, tallow pot (fireman); jerry gang, paperweight (clerk), rag (flagman), rail, razorback, snipe, stinger, switch hog; yard bull, yard goat (guard); dishwasher (engine wiper), dog chaser (relief), donkey, gandy dancer (section hand); general, ringmaster, dinger (yardmaster); grunt, snake, bookkeeper (flagman), cinder crusher, cherry picker (switchman), boom stick (itinerant worker), chambermaid (roundhouse machinist), detainer (dispatcher), cinder dick (detective), cinder bull (R.R. police).

RAILROAD CROSSING SIGN n. clothes tree.

RAILROAD FREIGHT CAR n. riff, reefer, freezer (refrigerated); gon, gond, oilcan, boxer, can, rod, dise drag, gory (empty), gunboat, side-door Pullman, rattler.

RAILROAD LOCOMOTIVE n. bull, bull engine, hog, pig, goat (switch), battleship (heavy duty), battlewagon (tender), boiler, iron horse, smoker, calliope, camel, dinge, hay burner, jack, Johnson rod (mythical part), teakettle, pot, kettle, Mother Hubbard, yard goat, moose gooser.

RAILROAD SIGNAL n. eye, red eye, green eye, wig-wag.

RAILROAD TERMS AMTRAK, brass collar (R.R. official), bullfighter (empty freight car), bullpen (dormitory), barefoot (without brakes), car toad (service train), boom car (crane), cradle (gondola), crumb (work-crew bunk car), deck (passenger car roof), breeze (air brakes), first reader (conductor's notebook), garden (yard), gate, gun (warning torpedo), possum belly, jerk (branchline), shuffle them up, high-ball (high-speed), the cushions (first-class passenger car), deadhead (return empty), bumper (coupling).

RAILROAD TRAIN n. choo-choo, choo-choo train, Chattanooga, Chattanooga choo-choo, rattler, ball of fire, highballer, jack, rat, meat run, red ball, varnished car; cannonball, cannonball express (fast); AMTRAK, B. & O., Belt Line, Challenger, Commodore Vanderbilt, C.P.R., Orient Express, Daylight, Dixie Cannonball, Green Diamond, Owl, Pennsy, Twentieth Century Limited, Zephyr.

RAIMENT n. threads, togs, duds, outfit, rags, glad rags, getup, get-out, feathers, Barbie and Ken (conventional), California chic (expensive casual), vine, weeds, frame, flash, drapery, drapes, California black tie (any colorful variation of formal wear), Sunday best, hand-me-downs. See CLOTHING

RAIN n. precip, pouring; drips, light drips (shower), spit, it's raining cats and dogs, it's raining hammer handles, it's raining pitchforks, really coming down, deep water (heavy), gully washer, window washer, sheets, wet stuff, drownder, goose drownder, heavy dew, California dew, California sunshine, California weather (in Florida), Florida weather (in California), California orange juice, sky juice, cloud juice.

RAINCOAT n. mack, Fog, slicker.

RAISE n. move-up, step-up, boost, leg, leg-up, bump, jump, jump-up, holdup (salary), Mexican raise (promote without raise in pay), win one's wings, hike, hike upstairs.

RAISE v. 1. boost, look up, pick up, perk up, snowball, mushroom, shoot up, build up, fetch up, goose, goose up, hike, hike up, jack up, jump up, put up, run up, pyramid. 2. bring up, drag up.

RAISIN CAKE n. fly cake.

RAKE n. playboy, player, hound, poon hound, lech, wolf, tomcat, alley cat, cocksman, womanizer, sport, swinger, make-out artist, beastmaster (dates ugly women), chaser, woman chaser. See LECHER.

RALLY n. clambake, pep rally, meet, get-together, pow-wow. See also MEETING.

RALLY v. pick up, perk up, shape up, get back in shape, bounce back, make a comeback, come from behind, snap out of it, come along, get one's act together, turn around, turn things around. See IMPROVE. See also ASSEMBLE, INCITE.

RAMBLE v. 1. get sidetracked, get off the track, lose the thread, all over the map. 2. knock around, knock about, cruise, drift, bum around, traipse, bat around, percolate, ooze, patrolling (indecisively, aimlessly), ank. See WANDER.

RAMPAGE n. ruckus, mad, Irish, storm, wing-ding, wilding, conniption fit, blowup, boiling point, tear, tearing up the pea patch, more heat than light. See ANGER.

RANCID adj. strong, high.

RANDY adj. heavy, horny, hot, hot and heavy, turned on, rammy. See LASCIVIOUS.

RANGE n. run, run of, space, elbowroom, leeway, room to swing a cat.

RANGE v. knock around, knock about, bum around, drift, float, follow one's nose, traipse, bat around, bat about, hit the road, hit the trail, globe-trot, trek. See WANDER.

RANK adj. strong, high.

RANK n. pecking order, down the line, place, slot.

RANK v. tab, peg, pigeonhole, button down, put away, put down as, put down for, type-cast, rank out, size up, take one's measure.

RANSACK v. beat the bushes, leave no stone unturned, look all over hell, look high and low, search high heaven, shake, shake down, toss, turn inside out, turn upside down.

RANT v. carry on, go on, take on, blow one's roof, blow one's top, sizzle, pop off, sound off, get on a soapbox, spiel, spout, chew the scenery, stump, sport a bug on. See also ORATE.

RAPACIOUS adj. grabby, poligot, greedyguts.

RAPE n. short-arm heist, gangbang, gang shay, lineup.

RAPID adj. screaming, on the double quick, quick as a wink, double time, in nothing flat, really rolling, hell-bent, hell for leather, like a house on fire, like greased lightening, like a big-assed bird, like a BAB, like a bat out of hell, like shit through a goose, like a raped ape. See FAST.

RAPIST n. arm man, short-arm bandit, keister bandit, pussy bandit, short-arm heister, skin heister, diddler.

RAPPORT n. good vibes, good vibrations, simpatico, togetherness, soul, on the same wavelength, cotton to, in the groove, groovy, hit it off.

RAPTURE n. gone, far out, cool, Nadaville.

RAPTUROUS adj. flying, floating, dreamy, zero cool, gone, in Nadaville, groked, spaced-out, zoned-out, walking on air, on cloud nine. See ECSTATIC.

RARE adj. 1. scarcer than hen's teeth, numerous as chicken lips. 2. seen a cow wounded worse than this and get better.

RASH adj. foolheaded, pay no mind, off the deep end, out on a limb, play with fire, stick one's neck out, leave oneself wide open. See RECKLESS.

RATE v. put away, put down as, put down far, tab, button down, peg, pigeonhole, typecast, size up, score, rank out, take one's measure, stand in with, redline (insurance rate zoning). See also APPRAISE.

RATIFICATION n. fuckin'-A, go ahead, green light, okay, OK, stamp of approval.

RATIFY v. bless, okay, go for, give the nod, give the go-ahead, give the green light, give the stamp of approval, rubber-stamp. See APPROVE.

RATION n. shore, bite, divvy, cut, cut of the melon, P.C., p.c., piece, piece of the action, piece of the pie, crack, drag. See SHARE.

RATIONAL adj. together, got it together, cool, have horse sense, commonsensical, all there, have all one's marbles, have both oars in the water. See REASONABLE.

RATIONALE n. the big idea, the idea, the whole idea, the what-for, the why-for, the why and wherefore, story, song and dance, sour grapes. See EXCUSE.

RATTLE v. get to, discomboberate, rattle one's cage, throw, psych out, fuck with one's head, put one on a crosstown bus, put off, flummox. See CONFUSE.

RATTLED adj. unglued, come unzipped, come apart, defrosted, all shook up, mucked-up, mixed-up, floored; farmisht, farshimmelt (Yid.), thrown, fussed rattlebrained, haywire, hissy, bamboozled. See CONFUSED.

RAVAGE v. wipe out, trash, total, cream, sink, smash, rack up, put in the toilet, take a hit, take apart, take a joint apart, tear down, break the lease, blue ruin, make hash of, fix one's wagon, play hob with. See DESTROY. See also LOOT, SEDUCE.

RAVE v. 1. carry on over, make a to-do over, take on over, fall all over one, go on about, whoop it up for. 2. freak out, flip one's lid, blow one's top, blow one's stack, go ape, go bananas, go bonkers, go off one's head, come unglued, come unzipped. See CRAZY, GO.

RAVENOUS adj. dog-hungry, empty, have a tapeworm, munchies (follows marijuana use), starved to death, could eat a horse, could eat the asshole out of a bear, could eat the asshole out of a bear without ketchup.

RAVISHER n. arm man, short-arm bandit, keister bandit, pussy bandit, short-arm heister, skin heister, diddler.

RAVISHING adj. devastating, ten, 10, drop-dead gorgeous, dyno, dishy, dream puss, glam, wukka, whistle bait, stone fox, head rush, knock one's eyes out, scrumptious, stunner, stunning, beaut, raving beauty, hot shit, knockout, knock one's eyes out, centerfold, living doll, oh yeah. See BEAUTIFUL.

RAY n. glim, dimmer.

RAZE v. wipe out, total, take the joint apart, break the lease, blue ruin, zap. See DESTROY.

RAZOR n. hook.

REACH v. wind up at, make it, make the scene, hit, hit town, blow in, sky in, breeze in, roll in, check in, sign in, time in, clock in, ring in, show, show up, roll up, bob up, buzz (to announce an arrival). See ARRIVE.

REACT v. 1. feel for, feel in one's bones, feel in one's guts, be turned on to, hear one, get in touch, have a funny feeling, have heart, have a hunch, have good vibes, have vibes, blow a hype, freak out, spazz, spazz out. 2. answer back, talk back, backtalk, shoot back, snappy comeback, come back at, get back at, come right back at, back at you. See ANSWER.

REACTION n. take, take it big, double-take, hit, cooler, knee-jerk reaction (expected), vibes, feedback, comeback, snappy comeback, sass, lip, backtalk, crackback, wisecrack, kick, kick back, mug (comic). See also RESULT.

REACTIONARY n. right, right-winger, radical right, Bircher, diehard, hard hat, lunatic, fringe, redneck. See CONSERVATIVE.

REACTIVATE v. take out of mothballs, demothball.

READILY adv. 1. at the drop of a hat, no sweat, hands down, like nothing, nothing to it, slick as a whistle, swimmingly, piece of cake. 2. toot sweet, in half a mo, in half a tick, in a jiff, in a jiffy, in half a jiffy, quick as a wink, before one can say Jack Robinson, abracadabra. See IMMEDIATELY.

READY adj. revved, revved-up, wired, squared away, bagged, fixed, have all the pieces in place, in place, in the slot, on deck, gaffed, rigged, set up, up on, psyched-up, down, ripe, crisp, cut-and-dry, got it covered, all bases covered, game for, waitin' on, ready for prime time, at the ready, hot to trot, loaded for bear. See PREPARED.

READY v. 1. prep, warm up, ready up, gear up, psych oneself up, get set for, clear the decks, pave the way, put through the grind, put through the mill. 2. brief, fill in, fill one in, put on to, put one in the picture, wise up, give a pointer to, let in on the know, keep one posted, post. See PREPARE.

REAL adj. it, for real, real stuff, genuine article, the real goods, absolute, real people, real world, live, in the flesh, honest-to-God, card-carrying, all wool and a yard wide. See SINCERE.

REAL ESTATE SALES n. fizzbo, FSBO (for sale by owner); gazundering (buyer tries to lower price before escrow closes), gazumping (seller raises price before escrow closes).

REALISTIC, BE v. get real, get a life, get a clue.

REALITY n. brass tacks, name of the game, bottom line, nuts and bolts, down to earth, the real world, no shit, straight shit, how it is, how things are, the way of it, what's what, where it's at, what it is, like it is, in living color, the word. See ACTUALITY.

REALIZATION n. aha reaction, slow take, take, double-take, take it big, see the light, flash on it, get one's drift, it hit me, it just come to me, it dawned on me.

REALIZE v. get, get it, got it, gotchya, get the idea, get the picture, catch, catch on, pick up, get through one's head, tumble, dig, see daylight, came the dawn. See UNDERSTAND.

REALLY adv. absofuckinglutely, cert, no shit, amen, why sure, fer sure, you know, you're not kidding, no buts about it, indeedy, helluv, for real, really truly. See ABSOLUTELY.

REALM n. territory, turf, stomping grounds, stamping grounds, neck of the woods. See also NEIGHBORHOOD, DISTRICTS.

REAR v. bring up, fetch up, drag up, raise up.

REASON n. cover, stall, song and dance, jive, the big idea, the whole idea, sour grapes, the what-for, the why and wherefore, the why-for. See EXCUSE.

REASONABLE adj. together, got it together, glued (antonym: unglued), resonate (that resonates), cool, cool as a cucumber, have horse sense, commonsensical, all there, in one's right mind, got all one's marbles, have all one's marbles, have all one's buttons, right, right in the head, have both oars in the water, play with a full deck. See also CHEAP.

REASSIGN v. bump (worker), kick upstairs.

REASSIGNMENT n. shake-up.

REASSURE v. buck up, pick up, brace up, chirk up, perk up, give a lift, snap out of it, let the sunshine in. See SUPPORT.

REBATE n. kickback, payola, drugola, gayola, a payback.

REBATE v. kick back, give up.

REBEL n. Johnny Reb, young Turk.

REBEL v. drop out, opt out, cop out, get out of line, rock the boat, make waves, leave the beaten path, kick over, kick over the traces.

REBELLIOUS adj. ornery, out of line, stoner. See also DISCONTENTED.

REBUFF n. nix, turndown, ice, no way José, November Foxtrot Whiskey (no fucking way), nothing doing, kick in the ass, kick in the teeth, cold shoulder, cut, go-by, hard time (sexual). See REJECTION.

REBUFF v. pass up, cut, drop, ice, cold-shoulder, high-hat, blow off, brush off, fluff off, give one the fluff. See REJECT.

REBUFFED adj. burned, cut, dead, feel adrift, killed, nixed, dumped, thrown-over, passed-over, passed on, put-down, turned-down, got it in the neck, out in the cold, left at the church. See REJECTED.

REBUILD v. pick up the pieces, face-lift, retread, rehab.

REBUKE n. put-down, gig, comeuppance, rap, slap in the face, bawling out, calling down, going over, ragging, what-for, hard time. See ADMONISH. See also SCOLDING.

REBUKE v. chew, chew ass, chew out, chew out one's ass, eat out, eat out one's ass, have someone's ass, kick ass and take names, fire on, rip on, ball out, bawl out, ream, ream out, ream ass, read one out, cuss out, dog on, go after, rip, zap, cap on, lay into, lay out, rank out, straighten out, serve one out, pay, pay out, sound off, lean on, sit on, jump on, jump all over, jump down one's throat, jump on one's shit, climb, climb on, climb all over, climb one's frame, light into, land on, can, tie the can on one, knock, drop the boom, lower the boom, jaw, jawbone, rake, rake up one side and down the other, take up one side and down the other, rake over the coals, haul over the coals, trim, have one on the carpet, have one on the mat, call on the carpet, dance the carpet, have one on the mat, call to task, smack down, slap down, call down, dress down, put down, burn down, burn one down, come down on, come down on hard, take down, take down a peg, down-mouth, ding, gig, growl, glue, rap, rap one's knuckles, slap on the wrist, put the slug on one, sock it to one, stick it to one, go upside one's haid, read the riot act, throw the book at one, speak to, tell a thing or two, tell off, tell where to get off, tee off on one, attend to, give it to, give what for, give a bawling out, give a going over, give a piece of one's mind, give one the business, give one both barrels, give one the deuce, give one the devil, give one the dickens, give one hell, give one hail Columbia, give one his lumps, give one his comeuppance, cloud up and rain on one, let one have it, let fly, fix, fix one's clock, skin, skin alive, scorch, blister, roast, fry, clobber, tear into, draw the line, lambaste, mop up the floor with, wipe up the floor with, jack up, hoist, rag, dig at, settle, settle one's hash, settle the score, campus.

REBUT v.   come back at, get back at, take on, cross, top. See REFUTE.

RECALL v.   flash, flash on, nail it down, rings a bell, it struck a note, all of a sudden it came to me, came to me that, came to me like it was yesterday.

RECANT v.   back off, dial back, go back on one's word, weasel out, worm one's way out, worm out of, welsh, renig, nig, back-water, crawfish, crawfish out, eat crow, eat humble pie.

RECAPITULATE v.   recap, rehash, replay, go over the same ground, go the same round. See REPEAT.

RECAPTURE v.   reel one back in. See also REMEMBER.

RECEIPTS n.   take, take-in, cash flow, revenue stream, bottom line, net, velvet, cush, get, gate, handle, melon; brocas, cactus, dust, ends, bread, lace (large profits). See INCOME.

RECEIVE v.   pull, pull down, snag, grab, cop, get one's hands on, get hold of, latch on to. See GET. See also WELCOME.

RECEIVER OF STOLEN GOODS n.   fence, neighborhood connection, shade, shifter (handler).

RECENT adj.   today, contempo, newy, hot off the fire, hot off the griddle, hot off the press, just out, up-to-date, the latest. See NEW.

RECEPTIVE adj.   ready, pushover. See also READY.

RECESS n.   break, coffee break, break-off, come up for air, breather, breathing spell, downtime, letup, five, ten, time-out, freeze, cutoff, layoff, letup; happy hour, attitude adjustment hour (cocktail hour).

RECESS v.   take a break, take a breather, take five, take ten, take a smoke, put on hold, call time, break it off, break it up, drop, drop it, pigeonhole, shake, sideline.

RECESSION n.   bust, hard times, bad times, bear market, bottom out, slide. rainy days, rainin', dead-cat bounce (false sign of recovery), the big trouble (the 1930s). See DEPRESSION.

RECIDIVIST n.   repeater, habitual, go back for seconds, two-time loser, three-time loser, four-time loser, glutton for punishment.

RECIPROCATE v.   scratch one's back, you scratch mine and I'll scratch yours, make up for, pay one's dues, tit for tat, square.

RECITE v.   get on a soapbox, spiel, spout, chew the scenery, stump. See ORATE.

RECKLESS adj.   foolheaded, squirrely, harebrained, dingy, dingy-dingy, flaky, kooky, sappy, screwy, pay no mind, any old way, any which way, fast-and-loose, helter-skelter, harum-scarum, devil-may-care, off the deep end, step off the deep end, out on a limb, play with fire, stick one's neck out, leave oneself wide open, go to sea in a sieve, go for broke, cowboy. See also CARELESS.

RECKLESS DRIVER n.   cowboy, bonzai, squirrel.

RECKLESSLY adv.   like crazy, like mad.

RECKON v.   tot, tot up, tote, tote up, run down, tick off, count heads, count noses, count the house, cut ice, cut some ice, keep tab, keep tabs, dope out, figure in, figure out, take account of, take one's measure, reckon up, square.

RECKONING n.   bad news, check, checkeroo, grunt, IOU, score, tab. See ACCOUNT.

RECOGNITION n.   1. strokes, cow sociology, pat on the back, pat on the head, PR, puff, puffing up, pumping up, low profile (avoid), rave, one's stock has gone up, plum (job, rank, or title). See COMMENDATION. 2. tumble, double-take (sudden second look), high sign. See also REALIZATION.

RECOGNIZE v.   flash on, make, peg, tab, tag, make one, spot, nail, lamp, button down, aim, finger, put the finger on, put one's finger on something, put down for, ring a bell, tumble to; not give one a flop, pass up, not give one a rumble or tumble (fail to). See also UNDERSTAND; REMEMBER.

RECOLLECT v.   flash, flash on, nail it down, rings a bell, it struck a note, all of a sudden it came to me, came to me that, came to me like it was yesterday.

RECOLLECTION n.   flashback, flash-on.

RECOMMEND v.   steer, tout, plug, put next to, put on to, put one wise, tip, tip off, get behind, push, spread it around, post. See ADVISE.

RECOMMENDATION n.   steer, bum steer, C.F., proposal, feeler, pass, proposition, tip, kibitz, flea in the ear, two cents' worth, plug, say-so.

RECOMPENSE n.   tip, toke (gambling), chip, cue, somethin', a little somethin'; subway, bus ride (nickel or dime tip); sweetener, grease, salve, palm oil, gravy, zukes. See also COMPENSATION.

RECOMPENSE v.   1. comp, cough up, ante up, put out, spring for, kick in, swing for bread, fork up, square, square things, sweeten the pot, tickle the palm, pay up, take care of. 2. chicken, schmear, grease, grease one's palm, oil, oil one's palm, fix, fix the alzo, put in the fix, piece one off, gaff, fit the mitt, put in the bag, put in the zingers, buzz, crack business, do business, see, see the cops, buy, buy off, reach, get at, get to. See PAY.

RECONCILE v. cool, fix up, bury the hatchet, make up, make it up, kiss and make up, make matters up, patch things up, get together on, come together. See PACIFY. 2. come around, trade off, strike a happy medium, meet halfway, can't fight 'em join 'em, come to school, come to the party, don't make waves, fit in, when in Rome do as the Romans do. See CONFORM.

RECONDITION v. fix up, doll up, face-lift, retread, rehab, retrofit, spruce, spruce up, do, do up.

RECONNAISSANCE n. recon, recce, recco, look-see.

RECONNOITER v. recon, case, spy out, stake out, check around, look around, smell around, see what cooks, see what's going down, see what's coming down, see what's happenin'. See also INVESTIGATE.

RECONSIDER v. run that by one one more time, run through, go over, hash over, rehash, polish up, rub up, brush up. See REVIEW.

RECONVERSION n. switch, switchover, born-again.

RECONVERT v. switch, switch over, see the light.

RECORD n. 1. comic book, funny book, the book on one, jacket, swindle sheet, ICE (Incidental Company Expenses: padding), track record, paper trail. See also DIRECTORY. 2. disc, platter, licorice pizza, manhole cover, vinyl, side, wax, cylinder, tunes (album), demo (audition).

RECORD v. wax, cut a wax, cut a track, can, tape, dub, lay it down, lay down some tracks.

RECORDING DEVICE n. VCR, tap, wiretap, bug, tape.

RECORDING TERMS bloop, tape, dub, mix, cut, cut a take, cut a side, make a take, charts, spin, side, thirty-three, forty-five, LP, single; grammy, gold (awards), groove yard (storage).

RECORD SOUND n. wow, flutter, hiss, rumble.

RECORD SPINNER n. D.J., deejay, disc jockey, platter pusher.

RECOUNT v. 1. play back, rehash, recap, echo, run that by one once more, say again, chew one's cabbage twice. See REPEAT. 2. run down, run through, track, picture, unload, blab, let one's hair down, verbalize, lay it on one, put it on the street, let it all hang out, bring it out into the daylight, bring it out into the open, spit it out, let one's hair down, spin a yarn, break a story. See RELATE.

RECOUP v. get out from under, get well, make well, make up for.

RECOVER v. bounce back, make a comeback, snap out of it, get out from under, get well (monetarily), be out of the woods, turn the corner. See IMPROVE.

RECREATION n. rec, R. and R., fun and games, playtime, big time, high time, high old time, picnic, merry-go-round, field day, ball, laughs, lots of laughs, grins. See also ENTERTAINMENT.

RECREATIONAL VEHICLE n. RV, moho.

RECRUIT n. draftee, boot (N.), rookie, tenderfoot, yardbird, chicken; barber bait, big Joe, big John, john, Johnny dogface, bimbo, bozo (WWII); plebe, Mr. Dumb-John (Naval Acad.); Mr. Dooley (A.F. Acad.), croot, dude, jeep, rubber sock, poggie. See also NOVICE.

RECRUIT v. sign on, sign up, take on, call up, poggie.

RECRUITER n. headhunter, people plucker, scout, talent scout.

RECTIFY v. 1. debug, doctor, fly-speck, launder, scrub, clean up, pick up, shape up, fix up, go over, fiddle with. 2. make up for, pay one's dues, square, square up, square the beef. 3. straighten up and fly right, straighten out, clean up one's act, get on the ball, recalibrate, dial back, turn things around. See CORRECT.

RECTOR adj. padre, the rev, Holy Joe, sky pilot, gospel ghee, sin hound, buck, Bible basher, gospel pusher, salvation rancher, glory roader. See CLERGYMAN.

RECTORY n. aquarium (Catholic).

RECTUM n. rear, rear end, ass, asshole, ying-yang, brown hole, back way, tube, exhaust pipe, Hershey bar route, little brown eyeball, crack. See ANUS. See also BUTTOCKS.

RECUPERATE v. bounce back, make a comeback, snap out of it, pull out of it, get well (monetarily), pick up the pieces, be out of the woods, bottom out, be on the mend, turn the corner. See IMPROVE.

RECURRING adj. string, roll, on a roll, run, streak, come again, row, chain, two-time, three-time, two-time loser (usually criminal).

REDECORATE v. doll up, fix up, gussy up, spruce, spruce up, do, do up, redo, face-lift, retread, rehab.

RED-HAIRED adj. rusty, red, carrot-top, bricktop.

REDISTRICT v. remap, gerrymander.

REDRESS v. make up for, pay one's dues, square, square up, square the beef, recalibrate, dial back, turn around, turn things around, turn over a new leaf. See CORRECT.

REDUCE v. cut, cut down, cut to the bone, nutshell, put in a nutshell, boil down, snip, trim, chop, get to the meat, cut back, roll back, lowball, dig in, tighten one's belt, downsize, leblang (The. ticket price), knock off, bump, bust, rif, bench. See also DIET.

REDUCTION n. cutback, rollback.

REEKING adj. stinko, stinking, stinky, whiffy, nosy, strong, loud (strong), high.

REELECTION, LOSE FOR v. go toes up.

REENLIST v. re-up.

REEXAMINE v. check, check over, double-check, cool something over, run it by one again, recap, rehash, hash over, go over, go over with a fine-tooth comb, go over the same ground, go the same round. See REVIEW.

REFEREE n. zebra, ref, homer (favors the home team). See also ARBITRATOR.

REFERENCE n. source, resource, commercial, plug.

REFERENCE POINT n. checkpoint, where one is at, where one's head is at, P.O.V. (point of view).

REFERRAL n. Ping-Pong (Medic., patient), reference.

REFILL v. hit, hit again.

REFINE v. dink, tweak, butcher.

REFINED adj. highbrow, hoity-toity, spiffy, classy, snazzy, posh, flossy, plush, plushy, ritzy, swanky, snarky, swell-elegant, nobby, blowed in the glass (hobo).

REFINERY n. cat plant.

REFLECT v. head trip, float, noodle, noodle it around, cool something over, stew, stew over, chew over, chew the cud, skull-drag. See THINK.

REFLEX n. gut reaction, knee-jerk reaction, take, double-take.

REFORM n. housecleaning, clean sweep, shake-up.

REFORM v. shape up, clean up, clean up one's act, get one's act together, get with it, get on the ball, turn over a new leaf, turn around, turn things around, switch, switch over, straighten up and fly right, go straight, straighten out, upgrade, make first-rate, mat down, come along, come to school, hit the legit, go up-and-up, get religion, sprout wings, see the light, come to Jesus, hit the sawdust trail.

REFORMED adj. born-again, got religion, newborn Christian, saw the light, a different person, a changed person.

REFORM SCHOOL n. college, juvey.

REFRAIN v. 1. take the pledge, take the cure, go on the wagon, go on the water wagon. 2. pass, pass up, sit out, sit on one's ass, sit on one's duff, give the go-by. See ABSTAIN.

REFRESHER n. go juice, pick-me-up, pickup, shot in the arm.

REFRESHMENT n. bite, feed, nosh, snack, spread, drink, pick-me-up. See also FOOD, DRINK.

REFRIGERATOR n. fridge, frige, cooler, ice box, dugout, reefer.

REFUELING PLANE n. flying gas station, tanker, buddy store (Vietnam).

REFUGE n. hideaway, hideout, hole in, hole up, safe house, blowout center, ivory tower, den.

REFUGEE n. boat people, defector, D.P., displaced person.

REFUND n. kickback, give up, payola, drugola, gayola. See also RESTITUTION.

REFURBISH v. doll up, fix up, gussy up, spruce, spruce up, redo, rehab, retread, face-lift.

REFUSAL n. nix, pass, turndown, no way José, November Foxtrot Whiskey (no fucking way), like hell I will, cold shoulder, go-by, splash, back up (refuse to do something), hard time (sexual). See DENIAL.

REFUSE n. gosh, hogwash, junk, dreck, shit.

REFUSE v. nix, turn down, ding, not buy, spike, back up (to do something), piss on, brush off, fluff off; plead a five, take the fifth (use the fifth amendment right to refuse to answer); stonewall. See REJECT.

REFUSE CREDIT v. lower the boom, cut off, cut up one's card.

REFUSED adj. nixed, burned, cut, dead, killed, turned down, put down, passed on, passed over, thrown over, left at the church, got it in the neck, kicked in the ass, punched out, out in the cold, feel adrift, thank you but no thank you.

REFUTE v. shoot down, shoot full of holes, top, squelch, poke full of holes, blow sky high, knock the bottom out of, knock the chocks out from under, knock the props out from under; burn, burn down, pass, pass on, pass by, throw out, turn thumbs down on, thumb down, kill.

REGAIN v. get out from under, get well, make well.

REGARD v. flash, flash on, eye, eagle eye, eyeball, beam, spy, dig, read, lamp, pipe, rap, rumble, check this out, bus it (Af. Am.), lay one's glims on, get a hinge, give the eye, get a load of, pipe. See SEE.

REGIMENTATION n. pecking order, down the line.

REGION n. territory, turf, hood, neck of the woods, stomping ground, ghetto, inner city, the jungle (crowded city), skid row, slum, zoo, high-rent district, burb, slurb. See DISTRICTS.

REGISTER v. sign on, sign up, sign up for, weigh in.

REGISTRATION n. sign-up.

REGRESS v. backslide, roll back.

REGRET v. kick oneself, cry over spilled milk.

REGULATE v. pull the strings, pull the wires, pull things together, shape up, straighten up, deal with. See MANAGE.

REGULATION adj. up to code, G, according to the book, according to Hoyle, kosher, S.O.P.

REGULATIONS n. regs, the book, by the numbers, by the book, chapter and verse, no-no's, bible (authoritative book).

REGURGITATE v. barf, puke, zuke, be sick, throw up, upchuck, urp, whoops, boag, water buffalo, yak, yank, Ralph, Ralph up, talking to Ralph on the big white phone, to the curb, reverse gears, shoot one's cookies, flash one's cookies, blow one's lunch, the technicolor yawn, drive the porcelain bus. See VOMIT.

REHABILITATE v. rehab.

REHABILITATION n. rehab.

REHEARSAL n. dry run, runthrough, call, shakedown, shakedown cruise, tryout, workout, dress, blocking.

REHEARSE v. run lines, run through, walk through, take it from the top, tune up, dry run, hone, warm up, work out. See also PRACTICE.

REIGN v. head up, boss, helm, ride herd on, sit on top of, run, run things, run the show, be in the driver's seat, rule the roost. See MANAGE.

REIMBURSE v. square, square things, make up for, pay one's dues.

REIMBURSEMENT n. payoff, kickback. See also PAYMENT.

REINFORCE v. 1. boost, stroke, build up, pick up, lend a hand, hype, hold a brief for, go to bat for, stand up for, back up, carry one, prop, prop up. See SUPPORT. 2. beef up, soup up, punch up, heat up, hot up, hop up, jazz up, juice up, build up, add fuel to the fire.

REITERATE v. play back, rehash, recap, recheck, double-check, check and double-check, come again, ditto, echo, one more time, una mas, run that by one once more, say again, go over the same ground, go the same round, chew one's cabbage twice.

REITERATION n. recap, rehash, replay, playback, echo.

REJECT v. 1. eighty-six, adios, heave-ho, dog, junk, throw away, throw out, throw on the junk heap, chuck, chuck out, round-file. See DISCARD. 2. pass by, pass on, pass up, Pasadena, blow off, nix, not (used at end of a positive sentence), splash, put down, turn down, turn thumbs down on, spike, blackball, ice, ice out, kill, chop, burn, burn down, shoot down, neg, not buy, not hear of, break with, ain't with that (Af. Am.), back up (refuse to do something), blackball, roof, cut, snip, zing, ding, piss on, shit on, drop, cold-shoul-der, high-hat, dump, ditch, air, flush, brush off, fluff off, give one the fluff, send one to the showers, hand one his walking papers, give one the air, give one the go-by, give one the gate, give one the wind, stay away from, swear off, kick in the ass, kick in the teeth, slap in the face, buck, hell no, like hell I will, thank you but no thank you, not touch one with a ten-foot pole.

REJECTED adj. out in the cold, nixed, burned, iced, cut, dead, killed, turned down, put down, passed on, passed over, thrown over, left at the church, got it in the neck, kicked in the ass, punched out, feel adrift.

REJECTION n. turndown, nix, not (used at end of a positive sentence), put down, pass, pass on, Pasadena, ding, thumbs down, spike, no go, no dice, no way, no way José, November Foxtrot Whiskey (no fucking way), fuck that noise, bump that, yank on that, nothing doing, you should live so long, the gate, bounce, grand bounce, kick in the ass, kick in the teeth, slap in the face, lumps, include me out, over my dead body, bite me, like hell I will, I'll see you in hell first, fubis (fuck you buddy, I'm shipping out), brushoff, call-down, cold shoulder, cut, go-by, hard time (sexual), walking papers.

REJOINDER n. lip, sass, topper, talk back, backtalk, snappy comeback, wisecrack. See ANSWER

REJUVENATE v. doll up, face-lift, retread, rehab, spruce, spruce up, do, do up.

RELATE v. 1. run down, run through, track, picture, sing, spill, spill the beans, unload, bull, bullshit, throw the bull, shoot the bull, shoot the shit, shoot the bullshit, shoot, shoot the breeze, shoot the lemon, let one's hair down, sling the crap, fess, fess up, verbalize, put one in the picture, lay it on the line, lay it out for, let in on, let in on the know, let it all hang out, bring it out into the daylight, bring it out into the open, get it off one's chest, get it out of one's system, give with, give a pointer to, give one the word, break it to one, clue one in, break a story, spin a yarn. 2. connect, contact, have truck with, make up to, in, in with, run with, swing, swing with, be one of the boys. See COMMUNICATE. 3. get your jib on, get your mac on, get your scam on, get your skippies on (try and start a relationship). 4. stack up against, match up, hang (how does that hang?), hold a candle to.

RELATION n. 1. tie-in, network, hookup. 2. kinfolk, kissin' cousin, shirttail kin, shirtail relatives, blood.

RELATIONSHIP n. tie-in, network, hookup. See ASSOCIATION.

RELATIVES n. folks, P's, peeps, rents (parents), home folks, kinfolk, kissin' cousin, shirttail kin, shirtail relatives, blood.

RELAX v. chill out, chillin', take a chill pill, chill hard, unlax, break, breeze, knock off, gel, come up for air, kick back, kick in, take a blow, blow on it, suck it easy, get naked, be sword (street talk), easin', lampin', hangin', take a break, take a breather, take five, take ten, take it easy, take time out, take the air out of the ball, at ease, neg, veg out, veg off, caulk off, catch forty winks, flake out, flop, goof off, recharge one's batteries, coast, cool it, cool out, cool your jets, eyes to cool it, chiz, don't sweat it, go with the flow, hang easy, hang loose, lay back, let go, let it all hang out, let it all happen, let it all out, mellow out, mellow up, lighten up, ease up on, give some slack, go easy on, let up on.

RELAXED adj. cas, cazh, cool, loose, loose as a goose, mellow, folksy, homey, haimish (Yid.), laid-back, let one's hair down. See CASUAL.

RELEARN v. go over, brush up, run through, take a refresher.

RELEASE n. 1. handout, the dope, the goods, scoop, leak, poop, poop sheet, shirttail (brief news story), skinny. 2. lifeboat, lifesaver, clemo, commute, spring, floater, forty-eight, forty-eighter, turnout, twenty-four, walkout, a D.O.R. (on one's own recognizance).

RELEASE v. 1. go easy on, let up on, wipe the slate clean, lifeboat, hand out clemo, commute, spring, put out on the street, turn out, bail out, get a floater, get hours, get a twenty-four. See FREE. 2. blow one's mind, blow on it, leak, let go, let off steam, unlax.

RELEASED adj. out, back on the street, beat the rap, sprung, walked, let off, let go.

RELEASE FROM CUSTODY n. spring, turnout, floater, forty-eight, forty-eighter, twenty-four, walk-out, a D.O.R. (on one's own recognizance).

RELEASE FROM CUSTODY v. spring, turn out, bail out, get a floater, get hours, get a twenty-four, put on the street, put on the pavement, put on the sidewalk, put on the bricks.

RELEASE INTESTINAL GAS v. fart, crack a fart, rip, rip one, toot, fluff, let one go, let one rip, break wind, cut one, cut the cheese, leave one, let one fly, queef, step on a frog, backfire, nose closer, the butler's revenge (silent).

RELEGATE v. kiss off, buck off.

RELENT v. lighten up, ease up on, give some slack, go easy on, let up on, fold, quit, cool it, cool out, lay back, hang loose, cave in, give up, give in, say uncle, cry uncle, pull in one's horns, go along with, let go, let it all hang out, let it all happen, mellow out. See also SOFTEN, RELAX, SURRENDER.

RELENTLESS adj. dead set on, hell bent on, bound, bound and determined, stop at nothing, go for broke, hang in, hang tough, mean business. See DETERMINED.

RELEVANT adj. on the button, on the nose, on target, right on, that's the ticket, just what the doctor ordered.

RELIABLE adj. there, count on one, one who always delivers, one who always comes through, always there in a pinch, rock, Rock of Gibraltar. See TRUSTWORTHY.

RELIEF n. light at the end of the tunnel, fix, quick fix.

RELIEVE v. 1. take a load off, take a load off one's mind, take the load off one's chest. 2. yank, pull.

RELIEVED adj. cool, breathe easy, got it off one's chest, load off one's mind.

RELIGIOUS adj. born-again, got religion, knee bender, Jesus lover, Jesus freak, Mary, Holy Joe, Jasper, goody, goody-goody, goody two-shoes, scoutmaster.

RELINQUISH v. give up, swear off, quit cold turkey, take the oath, drop, drop out, drop like a hot potato, opt out, back down, stand down, kiss good-bye, dump, cut loose, kick, ditch.

RELY ON v. 1. bank on, bet on, bet one's bottom dollar on, gamble on, lay money on. See BELIEVE. 2. ride on one's coattails, carry the load, carry the mail.

REMAIN v. sit tight, stay put, stick around, squat, nest, bunk, hang, hang out, perch, put on hold, roost, hold the fort, freeze, deep-freeze.

REMAINDER adj. bottom of the barrel, leftovers, pot likker.

REMAINS n. 1. cold meat, dead meat, stiff, croppy, cage. 2. broken arm (table scraps). 3. leftovers, pot likker.

REMARK n. backtalk, crack, one's two cents' worth, comeback, wisecrack.

REMARK v. 1. mouth off, crack, spring with a crack, wisecrack. See SPEAK. 2. flash on, get a load of, pick up on, spot, take in, catch. See SEE.

REMARKABLE adj. killer, a gas, 10, ten, super, smashing, gnarly, mega-gnarly, motherfucker (Obsc.), zero cool, chilly most, wicked, nose cone, gilt-edged, splash, primo, world-class, cosmic, solid, Jake, ginchy, slammin', fabu, mongo, greatest, cherry, deffest, dope, dual, fierce, fresh, fully on, fully, mint, nitro, on the strength, raw, sick, stupid fresh, lampin', happenin', cranking, fat. See EXCELLENT.

REMEDY n. fix, quick fix.

REMEDY v. 1. launder, debug, doctor, fly-speck, scrub, clean up, pick up, shape up, fix up, go over, fiddle with. 2. make up for, pay one's dues, square, square up, square the beef. 3. straighten out, clean up one's act, get one's act together, upgrade, recalibrate, dial back, turn things around. See CORRECT.

REMEMBER v. flash, flash on, nail it down, rings a bell, it struck a note, all of a sudden it came to me, came to me that, came to me like it was yesterday.

REMEMBRANCE n. flashback, flash-on.

REMISS adj. pay no mind, looking out the window, out to lunch, asleep at the switch, asleep on the job, daydreaming, woolgathering, slapdash, any old way, any which way, by halves. See CARELESS.

REMODEL v. redo, rehab, retrofit, doll up, face-lift, retread, fix up, gussy up, spruce, spruce up, do, do up.

REMONSTRATE v. pitch a bitch, beef, sound off, rain, push out one's lips. See COMPLAIN.

REMOTE adj. 1. cold, cool, cool cat, on ice, dog it, dog up, laid-back, offish, standoffish, put on airs, stuck-up, uppity. See ALOOF. 2. gone (from reality), turned off, out to lunch, spaced-out. 3. clear to hell and gone, to hell and gone, far piece, long chalk, boondocks, boonies, tullies, B.F.E., butt fucking Egypt, B.F.A., butt fucking Africa, on the dance floor but can't hear the band, God knows where, middle of nowhere. See FAR.

REMOTE CONTROL n. clicker.

REMOVAL n. ax, boot, bounce, bum's rush, kicking out, old heave-ho, pink slip, the gate, early retirement, executive fallout (business), the bullet, walking papers, walking ticket. See DISMISSAL.

REMOVE v. 1. junk, chuck, chuck out, adios, eighty-six, 86, deep six, dog, heave-ho, throw away, throw overboard, throw on the junk heap. See ERADICATE. 2. kick out, boot out, drum out, bounce, give one the old heave-ho, adios one, send packing, show the door, give the gate, give one his walking papers, give 'em the 1–2–3, ice out, lock out (labor dispute), wash out, shut out. See EJECT. 3. liquidate, wipe out, sanitize, sterilize, compromise (espionage use), scratch, dust, waste, off, knock off. See KILL. 4. drag, drag down, take down (bet).

REMOVED adj. 1. unfrocked (any profession), drummed-out, turned-off, dropped, washed-out, washed-up, all washed up, scratched, scrubbed, dogged, adiosed, eighty-sixed, offed, wasted. 2. gone (from reality), far out, out of it, out to lunch, play it cool, spaced-out.

REMUNERATE v. spring for bread, shell out, come down with, cough up, ante up, plank up, pony up, dish it out, fork up, post, pay off, pay up, pay to the tune of, do business. See PAY.

REMUNERATION n. 1. bread, sugar, bacon, bring home the bacon, take, take-home, eagle shit, peanuts, coffee and cakes (small); fogy, fogey (Mil.); double dipping (compensation from two government agencies). 2. walking-around money, cash on the nail, hush money, street money, grease, schmear, under the table, on the take, juice. 3. toke (gambling), tip, chip, cue, somethin', a little somethin'; subway, bus ride (small tip), palm oil, gravy, zukes. 4. strokes, brownie button (Hum.), feather in one's cap, plum, what's in it for one. See COMPENSATION.

REMUNERATIVE adj. sweet, in the black, going, going concern, paid off.

RENDEZVOUS n. 1. date, heavy date, blind date, gig, double date, meet; miss a meet, stand one up, stand one on a corner (fail to keep a); zero hour; creep, triff, treff (secret). 2. love nest, spot, matinee, noonie, one-night stand, quickie, your place or mine.

RENEGADE n. rat, rat fink, double-crosser, Benedict Arnold, hairball, fifth columnist, quisling, snake, snake in the grass. See also TRAITOR.

RENEGE v. back off, fudge, dial back, go back on one's word, weasel out, worm one's way out, worm out of, welsh, renig, nig, back-water, crawfish, crawfish out, eat crow, eat humble pie.

RENEW v. doll up, fix up, gussy up, spruce, spruce up, do, do up, redo, face-lift, retread, rehab.

RENEWAL n. face lift, born again, fresh start, retread.

RENEWED adj. born again.

RENOUNCE v. 1. swear off, take the pledge, get on the wagon, get on the water wagon. 2. drop out, opt out, dump, throw over, toss over, throw overboard, walk out on, wash one's hands of, change one's tune, change one's song, chuck, cop out, sell out, leave flat, ditch, run out on, shake, ding, piss on, put down. See also ABJURE. 3. shit on, shove it, stick it, stow it, heave-ho, hell no, like hell I will, nix, stick it up one's ass, shove it up one's ass, kiss good-bye, take some hide and hair.

RENOVATE v. doll up, fix up, gussy up, spruce, spruce up, do, do up, face-lift, retread.

RENOWNED adj. big-name, biggie, big-league, celeb, star, superstar, name, number one, a somebody, w.k. (well known), face, in the limelight, make a splash, page-oner, monster, face card, major-league, hooper-dooper. See CELEBRATED; CELEBRITY.

RENT PARTY n. percolator, shake.

REORGANIZATION n. housecleaning, sweep, clean sweep, sweep with a broom, shake up, hatchet man (reorganizer).

REPAIR v. fix up, doctor, fiddle with, face-lift, retread, debug, red-line (Mil.), easy fix.

REPAIR SHOP n. fix-it shop.

REPARATION, MAKE v. make up for, make good, square things, pay one's dues.

REPAST n. chow, chow time, feed, bite, snack, snack time, takeout, BBQ, barbecue, rib joint, slab house, cookout, tailgate party, brunch, do lunch, din-din, square meal, blue plate, black plate (soul food), Chinx (Chinese), pot luck, coffee and, sit-down dinner. See MEAL.

REPAY v. square, square things, square a beef, make up for, pay one's dues, scratch one's back, you scratch mine and I'll scratch yours. See also PAY.

REPEAL v. scrub, nix, call off, call all bets off, renig, kill, shoot down, shoot down in flames, wipe out, blow the deal, forget it, get off the hook, X out, kibosh, put the kibosh on, zap, kayo, KO, wash out, opt out, back out, back out of, backpedal, back-water, weasel out, worm out of, crawl out of, wangle out of, crawfish out, pull the plug, pull in one's horns, draw in one's horns, draw in one's claws, cut loose, stand down, quit cold, leave flat, throw over.

REPEALED adj. scrubbed, killed, shot, shot down, shot down in flames, washed-out, wiped-out, all bets off, all off, kaput, zapped.

REPEAT v. play back, rehash, recap, recheck, double-check, check and double-check, again, come again, ditto, echo, do like, go like, make like, one more time, una mas, run over, run that by one once more, say again, go over the same ground, go the same round, chew one's cabbage twice.

REPEATED adj. string, run, streak, row, straight (seven straight=seven in a row), chain, come again, two-time, two-time loser, three-time.

REPEATER adj. backslider, two-time loser. See also RECIDIVIST.

REPEL v. 1. gross out, turn off, scuzz one out, give one a pain, give one a pain in the neck, give one a pain in the ass. 2. brush off, cut, high-hat, cold-shoulder, cool, cool off, cool down, put down, turn down, turn thumbs down, not buy, not hear of, kick one in the ass, kick one in the teeth, slap one in the face, back up (refuse to do something), no go, nothing doing. See also REJECT.

REPELLED adj. grossed-out, turned-off, ech, eeeooo, gives one a pain in the ass. See DISGUSTED.

REPELLING adj. gross, grossed-out, grody, grody to the max, gagger, scank, pukey, pukoid, scurvy, skewy, icky, yecchy, yucky, turn-off. See DISGUSTING.

REPERCUSSION n. fallout, reaction, chain reaction, flak (bad), follow-up, follow-through, can of worms, spin-off, waves, feedback, kickback, shit hit the fan, it's your funeral. See RESULT.

REPERTOIRE n. schtick, book, rep, routine.

REPERTORY n. routine, rep, rep show, rep company (The.), shtick, gag, stunt, bit, chaser, afterpiece, stand-up comedy, dumb act (without words), hoke act.

REPLACE v. pinch-hit for, sub, sub for, swap places with, sit in, stand in, back up, fill in, take over, front for, ring, ring in, take out, step into the shoes of.

REPLACEMENT n. backup, spare, sub, stand-in, fill-in, pinch hitter, pinch runner, off the bench, bench warmer, ringer, second-string, third-string, switcheroo; newby, new-fer (both Mil.); dog chaser (R.R.).

REPLACEMENT DEPOT n. repple depple, rep dep, reppo depot.

REPLICA n. dupe, carbon, clone, ditto, mimeo, stat, xerox, repro, lookalike, workalike, flimsy, chip off the old block.

REPLICATE v. 1. knock off, fax, dupe, xerox, carbon, clone, mimeo, ditto, stat, repro. 2. act like, do, do like, go like, make like, mirror, take off as, do a take-off, play the ——— (affect a role). 3. steal one's stuff, pirate, knock off, bite, take a leaf out of one's book.

REPLY n. feedback, comeback, vibes, snappy comeback, sass, lip, backtalk, crackback, wisecrack, cooler, knee-jerk reaction (expected). See also RESPONSE.

REPLY v. answer back, shoot back, come back at, get back to one, be in touch with one, feedback, field the question, sass, squelch, top, crack. See ANSWER.

REPORT n. rundown, handout, the dope, the goods, picture, scoop, poop, ABC's, blow-by-blow, make, break, beat, earful, ear duster, chip, hash, haymaker, hot shot, hot wire; kick in the ass, shot in the ass (bad); are you ready for this?, page-oner, the latest, shirttail (brief news story), what's happenin'?, what's going down?, latrine rumor, scuttlebutt; black plague, dirty tricks, nut cracking, rat fucking (unfounded). See also NEWS.

REPORT v. put it out, put it on the street, spread it around, pass the word, drum, call, trumpet, track (narrate a sequence of events), debrief, break a story, weigh in. See also ANNOUNCE.

REPORTER n. animal (political campaign), jib-rat (reports war from distance), commuter hooter (traffic), columnist, anchor, anchorman, anchorwoman, newscaster, leg man, news hen, cub, stringer, ink slinger, scrivener, scribe, pen driver, pen pusher, pencil driver, pencil pusher, scratcher.

REPORTER, NEWSPAPER n. scribe, scrivener, columnist, stringer, leg man, news hen, cub, pen driver, pen pusher, pencil driver, pencil pusher, scratcher, ink slinger.

REPORTER, TV n. anchor, anchorwoman, anchorman, newscaster, leg man, stringer, jib-rat (reports war from distance).

REPOSSESS v. repo.

REPRESENT v. 1. front for, rep, stand in for, pinch hit for, sub, carry the water. 2. picture, run through, run down, track.

REPRESENTATIVE n. 1. hired gun, rep, front. 2. nature of the beast, that's one all over, just like one, what you see is what you get, WYSIWYG.

REPRESENTING adj. repping, fronting for, standing in for.

REPRESS v. 1. ice, put on ice, cool, cool off, cool out, cool down, bottle up, cork, cork up, box in, get one in a box, hog-tie, tie up, jam up, bring to a screaming halt, gridlock, lock up, put a lock on, put a stopper in, black out, put the lid on, keep the lid on, keep buttoned up, keep under one's hat, keep under wraps, put a half nelson on, bum out, bum one out, put the chill on, put the damper on, put the kibosh on, queer, kill, spike, squash, squelch, scrub, gag, muzzle, shut up, can it, ding, zing, nix, hush up, throw a monkey wrench into, throw cold water on, throw a wet blanket on, cut off one's water, turn off one's water, put off, turn off, put on hold, hold down, strong-arm, put the arm on, twist one's arm, pressure, put under pressure, put the heat on, put down, Chinese solution (brutal, as in Tienanmen Square), crack down on, clamp down on, shut down, sit on, put the scare on, throw a scare into, put the screws on, take care of, kid out of, talk out of, cramp one's style, hedge in, not go off the deep end. 2. bleep, blue-pencil, cut, decontaminate, launder, sanitize, sterilize, clean up. 3. keep it down, soft-pedal, dummy up, dry up, clam up, close up like a clam, pipe down, shut one's trap, shut one's mouth, shut one's face, button up, button one's lip, sit on, decrease the volume, mum's the word, drink one's beer. See also SILENCE.

REPRESSED adj. hung-up, uptight, tight-assed, square.

REPRIEVE n. lifesaver, anchor, lifeboat, clemo, commute, spring.

REPRIEVE v. let one off this time, let it go, let up on, lifeboat, hand out clemo.

REPRIMAND n. rap, rap on the knuckles, gig, comeuppance, rag, rag on, slap on the wrist, piece of one's mind, bawling out, calling down, jacking up, going over, ragging, grooming, what for, hell to pay, hard time, assbite. See ADMONITION. See also SCOLDING.

REPRIMAND v. kick ass and take names, have someone's ass, fire on, rip on, chew out, eat out, bawl out, ream out, light into, lower the boom, have one on the carpet, have one on the mat, call on the carpet, call down, dress down, come down on, rap one's knuckles, slap on the wrist, tell off, give what for, give a piece of one's mind, give one the dickens, give one hail Columbia. See REBUKE.

REPRINT n. stat, dupe, xerox, carbon, mimeo, ditto, knockoff (illegal).

REPRISE v. come again, one more time, uno mas.

REPROACH v. fire on, rip on, chew out one's ass, bawl out, ream, cuss out, lay out, dog on (verbal), sit on, light into, jaw, jawbone, rake, trim, call to task, call down, dress down, attend to, give what for, give a going over, give one the devil, give one his comeuppance, rag on. See REBUKE.

REPROBATE n. corn dog, Captain Cheddar, sleaze-ball, bad egg, heel, shit, turd, stinker, louse, rat, creep, black sheep, rotter, rounder. See SCOUNDREL.

REPRODUCE v. knock off, pirate, clone, carbon, dupe, mimeo, stat, xerox, ditto; bite, steal one's stuff (illegally). See COPY.

REPRODUCTION n. stat, clone, fax, ditto, dupe, mimeo, xerox, carbon, carbon copy, repro, flimsy, look-alike, fake, not what it's cracked up to be, twin, chip off the old block. See COPY.

REPRODUCTIVE FLUID n. come, cum, cream, spew, spoo, spooch, splooge, jisum, jizum.

REPROOF n. rap on the knuckles, slap on the wrist, comeuppance, piece of one's mind, calling down, jacking up, going over, ragging, what-for, hell to pay, hard time. See ADMONITION.

REPROVE v. hit, hit on, trash, ping (Mil.), zing, zap, knock, pan, slam, slug, slog, bag on (Hum.), base on, blast on, eat out one's ass, read one out, jump on one's shit, give a going-over, give one his comeuppance, needle, give one the needle, give one the raspberry, let one have it, cut down to size, sock it to one, stick it to one, swipe at, snipe at, take a dim view. See SCOLD.

REPUBLICAN PARTY n. GOP, G.O.P., Grand Old Party.

REPUBLICANS n. GOP, G.O.P., Good Old Party, Grand Old Party, Gypsy Moths, Ripons.

REPUDIATE v. break with, nix, not (used at end of a positive sentence), be agin, dump, fly in the face of, flush, wash one's hands of. See REJECT.

REPUDIATED adj. burned, cut, dead, feel adrift, killed, thrown over, passed over, passed on, put down.

REPUDIATION n. nix, not (used at end of a positive sentence), slap in the face, stick it up your ass, forget you, bag that, get bent, bite off, over my dead body, you should live so long, not a chance. See DENIAL.

REPUGNANCE n. allergy to, no use for.

REPUGNANT adj. creepy, sleazy, sleazeball, sludge-ball, gagger, slime bucket, shower scum, maggoty, bad case of the uglies, it rots, poxy, scurvy, scuzzo, scuzzy, shitsky, skewy, gross, grody, bunk, mutant, beastly, lame, pail, bucket, rum-dum, low rider, nic-nac, punk, gunsel, cocksucker. See UNDESIRABLE. See also UGLY.

REPULSE n. nix, turndown, thumbs-down, no way José, nothing doing, kick in the ass, kick in the teeth, slap in the face, lumps, brushoff, cold shoulder, go-by, the gate, hard time (sexual). See REJECTION.

REPULSE v. put down, brush off, heave-ho, nix, ice, fluff off, kick in the teeth. See REJECT. 2. gross out, turn off, scuzz one out, give one a pain, give one a pain in the neck, give one a pain in the ass.

REPULSIVE adj. 1. creepy, stinky, gagger, sleazy, sleazeball, sludgeball, slime bucket, maggot, spastic, funky (Af. Am.), cruddy, dorky, earth pig, shower scum, grimbo, gross, grody, bunk, off-putting. See UNDESIRABLE. 2. limburger (girl no one will date), pig, mole, dog, airedale, turd poodle, animal, beast, beat, plug-ugly, butt-ugly, scugly (Af. Am.), scag, scurvy, scuzzo, scuzzy, shitsky, shitburger, bad case of the uglies, bat, boo hog, bama, barfola; paper-bag case, double-bagger, triple-bagger, hagged out (Fem.), fart face, pruneface, homely as a mud fence. See UGLY. See also UNDESIRABLE PERSON.

REPUTABLE adj. Christian, true Christian, mensch, pillar of the church, salt of the earth. See VIRTUOUS.

REPUTATION n. rep.

REQUEST v. put in for, hit, hit up, touch, bite, bum, hustle, promote, make, mooch, schnor, score, sponge, nick, burn, pivot, pling, knock, make a touch, put the touch on, put the bite on, put the bee on, put the sleeve on, hold out for, pop the question, whistle for (but won't get). See also BEG.

REQUESTS n. commercials (band or orchestra).

REQUIRING adj. hurting for, needy. See also DESIRE.

REQUISITION v. put in for, dibs on something. See also APPROPRIATE.

RESCIND v. call off, call all bets off, scrub, nix, not (used at end of a positive sentence), renig, forget it, X out, wash out, back out of, backpedal, backwater, weasel out, worm out of, crawl out of, wangle out of, crawfish out, pull the plug, pull in one's horns. See REPEAL.

RESCUE v. bail one out, save one's ass, save one's neck, save one's bacon, give one a break, get one out of hock, get one off the hook, spring, pull something out of the fire, pull one's chestnuts out of the fire.

RESEARCH n. legwork, cut and try, R and D, fishing expedition, bottoms-up research (in depth).

RESEARCH v. cut and try, give it a go, fool around with, play around with, mess around.

RESEARCH CENTER n. think tank, skunk works (usually secret), lab, chem lab.

RESEARCHER n. numbers cruncher, mad doctor.

RESEMBLANCE n. two of a kind, look-alike, birds of a feather, like of, likes of, peas in a pod, ringer, dead ringer, spitting image, carbon, carbon copy, double.

RESEMBLE v. favor, double.

RESENT v. feel sore, have one's nose out of joint, rubbed the wrong way, put off by.

RESENTFUL adj. crabby, cranky, grousing, grouchy, sore, uptight, have one's nose out of joint, beefing, bugged, pissed, pissed-off, a bug up one's ass, on one's ear, get up on one's ear. See also DISCONTENTED.

RESENTMENT n. a bug up one's ass, rise, fog.

RESERVATION n. 1. string, string to it, catch, joker, kicker, fine print, fine print at the bottom with a grain of salt. See RESTRICTION. 2. res. See also APPOINTMENT.

RESERVE n. ace in the hole, stash, stache, plant, drop, nest egg; the bank, bankroll, nut, backing, budget, rainy day, sock, mattressful. See also ASSETS.

RESERVE v. 1. stash, stache, ditch, duck, plant; squirrel, squirrel away. 2. hold (hold the mayo), hold out on. 3. book, put a hold on, lay away. See SAVE.

RESERVE ASSET n. ace in the hole, ace up one's sleeve, on a string.

RESERVE, IN adj. deep, on a string, depth, string one along.

RESERVE OFFICERS TRAINING CORPS n. ROTC, Rotacy, Rot corps, Rot see, Rotasie.

RESERVED adj. 1. cool, cool customer, cold fish, ice in one's veins, icicle, clam, tight-lipped. See also SHY. 2. booked, held, laid-away.

RESERVED-SEAT TICKET n. hard ticket.

RESIDE v. bunk, bunk out, hang out, crash, nest, perch, roost, squat, locate, park, hole up, hang up one's hat, hang up one's shingle. See INHABIT.

RESIDENCE n. pad, crash pad, box, cave, condo, co-op, coop, domi, dommy, digs, dibs, roof over one's head, hole, home plate, rack, hooch, (Vietnam), roost. See HOUSE.

RESIDENT n. cliff dweller (apartment), dug-in, home guard, townie.

RESIDUE n. leftovers, pot likker.

RESIGN v. ankle, quit cold, quit cold turkey, drop, bow out, chuck, chuck it, fold, take a walk, give up, hang it up, throw in the towel, throw in the sponge, throw over, toss over, walk out on, wash one's hands of, pull the plug, punk out, pull the pin, pull out, cave in, cry uncle, chicken out, drop out, give up the ship, kiss good-bye, binch (job), pack in, pack it in, knock off, stand down, cry off, come off, drag it, hang up one's spurs, run out on, walk out on, bail out, opt out, cut loose, kick, swear off, cop out, bag it.

RESILIENCE n. bounce, vim and vigor, zip, staying power.

RESILIENT, BE v. roll with the punches, snap back, bounce. See also CHEERFUL.

RESIST v.   1. be agin, go agin, buck, stonewall, cross, lock horns with, face off, fight off, go one on one, turn thumbs down on. See OPPOSE. 2. fly in the face of, cross, make my day, go on make my day, hang tough, take one on, call one's bluff, stand up and be counted, not take lying down, stick to one's guns. See CONFRONT. 3. tangle with, tangle ass with, buck, bump heads with, cross swords with, lock horns with, put up an argument. See FIGHT. 4. beef, bitch, leed, make a stink, gripe, griping, pop off, gritch, sound off, squawk, put up a squawk, kvetch, bellyache, blast, crab, cut a beef. See COMPLAIN.

RESISTANT adj.   hard-nosed, hardliner, a wall, stonewall, like talking to the wall, like water off a duck's back, like getting blood from a turnip.

RESOLUTE adj.   dead set on, hang tough, stick to one's guns, mean business, mean serious jelly, no bird turdin', be out for blood. See DETERMINED.

RESOLUTION n.   all the right moves, pay dirt, the ticket, the nod, the call, quick fix, Band-Aid (temporary, too little).

RESOLUTION TRUST COMPANY n.   R.T.C.

RESOLVE v.   deal with, make a deal, chill, dope, dope out, pan out, figure out, crack, lick, done deal, iron, iron out, nail down, cinch, clinch, unzip, work through, hit it on the nose.

RESORT n.   tourist trap, hideaway, hideout, fat farm, banana belt, Borscht Belt.

RESOURCE n.   the bank, bankroll, nut, nest egg, rainy day, sock, mattressful, kitty, stake, backing, budget, ace in the hole, ace up one's sleeve (hidden), stuff, the goods, basics. See ASSETS. See also MONEY.

RESPECTED adj.   touted, highly touted, okay people, score, aces with, in with, daddy (The.).

RESPITE n.   time, time out, five, take five, downtime, break, coffee break, breather, breathing spell, freeze, piss call (Mil.); happy hour, attitude adjustment hour (cocktail hour), letup, layoff.

RESPOND v.   1. feel for, feel in one's bones, feel in one's guts, be turned on to, hear one, get in touch, have a funny feeling, have heart, have a hunch, have good vibes, have vibes. 2. answer back, talk back, shoot back, come back at, get back to one, be in touch with one, feedback, field the question, crack. See ANSWER.

RESPONSE n.   vibes, feedback, comeback, snappy comeback, sass, lip, backtalk, crackback, wisecrack, kick, kickback, mug (comic), take, take it big, double-take, hit, cooler, knee-jerk reaction (expected), gut reaction.

RESPONSIBILITY n.   where the buck stops, rap, take the rap, one's ass, one's neck, albatross, albatross around one's neck, can, carry the can, holding the bag, holding the sack. See also DUTY.

RESPONSIBLE adj.   1. taking care of business, TCB, minding the store, on the hook, carry the load, on one's back. 2. straight-arrow, there, count on one, right guy, rock, Rock of Gibraltar. See TRUSTWORTHY.

REST n.   1. break, coffee break, lunch break, breakoff, cutoff, layoff, letup, come up for air, blow, breather, breathing spell, five, ten, time out, downtime, goof-off time, time to burn, time to kill, one's own sweet time, piss call (Mil.), snooze, bunk fatigue (WWII), R and R. 2. leftovers, pot likker, bottom of the barrel.

REST v.   chill out, chillin', take a chill pill, cool your jets, unlax, veg out, kick in, knock off, blow on it, chiz, take a blow, take a break, at ease, flake out, kick it back, lay back, let it all hang out. See RELAX.

RESTATE v.   recap, rehash, go over the same ground, go the same round. See REPEAT.

RESTAURANT n.   eatery, pit stop, drive-in, hamburger heaven, burger joint, after joint, short-order joint, grease joint, ham joint, fast-food joint, rib joint, slab house; scarf and barf, pork and puke (fast-food restaurant), McDucks, Mickey-D's, chop suey joint, Chinks, Chinx, hash house, chop house, soup house, slop house, sloppy Joe, hideaway, ham and eggery, coffee bar, coffeepot, beanery, bean wagon, chuck wagon, dog wagon, greasy spoon, grease ball, grease trough, bistro, water hole, noshery, hashery, hash foundry, doughnut foundry, doughnut factory, doughnut house, doughnut joint, goulash, chew and choke, cook shack, caf, quick and dirty, Coney Island; micro, brew pub (contains small brewery).

RESTAURANT TERMS   draw one (coffee), BLT (bacon lettuce and tomato), hold ——— (e.g., hold the mayo), burn one (Coke), stretch it (large), hang a draw (large root beer), squeeze one (orange juice); fish eggs, eight eyes (tapioca pudding); sweep up the kitchen for one (hash), Adam and Eve on a raft (poached eggs on toast), wreck 'em (scramble eggs), eighty-six (out of item); on wheels, to go (take out).

RESTITUTION, MAKE v.   square things, pay one's dues, make up for, make good. See also REFUND.

RESTLESS adj.   jittery, jumpy, strung-out, twitty, bundle of nerves, yantsy, antsy, antsy-pantsy, ants in one's pants, itchy, in a dither, on edge, rarin' to go, on pins and needles, on tenterhooks. See ANXIOUS.

RESTLESSNESS n.   ants, ants in one's pants, antsy, antsy-pantsy, fantobs.

RESTORATIVE n.   go juice, pick-me-up, pickup, shot in the arm.

RESTORE v. doll up, fix up, gussy up, spruce, spruce up, do, do up, face lift, retread, rehab, pick up the pieces. See also FIX.

REST PERIOD n. five, take five, take ten, time, time out, break, coffee break, breather, breathing spell, freeze, piss call (Mil.); happy hour, attitude adjustment hour (cocktail hour), letup, goof-off, fuck-off, layoff.

RESTRAIN v. cool, cool off, cool out, cool down, keep the lid on, bottle up, cork, cork up, box in, get one in a box, cuff, hog-tie, tie up, jam up, gridlock, lock up, put a lock on, put a stopper in, bring to a screaming halt, put a half nelson on, put the chill on, kill, spike, throw a monkey wrench into, throw cold water on, throw a wet blanket on, cut off one's water, turn off one's water, put off, turn off, hold, hold down, strong-arm, put the arm on, twist one's arm, pressure, put under pressure, put the heat on, shut down on, sit on, sit down on, put the scare on, throw a scare into, put the screws on, take care of, kid out of, talk out of, cramp one's style, hedge in, not go off the deep end. See also HINDER.

RESTRAINED adj. 1. cool, cool and collected, laid-back, dealing with, got a handle on it, hip, ice man, in charge, in the driver's seat. See CALM. 2. hung-up, a narb, square, tight-assed, uptight, iced, chilled, bottled-up, corked-up, hog-tied. See JAILED.

RESTRAINT n. 1. hang-up, catch, lock, excess baggage, stumbling block, foot dragging, glitch, joker, one small difficulty. 2. juice, string, rope, weight. See HINDRANCE. See also PROHIBITION.

RESTRICT v. 1. ice, put on ice, put away, send up. See JAIL. 2. cool down, hold down, hold back, hang up, bottle up, cork up, box in, hog-tie, gridlock, lock up, put a half nelson on, hedge in. See RESTRAIN.

RESTRICTED adj. 1. hog-tied, iced, chilled, bottled-up, corked-up, held-down, held-back, hung-up, in a box, boxed-in, shut-down, fenced-in, hedged-in. 2. top secret, eyes only, for your eyes only, hush-hush, inside info, on the QT, under wraps, keep buttoned up, skunk works (secret manufacturing plant or laboratory). See SECRET.

RESTRICTION n. no-no, off limits, out of bounds, closed down, closed up, hang-up, catch, lock, excess baggage, stumbling block, foot dragging, glitch, joker, one small difficulty, string to it, kicker, fine print, fine print at the bottom, with a grain of salt.

REST ROOM n. can, john, Men's, Ladies', ladies' room, women's room, girls' room, little girls' room, ruth, powder room, men's room, boys' room, little boys' room, reading room, library, head, facilities, amenities, throne room, where the dicks hang out. See TOILET.

RESTUDY v. go over, brush up, polish up, rehash, rub up.

RESULT n. upshot, chain reaction, waves, flak (bad), score, blow-off, spin-off, payoff, punch line, fallout, follow-up, follow-through, kickback, shit hit the fan, verdict isn't in on that, can of worms, bottom line.

RÉSUMÉ n. brag sheet.

RESURGENT adj. born-again.

RETALIATE v. get even with, settle the score, settle one's hash, square accounts, fix one's wagon, give one tit for tat, get back at, turn the tables on, give one a dose of one's own medicine.

RETALIATION n. tit for tat, eye for an eye, get even.

RETARD v. gum up the works, bog, bog down, lose steam, back off, let up, hang up, hold up, bring to a screaming halt, flag one, shut off, shut down, shut 'em down, close off, choke, choke off, put on the shelf (Bus.), put on the back burner, stall, drag one's heels, drag one's foot, saddle with, weigh down, hang like a millstone round one's neck, throw a monkey wrench into the works, upset one's apple cart, down one, take one down, take care of, take the wind out of one's sails, crimp, put a crimp in, cramp one's style.

RETARDED adj. exceptional, retardo, pinhead, lamebrain, birdbrain, harebrained, rattlebrain, scatterbrain, dopey, dumbo, dum-dum, dumbbell, dumb Dora, dumbhead, blockhead, fathead, bonehead, knucklehead, rubblehead, rockhead, numbskull, rattleweed, yo-yo, sappy, not all there, soft in the head, weak in the upper story, Barbie and Ken, gorked. See also FEEBLEMINDED.

RETELL v. play back, rehash, recap, come again, ditto, echo, one more time, una mas, run that by one once more, say again, go over the same ground, go the same round, chew one's cabbage twice. See REPEAT.

RETICENT adj. clam, clammed-up, dried-up, dummied-up, garbo, tight-lipped, close-mouthed.

RETIRE v. 1. crash, flake out, flop, turn in, crawl in, get some shut eye, get forty winks, grab a few winks, hit the hay, hit the pad, hit the nod, hit the sack, sack, sack up, sack out, bat-cave, pad out, make some z's, knock a nod, knock the pad, go night-night, go bye-bye, go beddy-bye. 2. get the gold watch, hang up the gloves, hang it up, call it quits, pull the pin. 3. get the hell out, make oneself scarce, vamoose, highball, dog it, skip, skip out, powder, take a powder, take a run-out powder, fade, fade out, do a fade.

RETIRED adj. on the shelf, out of circulation, out to pasture, over-the-hill, passed it, a once was, has-been, hung up one's spurs, old-timer.

RETOOL v. switch, switch over, upgrade, modernize.

RETORT n. backtalk, comeback, crack, crackback, wisecrack, dirty crack, smart crack, nasty crack, snappy comeback, topper, cooler, lip, parting shot. See ANSWER.

RETORT v. talk back, back talk, shoot back, snappy comeback, come back at, come right back at, sass, squelch, top, crack. See ANSWER.

RETRACT v. welsh, renig, nig, back off, call off, call off all bets, dial back, forget it, go back on one's word, weasel out, worm one's way out, worm out of, back-water, crawfish, crawfish out, eat crow, eat humble pie, eat one's words, eat one's hat.

RETREAT n. blowout center, ivory tower, hideaway, hideout, den, place to hole up, hole in, hole up, safe house.

RETREAT v. 1. back down, back out, back out of, fold, quit, cave in, give in, go along with, opt out, flake, backpedal, back-water, backslide, weasel out, crawl out of, pull the plug, pull in one's horns, draw in one's horns, draw in one's claws, cut loose, stand down. 2. bail out, turn chicken, chicken out, check out, drop, drop out, cut out, cut and run, tail between one's legs, get the hell out, run like a scared rabbit, do a vanishing act, get small (from a crime), fade, fade out, do a fade, fade away, drift away. See GO.

RETRENCH v. tighten one's belt, dig in, roll back, cut corners, pull together, circle the wagons.

RETRIBUTION n. comeuppance, just deserts, what-for, what one has coming, tit for tat, eye for an eye.

RETROGRESS v. backslide.

RETURN n. 1. ball's in your court, callback, call-in, comeback (merchandise to store). 2. gravy, bottom line, net, velvet, pay, cush, get, gate, handle, peanuts (small), take, take in; brocas, cactus, dust, ends, bread, lace (large profits). See INCOME.

RETURN v. 1. bounce back, double back, back at you, call in, show up, dust 'em off (after absence). 2. clean up, clear, score, cash in on, make a good thing of, make a killing, make it big, make hay. See EARN.

RETURNED n. returnee.

REUNITE v. kiss and make up, fix up, patch up, patch things up, make up, make it up, make matters up.

REUSE v. rejase, recycle.

REVEAL v. 1. flash (also used in cards), do a fruit salad (expose genitals), debunk, blow one's cover, blow the lid off, drop a bomb, give the show away, go public. See EXPOSE. 2. talk, leak, tip off, tip one's hand, let the cat out of the bag, put hep, put hip, put it on the street, come out of the closet, open up, fess, fess up, croon, sing, sing like a canary, belch, snitch, squeal, spill, spill the beans, have a big mouth, blab, break, break a story. See CONFESS.

REVEL n. bender, rage, bat, binge, ball, bash, bust, beer bust, kegger, buzz, drunk, jag, caper, go, tear, toot, blow out, hoopla, whoopee, jamboree, wing-ding, shindig, brannigan, rip, merry-go-round, paint the town red, on the town, ca-rousing, growler rushing, hell around, hell bender, high jinks, whooper-dooper, big time, high time, high old time, larking, field day. See also PARTY.

REVEL v. 1. let go, let loose, cut loose, make whoopee, whoop it up, suck it up, rage, go clubbing, go on a rip, go on a tear, go on a toot, go on a bat, go on a bender, go on a low-flying mission, go on a bombing mission, binge, go on a binge, go on a bust, go on a spree, go on R. and R., lark, go on a lark, go places and do things, step out, paint the town, paint the town red, go on the town, go on the merry-go-round, go the dizzy rounds, carry on, hit the high spots, pub-crawl, run around, kick up one's heels, fool around, horse around, monkey around, kid around, hell around, raise hell, raise a rumpus, raise a storm, raise the devil, raise the deuce, raise the dickens, raise the roof, tear up the pea patch, blow off the lid, cut capers, cut up, cut a dido, cut a few touches, cut up a few touches, live a little, live it up, make a day of it, make a night of it, down the primrose path, see the sights, step out. 2. groove on, have a ball, balling, funk, grok, dig, dig one or something, dig the most, rat fuck, R.F., get some grins, adore, be big on, get off on, get high on, get naked (not necessarily sexual), flip, flip for, flip over, freak out on, get a charge out of, get a kick out of, get a lift out of, get a boot out of, get a bang out of, drop the bomb, just for kicks, just for laughs, knock oneself out, have oneself a time, eat up, eat it up, savvy, with it, kvell (Yid.).

REVELATION n. the latest, what's happenin', what's going down, leak, catch, break, beat, blow-by-blow, scoop, poop, chip, dope, earful, ear duster, clue, tip, cue, eye-opener, joker, kicker, bolt from the blue, bolt out of the blue, hash, haymaker, hot shot, hot wire; kick in the ass, shot in the ass (bad), are you ready for this?, page-oner, handout, showdown. See also SURPRISE.

REVELER n. good-time Charlie, playboy, man about town.

REVENGE n. tit for tat, eye for an eye.

REVENGE v. get even with, settle, settle with, settle the score, settle one's hash, settle accounts, square accounts, square, square things, fix, fix one's wagon, give one tit for tat, come back at, get back at, dish it back, hit back at, get hunk, kick back, stick it to one, stick it in and break it off, turn the tables on, give one what is coming to one, give one a dose of one's own medicine, give back as good as one got, defrosted.

REVENUE n. cash flow, revenue stream, net, velvet, pay, payoff, gravy, bottom line, cush, split, get, gate, handle, melon, strength, take, take-in; brocas, cactus, dust, ends, bread, lace (large profits). See INCOME.

REVEREND n. padre, the rev, Holy Joe, sky pilot, preacher man, fire proofer, fire escape, fire insurance agent, shepherd, buck, glory roader. See CLERGYMAN.

REVERIE n. trip, head trip, mind trip, castle in the air, fool's paradise, pipe dream, stare into the middle distance, pie in the sky.

REVERSAL n. 1. about-face, turn around, switcheroo, flip-flop, bottom out. 2. a bath, take a bath (financial).

REVERSE v. backtrack, backpedal, flip-flop, double back, put the cart before the horse, turn the tables, renig.

REVERSED adj. ass over elbows, arsy-varsy, ass backwards, bass ackwards, back asswards, topsy-turvy, catawampus.

REVERSED COLLAR n. dog collar.

REVERSE ORDER n. ass backwards, bass ackwards, back asswards, arsy-varsy, flip-flop.

REVERSE SIDE n. flip side, other side of the coin.

REVERT v. backslide, about-face, flip-flop, fall off the wagon.

REVIEW n. blurb, mention, notice, pan (bad), write-up. See also CRITICISM.

REVIEW v. 1. cool something over, chew over, chew the cud, check, check out, check over, cop, crack one's brains, hammer, hammer away at, bat it around, kick around, knock around, run it up the flagpole, run it by one again, run through, debrief, recap, rehash, hash over, go over, go over with a fine-tooth comb, go over the same ground, go the same round, revisit, brush up, polish up, rub up. 2. rave, pan, boo, base on, take down, put down, come down on, come down hard on, slice up, rip, bag on (Hum.), chew on, skin alive, lay out, needle, give one the needle, Bronx cheer, slam, bad-mouth, poor-mouth, trash, ping (Mil.), zing, zap, knock, rap, sock it to one, swipe at. See also CRITICIZE.

REVIEWER n. aisle-sitter, Monday morning quarterback, nitpicker, zapper, culture vulture, crix (Pl.).

REVILE v. dump on, rank out, dog on, rake over the coals, scorch, blister, tear into, lambaste, slam, rag, rag on, crack on (Hum., Af. Am.), give a black eye, swipe, roast, slag, shade, throw shade, skin alive. See SCOLD. See also RIDICULE.

REVISE v. dial back, recalibrate, blue-pencil, cut, debug, flyspeck, launder, scrub, clean up, tighten, go over, boil (bottom to top), bake (top to bottom). See EDIT.

REVIVAL n. retro.

REVIVAL MEETING n. shout.

REVIVE v. come around, come round, come back, come from behind, jump start, bounce back, make a come-back, pull out of it, snap out of it, turn the corner, be out of the woods, get back in shape, get a lift, perk up, brace up.

REVOKE v. call off, call all bets off, scrub, nix, not (used at end of a positive sentence), back out of, backpedal, back-water, Indian gift, See REPEAL.

REVOKED adj. scrubbed, killed, dusted, shot, shot down, shot down in flames, washed out, wiped out, all bets off, all off, kaput, zapped.

REVOLT v. 1. kick over, kick over the traces, drop out, opt out, cop out, get out of line, rock the boat, make waves, leave the beaten path. 2. gross out, turn off, scuzz one out, give one a pain, give one a pain (somewhere).

REVOLTED adj. grossed out, scuzzed out, turned off. See DISGUSTED.

REVOLTING adj. stinky, rotten, scurvy, gross, grody, grody to the max, mutant, godawful, scuzzo, scuzzy, shitsky, sleazy, sleazeball, sludgeball, bad case of the uglies, pukey, pukoid, gummy. See DISGUSTING.

REVOLUTIONARY n. Reb, Yankee Doodle, Commie, red, ratfuck.

REVOLUTIONARY adj. avant-garde, breaking new ground, breaking new snow, new wrinkle, newfangled, new-fangle, newfangled contraption.

REVOLVER n. blaster, burner, gat, artillery, cannon, piece, iron, rod, jammy (Af. Am.), snubby, snub-nose, Saturday night special, wheel gun, bean shooter, peashooter, popper, pop, equalizer, difference, speaker, Mr. Speaker, persuader, convincer, hardware, heater, heat, Betsy, roscoe, mahoska. See GUN.

REWARD n. fringe benefit, goodies, perk, perks, strokes, brownie button (Hum.), feather in one's cap, plum, sweetening, sweetener, grease, salve, palm oil, gravy, zukes, what's in it for one, tip, toke (gambling), chip, cue, somethin', a little somethin'; subway, bus ride (nickel or dime tip). See also BRIBE.

REWARD v. stroke, sugar-coat, slip one a buck, take care of, oil one's palm, piece one off.

RHAPSODIZE v. carry on over, make a to-do over, take on over, fall all over, go on about, whoop it up for, turn on.

RHETORIC n. hot air, balderdash, gobbledegook, gobbledygook, big talk, tall talk.

RHEUMATISM n. rheumatics, rheumatiz.

RHINOCEROS n. rhino.

RHODE ISLAND Little Rhody, Mini State, Ocean State, Plantation State.

RHYTHM n. beat, downbeat, bounce, brown off (break).

RHYTHM AND BLUES n. R and B.

RIBALD adj. dirty, filthy, feelthy, blue, low-down and dirty, rough, raunchy, raw, purple, salty, off-base, off-color, out of line. See OBSCENE

RIBALDRY n. scuz, smut, sleaze, cussing, dirty talk, porn, X-rated, hot stuff, jack-off material. See OBSCENITY.

RIBS n. slats. See also SPARE RIBS.

RICE n. weevil.

RICE WINE n. saki, bamboo juice (WWII).

RICH adj. up in the bucks, in the bucks, in the chips, the haves, rollin' in it, rolling in dough, money to burn, stinking rich, bifftad, well-heeled, plush, flush, loaded, made one's pile, uptown, upscale. See WEALTHY.

RICHES n. the life of Riley, velvet, high on the hog, on top of the heap, bed of roses, in clover, on Easy Street, in the lap of luxury. See WEALTH.

RICHMOND, VIRGINIA Grantsville.

RICKETY adj. rocky.

RID v. 1. 86, eighty-six, junk, adios something, adios it, adios one, fire, dog, heave-ho, throw on the junk heap, toss onto the scrap heap, scrap, chuck out, round file. See DISCARD. 2. give one the heave-ho, give one the bum's rush, give one the brush, give one the brush-off, give the mitten, give the hook, gate, give the gate, give the air, give 'em the hook, give 'em the 1–2–3, bounce, chase, duke out, boot out, kick out, kick it, muscle out, throw out on one's ear, French walk, send packing, show the door, lug, roust, put the skids to, skid (rid self of undesirable persons). See EJECT. 3. chill, put the chill on, dust off, fluff off, kiss off, California kiss-off, kiss good-bye, chop out, take one for a ride. See KILL. 4. shake, shake one, can, dump, ditch. See DISCHARGE.

RIDDLE n. sixty-four-dollar question, twister, teaser, sticker, floorer, stumper, mind boggler, hard nut to crack, tough nut to crack, tough proposition.

RIDE n. lift, commute, hitch, pickup, joyride, spin, whirl, run, burnout (high speed), airing, Sunday drive.

RIDE v. cruise, roll, tool, bomb around, hitch a ride, thumb a ride, hitchhike, go for a spin, go for a whirl. See DRIVE.

RIDE A HORSE v. fag along (fast), up, on top, in the irons, back in the saddle, beefsteak (badly).

RIDE FREIGHT TRAINS v. ride the rails, ride the rods, hit the rods, grab a handful of rods, grab an armful of box cars, hop a ride, hop a freighter, hop a rattler, catch a rattler.

RIDER n. drop, line load (taxi), seat cover, deadhead (free).

RIDICULE n. put-on, putdown, rank out, cap, hack on, dump, dirty dig, crack, slam, swipe, jab, dig, comeback, parting shot, brickbat.

RIDICULE v. kid, kid around, jive, needle, cap, rag, razz, rib, roast, jolly, josh, bag on (Hum.), goof on, ride, base on, slice up, pan, pooh-pooh, guy, put on, put down, take down, slap at, swipe at, dig at, do a number on, flip on the bird, give one the bird, give one the Bronx cheer, give one the razzberry, make sport of, yank one's crank, pull one's leg. See also TEASE.

RIDICULOUS adj. ridic, bodacious, bogus, jerky, nerky, nutty, wacky, squirrely, harebrained, daffy, goofy, slappy, slaphappy, whip-silly, foolheaded, horse's ass, horse's collar, horse's neck, horse's tail, sappy. See also FOOLISH; IMPOSSIBLE.

RIFLE n. artillery, equalizer, difference, persuader, convincer, hardware, Winchester, pop gun, B.A.R., flint-lock, flint stick, aught two, breechloader (19th Century), blowpipe, long rod, peashooter, smoke pole, smoke wagon, slim, stick, boom stick, tool, noise tool, works, business, iron betsy, boom boom (WWII), prod, crowd-pleaser (police), scatter-gun, bear insurance. See also GUN.

RIFLE v. rip, rip off, grab, smash and grab, take, tip over. See LOOT.

RIFLEMAN n. dogface, G.I. doughfoot, B.A.R. man, bolo (unskilled, Army 1930).

RIGGED adj. in the bag, it's in the bag, fix is in, boat race (horse race).

RIGHT adj. 1. on the nose, on the money, right on, righteous, right you are, right as rain, righto, hit the nail on the head, fuckin' A, amen, right stuff, keerect, reet, cooking on the front burner, according to Hoyle. See CORRECT. 2. that dog'll hunt, hold up, stand up, go, hold water, hold together, stick together, hold up in the wash, wash, fly, no buts about it, no ifs ands or buts, 3. right wing, neo-con, extreme right, rightist, hard right, radical right, skinhead, Birchite, John Bircher, Black Shirt, Brown Shirt, Ku Kluxer, lunatic fringe, McCarthyism, Posse Comitatus, storm trooper. See CONSERVATIVE.

RIGHT v. 1. shape up, fix up, debug, doctor, fly-speck, launder, scrub, clean up, pick up, go over, fiddle with. 2. make up for, pay one's dues, square, square up, square the beef. 3. Babylon (Af. Am.), straighten out, go straight, clean up one's act, make first-rate, recalibrate, dial back, turn around, turn things around. See CORRECT.

RIGHTEOUS adj. candy-ass, Christian, buzz killer, goody-goody, goody two-shoes, nice Nellie, Crabapple Annie, bluenose. See VIRTUOUS.

RIGHTFUL adj. legit, kosher, card-carrying, honest to God, twenty-four-carat, on the level, on the up-and-up, hold water, hold up in the wash. See LEGAL.

RIGHT-HANDED adj. righty.

RIGID adj. 1. locked-in, head in concrete, set in concrete, stuck in concrete, buried in concrete, chiseled in stone, rock-ribbed, dig in one's heels, hold the line, hang tough, tough nut to crack, bullheaded, dead set on. See STUBBORN. See also STRICT. 2. chickenshit, crab, hardliner, by the book, stiff, tough, rough. See PARTICULAR.

RING n. 1. hoop, band, handcuffs (wedding), rock, sparkler. 2. mob, clan, tribe, troupe, bunch, crowd, combination, combo, rat pack, syndicate, outfit, those one runs with. See ASSOCIATION.

RIOT n. free-for-all, brawl, all hell broke loose, to-do, row, stir, flap, fuss, big stink, run-in, rhubarb, rowdydow, rumble, rumpus, ruckus, ruction, shindy, shivaree, commo, dustup, hoopla, hassle, fofarraw, mix-up, kick-up, snarl-up, wingding, raise Cain, raise sand, fuzzbuzz, haroosh, big scene, gin, branigan, donnybrook, hey rube, dance, hoedown, jump, jackpot, stew; bingo, rockin' (prison). See also FIGHT.

RIOT v. throw rocks, kick over, kick over the traces. See also LOOT.

RIOTOUS adj. on a tear, raising a rumpus, raising a ruckus, raising the roof, kicking up a row, kicking up a shindy, off-base, out-of-line, out-of-order.

RISE v. 1. take off, perk up, pick up, bottom out, go through the roof, uptick (small). 2. rise and shine, roll out, turn out, pile out, hit the deck, show a leg, drop your cocks and grab your socks, keep bankers' hours (late). See AWAKEN.

RISK n. flier, flyer, flutter, header, plunge, spec, stab, on (on a horse), shot in the dark, brinksmanship. See WAGER.

RISK v. take the action, take a flyer, play, get down, lay it on the line, put it on the line, put up, put up or shut up, put one's money where one's mouth is, put on the spot, tackle, take on, take a plunge, plunge, play the market, take a header, have a fling at, give a fling, take a fling at, have a go at, give a go, give a whirl, take a crack at, take a whack at, make a stab at, have a shot at, jump off the deep end, stick one's neck out, stick one's neck in the noose, play into one's hands, go out on a limb, go the limit, go whole hog, go on the hook for, go for the long ball, shoot the works, ball the jack, make book, book the action, shoot one's wad, grift, on the grift, stake, backstrap, cheesebox, parlay, cap (add illegally), lay off (relay bet), spitball, chance it, skate on thin ice. See also WAGER.

RISKY adj. dicey, iffy, rocky, touchy, touch-and-go, longshot, chancy, fat chance, in the tube, not a prayer, on a wing and a prayer, on slippery ground, on thin ice, out on a limb, go out on a limb, on the spot, hanging by a thread, off the deep end, go off the deep end, step off the deep end, go for broke, leave oneself wide open, play with fire, hot potato,

one could get burned, too hot to handle, a snowball in hell, hasn't got a Chinaman's chance, go to sea in a sieve.

RISQUÉ adj. dirty, filthy, blue, off-base, off-color, out-of-line, X-rated, stag, jiggle, jiggly, spark. See also OBSCENE.

RIVAL n. opposish, oppo, opposite number, bad guy, bandit, buddy-buddy (sarcasm), buddy fucker, crip, meat, me and you, angries, dark horse (unknown).

RIVAL v. jockey for position, scramble for, go for, go after, in the hunt. See also EQUAL.

RIVALRY n. competish, rat race, dog-eat-dog, a regular jungle out there, do or die, one on one, a dick-measuring contest (needless).

RIVER n. drink.

RIVET n. bullet.

ROAD n. pike, rip strip, dragway, main drag, main stem, main line, back alley, back street, straightways, super slab, pavement, the bricks, byway, trail, stroll, groove, aisle, bowling alley, world's longest parking lot, four-lane parking lot, roller coaster, kidney buster, washboard, boardwalk (rough), licorice stick.

ROAD HAZARD n. pothole, chuckhole, church hole.

ROAM v. bum, bum around, drift, follow one's nose, traipse, knock about, bat around, take to the road, hit the road, globe-trot, trek. See WANDER.

ROAR v. holler, holler out, blast.

ROB v. rip off, mug (rob and beat), appropriate, boost, scrounge, pinch, promote, buzz, cop, kipe, liberate, graze (steal and eat food in a supermarket), take a five-finger discount (shoplift), lift, palm, moonlight requisition, snatch, snitch, swipe, snipe, get busy, rough off, house (money), gaffle, glom, glaum, glahm, glue, skim, hijack, heist, hoist, high-grade, elevate, make, make off with, burn, annex, borrow, touch, bag, nip, snare, stick up, kick over, tip over, knock off, knock over, shoot a jug, put up, root, put the arm on, take off, pluck, put a hand in the till, put a hand in the cookie jar, have one's hand in the cookie jar, loid, make an entry, make an in, push in, penetrate, blow a safe, burgle, clip a joint, crack a crib, crack a safe, slough, cold slough, hot slough, jimmy, shack, work in a bank and take home samples, give one a haircut, take to the cleaners, sting, score, clip, crash, cream, clout, charge, jackroll, hustle, kife, crook, crab, crib, cabbage, steal one blind, hook, hooky, maverick, nick, move, salvage, smooch, go south with something, get paid (successful), fall (unsuccessful).

ROBBER n. punk, holdup man, stickup man, mugger; lush diver, lush roller (of drunkards), prowler, crook, gonif (Yid.), operator, safecracker, booster, See THIEF; BURGLAR.

ROBBERY n. rip-off, snatch, snitch, caper, heist, grab, filch, pinch, lift, job, hustle, boost, stickup, holdup, holdup job, stickup job, car jacking, liberation, annexation, moonlight requisition, knock-over, break-in, push-in, crashing in joints, pushing joints, crib crime, crib job, cream, weed (from employers), mugging, cowboy job (amateur), coffee-and-cake time (right time and place), hoist, stand, jug heist, jug rap, hijacking, owl job, prowl, on the prowl, safeblowing, safecracking, second-story work, shack, sting, cattle lifting, cattle rustling. See also BURGLARY, SAFE OR VAULT.

ROBBERY COMMAND interj. hands up, stick 'em up, hold 'em up, get 'em up, reach, reach for the ceiling, hands up and your head down, look at me and you're dead, hang your nose on the wall, belly the wall, belly up, dance, elevate.

ROBOT n. mobot, steel-collar worker, autofacturing, cyborg, cybernaut, droid.

ROBOTYPE n. robo.

ROBUST adj. 1. in the pink, fit as a fiddle, in good shape, crunchy granola, got the horses to do it, powerhouse, industrial, bull, built like a brick shithouse, muscle man, buffed, he-man, hoss (muscular), hulk, hunk, beauhunk, tiger, Turk, strong as a lion, strong as an ox, strong as a horse. 2. zippy, zappy, snappy, peppy, live, wicked, husky, hefty, beefy, full of piss and vinegar. See STRONG. See also HEALTHY.

ROCHESTER, MINNESOTA Doctor Town.

ROCK n. alley apple, ground apple, ground biscuit, Irish confetti, love letter (thrown).

ROCKET n. bird, mouse (small); screaming meemie (small, Army use), vehicle, RV (reentry vehicle), PAM (payload assist module), Roman candle.

ROCKET BOMB n. doodlebug, bumblebomb, buzzbomb.

ROCKET EMERGENCY BUTTON n. chicken switch, chicken button, egads switch, egads button.

ROCKET FUEL n. plasma, lox (liquid oxygen), LH (liquid hydrogen), SRM (solid rocket motor), SRB (solid rocket booster), SSME (space shuttle main engine), ET (external tank).

ROCKET LAUNCH n. count-down, blast-off, insertion, moon shot, shot.

ROCKET LAUNCHER n. Minnie Mouse launcher, mousetrap.

ROCK 'N' ROLL adj. R and R, R 'n'R, fish music.

RODS n. macaroni.

ROGUE n. hooligan, booger, bugger, black sheep, cut up, scalawag, bounder, rotter, rounder, bad news, bad egg, bad'un. See SCOUNDREL.

ROLE n. stint, act, bit, game, piece, spiel, whatever one is into.

ROLE, THEATER n. star, villain, hero, heroine, juvenile, fat part, bit, bit player, bit part, walk-on, spear carrier, one-side part, super, extra, atmosphere, scenery chewer, top banana, second banana, third banana, baggy-pants comic, straight man.

ROLL CALL n. head count, nose count.

ROLLER SKATER n. blader (in-line).

ROLL SKATES n. blades, roller blades (in-line).

ROLLER SKATING n. blading (in-line).

ROMAN CATHOLIC n. RC; papish, papist, papistic, Romish (all Derog.).

ROMANCE n. affair, fling, carrying on, hanky-panky, holy bedlock, a thing together, a relationship, playing around, goings-on. See also AFFAIR.

ROMAN COLLAR n. dog collar.

ROMANIAN n. Romaniac (Derog.).

ROMANTIC adj. syrupy, drippy, soapy, soppy, soupy, tear-jerker, gushing, hearts and flowers, corny, off-the-cob, mushy, shmaltz, schmalzy. See SENTIMENTAL.

ROMANTICISM n. deep sugar, glop, hearts and flowers, schmaltz, mush, slush, slop, goo, sob story, tear-jerker.

ROMANTICIZE v. build castles in the air, build castles in Spain, talk through one's hat, look at the world through rose-colored glasses.

ROMP v. fool around, kid around, hell around, cut up, kick up one's heels, whoop it up, let loose, go on the town. See REVEL.

ROOF n. tar beach.

ROOK v. rip off, jerk one around, screw, shaft, frig, hose, rim, dick, dick one around, fuck one over, jive, shuck, shuck and jive, fleece, flam, flimflam, burn, bilk, clip, con, chisel, gouge, gyp, stiff, sting, sucker, mooch (commodity scam), hold up, hype. See CHEAT.

ROOKED adj. suckered, sandbagged, fell for, fucked over, been had, taken, get played (Af. Am.), stuck, aced-out, snookered, shafted, got a haircut, screwed, dicked, gaffled, hosed, get hosed, boned. See CHEATED.

ROOM n. 1. elbowroom, wiggle room, room to swing a cat. 2. pad, crash pad, cinch pad; cradle, hat (Af. Am.); box, flop, joint, cave, den, crib, cubby, cubby hole, go-down, balloon room (marijuana), rack, birdcage, heave, hot bed, padhouse, scatter, setup, walk-up, turf. See also APARTMENT.

ROOMMATE n. roomie, roomy, bunkie, chum, old lady, old miss, old man, O.M., wife. See also FRIEND.

ROOT BEER n. black cow, fifty-five.

ROOT BEER SODA n. black cow, root beer float.

ROSTER n. head count, nose count. See also LIST.

ROSTRUM n. soapbox, stump, bally stand (circus).

ROT v. go to pot, go downhill, use it or lose it. See DETERIORATE.

ROTTEN adj. stinking, gross, strong, high, loud. See also CORRUPT.

ROUÉ n. high liver, player, operator, heavy hitter, lech, dirty old man, sport, swinger, rounder. See LECHER.

ROUGH adj. 1. hairy, hellish, mean, aggro, tough, tough customer, roughneck, hard-boiled egg, ballsy, in your face. bad guy, bad actor, hooligan, commando, welcome to the NFL. 2. cheap, loud, loudmouth, loudmouthed, foulmouth, foulmouthed. See TOUGH. See also DIFFICULT.

ROUNDABOUT adj. go round the barn, went by way of, long way, long way home.

ROUSE v. 1. fire up, key up, steam up, stir up, work up, craze, bug, trigger, rabble-rouse, make waves, utz (Yid.), needle, go on make my day, ask for it, rile. See INCITE. 2. heat up, pep up, wake up, zip up, buck up, turn on the heat, run a temperature, get hot under the collar, jazz, jazz up, juice, send, grab, open one's nose. See EXCITE.

ROUT n. beating, whipping, licking, trimming, shellacking, trashing, smearing, clobbering, embarrassment, shutout, washout, disaster, roof fell in (sudden), upset, shuck, total shuck, come down. See DEFEAT.

ROUT v. bury, bash, trash, shred, smoke, blank, skunk, murder, kill, dog on, trounce, swamp, scuttle, shellack, bulldoze, roll over, torpedo, meatball, beat all hollow, finish, blow one out of the water, drub, larrup, whomp, whip, wipe, total, cream, zap, paste, kick ass, shut out, wipe up the floor with, wipe off the map. See DEFEAT.

ROUTE n. 1. rut, groove. 2. the bricks (hobo, police, union), beat, run. 3. pike, rip strip, dragway, super slab, pavement, the bricks, byway, trail, stroll, groove, aisle, bowling alley, four-lane parking lot, roller coaster, kidney buster, washboard, boardwalk (rough), shortcut, bee line.

ROUTINE n. same old shit, SOS, same old same old (Af. Am.), shtick, sked, grind, daily grind, groove, channels, cut-and-dried, G.I., red tape, donkey work. See also ACT, AVERAGE.

ROVE v. bum, bum around, drift, float, follow one's nose, hopscotch, knock around, bat about, trek. See WANDER.

ROVER n. floater, bum, gad, gadabout, globe-trotter. See also VAGRANT.

ROW n. baldheaded man's row, crotch row (row A, The). See also ARGUMENT, FIGHT.

ROW v. sky an oar.

ROWDINESS n. rowdydow, rowdy-dowdy, a rhubarb.

ROWDY adj. hell-raising, rambunctious, rootin'-tootin', roughhouse, hoopla, rowdy-dowdy, cowboy, loudmouth, ziggy, harum-scarum, off-base, out-of-line, out-of-order.

ROWDY n. bullyboy, bucko, hellcat, hell-raiser, hellion, terror, holy terror. See also THUG, VILLAIN.

RUBBISH n. hogwash, gash, junk, dreck, shit.

RUDE adj. fresh, cheeky, sassy, snippy, short, smart-alecky, smart-ass, base, brassy, lippy, gally, chutzpadik, cocky, out-of-line, off-base, cut, cold-shoulder, give one the business, roll over one. See INSOLENT.

RUDIMENTARY adj. basic, ABC's, three r's, primo. See BASIC.

RUDIMENTS n. ABC's, three R's, nuts and bolts. See BASICS.

RUE v. cry over spilled milk, kick oneself.

RUFFIAN n. mug, mugger, gorilla, ape, bodyguard, pug, heavy, goon, bullyboy, bucko, roughneck, tough cookie, bruiser, ugly customer. See THUG.

RUFFLE v. throw into a tizzy, get to, discomboberate, discombobulate, rattle one's cage, fuddle, put one on a crosstown bus, stump, floor, put off, flummox. See CONFUSE.

RUG n. wall-to-wall.

RUGGED adj. 1. heavy, hairy, uphill, mean, murder, pisser, bitch, son of a bitch, SOB, hellish, tough one, tough proposition, ballbuster, large order, no picnic, heavy sledding. See DIFFICULT. 2. hairy, tough, tough customer, roughneck, hard-boiled, ballsy, I'm shakin' (sarcastic response to threat), enforcer, commando, welcome to the NFL. 3. gutsy, gutty, nervy, spunky, tough it out, cool hand, beefy, hairy, hefty, husky, mean, strong as a horse, strong as a lion, strong as an ox, wicked. See TOUGH.

RUIN n. wasteland. See also FAILURE.

RUIN v. 1. trash, total, cream, dust, torpedo, kill, ax, sink, smash up, pile up, rack up, take apart, break the lease, blue ruin, blow sky high, blow out, put out of commission. See DESTROY, WRECK. 2. ding, wing, tweak, total, take a hit, crumb, crumb up, louse up, mess up, muck up, make hash of, snafu. See DAMAGE. 3. settle one's hash, put in the toilet, kibosh, put the kibosh on, fix, fix one's wagon, poke full of holes, do, do a number on one, do in, get, finish, finish off, blow one's doors off, cook one's goose, destabilize, shoot down, shoot down in flames, clip one's wings.

RUINATION n. belly up, go belly up, toes up, toes, go under, chapter 7, chapter 11, chapter 13, close the doors, in the tub, take a bath, the skids, on the skids, hit the skids.

RUINED adj. 1. gutted, queered, busted, dusted, dinged, totaled, gone, cooked, sunk, shot, flubbed, fragged, kaput, on the fritz, down, on downtime, on the blink, on the bum, out of action, no-go, run down, had it, glitched, gremlins, queered, bobbled, bitched, bitched-up, buggered, buggered-up, racked-up, screwed-up, fouled-up, fucked-up, fucked, loused-up, gummed-up, balled-up, bollixed-up, messed-up, hashed-up, mucked-up, all fucked up, all fouled up, fubar (fouled up beyond all recognition), fubb (fouled up beyond belief), fumtu (fouled up more than usual), tuifu (the ultimate in foulups), nabu (nonadjusting ball-up), sapfu (surpassing all previous foul-ups), snafu (situation normal all fouled up), susfu (situation unchanged still fouled up), tarfu (things are really fouled up), blow it, blow it big time, down the tube, down the drain, down the toilet, in the toilet, done for, done in, gone to the dogs, gone to pot, gone to rack and ruin, gone to bad, gone to hell, gone to the devil, gone to perdition, gone to glory, up in smoke. See also DESTROYED. 2. broke, flat, flat broke, busted, totaled, cleaned out, on one's ass, on the rocks, to the curb, down and out, blown out, down to one's last cent, down to one's last penny, in dire straits, on the rims, go to the wall. See DESTITUTE. See also BANKRUPT.

RULE v. sit on top of, run, run things, run the show, hold the reins, lay down the law, be in the driver's seat, take over, crack the whip, rule the roost, keep under one's thumb. See MANAGE.

RULES n. chapter and verse, by the book, by the numbers, no-no's, bible (authoritative book).

RUM n. myrrh.

RUMANIAN n. Rumaniac. (Derog.).

RUMINATE v. stew over, chew over, rack one's brains, brainstorm, head trip, use one's head, noodle, noodle it around, crunch, figger. See THINK.

RUMMAGE v. look all over hell, look high and low, beat the bushes, leave no stone unturned, geek out (seek crumbs of cocaine), search high heaven, shake, shake down, toss, turn inside-out, turn upside-down.

RUMMY TERMS run (consecutive order), knock, schneider, blitz (win all the points), a laydown, bait.

RUMOR n. scuttlebutt, talk, grapevine, clothesline, back-fence talk, earful, latrine rumor, wire, hot wire, vanilla. See GOSSIP.

RUMOR, UNFOUNDED n. black plague, dirty tricks, nutcracking, rat fucking.

RUMP n. buns, fanny, ass, behind, backside, bottom, bum, butt, bubblebutt (large and rounded), can, moon, tail, keister, derriere, prat, seat, rear end, tushy, tuchis, duff. See BUTTOCKS.

RUMPLED adj. messed-up, mussed-up, messy, mussy, mangled, thrashed, sloppy, slobbed out, grungy, grubby, scuzzed, scuzzed-up, beat-up.

RUN v. 1. cut ass, haul ass, bag-ass, barrel, barrel-ass, tear-ass, shag-ass, jog, joggin', stir one's stumps, nip off, tear off, tear out, dig out, book, book it, light, light off, light out, get going, highball, trot along, hightail, make tracks, hop it, hoof it, hotfoot, hotfoot it, smoke, scamper, rabbitfoot, greyhound, leg, leg it, step, step along, step it, get to steppin', knees pumpin', pick 'em up and lay 'em down, locomoting, move, pedaling with both feet, scramble, slide (Af. Am.), hit the grit, scratch gravel, pack the mail. 2. split, take off, fuck off, hightail, hotfoot, color me gone, air out (Af. Am.), bone out, motor, motorvate; le-go, sko (let's go); bolt (quickly), blow, blow this joint, blow this pop stand, break camp, hoof it, run like a scared rabbit, step on it, step on the gas, cut and run, cut out, roll out, get-git, take off in a cloud, take off in a cloud of sour owl shit, take off like a big-ass bird, take off like a B.A.B., smoke, haul it. See GO. 3. run things, run the show, pull the strings, mastermind, head up, boss, helm, ride herd on, kick ass, kick butt, be in the driver's seat, be in the saddle, take the conn. See MANAGE. 4. politick, press the flesh, stump, take the stump, stump the country, hit the campaign trail, whistle-stop, take to the hustings, shake hands and kiss babies, ring doorbells.

RUN AGROUND v. pile up (boat).

RUNAWAY n. lammister, hot, wanted.

RUNDOWN adj. beat-up, ratty, tacky, frowzy, fruit, dog-eared, used-up in a bad way, ramshackle. See also UNHEALTHY, TIRED.

RUNNING START n. hit the ground running.

RURAL COMMUNITY n. jerktown, jerkwater town, tank town, Hickville, South Succotash, boondocks, boonies, sticks, stix, bushes, bush league, pumpkin, wide place in the road. See SMALL TOWN.

RUSE n. game plan, game, little game, angle, dodge, twist, switch, stunt, scenario, shenanigans, curveball, booby trap. See STRATAGEM.

RUSH n. rush act, bum's rush, blitz, blitzkrieg.

RUSH v. hustle, shake a leg, roll, tool, fire up, hotfoot, barrel-ass, tear-ass, step on the gas, open 'er up, put on the afterburners, get the lead out of one's ass, get cracking, go like greased lightening, go like a big-assed bird, streak, eat up the road. See SPEED. See also GO.

RUSSIA n. Russky, the original borscht belt; Iron Curtain, behind the Iron Curtain (Obs.).

RUSSIAN n. Roosky, Russky, Russkie, Moscovite; comrade, Red, red, Tovarich.

RUSSIAN PLANE n. Mig.

RUSSIAN SATELLITE n. sputnik, muttnik.

RUST n. cancer.

RUSTIC n. plow jockey, country boy, country cousin, hillbilly, hick, hayseed, hay shaker, cornfed, rube, pecker-wood (So.), hecker, wahoo, yahoo, brush ape. See YOKEL.

RUT n. daily grind, grind, groove, hang-up, same old shit, SOS, cut-and-dried, red tape.

RUTHLESS adj. cutthroat, go for the jugular, killer instinct, mean machine, dog-eat-dog, hatchet job, take no prisoners, it's a regular jungle out there. See also CRUEL.

RYE BREAD n. with whiskey (sandwich on rye).

S

S. n. Sierra, Sugar.

SABOTAGE v. torpedo, crab, take out, blue ruin, blow sky high, do, do one in, do in, Dutch, screw up the works, queer, queer the works, throw a monkey wrench into the works, toss a monkey wrench into, throw a monkey wrench in the machinery, throw a wrench in the machinery, put a spoke in one's wheels, put something out of action, put out of commission, put the skids under one, gum up, gum up the works, foul up, fuck up, rack up, louse up, mess up, muck up, ball up, bollix, bollix up, bugger, bugger up, jim, pickle, mess with, do a number on, do in, deep-six (evidence). See also DISABLE.

SACRAMENTO, CALIFORNIA Sac, Sacto.

SAD adj. blue, hurting, in the dumper, down in the mouth, tear-jerker, in pain, gloomy Gus, sad sacky. See UNHAPPY.

SADDEN v. drag, turn one off, bum out, down, bring one down, damper, put a damper on, buzz crusher, faze, throw cold water on, throw a wet blanket on, act like a wet blanket. See DEPRESS.

SADDLE n. pimple.

SADISTIC adj. into SM, into leather, S, SM.

SADNESS N. blahs, blah-blahs, blues, blue devils, blue funk, crumbed, funk, bummer, downer, down trip, letdown, dolefuls, dismals, dumps, mumps, mopes, mokers, mulligrubs, tsures, heartache.

SADOMASOCHISM n. SM, S and M, B/D (bondage and discipline), C/P (corporal punishment), D/T (dominance training), leather sex, heavy leather, into domination, into leather, into submission, nice and nasty, R/S (rough stuff), Sadie-Maisie, slaves and masters; water sports, showers, golden showers (urinating on partner); brown showers (defecating on partner), dominatrix, governess, maitresse, Mom, S and M woman; drag, gear, uniforms (clothing).

SAD SONG n. tear-jerker, weeper, blues.

SAD STORY n. sob story, tear-jerker, weeper, downer.

SAFARI n. snofari (snow).

SAFE adj. home-free, safe-and-sound, coast is clear, cuchee, cushy, sitting pretty, buttoned-down, buttoned-up, out-of-the-woods.

SAFE n. peter, pete, box, pete box, crib, coffin, gopher, jug, keister, pocket, sock, trap (hidden).

SAFE BURGLARY n. box work, heavy, heavy time, taking boxes, cracking cribs, knocking off peters, peter racket, busting petes, pete job, pete work, the rip.

SAFE-DEPOSIT BOX n. damper.

SAFEGUARD v. ride shotgun for, shotgun.

SAFE OPENER n. boxman, safecracker, heavy G, heavy man, jug heavy, mechanic, gopher, pete blower, peteman, peterman.

SAFE-OPENING DEVICE n. can opener, hard ass, ripper, stick (blow); pull the box, punch the box.

SAFE SITE n. deep cover, safe house.

SAFETY BELT n. scare strap, submarine belt.

SAGACIOUS adj. cool, tuned in, all woke up, sharp, shark, smoothie, whiz, been there, have smarts, street smart, foxy, have savvy, have one's head screwed on right, wise to, hip, in the picture, on the beam. See SHREWD.

SAGE adj. deep, double-dome, beard, big-think, pundit, savvy, have the smarts, tool, power tool, cereb, got it all together, got one's boots on, know what's what. See INTELLIGENT.

SAIL n. skyscraper, rag.

SAIL v. give her beans, gunkhole, gunkholing (inlet sailing).

SAILING TERMS crush (win a race), hammered (lose a race), gear buster (tough race), blade (small sail), bulletproof (strong material), furniture store (elegantly decorated), hike out, hiking board, hiking seat, hiking stick, hiking strap, tack, reach, cruise, jibe, fall off (angle the boat), harden up, slam-dunk (tack next to another boat), hobbyhorses (rock), bad air (wind disturbed), gagger (windy day), header (wind shift), knockdown (strong gust), hole (windless area), bone in her teeth (foamy bow wave), rooster tail, sewer (below deck), foulies (foul weather gear), rail meat (passengers), veggies (seaweed).

SAILOR n. mate, shipmate, gob, swab, swabbie, swabber, bluejacket, jack, jacky, jack afloat, jack tar, tar, salt, old salt, sea dog, water dog, bullet bait (untrained), cannon fodder, feather merchant (office job), flange face, flatfoot (not common), geep, home guard (married), sand pounder, lobscouser, nuc (nuclear sub or vessel), limey, limejuicer (English), OD, AB, shellback, barnacle back, yachtie.

SALABLE THING n. hot cake, hot item, hot ticket.

SALACIOUS adj. dirty, blue, purple, X-rated, raunchy, raw, hot, heavy, hot stuff, stag, steamy, off-color, low-down. See OBSCENE.

SALAD n. grass, rabbit, rabbit food.

SALAMI n. horse cock, donkey dick (Mil.).

SALARY n. bread, eagle shit, scale, take, take-home, bring home the bacon. See COMPENSATION.

SALE, GO ON v. hit the shelves.

SALES BILL OR CHECK n. beef, tab, big ticket (expensive).

SALESPERSON n. peddler, drummer, bell ringer, —— dog (e.g., shoe dog), mooch (commodity scam), slammer, yakker, medicine man, pitchman, skig, spieler, tinge, Arab, bag guy (balloon), butch, butcher, hawker, farm salesman (pharmaceutical).

SALES TALK n. pitch, sales pitch, story, sell, hard sell, soft sell, bally, ballyhoo, spiel, spiff (commission), belly stand, bally stand, belly platform, grind (circus).

SALMON n. deep-sea turkey, goldfish (canned); lox, nova (Nova Scotia smoked), squaw candy (smoked).

SALOON n. gin mill, rum room, dive, joint, juice joint, beer joint, tap room, bucket shop, suds shop, alehouse, speakeasy, water hole, chain locker (dockside). See BAR.

SALT n. sand.

SALT LAKE CITY, UTAH Big Salty.

SALT PORK n. sow belly.

SALUTATION interj. hi, hey, hey, homie, yo, ciao, gimme five, gimme ten, 'sup?, what up?, what's up?, checkin' in, how do?, how's it happenin'?, what's happenin'?, what it is?, what does it look like?, what's shakin'?, what do you know?, what's going down?, what's coming down?, what's the drill?, what's the scam?, what cooks?, what gives?, hi ya, how you doin'. See HELLO.

SALUTE n. tumble, blow, high-five, howdy, highball, pump handle.

SALUTE v. highball, tumble, flag, give one the key to the city, roll out the red carpet. See GREET.

SALVAGE YARD n. chop shop (illegal), dump.

SALVATION ARMY n. Sal, Sally, Sally Anne.

SAME adj. xerox, dupe, clone, carbon, carbon copy, copy cat, ditto, double, ringer, dead ringer, look-alikes, work-alike, capatible (P.C. compatible), like two peas in a pod, six of one and half a dozen of the other, spit and image, spittin' image, one beat, S.O.S. (same old shit), same difference, same old same old (Af. Am.), no matter how you slice it cut it or dice it.

SAN ANTONIO, TEXAS Chili Switch.

SAN BERNARDINO, CALIFORNIA Berdoo, San Berdoo.

SANITARIUM n. funny farm, funny house (alcohol or drugs), fat farm.

SANCTIMONIOUS adj. goody, goody-goody, goody two-shoes, Holy Joe, holier than thou, stuffy, noble, square John.

SANCTION n. green light, get the green light, okay, OK, get the nod, go-ahead, get the go-ahead, the word. See APPROVAL.

SANCTION v. bless, okay, get behind, go for, hear it for, give the nod, give the go-ahead, give the green light. See APPROVE.

SANCTIONED adj. legit, okayed, kosher. See ACCEPTED.

SANCTUARY n. hideout, hideaway, hole in, hole up, place to hole up, den, safe house, blowout center, ivory tower.

SANDALS n. flip-flops, slaps, mules, thongs, Jesus sandals (Birkenstock).

SAN DIEGO, CALIFORNIA Dago (Derog.), Swabby Town.

SANDWICH n. burger, san, dog, hot dog, Coney Island, Texas hot wiener, chili dog, submarine, hero, Italian hero, Cuban hero, po-boy, poor boy, cowboy, double-decker, open-face, grinder, falafel, pocket, highpockets, Philly (steak sandwich), hoagie, croissandwich, B.L.T. (bacon, lettuce and tomato), B.T. (bacon and tomato), slab, ball lump, dukee, skyscraper, torpedo, wedge, Dagwood.

SANE adj. together, got it together, glued (antonym: unglued), commonsensical, all there, in one's right mind, got all one's marbles, have all one's buttons, have both oars in the water. See REASONABLE.

SAN FRANCISCO, CALIFORNIA Frisco, San Fran, Baghdad by the Bay, Bay City, Quake City.

SANITARY NAPKIN n. rag, Kotex.

SANTA BARBARA, CALIFORNIA Channel City.

SARCASM n. wisecrack, comeback, woofing, grind, put-down, cut, dig.

SARCASTIC adj. bitchy, cussed, mean, rank, ornery, salty, stanky (Fem.), needle, evil, crack, crimpers (U.), hooks, sticking the zingers in (remark), wise-guy, smart-ass, smart-aleck, smart-alecky, smarty, woofer (sarcastic person), weisenheimer, wiseheimer. See also DERISIVE.

SATAN n. fiend, hellion, little devil, debbil, the Deuce, the Dickens, Old Harry, Old Ned, Old Gentleman. See DEVIL.

SATED adj. full up, fed up, fed to the gills, fed to the teeth, bellyful, skinful, snootful, stuffed to the gills, topped-off, packed. See also JADED.

SATELLITE n. eye in the sky, spy in the sky, bird, Domsat, Comsat, Intelsat, Syncom, Telstar.

SATELLITE TRANSMISSION n. bird feed, feed, get on the bird.

SATIATED adj. fed up, fed to the gills, fed to the teeth, stuffed to the gills, bellyful, skinful, snootful, up to here, much of a muchness. See also FULL.

SATIRE n. takeoff, play on, put-on, spoof, cheese.

SATIRIZE v. put on, send up, sheik, take off, spoof, kid, roast.

SATISFACTION n. kick, kicks, sure shock, get off, get off on, a rush, hit, velvet.

SATISFACTORY adj. cool, A-okay, fucking-A, jake, hunky-dory, ducky, on the ball, up crazy, groovy, not half bad, on the beam. See ACCEPTABLE.

SATISFIED adj. 1. sold on, can't complain, have no kick coming, I'm straight, happy camper, hit the spot, just the ticket, just what the doctor ordered. See HAPPY. 2. skinful, snootful, bellyful, no more room, fed up, fed to the teeth, fed to the gills, stuffed to the gills.

SATISFY v. fill the bill, make a hit, hit the spot, hit the bull's-eye, go over big, do the trick, hack it, make it, make the grade, score, pass in the dark, sell, sell one on, get by, get one's jollies, get one's kicks, get off, get off on, be just the ticket, be just what the doctor ordered, thanks I needed that.

SATYR n. playboy, dude, operator, speed, cruiser, heavy hitter, letch, beastmaster (dates ugly women), old goat, wolf, hound, poon hound, tomcat, alley cat, sport, swinger, killer, cunt-chaser, tail-chaser, rounder, Don Juan. See LECHER.

SAUCE n. gunk, dip, glob, glop, goo, goop, goup.

SAUCY adj. fresh, sassy, flip, smarty-pants, cheeky, nervy, minx, hussy, saucebox, pup, puppy, bold as brass. See INSOLENT.

SAUERKRAUT n. kraut, hog, liberty cabbage, shrubbery.

SAUNTER v. ankle, ank, toddle, sashay, traipse, trapse, traipse around, trill, ooze, strut one's stuff, mope, mooch, boogie, diddy-bop, pimpin', percolate, tool, stump it. See WALK.

SAUSAGE n. dog, hot dog, hot dawg, wienie, weenie, frank, tube steak, special, balloon, beenie, bowwow, bun pup, Coney Island pup, puppy, pimp stick, beagle gut; donkey dick, horse cock (Mil.); beagles (prison).

SAVAGE adj. bad-ass, wild-ass, kill-crazy, hog-crazy. See also VIOLENT.

SAVAGELY adv. in cold blood, something fierce, something terrible.

SAVANT n. brain, egghead, hard-boiled egghead (tough-minded), scrambled egghead (fuzzy-minded), mc squared, gnurd, gnome, corn dog, grind, pencil geek, power tool, throat, wonk, auger, bookworm, cereb, cutthroat, grub, ink squirter, spider, squid, tool, weenie.

SAVE v. 1. scrimp, skimp, penny-pinch, cut corners, cut to the bone, go easy on the pocketbook, make ends meet, roll back, tighten one's belt, rub the print off a dollar bill, rub the picture off a nickel, save for a rainy day, put away for a rainy day, squirrel, squirrel away, sock away, salt away, salt down, rat hole, stache, stash. 2. bail one out, save one's ass, save one's neck, save one's bacon, give one a break, get one out of hock, get one off the hook, spring, pull something out of the fire, pull one's chestnuts out of the fire.

SAVED adj. let off, bailed out, off the hook, out of hock.

SAVINGS n. kitty, nest egg, stake, rainy-day account, sock, little something put away, mattressful, ace in the hole. See ASSETS.

SAVOIR FAIRE n. know-how, savvy, the big stick.

SAVORY adj. delish, grinds, yummy, nummy, divine, heavenly, scrumptious, sweetened, sugar-coated.

SAVORY n. sweets, cush, g'dong, gedunk, hickey.

SAW n. brad (small).

SAWDUST n. macaroni, chewed fine.

SAXOPHONE n. sax, ax, axe, pipe, barry, big pipe (baritone), small pipe (alto), fishhorn, foghorn, gobble pipe, peck horn.

SAY n. own say-so, own sweet way, say-so.

SAY v. go, goes, gab, rap, mack (Af. Am.), yak, yock, verbalize, spiel, jaw, lip, modjitate, splib, splib de wib, slide one's jib, shoot, flap, run one's mouth, blow, trash. See SPEAK.

SAYING n. daffodil.

SCAMP n. turd, fart, stinker, bastard, black sheep, cut up, scalawag, bounder, a dick, rotter, rounder, sleazeball, low life, bad news, bad egg, bad'un. See VILLAIN.

SCAN v. flash, flash on, get a hinge, take a hinge, take a squint, look-see, have a look-see, take a gander, take a tumble, tumble, give a thing a toss, give the once-over, once over lightly, hit the high spots, thumb through. See also SCRUTINIZE.

SCANDAL n. dirt, dirty linen, dirty wash, dirty laundry, dirty shame, low-down dirty shame, crying shame, burning shame, mud, slime, dynamite, sizzler, scorcher, skeleton, family skeleton, skeleton in the closet, skeleton in the cupboard, Watergate, Irangate, ——— gate (anything before gate). See also GOSSIP.

SCANDALMONGER n. busybody, yenta (Yid.), cat, muckracker, mudslinger, sleazemonger, source, tabby, tattletale, snitcher, snitch, chalk hat, fork tongue, mouse, punk, ringtail, shamus, songbird, polly, weasel, yodeler, blab, blabber, blabbermouth, peacher.

SCANDALOUS adj. hot, too hot to handle, red-hot.

SCANDINAVIAN n. Scandahoovian, Scandinoovian, squarehead, herring choker (all Derog.).

SCANT adj. scarce as hen's teeth, numerous as chicken lips, slim pickings.

SCAPEGOAT n. fall guy, goat, patsy, sucker, whipping boy, the one left holding the bag.

SCAR n. crater, track.

SCARCE adj. numerous as chicken lips, scarcer than hen's teeth, slim pickings.

SCARCELY adv. by the skin of one's teeth, pretty near, practically, craptically.

SCARE v. scare shitless, scare stiff, scare the pants off one, scare hell out of, scare the shit out of, scare silly, scare the bejesus out of one, scare to death, throw a scare into, spook, chill, lean on, nut on one, woof, push around. See FRIGHTEN.

SCARED adj. scared stiff, scared witless, scared spitless, scared shitless, scared still, scared silly, run scared, shit green, brick, shit a brick, jump out of one's skin, piss in one's pants, have cold feet, D and D (deaf and dumb, afraid to testify). See AFRAID.

SCARF n. a do rag (for hair, Af. Am.).

SCARS n. tracks.

SCATTER v. break up, break it up, bust up, scramble, split up, take off in all directions.

SCATTERED adj. all over the lot, all over the place, from hell to breakfast, every which way.

SCAVENGE v. scrounge, graze (steal and eat food in a supermarket), take a five-finger discount (shoplift), moonlight requisition.

SCENARIO n. book, the words, pages, sides, the shit. See also STORY.

SCENE n. bit, blackout, piece, routine, shtick, spot. See also ACT.

SCENE-STEAL v. upstage, ham it up.

SCENT n. smell well, smell good.

SCHEDULE n. lineup, sked, hit list (list of what has to be done), what's on tap.

SCHEDULE v. line up, get on line, sew up, set, set up, pencil in. See also ROUTINE.

SCHEME n. game, little game, game plan, layout, gimmick, angle, action, big picture, picture, pitch, proposition, proposish, dodge, setup, put-up job, lay of the land, what's cookin', how one figures it, what's the action, where one's heading, play, scenario, scene, story, bit, child, brain child, slant, trick, twist, switch, hustle, hype, booby trap, fix, frame, frame-up, hookup, skulduggery, bug in one's ear.

SCHEME v. finagle, angle, jockey, play games, pull strings, pull wires, figure, figger, hustle, hatch, operate, promote, wangle, quarterback, mastermind, craft, line up, ready up, cook up, dream up, trump up, whip up, come up with, lay out, work something out, get set for, fix to, put in a fix, be in cahoots with, get in bed with, work hand in glove with, rig, dodge, set up, frame, frame up, buy off, pack, pack the deal, stack the deck, stack the cards, put in the bag, put out a contract.

SCHEMER n. operator, finagler, wangler, wire-puller, mastermind, brain, velcroid (sticks to important people).

SCHIZOID adj. schizo, schizzy. See also CRAZY.

SCHIZOPHRENIA n. schiz, schizo.

SCHIZOPHRENIC adj. schiz, schizo, schizzy.

SCHOLAR n. brain, brains, brainy, propeller head, egghead, hard-boiled egghead (tough-minded), scrambled egghead (fuzzy-minded), professor, mc squared, tack, gnurd, gnome, grind, corn dog, pencil geek, power tool, throat, wonk, gweeb, auger, book smart, bookworm, cereb, cutthroat, grub, ink squirter, spider, squid, tool, weenie, poler, wig.

SCHOLARSHIP n. full ride.

SCHOOL n. alma mater, old Siwash, brainery, aggie, cow college, fem sem, Ivy League, halls of ivy, knowledge box, juku, cram school.

SCHOOL BUS n. iron pimp, brain train, kiddie car.

SCHOOL COURSE n. gut course, pipe course, snap course, cake, a mick, slider (easy); hard-core, killer, grinder (hard); dead whore (easy college test).

SCHOOL GRADES n. ace (A); flunk, fade, flag (F); hook (C); gentleman's C; dog (D); eagle; (E) (no grade, take again).

SCHOOL NOTES AND BOOKS n. bricks and mortar, hork (borrow or steal notes).

SCHOOL, PRIVATE n. hen pen (girls).

SCHOOL, PUBLIC n. blackboard jungle, jail, knowledge box, konk class.

SCHOOLTEACHER n. baby-sitter, prof, professor, guru, teach, Dr. Nytol (boring), grind, slavedriver.

SCHOOLWORK n. McPaper (poorly done), bite (copied without permission), tick (talk in class unprepared).

SCIENCE n. sci.

SCIENCE FICTION n. sci-fi, Scientifiction, skiffy, s.f., space fiction, space opera.

SCIENCE FICTION ACRONYMS UFO (Unidentified Flying Object), SETI (Search for Extra-Terrestrial Intelligence), ALF (Alien Life Form), BEM (Bug-Eyed Monster), CE (Close Encounter with an alien ship), CE2 (alien ship reacts), CE3 (Close Encounter with alien ship's occupants), FTL (Faster Than Light), LGM (Little Green Men).

SCIENCE FICTION TERMS ufology (study of UFOs), big bang (creation of the universe), big crunch (universe ends by implosion), Bowash (future supercity sprawl, Boston to Washington), Sansan (supercity San Diego-San Francisco), Chipitts (Chicago to Pittsburgh), moontel (moon hotel), cyberculture (automated society), waldo (mechanical hands), transphotic (travel faster than light), earth grazer (asteroid near-miss), exobiota (extra-terrestrial life), fanzine (sci-fi fan magazine), ish (used as a suffix meaning issue), nextish (next issue).

SCIENTIST n. propeller head, prof, professor, guru, technokraut (Ger.).

SCION n. chip off the old block, sun and air, junior, June bug, sprout.

SCOFF n. put-on, put-down, dig, dirty dig, cap, crack, slam, slap, swipe, jab, comeback, parting shot, brickbat, backhanded compliment, left-handed compliment.

SCOFF v. dig at, rank out, slap at, swipe at, pooh-pooh, rag, roast, josh, ride, pan, bag on (Hum.), give one the bird. See RIDICULE.

SCOLD n. bitch, hellion, battle-ax, fishwife, biddy, old biddy, screech, she-devil, she-wolf, wet hen.

SCOLD v. kick ass and take names, fire on, rip on, chew ass, chew out, eat out, ream out, lay out, jump down one's throat, climb all over, light into, rake up one side and down the other, slap down, sock it to one, read the riot act, give a going over, cloud up and rain on one. See REBUKE.

SCOLDING n. piece of one's mind, bit of one's mind, chewing, chewing-out, cussing-out, going-over, what-for, rap on the knuckles, slap on the wrist, bawling-out, set-down, calling-down, dressing, dressing-down, the business, catch, catch it, catch hell, speaking-to, talking-to, jacking-up.

SCOOP n. pooper-scooper (for dog droppings).

SCOPE n. 1. elbowroom, leeway, run, run of, space, room to swing a cat. 2. cup of tea, strong suit, long suit, bag, thing, weakness.

SCORE n. 1. points, tab. 2. charts (Mus.).

SCORE v. 1. get on the board, put something on the board, get something on the board, make it, get Brownie points, ring the bell, ring the gong, get into pay dirt, ace (high), knotted (tie), hang-up (sports). 2. count heads, count noses, cut ice, cut some ice, dope out, figure in, keep tab, keep tabs, run down, take account of, tote, tote up. 3. connect, click, put across, put over, get fat, get into pay dirt, go over big, break out with, bust out with (surprisingly or suddenly), make out, make a killing, make the grade, hit it big, hit pay dirt, luck in, luck out, pull off, take the cake, get Brownie points. See SUCCEED. 4. fire on, rip on, chew out, eat out, bawl out, tell where to get off, give what-for, give a going over, climb all over one, come down on, give one Hail Columbia. See REBUKE.

SCORELESS adj. bageled.

SCORE, MUSICAL n. charts.

SCORN v. put down, run down, do a number on, trash, thumb one's nose at, cap, shade, throw shade, rubbish, wipe out, BFD (big fucking deal).

SCOTCH v. spike one's guns, queer, crab, louse up, foul up, fuck up, snafu, bollix up, gum up, put a crimp in, upset one's applecart, knock the bottom out of. See HINDER.

SCOUNDREL n. corn dog, bub, sleazeball, slime bucket, barf bag, maggot, bad-ass, creep, low-ife, bad news, bad egg; prick, dick, shitheel, shower scum, M.F., mofo, motherfucker, mother-humper, mother-jumper, mother-jammer, mammy-jammer, mother-lover, mother-rucker (all Obsc.); black sheep, cutup, scalawag, bounder, rotter lame, rum-dum, low rider, nic-nac, punk, gunsel, cocksucker, rounder. See VILLAIN.

SCOUR v. beat the bushes, leave no stone unturned, look all over hell, look high and low, turn inside out, scratch around, track down. See SEARCH.

SCOUT v. case, case a joint, spot, spy out, check out, stake out, recon, get a load of, take in, bus it (Af. Am.), get an eyeful of, set eyes on, clap eyes on, eyeball, have a look-see. See also RECONNOITER, INVESTIGATE.

SCOWL n. dirty look, bad eye.

SCOWL v. look daggers, dog eye, bad eye, cloud up and rain on one, make a face, act the lion tamer, make a kisser, push out one's lips at. See FROWN.

SCRAMBLE EGGS v. shipwreck, wreck a pair.

SCRAP n. butt, end, stump, gob, glob, chunk, hunk, lump, smithereen, bite, cut, slice; junk, leftovers, odds and ends, bits and pieces, cats and dogs, broken arm (table scraps). See also ARGUMENT.

SCRAP v. junk, throw on the junk heap, dog, retire, chucker out, adios, kiss off. See DISCARD. See also ARGUE, FIGHT.

SCREAM n. holler, blow.

SCREAM v. holler out, beller, holler.

SCREEN v. scrub.

SCREW n. blower, fan, prop, windmill.

SCRIBE n. scribbler, scripter, scratcher, news hen, telewriter (TV), ink slinger, ink spiller, pen pusher, pencil driver. See WRITER.

SCRIMP v. penny-pinch, tighten one's belt, get more bang for the buck, rub the print off a dollar bill, rub the picture off a nickel. See STINT.

SCRIPT n. book, pages, sides, the words, the shit.

SCROTUM n. bag, basket, the family jewels, future.

SCRUB v. soogie, sujee, soujge, soogie-moogie, sujee-mujee (mostly N. and maritime).

SCRUPULOUS, BE v. mind one's p's and q's, think twice. See also PARTICULAR.

SCRUTINIZE v. check, check out, check over, peg, scope, burn up, pike off, smoke, candle, kick tires. put under a microscope, get a load of, get down to nuts and bolts, take the measure of. See SEE. See also SURVEY.

SCRUTINY n. look-see, double O, double OO, close-up, the eye, eyeball, eyeball inspection, long hard look, size-up, watchpot.

SCUFFLE v. mix-up, brawl, jump, go, rowdydow, rumpus, ruction, ruckus, shindy, scrap, dust-up, fuss, wrangle. See FIGHT.

SCULPTURE v. sculp, sculpt, model.

SCURRY v. hotfoot it, dust, barrel, step along, rip, zip, whiz along, get going, get a hustle on, get a wiggle on, pedaling with both feet, hop along. See SPEED.

SEA n. drink, big drink, big pond, deep, briny deep, the briny, the pond, Davy Jones' locker, sink, splash, bounding main.

SEALED WITH A KISS adj. S.W.A.K., SWAK.

SEAMAN n. swab, swabbie, mate, gob, bluejacket, jack, salt, old salt, sea dog, yachtie. See SAILOR.

SEARCH n. 1. skin search, shake down, frisking, bag job (illegal). 2. legwork, on the prowl, chase, fishing expedition.

SEARCH v. 1. beat the bushes, really get into it, leave no stone unturned, look all over hell, look high and low, search high heaven, geek out (seek crumbs of cocaine), shake, shake down, toss (search a premises), turn inside out, turn upside down, dog, bird-dog (scout), scout, scratch, scratch around, scratch for, track down, nose around. 2. frisk, pat one down, pad down, skin-search, feel out, jack up (body), furp up, fan. 3. chase, comb the streets, throw out the dragnet, fan, put the feelers on one, prowl, prowl around, sniff around. 4. penetrate, break in, toss (search a premises illegally).

SEASICK adj. feeding the fishes, hanging over the side, riding the rail, blue around the gills, green around the gills. See also VOMIT.

SEASON v. hot it up, pep it up, zip it up, zap it up.

SEASONED adj. longtime, vet, been through the wars, pro, old pro, been around the block, been around the block a few times. See SOPHISTICATED. See also SKILLED.

SEASONING n. guts, kick, zip, zap.

SEAT n. crotch row (row A), McCoys (choice, The.).

SECONAL n. red devil, R.D., red bird, red, Sec, sex, Seccy, Seggy, Secos, pink lady, marshmallow reds.

SECOND adj. deuce it (come in second), place, runner-up, second-fiddle, second-stringer, second-off.

SECOND n. sec, split second, tick, half a mo, half a shake, bat of an eye, shake, two shakes, two shakes of a lamb's tail, jiff, jiffy, half a jiffy, nothing flat.

SECONDARY SCHOOL n. hi, hi school, high school, prep school, senior hi, senior high.

SECONDARY SCHOOLER n. preppie, hi-schooler, high-schooler.

SECONDHAND adj. hand-me-down, reach-me-down, cheapie, secondhand Rose.

SECRET adj. hush-hush, strictly hush-hush, top secret, eyes only, for your eyes only, classified, classified info, family jewels (Govt., CIA), code word (extra-secret), inside, inside info, on the QT, under one's hat, hold out on, under the sheets, under wraps, undercover, doggo, incog, covered-up, holed-up, pull the ladder up behind one, keep buttoned up, planted, closet, stashed, close to one's chest, something up one's sleeve, for the cuff, for the hat, creep (mission); tref, triff, wildcat (plan).

SECRET n. classified info, inside info, skunk works (secret manufacturing plant or laboratory, originally Lockheed).

SECRETARY n. sec, girl, gal Friday, girl Friday, pink collar, pink-collar worker, desk jockey, coffee bitch. See also CLERICAL WORKER.

SECRETE v. 1. stash, stash away, stache, ditch, duck, plant, squirrel, squirrel away, hike, put in the hole, stick in the hole. 2. bury, whitewash, sweep under the rug, cover, cover up, duck, stonewall, finesse it, palm, paper over, hold out on, keep buttoned up, keep it under one's hat, keep under wraps, 3. hide out, hole up, play dead, lie doggo, lie low, lay low; on the down low, on the d.l. (Af. Am.); sit tight, tunnel, plant, cool off, duck out of sight, take it on the lam, do a crouch, flatten out, out, hit the shade, hit the mattresses.

SECRETED adj. planted, stashed, doggo, under wraps, holed-up.

SECRETIVE adj. tight-lipped, close-mouthed, garbo, tight chops, clam, clam up, clammed-up, dried-up, dummied-up, buttoned-up, button up one's lips, zip one's lip, on the q.t., between one and the lamppost.

SECRETIVELY adv. on the quiet, on the q.t., on the sly, in a hole-and-corner way, in holes and corners. wildcat, play close to the chest.

SECTION n. 1. Tin Pan Alley, the Great White Way, West End, Wall Street, Las Vegas Strip, Sunset Strip, SoHo, NoHo, high-rent district, garment district, red-light. See DISTRICTS. 2. chunk, gob, glob, hunk, lump, smithereen. 3. slot, wing. 4. seg, bite, end, split, drag, piece.

SECTION v. whack up, bump into, size into (chips); divvy, divvy up, slice, slice up, slice the melon, cut the pie, split up, cut up, piece up. See DIVIDE.

SECURE adj. 1. nailed-down, on ice, got a lock on something, license to print money, sure thing, as sure as shooting, cinch, all sewed up, cold lay, bet your ass, shoo-in, ironclad contract, rain or shine. See CERTAIN. 2. solid as a rock, anchored, nailed, hard nut to crack, locked, locked-in. 3. buttoned-down, buttoned-up, button up one's lip, coast is clear, cushy, home-free, safe and sound, out of the woods. 4. sitting pretty. See WEALTHY.

SECURE v. 1. access, promote, wangle, get one's hands on, glom on to, pick up, lock up, rack up, buy up, buy out. See GET. 2. feather one's nest, line one's nest. 3. back, back up, cosign, cover, cover up, cover one's ass, cover all bases, ride shotgun for, stand up for, stick up for. 4. button, button down, anchor, nail, nail down, freeze to, stay put, tack on, tack down, slap on, hook on, hook up, hitch on, hitch up, slough, stick like a barnacle. 5. lock, lock up, lock and win, have a lock on. See ASSURE. See also GUARANTEE. 6. sign on, sign up, hook, take on, catch.

SECURED adj. nailed-down, in the bag, on ice, cinched. See CERTAIN.

SECURITIES n. baby bond (less than $1,000 denomination), convertible, Ginnie Mae, Fannie Mae, Freddie Mac, Muni, municipals, James Bond (matures in 2007), Bo Derek (Treasury bond maturing in the year 2010); double-barreled bond (two sources of repayment), T-Bill; paper, wall paper (defunct); blue chips, blue-chip performer (solid), cats and dogs, stiffs, strips, fancies, high flyer, air pocket stock (dropping), over the counter, downturn, making a Dow line; bear market, bearish market, bottom out (low); bull market, bullish market, top side, top out (high); buy sign, sell sign, wash out, get caught.

SECURITIES, STOLEN n. stiff.

SECURITY GUARD n. company cop, lookout, lay chickie, bugster, rent-a-pig, rent-a-cop.

SEDATE adj. laid-back, cool, cool as a cucumber, not crack a smile, wipe the smile off one's face, cold sober, sober as a judge. See SERIOUS.

SEDATIVE n. downer, dope, goofball, knockout drop, Mickey Finn, pill, pain-killer, pain pill, sleeper, barb, yellow jacket, yellow, nemmie, red, red devil, M, morph.

SEDIMENT n. gook, gunk, black mayonnaise (harbor).

SEDUCE v. hit on, make a move on, put a move on, scam on, put the rush on, crack on, pull, grab, draw, kill, slay, bait, mousetrap, shill, steer, tout, go for it, give one the come-on, come on to one, sweep off one's feet, vamp, hook, make it with one, make out, suck in, rope in, score, reach home plate, get lucky, get over. See LURE. See also ATTRACT.

SEDUCER n. poon hound, speed, mother, cruiser, heavy hitter, heavy cake, operator, smoothie, lookin' to get lucky, lookin' to score, on one's tit, on my jock, letch, lech, old letch, old goat, dirty old man, wolf, vamp, man trap, velvet trap, party girl, player, pusher, C.S.P. (casual sex partner), swinger, sheik, dude, tomcat, cat, sharp cat, gay cat, sport, scorer, lover boy, joy boy, party boy, killer, lady-killer, ladies' man, man on the make, make-out artist, chaser, broad chaser, woman chaser, skirt chaser, cunt chaser, tail chaser, masher, rip, rounder, gay deceiver, gay dog, hound, whorehound, gash hound, tea hound, blade, Lothario, Don Juan, Casanova, good-time Charlie, parlor snake, campus butcher, lounge lizard, cake-eater, poodle faker, prom trotter, sailor, stick daddy (police), bun duster, arm man, diddler, keister bandit, short-arm bandit, short-arm heister, skin heister, pussy bandit, candy kid (1925), fancy Dan, furper (1930), drugstore cowboy.

SEDUCTIVE adj. stacked, whistle-bait, piece, piece of ass, flavor (Af. Am.), sex kitten, mink, tip, hot shit, centerfold, zimmer, good enough to eat up. See BEAUTIFUL.

SEDUCTRESS n. hooker, flirt, maneater, operator, C.S.P. (casual sex partner), party girl, player, swinger, vamp.

SEDULOUS adj. grind, nose to the grindstone, plugger, springbutt, eager beaver, whiz, work one's tail off. See INDUSTRIOUS.

SEE v. 1. flash, flash on, scope, clock, glom, glim, gun, gawk, beam, peg, spot, spy, dig, read, bus it (Af. Am.), lamp, candle, pipe, rap, rumble, spot, catch, focus, eye, eagleeye, eyeball, check, check over, check up, clap eyes on, lay eyes on, set eyes on, lay one's glims on, hold the glims on, take in, get a load of, get an eyeful of, get a hinge, take a hinge, take a squint, have a look-see, take a gander, take a tumble, tumble, give the once-over, give the double-O, give the OO, check, check out, check something out, pin, size up, burn up, pike off, smoke, rubber, rubberneck, kibitz, 87 1/2 (look at a girl, restaurant), give the eye, give one the eye, give one the beady eye, give one the fish eye, give with the eyes, give a ghee a toss, give a thing a play, give a thing a toss, get a load of, pipe, put the squint on, keep tab, keep tabs on, keep one's eyes peeled, pick up on, gap, jap (crime). See also SPY, SURVEY. 2. catch, catch on, get, get it, read, get the picture, blow wise, get hip, collar the jive, capeesh, fershtay, see daylight, dig, I know where you're comin' from, take in. See UNDERSTAND.

SEEDY adj. beatup, ratty, ratty-tatty, tacky, frowzy, fruit, dog-eared, used up, in a bad way.

SEEK v. 1. beat the bushes, leave no stone unturned, geek out (seek crumbs of cocaine), look high and low, toss (search a premises), scout, scratch, scratch around, scratch for. See SEARCH. 2. comb the streets, throw out the dragnet, fan, put the feelers on one, chase, prowl, prowl around, sniff around, track down, nose around, fish, fishing expedition.

SEESAW n. teeter-totter, jinky board, joggling board.

SEETHING adj. steamed-up, boiling over, see red, browned-off, blow one's stack, mad as a hornet, mad as a wet hen, apeshit, have a shit hemorrhage, hit the ceiling, hot, flipped one's wig, on the warpath, got a wild hair up one's ass, red-assed, loaded for bear. See ANGRY.

SEGMENT n. seg, hunk, chunk, bite, end, finger, piece, slice, split, cut, cut of the melon, cut of the pie. See SHARE.

SEGMENT v. divvy, divvy up, slice, slice up, cut the pie, split up, cut up, piece up. See DIVIDE.

SEGREGATION n. feel a draft (recognition of), glass ceiling (invisible barrier to promotion), Jim Crow, Jim Crowism, outseg, seg.

SEGREGATIONIST n. seg, seggie, Ku Kluxer.

SEIZE v. 1. snag, glom on to, latch on to, pick up, take up. See TAKE. See also APPROPRIATE. 2. bust, collar, pick up, pinch, bag, grab, nab, nail, snag, put the arm on, put the claw on, put the cuffs on. See ARREST. 3. grab, shanghai, snatch, put the snatch on one, sneeze, hijack, highjack, skyjack, dognap (dog abduction).

SEIZURE n. 1. collar, mitt, bust, brodie, drop, glom, grab, hook, pinch, run-in, snatch. See ARREST. 2. wing-ding, falling sickness.

SELECT adj. world-class, number one, numero uno, gonest, mostest, baaaadest, boss, cool, meanest, terrible, tops, savage, winner. See BEST. See also ELITE.

SELECT v. name, slot, opt, tap, tab, tag, make, peg, aim, creaming (selecting the best), finger, lay one's finger on, put one's finger on, put one's finger on something, put the finger on, button down, pin down, put down for, go down the line, say so, fish or cut bait, take it or leave it.

SELECTIVE adj. choicy, choosy, pernickety, persnickety, picky, picky-picky, fussy. See PARTICULAR.

SELF n. number one, numero uno, yours truly, me myself and I.

SELF-CENTERED adj. stuck on oneself, on an ego trip, hubcap, look out for number one, look out for numero uno, take care of number one, out for yours truly, shirt up, single-o. See CONCEITED.

SELF-CENTERED PERSON n. grandstander, hotdogger, blowhard, know-it-all, big I am, big I love me, big-timer, swelled head, be on an ego trip, go on an ego trip, think one's shit doesn't stink. See BRAGGART.

SELF-CONFIDENT PERSON n. hotshot, hotdogger, know-it-all. See also ARROGANT; CERTAIN.

SELF-CONTROLLED adj. cool, cool as a cucumber, keep one's cool, together, have one's act together, glued (antonym: unglued), keep one's shirt on, keep a stiff upper lip, not turn a hair, unflappable, commonsensical, ah-ah head, roll with the punches. See also ASSURED; CALM.

SELF-DECEPTION n. jive turkey, bury one's head in the sand, in denial, kid one's self, talk oneself into it.

SELF-DESTRUCTION n. O.D., take oneself out, take a rope, wrap-up, solitaire, Brodie (off a bridge), gorging out, hang-up, hit oneself in the bonnet, hit oneself out, pack in, string up, swing, back-gate commute.

SELF-GRATIFICATION n. ego trip, dolce vita.

SELF-IMPORTANT adj. cocky, puffed-up, ego-tripping, king shit, big head, on one's high horse, full of hot air, hotshot. See CONCEITED.

SELF-INDULGENT, BE v. look after number one, look after numero uno, take care of number one, take care of numero uno, shirt up, single-o. See also INTEMPERATE.

SELFISH adj. hog, got the gimmies, look out for number one, look out for numero uno, out for yours truly, take care of number one, take care of numero uno, shirt up, single-o.

SELF-POSSESSED adj. laid-back, cool, cool as a cucumber, keep one's cool, keep one's shirt on, not turn a hair, unflappable. See CALM. See also ASSURED.

SELF-RELIANCE n. guts, stock, store, sure bet, walking tall.

SELF-RELIANT adj. gutsy, iceman, got the faith baby, cocksure, sure as shit, gamble on, racked. See also SELF-SUFFICIENT.

SELF-RIGHTEOUS adj. goody, goody-goody, goody two-shoes, holier than thou, Holy Joe, noble, square John.

SELF-START v. bootstrap.

SELF-SUFFICIENT adj. on one's own, on one's own hook, one's own sweet way, do one's own thing, paddle one's own canoe, look out for number one. See INDEPENDENT.

SELL v. push, drum, hustle, pitch, move, unload, dump, hit on, go clean, sell out, soft-sell, hard-sell, soft-soap, sweet-talk, snow, close, close the deal, clinch the deal, done deal, puff, boost, plug, ballyhoo, spiel, jam, beat the drum, thump the tub, put on the map. See also ADVERTISE, PERSUADE.

SELTZER n. mixer, soda back (on the side), penny plain, two cents plain. See also CARBONATED WATER.

SEMEN n. come, cum, wad, load, cream, spew, spoo, spooch, splooge, home brew, hocky, hookey, jack, jism, jisum, jizz, love liquid, juice, baby juice, love juice, man juice, pecker tracks, jazz, yogurt, protein, blecch, scum, sugar, crud (dried).

SEMICONSCIOUS adj. not all there, out of it, one's bell rung, punchy.

SEMILIQUID adj. slurpy, gloppy, gooey, gooky, goopy, gunky.

SEMINAL FLUID n. come, cum, cream, spew, spoo, spooch, splooge, hocky, home brew, hookey, jack, jism, jisum, jizz, pecker tracks, protein, scum, sugar, crud (dried).

SEMINARY n. alma mater, old Siwash, brainery, aggie, cow college, fem sem.

SENATE n. the Hill.

SENIOR n. golden ager, senior citizen, gray, gray-haired, blue-haired, wrinklie, P.'s, peeps, pops, gramps, granny, creak, back number, relic, old fossil, old geezer, old folks, old-timer, —— years young, A.K., alte kocker, mossback, gerk (fool). See AGED.

SENIOR HIGH SCHOOL n. hi, hi school, high school, prep school, senior hi, senior high.

SENIORITY n. pappy guy, grandfather in.

SENSATION n. 1. vibes, high, rush, head rush, kick, charge, boot, bang, lift, jollies, gut reaction, where one lives. 2. barnburner, flash, hit.

SENSATIONAL adj. 1. sensay, sensaysh, killer, zero cool, the most, mostest, chilly most, mind-blowing, out-of-this-world, turn on, gone, real gone, solid sender, sizzler, scorcher, drop dead, cliff-hanger, dynamite, hot off the press, one for the book, page-oner, something to write home about, page-turner, thriller. See FABULOUS. 2. blue, purple, dirty, low-down and dirty, off-color, flaming (obscene computer conversations). rough, salty, raunchy, X-rated. See OBSCENE.

SENSE n. 1. drift, point, meat, stuff, heart, key, get to the point, nitty-gritty, nub, nuts and bolts, bottom line, punch line, name of the game, the way of it, nature of the beast. 2. guts, gut reaction, vibes, where one lives.

SENSE v. 1. have a hunch, have vibes (good or bad), get vibes (good or bad), feel in one's bones, feel in one's guts, have a funny feeling, be turned on to. 2. read, savvy, dig, take in, pick up, be with it, chilly, be with one, catch, catch on, catch the drift, get, get the drift, get the hang of, get the idea, get the picture.

SENSELESS adj. 1. gorked, loxed out, veged out, dead, dead to the world, out cold, out of it, out to lunch, out like a light, on the nod. See UNCONSCIOUS. 2. double-talk, doublespeak, hot air, piss and wind, that doesn't chop any wood, that doesn't cut any ice. 3. cockeyed, batty, daffy, goofy, flaky, kooky, loony, sappy, wacky, whacko, hare-brained, balloon-brained, helium-headed, airheaded, cone-head, zombie, cockamamie, screwy, nutty. See FOOLISH.

SENSIBILITY n. gut reaction, vibes, where one lives.

SENSIBLE adj. together, got it together, resonate (that resonates), cool, cool as a cucumber, have horse sense, commonsensical, all there, in one's right mind, got all one's marbles.

SENSITIVE adj. choked, yantsy, feel stuff, touchy-feely, get the vibes, sympatico, hyper, nervy, twitty, tightened-up, wired-up, uptight, hung-up, wreck, nervous wreck, bundle of nerves, have one's teeth on edge, on the ragged edge, tetchy, goosy, jumpy as a cat on a hot tin roof, shot to pieces, all-overish, rabbit ears, hit one where one lives, thin-skinned, grumpy, ugly, crabby, grouchy, got up on the wrong side of the bed, bitchy, turd poodle, cantankerous, can't even look at one cross-eyed.

SENSITIVITY TRAINING n. acidless trip, bod biz.

SENSUAL adj. hot, heavy, hot and heavy, hot stuff, rough, rough stuff, steamy, blue, purple, flaming (obscene computer conversations). X-rated. See LASCIVIOUS.

SENSUOUS adj. slinky, gully low, low-down, low-down and dirty.

SENTENCE n. time, hitch, stretch, term, up, up the river, trick, knock, rap, jolt, icebox, fall, good time, getup, sleep, vacation, curtains for; big bit, buried (long); all, do it all, the clock, the book (life); sleeping time (short); newspaper, magazine; calendar, boppo, boffo (one year). See PRISON SENTENCE.

SENTENCE v. put away, send up, send up the river, ice, put on ice, throw the book at, put one away, take one away, take the fall, break one's license, clean up the calendar, settle, slough, slough up, railroad, walk (escape punishment). See also FINE.

SENTIMENT n. mush, slush, slop, goo, glop, deep sugar, schmaltz, hearts and flowers.

SENTIMENTAL adj. syrupy, drippy, soapy, softie, soft on, soppy, soupy, slush, tear-jerker, teary, beery, sticky, gummy, gooey, sappy, sloppy, gushing, namby-pamby, hearts and flowers, corny, cornball, off the cob, hoke, hokey, hokum, icky, mushy, shmaltz, schmalzy, lovey-dovey, big, big for, crazy for, crazy about, crazy over, nutty about, nutty over, all over one.

SENTINEL n. lookout, weather eye, eagle eye, spotter, tip, lay butzo, lay chickie, zex man, jigger, outside man, hawk, gap. See LOOKOUT. See also GUARD.

SEPARATE v. 1. split, split up, break, break off, break up, kiss off, wash up, rat-fuck, pull out, X, dedomicile, untie the knot, Reno-vate, go to Reno, go pffft. 2. break it off, break it up, boot, drop, drop it, put daylight between, sideline, want out. See also DISENGAGE.

SEPARATED adj. on the outs, in bad with, on one's shit list, at outs, at loggerheads, at sixes and sevens.

SEPARATION n. breakup, dedomiciling, pffft, phfft, go phftt, split, splitsville, split-up, on the rocks, marriage on the rocks, come to a parting of the ways, couldn't make it, on the out-and-out, washed-up. See also DIVORCE.

SEQUEL n. spin-off, son of ——— (e.g., son of Dracula), The ——— Out West (The Draculas Out West), II (Rocky II).

SEQUENCE n. skein, run, streak, pecking order, down the line, time line, track.

SERB n. itch, itchy, tug (Derog.).

SERENDIPITY n. luck out, luck into, find.

SERENE adj. laid-back, cool, cool as a cucumber, ah-ah head, unflappable. See CALM.

SERENITY n. cool.

SERGEANT n. sarge, top, topkick, third lieutenant, third looey, three-striper, first man.

SERIAL n. soap, soap opera.

SERIES n. skein, time line, run, string, streak.

SERIOUS adj. 1. heavy, heavy number, meaningful, jelly, serious jelly, serious talk, serious shit, cosmic, no shit, no bird turdin', no fooling, am I laughing?, chill out, buckle down, getting it straight, not playing around, playing for real, playing hard ball, playing for blood, have blood in one's eye, be out for blood, dropping the green flag, smoking, get down, strictly business, mean business, taking care of business, TCB, get down to business. 2. deadpan, draggy, downbeat, sourpuss, am I laughing?, I kid you not, not crack a smile, wipe the smile off one's face, wipe it off, frozen-faced, cold sober, sober as a judge. 3. big-league, major-league, high-powered, double-barreled, high-cotton, heavyweight, heavy stuff, nuclear, matter of life and death, something, something else, chips are down, money talks bullshit walks, we're not talking about nutmeg here, not to be sneezed at. 4. bound, bound and determined, set, dead set on, bent on, hell bent on, make no bones about it, go for broke.

SERIOUSLY adv. get real, get a life, for real, get a clue, for serious, cool it, cut the comedy, quit horsing around, straighten out, save it, simmer down.

SERMON n. angel food.

SERVANT n. help, live-in, girl, woman, cleaning woman, cleaning lady, man, boy, houseman, houseboy, pratt boy, biddy, cabin girl (chambermaid), pillow puncher, dog robber (Army orderly), flunky, tweeny, furp, peon, serf, slave, slavey, pancake (Uncle Tom).

SERVE v. do for, hit (drink). See also HELP.

SERVE FOOD v. sling hash, chase.

SERVICEMAN n. dogface, G.I., GI Joe, grunt, leg (infantry, Vietnam), sad sack, buck-ass private, doughboy, footslogger, jazzbo (Af. Am.), Yank, cannon fodder. See SOLDIER.

SERVICE STRIPE n. hash mark, Hershey bar.

SERVILE, BE v. dance, dance to one's tune, eat crow, eat humble pie, eat shit; handkerchief head, Stepin Fetchit, Uncle Tom (Af. Am.). See SUBSERVIENT. See also SUBMISSIVE.

SESSION n. clambake, confab, affair, meet, get-together, huddle, buzz session, rap, rap session, bull session, bitch session, jam session, showdown, put heads together. See MEETING.

SET adj. locked-in, stuck in concrete, chisled in stone, solid as a rock, brick wall, ironclad, pat, dig in one's heels, stick to one's guns, hang tough, stiff-necked, unflappable, dead set on. See STUBBORN.

SET n. crew, gang, bunch, crowd, mob, the boys, the boys uptown, Old Boy network, those one runs with, rat pack. See ASSOCIATION.

SET v. plank, plank down, park, plunk, plop.

SETBACK n. whole new ball game, about-face, switcheroo, flip-flop, back to square one, back to the drawing board, bottom out; bath, take a bath (Fin.).

SETDOWN n. comeuppance, take-down, put-down, touché. See BELITTLED. See also ADMONITION.

SET DOWN v. take down, put down, put one away, get one's comeuppance, top, burn, burn down, burn one down, cap, slice up, shoot one down, prick one's balloon, take the wind out of one's sails. See BELITTLE. See also ADMONISH.

SET THE TABLE v. set up.

SETTING n. location, jungle, zoo. See also LOCATION.

SETTLE v. 1. pay up, pay off, pick up the tab, pony up, ante up, come through, come across, come down with the needful, come up with the necessary, cash out, spring for, make good. See PAY. 2. call the shots, cinch, clinch, make a deal, nail down, take a decision. See DETERMINE. 3. square, square things, square up, square the beef, make up for, sugar-coat, pay the piper, pay one's dues, take care of. 4. cool it, grease, back off, pour oil on troubled waters, fix up, bury the hatchet, make up, make it up, make matters up, even the score, have a showdown. See PACIFY. 4. locate, park, hang up one's hat, hang up one's shingle.

SETTLED adj. on ice, in the bag, nailed down, all locked up, no buts about it, clinched, taped, for sure, que sera sera, the way the ball bounces. See DETERMINED.

SETTLEMENT n. 1. payoff, deal, showdown, cash on the barrelhead, cash on the line, cash on the nail. 2. cop out, deal, fifty-fifty, half and half, happy medium, sellout, trade-off. See also AGREEMENT.

SEVEN n. sevener.

SEVER v. chiv, shiv.

SEVERANCE PAY n. golden parachute, tin parachute (nonmanagement employee), golden handcuffs (deferred).

SEVERE adj. heavy, hefty, hard-shell, hairy, hard-nosed, mean, tough, wicked, hellish, jump off the deep end. See also DIFFICULT.

SEX APPEAL n. S.A., it, hot pants, chemistry, creamy, bedroom eyes, come on, bitchy, it girl, oomph, oomph girl, what it takes.

SEX APPEAL, LACK OF n. cold tit, turn-off, iceberg, cold fish, cold biscuit, dog.

SEX, GROUP n. gang bang, gang shag, gang shay, sloppy seconds, group grope, bunch punch, daisy chain, pulling a train. See GROUP SEX.

SEXIST n. MCP, male chauvinist pig.

SEX OFFENDER n. shut-eyes, short-eyes (child molester).

SEX, ORAL n. face, face job, head, skull (Af. Am.), French job, fruit cup, fur burger, muff dive, seafood, eating at the Y, eat out, suck, blow job, perm, deep throat, shot upstairs, sixty-nine, penilingism, bone gobbler, bumper head, head hunter, packin' mud, peter puffer.

SEX, ORAL v. eat it, give a face job, give face, give head, give skull (Af. Am.), give cone, go down on, eat pussy, go for sushi, muff dive, sit on one's face, sixty-nine, suck, cock-suck, suck off, blow, give a blow job, slob the knob (Af. Am.), talk to the mike, give one a perm, deep throat, cop a joint, clean the pipe, polish the knob, French, French kiss. See also FELLATIO.

SEXUAL ADVANCE v. hit, hit on, feeler, proposition, pass, vamp, scamming, come on to, come hither, come-hither look, bat eyes at. See FLIRT.

SEXUAL ATTRACTIVENESS n. candy, lickerish, sweet tooth.

SEXUAL CLIMAX n. cum, come, come off, blow, spew, spooch, splooge, bust one's nuts, go off, get it off, get off, get a nut, get one's nuts off, get one's rocks off, score, shoot, shoot off, shoot one's wad, haul one's ashes, go over the mountain, get over the mountain, go for the moon, explode, cookies, pop one's cookies. See also EJACULATE.

SEXUAL DESIRE n. hots, hot pants, cream for, hard-on for, wide-on (Fem.), bag, itch, in heat, lech, nasties, the urge, sweet tooth, cup of tea, druthers, go down the line, flash groove, turn-on, weakness, fire in the belly, yen, yen-yen, big eyes, zazzle.

SEXUAL ENTERTAINMENT n. circus, dig, exhibition, exhibish, gazupi, peepshow, trick-a-track, trip to the Red Sea, show.

SEXUAL EXPLOITATION n. SexPo, sexploitation.

SEXUAL INTERCOURSE n. fuck, jazz, screw, lay, hump, boff, I. & I. (Mil., intoxication and intercourse), bonk, boink, nookie, nooky, plowin', poke, ass, piece of ass, bang, action, balling, jelly, cock, leg, stroking, roll in the hay, have one, go the limit, quickie, McQ. (quickie), score, devirginize (first time), any (get any?), getting run, shot of crack, yum-yum, bouncy-bouncy, rocking chair, the business, the old in and out, meat injection, beef injection, oil change, missionary position, one-night stand, bed and breakfast, noonie, nooner, matinee, parallel parking, laying pipe, horizontal, horizontal bop, horizontal hulu, horizontal mambo, night baseball, fooling around, scrappin', laps around the track, bush patrol, ground rations, ball, freaking, dork, diddle, deliver, jive, jig-jig, gig, jing-jang, shtup, yentz, plow, slam, jump, jump on one's bones, bump bones, homework, work, trim, tumble, tip, hit, porking, a hormone fix, horsing, bare-back, bareback rider, ride, canoe, crawl, cook, cush, pound, pussywhippin', frisk, jiggle, knock, batter, gombo, grind, mug (Af. Am.), lallygag, lollygag, one shot, pluck, pom-pom (WWII), rock, roll, rock and roll, dating, date-rape, easy make, a little heavy breathing, he'n and she'n, she'n and she'n, he'n and he'n, fun and games, wing-ding, the deed, the dirty deed, frail job, sex job, flesh session, beating someone with an ugly stick, getting beat with an ugly stick, getting your plumbing snaked, getting your rocks off, getting your ashes hauled, the limit, belly ride, belly-to-belly, in the box, in the saddle, wall job (standing up), wham, wham bam thank you ma'am, slam bam, slam bam thank you ma'am, ram bam thank you ma'am, bunny fuck, dry fuck, dry hump, dry run (contraceptive used), ear sex (phone), dog fashion, dog style, shot, shot downstairs, shot at the front door; shot at the back door, asshole fucking, Greek, the Greek way, Greek fashion, Hershey bar route, tube, lay tube, corn hole, bugger, bufu, shirtlift, brown, brown-hole, bunghole, back door (anal); French, French way, half and half, head, bush patrol, lunch, box lunch, eat at the Y, go down, blow job, fudge, futy, fingerfuck, snog up (snuggle), petting party, body rub, half hour, pleasure immersion, keeping company, tea party (bathroom sex), like the birds and the bees; group grope, gang bang, gang shag, gang shay, bunch punch, daisy chain, doing, a scene, pulling a train; sixty-nine, head, mustache ride, blow job, donor (male partner).

SEXUAL INTERCOURSE v. fuck, screw, lay, hump, ball, nail, bang, hook up, boink, boff, jump, juice, juke, bump, boost, boogaloo, bootie, bootie drought (lack of), fuckstrated (frustrated sexually), cook up with, get laid, get together, get busy, get down, grab, grab on, grease, hound, jab, knock boots with, make (someone) scream, maul, penetration, pile, plug, ride the hobby horse, romp, fomp, rock (someone's) world, slam, square (someone's) circle, thump, dig, tax, jazz, score, dork, pork, diddle, deliver, hobble, jive, jam, lay pipe, bed down, go to bed with, dog, do the do, do the wild thing, do you up, do the old in and out, bust you out, do damage, get done, camel walk (Af. Am.), make the sheets sing, go the limit, spread for, come through, turn out, give it to one, do it, do the deed, do the dirty deed, do the nasty, do night laps, do the funky Alphonso, do the ootie-ootie, scrump, belly-to-belly, get it, get it on, get it up, get some, get in, get down to basics, get horizontal, sling up with, get one's ashes hauled, get one's nuts cracked, get one's oil changed, get one's banana peeled, get to first base, get a taste, get it off together, rubbing the bacon, jig-jig, gig, jing-jang, shtup, yentz, plow, hoe hoppin' (promiscuous, Af. Am.), jump, jump in the sack, jump on one's bones, bone dance, bump bones, bone, bone down, shake one down, poke, work, trim, tumble, tip, hit, beat someone with an ugly stick, get beat with an ugly stick, bareback, ride, canoe, crawl, cook, cush, pound, pussywhippin', frisk, jiggle, knock, batter, gombo, grind, mug (Af. Am.), liberate (with native of occupied country), lallygag, lollygag, lap-clap, one-shot, pluck, pluke, pom-pom (WWII), rock, roll, rock and roll, date, make it, make out, put out, go all the way, fool around, honey fuck, wing-ding, fire her up, ring one's bell, dip one's wick, empty one's trash, hide the salami, hide the weenie, parallel park, throw a bop into one, change one's luck, wham, wham bam thank you ma'am, slam bam, slam bam thank you ma'am, ram bam thank you ma'am, bunny fuck, dry fuck, dry hump, dry run (contraceptive used), fire blanks, laps around the track, see

a man about a dog, see a dog about a man, have a party, go down the line, visit the red-light district, lay your cane in a dusty corner (senior citizens), French, give head; give skull, slob the knob (Af. Am.); pearl dive, lunch, eat at the Y, go down, blow job, perm, fudge, futy, finger-fuck, freak off (unconventional), keep company, make like the birds and the bees; group grope, gang bang, gang shag, gang shay, moresome (three or more), daisy chain, do a scene, pull a train.

SEXUAL INTERCOURSE, ANAL n. corn hole, bugger, brown, brown hole, bunghole, asshole fucking, the Greek way, Greek fashion, Greek, bugger, bufu, shirtlift, Hershey bar route, up the chocolate highway, tube, lay tube, back door, shot at the back door.

SEXUAL INVITATION n. pass, proposition, bat one's eyes at, come hither, come-hither look, come-on, feeler, make eyes at, vamp. See FLIRT.

SEXUALLY AROUSED adj. turned-on, horny, honked, hungry, creaming, creaming one's jeans, wet and willing, hot, hot for, hot pants, red-hot, the hots, having the hots, hot as a firecracker, hot to trot, hot in the biscuit, hot and bothered, in the mood, hot in the ass, ready, rooty, rammy; have a hard-on, have a woody, sport a woody (erection); wide-on (Fem.), have a lech on, steamed up, blue balls (male frustrated). See also AMOROUS PLAY.

SEXUALLY ATTRACTIVE chicken delight (young), grills one's cheese, fresh nugs, hot stuff, armful, sex kitten, stone fox, slim, zimmer, chemistry, cutie, cute trick, it, oomph, pinup, playmate, make one's teeth fall out, a turn-on, traffic stopper.

SEXUALLY DEPRIVED adj. hard-up, cock-strong, fuckstrated.

SEXUALLY OBSESSED adj. cunt-struck, dick-brained, fuck-brained, fuck freak.

SEXUAL PARAPHERNALIA n. dildo, vibe, whips, chains, French tickler, leather.

SEXUAL PURSUIT n. pussy patrol, cruising, lock it in cruise mode, put it in cruise mode, do the street, troll, trim hunt, cunt hunt, beaver hunt, beaver patrol, give one the eye, give one the cyclops, take in the sights, go for the cheese.

SEXUAL RELATIONS n. fuck, screw, lay, nail, hump, boff, ass, bang, balling, do night laps, do the ootie-ootie, get down to basics, get horizontal, laying pipe, bone dance, dork, diddle, shtup, boogaloo, do the wild thing, get down, hoe hoppin' (promiscuous, Af. Am.), dating, getting it on, a little heavy breathing, fun and games, rubbing the bacon, wing-ding, the deed, the dirty deed, do the nasty, frail job, sex job, the limit, belly-to-belly, in the box, in the saddle, camel walk (Af. Am.), parallel park, bed and breakfast, bouncy-bouncy. See SEXUAL INTERCOURSE. See also AMOROUS PLAY.

SEXUAL SURROGATE n. hipsie.

SEXY adj. 1. dirty, filthy, blue, off-base, off-color, out-of-line, steamy, hot stuff, adult, mature. See OBSCENE. 2. horny, hot, hot for, hot pants, turned on, rammy, nasty. See LASCIVIOUS.

SEXY FEMALE n. hot number, hot mama, hot, hot stuff, hot pants, hot baby, hot patootie, hot tamale, sheba, stone, stone fox, foxy, foxy lady, pinup, pinup girl, sweater girl; poontang, brown sugar (Af. Am. or mulatto); sex job, sex pot, sex kitten, sizzler, scorcher, slinky, stuff, tease, teaser; cock teaser, CT (Obsc.); tomato, table grade, trade, vamp, bint, cobra, glamour girl, oomph, oomph girl, nymph, nymphet, jailbait, San Quentin quail.

SEXY MALE n. beefcake, Clydesdale (attractive), tasty, hunk, hunky, beauhunk, tuna, hoss (muscular), industrial, fox, beefcake, beef-a-roni, Greek god, demigod, drool over, crushman, mazeh (Yid.), good fuck, good lay, hot ticket, hound, cock hound, lady-killer, man about town, Sam, satisfier, stud, tomcat, trade, wolf.

SHABBY adj. beat-up, crummy, raunchy, tacky, ratty, ratty-tatty, ramshackle, rinky-dink, rinky-tinky, slummy, frowzy, fruit, dog-eared, used-up, in a bad way.

SHACKLE v. hog-tie, tie up, lock up, cool out, put the chill on, bottle up, cork up, hold down, cuff. See RESTRAIN.

SHACKLES n. darbies, derbies, cuffs.

SHACKS n. shanty town, Hooverville, shanties.

SHAKE v. jitter, shiver, have the shakes, have the jitters, have the shivers, have the quivers, have the cold shivers. 2. shimmy. 3. bring one up short, give one a turn, throw, throw one a curve, make waves, knock the chocks from under one, knock the props from under one. See DISTURB.

SHAKE HANDS v. press the flesh, shake, gimme five, gimme ten, high five, low five, gimme some skin, slip me some skin, knock one some skin, lay it there, put it there, mitt, pump the stump, touch gloves (boxing). See also GREET.

SHAKEN adj. shook, shook-up, bowled down, bowled over, discombobulated, discomboberated, defrosted, hissy, come apart, come apart at the seams, crack up, have the jitters. See DISTURBED.

SHAKILY adv. herky-jerky.

SHALLOW adj. half-assed, half-baked. See also SUPERFICIAL.

SHAM n. bunco, flimflam, jive, shuck, cover-up, snow job, whitewash, whitewash job, a cheat, smoke. See TRICK.

SHAM v. fake, fake it, jive, shuck and jive, put up a front, sucker one, do a number, goof on, make like. See PRETEND.

SHAME v. take down, take the shine out of, cut down to size, do a number on, give a black eye, dump on, shoot one down. See HUMILIATE.

SHAMED adj. drummed-out, lost face, come out moldy, eat crow, eat dirt, sing small, draw in one's horns. See DISGRACED.

SHANKS n. gams, gambs, hams, pins, pegs, stems, props, shafts, stilts, trotters. See LEGS.

SHAPE n. bod, chassis, classy chassy, build, built, built like a brick shithouse, V-man, bag of bones, frame.

SHAPE v. throw together, bring together, fudge together, knock together. See also PLAN.

SHAPELESS adj. baggy, blobby.

SHAPELY adj. curvy, stacked, well-stacked, busty, zaftig, built, built for comfort, built like a brick shithouse. See also BEAUTIFUL.

SHARE n. points, split, end, bite, seg, cut, cut in, cut up, melon, cut of the melon, divvy, crack, lagniappe, plum, taste, halver, lion's share, bigger half, big end, fifty-fifty, even-steven, drag, rake-off, p.c., piece, piece of the action, piece of the pie, slice, slice of the melon, slice of the pie, cut of the pie, fingers, finger in the pie, bit, chunk.

SHARE v. 1. divvy, divvy up, go halfies, go halvers, slice up, cut the pie, slice the melon, slice, crack, split up, piece up, whack up, bump into, size into (chips), buck it over. See DIVIDE. 2. be into, be in on, sit in, sit in on, have a finger in, have a finger in the pie, get into the act.

SHARECROPPER n. halfer.

SHAREHOLDER n. coupon clipper. See also INVESTOR.

SHARING n. togetherness.

SHARK n. sea lawyer.

SHARP adj. 1. on the ball, quick, quick on the trigger, quick on the uptake, smart as a whip, smart as a tack, sharp as a tack, foxy, crazy like a fox, not born yesterday, have smarts, have savvy. See SHREWD. 2. snippy, ornery, salty. 3. shady, bent, slick, slippery, snake-in-the-grass, two-faced, feather legs, speak with forked tongue. See DECEITFUL.

SHARPEN v. punch up, soup up, heat up, hop up, hot up, jazz up, pour it on, add fuel to the fire. See STIMULATE.

SHARPER n. 1. carder, cardsharp, card shark, mechanic, high roller, plunger, player, desperado, boneshaker, Broadway boy (small-time). See GAMBLER. 2. shark, sharpie, bunco, bunco steerer, bunco artist, clip artist, double-dealer, operator, slick operator, horse trader. See CHEATER.

SHATTER v. total, kablooey, scrunch, crunch, rack up, bust to bits, break to smithereens, make mincemeat of, smash to smithereens. See also DESTROY.

SHATTERED adj. totaled, busted, in smithereens, kablooey, scrunched. See also DESTROYED.

SHAVE v. knock off, knock off the whiskers, chiv, shiv.

SHAVE (FACE OR HEAD) n. scalping, scraping.

SHEEP n. wool on the hoof, wool on the run, woolly, lawnmower.

SHEET n. white lilies, lily whites, dreamer.

SHELL n. flak, G can, screaming mimi, Black Maria (WWII).

SHELTER n. 1. pad, crib, condo, co-op, coop, joint, den, domi, dommy, digs, diggings, roof over one's head, hole in the wall, cave, home plate, pen, dice house, rack, roost, turf. See HOUSE. 2. umbrella, fix, hat, insurance.

SHELTER v. cover up, cover.

SHELVE v. put on the back burner, put on ice, pigeonhole, cool it, sideline, wooden stake (executive), bird-dog (bureaucratese). See DELAY.

SHELVED adj. pigeonholed, passed up, sidelined, sidetracked, put-up, hung-up, held-up, put on hold, put on the back burner, scrubbed, slowed-up, tied-up, stabbed.

SHEPHERD v. baby-sit, keep tab on, keep tabs on, ride herd on. See also ESCORT; MANAGE.

SHERIFF n. cop, fuzz, bubble-gum man, bull, shamus, arm, pig, oink, clown (rural), the man, star, badge, county Joe, county mounty, county mountie, hick dick, long arm of the law, bear, Smokey, Smokey the Bear, local boy, road ranger. See POLICE OFFICER.

SHIELD n. Chinese wall.

SHIELD v. cover, cover up, cover one's ass, cover all bases, go to bat for, go to the mat for, ride shotgun for, shotgun, stonewall.

SHIFT v. 1. switch, switch over, shift gears, blow hot and cold, flip-flop, shilly-shally, waffle, hem and haw, drift, cook, bottom out, transmogrify, dial back, recalibrate, yo-yo. See also AVOID; VACILLATE. 2. turn over a new leaf, turn the corner, turn the tables, turn one around, do up, about face, flip-flop, sing a different tune. 3. swap places with, fill in, take over, step into the shoes of.

SHIFT BLAME v. pass the buck, buck it on.

SHIFT GEARS v. double-clutch, mash in.

SHIFTILY adv. on the quiet, on the q.t., in a hole-and-corner way, in holes and corners.

SHIFTY adj. shady, cagey, foxy, sneaky, crooked stick, slick, sharp, shifty-eyed, Honest John, doberman (Af. Am.), slimy, trust one as far as one can swing a cat, trust one as far as one can throw an elephant. See DISHONEST. See also SHREWD, DECEITFUL.

SHILL n. booster, pusher, bunco steerer, blow-off, nark, come-on man, plant, deek, puffer, stoolie, stool pigeon.

SHINE n. glitz, flash, show, zap.

SHINE v. buff up.

SHIP n. steamer, liner, tramp, tub, bathtub, bucket, rust bucket, hooker, can, ol' lady, wagon, battlewagon, fig (frigate), jeep, oil burner, sieve, bateau, limey (English ship), rogue ship (extremely dusty, cement, etc.).

SHIP v. drop (merchandise). See also HAUL.

SHIPMATE n. matie, matey.

SHIP'S DECK n. mat (Usu. aircraft carrier).

SHIP'S FUNNEL n. smokestack, stack, noble, Charlie Noble.

SHIP'S STORE n. slop chest.

SHIPWRECK v. pile up.

SHIRK v. 1. fuck off, goof off, fluff off, flub off, flub, flub the dub, sluff off, goldbrick, dog, dog it, fuck the dog, featherbed, lie down on the job, blow off, find Rover (work). 2. get around, dodge.

SHIRKER n. fuck-off, goof-off, buck passer, goldbrick, clock-watcher, coffee cooler, featherbedder, deuce, welsher, skimper.

SHIRT n. boiled rag, boiled shirt, fried shirt.

SHIVER v. have the shakes, have the quivers, have the shivers, have the cold shivers, get goose bumps.

SHIVERING n. shivers, cold shivers, shakes, heebie-jeebies, willies.

SHOCK n. jolt, whammy, double whammy, eye-opener, turn, shot in the ass, kick in the ass, bolt out of the blue, from out in left field. See also SURPRISE.

SHOCK v. rock, gork, floor, shake one up, give one a turn, bowl over, throw one a curve, knock one over with a feather. See SURPRISE.

SHOCKED adj. shook, shook-up, all shook up, rocked, gorked, defrosted, thunderstruck, floored, thrown, unglued, flabbergasted, bowled over, hit like a ton of bricks, bit one in the ass, sticker shock (auto price). See SURPRISED.

SHODDY adj. cheesy, borax, budget, schlocky, drecky, gummy, ticky-tacky, ratty-tatty, sleazy, junk, jeasley, slimpsy, below the mark, not up to scratch, not up to snuff, quick and dirty, plastic, comin' apart at the seams. See CHEAP.

SHOEHORN n. slipperslide (So.).

SHOE LIFTS n. lifties, Adler Elevators (1930–1950).

SHOES n. sneakers, joints, tennies, boats, canal boats, clodhoppers, gunboats, barkers, spikes, platforms, slides, stompers, tooting stomps, wedgies, weejuns, pinchers, treaders, dagger points, earth pads, monkey boots (ankle boots), fiddle cases, violin cases, floorburners, stumpers, goldies, ground grabbers, kemels, kicks, kickers, bottoms, brogans, wing tips, flats, Chicago flats, St. Louis flats, creepers, crabs, clunks, clunkers, coffins (large), flip-flops, marshmallow shoes, white ducks, jelly shoes, pyramids, camp (dress), easy walkers, ends, golashes, gruesome twosome (Army); air hose (wearing shoes without stockings).

SHOE SALESMAN n. shoe dog.

SHOE STORE n. bootique.

SHOE WIDTHS n. A: Al. B: Benny. C: Charley. D: Dave, David. E: Eddy, Edgar.

SHOOT v. zap, smoke, blast, gun, buck (street talk); grease hose, hose down (automatic fire), hemstitch (machine gun), trigger, pull the trigger, squeeze one off, open up, shoot 'em up, let go with, let fly, throw lead, throw slugs, turn on the heat, pop at, take a pop at, turkey shoot (helicopter, Vietnam), drop the hammer, fog away, bang away, beat to the draw, burn down, gun down, put a slug in, give 'em both barrels, give one lead poisoning, get the drop on.

SHOOTING n. fireworks, gunplay, heat, give one the heat, shootout, firefight, bustin' (exit shooting), ride on (drive by shooting), drive by (attack from car), divorce (domestic shooting).

SHOP n. supermarket, superette, super, deli, stand, chain store, outlet, outlet store, co-op, discount house, head shop, ma and pa grocery, mom and pop grocery, bodega (liquor or N.Y.C. grocery), the grab, schlock joint, five-and-ten, five-and-dime.

SHOPLIFT v. swipe, boost, lift, kipe, snatch, grab, hook.

SHOPLIFTER n. booster, derrick, dragger, hoister, crotch walker, pennyweighter, skinworker.

SHOPLIFTING n. five-finger discount, people's crime.

SHOPPER n. chump, easy make, float, front, head, mark, believer, pigeon, sucker, walk-in.

SHOPPING CENTER n. mall.

SHOPTALK n. lingo, officialese, federalese, doublespeak, hillspeak, bafflegab, bunkum, buzzwords, gobbledygook, mumbo-jumbo.

SHORE LEAVE n. liberty, Cinderella liberty (till midnight), forty-eight (weekend).

SHORT adj. 1. boiled-down, in a nutshell, short and sweet, make a long story short, cut to the bone. See also SHORT PERSON. 2. snippy, snappy.

SHORT-CHANGE v. duke (circus).

SHORTCOMING n. bug, catch, not come up to scratch, not make it, warts and all.

SHORT DISTANCE n. pretty near, within a whoop and a holler, within a stone's throw, in spitting distance, just up the road a piece, in the ball park, hair's breadth, practically, close by. See NEAR.

SHORTEN v. cut, cut down, cut to the bone, nutshell, put in a nutshell, boil down, trim, get to the meat, chop, snip, blue-pencil.

SHORT PERSON n. peanut, runt, trial size, shorty, shrimp, peewee, small fry, wart, mite, pint-sized, half-pint, short pint, squirt, duck-butt, dusty-butt, tad, teeny, teenyweeny, sawed-off, knee-high, knee high to a grasshopper.

SHORTS n. Bermudas, cut-offs, kneebusters, clamdiggers, baggies, jammies. See also PANTS.

SHORT-TERM adj. short-stop, in for a cup of coffee (Bsbl.).

SHORTWAVE RADIO TERMS ham, send, 10-4, over and out, do you read me?, pound brass (key), C.Q. (call), Mayday!

SHOT adj. smoked, caught slugs, caught it, bought it, take a hit.

SHOTGUN n. artillery, blaster, boom-boom, scatter, scattergun, iron, hardware, breakdown, gage, gauge, Betsy, slim, boom stick, works, business, copper-dropper, crowd-pleaser (police), bear insurance. See also GUN.

SHOULDERS n. brace of broads.

SHOUT v. holler, holler out, blow, yawp.

SHOVE v. boost, buck.

SHOVEL n. banjo, Irish banjo, Irish fan, jo, hemo jo, joe, muck stick, clam shovel (short), pooper-scooper.

SHOW n. expo, exbo, exhib, exhibish, grandstand play, showboat, flash (gaudy merchandise or prize), shine, splash, front, fireworks, do a fruit salad (expose genitals). See DISPLAY.

SHOW v. flash, hot dog, sport, streak, show time, let it all hang out, show off, showcase, do one's stuff, wave it around. See DISPLAY.

SHOW BUSINESS n. show biz, the Industry, the theater, Broadway, Off Broadway, Off-Off.

SHOWER v. drips, light drips, spit, it's raining cats and dogs, it's raining hammer handles, it's raining pitchforks, pour, really coming down. See also RAIN.

SHOWER BATH n. rain locker.

SHOW GIRL n. chorine, gypsy, pony, floor lamp, parade girl, Ziegfeld girl, in the line. See also DANCER.

SHOWY adj. 1. glitzy, flossy, flashy, loud, screaming, flaky, jazzy, snazzy, zappy, pizzazz, frou-frou, gussied up, kitschy, lit up like a Christmas tree. 2. splashy, splurgy, splendiferous, splendacious, tony, classy, chichi, spinach (excessive), frontin' (Af. Am.), putting on the dog, putting on the Ritz. See PRETENTIOUS.

SHRAPNEL n. shrap.

SHREVEPORT, LOUISIANA Sugar Town.

SHREW n. bitch, turbobitch, hellion, battle-ax, fishwife, biddy, old biddy, screech, she-devil, she-wolf, wet hen.

SHREWD adj. 1. cagey, foxy, crazy like a fox, sharp, sharpie, sharp stuff, shark, ringer, slicker, slick, slippery, smooth, smoothie, cute, cutie, fly, smarts, got the smarts, street smarts, streetwise, wised-up, inside, on the inside, have the inside track, in the know, be up on, on the beam, on top of, the smart money, ear to the ground, playing politics, double digs, sly-boots, hot tamale, hot, hotshot, Philadelphia lawyer. 2. bright, brain, double dome, gasser, wiz, wizard, gray matter, nifty. See INTELLIGENT.

SHUDDER v. jitter, judder.

SHUDDERING n. cold shivers, shakes, shivers, heebie-Jeebies.

SHUFFLE CARDS v. break the deck, wash.

SHUN v. cut, cut dead, dodge, duck, blow off, ditch, duck out of, pass up, get around, palm off, chill, shine one on, freeze, ice, cold-shoulder, give the cold shoulder to, give one the runaround, give the go-by, give a miss to, give a wide berth, stay shy of, steer clear of, have no truck with, not touch with a ten-foot pole, hide out, shake, shake off, stall off. See also AVOID, SNUB.

SHUNT v. get around, circumlocute, bend the rules.

SHUT v. fold, fold a joint, fold up, wrap a joint up, close down, shut down, ring down, drop the curtain, shutter. See CLOSE.

SHY adj. mousy, rabbity, dolo, wallflower, loner, lone wolf, Herman the hermit.

SIBLING n. sib, sis, sissy, bro, breed, bub, bubba, bud, buddy, rack (off the same rack).

SICK adj. peaked, run-down, down with, got the bug, feeling rotten, poorly, under the weather, barfy, green around the gills, blue around the gills. See ILL.

SICKEN v. feel awful, feel under the weather, gross out, look green around the gills, not feel like anything, come down with, take one's death.

SICKENING adj. gross, grossed out, faust, grody, grody to the max, it stinks; motherfucking, mother-grabbing (Obsc.); pukey, pukoid, rotten, scuzzed-out, stinking, turn-off.

SICK LIST n. binnacle list (N.), sick call (Mil.).

SICKLY adj. seedy, draggin', draggin' one's ass, rocky, down, run-down, laid low, below par, peaky, peaked, poorly, out of action, out of shape, good and flabby, Four F.

SICKNESS n. crud, creeping crud, bug, growth, the runs, trots, what's going around, the flu, the pip, dose, double scrudfantods, fascinoma (Medic.), burned (V.D.), willies (mythical).

SIDE EFFECT n. fallout.

SIDELINE n. left field, moonlighting, bench. See also AVOCATION.

SIDESHOW n. bally show, kid show, kid top (tent).

SIDESHOW FREAK n. geek.

SIDESTEP v. pussyfoot, duck, stutter-step, juke.

SIDEWALK n. bricks, byway, cruncher, pavement, turf.

SIGHTSEEING n. rubbernecking, slumming, seeing how the other half lives, flightseeing (from a plane). See also TRAVELING.

SIGHTSEER n. rubberneck, rubbernecker, jet-setter, globe-trotter. See also TRAVELER.

SIGN n. high sign, nod, wink.

SIGN v. ink, put one's John Hancock on, put one's John Henry on, rubber-stamp.

SIGNAL n. high sign, sign, nod, wigwag, wink, bleep, Mayday, SOS. See ALARM.

SIGNAL v. give the nod, flag, flash, give the high sign, wink.

SIGNALING DEVICE n. beeper, bleeper, wigwag, flasher.

SIGNATURE n. autograph, sig, X, fist, ink, John Hancock, John Henry, on the dotted line.

SIGNIFICANCE n. meat, point, heart, nub, key, score, stuff, bottom line, name of the game, nitty-gritty, nuts and bolts, the way of it, nature of the beast, drift, punch line, kicker (point of a story, joke, etc.).

SIGNIFICANT adj. heavy, meaningful, power, serious jelly, serious shit, high-cotton, cut ice, carry a lot of weight, the juice, the force. See IMPORTANT.

SIGNIFY v. send a message, talking (I'm talking big bucks), sign, high sign, flash, give the nod, wink. See also INDICATE.

SIGN OFF v. blow out, close down, wrap, wrap up.

SILENCE interj. shut up, knock it off, hold it down, take it down a thousand, bag it, bag your face, can it, button your lip, zip your lip, put a zipper on it, zipper up, hang up, lay off, spit, clam up, dummy up, dummy up and deal (gambling), bag your head, cool it, forget it, skip it, drop it, come off it, never mind, mum's the word, blow your nose, chop, fold up, get hep, get hip, get under the bed. See also TALKING, STOP.

SILENCE n. dead air.

SILENCE v. gag, ice, muzzle, squelch, squash, shut up, cool it, can it, keep it down, stifle it, hush-hush, soft-pedal, dummy up, dry up, clam, clam up, close up like a clam, pipe down, hold it down, take it down a thousand, shut one's trap, shut one's mouth, hush one's mouth, shut one's face, button up, button one's lip, sit on, sit down on, forget it, never mind, decrease the volume, lump it, save one's breath, mum, mum's the word, bottle up, breeze off, cut the mouth, drink one's beer, see the chaplain, chuck it, put the damper on, put the kibosh on, put the lid on, put a lid on that garbage, keep the lid on, put a half nelson on, cork, cork up, shut down on, jump on, crack down on, clamp down on, hog-tie. See also REPRESS.

SILENT adj. clammed-up, closed up like a clam, buttoned-up, iced, keep one's trap shut, keep one's yap shut, not let out a peep, not say boo, saved one's breath, dried-up, dummy up, dummied-up, garbo, tight-lipped, like a grave, could hear a pin drop, cool, cool as a cucumber, keep one's cool, keep one's shirt on, unflappable, not turn a hair, ah-ah head.

SILK n. worm.

SILLINESS n. poppycock, tommyrot, narrishkeit, twaddle, stuff and nonsense, claptrap, total cahcah, flapdoodle, balloon juice, horsefeathers, fudge. See NONSENSE.

SILLY adj. jerky, nerky, squirrely, dingy, flaky, kooky, dippy, punchy, slappy, slaphappy, bubbleheaded, sappy. See FOOLISH.

SIMILARITY n. spitting image, like of, likes of, look-alikes, peas in a pod, two of a kind, ringer, dead ringer, birds of a feather.

SIMPLE adj. 1. snap, slam dunk, no sweat, no problem, no biggie, no brainer, like nothin', doable, picnic, biscuit, easy as pie, turkey shoot, cake, cakewalk, a piece of cake, sleepwalk, walk, walkover, breeze, child's play, lead-pipe cinch. See EASY. 2. vanilla, clean, what you see is what you get. 3. folksy, homey, haimish, open-and-shut, meat-and-potatoes man. See PROSAIC.

SIMPLETON n. dork, dorf, nerd, nurd, lop, loser, dickhead, dickweed, dickwad, simp, droid, dogburger, birdbrain, bimbo (girl), full hank, yo-yo, twit, putz (Yid.), yutz, lowbrow, twillie, dodo, dumbo, dumb bunny, dumbfuck, dumbshit, mungshit, ninny, airbrained, airhead, heliumheaded, butthead, bubbleheaded, conehead, deadhead, deadass, feeb, zombie, lorg, gump, hamburger, jel, knows from nothing, doesn't know from A to B, doesn't know enough to come in out of the rain, punter (easily defrauded), stoop, dimwit, one doughnut shy of a dozen, his elevator doesn't go all the way to the top, isn't playing with a full deck, a low-watt bulb, a few sandwiches short of picnic, gink, farmer, jay, gerk (old). See STUPID.

SIMPLIFY v. get down to basics, break it down, cut the shit, cut the bullshit, cut the frills, cut the bells and whistles, get down to the meat, hit the high spots, clean it up, lay out, spell out, draw one a picture, dumb down, put one straight, let daylight in, let sunlight in, make clear, make perfectly clear, KISS (keep it simple, stupid). See also EXPLAIN.

SIMULATE v. 1. act like, do, do like, go like, make like, mirror, take off as, do a takeoff, put on, put on an act, send up, play the ——— (affect a role). 2. knock off, steal, pirate, fake, phony, steal one's stuff, bite, lift, borrow, crib, take a leaf out of one's book. See IMITATE. 3. put up a front, put on a false front, fake, fake it, make like, let on, let on like, chomp, play possum. See PRETEND.

SIMULATED adj. fake, faked, phony, queer, bogue, bogus, bogosity, bogotified, hokey, ersatz, plastic, pirate goods, pirate labels, bite, soft-shell, not what it's cracked up to be. See COUNTERFEIT.

SIMULATION n. 1. spitting image, spit and image, look-alike, work-alike, ringer, dead ringer, copycat, carbon, carbon copy, double, ——— compatible (P.C. compatible). 2. queer, fake, bogue, pseud, ersatz, pirate, pirate goods, pirate labels. See COUNTERFEIT. 3. takeoff, put-on.

SIMULTANEOUSLY adv. in sync, dead heat, on the beat, with the beat.

SINCE adv. from away back, back, back when, since God knows when, since Hector was a pup. See PAST.

SINCERE adj. up front, open, like it is, call it like it is, the real deal (Af. Am.), lay it on the line, on the up-and-up, on the level, dead level, the emess, what you see is what you get, blowed in the glass, it, honest to God, honest Injun, sure enough, twenty-four-carat, mellow, square, square John, square shooter, true blue, righteous, Christian, kosher, Boy Scout, fly right, Mr. Clean, spiffy, saint, down-home, regular, legit, on the legit, real, for real, playing for real, the real goods, real people, okay people, L7, granola head, straight, straight-arrow, straight-edge, shoot straight, straight shooter, straight from the shoulder, straight out, straight dope, straight stuff, straight shit, straight up, third-rail, talk like a Dutch uncle, call a spade a spade, put all one's cards on the table, make no bones about it, talk turkey, all wool and a yard wide, card-carrying, salt of the earth, no fooling, no shit, no bird turdin'. See also TRUSTWORTHY.

SING v.   groan, moan, scat, shout, throw a tonsil, chirp, croon, do a canary, canary, yodel, give out, belt out, line out.

SINGER n.   crooner, groaner, canary, chanteuse, monster (popular), songbird, thrush, warbler, bad pipes (bad), belter, coon shouter, folkie, shouter (gospel).

SINGING GROUP n.   group, barbershop quarter.

SINGING STYLES n.   blues, rhythm and blues, R & B, bebop, punk, country, western, country western, down home, Rock 'n' Roll, R and R, shout (gospel), scat, croon.

SINGLE PERSON n.   single, solo, single-o, swingle, swinger, loner, Crusoe, Robinson Crusoe, ace (restaurant). See also UNMARRIED.

SINGULAR adj.   1. special, onliest, strange one, oddball, an original, cool, dolo, rare bird, loner, three-dollar bill. See UNIQUE. 2. breaking new snow, avant-garde.

SIOUX FALLS, SOUTH DAKOTA the Sioux.

SIRE n.   old man, O.M., dad, daddy, big daddy, daddio, daddums, pa, papa, pappy, pap, pop, pops, poppa, padre, pater, governor, guv, warden.

SIREN n.   maneater, man trap, flirt, velvet trap, operator, C.S.P. (casual sex partner), party girl, player, swinger, vamp. See also SEDUCER.

SISSY adj.   faggy, swishy, pantywaist, cream-puff, sissified, cookie pusher, goody-goody, pretty boy, weak sister, Mama's boy (all Derog.) See EFFEMINATE.

SISTER n.   sis, sissie, sissy, moose, hood (Rel.).

SIT v.   squat, cop a squat, make a lap, park, park it, park yer carcus, put it there, grab a chair, grab a seat, take a load off, take a load off one's feet, give one's feet a rest.

SIT DOWN interj.   park it, set, sit your ass down, put it there, park yer carcus.

SITE n.   scene, spot, slot, X marks the spot, armpit (undesirable), hangout, lay, layout, fix.

SITUATION n.   scenario, situash, hap, like it is, where it's at, size of it, how things stack up, scene, ball game. See CONDITION.

SIX n.   sixer, Captain Hicks, sise.

SIXTY-FOUR n.   sixty-fourmo, 64mo.

SIZABLE adj.   humongous, mungo, humungous, humungoid, gross, monstro, moby, honking, big mother, beefy, hefty, bonzai, seagoing, jumbo, whopping, tidy. See BIG.

SKATEBOARD n.   boogie-board, deck.

SKATEBOARD TERMS boarder, skater, skate rat, skater boy, thrasher, boarding stick, deck (board), thrash (spin or any good move), blazin' (doing well), dag (slow down), backyard ramp, scab (short ramp), ollie grab, catch air (become airborne), curb slapping (jumping on or off curbs), face paint, slam, get in a pile, buried, ate it, loft (hang time), queeve (tire), scrub (on streets and curbs), sketch (mess up) unruly, shreddin' (aggressive), grabbin' air (airborne), wilson, bail; slapped, face plant (fall); skate rock (skateboard dancing to music), road rash, munchie, dog bio, bionic (good), beef (injury from fall); fifty-fifty, no comply, nose grind, nosepick grind, Ollie, pulled, shove-it, work, hand plant (stunts); goofy-footed (leads with left foot), half pipe, funbox (platform), truck (pivoting device); fakie, revert, poser (pretender); teller (exaggerates skill).

SKATER, ROLLER n.   blader (in-line).

SKATES, ROLLER n.   blades (in-line), roller blades.

SKATING, ROLLER v.   blading (in-line).

SKELETON n.   Mr. Bones, cage.

SKETCH n.   1. blackout, bit, piece, after piece, routine, shtick, spot, stand-up routine, stand-up comedy, dumb act (without words), hoke act. 2. doodle (meaningless pattern).

SKETCH v.   1. run down, run through, picture. 2. doodle (meaningless pattern).

SKI n.   slats, sticks, boards, bad dog (stunt performer), schuss boom (speed), shuss boomer (fast skier), sitzmark, cement (heavy, wet snow), mogul (snow mound).

SKID n.   gilhooley (auto racing).

SKID v.   drift (four-wheel).

SKIER n.   ski bum, schuss boomer, ski bunny, snow bunny, wanker-two-planker.

SKILL n.   1. one's thing, bag, dodge, line, what one does, what one's into. 2. the stuff, the right stuff, what it takes, cutting it, cutting the mustard, clout, makings, making the grade, moxie, smarts, savvy, the goods, up to it, up to snuff, up one's alley, chops, meal ticket, oil, thing, bit, something on the ball, throwin' stuff (Bsbl.), A, 1-10 (degree, he's a 4), know one's way around, know the ropes, know the score, know-how, know one's onions, know one's stuff, has what it takes, on the ball, plenty on the ball, something on the ball, a bump for, the formula, green thumb.

SKILLED adj.   sharp, sharp as a tack, smart as a whip, fly, brainy, brain, brains, savvy, wised-up, hep, hepster, hip, hipster, hip to the jive, hipped, cool, sharp, tuned-in, into, really into, go-go, with it, chilly, all woke up, groovy, in the picture, got it up here, a lot of nifty, slick, smooth, crack, crackerjack, cute, no slouch, no dumbbell, no dummy, nobody's fool, not born yesterday, quick on the trigger, quick on the uptake, heads-up, on the ball, on the beam, up to speed, up to snuff, phenom, pro, there, whiz, whiz kid, whiz-bang, wizard, boss player, shine at, shine in, enough ducks in a row, hot, hotshot, know one's stuff, know the ropes, know one's way around, know all the ins and outs, know the score, know all the answers, know what's what, know one's onions, know it all, know one's business, know one's p's and q's, in the know, have know-how, have a bump for, have plenty on the ball.

SKILLET n. spider.

SKILLFUL adj. smooth, mellow, good hands, savvy, sharp, slick, there, crack, crackerjack, cute, clean, heads-up, on the ball, on the beam, all-around, up-to-the-mark, up-to-snuff, up-to-speed, tuned-in, no slouch, up one's alley, have know-how, know one's onions, know one's stuff, know one's business, know one's oats, know one's beans, know one's bananas, know one's goods, know one's fruit, know one's groceries, know one's oil, big-league, enough ducks in a row, won one's spurs.

SKIM v. 1. smooth along, skate. 2. get the cream, give the once-over, hit the high spots, once over lightly, thumb through.

SKIM-BOARDING TERMS A-frame (wave cross-wash), doghouse (wave churning in one spot), gull, heathen (a skimmer who steals your wave), gumby (one foot on board maneuver), Kryptonic, all-time, classic epic (perfect skim conditions), 911 (a dangerous skimmer); sider, side wash (wave running parallel to shore); charge, slash (turn back sharply on a wave), tooled (injured), wanker (inexperienced skimmer), weed (a bad fall), widdly, westy loop (somersault over a wave).

SKIMP v. scrimp, penny-pinch, cut corners, cut to the bone, make ends meet, roll back, tighten one's belt. See STINT.

SKIN n. rind, bark, enamel, onion skin (dry).

SKIN DIVER n. frogman, snorkeler, scuba diver, snuba diver (air by hose from a raft).

SKIP v. 1. hippety-hop. 2. cut, pass up, blow off, knock off.

SKIRT n. maxi, maxiskirt (long); midi, midiskirt (mid-length); mini, miniskirt (short), drap, handkerchief hem. See also CLOTHING.

SKITTISH adj. 1. feeling one's oats, full of beans, full of piss and vinegar, full of ginger, peppy, zippy. See SPIR-ITED. 2. rabbity, jumpy. See also FEARFUL, EXCITED, SENSITIVE.

SKULK v. pussyfoot, prowl, gumshoe, snake, case, get around, mooch around, mooch in, mooch out.

SKULL n. biscuit, headbone, ivory.

SKULLDUGGERY n. game, little game, double-cross, fast one, double shuffle, shenanigans, dirty tricks. See TRICK.

SKUNK n. polecat, wood pussy.

SKY n. lid, the blue, the wild blue yonder.

SKYSCRAPER n. cloud buster, high-rise.

SLACK v. goof off, fluff off, fuck off, fake off, flub off, flub, flub the dub, goldbrick, dog, dog it, fuck the dog, featherbed, lie down on the job, find Rover (work). See also RELAX.

SLACKER n. buck passer, clock watcher, fuck-off, goof-off, goldbrick coffee cooler, featherbedder, blow-off, deuce, welsher, skimper.

SLAIN adj. done for, wasted, chilled, totaled, wiped-out, rubbed-out, snuffed, gone, had it. See KILLED.

SLANDER n. dirt, dirty linen, mud, slime, rap, slam, smear, hit, knock, black eye. See DEFAMATION.

SLANDER v. rap, take a rap at, take a swipe at, pan, slam, smear, hit, rag, rag on, bag on (Hum.), rip on, blister, roast, slag, snappin (Af. Am.), scorch, crack, peg, dump, dump on, shit on, hit on, shade, throw shade, mudsling, run down, put down, tear down, shoot down, cut down to size, cut up, cut-rate, cut to the quick, slice up, chop, zing, give one a zinger, needle, give one the needle, dozens, play dirty dozens, sound dozens, sound, signifying, signify'n', shucking and jiving, S'ing n' J'ing, woofing, knock, knock down, knock one off his perch, poor-mouth, bad-mouth, bitter-mouth, cap, back cap, backbite, rip, rip up and down, rip up the back, cut, skin alive, give one a black eye, make one lose face, pooh-pooh, rubbish, sour grapes, curdle, kick one around, do a number on, mark wrong, mark lousy, put the crimpers in, put the hooks in, put the needles in, put the zingers in, sizzle, put away, hurt one where one lives, hit one where one lives, hurl brickbats at, make one sing small. See also SLUR.

SLANDERER n. knocker, mudslinger, backbiter.

SLANG n. jive, jive talk, lingo, street talk, weasel words, talk that talk (Af. Am.), flash (thieves). See also LANGUAGE.

SLANTED adj. slaunchways, slaunchwise.

SLAP n. splap, potch, zetz, crack, slam, smack.

SLAPDASH adj. slam-bang, slap-bang. See also CARE-LESSLY.

SLAPSTICK n. baggy-pants comedy, pratfall comedy, afterpieces, boffo schtick, stationhouse bits. See also FARCE.

SLASH v. carve, carve initials in one, chop, chop down, clip, chiv, shiv, slice, stick, cut, cut a new kisser for, open up. See also WOUND.

SLATE n. lineup, ticket (Pol.).

SLATE v. line up, get on line, pencil in, set up.

SLAUGHTER n. offing, wasting, taking out, a ride, liquidation, chill, kiss-off. See KILLING.

SLAUGHTER v. beef up (cow).

SLAY v. liquidate, neutralize, waste, do, do in, hit, snuff, burn, cook, chill, ice, off, compromise (espionage use), cool out, take out, rub out, erase, knock off, blow away. See KILL.

SLAYER n. hit man, trigger man, piece man, torpedo, enforcer, gorilla, gun, gunsel, hatchet man. See KILLER.

SLAYING n. chill, big chill, offing, hit, knock-off, rub-out, the works, waste. See KILLING.

SLED n. belly whopper, pig sticker.

SLEDDING, GO v. belly-flop, belly flopper, belly whopper, belly-bust, belly busting, belly bumping, belly smacking.

SLEEP n. catnap, forty winks, microsleep, snooze, few Zs, winks, shut-eye, the nod, sleepville, rack duty, rack time, sack time, sack duty, duty time, pad duty, bat cave, blanket drill, bunk fatigue, bunk habit, in the arms of Morpheus, bye-bye, beddy-bye, beauty sleep.

SLEEP v. make some z's, grab a few z's, bag some z's, cop some z's, log some z's, blow z's, snooze, zizz, saw logs, saw wood, rack, rack time, get some shut-eye, get some sack time, sack up, sack in, sack out, conk out, zonk out, fall out, flack out, flake out, flake down, pad out, rack out, tube out, catnap, cooping (police), doss, doz, crash, calk off, drop off, dope off, cork off, knock off, grab some shut-eye, huddle, knock a nod, cop a nod, dig oneself a nod, collar a nod, catch a wink, take forty winks, blanket drill (Army), bunk fatigue (WWII), duty time, flop, kip, pound one's ear, pad down, cup, get horizontal, rest in the arms of Morpheus, plow the deep, in dreamland, sleep in (late).

SLEEPER n. lark, slug, limax, bunk lizard, goldbrick.

SLEEP, GO TO hit the hay, hit the sack, hit the pad, knock the pad, mixout, Z-out, catch some Z's, sack out, flack out, flake out. See RETIRE.

SLEEPING adj. bagging some Z's, making z's, sawing wood, collaring a nod, dead to the world, flaked-out, out of it. See ASLEEP.

SLEEPING BAG n. flea bag, fart sack.

SLEEPING PAD n. corking mat (N., WWII).

SLEEPING PILL n. goofball, goofy ball (Nembutal), dope, knockout drop, Mickey Finn.

SLEEPY adj. dopey, out of it, sleepy-head, snoozy, stretchy, on the nod, eye trouble, in sleepville, blah, blahs, drippy, wimpy, draggy.

SLENDER adj. skinny, twiggy, skeleton, stick, beanpole, beanstalk, stilt, broomstick, gangleshanks, long drink of water. See THIN.

SLEUTH n. dick, tec, private eye, P eye, narc; Pink, the Eye (Pinkerton detective or Pinkerton National Detective Agency); shoe, gumshoe, op, house dick, Hawkshaw, door knocker, beagle. See DETECTIVE.

SLICE v. whack, hack, chiv, shiv.

SLICK adj. 1. smooth, streetwise, foxy, crazy, like a fox, smarts, street smarts, cagey, fancy footwork, full of fancy footwork, slippery, slick Willie, sly-boots. See SHREWD. 2. greasy.

SLIDE v. smooth along, skate, scooch.

SLIDE RULE n. stick, slipstick, cheat stick, guess stick, swindle stick.

SLIDE TROMBONE n. sliphorn.

SLIGHT adj. skinny, twiggy, skeleton, stick, shadow, bag of bones, stack of bones, hatrack, broomstick, rattlebones. See THIN. See also AMOUNT, SMALL.

SLIGHT n. put-down, brush-off, call-down, cold shoulder, chill, freeze, cut, go-by, kick in the ass. See also REJECTION.

SLIGHT v. cut, cut dead, brush off, give one the brush, high-hat, not give one the time of day, chill, cool, cold-shoulder, give one the cold shoulder, shine one on, freeze, ice out. See SNUB. See also NEGLECT; REJECT.

SLIGHTED adj. in the cold, out in the cold, passed-up, sidelined. See SNUBBED. See also REJECTED.

SLIGHTLY adv. somewhat, pretty, kind of.

SLIM adj. skinny, slinky, stick, twiggy, shadow, beanpole, stilt, hatrack, broomstick. See THIN.

SLIME n. goo, gooey, glop, gloppy, Mississippi mud, gunk, scrunge.

SLIMY adj. scummy.

SLING v. heave, chuck, chunk, fire, lob, peg, pitch, toss.

SLINGSHOT n. flipper.

SLINK v. mooch around, mooch in, mooch out, gumshoe, pussyfoot, snake. See also SKULK.

SLIP n. flub, fluff, muff, boner, boo-boo, bobble, goof, foul-up, fuck-up, screw-up, slip-up, plumb (serious), blow it, blow it big time, howler, flap (social), fox paw, fox pass, gaffe. See MISTAKE.

SLIP v. 1. smooth along, skate. 2. let ride, let slide, slip up. 3. goof, goof up, slip up, flub, fluff, muff, make a boner, make a boo-boo, make a blooper, drop the ball, stumble, juke, put one's foot in it, put one's foot in one's mouth, stub one's toe. See ERR.

SLIPPERS n. skivvies, mules, scuffs, Jesus sandals (Birkenstock), thongs, flip-flops, zoris. See also SHOES.

SLIPPERY adj. 1. cagey, crazy like a fox, foxy, slick, smooth. See SHREWD. 2. greasy, skating-rink.

SLIPSHOD adj. sloppy, slapdash, junky, fly-by-night, messy, half-assed, do by halves, any old way, mess around, honky-tonk, cold haul, a lick and a promise. See CARELESS. See also SLOVENLY.

SLOG v. 1. plug, plug along, plug away, dig, grind, hammer, slave, sweat, sweat and slave, bear down on it. See PLOD. 2. hoof it, go by hand, boot it, stump it, beat the rocks, press the bricks. See WALK.

SLOPING adj. slaunchways, slaunchwise.

SLOTHFUL adj. drag-ass, lox, sack artist, underachiever, Stepin Fetchit. See also LAZY.

SLOT MACHINE n. one-arm bandit, one-armed bandit, slot, slots.

SLOVENE n. Krainer, Krajner, Greiner, Griner, Grinder (Derog.).

SLOVENLY adj. sloppy, slobbed-out, mangled, thrashed, grubby, grungy, groaty, grotty, grody, grunch, grunge, grubby, tacky, chili bowl, icky, scuzzy, scuzzed, scuzzed-up, sleazy, sleazeball, sludgeball, mess, messed-up, mussed-up, messy, mussy, bloody mess, holy mess, unholy mess, rat's nest, topsy-turvy, arsy-varsy, discombobulated, slob, fat slob, rag-mop, scraggly, piggy, pigpen, dip, jeeter, poky, seedy, draggle-tailed, drabble-tailed, down at the heel, out at the heels, out at the elbows. See also SLIPSHOD.

SLOW adj. 1. pokey, slowpoke, drag, draggy, drag ass, foot dragger, schlepper, underachiever, Valium picnic (slow day), banana boat, klupper, slower than the seven-year itch, Stepin Fetchit, stick-in-the-mud, molasses in January, lox, sack artists. 2. draggy, ho-hum, bor-ring, a yawn, big yawn, bore one stiff, dullsville, noplaceville, phoned-in, big deal, no big deal, flat. See BORING.

SLOW v. bog, bog down, lose steam, back off, let up, anchor it, brake, hit the brakes, put on the brakes, lay down rubber, leave a stripe, let down the flaps, give one the wind (suddenly), back off the pedal, lay back, cool it, choke, choke in, choke up, ease off. See also DELAY, HINDER, RETARD.

SLOWLY adv. flaps down, stick in the mud, get no place fast, mosey, toddle, plug along, poke along, schlep, drag tail (also move with difficulty), drag ass, drag one's tail, slo-mo, have lead in one's pants, overland route, by pony express, slowpoke, move like a slug, foot dragger, slower than the seven-year itch, in short pants, skuffling.

SLOW-MATURATION n. late bloomer.

SLOW-WITTED adj. dorky, dorf, nerdy, droid, ditzo, dickhead, Fred, Barney, Wilma, beau, out to lunch, lunchie, lunchbox, lunchsack, vacant lot, Z-head, McFly, feeb, lorg, gump, lamebrain, birdbrain, fuckbrained, beanbrain, four-letter man (dumb), deadass, hamburger, jel, stoop, stupe, spaz, thick, lob, dill, dud, ninny, nincompoop, airhead, helium-head, butthead, balloonhead, conehead, meatball, bonehead, Barbie and Ken, nuthin' upstairs, weak in the upper story. See STUPID.

SLUDGE n. gook, gunk, glop.

SLUGGISH adj. 1. dopey, laid-back, blah, drippy, moony, sleepyhead, stretchy, have spring fever. See LANGUID. 2. pokey, draggy, drag-ass, schlepper, slower than the seven-year itch, lox, slower than molasses in January. See SLOW.

SLUM n. inner city, back alley, back street, hogsville, skid row, shanty town.

SLUMBER n. forty winks, sleepville, sack time, sack duty, duty, duty time, pad duty, bat cave, bunk habit, beauty sleep. See SLEEP.

SLUMBER v. make some z's, log some z's, saw logs, saw wood, get some sack time, grab some shut-eye, catch forty winks, blanket drill (Army). See SLEEP.

SLUMP n. 1. hard times, bad times, bust, crash, rainy days, rainin', bear market, bottom out, slide, Black Monday (Oct. 19, 1987), Black and Blue Monday (Oct. 26, 1987), the big trouble (the 1930s). 2. blue devils, blue funk, funk, downer, dumps, down trip, letdown, hit the skids, die on the vine. See DEPRESSION.

SLUR n. put-down, zinger, cap, brickbat, rap, slam, knock, black eye, hit, dirty dig, dump, dozens, dirty dozens, woofing. See DEFAMATION.

SLUR v. put down, dump on, flip one the finger, give one the finger, give one five fingers, cap, shade, throw shade, chop, blister, roast, scorch, cut up, do a number on, zing, give one a zinger, burn, slice up, give one the cold shoulder, give one a backhanded compliment, give one a left-handed compliment, give one a black eye, give one a dirty dig, thumb one's nose, slap in the face, hurl brickbats at, dozens, play dirty dozens, sound dozens, sound, signify, signify'n', shucking and jiving, S'ing n' J'ing, woofing, eighty-six, hurt one where he lives, hit one where he lives, hit on, blow off, cut, cut to the quick, skin alive, cap, curdle, gross out, miff, push, kick one around, pooh-pooh. See also SLANDER.

SLUSH n. gook, gunk, glop.

SLY adj. smooth, foxy, smarts, street smarts, streetwise, crazy like a fox, cagey, fancy footwork, slick, slippery, greasy, greaseball, fishy, sly-boots, shady, sharp, snake in the grass, cheatin' heart, not kosher, Honest John, feather legs, speak with forked tongue. See also SHREWD.

SLYLY adv. undercover, under wraps, hush-hush, strictly hush-hush, on the q.t., on the quiet, on the sly, in a hole-and-corner way, in holes and corners.

SMALL adj. teeny, teeny-weeny, teensy, teensy-weensy, mini, minny, eentsy-weentsy, bitty, bitsy, little bitty, little bitsy, itsy-bitsy, itsy-witsy, shrimp, wee, peewee, peanut, runt, short, small-fry, small-time, dinky, measly, banty, tomtit, shot, shit, chickenshit, horseshit, bullshit, chippie, button, yea big, yea high, wart, mite, piddling, two-bit, two-by-four, pint-sized, half-pint, knee-high, knee-high to a grasshopper, penny ante, tad, titch, tich; jerkwater, one-horse (town).

SMALL PLACE n. hole in the wall, pigeonhole, cubbyhole, tight pinch, tight spot, tight squeeze.

SMALL TOWN n. jerkwater town, hick town, rube town, hoosier town, one-horse town, tank town, tank station, duckburg, South Succotash, East Jesus, Podunk, jumping-off place, hickville, burg, whistle stop, whistle snort, noplaceville, filling station, wide place in the road, hideaway, the bushes, the boondocks, boonies, sticks, stix, B.F.E., butt-fucking Egypt, B.F.A., butt-fucking Africa, bush leagues, pumpkin, the rhubarbs.

SMART adj. 1. brain, brainy, propeller head, cereb, egghead, brill, got the smarts, have the smarts, smart as a whip, book-smart, whiz, whiz kid, bright, technotrash (social idiot), long-haired, skull, genius, rocket scientist, Einstein. See INTELLIGENT. 2. sharp, sharp as a tack, tack, dap, last word, latest thing, nobby, natty, dressed to kill. See STYLISH.

SMASH v. 1. bust to bits, scrunch, crunch, make mincemeat of, break to smithereens, smash to smithereens, trash, squash, squish, smash up, take a joint apart, break the lease, put something out of action, put out of commission, bend the goods. See DESTROY.

SMEAR v. pan, slam, hit, blister, rag, rag on, bag on (Hum.), scorch, rap, mudsling, poor-mouth, bad-mouth, peg, rip up the back, give a black eye, pooh-pooh, rubbish, sour grapes, do a number on, put the zingers in. See SLANDER.

SMELLING SALTS n. dope.

SMELLY adj. stinko, whiffy, nosy, strong, stinking, stinky, funky, loud (strong), P.U., what died?

SMELT n. hooligan.

SMILE v. crack a smile, grin from ear to ear, grin like a Cheshire cat, grin like a Chessy cat.

SMIRK v. grin like a Cheshire cat, grin like a Chessy cat.

SMOCK n. Mother Hubbard.

SMOKE v. light up, burn, blow, drag, take a drag, inhale, pull, do up, puff, poke, toat, toke, smoke a toke, smoke a bowl, torch up, hit, take a hit, blow a stick, blow major jaw (smoke buds), blow smoke rings, chain-smoke, dinch (extinguish cigarette), have a pipeful, fog, fog up, French inhale, fume, fumigate.

SMOKE AND FOG n. smog.

SMOKE AND HAZE n. smaze.

SMOKED ALASKAN SALMON n. squaw candy.

SMOKER n. ashtray, chain smoker, fag hag (Fem.) (Derog.), chimney.

SMOKING ROOM n. butt room.

SMOOTH v. 1. cool, cool out, cool it, cool off, stroke, pour oil on troubled waters, take the edge off, take the sting out of, put the lid on. See PACIFY. 2. grease the wheels, run interference for, open doors, walk through, hand-carry.

SMOOTHLY adv. swimmingly, like nothin', soft touch, velvet, pie, cherry pie, easy as pie, duck soup, a piece of cake, fluff, breeze, walkover, waltz, slick as a whistle. See also EASY.

SMOTHER v. douse, kill (fire or cigarette), choke, knock down, stamp out. See also REPRESS.

SMUG adj. stuffy, top-lofty, hoity-toity, hot shit, hot stuff, hotshot, cock of the walk, think one is it, think one's shit doesn't stink. See CONCEITED.

SMUGGLE v. move the laundry, rum-run, run-rum, snake one in, whip over, push.

SMUGGLE LIQUOR v. run-rum, rum-run, whip over.

SMUGGLER n. bootlegger, legger, rum runner, monkey runner, sneaker (motorboat), coyote (illegal aliens).

SMUTTY adj. raw, raunchy, X-rated, filthy, in the gutter, off-color, flaming (obscene computer conversations). rough, rough stuff, salty. See OBSCENE.

SNACK n. bite, finger food, gorp, nash, nosh, nibble, midnight snack, snack time, eats, grub, pecks, peckings (Af. Am.), pick-me-up, yum, yum-yum, goodies, munchies, zoo-zoos. See also FOOD, MEAL.

SNACK BAR n. fast food, quick-and-dirty, short-order.

SNAG n. glitch, bug, fix, hole, pickle, scrape, stew, hang-up, spot, tight spot, crunch, Catch-22, joker, cropper, up a tree, tail in a gate, tit in a wringer, puzzler. See DIFFICULTY.

SNAG v. pick up, hook, nail, net, gaff, put the claw on, haul in. See GRAB.

SNAKE CHARMER n. geek.

SNAPPISH adj. snippy, snappy, short.

SNAPSHOT n. pic, pix, photo, snap, shot, print, glossy.

SNARE v. bag, net, land, get one's fingers on, corral, pull in, round up. See GRAB. See also ARREST.

SNATCH v. snag, snarf (with or without permission), collar, bag, glom, glom onto, put the snatch on, clap hands on, get one's fingers on, get one's hands on. See GRAB.

SNEAK v. pussyfoot, gumshoe, prowl, snake, case, get around, mooch around, mooch in, mooch out.

SNEAK ATTACK n. Pearl Harbor.

SNEAKILY adv. on the quiet, on the q.t., gumshoeing, pussyfooting, in a hole-and-corner way, in holes and corners.

SNEER n. put-down, put-on, dump, rank-out, dig, dirty dig, crack, slam, swipe, jab, comeback, parting shot, brickbat, bazoo, raspberry.

SNOB n. Brahmin, highbrow, high hat, smarty pants, stiff neck.

SNOBBISH adj. snooty, uppity, uppish, swanky, snotty, tony, dicty, put on airs, stuck up, hoity-toity, persnickeity, sniffy, snippy, high-hog, high-hat, high-hatted, hinkty, toplofty, high-nosed, sidity, sidity. See also ARROGANT.

SNOOP n. nosy Parker, busybody, Paul Pry, Peeping Tom, gumshoe.

SNOOPING adj. nosing around, peeping. See also INQUISITIVE.

SNORE v. saw gourds, saw logs, saw wood, make Z's. See also SLEEP.

SNOUT n. smeller, schnoz, schnozzola, schnozzle, hooter, beak, bugle, horn, honker, snoot, nozzle, bazoo, banana, bill, beezer, boke, conk, handle, sniffer, snuffer, whiffer.

SNOW n. powder, whiteout, dandruff, fluff stuff, cement (heavy wet), corn (man-made), termination dust (first of season, Alaska).

SNOWBOARD TERMS macking (fast), stalefish, Canadian bacon (jump), bone out, disaster slide, slip the pipe, fakie (ride backward), Mr. Wilson (fall), cut (outdated move), half pipe, (chute), wanker-two-planker.

SNOWMOBILE n. snowgo.

SNOWSTORM n. whiteout.

SNUB v. cut, cut dead, D.K., brush off, give the brush, give the go-by, pass up, high hat, chill, put the chill on, ice, ice out, frost, burr, cool, play it cool, act cool, leave out in the cold, put the freeze on, not give one the time of day, not give one a flop, not give one a rumble, not give one a tumble, look right through, cold-shoulder, give one the cold shoulder, cold-duke, freeze, duck, fluff, give one the fluff, fluff off, kiss off, scratch, scratch off the list, upstage, shine one on, kick in the ass. See also SHUN.

SNUBBED adj. cold-shouldered, cut, out in the cold, chilled, brushed-off, fluffed-off, get it in the neck, kicked in the ass, slapped in the face. See also REJECTED.

SNUFF n. dust, heifer dust (Obs.), snoose.

SNUG adj. comfy, cushy, snug as a bug in a rug, homey, tight.

SOAKING n. dunking.

SOAP n. soogie, sujee, soujge.

SOB v. blubber, bawl, break down, boo-hoo, weep bitter tears, turn on the waterworks, cry one's eyes out, cry me a river. See CRY.

SOBER adj. 1. on the wagon, on the water wagon, cold sober, sober as a judge, able to walk the chalk line, dry, took the pledge. 2. strictly business, heavy, heavy number, am I laughing?, not playing around, sourpuss, frozen-faced. See SERIOUS.

SOCIABLE adj. mix, get-together, right nice, right neighborly, downright neighborly, white, regular, square shooter, sucking around, kissing up to, get with it, break the ice, clubby, clubbable. See also COMPANIONABLE.

SOCIAL DISEASE n. AIDS, VD, clap, dose, dose up, dose of clap, old dose (neglected case), package, picked up something, picked up a nail, brothel sprouts, Cupid's itch, Venus's curse, crotch pheasants, lobster tails, full house (combination), short-arm inspection (examination of males for). See VENEREAL DISEASE.

SOCIAL GATHERING n. get-together, ball, bash, blast, bust, kegger, clambake, crush, shindig, rub, jump, mingle, blowout, coffee klatch, shindy, merry-go-round, wing-ding, jam, do, free-load, gig, scene. See PARTY.

SOCIAL GRACE n. polish.

SOCIALIST n. left-winger, left, lefty, lefto, Old Left, left of center, pink, pinko, parlor pink, radish, fellow traveler, linky-dink, bleeding heart, do-gooder, innocent (Af. Am.), knee-jerk reaction, comsymp, Wobbly.

SOCIALIZE v. pal up, pal around, mix, tie up with, gang up, hang around with, run with, chum with, chum together, chill hard, make the rounds, floss around, on the go, gadabout. See also FRATERNIZE.

SOCIALLY ACCEPTABLE adj. housebroken, in.

SOCIALLY ADROIT PERSON n. operator, swinger, player, street smart, streetwise.

SOCIAL OUTCAST n. fuckface. See also DISLIKED PERSON.

SOCIAL PERSON n. elbow bender, glad hander.

SOCIAL REGISTER n. blue book.

SOCIAL WORKER n. streetworker.

SOCIETY n. 1. the 400, the four hundred, beautiful people, Eurotrash, glitterati, upper crust, high-rise boys, high society, main line, jet set. See ELITE. 2. hookup, tie-in, tie-up, gang, mob, ring, clan, outfit, syndicate. See ASSOCIATION. 3. jungle, zoo, rat race.

SOCIOECONOMIC GROUPS n. baby boomer, blue collar, white collar, dik (double income, have kids), dink (double income, no kids), sik (single income with kids), sink (single income, no kids), zink (zero income, no kids), nilok (no income, lots of kids), OTNM (over thirty never married); WOOP, woopie (well-off older people); YUP, yuppie (young urban professional), buppie (black urban professional), guppie (gay urban professional), huppie (Hispanic upwardly mobile professional), RUB (rich urban biker), yumpie (young, upwardly mobile professional), yuffie, (young urban failure), yavis (young, attractive, verbal, intelligent, successful), domo (downwardly mobile professional), tafy (technically advanced family), the establishment, upper ten thousand, the 400, Four Hundred.

SOCIOLOGY n. soc, sosh.

SOCKS n. bobby socks, bobby sox.

SODA n. pop, club soda, clear soda, soda back (chaser), seltzer, sizz water, fizz water, penny plain, black cow, double chocolate. See SOFT DRINK.

SODA FOUNTAIN WORKER n. jerk, soda jerk, soda jerker, squirt, ninety-eight (Manager).

SODOMIST n. bugger.

SODOMY n. 1. goin' up the mustard road, ace fuck, butt, bufu, brown, brown hole, corn hole, burgle, Greek, bugger, shirt lift, Hershey bar way, tube, lay tube, sit on it, ride the deck, up the old dirt road, bite the brown, reem, rim job (all Obsc.). See also SEXUAL RELATIONS. 2. suck, cock-suck, sucky-suck, blow, blow job, go down on, head, give head, a shot upstairs, gobble, peter puff, play the skin flute (all Obsc.). See FELLATIO. 3. face, face job, hat job, French job, box lunch, fur burger, muff dive, eating at the Y (all Obsc.). See CUNNILINGUS.

SOFA n. davenport, sofa bed, daybed.

SOFT adj. 1. gone to seed, not what one used to be, out of condition, out of shape, run to seed, rusty, good and flabby. 2. cool, mellow, gravy.

SOFT DRINK n. Coke, pop, club soda, clear soda, white soda; chaser, back soda, soda back (chaser); seltzer, sizz water, fizz water, fizzy stuff, penny plain, for two cents plain, ammonia, maiden's delight (cherry), mixer, cream, egg cream, phosphate, black cow, double chocolate, float, cooler, bug juice.

SOFT-DRINK POWDER n. flukum, flookem, flookum.

SOFTEN v. take the edge off, take the bite out, take the sting out, soft-pedal, cool, cool it, cool out, fix up, make up, make it up, make matters up, patch things up, get together on, come together, meet halfway, pour oil on troubled waters.

SOFTHEARTED adj. softie, teddy bear, pussycat, nice guy, Joe Nice Guy, Mr. Nice, marshmallow. See also KIND.

SOIL v. sleaze up, crumb up, muck up, crud, mess, mess up, muss, muss up.

SOILED adj. cruddy, grungy, scrungy, raunchy, messy, messed-up, mussed-up, sleazy, sleazed-up. See DIRTY.

SOJOURN v. hang out, bunk, nest, perch, roost, squat, bunk out, crash. See INHABIT.

SOLDIER n. grunt, G.I., GI Joe, Joe, Joe Blow, Blow Joe, dogface, doughfoot (WWII), E.M. (enlisted man), draftee, doughboy (WWI, Mexican War), footsoldier, footslogger, hump, paddlefoot, buck-ass private, trooper, leg (infantry, Vietnam), red legs (artilleryman, WWI), retread (recalled to duty), sad sack, snuff, yardbird, bunion breeder, gravel agitator, gravel pounder, gravel crusher (WWI), Yank, jazzbo (Af. Am.), bullet bait, cannon fodder, fuck-off, government inspected meat (homosexual use), lifer (career), Fed (Union), bluebelly (Union soldier, Derog.), dolly dancer (easy duty), barracks lawyer, guardhouse lawyer, galoot, crunchie, clerks and jerks (rear echelon).

SOLD-OUT adj. SRO, sellout, go clean, clean house.

SOLE adj. onliest, ace (Rest.). See ALONE.

SOLELY adv. onliest. See ALONE.

SOLEMN adj. 1. heavy, heavy number, matter of life and death, no fooling, chill-out, mean business. 2. downbeat, am I laughing?, cold sober, sober as a judge. See SERIOUS.

SOLICIT v. 1. hit on, pop the question, whistle for (but won't get). 2. run a stable, have a string of hustlers, have a sister-in-law, steer, tout. 3. panhandle, bum, hustle, sponge, schnor, cadge, touch, mooch, promote, put the bite on, pass the hat, hit up. See BEG.

SOLICITOR n. 1. mouthpiece, shyster, ambulance chaser, legal eagle, beagle, lip, tongue, squeal, spieler, spouter, springer. See ATTORNEY. 2. mack, mackman, macko man, mac, mackerel, maggot, dude, hustler, Johnny Ponce, pee eye, P, brother-in-law, honey man. See PIMP, PROSTITUTE.

SOLICITOUS adj. worried sick, worried stiff, heart in the right place, beside oneself, all-overish. See also CONSIDERATE.

SOLICITUDE n. tender loving care, TLC.

SOLID adj. 1. solid as a rock, Rocka Gibraltar, Rock of Gibraltar, Rock of Gib, brick wall, set in concrete, stuck in concrete, buried in concrete, chiseled in stone. 2. unflappable, set, stay put, hard-core, hard-line, rock-ribbed. See STUBBORN. 3. sound as a dollar, in the black. See also WEALTHY. 4. big-time, big-league, major-league, heavyweight, high-powered, double-barreled. See IMPORTANT. 5. husky, buffed, hefty, hoss (muscular), industrial, heavy, hunk, hulk. See STRONG.

SOLITARY adj. loner, lone wolf, dolo, solo, stag, all by one's lonesome, in solitary, chew something alone, traveling light. See ALONE.

SOLITARY CONFINEMENT n. bury, plant, ice, put on ice, put in the hole, salt, throw the key away, do penance, slap in the box, hit the box, hit izo, hit isolation, hit the beach, hit the icebox, hit the plant, a month in Congress, P and Q (peace and quiet), on the shelf, tending the bar (standing handcuffed), time out.

SOLO adj. dolo, loner, single, single-o, swingle, go it alone, Crusoe, Robinson Crusoe, ace (alone in Rest.), get off (swing music: improvised). See also ALONE.

SOLUTION n. quick fix, all the right moves, on target, pay dirt, the ticket, the nod, the call, Band-Aid (temporary, too little).

SOLVE v. dope, dope out, chill, pan out, figure out, crack, lick, deal with, make a deal, iron, iron out, nail down, cinch, clinch, unzip, work through, hit it on the nose.

SOLVENT adj. sound as a dollar, in the black. See also WEALTHY.

SOMALIS Sammies, Skippies (U.S. Army).

SOMBER adj. dragged, ass in a sling, blue, got the blue devils, down, hang crepe, hurting, carry a heavy load, gloomy Gus, not crack a smile, wipe the smile off one's face, prune-faced, sourpuss. See UNHAPPY.

SOMERSAULT v. endo.

SOMETIMES adv. once in a blue moon, once in a coon's age, every now and then, every once in a while, every so often.

SOMNOLENT adj. dopey, out of it, sleepyhead, snoozy, stretchy, on the nod, eye trouble, in sleepville, blah, blahs, drippy, wimpy, draggy. See also LANGUID.

SON n. chip off the old block, junior, sprout, sun and air, June bug.

SONG n. tune, oldie, golden oldie, holler, holler song, torch song, belly music, chart-busting hit.

SONGWRITER n. cleffer, songster, tunesmith, tunester.

SONOROUS adj. leather-lunged. See also LOUD.

SOON adv. by 'n' by, in a short, short-short, coming down the pike.

SOOTHE v. cool, cool off, stroke, butter up, make nice, play up to, pour oil on troubled waters, square, take the edge off, take the sting out of, make matters up, patch things up. See PACIFY.

SOOTHING adj. cool, mellow, flannel (manner). See also TRANQUILIZER.

SOPHISTICATE n. cat, sharp cat, hepcat, hip cat, tomcat, hipster, dude, sport, swinger, slicker, city slicker, man about town. See also VETERAN.

SOPHISTICATED adj. fly, with it, chilly, chilly most, wised-up, wise to, hep to, hep, hip, hip cat, hepcat, sharp cat, tomcat, been there, dude, on to, on the beam, down by law, uptown, go-go, in, into, really into, groovy, swinging, mod, up to speed, street smart, streetwise, uppity, executive, sport, city slicker, laid-back, cool, cool-and-collected, on, switched-on, kicked around, been around, been hit before, been there before, been around the block, been around the block a few times, didn't come into town on a load of hay, wasn't born yesterday, cut a few touches, in the know, knows the score, knows the ropes, knows which side is up, knows which side his bread is buttered on, knows which side his head is battered on, dolce vita.

SOPHOMORE n. soph.

SORCERY n. evil eye, stink eye, go, hoodoo, voodoo, jinx, whack, whammy, hocus-pocus, mumbo-jumbo, abracadabra.

SORE THROAT n. bad pipes.

SORORITY HOUSE n. house, frau shack, soror house, snake house, zoo, animal farm, bull pen.

SORORITY MEMBER n. soror, Suzie Sorority, Sue, Sorority Sue, Muffy, Buffy, sister, rushee, Rhonda Rushee, pheeze (pledge).

SORROW n. heartache, blues, tsuris, rain, rainin', trouble, big trouble, bad news. See MISERY.

SORROW v. carry on, eat one's heart out, hang crepe, sing the blues, take on, cry me a river. See MOURN.

SORROWFUL adj. in pain, crying the blues, sob story, sob stuff, tear-jerker, weeper, teardrop special, sing the blues, hang crepe, bummed-out, hurting, in the pits, carry a heavy load, raining on one's parade, sad-sacky. See UNHAPPY.

SORT n. likes, likes of, lot, number.

SORT v. peg, pigeonhole, type-cast, tab, button down, put down as, put down for, size up, put in shape, put to rights, put in apple-pie order. See also ARRANGE.

SOT n. drinker, heavy drinker, drunk, big drunk, boozer, boozehound, dipso, brown bagger, souse, sponge, lush, wino, juicehead, town drunk, stiff, juicer. See DRINKER.

SOUND adj. 1. up to snuff, up to the mark, wrapped tight, alive and kicking, in fine whack, in the pink, sound as a dollar, right as rain. See HEALTHY. 2. cool, together, got it together, glued (antonym: unglued), commonsensical, all there, in one's right mind, have all one's marbles, have all one's buttons. See REASONABLE. 3. legit, kosher, wash, fly, go, signify, stand up, hold up, hold water, hold together, hang together, hold up in the wash, all there.

SOUND n. flutter (frequency distortion), howlback (noise).

SOUNDPROOF n. dead room.

SOUP n. dishwater, bowl, splash, water, bilge water.

SOUP STOCK n. pot liquor, pot likker (residue).

SOURCE n. horse's mouth, connection, tipster, tout.

SOUTH n. Dixie, the cotton curtain, 'Bama, below the Mason-Dixon line, down home, Old South, Galilee, sunny South, way down South, Deep South.

SOUTH AMERICAN n. Latino, south of the border; greaseball, spic (Derog.).

SOUTH BEND, INDIANA Irish City.

SOUTH CAROLINA Free State, Gamecock State, Palmetto State, Rice State, Swamp State, Sand-Lapper.

SOUTH CAROLINA RESIDENT n. clay eater.

SOUTH DAKOTA Coyote State, Sunshine State.

SOUTHEAST ASIA TREATY ORGANIZATION n. SEATO.

SOUTHERN adj. down-home, cornpone.

SOUTHERN CALIFORNIA So Cool.

SOUTHERNER n. good ole boy, Dixiecrat; cracker, magnolia blossom, Bubba (white male), redneck, ridge runner, chiv, cornpone, grits, hard-boot, hardhead, jig chaser, peckerwood, white trash, clay eater, Reb, Rebel (all Derog.).

SOUTHERN HEMISPHERE n. Third World, the South.

SOW n. porker, porky, cob roller (young or small).

SPA n. fat farm, watering hole.

SPACE n. 1. slot, spot, zone, turf, territory. 2. elbowroom, wiggle room, room to swing a cat, leeway. 3. outer space, deep space. 3. air, lead (space between lines).

SPACE OBJECTS n. space junk, garbage.

SPACESHIP n. starship, bird, Roman candle, RV (re-entry vehicle), PAM (payload assist module), flying saucer, LEM, LM, UFO.

SPACESHIP SEA LANDING n. splashdown.

SPACE SHUTTLE n. Ace Trucking Company.

SPACE SUIT n. penguin suit; tinman, AX-5, Mark-3 (aluminum), spaghetti suit (underwear).

SPACE TERMS lift-off, all systems go, A-OK, stability envelope (normal limits), RV (reentry vehicle), PAM (payload assist module), SRM (solid rocket motor), SRB (solid rocket booster), SSME (space shuttle main engine), ET (external tank), decay (lose momentum), fly-by-wire (automatic pilot), chicken switch (abort switch), chicken button (pilot eject switch), touchdown (landing); scrub, backout (cancel mission); space junk (debris in space).

SPADE n. muck stick, pooper-scooper, banjo, clam shovel (short), Irish banjo, Irish fan, jo, hemo jo, joe.

SPAGHETTI n. worms, carbos, lead pipe, spa-gay-me, pisghetti.

SPANIARD n. spic, spick, greaseball, hatchet thrower, hombre (all Derog.).

SPANK v. whup, whup ass, buttwoop (Af. Am.), whale, whop, wallop, swinge, lick, larrup, clobber, welt, trim, flax, lather, leather, hide, paddle, paddle one's ass, botch, potch, fan, tan, tan one's hide, take it out of one's hide, take it out of one's skin, dust one's pants, dust one's trousers, give a dose of birch oil, give a dose of strap oil, give a dose of hickory oil, give a dose of hazel oil. See also HIT.

SPANKING n. licking, paddling, larruping, walloping, whupping, buttwoopin' (Af. Am.), whaling, lathering, leathering, hiding, tanning, dose of strap oil, dose of hazel oil, dose of hickory oil, dose of birch oil. See also BEATING.

SPARE adj. 1. skinny, stick, twiggy, shadow, beanstalk, stilt, hatrack, broomstick. See THIN. 2. widow. 3. fifth-wheel, option, all the options, spare tire, back up, gash, lagniappe, bells and whistles. See also EXTRA.

SPARE v. let go, let off, let off the hook, bail one out, save one's ass, save one's neck, save one's bacon, give one a break, get one out of hock, get one off the hook, spring, pull something out of the fire, pull one's chestnuts out of the fire. See also FORGIVE.

SPARED adj. off the hook, let off, bailed out, out of hock.

SPARE RIBS n. ribs, piano, first lady (Eve), rack, baby backs.

SPARE TIME n. goof-off time, fuck-off time, time to burn, time to kill, one's own sweet time.

SPARKLE n. glitz, flash, show, zap.

SPASM n. yank, yerk.

SPASMODIC adj. choppy, herky-jerky, fits and starts.

SPASMODICALLY adv. by bits and pieces, by fits and starts, herky-jerky. See ERRATICALLY.

SPASTIC adj. spaz, spas, herky-jerky.

SPAT n. tiff, hassle, static, brush, flap, words, run-in, fuss, bone to pick, bone of contention. See ARGUMENT.

SPAY v. alter, fix, neuter.

SPEAK v. 1. go, gab, rap, mack (Af. Am.), yackety-yack, yada-yada, yada, yatata-yatata, yak-yak, yak, yack, yock, yuk, yuck, yam, yap, yawp, yaup, yatter, patter, natter, wig, spout, spout off, spiel, jaw, lip, chin, gas, chaff, chew, chew over, chew the fat, chew the rag, rag around, modulate, modjitate, splib, splib de wib, slide one's jib, sing, spill, spill the beans, bull, bullshit, throw the bull, shoot the bull, shoot the shit, shoot the bullshit, shoot, shoot the breeze, shoot the lemon, shoot one's wad, shoot off one's mouth, shoot off one's trap, shoot off one's yap, shoot off one's face, shoot one's bazoo off, shoot one's kisser off, let off steam, blow off steam, unload, blab, blab off, pop off, noise off, sound off, flip one's lip (idle), flap, flap one's lip, flap one's jaw, flap one's chops, flap one's jowls, grind, gum, let one's hair down, jibber-jabber, mushmouth, rattle, schmoose, schmoozle, fat mouth, run one's mouth, run off at the mouth, diarrhea of the mouth, have verbal diarrhea, fold one's ear, bend one's ear, interact, interface, network, reach out, relate, talk one's ear off, do a barber, woof, beef, chop it up, chop up jackpots, slice chops, cut up jackies, crack, spring with a crack, cut it up, kick the gong around, punch the gun, sling the crap, sling the lingo, blow, blow hot air, blow change (radical), blow off one's mouth, blow off one's trap, blow off one's yap, bat one's gums, beat one's gums, chew one's gums, bump one's gums, beat around the bush, beat the drum, beat one's chops, bat the chat, bat the breeze, breeze, buzz, chip the ivories, sass, trash, knock, blitz, bad-mouth, bad-talk, sweet-talk, fast-talk, drool, open one's face, some pig, gobble, talk turkey, wag the tongue, parley-voo, twiddle, touch, keep in touch, touch base, have truck with, visit, visit with. 2. grok, back channel (secretly), pitch, spiel, spout, stump, get across, get on a soapbox.

SPEAKEASY n. speak, gin mill, saloon, boozery, blind pig. See also BAR.

SPEAKER n. spieler, spouter, tub thumper, jawsmith, soapboxer, soapbox orator, chalk talker, roaster (uncomplimentary tribute).

SPEAK LOUDER v. increase the volume, take it up a notch.

SPECIAL adj. 1. killer, A number one, 10, ten, super-duper, smashing, gnarly, unreal, zero cool, wicked, out-of-this-world, out-of-sight, flash, primo, crack, solid gold, beautiful, mean, lampin', not too shabby, heavy, terrible,

state of the art, this is some kinda ———. See EXCELLENT. 2. world-class, job, wizard, high-cotton, splash; mother, motherfucker, muthah, muthahfuckah (Obsc.); skull, brain, grind. See also BEST. 3. nature of the beast, that's one all over, just like one.

SPECIAL FORCE n. SWAT team, commandos, flying squad, goon squad, rangers.

SPECIALIST n. pro, old pro, hired gun, old hand, old war-horse, maven, trained seal, bone man, heart man, big nose man, high priest, guru. See AUTHORITY.

SPECIALIZE v. do one's thing, be into, go in for, have a weakness for, get down to brass tacks, get down to cases.

SPECIAL, TV n. spec.

SPECIALTY n. strong suit, long suit, bag, case, cup of tea, game, number, racket, thing, up one's alley, weakness. See also OCCUPATION.

SPECIAL WEAPONS AND TACTICS n. SWAT, SWAT team.

SPECIES n. likes, likes of, lot, number.

SPECIFIC adj. on the button, on the numbers, on the money, on target, on the nose, on the noggin, right on, dead on, bull's eye, good eye, dot the I's and cross the T's, draw it fine, cut it fine, lay pipe, hit the nail on the head, flat-out, straight-out, nailed down, downright.

SPECIFICATIONS n. specs, Mil specs (Mil.).

SPECIFY v. 1. name, slot tab, tag, make, peg, finger, lay one's finger on, put one's finger on, put one's finger on something, put the finger on, button down, pin down, put down for. 2. spell out, lay out, tick off, draw one a picture, paint a picture, take it line by line, cross the T's and dot the I's, sweat the details, fine-tune, get down to brass tacks. See PARTICULARIZE.

SPECKS n. itsy-bitsy pieces, chewed fine.

SPECTACLE n. circus, ball, to-do.

SPECTACLES n. specs, shades, sun specs, cheaters, frames, rims, glims, grannies. See GLASSES.

SPECTACULAR adj. razzle-dazzle, eye-opener, show stopper, butchy, bitchin', twitchin'. See also PRETENTIOUS, ASTONISHING.

SPECTATOR n. 1. kibitzer, nark, sidewalk superintendent, gaper, watcher. 2. moviegoer, playgoer, showgoer, theatergoer, fan, sports fan, standee, clacker, clapper, deadhead, paper (free pass), one who catches a show, fence-hanger.

SPECTER n. haint, hant, spook, things that go bump in the night.

SPECULATE v.   1. spec, play, play the market, plunge, take a flier, take a fling at, make book, stick one's neck out, go on the hook for, ball the jack. See WAGER. 2. figger, cool something over, brainstorm, breakout meeting (brainstorm session), kick around, run it up the flagpole, head trip, chew over, pipe-dream, build castles in the air. See THINK. 3. guesstimate, windshield appraisal (superficial, from a car), dope, dope out, figger, figure, figure out, size up, call it, call the turn, call one's shots, call the shots, read, read between the lines, make book, have a hunch, SWAG (slightly wild-assed guess), in the cards, it's looking to, see it coming, crystal-ball it, psych it out, be afraid.

SPECULATION n.   1. guesstimate, hunch, shot, shot in the dark, SWAG (slightly wild-assed guess), sneaking suspicion, stab, stab in the dark. 2. flyer, backing, in on the ground floor, inside, piece, plunge, right money, smart money, spec, stab; flutter, hunch, shot, shot in the dark, bear market, bearish market (low); bull market, bullish market (high). See also WAGER.

SPECULATIVE adj.   dicey, iffy, touchy, touch-and-go, long-shot, chancy, fat chance, hasn't got a Chinaman's chance, a prayer, on a wing and a prayer, on slippery ground, on thin ice, out on a limb, on the spot in the tube, hanging by a thread, off the deep end, go for broke, leave oneself wide open, play with fire, hot potato, one could get burned, too hot to handle, a snowball in hell, up for grabs, go to sea in a sieve. See also DOUBTFUL.

SPECULATOR n.   high roller, plunger, spec, player, dealer, wheeler-dealer sharper, crap shooter, boneshaker, gunslinger, the bankroll, staker. See GAMBLER.

SPEECH n.   1. lingo, bafflegab, doublespeak, doubletalk, gobbledygookese, Hillspeak (Washington, D.C.), officialese, psychobabble, Urbabble (city Govt.), Yerkish (artificial), Yinglish (English using many Yiddish words), talkin' white (Af. Am.). 2. spiel, chalk talk, pep talk, pitch, stem winder (excellent), soapbox oration, skull session. 3. yack-yack, gab, gas, talkee-talkee, jive, chin music, spiel, lines, rag chewing, gum beating. See TALK.

SPEECHLESS adj.   clammed-up, closed up like a clam, buttoned-up, iced, keep one's trap shut, keep one's yap shut, not let out a peep, not say boo, saved one's breath, dried-up, dummy up, garbo, tight-lipped, D. and D. (deaf and dumb, afraid to testify), like a grave, could hear a pin drop, cool, cool as a cucumber, keep one's cool, keep one's shirt on, unflappable, not turn a hair, ah-ah head.

SPEED n.   clip, lick, ton.

SPEED v.   1. put the pedal to the metal, gun, rev, rev up, open 'er up, drop the hammer down, hammer on, haze the tires, hook up, stand on it, wheelie, wheelstand, peel rubber, hop up, put on the afterburners, wing it, clip, jole, spank along, cut along, get a move on, get moving, get going, get the lead out, get the lead out of one's ass, get one's ass in gear, get cracking, get a hustle on, get a wiggle on, get a hump on, let's move it, haul, haul ass, haul the mail, hustle, hustle up, chop chop, what's keepin' ya?, fog, whale one's butt, shake a leg, shake it up, bounce, dust, roll, tool, fire up, hotfoot it, bear down on it, hump it, hump oneself, barrel-ass, tear ass, shag ass, stir one's stumps, in a jiffy, snap, snap shit, snap to it, snap into it, snap it up, step, step along, step on the gas, step up, step on it, step on its tail, railroad, railroad through, break one's neck, fall all over oneself, hop to it, charge, go like greased lightening, go like a big assed bird, go like a BAB, go hell-bent for election, go full blast, full gate, full bore, go like hell, go like a bat outta hell, go to the whip, crackin' the whip, floor, floor it, push, push it, push it to the floor, push it to the floorboard, put it to the floor, flying, burn rubber, burn up the road, burn the breeze, burn leather, lay scratch, lay rubber, lay rubber down, split the breeze, streak, truckin', wheeling it, whistling, diggin' one's spurs, hit the high spots, flat out, let 'er out, let it out, let it all hang out, slack out, hang your leg on it, drag, locomoting, move, pedaling with both feet, rolling, shoveling coal, smoking, give one or something the goose, give it the gun, give 'er the gas, give it the juice, really rolling, highball, make tracks, carry the mail, hop along, run like a scared rabbit, run like mad, breeze, breeze along, tear up the track, tear up the road, eat up the track, eat up the road, scorch, sizzle, rip, zip, whiz, whiz along, nip, zing, ball the jack, scat, beat the band, bend the needle, flash, don't spare the horses, lay a batch, blip, prune, soup up, hurry up, knock the gun, jazz up. 2. hand-carry, hand-walk, walk it over, walk it through, handle personally, cut red tape, fast track, grease the wheels, run interference for, run with the ball, railroad.

SPEEDER n.   lead foot, heavy foot, hell driver, hummer, hustler, scorcher, sizzler, speed demon, speed maniac, speed merchant.

SPEEDY adj.   sizzler, speedball, fly, make it snappy, shake a leg, stir your stumps, haul ass, highball, speed boy, speed merchant, like sixty, like crazy, like a scared rabbit, beat the devil, beat the deuce. See FAST.

SPELL n.   1. evil eye, stink eye, hoodoo, voodoo, jinx, whack, whammy, hocus-pocus, mumbo-jumbo, abracadabra. 2. jag (crying jag).

SPEND v.   1. drop some iron, pay down, put down, pay to the tune of, cough up, pony up, ante up, come through, come across, come down with, blow, cash out, shell out, spring for, throw money at, throw money around, piss it away. 2. square, square things, square up, square the beef, sweeten the pot, tickle the palm, pay the piper, pay one's dues, pay through the nose, slip one a buck, schmear, grease, fix the alzo, piece one off, do business, buy off, reach, get to. See PAY. 3. run through, go through, live high on the hog, spend like a drunken sailor, spend money like water, spend money like it was going out of style, spend like there was no tomorrow. See SQUANDER.

SPENDER n. sport, big sport, live one, live wire, fast one with a buck, high roller, big-time spender, last of the big-time spenders, good-time Charlie.

SPENT adj. 1. blown, blown out, diddled away, pissed away, thrown away, down the drain, down the tube, down the rathole, down the spout, down the toilet. 2. pooped, had it, creased, fagged-out, dragged, dragging one's ass, dead, beat-up, shot, hacked, dog-tired, cooked. See TIRED.

SPERM n. come, cum, scum, cream, jism, jisum, jizz, spew, spoo, spooch, splooge, blecch, crud (dried), hocky, home brew, hookey, jack, pecker tracks, protein, sugar.

SPERM BANK n. spoo bank.

SPEW v. 1. let fly, blow, spritz, hawk. 2. barf, puke, zuke, throw up, upchuck, urp, yak, boag, reverse gears, whoops, Ralph up, York, buick, feed the fish, blow one's groceries, kiss the porcelain god, drive the bus. See VOMIT.

SPHERE n. 1. big blue marble, apple, real estate, spaceship earth. 2. apple, pellet, pill. 3. bag, cup of tea, strong suit, long suit, thing, racket. 4. hood, neck of the woods, stomping ground, old stomping grounds, territory, turf, ghetto, inner city, jungle, shanty town, skid row, slum, zoo.

SPICE n. guts, kick, zip, zap.

SPICE v. hot it up, pep it up, zip it up, zap it up.

SPICY adj. 1. zippy, peppy, shotgun. 2. hot, too hot to handle, red-hot, blue, dirty, filthy, off-base, off-color, out-of-line, X-rated, jiggle, jiggly, spark. See also OBSCENE.

SPINACH n. marsh grass, Popeye, seaweed.

SPINSTER n. old maid, single, single-o, cherry, canned goods, bug.

SPIRIT n. 1. jazz, oomph, gumption, balls, guts, heart, nerve, stomach, what it takes, grit, true grit, spunk, backbone, moxie, starch, clock, corazón, Dutch courage (intoxicated). 2. spook, haint, hant, fiend, hellion, little devil. See also DEVIL.

SPIRITED adj. perky, bouncy, chirpy, chipper, peppy, grooving, zingy, zappy, zippy, snappy, jumping, jacked, jaked, jazzed, hyper, swinging, swingle, rocking, salty, juiced up, upbeat, burning, red-hot, powerhouse, bull, push, punch, fireball, ball of fire, hot to trot, hotshot, all out, go-getter, go-go, on the go, full tilt, full of go, full of pep, full of beans, full of vinegar, full of piss and vinegar, full of ginger, full of hops, full of prunes, in full swing, feeling one's oats, got the horses to do it, steamroller, get up a head of steam, Norwegian steam, spanking, punchy, gutsy, have lead in one's pencil, come on strong, come on like gangbusters, take over, take charge, fair hell.

SPIRITLESS adj. 1. dopey, drippy, blah, flat, have spring fever, moony, flat tire, zero, big zero, don't give a shit, don't give a damn, could care less, draggy. See INDIFFER-

ENT. 2. dick in the dirt, down, down in the mouth, low, bummed-out, flaked-out, have the blahs, droopy, mopey. See DEPRESSED. 3. dull as dishwater, ho hum, bor-ring, yawn, big yawn, dead, nowhere, noplaceville, Nadaville, nothing, nothing doing, tired. See BORING. 4. stick-in-the-mud, wet blanket, beige, drip, grass, grass out, Irving, Melvin, party-pooper, buzz killer, wonky.

SPIRITS n. hard liquor, likker, alky, doctor, idiot oil, hootch, booze, moonshine, mountain dew, red-eye, sauce, panther piss, medicine, mouthwash, poison, firewater, embalming fluid, giggle water, hard stuff. See LIQUOR.

SPIRITUAL n. shout.

SPIT v. let fly, hawk, hawking loogies (phlegm), spritz.

SPITE n. peeve, pet peeve, bone to pick.

SPITE v. hang up, foul up, fuck up, louse up, cramp one's style, snooker, crab, fake out, give one the business, upset one's apple cart, spike one's guns, get even with one, do one dirt. See THWART.

SPITEFUL adj. bitchy, cussed, catty, evil, waspish, dirty, mean, stanky (Fem.), ornery, accidentally on purpose, do one dirt. See MALICIOUS.

SPITTOON n. gaboon, goboon, garboon.

SPLENDID adj. splendiferous, splendacious, magnif, magnifico, aggro, plush, posh, swanky, splashy, splurgy, fab, fat, elegant, mad, solid gold. See MAGNIFICENT.

SPLINTER v. break to smithereens, smash to smithereens, bust to bits.

SPLIT v. whack, hack, chiv, shiv. 2. split up, divvy, divvy up, go halfies, go halvers, go fifty-fifty, go even-steven, crack, slice up, cut the pie, cut the melon, slice the melon. See DIVIDE.

SPOIL v. bitch up, fuck up, hash up, ding, mess up, muck up, make hash of, crumb, crumb up, put in the toilet, play hob with, queer, put the skids under one, blow up in one's face, cut the ground out from under, put out of commission, screw up the works, put a spoke in one's wheels, trash, squash, smash, take apart, zing, break the lease, cook one's goose, blow one's doors off, bend the goods. See DESTROY; RUIN.

SPOILED adj. 1. screwed-up, fouled-up, fucked-up, loused-up, messed-up, hashed-up, dusted, busted, kaput, dinged, bent, totaled, sunk, shot. See DAMAGED. 2. spoiled rotten. 3. strong, high, loud, gross, stinking, bum, rummy.

SPOILS n. take, graft, goods, hot goods, hot items, swag, squeeze, boodle, make, cut, loot, pickings, booty, melon, pie.

SPOILSPORT n. party-pooper, drag, drip, buzz crusher, buzz killer, wet blanket, crepe hanger, sourpuss, sourbelly, sourball, dog in the manger, bogart, bogarde (keep possession), gloomy Gus, killjoy, stick-in-the-mud, moldy fig, worry wart, Calamity Jane, calamity howler.

SPOKANE, WASHINGTON Spoke.

SPOKESPERSON n. mouthpiece, hired gun.

SPONGER n. bummer, cheapskate, cadger, beat, deadbeat, freeloader, lounge lizard, moocher, schnorer, sponge, hanger-on, hose. See also PARASITE.

SPONSOR n. backer, angel, greenback, rabbi, Chinaman, fairy godfather, fairy godmother, grubstaker, lady bountiful, meal ticket, Santa Claus, staker, sugar daddy. See FINANCIER.

SPONSOR v. bankroll, angel, the bank, grubstake, stake, greenback, back. See FINANCE.

SPONTANEOUS adj. off the cuff, off the top of one's head, ad lib, up front, shoot from the hip, off the hip, spitball, pop off, cold turkey, down, get down, all hanging out, free-spirited, far out, stretched out, break loose, cut loose, loose wig, let down one's hair. See also IMPULSIVE.

SPOON n. shovel, bug (industrial or baker).

SPORADICALLY adv. by fits and starts, by bits and pieces, hit or miss, helter-skelter. See ERRATICALLY.

SPORT n. rec, action, ball, big time, fun and games, get some grins, grins, high old time, high time, hoopla, laughs, lots of laughs, picnic, whoopee. See also GAMBLER.

SPORT v. fool around, monkey around, hell around, step out, paint the town red, go places and do things, go on a spree, whoop it up, kick up one's heels, raise hell. See REVEL.

SPORTING adj. square-dealing, square-shooting, straight-shooting. See FAIR.

SPORTS BROADCASTING TERMS color, color-caster, color man, play-by-play, play-by-play man.

SPORTS DEFEAT n. blown out, blown away, shut-out, down, dump, pasting, sieve, horse collar (zero); sudden death, sudden death finish (tiebreaker); tank, go into the tank (intentional loss).

SPORTS, GAMBLING n. action, point spread, favorite, long shot, underdog, make book, lay off, overlay, odds-on favorite, vigorish.

SPORTS INJURY n. charley horse (leg muscle injury), iron man (plays in spite of injury).

SPORTSMAN n. 1. animal, jock, superjock, ape, muscle head, muscle man, meathead, shoulders, Neanderthal. See ATHLETE. 2. high roller, K.G. (known gambler, police use), big timer, sharper, sport. See GAMBLER.

SPORTSMANLIKE adj. square-dealing, square-shooting, straight-shooting. See FAIR.

SPORTS PERFORMANCE n. grandstander, grandstand play, hot dog, hot dogging, show time (showing off); groove (groove your swing), header (fall headfirst); heads-up play, heads up player (wide awake); real pro, journeyman, hustle, iron man (durable competitor), up (ready for anything, winning), on (at one's best), troops (good players); clutch player, money player (best under stress); choke (psychological disadvantage); picture book, picture-perfect (classic); sandbag (fake early weakness, then overwhelm the opponent), scrappy (spirited), telegraph (reveal next move), dog it, go flat out, pull it out, full bore, hot, hustle, make a run at, break it open, September swoon, barnburner (exciting contest), snakebit (playing in bad luck).

SPORTS, PSYCHOLOGICAL TERMS choke, choke up, clutch, clutch up (all poor performance under tension); psych, psych out (distract an opponent); charge up, psych up (inspire); sucker play (entrap).

SPORTS RECORDS n. the gold (gold medal), lifetime, world-class, all-American all-time (best ever), cellar (last place).

SPORTS SCORING n. card (score card), blow out (overwhelm the opponent), chalk up, chalk up one (score), draw first blood, the gold (gold medal), horse collar (zero); ice, on ice (assured victory); a laugher (lopsided victory), make a run at (concentrated effort to outscore opponent), point spread (betting odds), run away, run away and hide (outdistance opponent), run off (score consecutive points); sudden death, sudden death finish (tiebreaker); burn (score or win).

SPORTS SPECTATOR n. backer, booster, bench (players' seat), blackout (local television broadcast restriction), bleachers, bleacherite, fan, scout (sports spy).

SPORTS SUBSTITUTE n. backup, backup player, bench, bench jockey, extra horses, ringer (illegal), sideliner, sub, bull pen, reliefer, fireman.

SPORTS TERMS meet (contest), barnburner (exciting contest), away (play at opponent's arena), host (the Yanks host Detroit), beat out, break it open; dominate, walkaway, walkover, win (victory); the gold (gold medal), cellar (last place), paste (defeat); shut out, sieve (scoreless); stiffener, dead heat, scrub (tie); ref, ump, zebra (referee); call (referee's decision); call time, chalk talk (discussion of plays), starter, vet, rookie (first-year player), jayvee (junior varsity), homebrew (locally bred player), redshirt (elegibility extended), while hope (Caucasian contender), ringer (high-rated player illegally entered), suit up (ready to play), benched, cut (remove player from team), thin (no reserve players); first string, front line (starting players); firepower, horses (power), book (data on opponents), free-wheeling (formless style of play), dog (guard opponent closely), that dog can run (fast man); bobble, foozle (error); bum, clutch, turnover, kick (error), choke, choke up; chapter, canto, frame, lap (division); round, stanza (time period); get, gate, take (receipts); card (scorecard program), wild card (playoff qualifier), October classic (World Series), greenie (stimulant pill), enduro (endurance race), jock, jog, jogger, jogging, spikes (shoes worn for certain sports), black belt (karate expert), action (gun mechanism for loading and firing), wave (crowd stands up and cheers, in sections).

SPORTS, WINNING n. top dog, sudden death, sudden death finish (tiebreaker); sweep (the Lakers swept the series), up, the upper hand; blow out of the water, blow out (overwhelm an opponent); chalk up one, clinch, edge, the gold (gold medal), ice (they had the game iced), on ice, a laugher (18 to 1, it was a laugher), run away, run away and hide (outdistance).

SPOT n. where one is at, X marks the spot, hangout, joint, lay, layout, plant, office, dump, digs, scene, slot, hole, pad, crib, crash pad, roof over one's head, hooch (Vietnam), digs, the pits, armpit, barf city (undesirable). See also BLEM-ISH, LOCATION, HOUSE, BAR.

SPOTLIGHT n. center stage.

SPOUSE n. man, my man, old man, main man, man on the hitch, ace lane, breadwinner, buffalo, old lady, O.L., mama, missus, better half, little woman, the wifey, missus, little missus, wiff, chief of staff, rib, ball and chain, block and tackle, roommate, front office, golf widow, grass widow, glass widow (husband is alcoholic), headache, War Department, mat, hat, sea gull, slavedriver, squaw, headquarters, apron, main queen, old saw, first sergeant, fishwife, fag bag (married to homosexual).

SPRAY v. dust (crops), spritz, shoot (paint).

SPREE n. bat, bender, binge, ball, bash, bust, beer bust, kegger, buzz, drunk, jag, caper, go, tear, toot, blowout, hoopla, whoopee, jamboree, wingding, shindig, brannigan, rip, merry-go-round, paint the town red, on the town, carousing, growler rushing, hell around, hell bender, high jinks, whooper-dooper, big time, high time, high old time, larking, field day. See also PARTY; REVEL.

SPRIGHTLINESS n. piss and vinegar, bounce, zip, zap.

SPRIGHTLY adj. jacked, jaked, jazzed, perky, bouncy, chirpy, chipper, peppy, grooving, zingy, zappy, zippy, jumping, hyper, swinging, go-go, full of ginger, feeling one's oats. See SPIRITED.

SPRING v. hippety-hop.

SPRINKLE v. dust (crops), spritz.

SPRUCE adj. classy, dap, nifty, snazzy, spiffy. See also STYLISH, CLEAN.

SPRY adj. 1. quick on the draw, quick on the trigger, twinkle-toes. 2. zappy, zippy, rocking, go-go, on the go, full of go, full of pep, full of ginger, in full swing, feeling one's oats. See also SPIRITED.

SPUR n. fire in the belly, needle, goose, trigger, turn-on.

SPUR v. goose, goose up, fire up, key up, work up, work up into a lather, put up to, spark, egg on, turn on, trigger, sound. See STIMULATE.

SPURIOUS adj. hyped-up, bogue, bogus, bogosity, bum, bent, phony, falsie, plastic, fake, faked, framed, made out of whole cloth, not what it's cracked up to be, pirate goods, bite, Hollywood. See COUNTERFEIT.

SPURN v. pass by, steer clear of, nix, turn down, turn thumbs down on, not buy, not hear of, have no truck with, back up (refuse to do something), cut, piss on, shit on, drop, cold-shoulder, dump, air, flush, give one the air, give one the wind, thank you but no thank you. See REJECT. See also SNUB.

SPURNED adj. nixed, burned, cut, turned-down, put-down, passed-over, left at the church, out in the cold. See REJECTED. See also SNUBBED.

SPURS n. pothooks.

SPURT n. spritz.

SPURT v. spritz.

SPY n. agent, spook, mole, gray man (inconspicuous, the perfect agent), beekie, snark, buddy fucker, humint, operative, plant, rug merchant, sheep dip (Mil. disguised as civilian), vacuum cleaner (informant who supplies overabundant details), cousin (British Intelligence. Also Israeli Intelligence reference to an Arab), cutout (secret intermediary) CI-nick (counter-intelligence, pronounced see-nick), piano player (radio operator), sleeper, company brown nose, keek (industrial); enemy; ac-op (active opposition); sold (betrayed by his own people), barbarians, Indians, visiting team, ELINT (information gathered by spy satellites). See also OPERATIVE.

SPY v. case, case a joint, spot, spy out, stake out, recon, get a load of, take in, bus it (Af. Am.), get an eyeful of, set eyes on, clap eyes on, eyeball, have a look-see. See also RECONNOITER.

SPYING DEVICE n. asset, bug, harmonica bug (telephone listening device—may also be explosive), babbler (counterbugging device), fumigate, sweep (search for listening devices), wire, black box (generic name for electronic devices), music box, musician (wireless transmitter), body mike, eye in the sky, spy in the sky.

SPY SATELLITE n. eye in the sky, spy in the sky.

SPY TERMS toss (search a premises), the loot (info gained through intelligence operation), noise (useless information to confuse relevant information), flaps and seals (course of instruction in surreptitious letter opening); honey trap, lady (woman sent to compromise the opposition); legend (fictional cover story), lion tamer (one who deals with a former agent who threatens trouble), naked (alone without help), biographic leverage (blackmail), black-bag job (bribery or burglary), family jewels (illegal activities by CIA); demote maximally, terminate (purge by killing); measles (murder that looks like natural causes), BO, Bug out (kill with toxic), BBs, L-pill (suicide pill), nasty (national security), cop (cover protection), knuckle dragger (paramilitary working with CIA), phew (psychological warfare), run a wire (install tap or microphone), dry cleaning (avoiding pursuit or testing to see if being followed), make (identifying one's surveillant), pest, pest control (hiring security), humint (human intelligence), sigint (electronic intelligence); wet operation, wet squad, wet work (involving shedding blood); granny (non-Agency employee whose premises are used for observation), Aunt Minnie (tourist photo that includes a strategic location), letter-drop (secret message depository).

SQUABBLE n. hassle, flap, spat, tiff, words, row, scrap, scene, set-to, fuss, flack session, rhubarb, wrangle. See ARGUMENT.

SQUABBLE v. lock horns, row, scrap, bump heads, cross swords, pick a bone, put up an argument. See ARGUMENT.

SQUAD CAR n. fuzzmobile, black-and-white, skunk wagon, bear car, bearmobile, buzz, buzzer, screaming gasser, whistler, catch car; brown bag, plain wrap (unmarked); cherries (flashing lights), buggy whip (transmitter).

SQUALID adj. cruddy, crudded-up, crumby, crummy, crummed-up, crusty, grungy, icky, yecchy, yucky, barfy, vomity, pigpen, barn, stable, stinking, stall, scuzzy, skank, raunchy, sleazy, sleazed-up, mucked-up. See also SLOVENLY.

SQUANDER v. blow, fork out, put out, shell out, spring for, go for a meg, throw money at, throw money around, piss it away, blow out, cash out, diddle away, run through, go through, live high on the hog, spend like a drunken sailor, spend money like water, spend money like it was going out of style, spend like there was no tomorrow. See also PAY.

SQUANDERED adj. blown, pissed away, thrown away, diddled away, down the drain, down the toilet, down the rathole, down the spout, tubed, down the tube.

SQUASH v. 1. scrunch, squish, 2. squelch, ice, kill, put the kibosh on, put the lid on, shut down on, put the damper on. See REPRESS. See also SILENCE.

SQUEAMISH adj. barfy, pukish, puky, rocky, sick as a dog. See also FASTIDIOUS.

SQUEEZE n. crisis mode, clutch, crunch.

SQUEEZE v. lean on, scrunch, squish, juice. See also PERSUADE.

SQUELCH v. black out, sit on, kibosh, kill, put the kibosh on, put the lid on, settle one's hash, squash. See also SILENCE.

SQUINT v. squinch, scrunch up one's eyes.

SQUIRT v. spritz.

ST. LOUIS, MISSOURI Big Arch, the Gateway.

ST. PAUL, MINNESOTA Twin City.

STAB v. carve, knife, cut, open up, slice, stick, jag, brand, carve initials in one, chiv, shiv, chop, chop down, clip, shank, cut a new kisser for. See also WOUND.

STABILIZE v. firm up, pour oil on troubled waters, cool, freeze. See also PACIFY.

STABLE adj. 1. set, sot, stay put, together, brick-wall, solid as a rock, set in concrete, chiseled in stone, Rock a Gibraltar, Rock of Gibraltar, Rock of Gib, anchored, nailed, nailed-down. See also PERMANENT; TRUSTWORTHY. 2. unflappable, cool, keep one's cool, cool as a cucumber, keep one's shirt on, not turn a hair, without a nerve in one's body, together. 3. set, going concern.

STADIUM n. bowl, gridiron (Ftbl.), diamond (Bsbl.), ring, pit, dome.

STAFF n. crew, troops, help, shop, flunky, furp, space cadet (young), apparatchik, squeak, home guard, peon, savage, serf, slave, slavey, girl Friday, gal Friday, man Friday.

STAGE n. show biz, legit, Broadway, off Broadway, boards, straw-hat circuit, the Fabulous Invalid, Toby Show. See THEATER.

STAGE v. mount, put on.

STAGEHAND n. deck hand.

STAID adj. stuffy, not crack a smile, wipe the smile off one's face, cold sober, sober as a judge.

STAKES n. pot (games). See also WAGER.

STALE adj. 1. flat, flat as a pancake. See INSIPID. 2. tired, out, played out (Af. Am.), old hat, past it, passé, bent, back-number, moth-eaten, moldy fig, yesterday, corny, dinosaur, horse-and-buggy. See also DATED.

STALEMATE n. standoff, Mexican standoff, gridlock, deadlock, Catch-22, damned if you do and damned if you don't.

STALL v. play for time, conk out, die, piddle-diddle (So.), See also DELAY.

STALWART adj. 1. double-barreled, hoss, powerhouse, steamroller, mover and shaker, wavemaker, have lead in one's pencil, juice, force, come on strong, walk heavy, walk tall. See also STRONG. 2. gutsy, gutty, gritty, nervy, spunky, tough it out, cool hand, ain't scared of shit. See FEARLESS. 3. dead set on, bound, bound and determined, brick wall, stonewall, dig in one's heels, solid as a rock, hang tough. See STUBBORN.

STAMINA n. backbone, grit, guts, gutsiness, heart, moxie, starch, cool, hanging in there, hang tough, legs, intestinal fortitude, staying power, sitzfleisch.

STANCE n. 1. say-so, slant. 2. brace, brush (Army).

STAND n. 1. bally stand (circus), soapbox, stump. 2. P.O.V. (point of view), slant, sound, take, twist, angle, two cents' worth, say-so, where one is at, where's one's head is, another country heard from.

STAND v. stand for, stand the gaff, stand up, stand up to it, suck it up, handle, live with, bear with, put up with, hang in, hang in there, hang tough, hang on, stay the course, take it on the chin, be big, grin and bear it. See ENDURE.

STANDARD adj. everyday, garden variety, vanilla, strictly union, boiler plate, run-of-the-mill, starch. See AVERAGE.

STANDARDIZE v. homogenize.

STANDARDIZED adj. PX.

STANDING n. the scene, how the land lies, lay of the land, how things stack up, how things stand, place, slot, pecking order, like it is, where it's at, size of it.

STANDSTILL n. gridlock, box, corner, dead end, hole, standoff, Mexican standoff, damned if you do and damned if you don't.

STAR n. superstar, monster, topliner, headliner, luminary, box office, celeb, face, in the limelight, prima donna, right up there; eight-hundred-pound gorilla, eight-hundred-pounder, gorilla (TV news). See CELEBRITY.

STARE n. fish-eye, gun.

STARE v. gawk, glom, glim, gun, eye, eyeball, get an eyeful, give the eye, eagle-eye, beam, pipe, focus, hold the glims on, take in, get a load of, get an eyeful of, pin, rubber, rubberneck, 87 1/2 (look at a girl, Rest.), give one the eye, give one the beady eye, give one the fish eye, give with the eyes, eyeballs buggin' out like percolator tops, take a picture (stop), keep one's eyes peeled. See also SEE.

START n. opener, openers, preem, bow, square one, day 1, day one, phase zero, the git-go (Af. Am.), first crack out of the box, countdown, for starters, flying start, running start, hit the ground running, jump-start, jump-off, kickoff, takeoff, start-off. See BEGINNING.

START v. open, open up, bow, come out, roll 'em, start the ball rolling, phase in, get one's feet wet, get the show on the road, get cracking, get off the dime, take it from the top, from the gate; break one's cherry, devirginize (first time), kick off, kick in, kick it, hit out, head out, ring in, blast away, hang up one's shingle. See BEGIN.

START, FALSE n. jump the gun.

STARTLE v. 1. scare to death, scare the shit out of, spook, put the chill on, give one a turn, make one jump a mile, spring something on one. See FRIGHTEN. 2. rock, gork, floor, shake one up, blow away, blow one's mind, from out in left field, hit them where they ain't, knock one over with a feather. See SURPRISE.

STARTLED adj. spooked, frozen, pucker-assed, jumped a mile, jumped out of one's skin, given a turn, given a jar, given a jolt. See FRIGHTENED; SURPRISED.

STARTLING adj. hairy, hair-raising, grabber, scary, spooky mind-blowing, stunning, hell of a note, helluva note. See also IMPRESSIVE.

STAR TREK FAN n. Trekkie, Trekker.

STARVED adj. skinny, dog-hungry, empty, peaked, peaky, rattleboned, skin and bones.

STARVING adj. empty, dog-hungry, fly light, grits time, have a tapeworm, munchies (after marijuana use), starved, starved to death, could eat a horse, could eat the asshole out of a bear.

STATE n. 1. Big Brother, D.C., the digger, the mighty dome, the Feds, the Union, Uncle Sam, U.S., U.S.A., US of A, Washington. 2. situash, like it is, where it's at, the size of it, way of the world, how the land lies, fix (stationary). See CONDITION. 3. cherry (perfect), mint, showroom perfect, —— city (fat city).

STATE DEPARTMENT n. Foggy Bottom, State.

STATE DEPARTMENT OFFICIAL n. cookie pusher.

STATELY adj. highfalutin, high-minded, high-nosed, high-toned, stiff-necked. See also MAJESTIC; POMPOUS.

STATEMENT n. story, ABC's, blow by blow, rundown, make, picture, bomb, spiel, pitch, say-so, two-cents' worth. See also ACCOUNT.

STATE OF AFFAIRS n. stacks up, shapes up, how things stack up, how things stand, like it is, where it's at, way things are, how it goes, size of it, how the land lies, lay of the land.

STATE OF MIND n. 'tude, where one's at, where one's coming from, where one's head is at, mind-set.

STATE OF NEW YORK MORTGAGE AGENCY n. Sonny Mae.

STATES' RIGHTS DEMOCRATIC PARTY n. Dixiecrats.

STATIC n. background, buckshot, breaking up, covered-up (radio).

STATIONARY adj. anchored, nailed, nailed down, pat.

STATION WAGON n. woody.

STATISTICS n. stats, sadistics (Stu.).

STATUETTE n. Oscar, Emmy, Grammy, Tony (any small statue, especially an Academy Award).

STATUS n. where it's at, where one is at, the way it shapes up, lay of the land, black eye (low). See CONDITION.

STAY v. sit tight, stay put, let it ride, stick around, squat, nest, bunk, hang, hang out, hang in, hang around, hang about, perch, roost, save it, sweat it, sweat, sweat it out, hold the fort. See also WAIT, STOP, DELAY, INHABIT.

STEADFAST adj. unflappable, bound, bound and determined, brick wall, stick it out, stand by one's guns, solid as a rock, hang tough, Rock of Gibraltar. See STUBBORN. See also LOYAL; TRUSTWORTHY; DETERMINED.

STEADY adj. solid as a rock, Rocka Gibraltar, Rock of Gibraltar, Rock of Gib, brick wall, set in concrete, stuck in concrete, buried in concrete, chiseled in stone. See also LOYAL; TRUSTWORTHY.

STEAK n. shoe leather (tough), rubber, chew it (rare).

STEAL v. rip off, appropriate, boost, scrounge, graze (steal and eat food in a supermarket), pinch, promote, buzz, cop, kipe, rough off, rouge, liberate, lift, take a five-finger discount (shoplift), punk, jack, moonlight requisition, house (money), snatch, snitch, swipe, snake, snipe, glom, glaum, glahm, glue, skim, high-grade, hijack, skyjack, heist, hoist, elevate, make, make off with, burn, annex, borrow, touch, palm, bag, nip, snare, stick up, kick over, tip over, knock off, knock over, shoot a jug, truck-lift, boost a car, gleep a cage (auto), put up, root, rack, scuffle, throw, throw up, tumul, put the arm on, take off, pluck, put a hand in the till, put a hand in the cookie jar, have one's hand in the cookie jar, work in a bank and take home samples, give one a haircut, take to the cleaners, sting, score, clip, crash, cream, clout, charge, mug (rob and beat), jackroll, hustle, kife, crook, crab, crib, cabbage, gaffel, sneeze, wease, bit, O.P.P. (other people's property), steal one blind, hook, hooky, maverick, nick, move, salvage, smooch, go south with something, fall (unsuccessful). See also APPROPRIATE; ROB; CRIME; CRIME; COMMIT A.

STEALING, DOG n. dognapping, pooch snatch, yip snatch.

STEALTHILY adv. on the q.t., on the quiet, on the sly, in a hole-and-corner way, in holes and corners, undercover, under wraps, hush-hush, strictly hush-hush.

STEALTHY adj. undercover, tref, triff, under wraps; hush-hush, skunk works (secret manufacturing plant or laboratory); creep (mission).

STEAM CALLIOPE n. horse piano.

STEAMER n. crock, tub, rust bucket, tramp. See also SHIP.

STEER v. take the wheel, helm, captain, skipper, take her, take over, take the conn, herd, shepherd, ride herd on, sit on top of, run, run things, take the reins, pull the strings, pull the wires. See MANAGE.

STEERING CONTROL n. joy knob, joystick, wheel.

STENOGRAPHER n. steno, girl, girl Friday, man Friday.

STEREOTYPE n. boilerplate.

STERILE adj. no lead in the pencil, no toothpaste in the tube, fire blanks.

STERN adj. crab, chickenshit, by the book, stiff, tough, tough nut, tough nut to crack, burnt, rough, burly, hard-nosed, hard-core, hard-shell, hard-line, hard-boiled, hard-headed, bulletheaded, bullhead, bullheaded, pigheaded, muleheaded, mulish, mule, stubborn as a mule, stiff-necked, dyed in the wool, hang in, hang in there, hang tough.

STEROIDS n. roids, oids, acid, sauce, juice, gorilla juice, stack (mixture), D-ball (Dianabol), Bol (Bolosterone), Test (Testosterone); 'roid boy, juicer (user), joyrider (non-athlete user); 'roid rage, 'roid mania (bad reaction), 'roid slip (medical chart).

STETHOSCOPE n. ears.

STEVEDORE n. dock walloper, roustabout.

STEW n. mulligan, coll, lorelei, salamagundi, slumgullion, Black Mike (hobo).

STEWARDESS n. stew, cow pilot.

STICK n. nightstick, billy, billy club, blackjack, club, sap, sap stick. See CLUB.

STICK v. freeze to, stay put, hold on like a bulldog, stick like a barnacle, stick like a leech, stick like a wet shirt, cling like ivy, cling like a burr, stick like a limpet.

STICKLER n. 1. nitpicker, picky, picky-picky, smitty, ace, comma counter, fussbudget, fusspot, granny, old maid, pernickety, persnickety. See PARTICULAR. 2. hard-nosed, hard-core, hard-shell, hard-line, locked-in, pat, stand-pat, stay put, stick to one's guns, stiff-necked, stuffy, sticky, set, sot, dead set on. See STUBBORN.

STICKY adj. gooey, gloppy, globby, gook, gooky, goonk, gummy, gunk.

STIFFNESS n. charley horse, charley, tennis elbow.

STIFLE v. 1. gag, ice, muzzle, squelch, squash, shut up, dry up, clam up, hold it down, take it down a thousand, shut one's face, bag it, bag one's face, button up, sit on, put the lid on, cork up, clamp down on. 2. torpedo, kill, queer, spike, squash, squelch, hush up, black out, put in the toilet, keep under wraps, ding, zing, hog-tie, tie up, jam up, bring to a screaming halt, put a stopper in, throw cold water on, cut off one's water, put the heat on, crack down on. See RE-PRESS.

STIFLING adj. broiler, roaster, scorcher, sizzler, swelterer, sticky, steamy, steam box, sweaty, sweat box, close, one can fry eggs on the sidewalk, hotter than blue mud.

STIGMA n. black eye, lost face.

STIGMATIZE v. trash, crud up, crumb up, scuzz up, skank, muck up, sleaze up, mess up, piss on, blackball, give one a black mark, give one a black eye, make one lose face.

STILL adj. buttoned-up, clammed-up, closed up like a clam, iced, sealed-lipped, close-mouthed, not let out a peep, not say boo, saved one's breath. See SILENT.

STILL n. barrelhouse, boiler, plant, groundhog, sneaker.

STILL v. gag, muzzle, squelch, squash, shut up, soft-pedal, dummy up, clam up, sit on, decrease the volume, bottle up, cut the mouth, drink one's beer, put the damper on, put the lid on, cork up, shut down on. See SILENCE.

STIMULANT n. doll, spark plug, rit, upper, pellets, pick-me-up, shot in the arm, fast one, coke, snow, pep pill, jolly bean, bennie, benzie, dexie, heart, football, purple heart, meth speed, crystal, businessman's trip. See also DRUGS, TONIC.

STIMULATE v. jazz, jazz up, juice, juice up, turn on the juice, send, grab, spark, trigger, hook, fuss, bug up, pep up, put pep into, perk up, snap up, wake up, zip up, put zip into, key up, fire up, steam up, stir up, work up, work up into a lather, work into a stew, work into a tizzy, work into a pucker, pick up, chirk up, wig out, adjy, flip, egg on, turn on, turn one on, switch on, turn on the heat, give one a hotfoot, race one's motor, open one's nose, make waves, rabble-rouse, needle, put the needles in, throw wood on the fire, add fuel to the flames. See also EXCITE.

STIMULATED adj. charged, charged up, higher 'n a kite, hyper, revved, revved-up, steamed-up, juiced-up, jacked-up, headin' up the mountain (sexual), rooty, ready to cook. See EXCITED.

STIMULUS n. upper, charge, large charge, bang, kick, needle, fireworks, flash, jollies, turn-on, razzle-dazzle, kick in the ass, eye-opener. See also DRUGS; SPUR.

STINGY adj. cheap, cheapskate, close, penny-pinching, nickel-nursing, tight, tightwad, tight-fisted, so tight one squeaks, last of the big spenders, last of the big-time spenders, fast man with a buck, a regular Jack Benny, tight as a drum, tight as O'Reilly's balls, tight as Kelsey's nuts, skinflint, Scotch, sticky-fingered, crumb, bog pocket, dead one,

squeezing the eagle, piker, chintzy, chinchy, scrimpy, skimpy, pinch-fisted, hard-fisted, pinchy.

STINK v. reek.

STINKING adj. stinko, whiffy, nosy, strong, phew, P.U., high, atomic atmosphere.

STINT v. scrimp, penny-pinch, cut corners, cut to the bone, go easy on the pocketbook, make ends meet, roll back, tighten one's belt, rub the print off a dollar bill, rub the picture off a nickel, save for a rainy day, sock away, squirrel, stash.

STIPEND n. bread, take, take-home, sugar, shake, soap, touch, bacon, bacon and eggs, eagle shit; peanuts, coffee and cakes (small); double dipping (compensation from two government agencies). See COMPENSATION.

STIPULATE v. spell out, name, slot, tab, tag, make, peg, finger, lay one's finger on, put one's finger on, put one's finger on something, put the finger on, fine-tune, button down, pin down, put down for.

STIPULATION n. joker, kicker, string, string to it, a string attached to it, small print, fine print, fine print at the bottom, small fine print, small fine print at the bottom.

STIR n. scene, to-do, fuss, dustup, flap, row, fuzzbuzz (commotion), fuzzbuzzy, kick-up. See TURMOIL. See also EXCITEMENT; ACTION.

STIR v. adjy, psych, spook, get to, flip out, craze, bug, bug up, fire up, work up, rabble-rouse, stir up, make waves, make a scene, make a fuss, steam up, throw wood on the fire, add fuel to the flames, rile. See DISTURB. 2. jazz up, juice up, spark, trigger, pep up, zip up, switch on, turn on the heat, race one's motor, open one's nose. See EXCITE.

STIRRED adj. hyper, charged, wired, wired-up, fired-up, revved, revved-up, keyed-up, all keyed up, steamed-up, hopped-up, worked-up, turned-on; horny, rammy (sexual); stoned, shook-up, hot-and-bothered, in a tizzy. See EXCITED.

STIRRING adj. marvy, like wow, mind-blowing, mind-bending, out-of-this world, turned on by, large, large charge, solid, solid sender, something, something else, something to shout about, something to write home about, sizzler, scorcher, big splash, out-of-sight, flashy, showy, bang-up, feel in one's guts, grabbed by. See EXCITING.

STOCKBROKERAGE n. boiler room, bucket shop, brokerage, wire house.

STOCK CAR n. stocker.

STOCK EXCHANGE n. Big Board, Exchange, over the counter, OTC, the market, the Street, Wall Street.

STOCKHOLDER n. lamb (new investor), IPO (initial public offering), ESOP (employee stock ownership plan), mullets, coupon clipper.

STOCKINGS n. nylons, first national bank (woman's), gam cases, leg sacks; air hose (wearing shoes without stockings).

STOCK MARKET DECLINE n. correction, dip, downturn, adjustment, crash, crashlet, falling out of bed, nosedive, plummet, sell-off, Black Monday (Oct. 19, 1987), Black and Blue Monday (Oct. 26, 1987), meltdown (Oct. 1987 crash), slide.

STOCK MARKET TERMS bear market, bearish market (low); bull market, bullish market, top side, top out (high); bottoming out, making highs, touch bottom, downturn, making a Dow line, buy sign, sell sign, triple witching hour (third Friday of calendar quarter when stock options, stock-index options and stock-index futures expire), wash out, get caught, pull back, a squeeze on profits, shallow river running deep (rising price, basis unknown), recapture (recoup investment), IPO (initial public offering), ESOP (employee stock ownership plan), arbs (arbitrageurs), boot (acquisition includes cash), socks and stocks (nonbanking company such as Sears offering financial services).

STOCK OPTION n. alligator spread (profitless), LYON (liquid yield option note), going naked (short sale), guts (buying and selling simultaneously), strangle (guts situation failing), triple witching hour (third Friday of calendar quarter when stock options, stock-index options and stock-index futures expire).

STOCKS n. blue chips, IPO (initial public offering), ESOP (employee stock ownership plan), cats and dogs, pups, paper, wallpaper (defunct), over the counter, convertible, fancies, high flyer, slam-dunk (sure thing), Buck Rogers (sudden rise), bullet, home run (large capital gain), war babies (defense), yo-yos (fluctuate wildly), Motors (General Motors), fallen angels (out-of-favor stocks at bargain prices), Knockout (Coca-Cola). See also BONDS.

STOCK TICKER n. tape, ticker.

STODGY adj. square, squaresville, L7, a narb, narbo, duddy, fuddy-duddy.

STOICAL adj. cool, cool as a cucumber, keep one's cool, keep one's shirt on, not turn a hair, roll with the punches, unflappable.

STOKER n. bakehead, smoke agent.

STOLEN AUTOMOBILE n. hot car, a short, bent one, rinky, trap, slick, gondola (not common); consent job, owner's job (insurance fraud, theft of); move a job, push hot boilers, push hot ones (dispose of), on the schlep (stealing).

STOLEN MERCHANDISE n. make, take, stuff, swag, bull's wool, five-finger discount, poke, waif (abandoned in flight); shrinkage, seepage (amount stolen from supermarket).

STOMACH n. tummy, tum-tum, gut, pot, pot gut, pus gut, belly, potbelly, melon belly, swag belly, banjo-belly (So.), beerbelly, keg, pail, tank, solar plexus, spare tire, corporation, alderman, breadbasket, briskit, bay window, kishkes, crammer, kitchen, labonza, pantry, balcony, basement, bay, bag, basket, dinner pail, feedbag, feedbox, front porch, locker, navy chest, garbage can, chicken cemetery, below the belt, German goiter, Milwaukee goiter.

STOMACH v. live with, bear with, put up with, roll with the punches, bite the bullet, hang in, hang on, sweat it, take it, grin and bear it. See ENDURE.

STOMACHACHE n. bellyache, gutache, tummyache.

STONE n. 1. brickbat, egg, Irish confetti (Derog.). 2. rock, sparkler, ice, Christmas, glass, paste, hardware, pennyweight, junk jewelry (cheap or fake).

STOOL n. 1. squatter, seat. 2. BM, caca, crap, dingleberry, honey, shit, turd. See BOWEL MOVEMENT.

STOP n. freeze, break, break-off, cutoff, layoff, letup, screaming halt, shuddering halt, grinding halt.

STOP v. gronk out, wind, wind up, wrap, wrap up, sew up, scrub, kill, chop, pack in, kick, kick over, kick the habit, kayo, KO, drop, drop it, drop and go (dockworker use), blow off, kiss off, turn it off, knock off, knock it off, nip it, check it, chuck it, hold it, cool it, quit cold, cold turkey, quit cold turkey, close up, close out, can it, can, cut (film), cut the crap, cut the shit, cut off (Bsbl.), cut off one's water, turn off one's water, break off, break it off, sign off, choke, choke off, gag, bottle up, hush-hush, ice, muzzle, put the damper on, stall, stuff it, shove it, break it up, cut it out, cut out the something, cut one some slack, give it a rest (stop talking), lay off, cry off, come off, come off it, back off, leave off, call off, call all bets off, call it a day, call it quits, cave in, throw in the sponge, throw in the towel, throw over, cry uncle, take the cure, give up, let up, cork, cork up, put a cork in it, pack it in, fold, fold one's hand, drop out, butt out, tune out, punk out, chicken out, peter out, bow out, pull the pin, pull the plug, pull the plug on one, get on the wagon, come to a screeching halt, come to a screaming halt, come to a grinding halt, come to a shuddering halt, stop on a dime, put on the brakes, put the lid on, put the finisher on, kibosh, put the kibosh on, put a stop to, clamp down on, put to bed, drop anchor, shut out, shut off, shut down, shut 'em down, stand down, ring down, drop the curtain, cash in one's chips, flag one, freeze, stow it, drag it, pig it, hang it up, hang up one's spurs, binch (job), hold one's horses, want out.

STOPGAP n. Band-Aid, temp, quick fix, throwaway.

STOP HARASSING v. cool it, get a job, get out of my face, get real, get a life, lay off, knock it off, butt out, get off one's back, sign off, cut one some slack, cut the crap, cut the shit, change your act, don't bug one, all right already, give it a rest, come off it, stop hocking, stop hocking a charnik (Yid.).

STOPPAGE n. down, downtime, shutdown, walkout, lockout, sit-down.

STOPPED adj. dropped, sidelined, shut-out, gronked-out, shut-down, dusted, stonewalled, iced, scrubbed, killed, shot, shot-down, shot down in flames, washed-out, wiped-out, all bets off, all off, kaput, zapped, dead in the water.

STORAGE BATTERY n. can (WWII).

STORE n. supermarket, superette, deli, super, chain store, outlet, outlet store, discount house, co-op, mom and pop, Ma and Pa, bodega (liquor store or N.Y.C. grocery), stand, down to the corner for a bottle, the grab, schlock joint, five-and-ten, five-and-dime.

STORE v. stash, stache, plant, park, squirrel, squirrel away, sock away, salt away, salt down, rathole, put away for a rainy day. See SAVE. See also ACCUMULATE.

STOREHOUSE n. Fort Knox, stash house.

STORM n. blow, coming down, gully washer, heavy wet, heavy dew, precip, raining cats and dogs, raining puppies and kittens, whiteout.

STORM v. 1. come down, rain cats and dogs, rain puppies and kittens, blow. 2. blow one's top, sizzle, sound off, burn up, steam up, tear, tear up the pea patch, carry on, go on, take on. See RAGE. 3. gang up on, come at, come down on, rip, rip into, rip up, rip up one side and down the other, blitz, fly in the teeth of, pull a Jap (surprise).

STORMY adj. wet, blowy, gully washer, raining cats and dogs, raining puppies and kittens, coming down.

STORY n. yarn, book, beat, scoop, clothesline, cliffhanger, bodice-ripper (romance), splatterpunk (violent, lurid), potboiler, spyboiler, gag, long and the short of it, megillah, spiel, wheeze, heavy lard, chestnut, old chestnut, old wives' tale, old saw, old touches, touches. See also JOKE.

STOUT adj. fat-assed, lard-assed, beef trust, Mr. Five by Five, built for comfort, zaftig. See FAT.

STOVE n. hot plate, belly stove, coal pot.

STOW v. stash, stache, jam, jam-pack, pack 'em in, pack like sardines, sardine, ram in, chock, chockablock, stuff, fill to the brim, top off. See also SECRETE.

STRADIVARIUS n. Strad.

STRAFE v. on a rhubarb.

STRAGGLE v. get noplace fast, poke, poke around, tail, go all over the map, goof off, rat fuck, R.F. See DAWDLE.

STRAIGHT adj. on the beam, slam-bang, beeline, as the crow flies, down the alley, down the pipe, in the groove.

STRAIGHTEN HAIR v. fry (Af. Am.).

STRAIGHTFORWARD adj. up front, open, mellow, like it is, call it like it is, lay it on the line, right on, level, what you see is what you get, square shooter, Mr. Clean, spiffy, straight arrow, talk like a Dutch uncle, call a spade a spade, talk turkey, all wool and a yard wide. See SINCERE.

STRAIN n. pressure cooker, burnout, brain fog. See also NERVOUSNESS.

STRAIN v. sweat, sweat it, push, hassle, scratch, grind, dig, plug, peg away, hammer away, hustle, hump, hump it, hump oneself, bust a gut, bust one's ass, break one's neck, break one's back, bear down, put one's back into it, go for broke. See STRUGGLE.

STRAINED adj. uptight, choked, get off my case, get outta town, give me a break, cut me some slack, strung out, unglued, in crisis mode, wreck, nervous wreck, bundle of nerves, wired, wired up, clutched up, basket case, sweating bullets, agita, in a state, hard put to it, at the end of one's rope. See TENSE.

STRAIT n. bottleneck, choke point. See also PREDICAMENT.

STRAITJACKET n. camisole, jacket, tuxedo.

STRAITLACED adj. a narb, narbo, square, squaresville, L7, cubular, uptight, candy-ass, tight-assed, stuffy, stick, Barbie and Ken, in line, granola head, straight, straight-arrow, straight-edge, short haircut, Bible thumper, Christer, Jesus freak, nice Nellie, Crabapple Annie, prune, goody-goody, goody two-shoes, old maid, bluenose, crab, chicken, chickenshit, by the numbers, by the book, according to the book, according to Hoyle, stiff, rock-ribbed, hard-nosed, hard-core, hard-shell, hardline, hardheaded, bulletheaded, bullhead, bullheaded, pigheaded, muleheaded, mulish, mule, stubborn as a mule, horse, Turk, stiff-necked, stuffy, sticky, set, sot, unflappable, dead set on, dyed-in-the-wool.

STRANDED adj. godforsaken, passed up, left in the lurch, sidelined, sidetracked, on the rocks, out in left field, left high and dry, left at the altar, left God knows where.

STRANGE adj. freaky, freaked out, archfreak, flake, flaky, fringy, kinky, kooky, cooky, quirky, bogus, camp, coocoo, semi-dork, dorf, geeky, glick, wombat, creepo, yo-yo, nut, nutcake, nutroll, oddball, banana truck, foul ball, goofball, whack, whacko, random, weird, for weird, weirdo, weirdie, fly ball, case, hippy, beat, beatnik, beat generation, offbeat, off the beaten track, dudical, radical dude, gooney bird, screwball, loner, dolo, chirp, queer fish, queer duck, strange duck, rare bird, jayhawk, three-dollar bill, crackpot, gonzo, queer potato, jell brain, twerp, character, fantasmo, bent, bunk, grody, grody to the max, gross, special, avant-garde, funky, wrinkle, new wrinkle, cool, speed, far out, way out, out-of-sight, wild, crazy, funny, funny-looking, off the wall, out in left field, trippy, not wrapped real tight, gooey, gooney, gasser, meshuga, meshugana, potty, cockeyed, queer in the head, herky, screwy, aired-out, jelled, shaky, creepy, wacky, whacky, whacked out, wakilana, nutty, nutty as a fruitcake, fruity, fruitcake, spacey, cockamamie. See also ECCENTRIC.

STRAPPING adj. husky, hefty, beefy, buffed, industrial, gorilla, hunk, hulk, powerhouse, hoss (muscular), muscle man, he-man, bruiser, big bruiser, ox, beefcake, beef-a-roni, crushman, built like a brick shithouse. See STRONG.

STRATAGEM n. angle, dodge, slant, take, trick, twist, switch, pitch, proposition, setup, layout, lay of the land, action, what's the action, play, scenario, scene, story, bit, child, brain child, game plan, game, little game, gamesmanship, one-upmanship, booby trap, grift, racket, con, gimmick, what's cookin', how one figures it. See also PLAN.

STRATEGIC ARMS LIMITATION TREATY n. SALT.

STRATEGIC ARMS REDUCTION TALKS n. START.

STRATEGIC DEFENSE INITIATIVE n. Star Wars, SDI.

STRATEGIST n. mastermind, brain, finagler, operator, wire-puller.

STRATEGY n. game plan, layout, angle, action, play, scenario, scene, story, brain child, hardball (tough political), how one figures it, what's the action. See PLAN.

STRAY n. mudlark, ragamuffin, drop, fetch, guttersnipe, rustle.

STRAY v. get sidetracked, circumlocute, all over the map. See WANDER.

STREAM n. spritz.

STREAMLINE v. cut the shit, cut the bullshit, cut the frills, cut the bells and whistles, clean it up, break it down, get down to basics, get down to the meat. See SIMPLIFY.

STREET n. pavement, bricks, main drag, main line, turf, back alley, byway, trail, stroll, groove. See ROAD.

STREET PEOPLE n. player, bum, pusher, hooker, alley cat, pimp, operator, drifter, runaway, throwaway, squatter, hippie.

STRENGTH n. 1. pow, juice, sock, kick, the force, beef, clout, might and main, the heavy artillery, powerhouse, strong arm, steamroller. 2. upper hand, whip hand, connection, hooks, in, license, wire, guts, intestinal fortitude, string, ropes, weight. See POWER.

STRENGTHEN v. beef up, soup up, charge up, punch up, heat up, hot up, hop up, jazz up, juice up, build up, step up, pour it on, add fuel to the fire, needle, spike (drink).

STRESS n. crisis mode, pressure cooker, clutch, crunch, heat, albatross, around one's neck, choke, if you can't stand the heat get out of the kitchen (react to).

STRESS v. underline, spot, spotlight, limelight, resonate, headline, hit.

STRESSED adj. get off my case, get outta town, give me a break, cut me some slack, don't sweat me (Af. Am.), uptight, choked, clutched, clutched-up, strung-out, unglued, hyper, in crisis mode, spooked, wreck, nervous wreck, bundle of nerves, wired, wired-up, yantsy, shot to pieces, basket case, agita, hung up with, up the wall, don't trip, in a tizzy, in a state, on edge, worried sick, worried stiff, biting one's nails, at the end of one's rope. See TENSE.

STRESSFUL adj. bummer, downer, bad scene, grabber.

STRETCH v. 1. pad, fill, spin out, string out, drag out, run out, stretch out, build up, beef up, drag one's feet. 2. build up, boost, pyramid, lay it on, spread it on, make a mountain out of a molehill, make a federal case out of something. See EXPAND.

STRETCHED adj. spun-out, strung-out, dragged-out, padded, run out, boosted, hiked, hiked-up, built-up, beefed-up, jacked-up.

STRETCHER BEARER n. body snatcher (WWII).

STRETCHER CASE n. carry, have to scrape one off the pavement.

STRICKEN adj. 1. hurting, bleedin', damaged, winged, nicked, zinged, cut, grabbing, bunged-up, busted-up, put away, walking wounded, have to scrape one off the sidewalk. See also ILL. 2. all torn up, cut up, hit where one lives, shook, shook-up, screwed-up, miffed, miffy, defrosted, burned, burned one's ass, shot-down, have one's nose out of joint, sore, uptight. See also UNHAPPY, UNNERVED.

STRICT adj. 1. tight-assed, square, cubular, uptight, stuffy, in line, straight, straight-arrow, short haircut, bluenose, chickenshit, by the numbers, by the book, according to the book, according to Hoyle, burnt, sticky, set, sot, unflappable, dead set on, hardliner. 2. picky, picky-picky, nitpicker, stickler, ace, comma counter, fussbudget, fusspot, fancy pants, fuddy-duddy, granny, old woman, old maid, pernickety, persnickety. See STERN.

STRICTURE n. hang-up, catch, stumbling block, glitch, joker, one small difficulty, bottleneck, choke point. See HINDRANCE.

STRIDE n. clip, lick. See also WALK.

STRIDE v. leg it, hoof it, stomp, pound the beat, pound the pavement, boot it, stump it, traipse, trapse, traipse around, ooze, strut one's stuff, beat the rocks, press the bricks, broom, drill. See also WALK.

STRIFE n. 1. blowup, blowoff, spat, hassle, row, words, rhubarb, ruckus, ruction, rumpus, run-in, static, flap, fuss, flak, wrangle. See ARGUMENT. 2. brawl, brush, scrap, scene, set-to, rumble, knockdown, knockdown and drag-out, mix-up, jihad, battle royal, stew, shindy, catamaran. See FIGHT.

STRIKE n. 1. walkout, sit-down, sit-in, tie-up, hit the bricks, lockout, holdout, sick-in, sick-out, blue flu (police), skippy strike, quickie; outlaw strike, wildcat (unsanctioned). 2. blitz, push. 3. belt, chop, bam, boff, bop, biff, bash, swat, sock, slug, zap, zetz, wallop, lollop, haymaker, bonk, blindside (unexpected). See HIT.

STRIKE v. 1. walk out, sit down, sit in, skippy strike, locked out, wildcat strike, outlaw strike, hit the bricks, tie up, sick in, sick out, blue flu, hold out. 2. boff, bash, whop, whack, bonk, conk, bop, biff, bean, belt, bung, sock, slug, smack, poke, clip, wallop, throw a punch, sock it to one, plant one, haul off on one, let one have it, land a haymaker. See HIT. 3. bleep, bleep out, blue-pencil, cut, knock out, X out, trim, gut, clean up, launder, sterilize, sanitize, decontaminate, snip, pass up, drop, rub, squash, squelch.

STRIKEBREAKER n. scab, fink, rat, rat fink, goon, goon squad, flying squad, flying squadron, scissorbill, boll weevil, missionary worker.

STRIKER n. holdout, picket.

STRIKING adj. 1. flashy, jazzy, splashy, make a big splash, showy, splurgy, candy, classy, flossy, toney, high-toned, belled, duded-up, hotshot, stand out, spot one like a lead dime, stick out, stick out like a sore thumb, somebody. 2. bitchin', twitchin', killer, boss, stunning, primo, A number one, 10, ten, supercolossal, smashing, mean, gnarly, unreal, motherfucker (Obsc.), zero cool, far out, out-of-this-world, out-of-sight, corking, doozie, dynamite, dyno, in orbit, something, something else, mind-blowing, groovey, heavy, hottie, freak, fly-girl, fly-boy, too much. See FABULOUS. See also BEAUTIFUL, POWERFUL.

STRING MUSICIAN n. fiddler, banjo picker, picker, strummer, thrummer, twanger.

STRINGENT adj. 1. ironclad, chickenshit, by the numbers, by the book, according to the book, according to Hoyle, stiff, tough, rough, brick wall, stick to one's guns, put one's foot down, hard-nosed, set, sot, dead set on, hardliner, dyed-in-the-wool. See STERN. 2. nitpicking, picky, picky-picky, stickler, pernickety, persnickety. See PARTICULAR.

STRIP v. slip out of, take it off, peel, shuck, husk, get all naked, do a striptease, do a strip, strip to the buff.

STRIPPED adj. bare-assed, B.A., bald, naked as a jay-bird, nudie, in one's birthday suit, in the altogether, in the buff, buffo, in the raw, wear a smile. See NUDE.

STRIPTEASE n. strip, stripper, tits and ass, T and A, bumps, grinds, bumps and grinds; pastie, pasty, g-string (costume).

STRIPTEASER n. burlesque queen, exotic dancer, peeler, stripper, stripteuse.

STRIVE v. sweat, sweat it, sweat and slave, tackle, take on, cut and try, buck, hassle, dig, plug, peg away, bust a gut, break one's ass, bear down, put one's back into it, bend over backward, knock oneself out, go all out, go for broke, go the limit, pour it on, work one's head off, mouse milking (maximum time for minimum return). See APPLY ONESELF; ATTEMPT. 2. jockey for position, scramble for, go for the throat, go for the jugular, go after, make a play for, push, push for, shoot for, shoot at, shoot the works. See also CONTEST. 3. take on, fly in the face of, be agin, cross, buck, nix, have a bone to pick, put up an argument, put up a fight, mix it up with, tangle with, bump heads with, cross swords with, lock horns with, stick it to one, push around. See FIGHT.

STRIVING adj. in there, in there pitching, hanging in, going for it.

STROLL v. ankle, ank, toddle, sashay, traipse, trapse, traipse around, ooze, cruise, air out, mope, mooch, trill, percolate. See WALK.

STRONG adj. 1. husky, hefty, heavy, beefy, buffed, gorilla, hunk, hulk, bull, powerhouse, industrial, muscle man, he-man, bruiser, ox, beefcake, beef-a-roni, crushman, bone crusher, enforcer, hard-boiled, hooligan, tough customer, plug-ugly, roughneck, big stiff, ballbreaker, ballbuster, backbreaker, built like a brick shithouse, got the horses to do it, hoss, strong as a horse, strong as a lion, strong as an ox, sturdy as an ox. 2. hardball, hard-nosed, wicked, mean, aggro, hairy, ballsy, Chicago, bitch, handful, push, punch, go-getter, go-go, ball of fire, hotshot, steamroller, get up a head of steam, Norwegian steam, spanking, punchy, gutty, gutsy, mover and shaker, wavemaker, full of piss and vinegar, full of beans, full of hops, have lead in one's pencil, come on strong, come on like gangbusters, take over, take charge, fair hell. See also POWERFUL.

STRONGBOX n. box, crib, coffin, gopher, jug, keister, pete, peat, pete box, pocket, sock, trap (hidden).

STRONG-WILLED adj. 1. hang tough, tough nut, tough nut to crack, head in concrete, stand one's ground, mule-headed, set, sot, unflappable, dead set on, cussed, ornery, murder (he's murder). See STUBBORN. 2. gutsy, got the horses to do it, powerhouse, go-getter, steamroller, movers and shakers, wave makers, take over, take-charge, fair hell, moving out. See STRONG. 3. bound, bound and determined, hang tough, take no prisoners, unflappable, set, dead set on, hell bent on, stand by one's guns, put one's foot down, strictly business, mean serious jelly, no shit, no bird turdin', not playing around, no fooling, have blood in one's eye, be out for blood. See DETERMINED.

STRUCTURE n. 1. pile o' bricks, rockpile, cage, the blindfold lady (court). 2. pecking order, T.O. See also ORGANIZATION.

STRUCTURED adj. glued (antonym: unglued), together, all together, have all the pieces in place, have one's act together, have one's shit together, have one's head together, have one's head screwed on right. See ORGANIZED. See also ORGANIZATION.

STRUGGLE n. 1. grind, daily grind, grindstone, rat race, the salt mines, uphill battle, 2. hassle, wrangle, beef, brush, rumble, roughhouse, free-for-all, donnybrook, flap, jihad, jump, mix-up, jam, run-in, go, rowdy-dowdy, row, rumpus, ruction, ruckus, stew, shindy, set-to, scrap, when push comes to shove. See FIGHT.

STRUGGLE v. 1. sweat, sweat and slave, sweat it, hustle, scratch, slave, grind, dig, plug, plug away, hassle, take on, have one's nose to the grindstone, bust a gut, bust one's conk, back to the salt mines. See WORK. See also APPLY ONESELF. 2. buck, brawl, hassle, scrap, row, kick up a row, roughhouse, pluggin', scruff up, romp, slug, smack, shuffle, put up a fight, tangle ass with, bump heads with, cross swords with, lock horns with, go up against, be agin. See FIGHT. 3. fly in the face of, fly in the teeth of, tummel, raise sand, pettifog, put up an argument. See ARGUE. 4. make a run at, tackle, take on, look to, make a try, cut and try, try on for size, do it or bust a gut, bust one's ass, break one's ass, break one's neck, break one's back, break one's heart, try one's damnedest, give it the old college try, try on for size, give it a try, give it a go, give it one's best shot, take one's best shot, give it a whirl, give it one's all, give it all one's got, bend over backward, lay oneself out, push, knock oneself out, take the bull by the horns, take a shot at, take a fling at, take a crack at, take a whack at, take a cut at, take a stab at, make a stab at, have a go at, have a fling at, have a shot at, on the make, pitch into, in there pitching, in it to win it (Af. Am.), do one's level best, go all out, go for it, go for broke, go the limit, shoot the works. 5. buckle down, push, hump it, hump oneself, bear down, put one's back into it, bend over backward, pour it on, work one's head off. See ATTEMPT. 6. go to pieces, come a-cropper, phumpher, crash, crack up, flop, blow the gig, get hung up, make a hash of. See FLOUNDER.

STRUMPET n. hooker, call girl, hustler, ho, working broad, working girl, skeezer, nok, model, pro, lot lizard (truckstop parking lot), roller (robs drunks), floozie, chippie, prosty, alley cat, tart, baggage, B-girl, bimbo, bimbette (young, sexy), broad, chacha, fallen woman, ass peddler, hussy. See PROSTITUTE.

STRUT v. sashay, boot, ank, boogie, show off, grandstand, hot-dog, put up a front, put on airs, put on, put on the dog, ritz it, look big, shoot the agate, swank, play to the gallery, parade one's wares, strut one's stuff, style (Af. Am.). See also WALK.

STUBBORN adj. hard-nosed, hard-core, hard-shell, hard-ass, hard-line, take no prisoners, hang in, hang in there, hang tough, tough nut, tough nut to crack, hard nut to crack, burly, Turk, locked, locked-in, head in concrete, set in concrete, stuck in concrete, buried in concrete, chiseled in stone, solid as a rock, Rock of Gib, Rock of Gibraltar, rock-ribbed, brick wall, pat, stand-pat, stay put, stand one's ground, hold one's ground, dig in one's heels, stick it out, stick to one's guns, put one's foot down, hold the fort, hold the line, do-or-die, mean business, come hell or high water, money talks bullshit walks, hard as nails, hardheaded, bulletheaded, bullhead, bullheaded, pigheaded, muleheaded, mulish, stubborn as a mule, stiff-necked, sticky, set, sot, unflappable, dead set on, bitter-ender, dyed-in-the-wool, has one's Dutch up, cussed, ornery, murder (he's murder).

STUDEBAKER n. Studie, Studey.

STUDENT n. wonk, tool, power tool, dweeb, gweeb, grind, greasy grind, conch (serious), corndog, mc squared, gunner, wienie, grub, throat, super strap, swat, brown bagger, mug, file boner, plug, plugger, dig, poler, brain, cereb, skull, four-pointer, five-pointer, bookbuster, swot, digithead, curve-killer (superior), poindexter (good), squid, flunky (failing), shark, coed, undergrad, grad, doc, postdoc, prep, preppie, grandfather (senior), soph (sophomore); frosh, dewdrop, rat (freshman); rhinie (prep-school freshman), bone, boner, Flunkenstein, jock, jockey, horse (athlete), big man on campus, B.M.O.C., big-time operator, B.T.O., big wheel, key, key swinger, frat (square), ginny (glamorous), Joe College, blood (college); Joe Yale, white shoe (Ivy League); aggie (agricultural), Christer (prude, nondrinker), Jasper (theological), donkey (Rel.), hookie (noninvolved); full nun, full monk (obedient); cad, crib (cheats), dryball, doughball, mothball, party boy, party girl, calico, cosmo (foreign), zoomer (returns after hiatus), fossil (longtime student), over-the-counter (late registrant).

STUDENT DOCTOR n. tern.

STUDENT LOAN MORTGAGE ASSOCIATION n. Sally Mae.

STUDENT NONVIOLENT (OR NATIONAL) COORDINATING COMMITTEE n. SNCC, Snick.

STUDIOUS adj. wonk, tool, power tool, cereb, mc squared, conch (serious); swot, bookworm, study dweeb, gweeb, digithead, floppy disk (studies too much), throat, cutthroat, gome, grub, gunner, egghead, Eggbert, Merv, Poindexter, pencil geek, pencil neck, smack, poler, professor, squid, weenie, wig.

STUDY v. 1. crack the books, hit the books, cook the books, pound the books, heavy booking, book it, go book, megabook, megastudy, grind, plug, shed, speed, pour it on, power study, bone, bone up, pull an all-nighter, make love to the books, burn, burn the midnight oil, bury oneself in, blitz, bust ass, cram, cram session, skull practice, skull drag, dig, dust 'em off, rack, rush the attic, bag some food for the brain, cruise a subject, wade through, plunge into, polish up, kick around, knock around, worm, hard-wire (by rote), get down, get down pat, get down cold, get hold of, get into one's head, pick up, pick up on, learn the ropes, learn backwards and forwards. 2. check, check out, check it out, check over, check up, look-see, double-O, OO, eye, gun, glim, case, keep tab, keep tabs on, peg, scope, read, scout it out, squack, spot, burn up, eagle-eye, pike off, smoke, candle, case. See also SEE. 3. figure, figure out, sort out, kick around, bat it around, brainstorm, head-trip, float, stew over, chew over, run it by one again. See THINK.

STUFF n. 1. junk. 2. goods, schmatte. 3. bottom line, nitty-gritty, nuts and bolts, heart, meat.

STUFFED adj. 1. packed, jam-packed, full up, topped-off, up to here, fit to bust, packed like sardines, sardined. See CROWDED. 2. fed up, fed to the gills, fed to the teeth, stuffed to the gills, skinful, snootful, bellyful, with a bellyful, with a skinful, with a snootful.

STUN v. rock, gork, floor, bowl over, shake one up, give one a shot, give one a turn, blow away, blow one's mind, throw one a curve, knock one over, set on one's ass. See SURPRISE.

STUNNED adj. shook-up, all shook up, gorked, punchy, slaphappy, bug-eyed, thunderstruck, floored, thrown, defrosted, unglued, flabbergasted, boggled, bowled-over, whomper-jawed, hit like a ton of bricks, caught with one's pants down. See SURPRISED.

STUNTED adj. dinky, measly, banty, shrimp, wee, peewee, peanut, runt, short, small-fry, small-time, tomtit, shot, yea big, yea high, wart, mite, piddling, two-bit, two-by-four, pint-sized, half-pint, knee-high, knee-high to a grasshopper.

STUNT MAN n. bump man.

STUPEFIED adj. gorked, glazed, MEGO (my eyes glaze over), gone, dopey, out of it, out to lunch, spaced, spaced-out, spacey, trippy, tweeked-out, woozy, foggy, in a fog, wandering around in a fog, punchy, punch-drunk. See DAZED.

STUPEFY v. rock, gork, zone out, floor, blow away, blow one's mind, bowl over, bowl down, set on one's ass, set back on one's heels, put one away. See SURPRISE.

STUPENDOUS adj. fab, glor, killer, it's to die for, rad, way rad, fantasmo, fat, super, superfly, too much, the utmost, unreal, zero cool, dynamite, marvy, major, terrif, bitchin' twitchin', mongo, a gas, seven-ply gasser, pisseroo, shirty, aggressive, the greatest, skrouk, smashing, something else, hot shit, cherry, deffest, dope, dual, fat, fierce, fresh, fully on, fully, mint, nitro, on the strength, raw, sick, stupid fresh, out-of-this-world, out-of-sight. See FABULOUS. See also BIG; IMPORTANT.

STUPID adj. exceptional, dorf, dork, dorkmunder, megadork, droid, dogburger, hamburger, nerd, nurdy, ditzo, penis wrinkle, vacant lot, Z-head, numb nut, full hank, boofa, bofa, lop, cob, Fred, Barney, Wilma, biff, dimbo (girl), feeb, loser, winner, twillie, cheese dong, cheesy, cheezy, goob, lump, dickweed, dickwad, remo, sped, sub-human, mouth breather, mental giant, mental midget, skadoodle, knuckle dragger, asshole, assface, deadass, McFly, chili bowl, punter (easily defrauded), jel, lamebrain, birdbrain, birdie (teenage), clambrain, air-brained, beanbrain, scatterbrain, fuck-brained, rattlebrain, rattleweed, lorg, gump, yo-yo, nebbish, out to lunch, lunchie, lunchbox, lunchsack, Barbie and Ken, knob, doorknob, out of it, zonked out, nobody home, light's on but nobody's home, pod people, troll, rummy, tool, jerk, putz (Yid.), yutz, lowbrow, bogus, beau, dodo, dummy, dumbo, dimbo, dumdum, dumbfuck, dumbbell, dumb bunny, dumb cluck, dumb Dora, dumbhead, dumb ox, dumbshit, mungshit, four-letter man (dumb), blonde, dye-job, bonetop, boob, birk, box, oofus, doofus, gink, ninny, nincompoop, zombie, Gumbeyhead, airhead, helium head, algae head, bubblehead, balloonhead, meathead, musclehead, blockhead, broomhead, pointyhead, cone-head, buckethead, bullhead, bumhead, butthead, butterhead, banana head, squarehead, mush head, cementhead, dungeon head, pumpkinhead, saphead, lunk-head, muttonhead, fathead, bonehead, knucklehead, shithead, dough head, hammerhead, jughead, blubberhead, cheesehead, chickenhead, chucklehead, mallet head, lardhead, peahead, pinhead, puddinghead, woodenhead, rubblehead, rockhead, stupidhead, dunderhead, blunderhead, chowderhead, cabbagehead, beetlehead, po-tato head, deadhead, flathead, numbskull, numb head, numb-brained, a few bricks shy of a load, one doughnut shy of a dozen, his elevator doesn't go all the way to the top, isn't playing with a full deck, a low-watt bulb, a few sandwiches short of a picnic, one sandwich short of a picnic, belt does not go through all the loops, doesn't have both oars in the water, not all there, minus some buttons, missing a few buttons, not have all one's buttons, missing a few marbles, not have all one's marbles, lost one's marbles, non compos, non compos mentis, knows from nothing, doesn't know from nothing, doesn't know the time of day, doesn't know from A to B, doesn't know A from izzard, doesn't know which way is up, doesn't know from straight up, doesn't know enough to come in out of the rain, case, turkey, jive turkey, goop, stoop, stupe, thick, loogan; schlemiel, schlamozzle, schlump, schlub, schmendrick, shmoe, shmoo, schnook, schmuck (Yid.), stiff, big stiff, clod-pated, dip, dipshit, dipstick, deadneck, dildo, dill, load, lob, packhorse, droop, dud, Elmer, gasser, gonus, good fellow, goofy, goofus, goofball, goon, goopus, got a hole in the head, leak in the think tank, nuthin' upstairs, jackass, knuckle, bloke, bohunk, baloney, captain of the head, Caspar, soft in the head, half-baked, boob, sappy, slaphappy, fat dumb and happy, mess, mutt, muttontop, meat, meatball, mope, weak in the upper story, simp, klutzy, jaggie, head up, jay, jiggens, juggins, lead-footed, marble dome, newt, nitwit, nougat, one-eye, chump, clam, clock, cluck, cluckhead, world's prize cluck, clunk, dopey, dunce, dead ass, dimwit, dodunk, dub, fish, flub, farmer, melon farmer, shit stick, popcorn, sausage, duck soup, slow on the uptake, slow on the draw.

STURDY adj. 1. husky, hefty, heavy, beefy, buffed, gorilla, hulk, bull, hoss (muscular), powerhouse, muscle man, he-man, strong-arm, bruiser, strong as an ox, strong as a horse, beefcake, beef-a-roni, crushman, bone crusher, built like a brick shithouse. See STRONG. 2. hard-boiled egg, tough, roughneck, ballbreaker, ballbuster. backbreaker. See TOUGH.

STUTTER v. dribble.

STYLE n. bag, cup of tea, druthers, flash, groove, number, thing, type, turned on to, bump for, plenty on the ball, something on the ball, shine at, shine in, dash, splash, splurge. See also FLAIR.

STYLISH adj. faddy, trendy, mean, cosmo, happenin', bust fresh, in, in the mainstream, in thing, the thing, latest thing, latest wrinkle, new wrinkle, newest wrinkle, last word, mod, now, really now, the rage, mockin' it, spinach, up-to-the-minute, up-to-speed, in-the-swim, corporate (business), masscult, fashion plate, chichi, chic, natty, dap, sharp, snazzy, beautiful, clean, go-go, hip, hep, Captain Hipness, ragging, mellow-back, swinger, swingle, upscale, uptown, ritzy, plush, posh, spiffy, classy, high-class, tony, nifty, swanky, swell, nobby, city slicker, kicky, to be bad, dicty, duggy, doggy, dog it, go-getter, jazzy, jazzbo, reat, sharpie, tabbed, cheesy, cat's meow, knock one's eye out, dressed to kill, dressed to the teeth, dressed to the nines, clotheshorse, catch on, in-spot, happening place, groovy hangout, hot spot.

STYLUS n. ballpoint, stick.

STYMIE v. hang up, hold up, choke off, cut off, queer, crab, crimp, cramp one's style, throw a monkey wrench into the works, stall, stonewall. See PREVENT. See also HINDER. 2. shelve, put on the shelf, put on the back burner, put on hold, put on ice, hold off, hang fire, pigeonhole, corner, dead-end, give one the runaround (repeatedly). See DELAY.

SUBCONTRACT v. farm out.

SUBCULTURE n. punk, street people, hippy, yippie, underground.

SUBDEBUTANTE n. subdeb, deb.

SUBDUE v. 1. break, break in, bust, gentle. See SOFTEN. 2. squash, squelch, goof up, queer, sideways over a cliff, put down. 3. drub, trash, whip, smoke, drop, deck, clobber, cream, zap, waste, take the wind out of one's sails, take down, put down, smack down, shut down, shut out, rank out. 4. bury, blank, skunk, trim, trounce, fix one's wagon, scuttle, shave, massage, shellack, roof fell in (sud-den), squelch, squash, make one say uncle, do in, lick to a frazzle, beat all hollow, shut off, blow away, blow one out of the water, put away, settle one's hash. See DEFEAT.

SUBJECT n. guinea pig.

SUBJUGATE v. ride herd on, henpeck, crack the pussy-whip (Fem.), wear the pants, wear the trousers, rule the roost, keep under one's thumb, lead by the nose, kick one around, throw one's weight around, throw a lot of weight, twist around one's little finger, wind around one's little finger, have the upper hand, have the whip hand, have it covered, have the say-so, hold the reins, pull the ropes, pull the strings, pull the wires, wire-pull, reel one back in, bring to heel, box in, get one in a box, get one's hook into, sit on top of, break, break in, bust, gentle.

SUBJUGATED adj. in one's power, in one's pocket, in one's clutches, under one's thumb, at one's mercy, at one's beck and call, at one's feet, a slave to, led by the nose, putty in one's hands, wimpy, wet rag, wet sock, tied to one's apron strings, dance to one's tune, peon, serf, slave, slavey, pratt boy, worker bee.

SUBLIME adj. killer, fab, fantasmo, fat, mongo, super, super-fly, gross, evil, terrible, too much, the most, zero cool, heavy, dynamite, marvy, terrif, solid gold, outrageous, far out, the greatest, stunner, heavenly, out-of-this-world, out-of-sight. See FABULOUS.

SUBMARINE n. navy shark, pig boat, tin can, tin fish, tin shack, boomer (nuclear missiles).

SUBMARINE TERMS Christmas tree (control panel), the creeps (itch from low pressure), pull the plug (submerge).

SUBMERGE v. dunk, pull the plug (submarine).

SUBMERSE v. dunk.

SUBMERSION n. dunking.

SUBMISSIVE adj. yes-man, ass-kisser, on a string, henpecked, tied to one's apron strings, on a leash, weak sister, Milquetoast, Caspar Milquetoast, tail between one's legs, schnook, dance, dance to one's tune, eat crow, eat humble pie, eat shit, putty in one's hands, wimpy, wet rag, wet sock, when in Rome do as the Romans do.

SUBMIT v. 1. cave in, give in, say uncle, cry uncle, fold, quit, throw in the sponge, pack it in, kiss ass, eat crow, eat dirt, knuckle under, kowtow, lie down and roll over for, give away the store. See SURRENDER. 2. go with the flow, don't make waves, don't rock the boat, play the game, play ball with, shape up, not get out of line, go social. See COMPLY. 3. make a pitch, proposition, put a feeler out, pop the question.

SUBORDINATE n. peon, serf, slave, slavey, girl Friday, man Friday, low man on the totem pole, second fiddle, second string, third string, flunky, stiff, dweeb, space cadet (young), apparatchik. See INFERIOR.

SUBORDINATION n. pecking order, down the line.

SUBPOENA n. papers, plaster.

SUBSCRIBE v. 1. hold a brief for, hold with, back, bless, boost, give the nod, give the go-ahead, give the green light, give one's stamp of approval, get behind, okay, go along with, put one's John Hancock on, thumbs up, take, take kindly to, yes one, ditto, rubber-stamp. See ENDORSE. 2. ante up, pony up, get it up, put up, put something in the pot, sweeten the pot, sweeten the kitty, do one's part. See GIVE. 3. sign on, make a deal, firm a deal, cut a deal, okay, OK, buy, set, play ball with.

SUBSCRIBER n. angel, Santa Claus, sugar daddy, fairy godmother, lady bountiful, giver, heavy hitter, maxed-out (political limit).

SUBSERVIENT adj. 1. bush-league, low in the pecking order, flunky, furp, handkerchief head, Stepin Fethit, Uncle Tom (Af. Am.). See INFERIOR. 2. in one's power, in one's pocket, in one's clutches, under one's thumb, at one's mercy, at one's beck and call, at one's feet, dance, dance to one's tune, eat crow, eat humble pie, eat shit, a slave to, led by the nose. See SUBJUGATE.

SUBSIDIARY n. branch, subsid.

SUBSIDIZE v. angel, back, the bank, greenback, bank-roll, juice, grubstake, pick up the check, pick up the tab, stake, prime the pump, knock (Af. Am.) See FINANCE. See also GIVE.

SUBSIST v. 1. get along, just makin' it, get by. 2. hang in, hang in there, hang tough, hang on, stick, stick it out, stick with it, ride out. See also MANAGE.

SUBSISTENCE n. the wherewithal, bread, bread and butter, the bacon, the necessary.

SUBSTANCE n. 1. point, stuff, nub, bottom line, ABC's, nitty-gritty, nuts and bolts, brass tacks, coal and ice, guts, innards, name of the game, the way of it, nature of the beast, drift, heart, meat. 2. hunk, chunk, gob.

SUBSTANDARD adj. crap, junk, shit, G, lemon, Mickey Mouse, piss-poor, schlocky, bottom-of-the-barrel, sleazy, slimpsy, below the mark, not up to scratch, not up to snuff, seconds. See IMPERFECT.

SUBSTANTIAL adj. 1. sound as a dollar, solid as a rock. 2. heavy, heavyweight, big-league, major-league, we're not talking about nutmeg here, big deal. 3. biggie, Mr. Big, big gun, big noise, big shit, big timer, big wheel, bigwig, real cheese, movers and shakers, high-muck-a-muck, tycoon, baron, brass, V.I.P., connection, wire, godfather, a somebody, double-barreled, big daddy, major-league, big-league. See IMPORTANT. 4. legit, card-carrying, sure enough, honest-to-God, twenty-four-carat, all wool and a yard wide, for real, righteous.

SUBSTANTIATE v. 1. check out, check up, check up on, debunk (prove false). 2. try, try out, try on. See also TEST; CONFIRM.

SUBSTANTIVE adj. heavy, meaningful, meaningful experience. See also BASIC.

SUBSTITUTE n. backup, sub, spare, stand-in, fill-in, pinch hitter, pinch runner, off the bench, bench warmer, ringer, redundancy, second-string, third-string, switcheroo, dog chaser (R.R.); front.

SUBSTITUTE v. pinch-hit for, sub, sub for, swap places with, sit in, stand in, back up, fill in, take over, front for, ring, ring in, take out, step into the shoes of, cover for.

SUBSTITUTION n. switcheroo, sub.

SUBTERFUGE n. 1. game plan, game, angle, dodge, slant, trick, twist, switch, pitch, proposition, setup, layout, lay of the land, what's the action, play, scenario, scene, story, bit, child, brainchild, little game, gamesmanship, one-up-manship, booby trap, grift, racket, con, jazz, jive, shuck, total shuck, balls, bunco, hooey, hocky, hoke, hokey-pokey, hokum, hogwash, malarkey, marmalade, spinach, banana oil, baloney, bulldog, garbage, snow job, whitewash, white-wash job, doesn't wash, plant, hookup, put-on, spoof, shell game, skin game, trick, fool, fast one, runaround, cutie, claptrap, line of cheese, borax, song, song and dance, string, smoke, blow smoke up one's ass, tripe, vanilla, gimmick, what's cookin', how one figures it. 2. cover, cover up, cover story, fig leaf, clean up, cop out, fish tale, fish story, cock-and-bull story, tall story, tall tale, fairy tale, whopper, yarn, dirty lie, terminological inexactitude, Mother Machree, Mother McCrea, routine, stall. 3. con, con game, short con, big con, big store, hustle, hassle, sting, bunk, bunco, flam, flimflam, flimflammery, jip, gyp, scam, racket, dodge, stunt, fast shuffle; ride-out, squat (fraudulent auto accident), all hat and no cattle (Texas), bait and switch. See TRICK.

SUBTRACT v. knock off, take away.

SUBTRACTION n. deduck (income tax item), cut.

SUBURB n. slub, slurb, burb, spread city, bedroom community, sticks, stix, Peter Pan suburb (no planning for elderly), burbed-out (looks suburban).

SUBWAY n. hole, hole in the ground, metro, tube.

SUCCEED v. put across, put it together, put over, click, connect, pull it off, pull it out (despite adversity), get over, get well, get fat, get rich, get ahead, get away with, get on, get something on the board, get there, get into pay dirt, get the breaks, break the bank, go places, go to town, go great guns, go over, go over big, go crazy large (Af. Am.), win out, check out, make out, make the cut, make it, make a killing, make hay, make well, make the grade, make good, make a noise in the world, be heard from, make a hit, hit, hit it big, hit the jackpot, hit the bull's-eye, hit pay dirt, strike it rich, strike oil, strike gold, strike a vein, make a lucky strike, strike it lucky, luck, luck in, luck out, kick it live (Af. Am.), fall into the shithouse and come up with a five-dollar gold piece, shit in high cotton, ace, ace the easy, hold aces, turn up trumps, move out, take off, fly, skyrocket, flash in the pan (brief), ring the bell, score, hang up (sports), win hands down, win going away, win in a walk, win in a waltz, waltz off with, breeze home, romp home, romp off with, run with the ball, blow away, blow out of the water, cream, clean sweep, skunk, KO, knock one for a loop, walk over, blow one away, blow one out of the water, have one by the balls, have one by the short hairs, have one by the tail, be a gas, be a gasser, bring home the bacon, bring home the groceries, have it made, turn the trick, got it made, pull off, bring off, carry off, catch on, pass muster, fill the bill, get by, pass in the dark, arrive, nail it, hack it, win one's spurs, do the job, do oneself proud, do all right by oneself, do a land-office business, come on, come along, be fat dumb and happy, live high on the hog, live off the fat of the land, live the life of Riley, live on Easy Street, live in clover, live on velvet, have one's place in the sun, come out on top of the heap, lie on a bed of roses, take the cake, get Brownie points, break the back of, light at the end of the tunnel, over the hump.

SUCCEEDING adj. 1. on fire; go crazy large, large and in charge (Af. Am.); 2. next off, next up, next in line for.

SUCCESS n. 1. winner, grand slam, slam dunk, big hit, sockeroo, killing, laugher, hot run, daily double (series of successes), sleeper (unexpected), howling success, pay dirt. See TRIUMPH. 2. boom, good times, gravy train, land-office business, high on the hog, on top of the heap, bed of roses, clover, Easy Street, lap of luxury, the life of Riley, velvet.

SUCCESSFUL adj. on fire, hot, smoking, really smoking, really popping, gone crazy large (Af. Am.), it cooks, got legs, chill, have it made, have a mint, have the wherewithal, have one's place in the sun, loving life, loving it, caught the gold ring, on Easy Street, on velvet, on top of the heap, on a bed of roses, everything's coming up roses, high on the hog, right up there, up in the bucks, in the bucks, in the money, in the chips, in the lap of luxury, in clover, rolling in clover, a pig in clover, on a roll, really rolling, rollin' in it, rollin' in dough, rolling in money, lousy with money, tall money, money to burn, livin' large, clockin', really cooking, cooking with gas, lousy rich, stinking rich, stinky pie rich, holding, well-heeled, well fixed, well-to-do, well-set-up, set up, sitting pretty, sit fat, fat, fat city, fat cat, arrived, plush, lush, flush, loaded, booming, going strong, going great guns, gold mine (successful business), mining the gold, Midas touch, golden, made it, made it big, made one's pile, did all right by oneself, home free, laughing all the way to the bank, ride the gravy train, gravy boat, jammy, good ticket, yuppie (young urban professional), buppie (black urban professional), huppie (Hispanic upwardly mobile professional), yumpie (young upwardly mobile professional), yavis (young attractive verbal intelligent successful), dicty, big, biggie, big shot, long hitter, king of the hill, duke of the catwalk,

Daddy Warbucks, scissorbill, swell, lace curtain, coupon clipper, big butter-and-egg man, rich as Croesus, the establishment, big boys, the 400, upper class, the beautiful people, main-line, large, oofy, uptown, upscale, piss on ice; greasing it out, sleazeball, sleazing (tennis shots).

SUCCESSFULLY adv. with a bang, swimmingly.

SUCCESSION n. pecking order, down the line, time line.

SUCCINCT adj. short and sweet, in a nutshell, make a long story short, boiled-down, cut to the bone.

SUCCOR v. back up, give a leg up, give a lift, lend a hand, go to bat for, go to the mat for, bail out, hold one's end up, boost, buck up, brace up, up. See AID.

SUCCULENT adj. yummy, yummy in the tummy, nummy, delish, divoon, devine, heavenly.

SUCCUMB v. 1. go, kick off, kick the bucket, buy the farm, pass away, croak, meet one's maker, give up the ghost, breathe one's last, go west, pop off, cash in one's chips, turn it in, check out, up and die. See DIE. 2. fold, quit, cave in, give in, give into, say uncle, cry uncle, toss in the towel, throw in the sponge, pack it in, eat crow, eat dirt, eat humble pie, knuckle under. See SURRENDER. 3. go with the flow, don't make waves, don't rock the boat, play the game, shape up, clean up one's act, straighten up and fly right, stay in line, not get out of line, when in Rome do as the Romans do. See COMPLY.

SUDDEN adj. flash, from out in left field, from out of the blue, like a bolt from the blue.

SUE v. drag into court, haul into court, see one in court, have the law on, take the law on, take out after, have up, put one away, pull up.

SUFFER v. live with, bear with, put up with, bite the bullet, sweat, sweat it, wait out, take it, sit and take it, take it on the chin, grin and bear it, not let it get one down, bleed, hurt, carry the torch for one (love), eat one's heart out (envy). See ENDURE.

SUFFERING adj. hurting, grabbing, bleeding, stab in the ———, making like the anvil chorus in one's skull, who needs it, this I need yet, need it like a hole in the head, take some hide and hair, biting the bullet, carrying the torch, torching. See also DISTRESSED.

SUFFICE v. fill the bill, make a hit, hit the spot, go over big, do the trick, hack it, make the grade, get by, be just the ticket, be just what the doctor ordered. See SATISFY. See also QUALIFY.

SUFFICIENCY n. a ton, mucho, mucho-mucho, heavy, stinking with, oodles, oodles and oodles, beaucoup. See also ENOUGH.

SUFFICIENT adj. up to one's ass in, no end, a dime a dozen, a mess, aplenty, drug on the market, galore, money to burn, bellyful, had it, up to here, that's it, all right already, enough already, enough of that shit, fed up, have a skinful, have a snootful, sick and tired of, punched-out, last straw.

SUGAR n. dirt, dominoes (cubes), sand, white gold, sawdust.

SUGGEST v. steer, tout, plug, let in on, put on to something hot, put a bug in one's ear, put in one's two cents, tip, tip off, give one a tip, fold an ear. See ADVISE. See also PROPOSE. 2. favor, double for.

SUGGESTIBLE adj. believer, sucker, patsy, mark, easy mark, pigeon grape (waiting to be squeezed), duck, sitting duck, pushover, swallow anything, swallow whole, be taken in, wide-open. See SUSCEPTIBLE.

SUGGESTION n. 1. hot lead, lead, tip-off, tip, steer, telltale, bum steer (false). 2. tad, touch, titch, smell, two cents' worth. 3. angle, gimmick, big idea (unwelcome), feeler, pitch, proposition, proposish, game plan, setup, how one figures it, bit, brain child, sneaking suspicion.

SUGGESTIVE adj. blue, dirty, filthy, off-base, off-color, out-of-line, jiggle, jiggly, C.F.M. (come fuck me: sexually suggestive clothing), spark. See also OBSCENE.

SUICIDE n. OD, take oneself out, take a rope, wrap-up, solitaire, Brodie (off a bridge), gorging out, back-gate commute.

SUICIDE, COMMIT v. check out, pack in, OD, Brodie (off a bridge), gorge out, hang up, hit oneself in the bonnet, hit out, hit oneself out, swing, take a back-gate commute, swing, string up, take a rope, pack in, wrap up.

SUIT n. threads, set of threads, vine, flute, gray flannel, front, getup, rig, zoot suit, ice-cream suit (white), drapes, set of drapes, drape, drape shape, drape shape with a reet pleat, flash, frame, frock, sock frock. See also CLOTHING.

SUIT v. 1. fit in, go by the book, roll with the punches, swim with the tide, come up to scratch, do it according to Hoyle, play the game, toe the mark. See CONFORM. 2. make it, make the cut, make the grade, cut the mustard, check out, hack it, pass muster, fill the bill, get by, pass in the dark. See SUCCEED.

SUITABLE adj. 1. user-friendly, handy, all-around. 2. right stuff, keerect, reet, reat, all reet, all root, all rightee, allrightie, all righty, easy, I can live with that, not half bad, cool, coolville, crazy, copacetic, kopasetic, O.K. okay, A-O.K., A-okay, fucking-A, okey-dokey, okey-doke, ding-ho, ding-how, ding-hau, ding-hao, swell, dory, okey-dory, hunky-dory, right, righteous, hit the nail on the head, an A., S.O.P., kosher, according to Hoyle, up to code, up to snuff, it's the berries, in the groove, groovy, dead on, right on, on the nose, on the button, on the numbers, on the money, right on the money, on the ball, on the beam, on target, on track, on the right track, hitting on all six, all to the mustard, just what the doctor ordered, that's it, that's the idea, that's the ticket, that's the thing, that's just the thing, that's the very thing.

SUITCASE n. jiffy bag, keister, valpack, tote bag, garment bag, duffel, duffle bag, A & P suitcase (grocery bag used to hold clothing), carry-on.

SUITOR n. old man, squeeze, main squeeze, main dude, main man, boy friend, B.F., ace, big moment, papa, sweet papa, date mate, honey, hon, back-door man. See BOY FRIEND.

SULKY adj. mopey, moony, downer, taken down, down-in-the-mouth, out-of-sorts. See UNHAPPY.

SULLEN adj. bitchy, mean, ornery, out-of-sorts, grouchy, grumpy, cranky, bear, ogre, stanky (woman), ugly, ugly customer, turd poodle, uptight, pushing out one's lips, got up on the wrong side of the bed. 2. mopey, moony, low, ass in a sling, dick in the dirt, in a blue funk, a downer, bummed-out, hurting, off one's feed, killjoy, prune-faced. See MELANCHOLY.

SULLIED adj. dirty, exposed, mucked-up, cruddy, scuzzy, raunchy, sleazy, sleazed-up, crudded-up, crummed-up. See DIRTY.

SULLY v. 1. sleaze up, crumb up, muck up, crud, mess, mess up, muss, muss up. 2. put down, pan, knock, slam, hit, rap, slice up, give one a black eye, make one lose face. See SLANDER.

SULTRY adj. 1. sticky, stuffy, close, broiler, roaster, scorcher, sizzler, swelterer. 2. heavy, hot and heavy, hot stuff, steamy, flaming (Obsc., computer conversations). blue, purple, X-rated, low-down, low-down dirty, low-down and dirty, turned-on, nasty. See also OBSCENE.

SUM n. fixins', fixings, shebang, the whole enchilada, the works, the whole megillah, whole shebang, whole schmeer, whole works, lump sum (money). See WHOLE.

SUMMARIZE v. 1. rehash, recap, run down, run over, run through, make a long story short, get down to cases, get down to brass tacks. 2. cut, cut down, cut to the bone, nutshell, put in a nutshell, boil down, trim, get to the meat, chop, snip.

SUMMARY n. 1. rundown, run-through, recap, rehash. 2. money quote (one sentence), short and sweet, boiled down, in a nutshell, make a long story short.

SUMMER n. heat time, heavy heat stretch, riot time.

SUMMER DAY n. broiler, roaster, scorcher, sizzler, swelterer, sticky, close, one can fry eggs on the sidewalk.

SUMMER STOCK n. strawhat, strawhat circuit.

SUMMIT n. tops, the max, the most, up there, really up there.

SUMMON v. beep.

SUMMONS n. papers, plaster, greetings.

SUMPTUOUS adj. posh, plush, ritzy, swank, swanky, splendiferous, splendacious, with all the extras, ultra-ultra, out-of-this-world, out-of-bounds. See LUXURIOUS.

SUN n. rays, Old Sol, Ol' Sol, big red (Gulf War), bean, Betsy, Betsey, pumpkin.

SUNBATHE v. bag some rays, tan.

SUNGLASSES n. shades, sunshades, glims, tints, looks, loks, mask, peepers, specs, wraparounds. See also GLASSES.

SUNRISE n. crack of dawn, bright, early bright, day peep, sunup.

SUNSHINE n. rays, UV.

SUPERABUNDANT adj. lousy with, crawling with, ton, mucho, mucho-mucho, no end, up to one's ass in, up the ying yang in, mess, loaded, scads, shithouse full, shitload, shit bag, fat, wad, heaps. See AMOUNT; LARGE.

SUPERANNUATED adj. on the shelf, out of circulation, over the hill, put out to pasture, out, played-out (Af. Am.), back-number, has-been, old-hat, foozle, fossil, passed it, a once-was, hung up one's spurs, old-timer.

SUPERB adj. killer, aces, mega-gnarly, zero cool, aggro, rad, way rad, fab, bump'n', state of the art, tops, stunning, solid, greatest, lampin', the real George, hummer, in orbit, Jake, ginchy, slammin', fabu, cherry, deffest, dope, dual, fat, fierce, fresh, fully on, fully, mint, nitro, on the strength, raw, sick, stupid fresh, key, cranking, rattling, rocking, this is some kinda ———, the best. See EXCELLENT.

SUPERCILIOUS adj. high-and-mighty, on one's high horse, dog it, put on airs, toplofty, smitty, sniffy, snooty, snotty, hoity-toity, uppish, uppity, bossy, high-toned, smart, cocky, gally, nervy. See ARROGANT.

SUPERFICIAL adj. flash, flash in the pan, glib, half-assed, half-baked, half-cocked, paper-thin, ditsy, bubbleheaded, Barbie and Ken, Muffy, Fifi, Heather, foof, quick fix, slick, tip of the iceberg.

SUPERFICIALLY adv. hit the high spots, once over lightly, skim, lick and a promise.

SUPERFLUITY n. overruns, the limit, he's the limit, too much. See also PLENTY.

SUPERFLUOUS adj. fifth-wheel, blivit.

SUPERINTENDENT n. 1. super, sitter, house-sitter. 2. head, headman, hired gun, Big Brother, boss, bosshead, pit boss, pusher, straw boss, slavedriver, governor, bull, bull of the woods, swamper, crumb boss (hobo and logger), zookeeper (racing). See also EXECUTIVE.

SUPERIOR adj. 1. killer, in spades, super, mega-gnarly, cool, zero cool, winner, rad, radical, state-of-the-art, gilt-edged, righteous, tops, top-of-the-line, key, first-class, golden, heavy, bad, marvy. See EXCELLENT. 2. cool, cocky, biggety, bossy, dicty, sniffy, snooty, snotty, uppity, upstage, stuck up, gold-card, king-shit, high-and-mighty, high hat, highfalutin, put on airs, have one's glasses on (Af. Am.), throw one's weight around, smarty-pants, wise-ass. See ARROGANT. 3. have one by the balls, have one by the tail, have one by the short hairs.

SUPERIOR n. CEO, C.O., exec, suit, key player, chief, bossman, czar, head honcho, the brass, VIP, Mr. Big, big cheese, big gun, big wheel, big player, big chew, top dog, bowwow, superfly, rabbi, higher-up, higher-ups, guru, buddy seat, the say, the word. See EXECUTIVE.

SUPERIORITY n. edge, ahead, over, top, on top, bulge, spark. See ADVANTAGE.

SUPERLATIVE adj. number one, numero uno, A, A-1, ten, 10, world-class, greatest, gonest, hundred-proof, mostest, baaaadest, first chop, def, super, gilt-edge, all-time, tops, top dog, endsville, the end, solid gold, winner. See BEST.

SUPERNUMERARY n. spear carrier, extra, supe, super, walking gentleman, walking lady, walk-on, atmosphere. See also ACTOR.

SUPERSTAR n. box-office champ, big box office, box office, B.O., box-office name, champ, one to pull 'em in, sure sell, bankable one, draw, big draw, big name, monster, celeb, name, household name, number one, prima donna, great, large, talent, right up there, big-timer, biggie. See CELEBRITY.

SUPERVISE v. run, run things, run the show, ride herd on, sit on top of, call the shots, call the play, be in the driver's seat, be in the saddle, deal with, crack the whip. See MANAGE.

SUPERVISOR n. super, boss, suit, brass hat, Big Brother, head, top dog, big weenie, big cheese, bull of the woods, king of the hill, big shot, big shit, pit boss (gambling), straw boss, slavedriver, zookeeper (racing). See also EXECUTIVE.

SUPPER n. din-din, chow, chow time, bite, eats, feed, feed bag, ribs (hot), hots (hot meal, Mil.), grub, takeout, sit-down, blue plate, black plate (soul food), cook out, barbecue, BBQ, Chinx (Chinese, Derog.), potluck. See also FOOD.

SUPPLANT v. pinch-hit for, sub for, swap places with, sit in, stand in, back up, fill in, take over, front for, ring, ring in, take out, step into the shoes of.

SUPPLANTED adj. has-been, out.

SUPPLEMENT n. spin-off, options, all the options, bells, bells and whistles, padding, spare tire, fifth wheel, widow, gash, lagniappe, goody, perk. See also ADDITION.

SUPPLEMENT v. beef up, soup up, charge up, pad, bump, bump up, punch up, heat up, hot up, hop up, jazz up, juice up, build up, step up, pour it on, add fuel to the fire. See ADD.

SUPPLY v. heel (money), fix up, fix up with, drop (usually illegal or contraband goods), give with, pony up, put up, put out, get it up, kick in, come across with, come through, duke, weed, stake, put a buck one's way. See GIVE.

SUPPLY BASE n. buddy store (Vietnam).

SUPPORT n. 1. backup, backing, the wherewithal, bread, bread and butter, the bacon, the necessary. 2. security blanket, old standby, standby, juice, on the reservation (Pol.). 3. lift, shot in the arm, shot in the ass. See also ASSIST.

SUPPORT v. 1. buck up, brace up, boost, stroke, juice, juice up, key up, psych up, egg on, turn on, build, build up, chirk up, perk up, pick up, put up to, give a boost to, give a leg up, give a lift, lend a hand, plug, hype, ballyhoo, push, goose, hold a brief for, go with, go for, go to bat for, go to the mat for, go down the line for, go the route for, make a pitch for, beat the drum for, plump for, run interference for, grease the wheels for, thump the tub for, root for, stump for, get on the bandwagon, front for, stand up for, stick by, stick up for, ride shotgun for, take care of one, open doors, up, back, back up, pat on the back, toss a bouquet, give a bouquet, give a posy, give the man a big cigar, hand it to, give one the spotlight, gold star, puff up, trade last, TL, hear it for, hats off to, bail out, tin-cupping (seeking management support), carry one, prop, prop up, hold one's end up. 2. angel, the bank, bankroll, grubstake, stake, greenback, back, juice, pick up the check, pick up the tab, knock (Af. Am.), lay on one, piece one off, prime the pump, go for. See FINANCE. 3. turn on, spark, trigger, zap, beef up, soup up, punch up, fire up, add fuel to the fire, heat up, hot up, hop up, jazz up, build up, juice, juice up, get it up, work up, give a lift, put one on top of the world, put one on cloud nine, brace up, chirk up, buck up, pick up, perk up, zip up, snap up. 4. live with, bear with, put up with, handle, lump it, suck it up, bite the bullet, hang in, hang in there, hang tough, hang on, stick it out, ride out, sit and take it, sweat out, wait out, stay the course, stand up to it, be big, grin and bear it. See ENDURE.

SUPPORTER n. 1. backer, greenback, angel, staker, grubstaker, meal ticket, rabbi, Chinaman, fairy godmother, lady bountiful, sugar daddy, Santa Claus. 2. fan, freak, booster, frenzies, nut, buff, hanger-on, sideman, ho-dad, ho-daddy, go in for, go out for, have a go at, plaster, shadow, echo, stooge, flunky, tail.

SUPPOSE v. 1. be afraid, have a hunch, have a sneaking suspicion, take as gospel truth, take stock in, swear by. See BELIEVE. 2. go out on a limb, take a stab, take a stab in the dark, take a shot, take a shot in the dark, figure, size up, guesstimate, SWAG (slightly wild-assed guess). 3. cook up, dream up, make up, think up, trump up, head trip, spark, toss out, spitball, brainstorm, take it off the top of one's head, talk off the top of one's head.

SUPPOSITION n. guesstimate, hunch, SWAG (slightly wild-assed guess), shot, shot in the dark, sneaking suspicion, stab, stab in the dark.

SUPPRESS v. black out, kill, squash, squelch, hush up, bag, put the lid on, crack down on, keep under wraps, keep buttoned up. See REPRESS.

SUPPRESSED adj. 1. tight-assed, hung-up, a narb, square, uptight. 2. bottled-up, corked-up, bagged, squashed, squelched, blacked-out, kept under wraps, hushed-up, shut-down, killed, buttoned-up. See also SECRET. 3. in one's power, in one's pocket, in one's clutches, under one's thumb, at one's mercy, at one's feet, putty in one's hands, dance to one's tune, slavey. See SUBJUGATED.

SUPPRESSION n. no-no, a don't, off limits, outa bounds, bleeper, blankety-blank (word or expression), blackout, hush-up, clampdown, crackdown.

SUPREME COURT n. Nine Old Men, SCOTUS (Supreme Court of the United States).

SURCEASE n. breather, breathing spell, break, coffee break, five, ten, come up for air, downtime, time out, break-off, cutoff, layoff, letup, screaming halt, shuddering halt, grinding halt, freeze. See also END; STOP.

SURE adj. 1. sure enough, sure as fate, sure as shooting, sure as God made little green apples, sure as hell, sure as the devil, sure as I live and breathe, sure as death and taxes, sure as can be, sure as shit, sure thing, surest thing you know, surefire, for sure, fer sher, fer shirr, that's for sure, for damn sure, for danged sure, dead sure, for a fact, for a fact Jack, for certain, on ice, cold, down pat, nailed-down, got the faith baby. See CERTAIN. 2. iceman, ice in one's veins, gutsy, high, all puffed up, pumped-up, looking at the world through rose-colored glasses. See ASSURED; CONFIDENT; COCKSURE.

SURELY adv. absofuckinglutely, posolutely, absitively, cert, amen, sure, why sure, fer sure, fer sher, and no mistake, you know, you know it, you better believe it, you betcha, you betcher life, you bet, you can say that again, you're darn tootin', no catch, no kicker, no buts about it, no ifs ands or buts, is the Pope Catholic?, does a bear shit in the woods?, indeedy, yes indeedy, for real, no shit, right-o. See ABSOLUTELY.

SURFBOARD n. double-ender, gun, deck, boogie-board, hot-dogging board, spoon, stick, popout, quiver (assortment of boards).

SURFEIT n. bellyful, had it, skinful, snootful, up to here, dose, much of a muchness. See also FULL.

SURFEITED adj. done it all, been around twice, sick and tired of, had it up to here, fed up, fed to the teeth, fed to the gills, stuffed to the gills, skinful, bellyful, snootful.

SURFER n. surf Nazi (skilled), ripper (good), boogie boarder, sponger, sponge head; gut slider, gremlin, gremmie (beginner); thrasher, hot dogger; hodad, poser (pretends to be), aggro (uptight), half-men (use knee boards), kook (spoils a wave), soul surfer (for joy), shredder (uses short board), grommett (young child), caddy, surf bum, wahine (Fem.), a non, beach bunny, Debbie (non-surfer), Martian (stranger).

SURFING STYLES n. hang five, hang ten, hot dog, goofy foot (left foot forward), reverse kickout, ride the nose, kick out and shoot the curl, rip (surf well).

SURFING TERMS back out, bomb, bomb out, wipe out, gas out, get the ax, grab a rail, kamikaze (voluntary wipe), pull out, left slide, pearling (nose-down dive), kick out and shoot the curl, catch a rail; like going to church, in the Pope's living room (a great ride), stylin' (doing well), wig out (nervous), slap (crash), take gas, get dogged, womb (wave when surfer is inside it), soup, drilled (pounded by a wave), cowabunga, beach bunny, gun, heavy, toe a stick, skim board, pipe, tube, greenback, haken (surf and eat), wetties (wetsuit), ho dad; kneebusters, clamdiggers, baggies, jammies (pants); val (inland dweller), gnarly (radical), goofy-footed (starts with left foot), goob (a nonentity), nuch (not much) zup, yabba-dabba-doo (greeting).

SURFING WAVES n. the green, surf's up, heavy, blown out, junk surf, looper, soup (foam), gnarly (dangerous), wake surf, tasty waves, like death, wall up (the waves walled up to ten feet before curling).

SURGE n. jump start.

SURGEON n. bones, sawbones, bone bender, bone breaker, M.D., doc, big eye man, big nose man, big heart man, medic, medico, croaker, stick croaker, butcher, blade, knife man, knife-happy, body-and-fender man (plastic).

SURGERY n. 1. procedure, go in, go under the knife. 2. OR (operating room), the pit.

SURMISE n. a stab, a stab in the dark, out on a limb, a shot, a shot in the dark, guesstimate, windshield appraisal (superficial, from a car), hunch, SWAG (slightly wild-assed guess), sneaking suspicion.

SURMISE v. have a sneaking suspicion, take a stab, take a shot, take a shot in the dark, guesstimate, spitball. See SPECULATE.

SURPASS v. blow one's doors off.

SURPLUS n. overruns, the limit, too much, drug on the market.

SURPRISE n. whammy, double whammy, glork, jolt, bolt out of the blue, from out in left field, eye-opener, curveball, ace in the hole, bite one in the ass, kick in the ass, shot in the ass, sleeper (unexpected success), sticker shock (auto price).

SURPRISE v. 1. rock, glork, floor, shake one up, give one a shot, give one a turn, blow away, blow one's mind, bowl over, bowl down, strike all of a heap, flabbergast, put one away, make one jump out of his skin, spring something on one, from out in left field, throw one a curve, hit them where they ain't, knock one over, knock one over with a feather, set on one's ass, set back on one's heels, put one away, throw on one's beam ends. 2. drop in on.

SURPRISED adj. shook, shook-up, all shook up, rocked, glorked, discombobulated, discombooberated, bug-eyed, thunderstruck, floored, thrown, fussed, gassed, shit, shit blue, shit green, unglued, come unglued, come unzipped, come apart, come apart at the seams, fall apart, fall out, flatfooted, caught flatfooted, galley west, higgledy-piggledy, skimble-skamble, in a flush, shot, shot to pieces, kerflumixed, flummoxed, flabbergasted, boogily-woogily, bowled down, bowled over, hit like a ton of bricks, struck all of a heap, thrown off one's beam ends, caught off base, caught with one's pants down, bit one in the ass.

SURPRISE ENDING n. joker, catch, kicker, payoff.

SURPRISING adj. mind-blowing, stunning, grabber, hell of a note, megadual.

SURRENDER v. 1. cave in, give up, give in, fold, quit, say uncle, cry uncle, toss in the towel, toss in the sponge, throw in the towel, throw in the sponge, toss it in, pack in, pack it in, buckle under, lump it, gleek it, eat crow, eat dirt, eat humble pie, come out moldy, pull in one's horns, knuckle to, knuckle under, drop, kowtow, lie down and roll over for, roll over and play dead, go along with. 2. come across, come across with, give out, put out (sexual); fork over, give away the store. See also GIVE UP.

SURREPTITIOUSLY adv. undercover, under wraps, hush-hush, strictly hush-hush, on the q.t., on the quiet, on the sly, in a hole-and-corner way, in holes and corners.

SURROUNDED adj. boxed-in.

SURVEILLANCE n. bug, bugging, eye in the sky, spy in the sky, ELINT (information gathered by spy satellites), stake-out, tail, tap, track, wiretap, body mike.

SURVEY v. 1. case, case the joint, eye, eyeball, scope, read, check, check out, check over, check up, size up, spy out, stake out, bus it (Af. Am.), give it the once-over, kick tires, scout it out, squack, candle, put under a microscope, get down to nuts and bolts, take the measure of. See SEE. See also RECONNOITER. 2. put out a feeler, test the waters, see which way the wind blows, send up a trial balloon. 3. do the street, troll, give one the eye, give one the cyclops, take in the sights, go for the cheese, scoop (admiringly).

SURVIVE v. 1. cut it, make the cut, handle, lump, lump it, live with, bear with, put up with, roll with the punches, bite the bullet, hang in, hang in there, hang tough, hang on, hang on for dear life, hang on like a bulldog, hold on like a bulldog, hang on like a leech, stick like a leech, stick like a barnacle, stick like a limpet, stick like a wet shirt, stick, stick it out, stick with it, win out, ride out, get by, go the limit, sit tight, sit and take it, sweat, sweat it, sweat it out, sweat out, staying power, stay the course, hack it, take it, stand for, stand the gaff, stand up, stand up to it, shape up, show one's mettle, show one's stuff, be big, be big about, pay dues, grin and bear it, not let it get one down, tough it out, go the limit, go all the way, see through, see it through, carry through, see it out, not give up the ship, never say die. See also ENDURE; PERSIST. 2. bounce back, make a comeback, come around, come round, come back, come from behind, pull out of it, snap out of it, turn the corner, be out of the woods, get back in shape. See IMPROVE.

SUSCEPTIBLE adj. believer, sucker, patsy, mark, easy mark, pigeon, clay pigeon, grape (waiting to be squeezed), duck, sitting duck, pushover, tool, sucker for, fall for, tumble for, swallow anything, swallow whole, swallow hook line and sinker, be taken in, stick one's neck out, out on a limb, ready to be taken, putty in one's hands, wide-open, sucker for a left.

SUSPECT adj. pseudo.

SUSPECT v. be afraid, expect, have a hunch, have a sneaking suspicion, smell a rat. See also BELIEVE.

SUSPEND v. 1. can, fire, lay off, ax, give the ax, give the air, give one his walking papers, cut loose (dockworker use), sack, pink-slip, show the door, downsize, drum out, throw out on one's ear. See DISCHARGE. 2. shelve, put on the back burner, put on hold, put on ice, put off, hold off, hold up, hang, hang up, hang fire, blow things off, pigeonhole. See DELAY.

SUSPENDERS n. braces, galluses, gaters, pulleys, stretches.

SUSPENSEFUL adj. blood-and-thunder, thriller, chiller, cliff-hanger, cloak-and-dagger, page-turner, pot-boiler, spyboiler, grabber, white-knuckle, twisting in the wind.

SUSPENSION n. 1. ax, pink slip, sack, boot, the gate, door, layoff, rif (reduction in force), walking papers, the bullet, payroll adjustment, released resources, reshaping, old heave-ho. See DISMISSED. 2. break, coffee break, break-off, breather, breathing spell, downtime, letup, five, ten, timeout, freeze, cutoff, layoff, letup, happy hour, attitude adjustment hour (cocktail hour).

SUSPICION n. funny feeling, hunch, sneaking suspicion. See also INTIMATION.

SUSPICIOUS adj. 1. cagey, leery, been hit before, not born yesterday, on the lookout, with a weather eye open, with one's eyes peeled. See CAUTIOUS. 2. uptight, green-eyed, jelly. 3. fishy, funny, not kosher, reachy, won't wash, phony, rings phony, too much, something's rotten in Denmark, stink to high heaven.

SUSTAIN v. 1. angel, bankroll, grubstake, stake, the bank, back, greenback, juice, pick up the check, pick up the tab, knock (Af. Am.), piece one off, prime the pump, go for. 2. buck up, brace up, lend a hand, plug, go with, front for, stand up for, stick up for, carry one, prop up. See SUPPORT. 3. beef up, soup up, punch up, heat up, hot up, hop up, jazz up, juice up, build up, stick to one's ribs, add fuel to the fire. 4. live with, bear with, put up with, bite the bullet, hang in, take it, stand up to it. See ENDURE.

SUSTENANCE n. the wherewithal, bread, bread and butter, the bacon, the necessary.

SWAGGER v. sashay, boot, ank, boogie, show off, grandstand, hot-dog, put up a front, put on airs, put on, put on the dog, ritz it, look big, shoot the agate, swank, play to the gallery, parade one's wares, strut one's stuff, style (Af. Am.). See also WALK.

SWAIN n. main dude, main man, main squeeze, squeeze, sweet back (Af. Am.), my guy, my man, old man, stud, John, ace, ace lane, beau, big moment, flame, heart-throb. See BOY FRIEND.

SWALLOW n. shot, belt, swig, gulp, chugalug.

SWALLOW v. belt, chugalug, drop (drug), rock one back, throw back, swig, toss one back, slurp, scarf down, gorm, gorp, wolf, wolf down, inhale, gobble, gulp, bolt, dispatch, dispose, swabble, tuck in, tuck away, put away, put it away, pack it away, surround oneself outside of, put oneself outside of. See also ENDURE.

SWAMP DWELLER n. swamp angel.

SWARM n. jam, jam up, mob, push, turnout, blowout, crush, everybody and his brother, everybody and his uncle, loaded to the rafters, wall-to-wall people.

SWARMING adj. alive with, crawling with, thick with.

SWAY v. 1. soften up, work on, turn one's head around, brainwash, mind-fuck, eat one's mind, crack one, put across, sell, sell one on, suck in, hook. See PERSUADE. 2. impact on, lead by the nose, pull ropes, pull strings, pull wires, throw one's weight around, whitewash, wire-pull, get one's hooks into, hold one's feet to the fire, twist one's arm. 3. yo-yo, blow hot and cold, shilly-shally, hem and haw.

SWEAR v. 1. cuss, damn, darn, drat, flame, talk dirty. 2. cross one's heart and hope to die, swear till one is blue in the face, swear up and down, swear on a stack of bibles, say-so.

SWEARING n.   dirty word, cuss, cussing, cuss word, four-letter word, swearword, no-no, dirty name, French, pardon my French, dirty language, dirty talk.

SWEARWORD n.   four-letter word, cuss word, bleeper.

SWEAT v.   get all in a lather, sweat like a horse, sweat like a trooper.

SWEATER n.   pullover, pull-on, poorboy, bulky, sloppy Joe, cardigan.

SWEATY adj.   sticky, stinky, wet, drippy, bathed in sweat, perspiry.

SWEDE n.   Viking; squarehead, herring-choker, Olaf, Ole, Scandie, Swenska (all Derog.).

SWEEPER n.   mop jockey, broom jockey.

SWEEPING adj.   across-the-board, wall-to-wall, big-time, in a big way. See also WHOLE.

SWEETENING n.   dirt, dominoes (cubes), sand, white gold.

SWEETHEART n.   old lady, old man, squeeze, main squeeze, main queen, main dude, main man, my guy, my man, wrap (girl), best girl, dream girl, girl friend, G.F., boy friend, B.F., jane, stud, John, ace, ace lane, beau, best fella, significant other, number one, numero uno, hat, mat, big moment, heartthrob, heartbeat, body and soul, one and only, hamma, mama, sweet mama, chick, papa, sweet papa, sweet back (Af. Am.), daddy, sugar, sugar daddy, Casanova, Lothario, Don Juan, date mate, companion, constant companion, couple, gruesome twosome, flame, passion ration, sugar bowl, nectar, gooey nectar, honey, hon, jelly roll, kissing cousin, baby, total babe, lovebird, turtle dove, lambie pie, back-door man, honey man, money honey, generous keeper, gold mine, big game, biscuit roller, rave, masher, mule skinner, oyster, armpiece, baby cake, cake, candy leg, gussie mollie (not common), patootie, hot patootie, sweet patootie, josan (Korean War), snoff, corn bread, home cooking, stone marten (beautiful).

SWEET POTATOES n.   sweets.

SWEET ROLL n.   Danish, coffee and, mud ball.

SWEETS n.   cush, g'dong, gedunk, hickey, goodies, yum-yum.

SWELTERING adj.   broiler, roaster, scorcher, sizzler, swelterer, sticky, stuffy, close, one can fry eggs on the sidewalk.

SWIFT adj.   screaming, sizzler, speedball, pronto, snappy, barreling, on the double, balls out, get a move on, get cracking, move your tail, in nothing flat, in jig time, step on it, make it snappy, shake a leg, pour it on, like mad, like crazy, like shit through a goose. See FAST.

SWIM v.   dog-paddle, skinny-dip.

SWIMMER n.   fanny dipper.

SWIMSUIT n.   bikini, monokini (topless), string, floss (thong-backed), tank suit.

SWINDLE n.   hustle, con, sting, flam, gyp, scam, racket, shady deal, crooked deal, fast shuffle, royal fucking, jive, shuck, hoke, dirty pool, frame-up, double-cross, shell game, skin game, fast one; rideout, squat (fraudulent auto accident). See CHEAT.

SWINDLE v.   sting, rook, screw, shaft, frig, fudge, hose, hump, rim, rip off, mooch (commodity scam), jerk one off, blow smoke up one's ass, dick, dick one around, fuck one over, jive, shuck, shuck and jive, run a game on, fleece, flam, flimflam, clip, con, chisel, gouge, scam, stiff, sandbag, pluck, take, sucker, suck in, stack the deck, sting, skin, skunk, gank, set up, frame, promote, hold up, soak, fox, ice, score. See CHEAT.

SWINDLED adj.   sucked-in, fell for, jerked around, jobbed, fucked, boned, fucked-over, taken, been taken, taken for a sleigh ride, clipped, stung, got the shaft, got the short end of the stick, got a haircut, screwed, hosed, get hosed, dicked, gaffled, tattooed, laid relaid and parlayed, bearded. See CHEATED.

SWINDLER n.   shark, sharp, sharpie, mechanic, burn artist, con man, chisler, doberman (Af. Am.), flimflammer, gyp, gyp artist, crook, double-dealer, whip, operator, cheese-eater. See CHEATER.

SWINE n.   porker, porky, cob roller (young or small).

SWITCHBOARD n.   phones, board, PBX.

SWITCH OFF LIGHTS v.   save 'em, dim the glims, kill the lights.

SWOON v.   black out, go out like a light, keel over, pass out, freak out, flicker (also pretend).

SWORD n.   pig-sticker.

SYCOPHANCY n.   soft soap, bullshit, jive, snow, snow job, baked wind, abreaction route, soap, con, promote, applesauce, balloon juice, banana oil, hot air, malarkey. See FLATTERER; TOADY; MINION.

SYCOPHANT n.   ass kisser, A.K., kiss-ass, ass sucker, ass wipe, butt wipe, bun duster, bootlick, bootlicker, foot-licker, ass licker, tuchis licker, yes-man, nod guy, schmeikler, fan, groupie, gofer, back slapper, back scratcher, glad-hander, handshaker, greaser, stroker, apple polisher, apple shiner, Simonizer, brownie, brown tongue, brown nose, brown noser, those aren't freckles on his nose, fart sniffer, cocksucker (all Obsc.); egg sucker, earbanger, heeler, ho-dad, ho-daddy, honey cooler, politician, flunky, flunky-stooge, stooge, hanger-on, waterboy, lackey, sideman.

SYMBOL n. logo.

SYMPATHETIC adj. 1. softhearted, old softie, old softy, heart in the right place; bleeding heart, all heart (Derog.). 2. grokking, on the same beam, on the same wavelength, simpatico, tuned-in, cool, down, have a heart, hip.

SYMPATHIZE v. tune in, grok, I hear ya, can get behind it, be on the same wavelength, pick up on, feel for, be there for one.

SYMPATHY n. heart, grandstand play.

SYMPOSIUM n. confab, rap, rap session, buzz session, clambake, gam, powwow, think-in, chinfest, talkfest, talkee-talkee, skull session. See also MEETING.

SYNAGOGUE n. Amen Corner, dirge factory, God box.

SYNCHRONIZE v. 1. lip-sync, sync, sync up. 2. get it together, get one's act together, team up, pull together, jive, click.

SYNCHRONIZED adj. in sync.

SYNCOPATE v. play jazz, play jive, play rag, play swing.

SYNCOPATED adj. jazzed, jazzed-up, hot, jazzy, ragtimy, swingy.

SYNDICATE n. organization, megacorp, multinational, multinationals, bunch, crew, crowd, gang, mob, plunderbund, outfit, ring.

SYNOPSIS n. 1. recap, capsule, rundown, runthrough. 2. money quote (one sentence), short-and-sweet, boiled-down.

SYNOPSIZE v. 1. run over, run through, run down, rehash, recap, make a long story short, get down to cases, get down to brass tacks. 2. cut, cut down, cut to the bone, nutshell, put in a nutshell, boil down, trim, get to the meat, chop, snip, blue-pencil.

SYNTHETIC adj. ersatz, hokey, plastic.

SYNTHETIC FUEL n. synfuel.

SYPHILIS n. VD, syph, syff, siff, dose, boogie, chankers, shankers, chank, shank, crud, blood disease, sigma phi (medical), the French sickness, old Joe, the ral, ral up, rahl, rahl up, the rail, Cupid's itch, Venus's curse. See also VENEREAL DISEASE.

SYRINGE n. harpoon (drug use), needle.

SYRUP n. machine oil, googlum, goozlum, goop, glop.

SYRUPY adj. goo, gooey, goop, goopy, glop, gloppy, goozlum.

SYSTEM n. the Company, the Establishment, the Man, channels, cut-and-dried, G.I., red tape, same old shit, SOS, shtick, sked, grind, daily grind, environment.

SYSTEMATIZE v. pull things together, shape up, straighten up and fly right, get all the pieces in place, get one's act together, get one's head together, get one's shit together, tighten up, unzip.

SYSTEMATIZED adj. together, all together, glued (antonym: unglued), have one's act together, have one's shit together, have one's head together, have one's head screwed on right.

T

T n. Tango, Tare.

TAB n. logo.

TABLE v. shelve, put on the shelf, put on the back burner, put on hold, put on ice, put off, hold off, hold up, hang, hang up, hang fire, pigeonhole, cool, cool it. See DELAY.

TABLE OF ORGANIZATION n. dotted-line responsibility, T.O.

TABLET n. scratch pad, scratch.

TABOO n. no-no, a don't, off limits, out of bounds, bleeper, blankety-blank (word or expression), thou shalt not.

TACHOMETER n. tach.

TACITURN adj. clammed-up, dried-up, dummied-up, garbo, tight-lipped.

TACKLE v. take on, make a run at, cut and try, try on for size, give it a try, give it a go, give it a whirl, take a shot at, take a fling at, take a stab at, pitch into, go for it. See ATTEMPT.

TACTICS n. channels, red tape, hardball (Pol., playing tough), by the numbers, by the book.

TAG n. logo.

TAILOR n. Abie, schneider (Derog.); needleworker.

TAINT v. 1. doctor, doctor up, spike, water, water down, cut, cook. 2. trash, crud up, crumb up, scuzz up, skank, muck up, sleaze up, mess up, piss on. 3. give one a black eye, make one lose face.

TAINTED adj. 1. cooked (radiation), dirty, exposed, mucked-up, doctored. 2. strong, high, loud, gross, stinking.

TAKE v. 1. get, get one's fingers on, grab, glom, glom onto, nab, nail, snarf (with or without permission), snag, bag, pick up, take in, haul in, pull in, swoop, carve out. See SEIZE. See also APPROPRIATE. 2. rip off, snarf, boost, cop, liberate, lift, contifisticate, snatch, snitch, make off with, annex, borrow, touch, nip, snare, pluck, salvage. See STEAL. 3. lug, pack, piggyback, ride, shlep, shlep along, tote, truck, back, birdie-back, buck, gun, heel, hump, jag, shoulder, move. 4. stand for, lump it, live with, bear with, put up with, suck it up, hang in, hang in there, hang tough, hang on, stick it out, ride out, take it, take it on the chin, be big, be big about, grin and bear it. See ENDURE. 5. do (do drugs).

TAKE BLAME v. take the rap, take the fall.

TAKE COVER v. hide out, hole up, play dead, lie doggo, lie low, lay low, tunnel, plant, cool off, duck out of sight, do a crouch, flatten out, hit the shade, hit the mattresses. See HIDE.

TAKEOUT adj. to go, on wheels, let it walk.

TALE n. yarn, clothesline, long and the short of it, megillah, cliff-hanger, potboiler, chestnut, heavy lard, touches, book. See STORY.

TALEBEARER n. rat, fink, rat fink, narc, nark, finger, snitch, squealer, stoolie, stool pigeon, snout, canary, songbird, yellow dog (gang), weasel, blabbermouth, tattletale, whistle-blower, fat mouth, preacher, deep throat. See INFORMER. See also GOSSIPER.

TALEBEARING n. scuttlebutt, talk, grapevine, clothesline, back-fence talk, back-fence gossip, latrine rumor, wire, hot wire, whispering campaign, black plague, dirty tricks, nut cracking, rat-fucking, dirty linen, dirty wash. See GOSSIP.

TALENT n. the goods, the stuff, the right stuff, star power, what it takes, the formula, know-how, up one's alley, savvy, fly, with it, green thumb, smarts, something on the ball, plenty on the ball, a bump for, have a way with, have a knack for, have a head for, bag, thing, bit, chops, dash, splash, splurge, throwin' stuff (Bsbl.), meal ticket. See also SKILL.

TALENTED adj. sharp, sharp as a tack, smart as a whip, killer, A, 1–10 (degree, he's a 9), fly, brainy, brains, savvy, wised-up, hep, hepster, hipster, hip to the jive, hipped, cool, sharp, tuned-in, into, go-go, with it, all woke up, got it, got it up here (head), a lot of nifty, class act, slick, smooth, crack, crackerjack, cute, no slouch, no dumbbell, no dummy nobody's fool, not born yesterday, quick on the trigger, quick on the uptake, heads up, something on the ball, on the ball, on the beam, up to speed, phenom, pro, there, whiz, whiz kid, whiz bang, wizard, gasser, boss player, shine at, shine in, enough ducks in a row, hot, hotshot, book smart, know one's stuff, know the ropes, know all the ins and outs, know the score, know all the answers, know what's what, know one's onions, know it all, know one's business, P's and Q's, know one's p's and q's, have know-how, have the goods, have the stuff, have the right stuff, have what it takes, have a bump for, have it on the ball, have plenty on the ball.

TALENT POOL n. stable.

TALENT SCOUT n. ivory dome.

TALISMAN n. gig, security blanket, gigi, gee-gee.

TALK n. buzz session, hash session, rap, rap session, rapping rash; lines, mack, lip music (Af. Am.), yak, yakkety-yak, yack-yack, yatata-yatata, yawp, blah-blah, chinfest, chit-chat, gab, gas, guff, lip, hot air, small talk, straight talk, pillow talk (confidential), talkee-talkee, talkfest, gabfest, bullfest, bull, bull session, bullshit, B.S., bilge, jazz, jive, garbage, gam, gobbledygook, podspeak (meaningless automatic response), apple butter, fluff, malarkey, mush, chin music, chin-jaw, flap-jaw, flap (urgent), riff, some pig, clambake, eyeball-to-eyeball encounter, confab, huddle, pow-wow, earful, bibful, spiel, rag-chewing, gum-beating, visit. See also SPEECH.

TALK v. 1. gab, rap, mack (Af. Am.), yackety-yak, yap, spout, spout off, spiel, modulate, modjitate, splib, splib de wib, slide one's jib, blab, noise, noise off, shoot the wind, drool, flip one's lip (idle), run one's mouth, fat-mouth, talk one's ear off, cut up jackies, sling the lingo, blow, beat one's gums, yammer, bad-talk, sweet-talk, fast-talk, talk turkey. 2. contact, interact, interface, network, reach out, relate, touch, touch base, keep in touch, have truck with, grok, groupthink, go into a huddle, huddle, take a meeting, give a meeting, have a meet, confab. 3. pitch, spiel, stump. See SPEAK. 4. fess, fess up, rat, rat on, fink, fink on, croon, sing, sing on, sing like a canary, belch, snitch, squeal, stool, spill, leak, blow the whistle, drop a dime on one, put it on the street. See CONFESS; INFORM.

TALKATIVE adj. gabby, gabber, talker, great talker, fast talker, yacker, yacky, yakkety-yak, gift of gab, shoots the gab, gasbag, gasser, CBS, blowhard, windy, long-winded, windbag, bag of wind, windjammer, bullshitter, barber, flip, loudmouth, big-mouthed, bucket mouth, blabbermouth, chatty Cathy, gum-beater, ear-bender, rattle on, spieler, all jaw, flap jaw, ratchet jaw, ratchet mouth, hot-air artist, thick-slung, slick tongue, slick, slicker, smooth, smoothie, old smoothie, smooth apple, smooth operator, smooth article, ear duster, drooler, beefer, gossipy, waxer, have verbal diarrhea, diarrhea of the mouth.

TALK BACK v. give one the lip, lip, sass.

TALKER n. windbag, gabby, jawsmith, soapboxer, soapbox orator, spieler, spouter.

TALKING, STOP v. give it a rest, hang it up, shut up, shut one's trap, shut one's head, shut one's face, shut one's mouth, hush one's mouth, put up or shut up, bag it, bag your face, beat it, go away, pipe down, bite one's tongue, hold one's tongue, cut it out, clam up, close up, hang up, dummy up, fold up, dry up, choke, choke in, choke up, drag in one's rope, pull in one's ears, rest one's jaw, sign off, ring off, lay off, roll up one's flaps, stow it, save it, chuck it, can it, stifle, stifle it, step on it, put a lid on it, button one's lip, zip, zip one's lip, bag one's lip, bag one's head, be cool, cool one's chops, drink one's beer.

TALK SHOW n. confrontalk, chatcom (with comedian), slimetime.

TALK-SHOW HOST n. talk jockey, T.J., t.j., shock jock.

TALL AND SLIM adj. twiggy, long drink of water, Long John, skeleton, stringbean, bean pole, beanstalk, broomstick, clothes pole, hatrack, stilt, stick. See THIN.

TALL adj. tall drink of water, long drink of water, flanker (West Point), highpockets, bean pole, beanstalk, stick, longlegs, longshanks, Long John.

TALLY n. score, tab.

TALWIN n. blue jeans and T-shirts, T's and blues, tricycles and bicycles, tops and bottoms (all mixed with pyribenzamine).

TAME v. break, break in, bust, gentle.

TAMPA, FLORIDA Big T, Cigar City.

TAMPER v. doctor, doctor up, phony up, flake (plant false evidence), pencil-whip (documentation), fiddle around with, fiddle with, plant, spike, water, water down, baptize, irrigate, cook, cut, needle.

TAMPERED adj. doctored, cooked.

TAMPON n. pon, cork.

TANG n. kick, zip.

TANK n. alligator, duck (amphibious); bus (WWI), doodle bug, hell buggy, iron horse, treadhead (driver).

TANKER n. crock, tub, rust bucket, tramp, buddy store (Vietnam). See also SHIP.

TANTRUM n. cat fit, duck fit, conniption, conniption fit, shit fit, shit hemorrhage, dander up, Irish, Irish up, in a huff, in a pet, in high dudgeon, on a tear, have a devil in one, possessed by the devil. See TEMPER.

TAPE, DUCT n. duck tape, racer's tape, 200-mph tape, two hundred miles per hour tape, gray tape, silver tape.

TAPE PLAYER n. deck, boom box, boom, box, thunderbox, ghetto blaster, hi-fi, stereo, third-world attaché case.

TAPIOCA PUDDING n. cat's eye, fish eyes, fish eggs, fish eyes and glue.

TARDY adj. hung up, held up, in a bind, jammed, jammed-up, strapped for time, snooze you lose.

TARGET n. ground zero, sitting duck (easy), Maggie's drawers (missed, Mil.).

TARGET v. get one in the cross-hairs, zero in on.

TARPAULIN n. tarp.

TARRY v. get noplace fast, put on hold, hold the phone, stall, hang around, hang in, hang about, goof around, stick around, mooch around, monkey around, fuck the dog, cool one's heels, sit on one's ass, jelly, tool tail, piddle-diddle (So.), warm a chair. See LINGER.

TART adj. snippy, snappy, short.

TASK n. gig, grind, daily grind, grindstone, scutwork, donkeywork, hemo jo (hard labor). See WORK.

TASK, DIFFICULT n. grind, daily grind, rat race, elbow grease, shitwork, donkeywork, gruntwork (Army), scud, scut, workout, ballbreaker, ball racker, ballbuster, bone breaker, backbreaker, ass breaker, conk buster, bitch, bitch kitty, son of a bitch, fun and games.

TASK, EASY n. lead-pipe cinch, breeze, piece of cake, pie, meat, white meat, doable, wrap-up, cakewalk, sleepwalk, walkover, chicken, clay pigeon, angel teat, around-the-bend (almost completed), alyo (routine).

TASKMASTER n. Big Brother, boss, head, head man, head honcho, bosshead, super, skipper, old man, papa, Big Daddy, Big Brother, top dog, top hand, topkick, mother, the man, boss man, boss lady, bull, bull of the woods, ball breaker, straw boss, slavedriver, pusher, Elmer. See also EXECUTIVE.

TASS n. Rita (Russian Information Telegraph Agency).

TASTE n. 1. bag, cup of tea, druthers, flash, groove, thing, turned on to, type, weakness. See INCLINATION. 2. chaw, chomp, gob.

TASTEFUL adj. spiffy, classy, snazzy, posh, plush, plushy, ritzy, uptown, swank, swanky, snarky, swellelegant, splendiferous, splendacious, nobby.

TASTE, BAD adj. tacky, gross, budget, bad form, off-base, off-color, humbug, borax, taboo, blue, skank.

TASTELESS adj. 1. cheap, loud, skank, tacky, raunchy, dirty, low-down and dirty, off-color, rough. See VULGAR. 2. blah, draddy, plain vanilla, nowhere, flat, pablum, zero, big zero. See INSIPID.

TASTY adj. delish, grinds, divine, divoon, heavenly, scrumptious, sweetened, sugar-coated, nummy, yummy, yummy in the tummy.

TATTERED adj. ratty-tatty, beat up, tacky, dog-eared, frowzy.

TATTLE v. blab, blabber, leak, talk, crack on, peach, spill, spill it, spill the beans, give away, give the show away, have a big bazoo, have a big mouth, do one dirt, snitch. See INFORM. See also GOSSIP.

TATTLETALE n. 1. sleazemonger, yenta, polly, satch, gasser, load of wind, windbag, busybody, tabby. See GOSSIP. 2. snitch, snitcher, squealer, blab, blabber, blabberer, blab-bermouth, tattler, telltale, whistle-blower, whistler, fat mouth, peacher, squealer. See INFORMER.

TAUNT n. put down, rank out, dump, cap, dig, dirty dig, dozens, dirty dozens, crack, slap, slam, swipe, jab, comeback, parting shot, brickbat, backhanded compliment, left-handed compliment.

TAUNT v. play dozens, play dirty dozens (Af. Am.), bag on.

TAVERN n. beer joint, taproom, grocery, the nineteenth hole, gutbucket, bucket shop, suds shop, slop, slop-shop (beer), office, draft board, guzzlery, guzzery, guzzle shop, dram shop, grog shop, grog mill, gin mill, fillmill, hideaway, room, rum room, night spot, nitery, dive, joint, after-hours joint, juke joint, juice joint, hop joint, barrel house, gashouse, alehouse, beerhouse, mug house, washer, cheap John, creep dive, deadfall, honky-tonk, speakeasy, blind pig, blind tiger, scatter, gargle factory, water hole, chain locker (dockside). See also BAR.

TAWDRY adj. tinhorn, showy, glitzy, flossy, flashy, splurgy, loud, junky, jeasley, jazzy, gussied-up, lit up like a Christmas tree, sporty. See GAUDY.

TAX n. nick, bite, sintax (tobacco and liquor), Irish dividend, zero out (not paying taxes).

TAX BENEFIT n. write-off, ITC (investment tax credit), shelter.

TAXICAB n. cab, checker, gypsy (without license), hack, taxi, yellow, dimbox, short.

TAXICAB DRIVER n. cabby, hack driver, hackie, hacker, jockey, skip, boulevard westerner, boulevard cowboy.

TEA n. Boston coffee, belly wash, dishwater, brew, nux, boiled leaves (not common).

TEACH v. break in, let in on the know, put through the grind, put through the mill, show one the ropes, pull one's coat, drum, drum into. See INSTRUCT.

TEACHER n. prof, teach, tweet, baby-sitter, Dr. Nytol (boring), grind, guru, nerdmeister, slavedriver, snap. See also SCHOLAR.

TEACHING n. chalk talk, skull session.

TEAM n. varsity, junior varsity, frosh, pro, first string, second string, third string. See also COUPLE.

TEAMMATE n. buddy, buddy-buddy, playmate, sidekick, sidekicker, pard, pardner.

TEAMSTER n. skinner, trucker, hair pounder.

TEARFUL adj. blubbery, weepy, cry one's eyes out, cry, good cry.

TEAR GAS n. bug juice, eyewash.

TEARS n. waterworks, weeps.

TEASE n. kibitzer, front, nag, clown, nudge, nudzh, noodge, nudge, nudnik, teaser; cock teaser, C.T., prick teaser, P.T. (all Obsc.).

TEASE v. ride, razz, roast, roust, jive, snap, guy, needle, give one the needle, crack on (Hum., Af. Am.), dog on, pick on, goof on, bug, hack, worry, wig, dog, cap, rag, rag on, get in one's face, yank one's crank, rib, spoof, jeffin', talking out of one's neck, dump on, put down, put one on, sound, rank out, slap at, slam, play dozens, hurl a brickbat, pooh-pooh, shiv, chiv, chivey, chivvy; noodge, nudge, nudzh, utz (Yid.); kibitz, kibitz around, horse around, funnin', send up, sheik, be on the back of, be at, give a bad time to, swipe at, dig at, josh, poke fun at, clown, clown around, fool, fool around, jack around, jack someone around, kid, kid around, play games, pull one's leg, jolly, fake one out, give one hemorrhoids, give a bad time to, give one a hard time, give one the business, get under one's skin, fuzzbuzz, drive one bananas, drive one up a tree, rattle one's cage, fart around, futz around, push one's button, push all the buttons, push the right button, mess with, bone, all right already (stop). See also JOKE.

TEATS n. boobs, boobies, kajoobies, bubs, tits, titties, hooters, tatas, bodacious tatas (large), knockers, bazooms, cans, eyes, globes, headlights, knobs, maracas, cantaloupes, melons, pair, balloons, mosquito bites (small). See BREASTS.

TECHNICAL adj. hi-tech (style), techie.

TECHNICAL INSTITUTE n. tech.

TECHNICALITY, LEGAL n. teck.

TECHNICIAN n. techie, tekky, tollie, technotrash, technoslut, technoweenie (socially inept).

TECHNOLOGY n. tech, hi tech.

TEDIOUS adj. draggy, dull as dishwater, ho-hum, borring, noplaceville, deadsville, snooze, cheesy, pablum. See BORING.

TEENAGER n. mall brat, mall rat, teen, teeny, teenybop, teenybopper, creepybopper, weenie, teenie, teeniebop, weenie bopper, Valley girl, alternateen (into counterculture), jive (associated with jive music, movie, etc.), bobby soxer, petiteen, subdeb, sweet sixteen, twixt teen, jailbait, San Quentin quail, juve, juvenile delinquent, JD, punk, punk kid, punker, punk rocker, bubblegum, bubblegummer, bubblegum rocker, man, boyo, yoot, cokey, duck, gunsel, monkey, pecker, pisser, young fry, young blood, salad days; twink, twinkle, twinky (homosexual).

TEETH n. china, chops, choppers, fangs, snappers, buck, barn doors (prominent), chewers, crockery, dominoes, gummers, ivories, porcelain.

TEETOTALER n. A.A., dry, on the wagon, on the water wagon, on the dry, fence-sitter, wet blanket, Christer.

TEGUCIGALPA, HONDURAS Tegoose, Goose City.

TELEGRAM n. wire.

TELEGRAPH v. wire, send a wire, telex, cable.

TELEGRAPHER n. sparks, op, brass pounder, lightning slinger, dit-da artist, fist (touch), glass arm (cramped).

TELEGRAPH KEY n. bug (semiautomatic).

TELEGRAPH OPERATOR n. sparks, op, brass pounder, dit-da artist, lightning slinger, fist (touch), glass arm (cramped).

TELEPHONE n. phone, horn, Ma Belle, digits, ship-to-shore (cordless), Ameche, double L, voice line; hot line (emergency); blue box, black box (illegal calling devices).

TELEPHONE v. phone, buzz, ring, call, get one on the line, get one on the horn, it's your nickel (you talk), voice (talk), ring off the hook, jingle, tinkle, put in a call, make a call, call up, ring up, give a ring, give a buzz, give one a jingle, touch base with, reach out and touch someone, blast, contact, pick up (answer), get back to, electric doughnut (known only by phone conversation), phonie (addicted to telephone), ring off (hang up).

TELEPHONE BOOK n. little black book, phone book, Yellow Pages, fluff log.

TELEPHONE CALL n. buzz, call, phone call, ring.

TELEPHONE LINE n. clothesline.

TELEPHONE SERVICE LINE n. WATS line.

TELESCOPE n. sniperscope, snooperscope.

TELETHON n. begathon.

TELETYPING n. mux.

TELEVISION n. tube, boob tube, TV, vid, video, screen (Af. Am.), telly, box, idiot box, tubaruba, goggle box, big eye, eye, one-eyed monster, cyclops, baby-sitter, flickering blue parent, kidvid (children's), checkout channel (in markets), the Business,

TELEVISION PROGRAM n. spec, spex, special, infotainment (news), infomercial (program-length commercial), spectacular, miniseries, soap, soaper, sudser, talk show, slime-time (talk show), sitcom, pilot; tabloid TV, trash TV, grunt shows (lurid); docudrama, dromedy, kidvid, music video, MTV, skein (series), freevee, living-room gig, late show, late late show, reruns, telethon, begathon (telethon), sweeps (rating period), sweeps week.

TELEVISION PROGRAM, ORIGINAL n. pilot.

TELEVISION RECEPTION n. snow, snowstorm, blooping, ghost.

TELEVISION REMOTE CONTROLLER n. clicker, driver, zapper, remote, buttons, thingie; channel surfer, traveler (channel changer), couch commander (person with control).

TELEVISION TERMS, TECHNICAL garbage can (microwave relay transmitter), ghost, ike (iconoscope), live eye (camera), bloom (glare from a white object), gobo (back screen), crawl (rolling credits), slot (time period), sound bite (brief news quote), talking head, blizzard head (blonde actress).

TELEVISION, VIEW v. catch a show, eye the big eye, see what's on, tube, tube it, tube it up, tube out, tube up; sweeps, sweeps week (audience rating survey period).

TELEVISION WATCHER n. vidiot, couch potato, sofa spud, spec tater, channel surfer, traveler (channel changer), infomaniac (news addict).

TELEVISION WRITER n. telescripter, telewriter, teleplaywright, scripter.

TELL v. 1. spout, spout off, jaw, splib de wib, spill, spill the beans, unload, blab, run one's mouth, crack, open one's face, wag the tongue. See TALK. 2. stab one in the back, rat, rat on, fink, fink on, croon, sing, chirp, talk, snitch, belch, squeal, squeal on, squawk, stool, spill, belch, blow, blow the whistle, tip off, yellow-dog (gang), drop a dime on one. See INFORM. 3. fess, fess up, come clean, come through, come out, come out of the closet, put it on the street, let it all hang out, let one's hair down, bring it out into the daylight, bring it out into the open, open up, own up, cough up, get it off one's chest, get it out of one's system, give away, give the show away, blab, blabber, blab off. See CONFESS.

TEMPER n. 1. miff, pet, stew, tiff, snit, cat fit, conniption, conniption fit, shit hemorrhage. dander, dander up, Irish, Irish up, short fuse, slow burn, in a huff, in a pet, in a sniff, in a snit, in a tizzy, in a stew, in a pucker, in a wax, in high dudgeon, duck fit, tear, on a tear, have a devil in one, possessed by the devil, foaming at the mouth. 2. where one's at, bit, in the groove, one's bag, scene, soul.

TEMPER v. 1. soft-pedal, cool, cool out, take the edge off, take the bite out, take the sting out. See SOFTEN. 2. tweek, give it a tweek (small), fine-tune, take it in a little, mid-course correction, monkey around with, bottom out, switch, switch over, about-face, flip-flop, turn over a new leaf, turn the corner, turn the tables, turn one around, revamp, transmogrify.

TEMPERAMENTAL adj. bitchy, cussed, mean, ornery, tetchy, thin-skinned, scrappy. See also EMOTIONAL, IRRITABLE, CAPRICIOUS.

TEMPLE n. Amen Corner, dirge factory, God box.

TEMPO n. beat, bounce, downbeat, brown-off (break).

TEMPORARY adj. temp, here today gone tomorrow, Band-Aid, quick fix, fly-by-night, hit or miss, Mickey Mouse, rinky-dink, slapdash, throwaway, haywire.

TEMPORIZE v. fudge, play for time, vamp, hedge one's bet, gardening, hom-rim it, pussyfoot, trade off, make a deal, meet halfway, go fifty-fifty, can't fight 'em join 'em, strike a happy medium, back and fill, play ball with. See also HEDGE.

TEMPT v. 1. bait, mousetrap, give one the come on, give one a come-hither look, vamp, hook, bat one's eyes at, bat the eyes at. See ATTRACT. See also LURE. 2. schmeer, schmeikle, butter, butter up, honey, soap, oil, dooze, kid along, play up to, get around, turn one's head around, eat one's mind, crack one, or something, con, duke in, promote, swindle in, sell, sell one on, hard-sell, soft-sell, fast-talk, snow, snow under, jolly, hand one a line. See also PERSUADE.

TEMPTED adj. on the hook, sucked in, hooked, roped in.

TEMPTER n. cruiser, heavy hitter, operator, wolf, vamp, man trap, velvet trap, swinger, sheik, sport, lady-killer. See SEDUCER.

TEMPTING adj. delish, yummy, yummy in the tummy, nummy, divine, heavenly, scrumptious.

TEMPTRESS n. hooker, flirt, man-eater, operator, C.S.P. (casual sex partner), party girl, player, swinger, vamp.

TEN n. both hands, two-fives; Dixie, sawbuck (money).

TENACIOUS adj. mulish, stubborn as a mule, the game ain't over till the last man is out, game, spunky, dead set on, bent on, hell bent on, mean business, bound, bound and determined, set, sot, stand by one's guns, stick to one's guns, going the whole hog, going all the way, going for broke, stick like glue, stick it out, dig in one's heels. See DETERMINED. See also STUBBORN.

TENACITY n. 1. stick-to-itiveness. 2. balls, guts, gutsiness, guttiness, heart, nerve, stomach, what it takes, grit, true grit, spunk, backbone, moxie, starch, clock, corazon, chutzpah, intestinal fortitude, Dutch courage (intoxicated).

TEND v. sit, baby-sit, watch over, watch out for, keep an eye on, keep tabs on, keep on a leash, ride herd on, poke, punch, check out, do for. See HEED.

TENDENCY n. thing, thing for, bag, groove, turned on to, flash, weakness for, cup of tea, druthers, type, mind-set. See INCLINATION.

TENDER adj. lovey-dovey, mushy, all over one, tender loving care, TLC, all heart (Derog.), bleeding heart, heart in the right place, old softie, softhearted. See also AFFECTIONATE.

TENDER n. feeler, hit, proposish, proposition, pass, pitch, action.

TENDER v. make a pitch, make a pass, pop the question, proposition, speak one's piece, put a feeler out, hit, hit on. See also GIVE.

TEND TO BUSINESS v. mind the store, watch the store, who's minding the store?, who's watching the store?, take care of business, TCB.

TENNESSEE Monkey State, Volunteer State.

TENNESSEEAN n. mudhead.

TENNIS, SCORING n. ad (advantage), ad in, ad out, deuce (tied at 40), break (win a game against opponent's serve), break point (opportunity to break opponent's serve), line ball, line call.

TENNIS TERMS kill, cave, cream, dust, powder, tube, eat their lunch, on their heads (beat); dink, garbage (soft tricky returns); sweet spot, hack, hacker; passing shot, put-away (scoring opportunities); overhead, overhead smash, ace (untouched serve), daisy cutter, deef (default), tree, zoning (excellent play), tanking (lose on purpose); greasing it out, sleezeball, sleezing (easy or lucky); clip, hook, roast (cheat), furniture (racket frame), exho (exhibition), Wimby (Wimbledon).

TENOR n. Irish nightingale, whiskey tenor.

TENSE adj. wired, wired-up, clutched, clutched-up, uptight, jittery, jumpy, the jumps, jitters, shaky, bugged, choked, zonkers, pissin', shittin', shittin' bricks, white knuckles, strung-out, hyper, twitty, fidgety, wreck, nervous wreck, bundle of nerves, nervy, all-overish, have a short fuse, butterflies, butterflies in one's stomach, butterflyish, coffee head, the jams, the jims, the jimmies, jim-jams, heebie-jeebies, the screaming meemies, the meemies, fall apart, torn down, shot to pieces, basket case, agita, hung up with, tightened-up, up the wall, in a lather, in a stew, in a sweat, sweaty, sweat it, sweating bullets, in a swivet, in a tizzy, in a state, in a dither, on edge, on the ragged edge, have one's teeth on edge, on pins and needles, on tenterhooks, on the gog, jumpy as a cat on a hot tin roof, have kittens, cast a kitten, having the leaps, worried sick, worried stiff, biting one's nails, beside oneself, put to it, hard put to it, at the end of one's rope. See also AFRAID; APPREHENSIVE; NERVOUS.

TENSION adj. cliff-hanging, white-knuckle, jitters, jumps, shakes, ants, ants in one's pants, a real nail-biter, pins and needles, worriment. See ANXIETY.

TENT n. dog tent, pup tent, top, big top, boudoir, pyramid (Army, WWII).

TEQUILA n. cactus juice.

TERM n. one's watch (of office), hitch, stretch, time. See also PRISON SENTENCE.

TERMINAL adj. 1. ass-end, that's all she wrote, and that was all she wrote, and that was it, curtains for, last hurrah, bitter end, period, the chips are down. See ULTIMATE. 2. done for, on one's last legs, on the way out, checking out, at the end of one's rope, MFC (measure for coffin), heading for the last roundup, one's number is up, one foot in the grave, one foot in the grave and the other on a banana peel.

TERMINATE v. wrap, wrap up, nuke, scrub, scratch, fold, wind up, sew up, drop and go (dockworker use), clinch, hang it up, shutter, close, wash out, close out, close down, shut down, pull the pin, pull the plug, put the lid on, bite the dust, cap, can it, cut off one's water, blow the whistle on, call it a day, kayo, get down to the short strokes. See FINISH.

TERMINATED adj. wrapped up, wound up, buttoned up, washed up, set, wired, fixed, dusted, history, all over but the shouting, fini, kaput, wiped out. See FINISHED.

TERMINATION n. wrap-up, windup, mop-up, dust, blow-off, kiss-off, fag end, thirty, -30-, curtain, curtains, down to the short strokes, end of the line, when the balloon goes up, when the fat lady sings. See END.

TERMS n. what it is, the size of it, nitty-gritty, small fine print at the bottom, string, string attached, string to it, ball game, catch, Catch-22,———city (e.g., fat city), fine print, bottom line, joker, kicker. See CONDITION.

TERRA FIRMA n. real estate, dust, old sod.

TERRIBLE adj. hellish, sucks, sux, sucky, bald, beat, pail, bucket, it rots, poxy, grody, grody to the max, gross, dead ass, rat's ass, barfy, burnt, grunge, grungy, scuzzy, sleazy, sleazeball, shitty, cocksucking, something fierce, wicked, heavy, bummer, downer, hairy, bad news, the pits. See BAD.

TERRIFIED adj. scared stiff, scared out of one's head, scared out of one's mind, scared witless, scared shitless, shitting peas, shit green, brick, shit a brick, run scared, petrified, D and D (deaf and dumb, afraid to testify), jumped out of one's skin, bowled-over. See FRIGHTENED.

TERRIFY v. chill, chill off, put the chill on, spook, scare stiff, scare the pants off one, scare the shit out of, scare silly, make one jump out of his skin, lean against, put on the arm, put the heat on. See FRIGHTEN.

TERRIFYING adj. hairy, hair-raising, hellish, furry, nightmare, scary, white-knuckle, spooky. See FRIGHTENING.

TERRITORY n. turf, hood, neck of the woods, stomping ground, old stomping grounds, stamping grounds, the block, the street, neck of the woods. See NEIGHBORHOOD. See also DISTRICTS.

TERSE adj. 1. in a nutshell, short and sweet, make a long story short, boiled down, cut to the bone. 2. tight-lipped.

TEST n. 1. exam, final, oral, orals, blue book, comp (comprehensive), cream (successful); drop quiz, shotgun quiz, pop test, pop quiz (unannounced); prelim. 2. dry run, try, go, fling, shot, crack, whack, stab, lick, tryout, try on, beta test, trial balloon, feeler, workout, acid test, shakedown, shakedown cruise, whiz, showcase, have a fling at, run that by.

TEST v. 1. cut and try, try on, try it on for size, give a tryout, give a workout, give it a go, shake down, prove out, mess around, fool around with, play around with, run it up the flagpole and see if anyone salutes, see how the cookie crumbles, see how it flies, see how the ball bounces, run this (idea) by one. 2. hang (how does that hang?), hold a candle to, stack up against, match up.

TEST ANSWERS n. cheat sheet, bicycle, pony, crib, gouge, hobby, horse, jack, jockey (student who cribs).

TESTEE n. guinea pig.

TESTES n. balls, nuts, rocks, cajones, nads, boo-boos, ears, diamonds, family jewels, bag, ballocks, basket, bullets, chestnuts, clangers, gajoobies. See also GENITALIA, MALE.

TESTICLES n. 1. balls, nuts, rocks, stones, cajones, nads, nards, eggs, marbles, boo-boos, ears, diamonds, family jewels, bag, ballocks, basket, racked, racked up (hit). See also GENITALIA, MALE. 2. Rocky Mountain oysters, mountain oysters (lamb, pork, beef testicles used as food), prairie oysters, bull fries, swinging steak, bull balls, bull nuts (beef).

TESTIFY v. 1. go to bat against, rat on, belch, squeal on, sing. 2. swear up and down, swear on a stack of bibles, swear till one is blue in the face, cross one's heart and hope to die, say so.

TESTIMONIAL n. say-so, plug.

TEST PILOT n. blue suiter (A.F.), white suiter (civilian).

TESTY adj. bitchy, mean, ornery, tetchy, out-of-sorts, cantankerous, grouchy, grumpy, crabby, cranky, uptight, thin-skinned, pushing out one's lips, ready to fly off the handle, edgy, got up on the wrong side of the bed. See IRRITABLE.

TEXAN n. Tex, chub, Bubba (white male), redneck, shit kicker, country boy, longhorn.

TEXAS Lone Star State.

TEXT n. words, book.

THANKS n. gramercy, thank you much, thanks a million, mercy buckup, messy bucket, merky bucket,

THE art. a, uh.

THEATER n. 1. the movies, movie, movie theater, drive-in, skin house, stroke house (pornographic). See MOTION PICTURE THEATER. 2. Broadway, off-Broadway, main stem, main kick, house, four walls, black box (small, modern), legit, legiter, boards, deluxer, paper house, barn, straw hat, strawhat circuit, the Fabulous Invalid, opera house, garlic opera (old, cheap); the big time, two-a-day, the circuit

(vaudeville); T and A, tits and ass, strip joint, burleque, burlycue, leg show, grind house, honky-tonk, mousetrap, jiggle, a circus (Obsc. girlie shows); minstrel show, cork opera, Toby show.

THEATERGOER n. buff, fan, standee. See AUDIENCE.

THEATRICAL adj. hammy, schmaltzy, tear-jerking, scenery-chewing.

THEATRICAL AGENT n. flesh peddler, ten percenter.

THEATRICAL BUSINESS n. show biz, B.O., box office, take, angel, butter and egg man, paper, Annie Oakley, pack in, pack them in, SRO (standing room only), fairy godfather, ghost, paper the house, paper house, split week, roadie (manager), four-wall (lease).

THEATRICAL PROPERTY n. prop, props.

THEFT n. rip-off, snatch, snitch, touch, caper, heist, grab, filch, pinch, lift, job, hustle, boost, stickup, holdup, holdup job, annexation, break-in, weed (from employers). See ROBBERY.

THEOLOGICAL SCHOOL n. angel factory.

THEORY n. shot, shot in the dark, stab, judgment call, op, say-so, slant, two cents' worth.

THERAPIST n. shrink, head shrinker, couch doctor, guy with the net, guy in the white coat, sexpert (sex), bug doctor (prison), guru, wig picker, squirrel, avatar.

THERAPY, GROUP n. blowout center, who you're screaming with.

THESPIAN n. thesp, star, straight man, feeder, stooge, foil, legiter, ham, hambone, ham-fatter, trouper, lead, bit player, moppet (child), talent, mugger. See ACTOR.

THICK adj. gooey, gloppy, globby, gooky, gozzle, goupy, gunky, goonky, gummy, clabbered, loppered.

THICKEN v. goonk up, gum up, clabber, lopper.

THIEF n. holdup man, stickup man, punk, mugger, jigger; push-up ghee, stickup ghee, throw-up ghee (armed); lush diver, lush roller (of drunkards); prowler, crook, scrounger, off artist, lifter, derrick, sniper, clip, gonif, ganef, gon, heel, high-grader, jackroller, operator, pack rat, alley rat, second-story man, second-story worker, porch climber, cold-slough worker, hot-slough worker, crasher, flat worker, fly, midnight, midnighter, moonlighter, owl, shacker, spider (burglar); iceman, crib man, loid man, cracksman, safecracker, screwman, pete man, peterman, pete blower (safecracker); yegg, reader; gopher, one of a gopher mob, damper mob, heavy, jug heavy, one of a jug mob (bank robber); light-fingered, sticky-fingered, sticky fingers, five-finger, five-fingers, footpad, cannon, booster, gun, grifter, heister, heist man, hist man, hijacker, chain man (watch thief), pennyweighter (jewel thief); loft man, one of a loft mob, loft worker, worm worker (specialist in fur and silk lofts).

THIN adj. skinny, skin and bones, skeleton, cadaver, pinner, peaked, peaky, slinky, stick, twiggy, shadow, bag of bones, stack of bones, beanpole, beanstalk, stilt, hat rack, broomstick, clothes pole, rattlebones, gangling, gangly, gangleshanks, spindleshanks, spindlelegs, lath-legs, stick-legs, bird-legs, turkey legs.

THIN v. water, water down, baptize, irrigate, cook, cut, spike, needle, lace, doctor, doctor up, phony up, shave.

THING n. thingy, thigamajig, thingamajig, thinguma-jugfer, thingum, thingummy, thingadad, thingumabob, thingumadad, thingumadoo thingamadodger, thinga-madudgeon, thingamananny, thingamaree, thang, gismo, gadget, shtick, widget, black box, job, jobby, contraption, dealie bob, sucker, bugger; mama, mother, motherfucker, mofo, mother-jumper (Obsc.); whatchamacallit, whatzis, whoziz; props, shit, junk. See APPARATUS.

THINK v. flash on, feel, spark, spitball, sweat, figger, figure, figure out, crunch, sort out, noodle, noodle it around, percolate, perk, float, head-trip, use one's head, use one's noodle, track, hammer, hammer away at, um, craft, take stock in, hone in, knuckle down, skull practice, skull drag, cool something over, hash, rehash, hash over, stew, stew over, sweat over, chew over, chew the cud, crack one's brains, rack one's brains, get one's head together, put on one's thinking cap, brainstorm, breakout meeting (brain-storm session), kick around, knock around, kick it around, knock it around, bat it around, run it up the flagpole, run it by one again, pour it on, dream up, make up, think up, trump up, take it off the top of one's head, blow change (radical). See also RECALL.

THINKER n. the brain, genius, egghead, hard-boiled egghead (tough-minded), scrambled egghead (fuzzy-minded), beard, big think, double-dome, ivory dome, high-brow, long-hair, pointy head, good head, skull, thumbsucker, professor, wig, trig wig (fast), Einstein, gas-ser, gray matter, whiz, wizard, avant-garde. See INTELLEC-TUAL. See also SCHOLAR.

THINNED adj. watered, watered-down, baptized, irri-gated, cooked, cut, spiked, needled, laced, doctored, doc-tored-up, phonied-up, shaved.

THIRSTY adj. cotton-mouthed, mouth full of cotton, dry as dust.

THIRTEEN n. baker's dozen, devil's dozen, long dozen.

THIRTY-TWO n. thirty-twomo, 32mo.

THORN n. sticker.

THOROUGH adj. slambang, all out, whole hog, go the limit, do up brown, open all stops, from A to Z, plenty, royal, hanging in, tough, heart and soul into, all the way, go big time, whole hog, to a fare-thee-well, galley west, the works, not overlook a bet, move heaven and earth, leave no stone unturned, six ways to Sunday, you name it, from hell to breakfast, from soup to nuts.

THOROUGHBRED adj. graded.

THOROUGHFARE n. rip strip, dragway, pavement, the bricks, byway, aisle, bowling, alley. See ROAD.

THOROUGHLY adv. all (all dolled up), from A to Z, top to bottom, whole hog, slambang, smack, smack out, flat out, flat-ass, tote, from soup to nuts. See COMPLETELY.

THOUGHT n. brainchild, brainstorm, brain wave, child, spark, spark plug, flash, bell-ringer, deep think, it hit me, big idea, how one figures it, op, two cents' worth. See IDEA.

THOUGHTFUL adj. cool, mellow, play it cool. See also SERIOUS.

THOUGHTLESS adj. pay no mind, out to lunch, asleep at the switch, daydreaming, woolgathering, any old way, go off half-cocked, devil-may-care. See CARELESS. See also VACUOUS. 2. flaky, mad, ad lib, winging it, off the wall, off the cuff, off the hip, off the top of one's head, shoot from the hip, spitball, play by ear, dash off, strike off, knock off, toss off, toss out. See IMPULSIVE.

THOUSAND n. G, grand, K, M, thou, yard, horse (dol-lars).

THRASH v. 1. bash, trash, drub, dog on, lather, larrup, leather, lambaste, cane, work over, whip, tan one's hide, take it out of one's hide, take it out of one's skin, clobber, kick ass, wipe out, dot (precise blow), beat up, beat the bejesus out of one, beat the shit out of one, whale the daylights out of one, punk, jack, whale, wallop, welt. See HIT. 2. bury, blank, plunk, skunk, schneider, murder, kill, cook, trim, trounce, fix one's wagon, shellack, bulldoze, roll over, torpedo, meatball, make one say uncle, beat all hollow, finish off, rack up, blow out, pin one's ears back. See DE-FEAT.

THREADBARE adj. beat-up, ratty, tacky, frowzy, dog-eared, used-up, in a bad way.

THREAT n. wolf ticket, fix, fix one's wagon, else, or else, I'm gonna break your face, he's gonna have me popped, defi, defy.

THREATEN v. enforce, lean on, flex one's muscles, whip one around (intellectually), walk heavy, put on the arm, put the heat on, hang tough, spook, chill off, shine one on, woof, bulldoze. See INTIMIDATE.

THREATENED adj. feel the heat, heat's on, hot, spooked, frozen, goose-bumpy, shit in one's pants, panicked, run scared, shake in one's boots, given a turn, given a jar, given a jolt. See also FRIGHTENED.

THREATENING adj. in the cards, in the wind, at hand, see it coming, it's looking to, the noose is hanging, snake-in-the-grass.

THREE n. trey, ace-deuce.

THREE-DIMENSIONAL adj. 3D.

THRIFTY adj. 1. dirt cheap, cheap as dirt, dog cheap, cheapie, el cheapo, steal, a real steal, buy, a real buy, low-budget, low-cost, cost nothing, cost next to nothing, more bang for the buck, bought for a song, cut-rate, low-tariff. 2. tight, so tight one squeaks, penny-pinching, pinchy, close, close-fisted, chinchy, chintzy, scrimpy, skimpy, stingy, on the rims, run on the rims, bog pocket, Scotch, nickel-nurser, last of the big spenders.

THRILL n. rush, upper, blast, wallop, belt, boot, blow one's mind, blown away, charge, large charge, bang, get a bang out of, kick, kicks, for kicks, turn on, circus, fireworks, flash. See EXCITEMENT.

THRILL v. 1. juice, send, grab, spin one's wheels, key up, fire up, steam up, stir up, turn one on, switch on, get it up, get hot under the collar, race one's motor, open one's nose. See EXCITE. 2. freak out, wig out, blow one away, turn on, knock out, knock dead, knock the socks off one, send, slay, score, wow, just what the doctor ordered, go over big. See DELIGHT.

THRILLED adj. high, hyper, jacked, jaked, jazzed, turned-on, freaked-out, charged, hopped-up, sent, gassed, flipped, backflips, flipping, blew one's mind, mind-blowing, in seventh heaven, on cloud nine, walking on air, got one's grits, got one's jollies, set up, handsprings, lookin' good, pleased as Punch, sold on, tickled pink, tickled to death, wowed, a rush. See also EXCITED.

THRILLING adj. frantic, wild, fab, killer, zero cool, boss, mad, like wow, mind-blowing, mind-bending, turn on, kicky, knockout, live one, large, large charge, nervous, swinging, lush, sizzler, scorcher, thriller, sensay, sensaysh. See EXCITING.

THRIVE v. get well, get fat, get there, go great guns, make hay, make well, make out, put it together, home free, hack it, do all right by oneself, live off the fat of the land. See SUCCEED.

THRIVING adj. have it made, have a mint, have the wherewithal, on top of the heap, living high on the hog, loving life, loving it, right up there, livin' large, clockin', up in the bucks, in the chips, really rolling, money to burn, really cooking, lousy rich, well-fixed, well-set-up, sitting pretty, fat dumb and happy, arrived, booming, going strong, going great guns, mining the gold, home free, laughing all the way to the bank, oofy, uptown. See SUCCESSFUL.

THROAT n. pipes, gargle, google, goozle, guzzle.

THROB n. pitapation.

THROB v. go pit-a-pat, tick.

THRONG n. blowout, mob, push, turnout, crush, jam, jam-up, everybody and his brother, everybody and his uncle, loaded to the rafters, wall-to-wall people, sellout.

THROTTLE n. gun.

THROUGH adv. wrapped up, fini, wound up, buttoned up, history, done to a T, in the bag, nailed down, on ice, all over but the shouting, signed sealed and delivered. See FINISHED.

THROW v. chuck, chunk, fire, heave, lob, peg, pitch, sling, toss; gollum (frisbee, wild throw).

THROW AWAY v. lose, chuck, deep-six, eighty-six, junk, nox out, give the old heave-ho, throw on the junk heap. See DISCARD.

THRUST n. boost, speedup, blitz, jump, push.

THRUST v. chuck, chunk, fire, heave, lob, peg, pitch, sling, toss, hump, boost, buck, charge, bear down on it, push it, give it the gun, pour it on, zing, go to town on, railroad through.

THUG n. mug, mugger, hood, hoodlum, gorilla, ape, bodyguard, pug, sleazeball, heavy, clipper, big boy, bad actor, goon, greaser, bullyboy, bucko, hellcat, hellraiser, hellion, holy terror, roughneck, tough cookie, critter, bruiser, ugly customer, plug-ugly, hooligan, strong-arm man, muscle man, hit man, hatchet man, hatchet boy, sidewinder.

THUNDERBIRD (CAR) n. T-Bird.

THUNDEROUS adj. leather-lunged. See also LOUD.

THWART v. crimp, cramp, put a crimp in, cramp one's style, queer, stymie, skin, snooker, crab, hang up, hold up, foul up, fuck up, louse up, snafu, bollix, gum up the works, fake out, flummox, stump, cross, cross up, double-cross, give one the business, throw a monkey wrench into the works, upset one's apple cart, spike one's guns, steal one's thunder, trash, take one down, take care of, take the wind out of one's sails, knock the bottom out of, knock the chocks from under one, knock the props from under one, down one, ditch, give the slip, skip out on, duck, dodge, get around, give the runaround, run circles around, run rings around. See also HINDER.

THWARTED adj. hung up on, stymied, through the mill, up the wall, faked-out, put away, skinned, queered, crabbed, fouled-up, fucked-up, bollixed-up, crimped, cramped, stonewalled, flummoxed. See also DEFEATED.

TICKET n. admish, board, stub, twofer (half-price), pasteboard, chit, deadwood (unsold); pass, freebee, paper,

Annie Oakley, Chinee ducat, comp (free); throwaway (traffic), DWI (driving while intoxicated) dookie (meal ticket), duck (social event); bid, invite (invitation).

TICKET BROKER n. scalper.

TICKET SELLER n. pitchman.

TICKET TAKER n. chopper, ducat snatcher.

TIDINGS n. info, poop, skinny, hot skinny, lowdown, dirt, dope, dope sheet, inside dope, the know, whole story, the latest, what's happenin', what's going down, earful, hot wire, are you ready for this? See NEWS.

TIDY adj. apple-pie, apple-pie order, neat as a button, neat as a pin, Bonnie Brillo (neat person), tacked-down (Af. Am., neatly dressed), slick, to rights, all policed up, in good shape, shipshape.

TIDY v. put in shape, put in good shape, whip into shape, put to rights, put in apple-pie order, clear the decks, fix up, police, police up, spruce, spruce up, have all the pieces in place, get one's act together, get one's head together, get one's shit together, pull things together, shape up, straighten up and fly right, frame. See also CLEAN.

TIE n. 1. dead heat, push, photo finish, standoff, Mexican standoff. 2. four-in-hand, string. 3. tie-up, tie-in, tie-in tie-up, hookup, network, outfit, gang. See ASSOCIATION.

TIE v. 1. hog-tie, put a half nelson on, put a lock on, lock up. 2. push (bet).

TIE PIN n. prop.

TIGER n. big cat, cat, stripes.

TIGHT adj. quick.

TIGHT-LIPPED adj. clammed-up, dried-up, dummied-up, garbo. See SILENT.

TIJUANA, MEXICO T.J.

TILTED adj. raked (auto), slaunchways, slaunchwise.

TIMBER n. load of sticks.

TIMBERLAND n. big sticks.

TIME n. ticks, half a mo, half a shake, jiffy, zero hour, bells (nautical), bite (TV news), age, ages; on the button, right on the button, on the nose (on time); at this moment in time, ol' man Mose, coon's age, a dog's age, many a moon, a month of Sundays, once in a blue moon, hitch, stretch, since Hector was a pup, up at the crack of one's back, on the dot; fucking off, goofing off, fucking the dog (kill time), bad time, hard time, movin' through (time passage); count one's thumbs, twiddle one's thumbs (waiting); time to bail, time to book (time to go).

TIME v. clock.

TIMELY adj. with it, now, chilly, up-to-the-minute, hard-hitting, high-powered.

TIMELY adv. at the eleventh hour, in the nick of time.

TIME PERIOD n. time frame, window, bite (TV news), float (Fin.).

TIMEPIECE n. ticker; turnip, kettle turnip (pocket); chroniker, Albert (with chain), Big Ben, totter.

TIMID adj. rabbity, mousy, have cold feet, 'fraidy cat, scaredy cat, run scared, wimpy, wet sock, wet rag, goosebumpy, weenie, jellyfish, chicken, chickenhearted, lily-livered, milksop, Caspar Milquetoast, weak-kneed, weak sister, sissy, baby, big baby, pucker-assed, candy-ass. See FRIGHTENED. See also COWARDLY, SHY.

TINFOIL n. Christmas, window (WWII, dropped to confuse radar).

TINKER v. mess around, monkey around, fiddle with, potchky (Yid.). See DABBLE.

TINY adj. mini, teeny, teeny-weeny, teensy, teensy-weensy, bitty, bitsy, itsy-bitsy, wee, peewee, tomtit, yea big, pint-sized, knee high to a grasshopper. See SMALL.

TIP n. 1. toke, chip, cue, somethin', subway, bus ride (nickel or dime), lagniappe, one-way (five cents), sweetener. See GRATUITY. 2. tip-off, steer, bum steer, kibitz, flea in the ear, one's two cents' worth, word to the wise, wise up; feedbag information, feedbox information (horse racing), on the Bill Daley.

TIPPLE v. hit the bottle, bend one's elbow, tip one's elbow, crook one's elbow, wet one's whistle, dip the beak, hang a few on, swig, irrigate. See DRINK.

TIPPLER n. barfly, juicer, guzzler, tosspot, soak, elbow-bender, elbow-crooker, pretzel-bender, bottle baby, bottle sucker. See DRINKER.

TIPSTER n. tout.

TIPSY adj. tight, crocked, loopy, high, high as a kite, tied one on, loaded, feeling no pain, on a toot, lubricated, mellow, wet, lit, lit up like a Christmas tree, boozy, buzzey, piffled, addled, tiddly, happy, beery, flying with one wing low, groggy, had one or two, irrigated, D.O.A., seeing pink elephants, woozy, had one too many. See DRUNK.

TIRE v. fade, fag, fold, tucker, poop, poop out, burn out, fag out, tucker out, knock out, peter out, fizzle, fizzle out, conk out, peg out, cave in, go soft, go to pieces, come apart at the seams, die on the vine, be on one's last legs.

TIRED adj. 1. dopey, out of it, sleepyhead, snoozy, stretchy, on the nod, eye trouble, in sleepville, blah, blahs, drippy, wimpy, draggy. 2. bushed, had it, hung, pooped, too pooped to pop (too tired for sex), dusted, wimped out, out of gas, out of juice, knocked out, wiped out, wrung out, burned out, burnt, blown out, creased, crispy, played out, crapped out, down and out, flaked out, wore out, worn out, gave out, petered out, pegged out, dragged out, crumped out, conked out, fagged, fagged out, tuckered out, washed out, whacked out, zonked, dragged, dragging one's ass, draggin' ass, have one's ass in a sling, a wreck, worn to a frazzle, foozled, nearly dead, dead, dead tired, dead beat, beat, beat to the ground, beat down to the ankles, beat to the socks, beatsville, pissed-up, used-up, done-up, done in, all in, in a bad way, on one's last legs, whipped, whupped, licked, guffed, dished, punchy, low, crumped, shot, shot one's load, shot down, at the end of one's rope, at row's end, hit the wall (marathon), clanked, clanked out, hacked, bone-tired, bone-weary, dog-tired, dog-weary, ratty, cooked. 3. fed up, up to here, had it up to here, done it all, been around twice. See also JADED.

TIRELESS adj. grind, plugger, springbutt, eager beaver, work one's tail off, ball of fire, fireball, hyper, jumping, on the go, perky. See also SPIRITED.

TIRES n. duals (includes wheels), rags, runners, skates, whitewalls, slicks, radials, shoes, skins, flats, flat hoops, sore feet (punctured), pumpkins (flat).

TIRESOME adj. 1. uncool, heavy, hefty, that bugs me, gives one a pain, pain in the neck, pain in the ass, bitch, son of a bitch, son of a gun, a bit much, too much. 2. bor-ring, ho-hum, drag, draggy, yawn, big yawn, yawner, nowhere, bore one stiff, tired, wonky, cheesy, gummy. See BORING.

TITILLATE v. 1. turn on, switch on, grab, hook. 2. crack one up, break one up, fracture one, get one's kicks, get one's jollies, tickle pink. See EXCITE. See also AMUSE, ENTERTAIN.

TITILLATED adj. caught, hooked, into, sold, turned-on, tickled pink.

TITLE n. handle, handle to one's name, tag, brand, flag (assumed), front name, label, tab, moniker, what's-his-name, what's-his-face.

TOADY n. A.K., ass-kisser, bootlick, kiss-ass, ass sucker, ass wipe, butt wipe, ass-licker, tukis licker, brownie, brown noser, fart sniffer (Obsc.); yes-man, nod guy, schmeikler, groupie, gofer, waterboy. See SYCOPHANT.

TOADY v. soft-soap, jolly, oil, lay it on, lay it on thick, lay it on with a trowel, play up to, butter up, sweeten up, brown-nose, suck around, suck ass, kiss ass, kiss butt, bootlick, fall all over, kowtow. See FLATTER.

TOAST n. shingle, down.

TOASTED adj. down.

TOASTMASTER n. the chair, MC, emcee.

TOASTS n. cheers, cheerio, prosit, here's looking at you, here's to ya, l'chayim, sante, salud, bottoms up, mud in your eye, down the hatch, chugalug, absent friends.

TOBACCO n. weed, filthy weed, plug, bull, hay, alfalfa, Bull Durham, dust, freckles, gage, commo (prison); wad, cheekful, chaw (chewing), rock hound candy, pinch (snuff), niggerhead, coal pot (pipe), bug juice (residue).

TOBACCO CHEWER n. bell-ringer.

TODDLER n. kid, babe, bottle baby, babykins, bambino, tot, tad, in diapers, nipper, button, little darling. See BABY.

TOES n. piggy, ten.

TOGETHER adv. in sync, on the beat, with the beat, witha one witha two witha three, witha one anda two anda three. See also COMPATIBLE.

TOIL n. grind, scutwork, donkeywork, hemo jo (hard labor), shitwork, chickwork (household), elbow grease, gig, nine-to-five shit. See WORK.

TOIL v. sweat it, plug away, peg away, put one's nose to the grindstone, beat one's brains out, bust a gut, work one's head off, mouse milking (maximum time for minimum return). See WORK.

TOILET n. can, Cannes, john, johnny, johnny house, restroom, Men's, Ladies', ladies' room, women's room, girls' room, little girls' room, ruth, powder room, men's room, boys' room, little boys' room, telephone, reading room, blue room, library, head, facilities, amenities, comfort station, terlit, piss house, shithouse, shitter, crapper, crappery, crap-house, WC (water closet), loo, sandbox, play in the sandbox (go to), biffie, biffy, bippy, bank, chamber of commerce, altar, altar room, holy of holies, chapel, throne, throne room, donagher, donniker, Andy Gump, bucket, privy, two-holer, fireless cooker, out back, Chic Sale, back, backhouse, honeywagon, honeypot, honey house, pisspot, pot, potty, potty chair, puke hole, cat box, thunder box, thunder mug, joe, jane, flusher, kazoo, gazoo, gazool, showers, cacatorium, necessarium, where the dicks hang out, old soldiers' home.

TOILET PAPER n. T.P., teepee, ammunition, sandpaper (Mil.).

TOILET PAPER BALLS n. dingleberries.

TOLEDO, OHIO Scale City.

TOLERANT adj. big, soft-shell, easy with, easy on.

TOLERATE v. bear with, live with, go along with, string along with, put up with, suck it up, hear of, stand for, sit still for, stomach something, grin and bear it, sit and take it, stay the course, stand for, stand the gaff, stand up, be big, be big about, not let it get one down. See also ENDURE.

TOLL BOOTH n. cash register, piggy bank.

TOLUENE n. tolly.

TOMATO n. love apple, tommy.

TOMATO SOUP n. red noise.

TOMB n. cold storage, dustbin.

TOMFOOLERY n. monkeyshines, shenanigans, hijinks.

TONE n. football (whole musical note), lick (Mus.).

TONE-DEAF adj. tin-ear.

TONGUE n. stinger.

TONGUE KISS n. tongue sushi, French kiss, soul kiss.

TONIC n. pick-me-up, pick-up, shot in the arm, go juice. See also DRINK.

TOO BAD adv. tough nuggies, tough shit, TS.

TOOL n. gismo, gadget, widget, job, contraption, dealie bob; sucker, bugger, mother, motherfucker, mofo (Obsc.); whatchamacallit, whatsis, jigamaree, dojigger, Armstrong (requires strength). See APPARATUS.

TOOTHPICK n. lumber.

TOOTHSOME adj. delish, grinds, yummy, divine, heavenly, scrumptious, sweetened, sugar-coated, yummy in the tummy.

TOP v. 1. cap (add to bet), piggyback. 2. bury, smoke, skunk, schneider, trounce, swamp, shellack, bash, trash, drub, total, clobber, cream, beat all hollow, plow under, blow out, run rings around, run circles around, put away, shut out, rank out, wipe out, put one in the cookie jar, put one in the popcorn machine. See DEFEAT. 3. ace, ace out, beat one's time, fox, outfox, goose, con, short con, vend run, fake out, juke, cop a heel on, cop a sneak on, pull a quickie on, pull a fast one, finagle, work one's points. See also EXCEL.

TOPCOAT n. car coat, horse blanket, threads, benny, binny, Benjamin, flogger, fog.

TOPEKA, KANSAS Railroad City.

TOPER n. wino, big drunk, brown bagger, lush, souse, stew, boozer, boozehound, alky, juice head, dipso, rummy, shikker, tosspot, soak, sponge, elbow-bender, bottle baby. See DRINKER.

TOP FORM n. up, wrapped tight, ready, fine-tuned.

TOPPING n. glop, gunk, ice.

TOPPLE n. header, spill, nose-dive, pratfall, belly buster, belly flop, belly whopper, pancake landing.

TOPPLE v. take a header, spill, tip over, belly up, nose-dive, lose it, do a pratfall, fall down and go boom, land on one's ass, hit the dirt, come a-cropper, go ass over teakettle.

TOP SECRET adj. hush-hush, classified, under one's hat, under wraps, eyes only, for your eyes only, closet, family jewels (Govt., CIA), pull the ladder up behind one, something up one's sleeve, wildcat (plan), skunk works (secret manufacturing plant or laboratory). See SECRET.

TORMENT v. give a bad time to, drive one bananas, hassle, hound, give a hard time to, put the heat on, drive up the wall, put the squeeze on one, put one through the wringer, play cat and mouse, rub salt in the wound, bone, break one's balls. See ANNOY.

TORNADO n. twister.

TORONTO, ONTARIO Home of the Chirps, Home of the Chirpers, TO.

TORPEDO n. fish, tin fish, torp, firecracker, pickle, pineapple (Ger.), torp.

TOSS v. 1. heave, lob, peg, pitch, sling, chuck, chunk, fire; gollum (frisbee, wild throw). 2. chuck, lose, deep-six, eighty-six, junk, nox out, give the old heave-ho, throw on the junk heap. See DISCARD.

TOT n. kid, little kid, shaver, little shaver, rug rat, drape ape (Stu.), house ape, squirt, little squirt, little guy, little bugger, little dickens, little darling, cub, sonny, sprout, bambino, nipper, tad, ankle biter. See CHILD. See also BABY.

TOTAL n. jackpot, the works, whole enchilada, whole ball of wax, whole nine yards, whole shebang, whole works, everything including the kitchen sink, lock stock and barrel. See WHOLE.

TOTAL v. tot, tot up, tote, tote up, reckon up, go (gambling).

TOTALIZATOR n. tote, tote board, big board.

TOTALLY adv. top to bottom, go big time, whole hog, full blast, stone (stone deaf), smack out, flat out, flat-ass, tote, from soup to nuts. See COMPLETELY.

TOUCH v. 1. frisk, feel up, put the feelers on one or something, grab ass, fool around, paw, playing footsie. See also CARESS. 2. reach, get in touch, touch base, keep in touch, interact, connect, grok, reach out, relate, get across. See COMMUNICATE. 3. get to, grab, stroke, feel out, have a funny feeling, have heart, have good vibes, have vibes, get vibes, know where one is coming from.

TOUCHED adj. turned on by, turned on to, got to, grabbed, feel for, feel in one's guts.

TOUCHING adj. stunning, stunner, mind-blowing, out of this world, feel in one's guts, grabbed by. See MOVING.

TOUCHY adj. 1. goosy, jumpy as a cat on a hot tin roof, yantsy, wired-up, uptight, hung-up, wreck, nervous wreck, bundle of nerves, thin-skinned, bitchy, cantankerous, mean, ornery, can't even look at one cross-eyed. See SENSITIVE. 2. unhealthy, widow maker, heavy, dicey, iffy, chancy, in the tube, too hot to handle, hot potato, on thin ice, on slippery ground, touch-and-go. See DANGEROUS.

TOUGH adj. 1. hairy, mean, tough customer, rough-neck, wicked, hard-nosed, hard-shell, hard-boiled, I'm shakin' (sarcastic response to threat) hardball, ballsy, ballbuster, ballbreaker, eat nails, bad guy, bad actor, John Wayne, burly, bogard, down, enforcer, hooligan, plug-ugly, stiff, cob, commando, Chicago, welcome to the NFL, gutsy, gutty, nervy, spunky, cool hand, beefy, hefty, husky, strong as a horse, strong as a lion, strong as an ox, wicked. 2. uphill battle, heavy, bitch, hellish, tough nut to crack, toughie, hard row of stumps, the hard way, handful, ballbreaker, back-breaker, bear, honey, no piece of cake, heavy sledding. See DIFFICULT.

TOUPEE n. rug, toup, piece, sky piece, sky rug, fur, brush, divot, mucket, doily, dome doily, scalp doily, head-piece, muff, head falsie.

TOUR n. junket, hop, swing, jaunt, cruise, trek, over-night, weekend, getaway, Cook's tour. See TRAVEL. 2. the road, the circuit; stump, whistle-stop, mashed-potato circuit, rubber-chicken circuit (Pol.). 3. hitch, stretch, time.

TOUR v. 1. jet around, go on Apex, hop, city-hop, country-hop, globe-trot, cruise, do the continent, do Europe (or wherever), junket, Cook's tour, Cook's Tour, swing, barnstorm. See TRAVEL. 2. go on the road, stump (Pol.).

TOURING adj. globe-trotting, rubbernecking, cruising, doing the continent, on the road, on the circuit, on the go, barnstorming, stumping, flightseeing (from a plane). See TRAVELING.

TOURIST n. jet-setter, globe-trotter, rubberneck, rubbernecker, dude (bus), snowbird, snowflake, sunflower.

TOUSLED adj. beat-up, mangled, thrashed, messed-up, mussed-up, messy, mussy, sloppy, grungy, grubby, scuzzed, scuzzed-up.

TOUT v. let in on, let in on the know, steer, boost, give a boost to, push, put next to, put on to, put on to something hot, put one in the picture, put hep, tip, tip off, give one a tip. See ADVISE.

TOW CAR n. draggin' wagon, the motor club.

TOWER n. cloud buster, high-rise.

TOWN n. burg, apple, Big Town, big time, boomer, boomtown, dump, tough town, wide-open joint, tank town, tank station, wrong tank, right tank, slab, two-stemmer, urb, patch, jerkwater town, hick town, rube town, duckburg, hoosier town, one-horse town, ghost town, South Succotash, East Jesus, Podunk, jumping-off place, hickville, whistle-stop, whistle-snort, noplaceville, filling station, wide place in the road, hideaway, the bushes, the boondocks, boonies, sticks, stix, bush leagues, pumpkin, the rhubarbs.

TOWNSPERSON n. townee, towner, local local. See also CITY DWELLER.

TOW TRUCK n. hooker, draggin' wagon, the motor club.

TOW TRUCKING TERMS TA (traffic accident), capping (recommending a lawyer, illegal), prowling (cruising for accidents), posting up (parking while waiting for a call), jumping a call (racing police to an accident, illegal), fading (beating the competition to the scene), PR (person reporting).

TOY v. fool with, play games with, dilly-dally, play around, fool around, jerk off, lead one on, string one along. See DALLY. See also DABBLE.

TRACK n. boards (indoor), groove, rut.

TRACK v. 1. dog, bird-dog (scout), scout, beat the bushes, run down, leave no stone unturned, track down. See SEARCH. 2. shadow, tail, trail, tail down, hot on one's tail, go after, dog one's heels, stick to. See FOLLOW.

TRACK-AND-FIELD TERMS anchor, anchorman (heavy man in tug-of-war or last runner in relay race), anchor leg (last segment of relay race); breast the tape (win), bunch-start (crouch), hand-off (relay race conversion).

TRACT n. broadside, flyer, handout.

TRACTABLE adj. putty in one's hands, game, go along with, hang loose, roll with the punches. See also FLEXIBLE.

TRACTOR n. cat, cat skinner (operator), horse, kitty cat.

TRADE n. bag, gig, day gig, beeswax, biz, game, gesheft, line, line of business, dodge, what one is into, thing, nine-to-five shit, racket. See OCCUPATION. 2. Wall Street, the Exchange, the Big Board, over-the-counter.

TRADE v. dicker, hack out a deal, hammer out a deal, make a deal, work out a deal, wheel and deal, hondle, horse-trade, swap. See NEGOTIATE.

TRADEMARK n. logo.

TRADER n. dealer, middleman, big-time operator, BTO, big wheel, wheeler-dealer, tycoon, cockroach (small), nickel-and-dime operator, small potatoes, tradester, robber baron, big butter-and-egg man, peddler, drummer, bell ringer, ——— dog (e.g., shoe dog), medicine man, pitch-man, skig, spieler, tinge, Arab, bag guy (balloon), butch, butcher, hawker.

TRADITIONAL adj. trad. See also CONVENTIONAL.

TRAFFIC CITATION n. ticket, tag, DWI (driving while intoxicated), coupon, green stamps, bit on the britches, Christmas card, feed the bears.

TRAFFIC JAM n. gridlock, gawker's block, gaper's block, curiosity creep, slow-and-go, jam, parking lot, stall ball, level F, cone zone (working area), greenlock (in national parks).

TRAFFIC SIGN n. magic marker.

TRAFFIC TERMS make the light (go through on green or yellow), run a light (go through on red); ticket, tag, coupon (court summons), pulled over, joyride, cruisin', Sunday driver (inept), Hollywood stop (roll through a legal stop); sleeping policeman, speed bump (a bump placed to slow speeding cars).

TRAFFIC WITH v. 1. interact, interface, contact, network, reach out, relate, touch, touch base, have truck with, connect with. See COMMUNICATE. 2. dicker, make a deal, cut a deal, work out a deal, horse trade, swap, swap horses. See also NEGOTIATE.

TRAGEDY n. bad scene, bummer, curtains, downer, grabber, total shuck, Waterloo, the worst, blue ruin, shit hit the fan. See DISASTER. See also MISFORTUNE.

TRAIL n. byway, aisle, stroll, groove, rut.

TRAIL v. 1. dog, leave no stone unturned, take out after, track down. See SEARCH. 2. shadow, tail, shag, hot on one's tail, on one's quiff (closely), dog one's heels, tag after, spook. See FOLLOW. 3. get noplace fast, poke, poke around, poke along, schlep along, play catchup, string along, tag along.

TRAILER CAMP n. mo-camp.

TRAILER PARK n. galvanized ghetto.

TRAIN n. choo-choo, choo-choo train, rattler, ball of fire, highballer, jack, rat, meat run, milk run, red ball, cannonball, AMTRAK. See RAILROAD TRAIN.

TRAIN v. 1. tune up, lick into shape, get in shape, work out, warm up, put through the grind, put through the mill, run through, walk through, take it from the top, dry run, hone, sharpen, break, break in. See also PREPARE. 2. brainwash, break, break in, put one in the picture, put one wise, wise one up, show one the ropes, update, level, clue one in, give a pointer to, drum, drum into.

TRAIN CONDUCTOR n. big O, big ox, brains, captain, chopper, con, dude, drummer, grabber, kayducer.

TRAINED adj. up-to-snuff, up-to-speed, up-to-code, been through the mill, from way back, pro, vet, war-horse, won one's spurs, one of the old school, old-timer, has knowhow, knows the ropes, knows one's onions, knows one's ps and qs. See also KNOWLEDGEABLE.

TRAINEE n. tenderfoot, boot, rookie, flunky, heel, heeler (reporter), peg boy, pratt boy. See NOVICE. See also RECRUIT.

TRAINER n. old man, skipper.

TRAINING n. workout, warm-up, sharpening up, shaping up, an edge, readying, breaking-in, daily dozen, chalk talk, skull session. See also PREPARATION.

TRAINING CENTER n. boot camp.

TRAIT n. nature of the beast, thing, one's thing, the way of it, the name of that tune, that's one all over, just like one. See also CHARACTERISTIC.

TRAITOR n. Benedict Arnold, fifth columnist, quisling, rat, rat fink, fink, double-crosser, snake, snake in the grass, narc, snitch, squealer, stoolie, stool pigeon, snitcher, snout, tattletale; yellow dog, whistle-blower (U.). See INFORMER.

TRAITOROUS adj. double-crossing, snake-in-the-grass, two-faced, two-timing, low-down and dirty, dirty work, cheatin' heart, slick, slippery, speak with forked tongue.

TRAMP n. bum, on the bum, king of the road, bo, stiff, bindleman, floater, ragbag, road agent. See VAGRANT.

TRAMP v. hoof it, go by hand, burn shoe leather, hit the road, press the bricks, air out, beat the rocks, navigate, count ties (hobo). See WALK.

TRANCE n. Nadaville, gone, far out, cool, gauze, glaze, MEGO (my eyes glaze over).

TRANQUIL adj. cool, cool as a cucumber, keep one's cool, keep one's shirt on, not turn a hair, unflappable, ah-ah head, all quiet on the Potomac, all quiet on the western front.

TRANQUILIZER n. trank, tranx, backwards, volume, dope, goofball, knockout drop, Mickey Finn, housewife's delight. See also SEDATIVE.

TRANSACT v. 1. hammer out a deal, hack out a deal, cut a deal, work out a deal, wrap up, close, sew up, button down, button up, jell, take care of, clinch. See NEGOTIATE. See also FINISH. 2. move, make one's move, effectuate, TCB (take care of business), take a flyer (impulsively), break out with, bust out with (surprisingly or suddenly), pull off, move on (to something else), fish or cut bait, get with it, shit or get off the pot, perk, tick, operate, run with the ball, do one's stuff. See ACT.

TRANSACTION n. goings-on, carrying on, hanky-panky, hap, happening, ongoing, play, irons, irons in the fire, done deal, little deal (often unethical).

TRANSACTIONAL ANALYSIS n. TA.

TRANSCENDENTAL MEDITATION n. TM.

TRANSFIX v. nail down, pin down, stick.

TRANSFORM v. 1. switch, switch over, doctor, phony up, shift gears, cook, transmogrify, revamp. 2. turn over a new leaf, turn the corner, turn the tables, turn one around, do up, about face, flip-flop, sing a different tune. See CHANGE.

TRANSFORMATION n. about-face, flip-flop, switch, switchover, transmogrification.

TRANSFORMED adj. born again, got religion, new-born Christian, saw the light.

TRANSITORY adj. fly-by-night, flash in the pan, here today gone tomorrow.

TRANSMIT v. 1. duke, weed, pass it over, get across, get the message, back channel (secretly). 2. drop a line, drop a note, give one a ring, give one a jingle, give one a call, get one on the horn. See also DELIVER; DISPATCH.

TRANSMITTER n. rig.

TRANSPIRE v. gel, jell, shake, smoke, come down, what's coming down?, go down, what's going down?, what goes?, where's the action? See OCCUR.

TRANSPORT v. lug, pack, back, piggyback, birdie-back, fishy-back (by water), ride, shlep, shlep along, tote, truck, buck, gun, heel, hump, jag, shoulder, move.

TRANSPORT DRUGS v. carryin', carry the mail, body pack.

TRANSPOSE v. flip-flop, back-track, double back, turn the tables, put the cart before the horse, put ass backwards, put bass ackwards, put ack basswards.

TRANSVESTITE n. TV, T.V.

TRANSVESTITE CLOTHING n. drag (also transvestite party).

TRAP v. rope in, suck in, box in, get one in a box, collar, corral, grab, hook, land, nail, bag, nab, lay for. See also AMBUSH.

TRAPEZE ARTIST n. flyer.

TRAPPED adj. dog meat, nabbed, nailed, cornered, in a box, in a hole, up a tree, jammed-up, on the peg, stiffed in, swamped. See CAUGHT.

TRASH n. gash, hogwash, junk, dreck, shit.

TRASH COLLECTOR n. san man.

TRAVEL n. hop, swing, jaunt, cruise, junket, trek, overnight, weekend, Cook's tour.

TRAVEL v. jet, jet in, jet out, sky in, sky out, jet around, get around, knock around, knock about, belt around, bat around, bat about, swing, go places, go on Apex, on the go, take off, hop, city-hop, country-hop, globe-trot, tripping, cruise, hit the road, on the road, on the move, on the trail, hit the trail, traipse, trek, do the continent, do Europe (or wherever), jaunt, junket, junketing, overnight, weekend, beat one's way, barnstorm, bum, bum around, bum a ride, thumb, thumb a ride, lam, hitch, hitchhike, hitch a ride, hopscotch, breeze, dog it, drive in, hit the dirt, hit the grit, walk the tracks, count ties.

TRAVELER n. jet-setter, globe-trotter, frequent flyer, deadhead (free), seat-cover, dude (bus), drop, line load (taxi), rubberneck, rubbernecker, snowbird, snowflake, sunflower.

TRAVELING adj. on the road, on the circuit, on the go, on the jump, on the gad, on the bum, jetting, globe-trotting, cruising, doing the continent, rubbernecking, knocking around, knocking about, batting around, batting about, barnstorming, stumping.

TRAVELING CASE n. jiffy bag, tote, tote bag, carry-on, valpack, keister.

TRAVESTY n. take-off, play on, put-on, roast.

TREACHEROUS adj. double-crossing, snake in the grass, two-faced, two-timing, slick, slippery, speak with forked tongue. See DECEITFUL. See also DISHONEST.

TREACHERY n. dirty dealing, dirty work, dirty pool, dirty trick, double-cross, sellout, put-on, scam, fake, flam, flim-flam, racket, dodge, royal fucking, royal screwing, bunco, bunko, fast shuffle, double shuffle, gyp, jip, double banker, diddle, diddling, grift, shell game, skin game, Judas kiss, stab in the back, two-timing, crocodile tears, soft soap, sweet talk, spoof, whitewash job, cake cutter (circus). See also CHEAT.

TREASURER n. ghee with the boodle, payoff ghee.

TREASURY n. damper, Fort Knox.

TREASURY AGENT n. narc, T man.

TREASURY SECURITY n. T-Bill, baby bond (less than $1,000 denomination), James Bond (matures in 2007); Bo Derek, ten (Treasury bond maturing in the year 2010); double-barreled bond (two sources of repayment). See also BONDS.

TREAT n. cush, sweets, g'dong, gedunk, hickey.

TREAT v. 1. doctor. 2. blow, blow one to, on one, on the house, I'll get it (pay the check), I'm buyin', pick up the check, pick up the tab, pop, pop for, spring for, stand for, set up, stake.

TREATED BY adj. on (it's on me), on the house.

TREE n. twig.

TREK v. hit the trail, beat one's way, hit the dirt, hit the grit, on the road, on the move, on the trail. See also TRAVEL.

TREMBLE v. have the shakes, have the quivers, have the shivers, have the cold shivers, jitter, shake, shiver.

TREMENDOUS adj. humongoid, humongous, humongo, mungo, monstro, honking, big mother, super-colossal, jumbo, blimp, butt-kicking, barn door, whale of a, whopper, whopping. See BIG.

TRENCH n. foxhole, dug in, bughouse (WWI).

TRENCHCOAT n. mack, Fog.

TREND n. 1. the rage, in, in-thing, the latest thing, kick, newest wrinkle, swim. See RAGE. 2. drift, swing.

TREPIDATION n. goose bumps, creeps, cold creeps, cold shivers, jitters, worriment, pucker-assed, asshole-puckerin', asshole suckin' wind. See FEAR. See also AGITATION.

TRESPASS v. 1. mix in, butt in, chisel in, horn in, muscle in, stick one's nose in, poke one's nose in, kibitz, put in one's oar, put one's two cents in, shove in one's oar. 2. crash, crash the gates, penetrate (secret agent).

TRESPASSER n. buttinski, buttinsky, crasher, gate-crasher.

TRIAL n. 1. try, go, fling, fling at, shot, crack, whack, stab, lick, R and D, showcase, tryout, try on, workout, dry run, trial run, shakedown, shakedown cruise, run that by. 2. downer, drag, bitch, headache, tsuris, pain, pain in the ass, pain in the neck, nag, nudge, nudzh, noodge, worriment, worriation, hang-up, rough go, handful, blister, pill, botheration. See also PREDICAMENT.

TRIAL BY JURY, UNDERGO v. go up, go to bat.

TRIBULATION n. bummer, downer, shit, deep shit, tough shit, TS, bad scene, drag, hard time, hard knocks, up against it, nightmare, rain, rainin', rainy day, double whammy, headache, tsuris, they're peeing on us and telling us it's raining, next week East Lynne.

TRICK n. dodge, stunt, bait and switch, the pilgrim drop, handkerchief, switch, bum steer, curveball, dirty pool, dirty trick, taradiddle, diddling, fix, Barney, frame, frame-up, plant, flake (plant false evidence), hookup, put-on, spoof, cross, double-cross, double-X, XX, double banker, double shuffle, fast shuffle, shell game, skin game, fast one, runaround, cutie, smoke, hanky-panky, hocus-pocus, hugger-muggery, double trays, dipsy-doodle, shenanigans, monkeyshines, monkey business, funny business.

TRICK v. rook, screw, shaft, frig, fudge, deke, hose, job, jerk one off, jerk one around, dick, dick one around, fuck one over, shine one on, low-ball, jive, shuck, shuck and jive, goof on, run a game on, snake one in, disinform, sell wolf cookies, fake, fake it, fake one out, flam, flimflam, scam, sandbag, throw a game, play games with, play the nine of hearts, play for a sucker, double-shuffle, double-deal, second-deal, deal from the bottom, shave a deck, set up, hocus, hocus-pocus, slip one over on. See CHEAT.

TRICKED adj. jerked around, foxed, disinformed, been had, mousetrapped, strung along, set up, suckered, sucked in, sold, sold a bill of goods, get played (Af. Am.), bearded, fell for, took the bait, roped in, double-crossed, diddled, shaved, buffaloed, hippoed.

TRICKERY n. con, sting, flimflam, gyp, scam, dodge, stunt, razzle-dazzle, fast shuffle, royal fucking, royal screwing, bait and switch, shell game, skin game, Murphy game, the old army game, hocus-pocus, shenanigans, monkey-shines, monkey business, funny business, limb, shit kicker; tap, tap game (advertising). See TRICK.

TRICKSTER n. card, phony, play actor, shark, sharp, hustler, mechanic, faker, flimflammer, flimflam man, gyp, jip, gyp artist, gypster, con artist, clip artist, burn artist, double-dealer, two-timer, two-faced, smoothie, smooth apple, smooth article, smooth operator, operator, suede-shoe operator, slick operator, diddler, fast talker, slicker.

TRICKY adj. foxy, cagey, crazy like a fox, fancy foot-work, full of fancy footwork, slick, slippery, slyboots, smarts, smooth, street smarts, streetwise, shady, greasy. See also DECEITFUL; SHREWD.

TRIFLE n. squat, diddly-squat, diddly-shit, beans, borscht, fly speck, minimal to the max, from nothing, two-bit, big deal, big fucking deal, BFD, no big shit, no biggie, no great shakes. See NOTHING. See also AMOUNT; SMALL.

TRIFLE v. dilly-dally, monkey, play around, lollygag, jerk off, play games with. See DABBLE. See also DALLY.

TRIFLING adj. pissy-assed, dinky, big zero, big deal, big fucking deal, BFD, no big deal, no biggie, no big thing, no big shit, no count, measly, chickenshit, bupkes, small spuds, forget it, makes no never mind, little go. See UNIMPORTANT.

TRIM adj. 1. in good shape, in fine fettle, slick. 2. neat as a button, neat as a pin, apple pie, apple-pie order, Bonnie Brillo (neat person), slick, all policed up, in good shape, shipshape.

TRIM n. gingerbread, bells and whistles, gewgaws, garbage (food). See ORNAMENT.

TRIM v. 1. doll up, fix up, gussy up, spruce up, pretty up. See ORNAMENT. 2. cut, cut down, cut to the bone, put in a nutshell, boil down, get to the meat, chop, snip, blue-pencil, boil (bottom to top), bake (top to bottom).

TRIMMING n. fuss, gingerbread, gewgaws, bells and whistles, options gadget, jazz, widget. See ORNAMENT.

TRINKETS n. gewgaws, junk jewelry, brass (cheap or fake), stones, rocks, sparklers, ice, Christmas, glass, hardware, pennyweight.

TRIP n. trek, hop, swing, jaunt, cruise, junket, overnight, weekend, Cook's tour. See TRAVEL.

TRIP, GO ON A v. jet, jet in, jet out, sky in, sky out, jet around, knock around, go places, take off, tripping, cruise, hit the road, on the move, hit the trail, trek, do the continent, do Europe (or wherever), junket. See TRAVEL.

TRITE adj. corn, corny, cornball, corn-fed, hokum, hokey, tripe, chestnut, old chestnut, old saw, old song, old story, familiar tune, garden variety, everyday, dime-a-dozen, rum-dum, run-of-the-alley, run-of-the-mill, boiler plate, pulp, slick, bromide, Clyde, old-hat.

TRIUMPH n. KO, slam dunk, win, big win, win all the marbles, do a Rocky, grab the gold, nose out, beat the competish, rake in the pot, bring home the bacon, bull's-eye, slam, grand slam, homer, hole in one, hit, big hit, smash hit, bomb, bombshell, score, sell, sock, socko, sockeroo, boff, boffo, splash, takeover, walkaway, walkover, kill, killing, clean sweep, picnic, laugher (lopsided score), wow, pushover, sitting duck, winning streak, hot run, daily double (series of successes), one-two sweep (win two things at once), sleeper (unexpected), easy digging, pay dirt, howling success, roaring success, gas, gasser, riot, sensation, gold star, feather in one's cap, cinch, lead-pipe cinch, shoo-in, sure thing, sure bet, splashed the Zeros (A.F. WWII).

TRIUMPH v. win out, make a killing, strike it lucky, win hands down, clean sweep, skunk, take it all, schneider, sweep, trounce, beat the game, beat the system, blow out, sink the opposition, win all the marbles, take the cake, get the last dance. See WIN.

TRIUMPHANT adj. lookin' good, set up, luck out (against all odds), on top of the heap. See VICTORIOUS. See also SUCCESSFUL.

TRIVIA n. chickenshit, chicken feed, peanuts, small beer, small change, not count for spit. See also TRIFLE.

TRIVIAL adj. big deal, big fucking deal, BFD, no biggie, no big shit, no great shakes, pissy-assed, dinky, measly, two-bit, tinhorn, chickenfeed, bupkes, makes no never mind, nutmeg, nit-picking, picky-picky, little go, flyspeck. See UNIMPORTANT.

TRIVIALITY n. small potatoes, small beer, small change, small pot, minimal to the max, big deal, no big deal, big shit, no big shit, no biggie, no big thing, no matter; ain't no thang, ain't no thing but a chicken wing (Af. Am.), drop in the bucket, drop in the ocean, no great shakes, flying fuck, mere bagatelle. See also FOOLISHNESS; UNIMPORTANT.

TROLLOP n. hooker, call girl, hustler, ho, working girl, skeezer, model, pro, floozie, chippy, prostie, lot lizard (truckstop parking lot), alley cat, roller (robs drunks), tart, bag, baggage, B-girl, broad, chicken rancher, bawd, jade. See PROSTITUTE.

TROMBONE n. slip horn, slipstick, slush pump, T bone, trom, bone, gas pipe, grunt horn, piston, push pipe, syringe.

TROPHY n. the cookies, feather in one's cap, gold star, the gold, Oscar, blue ribbon.

TROPICAL adj. sticky, steamy, close, sweat box, hotter than blue mud.

TROTSKYITES n. Trots.

TROUBLE n. shit, deep shit, serious jelly, serious shit, bad news, bad scene, clutch, hang-up, jam, in a jam, crisis mode, in crisis mode, in deep doo-doo, in a clutch, in a mess, in a pickle, scrape, in a scrape, in a spot, in a tight spot, in a hot spot, on the hot seat, hot water, in deep water, in heavy water, stew, in a stew, in over one's head, trouble in River City, up a tree, up the creek, up the creek without a paddle, up shit creek, up shit creek without a paddle, drag, bind, double bind, rough go, heavy sledding, rainin', spot, ticklish spot, tricky spot, tight spot, tight squeeze, lose-lose situation, no-win situation, gasser, pisser, rat's nest, snake pit, box, crunch, catch, Catch-22, bitch, handful, headache, bummer, downer, worriment, botheration, grabber, hooker, double trouble, behind the eight ball, boxed in, in a box, in a fix, in a hole, snafu, pain in the ass, pain in the neck, between a rock and a hard place, tail in a gate, tit in a wringer, mix, mess, holy mess, unholy mess, nightmare, kettle of fish, fine kettle of fish, a fine mess you've got us into, how-do-you-do, fine how-do-you-do, it's your funeral, hobble, pickle, pretty pickle, pretty pass, squeeze, sticky wicket, hard row to hoe, hard row of stumps, hard time, hard pull, heat's on, a mountain out of a molehill, heavy load to haul, the devil to pay, hell to pay, bug, glitch, puzzler, can of peas, can of worms, Pandora's box, green hornet (Mil.), honey, hot potato, your court (your problem), stinker, tsuris, tumul, what's with, sixty-four-dollar question, twister, sticker, floorer, stumper, tar baby, bugaboo, crimp, crimp one's style, hump, stinger, hot grease, jackpot, mess up, screw up, need it like a hole in the head, next week East Lynne, rub, push comes to shove, when things get tough, toughie, tough proposition, tough nut to crack, tough going, hard going, joker, scuffle, put on the spot, hit a snag, a holdup, cropper, come a-cropper, one small difficulty.

TROUBLE v. adjy, psych, spook, get to, flip out, craze, bug, bug up, burn up, fire up, make waves, make a scene, make a fuss, fuss, fuzzbuzz, give one a bad time, give one a hard time, make it a tough go, stir up, chap, drive one bananas, drive one up a wall. See DISTURB.

TROUBLED adj. uptight, tightened-up, bugged, choked, clutched, clutched-up, bummed-out, burned-up, hung-up, miffed, peeved, riled, rubbed the wrong way, discombobulated, in crisis mode, in a lather, in a stew, on edge, on pins and needles, on tenterhooks, worried stiff, biting one's nails, beside oneself, put to it, hard put to it, at the end of one's rope. See also ANXIOUS; DISTURBED.

TROUBLE, IN adj. in crisis mode, in the soup, in deep, in deep shit, in deep kim chee, in deep water, in deep doo-doo, in heavy water, in sour, in over one's head, in the barrel, in the center, in a crack, in the middle, in a jackpot, in a swindle, in a heavy place, in Dutch, in a jam, in a scrape, in a mess, in a hole, in a corner, in a box, in a bind, in a fix, in a pickle, in a pretty pickle, in a spot, in a tight spot, toast, fucked, hurting, coming undone, coming unglued, coming unzipped, behind the eight ball, on a one-way street, on the shitlist, on the shit parade, on Queer Street, ass out, got one's ass in a sling, got one's ass in a bind, one's ass is grass, one's ass is new-mown grass, up against it, up the creek, up shit creek, up shit creek without a paddle, messed-up, screwed-up, hung-up, hard-up, jackied-up, jammed-up, all balled up, all bollixed up, fighting to keep one's head up, bust, out on a limb, out of one's depth, out of line, have a case, looks like curtains, sack, satchel, swamped, under the gun, panic is on, panicked-out, squeezed, hit a snag, come a-cropper, at the end of one's rope, scrape the bottom of the barrel, over a barrel, back to the wall, tryin' to stay alive, runnin' out of time, no more cards to play, buried, holding the bag, be a dead pigeon, put one's foot in it, paint oneself in a corner, it's your funeral.

TROUBLE, LOOK(ING) FOR v. fuck with, mess with, kick up a fuss, cruisin' for a bruisin'.

TROUBLEMAKER n. gremlin, gremmie, bag biter, wise guy, smart aleck, punk, smart ass, dog, eel, false alarm, muzzler, one who cries wolf, one who is pea soup, gummio, iceman, mutt, phony, loose cannon, shitheel, snake, weasel. See also AGITATOR.

TROUBLESOME adj. pesky, pestiferous, uphill, up-hill battle, wicked, mean, messy, heavy, hairy, hellish, stanky (Fem.), murder, pisser, burly, pain, pain in the ass, pain in the neck, from hell, rough, uncool, bitch, son of a bitch, son of a gun, stiff, tough, tough one, tough nut to crack, toughie, tough proposition, tough lineup to buck, tough job, rough go, hard job, hard pull, hard row to hoe, hard row of stumps, the hard way, hi-tech, handful, ballbreaker, ballbuster, conk buster, backbreaker, headache, large order, tall order, honey, no picnic, no piece of cake, sticky, sticky wicket, bear, can of worms, heavy sledding, it's your funeral.

TROUNCE v. 1. bash, trash, drub, dog on, flax, wax, punk, jack, lather, lambaste, whip, bust, dust, total, clobber, cream, paste, waste, smack down, shoot down, wipe out, wipe off the map, beat the shit out of one, put one in the hospital, jack one up. 2. bury, blank, skunk, schneider, murder, cook one's goose, blow one's doors off, trim, cap, top, fix one's wagon, swamp, scuttle, skin, shellack, roof fell in (sudden), roll over, tube, blow away, blow out, put away. See DEFEAT.

TROUPER n. ham, hambone, ham-fatter, lead, bit player, star, thesp, straight man, barnstormer, spear carrier, super, talent, walk-on. See ACTOR.

TROUSERS n. slacks, jeans, Levi's, ducks, whites, bells, hip-huggers, kneebusters, dungarees, pegs, pistols (pegged). See PANTS.

TRUANCY n. AWOL, cut, French leave, hookey.

TRUANT n. hookey, no-show, cutting, blitz, bag (Sch.), A.W.O.L., French, French leave, over-the-hill, out, out-of-pocket, out-of-touch.

TRUCK n. rig, wheels, four-by-four, four-by-eight, quarter-ton, eighteen-wheeler, semi, bobtail, Big Mack, oil burner (diesel), dump, box (trailer); draggin' wagon, dragon wagon, hooker (tow truck); but (Army, WWII), pickemup, gypsy, horse, cement mixer (noisy), kidney buster, bucket of bolts, scow, straight job, carry-all, fat load (overweight), beaver trap, bedbug hauler (moving van); freight box, bushel basket (freight); crate of sand (sugar), muck truck (cement), barn yard (cattle), big orange, bottle popper (beverage); branch bank, money bus, loot limo (armored); pig rig (hogs); portable barnyard, rolling ranch, bulldog, bull rack (animals); icebox, cold rig (refrigerator); fun run (empty); portable pipeline, thermos bottle (tank), gas station (tanker), go-devil, honey wagon (beer), mobile forest (logging); portable parking lot, mobile parking lot (auto); roach coach (catering and garbage), garbage truck (catering); salt shaker, sand blaster (salt); scrub brush (street cleaner). See also AUTOMOBILE.

TRUCK DRIVER n. trucker, teamster, hack hand, jeep jockey, spinner, skinner, boll weevil (inexperienced), bottle cap (tank), dump chump (dump), fat daddy, pop top (beverage), road runner, bird-dogger (unlicensed tow truck driver), truppie (family lives behind cab), gypsy, hair pounder (1925).

TRUCK STOP n. bookstore, chuck wagon, cook shack, water hole.

TRUCK TRACTOR n. bobtail (without semi-trailer), widow maker (double-trailered), horse.

TRUCULENT adj. ornery, scrappy, snorky, bitchy, turbobitch, cussed, salty, spiky, mean, cantankerous, fire-eater, have it in for, at loggerheads, trigger-happy. See BELLIGERENT.

TRUDGE v. plug along, schlep. See also WALK.

TRUE adj. 1. hold up, stand up, absolute, go, hold water, hold together, stick together, hold up in the wash, wash, fly, no buts about it, no ifs ands or buts. See also CORRECT. 2. true blue, true believer, dyed-in-the-wool, faithful but not blind. 3. for real, it, the real McCoy, real stuff, genuine article, real goods, in the flesh, honest-to-God, kosher, legit, on the level, on the up-and-up, twenty-four-carat. See SINCERE. 4. up front, right up front, straight, on the up-and-up, no lie, what you see is what you get, honest Injun, square John, square shooter, boy scout, Mr. Clean. See TRUSTWORTHY.

TRULY adv. indeedy, yes indeedy, amen, sure, why sure, sure thing, fer sure, you better believe it, no buts about it, on the money, on the nose, for real, really truly, cross my heart, cross my heart and hope to die, if I'm lyin' I'm flyin' (Af. Am), I'm not shittin' you, so help me. See ABSOLUTELY.

TRUMPET n. iron horn, horn, piston, plumber, plumbing, quail, screamer, squeeze horn.

TRUMPET PLAYER n. Gabriel, lip-splitter.

TRUNK n. keister.

TRUNKS n. baggies, jammies, clamdiggers, knee-busters (swimming); skivvies, boxers, shorts, jockey, jockeys (underwear). See also PANTS.

TRUST n. 1. gospel truth, stock, store. 2. megacorp, multinational, bunch, crew, crowd, gang, mob, plunderbund, outfit, ring.

TRUST v. bank on, bet on, bet one's bottom dollar on, gamble on, lay money on, string along with. See BELIEVE.

TRUSTFUL adj. believer, sucker, swallow anything, patsy, mark, easy, easy mark, wide-eyed, blue-eyed, yold. See GULLIBLE.

TRUSTWORTHY adj. 1. minding the store, on the hook, carry the load, on one's back. 2. there, count on one, one who always delivers, one who always comes through, always there in a pinch, surefire, all right, all-right guy, right guy, boy scout, down-home, up-front, right up front, on the up-and-up, on the level, Christian, fly right, Mr. Clean, spiffy, open, real people, saint, rock, Rock of Gibraltar, straight, straight-arrow, true-blue, oncer, kosher, third-rail, square John, square shooter, gimper (A.F.). See also SINCERE.

TRUTH n. dope, scoop, score, picture, whole story, low-down, brass tacks, meat and potatoes, name of the game, hangout route, nitty-gritty, point, stuff, nub, bottom line, the numbers, nuts and bolts, down-to-earth, the real world, the real deal (Af. Am.), for real, no shit, straight shit, straight stuff, straight up Babylon, that's word, word up (Af. Am), straight of it, straight goods, the goods, the case, scene, size of it, how it is, how things are, the way of it, what's what, where it's at, what it is, tell it like it is, nature of the beast, live, in the flesh, the real emess, the real McCoy, skinny, from the horse's mouth, that's a fact Jack, cross my heart and hope to die, if I'm lyin' I'm flyin' (Af. Am.), the goods, honest-to-God truth, God's truth, bible, the word, gospel, hold turkey, you ain't just whistling Dixie.

TRUTHFUL adj. on the up-and-up, on the level, like it is, call it like it is, honest Injun, raw (Af. Am.), square, square shooter, true-blue, righteous, Christian, kosher, boy scout, legit, straight, call a spade a spade, white, damn white, put all one's cards on the table, talk turkey. See SINCERE.

TRUTHFULLY adv. flat out, level, on the level, on the dead level, on the up and up, spring with the legit, spill the works, come out with it, straight, no foolin', say a mouthful (you said a mouthful), cross my heart, cross my heart and hope to die, if I'm lyin' I'm flyin' (Af. Am.), I'm not shittin' you, indeedy, no buts about it, really truly, so help me.

TRUTH, TELL THE v. level, level with, dead level, on the level, go the hangout route, blow soul, fack (Af. Am.), guts, play it straight.

TRY n. all one's got, crack, go, jelly go, one's all, one's damnedest, one's darnedest, one's best shot, shot, stab, try, whack. See ATTEMPT.

TRY v. make a run at, tackle, take on, make a try, cut and try, try on for size, in it to win it (Af. Am.), bust one's ass, break one's neck, give it all one's got, try one's damnedest, try one's darnedest, give it the old college try, try on for size, give it a try, bend over backward, go for it, go for broke, shoot the works. See ATTEMPT.

TRYST n. 1. date, heavy date, rendezvous, meet, zero hour, creep, triff, treff (secret). 2. love nest, spot, matinee, noonie, one-night stand, quickie. See RENDEZVOUS.

TRYSTING PLACE n. love nest, place, spot, your place or mine.

TUBA n. grunt box, grunt horn, grunt iron, oompah.

TUBERCULOSIS n. TB, con, galloping consumption, lunger (patient).

TUBING n. macaroni.

TUGBOAT n. tug, cider barrel (oceangoing).

TUINAL n. Christmas trees, double-trouble, rainbows, tooies, tuie, reds, blues, T.

TULSA, OKLAHOMA Oil City.

TUMBLE n. header, spill, nose dive, pratfall, belly buster, belly flop, belly whopper.

TUMBLE v. take a header, spill, nose-dive, lose it, do a pratfall, land on one's ass, go ass over teakettle, tip over, belly up, fall down and go boom, come a-cropper, take a belly whopper, hit the dirt.

TUMULT n. to-do, flap, fuss, row, stir, stink, big stink, rhubarb, rowdydow, rumble, rumpus, ruckus, ruction, jihad, commo, hell broke, loose, all hell broke loose, scene, big scene. See TURMOIL.

TUNE UP v. lick one's chops (music).

TUNNEL n. hole in the wall, Chunnel (under the English Channel).

TURBULENCE n. dirty air, bumps, bumpy, air pockets.

TURK n. Abdul, Arab, infidel (Derog.).

TURKEY n. buzzard, gobbler, turk.

TURMOIL n. 1. mix-up, topsy-turvy, every which way, galley west, hectic, discombobulation, flusteration, flustration. See CONFUSION. 2. flap, fuss, to-do, row, stir, stink, big stink, rhubard, rowdy-dow, rumble, rumpus, ruckus, ruction, shindy, shivaree, commo, dust-up, foofooraw, free-for-all, jihad, brawl, all hell broke loose, kick-up, wing-ding, raise Cain, raise sand, roughhouse, fuzz-buzz, haroosh, big scene, storm, blast, blow-up, flare-up, tear. 3. circus, fire-works, mess, razzle-dazzle.

TURN n. one's move, one's say, go, go-around, whack, bit, routine, shtick, act. See OPPORTUNITY.

TURN v. cut, hang a right, hang a ralph, hang a left, hang a louie, hang a huey, swivel, make a right, make a left.

TURNABOUT n. about-face, switcheroo, flip-flop.

TURNCOAT n. rat, rat fink, double-crosser, Benedict Arnold, fifth columnist, quisling, snake, snake in the grass. See also INFORMER.

TUSSLE n. brush, rumble, roughhouse, donnybrook, flap, gin, hassle, mix-up, go, row, rumpus, ruckus, shindy, set-to, scrap, wrangle. See FIGHT.

TUTOR n. baby-sitter, grind, guru, prof, slavedriver, snap, teach.

TUTOR v. put hip, put hep, let in on the know, let next to, put through the grind, put through the mill, update, ready, lick into shape, clue one in, lay it out for, drum, drum into. See INSTRUCT.

TUXEDO n. monkey suit, tux, black tie, clothes, monkey clothes, smoking, bib and tucker, soup and fish.

TV n. video, tube, idiot box, boob tube, big eye, baby-sitter, telly, telley.

TWEAK n. yank, yerk.

TWELVE n. boxcars, box cars (dice), twelvemo, 12mo.

TWENTY-FIRST CENTURY n. the ohs, the oughts, the zeros (first decade), the twenty hundreds.

TWENTY-FOUR n. twenty-fourmo, 24mo.

TWIN n. pod.

TWIST n. yank, yerk.

TWISTED adj. cockeyed.

TWIT v. jive, needle, rag, razz, rib, jolly, josh, ride, put on, make sport of, yank one's crank, pull one's leg. See RIDICULE.

TWITCH n. yank, yerk.

TWO n. deuce, doubleheader, double, double in brass, a couple, a pair, a team, a brace, twosome, duo.

TWOFOLD adj. twin, wear two hats, doubleheader (successful two ways), double in brass (two kinds of work), rule of twice, twofers.

TWOSOME n. duo, item, deuce it, couple, gruesome twosome, team, pair off, spic and span (Puerto Rican and Af. Am., Derog.).

TYLENOL n. four-doors, fours and doors (with codeine).

TYPE n. likes, likes of, lot, number.

TYPE v. tab, peg, button down, pigeonhole, put away, put down as, put down for, typecast.

TYPEWRITE v. hunt 'n' peck, touch, bat out, beat out.

TYPEWRITER n. chatterbox, desk piano, office piano.

TYPICAL adj. just like one, nature of the beast, that's one all over.

TYPIST n. steno, woodpecker.

TYPOGRAPHICAL ERROR n. typo, PE.

TYRANNIZE v. rule the roost, keep under one's thumb, throw one's weight around, bring to heel, bulldoze, henpeck, pussy-whip (Fem.), crack the whip, wear the pants. See DOMINEER.

TYRANT n. a Hitler, Simon Legree, slavedriver, czar.

TYRO n. newie, greeny, freshie, turkey, punk, rook, rookie, boot, new blood, new kid on the block, fish, greenhorn, tenderfoot, jice, first of May. See NOVICE.

U

U n. Uniform, Uncle.

UBIQUITOUS adj. wall-to-wall.

U-BOAT n. navy shark, pig boat, tin can, tin fish, tin shack.

UGLY adj. pig, dog, dogface, airedale, bowser, bowwow, mud puppy, animal; limburger (girl no one will date), dag, beast, beat, bat, boo hog, bama, barfola, chopped, crushed, wacked, buckled, paper-bag case; bagger, one-bagger, two-bagger, double-bagger, triple-bagger (all Fem.); grody, gross, plug, plug-ugly, butt ugly, buttly, scugly (Af. Am.), scag, coyote ugly, fugly, piss-ugly; hurt, hurting (very); troll, bushbitch, bush pig, skank, stanky, slag (slutty), hein, heinous, hellpig (fat girl), eddie, zarf (M.), gizzly, misty, ugly as sin, grimbo, hagged-out, hard on the eyes, fartface, bad head, beaujeeful, a face only a mother could love, face would crack a mirror, face would stop a clock, prune-face, homely as a mud fence, mud duck (girl), chromo, short on looks, schacks, boogie bear, from hunger, awful, grungy, death warmed over, gruesome twosome.

UKRAINIAN n. Galician, Galitizianer.

UKULELE n. uke, tipple.

ULTIMATE adj. the most, the mostest, max, maxi, bottom line, the end, drop dead ——— (anything), the livin' end, ass end, bitter end, tail ass (A.F.), curtains, curtains for, final curtain, blow off, capper, critical mass, payoff, last hurrah, swan song, far out, radical (not Pol.), nose cone, go over the mountain, shoot one's wad, the chips are down.

ULTRA adj. ultra-ultra, too-too, too much, all out, gone, glorkish, out-of-bounds, out-of-all-bounds, cosmic, out of this world, radical (not Pol.). See EXTREME. See also RADICAL.

ULTRANATIONALIST n. flag-waver, hundred percenter, hard hat, jingoist, patrioteer, superpatriot, wraps oneself in the flag. See also CONSERVATIVE.

UMBRELLA n. bumbershoot, mush, shower stick.

UMBRELLA THIEF n. mush faker.

UNABLE adj. uncool, not cut out for, can't hack it, can't cut it, can't cut the mustard, can't make the grade, can't fade that, sidelined, out of commission, no can do, hog-tied. See INCOMPETENT. See also INADEQUATE.

UNACCEPTABLE adj. not up to scratch, not up to snuff, doesn't hack it, won't do, half-assed, half-baked, lemon, seconds, crappy, drek, lousy, Mickey Mouse, piss-poor, rat-fuck, shlocky, sleazy, slimpsy, below the mark, beyond the pale, damaged goods, a reject, a clinker, God forbid, heaven forbid it, no way, by no means, not on your life, take it away, perish the thought, I'll be hanged if. See INADEQUATE.

UNACCOMPANIED adj. loner, lone wolf, doe, shag, stag, solo, onliest, Herman the hermit, Crusoe, Robinson Crusoe, traveling light. See ALONE.

UNADORNED adj. bare-bones, clean, vanilla, whitebread, what you see is what you get, folksy, homey, haimish, open-and-shut, no-frills, meat-and-potatoes. See PLAIN.

UNADULTERATED adj. neat, straight, uncut, right out of the bottle, legit, on the legit, honest-to-God, Christian, kosher, the emess, righteous, straight dope, straight from the horse's mouth, sure enough, too good to be true, twenty-four-carat, all wool and a yard wide, blowed-in-the-glass, clean. See also PLAIN.

UNAFFECTED adj. 1. on the natch, go organic. 2. folksy, homey, up front, laid back, no sweat, don't sweat it, cas, cazh, cool, cool cat. See NATURAL. See also CASUAL. 3. thick-skinned, hard-boiled, hardhearted, not to worry, I should worry, cold fish. See CALLOUS.

UNAFRAID adj. gritty, gutsy, game, gutty, spunky, nervy, stand tall, tough it out, I'm shakin' (sarcastic, response to threat), bigger'n life, fire-eater, hairy, cool hand. See FEARLESS.

UNALTERABLE adj. set in concrete, hard-nosed, tough nut, tough nut to crack, locked-in, take no prisoners, head in concrete, burly, solid as a rock, rock-ribbed, brick wall, bullheaded, pigheaded, stubborn as a mule, set, dead set on. See STUBBORN.

UNAMBIGUOUS adj. dead sure, dead to rights, for sure, fer shirr, for damn sure, for a fact Jack, posolutely, no buts about it, checked and double-checked, and no mistake, know damm well. See CERTAIN.

UNANTICIPATED adj. from out in left field, from out of the blue, bolt from the blue, sleeper, payoff.

UNAPPETIZING adj. grody to the max, gross, pukey, pukoid, yucky, icky, yicky, barfy, stinky, hocky, hooky, gooky. See UNSAVORY.

UNARMED adj. skinned, clean. See also DEFENSELESS.

UNASSAILABLE adj. bulletproof, covered.

UNATTACHED adj. loner, traveling light, solo, on one's own, paddling one's own canoe, batching it, stag, free-wheeling.

UNATTAINABLE adj. no-go, it won't fly, don't have the horses, not a prayer, not a Chinaman's chance, not a chance in hell, nonstarter, beating a dead horse, out of pocket, no got.

UNATTENDED adj. stag, solo, by one's lonesome, on one's own.

UNATTRACTIVE adj. gross, grody, grody to the max, grimbo, grimbibble, roachy, earth pig, pig, dog, bow-wow, beast, beat, limburger (girl no one will date), bat, boo-hog, bama, barfola; paper bag case, double bagger, triple bagger (all Fem.) cold biscuit, gizzly, hiddy, sad sack, scag, witch, flat-tire, no bargain, weird, yucky, icky, yicky, icky, wonky. See UGLY.

UNAUTHENTIC adj. phony, queer, fake, ersatz, bogus, pirate goods, pirate labels, plastic, not what it's cracked up to be. See COUNTERFEIT.

UNAUTHORIZED adj. under-the-counter, under-the-table, pirated, bite, no-no, crooked, off-base, out-of-line, out-of-bounds, over-the-line, racket, shady, dirty, wildcat.

UNAVAILABLE adj. out of pocket, eighty-six, 86, pie in the sky, no-got, ungettable.

UNAVAILING adj. 1. going nowhere, goin' round in circles, can't win for losin', go fight City Hall, save one's breath, not a prayer, not a snowball's chance in hell. 2. good-for-nothing, out of luck, out to lunch, neverwuz, total shuck, shooting blanks, not work, not come off, out of it, missed the boat, a day late and a dollar short, can't even get arrested, can't even write home for money, can't punch his way out of a paper, should have stood in bed. See USELESS.

UNAVOIDABLE adj. open-and-shut, sure as fate, sure as God made little green apples, sure as I live and breathe, all locked up, set, come hell or high water, and no mistake. See CERTAIN.

UNAWARE adj. 1. loxed-out, veged-out, gorked, stoned, zonked, zonked-out, zoned-out, z-head, spacey, spaced-out, out of it, out to lunch, strung out, out cold, out like a light, on the nod, doped, mooning, moony, pipe dreaming, daydreaming, woolgathering, not all there, not with it, dead, dead to the world. 2. unhep, unhip, in the fog, blind as a bat, doesn't know from nothing, D.K., doesn't have both oars in the water, wouldn't know it if it bit him in the ass, hasn't checked in, clueless, hasn't a clue, hasn't the foggiest, not know the score, not know the time of day, not know shit from Shinola. See IGNORANT.

UNBALANCED adj. kooky, flaky, wacky, head-case, unglued, unzipped, unscrewed, have a screw loose, have a lug nut loose, loose in the bean, loose in the upper story, nobody home, light's on but nobody's home, one sandwich short of a picnic, belt does not go through all the loops, doesn't have both oars in the water, out to lunch, cockeyed, cockamamie, freaky, off one's head, off one's trolley, missing a few marbles, touched in the head, leak in the think tank, not all there. See CRAZY.

UNBEARABLE adj. too much, a bit much, heavy-handed, the last straw, the straw that broke the camel's back, that's it, that blows it, enough already.

UNBELIEVABLE adj. phony, rings phony, thick, thin, reachy, bogus, won't wash, won't hold water, fishy, for the birds, full of holes, for real, pure bullshit, BS, blow it out your ear, lip gloss, too much, cockamamie, cockeyed, topsy-turvy, screw-loose, jerky, nerky, batty, squirrely, hare-brained, scatterbrained, rattlebrained, lamebrained, fuckbrained, birdbrained, dingy, flaky, freaky, wacky, kooky, dippy, bubbleheaded, foolheaded, goofus, gump, horse's ass, horse's collar, horse's neck, horse's tail, sap, sappy, screwy, off-the-wall, far-out, takes the cake, beats the Dutch, not on a stack of bibles.

UNBENDING adj. stand pat, stand by one's guns, stand one's ground, hold one's ground, hold the fort, hold the line, brick wall, stick to one's guns, dig in one's heels, take no prisoners, set in concrete, do or die, come hell or high water, hard as nails, hard nut to crack, locked-in. See STUBBORN.

UNBIASED adj. 1. straight, call 'em as one sees 'em, even-steven, level playing field. 2. color-blind, cold, cold turkey, the emess, on the fence, mugwumpian, mugwump-ish.

UNBURDEN v. own up, fess, fess up, out with it, get it off one's chest, let it all hang out, let one's hair down. See CONFESS.

UNBUTTON v. unslough, strip.

UNCANNY adj. spooky, spookish, scary.

UNCARING adj. thick-skinned, cold fish, cool cat, could care less, hard-boiled, hard as nails, dead-ass, don't give shit, just going through the motions, I should worry? See INDIFFERENT.

UNCEREMONIOUS adj. folksy, down-home, laid-back, easygoing, off-the-cuff, improv. See CASUAL. See also OFFHAND.

UNCERTAIN adj. 1. chancy, iffy, up for grabs, doubting Thomas, touchy, touch-and-go, on slippery ground, on ice, on thin ice, hanging by a thread. See also DANGEROUS. 2. wishy-washy, leery, pussyfoot around, run hot and cold, blow hot and cold, straddle, fence, shilly-shally, the jury's out. See DOUBTFUL.

UNCHALLENGING adj. snap, no sweat, no problem, no biggie, no brainer, nothing to it, like nothin', pushover, picnic, cinchy, easy as pie, duck soup, cake, cakewalk, sleepwalk, walk, walkover, piece of cake, breeze, slam-dunk, walkover, win in a walk, win hands down, kid stuff, child's play, lead-pipe cinch, clear sailing, free ride. See EASY.

UNCHECKED adj. runaway, wide open, loose, on the loose, let loose, cut loose, all out, funky, jag (laughing jag, crying jag), go to town. See also FREE; UNCONTROLLED.

UNCIRCUMCISED adj. blind, uncut.

UNCIRCUMSCRIBED adj. straight out, straight from the shoulder, no catch, no joker, no ifs ands or buts. See UNCONDITIONAL.

UNCIVIL adj. flip, fresh, nervy, cheeky, sassy, snippy, short, smart, smart-alecky, lippy, cocky, crusty, base, out-of-line, off-base. See INSOLENT.

UNCIVILIZED adj. 1. bad-ass, wild-ass, kill-crazy, hog-crazy. 2. boondocks, boonies, sticks, stix, B.F.E., butt-fucking Egypt, B.F.A., butt-fucking Africa, Wild West (anywhere west of N.Y.C.).

UNCLE n. unc, unk, uncs, unks, nuncle, nunks, nunky.

UNCLEAN adj. grungy, pig-pen, pig-sty, barn, stable, stall, scuzzy, skank, mucky. See DIRTY.

UNCLEAR adj. clouded, fuzzy, spacey. See OBSCURE.

UNCLOTHE v. peel, strip, strip to the buff, do a strip, do a striptease, get all naked, take it off, husk, shuck.

UNCLOTHED adj. bare-assed, B.A., peeled, naked as a jaybird, in one's birthday suit, in the altogether, buff, buffo, in the buff, in the raw, au naturel, skinny, wear a smile. See NUDE.

UNCOMMITTED adj. 1. cop out, don't care one way or another, don't give a shit, it's all the same to me, middle ground, middle-of-the-road, on the fence, fence-sitter, mugwumpian, mugwumpish. See NEUTRAL. 2. free-wheeling, free-spirited, on one's own, flake, break loose, cut loose, loose wig, nonstarter. See FREE.

UNCOMMON adj. 1. offbeat, kinky, kooky, funky, freaky, off-the-wall, far-out, way-out, out-of-sight, wild, radical (not Pol.), screwball. See also NEW. 2. scarcer than hen's teeth, numerous as chicken lips. See STRANGE.

UNCOMMUNICATIVE adj. hush-hush, tight-lipped, close-mouthed, tight chops, clammed-up, dried-up, dummied-up, buttoned-up, garbo, on the q.t., between one and the lamppost.

UNCOMPASSIONATE adj. cutthroat, go for the jugular, killer instinct, mean machine, dog-eat-dog, hatchet job, take no prisoners. See also UNSYMPATHETIC.

UNCOMPREHENDING adj. nerdy, in the dark, out to lunch, out of it, blind as a bat, doesn't know one's ass from a hole in the ground, search me, hasn't the foggiest, hasn't a clue, in the fog, doesn't have both oars in the water, hasn't checked in, clueless, lame, duck, lop, lophead, not know the score, not getting it, not be with it. See IGNORANT.

UNCOMPROMISING adj. hard-line, hard-core, locked, locked-in, set in concrete, chiseled in stone, take no prisoners, rock-ribbed, brick wall, dig in one's heels, stick to one's guns, hold the line, stand by one's guns, pigheaded, stubborn as a mule, stiff-necked. See STUBBORN.

UNCONCERNED adj. hard-boiled, hardhearted, hard as nails, could care less, don't give shit, don't give a hoot, it's all the same to me, that's your lookout, that's your pigeon. See INDIFFERENT.

UNCONDITIONAL adj. all-out, flat-out, open, wide open, flat-ass, straight-out, straight from the shoulder, what you see is what you get, no strings, no strings attached, no holds barred, no catch, no joker, no kicker, no joker in the deck, no ifs ands or buts, no buts about it, no small print, no fine print, no small fine print, no fine print at the bottom, downright.

UNCONNECTED adj. free-wheeling, on one's own, paddle one's own canoe, indie (film).

UNCONSCIOUS adj. out, gone, gone under, blacked-out, loxed-out, veged-out, wiped-out, gorked, stoned, zonked, zonked-out, spacey, spaced-out, out of it, out to lunch, strung out, bombed-out, out cold, out like a light, put away, on the canvas, knocked for a loop, hearing birdies, coo-coo, cooked, in a gauze, cold-cocked, flattened, feeling no pain, passed-out, passed out cold, on the nod, doped, mooning, moony, pipe-dreaming, daydreaming, woolgathering, not all there, not with it, dead, dead to the world, D.O.A., cockeyed, blotto, auger in, crump, crimped out (from drinking).

UNCONTROLLABLE adj. loose cannon, having a spaz attack, bull-goose loony, freaked, freaked-out. See also EXCITED.

UNCONTROLLED adj. apeshit, go ape, hemorrhage, jerked about, off the wall, bull-goose loony, on a tear, kicking up a row, burn one's candle at both ends, out of order. See UNRESTRAINED.

UNCONVENTIONAL adj. funky, freaky, kooky, beat, beatnik, offbeat, off the beaten track, radical dude, dudical, weirdo, weirdie, oddball, bogus, avant-garde, fringy, kinky, hippy, far-out, way-out, wild, crazy, off-the-wall, out-in-left-field, granola, crunchy-chewy. See ECCENTRIC.

UNCONVINCING adj. fishy, cut no ice, thin, thick, iffy. See also DOUBTFUL.

UNCOORDINATED adj. clunky, klutzy, flub-dub, all thumbs, butterfingers, ham-fisted, two left hands, two left feet, a newt, clodhopper, galoot. See CLUMSY.

UNCOUNTABLE adj. oodles, oodles and oodles, lots, zillion, jillion, bazillion, umpteen. See COUNTLESS.

UNCOUTH adj. cheap, loud, loud-mouthed, raw, skank, tacky, raunchy.

UNCOVER v. 1. hit upon, spark, strike (oil, gold), see the light, stumble on, spotlight, limelight. 2. dig up, let the cat out of the bag, crack, break, leak, giveaway, give the show away, drop a bomb, spill the beans, tip one's hand, let it all hang out, bring it out into the daylight, bring it out into the open, open up, blow one's cover, blow the lid off, blow the whistle, mooning (buttocks), streak. See EXPOSE.

3. catch flatfooted, catch red-handed, catch with one's pants down, catch with one's hand in the cookie jar. See DISCOVER. See also CAUGHT IN THE ACT.

UNCOVERED adj. 1. bare-assed, buck naked, naked as a jaybird, in one's birthday suit, in the altogether, in the raw, without a stitch on, au naturel. See NUDE. 2. ass out, neck stuck out, wide-open, sitting duck. See also CAUGHT.

UNCTUOUS adj. 1. greasy, plummy, smarmy. 2. slick, silky, gift of gab, great talker, smooth, smoothie, smooth apple, smooth operator, smooth article, waxer. See also HYPOCRITICAL, SANCTIMONIOUS.

UNDAUNTED adj. spunky, fire-eater, iceman, ice in one's veins, come on strong, got the faith baby. See FEARLESS.

UNDECIDED adj. iffy, fence straddle, fence hanger, on the fence, sit on the fence, run hot and cold, blow hot and cold, hedge, hedge off, shilly-shally, wimpy, wishy-washy, waffle, waffling, hem and haw, pussyfoot, pussyfoot around, betwixt and between, hanging fire, stuck, the jury's out, up for grabs, up in the air, between sixes and sevens, dippydro.

UNDEMONSTRATIVE adj. cool, cool customer, cold fish, ice in one's veins, icicle.

UNDENIABLE adj. absofuckinglutely, posolutely, absitively, sure thing, for a fact, on ice, have down cold, no buts about it. See CERTAIN.

UNDEPENDABLE adj. 1. fly-by-night, wrong number, loose, no-good, N.G., no account, no bargain, trust one as far as one can swing a cat, trust one as far as one can throw an elephant. See DISHONEST. 2. honest John, rat, fink, rat-fink, stool pigeon, stoolie, shitheel, shit hook, worm, tinhorn, bum, clown, convict. See also DANGEROUS.

UNDERACT v. throw away.

UNDERCAPITALIZED adj. on a shoe string, hand-to-mouth operation.

UNDER CONSIDERATION adv. on the table, on the line, in the works, on the boards, on the fire, jury is out.

UNDERCOVER adj. under wraps, creep (mission), tref, triff, hush-hush, doggo, incog, q.t., on the q.t., on the quiet, in a hole-and-corner way, in holes and corners, wildcat, skunk works (secret manufacturing plant or laboratory). See also SECRET.

UNDERGARMENTS n. undies, underthings, unmentionables, bra, briefs, bikinis, panties, bodystocking, teddy, woolies, shorts, jockey shorts, jockeys. See UNDERWEAR.

UNDERGRADUATE n. undergrad.

UNDERGROUND adj. on the q.t., on the quiet, in a hole-and-corner way, in holes and corners, on the sly, undercover, under wraps, hush-hush, strictly hush-hush. See also SECRET.

UNDERHANDED adj. 1. shady, double-crossing, snake in the grass, two-faced, two-timing, dirty-dealing, dirty pool, slippery. 2. undercover, under wraps, hush-hush, strictly hush-hush, on the q.t., on the quiet, on the sly, in a hole-and-corner way, in holes and corners, wildcat. See DECEITFUL. See also SECRET.

UNDERLING n. peon, serf, slave, girl Friday, gofer, dweeb, yes-man, stooge, running dog, low man on the totem pole, second fiddle, second string, third string, flunky, spear carrier, second banana. See INFERIOR.

UNDERLYING adj. bottom-line, nitty-gritty, where it's at, name, name of the game, cold, cold turkey, nub, meat-and-potatoes, coal-and-ice. See BASIC.

UNDERMINE v. blow sky high, knock the bottom out of, knock the chocks out from under, knock the props out from under, poke full of holes, shoot full of holes, clip one's wings, soften up, sandbag, torpedo (a plan), toss in a monkey wrench. See also SABOTAGE.

UNDERPLAY v. downplay, play down, gloss over, soft-pedal, throwaway, cover up, lay back, play it cool, make light of, take it lightly, take it like water off a duck's back, not bat an eye, not blink an eye, just stand there with a mouth full of teeth.

UNDERPRICED adj. dirt cheap, cheap as dirt, dog cheap, cheapie, el cheapo, steal, a real steal, buy, a real buy, low-cost, cost nothing, cost next to nothing, more bang for the buck, bought for a song, cut-rate, low-tariff, price is right.

UNDERPRIVILEGED adj. truly needy, hard-up, disadvantaged, deprived, underdeveloped (nation or district), oofless, down-and-out, have-nots, in dire straits, in Queer Street, seen better days, bag lady, piss-poor, dirt-poor, poor as a church mouse, cold in hand (Af. Am.), for the yoke. See also DESTITUTE.

UNDERREACT v. lay back, play it cool, make light of, take it lightly, not bat an eye, just stand there with a mouth full of teeth. See UNDERPLAY.

UNDERSIZED adj. mini, minny, teeny, teeny-weeny, bitty, bitsy, shrimpy, wee, peewee, runty, small fry, measly, piddling, pint-sized, half-pint. See SMALL.

UNDERSTAND v. get, get it, grok, gotcha, get the idea, get the point, get the picture, get a handle on it, get the hang of it, get next to, get next to oneself, get jerry, get through one's head, get through one's thick head, get into, get into one's head, get it into one's thick skull, hive (West Point), get across, get over, get it down, have down cold, have down pat, get down pat, get down cold, get the hang of, get the message, get the drift, catch the drift, catch, catch on, flash, flash on, latch on, latch on to something, get hold of, pick up, pick up on, wise up, wise up to, blow wise, get wise to, hep to, hep up, hip up, soak up, get hep, get hip, get hip to the lay, be hip to, follow, track, feature, cop, collar, collar the jive, colly (Af. Am.), compy, wake up and smell the coffee, take, take in, tumble, tumble to, quick on the draw, quick on the uptake, savvy, capeesh, fershtay, can you relate (Af. Am.), dig, I dig you, make, pin, copy, read, I read you, read someone loud and clear, hear, hear it, I hear you, I hear you talkin', I know where you're coming from, see the light, see daylight, are one's boots laced?, have one's boots laced, peg, peg a set up, figure out, be with it, be with one, be on the beam, right on, right-o, give one some slack, rumble, know what's what, know one's ass from one's elbow, know a rock from a hard place, know crossways from crosswise, have dead to rights, have one's number.

UNDERSTANDABLE adj. clear as the nose on one's face, plain as the nose on one's face, open-and-shut. See APPARENT.

UNDERSTANDING adj. tuned-in, cool, down, simpatico, on the same beam, on the same wavelength, chilly, grokking, have a heart.

UNDERSTANDING n. 1. aha reaction, savvy, hep to, wise to, see the light, flash on it, get one's drift, I got it, it hit me, it just come to me, double-take, slow take, take, take it big, get it through one's thick skull. 2. handshake, deal, dicker. See AGREEMENT.

UNDERSTATE v. throw away.

UNDERSTATED adj. low-profile, soft-pedaled, glossed over.

UNDERSTOOD adj. roger, roger-dodger, grokked, gotcha, got, got it, got the picture, hep to, on to, pat, down pat, wise to, pegged, dug, clicked, know where one is coming from, picked up on, dawned on one, light dawned.

UNDERSTUDY n. backup, backup man, pinch hitter, stand-in, sub. See also SUBSTITUTE.

UNDERSTUDY v. back up, pinch-hit for, stand in for, sub, take over for, fill in for. See also SUBSTITUTE.

UNDERTAKE v. tackle, take on, make a run at, give it a try, give it a go, give it a whirl, take a shot at, have a go at, go in for, go for broke. See ATTEMPT.

UNDERTAKEN adj. in the hopper, in the pipeline, in the works, taken-on.

UNDERTAKER n. body snatcher, crepe hanger, black coat, Digger O'Dell.

UNDERTAKING n. 1. go, jelly go, crack, fling, shot, stab, try, whack, header. See ATTEMPT. 2. proposition, deal, racket, thing, grift, play, beeswax, job, what one is into, biz, gesheft, outfit, setup, shop, turnkey operation, carrying on, goings-on, hap, happening. See also ENTERPRISE.

UNDERWEAR n. undies, underthings, unmentionables, bra, briefs, bikinis, panties, bodystocking, teddy, stepins, drawers, BVD's, beeveedees, woolies, skivvies, shorts, jockey shorts, jockeys, big eighths (Af. Am.); longies, John-L's, long-handle underwear, long Johns, long ones (long).

UNDERWEIGHT adj. skinny, skeleton, shadow, bag of bones, stack of bones, rattlebones, gangly. See THIN.

UNDERWORLD n. the rackets, the mob, the syndicate, Mafia, Cosa Nostra, Black Hand, blaht, blot. See also HELL.

UNDERWRITE v. stake, angel, bankroll, grubstake, bank, back, greenback. See FINANCE.

UNDESIRABLE adj. 1. rotted, rottissimo (very bad), Rotterdam, it rots, fat city, motherfucking, mother-grabbing, nowhere, sucks, sux, sucky, it sucks, gagger, poxy, pail, bucket, grody, grody to the max, gross, grossed-out, uncool, rotten, beastly, sleazy, yucky, icky, yicky, hairy, bitchy, wanker, goonk, bummer, bum trip, bad news, bad scene, Velveeta, Captain Cheddar, Cap'n Chedda, godawful, goshawful, left-handed, eighteen-carat, murder, nuts, poison, rough, sad, fierce, something fierce, hard time, lousy, who needs it, need it like a hole in the head, this I need yet?, from hunger, for the birds, NIMBY (not in my back yard), NIMTOO (not in my term of office), NIMEY (not in my election year), excess baggage, drug on the market. 2. blackballed, cold-shouldered, left out in the cold, not in the picture, baldhead, shut-out.

UNDESIRABLE PERSON n. asshole, assface, asswipe creep, penis wrinkle, gagger, mutant, dorf, dork, megadork, megabitch, barf bag, rat, wanker, wrongo, drip, stinker, stinkpot, shit, shithead, sleaze, sleazeball, sludgeball, slime bucket, cocksucker, elrod, scoob, goob, goober, goobatron, yernt, cheesehead, cheeseface, Captain Cheddar, nothingburger, bunk, maggot, turkey, jerk, fink, gross, scrub, scurvy, scuzzo, scuzzy, shitsky, shitburger, shower scum, dag, loser, louse, lousy, hamburger, meatball, droid, geekoid, nerd, nurd, twink, woofie, dexter, full hank, lop, narc, spud, squid, cull, schmo, shmoe, weirdo, goon, glick, bad case of the uglies, banana, out, out of it, dumb cluck, dummy, mince, mole, nothing, simp, spastic, weenie, wimp, cotton-picker, dipstick, arrowhead, for the birds, twerp, twirp, yo-yo, corndog, zombie, corpse, droop, herkle, prune, specimen, roach, toad, phrog, potato digger, won't give one the time of day, gives one a pain, gives one a pain in the neck, gives one a pain in the ass, gripes one's ass, wallflower, can't see one for dust, ho-dad, ho-daddy, funky, lame, rum-dum, low rider, nic-nac, punk, gunsel, Joe Sad (Af. Am.).

UNDESIRED adj. lousy, who needs it, need it like a hole in the head, this I need yet?, from hunger, for the birds, NIMBY (not in my back yard), excess baggage, drug on the market.

UNDETERMINED adj. iffy, on the fence, run hot and cold, blow hot and cold, hedge off, shilly-shally, betwixt and between, hanging fire, the jury's out, up for grabs. See UNDECIDED.

UNDEVELOPED adj. half-assed, half-baked, half-cocked.

UNDEVIATING adj. as the crow flies, beeline, down the alley, down the pipe, in the groove, on the beam, slambang.

UNDILUTED adj. neat, straight, uncut, right outta the bottle, all wool and a yard wide, honest-to-God, twenty-four-carat.

UNDISGUISED adj. barefaced, plain as the nose on one's face, under one's nose, big as life, out in the open, open-and-shut, if it were a snake it would bite you. See OBVIOUS.

UNDISTINGUISHED adj. vanilla, plain vanilla, garden variety, rum-dum, run-of-the-alley, run-of-the-mill, starch, no great shakes. See AVERAGE.

UNDIVIDED adj. jackpot, the works, lock stock and barrel, whole enchilada, whole ball of wax, whole nine yards, whole shebang, whole shooting match, everything including the kitchen sink. See WHOLE.

UNDO v. 1. adjy, get to, flip out, craze, bug, make waves, make a scene, make a fuss, give one a turn, give one a bad time, give one a hard time, put the needles in, stir up, rattle, discomboberate, discombobulate. See AGITATE. 2. queer, crimp, cramp, stymie, skin, snooker, crab, hang up, hold up, fuck up, bollix, gum up the works, upset one's apple cart, spike one's guns, take care of. See CANCEL. See also DEFEAT. 3. psych out, unglue, unzip, get to, blow up, blow out, take apart, take the steam out, send up, send up the balloon.

UNDONE adj. 1. rattled, thrown, fussed, defrosted, shook-up, creeped-out, hissy, lost one's cool, shot, shot to pieces, psyched-out, unglued, unscrewed, unzipped. 2. sunk, gone, goner, dead duck, toast, can't win for losin', no more cards to play, at the end of one's rope, one's ass is grass,

ass-out, in deep shit, bust, runnin' out of time, got one's back to the wall, fighting to keep one's head up. See also DEFEATED.

UNDRESS v. strip, strip to the buff, do a strip, do a striptease, peel, get all naked, slip out of, take it off, husk, shuck.

UNEARTH v. hit upon, spark, strike (oil, gold), see the light, stumble on, dig up, spotlight, limelight.

UNEARTHLY adj. spooky, spookish, scary.

UNEASY adj. uptight, jittery, jumpy, strung-out, unglued, hyper, spooked, wreck, nervous wreck, bundle of nerves, yantsy, antsy, in a state, in a dither, on edge, biting one's nails. See ANXIOUS. See also DISTURBED; TROUBLED.

UNEDUCATED adj. lowbrow, galoot, ignoramus.

UNEMOTIONAL adj. 1. cool, laid-back, flat, cold, cold fish, cool cat, ice man, mean machine, thick-skinned, dead-ass, deadpan. See CALLOUS. 2. wimpy, blah, go along for the ride, go with the flow.

UNEMOTIONALLY adv. in cold blood, deadpan, with a poker face, with a straight face.

UNEMPLOYED adj. at liberty, between engagements, on layoff, on the shelf, on the bench, on the beach, on the dole, on the turf, out of the rat race, cut loose (dockworker use), out of action, out of the swim, down, closed-down, bum, in short pants, shuffler, skuffling.

UNENCUMBERED adj. traveling light, no strings, fancy-free. See FREE.

UNENDURABLE adj. too much, bit much, enough already, had it up to here, last straw, straw that broke the camel's back, that's it, that blows it.

UNENLIGHTENED adj. uncool, unhep, unhip, mushroom, in the fog, doesn't have both oars in the water, hasn't checked in, clueless, hasn't a clue, in the dark, out to lunch, doesn't know one's ass from first base, hasn't the foggiest, not know a rock from a hard place, not know shit from Shinola. See IGNORANT.

UNENTERTAINING adj. draggy, draddy, ho-hum, bor-ring, bore one stiff, yawn, big yawn, zero, big zero. See BORING.

UNEQUAL adj. dif, diff, poles apart, weird, whale of a difference, like night and day, march to the beat of a different drummer.

UNEQUIVOCAL adj. flat-out, flat-ass, tell it like it is, straight-out, straight dope, right-on, open-and-shut. See CERTAIN.

UNEQUIVOCALLY adv. no strings attached, no holds barred, no catch, no kicker, come hell or high water, cert, amen, you better believe it, you betcher life, in spades. See ABSOLUTELY.

UNESSENTIAL adj. minimal to the max, gadget, never mind, no matter, chickenfeed, chickenshit, macht nichts, mox nix, makes no never mind, no great shakes, mere bagatelle, row of buttons, row of pins. See UNIMPORTANT.

UNETHICAL adj. bent, shady, sharp, wrong, double-crossing, mother-dangle, motherfucking, mother-rucking, hanky-panky, snake-in-the-grass, two-faced, two-timing, dirty, low-down and dirty, dirty work, dirty-dealing, dirty pool, dirty trick, crooked, crooked stick, cheatin', cheatin' heart, fishy, gyp, not kosher, wrong number, wrong gee, Honest John, doberman (Af. Am.), feather-legs, slick, slippery, speak with forked tongue, sellout, put-on, scam, fake, ride-out, squat (fraudulent auto accident), flam, flim-flam, shell game, skin game, fly-by-night, Judas kiss, stab in the back, crocodile tears, whitewash job. 2. on the sly, in a hole-and-corner way, in holes and corners.

UNEXCEPTIONAL adj. so-so, fair, fair-to-middling, run-of-the-mill, garden variety, no great shakes, strictly union, vanilla. See AVERAGE.

UNEXCITABLE adj. cool, cool as a cucumber, keep one's cool, keep one's shirt on, not turn a hair, roll with the punches, without a nerve in one's body, unflappable. See IMPERTURBABLE. See also CALM.

UNEXCITING adj. draggy, draddy, dull as dishwater, ho-hum, bor-ring, yawn, big yawn, nowhere, beige, cheesy, noplaceville, Nadaville, dullsville, flat-tire, flat as a pancake, pablum, dog. See BORING.

UNEXPECTED adj. random, from out in left field, from out of the blue, bolt from the blue, sleeper, payoff.

UNEXPLODED adj. dud, UXB.

UNFAILING adj. straight-arrow, dyed-in-the-wool, there, count on one, one who always delivers, one who always comes through, always there in a pinch, rock, Rock of Gibraltar, Rocka Gibraltar, Rocka Gib, the Rock. See TRUSTWORTHY.

UNFAIR adj. fix, fixed, bogus, low, low blow, below the belt, hitting below the belt, not cricket, wired, stinks, reeks, raw, raw deal, dirty, dirty trick, dirty pool, low-down, low-down and dirty, cheap shot, cold duck, dog, feather-legs, half a shake.

UNFAITHFUL adj. double-crossing, snaky, snake-in-the-grass, worm, two-faced, two-timing, cheat on, cheating heart, moonlighting, chippy on one, sneakin' deacon, stepping out on one, tip, witch, doggin', dog one around, working late at the office, yard on. See also INFIDELITY.

UNFALTERING adj. dead set on, bent on, hell bent on, mean business, bound, bound and determined, stick at nothing, set, sot, unflappable, bulletheaded, pigheaded,

stiff-necked, mulish, stubborn as a mule, the game ain't over til the last man is out, sticking to one's guns, hanging in, going all the way. See also CERTAIN.

UNFASHIONABLE adj. played-out (Af. Am.), tired, out, not with it, old hat, passé, back number, moth-eaten, moldy fig, corny, horse-and-buggy, ricky-tick, gasser. See DATED.

UNFASTEN v. unslough, strip.

UNFATHOMABLE adj. too deep for one, heavy, clear as mud, it beats me, I pass, tough nut to crack. See OBSCURE.

UNFAVORABLE adj. on the debit side, debit side, down side, the bad news.

UNFEELING adj. dead-ass, deadpan, cold, cold fish, cool cat, cold-blooded, iceman, thick-skinned, with a straight face, poker face. See CALLOUS.

UNFINISHED adj. half-assed, half-baked, half-cocked, holiday (task).

UNFIT adj. 1. draggin', draggin' one's ass, rocky, seedy, down, run-down, laid low, below par, peaky, peaked, poorly, outta action, out of shape, good and flabby, Four F. See also ILL. 2. uncool, not cut out for, can't hack it, can't cut it, can't cut the mustard, can't make the grade, can't fade that, sidelined, out of commission, hog-tied. See also INAPPROPRIATE. 3. out to lunch, bringdown, amateur night, amateur night in Dixie, not have it, Mickey Mouse, bush, bush-league, haywire, dead one, lame-brained, a newt, dub, flub-dub, half-assed, half-baked, fumble-fist, butterfingers muff. See INCOMPETENT.

UNFITTING adj. off-base, off-color, bad form, out-of-line, humbug, garbage.

UNFLINCHING adj. spunk, spunky, bodacious, brass, brassy, bold as brass, I'm shakin' (sarcastic response to threat), ballsy, gutsy, gutty, guttiness, gutsiness, grit, gritty, nerve, nervy, chutzpahdik, tough it out, fire-eater, cool hand, iceman, ice in one's veins. See also FEARLESS; STUBBORN.

UNFORESEEN adj. from out in left field, bolt from the blue.

UNFORMED adj. baggy, blobby.

UNFORTUNATE adj. 1. jinxed, hoodooded, voo-dooed, behind the eight-ball, jonah, joner, snake-bit, scrub, loser, sure loser, winner, real winner, fuck-up, sad sack, dick in the dirt, schlemiel, schlemazel, hardcase, down on one's luck, tough luck, rotten luck, shit out of luck, S.O.L., lame, bad break, rotten break, tough break, out-of-luck, hard-luck guy, flop, bust, loser, goner, dead, dead duck, beat, dead-beat, dead pigeon, squid, bum, turkey, poor fish, in the toilet, in deep water, in the dumper, in above one's head, blown out of the water, down, down the drain, down-and-out, out of it, clambake, also-ran, losing streak, went down like the Titanic, get nowhere, never passed, never passed go, a day late and a dollar short, missed the boat, on the skids, back to the drawing board, can't even get arrested, can't even write home for money, can't punch his way out of a paper bag, should have stood in bed, fall on one's face, fall flat on one's face, fall on one's ass, washout, washed-out, washed-up. 2. down the drain, down the chute, down the toilet, abortion, hurting, clinker, cruller, brodie, foldo, chapter eleven, go chapter eleven, behind the eight-ball, lumpy, on the rocks.

UNFOUNDED adj. bullshit, hot-air, piss-and-wind, off-base, cockeyed, who sez?, my eye, just talk, whataya talkin', you're talkin' like a man with a paper ass, where'd ya get that shit?, pie in the sky. See GROUNDLESS.

UNFRIENDLY adj. 1. cool, cold, cold fish, loner, lone wolf, laid-back, stuck-up, uppity, offish, standoffish. See ALOOF. 2. scrappy, bitchy, salty, spiky, cantankerous, fire-eater, have a chip on one's shoulder, at outs, on the outs, allergic to, down on, turned off by. See ANTAGONISTIC.

UNGAINLY adj. klutzy, clunky, all thumbs, bogus, butterfingers, two left hands, two left feet, a newt, galoot. See CLUMSY.

UNGENEROUS adj. stingy, penny-pinching, close, tight, tightwad, last of the big spenders, tight as a drum, skinflint, skin, screw, Scotch, piker, chintzy, scrimpy, skimpy. See STINGY.

UNGRAMMATICAL, BE v. murder the King's English, murder the Queen's English, Mrs. Malaprop.

UNHAMPERED adj. no strings attached, no strings, no holds barred, no catch, no joker, no kicker, no joker in the deck. See UNCONDITIONAL. 2. footloose, footloose and fancy-free, free-wheeling, break loose, cut loose, loose wig, on one's own, shoot the moon, all hanging out. See FREE.

UNHANDY adj. klutz, clunker, dub, jerk, flub-dub, amateur, amateur night in Dixie, a newt, all thumbs, butterfingers, two left hands, two left feet, not cut out for. See CLUMSY.

UNHAPPY adj. 1. crumbed, dragged, ripped, low, defrosted, destroyed, dragging ass, ass in a sling, have one's ass in a sling, dick in the dirt, blue, blue funk, in a blue funk, funky, grim, got the blue devils, in the toilet, in the dumper, in the dumps, down, a downer, on a downer, let down, taken down, taken down a peg, taken down a peg or two, down in the dumps, in the doleful dumps, down-and-out, down in the mouth, downbeat (movie, song, etc.), low-down, crummy, cleek, pruneface, sob story, sob stuff, tearjerker, weeper, teardrop special, make like an alligator, have the blues, singing the blues, crying the blues, hang crepe, on a bummer, bummed-out, flaked-out, put away, carry the torch, hurting, bleeding, in pain, in the pits, shook, shot-down, should have stood in bed, carry a heavy load, off one's

feed, rhino, have the mulligrubs, have the dolefuls, have the blahs, clanked, clanked-up, cracked-up, tore-up, all torn up, droopy, mopey, moony, gloomy Gus, wet blanket, raining on one's parade, sad-sacky, killjoy, pruneface, prunefaced, sourpuss, spring fever. See also DESPAIRING. 2. not a happy camper, unhappy camper, sour, beefing, bitching, kicking, bellyaching, crabbing, crabby, kvetching, cranky, griping, grouchy, grousing, raining on one's parade.

UNHEALTHY adj. draggin', draggin' one's ass, rocky, seedy, down, run-down, laid low, below par, peaky, peaked, poorly, out of action, out of shape, good and flabby, 4-F. See also ILL.

UNHEEDING adj. 1. slapdash, sloppy, any old way, any which way, helter-skelter, devil-may-care, leave oneself wide open, play with fire, go overboard. See CARELESS. 2. out-to-lunch, asleep at the switch, pay no mind, looking out the window, daydreaming, mooning, helium-headed, air-headed. See PREOCCUPIED.

UNHINDERED adj. 1. no strings, no strings attached, no holds barred, no catch, no joker, no kicker, no joker in the deck. 2. footloose, footloose and fancy-free, free-spirited, free-wheeling, loose wig, on one's own, let down one's hair, all hanging out. See FREE.

UNHINGED adj. bent, unglued, unzipped, unscrewed, dingy, dingaling, loose in the upper story, schizy, schizzed out, schizoid, psycho, psyched-out, freaked-out, got a wild hair up one's ass, flipped-out, out of one's gourd, in the ozone, cracked-up, off one's nut, off one's rocker, off one's trolley, have a lug nut loose, cutting out paper dolls, cuckoo, gone, not all there, round the bend, squirrely. See CRAZY.

UNHURRIED adj. draggy, pokey, slowpoke, schlepper, banana boat, slower than the seven-year itch. See SLOW.

UNIDENTIFIED FLYING OBJECT n. UFO, flying saucer, spaceship.

UNIFICATION CHURCH MEMBER n. Moonie.

UNIFORM adj. xerox, carbon copy, ditto, double, dead ringer, lookalike, like two peas in a pod, spit and image, spittin' image, one beat, same difference.

UNIFORM n. khakis, the suit, olive drab, O.D., bag, in the bag (in uniform), pickle suit (marine), getup, monkey clothes, monkey jacket, state o, tar bucket, tit cap, harness, sailor suit, soldier suit, stripes (prison).

UNIMAGINATIVE adj. bromidic, pablum, zero, vanilla, square, L7, ho hum, dull as dishwater, flat, flat as a pancake, white-bread, dime-a-dozen, noplaceville, droid (person), a narb, narbo, camel, meat-and-potatoes man. See PROSAIC.

UNIMPEDED adj. 1. no holds barred, no catch, no joker, no kicker, no joker in the deck, no strings, no strings attached. See UNCONDITIONAL. 2. footloose, footloose and fancy-free, free-spirited, free-wheeling, break loose, cut loose, loose wig, wide open. See FREE.

UNIMPORTANT adj. 1. diddly, squat, diddly-squat, diddly-poo, doodly-squat, shit, beans, Jack, borscht, 86, nada, nix, zero, big zero, zip, zippo, zip city, zilch, nothing, cipher, goose egg, collar, horse collar, dunnage (dockworker use), flyspeck, flea, chit, chirp, chromosome, crum, crumb, drip, dinky, measly, minimal to the max, from nothing, Mickey Mouse, gadget, rinky-dink, nutmeg, two-by-four, two-bit, nickel-and-dime, penny-ante, peanuts, pissy-tailed, pissy-assed, piss-assed, scratch, big deal, big fucking deal, BFD, no big deal, big shit, no biggie, no big thing, no skin off one's nose, never mind, no matter; ain't no thang, ain't no thing but a chicken wing (Af. Am.); chickenfeed, chickenshit, flying fuck, bupkes, hump, shot, tinhorn, bottom-rung, lower-rung, small potatoes, small spuds, small beer, small change, small-time, small pot, pokerino, pinchy, one-horse, nowhere, drop in the bucket, drop in the ocean, sucking wind, little go, mox nix, makes no never mind, no great shakes, mere bagatelle, frig it, chuck it, drop it, forget it, let it pass, skip it, doesn't amount to a bucket of warm piss, not worth a hill of beans, not worth a row of beans, row of buttons, row of pins, damn, darn, tinker's dam, hoot, got other fish to fry, other fish in the sea, other pebbles on the beach, raggedy act, harlot's hello. 2. empty suit, herb, wimpy, wuss, jerky, sad-sack, lop, semi-dork, nebbish, squirt, twerp, shrimp, squid, scrub, runt, little guy, small potatoes, small fry, low-level Munchkin, cipher, zilch, zip, zippo, zero, big zero, nobody, Mr. and Mrs. Nobody, Brown Jones and Robinson, John Doe and Mary Roe, Jane Doe and Richard Roe, Tom Dick and Harry, spear carrier, pushover, winner, real winner, dog, scrub, loser, real loser, punk, tinhorn, flat tire, dud, skag, pipsqueak, whippersnapper, whiffet, flash-in-the-pan, man with a paper ass, jackstraw, man of straw, gerk (old).

UNIMPRESSIVE adj. big zero, underwhelming, nowhere, dog, scrub, loser, real loser, winner, real winner, cut no ice, big whip, big deal, no big deal, no biggie, big shit, no big shit, downer, dullsville, flat, flat-tire does nothing for one. See also SMALL, UNIMPORTANT.

UNINFORMED adj. uncool, unhep, unhip, in the fog, doesn't have both oars in the water, wouldn't know it if it bit him in the ass, hasn't checked in, clueless, hasn't a clue, hasn't the foggiest, airhead, helium-head, a mushroom, in the dark, doesn't know from nothing, doesn't know one's ass from first base, doesn't know one's ass from a hole in the ground, a big know-it-all, not be with it. See IGNORANT.

UNINHIBITED adj. footloose, footloose and fancy-free, free-wheeling, off the cuff, all hanging out, break loose, cut loose, loose wig, no holds barred, fly kites, let down one's hair, off the wall. See SPONTANEOUS.

UNINITIATED adj. cherry.

UNINSPIRED adj. phoned in, corny, bromidic, old hat, everyday, square, L7, ho-hum, yawn, big yawn, flat, flat as a pancake, flat-tire, camel. See PROSAIC.

UNINSURED, REMAIN v. go bare.

UNINTELLIGENT adj. ditzo, dorkmunder, dorf, doofus, remo, sped, vacant lot, nerdy, numb-nut, numb-brained, lamebrain, birdbrain, nobody home, droid, beau, biff (girl), McFly, dummy, dumbo, dum-dum, dumb bunny, dumb cluck, mungshit, mouth breather, mental giant, lorg, gump, jel, bone-top, boob, nincompoop, musclehead, blockhead, fathead, bonehead, doesn't know from A to B, doesn't know which way is up, stoop, stupe, got a hole in the head, leak in the think tank, nuthin' upstairs, jackass, Barbie and Ken, dimwit, deadass. See STUPID.

UNINTELLIGIBLE adj. clear as mud, double-Dutch, Greek, unreadable, breaking up (radio signal). See OBSCURE.

UNINTERESTED adj. don't give shit, don't give a shit, don't give a damn, don't give a hoot, phone it in, could care less, bored stiff, hard-boiled, hardhearted, dead-ass, just going through the motions, walk through it, what's the diff?, what the hell?, so what?, so what else is new?, it's all the same to me, that's your lookout, that's your pigeon, I should worry, clock-watcher, turned off. See also INDIFFERENT.

UNINTERESTED, BE v. not give a damn, not give a shit, so?, so what?, what's the diff?, what the hell, clock watcher. See INDIFFERENT.

UNINTERESTING adj. 1. draggy, cheesy, dull as dishwater, blah, ho-hum, bor-ring, big yawn, nowhere, noplaceville, Nadaville, Dullsville, nothing, tired, flat, big zero. See BORING. 2. beige, drip, grass, grass-out, Irving, Melvin, party-pooper, stick-in-the-mud, wet blanket, wonky.

UNINTIMIDATED adj. I'm shakin' (sarcastic response to threat) in your face, gutsy, gritty, nervy, spunky, ballsy, brassy, bold as brass, fire-eater, ice in one's veins, come on strong, cocky, cocksure, cool hand. See FEARLESS.

UNINVITED adj. buttinsky, crasher, gate-crasher.

UNINVOLVED n. hands-off (usually management).

UNION n. 1. local, syndicate. 2. tie-up, tie-in, tie-in tie-up, hookup. See ASSOCIATION.

UNION CARD n. pie card.

UNION LABEL n. bug, union bug (printing).

UNION MEETING n. chapel, chapel meeting.

UNION MEMBER n. brother, sister, pork chopper, Jimmie Higgens.

UNION ORGANIZER n. labor skate.

UNIQUE adj. 1. onliest, funky, offbeat, off the beaten track, bent, weird, weirdo, dudical, radical dude, grody, grody to the max, strange one, oddball, goofball, special, wrinkle, new wrinkle, an original, cool, fringy, flaky, far-out, way-out, out-of-sight, wild, crazy, off the wall, out in left field, trippy, fly ball, gooney, gooney bird, rare bird, loner, three-dollar bill, gonzo, character, scarcer than hen's teeth, numerous as chicken lips. 2. unreal, out-of-sight, standout, best ever, primo, something else, far out, the most, the utmost, the end. See EXCELLENT. 3. state-of-the-art, the leading edge, the cutting edge, breaking new snow, avant-garde, last word, the latest, latest thing, latest wrinkle. See NEW.

UNIT n. crew, bunch, crowd, gang, mob, outfit, ring.

UNITE v. 1. tag on, tack on, slap on, hitch on, piggyback, plug into, cross-dissolve (film), cue in (scripts, mss., songs), dub, hook in, marry (film), mix (recording). 2. hook up, go partners with, pool, take up with, get in with, get together, join up with, meld with, play ball with, throw in with, gang up with. See ASSOCIATE.

UNITED adj. hooked up with, in cahoots with, joined up with, lined up with, partners with, thrown in with, tied in with, plugged into.

UNITED NATIONS CHILDREN'S FUND n. UNICEF.

UNITED NATIONS EDUCATIONAL, SCIENTIFIC, AND CULTURAL ORGANIZATION n. UNESCO.

UNITED STATES n. States, U.S., U.S.A., stateside, lower forty-eight, Lower 48, Mainland, CONUS (continental United States), coast-to-coast, Uncle Sam, Uncle Sap, Uncle Sham, Uncle Sugar, Uncle Sucker, Uncle Whiskers, Whiskers, Mr. Whiskers, the old man with the whiskers, Yankee land, Brother Jonathon, melting pot, Babylon (Af. Am.).

UNITED STATES ARMY n. green machine, ultimate weapon (infantry soldier).

UNITED STATES ARMY RANKS n. brass, brass hat, gold braid, barbed wire, skipper, skip, old man, buck general (brigadier); chicken colonel, bird colonel, buzzard colonel (colonel); lieut, looey, butter bar, brown bar (1st Lt.); second looey, shavetail, 90-day wonder (2nd Lt.); butcher (M.D.), buggy bitchers (field artillery, cavalry 1930), regs, the book, mustang (officer risen from the ranks), ossifer, goat, dust-dust (newly promoted); NCO; sarge (sergeant), two-striper (corporal), one-striper, poor fucking civilian, PFC (private first class), kick, topkick, buckass private.

UNITED STATES CAPITOL n. the Hill.

UNITED STATES DEPARTMENT OF HOUSING AND URBAN DEVELOPMENT n. HUD.

UNITED STATES DEPARTMENT OF STATE n. Foggy Bottom, State.

UNITED STATES FLAG n. Stars and Stripes, red white and blue, Star-spangled Banner, Old Glory, Old Betsy, Stars and Bars (Confederacy).

UNITED STATES GOVERNMENT n. feds, Uncle Sam, Uncle Sugar, Washington.

UNITED STATES MARINE BASE n. green machine.

UNITED STATES NAVY RANKS n. scrambled eggs (commander and up), crow (chief or captain), broken striper (warrant officer), buffer (chief boatswain's mate); hack driver, C.P.O. (chief petty officer).

UNIVERSAL adj. multinational, anational.

UNIVERSITY n. Alma Mater, old Siwash, brainery, aggie, cow college, fem sem, kindergarten, Ivy League, halls of ivy.

UNIVERSITY COURSE, EASY n. piece of cake, crip course, breeze, snap, crib course, gut course, Sandbox 101, skate, slide.

UNIVERSITY GRADES n. A: ace, smoke, blitz, kick butt. B: B-out. C: hook, D: donut, dog. F: bomb, blow, punch-out, wave.

UNJUST adj. fixed, raw deal, dirty pool, bogus, stinks, reeks, low-down and dirty, hitting below the belt, cheap shot. See UNFAIR.

UNKEMPT adj. sloppy, grubby, grungy, mangled, thrashed, chili bowl, nappy, scuzzy, scuzzed-up, messed-up, mussed-up, messy, mussy, seedy, down-at-the-heel, out at the heels, out at the elbows. See SLOVENLY.

UNKNOWN adj. 1. unk-unks, pig in a poke, X, X factor, whatsis, what's-its-name, whatzit. 2. incog, certain person, Joe Doaks, Jane Doe, John Doe, Cheap John, Joe Blow, Mr. X, George Spelvin, so and so, such and such, whatchamacallit, what d'ye call em, what's his name, what's his face, you know who, bearding. 3. off the map, over the edge, off the street, points west.

UNLICENSED adj. wildcat, bandit (taxicab).

UNLIKE adj. diff, poles apart, far cry, funky, offbeat, weird, whale of a difference, like night and day, march to the beat of a different drummer.

UNLIKELIHOOD n. long shot, hundred-to-one shot, it don't figure, not in the cards, nonstarter, not a chance in hell, outside chance. See IMPROBABILITY.

UNLIMITED adj. wide-open, no strings, no strings attached, no holds barred, no end of, no end to, no catch, no joker, no kicker, no joker in the deck, no ifs ands or buts, more than you can shake a stick at. See also COUNTLESS.

UNLOAD v. off-load, dump, get it off one's chest, take the load off one's chest, take a load off, take the load off one's mind. See also SELL.

UNLOCK v. loid, jimmy.

UNLUCKY adj. hoodooed, behind the eight-ball, snakebit, hard-luck guy, salty (gambling), down on one's luck, tough luck, rotten luck, bad break, left-handed, poor fish, dead pigeon. See UNFORTUNATE.

UNMAN v. cut off one's balls, deball, fix, alter.

UNMANLY adv. 1. faggy, swishy, pansy, pantywaist, old woman, sissy, goody-goody, pretty boy, weak sister, mama's boy (Derog.). See EFFEMINATE. 2. wimpy, yellow-bellied, 'fraidy cat, scaredy cat, rabbity, mousy, jellyfish, chicken, lily-livered, Caspar Milquetoast, wet sock, wet rag, weak sister, nerd, candy-ass, pucker-assed. See COWARDLY.

UNMARKETABLE adj. stuck with, white elephant, gotta eat it.

UNMARRIED adj. single, single-o, bach, old bach, old maid, cherry, canned goods, bug.

UNMASK v. give away, give the show away, drop a bomb, spill the beans, out, come out, come out of the closet, let it all hang out, bring it out into the open, blow one's cover, spring, spring one's duke, debunk, blow the lid off, blow the whistle. See EXPOSE.

UNMETHODICALLY adv. any old way, any which way, hit or miss, slapdash, half-assed, all over the shop. See ERRATICALLY.

UNMINDFUL adj. out-to-lunch, pay no mind, asleep at the switch, woolgathering, popcorn-headed, airheaded. See FORGETFUL.

UNMISTAKABLE adj. no buts about it, no ifs ands or buts, open-and-shut, for certain, absofuckinglutely, posolutely, absitively, dead sure, dead to rights. See CERTAIN.

UNMOVED adj. unflappable, hard-boiled, hard-hearted, hard as nails, not turn a hair, could care less, strong-faced, rhinoceros hide, dead-ass, butter wouldn't melt in one's mouth, poker-faced, don't give shit, so what? See INDIFFERENT.

UNNAMED adj. 1. X, X factor, brand X, whatsis, what's-its-name, whatzit, unk-unks, pig in a poke. 2. incog, Jane Doe, John Doe, Joe Blow, Mr. X, whatchamacallit, what's-his-name, what's-his-face, bearding. See ANONYMOUS.

UNNATURAL adj. 1. weird, for weird, weirdo, odd-ball, queer in the head, queer potato, strange duck, bent. See also ECCENTRIC. 2. hammy, schmaltzy, phony, bogus, gone Hollywood, camp around, chichi, putting on the dog, airish, play the ———. See AFFECTED.

UNNECESSARY adj. deadwood, excess baggage, Mickey Mouse, need it like a hole in the head, this I need?, who needs it.

UNNERVE v. 1. psych, psych out, spook, get to, bug, needle, put the needles in, ride, rattle, floor, throw, discomboberate, discombobulate, give one a turn, give one a bad time. See DISTURB. 2. chill, scare the pants off one, scare hell out of, bowl over, buffalo, whip one around (intellectually), put one through the wringer, bad-eye. See FRIGHTEN.

UNNERVED adj. thrown, psyched out, unglued, unscrewed, unzipped, spazzed out, choked, come apart, come apart at the seams, shot, shot to pieces. See also FRIGHTENED.

UNNOTEWORTHY adj. 1. no great shakes, strictly union, so-so, run-of-the-alley, run-of-the-mill, garden variety, humdrum, rum-dum, vanilla, two-bit, one-horse. 2. pipsqueak, Tom Dick and Harry, Mr. and Mrs. Nobody, nobody, spear carrier, small fry, small beer, small change, small potatoes, chromosome, twerp, flyspeck. 3. never mind, mox nix, makes no never mind, no matter, not worth a hill of beans, no big deal, no biggie. See UNIMPORTANT.

UNNOTICEABLE adj. low-keyed, low-profile, soft-pedaled.

UNOBSTRUCTED adj. wide-open.

UNOBTAINABLE adj. 1. ungettable, pie-in-the-sky, blue-sky, no got. 2. out-of-pocket.

UNOBTRUSIVE adj. low-keyed, low-profile, soft-pedaled.

UNOBTRUSIVELY adv. under wraps, hush-hush, strictly-hush hush, on the q.t., on the quiet, on the sly, undercover, in a hole-and-corner way, in holes and corners.

UNORGANIZED adj. hit-or-miss, willy-nilly, any old way, any which way, helter-skelter, higgledy-piggledy, slapdash, all over the shop. See also UNPREPARED; ERRATICALLY.

UNORTHODOX adj. kinky, hippy, flaky, quirky, beat, beatnik, beat generation, Bohemian, off the beaten path, weirdo, geeky, avant-garde, po-mo (postmodern), fringy, far-out, way-out, crazy, rare bird, three-dollar bill. See ECCENTRIC. See also NONCONFORMIST.

UNPAID adj. what is coming to one, what one has coming, comeuppance.

UNPAINTED adj. holiday (spot missed).

UNPALATABLE adj. grody, grody to the max, gagger, gross, pukey, pukoid, yucky, icky, yicky, barfy, slimy, fishy, synthetic, gooky. See UNSAVORY.

UNPARALLELED adj. world-class, greatest, ten, 10, gonest, hundred-proof, mostest, baaadest, all-time, all-time haymaker, tops, the most, the end, solid gold, winner, champ. See BEST.

UNPERTURBED adj. cool, cool as a cucumber, keep one's cool, keep one's shirt on, unflappable, not turn a hair, ah-ah head. See CALM.

UNPLANNED adj. off-the-wall, improv, ginned up, ad lib, fake it, off the top of the head, play it by ear, cold, caught flatfooted, caught off base. See IMPROMPTU.

UNPLEASANT adj. rotted, rottissimo (very bad), Rotterdam, sucks, sux, sucky, it sucks, bunk, wack, whacked, grody, gross, uncool, yucky, bad news, bad scene, poison, sad, fierce, hard time, lousy. See UNDESIRABLE.

UNPLEASANT PLACE n. hellhole, hole, joint, dump.

UNPOPULAR PERSON n. geek, geekoid, barney, creep, scrounge, nightie (nightmare), smack (overachieving geek), rat, barf bag, drip, stinker, stinkpot, shit, shithead, hairball, corn dog, elrod, scoob, goob, goober, goobatron, yernt, turkey, fink, gross, scrub, scurvy, scuzzo, scuzzy, shitsky, shitburger, shit breath, quimp, remo, turdface, dag, loser, dexter, full hank, lop, narc, spud, squid, louse, wanker, cheesehead, cheeseface, Captain Cheddar, droob, drube, nob, social zero, twink, woofie, cull, mutant, weirdo, goon, bad case of the uglies, out, out of the loop, out of it, nothing, nothingburger, bunk, arrowhead, for the birds, roach, toad, won't give one the time of day, gives one a pain, gives one a pain in the neck, gives one a pain in the ass, wallflower, can't see one for dust, ho-dad, ho-daddy, lame, rum-dum, low rider, nic-nac, punk, gunsel, Joe Sad (Af. Am.), below the salt. See also DISLIKED PERSON.

UNPREDICTABLE adj. 1. from out in left field, bolt from the blue. 2. chancy, iffy, up for grabs, touchy, touch-and-go, fluckey, on slippery ground, on ice, on thin ice, hanging by a thread, the jury's out. See DOUBTFUL. See also RISKY.

UNPREJUDICED adj. 1. call 'em as one sees 'em, straight, even-steven. See FAIR. 2. colorblind, cold, cold turkey, the emess, on the fence, mugwumpian, mugwumpish.

UNPREPARED adj. flatfooted, caught flatfooted, cold, caught off base, caught napping, caught with one's pants down, a day late and a dollar short, improv, ginned-up, ad lib, vamp, fake, fake it, wing it, off the wall, off the cuff, off the hip, off the top of the head, play it by ear, go off half-cocked. See also IMPROMPTU.

UNPRETENTIOUS adj. folksy, down, down home, home folks, homey, haimish, with the bark on, all hanging out, up front, free-spirited, get down, let down one's hair, stretched-out, cas, cazh, laid-back.

UNPRINCIPLED adj. 1. bent, shady, double-crossing, doberman (Af. Am.), snake in the grass, two-faced,

two-timing, low-down and dirty, dirty-dealing, crooked stick, cheatin' heart, speak with forked tongue. 2. on the sly, in a hole-and-corner way, in holes and corners. See UNETHICAL.

UNPROCURABLE adj. ungettable, pie in the sky, no got.

UNPROFITABLE adj. in the red, red ink, total shuck, debit side, on the debit side, down side, the bad news, wild goose chase. See also USELESS.

UNPRONOUNCEABLE WORDS n. jawbreakers, jaw crackers, tongue twisters.

UNPROSPEROUS adj. 1. stony, flat, broke, hard-up, strapped, tapped, on the rocks, on one's uppers, hurting, feeling the pinch, down-and-out, seen better days, on the rims. See DESTITUTE. 2. missed the boat, on the skids, behind the eight-ball, foldo, washout, washed up, go under, go chapter eleven, flop, fall down on the job. See UNSUCCESSFUL.

UNPROTECTED adj. naked, ass out, neck stuck out, sitting duck, wide-open, on the line, on the spot, out on a limb, up the creek without a paddle, Achilles heel.

UNPUNISHED, GO v. get away with, get away with murder, get a slap on the wrist, walk.

UNQUALIFIED adj. 1. bush, bush-league, amateur night, nonstarter, didn't make the cut, can't cut it, not cut out for. See INCOMPETENT. 2. flat-out, no catch, no joker, no kicker, no small print, no fine print at the bottom, no ifs ands or buts. See UNCONDITIONAL.

UNQUESTIONABLE adj. open-and-shut, absofuckinglutely, posolutely, absitively, for certain, cold, have down cold, pat, down pat, no buts about it, no ifs ands or buts, bet one's bottom dollar on, checked and double-checked, and no mistake. See CERTAIN.

UNRAVEL v. dope, dope out, pan out, figure out, crack, lick, deal with, unzip, iron out, work through, hit it on the nose. See also EXPLAIN, SIMPLIFY.

UNREADY adj. cold, flatfooted, caught flatfooted, caught off base, caught napping, caught with one's pants down, go off half-cocked. See UNPREPARED.

UNREALISTIC adj. gone, reachy, play with oneself, pipe dream, float, floating on clouds, on cloud seven, on cloud nine, pie in the sky, castles in the air, Disneyland, blue-sky. See also IMPOSSIBLE.

UNREASONABLE adj. 1. far-out, way-out, overkill, out-of-bounds, out of all bounds, throw out the baby with the bath water, up the butt, up the ying-yang, too-too, too much. See EXTREME. 2. all wet, off the wall, off-base, off the beam, full of beans, full of hot air, smoking your socks, miss by a mile, have another think coming. See WRONG. 3. pricey, cher, dear, steep, stiff, posh, heavy sugar, an arm and a leg, up to here (elbow), holdup, highway robbery, important. See EXPENSIVE.

UNREFINED adj. cheap, loud, loud-mouthed, raw, skank, tacky, raunchy, rough. See also COARSE.

UNREGULATED adj. open, wide-open.

UNREHEARSED adj. improv, ginned up, ad lib, winging it, vamping, off the top of the head, off the hip, played by ear, tossed off, tossed out, spitballed. See IMPROMPTU.

UNRELENTING adj. bound, bound and determined, hard-nosed, hard-line, take no prisoners, hang tough, rock-ribbed, brick wall, pat, stand pat, stand one's ground, stick to one's guns, staying power, hardheaded, bullheaded, stiff-necked, set, dead set on, murder (he's murder). See STUBBORN.

UNRELIABLE adj. bent, shady, fishy, sneaky, slick, sharp, shifty, shifty-eyed, loose, fly-by-night, Mickey Mouse, no account, slimy, trust one as far as one can swing a cat, trust one as far as one can throw an elephant. See DISHONEST. See also DANGEROUS.

UNREMARKABLE adj. 1. no great shakes, nowhere, strictly union, so-so, fair-to-middling, run-of-the-alley, run-of-the-mill, garden variety, vanilla. 2. wimpy, pipsqueak, Tom Dick and Harry, nobody, small change, small potatoes, drip, twerp, flea, hoddy-doddy, 3. not worth a hill of beans, row of pins, nutmeg, little go, big zero, no big deal, no biggie, no big thing, no big shit. See UNIMPORTANT.

UNREQUITED LOVE n. torch, carry a torch.

UNRESERVED adj. 1. open, call it like it is, shoot straight, call a spade a spade, put all one's cards on the table, make no bones about it, talk turkey. See FRANK. 2. all-out, flat-out, flat-ass, no holds barred, no joker in the deck. See UNCONDITIONAL.

UNRESOLVED adj. run hot and cold, blow hot and cold, shilly-shally, waffling, pussyfoot around, betwixt and between, hanging fire, the jury's out, between sixes and sevens. See UNDECIDED.

UNRESTRAINED adj. 1. free-wheeling, free-spirited, break loose, cut loose, loose cannon, loose wig, having a spaz attack, freaked-out, don't give a damm, shoot the moon, fly kites, flake. See FREE. 2. on a tear, blizzed, raising a rumpus, raising a ruckus, kicking up a row, kicking up one's heels, burn one's candle at both ends, drive in the fast lane. See UNCONTROLLABLE.

UNRESTRICTED adj. 1. wide-open, all-out, flat-out, no strings attached, no fine print at the bottom, no holds barred, no catch, no ifs ands or buts. See UNCONDITIONAL. 2. free-wheeling, break loose, cut loose, let down one's hair, go to town, all hanging out. See FREE.

UNREWARDING adj. fungo, should have stood in bed, wild-goose chase. See USELESS.

UNRUFFLED adj. cool, cool as a cucumber, keep one's cool, keep one's shirt on, unflappable, not turn a hair, ah-ah head. See CALM. See also DISPASSIONATE.

UNRULY adj. off-base, out-of-line, on a tear, raising a rumpus, raising a ruckus, raising the roof, kicking up a row, kicking up a shindy, out-of-order. See also UNRESTRAINED, VIOLENT.

UNSAFE adj. widow maker, on thin ice, on slippery ground, on a wing and a prayer, out on a limb, touchy, touch-and-go, hanging by a thread. See DANGEROUS. See also DOUBTFUL.

UNSALABLE adj. white elephant, stuck with.

UNSANCTIONED adj. under-the-counter, under-the-table, pirated, bit, no-no, crooked, heavy, off-base, out-of-line, out of bounds, over the line, racket, shady, dirty, wildcat.

UNSATISFACTORY adj. whacked, lame, bonk, seconds, damaged goods, crappy, junk, shit, piece of shit, rat's ass, piss-poor, schlocky, sleazy, ticky-tacky, slimpsy, minus, no good, from hunger, for the birds, Mickey Mouse, it sucks, not up to scratch, not come up to scratch, not up to snuff. See INADEQUATE.

UNSAVORY adj. 1. gagger, grody, grody to the max, gross, grungy, yucky, icky, yicky, barfy, pukey, pukoid, raunchy, creepy, cruddy. rough, sad, stinky, stinking, lousy, slimy, shady, fishy, sneaky, slick, sharp, shifty, synthetic, tough nuggies, tripe, hocky, hooky, gooky. 2. bad-assed, creep, shifty-eyed, wrong, wrong number, wrong gee, not kosher, doin' dirt, dirty, low-down and dirty, dirty work, no-good, N.G., no account, barf bag, shit heel, shit hook, bum, worm, convict, copperhearted, eighteen-carat, crum, crumb, hellish, hell of a note, hipper-dipper. See also NASTY.

UNSCRAMBLE v. 1. dope, dope out, pan out, figure out, crack, lick, deal with, unzip, work through, hit it on the nose. 2. break it down, get down to basics, get down to the meat, clean it up, lay out, spell out, make perfectly clear. See SIMPLIFY.

UNSCRUPULOUS adj. 1. shady, sharp, double-crossing, two-faced, two-timing, low-down and dirty, dirty-dealing, doberman (Af. Am.), crooked stick, featherlegs, slippery, fly-by-night. 2. on the sly, in a hole-and-corner way, in holes and corners. See UNETHICAL.

UNSEATED adj. unfrocked (any profession), drummed out, turned off, blackballed.

UNSECURABLE adj. ungettable, pie in the sky, no got, out-of-pocket.

UNSEEING adj. 1. blind as a bat. 2. in the dark, wouldn't know it if it bit him in the ass, not know the score, not know the time of day, not know shit from Shinola, doesn't know from nothing. See IGNORANT.

UNSENTIMENTAL adj. hard-boiled, hard-headed, commonsensical.

UNSETTLE v. 1. psych out, spook, get to, flip out, bug, fuss, fuzz-buzz, give one a bad time, give one a hard time, make it tough for all, chew on, needle, push one's key, rattle, floor, throw. See DISTURB. 2. bollix, gum, gum up the works, put off, fuddle, throw a monkey wrench into the works, upset one's apple cart, take the wind out of one's sails, knock the props from under one, down one. See UPSET.

UNSETTLED adj. 1. betwixt and between, hanging fire, on ice, the jury's out, up for grabs, waffling. See UNDECIDED. 2. rattled, thrown, fussed, defrosted, shook-up, all shook up, antsy, fidgety, on pins and needles, all hot and bothered, Chinese fire drill. See CONFUSED. 3. dragged, got the blue devils, bummed-out, flaked-out, psyched-out, out of sorts, buggin', shot to pieces, going to pieces, droopy, mopey. See UNHAPPY.

UNSEXED adj. cut off one's balls, deballed, fixed, altered.

UNSHAKEBLE adj. set, sot, dead set on, set in concrete, pat, stand-pat, brick wall, locked in, unflappable, bound and determined, stand one's ground, dig in one's heels, hang tough. See STUBBORN. See also DETERMINED.

UNSIGHTLY adj. grody, gross, plug-ugly, ugly as sin, grimbo, beat, hagged out, scag, hard on the eyes, beaujeeful, chromo, short on looks, crappy, cruddy, death warmed over. See UGLY.

UNSKILLED adj. virgin, green, greenhorn, green ass, wet behind the ears, rookie, boot, hayseed, raw, fish, first of May, ham, amateur, amateur night, amateur night in Dixie, bush, bush leaguer, crufty, sour apples (can't do something for sour apples), cokey (Af. Am.). See also INCOMPETENT.

UNSMILING adj. sourpuss, frozen-faced, not crack a smile, wipe the smile off one's face. See SERIOUS.

UNSOCIABLE adj. cool, cool cat, cold, cold fish, loner, lone wolf, dolo, dog it, dog up, stuck-up, uppity, laid-back, offish, standoffish. See ALOOF.

UNSOLICITED adj. through the transom, under the door.

UNSOPHISTICATED adj. go organic, on the natch, low-tech, folksy, haimish, homey, corny, cornball, corn-fed, off the cob, on the cob, Golden Bantam, cracker barrel, soul-free, mossback, uncool, duck, clean, a narb, narbo, cube, square, L7, cob, bama, raw, boob, hayseed, buster, Jasper, Babbitt, rookie, green, greenhorn, green ass, nowhere, out to lunch, eight-ball, wide-eyed, wet behind the ears, not dry behind the ears, kid, babe in the woods, Bambi, blue eyes, blue-eyed, kid, lily white, mark, easy mark, pigeon, Clyde, Ed, Elk, fish, first of May, gunsel (boy), sophomore, bush, bush leaguer, country, country girl, country boy, hick, shitkicker, chintzy, clodhopper, hoosier, jay, jellybean, clown, lame, swallow anything, swallow hook line and sinker, take the bait, go for, fall for, tumble for, don't know shit from shoe polish, don't know shit from Shinola, don't know one's ass from a hole in the ground, don't know one's ass from first base, don't know crossways from crosswise, don't know from nothin', don't know what day it is. See also PLAIN, RUSTIC.

UNSPORTSMANLIKE adj. cheap shot, hitting below the belt, not cricket, raw deal, dirty pool, bogus, stinks, reeks, low-down, low-down and dirty, half a shake. See UNFAIR.

UNSTEADY adj. 1. yo-yo. 2. rocky, dicey, iffy, chancy, on thin ice, on slippery ground, on a wing and a prayer, out on a limb, Baker flying (N.), touchy, touch-and-go, hanging by a thread. See RISKY.

UNSUBSTANTIAL adj. gimcrack, gimcracky, Mickey Mouse, rocky, rickety, rink-dink, held together by spit, held together by chewing gum, house of cards. See FLIMSY.

UNSUCCESSFUL adj. 1. dead, dead duck, beat, squid, turkey, good-for-nothing, foul ball, toast, loser, roof fell in (sudden), never-wuz, also-ran, stiff, stifferoo, booby, can't even get arrested, flash in the pan. See FAILURE. 2. down, down the drain, down the chute, down and out, down the toilet, in the toilet, in the dumper, washout, washed out, washed up, nowhere, bust, flop, floppo, flopperoo, bomb, blank, bloomer, shellacking, stinkeroo, fluke, flummox, flookum, clambake, false alarm, dud, disaster, abortion, that dog won't hunt, not work, not come off, a day late and a dollar short, flunk, flunk out, crap out, strike out, never passed go, A for effort, a miss, near miss, missed the boat, no dice, no-go, back to the drawing board, phftt, on the skids, on the rocks, should have stood in bed, go under, cropper, pratfall, muss up, piss up, fuck up, foul up, snafu, put down, come down, went down like the Titanic, wet smack, misfire, drew a blank, blown out of the water, header, in over one's head, in deep water, fall on one's face, fall flat on one's face, fall on one's ass, flat failure, also-ran, dull thud, brodie, total loss, foozle, lamo, stinker, lead balloon (idea went over like a lead balloon), lemon, fizzle, frost, bagel, botch, clunker, dog, enema, hash, jumble, pancake, turd, turkey. 3. foldo, belly up, toes up, toes, chapter 7, chapter 11, chapter 13, broke.

UNSUITABLE adj. cockamamie, bad form, off-base, off-color, humbug, out-of-line. See also UNDESIRABLE.

UNSUPPORTED adj. left twisting in the wind, left holding the bag. See also GROUNDLESS.

UNSURE adj. 1. iffy, up for grabs, touch-and-go, on slippery ground, on thin ice. 2. wimpy, pussyfoot around, blow hot and cold, on the fence, betwixt and between, between a rock and a hard place. See DOUBTFUL.

UNSURPASSED adj. number one, numero uno, A, A-1, A-number 1, ten, 10, out-of-sight, out-of-this-world, gonest, crack, def, tops, winner, champ. See BEST.

UNSUSPECTING, BE v. fall for, bite, be taken in, swallow hook line and sinker, patsy, easy mark. See GULLIBLE.

UNSYMMETRICAL adj. agee, agee-jawed, wamper-jawed, jack-deuce.

UNSYMPATHETIC adj. 1. tough nuggies, tough shit, TS, too bad, that's the way the ball bounces, that's the way the cookie crumbles. 2. cool, chill, cold, cold fish, cold-blooded, iceman, arctic, hard instinct, mean machine, butter wouldn't melt in his mouth. See also UNCOMPASSIONATE, CALLOUS, PITILESS.

UNSYSTEMATICALLY adv. any old way, any which way, hit or miss, willy-nilly, by fits and starts, helter-skelter, higgledy-piggledy. See ERRATICALLY.

UNTALKATIVE adj. clammed-up, dried-up, dummied-up, garbo, tight-lipped. See SILENT.

UNTIDY adj. sloppy, slobbed-out, mangled, thrashed, grungy, grubby, scuzzed-up, mess, messed-up, mussed-up, messy, mussy, looks lived in, bloody mess, holy mess, unholy mess, rat's nest, pigpen. See SLOVENLY.

UNTIMELY adv. previous, a bit previous, bright and early, early bird, early on.

UNTIRING adj. grind, plugger, springbutt, eager beaver, ball of fire, fireball, hyper, jumping, go-go, perky. See also SPIRITED.

UNTITLED adj. 1. X, X factor, whatsis, what's-its-name, whatzit, unk-unks, pig in a poke. 2. a certain person, Joe Doakes, Jane Doe, John Doe, Cheap John, Joe Blow, Mr. X, George Spelvin, so and so, such and such, whatchamacallit, what-d'ye-call-em, what's-his-name, what's-his-face, you know who.

UNTRUE adj. 1. it won't fly, it stinks, crock, crock of shit, hogwash, no such animal. 2. two-timing, cheating heart, moonlighting, chippy on one, doggin', sneakin' deacon, step out on one, tip, working late at the office. See UNFAITHFUL.

UNTRUSTWORTHY adj. rat, fink, rat fink, stool pigeon, stoolie, crooked, shady, sneaky, sharp, shifty, shifty-eyed, Honest John, doberman (Af. Am.), trust one as far as one can swing a cat, trust one as far as one can throw an elephant. See DISHONEST.

UNTRUTHFUL adj. fishy, jivey, jive-assed, shuckin' and jivin', two-faced, shuck, gil, Hollywood, reach-me-down, put-on, slick, sincere, snide, phony, bogus, fake, cry crocodile tears.

UNUSABLE adj. crashed, down, gronked, busted, dusted, out-of-order, out of commission, kaput, haywire, no go. See DAMAGED.

UNUSUAL adj. 1. kooky, kinky, funky, far out, way out, out-of-this-world, out-of-sight, out in left field, offbeat, off the beaten track, bent, melba, quirky, weird, wild, crazy, radical (not Pol.), off the wall. See STRANGE. 2. funky, gnarly, mega-gnarly, unreal, rat-fuck, cool, zero cool, cold, wicked, nose-cone, catch, find, stellar, dream, lollapaloosa, not too shabby, something, something else, state of the art, too much, the utmost, shirt, shirty, tawny. See also EXCELLENT, NEW. 3. scarcer than hen's teeth, numerous as chicken lips.

UNUSUALLY adv. awful, awfully, real, really, daisy, mighty, plenty, so, so much, too much, terribly, terrifically, almighty, powerful, right.

UNVARNISHED adj. 1. vanilla, folksy, homey, haimish, open-and-shut, meat and potatoes, clean, white-bread, what you see is what you get. See PLAIN. 2. it, for real, the real McCoy, real stuff, genuine article, the real goods, honest-to-God, legit. See GENUINE.

UNVEIL v. out, come out, come out of the closet, bring it out into the daylight, let it all hang out, spring, spring one's duke, tip one's hand, tip one's duke, open up, give the show away. See EXPOSE.

UNWANTED adj. lousy, who needs it, need it like a hole in the head, this I need yet?, from hunger, for the birds, NIMBY (not in my back yard), excess baggage, drug on the market.

UNWAVERING adj. set, dead set on, buried in concrete, solid as a rock, Rock of Gibraltar, pat, stand-pat, stay put, brick wall, unflappable. See STUBBORN.

UNWED adj. single, single-o, bach, old bach, old maid.

UNWELCOME adj. 1. left out in the cold, black-balled, cold-shouldered, not in the picture, baldhead, shut-out. 2. lousy, who needs it, need it like a hole in the head, this I need yet?, from hunger, for the birds, NIMBY (not in my back yard), excess baggage, drug on the market.

UNWELL adj. draggin', draggin' one's ass, peaky, run down, down with, got a bug, got the bug, rocky, punk, feeling rotten, poorly, feeling awful, under the weather, below par, off one's feed, sick as a dog, laid low. See ILL.

UNWORKABLE adj. crashed, down, go down, out of whack, out of kilter, out of order, out of commission, kaput, on the fritz, conked-out, no go. See DAMAGED.

UNWORLDLY adj. 1. low-tech, folksy, haimish, homey, corny, cornball, corn-fed, off the cob, on the cob, Golden Bantam, cracker barrel, mossback. 2. uncool, clean, a narb, narbo, cube, square, L7, duck, boob, hayseed, green-ass, eight-ball, not wrapped too tight, wide-eyed, wet behind the ears, babe in the woods, Bambi, bush-league, country, hick, shit kicker, don't know shit from Shinola, don't know one's ass from a hole in the ground. See UNSOPHISTICATED.

UNWRAPPED adj. bald.

UNYIELDING adj. hard-nosed, hard-core, hard-shell, hard-line, tough nut, take no prisoners, locked in, dig in one's heels, hold the fort, hold the line, hardheaded, pigheaded, burly, stiff-necked, dead set on. See STUBBORN.

UPBRAID v. kick ass and take names, fire on, rip on, chew, chew ass, chew out, eat out, bawl out, cuss out, lay into, jump down one's throat, climb all over, rake, rake up one side and down the other, take up one side and down the other, rake over the coals, have one on the carpet, call to task, dress down, read the riot act, tell where to get off, give one hail Columbia, let one have it, settle one's hash. See REBUKE.

UPHEAVAL n. 1. blue ruin, shit hit the fan. See also DISASTER. 2. about-face, flip-flop, turnaround, switch, switchover, new ball game, new deal, new shuffle.

UPHOLD v. stick by, stick up for, back up, pat on the back, hear it for, prop up, hold one's end up, hold a brief for, boost. See SUPPORT.

UPLIFT n. uptick, upping, boost, pickup.

UPLIFT v. 1. buck up, pick up, brace up, chirk up, perk up, give a lift, put one on top of the world, put one on cloud nine, snap out of it, let the sunshine in. 2. hear it for, sound off for, root for.

UPLIFTED adj. flying, float, float on air, cloud seven, cloud nine.

UPPER CLASS n. the 400, the four hundred, the beautiful people, glitterati, upper crust, blue blood, FFV's (First Families of Virginia), high society, smart set, jet set, Eurotrash, our crowd, the establishment. See ELITE.

UPPERMOST adj. 1. big-shot, big-shit, high up, higher ups, high muck, high-muck-a-muck, high pillow, top brass, big number, big wheel, head honcho, main squeeze. See EXECUTIVE. 2. world-class, greatest, out-of-sight, out-of-this-world, bitchin', twitchin', boss, tops, the most, A-list, endsville, the end, master (Af. Am.), solid gold, winner. See BEST. See also EXCELLENT.

UPRIGHT adj. up front, straight, straight-arrow, square shooter, true blue, righteous, Christian, kosher, Mr. Clean, real people, third-rail, all wool and a yard wide. See VIRTUOUS.

UPROAR n. to-do, flap, fuss, row, stir, stink, big stink, rhubarb, hoo-ha, hubba-hubba, hullabaloo, rowdydow, rumble, rumpus, ruckus, ruction, shindy, shivaree, commo, dust-up, fofarraw, free-for-all, brawl, jihad, all hell broke loose, kickup, wing-ding, raise Cain, raise sand, roughhouse, buzz-buzz, fuzz-buzz, haroosh, big scene. See also TURMOIL.

UPSET adj. 1. rattled, thrown, fussed, defrosted, shook up, antsy, creeped-out, hissy, jittery, jumpy, charged-up, in a botheration, in a stew, fidgety, on pins and needles, lost one's cool. See DISTURBED. 2. dragged, low, ass in a sling, dick in the dirt, blue, got the blue devils, buggin', sob story, sob stuff, tearjerker, weeper, teardrop special, flaked-out, psyched-out, shot to pieces, all torn up, broken up, cut up, unglued, unscrewed, unzipped, come apart at the seams. See UNHAPPY.

UPSET n. foul-up, fuck-up, screw-up, mishmosh, mishmash, goulash, mess and a half, don't trip, flusteration, flustration, stew, sweat, tizzy, hassle, free-for-all. See TURMOIL.

UPSET v. 1. adjy, psych, spook, get to, flip, flip out, craze, curdle, bug, bug up, fire up, key up, egg on, turn on, pick on, make waves, make a scene, give one a turn, give one a hard time, stir up, rattle, floor, throw. See DISTURB. 2. queer, crimp, cramp, put a crimp in, cramp one's style, stymie, skin, snooker, crab, hang up, hold up, foul up, fuck up, louse up, snafu, bollix, gum, gum up the works, fake out, put off, flummox, buffalo, bamboozle, fuddle, stump, cross, cross up, double-cross, give one the business, throw a monkey wrench into the works, upset one's apple cart, spike one's guns, steal one's thunder, trash, take one down, take care of, take the wind out of one's sails, knock the bottom out of, knock the chocks from under one, knock the props from under one, down one, ditch, give the slip, skip out on, duck, dodge, get around, give the runaround, run circles around, run rings around.

UPSETTING adj. downer, drag, bummer, bad scene, buzz crusher, bringdown, bring one down, slump, blue funk, crash.

UP TO DATE adj. now, today, state-of-the-art, avant-garde, the leading edge, the cutting edge, at the cutting edge, fly, with it, chilly, what's happening, what's in, the in-thing, contempo, po-mo (postmodern), last word, the latest, newfangled. See NEW.

URBANITE n. city slicker, cliff dweller, cave dweller, subway rider, strap-hanger, street people, Broadway baby, townee, towner.

URCHIN n. J.D. (juvenile delinquent), punk, snot-nose, snot-nose kid, holy terror, guttersnipe, mudlark, raggedy muffin. See also CHILD.

URETHRA n. plumbing, pipe.

URGE n. itch, hard-on, wide-on (Fem.), nasties, beaver fever, sweet tooth, druthers, weakness, fire in the belly, the munchies (food), yen. See DESIRE.

URGE v. fire up, put up to, turn on, egg one on, goose, bug, sell one on, work on, put the bee on, hold one's feet to the fire, twist one's arm, lay a rap, lay it on thick. See PERSUADE, PUSH.

URGENT adj. heavy, heavy number, heavyweight, heavy stuff, serious jelly, fire in the belly, heat's on, hurry-up call, matter of life and death, chips are down, like all-get-out, hot flash, touch-and-go, touchy.

URINAL n. duck (bed). See also TOILET.

URINATE v. pee, pea, piss, leak, take a leak, go, go wee-wee, go pee-pee, tinkle, wee, wee-wee, make wee-wee, make pee-pee, pish, number one, make number one, spend a penny, powder one's nose, go to the john, go to the can, go to the Chic Sale, lift a leg, drain one's radiator, drain the dragon, drain the main vein, drain the dew, drain the dew from one's lily, pump ship, wet one's pants, call, nature's call, let fly, piddle, make water, make a pit stop, take a whizz, sis-sis, siss, see a man about a dog, go play in the sandbox, answer nature's call, answer the call, one's back teeth are floating (urgent need to).

URINE n. pee, pee-pee, number one, piddle, pish, piss, tinkle, wee, wee-wee.

USE n. one's bag, thing, Jones, into, hang-up, shot, kick.

USE v. 1. truck with, sign on, sign up, take on, ink, bring on board, come on board. 2. pick one's brains, mine, trip on one. 3. eat up (use entirely), chew up.

USED adj. previously owned, secondhand.

USED CAR n. cream puff (good), lemon (bad).

USED-UP adj. down the tube, petered out, eighty-six, 86, out, cashed, cheapie, hand-me-down, reach-me-down, secondhand, secondhand Rose, shot, experienced, had, re-cycled.

USELESS adj. 1. junk, rat's-ass, no-good, N.G., dust, lousy, hill of beans, crap, lemon, dreck, two-bit, diddly, diddly-poo, doodly, doodly-poo, down, on down time, on the blink, on the bum, out of action, no-go, run-down, dead-ass, dinger, busted, had it, on the fritz, kaput, garbage, bone (street talk), white elephant, humpty-dumpty, hump, jeasley, no bargain, ice, pretzels, shitbox, shitbag, shitburger, ain't worth shit, ain't worth the powder to blow it to hell, ain't worth a hill of beans, ain't worth a hoot, ain't worth a plugged nickel, go tits up, blah, stiffo, tin, wood, dead wood, dreck, dud, foul ball, flat tire. 2. total shuck, that dog won't hunt, wombat (waste of money, brains and time), goin' round in circles, in a vicious circle, spin one's wheels, on a treadmill, going nowhere, goner, gone goose, dead duck, wild-goose chase, on a wild-goose chase, no way, can't win for losin', no-win situation, shoulda stood in bed, go fight City Hall, might as well talk to the wall, go hit your head against the wall, locking the barn after the horse is stolen, looking for a needle in a haystack, save one's breath, not a ghost of a chance, not a Chinaman's chance, not a prayer, not a snowball's chance in hell, not till hell freezes over, who needs it?, I need it like a hole in the head, this I need yet? See also INEFFECTIVE.

USUAL adj. 1. same old shit, SOS, same old same old (Af. Am.), sked, grind, daily grind, groove, channels, cut-and-dried, playing it safe, in the groove, in a rut, chicken, according to Hoyle. 2. garden variety, everyday, plastic, cotton-pickin', so-so, vanilla, mainstream, run-of-the-mill. See AVERAGE.

USURER n. shark, loan shark, shylock, shy, juice dealer.

USURP v. 1. take over, annex, grab, grab hold of, glom on to, clap hands on, get one's fingers on, get one's hands on, swipe, kipe, highjack, hijack, high-grade. See APPROPRIATE. 2. worm in, worm one's way in, squeeze in, elbow in, horn in, chisel in, muscle in, work in, barge in, butt in.

UTAH Beehive State, Mormon State.

UTENSIL n. gismo, gadget, widget, sucker, motherfucker, mofo, grabber, gimmick, whatchamacallit, what's it, whatchee, thingamajig, thingumabob, dojigger, domajig, dohickey, dingbat, dingus, goofus, gasser. See APPARATUS.

UTENSILS n. fighting tools (knife, fork and spoon, WWII), tools (table).

UTILITARIAN adj. commonsensical, hard-headed, nuts and bolts.

UTMOST adj. 1. worst-case scenario, glorkish, ultra-ultra, out-of-bounds, out-of-sight, out-of-this-world, last straw, the straw that broke the camel's back, too-too, too much, bitter end, the pits, the dogs, the least. See EXTREME. 2. world-class, number one, numero uno, ten, 10 ace-high, aces, the most, mostest, greatest, baaaadest, key, bitchin', twitchin', bump'n', stokin', tubular, vicious, wailing, whaling, dope on a rope, hype, stink, stone, stone groove, tops. See BEST.

UTOPIA n. Erewhon, pie in the sky, Shangri-la.

UTOPIAN adj. pie-in-the-sky.

UTTER v. go, spiel, jaw, lip, chin, gas, chaff, modulate, modjitate, splib, splib de wib, slide one's jib, cut it up, verbalize, mouth. See TALK.

V

V n. Victor.

VACANT LOT n. prairie (Midwest).

VACATION n. two weeks with pay, vaykay, getaway, gafiate, time off, layoff, a few days off, eyes to cool it, liberty, gone fishing.

VACATIONER n. jet-setter, globe-trotter, out-of-towner, punter (easily defrauded); snowbird, snowflake, sunflower (south for the winter).

VACCINATE v. give a shot, shoot, give one the square needle, give one the hook, hook, stick one.

VACCINATED adj. stabbed in the ass, got the hook, got the square needle, binged (WWI).

VACCINATION n. shot, shot in the arm, shot in the ass, stab in the ass, booster, booster shot.

VACILLATE v. straddle, fence-straddle, fence hanger, on the fence, sit on the fence, yo-yo, hot and cold, run hot and cold, hedge, hedge off, blow hot and cold, shilly-shally, back and fill, wimpy, wishy-washy, waffle, hem and haw, pussyfoot around.

VACILLATING adj. wishy-washy, waffling.

VACUOUS adj. dead-ass, dorf, droid, ditzo, dickhead, dickweed, dickwad, doofus, vacant lot, Z-head, beanbrain, jel, light's on but nobody's home, dimbo, dumbfuck, dumbshit, subhuman, mouth breather, mental giant, mental midget, zombie, butthead, belt does not go through all the loops, doesn't have both oars in the water, beau, gink, droob. See STUPID.

VACUUM n. vac.

VACUUM CLEANER n. bagpipe.

VACUUM TUBE n. bottle.

VAGABOND n. floater, ragbag, on the bum, king of the road, bo, 'bo, road agent. See VAGRANT.

VAGINA n. pussy, cunt, vige, snatch, twat, beaver, crack, hole, joy hole, pit, cockpit, quiff, quim, purse, snapper, red snapper, snapping pussy, trim, ginch, box, fur, fur pie, furburger, furrow, gash, slash, nookie, poontang, poonage, poo-poo, vag, rosebud, tail, clam, bearded clam, tuna, lower lips, lotus, cabbage, coochie (Af. Am.), cookie, love muscle, love canal, love tunnel, chinchilla, kitty, monkey, pink eye, slice, slit, fireplace, oven, Holiday Inn, cock inn, Cape Horn, snack bar, sardine can, ace, ace of spades, coffee shop, mink, cuzzy, cooz, coozy, cooch, chacha, chocha,

twelge, futy, futz, gigi, giggy, geegee, jazz, jelly roll, jing-jang, nautch, notch, piece, cunny, honey pot, fruit cup, shaf, fern, muffin, muff, McMuff, Garden of Eden, mount, Mount Joy, receiving set, gold mine, moneymaker, altar of love, puka, meat, dark meat, white meat, pink, the Y, middle eye, Venus mound, Venus-flytrap, beauty spot, crack of heaven, cavern, vertical smile, baby factory (all Obsc.).

VAGINAL SECRETION n. gravy, cunt juice, oil of horn, vagina juice (all Obsc.).

VAGRANCY n. vag.

VAGRANT n. vag, tomato can vag, bum, on the bum, stumblebum, tramp, hard road freak, hobo, ragbag, bag lady, bag woman, dock rat, drifter, king of the road, bo, bust, stiff, stiffo, blanket stiff, bindlestiff, bindleman, deadbeat, dead one (ex), floater, dingbat, ding-dong, gay cat, jungle buzzard, road agent, on the burrola (U., 1930). See also BEGGAR.

VAGUE adj. 1. fuzzy, out to lunch, spacey. 2. doubletalk, doublespeak, hot air, that doesn't chop any wood, that doesn't cut any ice.

VAIN adj. puffed-up, stuck on oneself, ego-tripping, high-and-mighty, big head, have one's glasses on (Af. Am.), puffed up, big I am, stuck on oneself, think one's shit doesn't stink. See CONCEITED.

VAIN, IN adv. 1. total shuck, goin' round in circles, in a vicious circle, on a treadmill, going nowhere, wombat (waste of money, brains, and time), spin one's wheels, wild-goose chase. 2. no way, can't win for losin', no-win situation, go fight City Hall, not a ghost of a chance, not a prayer, not a snowball's chance in hell, looking for a needle in a haystack, save one's breath. See USELESS.

VALIANT adj. gritty, gutsy, gutty, spunky, nervy, game, stand tall, tough it out, bigger'n life, fire-eater, hairy, cool hand. See FEARLESS.

VALID adj. 1. legit, kosher, raw (Af. Am.), card-carrying, sure enough, honest-to-God, twenty-four-carat, all wool and a yard wide, on the legit, on the level, on the up and up, stand up, hold up, hold water, hold together, hang together, hold up in the wash, wash, go, fly, okayed. 2. for real, honest-to-God, the lowdown, the emess, righteous, out of the horse's mouth, straight from the horse's mouth.

VALIDATE v. give the nod, give the go-ahead, give the green light, give the stamp of approval, make something stick, okay, OK, sign off on, put one's John Hancock on, rubber-stamp. See CONFIRM.

VALIDATION n.   go-ahead, green light, okay, OK, mouthful (you said a mouthful), say-so, one's stamp of approval, Good Housekeeping Stamp of Approval, rubber stamp. See CONFIRMATION.

VALISE n.   jiffy bag, keister, valpack, tote bag.

VALIUM n.   housewife's delight, ums, V, volume, downer, dies, dis, dyes, vals, mello yello, mellow yellow, true blue.

VALOR n.   balls, guts, heart, nerve, stomach, what it takes, grit, true grit, spunk, backbone, moxie, starch, clock, corazón, Dutch courage (intoxicated).

VALOROUS adj.   gritty, gutsy, gutty, game, spunky. See also COURAGEOUS.

VALUABLE adj.   worth its weight in gold, worth a king's ransom, collectibles, high price tag, big price tag, what the traffic will bear, worth an arm and a leg, important. See also EXPENSIVE.

VALUATE v.   check, check out, dig it, eye, look over, peg, size, size up, dope out, take account of, kick tires, figure, figure in, guesstimate, windshield appraisal (superficial, from a car), have one's number, take one's measure.

VALUE v.   dope out, guesstimate, what the traffic will bear, figure, figure in, figure out, cut ice, cut some ice, keep tab, keep tabs, windshield appraisal (superficial, from a car), size up, take one's measure. See also APPRAISE.

VALUELESS adj.   diddly, diddly-shit, shitbox, shitbag, shitburger, ain't worth shit, ain't worth the powder to blow it to hell, ain't worth a hoot, ain't worth a plugged nickel, ain't worth a hill of beans, garbage, junk, dunnage (dockworker use), no-count, from hunger, white elephant, jeasley, tinhorn. See USELESS.

VAMPIRE n.   vamp.

VAN n.   cock wagon, sin-bin, See AUTOMOBILE.

VANDALIZE v.   trash, smash, smash up, foul up, crud up, scuzz up, mess up, rack up, take a joint apart, break the lease, blue ruin. See DESTROY.

VANGUARD adj.   leading-edge, cutting-edge, state-of-the-art, cool, far out, beat, beat generation, beatnik, way out, hep, hip, hipster, hippie, yippie, crazies, beard, cool cat, new wave. See also NEW.

VANILLA adj.   van.

VANISH v.   do a vanishing act, fade, fade out of sight, fade away, get small (from a crime), pull a Judge Crater.

VANITY n.   ego trip.

VAPID adj.   nowhere, the least, noplaceville, Nadaville, nothing, nothing doing, wiped out, flat-tire, zero, big zero. See INSIPID.

VARIABLE adj.   iffy, waffling, yo-yo, etched in sand.

VARIANCE n.   1. about-face, flip-flop, mid-course correction, switch, switchover, transmogrification. See MODIFICATION. 2. diff, different strokes, different strokes for different folks.

VARIETY n.   mishmash, mishmosh, mixed bag, combo, everything but the kitchen sink, duke's mixture (strange), stew, soup (liquid), lorelei.

VARIETY STORE n.   dime store, five-and-dime, five-and-ten, five-and-ten-cent store, Kress's, Woolworth's, drugstore.

VARNISH v.   cover up, soft-pedal, whitewash. See LIE. See also CONCEAL.

VARY v.   blow hot and cold, hem and haw, yo-yo, shilly-shally. See VACILLATE.

VAST adj.   humongoid, humongous, humungous, humongo, mungo, moby, bonzai; mother, motherfucker, big mother (Obsc.); big mama, big daddy, super, super-duper, supercolossal, seagoing, jumbo, lunker, blimp, barn door, butt-kicking, whale of a, whaling, whacking, walloping, lolloping, whopping, whopper. See also BIG.

VAUDEVILLE n.   the circuit, Orpheum Circuit, Orpheum time, two-a-day, six-a-day, the big time, small time, peeler. See also THEATER.

VAULT n.   biscuit, box, crib, peter, can.

VEER v.   1. cut, hang a right, hang a left, make a right, make a left, swivel, sideslip. 2. drift, get around.

VEGETABLES n.   veggies.

VEGETABLE SOUP n.   a splash out of the garden.

VEGETARIAN n.   sproutsy (Stu.), veggy, vegan.

VEHEMENT adj.   hot, hot for, blow-top, raising a rumpus, raising a ruckus, kicking up a row, kicking up a shindy, hopped up, catawamptious, come out swinging, come on like gangbusters, come on strong, enforcer, on the make, out for a rep, ball of fire, fireball, heller, hyper.

VEHEMENTLY adv.   like crazy, like mad, terrifically, really truly, fer sure, you know it, straight out, no buts about it, no ifs ands or buts, in spades, with bells on, with knobs on, with tits on, in a handbasket, I'll tell the world, I'll tell the cockeyed world, come hell or high water.

VEHICLE n.   1. wheels, van, jeep, bus, chine, mobe, wheel chair, boom car (loud radio or tape), jalopy, crate, junk heap, jitney, boat, buggy, muscle car, hot rod, chariot, flivver; Humvee, Hummer (Mil.). See also AUTOMOBILE. 2. four-by-four, four-by-eight, quarter ton, eighteen-wheeler, rig, semi, Big Mack, oil burner (diesel), dump, draggin' wagon pickemup, horse, kidney buster, scow, carry-all, freight box. See also TRUCK.

VEIL v. 1. cover up, wear cheaters, slap on some glims, flash the gogs, beard. 2. stonewall, whitewash, blow smoke, put up a front. 3. finesse it, launder, paper over, sweep under the rug. See COVER UP.

VEIN n. blue pipe, road maps (prominent).

VENAL adj. on the take, on the pad, open, wide-open, go with the money, money talks bullshit walks, meateater, racket up, something rotten in Denmark.

VENDOR n. peddler, drummer, bell-ringer, ——— dog (e.g., shoe dog), medicine man, pitchman, skig, spieler, tinge, Arab, bag guy (balloon), butch, butcher, hawker, cheap jack, Cheap John; candy man, travel agent (LSD), pusher (drugs), dealer.

VENEREAL DISEASE n. VD, AIDS, clap, claps, dose, dose up, dose of claps, old clap, old dose (neglected case), package, hammerhead clap, the drip, blue balls, crud, scrud, double scrud, syph, syff, siff, sigma phi (syphilis, Medic.), head cold, caught a cold, picked up something, picked up a nail, lulu (painful case), pissing razor blades, burn, shank, chanck, dog, old dog, ten-year-old dog, the rahl, rahl up, brothel sprouts, Cupid's itch, Venus's curse, crotch pheasants, lobster tails, full house (combination of), sct one up (infect), short-arm inspection (examination of males for). See also SYPHILIS; GONORRHEA.

VENERY n. 1. fuck, jazz, screw, lay, hump, boff, nookie, poke, piece of ass, bang, action, balling, shot, a hormone fix, I. & I. (Mil., intercourse and intoxication), roll in the hay, do the nasty, do night laps, do the ootie ootie, boogaloo, do the wild thing, do you up, bust you out, do damage, get done, get down, get down to basics, get horizontal, lay pipe, go the limit, score, yum-yum, dirty deed, beat someone with an ugly stick, get beat with an ugly stick, oil change, noonie, matinee, parallel parking, night baseball, fooling around, laps around the track, hoe hoppin' (promiscuous, Af. Am.), bush patrol. See SEXUAL INTERCOURSE. 2. high living, life in the fast lane, burn one's candle at both ends, go to hell in a handbasket. See DISSOLUTE.

VENGEANCE n. eye for an eye, tit for tat, get even.

VENOMOUS adj. bitchy, cussed, catty, evil, waspish, dirty, mean, ornery; turbobitch, stanky (Fem.), accidentally on purpose, do one dirt. See also ANTAGONISTIC; MALEVOLENT.

VENTURE n. 1. thing, thing one's into, baby, bag, bag one's into, biggie (major), deal, pet project, proposition, setup. See also BUSINESS. 2. flyer, flutter, header, plunge, on spec, spec, stab, shot, maximax (big return, big loss), maximin (small return, big loss), minimax (safe). See WAGER.

VENTURE v. take the action, take a flyer, play, get down, get on, lay it on the line, put up, take a plunge, play the market, have a fling at, give a whirl, take a crack at, make

a stab at, stick one's neck out, go out on a limb. See RISK. See also WAGER.

VENTURESOME adj. 1. dicey, chancy, on thin ice, out on a limb, off the deep end, in the tube, one could get burned. See DANGEROUS. 2. ambish, ballsy, bogard, come-on, come on like gangbusters, come on strong, gumption, spunk, balls, drive, hungry, guts, go-go, full of piss and vinegar, full of get-up-and-go, get-up-and-go, get-out-and-go, go-getter, pushy, fair hell, heller, moxi, taking it to 'em, take charge, takeover, take the bull by the horns, play hardball, play for keeps, ball of fire, hotshot, moving out.

VERACIOUS adj. up front, right up front, open, raw (Af. Am.), like it is, call it like it is, lay it on the line, on the up-and-up, on the level, the emess, no lie, what you see is what you get, honest-to-God, true blue, righteous, kosher, boy scout, Mr. Clean, straight-arrow, straight shooter. See TRUTHFUL.

VERACITY n. honest-to-God truth, the word, gospel, no shit, straight shit, straight stuff, straight goods, the real deal (Af. Am.), how things are, like it is, the real emess, the real McCoy. See TRUTH.

VERANDA n. gallery, front stoop, stoop.

VERBOSE adj. gabby, windy, long-winded, talker, great talker, yacker, windbag, bag of wind, load of wind, windjammer, barber, have verbal diarrhea, diarrhea of the mouth. See TALKATIVE.

VERIFICATION n. dope, goods, info, smoking gun (crucial), clincher, grabber, chapter and verse, straight stuff, from the horse's mouth. See PROOF.

VERIFY v. add up, check out, check up, check up on, double-check, dig it, eye, eyeball, peg, look-see, make sure, size, size up, crack on one or something, debunk (prove false), pan out, stand up, hold one up.

VERITABLE adj. for real, honest-to-God, the real McCoy, genuine article, the real goods, on the legit, on the level, the emess, straight dope, no buts about it. See TRUE.

VERMIN n. crabs, cootie, cutie, cootie garage (hair puffs in which cootie lives), grayback, seam squirrel, crum, shimmy lizard; crumby, lousy (afflicted with).

VERMONT Green Mountain State.

VERNACULAR n. jive talk, lingo, street talk, flash (thieves), gobbledygookcsc, Hillspeak (Washington, D.C.), psychobabble, Urbabble (city Govt.). See LANGUAGE.

VERSATILE adj. all-around, AC/DC, acdac, cosplug, switch hitter, go every which way, one who can do it all, hang loose, roll with the punches, putty in one's hands, fungible.

VERSED adj. hip, hip to the jive, savvy, fly, with it, all woke up, tuned-in, chilly, been there, in the picture, booted on, on the inside, in the know, enough ducks in a row. See KNOWLEDGEABLE.

VERTIGO n.   wooziness, woozy.

VERVE n.   go juice, bounce, snap, zap, zing, zip, pow, sock, pizzazz, splash, moxie, punch, vim, pepper, get-up-and-go, piss and vinegar. See EXUBERANCE.

VERY adv.   way, awful, awfully, gosh awful, wicked, mucho, mondo, mongo, something, real, really, but, butt, hella, helluva, crazy, mad, jolly, bloody, daisy, mighty, plenty, so, so much, too much, stone (stone deaf), downright (So.), terribly, terrifically, almighty, powerful, right.

VESSEL n.   steamer, liner, tramp, tub, bathtub, bucket, rust bucket, hooker, can, ol' lady, wagon, battlewagon, jeep, oil burner, sieve, bateau.

VESTIBULE n.   squat pad.

VESTMENTS n.   1. clericals. 2. threads, togs, toggery, duds, outfit, rags, glad rags, get-up, get-out, Barbie and Ken (conventional), vine, weeds, dry goods, California black tie (any colorful variation of formal wear), California chic (expensive casual), flash, rig, ready-made, drape, drapery, drapes, set of drapes, bib and tucker. See CLOTHING.

VEST POCKET n.   sky pocket.

VETERAN adj.   longtime, pro, vet, hep, hip, has what it takes, knows one's stuff, knows one's way around, knows the ropes, knows the score, knows which side is up, knows which side his bread is buttered on, knows which side his head is battered on, knows how, knows one's onions, up, wised up, up to snuff, up to speed, to the mark, up one's alley, from way back, one of the old school, won one's spurs, kicked around, been around, been around the block, been around the block a few times, been hit before, been there before, been through the mill, been through the wars, cut a few touches, wasn't born yesterday, didn't come into town on a load of wood.

VETERAN n.   vet, G.I., ex-GI, got his ruptured duck (WWII), war-horse, pro, old pro, old hand, old-timer, old salt, old sea dog, shellback. 2. cat, hepcat, hip cat, sport, city, slicker. See SOPHISTICATED.

VETERINARIAN n.   horse doctor, vet.

VETO n.   ding, zing, blackball.

VETO v.   kill, burn, burn down, shoot down, pass, pass on, pass by, throw out, throw away, chuck, chuck out, round file, heave-ho, dog, cut, ding, zing, nix, not (used at end of a positive sentence), put down, turn thumbs down, thumb down, blackball, not go for, adios it, eighty-six, 86, hell no. See also NEGATE.

VEX v.   bug, ride, be at, be on the back of, eat, shiv, noodge, brown off, tick off, piss one off, turn one off, cop an attitude (Af. Am.), go on make my day, give one a hard time,

get in one's hair, get under one's skin, drive one up a tree, rile, chap, hack, hassle, that grinds my gears, push one's key, push the right button, rub the wrong way. See ANNOY.

VEXATION n.   rise, botheration, downer, worriment, bad news, headache, pain in the ass, pain in the neck, tsuris. See ANNOYANCE.

VEXED adj.   bugged, hacked, steamed, uptight, clutched up, hacked, hacked-off, brassed-off, cheesed-off, pissed-off, peed-off, tee'd-off, browned-off, riled, aggro, rubbed the wrong way. See ANNOYED.

VIBRAHARP n.   vibes.

VIBRAPHONE n.   vibes, bells.

VIBRATION n.   judder, shimmy.

VIBRATO n.   wah-wah.

VICAR n.   padre, the rev, Holy Joe, sky pilot, sky scout, preacher man, buck, sin hound. See CLERGYMAN.

VICE-PRESIDENT n.   V.P., Veep, veepost.

VICE SQUAD n.   pussy posse, John squad.

VICINITY n.   1. hood, nabe, neck of the woods, territory, turf. See NEIGHBORHOOD. 2. around, pretty near, practically, in the ballpark of, in the neighborhood of. See NEAR.

VICIOUS adj.   bad-assed, bitchy, stanky (Fem.), cussed, dirty, mean, ornery, rough, tough, nuts, poison, bum, lousy, murderous, kill-crazy, doin' dirt, eighteen-carat, hellish. See also MEAN.

VICISSITUDE n.   flip-flop, about-face, turnaround, mid-course correction, switch, switchover, new ball game, new deal, new shuffle.

VICTIM n.   mark, easy mark, easy make, believer, pigeon, patsy, pushover, sucker, grape (waiting to be squeezed), turkey, vic, lame, mom, chump, mooch (commodity scam), a narb, square, clown, cousin, setup, soft touch, fall guy, sitting duck, babe in the woods, boob, schlemiel, stooge, cat's paw, jack, duck, goofus, gopher, jay, lobster, round-heeled, sweetheart, quick push, softie, sweet pea, tool, tourist, yuld, yold, yo-yo, apple, clay pigeon, angel (criminal), fish, sausage, fruit, lamb, Clyde, dumb john, Winchell, Bates, John Bates, Mr. Bates, babe, cinch, lead-pipe cinch, grunt, score, storch, greeny, greener, sap, saphead, prize sap, addict, eggs, comedown (pickpocket), mushroom (victim of drive-by shooting).

VICTIMIZE v.   jerk one around, jerk one's chain, fuck, frig, fuck one over, shuck and jive, run a game on, rope in, fleece, stick, burn, bilk, clip, con, chisel, gouge, stiff, sting, sucker into, double-shuffle, stack the cards, set up, snow under. See TRICK.

VICTIMIZED adj. stung, stuck, taken, been had, jobbed, fucked over, screwed, stiffed, ripped-off, hosed, get hosed, got a haircut, got trimmed, rooked, burned, boned, juiced, dicked, gaffled, snowed under, steamrolled, bulldozed. See TRICKED.

VICTOR n. champ, king o' the hill, number one, numero uno, the greatest, top dog, medalist, gold medalist, takes the gold, takes the cake, shoo-in, title holder. See also SUCCESSFUL.

VICTORIOUS adj. on top of the heap, arrived, fat, fat city, king of the hill, duke of the catwalk, loving life, loving it, blow one away, blow one out of the water, have one by the balls, have one by the short hairs, have one by the tail, have it made, lucked out (against all odds).

VICTORY n. clean sweep, grand slam, hole in one, win, do a Rocky, grab the gold, nose out, beat the competish, bring home the bacon, bull's-eye, slam, hit, killing, upset, pay dirt. See TRIUMPH.

VICTUALS n. grubbery, vittles, chow, bite, snack, grub, fast food, pogey, scoff, go juice, chuck, blue plate, black plate (soul food), pecks. See FOOD.

VIDEO CASSETTE RECORDER n. VCR, homevid, home video.

VIDEO MASTER OF CEREMONIES n. video jockey, V.J., veejay.

VIE v. scramble for, go for, go for broke, go for the throat, go for the jugular, go for the gold, jockey for position, buck, push, hassle, sweat, sweat it.

VIET CONG n. Charlie, V.C., Cong, Victor Charlie (also soldier).

VIETNAM Nam.

VIETNAMESE n. gook, dink, gink, chink, slope, banana (favors whites, yellow on the outside white inside), zip, wog (all Derog.).

VIETNAMESE HOUSE OR HUT n. hooch.

VIEW n. 1. judgment call, value judgment, op, say-so, slant, take, two cents' worth, vox pop, another county heard from, another country heard from. See also ATTITUDE. 2. close-up, C.U., slant, twist. 3. flash, gander, gun, hinge, glom, squint, slant, lamp, look-see, eyeball inspection, pike, swivel.

VIEW v. 1. flash, flash on, glom, glim, gun, beam, scope, spot, spy, dig, read, pipe, rap, eye, eagle-eye, clap eyes on, lay eyes on, set eyes on, get a load of, get an eyeful of, rubberneck. See SEE. 2. go slumming, slum, take in the sights.

VIEWER n. kibitzer, nark, sidewalk superintendent, watcher.

VIEWPOINT n. P.O.V. (point of view), slant, sound, twist, angle, take, two cents' worth, where one is at, where one's head is, another country heard from.

VIGILANT adj. on the ball, on the job, on one's toes, with a weather eye open, with one's eyes peeled, on the lookout, on the qui vive, got it covered, all bases covered, looking to, looking for, waiting on, the noose is hanging, at the ready, loaded for bear. See also ATTENTIVE.

VIGILANTES n. death squad.

VIGOR n. juice, bounce, zing, sock, kick, ginger, clout, punch, steam, hustle, the stuff, get-up-and-go, piss and vinegar, full head of steam. See POWER.

VIGOROUS adj. zippy, zappy, snappy, peppy, got the horses to do it, strong as a horse, strong as a lion, strong as an ox, ball of fire, steamroller, spanking, punchy, come on strong, come on like gangbusters, take over, take charge. See STRONG. See also HEALTHY.

VIGOROUSLY adv. turn on the heat, full on, full tilt, full swing, full steam ahead, all out, slam-bang, by storm, like gangbusters.

VILE adj. rat's-ass, bald, grungy, raunchy, scuzzy, sleazy, sleazeball, cocksucking, shitty, cruddy, burnt, cheesy, the pits, stinking, garbage, the least. See BAD.

VILIFY v. 1. pan, slam, blister, scorch, cap, rap, base on, mud-sling, knock, slice up, rip up the back, give a black eye, mark lousy. See SLANDER. 2. dump on, call down, dress down, put down, scorch, blister, tear into, slam, dog on, rag on, (Hum.), crack on (Hum., Af. Am.), dig at, give a black eye, roast, slag, skin alive. See SCOLD. 3. cuss, damn, darn, drat, flame, jinx, put the horns on, put the whammy on one, put the double whammy on one, give one a kine ahora (Yid.), hoodoo, hoodoo one, voodoo, voodoo one.

VILLAIN n. shit, shitheel, creep, corn dog, scoob, goob, goober, goobatron, yernt, nob, social zero, nothingburger, sleazeball, sleazoid, slime bucket, shower scum, barf bag, wrongo, buddy fucker, bad ass, bad guy, black hat, dirty dog, scalawag. See SCOUNDREL.

VILLAINOUS adj. bad-assed, rat's-ass, sucks, scuzzy, sleazy, sleazeball, bad news, murderous, poison, dirty, doin' dirt, low-down, no-good. See BAD.

VIM n. moxie, bounce, snap, zap, zing, zip, zippo, pow, sock, kick, pizzazz, the force, pepper, get-up-and-go, piss and vinegar. See POWER.

VINDICATION n. tit for tat, eye for an eye, the what-for, the why and wherefore, the why-for. See also EXCUSE.

VIOLA n. chin bass.

VIOLENCE n. storm, ruckus, ruction, rumble, rumpus, shivaree, wing-ding, blast, blow, blowup, flare-up, dust-up, flap, foofaraw, jihad, free-for-all, fuss, tear, hell broke loose, raise Cain, raise sand, roughhouse, rowdydow. See also ANGER.

VIOLENT adj.   kill-crazy, blowtop, flipped, ape, gone ape, got a wild hair up one's ass, on a tear, raising a rumpus, raising a ruckus, kicking up a row, kicking up a shindy, hitting out in all directions.

VIOLENTLY adv.   like crazy, like mad, bulldoze, take by storm, steamroll, steamroller tactics, strong-arm, strong-arm tactics, rockem and sockem, slam-bang, galley west, hell west and crooked (Obs.). See also VEHEMENTLY.

VIOLIN n.   Strad, fiddle, scratch box.

VIOLINIST n.   fiddler, mice, squeaker.

VIOLIN, PLAY THE v.   saw, scrape.

VIRGIN n.   cherry, cherry tree (tall), canned goods, bug, roni (young), old maid, damaged goods (nonvirgin).

VIRGINIA   Cavalier State, Mother of Presidents, Mother of States, Old Dominion.

VIRGINITY n.   unspoiled, clean, cop a cherry, cop her cherry, pop her cherry (take away).

VIRILE adj.   macho, he-man, hunk, beauhunk, tuna, Clydesdale (attractive), hoss (muscular), beefcake, beef-a-roni, Greek god, stud, industrial, mazeh (Yid.), jock, jock-strap, two-fisted, caveman, bucko, hairy, jelly, roll, tiger, two-fisted, colt, chrismo, chismo. See also MAN; POWERFUL.

VIRTUALLY adv.   around, give or take a little, guessti-mate, ball-park figure, in the ball-park of, in the neighbor-hood of, practically, something like, upwards of. See NEARLY.

VIRTUOSO n.   old pro, old hand, ol' professor, brain, pro, pundit, egghead, maven, ringer, shark, sharp, natural, ace, star, superstar, hotshot, hot stuff, tuned-in, whiz, wizard, crackerjack, champ, no slouch, know one's onions, know one's stuff, big-league, enough ducks in a row. See also AUTHORITY; PRODIGY; INTELLIGENT; MUSICIAN; CELEBRITY.

VIRTUOUS adj.   on the up and up, up front, right up front, on the level, honest-to-God, honest Injun, square, Square John, square shooter, true blue, righteous, Christian, kosher, boy scout, Mr. Clean, regular, legit, on the legit, for real, real people, okay people, saint, straight, straight-arrow, straight shooter, straight from the shoulder, straight out, straight dope, straight stuff, straight shit, third-rail, white, damn white, all wool and a yard wide, card-carrying, salt of the earth, a prince of a fellow, pillar of the church.

VIRUS n.   bug, plague, crud, creeping crud, trots turistas, runs, Montezuma's revenge, what's going around.

VISAGE n.   kisser, mug, pan, puss, map, phiz, phizog, biscuit, clock, mask, dial. See FACE.

VISCOUS adj.   gooey, gloppy, globby, gooky, gozzle, goupy, gunky, goonky, gummy.

VISIBLE adj.   plain as the nose on one's face, under one's nose, big as life, out in the open, barefaced, if it were a snake it would bite you. See APPARENT.

VISION n.   1. spook, haunt, hant, haint, things that go bump in the night. 2. trip, head trip, mind trip, castle in the air, fool's paradise, pipe dream, stare into the middle distance, pie in the sky. See also DREAM. 3. dazzler, dream, dreamy, dreamboat, dream puss, dream bait, angel, angel face, angel puss, head rush, stunner, stunning, look like a million, eye-filling, eyeful, a picture, pretty as a picture, centerfold. See BEAUTIFUL.

VISIONARY n.   stargazer, dreamer.

VISIT v.   swing by, fall by, fall down, fall up (Af. Am.), hit, play, pay a call, drop in, drop by, crash (uninvited). See also APPEAR.

VISITOR n.   out-of-towner, company, visiting fireman, punter (easily defrauded), ET (extraterrestrial), little green men, man from Mars.

VISUALIZE v.   dream up, get the picture, head trip. See also THINK; CREATE.

VITAL adj.   l. bottom-line, meat-and-potatoes, nitty-gritty, coal and ice, gutty, name, name of the game. See BASIC. 2. heavy, heavy number, meaningful, business end of, serious shit, serious jelly, matter of life and death, chips are down, underlined. See IMPORTANT.

VITALITY adj.   go juice, bounce, bang, zing, zip, sock, pizzazz, the force, clout, steam, the stuff, full of piss and vinegar, full of p & v. See POWER. See also SPIRITED.

VIVACIOUS adj.   bouncy, grooving, jumping, hyper, swinging, swingle, rocking, salty, upbeat, red-hot, fireball, ball of fire, go-go, full of go. See SPIRITED.

VIXEN n.   bitch, bitch kitty, ball breaker, battle-ax, fish-wife, hellion, hellcat, she-devil, she-wolf, biddy, old biddy, pain in the ass, screech, wet hen.

VOCAL CORDS n.   pipes.

VOCALIST n.   chanteuse, chantoosie, crooner, groaner, canary, warbler, songbird, thrush, nightingale, bel-ter, folkie, monster (popular), shouter (gospel), coon shouter (Derog.), bad pipes (bad).

VOCALIZE v.   groan, moan, chirp, canary, do a canary, croon, warm up, yodel, give out, belt out a song, belt out a number, scat, shout, throw a tonsil.

VOCATION n.   bag, gig, biz, game, gesheft, line, line of business, number, go, do, dodge, what one is into, thing, hang, nine-to-five shit, racket. See OCCUPATION.

VODKA n.   green serpent.

VOGUE, IN adj. faddy, trendy, fly, happenin', what's happening, bust fresh, in, in-thing, the thing, with it, chilly, mod, now, state-of-the-art, up-to-speed, the latest, last word, mod, now, the rage, up-to-the-minute; muffy, fifi, Heather, foof (trendy young woman). See STYLISH.

VOID n. black hole (into which things disappear).

VOID v. 1. ding, zing, nix, not (used at end of a positive sentence), wipe out, take out, knock out, KO, black out, torpedo, kill, queer, shoot down, shoot down in flames, wipe off the map. See CANCEL. 2. sterilize, sanitize, decontaminate, bleep, bleep out, cut, blue-pencil, knock out, X out, trim, gut, clean up, launder, snip, pass up, blow off, drop, rub, squash, squelch. 3. go, go to the can, go to the john, go caca, shit, crap, dump, poop, make poo-poo, shake a few clinkers out; pee, piss, leak, take a leak, make a pit stop, go, go wee-wee, go pee-pee, tinkle, make wee-wee, pish, drain the dragon, drain the main vein, drain the dew piddle, go play in the sandbox (urinate). See BOWEL MOVEMENT; URINATE.

VOLKSWAGEN n. Beetle, bug, Nazi go-cart, VW, V-dub.

VOLUBLE adj. gabby, windy, windbag, bag of wind, gasser, yacker, CBS, load of wind, windjammer, big-mouthed, bucket mouth, motor mouth, gum beater, all jaw, flap jaw, ear duster. See TALKATIVE.

VOLUME n. pump it up (turn up).

VOLUNTEER n. walk-on, buddy (companion to AIDS patient).

VOMIT n. puke, Ralphage.

VOMIT v. barf, puke, be sick, throw up, throw up one's guts, bring up, chuck up, upchuck, urp, boag, bison, water buffalo, yak, yank, reverse gears, whoops, rolf, Ralph, Ralph up, talk to Ralph, talk to Ralph on the big white phone, talk on the big white phone, talk into the porcelain phone, call Ralph, call Hughie, call Ruth, call Earl, talk to Earl, talk to John, talk to the seals, to the curb, York, Buick, sell Buicks, honk, boot, power boot, spule, spew, boff, bof, woof, zukc, shoot one's breakfast (etc.), shoot one's cookies, blow cookies, toss one's cookies, toss one's tacos, toss one's groceries, waste groceries, drop one's cookies, woof cookies, flash, flash the hash, flash one's cookies, flash one's food, feed the fish, lose it, lose one's lunch, launch one's lunch, blow one's lunch, lose one's doughnuts, lose one's groceries, spill the blue groceries, throw doughnuts, blow one's doughnuts, blow one's groceries, blow grits, blow beets, blow chunks, chunk, hurl, hurl chunks, chummy, spit beef, chew the cheese, the technicolor yawn, instant boot camp, marry your porcelain mistress, kiss the porcelain god, bow to the porcelain god, worship the porcelain goddess, worship the throne, pray to the porcelain god, pray to the enamel god, drive the bus, drive the porcelain bus, drive the big white bus, laugh at the carpet, air one's belly, heave, cast the gorge, heave the gorge, good stick (heroin-induced).

VOODOO n. hocus-pocus, mumbo-jumbo, hoodoo, abracadabra, hootchy-kootchy (practitioner).

VORACIOUS adj. dog-hungry, empty, fly light, grits time, have a tapeworm, munchies (follows marijuana use), starving, starved, starved to death, could eat a horse, could eat the asshole out of a bear, piggy, greedy-guts.

VOUCH v. 1. swear up and down, swear on a stack of Bibles, swear till one is blue in the face, cross one's heart and hope to die, say so. See SWEAR. 2. stand up for one, back, get behind one, okay, OK, sign for, cosign, put one's John Hancock on, rubber-stamp. hold one up, go to bat for. See also SUPPORT.

VOW v. cross one's heart and hope to die, swear till one is blue in the face, swear up and down. See SWEAR.

VOYAGE n. hop, swing, jaunt, cruise, junket, trek, overnight, weekend. Cook's tour. See TRAVEL.

VOYAGE v. jet around, go places, hop, city-hop, country-hop, globe-trot, tripping, cruise, hit the road, on the move, trek, do the continent, do Europe (or wherever), junket. See TRAVEL.

VOYAGER n. jet-setter, globe-trotter, deadhead (free), seatcover, dude (bus), drop, line load (taxi), rubberneck, rubbernecker, snowbird, snowflake, sunflower.

VOYEUR n. peek, freak, peeping Tom.

VULGAR adj. 1. cheap, loud, loud-mouthed, foul-mouth, foul-mouthed, raw, skank, tacky, raunchy, X-rated, hard-core, soft-core, blue, dirty, filthy, low-down and dirty, stag, in the gutter, flaming (obscene computer conversations), off-color, rough, rough stuff, salty. 2. garden variety, run of the mill, everyday, dime-a-dozen, plastic, cotton-pickin', chit, low.

VULGARITY n. raunch, flaming (Obsc., computer conversations).

VULNERABLE adj. 1. naked, pigeon, clay pigeon, sitting duck, ass out, neck stuck out, ready to be taken, wide-open, on the line, on the spot, out on a limb, tool, sucker for a left, Achilles heel. 2. soft (nuclear target).

VULVA n. pussy, cunt, snatch, vige, twat, beaver, crack, hole, quiff, quim, box, fur, fur pie, tail, clam, coochie (Af. Am.), nookie, nautch, piece, cunny, muff, receiving set, the Y (Obsc.). See VAGINA.

W

W n. Whiskey, William.

WAFER n. dry cush.

WAFFLE n. collision mat (N.).

WAG n. cutup, life of the party, madcap, trickster, card, a million laughs, kibitzer, funster, punster, quipster, wisecracker. See JOKER.

WAG v. fish-tail.

WAGER n. shot, shot at, get a shot at, long shot, shot in the dark, hundred-to-one shot, spec, break, breaks, big break, even break, odds-on, whack, whack at, go, go at, stab, stab at, have a fling at, prayer, hunch, in the running, fighting chance, outside chance, Chinaman's chance, as much chance as a snowball in hell, snowball chance, fifty-fifty, toss-up, flier, flyer, header, plunge, brodie, play, action, ante, down on, parlay, brinkmanship, maximax (big return, big loss), maximin (small return, big loss), minimax (safe); standoff, push (tie); hedge, hedge-off, layoff, handle (total).

WAGER v. play, plunge, put up, put up or shut up, lay on the line, put it on the line, put on the spot, put one's money where one's mouth is, parlay, take a flier, take a plunge, take a header, chance it, jump off the deep end, take the action, book the action, make book, get down, get down on, on (on a horse), play the ponies, play the market, spec, on spec, go the limit, go whole hog, shoot, shoot one's wad, shoot the works, go for a chunk, go out on a limb, go on the hook for, skate on thin ice, stick one's neck out, hustle, ball the jack, grift, on the grift, stake, backstrap, cheesebox, cap (add illegally); hedge, lay off (relay bet).

WAGES n. bread, sugar, take, take-home, bacon, bacon and eggs, bring home the bacon, eagle shit. See COMPENSATION.

WAGE SCALE n. going rate, scale, top of the show (TV), cheat stick, (worker, logger).

WAIF n. drop, fetch, guttersnipe, mudlark, raggedy-muffin, rustle.

WAIL v. sing the blues, cry the blues, blubber, go for a crying towel, beat one's breast, rain, carry on, howl, raise a howl. See LAMENT.

WAIST n. midsection, spare tire, bulge, battle of the bulge, brisket (fat). See also STOMACH.

WAIT n. hold, on hold, holdup, down, downtime.

WAIT v. cool it, cool one's heels, sweat, sweat it, sweat it out, sweat out, wait out, put on ice, put on hold, hold down, hold the phone, hold the line, hold on, hold everything, hold fire, save it, stall, dork off, hang, hang in, hang on, hang out, hang around, hang about, stick around, sit, sit tight, sit and take it, sit out, sit it out, sit on one's ass, sit on one's butt, sit on one's duff, warm a chair, lay dead, play dead, keep one's shirt on, hold your horses, see which way the cookie crumbles, champ, champ at the bit, chomp at the bit, wait for the other shoe to drop, piddle-diddle (So.), play the waiting game.

WAITER n. garçon, hasher, boy, carhop, coffee bean, punk, soup jockey. See also WAITRESS.

WAITING adj. 1. looking for, waitin' on, waiting for the other shoe to drop, the noose is hanging. 2. in the wings, in the cards, in the wind, at hand, see it coming, it's looking to.

WAITING ROOM n. squat pad, icebox, dugout, bull-pen, green room (The.).

WAIT ON TABLE v. hash, sling hash, deal them off the arm, gun.

WAITRESS n. hasher, girl, miss, biscuit shooter, carhop, coffee bean, curbie, heaver, soup jockey, topless. See also WAITER.

WAKE n. cold-meat party.

WAKE UP interj. rise and shine, roll out, pile out, turn out, hit the deck, show a leg, drop your cocks and grab your socks, piss call.

WAKE UP v. 1. rise and shine, roll out, turn out, pile out, hit the deck, show a leg, drop your cocks and grab your socks, keep banker's hours (late). See AWAKEN. 2. jazz up, juice up, pep up, zip up, key up, fire up, steam up, stir up, get it up, switch on, turn on the heat, rabble-rouse. See EXCITE.

WALK n. 1. constitutional, hump (Mil., with full equipment), legwork, schlep, traipse. 2. pavement, the bricks, byway, trail, stroll, aisle, boardwalk.

WALK v. leg it, hoof it, ankle, ank, toddle, hotfoot, go by hand, sashay, heel-toe express, boot, boot it, foot it, hump (Mil., with full equipment), burn shoe leather, shanks' mare, ride shanks' mare, stomp, pound the beat, pound the pavement, hit the road, hit the bricks, hit the dirt, hit the grit, move out, stump it, traipse, trapse, traipse around, ooze, strut one's stuff, cruise, air out, beat the rocks, gumshoe, navigate, mope, mooch, press the bricks, boogie, Spanish walk, walk Spanish, trill, hippety-hop, broom, diddy-bop, truck, percolate, count ties (hobo), drill, jaywalk.

WALKER n. boot jockey, gumshoe, jaywalker (illegal street crossing).

WALLET n. lizard, pig, poke, frame, leather, okus, skin, cush (found or stolen).

WALLOP v. bash, wham, bam, whop, whomp, whack, bushwhack, hide, tan, take it out of one's hide, take it out of one's skin, bop, boff, belt, sock, slug, slog, smack, clobber, zap, zetz, paste, take out, take a whack at, plant one, land a haymaker, beat the bejesus out of one. See HIT.

WALLOPING n. licking, larruping, whaling, lathering, leathering, hiding, tanning, shellacking, waxing, get one's lumps, strap oil, dose of strap oil. See BEATING. See also DEFEAT.

WANDER v. bum, bum around, cruise, drift, float, patrolling (indecisively, aimlessly), sashay, traipse, trapse, traipse around, knock around, knock about, bat around, bat about, hopscotch, percolate, air out, beat the rocks, press the bricks, gumshoe, take to the road, hit the road, hit the trail, hit the dirt, hit the grit, walk the tracks, count ties, ooze, mope, navigate, mooch, ank, boogie, follow one's nose, globe-trot, trek, circumlocute. 2. get off the track, get sidetracked, all over the map. See also DRIFT.

WANDERER n. drifter, bum, floater, gad, gadabout, globe-trotter. See also VAGRANT.

WANT v. have the hots for, cream for, lech for, itch for, hanker for, have eyes for, spoil for, yen for, give one's eyeteeth for, have one's mouth fixed for, die over. See DESIRE.

WANTING adj. 1. toast, outa gas, burned-out, cooked, not come up to scratch, not hack it, not make it, not cut out for, second-fiddle, second-stringer, third-stringer, low man on the totem pole. See also INADEQUATE; IMPERFECT. 2. short, come up short, minus, bupkis, chickenshit, too little too late, half-assed, half-baked. 3. horny, turned on, pash, sexy, heavy, rammy, hot, hot and heavy, hot baby, hot number, hot pants, hot patootie.

WANTON adj. 1. loose, fast, fast and loose, speedy, swinging, cheap, for free, chippy around, sleep around, bone addict, two-timing, extracurricular, spread like peanut butter, on the make, on my jock, put out, put the horns on, hobbler, punchboard, stanky tuna, no better than she should be. 2. filthy, dirty, blue, X-rated, raunchy, raw, hard-core, soft-core, hot, heavy, hot and heavy, hot stuff, rough, rough stuff, evil-minded, foul mouth, foul-mouthed, flaming (obscene computer conversations), salty, off-color, low-down, low-down dirty, low-down and dirty, purple, in the gutter; horny, cream jeans, hot pants, a lech on, lechin's. 3. on the take, on the pad, open, wide-open, meat eater, racket up, something rotten in Denmark, gone to bad, gone to the dogs, gone to hell, double-crossing. 4. flaky, kinky, fantasmo, gaga, punchy, yo-yo, any way the wind blows, blow hot and cold, up-and-down, every which way. 5. cussed, stanky (Fem.), evil, mean, ornery, accidentally on purpose, do one dirt.

WANTON n. swinger, pushover, C.S.P. (casual sex partner), roundheels, easy lay, slag, slagheap, hank, chippie, floozy, cuddle bunny, pigmeat (old). See LECHER.

WAR n. cold war, hot war, police action, strike, first strike, preemptive strike, surgical mission; ABC, alphabet, soup (atomic, biological and chemical warfare); the big one (WWI, WWII), the balloon goes up (start).

WAR ADVOCATE n. hawk.

WARBLE v. chirp, canary, do a canary, yodel.

WARDEN n. man, the Man, king, main ghee, skipper, belly robber, gut robber, big shot, big noise, big spud, strib, screw. See also JAILER.

WARDEN'S DEPUTY n. dogcatcher, whitecap.

WARDROBE n. threads, togs, toggery, duds, rags, vine, weeds, dry goods, drapery, drapes. See CLOTHING.

WAREHOUSE n. stash house.

WARES n. the goods, material, stuff, hot number, jive (gaudy), seconds.

WARM adj. toasty, sticky, close, broiler, roaster, scorcher, sizzler, swelterer, one can fry eggs on the sidewalk.

WARMHEARTED adj. clubby, mellow (close), tight, palsy, palsy-walsy, cozy, pally, right nice, right friendly, regular. See also KIND.

WARMONGER n. hawk, Dr. Strangelove, Strangelove.

WARN v. 1. lay it on one, lay it out for, let in on, put one wise, wise up, tip, tip off, post. See ADVISE. 2. flag, wave a red flag, highball, cloud up, give one the high sign, toot the tooter.

WARNING interj. fore, watch it, heads up, cheese it the cops, jiggers, beat it, look out, amscray. See ALARM.

WARNING n. 1. Mayday, SOS, high sign, sign, wigwag, wink, bleep, ixnay, tip, tip-off, burn notice (warning that a person is a liar), a bug in one's ear. See ALARM. See also PREMONITION. 2. speaking to, talking to, calling down, jacking up, chewing, cussing out, going over, set down, rap on the knuckles, slap on the wrist. See also SCOLD.

WARRANT n. 1. sticker, shingle, plaster, ticket, tag, chit, hooker, ducat, general, reader, reader with a tail. 2. go-ahead, green light, OK, okay, the word.

WARRIOR n. cannon fodder, bulletbait, G.I., GI Joe, dogface, doughboy, footslogger, grunt, paddlefoot, buck-ass private, trooper. See SOLDIER.

WART n. beauty spot.

WARY adj. cagey, leery, walk on eggs, handle with kid gloves, watch one's step, watch out, keep on one's toes, think twice, hedge one's bets, on the lookout. See CAUTIOUS.

WASH v. dobee, doby (do by hand), button chop, soogie, sujee, soujge, soogie-moogie, sujee-mujee, swab, swab down, (N. and maritime). See also CLEAN.

WASH CLOTHES v. boil up (hobo), button-chop.

WASH DISHES v. pearl-dive, do the dishes, bust suds, K.P., China clipper, bubble dance, bubble dancer (WWII).

WASHINGTON Chinook State, Evergreen State.

WASHINGTON, D.C. D.C., the Capital, Capital City, Chocolate City, the Hill, inside the Beltway, across the river.

WASHINGTON, D.C., TERMS boutique (consulting firm), Beltway bandit (consultant).

WASHROOM n. can, john, restroom, Men's, Ladies', ladies' room, women's room, girls' room, little girls' room, powder room, men's room, boys' room, little boys' room, head, facilities, piss house, crapper, WC (water closet), loo, sandbox, altar room, throne room, donagher, donniker, Andy Gump, bucket, privy, two-holer, out back, Chic Sale, honeywagon, honeypot, pisspot, pot, potty, potty chair, catbox, thunder box, thunder mug, joe, jane, showers, where the dicks hang out. See TOILET.

WASTE n. 1. gash, hogwash, junk, dreck, shit. 2. BM (bowel movement), crap, shit, caca, turd, dingleberry. See EXCRETION.

WASTE v. piss away, flush down the toilet, run through, spend money like it was going out of style, throw out the baby with the bathwater, kill the goose that lays the golden egg. See SQUANDER.

WASTEBASKET n. file, circular file, round file; file thirteen, file seventeen, skid box (WWII).

WASTED adj. blown, blown out, diddled away, pissed away, petered out, shot, down the toilet, down the tube, down the drain, down the spout, down the rathole, going in circles, out the window.

WASTE OF TIME n. total shuck, wild goose chase, goin' round in circles, spin one's wheels, can't win for losin', no-win situation, go fight City Hall, go hit your head against the wall, locking the barn after the horse is stolen, not a prayer, wombat (waste of money, brains and time). See USELESS.

WASTE TIME v. veg, vegetate, hang out, hang around, goof around, monkey around, fool around, dork off, fake off, goof off, screw off, fuck the dog, sit on one's ass, jelly, tool, tail, lie down on the job. See IDLE. See also DAWDLE.

WASTREL n. big-time spender, last of the big-time spenders, sport, good-time Charlie.

WATCH n. 1. swatch (brightly colored plastic), ticker, timepiece, turnip, kettle turnip (pocket), chroniker, Albert (with chain). 2. weather eye, peeled eye, eagle eye, gapper, hawk, spotter, tip, anchor, case, gap, jigger, jigger guy, jigger man, outside man, zex man, lay zex, lay butzo, lay jiggers, lay chickie, gander.

WATCH v. 1. scope, spy, pipe, focus, eye, eagle-eye, hold the glims on, take in, get a load of, have a look-see, give the once-over, check out, check something out, case, bus it (Af. Am.), rubber, rubberneck, scoop (admiringly), 87 1/2 (look at a girl, Rest.), keep an eye on, keep tab, keep tabs on. See SEE. 2. keep one's eyes peeled, keep a weather eye peeled, peel your eyeballs, pick up on, ride shotgun for, shotgun, burn up; gap, jap (U.); go slumming, slum, kibitz, take in the sights, Peeping Tom.

WATCHFUL adj. on the lookout, on the qui vive, on the ball, on the job, on one's toes, with a weather eye open, with one's eyes peeled, all ears, keep one's ear to the ground, glued, hooked, not miss a trick, not overlook a bet, see after, see to, mind one's p's and q's. See also CAUTIOUS.

WATCHMAN n. lookout, lay chickie, bugster; Charley, door knocker, stick (night watchman). See also GUARD; LOOKOUT.

WATCH OUT interj. fore, watch it, heads up, cheese it, cheese it the cops, chickie, chickie the cops, jigs, jiggers, jiggers the cops, beat it, bite, moose, look out, amscray, awlay, bleaso, butso, duck, freeze, bird dog.

WATER n. drink, the drink, aqua, H₂O, Adam's ale, Adam's water; eighty, eighty-two, eighty-six (glass of water), hobo cocktail, sky juice, splash, ammonia, fizz water, fizzy stuff, seltzer, for two cents plain (carbonated).

WATER v. doctor, doctor up, phony up, plant, spike, water down, baptize, irrigate, cook, cut, needle, lace, shave.

WATERMELON n. piss chunk.

WAVER v. yo-yo, waffle, hem and haw, pussyfoot around, run hot and cold, blow hot and cold, back and fill, shilly-shally, the jury's out, hedge, hedge off. See VACILLATE.

WAVES n. tasty waves (good surf), foam, breakers, rollers.

WAY n. 1. thataway, every which way, forty ways to Sunday, forty ways from Sunday, forty ways for Sunday. 2. bit, spitting distance, stone's throw, Sunday run, tidy step, whoop, two whoops and a holler, a shlep, sleeper jump, piece, far piece, fer piece, fur piece. 3. groove, thing, Jones, into, hang-up, bag, one's bag, shot, kick, style, hook. See STYLE. See also ROUTINE; PLAN.

WAYFARER n. jet-setter, globe-trotter, gadabout, deadhead (free), seat cover, dude (bus), drop, line load (taxi), rubberneck, rubbernecker, snowbird, snowflake, sunflower.

WAYLAY v. jump, lay for, bushwhack, dry-gulch, jap, pull a jap, box, get one in a box. See AMBUSH.

WEAK adj. 1. rocky, wussy, woozy, dopey, wishy-washy, out of gas, don't have the horses. 2. empty suit, paper tiger, turkey, weak sister, ouisha, herb, wimp, wimpy, wet rag, wet sock, dopey, laid-back, moony, basket case, chicken, gutless, jerky, nerd, nerdy, neb, nebbish, nobody, sad sack, shnook, slob, fish, poor fish, squid, clown, dud, fuddy-duddy, dead one, eight-ball, lameola, lame-brained, half-baked, rocky, blah, draddy, pablum, nothing, zero, zilch, diddly-bop, flub the dub, half-assed, pigeon, clay pigeon, sitting duck, lame duck, shooting blanks, out on a limb, out of gas, out of one's depth, in over one's head, don't have the horses, ready to be taken, wide-open, sucker for a left, putty in one's hands, what the cat dragged in.

WEAKEN v. 1. irrigate, cut, baptize. See DILUTE. 2. blow sky high, knock the bottom out of, knock the chocks out from under, knock the props out from under, poke full of holes, shoot full of holes. 3. break, crack, crack up, fade, fold, cave in, go soft, go to pieces, going down (Af. Am.), poop out, peg out, fizzle out, come apart at the seams, be on one's last legs, have one foot in the grave, have one foot in the grave and the other on a banana peel. See DETERIORATE. 4. clip one's wings, shake up, soften up, take the edge off, take the bit out, take the sting out.

WEAKENED adj. 1. draggin', draggin' one's ass, rocky, seedy, down, run-down, laid low, below par, peaky, peaked, poorly, out of action, out of condition, out of shape, good and flabby, 4F. 2. out of gas, out of juice, wiped, wrung-out, burned-out, played-out, nearly dead, used-up, veggie, in a bad way. See TIRED. 3. cut, spiked, watered-down, baptized, irrigated, needled, laced, shaved.

WEAKLING n. herb, wimp, wuss, wuss-puss, chicken, chickenheart, chicken liver, lily liver, white liver, yellow, yellow belly, paper tiger, poor tool, weak tool, droop, glass arm, candy ass, pecker ass, fraidy cat, scaredy cat, jellyfish, squid, cream puff, ladyfinger, skinny, softy, weak sister, sissy, panty waist, pantywaist, pushover, baby, big baby, crybaby, mamby-pamby, dancer, deuce, piker, mouse, milksop, Caspar Milquetoast, tootie fruitie, gutless, gutless wonder, drip, sad sack, neb, nebbish, nerd, turkey, doormat, cookie cutter, cookie pusher, punk, putty in one's hands, lame duck.

WEAKNESS n. wimp factor, soft spot, bag, cup of tea, a thing for, soft underbelly, glass chin, Achilles heel. See also LOVE.

WEALTH n. bed of roses, clover, velvet, Easy Street, lap of luxury, the life of Riley, high on the hog, on top of the heap.

WEALTHY adj. uptown, upscale, the haves, have it made, have a mint, have the wherewithal, have one's place in the sun, on Easy Street, on velvet, on top of the heap, on a bed of roses, everything's coming up roses, high on the hog, right up there, in the bucks, in the money, in the chips, in the lap of luxury, in clover, rolling in clover, on a roll, rollin', really rolling, rolling in dough, rolling in money, lousy with money, tall money, moneybags, money to burn, burner, really cooking, cooking with gas, lousy rich, stinking rich, filthy, filthy rich, holding, livin' large, clockin', bifftad, well-heeled, well-fixed, well-to-do, well-set-up, set up, sitting pretty, fat, sit fat, fat city, fat cat, arrived, plush, lush, flush, heavy sugar, big bucks, loaded, booming, going strong, going great guns, mining the gold, Midas touch, golden, made it, made it big, made one's pile, did all right by oneself, home-free, laughing all the way to the bank, ride the gravy train, gravy boat, jammy, good ticket, dicty, big, biggie, big-shot, long hitter, king of the hill, duke of the catwalk, like of Reilly, live off the fat of the land, Fat Daddy Greenbacks, Daddy Warbucks, scissorbill, swell, curtain, lace curtain, coupon clipper, big butter-and-egg man, rich as Croesus, the establishment, big boys, the 400, upper class, the beautiful people, main line, large, oofy, piss on ice.

WEAPON n. keeper, shit, knucks, dingbat, pig sticker, shank (homemade knife), prop, hardware, heat (gun), Z, Zip, (homemade gun).

WEAPONLESS adj. skinned, clean.

WEAR v. rig out, rig up, rag out, rag up, turn out, fit out, tog, suit up, doll up, dog out, dud, dude, dude up, dode (bad fit), sport.

WEARINESS adj. brain fag, burnout.

WEARING APPAREL n. threads, set of threads, togs, toggery, duds, outfit, rags, glad rags, getup, get out, Barbie and Ken (conventional), vine, weeds, dry goods, California black tie (any colorful variation of formal wear), California chic (expensive casual), flash, ready-made, tailor-made, bib and tucker. See CLOTHING.

WEARY adj. 1. bushed, pooped, out of gas, out of juice, had it, knocked-out, wiped-out, burned-out, blown-out, veggie, vegged-out, crispy, creased, flaked-out, zonked, draggin' ass, dead tired, dusted, wimped-out, beat, done in, all in, punchy, bone-tired, dog-tired, hit the wall (marathon). 2. ho-hum, so what else is new?, bored stiff, fed up, full up, up to here, had it up to here, done it all, been around twice. See TIRED. See also JADED.

WEARY v. fade, fold, fizzle, fizzle out, fag, tucker, poop, poop out, burn out, fag out, tucker out, knock out, peter out. See TIRE.

WEATHER TERMS bomb, gremlin (surprise weather change), chinook, snow eater (dry, warm wind off the Rockies to the east), Alberta clipper (a winter storm south out of Canada), cut-off low (slow moving unsettled condition).

WED v. middle-aisle it, get hitched, get spliced, say I do, ball and chain up.

WEDDING n. bells, shotgun wedding, hook.

WEE adj. teeny, peewee, peanut, small fry, banty, mite, pint-sized, knee-high. See SMALL.

WEEK n. double trey (workweek), stanza.

WEEP v. blubber, bawl, break down, boo-hoo, let go, let it out, turn on the waterworks, cry one's eyes out, cry me a river, crack-up. See CRY.

WEEPER n. crybaby, crying jag.

WEEPING n. waterworks, weeps.

WEIGH v. 1. kick around, bat it around, brainstorm, head trip, noodle, noodle it around, knock around, put on one's thinking cap, cop, track, run it up the flagpole, run it by one again, blow change, sort out, hash, rehash, hash over, stew, stew over, sweat, sweat over, cool something over, chew over, chew the cud. See ANALYZE. 2. hang (how does that hang?), hold a candle to, stack up against, match up. 3. heft.

WEIGH STATION n. chicken coop, pig pen.

WEIGHT n. 1. beef, beefiness, heft, heftiness, avoirdupois. 2. albatross, albatross around one's neck, excess baggage, schlepper, ball and chain. See HINDRANCE. 3. juice, string, ropes, drag, pull, clout, access, fix, grease, connection, in, a lot to do with, a lot to say about, inside track, wire-pulling. See INFLUENCE. 4. iron.

WEIGHT LIFTER n. iron pumper.

WEIGHTY adj. 1. heavy, hefty, beefy, lead-footed. See also FAT. 2. heavy, heavyweight, heavy stuff, heavy number, meaningful, mean business, matter of life and death, serious jelly, talk serious shit, cosmic, we're not talking about nutmeg here, money talks, no fooling, no shit, no bird turdin'. See SERIOUS. 3. big-league, major-league, walk heavy, big deal, carry a lot of weight, the juice, the force, underlined. See IMPORTANT.

WEIRD adj. weirdo, archfreak, semi-dork, dorf, creepo, freaky, funky, kinky, kooky, geeky, glick, birdie, flaky, wombat, quirky, off-the-wall. See STRANGE. See also ECCENTRIC.

WELCOME n. tumble, rumble, blow, high five, low five, hello, howdy, highball, red carpet, red-carpet treatment, welcome mat, key to the city.

WELCOME v. highball, tumble, flop, give one a flop, give one a toss, flag, shoulder, whistle for, whistle down, give one the glad eye, give one the glad hand, give one the key to the city, roll out the red carpet.

WELDER n. smoke-eater.

WELL adv. alive and kicking, wrapped tight, bright-eyed and bushy-tailed, chipper, together, up to snuff, up to the mark, fit as a fiddle, full of beans, full of piss and vinegar, in fine feather, in fine whack, in high feather, in the pink, sound as a dollar, right, right as rain, solid as a rock, beefy, husky, strong as a horse, strong as a lion, strong as an ox.

WELLBORN adj. born with a silver spoon in one's mouth, blue-blood, lace curtain, silk-stocking, upper-crust, upper-cut, FFV (first families of Virginia), 400, four hundred.

WELL-BRED adj. blue-blood, lace curtain, silk-stocking, upper-crust, upper-cut, FFV (first families of Virginia), 400, four hundred.

WELL-CONNECTED adj. in, wired, well-wired.

WELL-DRESSED adj. looking sharp, got one's stuff wired, tacked-down (Af. Am., neatly dressed), looking spiffy, looking classy, looking nifty, looking snazzy, looking swanky, looking posh, looking ritzy, looking swell, looking nobby, corporate (business), togged, togged-up, togged-out, togged to the bricks, slicked-up, rigged-up, rigged-out, ragged-up, ragged-out, duded-up, duded-out, decked-out, tricked-out, tricked-up, figged-out, figged-up, turned-out, dolled-up, fancied-up, gussied-up, slicked-up, spiffed-up, spruced-up, in fine feather, in high feather, in one's best bib and tucker, mellow back, dap, tabbed, laid out, tied back, clean back (Af. Am.), wearing one's best, dressed fit to kill, dressed to kill, dressed to the teeth, dressed to the nines, in one's Sunday best, Sunday go-to-church, Sunday go-to-meeting, putting on the dog. See also STYLISH.

WELL GROOMED adj. 1. classy, dap, nifty, snazzy, spiffy, smooth, corporate (business), got one's stuff wired, tacked-down (Af. Am., neatly dressed), dressed to kill, dressed to the teeth, dressed to the nines, sharp, swank, posh, ritzy, swell, nobby. See WELL-DRESSED. See also STYLISH. 2. Bonnie Brillo (neat person), neat as a pin, clean, pressed, in apple-pie order.

WELL-INFORMED adj. posted, hip, hep, hip to the jive, savvy, all woke up, in the picture, been there, booted on, wise to, inside, in the know, know the score, know-it-all, know all the answers. See INFORMED.

WELL-KNOWN adj. WK, w.k., celeb, star, superstar, name, somebody, VIP, face, in the limelight, make a splash, page-oner, large, right up there, big, big name, biggie. See CELEBRITY; CELEBRATED.

WELL-MEANING adj. softhearted, bleeding heart, old softie, heart in the right place, all heart (Derog.), have a heart.

WELL-WISHING n. send-off, royal send-off.

WELSH RAREBIT n. rabbit, bunny, blushing bunny (with tomato sauce or soup).

WELTER n. goulash, mishmash, mishmosh, garbage, everything but the kitchen sink.

WEST COAST n. Left Coast, the Coast.

WESTERN FILM n. horse opera, oater, shoot-'em-up, spaghetti Western (made in Italy), sukiyaki Western (Japanese version).

WEST INDIAN n. conch, jig, zig (all Derog.)

WEST POINT CADET n. gray-legs, yearling.

WEST VIRGINIA Mountain State, Panhandle State.

WHALE'S PENIS n. Pink Floyd.

WHAT pron. whu?, whuh?, come again?, howzat?, huh?, nu?, so?, what then?, I'll bite.

WHEEDLE v. soap, soft-soap, snow, jolly, oil, spread it on, lay it on, butter up, soften up, sweeten up, work on, brown-nose, suck ass, polish the apple, apple-polish, kowtow, buddy up, curry below the knee. See CAJOLE.

WHEEDLING n. snow, snow job, jive, smoke, baked wind, line, abreaction route, goo, hoke, eyewash, soap, soft soap, bullshit, con, sell, applesauce, balloon juice, snake oil. See FLATTERY.

WHIM n. fool notion, bee in one's bonnet, flea in one's ear, spur of the moment. See also DESIRE.

WHIMSICAL adj. flaky, kinky, fantasmo, impomanic, blow hot and cold, up-and-down. See CAPRICIOUS.

WHINER n. bitcher, bellyacher, griper, kvetch, plainer. See COMPLAINER.

WHIP n. bat (jockey).

WHIP v. 1. bash, trash, drub, lather, larrup, dot (precise blow), whop, whomp, hide, tan, tan one's hide, take it out of one's hide, take it out of one's skin, whip ass, beat the shit out of one, beat the living daylights out of. 2. bury, blank, skunk, schneider, murder, kill, cook, cook one's goose, blow one's doors off, trim, trounce, top, fix one's wagon, skin, shellack, tube, make one say uncle, do in, lick, beat all hollow, blow one out, run rings around, run circles around, put away, settle one's hash. See DEFEAT.

WHIPPED CREAM n. snowstorm, in a snowstorm, in the snow.

WHISKERS n. beaver, brush, muff, peach fuzz, pez, spinach, face spinach, face lace, bush, shrubbery, alfalfa, chin whiskers, Castro; gallaway, galways (stage Irishman).

WHISKEY n. hard liquor, likker, alky, alchy, doctor, idiot oil, hooch, booze, corn, cave corn, red-eye, moonshine, mountain dew, prairie dew, squirrel dew, sauce, mouthwash, wee drop, coffin varnish, brush whiskey, nigger pot (Derog.), damp bourbon poultice, dirty bird (Old Crow). See also LIQUOR.

WHISPER v. buzz, sotto.

WHITE HOUSE n. big white jail, cottage.

WHITE n. WASP, white bread, face, paleface, citizen, ball face (Af. Am.), vanilla, fay, ofay, ofaginzy, gringo, anglo, honky, white honky, white meat, whitey, the Man, Mister Charlie, Chuck, white trash, poor white trash, P.W.T., howley, haole (Hawaiian), egg (has Asian attitudes), kelt, keltch, blue-eyed, blue-eyed devil, round-eye, cracker, Florida cracker, Georgia cracker, soda cracker, great white father, gray, grey boy, hack, hay eater, peck, peckerwood, silk, silk girl, silk broad, fay chick, li'l Eva, marshmallow, Miss Ann, pale, lily-white, milk, Sylvester, bale of straw (blonde), beasts, buckra, fade, chalk, flake, gavacho, pack, whoogie, pink whoogie, Savana, wood, hack, hardhead, pink, jeff, Paddy, patty, patty boy, spook, steel, wig, jig chaser (all Derog.).

WHITEWASH v. launder.

WHOLE n. jackpot, the works, lock stock and barrel, hook line and sinker, fixin's, whole enchilada, whole ball of wax, whole nine yards, whole shebang, whole works, whole bit, whole deal, whole schmeer, whole show, whole shtick, megillah, whole megillah, whole shooting match, whole bunch, whole mess, caboodle, whole caboodle, whole kit and caboodle, whole hog, everything including the kitchen sink, lump sum (money), the picture, the big picture, you've seen my whole spring line, across the board, wall to wall.

WHOLESOME adj. right, right as rain, together, crunchy granola, all there, in the pink, fit as a fiddle, in fine feather, sound as a dollar. See HEALTHY. See also MORAL.

WHOLLY adv. from A to Z, from A to izzard, top to bottom, shoot the works, stone (stone deaf), totc, from hell to breakfast, all the way, all hollow. See COMPLETELY.

WHOOP n. holler.

WHOOP v. holler, holler out, blow.

WHORE n. hooker, call girl, hustler, ho, working broad, working girl, skeezer, nok, model, pro, lot lizard (truckstop parking lot), floozie, chippy, prosty, prostie, streetwalker, alley cat, baggage, broad, chicken rancher, chile whore, chacha, ass peddler, coozey, roller (robs drunks), vegetarian (won't perform fellatio). See PROSTITUTE.

WHOREDOM n. world's oldest profession, broad racket, the bottle, hustle, the life, in the life, turning a trick, on the turf, hitting the turf, stepping out, going out for a buck, white slavery.

WHOREHOUSE n. house, cathouse, can house, call house, massage parlor, rap parlor, poontang palace, snake ranch, chicken ranch, meat market, camp, zoo, joint, call joint, hook shop, rib joint, body shop, beaver base, service station. See BROTHEL.

WHOREMONGER n. mack, mackman, macko man, hard mack (violent), sweet mack, mac, mackerel, dude, flesh peddler, king bung, pee eye, P.I., ponce, Johnny Ponce, husband. See PIMP.

WHY adv. howcome? howcum?

WICKED adj. bad-assed, rat's-ass, sucks, scuzzy, sleazy, sleazeball, bad news, tough, tough nuggies, fierce, lousy, murder, poison, dirty, low-down. See BAD.

WICKED PLACE n. hellhole, hole, joint, den, den of iniquity, sink, sink of corruption.

WIDE-EYED adj. bug-eyed, pop-eyed, eyes like percolator tops.

WIDESPREAD adj. all over the lot, all over the place, from hell to breakfast, across the board, wall to wall.

WIENER n. hot dog, hot dawg, frank, wienie, weenie, tube steak, balloon, beenie, bow-wow, bun pup, Coney Island pup, pimp stick, puppy, special.

WIFE n. old lady, O.L., roommate, mama, missus, better half, little woman, the wifey, little missus, wiff, chief of staff, rib, ball and chain, block and tackle, front office, golf widow, grass widow, glass widow (husband is alcoholic), headache, War Department, mat, hat, seagull, slavedriver, squaw, headquarters, apron, main queen, old saw, first sergeant, baby, fishwife, fag bag (married to homosexual).

WIG n. rug, sky piece, toup, brush, doily, dome doily, scalp doily, headpiece, muff, head falsie, merkin (pubic hairpiece).

WILD adj. funky, gonzo, harum-scarum, hog-wild, rat fuck, wild-ass, like crazy, like mad, flaky, kill-crazy, hog-crazy. See also VIOLENT; UNRESTRAINED.

WILDERNESS n. boondocks, boonies, bush, B.F.E., butt-fucking Egypt, B.F.A., butt-fucking Africa, outback, sticks.

WILDLY adv. like crazy, like mad, something fierce, something terrible, helter-skelter, holus-bolus, hurry-scurry, ramble-scramble.

WILE n. angle, dodge, slant, trick, twist, switch, setup, game, little game, booby trap, grift, racket, con, gimmick, curveball, monkeyshines, shenanigans, stunt. See also CUNNING; TRICK.

WILINESS n. hustle, gamesmanship, one-upmanship, con, double shuffle, fast shuffle, fast one, runaround, song and dance, monkey business, funny business. See CUNNING.

WILLING adj. game, on, go along with. See also READY.

WILLINGLY adv. at the drop of a hat, game for.

WILY adj. 1. smooth, streetwise, street smarts, foxy, crazy like a fox, cagey, fancy footwork, slick, slippery, greasy, greaseball, sly-boots, sharp. See SLY. 2. nifty, Philadelphia lawyer, sharpie, sharp stuff, shark, ringer, slicker, smoothie, got the smarts, got one's boots on, tuned in, nobody's fool, not born yesterday. See INTELLIGENT.

WIMBLEDON n. Wimby.

WIN n. slam, grand slam, bombshell, score, walkaway, kill, killing, clean sweep, laugher, hot run, pay dirt, gold medal, gold star. See TRIUMPH.

WIN v. beat the competish, beat the game, beat the system, beat like a drum, beat all hollow, beat by a nose, nose out, edge out, shred, sneak past, upset, put the skids to, snow under, plow under, put the kibosh on, finish off, shut off, rack up, blow out, blow off, sink the opposition, pin one's ears back, have it knocked, have it locked, all locked up, lock-and-win situation, walk off with, walk away with, walk over, run away with, run rings around, run circles around, breeze in, rake in the pot, break the tape, grab the brass ring, grab the gold, catch the gold ring, clean on, clean one, clean out, clean up, clean sweep, break the book, put away, rake it in, make a payday, take one, take one to the cleaners, take it all, take all the marbles, take out, take one out, take care of, shoot down, shoot one down, shoot down in flames, shut down, shut out, lay one low, wipe out, wipe off the map, do a Rocky, bury, blast, blank, plunk, skunk, schneider, sweep, cook, cook one's goose, blow one's doors off, trounce, top, swamp, scuttle, sconce, skin, smear, shellack, whitewash, squelch, squash, steamroller, bulldoze, roll over, torpedo, tube, meatball, make one say uncle, do in, lick, lick to a frazzle, ring the bell, ring the gong, score, hang up, win hands down, win going away, win in a walk, win in a canter, win in a waltz, waltz off with, win all the marbles, win one's spurs, breeze home, romp home, romp off with, click, connect, put across, put it together, put over, get over, get well, get fat, get rich, get ahead, get away with, get something on the board, get there, get the last dance, get into pay dirt, get a break, get the breaks, break the bank, go places, go to town, go great guns, go over, go over big, win out, check out, make out, make the cut, make it, make a killing, make hay, make well, make the grade, make good, make a noise in the world, make a hit, hit, hit it big, hit the jackpot, hit the bull's-eye, hit pay dirt, strike it rich, strike oil, strike gold, strike a vein, strike a rich vein, make a lucky strike, strike it lucky, luck, luck in, luck out, fall into the shithouse and come up with a five-dollar gold piece, shit in high cotton, ace, ace the easy, hold aces, turn up trumps, move out, take off, fly, skyrocket, flash in the pan (brief), run with the ball, blow away, blow out of the water, cream, cream up, clean sweep, skunk, knock one for a loop, walkover, walkaway, pushover, picnic, winning streak, laugher, loving life, loving it, be a gas, be a gasser, bring home the bacon, bring home the groceries, home-free, have it made, turn the trick, pull off, bring off, carry off, catch on, pass muster, fill the bill, get by, pass in the dark, arrive, nail it, hack it, win one's spurs, put a feather in one's cap, do the job, do oneself proud, do all right by oneself, do a land-office business, come on, come along, be fat dumb and happy, live off the fat of the land, live the life of Riley, live on Easy Street, have one's place in the sun, come out on top of the heap, lie on a bed of roses, take the cake, get Brownie points, break the back of, end in sight, got it made, light at the end of the tunnel, over the hump, knock out, K.O., KO, kayo, waste, take the wind out of one's sails.

WIN APPROVAL v. go over, kill, slay, wow, have 'em eating out of one's hand.

WIND n. big blow, chinook, mistral, Mr. Hawkins, the hawk.

WINDBREAKER n. peacoat, Eisenhower. See also JACKET.

WIND CONE n. wind sock, condom.

WINDFALL n. gravy, goodies, perks, hat, ice, button, PM, spiff (salesman).

WINDOW n. gazer, burglar bars (barred).

WINDPIPE n. Sunday throat.

WINDSHIELD WIPERS n. slappers.

WINDY adj. hawk stretch.

WINE n. vino, grape, jug wine, juice, alley juice (cheap), white, blush (pink), Dago red (Italian or any cheap red, Derog.), mad dog (Mogen David), ink, red ink, King Kong, duck, smash, squeeze, plonk, plunk, pluck, plug, sneaky pete, split, vinblink, vinegar blink, pop wine, soda pop wine (fruit flavored).

WINE AND BARBITURATES n. ripples and reds.

WINK v. bat the eyes.

WINNER n. champ, king o' the hill, number one, numero uno, the greatest, top dog, medalist, gold medalist, takes the gold, takes the cake, shoo-in, title holder.

WINNINGS n. payoff, rake-off, velvet, gravy, cush, bundle, package, skim, take. See INCOME.

WINNIPEG, CANADA the Peg.

WINSTON-SALEM NORTH CAROLINA Tobacco City, Twin City.

WINTER VACATIONER n. snowbird, snowflake, sunflower.

WINTRY adj. snappy, colder than a well-digger's ass, freeze one's ass off, three-dog night, icebox (place). See COLD.

WIRE n. string.

WIRELESS ROOM n. shack, radio shack.

WIRETAP v. bug, tap, body-mike.

WISCONSIN Badger State, America's Dairyland.

WISE adj. sharp, with it, all woke up, posted, fly, savvy, have one's head screwed on right, not born yesterday, been there, tool, power tool, cereb, gray matter, wised-up. See KNOWLEDGEABLE.

WISEACRE n. smart aleck, smart ass, wisenheimer, wise guy.

WISECRACK n. one-liner, throwaway, topper, payoff, comeback, needle, nifty, rib, crack, smart crack. See JOKE.

WISECRACKER n. cutup, life of the party, madcap, trickster, card, million laughs, kibitzer, funster, punster, quipster. See JOKER.

WISH v. itch, itch for, hanker for, spoil for, give one's kingdom in hell for, give one's eyeteeth for, yen, yen for. See DESIRE.

WIT n. cutup, clown, life of the party, madcap, trickster, card, a million laughs, kibitzer, booger, bugger, jokesmith, gagman, gagster, funster, punster, quipster. See also JOKER.

WITCH n. bitch kitty, hellcat, ball breaker, she-devil, she-wolf, hootchy-kootchy.

WITCHCRAFT n. hoodoo, voodoo, evil eye, stink eye, jinx, whack, whammy, hocus-pocus, mumbo-jumbo, abracadabra.

WITH prep. by (by me).

WITHDRAW v. 1. bow out, ooze out, ease out, faze out, check out, drop out, bail out, pull out, break out (Af. Am.), get lost, make oneself scarce, exfiltrate, do a vanishing act, take a walk, book, time to book, get small (from a crime), fade, fade out, do a fade, fade away. See GO. 2. fold, quit, opt out, back out, back out of, backpedal, back-water, backslide, punt (Stu.), weasel out, fink out, crawl out of, worm out of, wangle out of, crawfish out, bail out, turn chicken, chicken out. See RETREAT. 3. call off, call all bets off, renig, forget it. See RETRACT.

WITHDRAWAL (DRUG) n. cold turkey, kicking the habit, sweating it out, taking the cure, becoming Mr. Fish, bogue, belly habit (pain), crash.

WITHDRAWAL SYMPTOMS n. sweats, cartwheel, circus, figure eight, twister, wing-ding.

WITHHOLD v. hold (hold the mayo), hold out on, kill, spike, keep it under one's hat, keep under wraps, keep buttoned up, dummy up, clam up. See also ABSTAIN.

WITHHOLD PAYMENT v. hold out, nick.

WITHOUT prep. hold (hold the mayo), cut (cut the onions).

WITHSTAND v. put up with, hang tough, hang on, win out, ride out, sit and take it, take it, stand the gaff, stand up to it. 2. fly in the face of, fly in the teeth of, brace, cross, meet eyeball to eyeball, take one on, stand up to, stick, stick fast, stick it out. 3. take out, face down, top, put the blocks to, put up a fight, put up a struggle, not take lying down. See ENDURE.

WITNESS n. wit, rapper, gawker, checkbook witness (paid).

WITNESS v. flash on, spot, spy, read, eyeball, take in, get a load of, get an eyeful of, have a look-see, pipe, pick up on. See SEE.

WITNESS CHAIR n. hot seat.

WITTICISM n. one-liner, laugh, throwaway, topper, payoff, funny, a haha, howl, hot one, needle, nifty, rib, rib tickler, knee-slapper, sizzler, spoof, story, whiz-bang, jive, crack, smart crack, wisecrack; an egg, an omelette, a bomb, bombed out, died, laid there, laid an egg (unfunny). See also JOKE.

WITTY adj. jokey, joshing, yokky, gagged-up, for grins, camp, campy, cool, crazy, priceless, screaming, screamingly funny, too funny for words, too killing for words.

WIZARDRY n. hocus-pocus, mumbo-jumbo, hoodoo, voodoo, evil eye, stink eye, go, jinx, whack, whammy, abracadabra.

WOE n. 1. heartache, blues, shit, deep shit, crisis mode, bad news, bad scene, clutch, hang-up, drag, rough go, heavy sledding, rain, rainin', crunch, bitch, nightmare, handful, headache, bummer, downer. See MISERY. 2. worriment, one's ass is grass, ass out, in deep water, in over one's head, up shit creek, up shit creek without a paddle, up against it, between a rock and a hard place. See TROUBLE; TROUBLE, IN.

WOEBEGONE adj. low, ass in a sling, dick in the dirt, blue, grim, got the blue devils, in the toilet, down-in-the-mouth, hang crepe, bummed-out, hurting, in pain, in the pits, shot-down, carry a heavy load, prune-faced. See UNHAPPY.

WOMAN n. chick, mama, hama, old woman, old lady (girlfriend), dame, doll, skirt, broad, studette (man chaser), freak mama, frill, frail, jane, tomato, mouse, twist, talent, kitten, kitty, sugar-wooga, rib, leg, li'l mama, she-stuff, she-she, chi-chi, femme, fox, stone fox, beddy, betty, bet, nugget, nuggy, gooey nectar, nectar, necky, squash blossom, fly chick, fly girl, tree (tall), cherry tree (tall virgin), granola (wears no makeup), brick house (big breasts), filet, hammer, burger, double burger, triple burger with cheese, beauty, my beauty, pin-up, cheesecake, cupcake, cutie, cutie pie, classis chassis, classy chassy, body, the body, bombshell, blonde, blond bombshell, brick, miniskirt, calico, sweater girl, bloomer girl, slick chick, chicken delight (young), spring chicken, cookie, bunny, ski bunny, snow bunny, babbling brook, peach, zimmer, eel, frail eel, babe, baby, baby doll, bird, pigeon, chicken, wren, fine fryer, fly chick, cub, gadget, jill, toots, tootsie, sis, kid, kiddo, slip, nun, cold tit (frigid), bantam, band, bezark, bag, bitch, turbobitch, bitch kitty, bad bitch, nothin'-ass bitch, bear, bear cat, ball breaker, hellcat, witch, barracuda (spiteful); harpy, battle, battle-ax; paper bag case, two-bagger, double-bagger, triple-bagger, Zelda, bucket, beetle, beast, beat, limburger (girl no one will date), boo hog, bama, barfola, pig, pigmeat (all ugly); sow, scow, heifer, cow, gaunch, ginch, pot, blimp, old maid, old bitch, old bag, bat, old bat, biddie, biddy, old biddy, hen, old hen, stewer, crow, old crow, blue hair (old), baggage, excess baggage; cunt, C, pussy, muff, gash, twat, twitch, snatch, ass, piece, piece of ass, piece of tail, nookie, meat, dark meat, white meat, tuna, (all Obsc.); squab, quail, San Quentin quail, jailbait, whistle bait, wench, gum drop, floozie, floozy, floogy, faloosie, demi-rep, lay, make, round heels, gimme, wet hen, alley cat, B-girl, bawd, biscuit, blister, baloney, barlow, barnacle, motorcycle, stallion (Af. Am.), pit popsie hose, groundcloth (promiscuous), frame dame, cover, bim, bimbo, bimmy, bimmo, bimbette (young, sexy), fish, jerry, mort, mott, moll, gun moll, jellybean, queen, queen bee, butterfly, doe (alone), mare, raggle, quasar, hip chick, head, head chick (fellationist), fine dinner (Obs.), bachelor girl, lobo; tomboy, les, lez, dyke, bull dyke, bull bitch, rug muncher, shemale.

WOMANISH adv. faggy, swishy, fruity (Derog.), ma, mother, old woman, Ethel, pretty boy, weak sister. See EFFEMINATE.

WOMEN'S ARMED SERVICES n. WAC, Wacs (Army), WAVE, Waves (N.), WAF, Wafs (A.F.), WAM (Marines).

WOMEN'S ARMY CORPS n. WAC, WACS, the First Skirt (commanding officer).

WOMEN'S LIBERATIONIST n. libber, women's libber, bra burner.

WOMEN'S RIGHTS n. women's lib.

WONDERFUL adj. awesome, killer, fab, fantasmo, def, rare, fat, froody, superfly, hellacious, boffo, evil, too much, a gas, it's to die for, unreal, cool, zero cool, heavy, major, dynamite, marvy, pisseroo, lampin', outrageous, tits, tawny, aggro, aggressive, prince, cherry, deffest, dope, dual, fierce, fresh, fully on, fully, mint, nitro, on the strength, raw, sick, stupid, fresh, massive, stokin', tubular, vicious, wailing, whaling, dope on a rope, hype, stink, stone groove, something else, something to brag about, something to shout about, something to write home about, hot shit. See FABULOUS.

WONT n. thing, Jones, into, hang-up, one's bag, shot, kick, hook.

WOO v. chase, run after, date, make time with, rush, spark, play up to. See COURT.

WOODEN LEG n. peg, pegleg.

WOODS n. big sticks, load of sticks.

WORDY adj. talky, yacky, yakkety-yak, gabby, shoots the gab, gassy, CBS, blowhard, windy, long-winded, windbag, bag of wind, windjammer, barber, chatty Cathy, gum beater, verbal diarrhea, diarrhea of the mouth. See TALKATIVE.

WORK n. line, line of business, bag, dodge, do, gig, day gig, go, hang, moonlight, nine-to-five shit, one's thing, what one does, slot, what one's into, rat race, grind, daily grind, grindstone, McJob (service job), the salt mines, shitwork, chickwork (household), gruntwork (army), scud, scut, scutwork, donkeywork, bull work, hemo jo (hard labor), lick, lick of work, stitch of work, racket, swindle gyppo, jippo, elbow grease. See also OCCUPATION.

WORK v. hustle, scratch, slave, sweat, sweat and slave, sweat it, buckle down, knuckle down, boogie, time to boogie (time to get started), grind, dig, plug, plug away, plug along, mouse-milking (maximum time for minimum return), hammer, peg away, cook, it cooks, percolate, perk, tick, moonlight, daylight, buck, hassle, take on, pour it on, put one's nose to the grindstone, beat one's brains out, bust a gut, bust one's conk, bust one's buns, knock oneself out, work one's head off, do for, do one's stuff, do one's thing, do one's number, do the trick, fill the bill, hit the ball, bear down on it, hold down a job, bull work, back to the salt mines, dog it (inferior), featherbed, jet up, mess around, make a buck, make change, hang out one's shingle, whittle, heel (Stu.). See also ACT.

WORKABLE adj. no sweat, cinch, snap, pushover, biscuit, piece of cake, setup, doable, breeze, that dog'll hunt, duck soup, pie, easy as pie, easy as falling off a log, simple as ABC. See also EASY.

WORKER n. help, breadwinner, suit (office worker), beaver, eager beaver, workhorse, stiff, working stiff, grind, greasy grind, nose to the grindstone, workaholic, company man, space cadet (young), apparatchik, cee gee, boll weevil, flunky, temp, pencil pusher, desk jockey, girl Friday, man Friday, nine-to-fiver, white collar, pink collar, bright collar (intelligent, well-educated, young), gold collar, hard hat, blue collar, heads (assembly plant), dirty neck, jerry, razorback, phantom (under assumed name), chump, dinner pailer, legit ghee, legit stiff, furp, home guard, peasant, peon, savage, serf, slave, slavey, scissorbill, square, Square John, square plug, up-and-up ghee, pork chopper, wearing two hats, dig, prentice, come along (temporary, inexperienced), fish, floater, glass arm, grease monkey, gyppo, jippo, ham-and-egger, gandy dancer, hunky chunk (Central European), deadwood (unnecessary), camello (Mex.).

WORKING adj. going, tasking, gigging (Af. Am), in full swing, hot, on track, on.

WORKING HOURS n. strictly 9-to-5, flex time (flexible hours).

WORKING PARENTS' CHILD n. latchkey child.

WORKOUT n. daily dozen, constitutional, aerobics, warm-up, jazzercise.

WORKPLACE n. the store, the office, shop, mines, salt mines, trenches, firing line, electronic cottage (home worker).

WORK SHIFT n. day, nine-to-five, graveyard, graveyard shift, moonlight, hoot owl, swing shift, lobster shift, tour, flex time (flexible hours).

WORK SLOWLY v. slow down, drag one's ass, drag one's foot, have lead in one's pants, dog it, jake it.

WORLD n. apple, big blue marble, real estate, spaceship earth.

WORLDLY adj. hep, hip, on to, uptown, swinging, mod, executive, cool, been around, been hit before, been around the block a few times, knows the score. See SOPHISTICATED.

WORLDWIDE adj. multinational, a-national.

WORN OUT adj. 1. bushed, pooped, too pooped to pop, had it, dusted, wimped out, out of gas, out of juice, knocked out, blown out, creased, wiped, wiped out, wrung out, burned out, wore out, pegged out, dragging ass, beat, hit the wall (marathon). See TIRED. 2. had it, busted, kaput, dinged, totaled, gone, glitched, shot, ratty-tatty, hand-me-down, reach-me-down, secondhand, experienced.

WORRIED adj. in crisis mode, uptight, creeped out, clutched, sweat it, sweat bullets, on edge, on pins and needles, on tenterhooks, worried stiff, biting one's nails, beside oneself. See DISTURBED. See also ANXIOUS; NERVOUS.

WORRIER adj. worry wart, nail-biter, nervous Nellie.

WORRY n. headache, crisis mode, nag, noodge, bitch, tsuris, pain, pain in the ass, pain in the neck, ants, nail-biter, worriment, worriation, cliffhanger, bad news. See ANXIETY. See also PREDICAMENT.

WORRY v. 1. bleed, take on, eat one's heart out, have a heart attack, stew, carry a heavy load, work oneself into a lather. 2. be at, be on the back of, get in one's face, eat, chivvy, noodge, nudge, nudzh, give one hemorrhoids, give a bad time to, give one a hard time, hassle, hound, dog, bulldog, nag. See ANNOY. See also DISTRESS.

WORSHIPPER n. booster, freak, buff, fan, groupie, skeezer (hip-hop), wannabee, rooter, bug, crazie. See DEVOTEE.

WORTHLESS adj. diddly-squat, ain't worth doodly-shit, ain't worth shit, ain't worth the powder to blow it to hell, piss-assed, stiffo, tripe, garbage, junk, beans, borscht, nada, big zero, measly, shitbox, shitbag, shitburger, minimal to the max, two-bit, nickel-and-dime, penny ante, peanuts, chickenshit, bupkes, pokerino, white elephant, dunnage (dockworker use), no prize package, not worth a hill of beans, from hunger. See USELESS.

WORTHY adj. A, A-1, aces, ace-high, winner, def, choice, gilt-edged, best ever, salt of the earth, top, tops, top notch, topflight, top-drawer, first-class, first-chop, first-rate, solid, not too shabby, something else, heavy, world-beater, the best. See ADMIRABLE.

WOUND v. 1. chop, scratch, ouch, bung, bung up, cut, cut one, cut up, jig cut, cut a new kisser for, open up, shiv, chiv, slice, stick, boo-boo (minor flesh), mark, rat mark, stool mark (knife), nick, brand, carve, carve initials in one, chop down, clip, zing, ding, total, wax, tweak. See also MISTREAT. 2. get, gotcha, zing, curdle, do, do in, do a number on, lean on, dump on, put down, burn, burn down, burn one down, rough up, hit one where one lives, hurl brickbats at, lay a bad trip on one, thumb one's nose at, gross out, mess up, shake up, cut, cut up, cut to the quick, total, wax, wing, nick, turn off, cool, chop, sound, dozens, sounding dozens, play dirty dozens, signify, signify shucking and jiving, S'ing'n' J'ing, miff, cap, pooh-pooh, get bent, blow off, give one a backhanded compliment, give one a left-handed compliment, give one the cold shoulder, hurt one where one lives, kick one around, mess around with.

WOUNDED adj. 1. hurtin', bleedin', damaged, winged, nicked, zinged, cut, bunged-up, busted-up, burned, burned one's ass, put away, screwed-up, walking wounded, have to scrape one off the sidewalk. 2. burnt-up, browned off, bleeding, all torn up, cut up, hit where one lives, shook, shook-up, miffed, miffy, shot down, have one's nose out of joint, sore, uptight.

WRANGLE n. blowup, brawl, flap, brannigan, donnybrook, row, rowdy-dow, ruckus, ruction, rumpus, scene, blow-off, dust-up, rumble, knockdown and drag-out, battle royal, flack session, rhubarb. See ARGUMENT.

WRANGLE v. brawl, buck, take on, lock horns, set to, row, bump heads, cross swords, have at it, pick a bone, kick up a row, tangle with, tangle ass with, pitch a bitch, put up a fight. See ARGUE.

WRATH n. mad, huff, dander, Irish, miff, stew, storm, wing-ding, conniption, cat fit, blowup, flare-up, boiling point, rise, more heat than light. See ANGER.

WRECK n. fender bender, rear ender, pile-up, stack-up, rack-up, crack-up, smash, smash-up, total. See ACCIDENT.

WRECK v. trash, total, cream, smash, smash up, pile up, rack up, crack up, take out, take apart, take a joint apart, break, break the lease, put out of commission, put in the toilet, bend the goods. See DESTROY.

WRECKED adj. gutted, busted, totaled, dusted, gone, cooked, sunk, shot, fragged, kaput, no-go, bitched-up, buggered, racked-up, hashed-up, mucked-up, down the tube, down the toilet, out the window, done in, gone to rack and ruin. See DESTROYED.

WRENCH n. knuckle buster (crescent).

WRESTLE n. rassle, grunt, grunt and groan.

WRESTLER n. pretzel bender, bone breaker, bone cracker, bone crusher, grunt, grunt and groaner. See also PRIZEFIGHTER.

WRETCH n. 1. sleazeball, sludgeball, sleazoid, creep, corn dog, elrod, scoob, goob, goober, goobatron, yernt, nob, social zero, nothingburger, prick, dick, barf bag, fart, rat, stinker, muthahfuckah, mofo, bad news, bad egg, bad'un, wrong'un, black sheep, bounder, bastard, son of a bitch, a dirty so-and-so, lame, rum-dum, low rider, nic-nac, punk, gunsel, low-life. See SCOUNDREL. 2. jinx, hoodoo, voodoo, eight-ball, jerk, jonah, joner, snake bit, scrub, loser, sure loser, winner, real winner, fuck-up, sad sack, schlemiel, schlemazel, hardcase, hard-luck guy, squid, flop, bust, loser, goner, dead, dead duck, beat, deadbeat, dead pigeon, bum, turkey, poor fish.

WRETCHED adj. ass in a sling, dick in the dirt, down-and-out, down-in-the-mouth, low, long face, singing the blues, crying the blues, bummed-out, hurting, in the pits, clanked, all torn up, raining on one's parade. See UNHAPPY.

WRINKLE v. prune up.

WRINKLES n. crow's feet.

WRIT, LEGAL n. paper.

WRITE v. push a pen, push a pencil, drive a pen, drive a pencil, drop a note, drop a line, script, scriven, pen, put pen to paper, put down, note down, dash off, toss off, bang out, bat out, knock out, knock out a few pages, shove out, knock off, knock off hen tracks on a roll-top piano (type), make hen tracks, ghost, ghost-write, Grub Street (hack), stain a paper, spoil a paper, shed ink, spill ink, sling ink, coin a phrase; comp, clef, tune. See also COMPOSE.

WRITE A LETTER v. drop a note, drop a line, drop a kite, knock out a tab, pen. See CORRESPOND.

WRITER n. scribbler, scribe, scripter, scrivener, scratcher, word slinger, wordsmith, freelance, pen driver, pen pusher, pencil driver, pencil pusher, ink slinger, ink spiller, ghost, ghost writer, spook, boo, knight of the pen, knight of the plume, knight of the quill; telewriter, teleplaywright (TV), legman, columnist, stringer, cub, newshen, play doctor, play fixer, Grub Streeter (also hack).

WRITING n. hen tracks, chicken tracks, bilge, scribble, stuff; AA (author's alterations, publishing), EA (editor's alterations).

WRITING PAPER n. the blank page, scratch.

WRITING TABLET n. scratch pad, scratch.

WRIT OF HABEAS CORPUS n.   hapas capas.

WRIT OF MANDAMUS goddamus.

WRONG adj.   off, way off, off base, off the beam, goofed, fluffed, duffed, boo-booed, smokin', blowing smoke, smoking your socks, put one's foot in it, put one's foot in one's mouth, muffed one's cue, fluffed one's lines, bletcherous, cretinous (computer), all wet, cockeyed, ass-backwards, back-asswards, bass-ackwards, 180 out (Mil.), that dog won't hunt, fouled-up, fucked-up, glitched-up, haywire, gone haywire, full of beans, full of hops, full of hot air, full of prunes, talking through one's hat, talking like a man with a paper ass, don't know one's ass from a hole in the ground, don't know one's ass from first base, don't know one's ass from one's elbow, don't know shit from Shinola, don't know from shit, don't know from nothing, nutty, off one's nut, that doesn't track, screwy, all wasted, bum, bum steer, wrong number, fell flat on one's face, fell flat on one's ass, dropped the ball, out in left field, miss by a mile, on a fool's errand, have another thing coming, count one's chickens before they're hatched, bark up the wrong tree, back the wrong horse.

WRONGDOER n.   turd, creep, shit, shithead, heel, shitheel, sleazeball, sleazoid, slime bucket, shower scum, barf bag, megabitch, maggot, prick, dick, fart, louse, rat, stinker, motherfucker, mofo, hood, hooligan, bad news, bad egg, low-life. See SCOUNDREL. See also CRIMINAL.

WROUGHT UP adj.   hyper, charged, wired, wired-up, got a wild hair up one's ass, amped, fired-up, keyed-up, all keyed up, steamed-up, hopped-up, worked-up, defrosted, freaked-out, flipped-out, creeped-out, spazzed-out, had a spaz attack, don't trip, all shook up, mind-blowing, mind-bending, in a lather, in a tizzy.

WYOMING Equality State, Suffrage State.

X

X n. X-ray, X ray.

X-RAY v. zap, film.

XYLOPHONE n. woodpile.

Y

Y n. Yankee, Yoke.

YACHT n. yatch, goldplater, stinkpot, a hole in the water, a hole in the water into which one throws money.

YACHTSMAN n. yachtie, yachty, yottie, yotty, skipper.

YAMS n. sweets.

YARN n. tall story, fish story, cock-and-bull story, cock and bull, tall tale, fairy tale, potboiler, string, line, line of cheese, song, song-and-dance, chestnut, old chestnut.

YAWN v. catch flies.

YEAR n. boffo (prison).

YEARN v. hurting for, hanker for, have eyes for, wild for, die over, got to have, yen for, carry a torch for, sweet on, have a crush on, have a case on, have it bad, eat one's heart out. See DESIRE.

YEARNING n. itch, yen, yen-yen, mash, pash, hankering, hots, hot pants, in heat, nasties, the urge, sweet tooth, flash groove, fire in the belly, the munchies (food), beaver fever. See DESIRE.

YELL n. holler, blow.

YELL v. blow at, holler, holler out, squawk.

YES interj. yeah, yeah man, yowzah, yeh, yep, yup, yessiree, si si, sweet, awesome, that'll work, A, fuckin' A, all right, all rightee, alrighty, all reet, reat, right, right on, right-o, rather, A-O.K., A-okay, O.K., okay, okey-dokey, okey-doke, okie bebe doakie, dory, okey-dory, hunky-dory, easy, works for me, ding-ho, ding-how, ding-hau, I can live with that, shoot, ducky, just ducky, solid, swell, absofuckinglutely, like you say, good deal, kee-rect, right you are, right as rain, for a fact, that's for sure, for sure, fer sher, fer shirr, shore, sure, sure thing, surest thing you know, you betcha, you bet, and no mistake, come hell or high water, no buts about it, no ifs ands or buts about it, check, for it, give the nod, thumbs up, indeedy, yes indeedy, Rodger Dodger, really truly, crazy, copacetic, uh-huh, um-huh, fine, amen, you better believe it, you said it, you said a mouthful, you can say that again, you're not kidding, you bet your life, you bet your ass, you bet your sweet ass, you bet your boots, you're damn tootin', you're dern tootin', you're the doctor, natch, yea-bo, Charlie, Uncle Charlie, George, jake, jake with me, like a shot.

YIELD v. 1. cave in, fold, quit, flake, back down, give up, give in, buy, say uncle, cry uncle, toss in the towel, throw in the towel, pack it in, eat shit, eat crow, eat dirt, eat humble pie, knuckle to, lie down and roll over for; come across, come across with, give out, put out (sexual). See SURRENDER. 2. go along with, go along with the crowd, go with the flow, don't make waves, don't rock the boat, play the game, fit in, toe the line, toe the mark. See COMPLY.

YIELDING adj. putty in one's hands. See also SUBMISSIVE.

YOKEL n. hillbilly, hick, plow jockey, country, country boy, country cousin, local yokel, hayseed, hay shaker, cornfed, boob, rube, shitkicker, clodhopper, clown, brush ape, busher, bush leaguer, clay eater (So.), cracker barrel, Bill Shears, Alvin, Reuben, galoot, gil, goober grabber, goofus, hay rube, hecker, hoosier, swamp angel, wahoo, yahoo, bucolic, woodhick, Herkimer Jerkimer.

YOUNG adj. juve, punk, yoot, Y-person, Y-people, bobby soxer, jailbait (Fem.), green, green ass, spring chicken, wet behind the ears, still wet behind the ears; YUP, yuppie (young urban professional), yuffie (young urban professional failure), yumpie (young upwardly mobile professional), yavis (young attractive verbal intelligent successful), boomerang kid (young adult living with parents again), salad days.

YOUNG ADULT n. Generation X, the Blank Generation, the Busters, twenty-somethings, twenty-nothings.

YOUNGER adj. kid (sister, brother).

YOUNG MAN n. kid, kiddo, shemp, toy boy, sonny, bub, punk, punk kid, yute, bud, buddy, rock, rocker, snag, stud, stud muffin, diesel, stallion, cock, colt, squirt, bugger, booger, chicken, wet behind the ears, man, cokey, duck, gunsel, monkey, pecker, pisser, lad, boy, boyo, boychick, buck, buster, Joe College, bummer, butch, chip, crasher, crock (disliked), junior; YUP, yuppie (young urban professional), yumpie (young upwardly mobile professional), rookie, dollface (good-looking), drape (hip clothing), fruit, buddy gee (1930), pachuco (1942, Mex.), jerk (1945), frat, gazooney, glad lad, chico, glamour puss, hell pup. See also BOY, YOUTH.

YOUNGSTER n. squirt, little squirt, yupster, kid, little kid, little guy, little bugger, shaver, little shaver, snotnose kid, juve, juvenile delinquent, JD, punk, punk kid, pup, puppy, cub, junior, J.R., sonny, sonny boy, bud, buddy, bub, bubba, young fry, small fry, chit.

YOUNGSTOWN, OHIO Baseball City.

YOUNG URBAN PROFESSIONAL n. YUP, yuppie, yumpie (young upwardly mobile professional), Y-people, buppie (Af. Am.), yavis (young attractive verbal intelligent successful), dewk (couple employed with kids); dinks, dinkies (double income, no kids), siks (single income, kids), dimps (double income, money problems), puppies (poor), yuffie (failure), guppies (gay), yummies (mommies), Yorkie (N.Y.), chuppie (Chicano), juppies (Jap.), yucas (Cuban-American).

YOUNG WOMAN n.   chick, chicken delight, betty, broad, studette (man chaser), babe, doll, jailbait, frail, skirt, pussy, piece, granola (wears no makeup), tomato, muffy, fifi, Heather, foof (superficial). See GIRL.

YOU'RE WELCOME interj.   de nada, no problem, no biggie, no sweat, think nothing of it, forget it, hey, doy tashey mashtay (Jap.).

YOURS pron.   it's you, you got it, got your name on it.

YOUTH n.   kid, Y-person, shaver, yupster, squirt, juve, juvenile delinquent, JD, punk, kiddo, shemp, snag, pup, sonny, sonny boy, bud, buddy, bub, bubba, bubble-gum rocker, teen, teenie, teeniebopper, weenie bopper, creepybopper, jive (associated with jive music, movies, etc.), mall brat, mall rat, Valley girl, petiteen, subdeb, sweet sixteen, twixt-teen, bobby-soxer, boyo, cokey, duck, gunsel, monkey, pecker, pisser, young fry, youngblood, wet behind the ears, what's wasted on the young, salad days; twink, twinkle, twinky (homosexual).

YUGOSLAVIAN n.   Hunkie, Hunky, Bohunk, Slav (all Derog.).

Z

Z n. Zulu, Zebra.

ZANY n. gagman, gagster, jokesmith, Joey, pale face, cutup, madcap, wisecracker.

ZANY adj. goofy, kooky, loony, crazy, sappy, camp, campy, jokey, joshing, yokky, boffo, gagged-up, for grins, whacked out, goofus, screamingly funny, tomfool, fool, foolheaded. See FOOLISH.

ZEALOT n. 1. fan, freak, groupie, hound, bug, crazies, nut, frenzie, junkie, punker (punk rock), culture vulture, fiend, demon, eager beaver, sucker for, fool. See DEVOTEE. 2. arm-waver, flag-waver, superpatriot, patrioteer, hundred percenter, jingoist, scoutmaster.

ZEALOUS adj. gung-ho, pushy, pushy hotshot, hot, hot for, hot to go, hot to trot, full on, hopped-up, ants, antsy, antsy-pantsy, ants in one's pants, catawamptious, itchy, keen, ripe, creaming to, ready for Freddie, fall all over oneself to, go great guns, come on like gangbusters, come on strong, enforcer, get-up-and-go, go-getter, on the make, out for a rep, ball of fire, eager beaver, fireball, spark plug, self-starting, full of get-up-and-go, heller, not let any grass grow under one's feet. See also ENTHUSIASTIC.

ZEBRA n. convict (circus).

ZEN BUDDHISM n. Zen, Zen hipster.

ZENITH n. blow-off, capper, topper, critical mass, pay-off, ape, bitter end, blow one's wad, far out, radical (not political), go over the mountain, shoot one's wad.

ZEPPELIN n. Zepp, blimp.

ZERO adj. zilch, nix, big zero, zip, zippo, zip city, zot, cipher, goose egg, duck egg, duck eggs, egg, bagel, shutout, nada, 86, scratch, minimal to the max, from nothing. See NOTHING. See also UNIMPORTANT.

ZEST n. guts, kick, zip, zap, moxie, pep, bounce, piss and vinegar.

ZESTFUL adj. 1. perky, bouncy, chirpy, chipper, peppy, zingy, zappy, zippy, jumping, hyper, jazzed, swinging, swingle, rocking, snappy, salty, revved, revved-up, juiced-up, upbeat, burning, red-hot, fireball, ball of fire. 2. hot, hot for, hot to go, hot to trot, rarin' to go, full of get-up-and-go, go great guns, gung-ho, hopped-up, spark plug, self-starter. See SPIRITED.

BIBLIOGRAPHY

Revised Edition

Abrams, Garry. "Fighting Words." *Los Angeles Times*, Jan. 27, 1991.

Adams, Ramon F. *The Cowboy Says It Salty*. Tucson: University of Arizona Press, 1971.

Agel, James, and Glanze, Walter D. *Cleopatra's Nose*. New York: Prentice-Hall Press, 1990.

Alexander, Clifton J., M.D., and Alexander, Sally. *How to Kick the Habit*. New York: Frederick Fell, 1972.

Alexander, Don, and Block, John. *The Racer's Dictionary*. Santa Ana, Calif.: Steve Smith Autosports, 1980.

Allen, Irving Lewis. *The Language of Ethnic Conflict*. New York: Columbia University Press, 1983.

Allen, Irving Lewis. *Unkind Words*. New York: Bergin & Garvey, 1990.

Allen, Jay Presson. *Just Tell Me What You Want*. New York: E. P. Dutton & Co., 1975.

Andrews, Malachi, and Owens, Paul T. *Black Language*. Berkeley: Seymour Smith Publishing, 1973.

Aponte, Wayne Lionel. "Talkin' White." *Essence*, Jan. 1989.

Banks, Carl J., Jr. *Banks Dictionary of the Black Ghetto Language*. Los Angeles: Saidi Publications, 1975.

Barnett, Lincoln. *The Treasure of Our Tongue*. New York: Alfred A. Knopf, 1967.

Barnhart, Clarence L., Steinmetz, Sol, and Barnhart, Robert K. *The Barnhart Dictionary of New English Since 1963*. New York: Barnhart/Harper & Row, 1973.

Barnhart, Clarence L., Steinmetz, Sol, and Barnhart, Robert K. *The Second Barnhart Dictionary of New English*. New York: Barnhart/Harper & Row, 1980.

Barnhart, David K. *Neo-Words*. New York: Collier Books, 1991.

Bentley, William K., and Coebett, James M. *Prison Slang*. Jefferson, N.C.: McFarland & Company, 1992.

Boatner, Maxine Tull, and Gates, John Edward. *A Dictionary of American Idioms*. Woodbury: Barron's Educational Series, 1975.

Bombeck, Erma. *Los Angeles Times*, Jan. 28, 1986.

Braithwaite, Fred (Fab 5 Freddy). *Fresh Fly Flavor*. Stamford, Conn.: Longmeadow Press, 1992.

Brandeth, Gyles. *The Joy of Lex*. New York: William Morrow & Company, 1980.

Burke, David. *Street Talk*. Los Angeles: Optima PrePress, 1991.

"Cagney and Lacey," TV segment, Jun. 18, 1984.

Carillo, Mary. "I Deef, You Deef, He Deefs." *World Tennis*, February 1982.

CB Fact Book and Language Dictionary. Milwaukee: DMR Publications, 1977.

Chapman, Bruce. *Why Do We Say Such Things?* New York: Miles-Emmett, 1947.

Claerbaut, David. *Black Jargon in White America*. Grand Rapids, Mich.: William B. Eerdman's Publishing Company, 1972.

Cohen, John. *The Essential Lenny Bruce*. New York: Ballantine Books, 1967.

Cohen, Sidney, M.D. *The Drug Dilemna*. New York: McGraw-Hill Co., 1969.

Cohen, Stanley. "Cop Talk—New York Style." *The Writer*, November 1980.

Collins, Glen. "Doing a Number on Words." *New York Times Magazine*, Feb. 13, 1977.

Cox, Terrance C., Jacobs, Michael R., Le Blanc, A. Eugene, and Marshman, Joan A. *Drugs and Drug Abuse*. Toronto: Addiction Research Foundation, 1983.

Cross, Donna Woolfolk. *Word Abuse*. New York: Coward, McCann Geoghegan, 1979.

"A Cursory Glossary to the Off-Beat Side of Now." *Harper's Bazaar*, Apr. 1965.

Dahl, Hartvig. *Word Frequencies of Spoken American English*. Essex: Verbatim Books, 1979.

Daily Variety, Mar. 10, Mar. 12, Nov. 19, 1986.

"Dear Abby," *Los Angeles Times*, Nov. 30, 1983.

Dennis, Paul, and Barry, Carolyn. *The Marijuana Catalogue*. Chicago: Playboy Press, 1978.

Dickson, Paul. *Words*. New York: Delacorte Press, 1982.

Dickson, Paul. *Slang!* New York: Pocket Books, 1990.

Dills, Lanie, and Silver, Robert M. *CB Slanguage Language Dictionary*. New York: Louis J. Martin & Associates, 1976.

Ditlea, Steve. "Word Processing." *Personal Computing*, October 1986.

Dohan, Mary Helen. *Our Own Words*. New York: Alfred A. Knopf, 1974.

Dreyfus, Patricia A. "Broker Babble." *Anchorage Daily News*, Nov. 19, 1984.

Dusek, Dorothy, and Girdano, Daniel A. *Drugs—A Factual Account* (3d ed.). Reading, Pa.: Addison-Wesley Publishing Co., 1980.

Eaton, Dian. *Is It True What They Say About Dixie*. Dan Mills, Ontario: Citadel Press, 1988.

Eble, Connie. *College Slang, 101*. Connecticut: Spectacle Lane Press, 1989.

Espy, Willard R. *Thou Improper, Thou Uncommon Noun*. New York: Clarkson N. Potter, 1978.

Fager, Chuck. "Hillspeak—The Secret Language of Policy Makers in Washington." *Christian Century*, May 13, 1981.

Fahey, Tom. *The Joys of Jargon*. Hauppaug, N.Y.: Barron's, 1990.

Fast, Howard. *The Outsider*. Boston: Houghton Mifflin, 1984.

Fast Times at Ridgemont High. Film. 1982.

Flamingo Hilton Gaming Guide. Las Vegas.

Fleming, Thomas J. "Space Language." *American Weekly*, Aug. 30, 1959.

Flexner, Stuart Berg. *I Hear America Talking*. New York: Van Nostrand Reinhold Co., 1976.

48 Hours. Film. 1982.

Free. *Revolution for the Hell of It*. New York: Dial Press, 1968.

Freeman, David. *A Hollywood Education*. New York: G. P. Putnam's Sons, 1986.

Funk, Charles Earle. *A Hog on Ice*. New York: Harper & Brothers, 1948.

Funk, Charles Earle. *Heavens to Betsy*. New York: Harper & Brothers, 1955.

Gannon, Frank. "A Portrait of the Artist as a Young Californian." *New Yorker*, Mar. 25, 1985.

A Glossary of Fund-Raising Terms. American Association of Fund Raising Counsel, National Society of Fund Raisers. National Association for Hospital Development.

Goldin, Hyman G., O'Leary, Frank, and Lipsius, Morris. *Dictionary of Underworld Lingo*. New York: Twayne Publishers, 1950.

Goldman, William. *Adventures in the Skin Trade*. New York: Warner Books, 1983.

Gozzi, Raymond Jr. *New Words*. Columbia, S.C.: University of South Carolina Press, 1990.

"Hardcastle and McCormick," TV segment, Nov. 13, 1983.

Holder, R. W. *The Faber Dictionary of Euphemisms*. London: Farber and Farber Ltd., 1989.

Holt, Alfred H. *Phrase Origins*. New York: Thomas Y. Crowell Company, 1936.

Homer, Joel. "Helpful Talk." *Atlantic Monthly*, November 1979.

Homer, Joel. "Big Business Talk." *Atlantic Monthly*, December 1979.

Homer, Joel. *Jargon*. New York: Times Books, 1979.

Infoworld Magazine, Dec. 3, Dec. 17, 1984; Mar. 24, 1986.

"Jack and Mike," TV segment, Nov. 11, 1986.

Jacobson, John D. *Toposaurus*. New York: John Wiley & Sons, 1990.

"Jeopardy," TV segment, Jun. 20, 1985.

Junker, Howard. "As We Used to Say in the Fifties." *Esquire*, August 1969; June 1983.

KABC Talk Radio, 4pm, Nov. 18, 1991.

KNBC News, Dec. 2, 1983; Sept. 12, 1984; Apr. 7, 1986; Sept. 30, 1986.

Kagos, Fred. *A Dictionary of Yiddish Slang and Idioms*. Secaucus, N.J.: The Citadel Press, 1966, 1967.

Kaufman, Diana. "Yo Parents! Check Out This Hot Stylin' Slang." *Anaheim Bulletin*, Feb. 1990.

KNXT News, May 19, 1984; Mar. 17, May 2, 1985.

"L.A. Speak," *Los Angeles Times*, January 1992-June 1993.

Lambodian, William. *Doublespeak Dictionary*. Los Angeles: Pinnacle Books, 1979.

Landy, Eugene E., Ph.D. *The Underground Dictionary*. New York: Simon and Schuster, 1971.

LeMay, Harold, Lerner, Sid, and Taylor, Marian. *The New New Words Dictionary*. New York: Ballantine Books, 1989.

Lerner, Sid, and Belkin, Gary S. *Trash Cash, Fizzbos and Flatliners*. Boston: Houghton Mifflin Company, 1993.

Levy, Steven. *Hackers*. Garden City, N.Y.: Anchor Press, Doubleday, 1984.

Limbacher, James L. *Sexuality in World Cinema*. Metuchen, N.J., and London: Scarecrow Press, 1983.

Lit, Hy. *Hy Lit's Unbelievable Dictionary*. Philadelphia: Hyski Press, 1968.

Los Angeles Times, May 27, 1982-Jan. 26, 1987.

Louria, Donald B., M.D. *The Drug Scene*. New York: McGraw-Hill Book Co., 1968.

"MacNeil-Lehrer Report," KCET, Jul. 26, 1984.

Mager, N. H. and S. K. *The Morrow Book of New Words*. New York: Willam Morrow and Company, 1982.

Major, Clarence. *The Dictionary of Afro-American Slang*. New York: International Publishers Co., 1970.

Maledicta, vols. IX (1986-87), X (1988-89).

Marketing Definitions. A Glossary of Marketing Terms. Compiled by the American Marketing Association.

Mason, Jackie. *How to Talk Jewish*. New York: St. Martin's Press, 1990.

Matthews, Mitford M. *American Words*. Cleveland and New York: The World Publishing Co., 1959.

McCarthy, Abigail. "Can We Rescue Language?" *Commonweal*, Jan. 28, 1983.

McFadden, Cyra. *The Serial*. New York: Signet Book/New American Library, 1978.

McLellan, Diana. "Slang-O-Rama." *Washingtonian*, March 1991.

McWilliams, Peter A. *The Personal Computer Book*. Los Angeles: Prelude Press, 1983.

Mencken, H. L. *The American Language*. New York: Alfred A. Knopf, 1963.

Meyers, Mike, and Ruzen, Robin. *Wayne's World Extreme Close-up*. New York: Cader Books, 1991.

Middleton, Thomas H. "Light Refractions." *Saturday Review*, Nov. 25, 1978.

Miller, Don Ethan. *The Book of Jargon*. New York: Macmillan Publishing Co., 1981.

Miller, Merl K., and Sippl, Charles, J. *Home Computers: A Beginner's Glossary and Guide*. Portland: Dilithium Press, 1978.

Morrow, Lance. "If Slang Is Not Sin." *Time*, Nov. 8, 1982.

Munro, Pamela. *U.C.L.A. Slang*. Los Angeles: Dept. of Linguistics, U.C.L.A., 1989.

Munro, Pamela. *U.C.L.A. Slang 2*. Los Angeles: Dept. of Linguistics, U.C.L.A., 1993.

Neaman, Judith S., and Silver, Carole S. *Kind Words, A Thesaurus of Euphemisms*. New York: Facts On File Publications, 1983.

Newman, Edwin. *Strictly Speaking*. Indianapolis/New York: Bobbs-Merrill Company, 1974.

Newman, Edwin. *A Civil Tongue*. Indianapolis/New York: Bobbs-Merrill Company, 1976.

"Nightline," TV segment, Oct. 23, 1985; Dec. 17, 1986.

Novak, William, and Waldoks, Moshe. *The Big Book of Jewish Humor*. New York: Harper & Row Publishers, 1981

O'Dair, Barbara. "Slanging Out." *Orange County Register*, Sept. 11, 1989.

Opdycke, John Baker. *Say What You Mean.* New York: Funk and Wagnalls Company, 1944.

Overmeyer, Eric. *Native Speech.* Play produced by LAAT. June 1983.

Partridge, Eric. *Slang Today and Yesterday* (4th ed.). New York: Barnes & Noble, 1970.

Partridge, Eric. A *Dictionary of Slang and Unconventional English.* New York: Macmillan Company, 1972.

Pei, Mario. *Words in Sheep's Clothing.* New York. Hawthorne Books, 1969.

Pei, Mario. *Double-Speak in America.* New York: Hawthorne Books, 1973.

Petievich, Gerald. *Money Men.* New York: Harcourt Brace Javanovich, 1981.

Pimp Talk: A Dictionary of Black Hustling Slang.

Porky's, Film. 1982.

Randall, Bernice. *When Is a Pig a Hog?* New York: Prentice-Hall, 1991.

Rawson, Hugh. A *Dictionary of Euphemisms and Other Doubletalk.* New York: Crown Publishers, 1981.

Reilly, Bill. *Big Al's Official Guide to Chicago.* Chicago: Contemporary Books, Inc., 1982.

Reversal of Fortune. Film. 1993.

Roberts, Hermese E. *The Third Ear: A Black Glossary.* Better Speech Institute of America, 1971.

Rogers, James. *The Dictionary of Clichés.* Avenel, N.J.: Wings Books, 1992.

Rosten, Leo. *The Joys of Yiddish.* New York: McGraw-Hill Book Company, 1968.

Rosten, Leo. *The Joys of Yinglish.* New York: McGraw-Hill, 1989.

Rusche, Sue. "The Drug Scene." *Los Angeles Times,* Nov. 11, 1984.

Safire, William. *On Language.* New York: Times Books, 1980.

Safire, William. *What's the Good Word?* New York: Times Books, 1982.

Safire, William. "On Language." *New York Times Magazine.* Mar. 6, 1983-Jan. 11, 1987; Oct. 27, 1991-May 23, 1993.

Sanders, Lawrence. *The Fourth Deadly Sin.* New York: G. P. Putnam Sons, 1985.

Sanoff, Alvin P. "Everything from Airheads to Zoids." *US News World Report,* Nov. 3, 1986.

Sassy Magazine, May 1991-June 1993.

Schell, Jonathan. "History in Sherman Park." *New Yorker,* Jan. 12, 1987.

Severn, Bill. *Place Words.* New York: Ives Washburn, 1969.

Sheldon, Sidney. *The Doomsday Conspiracy.* New York: William Morrow and Company, 1991.

Simmons, J. I., and Winograd, Barry. *It's Happening.* Santa Barbara, Calif.: M/L Marc-Laird Publications, 1967.

Simon, John. *Paradigms Lost.* New York: Clarkson M. Potter, 1976–1980.

Sitbon, Guy. "The Cocaine Society." *World Press Review,* February 1983.

Slansky, David. *Hold 'Em Poker.* Las Vegas: GBC Press.

Soukhanov, Anne H. "Word Watch." *Atlantic Monthly,* 1990.

Spears, Richard A. *Slang and Euphemism.* Middle Village: Jonathon David Publishers, 1981.

Spears, Richard, A. *Forbidden American English.* Lincolnwood, Ill.: Passport Books, 1990.

Spears, Richard, A. *Contemporary American Slang.* Lincolnwood, Ill.: National Textbook Company, 1991.

Spears, Richard A. *Slang and Euphemism* (2d rev. ed.). New York: Signet, 1991.

Spears, Richard, A. *Common American Phrases.* Lincolnwood, Ill.: National Textbook Company, 1992.

"Spencer for Hire," TV segment, Sept. 21, 1986.

Taylor, Marjorie A. *The Language of World War II.* New York: H. W. Wilson Company, 1944.

Testament. TV film, Nov. 26, 1984.

Thompson, Hunter S. *Fear and Loathing in Las Vegas.* New York: Fawcett Popular Library, 1971.

Thorndike, Edward L., and Lorge, Irving. *The Teacher's Word Book of 30,000 Words.* New York: Bureau of Publications, Teachers College, Columbia University, 1963.

Thorne, Tony. *The Dictionary of Contemporary Slang.* New York: Pantheon Books, 1990.

Time, Nov. 8, 1982; Jan. 3, 1983; Nov. 3, 1986.

Trudeau, Garry, "Doonesbury" comic strip. Jan. 6, 1985; June 6, Sept. 23, 1986; Dec. 18, 1986.

Truman, Margaret. *Murder at the Pentagon.* New York: Random House, 1992.

Tuotti, Joseph Dolan. *Big Time Buck White.* New York: Grove Press, 1969.

Urdang, Laurence, and LaRoche, Nancy. *Picturesque Expressions, A Thematic Dictionary.* Detroit: Gale Research Company, 1980.

Wambaugh, Joseph. *Fugitive Nights.* New York: William Morrow and Company, 1992.

Watts, Peter. A *Dictionary of the Old West.* New York: Alfred A. Knopf, 1977.

Webber, Elizabeth, and Feinsilber, Mike. *Grand Allusions.* Washington, D.C.: Farragut Publishing Company, 1990.

Webster's Sports Dictionary. Springfield, Mass.: G. & C. Merriam Company, 1976.

Wentworth, Harold, and Flexner, Stuart Berg. *Dictionary of American Slang* (2d supp. ed.), New York: Thomas Y. Crowell Company, 1975.

Wolkomis, Richard. "Slipping the Mitten to a Catawamptious Wally: The Slang Gap Revisited." *Smithsonian,* March 1983.

Wouk, Herman. *Inside, Outside.* Boston-Toronto: Little, Brown and Company, 1985.

Zamora, Jim Herron. "Why Valley Girls and Mutant Turtles Sound Like Surfers." *Wall Street Journal,* Sept. 27, 1990.